CLASSICAL AND MEDIEVAL LITERATURE CRITICISM

Guide to Gale Literary Criticism Series

For criticism on	Consult these Gale series
Authors now living or who died after December 31, 1999	*CONTEMPORARY LITERARY CRITICISM (CLC)*
Authors who died between 1900 and 1999	*TWENTIETH-CENTURY LITERARY CRITICISM (TCLC)*
Authors who died between 1800 and 1899	*NINETEENTH-CENTURY LITERATURE CRITICISM (NCLC)*
Authors who died between 1400 and 1799	*LITERATURE CRITICISM FROM 1400 TO 1800 (LC)* *SHAKESPEAREAN CRITICISM (SC)*
Authors who died before 1400	*CLASSICAL AND MEDIEVAL LITERATURE CRITICISM (CMLC)*
Authors of books for children and young adults	*CHILDREN'S LITERATURE REVIEW (CLR)*
Dramatists	*DRAMA CRITICISM (DC)*
Poets	*POETRY CRITICISM (PC)*
Short story writers	*SHORT STORY CRITICISM (SSC)*
Black writers of the past two hundred years	*BLACK LITERATURE CRITICISM (BLC)* *BLACK LITERATURE CRITICISM SUPPLEMENT (BLCS)*
Hispanic writers of the late nineteenth and twentieth centuries	*HISPANIC LITERATURE CRITICISM (HLC)* *HISPANIC LITERATURE CRITICISM SUPPLEMENT (HLCS)*
Native North American writers and orators of the eighteenth, nineteenth, and twentieth centuries	*NATIVE NORTH AMERICAN LITERATURE (NNAL)*
Major authors from the Renaissance to the present	*WORLD LITERATURE CRITICISM, 1500 TO THE PRESENT (WLC)* *WORLD LITERATURE CRITICISM SUPPLEMENT (WLCS)*

ISSN 0896-0011

Volume 42

CLASSICAL AND MEDIEVAL LITERATURE CRITICISM

Excerpts from Criticism of the Works of World
Authors from Classical Antiquity through the
Fourteenth Century, from the First Appraisals
to Current Evaluations

Jelena O. Krstović
Editor

Detroit
New York
San Francisco
London
Boston
Woodbridge, CT

STAFF

Lynn M. Spampinato, Janet Witalec, *Managing Editors, Literature Product*
Kathy D. Darrow, *Product Liaison*
Jelena Krstović, *Editor*
Mark W. Scott, *Publisher, Literature Product*

Elisabeth Gellert, *Associate Editor*
Mary Ruby, *Technical Training Specialist*
Deborah J. Morad, Kathleen Lopez Nolan, *Managing Editors, Literature Content*
Susan M. Trosky, *Director, Literature Content*

Maria L. Franklin, *Permissions Manager*
Edna Hedblad, *Permissions Specialist*
Shalice Shah Caldwell, *Permissions Assistant*

Victoria B. Cariappa, *Research Manager*
Tracie A. Richardson, *Project Coordinator*
Andrew Guy Malonis, Barbara McNeil, Gary J. Oudersluys, Maureen Richards, Cheryl L. Warnock, *Research Specialists*
Tamara C. Nott, *Research Associate*
Tim Lehnerer, *Research Assistant*

Dorothy Maki, *Manufacturing Manager*
Stacy L. Melson, *Buyer*

Mary Beth Trimper, *Composition and Prepress Manager*
Carolyn Roney, *Composition Specialist*

Randy Bassett, *Image Database Supervisor*
Robert Duncan, *Imaging Specialist*
Mike Logusz, *Graphic Artist*
Pamela A. Reed, *Imaging Coordinator*
Kelly A. Quin, *Imaging Editor*

Library of Congress Catalog Card Number 88-658021
ISBN 0-7876-4384-X
ISSN 0896-0011
Printed in the United States of America

10 9 8 7 6 5 4 3 2 1

Contents

Preface

Since its inception in 1988, *Classical and Medieval Literature Criticism* (*CMLC*) has been a valuable resource for students and librarians seeking critical commentary on the works and authors of antiquity through the fourteenth century. The great poets, prose writers, dramatists, and philosophers of this period form the basis of most humanities curricula, so that virtually every student will encounter many of these works during the course of a high school and college education. Reviewers have found *CMLC* "useful" and "extremely convenient," noting that it "adds to our understanding of the rich legacy left by the ancient period and the Middle Ages," and praising its "general excellence in the presentation of an inherently interesting subject." No other single reference source has surveyed the critical reaction to classical and medieval literature as thoroughly as *CMLC*.

Scope of the Series

CMLC provides an introduction to classical and medieval authors, works, and topics that represent a variety of genres, time periods, and nationalities. By organizing and reprinting an enormous amount of critical commentary written on authors and works of this period in world history, *CMLC* helps students develop valuable insight into literary history, promotes a better understanding of the texts, and sparks ideas for papers and assignments.

Each entry in *CMLC* presents a comprehensive survey of an author's career, an individual work of literature, or a literary topic, and provides the user with a multiplicity of interpretations and assessments. Such variety allows students to pursue their own interests; furthermore, it fosters an awareness that literature is dynamic and responsive to many different opinions. Early commentary is offered to indicate initial responses, later selections document changes in literary reputations, and retrospective analyses provide the reader with modern views. The size of each author entry is a relative reflection of the scope of the criticism available in English.

An author may appear more than once in the series if his or her writings have been the subject of a substantial amount of criticism; in these instances, specific works or groups of works by the author will be covered in separate entries. For example, Homer will be represented by three entries, one devoted to the *Iliad,* one to the *Odyssey,* and one to the Homeric Hymns.

CMLC continues the survey of criticism of world literature begun by Gale's *Contemporary Literary Criticism* (*CLC*), *Twentieth-Century Literary Criticism* (*TCLC*), *Nineteenth-Century Literature Criticism* (*NCLC*), *Literature Criticism from 1400 to 1800* (*LC*), and *Shakespearean Criticism* (*SC*).

Organization of the Book

A *CMLC* entry consists of the following elements:

- The **Author Heading** cites the name under which the author most commonly wrote, followed by birth and death dates. Also located here are any name variations under which an author wrote, including transliterated forms for authors whose native languages use nonroman alphabets. If the author wrote consistently under a pseudonym, the pseudonym will be listed in the author heading and the author's actual name given in parenthesis on the first line of the biographical and critical information. Uncertain birth or death dates are indicated by question marks. Single-work entries are preceded by a heading that consists of the most common form of the title in English translation (if applicable) and the original date of composition.

- The **Introduction** contains background information that introduces the reader to the author, work, or topic that is the subject of the entry.

- A **Portrait of the Author** is included when available.

- The list of **Principal Works** is ordered chronologically by date of first publication and lists the most important works by the author. The genre and publication date of each work is given. In the case of foreign authors whose works have been translated into English, the list will focus primarily on twentieth-century translations, selecting those works most commonly considered the best by critics. Unless otherwise indicated, dramas are dated by first performance, not first publication. Lists of **Representative Works** by different authors appear with topic entries.

- Reprinted **Criticism** is arranged chronologically in each entry to provide a useful perspective on changes in critical evaluation over time. The critic's name and the date of composition or publication of the critical work are given at the beginning of each piece of criticism. Unsigned criticism is preceded by the title of the source in which it appeared. All titles by the author featured in the text are printed in boldface type. Footnotes are reprinted at the end of each essay or excerpt. In the case of excerpted criticism, only those footnotes that pertain to the excerpted texts are included. Criticism in topic entries is arranged chronologically under a variety of subheadings to facilitate the study of different aspects of the topic.

- A complete **Bibliographical Citation** of the original essay or book precedes each piece of criticism.

- Critical essays are prefaced by brief **Annotations** explicating each piece.

- An annotated bibliography of **Further Reading** appears at the end of each entry and suggests resources for additional study. In some cases, significant essays for which the editors could not obtain reprint rights are included here. Boxed material following the further reading list provides references to other biographical and critical sources on the author in series published by Gale.

Cumulative Indexes

A **Cumulative Author Index** lists all of the authors that appear in a wide variety of reference sources published by the Gale Group, including *CMLC*. A complete list of these sources is found facing the first page of the Author Index. The index also includes birth and death dates and cross references between pseudonyms and actual names.

Beginning with the second volume, a **Cumulative Nationality Index** lists all authors featured in *CMLC* by nationality, followed by the number of the *CMLC* volume in which their entry appears.

Beginning with the tenth volume, a **Cumulative Topic Index** lists the literary themes and topics treated in the series as well as in *Nineteenth-Century Literature Criticism, Twentieth-Century Literary Criticism,* and the *Contemporary Literary Criticism* Yearbook, which was discontinued in 1998.

A **Cumulative Title Index** lists in alphabetical order all of the works discussed in the series. Each title listing includes the corresponding volume and page numbers where criticism may be located. Foreign-language titles that have been translated into English are followed by the titles of the translation—for example, *Slovo o polku Igorove (The Song of Igor's Campaign)*. Page numbers following these translated titles refer to all pages on which any form of the titles, either foreign-language or translated, appear. Titles of novels, dramas, nonfiction books, and poetry, short story, or essay collections are printed in italics, while individual poems, short stories, and essays are printed in roman type within quotation marks.

Citing *Classical and Medieval Literature Criticism*

When writing papers, students who quote directly from any volume in the Literary Criticism Series may use the following general format to footnote reprinted criticism. The first example pertains to material drawn from periodicals, the second to material reprinted from books.

T. P. Malnati, "Juvenal and Martial on Social Mobility," *The Classical Journal* 83, no. 2 (December-January 1988): 134-41; reprinted in *Classical and Medieval Literature Criticism,* vol. 35, ed. Jelena Krstović; (Farmington Hills, Mich.: The Gale Group, 2000), 366-71.

J. P. Sullivan, "Humanity and Humour; Imagery and Wit," in *Martial: An Unexpected Classic* (Cambridge University Press, 1991), 211-51; excerpted and reprinted in *Classical and Medieval Literature Criticism,* vol. 35, ed. Jelena Krstović; (Farmington Hills, Mich.: The Gale Group, 2000), 371-95.

Suggestions are Welcome

Readers who wish to suggest new features, topics, or authors to appear in future volumes, or who have other suggestions or comments are cordially invited to call, write, or fax the Managing Editor:

Managing Editor, Literary Criticism Series
The Gale Group
27500 Drake Road
Farmington Hills, MI 48331-3535
1-800-347-4253 (GALE)
Fax: 248-699-8054

Acknowledgments

The editors wish to thank the copyright holders of the excerpted criticism included in this volume and the permissions managers of many book and magazine publishing companies for assisting us in securing reproduction rights. We are also grateful to the staffs of the Detroit Public Library, the Library of Congress, the University of Detroit Mercy Library, Wayne State University Purdy/Kresge Library Complex, and the University of Michigan Libraries for making their resources available to us. Following is a list of the copyright holders who have granted us permission to reproduce material in this volume of *CMLC*. Every effort has been made to trace copyright, but if omissions have been made, please let us know.

COPYRIGHTED EXCERPTS IN *CMLC*, VOLUME 42, WERE REPRODUCED FROM THE FOLLOWING PERIODICALS:

Acta Asiatica, v. 20-21, 1971. Reproduced by permission.—*Allegorica,* v. 1, Spring, 1976. Reproduced by permission.—*Hebrew University Studies in Literature,* v. 2, Spring, 1974. Reproduced by permission. —*Journal of Chinese Philosophy,* v. 2, 1982; v. 9, 1982.; v. 10, 1983; v. 14, June, 1987. All reproduced by permission. —*Michigan Academician,* v. 5, 1972. Reproduced by permission.—*Romance Notes,* v. 11, Spring, 1970. Reproduced by permission.—*Studi Francesi,* n. 51, September-December, 1973. Reproduced by permission.—*Studies in Philology,* v. 63, January, 1966; v. 74, January, 1977. All used by permission of the publisher.—*The French Review,* v. xliii, March, 1970. Copyright 1970 by the American Association of Teachers of French. Reproduced by permission.—*Yale French Studies,* n. 45, 1970. Copyright © Yale French Studies 1970. Reproduced by permission.—*Zeifschrift fur Celtische Philologie,* v. 31, 1970 for "Aucassin et Nicolette and Celtic Literature" by G. W. Goetinck. Reproduced by permission of the author.

COPYRIGHTED EXCERPTS IN *CMLC*, VOLUME 42, WERE REPRODUCED FROM THE FOLLOWING BOOKS:

Chan, Wing-Tsit. From *Chu Hsi: A New Studies.* University of Hawaii Press, 1989. © 1989 University of Hawaii Press. All rights reserved. Reproduced by permission.—Chan, Wing-Tsit. From *Reflections on Things at Hand.* Columbia University Press, 1967. Copyright © 1967 Columbia University Press, New York. All rights reserved. Republished with permission of the Columbia University Press, 562 W. 113th St., New York, NY 10025.—Cobby, Anne Elizabeth. From *Ambivalent Conventions: Formula and Parody in Old French.* Rodopi, 1995. © Editions Rodopi V.V., Amsterdam - Atlanta, GA 1995. Reproduced by permission.— de Bary, William Theodore. From *The Message of the Mind in Neo-Confucianism.* Copyright © 1989 Columbia University Press, New York. All rights reserved. Republished with permission of the Columbia University Press, 562 W. 113th St., New York, NY 10025.—Dorman, Eugene. From *Homenaje Robert A. Hall, Jr.* Edited by David Feldman. Playor, 1977. Reproduced by permission.—Lawson, John. From *The Biblical Theology of Saint Irenaeus.* Epworth Press, 1948. Reproduced by permission.—Martin, June Hall. From *Love's Fools: Aucassin, Troilus, Calisto, and the Parody of the Courtly Lover.* Tamesis Book Limited, 1972. Reproduced by permission.—Pensom, Roger. From *Aucassin et Nicolette: The Poetry of Gender and Growing Up in the French Middle Ages.* Peter Lang, 1999. © Peter Lang AG, European Academic Publishers, Bern 1999. Reproduced by permission.—Smith, Joseph P. From *Ancient Christian Writers: The Works of the Fathers in Translation.* The Newman Press, 1952. Reproduced by permission.—Tiessen, Terrance L. From *Irenaeus on the Salvation of the Unevangelized.* The Scarecrow Press, Inc., 1993. Copyright © 1993 by Terrance L. Tiessen. Reproduced by permission.—Tillman, Hoyt Cleveland. From *Confucian Discourse and Chu Hsi's Ascendancy.* University of Hawaii Press, 1992. © 1992 University of Hawaii Press. Reproduced by permission.—Timothy, Hamilton Baird. From *The Early Christian Apologists and Greek Philosophy.* Van Gorcum & Comp. B.V., 1973. © by Koninklijke Van Gorcum & Comp. B.V., Assen, The Netherlands.—Unger, Dominic J. From *St. Irenaeus of Lyons: Against the Heresies,* Vol. 1. Paulist Press, 1992. Copyright © 1992 by Capuchin Province of Mid-America. Reproduced by permission.—Vinaver, Eugene. From *Medieval Studies in the Memory of Gertrude Schoepperle Loomis.* Slatkine Reprints, 1974. Reproduced by permission.

PHOTOGRAPHS APPEARING IN *CMLC*, VOLUME 42, WERE RECEIVED FROM THE FOLLOWING SOURCES:

Dancers, performing in Wendy Toye's Ballet "Aucassin and Nicolette," photograph by Sasha. © Hulton-Deutsch Collection/ Corbis. Reproduced by permission.—Gottfried von Strassburg (seated on a stage), with other figures, manuscript painting. The Library of Congress.

Aucassin et Nicolette

Thirteenth-century French poetry and prose.

INTRODUCTION

Aucassin et Nicolette, composed by an unknown author, relates the adventures of two lovers—Aucassin, the son of a French count, and Nicolette, a Saracen captive. Although the work has traditionally been regarded as an idyllic romance, many modern critics have deemed the tale a parody of courtly love. The form of *Aucassin et Nicolette* combines verse and prose, with the original manuscript also including musical notation. The novelty of this literary style remains an area of critical debate.

TEXTUAL HISTORY

Nothing is known about the author of *Aucassin et Nicolette,* and the poem can only roughly be dated to the thirteenth century. There is but a single extant manuscript.

PLOT AND MAJOR CHARACTERS

The title characters of the poem are unlikely lovers: Aucassin is the son of Count Garins of Beaucaire, and Nicolette is a beautiful Saracen captive. When the Count learns of his son's love for Nicolette, he forbids their marriage and imprisons the girl in a tower. As Aucassin still pines for his love, the Count imprisons his son as well. Nicolette escapes, finds her lover imprisoned, and flees in order to avoid capture. Upon his release from prison, Aucassin pursues Nicolette. Their adventures include an episode the the bizarre land of Torelore, in which the King is about to give birth, the Queen is commanding troops to a battle, and the war is being fought with cheese and fruit. Eventually, Aucassin and Nicolette are reunited.

MAJOR THEMES

Early critics of *Aucassin et Nicolette,* maintain that its primary emphasis is on ideal love and courtly values. Other, more recent critics, however, have found in the story elements that parody the same idyllic love and virtues. The literary conventions of the day, particularly the vapid heroes, heroines, and plots of traditional romance, are the object of the author's satire. Aucassin, as a courtly lover, is mocked in such a way that the role of the courtly lover in thirteenth-century French society is shown to be impractical and somewhat absurd.

CRITICAL RECEPTION

The form of *Aucassin et Nicolette* is described by its author as a *chantefable,* or "song-story," because it combines verse, prose, and music. That it is the only work of French literature of its time to be so named has caused many critics to examine the apparent novelty of this form. While John R. Reinhard admits that it is the only known work in French literature of the Middle Ages composed in such a manner, he points out that when the element of music is disregarded the form ceases to be unique. Reinhard maintains that although some critics attempt to identify the origins of this form in Oriental, Celtic, or Old Norse literature, it is more likely that the author made use of the literary traditions of Greece and Rome, which were readily available to him. Reinhard cites examples of Greek and Roman works in which prose and verse are similarly combined. G. W. Goetinck, on the other hand, states that it is possible that Celtic literature did in fact influence the author of *Aucassin et Nicolette.* Goetinck discusses a number of features in the poem reminiscent of Celtic literature. Like Reinhard, Tony Hunt also finds works in Latin literature in which both prose and verse are used. Hunt maintains that while *Aucassin et Nicolette* is not original in terms of form, its regularity and consistency of structure are unique.

In addition to discussion of *Aucassin et Nicolette*'s form, another area of critical debate is the issue of the work as parody. Generally, nineteenth- and early twentieth-century critics interpreted the poem as a straightforward romance. Andrew Lang describes the poem as a "sympathetically told love story," and Henry Adams finds in the work an emphasis on courtesy and courtly love. While many modern critics refute these claims, there are also recent scholars who deny that the work is parodic in nature. Eugene Vance argues that while the author utilizes the techniques of satire, satire is not the chief aim of the work. Rather, Vance describes *Aucassin et Nicolette* as a "sensitive attempt" to examine the role of literary language "in terms of the language itself." S. L. Clark and Julian Wasserman view the poem not as parody or satire, but as an allegory designed to demonstrate the absurd nature of human error. The progression of Aucassin, they argue, through adventures focused on the development of his decision-making skills is the means by which the allegory is presented. Yet a considerable number of critics find what they believe to be striking and obvious clues that suggest that the author intended *Aucassin et Nicolette* as parody. Robert Harden notes that the language, form, and particularly the author's use of character inversions, mock the insipid plots and characters of the typical medieval romance. Focusing his analysis on the Torelore episode, Darnell H. Clevenger maintains that these adventures may be viewed as a burlesque of chivalric valor and courtly love. Clevenger further states that the episode underscores the relative unimportance of the plot and emphasizes that the world (both real and fictional) is the main antagonist in *Aucassin et Nicolette*. Just as Harden stresses the importance of character inversion, June Hall Martin contends that the parody of one character in particular, Aucassin, unifies the episodes of the tale and highlights the author's criticism of courtly love. Anne Elizabeth Cobby identifies another layer of parody in *Aucassin et Nicolette*. Cobby's analysis reveals that the author manipulates the readers' expectations through the parodic references to contemporary literary genres, including the romance and the *chanson de geste,* and through the characterization of Aucassin and Nicolette. Aucassin, explains Cobby, is portrayed to an overstated level as the stereotypical courtly lover. While he conforms completely to the external values of this type of hero, he demonstrates a complete lack of the inner ideals usually associated with the courtly lover. Cobby further shows that while Nicolette is painted as a quintessential courtly heroine, her actions reveal her to be thoroughly unconventional. Cobby states that such contrasts stress the futility of labels. Solidifying her argument that the essentially parodic nature of *Aucassin et Nicolette* is revealed through the author's redirecting of his reader, Cobby points out that by the time Aucassin and Nicolette are reunited in the forest, we fully anticipate the thwarting of our expectations, yet now some of them are in fact fulfilled.

PRINCIPAL WORKS

Principal English Translations

Aucassin and Nicolette. A Love Story (edited and translated by Francis William Bordillon) 1887
Aucassin and Nicolette (translated by Andrew Lang) 1887
Aucassin and Nicolette (translated by Eugene Mason) 1910

CRITICISM

Andrew Lang (letter date 1889)

SOURCE: "*Aucassin and Nicolette*" in *Letters on Literature*, Longmans, Green, and Co., 1889, pp. 80-91.

[*In the following essay, originally written as a letter to Lady Violet Lebas, Lang reviews the form and plot of* Aucassin et Nicolette, *describing the work as a "sympathetically told love story."*]

To the Lady Violet Lebas.

Dear Lady Violet,—I do not wonder that you are puzzled by the language of the first French novel. The French of *Aucassin et Nicolette* is not French after the school of

Miss Pinkerton, at Chiswick. Indeed, as the little song-story has been translated into modern French by M. Bida, the painter (whose book is very scarce), I presume even the countrywomen of Aucassin find it difficult. You will not expect me to write an essay on the grammar, nor would you read it if I did. The chief thing is that 's' appears as the sign of the singular, instead of being the sign of the plural, and the nouns have cases.

The story must be as old as the end of the twelfth century, and must have received its present form in Picardy. It is written, as you see, in alternate snatches of verse and prose. The verse, which was chanted, is not rhymed as a rule, but each *laisse,* or screed, as in the *Chanson de Roland,* runs on the same final assonance, or vowel sound throughout.

So much for the form. Who is the author? We do not know, and never shall know. Apparently he mentions himself in the first lines:

> Who would listen to the lay,
> Of the captive old and gray;

for this is as much sense as one can make out of *del deport du viel caitif.*

The author, then, was an old fellow. I think we might learn as much from the story. An old man he was, or a man who felt old. Do you know whom he reminds me of? Why, of Mr. Bowes, of the Theatre Royal, Chatteris; of Mr. Bowes, that battered, old, kindly sentimentalist who told his tale with Mr. Arthur Pendennis.

It is a love story, a story of love overmastering, without conscience or care of aught but the beloved. And the *viel caitif* tells it with sympathy, and with a smile. 'Oh, folly of fondness,' he seems to cry; 'oh, pretty fever and foolish; oh, absurd happy days of desolation:

> When I was young, as you are young,
> And lutes were touched, and songs were sung!
> And love-lamps in the windows hung!

It is the very tone of Thackeray, when Thackeray is tender; and the world heard it first from this elderly nameless minstrel, strolling with his viol and his singing boys, a blameless D'Assoucy, from castle to castle in the happy poplar land. I think I see him and hear him in the silver twilight, in the court of some château of Picardy, while the ladies around sit listening on silken cushions, and their lovers, fettered with silver chains, lie at their feet. They listen, and look, and do not think of the minstrel with his grey head, and his green heart; but we think of him. It is an old man's work, and a weary man's work. You can easily tell the places where he has lingered and been pleased as he wrote.

The story is simple enough. Aucassin, son of Count Garin, of Beaucaire, loved so well fair Nicolette, the captive girl from an unknown land, that he would never be dubbed knight, nor follow tourneys; nor even fight against his father's mortal foe, Count Bougars de Valence. So Nicolette was imprisoned high in a painted chamber. But the enemy were storming the town, and, for the promise of 'one word or two with Nicolette, and one kiss,' Aucassin armed himself and led out his men. But he was all adream about Nicolette, and his horse bore him into the press of foes ere he knew it. Then he heard them contriving his death, and woke out of his dream.

'The damoiseau was tall and strong, and the horse whereon he sat fierce and great, and Aucassin laid hand to sword, and fell a smiting to right and left, and smote through helm and headpiece, and arm and shoulder, making a murder about him, like a wild boar the hounds fall on in the forest. There slew he ten knights, and smote down seven, and mightily and knightly he hurled through the press, and charged home again, sword in hand.' For that hour Aucassin struck like one of Mallory's men in the best of all romances. But though he took Count Bougars prisoner, his father would not keep his word, nor let him have one word or two with Nicolette, and one kiss. Nay, Aucassin was thrown into prison in an old tower. There he sang of Nicolette,

> Was it not the other day
> That a pilgrim came this way?
> And a passion him possessed,
> That upon his bed he lay,
> Lay, and tossed, and knew no rest,
> In his pain discomforted.
> But thou camest by his bed,
> Holding high thine amice fine
> And thy kirtle of ermine.
> Then the beauty that is thine
> Did he look on; and it fell
> That the Pilgrim straight was well,
> Straight was hale and comforted.
> And he rose up from his bed,
> And went back to his own place
> Sound and strong, and fair of face.

Thus Aucassin makes a Legend of his lady, as it were, assigning to her beauty such miracles as faith attributes to the excellence of the saints.

Meanwhile, Nicolette had slipped from the window of her prison chamber, and let herself down into the garden, where she heard the song of the nightingales. 'Then caught she up her kirtle in both hands, behind and before, and flitted over the dew that lay deep on the grass, and fled out of the garden, and the daisy flowers bending below her tread seemed dark against her feet, so white was the maiden.' Can't you see her stealing with those 'feet of ivory,' like Bombyca's, down the dark side of the silent moonlit streets of Beaucaire?

Then she came where Aucassin was lamenting in his cell, and she whispered to him how she was fleeing for her life. And he answered that without her he must die; and then this foolish pair, in the very mouth of peril, must needs begin a war of words as to which loved the other best!

'Nay, fair sweet friend,' saith Aucassin, 'it may not be that thou lovest me more than I love thee. Woman may not love man as man loves woman, for a woman's love lies no deeper than in the glance of her eye, and the blossom of her breast, and her foot's tip-toe; but man's love is in his heart planted, whence never can it issue forth and pass away.'

So while they speak

> In debate as birds are,
> Hawk on bough,

comes the kind sentinel to warn them of a danger. And Nicolette flees, and leaps into the fosse, and thence escapes into a great forest and lonely. In the morning she met shepherds, merry over their meat, and bade them tell Aucassin to hunt in that forest, where he should find a deer whereof one glance would cure him of his malady. The shepherds are happy, laughing people, who half mock Nicolette, and quite mock Aucassin, when he comes that way. But at first they took Nicolette for a *fée*, such a beauty shone so brightly from her, and lit up all the forest. Aucassin they banter; and indeed the free talk of the peasants to their lord's son in that feudal age sounds curiously, and may well make us reconsider our notions of early feudalism.

But Aucassin learns at least that Nicolette is in the wood, and he rides at adventure after her, till the thorns have ruined his silken surcoat, and the blood, dripping from his torn body, makes a visible track in the grass. So, as he wept, he met a monstrous man of the wood, that asked him why he lamented. And he said he was sorrowing for a lily-white hound that he had lost. Then the wild man mocked him, and told his own tale. He was in that estate which Achilles, among the ghosts, preferred to all the kingship of the dead outworn. He was hind and hireling to a villein, and he had lost one of the villein's oxen. For that he dared not go into the town, where a prison awaited him. Moreover, they had dragged the very bed from under his old mother, to pay the price of the ox, and she lay on straw; and at that the woodman wept.

A curious touch, is it not, of pity for the people? The old poet is serious for one moment. 'Compare,' he says, 'the sorrows of sentiment, of ladies and lovers, praised in song, with the sorrows of the poor, with troubles that are real and not of the heart'! Even Aucassin the lovelorn feels it, and gives the hind money to pay for his ox, and so riding on comes to a lodge that Nicolette has built with blossoms and boughs. And Aucassin crept in and looked through a gap in the fragrant walls of the lodge, and saw the stars in heaven, and one that was brighter than the rest.

Does one not feel it, the cool of that old summer night, the sweet smell of broken boughs and trodden grass and deep dew, and the shining of the star?

> Star that I from far behold
> That the moon draws to her fold,
> Nicolette with thee doth dwell,
> My sweet love with locks of gold,

sings Aucassin. 'And when Nicolette heard Aucassin, right so came she unto him, and passed within the lodge, and cast her arms about his neck and kissed and embraced him:

> Fair sweet friend, welcome be thou!
>
> And thou, fair sweet love, be thou welcome!

There the story should end, in a dream of a summer's night. But the old minstrel did not end it so, or some one has continued his work with a heavier hand. Aucassin rides, he cares not whither, if he has but his love with him. And they come to a fantastic land of burlesque, such as Pantagruel's crew touched at many a time. And Nicolette is taken by Carthaginian pirates, and proves to be daughter to the King of Carthage, and leaves his court and comes to Beaucaire in the disguise of a minstrel, and 'journeys end in lovers' meeting.'

That is all the tale, with its gaps, its careless passages, its adventures that do not interest the poet. He only cares for youth, love, spring, flowers, and the song of the birds; the rest, except the passage about the hind, is mere 'business' done casually, because the audience expects broad jests, hard blows, misadventures, recognitions. What lives is the touch of poetry, of longing, of tender heart, of humorous resignation. It lives, and always must live, 'while the nature of man is the same.' The poet hopes his tale will gladden sad men. This service it did for M. Bida, he says, in the dreadful year of 1870-71, when he translated 'Aucassin.' This, too, it has done for me in days not delightful.[1]

Notes

1. *Aucassin and Nicolette* has now been edited, annotated, and equipped with a translation by Mr. F. W. Bourdillon (Kegan Paul & Trench, 1887).

Henry Adams (essay date 1904)

SOURCE: "Nicolette and Marion" in *Mont-Saint-Michel and Chartres,* Houghton Mifflin Company, 1994, pp. 230-50.

[*In the excerpt below, Adams offers a brief overview of* Aucassin et Nicolette, *discussing the form and plot of the work. In particular, Adams notes that the* chantefable *emphasizes the virtues of courtesy and courtly love.*]

> C'est d'Aucassins et de Nicolete.
>
> Qui vauroit bons vers oir
> Del deport du viel caitif
> De deus biax enfans petis
> Nicolete et Aucassins;
> Des grans paines qu'il soufri
> Et des proueces qu'il fist
> Por s'amie o le cler vis.
> Dox est li cans biax est li dis

> Et cortois et bien asis.
> Nus hom n'est si esbahis
> Tant dolans ni entrepris
> De grant mal amaladis
> Se il l'oit ne soit garis
> Et de joie resbaudis
>   Tant par est dou-ce.
> This is of Aucassins and Nicolette.

> Whom would a good ballad please
> By the captive from o'er-seas,
> A sweet song in children's praise,
> Nicolette and Aucassins;
> What he bore for her caress,
> What he proved of his prowess
> For his friend with the bright face?
> The song has charm, the tale has grace,
> And courtesy and good address.
> No man is in such distress,
> Such suffering or weariness,
> Sick with ever such sickness,
> But he shall, if he hear this,
> Recover all his happiness,
>   So sweet it is!

This little thirteenth-century gem is called a "chante-fable," a story partly in prose, partly in verse, to be sung according to musical notation accompanying the words in the single manuscript known, and published in facsimile by Mr. F. W. Bourdillon at Oxford in 1896. Indeed, few poems, old or new, have in the last few years been more reprinted, translated, and discussed, than "Aucassins," yet the discussion lacks interest to the idle tourist, and tells him little. Nothing is known of the author or his date. The second line alone offers a hint, but nothing more. "Caitif" means in the first place a captive, and secondly any unfortunate or wretched man. Critics have liked to think that the word means here a captive to the Saracens, and that the poet, like Cervantes three or four hundred years later, may have been a prisoner to the infidels. What the critics can do, we can do. If liberties can be taken with impunity by scholars, we can take the liberty of supposing that the poet was a prisoner in the crusade of Cœur-de-Lion and Philippe-Auguste; that he had recovered his liberty, with his master, in 1194; and that he passed the rest of his life singing to the old Queen Eleanor or to Richard, at Chinon, and to the lords of all the châteaux in Guienne, Poitiers, Anjou, and Normandy, not to mention England. The living was a pleasant one, as the sunny atmosphere of the Southern poetry proves.

> Dox est li cans; biax est li dis,
> Et cortois et bien asis.

The poet-troubadour who composed and recited *Aucassins* could not have been unhappy, but this is the affair of his private life, and not of ours. What rather interests us is his poetic motive, "courteous love," which gives the tale a place in the direct line between Christian of Troyes, Thibaut-le-Grand, and William of Lorris. Christian of Troyes died in 1175; at least he wrote nothing of a later date, so far as is certainly known. Richard Cœur-de-Lion died in 1199, very soon after the death of his half-sister

Mary of Champagne. Thibaut-le-Grand was born in 1201. William of Lorris, who concluded the line of great "courteous" poets, died in 1260 or thereabouts. For our purposes, *Aucassins* comes between Christian of Troyes and William of Lorris; the trouvère or jogléor, who sang, was a "viel caitif" when the Chartres glass was set up, and the Charlemagne window designed, about 1210, or perhaps a little later. When one is not a professor, one has not the right to make inept guesses, and, when one is not a critic, one should not risk confusing a difficult question by baseless assumptions; but even a summer tourist may without offence visit his churches in the order that suits him best; and, for our tour, *Aucassins* follows Christian and goes hand in hand with Blondel and the châtelain de Coucy, as the most exquisite expression of "courteous love." As one of *Aucassins'* German editors says in his introduction: "Love is the medium through which alone the hero surveys the world around him, and for which he contemns everything that the age prized: knightly honour; deeds of arms; father and mother; hell, and even heaven; but the mere promise by his father of a kiss from Nicolette inspires him to superhuman heroism; while the old poet sings and smiles aside to his audience as though he wished them to understand that Aucassins, a foolish boy, must not be judged quite seriously, but that, old as he was himself, he was just as foolish about Nicolette."

Aucassins was the son of the Count of Beaucaire. Nicolette was a young girl whom the Viscount of Beaucaire had redeemed as a captive of the Saracens, and had brought up as a god-daughter in his family. Aucassins fell in love with Nicolette, and wanted to marry her. The action turned on marriage, for, to the Counts of Beaucaire, as to other counts, not to speak of kings, high alliance was not a matter of choice but of necessity, without which they could not defend their lives, let alone their counties; and, to make Aucassins' conduct absolutely treasonable, Beaucaire was at that time surrounded and besieged, and the Count, Aucassins' father, stood in dire need of his son's help. Aucassins refused to stir unless he could have Nicolette. What were honours to him if Nicolette were not to share them. "S'ele estait empereris de Colstentinoble u d'Alemaigne u roine de France u d'Engletere, si aroit il asses peu en li, tant est france et cortoise et de bon aire et entecie de toutes bones teces." To be empress of "Colstentinoble" would be none too good for her, so stamped is she with nobility and courtesy and high-breeding and all good qualities.

So the Count, after a long struggle, sent for his Viscount and threatened to have Nicolette burned alive, and the Viscount himself treated no better, if he did not put a stop to the affair; and the Viscount shut up Nicolette, and remonstrated with Aucassins: "Marry a king's daughter, or a count's! leave Nicolette alone, or you will never see Paradise!" This at once gave Aucassins the excuse for a charming tirade against Paradise, for which, a century or two later, he would properly have been burned together with Nicolette:—

> En paradis qu'ai je a faire? Je n'i quier entrer mais que
> j'aie Nicolete, ma tres douce amie, que j'aim tant. C'en

paradis ne vont fors tex gens con je vous dirai. Il i vont ci viel prestre et cil vieil clop et cil manke, qui tote jour et tote nuit cropent devant ces autex et en ces vies cruutes, et cil a ces vies capes ereses et a ces vies tatereles vestues, qui sont nu et decauc et estrumele, qui moeurent de faim et d'esci et de froid et de mesaises. Icil vont en paradis; aveuc ciax n'ai jou que faire; mais en infer voil jou aler. Car en infer vont li bel clerc et li bel cevalier qui sont mort as tornois et as rices gueres, et li bien sergant et li franc home. Aveuc ciax voil jou aler. Et si vont les beles dames cortoises que eles ont ii amis ou iii avec leurs barons. Et si va li ors et li agens et li vairs et li gris; et si i vont herpeor et jogleor et li roi del siecle. Avec ciax voil jou aler mais que j'aie Nicolete, ma tres douce amie, aveuc moi.

In Paradise what have I to do? I do not care to go there unless I may have Nicolette, my very sweet friend, whom I love so much. For to Paradise goes no one but such people as I will tell you of. There go old priests and old cripples and the maimed, who all day and all night crouch before altars and in old crypts, and are clothed with old worn-out capes and old tattered rags; who are naked and foot-bare and sore; who die of hunger and want and misery. These go to Paradise; with them I have nothing to do; but to Hell I am willing to go. For, to Hell go the fine scholars and the fair knights who die in tournies and in glorious wars; and the good men-at-arms and the well-born. With them I will gladly go. And there go the fair courteous ladies whether they have two or three friends besides their lords. And the gold and silver go there, and the ermines and sables; and there go the harpers and jongleurs, and the kings of the world. With these will I go, if only I may have Nicolette, my very sweet friend, with me.

Three times, in these short extracts, the word "courteous" has already appeared. The story itself is promised as "courteous"; Nicolette is "courteous"; and the ladies who are not to go to heaven are "courteous." Aucassins is in the full tide of courtesy, and evidently a professional, or he never would have claimed a place for harpers and jongleurs with kings and chevaliers in the next world. The poets of "courteous love" showed as little interest in religion as the poets of the eleventh century had shown for it in their poems of war. Aucassins resembled Christian of Troyes in this, and both of them resembled Thibaut, while William of Lorris went beyond them all. The literature of the "siècle" was always unreligious, from the "Chanson de Roland" to the "Tragedy of Hamlet"; to be "papelard" was unworthy of a chevalier; the true knight of courtesy made nothing of defying the torments of hell, as he defied the lance of a rival, the frowns of society, the threats of parents or the terrors of magic; the perfect, gentle, courteous lover thought of nothing but his love. Whether the object of his love were Nicolette of Beaucaire or Blanche of Castile Mary of Champagne or Mary of Chartres, was a detail which did not affect the devotion of his worship.

So Nicolette, shut up in a vaulted chamber, leaned out at the marble window and sang, while Aucassins, when his father promised that he should have a kiss from Nicolette, went out to make fabulous slaughter of the enemy; and when his father broke the promise, shut himself up in his chamber, and also sang; and the action went on by scenes and interludes, until, one night, Nicolette let herself down from the window, by the help of sheets and towels, into the garden, and, with a natural dislike of wetting her skirts which has delighted every hearer or reader from that day to this, "prist se vesture a l'une main devant et a l'autre deriere si s'escorça por le rousee qu'ele vit grande sor l'erbe si s'en ala aval le gardin"; she raised her skirts with one hand in front and the other behind, for the dew which she saw heavy on the grass, and went off down the garden, to the tower where Aucassins was locked up, and sang to him through a crack in the masonry, and gave him a lock of her hair, and they talked till the friendly night-watch came by and warned her by a sweetly-sung chant, that she had better escape. So she bade farewell to Aucassins, and went on to a breach in the city wall, and she looked through it down into the fosse which was very deep and very steep. So she sang to herself—

> Peres rois de maeste
> Or ne sai quel part aler.
> Se je vois u gaut rame
> Ja me mengeront li le
> Li lions et li sengler
> Dont il i a a plente.
> Father, King of Majesty!
> Now I know not where to flee.
> If I seek the forest free,
> Then the lions will eat me,
> Wolves and wild boars terribly,
> Of which plenty there there be.

The lions were a touch of poetic licence, even for Beaucaire, but the wolves and wild boars were real enough; yet Nicolette feared even them less than she feared the Count, so she slid down what her audience well knew to be a most dangerous and difficult descent, and reached the bottom with many wounds in her hands and feet, "et li san en sali bien en xii lius"; so that blood was drawn in a dozen places; and then she climbed up the other side, and went off bravely into the depths of the forest; an uncanny thing to do by night, as you can still see.

Then followed a pastoral, which might be taken from the works of another poet of the same period, whose acquaintance no one can neglect to make—Adam de la Halle, a Picard, of Arras. Adam lived, it is true, fifty years later than the date imagined for Aucassins, but his shepherds and shepherdesses are not so much like, as identical with, those of the Southern poet, and all have so singular an air of life that the conventional courteous knight fades out beside them. The poet, whether bourgeois, professional, noble, or clerical, never much loved the peasant, and the peasant never much loved him, or any one else. The peasant was a class by himself, and his trait, as a class, was suspicion of everybody and all things, whether material, social, or divine. Naturally he detested his lord, whether temporal or spiritual, because the seigneur and the priest took his earnings, but he was never servile, though a serf; he was far from civil; he was commonly gross. He was cruel, but not more so than his betters; and his morals

were no worse. The object of oppression on all sides,—the invariable victim, whoever else might escape,—the French peasant, as a class, held his own—and more. In fact, he succeeded in plundering Church, Crown, nobility, and bourgeoisie, and was the only class in French history that rose steadily in power and well-being, from the time of the crusades to the present day, whatever his occasional suffering may have been; and, in the thirteenth century, he was suffering. When Nicolette, on the morning after her escape, came upon a group of peasants in the forest, tending the Count's cattle, she had reason to be afraid of them, but instead they were afraid of her. They thought at first that she was a fairy. When they guessed the riddle, they kept the secret, though they risked punishment and lost the chance of reward by protecting her. Worse than this, they agreed, for a small present, to give a message to Aucassins if he should ride that way.

Aucassins was not very bright, but when he got out of prison after Nicolette's escape, he did ride out, at his friends' suggestion, and tried to learn what had become of her. Passing through the woods he came upon the same group of shepherds and shepherdesses:—

> Esmeres et Martinet,
> Fruelins et Johannes,
> Robecons et Aubries,—

who might have been living in the Forest of Arden, so like were they to the clowns of Shakespeare. They were singing of Nicolette and her present, and the cakes and knives and flute they would buy with it. Aucassins jumped to the bait they offered him; and they instantly began to play him as though he were a trout:—

"Bel enfant, dix vos i ait!"

"Dix vos benie!" fait cil qui fu plus enparles des autres.

"Bel enfant," fait il, "redites le cançon que vos disiez ore!"

"Nous n'i dirons," fait cil qui plus fu enparles des autres. "Dehait ore qui por vos i cantera, biax sire!"

"Bel enfant!" fait Aucassins, "enne me connissies vos?"

"Oïl! nos savions bien que vos estes Aucassins, nos damoisiax, mais nos ne somes mie a vos, ains somes au conte."

"Bel enfant, si feres, je vos en pri!"

"Os, por le cuer be!" fait cil. "Por quoi canteroie je por vos, s'il ne me seoit! Quant il n'a si rice home en cest pais sans le cors le conte Garin s'il trovait mes bues ne mes vaces ne mes brebis en ses pres n'en sen forment qu'il fust mie tant hardis por les es a crever qu'il les en ossast cacier. Et por quoi canteroie je por vos s'il ne me seoit?"

"Se dix vos ait, bel enfant, si feres! et tenes x sous que j'ai ci en une borse!"

"Sire les deniers prenderons nos, mais je ne vos canterai mie, car j'en ai jure. Mais je le vos conterai se vos voles."

"De par diu!" faits Aucassins. "Encore aim je mix conter que nient."

"God bless you, fair child!" said Aucassins.

"God be with you!" replied the one who talked best.

"Fair child!" said he, "repeat the song you were just singing."

"We won't!" replied he who talked best among them. "Bad luck to him who shall sing for you, good sir!"

"Fair child," said Aucassins, "do you know me?"

"Yes! we know very well that you are Aucassins, our young lord; but we are none of yours; we belong to the Count."

"Fair child, indeed you'll do it, I pray you!"

"Listen, for love of God!" said he. "Why should I sing for you if it does not suit me? when there is no man so powerful in this country, except Count Garin, if he found my oxen or my cows or my sheep in his pasture or his close, would not rather risk losing his eyes than dare to turn them out! and why should I sing for you, if it does not suit me!"

"So God help you, good child, indeed you will do it! and take these ten sous that I have here in my purse."

"Sire, the money we will take, but I'll not sing to you, for I've sworn it. But I will tell it you, if you like."

"For God's sake!" said Aucassins; "better telling than nothing!"

Ten sous was no small gift! twenty sous was the value of a strong ox. The poet put a high money-value on the force of love, but he set a higher value on it in courtesy. These boors were openly insolent to their young lord, trying to extort money from him, and threatening him with telling his father; but they were in their right, and Nicolette was in their power. At heart they meant Aucassins well, but they were rude and grasping, and the poet used them in order to show how love made the true lover courteous even to clowns. Aucassins' gentle courtesy is brought out by the boors' greed, as the colours in the window were brought out and given their value by a bit of blue or green. The poet, having got his little touch of colour rightly placed, let the peasants go. "Cil qui fu plus enparles des autres," having been given his way and his money, told Aucassins what he knew of Nicolette and her message; so Aucassins put spurs to his horse and cantered into the forest, singing:—

> Se diu plaist le pere fort
> Je vos reverai encore
>   Suer, douce a-mie!
> So please God, great and strong,
> I will find you now ere long,
>   Sister, sweet friend!

But the peasant had singular attraction for the poet. Whether the character gave him a chance for some clever mimicry, which was one of his strong points as a story-teller: or whether he wanted to treat his subjects, like the legendary windows, in pairs; or whether he felt that the forest-scene specially amused his audience, he immediately introduced a peasant of another class, much more strongly coloured, or deeply shadowed. Every one in the audience was—and, for that matter, still would be—familiar with the great forests, the home of half the fairy and nursery tales of Europe, still wild enough and extensive enough to hide in, although they have now comparatively few lions, and not many wolves or wild boars or serpents such as Nicolette feared. Every one saw, without an effort, the young damoiseau riding out with his hound or hawk, looking for game; the lanes under the trees, through the wood, or the thick underbrush before lanes were made; the herdsmen watching their herds, and keeping a sharp lookout for wolves; the peasant seeking lost cattle; the black kiln-men burning charcoal; and in the depths of the rocks or swamps or thickets—the outlaw. Even now, forests like Rambouillet, or Fontainebleau or Compiègne are enormous and wild; one can see Aucassins breaking his way through thorns and branches in search of Nicolette, tearing his clothes and wounding himself "en xl lius u en xxx," until evening approached, and he began to weep for disappointment:—

> Il esgarda devant lui enmi la voie si vit un vallet tel que je vos dirai. Grans estoit et mervellex et lais et hidex. Il avoit une grande hure plus noire qu'une carbouclee, et avoit plus de planne paume entre ii ex, et avoit unes grandes joes et un grandisme nez plat, et une grans narines lees et unes grosses levres plus rouges d'unes carbounees, et uns grans dens gaunes et lais et estoit caucies d'uns housiax et d'uns sollers de buef fretes de tille dusque deseure le genol et estoit afules d'une cape a ii envers si estoit apoiies sor une grande maçue. Aucassins s'enbati sor lui s'eut grand paor quant il le sorvit. . . .

"Baix frere, dix ti ait!"

"Dix vos benie!" fait cil.

"Se dix t'ait, que fais tu ilec?"

"A vos que monte?" fait cil.

"Nient!" fait Aucassins; "je nel vos demant se por bien non."

"Mais pour quoi ploures vos?" fait cil, "et faites si fait doel? Certes se j'estoie ausi rices hom que vos estes, tos li mons ne me feroit mie plorer."

"Ba! me conissies vos!" fait Aucassins.

"Oie! je sai bien que vos estes Aucassins li fix le conte, et se vos me dites por quoi vos plores je vos dirai que je fac ici."

As he looked before him along the way he saw a man such as I will tell you. Tall he was, and menacing, and ugly, and hideous. He had a great mane blacker than charcoal and had more than a full palm-width between his two eyes, and had big cheeks, and a huge flat nose and great broad nostrils, and thick lips redder than raw beef, and large ugly yellow teeth, and was shod with hose and leggings of raw hide laced with bark cord to above the knee, and was muffled in a cloak without lin-ing, and was leaning on a great club. Aucassins came upon him suddenly, and had great fear when he saw him.

"Fair brother, good day!" said he.

"God bless you!" said the other.

"As God help you, what do you here?"

"What is that to you?" said the other.

"Nothing!" said Aucassins; "I ask only from good-will."

"But why are you crying!" said the other, "and mourning so loud? Sure, if I were as great a man as you are, nothing on earth would make me cry."

"Bah! you know me?" said Aucassins.

"Yes, I know very well that you are Aucassins, the count's son: and if you will tell me what you are crying for, I will tell you what I am doing here."

Aucassins seemed to think this an equal bargain. All damoiseaux were not as courteous as Aucassins, nor all "varlets" as rude as his peasants; we shall see how the young gentlemen of Picardy treated the peasantry for no offence at all; but Aucassins carried a softer, Southern temper in a happier climate, and, with his invariable gentle courtesy, took no offence at the familiarity with which the ploughman treated him. Yet he dared not tell the truth, so he invented, on the spur of the moment, an excuse;—he has lost, he said, a beautiful white hound. The peasant hooted—

"Os!" fait cil; "por le cuer que cil sires eut en sen ventre! que vos plorastes por un cien puant! Mal dehait ait qui ja mais vos prisera quant il n'a si rice home en ceste tere se vos peres l'en mandoit x u xv u xx qu'il ne les envoyast trop volontiers et s'en esteroit trop lies. Mais je dois plorer et dol faire?"

"Et tu de quoi frere?"

"Sire, je le vos dirai! J'estoie liues a un rice vilain si caçoie se carue. iiii bues i avoit. Or a iii jors qu'il m'avint une grande malaventure que je perdi le mellor de mes bues Roget le mellor de me carue. Si le vois querant. Si ne mengai ne ne bue iii jors a passes. Si n'os aler a le vile c'on me metroit en prison que je ne l'ai de quoi saure. De tot l'avoir du monde n'ai je plus vaillant que vos vees sor le cors de mi. Une lasse mere avoie; si n'avoit plus vaillant que une keutisele; si li a on sacie de desous le dos; si gist a pur l'estrain; si m'en poise asses plus que demi. Car avoirs va et vient; se j'ai or perdu je gaaignerai une autre fois; si sorrai mon buef quant je porrai, ne ja por çou n'en plorerai. Et vos plorastes por un cien de longaigne! Mal dehait ait qui mais vos prisera!"

"Certes tu es de bon confort, biax frere! que benois sois tu! Et que valoit tes bues!"

"Sire, xx sous m'en demande on, je n'en puis mie abatre une seule maille."

"Or, tien," fait Aucassins, "xx que j'ai ci en me borse; si sol ten buef!"

"Sire!" fait il, "grans mercies! et dix vos laist trover ce que vox queres!"

"Listen!" said he; "By the heart God had in his body! that you should cry for a stinking dog! Bad luck to him who ever prizes you! When there is no man in this land so great, if your father sent to him for ten or fifteen or twenty, but would fetch them very gladly, and be only too pleased. But I ought to cry and mourn."

"And why you, brother?"

"Sir, I will tell you. I was hired out to a rich farmer to drive his plough. There were four oxen. Now three days ago I had a great misfortune, for I lost the best of my oxen, Roget, the best of my team. I am looking to find him. I've not eaten or drunk these three days past. I dare n't go to the town, for they would put me in prison, as I've nothing to pay with. In all the world I've not the worth of anything but what you see on my body. I've a poor old mother who owned nothing but a feather mattress, and they've dragged it from under her back, so she lies on the bare straw; and she troubles me more than myself. For riches come and go; if I lose to-day, I gain to-morrow; I will pay for my ox when I can, and will not cry for that. And you cry for a filthy dog! Bad luck to him who ever thinks well of you!"

"Truly, you counsel well, good brother! God bless you! And what was your ox worth?"

"Sir, they ask me twenty sous for it. I cannot beat them down a single centime."

"Here are twenty," said Aucassins, "that I have in my purse! Pay for your ox!"

"Sir!" said he; "many thanks! and God grant you find what you seek!"

The little episode was thrown in without rhyme or reason to the rapid emotion of the love-story, as though the jongleur were showing his own cleverness and humour, at the expense of his hero, as jongleurs had a way of doing; but he took no such liberties with his heroine. While Aucassins tore through the thickets on horseback, crying aloud, Nicolette had built herself a little hut in the depths of the forest:—

Ele prist des flors de lis
Et de l'erbe du garris
Et de le foille autresi;
Une belle loge en fist,
Ainques tant gente ne vi.
Jure diu qui ne menti
Se par la vient Aucassins
Et il por l'amor de li
Ne si repose un petit
Ja ne sera ses amis
          N'ele s'a-mie.
So she twined the lilies' flower,
Roofed with leafy branches o'er,
Made of it a lovely bower,
With the freshest grass for floor,
Such as never mortal saw.
By God's Verity, she swore,
Should Aucassins pass her door,
And not stop for love of her,

> To repose a moment there,
> He should be her love no more,
>   Nor she his dear!

So night came on, and Nicolette went to sleep, a little distance away from her hut. Aucassins at last came by, and dismounted, spraining his shoulder in doing it. Then he crept into the little hut, and lying on his back, looked up through the leaves to the moon, and sang:—

> Estoilete, je te voi,
> Que la lune trait a soi.
> Nicolete est aveuc toi,
> M'amiete o le blond poil.
> Je quid que dix le veut avoir
> Por la lumiere de soir
> Que par li plus clere soit.
> Vien, amie, je te proie!
> Ou monter vauroie droit,
> Que que fust du recaoir.
> Que fuisse lassus o toi
> Ja te baiseroi estroit.
> Se j'estoie fix a roi
> S'afferies vos bien a moi
>   Suer douce amie!
> I can see you, little star,
> That the moon draws through the air.
> Nicolette is where you are,
> My own love with the blonde hair.
> I think God must want her near
> To shine down upon us here
> That the evening be more clear.
> Come down, dearest, to my prayer,
> Or I climb up where you are!
> Though I fell, I would not care.
> If I once were with you there
> I would kiss you closely, dear!
> If a monarch's son I were
> You should all my kingdom share,
>   Sweet friend, sister!

How Nicolette heard him sing, and came to him and rubbed his shoulder and dressed his wounds as though he were a child; and how in the morning they rode away together, like Tennyson's "Sleeping Beauty,"—

> O'er the hills and far away
> Beyond their utmost purple rim,
> Beyond the night, beyond the day,

singing as they rode, the story goes on to tell or to sing in verse—

> Aucassins, li biax, li blons,
> Li gentix, li amorous,
> Est issous del gaut parfont,
> Entre ses bras ses amors
> Devant lui sor son arçon.
> Les ex li baise et le front,
> Et le bouce et le menton.
> Elle l'a mis a raison.
> "Aucassins, biax amis dox,
> "En quel tere en irons nous?"
> "Douce amie, que sai jou?"
> "Moi ne caut u nous aillons,

> "En forest u en destor
> "Mais que je soie aveuc vous."
> Passent les vaus et les mons,
> Et les viles et les bors
> A la mer vinrent au jor,
> Si descendent u sablon
>   Les le rivage.
> Aucassins, the brave, the fair,
> Courteous knight and gentle lover,
> From the forest dense came forth;
> In his arms his love he bore
> On his saddle-bow before;
> Her eyes he kisses and her mouth,
> And her forehead and her chin.
> She brings him back to earth again:
> "Aucassins, my love, my own,
> "To what country shall we turn?"
> "Dearest angel, what say you?
> "I care nothing where we go,
> "In the forest or outside,
> "While you on my saddle ride."
> So they pass by hill and dale,
> And the city, and the town,
> Till they reach the morning pale,
> And on sea-sands set them down,
>   Hard by the shore.

There we will leave them, for their further adventures have not much to do with our matter. Like all the romans, or nearly all, *Aucassins* is singularly pure and refined. Apparently the ladies of courteous love frowned on coarseness and allowed no licence. Their power must have been great, for the best romans are as free from grossness as the "Chanson de Roland" itself, or the church glass, or the illuminations in the manuscripts; and as long as the power of the Church ruled good society, this decency continued. As far as women were concerned, they seem always to have been more clean than the men, except when men painted them in colours which men liked best. . . .

John R. Reinhard (essay date 1926)

SOURCE: "The Literary Background of the *Chantefable*," in *Speculum*, Vol. 1, No. 2, April, 1926, pp. 157-69.

[*In the essay below, Reinhard asserts that the form of* Aucassin et Nicolette *did not originate with the work, but is indebted to the traditions readily available to the author—that is, to the literary traditions of Greece and Rome.*]

The new edition of ***Aucassin et Nicolette*** by Mario Roques[1] once more offers occasion for the discussion of its peculiar literary form, that of alternate prose and verse. In his Introduction, Roques briefly discusses "cette forme *originale* et *unique* dans la littérature du moyen âge,"[2] and after rejecting the various definitions of ***Aucassin*** as a "*roman*," a "*conte*," a "*nouvelle*," a "*fabliau*," and a "*récit*," he arrives at the conclusion that it is a "*mime*."[3] If a technical name must be found for the type of literature which ***Aucassin*** represents, why not call it, as did its author, a *cantefable*? If it is felt that this term needs explanation, we can find none better than that of Gaston Paris, who has definitely explained the *chantefable* as "ce mélange de prose et de vers, de morceaux où l'on *chante,* et de morceaux où l'on *dit et conte et fable.*"[4]

So far as we know, *Aucassin et Nicolette is* the only specimen of French literature in the Middle Ages which is composed of verse *andrsquoand* prose, and thus it is rightly called unique. But if we view the *chantefable* as being in its elementary form simply a literary style in which prose and verse operate together as a unit in narrative function, and if we disregard the special characteristic of musical notation on the manuscript of *Aucassin,* then we shall be able to match it with other pieces of literature written in this style in both earlier and later times. Examples of prose-and-verse in which the verse is purely adventitious and does not form an integral part of the narrative vehicle have not been included among the following quotations. That *Aucassin* represents a type of literature which in France was eventually attracted to the theatre, is a matter we shall not discuss. Our interest in the document lies not so much in its successors as in its literary antecedents, and these, we shall show, were of various types.

Scholars who have treated the various problems offered by *Aucassin et Nicolette* have not neglected the matter of its form.[5] A variety of opinion prevails on this subject. G. Gröber (*Grundriss,* II, i, 529) and H. Heiss[6] consider the form to be the invention of the author. Ten Brink explained the prose as having grown out of a commentary on the verse.[7] H. Suchier seems to consider the form as a transition stage between the verse novel and the prose novel.[8] Other scholars are of the opinion that the form of *Aucassin* derives from Arabic or other oriental literary models. W. Hertz[9] in his notes to *Aucassin et Nicolette* gives some oriental analogies. K. Burdach seems to hold this theory also.[10] It is very ably, though inconclusively, supported by L. Jordan,[11] whereas W. Suchier in the *Einleitung* to his ninth edition of *Aucassin et Nicolette* reverts to Gröber's opinion as to the form, while postulating an Arabico-Byzantine source for the story.[12] A still different opinion as to the origin of the mixed prose and verse form of *Aucassin* is held by W. Meyer-Lübke.[13] He discards the opinions of Gröber, Suchier, and Hertz, mentions the Provençal *razos* and the *Vita Nuova* as showing similar form. But when considering the origin of Old-French narrative, says Meyer-Lübke, we are inclined to look to the west and to the Celts, whose literature likewise shows prose interspersed with verse. He then quotes several passages (without references) from R. Thurneysen's *Sagen aus dem alten Irland.*[14]

But this scholar's Irish parallels prove no more than do Hertz's oriental analogues. Meyer-Lübke might have quoted—as he does not—numerous passages from Old-Norse literature, of which mixed prose and verse is one of the outstanding stylistic characteristics.[15]

That *Aucassin et Nicolette* owes its form to oriental, Celtic, or Old-Norse literature still remains to be proved by documentary evidence. On the other hand, it seems to be a reasonable conjecture that the mediaeval artistic author, where he did not invent—and he was not inventive, whatever other virtues he may have possessed—followed the guidance of familiar literary models. So far as the present writer is aware, the Mohammedan Empire, Ireland, Iceland, however many stories and plots they may have furnished, did not contribute any traditions of literary workmanship to the mediaeval world.[16] The mediaeval author did not deliberately look into far corners for literary guides: rarely did he possess the learning that would have enabled him to do so, even if he had thought of it. What he did do was, in our opinion, to make use of what lay ready to his hand—the literary traditions of antiquity in which he had been reared. The aim of this article is to show what literary traditions of Greece and Rome lay behind the prose-and-verse form of writing as illustrated by *Aucassin et Nicolette.*

If the form of *Aucassin et Nicolette* has piqued the interest of students of French literature, the form of the *Vita Nuova,* which Dante followed again in the *Convito,* has piqued that of students of Italian literature. From Dante and his contemporaries, Francesco da Barberino and Brunetto Latini, it is but a step to Sedulius Scotus (fl. *ca.* 850), and another step to Boëthius and Martianus Capella, with whom we have arrived at the borders of Roman literature. Continuing our search backward through the centuries we are halted by the hilarious personalities of Lucius Apuleius and Petronius Arbiter, with the latter's somewhat heavier contemporary, Seneca the Younger. But our search does not end here, for Cicero directs our attention to Varro and Menippus.[17]

With Menippus of Gadara, who flourished *ca.* 280 B.C., our quest comes to an end. He was the author, and apparently the originator, as far as the Occident is concerned,[18] of a type of literature in mixed prose and verse called after him the *Satura Menippea.*[19] In this style "he interspersed jocular and commonplace topics with moral maxims and philosophical doctrines, and may have added contemporary pictures, though this is uncertain." His works seem to have perished almost completely.[20] Still we may perhaps judge his style, even though imperfectly, from the Menippean Satires of Varro, who, as we have seen, imitated him.

The *Saturae Menippeae* of M. Terentius Varro (116-28 B.C.) are written in mixed prose and verse and sometimes alternate prose and verse. He treats all kinds of subjects just as they come to hand, "often with much grossness, but with sparkling point." Though the *Saturae* originally extended to one hundred and fifty books, only fragments now remain, comprising 591 lines in all. This fragmentary state makes illustration difficult, but the piece called *Est Modus Matulae* may serve our purpose. This seems to be an altercation between a partisan of wine-drinking and a prohibitionist who laments the bad example set by the gods.

> I. vino nihil iucundius quisquam bibit:
>   hoc aegritudinem ad medendam invenerunt,
>   hoc hilaritatis dulce seminarium,
>   hoc continet coagulum convivia

IV. dolia atque apothecas, tricliniaris, Melicas, Calenas
obbas et Cumanos calices

V. non vides ipsos deos, siquando volunt gustare vinum, derepere ad hominum fana et tamen tum ipsi illi
Libero simpuio vinum dari?[21]

Here we see prose and verse acting together in narrative
function in spite of the fragmentary state of the quotation.
A better illustration of the Menippean style is given by the
Apocolocyntosis of Seneca (3-65 A.D.). This
'Pumpkinification' of the Emperor Claudius "is a bitter
satire on the apotheosis of that heavy prince." When Claudius appears in heaven, Hercules is told off to interview
him.

VII. Tum Hercules 'audi me' inquit 'tu desine fatuari.
venisti huc, ubi mures ferrum rodunt. citius mihi verum,
ne tibi alogias excutiam.' et quo terribilior esset, tragi-
cus fit et ait:

'exprome propere, sede qua genitus cluas,
hoc ne peremptus stipite ad terram accidas;
haec clava reges saepe mactavit feros.
quid nunc profatu vocis incerto sonas?
quae patria, quae gens mobile eduxit caput?
edissere.'

. . . haec satis animose et fortiter, nihilo minus mentis
suae non est et timet μωρου πληγνν. Claudius ut vidit
virum valentem, oblitus nugarum intellexit neminem
Romae sibi parem fuisse, illic non habere se idem gra-
tiae: gallum in suo sterquilino plurimum posse. itaque
quantum intellegi potuit, haec visus est dicere:[22]

Here we see more clearly than in Varro that the verse continues and advances the narrative in prose. The fact that
the prose-and-verse style was used by Menippus, Varro,
Seneca, and, in a somewhat different fashion, by Petronius
as a vehicle for satire is not prejudicial to the purpose for
which these passages are quoted. We have already been
told that the form was used as a vehicle for drama in *Aucassin et Nicolette;* later we shall see it used as a medium
of literary criticism and didactics also.

In 65 A.D. Petronius Arbiter, declining to "endure the suspense of hope and fear," himself opened his veins in a
bath, bequeathing to his master Nero—so the story goes—a
fearful revenge in the *Satiricon.* The incident of En-
colpius's rage at the perfidy of Ascyltos and Giton will illustrate Petronius's use of the prose-and-verse style.

LXXX. . . . fulminatus hac pronuntiatione, sic ut eram,
sine gladio in lectulum decidi, et attulissem mihi dam-
natus manus, si non inimici victoriae invidissem.
egreditur superbus cum praemio Ascyltos et paulo ante
carissimum sibi commilitonem fortunaeque etiam si-
militudine parem in loco peregrino destituit abiectum.

nomen amicitiae sic, quatenus expedit, haeret;
calculus in tabula mobile ducit opus.
cum fortuna manet, vultum servatis, amici;
cum cecidit, turpi vertitis ora fuga.
grex agit in scaena mimum: pater ille vocatur,

filius hic, nomen divitis ille tenet.
mox ubi ridendas inclusit pagina partes,
vera redit facies, dum simulata perit.

LXXXI. nec diu tamen lacrimis indulsi. . . .[23]

By the time of Lucius Apuleius (125 (?)-200 (?) A.D.), the
prose-and-verse style was no longer a novelty in Latin literature. It may have been used in other Milesian tales—
now lost to use—than those of Petronius. The use made of
it in the *Metamorphoseon* represents rather a survival than
an active continuation of the style. Since there is only one
poem in the whole work (iv, 22)—and that an oracle,
which would naturally be pronounced in verse—space
need not be taken to quote from Apuleius here.

Somehow or other the style was kept alive in Latin literature for the next two hundred years, so that ca. 410-427
Martianus Capella was able to use it with vigor and effect
in his *de Nuptiis Philologiae et Mercurii.*[24] The following
passage from that fanciful allegory describes the bridal array of the *doctissima virgo* Philologia:

. . . At cingulum, quo pectus annecteret, sibi prudens
mater exsoluit et, ne Philologia ipsius Phronesis careret
ornatibus, eius pectori, quo uerius comeretur, appoint.
calceos praeterea ex papyro textili subligavit nequid
eius membra pollueret morticinum. acerra autem multo
aromate grauidata eademque candenti manus uirginis
onerantur.

et iam tunc roseo subtexere sidera peplo
coeperat ambrosium promens Aurora pudorem,
cum creperum lux alma micat, gemmata Dione
cum nitet, aurato uel cum fit Phosphorus astro.
tunc candens tenero glaciatur rore pruina
et matutina greges quatiunt in pascua caulas,
languida mordaces cum pulsant pectora curae
et fugit expulsus Lethaea ad litora somnus.

Ecce ante fores quidam dulcis sonus multifidis suauita-
tibus cietur, quem Musarum conuenientium chorus im-
pendens nuptialibus sacramentis modulationis doctae
tinnitibus concinebat.[25]

A greater man and a greater literary artist than Martianus
was Anicius Manlius Boëthius Severinus, ca. 480-524.
The richness of the *Consolatio Philosophiae* makes the selection of an illustrative passage difficult, but Prosa 2 (*ad
fin.*) and Metrum 2 of Book ii may serve our purpose. Attention is called to the fact that the prose and verse are exceptionally close knit, and that the latter not only advances
the narrative, but invests it with a dramatic intensity:

Nonne adulescentulus in Iouis limine iacere didicisti?
Quid si uberius de bonorum parte sumpsisti? Quid si a
te non tota discessi? Quid si haec ipsa mei mutabilitas
iusta tibi causa est sperandi meliora? Tamen ne animo
contabescas et intra commune omnibus regnum locatus
proprio uiuere iure desideres.

Si quantas rapidis flatibus incitus
　　　Pontus uersat harenas
Aut quot stelliferis edita noctibus

Caelo sidera fulgent
Tantas fundat opes nec retrahat manum
Pleno copia cornu,
Humanum miseras haud ideo genus
Cesset flere querellas.
Quamuis uota libens excipiat deus
Multi prodigus auri
Et claris auidos ornet honoribus,
Nil iam parta uidentur,
Sed quaesita uorans saeua rapacitas
Altos pandit hiatus.
Quae iam praecipitem frena cupidinem
Certo fine retentent,
Largis cum potius muneribus fluens
Sitis ardescit habendi?
Numquam diues agit qui trepidus gemens
Sese credit egentem.[26]

But we are still far from the year 1225. Is there anything between the beginning of the sixth century and the beginning of the thirteenth which bridges the gap? Did Martianus and Boëthius, representing the culmination of an anterior period, also fructify a suceeding one? Or did the tradition of the prose-and-verse style sink too far beneath the surface of literary usage to have any effect on such a work as *Aucassin et Nicolette*? The facts are that Martianus's manual was constantly studied in the schools, wherever there was a school, from Charlemagne's revival of studies throughout the Middle Ages. Indeed, the Schoolmen occupied themselves with a controversy over the respective claims of the Classics themselves and those of the Liberal Arts as represented by the *de Nuptiis*. It was a favorite book of Joannes Scottus (*ca.* 810-*ca.* 875), who wrote a commentary on it. In the same century Martianus was attacked by Prudentius, Bishop of Troyes, and Remi of Auxerre commented on him.[27] In the tenth century Walter of Speier shows acquaintance with his work; Notker Labeo († 1022) translated it. Saxo Grammaticus in the twelfth century copied his *prosimetrum* in the *Gesta Danorum*. Alain de Lille shows his influence in the *Anti-Claudianus*.

As in the case of Martianus, the tradition and influence of Boëthius was constant throughout the Middle Ages. Sedulius Scottus (fl. *ca.* 850) composed a *Liber de Rectoribus Christianis,* modelling the form on the *Consolatio*. He begins his work with a poem, and recapitulates the contents of each of the twenty prose chapters, except the last, in verse. King Alfred the Great made a translation of the *Consolatio* about 888. Provençal literature contains a version of it in 257 decasyllables, dated *ca.* 1000. Alfanus, Archbishop of Salerno (1058-1085), imitated Boëthius's verse. Notker Labeo translated some of his tracts. In the twelfth century his *prosimetrum* was copied by Bernard Silvester of Tours in his *de Mundi Universitate*. Alain de Lille (†1203) shows direct influence from the *Consolatio* in the mixed prose and verse of his *de Planctu Naturae*. It was translated into French in the twelfth century by Simon de Fraisne, and in the thirteenth by Jean de Meung. The book was the constant companion of Dante's maturity. If the Schoolmen had not read what lay behind them, namely, the literature of Rome, what would they have had to read?

Thus we see that the use in Latin of a style of literary composition in mixed prose and verse was constant in western Europe from the time of Cicero to the death of Alain de Lille in 1203. The author of *Aucassin* could hardly have avoided encountering the style at home: certainly he did not need to search for it abroad, in the literature of the Celts or the Arabs.

If, now, we were able to find a document written in this style which showed musical notation as well, we should have a still better model for *Aucassin et Nicolette*. It may be that such a document does exist in the *Psalter* of Louis the German, wherein certain *metra* from Boëthius's *Consolatio* have been set to music. This document, which is to be found in a Berlin manuscript, I have not been able to consult.[28]

But it was not only in Latin that *prosimetrum* was cultivated in western Europe. That *cursor mundi*, Brunetto Latini (1210-1294?), resorted to the use of it for didactic purposes in the work known to us as the *Tesoretto*.[29] He intended to write this key to the *Tesoro* entirely in verse, but in chapter five he tells us that, 'when he wishes to treat of things that would be obscure in verse, he will dispose the matter in prose so that it may be understood and learned.' Illustrations are not particularly good, but the following quotation from this chapter will show how these scraps of prose were inserted:

Che ad ogni creatura
Dispose per misura,
Secondo 'l convenete
Suo corso e sua semente;
Ma tanto ne so dire,
Ch' i' le vidi ubbidire,
Finire e 'ncominciare,
Morire e 'ngenerare.

E sappiate che tutte le cose che hanno cominciamento, cioè che furo fatte di alcuna materia, si aranno fine.[30]

The style was used for didactic purposes by Francesco da Barberino (1264-1348) also, in *Del Reggimento e Costumi di Donna*.[31] In this book of edification the author aims to instruct women in the way in which they should behave under various circumstances. A passage from *Parte prima* touching the problem of talkativeness will serve as an illustration.

III. Una donzella parlava' molto. Una fiata a tavola disse uno suo balio: "Tu parli per tutti quegli chessono a tavola." Disse ella: "Mesere, costoro sanno parlare, e però si possono posare; ma io non so, sichè mi conviene parlare per imprendere. . . ."

IV. Ritorno alla materia,
E dico, che non è sì da taciere;
Che altri non parli mai,
Sì c' altri non dicesse: "Ella non parla
Perch' ella è muta,"
Ma dico, da taciere è e da parlare,
Come lo luogo e lo tenpo richiede.[32]

Perhaps the most graceful and artistic use of the *prosimetrum* in modern times has been made by Dante (1265-

1321) in the *Vita Nuova* (*ca.* 1295). Dante's verse is usually but a repetition of what has already been told in prose,[33] or rather, the prose is only an amplified account of what has been said in rhyme. This is especially true in the *Convito* (*ca.* 1308) wherein, even more than in the *Vita Nuova*, prose is the medium of literary criticism of a given verse-text. In some instances in the *Vita Nuova*,[34] however, the verse continues the narrative and forms an integral part thereof:

> XX. Appresso che questa canzone fue alquanto divolgata tra le genti, con ciò fosse cosa che alcuno amico l'udisse, volontade lo mosse a pregare me che io li dovesse dire che è Amore, avendo forse per l'udite parole speranza di me oltre che degna. Onde io, pensando che appresso di cotale trattato bello era trattare alquanto d'Amore, e pensando che l'amico era da servire, propuosi di dire parole ne le quali io trattassi d'Amore; e allora dissi questo sonetto, lo qual comincia: *Amore e 'l cor gentil.*

> Amore e 'l cor gentil sono una cosa,
>   sì come il saggio in suo dittare pone,
>   e così esser l'un sanza l'altro osa
>   com' alma razional sanza ragione.
> Falli natura quand' è amorosa,
>   Amor per sire e 'l cor per sua magione,
>   dentro la qual dormendo si riposa
>   tal volta poca e tal lunga stagione.
> Bieltate appare in saggia donna pui,
>   che piace a gli occhi sì, che dentro al core
>   nasce un disio de la cosa piacente;
>   e tanto dura talora in costui,
>   che fa svegliar lo spirito d'Amore.
>   E simil face in donna omo valente.

Then follows the explanation.

> XXI. Poscia che trattai d'Amore ne la soprascritta rima, vennemi volontade di volere dire anche, in loda di questa gentilissima, parole, per le quali io mostrasse come per lei si sveglia questo Amore, e come non solamente si sveglia là ove dorme, ma là ove non è in potenzia, ella, mirabilmente, operando lo fa venire. E allora dissi questo sonetto, lo quale comincia: *Ne li occhi porta.*

The literary form of *prosimetrum* did not come to an end with Dante. Jacopo Sannazzaro (1458-1530) employed it in his *Arcadia* (1481-86). Here the poems are usually inserts in the form of musical compositions by some one of the assembled company, but there are also some verses used in the way illustrated above.[35] Sir Philip Sidney (1554-86), whose *Countess of Pembroke's Arcadia* (1580-81) appeared in 1590, followed Sannazzaro in this as in other things.[36] Shakespere often varies his blank verse with prose and lyrics. At the close of the sixteenth century Leroy, Gillot, Chrestien, Rapin, Pithou, Passerat and Durant united in writing, in prose and verse, *La Satire Ménippée* (1593), which, by its title, sends our thoughts back to Varro and Menippus.[37] Finally we may note that certain Italian *novellieri*, following the example of Boccaccio (1313-78) in the *Decameron*, adorned their prose with

canzoni. Such were Giovanni Fiorentino (*ca.* 1350-1406), Giovan Francesco Straparola (*ca.* 1480?-1565?) and Giraldi Cinzio (*ca.* 1504-73).[38]

We have now reached—and passed—the period in which ***Aucassin et Nicolette*** was composed, and I have endeavored to show by a sufficient, though not complete, series of examples that the *chantefable* does not stand alone, but forms a member of an extensive body of literature whose tradition was constant in western Europe down to the close of the Middle Ages. With such a persistent anterior and contemporary use of the *prosimetrum* style, the astonishing thing is, not that the author of *Aucassin* should have used it, but that it had no further fortune in France, as it had in Italy.[39]

Notes

1. *Aucassin et Nicolette: Chantefable du xiiie siècle*, éditée par Mario Roques (Paris: Champion, Classiques français du moyen âge, 1925).

2. The italics in this quotation are mine.

3. Roques, *op. cit.*, pp. iv-vi.

4. G. Paris, *Poèmes et Légendes du moyen âge* (Paris, 1900), p. 99.

5. See the bibliography listed by M. Roques on pp. xxix-xxxvi of the work cited above.

6. "Die Form der Cantefable," *Zs. f. franz. Spr. u. Lit.*, XLII (1912), 250 ff.

7. B. ten Brink, *Dauer und Klang* (Strassburg, 1879), p. iv.

8. H. Suchier-A. Birsch Hirschfeld, *Geschichte der französischen Literatur* (2. Aufl., Leipzig und Wien: Bibliographisches Institut, 1913), I, 226, 227. Although he does not say so, he may have had in mind the Ninus fragments and the *erotica* of Parthenius.

9. *Spielmannsbuch* (3d ed., Berlin, 1905), pp. 435-455.

10. *Sitzungsberichte der kgl. preuss. Akad. der Wissenschaften*, phil.-hist. Kl., 1904, p. 899; 1918, p. 1097, note 1.

11. "Die Quelle des Aucassin," *Zs. f. roman. Philol.* XLIV (1924), 291 ff.

12. H. Brunner, *Über Aucassin und Nicolette* (Halle, 1880), pointed out that Aucassin = Al-Kásim, the name of a Moorish king who ruled Cordova between 1018 and 1021.

13. "Aucassin und Nicolette," *Zs. f. roman. Philol.*, XXXIV (1910), 513 ff.

14. Better Celtic illustrations of prose mixed with verse, in which the latter is an indispensable and even dramatic part of the narrative, may be found in English in J. Dunn's translation of the *Táin Bó Cúalnge* (London: Nutt, 1914). For the Irish text of this, together with a German translation, see edition of E. Windisch, *Die altirische Heldensage Táin Bó Cúalnge* (Leipzig: Hirzel, 1905).

15. It would be tedious and pedantic to cite at length; one may mention *Howard the Halt, The Banded Men, The Ere-Dwellers,* and other pieces translated by Morris and Magnússon in the Saga Library. For a detailed study of prose-and-verse in Old-Norse literature the reader is referred to H. A. Bellows, *The Relations between Prose and Metrical Composition in Old Norse Literature* (Harvard diss., 1910). The present state of critical opinion—with the exception of Jordan's article mentioned above—has been admirably summed up by Roques, *op. cit.,* pp. vii-x.

16. The theory that derives Provençal poetry from Arabic poetry is now no longer largely credited.

17. *Academica,* i, 2. See also Quintilian, *Institutiones,* x, 1, 95, Aulus Gellius, *Noctes atticae,* ii, 18.

18. The *Book of Judges,* for example, is written in prose-and-verse.

19. C. Wachsmuth, *Sillographorum graecorum reliquiae* (2d ed., Leipzig, 1885), p. 79, writes: Hic igitur Menippus, quem acerbissime philosophos mortuous irridere videmus in Luciani scriptis, vivos irrisse audimus ex Diogene apud Lucian., *mort. dialog* I 1, conscripsit ad philosophos potissimum sigillandos satiras prosa oratione eam variavit immixtis diversi generis versibus parodiis facetiis. quod ita sese habere, etsi cetera omnia deessent testimonia, iam satis demonstraretur eo quod Varro Menippeus vocatus est ob saturas cynicas, quas ille Menippeas appellavit et composuit, ut ipse ait, 'Menippum imitatus, non interpretatus.'

20. I have not been able to find, as W. C. Wright directs in her *History of Greek Literature* (New York: American Book Co., 1907), p. 378, any fragments of Menippus under Bion in C. Wachsmuth's work cited above; I do find, however, this statement on p. 85 of the *Sillographorum:* "Fati autem invidia factum est, ut Menippi Meliagrique ϛπουδογελοίων librorum paene nihil sit relictum."

21. Cf. *Petronii Saturae et Liber Priapeorum,* 5th ed., F. Bücheler-W. Heraeus (Berlin: Weidmann, 1912), pp. 193, 194.

22. Bücheler-Heraeus, *ed. cit.,* pp. 256, 257.

23. Bücheler-Heraeus, *ed. cit.,* p. 56. A still better illustration is found in chapter CXXXI *ed. cit.,* pp. 102 ff.

24. Ed. A. Dick, *Martianus Capella* (Liepzig: Teubner, 1925).

25. *Ed. cit.,* pp. 48, 49.

26. Ed. H. F. Stewart and E. K. Rand (London: Loeb Library, 1918), pp. 180, 182.

27. John the Scot's commentary on Martianus, discovered by Hauréau among the ninth century MSS once belonging to the monastery of Saint-Germain-des-Prés (*Notices et Extraits des manuscrits de la Bibliothèque nationale* (Paris, 1862), XX (2), 1 ff.), further attests the familiarity with him in this century.

28. Cf. M. Manitius, *Geschichte der Lateinischen Literatur des Mittelalters* (München: Beck, 1911), I, 33 ("Fortleben der *Consolatio*").

29. I have not been able to consult a complete edition of this document; the edition of B. Wiese in *Zs. f. roman. Philol.,* VII (1883), 236 ff., reprinted in the *Bibliotheca Romanica,* Nos. 94, 95, contains no prose. I have used L. Gaiter, *Il Tesoro di Brunetto Latini volgarizzato da Bono Giamboni raffrontato col testo autentico francese edito da P. Chabaille, emendato con mss. ed illustrato* (Bologna, 1878), Vol. I, in the Introduction whereof certain extracts of prose and verse from the *Tesoretto* are found.

30. L. Gaiter, *op. cit.,* I, 173 ff.

31. Ed. Carlo Baudi di Vesme (Bologna, 1875).

32. *Op. cit.,* p. 28. See also *Parte nona,* pp. 273, 279.

33. *Cf. Liber de Rectoribus* of Sedulius, *supra,* p. 165.

34. Text quoted from *Le Opere di Dante,* edited by the Società Dantesca Italiana (Florence: R. Bemporad e Figlio, 1921), pp. 24, 25.

35. Cf. the end of Prosa VIII and Egloga VIII.

36. Cf. ed. E. A. Baker (reprinted by Routledge and Sons: London, 1921), p. 144.

37. J. C. F. Bähr, *Geschichte der Römischen Literatur* (Karlsruhe: 1868), I, 557, § 141, note 19, refers to the *Satira Menippea* of the Dutch classical scholar Justus Lipsius in *J. Lipsii Opera* (Antwerp, 1637 ff.), I, 417 ff. I have not been able to consult this work.

38. The works of these authors may be found in *Raccolta di Novellieri Italiani* (Firenze: Tipografia Borghi e Compagni, 1833-34), II, 2225 ff., 1287 ff., 1753 ff., except the *Piacevoli Notti* of Straparola, edited by G. Rua, Bologna, 1898-1908.

39. Rutebeuf's *Dit de l'Herberie,* consisting of a piece of prose and a piece of poetry, is not a *chantefable.* The *Satire Ménippée* ignores native mediaeval tradition and is inspired by classical antiquity. Examples of narrative *verse* interspersed with lyrics are afforded by *Cleomadès, Meliacin* and *Guillaume de Dole.* The Provençal *razo* contains a prose dedication to a poem. Further examples of a bastard sort of rhyme-prose may be found by consulting the Index of Manitius, *op. cit. supra, sub voce* "Reimprosa."

Robert Harden (essay date 1966)

SOURCE: "*Aucassin et Nicolette* as Parody," in *Studies in Philology,* Vol. 63, No. 1, January, 1966, pp. 1-9.

[*In the following essay, Harden contends that the use of inversion, particularly in terms of character, in* Aucassin et Nicolette *undermines the traditional plots and characters of the idyllic novel.*]

It has long been traditional to consider *Aucassin et Nicolette* as a piece of literature which, although offering some problems as to its actual literary genre, provided, as far as its protagonists were concerned, the purest example imaginable of characters motivated by idyllic love. Nevertheless, in spite of this generally acknowledged view, certain equivocal actions on the part of the youthful couple have always puzzled and morally distressed editors, translators and scholars in general. As a result of this, efforts have frequently been made to make both the principal characters and their behavior more respectable. Translators, both into modern French and into English, have been particularly guilty of this prudery. One of the early members of this group, A. Bida, for example, went so far, in his modern French version,[1] as to suppress an apparently inappropriate but yet very characteristic episode, that which took place in *Torelore,* on the grounds, presumably, that it was offensive and did not conform to his notions of the conduct of true lovers. With parallel objects in view, two translators into English, F. W. Bourdillon[2] and Andrew Lang,[3] either struggled, as in the case of the first, to rationalize into acceptable conduct some quite irrational and absurd actions on the part of the hero and his sweetheart, or, as in the case of the second, chose to distort the work through a bias of unrelieved sentimentality. In a similar, if indirect, way, other scholars, while primarily engaged in attempts to discover Arabic,[4] Byzantine,[5] epic,[6] classic[7] or folklore[8] origins for at least part of the tale, sought to bestow a certain noble gravity upon all the activities of the young couple. Likewise, Mme. Lot-Borodine, to whom it was a matter of prime concern to compress *Aucassin et Nicolette* into the mould of the idyllic novel, attempted valiantly to bring into line with her original concept of the work certain inconsistencies, to her way of thinking, in the plot. She was exceedingly disconcerted by two incidents in Aucassin's life which scarcely revealed him as an admirable lover. The first of these concerned his conduct during the aforementioned *Torelore* episode; the second, his behavior after the capture of his betrothed when he refused to search for her. Mme. Lot-Borodine noted that other scholars had faced the same dilemma and she cited, along with her own, their explanations. In the case of the first incident, she contented herself with the statement that the action 'a tout à fait l'air d'une bonne farce, introduite dans le récit pour en rompre la monotonie et égayer le public.'[9] In the case of the second she accepted, among others, the reasoning of M. Bourdillon who claimed that Aucassin's lack of gallantry was based on the fact that 'le seigneur de Beaucaire ne peut pas courir le monde, ainsi que l'avait fait le fils du comte de Beaucaire.'[10] It is evident that these explanations represented strained and unsatisfactory deductions on the part of both authors, determined to salvage the story for the sake of idealised love and utopian gallantry. Even Mario Roques who produced two separate and well-received editions of the *chantefable* and who hinted at some possible comic intention of the author when he said that the poet did not imitate the literature of the day 'sans quelque intention parodique,'[11] still persisted in referring to the work as 'cette naïve histoire."[12] It was Professor U. T. Holmes, Jr.,[13] to whom we are particularly in-

debted, who indicated most clearly that the author of *Aucassin et Nicolette* was consciously mocking the stock-in-trade of medieval writers whether it applied to genres, such as the saint's life and the epic, or to overworked themes such as the divided lovers' motive. He also saw parody in the use of the seven-syllable line instead of the usual eight-syllable line of ballad poetry. It is our intention to elaborate upon these suggestions and to indicate that the apparent lapses or inversions in the tone of the book and in the conduct of the protagonists are not exceptional but rather typical of the entire work and that this *chantefable* is above all a parody of the idyllic novel at least as far as plot and characters are concerned.

Inversion, especially in character, has always been an effective device for parody, one in which the great are made small and the small great, in which the solemn are made absurd and the absurd solemn, in which the ideal are made ridiculous and the ridiculous ideal. It is particularly telling when it is used within the rather rigid conventions of a form such as the idyllic novel where it throws into relief the exaggerated and fatuous nature of the hero's or heroine's conduct. It is, we believe, the very method and intention of the author of *Aucassin et Nicolette* as he mocks the vapid plots and equally vapid personages of the idyllic novel. An examination of the behaviour and thoughts of the two principal characters, we feel, can illustrate this, and we begin with the hero.

Our first view of Aucassin is scarcely prepossessing. We observe him as a petulant, mooning juvenile who throws a childish tantrum because his father denies him Nicolette. Neither Flor nor Pyramus, his ideal contemporaries, behaved with such lack of masculine dignity when they were deprived of their ladies as does Aucassin. Moreover, in an act which inverts both traditionally chivalric and filial virtues, he takes vengeance on his father by refusing to defend his homeland which is about to succumb to an invasion.[14] Left alone, he sets about musing on the pleasures of the afterworld, not however, of Heaven but of Hell, and as before, the author seizes the opportunity to depict an inverted idyllic hero. For, in what would appear to be a parody on the habitual manner of representing the yearnings of saints for the bliss of Paradise, the noble Aucassin cries out that he prefers the joys of a physical union in Hades in the company of other knights, clerks and their numerous sweethearts to a dull spiritual existence in Paradise.[15] He is, however, willing to bargain for his pleasure on earth so that when his father promises him his lady if he will fight, he is amenable under such circumstances to honoring his duty.

The battle sequence which follows is a wild satire on such often repeated scenes in the *chansons de geste.* But in the actual struggle it would seem that Aucassin quite forgets that his reunion with Nicolette depends on his victory at arms, for he neglects his horse and the business of riding. He allows his reins to fall and permits the animal to run helter-skelter into the midst of the fray, so that he is easily captured. Then, fearing he will be decapitated, he is moved

Dancers performing in Wendy Toye's ballet "Aucassin and Nicolette," at the Duke of York Theatre, London, England.

to make the inane observation that without his head he will be unable to speak to Nicolette. Suddenly, however, he is roused and begins to strike out indiscriminately, being compared unflatteringly, in an epic image, to a boar attacked by dogs. Then, just as capriciously, he gallops away from the field of battle with all possible haste. When Count Bougar de Valence rides up to him at a place far from the actual scene of combat, Aucassin, in a manner no genuine knight could condone, beats him over the head without the formality of a challenge and seizes him.[16] Such actions have all the impossible and hysterical valour of a Chaplinesque comedy.

Later when Aucassin's father refuses to fulfil his share of the pledge by which his son is to have Nicolette, the hero becomes a blatant traitor, releasing the enemy and urging war against his own people, an incredible piece of behaviour for a son, a knight and a king elect. For his action, he suffers the humiliation of being thrown into his father's prison.[17]

At this juncture, indeed, both the protagonists are in jail, Nicolette having been placed there as a precautionary mat-

ter. But while Aucassin mopes, presumably on the ground floor of his prison Nicolette has to knot sheets together in order to make a perilous descent from an upper room in her high, formidably solid tower, an exploit more suited surely to a male.[18] Furthermore, despite the danger of being burned alive if captured, she makes her way painfully to Aucassin's tower which by ironic contrast is in such a decrepit state that Nicolette can put 'sun cief par mi une creveure.'[19] From her uncomfortable and hazardous position on the ground outside his cell she can hear her lamenting lover and engages him in urgent conversation. But at such a moment which at the very least calls for no dalliance and in any genuine idyllic novel would have been followed by action, Aucassin indulges first in an exposition of the horrors of being cuckolded, a subject more suited to a farce or a *fabliau,* and then, in a discussion with his sweetheart as to who love more profoundly, men or women, which would seem to be a parody of the lyric form known as the *desbat.* With marvelous irony, considering Aucassin's inactivity, lack of initiative and less dangerous situation, the poet has him insist on the greater profundity of the male emotion in comparison to that of the female.[20] Moreover during this most inopportune intellec-tualising, Nicolette is almost captured. She is obliged to make a dolorous flight through the moat and into the beast-haunted forest.[21]

Eventually when it is believed that Nicolette is lost, Au-cassin is released from prison. But does he go at once in hot pursuit of his lady as if to verify the protested depth of his affection? No, he goes back to the castle and continues to brood until a knight reminds him finally that his sweet-heart could possibly be found if efforts to search for her were made.[22]

Having prepared and mounted his horse Aucassin finds that his journey takes him to the meeting place of the same shepherds with whom Nicolette had earlier talked. During the scene between them the poet takes the occa-sion to underline his satirical intent further. For he inverts the deference to be expected between one social order and another and has the shepherds address their lord's son with impertinent disdain and in saucy tones. The latter, in typical fashion, accepts the derision unprotestingly.[23]

Immediately following this incident occurs the celebrated encounter between Aucassin and the cowherd which in many ways duplicates the satric aspect of the preceding one. Here we have to picture to ourselves two huge males each weeping over the loss of his 'beast,' the *bouvier* for his ox and Aucassin for his *beste*. For in an evident at-tempt to link the two men in their love stories, the author has had Nicolette call herself a *beste*[24] when telling the shepherds what Aucassin is to seek in the forest. Each love tale mocks the other. As a lover, Aucassin is no supe-rior to the *bouvier*. Similarly, as objects of affection, there is, apparently, little choice between Nicolette and the ox.

Eventually, the hero finds Nicolette, in a shelter which, of course, she, not he, has built and thereupon he spends his time complaining of his misfortunes and injuries while she, the stoic, keeps her silence.[25] Furthermore, when they are about to flee from their precarious location, Nicolette quite justifiably asks their destination. To this Aucassin can only muster, 'que sai jou?'[26] Flor, Pyramus, Galeran de Bretagne, Guillaume of *L'Escoufle* and Guillaume de Pal-erne, all fellow lovers of the supposedly same idyllic school, never exercised such indecision or such lack of concern for the well-being of their ladies. Aucassin is a veritable anti-hero.

The aimless wanderings of the couple bring them to the kingdom of *Torelore*. There once again the poet selects an episode which is an inversion of accepted social conven-tions and as in the case of the *bouvier*, he also creates a character who parallels Aucassin in his conduct. For the hero, although he abuses the king of this curious land for his *couvade*,[27] has been equally negligent and inverted in his duties towards his lady, allowing her to instigate all the arrangements for their escape while he, like a female, ac-cepts protection and deference as his prerogatives.

Aucassin's lecturing and beating of the king is followed by a parody on justice in war in which the author once more inverts the hero's virtues as a knight and lover. For

he is shown to be capable of gaining a victory in battle only if he can viciously wield a sword against opponents whose sole weapons are baked apples, cheeses and eggs.[28]

Following this episode the couple are captured by Sa-racens and placed in separate boats. In typical fashion Nicolette, the real hero of the tale, has to submit to a con-tinuance of her miseries while Aucassin, lying in a boat which like him wanders about aimlessly, fortuitously reaches the security of his homeland.[29] There he assumes the rank of his deceased father and does absolutely noth-ing to find or rescue his sweetheart beyond the very be-lated proposal to send a messenger, ironically enough the disguised Nicolette, to search for her.[30] In this last gesture, if such it can be called, Aucassin reaches the zenith of his *proueces*[31] so sarcastically proclaimed in the opening verse.

As for Nicolette, much of the inversion in her character has already been exposed in discussing that of her lover. However the author on several occasions also burlesques the type of heroine, sweet, infinitely patient, impossibly pure which she is supposed to represent. On one occasion she is portrayed as a virtual saint in an obvious parody of the miracles attributed to such people. Aucassin tells of how one day she came to the bed of a pilgrim from Lim-ousin who was deathly ill. Gradually she lifted her gar-ment from various areas of her body until one leg was fi-nally exposed. At the sight of this limb the sick man was instantly cured and rose from his bed.[32] Such a tale is wor-thy of a *fabliau*.

Much closer to the general tone of inversion which has been noted in previous paragraphs is the episode dealing with Nicolette's escape from Carthage and her disguise as a *jongleur*. The first fact to observe is that once again it is she who is obliged to escape while her sweetheart reposes in comfort in his house, a total reversal of the usual situa-tion in idyllic novels where the hero customarily searches for his love who, although a prisoner, generally enjoys the sumptuous physical ease of an oriental court. The second is Nicolette's decision to assume the disguise of a male, that is, of a *jongleur* and not that of a *jongleresse*. Eventu-ally she even manages to apply to herself, in her complete absorption in her unnatural role, such masculine adjectives as *preus*.[33]

This parody by inversion of accepted character traits and dramatic situations may be also extended to the very names of the chief personalities. For Aucassin, the French hero, bears an Arabic name[34] whereas Nicolette, the North Afri-can heroine, bears a French one.

Finally the language and the form of **Aucassin et Nicolette** may also be enlisted in an attempt to underline our thesis. Reference has already been made to some of the elements in the plot which resemble those of the *fabliau*. With these in mind it does not seem entirely coincidental that the lan-guage of this genre is the same Picard dialect, in most cases, as that of **Aucassin et Nicolette,** that its tone is mocking and satiric and that it is frequently used to parody revered personages and types in the same fashion as we have found the case to be in the work under discussion here. As a consequence it does not appear exaggerated to assume that the author of *Aucassin et Nicolette* coming from the same region as the *fabliau* and writing in the same dialect, should also be influenced by the attitudes to life and literature which produced that genre.

The form of *Aucassin et Nicolette* with its distinctive combination of prose and poetry, along with fragments of music to be utilized in singing it, has been the subject of much speculation.[35] Again bearing in mind the Picard speech, we are moved to note that it was from the district of this dialect that the earliest secular dramas arose in Old French and that sometimes these works also combined dialogue, verse and music as in the case of the *Jeu de Robin et Marion*. As a consequence we would suggest that *Aucassin et Nicolette* has all the possibilities of histrionic interpretations, maybe as a dramatic monologue with vocal interpolations, maybe as part of a musical comedy or a satiric revue. Indeed we even begin to suspect that the creation of a special title, *chantefable* for this genre, was in some way a joke since it is apparently the only work of its kind to be classified under this distinctive form.

There has been no intention in this discussion to denigrate the qualities of *Aucassin et Nicolette* as a piece of literature. We have hoped rather that this examination would reveal the complete unity of tone, plot, and character in this entirely delightful work where the author attempts, principally by inversion, to parody, in particular, the extremes of the idyllic novel, and, in general, all that was, to his mind, sanctimonious, fatuously idealized, overworked and vainglorious in the literature of his day.

Notes

1. *Aucassin et Nicolette, chantefable du XIIe siècle,* traduite par A. Bida; révision du texte original et préface par G. Paris (Paris, 1878).

2. *Aucassin and Nicolette,* translated by F. W. Bourdillon (London: Kegan Paul, Trench, 1887), i-lxiii.

3. *Aucassin et Nicolette,* done into English by Andrew Lang (London: Nutt, 1904), i-xx.

4. L. Jordan, "Die Quelle des Aucassin und die Methode des Urteils in der Philologie." *Die Zeitschrift für die Romanische Philologie,* XLIV (1924), 291-307. *Aucassin et Nicolette,* kritischer Text mit Paradigmen und Glossar von Herman Suchier, Neunte Auflage bearbeitet von Walther Suchier (Paderhorn:Schöningh, 1921), xxiv-xxxiii.

5. O. M. Johnston, "Origin of the Legend of Floire and Blancheflor." *Matzke Memorial Volume* (Leland Stanford junior University Publications, 1911), 125-138.

6. *Aucassin et Nicolette,* éditée par Mario Roques (Paris: Edouard Champion, 1936), viii-x.

7. A. H. Krappe, "Two Ancient Parallels to Aucassin et Nicolette," *Philological Quarterly,* LV (1925), 159-181.

8. D. Scheludko, "Zur Entstehungsgeschichte von Aucassin et Nicolete," *Die Zeitschrift für die Romanische Philologie,* XLII (1922), 458-490.

9. Myrra Lot-Borodine, *Le roman idyllique au moyen âge* (Paris: Auguste Picard, 1913), p. 81.

10. *Ibid.,* p. 119.

11. *Op. cit.,* p. XI.

12. *Op. cit.,* p. VII.

13. *Aucassin and Nicolette,* translated by Edward Francis Moyer and Carey DeWitt Eldridge. Preface by Urban Tigner Holmes, Jr. (Chapel Hill, N. C.: Robert Linker, 1937), i-viii.

14. All citations are made from the editions of Mario Roques mentioned above. The Arabic numerals refer to the pages, the Roman numerals to the divisions of the work. 2, II.

15. 6, VI.

16. 10, X.

17. 12, X and XI.

18. 14, XII.

19. 14, XII, line 33.

20. 16, XIV.

21. 18, XVI.

22. 21, XX.

23. 23, XXII.

24. 19, XVIII, line 18.

25. 25, XXIV.

26. 29, XXVII, line 11.

27. 30, XXIX.

28. 31, XXX.

29. 33, XXXIV.

30. 37, XL.

31. I, 1, line 6.

32. 12, XI.

33. 35, XXXVII, line 1.

34. See Aucassin in the *Index des Noms Propres* of Mario Roques' edition.

35. Mario Roques, in the introduction to his edition, p. IV, provides a résumé of the opinions of numerous scholars concerning the form and possibly manner of public presentation of *Aucassin et Nicolette.*

Barbara Nelson Sargent (essay date 1969)

SOURCE: "Parody in *Aucassin et Nicolette:* Some Further Considerations," in *The French Review,* Vol. XLIII, No. 4, March, 1970, pp. 597-605.

[*In the essay below, Sargent examines two passages in* Aucassin et Nicolette *in which the author deliberately rejects medieval literary conventions. These examples, maintains Sargent, emphasize the author's humorous intentions.*]

Among those who have commented on *Aucassin et Nicolette* in the last few years there is general agreement that the *chantefable* was written, at least partially, with humorous intent. When it comes to the exact nature and scope of the humor, the agreement is much less marked. Some scholars have stressed the apparent satire of contemporary ideas and institutions: Christianity and the Catholic Church,[1] feudalism,[2] the whole complex of received ideas of the older generation.[3] Others have concentrated their attention on the verbal and structural aspects of the work that suggest parody. Three recent articles, by Alexandre Micha, Omer Jodogne, and Robert Griffin,[4] have examined in considerable detail the literary genres and rhetorical conventions that are subjected to mockery; and M. Jodogne has given a penetrating analysis of several of the techniques employed.[5]

Nevertheless, something may remain to be said concerning parody in this enigmatical work. Two of the most celebrated passages, Aucassin's statement of preference for Hell rather than Paradise and the full-length portrait of Nicolette, while making an initial impression of grace and charm, offer peculiarities of thought and expression that suggest a deliberate rejection of a number of medieval literary conventions.

The first passage comes as the viscount exhorts Aucassin to renounce Nicolette for the youth's own good, since the illicit love he craves would send his soul to Hell and never would he enter Paradise. Aucassin's answer is curious in several respects:

> . . . *En paradis qu'ai je a faire? Je n'i quier entrer, mais que j'aie Nicolete ma tresdouce amie que j'aim tant; c'en paradis ne vont fors tex gens con je vous dirai. Il i vont ci viel prestre et cil viel clop et cil manke qui tote jor et tote nuit cropent devant ces autex et en ces viés creutes, et cil a ces viés capes ereses et a ces viés tatereles vestues, qui sont nu et decauc et estrumelé, qui moeurent de faim et de soi et de froit et de mesaises; icil vont en paradis: aveuc ciax n'ai jou que faire. Mais en infer voil jou aler, car en infer vont li bel clerc, et li bel cevalier qui sont mort as tornois et as rices gueres, et li buen sergant et li franc home: aveuc ciax voil jou aler; et s'i vont les beles dames cortoises que eles ont deus amis ou trois avoc leur barons, et s'i va li ors et li argens et li vairs et li gris, et si i vont herpeor et jogleor et li roi del siecle: avoc ciax voil jou aler, mais que j'aie Nicolete ma tresdouce amie aveuc mi.*[6]

M. Micha has sensibly dismissed the interpretation, advanced by early commentators, that this passage represents the personal views of an "écrivain nonconformiste, une manière d'esprit fort"; he observes that "la sortie d'Aucassin sur le paradis n'a rien d'une profession de foi teintée de libertinage; c'est un morceau brillant et pittoresque, visiblement écrit avec plaisir" and probably not belonging to any established literary tradition.[7] M. Spitzer

too rejects the notion of a "paganisme latent" or an "esprit libertin" in this passage, which in his opinion is "la manifestation . . . d'un amour mystique dans le genre des troubadours qui déclaraient 'voir le paradis (ou Dieu)' en leur maîtresse."[8] This last expression, though, is rather remote from the thought of the *Aucassin* passage. Much closer to it is the sentiment voiced by Conon de Bethune:

> Bele doce Dame chiere,
> Vostre grans beautés entiere
>   M'a si pris
> Ke, si iere em Paradis,
> Si revenroie je arriere.[9]

Closer still is the troubadour Raimon Jordan, who would, though at the point of death, reject the chance of Paradise in favor of the chance to sleep one night with his lady:

> Que tan la desir e volh
> Que, s'er'en coita de mort,
> Non queri'a a Deu tan fort
> Que lai el seu paradis
>   M'aculhis
> Com que'm des lezer
> D'una noit ab leis jazer.[10]

There is indeed, in my view, a literary commonplace at the bottom of Aucassin's speech. Gaston Paris identified it, and considered that the writer had amplified it with some personal additions expressive of hatred of *jongleurs* and of worldly society for asceticism and gloomy priests. All he needed to have his character say was that "il ne se souciait pas du paradis sans Nicolette et que l'enfer lui plairait avec elle. . . ."[11] However, the commonplace referred to takes a queer form, is in fact negatived, owing to the special associations that here attach to Heaven and Hell. Indeed, no discussion of the passage in question has, to my knowledge, fully taken into account the very unorthodox picture given of the two regions. Aucassin is not saying that he finds Paradise in his beloved or that he would rather have her than eternal bliss without her. His attitude is rather this: "Paradise is an unpleasant place; I do not want to go there, *provided that I may have Nicolette.* Hell is a most agreeable place; I want to go there, *provided that I may have Nicolette.*" The representation of Heaven as peopled with the impoverished, misshapen, miserable devout, and Hell as filled with delightful people and desirable objects, may be somewhat startling, but is akin to notions expressed in other works of the period that reflect courtly standards. What is usually called, for lack of a better term, "courtly love" tacitly substituted a heretical system of values for the Christian system,[12] to the extent that love was named the source of all good and those who could not or would not engage in it were relegated, by literary convention, to something approximating Hell.[13] Thus far, *Aucassin et Nicolette* appears to concur with the courtly convention, which made a closed system in which love, courtesy, wealth, leisure, and nobility were supreme, and villainy, in all senses of the word, was beyond the pale. It seemingly agrees also with the teachings of the Church, which promised Paradise to all believers, especially the oppressed and wretched of the earth, provided they were abundant in faith and good works (the priests, the devout laity, the crippled and poor) while fulminating against luxury, display, private warfare, worldly entertainments, and adultery. But one notes that in this passage there is no mention of reward for the wretched devout after their decease, nor or punishment for the prosperous sinners. Transformation is no more alluded to than is recompense; one is left with the impression that the lame, the naked, the hungry, and the poor continue to be such in the afterlife, in the absence of any suggestion to the contrary. Similarly, to Hell go those who are valiant, learned, fair, gay, and amorous, and with them go silver and gold and costly furs, the good things of this life. Again, the inference is that these persons and things will continue as they were on earth.[14] If so, then we are faced with the anomaly of a paradise peopled not by glorious saints but by contemptible folk according to courtly standards; Aucassin feels an aristocratic aversion to them that he is at no pains to conceal. Hell, on the other hand, is populated by men and women he admires; and it boasts luxury and splendor. Thus Paradise is unpleasant and Hell is attractive. This is curious enough, but there is more. One could comprehend (though perhaps not approve of) an infatuated youth who stated, in a burst of enthusiasm, that he preferred Hell with his beloved to Paradise without her, meaning thereby that he would choose a highly unpleasant place with her rather than a delightful place without her.[15] What are we to make of a young man who says that he doesn't seek to go to an unpleasant place *provided that* (I so understand *mais que*[16]) he has his Nicolette, and that he wants to go to a delightful place provided, once again, that he has her? It seems to me that the problem is susceptible of only two solutions: either the author is attempting to show a character made incoherent by the force of his passions (love, frustration, resentment, and the like), or he is deliberately standing a literary convention on its head. Though Aucassin is frequently made to act and speak with a notable lack of sense,[17] I nevertheless incline toward the second explanation. Time and again, in other passages, the author presents situations, relationships, ideas, and expressions that are the contrary of what one would expect, from the reversal of the rôles of hero and heroine to the flat *non sequitur* ("mais si estoit soupris d'Amor, qui tout vaint, *qu'il ne voloit estre cevalers, ne les armes prendre, n'aler au tornoi, ne fare point de quanque il deust*").[18] In the very speech under examination there is another and perhaps more obvious example of the same technique. In his list of the admirable persons who go to Hell, Aucassin seems to be the spokesman for the normal courtly system of values, one of the best-known of which was the desirability of extramarital love. However, one of the essential traits of a *fin amant* according to the courtly code is faithfulness to one partner. Andreas Capellanus broad-mindedly counsels loving only one person at a time,[19] but the troubadours were less indulgent. Robert Griffin has shown that these poets not only condemned ladies who loved more than one man, but some of them specifically took to task ladies who had *two or three* lovers.[20] Aucassin's allusion to the "beles dames cortoises" is immediately contradicted by what follows: these amorous ladies are not, or not perfectly, *cortoises*. Just as

this detail flouts the convention of fidelity,[21] so the speech taken as a whole, if I understand it correctly, flouts another convention: that of the lover who will jib at no personal sacrifice in order to enjoy the presence and person of the beloved.

From this perspective, the Hell-Paradise speech is remarkable chiefly for its sheer perversity of thought and expression and what one might call the density of the parody; while developing the central notion (Aucassin's unheroic wish to make the best of two worlds), the author rapidly and deftly mocks the idea of punishment for sin, the traditional representation of Heaven and Hell, the actions and appearance of the devout, and the rule of faithfulness in love.

The oddities of the descriptive parts of the *chantefable* are less apparent to modern readers, even those acquainted with the medieval traditions of *descriptio*. The personal descriptions of hero and heroine are entirely normal; both are depicted according to the gothic ideal.[22] There is, no doubt, a certain tendency toward exaggeration: Nicolette's beauty is such that it lights up the forest, her skin is so white that white daisies in the moonlight seem black beside her feet, the very sight of her leg (obligingly exposed) not only cures a sick pilgrim but makes him better than ever. Luminous beauty, white skin, healing powers are frequently associated with medieval heroines; and one can scarcely make a claim for humorous exaggeration in the description in Section XII:

> *Ele avoit les caviaus blons et menus recerclés, et les ex vairs et rians, et le face traitice, et le nes haut et bien assis, et lé levretes vremelletes plus que n'est cerisse ne rose el tans d'esté, et les dens blans et menus; et avoit les mameletes dures qui li souslevoient sa vesteure ausi con ce fuissent deus nois gauges; et estoit graille par mi les flans qu'en vos dex mains le peusciés enclorre; et les flors des margerites qu'ele ronpoit as ortex de ses piés, qui li gissoient sor le menuisse du pié par deseure, estoient droites noires avers ses piés et ses ganbes, tant par estoit blance la mescinete.*

The portrait of Nicolette, in fact, could hardly be more conventional: an enumeration from head to foot of the qualities essential to feminine beauty.[23] Indeed, the author appears restrained in comparison with some of his contemporaries; Nicolette's skin is only extremely white, whereas that of Chrétien de Troyes' Enide is not only whiter than a lily, but her face is like a mirror[24] and her eyes radiate so much light that they resemble two stars. Nicolette's waist is so slender that two hands can span it; but Geoffroi de Vinsauf's prescriptions in the *Ars versificatoria* go even further: "Sit locus astrictus zonae, brevitate pugilli / Circumscriptibilis."[25] In point of fact, the conventional *romanciers* of the twelfth and thirteenth centuries go so far (following the theorists) in their outrageous claims for the supremacy of the beauty they are at the moment describing as to render parody impossible.[26]

The only oddity within the description is the fact that the young girl's extreme slenderness is later denied by the girl herself; in the Torelore episode she sings of the delights of love "quant mes dox amis m'acole / et il me sent grasse et mole."[27]

But the really puzzling thing about the description of the heroine is its position. Normally such a portrait is introduced into a medieval work for its affective value, not only for the reader but for another character in the text; *e.g.*, the hero, seeing for the first time a lady (whose beauty is at that moment either simply stated or fully depicted) falls in love with her. Matthieu de Vendôme, who has much to say about the technique of descriptions, cautions against their untimely use and prescribes the insertion of a picture of female beauty as a preliminary to a character's falling in love.

> *Amplius, si agatur de amoris efficacia, quomodo scilicit Jupiter Parasis amore exarserit, praelibanda est puellae descriptio et assignanda puellaris pulchritudinis elegantia, ut, audito speculo pulchritudinis, versimile sit et quasi conjecturale auditori Jovis medullas tot et tantis insudasse deliciis. Praecipua enim debuit esse affluentia pulchritudinis quae Jovem impulit ad vitium corruptionis.*[28]

This literary principle is a quite logical development from the commonplace of love's birth in the eyes, noted by Andreas Capellanus: "Amor est passio quaedam innata procedens *ex visione* et immoderata cogitatione formae alterius sexus. . . ."[29] This, however, is not the situation in *Aucassin et Nicolette;* there is no account of how the hero falls in love with the heroine, for their love is a "given" at the start of the story. The heroine, being loved, must be lovable; being lovable, she must be beautiful, and the author can spare himself the labor of enumerating her charms. If he wished to portray her nevertheless, the logical moment to do so would be when she first begins to take an active part in the narrative, moving and speaking "on her own." This moment occurs in Section V, well before the passage in question. There is, indeed, a description of Nicolette in V, which, though only four verses in length, is sufficient to confirm her beauty (mentioned earlier by Aucassin) and hence to establish her claim on the reader's sympathetic interest.

The fact remains that most medieval fiction that posits love at the outset simply omits the description of the heroine. If, exceptionally, her beauty is shown, it is to announce and explain her effect on characters other than her lover, as in *Floire et Blancheflor,* a possible source of the *chantefable* (the double full-length portrait of the lovers is postponed until they have been apprehended and brought before the Emir for trial, at which moment their beauty and pathetic plight make a deep impression on the spectators).[30] This situation, too, is lacking in *Aucassin.* The portrait of the heroine has no affective function; she is quite alone as she makes her way across the garden. The author could hardly have been ignorant of the conventional purpose of the portrait, since in the only other extended[31] personal description in the work, that of the plowman, he does show the effect of a character's appearance

on another character.[32] Nicolette's description, then, "pointless" according to conventional theory and practice, may signify a certain independence with regard to one more literary technique, perhaps even an outright rejection of it.

If these observations are valid, we have a somewhat clearer comprehension of what M. Micha has called the "ironie qui donne sa tonalité fondamentale à cette histoire d'amour"[33] and what M. Pauphilet termed (without examining in much detail) the "veine parodique" running through the entire work, the author having elected to "conter un roman d'aventures en tournant toujours le dos aux coutumes de ce genre."[34] M. Jodogne sums it up as "pastiche et parodie de l'amoureux, pastiche et parodie de trois genres littéraires" of which the chief is the idyllic romance; yet it "traite de façon badine les procédés et les thèmes du genre."[35]

Although it is impossible to be certain of the exact intentions of the author, either in specific passages or in the entire work, one may hazard a conjecture. It is that the creator of *Aucassin* was indulging in a light-handed and good-natured mockery of the whole art of fiction as practiced at the time, packing into a few dozen pages an astonishing number of "mistakes," *i.e.,* deliberate infractions of the rules of composition both as expounded by the theorists and as put into practice by writers of fiction.[36] The work appears to be a sort of thirteenth-century anti-novel, without the bitter and destructive quality that frequently marks the corresponding modern phenomenon. Since the conventions it so often and conspicuously flouts were still very much in vogue, we may have here some explanation of the fact that *Aucassin et Nicolette,* so much appreciated today, was apparently not successful in its time.

Notes

1. Hermann Suchier, ed., *Aucassin und Nicolette,* 10th ed. (Paderborn, 1932), p. 39.

2. Robert Griffin, "*Aucassin et Nicolette* and the Albigensian Crusade," *Modern Language Quarterly* XXVI (1965), 248.

3. Leo Spitzer, "Le Vers 2 d'*Aucassin et Nicolette* et le sens de la chantefable," *Modern Philology* XLV (1947-48), 11.

4. Micha, "En relisant *Aucassin et Nicolette,*" *Moyen Age* LXV (1959), 279-92; Jodogne, "La Parodie et le pastiche dans *Aucassin et Nicolette,*" *Cahiers de l'Association Internationale des Etudes Françaises* XII (1959), 53-65; Griffin, 243-56.

5. He has discovered three basic devices: "le jeu permanent de contrepied, l'exagération et la bouffonerie . . ." (op. cit., p. 60). The first of these terms, M. Jodogne acknowledges, comes from Alfred Pauphilet, *Le Legs du moyen âge* (Paris, 1950), p. 243.

6. Ed. Mario Roques, CFMA, 2nd ed. (Paris, 1954), VI. All quotations are taken from this edition.

7. *op. cit.,* p. 289. M. Jodogne agrees: "on comprend mal qu'on ait voulu entrevoir l'incrédulité religieuse

de l'auteur. . . ." He considers the passage as ironical (*op. cit.,* p. 58). Since parody is afoot in the *chantefable,* it is probably inevitable that the Church and its personnel and doctrines should have been brought in; these were favorite targets, especially for the Latin parodists. Helen Waddell made the general observation: "Medieval parody is graceless, even blasphemous. . . ." (*The Wandering Scholars,* 6th ed. [New York, 1955], p. 162).

8. *op. cit.,* p. 11.

9. *Les Chansons de Conon de Bethune,* ed. A. Wallensköld (Paris, 1921), VII, 11. 1-5.

10. *The Troubadour Raimon Jordan, Vicomte de Saint-Antonin,* ed. H. Kjellman (Uppsala-Paris, 1923), XIII, 11. 48-54.

11. *Poèmes et légendes du moyen âge* (Paris, 1900), pp. 109-110.

12. For a discussion of the conflict between the two systems, see A. J. Denomy, *The Heresy of Courtly Love* (New York, 1947).

13. As in the fifth dialogue of Andreas Capellanus' *De amore,* which represents the eternal reward granted to ladies who have loved rightly and the eternal punishment of those who have refused love as well as those who have been promiscuous. See Andreae Capellani regii francorum *De amore libri tres,* ed. E. Trojel (Copenhagen, 1892; reprint Munich, 1964), pp. 91-108.

14. That this inference is natural is borne out by M. Pauphilet's remark: ". . . Aucassin déclare qu'il aime bien mieux aller en enfer qu'au paradis, car la compagnie y *sera* beaucoup plus élégante." (Italics mine.) (*op. cit.,* p. 242.)

15. Werner Söderhjelm goes this far; Aucassin's declaration is, for him, ". . . un trait important, qui met particulièrement bien en relief son amour impétueux et son caractère indépendant." (*La Nouvelle française du XVe siècle* [Paris, 1910], pp. 109-110.)

16. I cannot agree with Mr. Griffin's suggestion concerning the interpretation of these lines: ". . . the subjunctive 'mais que j'aie Nicolete' could bear the meaning 'I would even go there provided I have Nicolete.'" (*op. cit.,* p. 251.)

17. There come to mind such passages as Aucassin's capture in battle and sudden exertions when it occurs to him that, decapitated, he will no longer be able to speak to Nicolette; also his quibbles about the relative strength of their respective loves when he might be forming a plan of escape, and his fall from a standing horse. Devoid of heroism, Aucassin also falls short of the courtly ideal of *mesure,* well discussed by Moshé Lazar in *Amour courtois et fin' amors* (Paris, 1964), pp. 28-32. M. Jodogne stresses, with much detail, the ridiculousness of Aucassin's words and actions (*op. cit.,* pp. 55-60).

18. Edition, p. 2.

19. Among the rules of love are: "III. Nemo duplici potest amore ligari," and "XVII. Novus amor veterem compellit abire" (*op. cit.,* pp. 310-11.). Faithfulness in love is for Guillaume de Lorris the last and great commandment; see *Le Roman de la Rose,* ed. E. Langlois, SATF (Paris, 1920), vv. 2233-64.

20. *op cit.,* p. 251.

21. And contradicts the faithfulness of the lovers themselves. Indeed, Aucassin reacts violently to the thought that Nicolette might become the mistress of another; see Edition, pp. 15-16.

22. Summarized by Edgar de Bruyne, *Etudes d'esthétique médiévale* (Bruges, 1946), II, 173 ff. For both men and women, the canon requires golden hair, bright eyes, rosy lips and cheeks, clear, white skin, long arms and hands, a straight and slender body. Certain other details, of course, vary according to sex. Alice Colby has recently made an extended study of the content and order of medieval personal descriptions in *The Portrait in Twelfth-Century French Literature* (Geneva, 1965); see especially pp. 25-72 for traits of ideal beauty.

23. Consult the precepts set forth by Geoffroi de Vinsauf in *Poetria nova,* published by Edmond Faral in *Les Arts poétiques du XIIe et XIIIe siècles* (Paris, 1924), pp. 214-15.

24. "Ce fu cele por verité / qui fu fete por esgarder, / qu'an se poïst en li mirer / ausi com an un mireor." (*Erec et Enide,* ed. Mario Roques, CFMA Paris, 1955, 11. 438-41.)

25. *Loc. cit.,* 11. 593-94. M. Micha is mistaken in considering this "un trait original, qui est une exagération jointe á une stylisation poétique. . . ." (*op. cit.,* p. 286).

26. Consider, from *Floire et Blancheflor:* "De sa bouche ist sa doce alainne, / Vivre en puet en une semainne: / Qui au lundi la beseroit / En la semainne fain n'avroit." (Ed. Margaret Pelan, Paris, 1956, 11. 2660-63.)

27. Edition, p. 33, 11. 4-5. The author is particularly fond of this sort of inconsistency; see the allusion in the Prologue to Aucassin's *proueces* (1. 6), belied by the youth's actions. Similarly, in the Hell-Paradise speech Aucassin expresses admiration of *li bel cevalier,* though elsewhere (pp. 2, 8) he emphatically states his lack of interest in becoming one. (Note that the qualifying phrase following *li bel cevalier* clearly indicates that the term has the same military, rather than social, connotations here as in the passages on pp. 2 and 8.)

28. *Ars versificatoria,* par. 40, in Faral, p. 119. Douglas Kelly has recently drawn attention to this principle of composition in "The Scope of the Treatment of Composition in the Twelfth- and Thirteenth-Century Arts of Poetry," *Speculum* XLI (1966), 274. Faral noted Matthieu's remarks on the subject in his *Recherches sur les sources latines des contes et romans*

courtois du moyen âge (Paris, 1913) and sums them up: ". . . la description . . . explique les événements, et . . . la beauté du héros justifie l'amour de la femme ou la beauté de la femme l'amour du héros" (p. 101).

29. *De amore*, p. 3.

30. Ll. 2610-79.

31. There is a brief description of Aucassin, but it comes at the beginning and serves merely to inform the reader that this character merits interest and sympathy.

32. Edition, p. 25. The hero, observing this hideous apparition, is frightened, as one might well expect. The plowman is perhaps to be ascribed to another possible source, the *Yvain* of Chrétien de Troyes, in which a similar character appears in an analogous situation. There, however, he advances the narrative by giving directions to the hero; in *Aucassin* he has no narrative function. Incidentally, the reader aware of the medieval equations beautiful = good, ugly = evil would expect this *vilain* to be very villainous indeed; yet he turns out to be a neutral, even slightly benevolent character.

33. *op. cit.*, p. 288.

34. *op. cit.*, pp. 248, 245.

35. *op. cit.*, pp. 64-65.

36. The closest parallel that suggests itself is Mozart's *Musikalischer Spass,* which aims at being as technically "wrong" as possible and yet results in an amusing and pleasing piece of work.

The problem of determining whether a parodist is seriously criticizing, or merely fooling, or engaging in a mixture of the two, is both common and exceedingly difficult to solve. Paul Lehmann discusses this question of intention in *Die Parodie im Mittelalter* (Munich, 1922), noting that ". . . Bissiges und Launiges nicht immer leicht zu trennen sind" (p. 228). In the second edition of this work, he inclines to the view that medieval parodists usually aimed at amusement (Stuttgart, 1963, p. 4). Even if this is true, it does not, of course, prove that mere amusement was the intention of any specific medieval parody.

Darnell H. Clevenger (essay date 1970)

SOURCE: "Torelore in *Aucassin et Nicolette,*" in *Romance Notes,* Vol. 11, No. 3, Spring, 1970, pp. 656-65.

[In the essay that follows, Clevenger avers that the episode of Aucassin et Nicolette *which takes place in the land of Torelore reveals the parodic nature of the work and emphasizes the writer's implicit assertion that the world and its laws and habits is the story's true antagonist.]*

The plot of the thirteenth-century *chantefable,* **Aucassin et Nicolette,** is quite simple. Aucassin, son and heir to Count Garin of Beaucaire, loves Nicolette, a Saracen slave purchased and then "adopted" by the Viscount of that same Beaucaire. The remainder of the story consists of one separation after another as the lovers flee their persecutors. During their travels they reach the inverted kingdom of Torelore, a country where the king is lying in childbed, the queen is leading the troops into battle, and the battle is being waged with good cheeses and baked apples. This episode at Torelore is the structural and symbolic center of the work. Without it the story would be incomplete. With it the work becomes a structure of three symmetrically interlocking pyramids, with Torelore as the central peak. Alone the episode stands as a burlesque of chivalry, of knightly valor and courtly love. As an integral part of the whole it determines the author's intended parody of the same. Moreover, it proves the basic unimportance of the plot, making the reader conscious, by one more in a series of tonal inversions or changes, that the world (the real as well as the fictional), its laws, customs and conventions, is the true antagonist of the story.

Nevertheless, not until recently have critics begun to recognize Torelore's ultimate significance. Kasper Rogger passed it off as an "intermezzo burlesque."[1] Albert Pauphilet did realize that it is the most outstanding example of the author's use of the "contre-pied" or inversion technique. However, he continues that "pour le progrès du roman, c'est une impasse, un épisode tellement statique qu'on n'en peut pas sortir, si ce n'est par une action extérieure."[2] Lately Omer Jodogne has been more than stylistic flair in the episode: "Cet épisode est nécessaire à la détermination de la valeur d'Aucassin," for it causes a softening of "ce que la satire avait de démesuré" against hero and love.[3] More recently Sister M. Faith McKean has shown an awareness of its true structural and symbolic value. She concludes that, as an interlude, it is the "key passage" for the love theme, one that underscores the reversal of the lovers' roles and the parody of courtly love.[4]

Torelore is not simply the "key" to the love theme, however. It is the key to the entire *chantefable.* As an interlude, it divides the story in half: the previous action occurring in Beaucaire, in flight, with Aucassin chasing and catching Nicolette; the succeeding action taking place in both Carthage and Beaucaire, with Nicolette following and catching Aucassin. The story opens with the siege of Beaucaire and Count Garin's attempt to separate the lovers. The Viscount imprisons Nicolette in a tower; the Count imprisons Aucassin in a cell. Nicolette escapes and, before fleeing into the forest, secretively visits Aucassin at his cell, where the two impersonally discuss the respective influence of love on man and woman, in spite of the more pressing matters of their own love and the proximity of pursuit, capture and death for Nicolette. Nicolette then continues her flight into the forest where she builds a bower of branches. Later Aucassin, being freed, follows her. At the bower, for the first time since the story opened, the lovers are together without interference, except for the possibility of pursuit. The first movement in the love theme is complete. After an interlude at Torelore, where they are free from the meddling of parental authority, but not from the world at large (the attempt of the nobles of Torelore to marry Nicolette to their prince), the lovers are again parted, being abducted by pirates, placed in different ships, and separated by a storm. Thus begins the second basic movement of the story.[5] This movement is parallel in structure to the first. The pirate raid on Torelore is similar to the siege of Beaucaire in much the same way that the storm parallels Count Garin's earlier role. During the storm, the lovers are blown to their respective homes, Carthage and Beaucaire. Afterwards the story again rises to an interlude. Nicolette, in minstrel disguise, escapes Carthage and returns to Beaucaire. There, in a scene reminiscent of the one at Aucassin's cell, she encounters Aucassin at court, relates their past love and adventures to him (without revealing her true identity), her fate at Carthage (without mentioning that she has escaped), and her fidelity. The lovers are together, as they were at the cell, but are kept apart by Nicolette's whim (she wishes to test her lover's faithfulness before revealing herself), as they were formerly kept apart by the bars on the cell window. Finally, Nicolette leaves the court and proceeds to the Viscountess' home, where she bathes eight days before sending her hostess after Aucassin; in the forest, earlier, she left a message with the herdsmen, allowing him three days to search for her. Of course Aucassin goes to her at the Viscountess', as he went to the bower, and the story ends in marriage.

Both movements thus terminate in symbolically ideal states of love, pagan and Christian, the bower and marriage.[6] They are parallel in structure (separation, interlude, resolution), and are complete and complementary units just as an act in a play or a chapter in a novel. However, two significant changes or inversions take place in the latter section. One, the inversion of the protagonists' roles, begun more humorously before Torelore, is definitely and totally completed after that episode. Nicolette assumes the male role as Aucassin does the female one. In the chase through the forest Aucassin was, symbolically, both knight and hunter. The nightwatchman, Nicolette herself, and the herdsmen all refer to her as prey. Aucassin calls her his lost greyhound. The journey itself seems to contain all the perils of the knight errant's trials of strength, in parody, especially in the case of the ugly ox driver. Aucassin's first trial is with the shepherds. He pays them for information in spite of their insulting ways. His next trial is with the ox driver, whom the author describes in such a way as to prepare us for a battle: he is hideous, gigantic, carries a huge club, and Aucassin approaches him with fear in his heart. The approaching battle dissolves into conversation, and the peasant's problems provide a humorous contrast to those of the hero (the loss of his ox and the loss of Aucassin's "white greyhound," his need for money and Aucassin's for love). Next Aucassin encounters his third trial at the very door of the bower: he falls while dismounting, dislocating his shoulder. After Torelore Nicolette becomes the hunter by traveling from Carthage to Beaucaire, in

male disguise, to search for Aucassin. Aucassin's earlier role is completely inverted, not only through contrast with Nicolette, but because he waits for her at Beaucaire, not because of the bars to a cell, but because of his own passivity, created by his love.

Two, there has also been an extreme change in tone after Torelore.[7] The mixture of reality, fantasy and folklore that created such caricatures as the ox driver is missing. The detail of description that made the love bower so delightful and the Beaucaire war such a travesty is absent. The burlesque quality of Aucasin's accident and the lighter humor in his description of Nicolette's healing powers, both are lacking. Remaining is the one tone that pervades the entire work, the rhythm of illogical or mysterious causality that creates the knight and the two storms, and does away with Aucassin's parents, at the appropriate moment.[8]

Between the above two movements stands Torelore. Several items, not the least of which is its central location, indicate this episode's importance structurally: it is the only episode in which natural phenomena directly intervene to affect the flight of the lovers (chance storms carry them both to and from the kingdom and thus separate it from the rest of their world); it, in relationship to Beaucaire, reverses the spatial movement found elsewhere in the story (arrival and departure in contrast to flight and return); it is the only place in the story where the world is abnormal and the actions of the protagonists normal; it is the first episode in which the lovers are together without interference or danger of pursuit; it is at Torelore where Aucassin and Nicolette meet their sole counterparts, the king and queen; and it is at Torelore where the world replaces the lovers as the direct object of the author's satire.

Throughout the story Aucassin's valor as man and knight is continuously ridiculed, both in his own actions and in contrast with those of Nicolette. He is hesitant, moody, incapable of an action not directly related to his love for her. When he does react, his reactions are negative, extremely violent or extremely passive, extremely charitable or extremely peevish, seldom being the appropriate reaction for the given situation. At Torelore this changes. He is aggressive and courteous rather than peevish and moody. He is somewhat violent and comic, but only by means of the contrast with the burlesque meekness of his opponents. Moreover, his lethargy disappears until he is again threatened with the loss of Nicolette. He has become a true knight, capable of acting in accordance with the necessity of the moment, and of reacting as man should, with moral and physical strength. Unfortunately the methods of his actions are determined by codes foreign to Torelore. Thus the superimposition of his former and later hesitancy onto his daredevil recklessness in Torelore implies a burlesque of valor, not of Aucassin. It redirects our attention to the motives for his actions, to his love for Nicolette, to the king's condition, and to some code of valor that we would expect of a knight. It reminds us that the inversion of his situation in love is the basic reason for the change in his conduct; that, therefore, love is the primary motivating force of the story, and as such is the ultimate butt of the author's satire. It is a gentle satire, however, and one directed more at a system of love than at love itself. The author's biting criticism is reserved for other conventions, such as honesty, war, filial love and feudal loyalty; in other words, for the human condition. Human conventions, in the story, create more harm than good, but only because they conflict with practice. The story is a humorous comment on the clash of the ideal with reality.[9]

As for Aucassin, his first question upon arriving at Torelore is whether or not there is a war in process. He presumably wishes to serve the king in order to win honors for himself and his mistress. When he does reach the battlefield the result is almost as much of a failure as was his earlier battle. He requests the king's permission to enter the struggle and immediately charges the wielders of baked apples and fresh cheeses, lopping off heads with his sword until the king begs him to desist and the enemy flees the field. At Beaucaire he was somewhat less aggressively energetic. He refused to enter the battle, although his own home and inheritance were being attacked and his honor was in danger, until Count Garin promised him a few kisses and words with Nicolette. When he did ride off to do battle, he rode as if in a dream, his thoughts full of his beloved. In that state of mind, meandering through the middle of the battlefield, he was dragged from his horse as unceremoniously as he later cudgels the king, and as the pirates, even later, truss him up and throw him into their ship. Not until his captors began plotting his death, an unchivalrous procedure, did he draw his sword and lay around him like a berserk housewife. He had realized that death would permanently separate him from Nicolette. After his escape, possibly still afraid of permanent separation through death, he fled the battlefield. On his way he met Count Bougars, leader of the enemy forces, and attacked him without warning, beating him to the ground and leading him, by the nosepiece of his helmet no less, to Count Garin. If the Count had upheld his promise, the victory would have been complete. He refused to allow Aucassin access to Nicolette, however, and Aucassin, in retaliation, petulantly made his captive swear to do all in his power to destroy Baucaire, thus reversing the expected oath in such a situation, as the battle itself reversed chivalric procedure and knightly conduct.

It is significant to note that, in both wars, Aucassin is victorious in battle. His victories are nullified by forces exterior to himself: the first by his father's treachery, and the second by the comic incompetence of the opposition and the king's reprimand. Ironically he is allowed to live in peace in Torelore in spite of the brutal beating he administers the king and his own bloody conduct in the war. Of the two kingdoms, at least insofar as Aucassin is treated, Torelore is preferable, just as the king is in some ways a morally better man than Count Garin. Furthermore, the absence of chivalry, (honor, loyalty, courtesy) at Beaucaire, and its presence in the war at Torelore, by contrast, implies a criticism of Beaucaire. It further suggests that the convention of chivalry is, if not itself ridiculous, at least

ridiculously inapplicable to normal human affairs. It functions, successfully, only in an abnormal situation.

It is further significant that the comic quality of Aucassin's actions at Beaucaire is produced by two conditions in his love affair, by separation from his beloved, and by his preoccupation with thoughts of her. The same is true elsewhere in the story. At his cell, and later at his court, Aucassin does nothing except mourn and weep for his beloved. He vows to commit suicide if she should ever adorn any bed but his own, instead of vowing revenge as a knight should. He vows to wait for her always, thus assuming the role of the woman who remains at home while her knight departs for the wars or in search of adventure. His fall from his horse is, moreover, caused by daydreams of Nicolette.

He, like the king, suffers from a lovesickness that has become a custom, or convention. The effect on his manhood is, to say the least, disparaging. The opposite is true of Nicolette for she assumes the role vacated by him. Love ennobles her as it degrades Aucassin. However, through her relationship to the queen, in whom love's effects are carried to a ludicrous extreme, Nicolette, as well as Aucassin, becomes more humorous with respect to the role she receives in the story, with respect to the convention that makes love the center (even if it is a lover's hell) of the universe and the beloved the very life of the lover. The king and queen have reversed the essential characteristics that distinguish man from woman. He is "pregnant." She is protecting the home through force of arms. The reversal of their roles is, symbolically, both physical and emotional. Much the same is true of the protagonists.

Nevertheless, the king and queen are but caricatures, not of the protagonists, nor of love, but of the most unimaginably extreme results of love. Furthermore, the story ends happily, without burlesque or parody. And the author never directly ridicules love or the protagonists. His descriptions of their love are often the most delightfully moving passages of the work, as is the case with Aucassin's verses at the bower, or Nicolette's to the king and nobles of Torelore. The same is true of their persons. At the very beginning, Aucassin is described as good, handsome, graceful, but under the influence of love. Nicolette's poignant beauty while crossing the moat, her bruised and bloodied hands and feet, and her fear of death lurking behind and before, make her quite feminine. Moreover, although their reversal of roles progressively increases toward the symbolic extreme, through their actions, their adventures before Torelore are either comic in nature, or contain comic overtones. Their later adventures can never seriously reflect upon themselves simply because of the parallel structure of the work and the central location of Torelore, for Nicolette's aggressiveness after that episode not only recalls her earlier efficiency, but also a picture of the queen and her legions competing to muddy the ford, and, through association, other more feminine characteristics of the heroine as well. Much the same is true of Aucassin in association with his own inefficiency and that of the king. When he goes to the Viscountess' home at Nicolette's bidding, we are reminded that he was the hunter in the forest. When Nicolette takes a bath before revealing herself to her lover, we are reminded of the mantel, her best, that she wore when she escaped the tower, on her way to visit her lover; we are reminded of the bower carpeted with flowers where she first awaited Aucassin. In all, we are reminded that the humor is tender when directed toward the protagonists, burlesque when directed toward their condition; satirical (the avarice of the herdsmen) or cynically missing (Count Garin's treachery and the Viscount's cruelty) when directed toward human reality; and that it is precisely at Torelore, where the extreme results of misguided love appear in the form of the king and queen, that our memories are re-directed toward the pleasant innocence of the protagonists' love.

Notes

1. Kasper Rogger, "Etude descriptive de la chantefable *Aucassin et Nicolette,*" II, *Zeitschrift für romanische Philologie,* 70 (1954), 41.

2. Albert Pauphilet, "*Aucassin et Nicolette,*" *Le Legs du Moyen Age,* chap. 8 (Melun: Librairie d'Argences, 1950), p. 244.

3. Omer Jodogne, "La Parodie et le pastiche dans *Aucassin et Nicolette,*" *Cahiers de l'Association internationale des études françaises,* 12 (1960), 61.

4. Sister M. Faith McKean, "Torelore and Courtoisie," *Romance Notes,* 3 (1962), 64.

5. Rogger, *op. cit.,* p. 19, with respect to the first movement of the story, concludes that it "constitute une unité, un tout parfait" and that it contains three basic divisions:

> La Ière partie raconte l'emprisonnement des deux amants: A, de Nicolette (II-VII); B, d'Aucassin (VIII-XI). La troisième partie relate l'évasion des deux amoureux: A, de Nicolette (XVI-XIX); B, d'Aucassin (XX-XXV). La deuxième partie est un intermède où apparaît Nicolette, la jeune fille victorieuse et entraînante. Cette partie *centrale* comprend non seulement le portrait triomphal de l'héroïne dans la rosée, mais aussi l'exposition des difficultés du jeune couple en particulier et du problème de l'amour en général.

My structural analyses of the second movement (the third part of the story), and of the story as a whole, are based on his conclusions.

6. It is evident that the bower represents, symbolically, an ideal pagan retreat for lovers, possibly the very "lovers' hell" that Aucassin mentions earlier. Rogger's (*op. cit.,* p. 7) discussion of the bower suggests this possibility: Les carrefours étaient le domicile des revenants, des diables, des mauvais esprits, le rendez-vous des sorciers et des sorcières; c'étaient les lieux où on se debarrassait de ses maladies . . . Mais c'étaient aussi les lieux propices aux filles amoureuses: là, elles se dévêtaient pour y attirer, magiquement, l'élu de leur cœur. Quelque chose de pareil devait faire le fond de la croyance folklorique qui a stimulé l'imagination de notre auteur.

The very spatial movement and tonal changes of the story are further suggestive of the same possibility. Beaucaire is a Christian country. Nicolette has been baptized there; both Count and Viscount mention this. The Viscount refers to the probability of Aucassin losing his soul if he should marry Nicolette. The elements of folklore, mythology and magic that Rogger (*op. cit.,* pp. 1-18) discusses do not actually enter the story until the scene in which Nicolette escapes, at night, from her tower, and they become progressively more evident as Aucassin approaches the bower. Torelore, of course, is the next step, from the depths of folklore to the depths of fantasy, for the tone of magic and myth terminates with the bower. After Torelore the earlier movement is reversed. Aucassin returns directly to Beaucaire, but Nicolette passes through Carthage, her own fatherland, and a country with a heretical faith, on her return trip to Beaucaire, a Christian country, and a Christian marriage. It is interesting that she returns with her face darkened with stain (there are a number of references to the whiteness of her skin, earlier, in Beaucaire) and that she bathes before marrying Aucassin. Could the former symbolize a religious relapse and the latter re-baptism? There must have been some association, for the medieval mind, between skin color and religious faith. In any case, both events coming together, immediately before her marriage and after her sojourn in Carthage, are quite suggestive. Furthermore, the contrastive placement of Nicolette's adventures in Carthage and Aucassin's in the forest, together with the Christian atmosphere at Beaucaire and the lack of it elsewhere, intimates a connection between the love bower and the later marriage, for they both unite the lovers at the end of two respective movements, flight and return.

7. Robert Harden, "*Aucassin et Nicolette* as Parody," *Studies in Philology,* 63 (1966), 3, states that the "apparent lapses or inversions in the tone of the book and in the conduct of the protagonists are not exceptional but rather typical of the entire work" and that this very use of inversion emphasizes the author's mockery of characters and themes. I would add that it is through inversion and parallelism that many of the symbolic relationships and meanings of the work become apparent. Parallel episodes, actions, scenes construct a system of associations which are delineated by the inverted aspect of some of the parallels. Torelore, of course, is the most outstanding example. The events there parallel events in both Beaucaire and Carthage, and thus establish a contrast between the three countries, a contrast which immediately includes the rulers of the countries also: Count Garin and Nicolette's father attempt to separate the lovers; the king does not. The parallel relationship of authority to "subject" once established, it becomes clear

that the king's decision is based on; one, a more tolerant or "humane" attitude toward love; or, two, and which seems more logical, his lack of filial connection to the protagonists. In either case the basic satire hidden in the relationship is directed at social attitudes toward love.

8. A. Micha, "En relisant *Aucassin et Nicolette*," *Le Moyen Age*, 4th ser., XIV (1959), 279-291, rejects Rogger's conclusion [*op. cit.*, I, 67 (1951), 421] that the part of the story following the bower of branches is heterogeneous to the part preceding it. Micha finds (pp. 279-280) that the change in style is due to a change of perspective, not of "intention profonde."

9. Paul Brians, "Medieval Literary Parody," (diss., Indiana Univ., 1968), p. 117, concludes that one of the main parodic devices of the author is the continuous intrusion of reality into the fictional world of romance. It is significant that the very clash of reality (actual procedure in human affairs) with the ideal (in this case, conventions in love and war), both before and during the flight of the lovers, is one of the author's basic means in parodying human conventions, through their ever increasing distance from reality (in other words, their extreme unreality), and, conversely, of satirizing that very reality from which the lovers flee. It is not so much a case of man's reality interfering with his ideals, or vice versa, for, in the work, neither are above ridicule. It is a case of a dual standard, neither aspect of which has common grounds for reconciliation with the other.

Eugene Vance (essay date 1970)

SOURCE: "The Word at Heart: *Aucassin et Nicolette* as a Medieval Comedy of Language," in *Yale French Studies,* No. 45, 1970, pp. 33-51.

[*In the following essay, Vance studies the form and language of* Aucassin et Nicolette *and suggests that the poem is an examination of the function of literary language.*]

Throughout the Latin middle ages there was speculation about the function of language and the potency of the word. Classical antiquity had provided a system of rhetoric and a mature theory of signs, but these were at once challenged and transformed in Christian culture by the doctrine that in the beginning God "spoke" the world of things, and after the Fall God spoke again in Christ the Word so that fallen man could again approach God. As St. Augustine said,

> All other things may be expressed in some way; He alone is ineffable, Who spoke, and all things were made. He spoke, and we were made; but we are unable to speak of Him. His Word, by Whom we were spoken, is His Son. He was made weak, so that He might be spoken by us, despite our weakness.[1]

In medieval Christian thought, problems of language remained central to problems of epistemology. In the Pauline tradition, language was to be understood as a system of signs pointing beyond themselves to an unknowable truth that is with God.[2] The word as sign is enigmatic. Language is a mirror through which mortals may gain imperfect knowledge. In the fallen language of mortals, words may signify, but only partially: *videmus nunc per speculum in aenigmate . . .*[3] Perfect knowledge, impossible to man on earth, will be without mediation, without signs, *facie ad faciem.*

In the later middle ages, speculation about the nature of language was intensified by a variety of cultural factors, such as the shift of learning from the monastery to the cathedral school and the university, the revival of classicism and the influx of Graeco-Arab translations, the decline of grammar in favor of logic, and of exegetical theology in favor of speculative theology. Like Abelard and St. Bonaventure, St. Thomas believed that the word as sign is conventional, and signification is possible through an act of the intellect.[4] The word refers to the concept, not to a universal. In the later scholastic period, thinkers attached great importance to relationships between the spoken word, the written word, and the concept. For Ockham and Duns Scotus, the written word is a sign, the spoken word is another; each is determined by convention and signifies the thing; we, for our part, must learn about the thing as a concept by dint of empirical experience.[5]

An intense concern with the nature of language was proper, then, to the disciplines of churchmen struggling to know God. But was this concern exclusively theirs? The answer is, of course, that medieval culture in *all* its forms remained deeply aware of the centrality and the potency of the word, and that the preoccupations of the churchmen did not oppose, but rather derived from, their experience as human beings in the culture of their time. We all know, for instance, that in feudalism, human relations—and indeed the structure of society itself—rested on a system of verbal oaths sanctified by ritual and relic. The French word for oath (*serment*) derives from the Latin *sacramentum*, which in its turn has been used to translate the Greek *mystérion;* in the interplay of these concepts we may witness the continuity between practical social rituals and the deepest areas of mystical belief in the medieval mind.[6]

The stream of cultural history has cross-currents, and medieval vernacular literature is similarly marked by a persistent consciousness of language as an all-embracing mode of action where the whole of human destiny is in play. However, the character of this consciousness of the word changed and evolved markedly during the twelfth and thirteenth centuries, particularly as vernacular literature gained in intellectual scope and shared with ecclesiastical writing many topics of common concern. Between *La Chanson de Roland* and the second part of *Le Roman de la rose*—that is, between the late eleventh and late thirteenth centuries—the consciousness of the word became explicit instead of implicit, reasoned instead of intuitive.

La Chanson de Roland may be described not only as a tragedy of feudal politics, or of heroic ideals, but as a tragedy of language. The oral tradition from which the poem derives is centered upon a heroic ethic whose formulas are most fully incarnate in Roland. They define his character, and Roland, through his deeds, is in a sense the true author of the poem:

> I will strike with Durendal, my sword,
> And you, my friend, shall strike with Halteclere . . .
> Never may a bad song be sung of them![7]

Charlemagne, a Roland grown old, a warrior who has glimpsed beyond the heroic code, has no language of his own to reverse the course of events in his doomed empire. Charlemagne's language consists either of gestures flung out of a dark, brooding silence, or else of pained outcries of wrath and despair that point up his helplessness. Though Charlemagne is at odds with the world he governs, his poem remains cognitively circumscribed by its traditional ethic. Oliver and Thierry are potential agents of reform, but their actions (probably interpolated late into the legend of Roland) are never allowed to alter the trajectory of events in the poem. The characters, like the poet, accept absolutely both the language of a warrior tradition and its ultimate social consequences: Charlemagne emerges alone at the end of the poem, tugging on his beard and weeping as before, but now his kingdom is ravaged and his anguish stands out as the supreme fact of the poetic world. Introspection tends to paralyze heroes, and *La Chanson de Roland* succeeds as tragedy precisely because the values implicit in the language of its code are never called into question; instead, they are lived out.

After *La Chanson de Roland* we may discern increasing self-consciousness in poets as they look ever more intently at the medium of their art. The impulse toward self-awareness that led poets to examine, and not just to master, literary language characterizes other spheres of medieval life as well. From the twelfth century on, kings pondered kingship, businessmen discovered finance, the faithful questioned belief. The manner in which poets gained consciousness of language as the medium of their art varied from poet to poet and from genre to genre. Chrétien de Troyes, for instance, discovered in the discipline of rhetoric the possibility of sustaining firm ironic distance between himself and his *matière*. The effect is to demand of the reader rigorously controlled emotions that make him aware of poetic invention as a deliberate process of the mind. As one critic has said,

> For most readers, there is likely to be an inverse relationship between the intensity of analytic activity and the degree of identification. Irony is a means of increasing the proportion of intellectual analysis; comedy (at least in Chrétien) suggests not so much analytic activity as moral judgment. Both establish aesthetic distance.[8]

A courtly lyric poet such as Thibaud de Champagne makes us aware of literary invention by means of a poetic that elicits from the reader simultaneous but conflicting responses. Exploiting a language whose outward appearance is conventional and even platitudinous, the poet reveals the specific qualities of his talent to the aristocratic *initiati* of a closed in-group through his exquisite manipulations of that language. Through the sweet guile of the poet, language finds itself betrayed by a transcendant *sur-langage,* the *signifiant* (to use descriptively the terms of Saussure) by the *signifié*. Because of the discrepancy, the reader is brought to an awareness of literary language as a precious but privileged realm of discourse distinct from all others. It is interesting that the anti-courtly lyric, which comprises a genre called *fatrasie,* takes courtly poetry to task precisely because of the excessive gap between *signifiant* and *signifié,* a gap that marks the aristocrat's wish to distance himself, through the word, from his social inferiors. The poet of *fatrasie* takes as his point of departure the same decorous conventions as the courtly poet; but then he assaults the preciosity of the *sur-langage* with the grotesque:

> Sweetly, I draw comfort
> From a half-dead cat
> That sings each Thursday . . .[9]

As Paul Zumthor notes, "Far from originating in individual revolt, the *fatrasie* asserts public dignity."[10] In short, conventional literary language became involved, during the thirteenth century, in a tug-of-war between opposing social consciousnesses.

During the thirteenth century, the matter of scholasticism began to preoccupy vernacular poets. It was now possible for a poet such as Jean de Meun to incorporate conscious linguistic theory into the poem itself. Soon after taking up the poetically conservative *Roman de la rose* where Guillaume de Lorris breaks off, Jean de Meun demolishes the spell of courtly decorum by causing the allegorical figure Reason to utter her famous *gros mots*.[11] As is not the case with the *fatrasie,* the cultural shock that results here from the collision of extreme opposites of linguistic conventions initiates a spirited debate about language in which Reason embarks upon a discourse on the word as an epistemological tool. The word, she claims, may have originated with God and may be, consequently, a faithful replica of the universal (as Plato had argued), yet men employ the word as a sign whose arbitrary nature is fixed by convention (as Aristotle and his followers had argued).[12] It is axiomatic that the action in literature whose authors demonstrate an acute consciousness of the character of language will be primarily verbal action. From the purely physical action of *La Chanson de Roland* we have come full swing to the almost purely verbal action in Part II of *Le Roman de la rose*. Warfare has given way to dialectics.

Self-awareness in the process of art, as in life, is perhaps most fully gained through self-division and conflict. "For what must be sole or whole must first be rent," says Crazy Jane, and I know of no better means of gaining insight into literary language than to set its resources against each other. *Aucassin et Nicolette,* about which we know little except that its unknown author wrote in the early thirteenth century in northern France, is in my opinion one of the most sensitive attempts on the part of a medieval author to probe the very materials out of which he constructs his tale. Its success in such a venture (unmatched by anything before *Don Quixote*) is striking because the author generates insight into the function of literary language *in the terms of the language itself,* rather than through extrinsic theories that alter the terms of our response by defining them.

For all its charm, **Aucassin et Nicolette** has perplexed those who ask of it the orthodox questions of modern medieval criticism. One notices, for example, in the fundamentally circular argument and in the exasperated rhetoric of a scholar as accomplished as Mario Roques, the inadequacy of prevailing routines of medieval criticism (theory of origins, genre theory, literary influence, etc.) in relating meaningfully to the poem:

> People have searched for distant origins for this naive story . . . they have made **Aucassin et Nicolette** Byzantine or Arabic, or both at once. Was this original and unique form in medieval literature, as we have inherited it, the invention of its author, an invention that perhaps found no success or stimulated no limitations? Or is it not, on the contrary, that **Aucassin et Nicolette** is the sole sample that remains of a genre once in favor? But how are we to define this genre, and what is **Aucassin et Nicolette?** Some make a romance, a tale, a novella, and even a fabliau out of it; and even if none of these names, taken in a precise sense, seems exactly to fit, they all express, at least, the idea that **Aucassin et Nicolette** is above all a story . . .[13]

The most fruitful scholarship concerning **Aucassin et Nicolette** derives from authors who primarily observe and describe, and such scholarship inevitably gravitates toward stylistic analysis.[14] In my opinion, the most interesting study to date is that of Simon Monsonégo, who turned **Aucassin et Nicolette** over to the computers and thereby made available a great fund of information whose worth is invaluable.[15] The role of linguistic and stylistic analysis has been to confirm that **Aucassin et Nicolette** is anything but a "naïve story," and that it reaches far beyond the role of mere entertainment. Indeed, it may be argued that the author's primary goal in **Aucassin et Nicolette** was to create not merely a comedy of love, but a comedy of language.

As is the case in so much medieval narrative, the plot of **Aucassin et Nicolette** is constructed upon the fixed nature of its characters, and a change of heart in any major character would cause the whole tale to collapse. Aucassin's love for Nicolette is such that

> From Nicolette the beautiful
> No man can separate him,
> Though his father does not approve
> And his mother threatens him.
>
>   (III)

Nicolette's love is reciprocal, but Aucassin's parents are opposed to union on social grounds, as his mother explains:

> She was cast out of Carthage
> And bought up from a Saracen.
> Since you wish to take a wife,
> Take a woman of high breeding.
>
>   (III)

In **Aucassin et Nicolette** the fundamental intractability of human nature provides an architecture for the stylistic and rhetorical juxtapositions that make this work unique.

At the same time, the typical nature of the characters tends to empty the plot of true human involvement and to invite us to consider the characters as emanations of literary language. Discourse, it seems, can create character and generate episodes, and in such circumstances the word tends to lose its primarily communicative function and to move into the center of dramatic interest. In other words, the author of **Aucassin et Nicolette** has created a story with the purpose, beyond that of entertainment, of juxtaposing a number of incompatible literary styles in such a way as to define them through contrast, as in a dialogue whose speakers are known in and through each other, where the objects of understanding are the participants themselves, and where stylistic interaction is at once the means of knowledge and its end.

The formal division of the text into alternating sung verse *laisses* and recited prose passages suggests from the very outset that **Aucassin et Nicolette** is more than a story and that its author perceives in literary language a fundamental multiplicity of functions. While it must be said that a work with alternating passages of prose and verse was not new in medieval literature, in the context of thirteenth-century culture such a hybrid had special significance. Vernacular prose was maturing, and not only was it giving rise to new forms (such as historiography), but it was also rivalling and even displacing poetry as a narrative vehicle, as in the prose of *Lancelot* and the Grail literature. In **Aucassin et Nicolette,** however, poetry enjoys a wider range of expression than prose: proportionately, for example, the vocabulary of the poetry is more extensive than that of the prose in the area of words that occur only once in the piece.[16] The lexical wealth of the verse lies, interestingly, in substantives and adjectives. The prose, by contrast, is proportionately strong in verbs and adverbs.[17] These differences point up statistically what we may observe in other ways: the verse proffers a world that is static and removed, where nominalizing language constitutes its own action; the prose, by contrast, proffers a world that is temporal and spatial, in which movement and action are compulsory. In other words, the opposition between verse and prose is not merely a formalistic device; indeed, it presupposes what may be called distinct ontological levels in the world of the poem. As we shall see, the interplay between the modes of experience postulated by the language of **Aucassin et Nicolette** functions dramatically in the way the characters perceive and respond to the world in which they move.

Aucassin and Nicolette draw their natures as lovers from the conventional, idealizing language of the courtly lyric. Thirteen of the twenty-one *laisses* are reserved for their dramatic presence and for their utterances, and only noble characters (except for the shepherd, who plays upon a noble style, and the author) are allowed to enter into the realm of verse. As incarnations of a courtly ethic, Aucassin and Nicolette derive from a poetic world that is now archaic, as the poet suggests from the outset:

> Who would like to hear good verses
> Amusement from the ancient past,
> About two pretty little youngsters,
> Aucassin and Nicolette,
> Of the hardships he endured
> And of the great deeds he did
> For his friend with the bright face . . .

(I)

That Nicolette speaks authentically, like Aucassin, in the elevated rhetoric of verse identifies her, despite the apparent disgrace of her birth, as infallibly noble in the audience's mind, for by the thirteenth century the rhetorical concept of the "high" style has come to signify as much the social standing of the speaker as the moral purpose of his discourse. Discourse, in other words, is now seen as a function of the decorum of type psychology, as Geoffrey of Vinsauf reveals in his *Documentum de modo et arte dictandi et versificandi:* "When one treats of great people or things, then the style is grandiloquent; when of humble people, humble; when of middle-class people, middle."[18] In the case of Nicolette, style has a dramatic function, for it identifies her as a noblewoman and justifies (and even explains), in the mind of the audience, the boundless love that Aucassin feels for her.

Aucassin and Nicolette derive their identity as nobles, then, from a conventional poetic style, and through the adventures of the characters this style will be tested and nearly destroyed by hardships proffered in a world of prose. The first of these arises when Aucassin's parents resort to preventive detention and have the two lovers thrown into separate cells,—prison, in medieval poetry, is a favorite contraceptive device. Although the parents provide the immediate pretext for Nicolette's imprisonment, it may be argued that imperatives also grow out of the necessity for the author to create dramatic situations that match the fundamentally rhetorical architecture of his work. In order for Aucassin and Nicolette to utter their initial complaints of love, they must first be separated. The prison provides exactly that anguishing but poetically inspiring distance commanded by the rhetorical assumptions of the *planctus.* At the same time, however, the courtly complaint is conventionally a seasonal utterance and it teleologically supposes that the urge to love motivates the vegetable and animal world as nature is quickened by spring. Accordingly, Nicolette's cell is, in her complaints, an exquisitely decorous place, an un-prisonlike, artful place that both occasions and complements the poeticizing of her imagination. Here is a case where motifs of lyrical poetic language create their own dramatic setting, if not the whole plot in which they occur:

> Nicolette is put in prison,
> In a vaulted chamber

> Fashioned with great art,
> Painted with great wonder.
> At the marble window sill
> The maiden leaned . . .
> She looked out on the garden
> And saw the rose in bloom
> And the birds with their outcry,
> And she began to exclaim:
> "Ah me! unhappy misery!
> Why am I in prison?
> Aucassin, my young lord,
> Truly, I am your love . . ."

(V)

Like Chaucer's Criseyde, however, Nicolette is not circumscribed by ephemeral rhetoric, and by the end of her complaint she is already resolving to take initiative that will ultimately prove salutory:

> "But, by God, the son of Mary,
> I won't be here for long,
> If I can manage!"

(V)

Aucassin, by contrast, effetely allows himself to dissolve in a rhapsody in which rhetorical excess is certainly condemning:

> Nicolette, beautiful being,
> Beautiful coming, beautiful going,
> Beautiful pleasure, beautiful speaking,
> Beautiful sporting, beautiful playing,
> Beautiful kisses, beautiful embraces . . .

(VII)

If by birth Aucassin and Nicolette possess an aristocratic style, the manner in which they employ language is at odds with the uncomprehending—or obstinate—world that surrounds them. Freed from prison, they are immured by language. Two parallel episodes underscore the opposition between their mode of discourse and that proper to the surrounding social world. In the first, Nicolette wanders through a forest searching for Aucassin. She happens upon a band of shepherds, whom she implores to bear a message to Aucassin should they encounter him. The message is artificial and figurative, and draws upon poetic symbolism of courtly romance for its meaning:

> "May God be with you, sweet children," she said, "tell him that there is a beast in this forest and that he should come hunting; and if he can capture it, he would not give one of its members for a hundred marks of gold, nor for five hundred, nor for any amount."

(XVIII)

By their answer, these shepherds reveal that they do not emanate from the aristocratic *pastourelle.* On the contrary, they are decidedly unreceptive to her literary use of language and they dispute the credibility of her message at its literal, rather than figurative, level.

> "Tell him that?" said one who was more outspoken than the others, . . . "there is no beast in this forest so

costly, neither stag, nor lion, nor boar, whose members are worth more than ten deniers, or even three at the very most; and you speak of such great amounts!"

(XVIII)

What looks at first like stupid literal-mindedness in silly shepherds is instead the wily impudence of a lower class finding its own voice in literature; for when destiny carries Aucassin along this same route a few moments later, the shepherds play at being "literary" shepherds, enacting the prettiest little *pastourelle* imaginable:

> Now the little shepherds gather,
> Esmerés and Martinés,
> Früelins and Johanés,
> Robeçons and Aubries.
> One says, "Good friends,
> Lord help Aucassin,
> By my faith, a fine young man,
> And the dainty maiden
> With the blond hair
> And the bright face and eyes
> Who gave us some money,
> With which we'll buy cakes,
> And knives and sheathes,
> And flutes and cornets,
> And crooks and pipes,
> Lord protect her!"

(XXI)

Unaware of the ruse, Aucassin thinks of Nicolette and bids the shepherds repeat the song so that he can decode it. However, the shepherds are in a foul temper because they feel abused by Aucassin's father, who happens to be their overlord and who is stingy with his land, and they balk at singing. No amount of money will induce the shepherds to oblige the young aristocrat with a song. However, for a good fee the shepherds' spokesman consents to deliver Nicolette's message in prose:

> "Sir, we will take the deniers, but I won't sing, for I've given my word; but I will tell it to you, if you wish."
> "Oh Lord," said Aucassin, "I'd rather hear it told than not at all."

(XXII)

The shepherd accordingly delivers the message in prose, ending with the truculent remark, "Now get on hunting, if you wish; or forget it, if you wish; whatever, I'm no longer obligated to her." Gone is the ingenuous shepherd of aristocratic literature, just as the black man of Uncle Tomism would vanish some six centuries hence. In this episode, the choice between modes of expression has risen to the dramatic surface of the tale to become an issue with the characters themselves. Thus, the author brings to consciousness the nature of literary language by portraying the social basis for its external expression.

In the second episode, Aucassin encounters a cowherd in the forest. This figure's animal features are modelled upon those of the cowherd who points the way to the perilous fountain in Chrétien's *Yvain;* hence its terms of reference lie in poetry. This cowherd, however, is no emanation from the poetic marvelous: rather, he is an insolent churl who cannot understand why a man as rich as Aucassin would ever have cause to weep. Unaffected by the cowherd's boorishness, Aucassin goes right on speaking in the veiled language of romance that the cowherd takes literally: "To be sure," said Aucassin, "I'll gladly tell you. I came with a white hound to hunt this morning in the forest, and I lost him: that is why I weep." (XXIV) The cowherd devastates the enigma of this discourse with an outburst of unfigurative contempt: "Now hear that!" he said, "By the heart in our Lord's belly! You weep for a stinking dog?" The cowherd then goes on to recount his own catastrophe, which is that he himself has lost Roget, his best plough-ox. The name of Roget, uttered so spontaneously, contrasts with that of Nicolette so artfully concealed in the enigmas of romance. Aucassin is swept with compassion and empties his purse into the cowherd's hand, but he never becomes concerned that he and the cowherd are caught up in separate systems of language, each of which proffers its own values and reality, neither of which we are asked to condemn. The breakdown of communication is the true subject of this episode, and nowhere in thirteenth-century vernacular literature do we find a passage demonstrating more clearly the notion prevailing elsewhere that language is an arbitrary system of signs fixed by social convention. The device whereby the audience finds its own response to literary language defined or at least reflected in that of a fictive audience (the shepherds and the cowherd) within the work foreshadows the ironic techniques of both the *Canterbury Tales* and *Don Quixote.*

The dialectic of poetry and prose is one means by which the author of **Aucassin et Nicolette** calls into question the nature of literary language, but there are others. For instance, he can manage modulations of tone within a single passage that elicit radical shifts of esthetic perspective in the reader. Two examples come to mind. The first occurs when Nicolette escapes from her prison, sneaks to Aucassin, and whispers to him through a crack in the wall of his cell. The situation derives from an essentially poetic world, by virtue of its implicit allusions to Ovid's tale of Pyramus and Thisbe, as well as to a number of episodes in romance narrative. A guard overhears their conversation, but he is himself "noble and courtly and valiant." When he sees Garin's soldiers approaching to seize Nicolette, he decides to sing a "song" of warning which the villainous soldiers will not comprehend. The song comprises fourteen lines, and the first seven indulge generously in the pathos of the lovers' own complaints. They are composed in the most elegant and ornamental courtly style:

> Young maiden with a noble heart,
> With a body so refined and appealing,
> With blond and shining hair,
> With bright eyes and open smile,
> I can see from your face
> That you have spoken to your lover,
> Who dies for you.

(XV)

The guard suddenly alters the tone of his song, however, as he apparently realizes that the elegant rhetoric of the courtly lyric is not an effective means of warning the young lady that soldiers are about to pounce on her. Accordingly, the last half of his song becomes baldly "unliterary" and takes on a telegram-like urgency that dispenses with all decorum and *sur-langage*. We may be certain that a poet performing this *laisse* would match the rhetorical shift with a similar shift in the tempo and style of his song:

> I am telling you and you can hear;
> Watch out for those soldiers
> Who have come here looking for you
> With swords unsheathed under their capes.
> They are a dangerous threat,
> And will do you great harm
> If you don't watch out!

(XV)

The second example is more subtle, and may be found in the complaint that Aucassin utters in prison. In the first line he compares Nicolette to a lily, and here we recognize an idealizing metaphor which strikes us above all with its utter conventionality: "Nicolette, lily! . . ." Metaphor in the medieval courtly lyric is not primarily descriptive. Privileged by the closed system of the strophe and ritualized through music, the word takes on an incantatory function that we may best call sacramental: it invokes and bestows the virtues of the object being compared upon the beloved who excites the comparison. In this case it is a lily, a symbol of purity and chastity. Such a metaphor of sight entails both light and distance, but it simultaneously defines the eye of the seer as one wholly embued with the conventional way of perceiving a beautiful young woman. The second line of the complaint reinforces the sublimation of Aucassin's desire by two formulas that are so orthodox ("sweet friend with the clear face") as to be empty, but the third line shifts to an image of taste. Now, desire of another sort is shortening the esthetic distance, for a metaphor of taste implies, however wishfully, physical contact, if not possession: "You are sweeter than grapes . . ." The fourth line extends the comparison to a point near bathos, where the motive of simple sexual desire becomes transparent: "or a sop of wine in a wooden bowl." Gone is the innocent lily; instead, the opposites of bread and wine sopping together in a wooden bowl. Surely we are meant to see here the dilemma of an excitable young man who is trying to maintain a high rhetorical style of discourse, but whose imagination intrudes with its own lustful imperatives. In brief, the author makes us conscious of conventional literary language by sabotaging its public nature and its formal decorum with metaphors generated in the compulsion of an unbridled, individuating imagination.

Like the poetry, the prose in Aucassin et Nicolette provides special potentialities for underscoring the nature of literary discourse, and in these we encounter some familiar techniques of satire. The most obvious of these, perhaps, is the rhetorical downgrading of *topoi* proper to the exalted figurativeness of courtly poetry. In romance, wounds incurred in the service of love, as well as the wounds of Eros, bid us to consider the woman as a physician, just as Christ, in devotional poetry, is the true physician for the sickness of sinners. In *Aucassin et Nicolette,* however, the author short-circuits the figurative content of such language and causes Aucassin to fall off his horse during a reverie and dislocate his shoulder. Nicolette soon appears on the scene, bestows some anaesthetizing kisses, then proceeds very literally to put his shoulder back in place. I shall only mention another obvious technique of challenging literary language that one finds in the prose of this work, which is to banalize, probably consciously, the conventions of formal rhetoric. For example, may we not discern in the following lines a rather heavy-handed *deliberatio* where Aucassin proves the obvious by way of the ridiculous?

> "Ah, God," he said, "sweet creature! are these my mortal enemies who lead me away to cut off my head? Since my head will be cut off, I will never speak to Nicolette again, to my sweet friend whom I so love. But I still have a good sword, and I still sit on a good horse . . ."

(X)

Perhaps the most effective means by which the author questions not only the style but the implied values of literary language is the introduction, in the episode of the castle of Torelore, of the *fabliau*. Aucassin and Nicolette are driven to the land of Torelore by a storm. Aucassin enters the castle and discovers the King lying in bed. Speaking in verse, the King proclaims that he has just given birth to a son. The shock value of such humor is immense, for at this moment we recognize that the ideal has met face to face with its natural enemy, the absurd. Each is founded on repudiation of what is middling and banal: yet each is most seriously threatened by the possibility of turning into the other. Most significant, Aucassin is confronted by nothing less than a grotesque apparition of the faults that he himself has demonstrated. The King of Torelore and Aucassin are both "unnatural" in that each has yielded those chivalric activities that constitute medieval manhood to a woman. Aucassin has been (and will remain) essentially passive during this tale, while Nicolette more than once provides the initiative that brings them together. Aucassin has been unwholesomely disposed to substituting words for action, and perhaps poetry for prose. Now, in the effeminate King he is confronted by the ultimate consequence of the transgression of his identity as a man. Aucassin properly flies into a rage and thrashes the King until he renounces his illusion, then Aucassin discovers that the Queen is out on the battlefield. The battle itself is another detail drawn from the *fabliau* and serves as a corrective for the excessively ritualized combats of chivalric romance, which, like rhetoric, displace action: the soldiers throw rotten fruit, eggs and cheese at each other. When Aucassin intervenes with a real sword, he is reprimanded: "'Sir,' said the King, 'you have gone too far—it is not our custom that we kill each other.'" Ironically, Aucassin's reactions to both spectacles of the absurd are exactly those that a thirteenth-century audience (particularly an audience of non-nobles) could have experienced when confronted by the tendencies toward over-preciosity in courtliness that Aucassin himself incarnates.

Although *Aucassin et Nicolette* often employs techniques of satire, satire is not its true goal. The thirteenth century was a time when many literary styles and forms were available, yet none could claim to be culturally comprehensive. *Aucassin et Nicolette* is a work where a series of deliberate stylistic transgressions serves to make conscious the nature of literary language at a moment when none, by itself, could suffice. Almost all of the major literary talents of the thirteenth and fourteenth centuries were touched by this artistic dilemma, and Dante alone emerged with a single, sustained work whose language and poetic could succeed as a comprehensive literary monument. Chaucer's career, by contrast, was an unending quest for style, and this quest is never far beneath the dramatic surface of the *Canterbury Tales.*

Cultural hybridism in which art is informed by a dialectic of styles is common in European literature. We have no good critical vocabulary to define or account for this esthetic of transgression, but it tends to erupt at moments of cultural turbulence such as the early seventeenth century, when hard-line Aristotelian genre-theory receded, or as the late eighteenth, when the romantics overthrew the strictures of neo-classicism. It is interesting to note, however, that in such literature, as in *Aucassin et Nicolette,* poetry and poetic experience somehow always remain central. With its perpetual anachronisms and solipsisms, poetic vision visits men and challenges them with experiences that confound everything probable and ordinary in life. Through the magic of the word, poetry galvanizes the rest of existence and creates characters who, in deriving their nature from poetry, test the value of poetry itself through their adventures in a world of prose. The successful reunion of Aucassin and Nicolette is a comic victory of love over the obstacles of life, but also that of a poetic language—an over-precious one, to be sure—over roguish, common parlance. The victory contains nothing absolute, however, and we may laugh because everyone in the poem finally gets exactly what he is looking for—love, money, heirs or whatever. Human nature remains faulty but intact, and we of the audience are not asked to judge. Rather, we leave the piece with a smile and, if we wish, an unanswered question that lay at the heart of every medieval debate on language: where does reality lie?

Notes

1. St. Augustine, *Enarratio in Psalmum XCIX* as quoted and translated by Marcia Colish, *The Mirror of Language,* New Haven, 1969, p. 35.
2. The classical sign (*signum*) differs, of course, from that of de Saussure, for whom the sign is composed of *signifiant* plus *signifié.*
3. St. Paul, I. Cor. 13.12.
4. Laurent Renaud. "Le langage de saint Bonaventure à Jean Duns Scot," *Actes du colloque Saint Bonaventure,* Montréal and Paris, 1969, pp. 141-8.

5. *Ibid.*
6. St. Thomas Aquinas, *Somme théologique, les sacrements, Quaestiones 60-65,* transl. Roguet, Paris, 1951, appendix II, p. 255-6.
7. l. 1462-6, cited from *La Chanson de Roland,* ed. Joseph Bédier, Paris, 1926; translations are my own.
8. Peter Haidu, *Aesthetic Distance in Chrétien de Troyes,* Geneva, 1969, p. 262.
9. Translated from Paul Zumthor, *Art et technique poétiques à l'époque romane,* Paris, 1963, p. 169.
10. *Ibid.,* p. 170.
11. Guillaume de Lorris et Jean de Meun, *Le Roman de la rose,* ed. Lecoy Paris, 1965, t. I, 1. 5507.
12. *Ibid.,* 11. 7069-7074.
13. Mario Roques, ed., *Aucassin et Nicolette,* Paris, 1963, pp. ix, VII. All references to the text are to this edition. Translations are my own.
14. See the critical bibliography in Roques's edition.
15. Simone Monsonégo, *Etude stylo-statistique du vocabulaire des vers et de la prose dans la chantefable Aucassin et Nicolette,* Paris, 1966.
16. *Ibid.,* p. 64.
17. *Ibid.,* pp. 39-44.
18. Translated from E. Faral, *Les Arts poétiques du XIIe et du XIIIe siècle,* Paris, 1924, p. 87.

G. W. Goetinck (essay date 1970)

SOURCE: "*Aucassin et Nicolette* and Celtic Literature," in *Zeitschrift fur Celtische Philologie,* Vol. 31, 1970, pp. 224-29.

[*In the following essay, Goetinck investigates the possibility of Celtic influence on the composition of* Aucassin et Nicolette.]

The sources of inspiration of the author of the thirteenth-century *chantefable,* the form and content of his creation, have provided material for much discussion. The possible influence of Arab literature was proposed, assailed, and eventually discounted[1]. There is another possibility which has not been so fully explored, the influence of Celtic literature through French works based on materials of Celtic provenance. There are several features in *Aucassin* which are reminiscent of Celtic literature and although there is no positive proof that the origin of the *chantefable* is to be found here, the similarities are worth examining.

The form of the *chantefable,* the use of both prose and verse to tell a story is not exclusive to Celtic literature,[2] but it is a familiar feature of Celtic literary tradition. Examples are to be found in the *englynion* sung by Efnysien, Math, and Gwydion in the *Mabinogi;* Trystan, Esyllt, Cai and Gwalchmai in the story of *Trystan ac Esyllt,* and in the verse known as *Canu Llywarch Hen* which contains the remnants of two sagas.[3] The tales of Finn, Cuchullin, and the *Acallamh na Senórach (the Colloquy of the Ancients)*, contain a considerable amount of poetry and the form of the *Acallamh*, 'prose interspersed with speech poems,' has been compared with **Aucassin et Nicolette**.[4] In the *chantefable* the poetry includes narrative, the *conteur* continuing his account in verse as well as in prose, but these passages differ from the Celtic tradition. Here the poems are used to express personal emotion or to narrate events in which the speaker either personally took part, or with which he was closely connected.[5]

The *bouvier* in **Aucassin et Nicolette** is reminiscent of those figures in Celtic literature whose function is to guide the hero toward his goal. He may meet them in a forest clearing, or in the open country, often seated on a mound. They are Otherworld figures, frequently of gigantic size, connected with animals, and often rough and impolite, though helpful. Two figures from Welsh literature spring to mind, Custennin the shepherd in *Kulhwch ac Olwen*, and the black man of the forest in *Owein*.

In *Kulhwch ac Olwen* the hero, accompanied by Arthur's men ". . . see a great flock of sheep without limit or end to it, and a shepherd tending the sheep on top of a mound, and a jerkin of skins upon him, and at his side a shaggy mastiff which was bigger than a nine year old stallion. It was the way of him that never a lamb has he lost, much less a grown beast. No company had ever fared past him that he did not do it harm or deadly hurt; every dead tree and bush that was on the plain, his breath would burn them to the very ground."[6] Custennin is not said specifically to be of unusual stature, although it would not be unreasonable to assume that he is. The only reference to size is made later when, accepting Kulhwch's ring, the shepherd discovers that it will not fit him. He is not said to be black, as is the *coydwr* in *Owein*, but he is clearly an Otherworld figure since he is seated on a mound and possesses a monstrous dog. His wife is a woman of unusual strength. She runs towards the visitors to embrace them and Cai thrusts a stake between her hands. She squeezes the stake so that it becomes a twisted withe.[7] Had Cai seen a woman of normal stature running towards them, it is not likely that he would have taken such a precaution, especially since he was, himself, exceptionally tall and powerful. Like the *bouvier*, Custennin is not a particularly happy man, neither is he soft spoken. He announces, "There is no affliction to do me harm save my wife." and later, ". . . because of my wife Ysbaddaden Chief Giant has wrought my ruin."[8] Ysbaddaden has killed all twenty three sons born to the shepherd and his wife, and the twenty fourth would have suffered the same fate had not Cai offered to protect him. Questioned about the owner of the sheep he is tending, Custennin begins, "Fools of men that you are!"

In *Owein* Cynon's host tells him that he will see, ". . . a mound in the middle of the clearing, and a big black man shalt thou see on the middle of the mound who is not smaller than two of the men of this world. And one foot

has he, and one eye in his forehead's core; and he has a club of iron, and thou canst be sure that there are no two men who would not find their full load in the club. But his is not an ugly disposition; yet he is an ugly man, and he is keeper of that forest. And thou shalt see a thousand wild animals grazing about him. And ask him the way to go from the clearing, and he will be gruff with thee, but even so he will show thee a way whereby thou mayest have that thou art seeking."[9]

In this case the herdsman is black, huge, and clearly an Otherworld figure. Like Custennin, he sits on a mound and has dominion over countless numbers of animals, in this instance of every conceivable species. He is far from polite to Cynon, addressing him as "little man", and when Cynon, unhorsed, is trudging back from his defeat by the Black Knight the *coydwr* does not spare his feelings. ". . . it is a wonder I did not melt into a liquid pool for shame at the mockery I got from the black man,"[10] he admits. Like Custennin, the *coydwr* does guide Cynon and help him attain his adventure. He does the same for Owain who does not return in defeat.

Chrétien's version of this encounter[11] differs in detail from the Welsh version, but it also differs completely in tone. In *Owein* it is the black man who dominates the scene, who is master of the forest, the animals, and Cynon. He is able to do this and be taken seriously by the storyteller and his audience because of the Celts' firm belief in the existence of the Other World and the powers of its inhabitants, powers far superior to those of men. Such is not the case in *Yvain*. Chrétien's *vilain* is ugly and misshapen and his appearance causes the same type of shock as that of a freak at a fair, but there is no suggestion of superior powers although he is feared by his beasts. His assertion "Je sui uns hon,"[12] only serves to emphasise his inferiority, and Calogrenant addresses him in the half-bullying, contemptuous tone in which he would address any peasant. The Welsh *coydwr* is not a man, nor is there any reason why he should claim to be one.

The way in which the *vilain* is described further confirms his inferiority, for his features are compared with those of animals and his big head, bigger than that of an old nag, his hairy, elephant-like ears, owl-like eyes, cat's nose, wolf's mouth, and boar's teeth do nothing to foster respect for him. Here is no Otherworld figure of forbidding appearance and redoubtable powers, but a miserably deformed creature, fit only to live with animals, to be laughed at, and treated with contempt.

The *bouvier* in **Aucassin et Nicolette** is, like the forester in *Owein* and the *vilain* in *Yvain*, huge and ugly. He has a club of considerable size, he is connected with animals, and the hero meets him in the forest. He is not said to be black, although he has a shock of black hair. The tone of the conversation is more akin to those in *Owein* and *Kulhwch* than that in *Yvain*. Aucassin may be the son of a count, but the *bouvier* is not a whit impressed. Like Custennin, he is the victim of misfortune, but he accepts his lot philosophically. He does not direct Aucassin to his goal as do Custennin, the *coydwr,* and the *vilain,* although he does meet him in the forest whilst the hero is on a quest.

Aucassin's love trance is more reminiscent of the episode in Chrétien's *Lancelot* where the hero, lost in dreams of Guenièvre, is hurled from his saddle, recovers, and defeats his attacker[13], than of the love trance in *Perceval* or the Welsh *Peredur.* In these romances the hero is lost in dreams of his love, but even in that state he is capable of trouncing those who attack him, and in the Welsh version he overthrows twenty four knights, one after another.

The sea voyage culminating in the visit to the strange kingdom of Torelore recalls the famous voyages of Celtic literature.[14] Those of Bran, Brendan, and Maél Dúin are amongst the best known. The hero would set sail with a company of men and during the course of a long voyage they would visit many strange islands and see many wonders.

Maél Dúin and his men visit thirty one islands including the island where there are ants as large as foals; the island where there is a fierce beast looking like a horse, but with clawed feet like a hound; the island of black mourners, weeping and wailing. One of Maél Dúin's foster brothers lands here, begins to weep, and has to be left behind. The island where the inhabitants shout, "It is they!", as if they feared the travellers; the island of women where they stay for a year before they succeed in escaping; the island of laughter where the people do nothing but laugh. Here again, one of Maél Dúins' foster brothers lands and has to be abandoned.

The visit to Torelore is of the same type as the Celtic voyages, but it is more in the style of a parody. There is nothing exciting or breathtaking in the king who stays in bed with child whilst his consort goes forth to a battle in which the weapons consist of cheeses, pieces of rotten wood, and eggs, and in which it is against the rules to kill anyone. There is quite a degree of amusement here, but it is mixed with a strong element of pity for those whose battle succeeds in giving Aucassin the appearance of an accomplished knight.

These episodes in *Aucassin et Nicolette* which recall similar episodes in Celtic literature are compositions of a far less significant scale than those which preceded them, but this has no bearing on the literary value of the *chantefable* since it was not the author's intention to write a saga. Its very brevity, frivolity, its ineffective hero, and its irreverent attitude toward religion, may well be a parody on the interminably long romances with their heroes of unfailing courage and prowess, and their attendance at church. Clearly the author was not directly inspired by Celtic literature, but by works based on material of Celtic provenance which, in addition to the well known romances, doubtless existed in many different versions told from court to court and from fair to fair by *conteurs* of the type mentioned with scorn by Chrétien in *Erec* and in *Per-*

ceval.[15] Some of these *conteurs* would have been Breton and they may have used, beside the rhymed romance form, a mixture of prose and verse similar to the style of the old Celtic sagas.

Notes

1. Mario Roques, ed. *Aucassin et Nicolette,* (Paris 1962), vii-x.
2. Eleanor Knott & Gerard Murphy, *Early Irish Literature,* (London 1966), 37. Also Roques, *Aucassin,* viii.
3. I. Williams, ed. *Canu Llywarch Hen,* (Cardiff 1953), xxxvii-xliii. Sir Ifor maintains that the greater part of the contents of the Black Book of Carmarthen derives from a number of sagas written in this style, from which the prose has been completely lost; *Llywarch,* xli.
4. *Early Irish Literature,* 37, 161-162.
5. Sir Ifor Williams, *Lectures on Early Welsh Poetry,* (Dublin 1944), 19; *Llywarch,* xxxviii; *Early Irish Literature,* 158.
6. Gwyn & Thomas Jones, *The Mabinogion,* (London 1950), 108.
7. Jones & Jones, 110.
8. Jones & Jones, 109.
9. Jones & Jones, 158.
10. Jones & Jones, 161.
11. T. B. W. Reid, ed. *Yvain,* (Manchester 1952), 278-408.
12. *Yvain,* 330.
13. Mario Roques, ed. *Le Chevalier de la Charette,* (Paris 1958), 3685-94.
14. *Early Irish Literature,* 113; "The earliest of them, the eighth-century *Immram Brain,* or 'Voyage of Bran' is essentially pagan in character. But by the ninth century the *Immrama* had been adapted to suit a Christian outlook and may describe the magic islands visited by Christian monks or penitents. On one of these Christianized *Immrama,* the ninth-century *Immram Maíle Dúin,* or 'Voyage of Máel Dúin' a late ninth- or early tenth-century Irish Latinist modelled his *Navigatio Brendani,* which, translated into many continental languages, became one of the most popular stories of the Middle Ages and played an important part in inspiring those real voyages which culminated in the discovery of America"
15. W. Roach, ed. *Perceval,* (Paris 1959), 8676-79; Mario Roques, ed. *Erec et Enide,* (Paris 1952), 13-22.

Edelgard DuBruck (essay date 1972)

SOURCE: "'*Omnia vincit amor*:' The Audience of *Aucassin et Nicolette*—Confidant, Accomplice, and Judge of Its Author," in *Michigan Academician,* Vol. 5, Fall, 1972, pp. 193-200.

[*In the following essay, DuBruck maintains that the author of* Aucassin et Nicolette *sought to appeal to the common people of the middle to lower classes of society in the late twelfth or early thirteenth centuries.*]

Since its first mention in modern times, in 1752, we know very little more about this charming piece of early thirteenth-century French literature than did the contemporaries of Lacurne de Sainte-Palaye, its first translator.[1] We do not know the author, we have no exact date, we have only one manuscript (BN #2168), which is partially damaged, and as for the audience to which it was addressed, any conjecture is as fair as it is unfair. Obviously, its remarkable structure attracted scholarly attention; its fictional content elicited investigations—none of them ultimately satisfactory—into the origins of its various motifs, and its rich endowment with parodic elements was uncovered more recently.[2] Unfortunately, though, the modern literary critic often does not hesitate to develop a kind of myopic vision, and, for the sake of explaining the entire work in terms of one principle, neglects the wonderful complexity of this little masterpiece.[3]

To show and elucidate the components of *Aucassin et Nicolete,* and still preserve its unity as a work of art, is my aim in this study. All this can be done, if one sees as the key to all the different attitudes, sentiments and thoughts displayed in our *chantefable* the audience to which it was addressed.

It is true that direct references of our author to his readers or listeners are rare. After an elaborate prologue of fifteen verses, in which he promises a good story, well told, which might have a salutary effect on everyone, all we find now and then is the formula "si que vous avés oï et entendu," and at the very end the simple words: "No cantefable prent fin; / N'en sai plus dire."[4] However, as the author let the story itself speak to his audience, it speaks to us, revealing many interesting details about his contemporaries. In fact, he never forgets that his audience is present: this is indicated by the periodic insertion of the phrase "si que vous avés oï et entendu," or a slight variation of it.[5] That he expects to be judged by his audience is clear from the prologue; but he seeks in the reader, also, a confidant, and perhaps even an accomplice.

Such a relationship between author and audience is by no means novel at the time, and Chrétien de Troyes' precedent comes to mind immediately.[6] What is new, however, is the type of confidence and complicity, and above all, the social stratum which is obviously addressed. The author of *Aucassin et Nicolette* speaks to the common man of the middle, lower middle and perhaps even the lowest class in the late twelfth and early thirteenth centuries in northern France, most likely in an area which was quickly urbanizing, changing from an agrarian to a materialistic, money-oriented economy. Within the accepted scale of social hierarchies, the common man was on a fairly low level, still looking up to secular and ecclesiastic aristocracy for guidance or just protection. Often caught in a mesh of conflicting loyalties, the common man's trust was not infrequently betrayed in one way or another. Whatever the project

was—crusade, fight for existence or fight for his daily living—he had little to gain, but everything to lose. The further the common people developed in their own physical and mental defenses, the more onerous did the older feudal ties prove to be.

What was the collective face—if there is such a concept—of thirteenth-century society like? Once neglected by historians of medieval French literature, this century becomes more and more interesting to us, as we discover its varied texture and the many different tendencies which urge their way forward to a more modern age. It saw the development of scholastic intellectualism as well as of popular piety, two strains so different and yet actually related to one another. It saw the failure of the crusades, the granting of the Magna Carta, a hitherto unequalled growth of the bourgeois population and the need to educate. Henceforth, the bourgeois will still eagerly absorb the aristocratic forms of literature, but he will not cultivate them further; rather, he will often make fun of them and eventually counterbalance them with a solid body of didactic writings. The man of the middle class begins to take possession of the world in which he lives, and this not only from the geographical point of view.

Most of the characters who people our *chantefable* are common men and women, burghers, merchants. Nicolete herself is a Moorish slave girl living in a bourgeois milieu. Her foster parents, Viscount and Viscountess, though noble, are burghers, as their property is in the city. Even Aucassin is, from the beginning, portrayed by his human, universal characteristics (his love for Nicolete), and not depicted within his aristocratic frame of reference. In chapter 8 the author makes it a point to mention the share of the "borgois" in the defense of Garin's chateau. There are references to such necessary burghers as the "escargaites de la vile" (chapter 14), or simply, "le gaite qui estoit sor le tor" (chapter 15). We encounter shepherds at mealtime, a serf who has lost the best of his master's oxen; we hear about the serf's mother who owned nothing but her mattress, and even that they took away from her: "Une lasse mere avoie, si n'avoit plus vaillant que une keutisele, si li a on sacie de desous le dos, si gist a pur l'estrain" (chapter 24). When Aucassin and Nicolete travel together, "passent . . . les viles et les bors" (chapter 27), till friendly merchants take them along. Nicolete eventually becomes a *jongleur* herself and takes shelter with a poor woman at the shore. A mariner gives her a ride in his boat.

As we analyze the role played by each of these common people in our story it becomes obvious that many of them have a favorable impact, whereas, with few nuances, the aristocracy (in the roles of Count Garins, his wife, and Bougars) fare negatively. To mention only one example, the serf opposes Aucassin's lament for Nicolete with his despair about his loss, the ox, all of which, even though the whole episode may be meant in jest and parody, makes a lot of sense in view of the precariousness of the serf's economic existence. After his words about his poor mother (see above)—what audience would at that moment still be interested in Nicolete? Yet, the serf settles the matter "philosophically": "Car avoirs va et vient" (chapter 24). We can surmise from this how popular the wheel-of-fortune allegory must have been with the lower classes.[7]

Although he is "lais et hidex," the serf is thus depicted favorably, and here we have an instance where physical ugliness is not necessarily allied to the morally and psychologically abject, as (upper-class) Platonism would have it in the Middle Ages. On the other hand, the lowest point in Count Garin's "career" is doubtless the moment when he is convicted of having lied to his son and broken his word (chapter 10). The wider implications of this scene—the moral failure of a parent, the human failure of a warring aristocracy whose chivalric ideals have become exclusive of any other motivation—will be discussed further on.

It is obvious from the preceding paragraphs that the author is trying to please the common man by drawing a portrait of his social level, and by drawing it in favorable terms. In addition, he maintains his interest by discussing problems arising between the lower and upper classes. Above all, there is the question: May Aucassin—or may he not—marry a Moorish slave girl. We know the negative attitude of his parents, and we witness the cautious dissuasion by the Viscount and his short "De ce n'avés vos que faire" (chapter 6). Another clash of classes occurs in chapter 22, when the shepherd refuses Aucassin's request with the proud words: "Por quoi canteroie je por vos, s'il ne me seoit?" Finally, the serf faces severe punishment for losing his master's ox, probably additional labor.

Thematically, following the current vogue of stories of love and adventure, the author tells such a story, but places it into a middle-class frame of reference. As for the form of narrative, he may well have had at his disposal several verse portions of a Spanish or Southern French romance which he builds skillfully into a prose tale: late in the twelfth century prose narration became fashionable among the middle class which was less illiterate than in former times and began to conquer its world even through the written word.

Indeed, the prose portions of our *chantefable* reveal much attention to detail in localities, decor and everyday utensils. As the first map makers put more and more detail into their portolan charts, our first prose writers tend to familiarize their middle-class readers with their fictional surroundings. Witness Nicolete's escape, the mechanics of which are depicted in all detail: "Ele se leva, si vesti un bliäut de drap de soie, que ele avoit molt bon; si prist dras de lit et touailes, si noua l'un a l'autre, si fist une corde si longe come ele pot, si le noua au piler de le fenestre, si n'avala contreval le gardin; et prist se vesture a l'une main devant et a l'autre deriére, si s'escorça par le rousée qu'ele vit grande sor l'erbe, si s'en ala aval le gardin" (chapter 12). She descends into what seems to be a burgher's garden; the only flower mentioned is the humble marguerite: ". . . et les flors des margerites qu'ele ronpoit as ortex de ses piés, qui li gissoient sor le menuisse du pié par deseure, estoient droites noires avers ses piés et ses ganbes, tant par estoit blance la mescinete" (ibid).

Any miraculous events are kept at a minimum (Nicolete's survival and return to her native land after shipwreck), or deftly told as a form of *dementia* (Nicolete's miraculous healing of a pilgrim, chapter 11). Verisimilitude seems to have been more important to our author than the mere desire to entertain; and why else would he have been intent on *le vraisembable* but because his middle-class audience had become skeptical after an overdose of adventure tales?

The element which may have pleased the middle and lower middle class reader most, however, was the rich admixture of the grotesque and the comical, such as, for example, the *couvade* and "battle" scenes in Torelore / Utopia (chapters 28-33). In chapter 10, Aucassin sounds like a frustrated Pulcinello when he exclaims: "Et puis que j'arai la teste caupée, jamais ne parlerai a Nicolete me douce amie que je tant aim" (laughter from the audience). The same type of joke can be found in chapter 14: "Et puis que vos ariiés jut en lit a home, s'el mien non, or ne quidiés mie que j'atendisse tant que je trovasse coutel dont je me peüsce ferir el cuer et ozirre!" In another scene, serious though the occasion was, one cannot help thinking that Aucassin's "ne m'alés mie sermonant, mais tenés moi mes covens" (to his father) must have elicited a sympathetic chuckle especially from the adolescent reader or listener. The imagery used for Nicolete's beauty in chapter 11 is frankly comical, if very middle class, because the reader expects, automatically, the traditional "sublime" epithets: "Plus es douce que roisins / Ne que soupe en maserin."

The *dementia* episode, when the sight of Nicolete's bare leg heals a pilgrim miraculously, can be satire or simple pastiche; but it also appeals to our type of audience which would rather hear a story with a sexual overtone directly, without the disguise of, say, allegory. Other points of emphasis on sexual detail are in the continuation of what seems to be a fairly stereotype *effictio* in chapter 12: "et avoit les mameletes dures, qui li souslevoient sa vesteüre, ausi con ce fuissent deus nois gauges." There is no doubt that this continuation turns the preceding part into a joke; it does not mean that our author necessarily wished to ridicule all such descriptions in the romances; he merely saw the comic (slightly salacious) possibilities of such a procedure, and he knew his audience, which in all probability enjoyed this passage to the fullest. In the same category, Aucassin's "philosophy of love" in chapter 14 is a slight sally against women in general: "Car li amors de le fenme est en son oeul, et en son le cateron de sa mamele, et en son l'orteil del pié; mais li amors de l'oume est ens el cuer plantée, dont ele ne puet iscir."

Middle-class satire of women was practiced almost simultaneously with their glorification, especially in the late Middle Ages. In this respect, *Aucassin et Nicolette* appears to be ahead of a trend, but so is the *Jeu de la Feuillée* where the same simultaneity can be observed (cf. Adam's double *effictio* of his wife). I am inclined to think that the author of *Aucassin* is male, and that he wishes to appeal here especially to the members of his own sex.

In the preceding pages we hope to have shown that the author of our *chantefable* tries in many ways to please his audience, to draw their attention, to discuss their problems, to make them laugh and thus to make them his confidant, as he, implicitly, is theirs. But there is more to our story: the author wants to lead them in an open attack against the upper classes and their favorite pastimes which are often so detrimental to the poorer folk. Thus, the audience becomes his accomplice, as he is theirs. For this purpose, he uses satire and parody. First of all, this early Cervantes attacks chivalry and warfare. Aucassin, as we all know, abhors fighting and thinks of nothing but his Nicolete. The people who do fight, Count Garins and Count Bougars, are depicted negatively. The battle in Torelore under the leadership of the queen is fought by means of roasted apples, eggs, fresh cheeses and mushrooms. When Aucassin, as a friend of the king, begins to strike the king's enemies, the latter intervenes hastily: "Il n'est mie costume que nos entrocions li uns l'autre" (chapter 32).

Our author has also his own ideas about nobility. Clearly, he prefers nobility of character to that of birth: "Avoi! péres, fait Aucassins, ou est ore si haute honers en terre, se Nicolete ma trés douce amie l'avoit, qu'ele ne fust bien enploiie en li? S'ele estoit enpereris de Colstentinoble u d'Alemaigne, u roïne de France u d'Engletere, si aroit il assés peu en li, tant est france et cortoise et debonaire et entecie de toutes bones teces" (chapter 2).

Repeatedly, he speaks up in favor of manual work and remuneration. The viscount, Nicolete's godfather, "li donra un de ces jors un baceler qui du pain li gaaignera par honor" (ibid); truly a "telling" statement, because our audience understands the implicit continuation of this sentence—i.e., not a nobleman who earns nothing, but takes what he needs, if need be, dishonorably. Money is mentioned frequently in the *chantefable,* and *richece* is a desirable goal. Aucassin's joy at the promise of his reward is expressed in this comparison: "Por cent mile mars d'or mier / Ne le fesist on si lié" (chapter 9); in a similar way, in chapter 18: if Aucassin could catch Nicolete, his wondrous "beste," "il n'en donroit mie un menbre por cent mars d'or, non por cinc cens ne por nul avoir." For money the shepherds are willing to relay Nicolete's message to Aucassin; they do, mentioning later the *deniers* she gave them, and what they bought. To get more information, Aucassin has to spend ten sous. In chapter 24, the ugly youth scoffs at Aucassin: "Mais por quoi plourés vos. . . ? Certes, se j'estoie ausi rices hom que vos estes, tos li mons ne me feroit mie plorer." For the poor man, happiness is *richece.* Aucassin gives him twenty sous to buy a nex ox.

The author also attacks some medieval religious attitudes encouraged by the church, specifically intolerance of any other faith. Nicolete, although of pagan origin, is lovely and morally stainless. She has been baptized as a Christian by her godparents, but socially she remains an outcast almost to the end. In turn, when she reaches her native Cartagena, she receives the highest honors, while Aucassin is about to be exiled. The healing incident told in Aucassin's *dementia* may be a satire of miraculous healings or not—in any case it is not original in the story but has been attested to in other romances. Finally, the author reverses the roles of hell and paradise in chapter 6, and he describes his ideal society which happens to be waiting for him in hell: "li bel clerc" (fellow intellectuals), "li bel cevalier," "li buen sergant" (middle class) and "li franc home" (middle class), "beles dames cortoises" (for the *deduit* of the cevalier, clerc, sergant or franc home, for Aucassin—and our author), "harpeor et jogleor" (like himself), and "li roi del siecle" (emphasis is on "del siecle" = secular). He abhors heaven, complete with priests, unhealthy, scurvy characters, half crippled, naked and famished ascetics: clearly, a bourgeois questioning of asceticism and its advisability as a *summum bonum.*

It has been said that the author attacks the concept of courtly love. This is only partially true. Aucassin is constantly preoccupied with Nicolete, but she is not inexorable or cruel; she is, indeed, in love with him herself. If anything, we have here a manifestation of Ovidian love, as in *Tristan,* or simply the concept of love one would find in an idyllic novel. It is the expression of love in sincerely poetic and sometimes quite naïve terms which is and was a main attraction of our *chantefable.*[8] The author not only destroys illusions; he also sets up new ideals in return. Aucassin is an individual who does not fit the mold of the knight who fights at the slightest provocation,—but to call him a coward and let it go under the label of parody is too easy a solution. Nicolete, on the other hand, is not the kind of woman who sits back and lets the man take over and make all the decisions. She takes the initiative and frees herself from prison. She wonders where they are going in the forest—a touch of realism—while Aucassin is too happy to be worried. What Nicolete admires in Aucassin has nothing to do with fighting or making decisions: at one point in the story she elaborates, calling him "gentix et sages, / Frans damoisiax honorables" (chapter 37).

That Aucassin is wise and tolerant and a true Christian is shown when he frees his father's enemy, Count Bougars.[9] His second humane action was to give twenty sous to the youth for his lost ox. Finally Aucassin, whose reputation must have endeared him to his father's subjects, is received with joy by them after Garin's death (chapter 34). It looks as if he was made in the image of the ideally wise ruler whom both our author and his audience may have known in their lifetime: Saint Louis. Thus, if certain accepted attitudes or upper-class ideals were attacked in *Aucassin et Nicolete,* the author seems to imply to his readers, who heartily agreed with his action, that something new has to replace whatever was worn out or unacceptable.

It would be wrong, however, to go to the other extreme and to insist, with Ménard, that parody cannot be proved to exist in the *chantefable* (op cit, n. 6, p. 521). There are definite traces of its various forms, but they are just one element in this complex work. Also, the author uses the customary safeguards of parodists and satirists, and in this, too, his audience has to be his accomplice, if he wishes to be understood. To mitigate the sting of his attack, he places the story in an exotic setting far away from northern France. In chapters 28-33, a utopian setting is inserted (story within a story), Torelore, with clear indications that it is meant to be a somewhat comical never-never-land with strange but very desirable customs. In his satire of the clergy, he carefully places his ideal society in hell—and what is wrong with that? Nicolete's "healing powers" are tested in a *dementia,* which is, like a dream, another security device.[10] Finally, we may have found a clue to the author's silence about himself, his complete absence from the text after the prologue: this, too, could be a security measure of a man who simply relates a story he has heard and who could claim innocence for any offensive detail in it.

For he knows he is going to be judged. Therefore the elaborate prologue which is, at the same time, intentionally inoffensive and betrays nothing of all the criticism and inversions, not even of the serious thoughts which we encounter throughout *Aucassin et Nicolete.* He refers to his story as "bons vers" and as "biax dis" (chapter 1), and it is still unclear—perhaps intentionally so—whether he reports someone else's story or his own, or whether he claims to recite what he has heard from the mysterious "viel antif," but is actually that person himself. He simply promises a good story, and the audience, in all probability, would agree that he kept his promise. Secondly, he assures the readers or listeners that the song will be "dox," courtly and well arranged ("bienasis"): he is an artist and knows that some in his audience may not be uncritical but well versed in the rules of his "trade," and that they also will welcome such innovations as the prose sections.

Finally, he predicts a certain salutary effect from his story:

> Nus hom n'est si esbahis,
> Tant dolans ni entrepris,
> De grant mal amaladis,
> Se il l'oit, ne soit garis,
> Et de joie resbaudis,
> Tant par est douce

(ibid).

Aucassin et Nicolete speaks indeed to everyone, no matter how grieved, how troubled, how poor, how disadvantaged and how desperate he is. Therefore the need for the many heterogeneous elements in the story. In these six last lines of the prologue the author addresses his real audience, the people he wishes to reach: the middle and lower classes. They shall be his confidant, accomplice, and judge.

If our findings have led us to accurate results, the audience must have accepted the author's story enthusiastically. I am disinclined to consider the fact that we have only one manuscript as proof for the work's unfavorable reception. I am also weighing the possibility of our finding, in due time, more *chantefables.* We should keep in mind that only a small part of the Middle Ages (approximately one

ninth, if a quantitative measure is at all appropriate) is known to us via extant manuscripts. Search and investigation must go on, especially in the East European countries, where many manuscripts are still stored and have not even been catalogued as yet. Secondly, the works that we do know reflect mostly the thoughts and attitudes of the upper classes, while we may perhaps never find out what the common man was thinking and doing, unless we develop a set of new research methods.

Be this as it may, the twentieth-century reader is just as enthusiastic about *Aucassin et Nicolete* as his thirteenth-century predecessor probably was. In an age of new sophistications and psychological complexities, of endless warfare, of women's liberation and parental problems, we understand the various episodes and thoughts linked up in the *chantefable.* With smiling intelligence we enjoy what seem to us the work's surrealistic touches, the grotesque, as well as the frankly comical incidents. If its unknown author had a message for us it would probably be to stop, in our criticism, the unilaterally analytical approach, to accept the work in all its marvelous complexity, to consider it something of a source book on social conditions in his time, and perhaps to avoid their imperfections. With his fine sense of realism, however, he would have known better than to expect great reforms from us.

Notes

1. (trans.), *Histoire ou Romance d'Aucassin et de Nicolette* (Paris, 1752).

2. Cf. D. Scheludko, "Zur Entstehungsgeschichte von *Aucassin et Nicolete,*" *ZRPh,* XLII (1922), 458-490; K. Rogger, "Etude descriptive de la chantefable *Aucassin et Nicolete,*" *ZRPh,* LXVII (1951), 409-457, and LXX (1954), 1-57; O. Jodogne, "La Parodie et le pastiche dans *Aucassin et Nicolete,*" *Cahiers de l'association internationale des études françaises,* XII (1960), 53-65; R. Harden, "*Aucassin et Nicolete* as Parody," *Studies in Philology,* LXIII (1966), 1-9; B. Nelson Sargent, "Parody in *Aucassin et Nicolette:* Some Further Considerations," *The French Review,* 43 (1970), 597-605.

3. To give one example, in Harden's treatment (v. n. 2, supra) Aucassin becomes "a petulant, mooning juvenile who throws a childish tantrum because his father denies him Nicolette" (p. 3). It is my intention to show that Aucassin is a much more complex character.

4. I am using the F. W. Bourdillon edition (Manchester, 1919, repr. 1930). All quotations from *Aucassin et Nicolete* will be taken from this edition.

5. Such contacts with the audience occur in chs. 6, 10, 11 ("si con vos porrés oīr"), 12, 18, 20, 24 ("Ne quidiés mie que les ronces et les espines l'espargnaiscent" and "tel con je vos dirai"), 28, 36 ("or lairons d'Aucassin, si dirons de Nicolete").

6. Cf. also, P. Ménard, *Le Rire et le sourire dans le roman courtois en France au moyen âge* (Paris, 1969), pp. 487 ff.

7. Harden's treatment of this episode is as follows: "Here we have to picture to ourselves two huge males each weeping over the loss of his 'beast,' the *bouvier* for his ox and Aucassin for his *beste* . . . Each love tale (sic) mocks the other. As a lover, Aucassin is no superior to the *bouvier*" (loc cit supra, n. 2, p. 6). Now, nothing in the text indicates that the *bouvier's* misfortune is a love tale. It is obvious that such a narrow point of view, even though correct in some detail, does an injustice to an episode which is filled with significance.

8. As P. Ménard has pointed out, the *aube* in ch. 15 and the star-song in ch. 25 are genuine samples of their genres, and nothing indicates that they were meant as parody. Their presence in the work leads us to the conclusion, however, that "l'auteur d'*Aucassin* nous semble fort bien connaître la tradition littéraire de son temps" (op cit, n. 6, supra, p. 519).

9. In their desire to establish a system of parodies in *Aucassin,* modern critics have either not discussed this episode or written it off as one of the absurd things that Aucassin did in his "cowardice" (cf. Harden, v. n. 2, supra, pp. 4-5). Note, on the other hand, that Aucassin's attitude comes as a reaction against Garin's failure to keep his promise.

10. I am indebted to Alan E. Knight for his *aperçus* on the dream device, as well as on social problems and their literary treatment ("The Medieval Theater of the Absurd," *PMLA,* LXXXVI, 1971, 183-189).

June Hall Martin (essay date 1972)

SOURCE: "Aucassin," in *Love's Fools: Aucassin, Troilus, Calisto, and the Parody of the Courtly Lover,* Tamesis Books Limited, 1972, pp. 23-36.

[*In the following essay, Martin argues that the parody of Aucassin as a courtly lover in* Aucassin et Nicolette *is the element that unifies the various episodes in the tale.*]

While almost all medieval literature is the object of far too little study, the thirteenth-century *chantefable,* **Aucassin et Nicolette,** is even more critically impoverished than most. Until fairly recently, scholars who had given attention to the text had concentrated primarily on certain linguistic difficulties, disputed readings of various lines or, at best, examinations of single motifs. In the past two decades, however, critics have begun to consider the text as a whole, and their investigations have led to a general agreement that **Aucassin et Nicolette** is not the sweet and simple tale it was once thought to be, but that it is intended to be humorous. Most notable among these recent studies are those of Albert Pauphilet (1950), Omer Jodogne (1959), and Robert Harden (1966).[1] Although their investigations differ in many respects, they agree on one fundamental point— that **Aucassin et Nicolette** is, in some sense, a parody. Pauphilet claims that the author of the *chantefable* is paro-

dying current literary themes of war, adventure and romance. Jodogne goes a step further in asserting (p. 65) that the work is both "pastiche et parodie de trois genres littéraires", the *roman idyllique,* from which the work takes its structure, the *chanson de geste* and lyric poetry. Harden agrees that the parody is directed towards the "vapid plots and equally vapid personages of the idyllic novel" (p. 3). But he, too, is unable to account for all situations within the rather narrow structure he suggests, and he is forced to compromise his position somewhat by admitting that the parody laps over into *chanson de geste, desbats,* and even *fabliaux.*

While these studies undoubtedly point in the right direction, that is, toward parody, in the final analysis they leave something to be desired, for they tend to obscure the fundamental unity of the text. The parody does not seem to lie in the disunity that a pastiche of several genres or themes would suggest. Nor, indeed, does the parody seem to be one of genres at all, except peripherally. There is a more fundamental unifying element, a character who ties together the actions and tones of the different episodes— Aucassin. Certainly the importance of Aucassin as a humorous figure in the *chantefable* has not gone unnoticed. Pauphilet has remarked that he is "un personnage sympathique, mais un peu pâle, qui prête souvent à sourire, mais sans hostilité de fond" (p. 246). Jodogne has attributed even greater importance to Aucassin's role, concluding that along with the pastiche and parody of the three literary genres previously mentioned there is also "pastiche et parodie de l'amoureux" (p. 65) whom he characterizes as "un insensé, un réfractaire au statut social, un pusillanime" (p. 59). Harden as well has noted the humorous role of Aucassin and asserts that he is "a veritable anti-hero" (p. 6). Rather than considering the parody of the hero as a secondary issue, or, as in the case of Jodogne, of no greater significance than the generic parodies, I would contend that it is precisely and primarily toward Aucassin that the parodist directs himself, his humor, his criticism, and, as Pauphilet has suggested, his sympathy. He has seized upon the figure of the courtly lover and has made an amusing quasi-critical commentary on the eccentricities of his behavior and his lack of practical function in the real world.[2] Virtually all the humor in the *chantefable* is centered, not around the situation nor the individual episodes *per se,* but around the behavior of the protagonist within each episode. Even the land of Torelore which is constructed around an inherently ludicrous situation is rendered more humorous by the thrashing about of Aucassin, who exhibits there a bravura he has not shown in the outside world.[3] Aucassin, and this episode merely tends to confirm it, is fundamentally a misfit. He shares with Don Quixote an existence in a world that is not especially prepared for him. The world of Aucassin should be one of dwarfs, magic rings, and strange, heroic adventures, for it is in this sort of world that he could properly function as a courtly lover. Placed in such a world as that of Beaucaire, which is by no means the "random, everyday, real world"[4] of Don Quixote but which does concern itself with practical considerations, Aucassin is remarkably inept at almost everything. He is as awkward as the young Perceval entering for the first time into the world of chivalry, and the only lover's "duties" he can properly perform are those of mourning, sighing, and weeping, which he does abundantly, precisely the behavior most likely to be picked up and put into perspective by the mocking pen of the parodist.

From the very beginning Aucassin is described in conventional courtly-love terms. The first *laisse* announces that the tale is about Nicolette and Aucassin, emphasizing the role of Aucassin:

> Qui vauroit bon vers oïr . . .
>
> des grans paines qu'il soufri
> et des proueces qu'il fist
> por s'amie o le cler vis.[5]

These last three lines sum up the essential actions of the traditional courtly lover who, as we see in a more or less ideal state in the romances of Chrétien, suffered "grans paines" and performed "des sproueces . . . por s'amie". That the parodist felt compelled to mention Aucassin's "proueces", which can only be read ironically, merely confirms the hypothesis that we are indeed dealing with a "courtly lover" called Aucassin. His physical description in the second division of the work is also traditional: "Biax estoit et gens et grans et bien tailliés de ganbes et de piés et de cors et de bras; il avoit les caviax blons et menus recercelés et les ex vairs et rians et le face clere et traitice et le nes haut et bien assis" (II, 10-14). Blond curls, grey eyes, and a well-made nose are almost as necessary to the courtly lover as his horse and sword.

The beginning of the tale finds Aucassin already in such an unbalanced state of development between *paines* and *proueces* that he is almost immediately recognizable as a parody or a bad copy of the conventional courtly lover. ". . . si estoit soupris d'Amor, qui tout vaint, qu'il ne voloit estre cevalers, ne les armes prendres, n'aler au tornoi, ne fare point de quanque il deust" (II, 15-18). He is not without literary precedent, however, for even within the works of Chrétien, as we have seen, this sort of conflict between love and prowess plays a significant role. Aucassin is in essentially the same position as Erec and Yvain shortly after their respective marriages. Such apparent recreancy is one of the pitfalls of love, one into which better men than Aucassin have fallen. But if the parody did not go beyond this point Aucassin would remain a mere caricature of a courtly lover. The success of the parody is derived not just from Aucassin himself, but from an essential conflict between our courtly lover and the other characters who inhabit Beaucaire, none of whom appears to know the rules of the courtly world. In Beaucaire, for example, one cannot even trust a father to keep his word. Aucassin makes a bargain with his father Count Garin, agreeing to don his armor and defend his land against an invading army in exchange for a kiss and a few words from Nicolette. But when Aucassin has fulfilled his promise and captured the enemy leader, Garin pretends to have forgotten

his pledge. How different this is from the world of Chrétien's heroes where a captured knight gives his word to return to Arthur's court and recount the story of his own defeat and fulfills his promise!

Aucassin often finds himself in situations which parallel episodes in Chrétien's romances. He behaves in many instances very much as Lancelot or Yvain before him has behaved, but the same set of rules is not followed by the other characters. For example, as Aucassin rides into battle, his mind is so preoccupied with thoughts of Nicolette that he drops his reins, totally oblivious of the fact that his horse has borne him into the thick of battle. The enemy captures him without warning. Lancelot, in search of Guenevere, finds himself in a similar situation which has been referred to in the introduction to the present study. He rides toward a forbidden ford, lost in thought:

> et ses pansers est de tel guise
> que lui meïsmes en oblie,
> ne set s'il est, ou s'il n'est mie,
> ne ne li manbre de son non,
> ne set s'il est armez ou non,
> ne set ou va, ne set don vient;
> de rien nule ne li sovient
> fors d'une seule, et por celi
> a mis les autres en obli;
> a cele seule panse tant
> qu'il n'ot, ne voit, ne rien n'antant.[6]

Struck down by the knight who guards the ford, Lancelot asks to be allowed to rearm and joust fairly with the knight who agrees willingly.

Having been taken prisoner by the forces of Bougar de Valence, Aucassin remembers suddenly that if his head is cut off he can no longer converse with Nicolette. He realizes then that they have neglected to take away his sword; and singlehanded he captures Bougar and takes him back to his father. But when he learns of his father's perfidy, he releases Bougar, demanding from him only a promise that he will do some evil toward Count Garin every day for the rest of his life. Bougar thinks he is joking: "Sire, por Diu, fait il, ne me gabés mie; mais metés moi a raençon: vos ne me sarés je demander or ni argent, cevaus ne palefrois, ne vair ne gris, ciens ne oisiax, que je ne vos doinse" (X, 66-69). Bougar is a practical man; he cannot understand Aucassin's request for a mere promise when he could have any ransom he asked. But Aucassin insists on the promise and Bougar agrees, although there is no evidence within the text that he fulfilled the agreement. Jodogne interprets the fact that we hear from Bougar no more as conclusive evidence that he has lied to Aucassin just as his father the Count had lied. "Ces deux personnages ne sont pas déloyaux; ils ont menti comme on ment à un malade, ou mieux à un fou qu'on voudrait interner. Ils sont très sages, en somme; ils ne veulent pas 'baer a folie'" (p. 60). For Jodogne Aucassin is "un fou au pays des sages", but such a conclusion seems to me a gross oversimplification. What we have here is a conflict of social systems. While it is true that Aucassin usually comes out looking a little foolish, the reader tends to smile *sympathetically,* for however often he is the butt of the joke, he is usually right. And he has little understanding of the materialistic world of Beaucaire.

Material values are brought into play also when Aucassin meets the various rustics in the woods. Jodogne has attributed their appearance in the *chantefable* to an intended parody of the *pastourelle,* but the rustic is by no means an unfamiliar figure in the romances of Chrétien. The giant herdsman in the *Yvain,* for example, is almost copied in the *Aucassin.*[7] Both are described as large and black; both are depicted as leaning upon a club. Even identical terms are used in the descriptions. For example, "leiz et hideus" in the *Yvain* becomes in the thirteenth-century Picardian dialect of the *Aucassin* "lais et hidex". Instead of being adorned with "danz de sengler aguz et rous", the rustic of the *Aucassin* has "uns grans dens gaunes et lais". Yvain's rustic is described as "apoiez fu sor sa maçue", while Aucassin's is "apoiiés sor une grande maçue". And both are clad in skins of cattle. The similarities of the descriptions, while Chrétien's is considerably more detailed, are rather remarkable.

Just as the descriptions of the rustics are strikingly similar, so, too, in some respects, are the actions of Calogrenant, the hero of this episode of the *Yvain,* and Aucassin. The notable exception is the vastly different greetings proffered by our two protagonists. Calogrenant, who would not be too surprised to meet such a monster in the woods, is primarily concerned with the moral position of the giant rustic. He exclaims:

> . . . Va, car me di
> se tu es boene chose ou non.[8]

Calogrenant's question shows a certain sophistication, a certain awareness of several possibilities, particularly when it is compared to Aucassin's innocent "Biax frere, Dix t'i aït!" (XXIV, 25). Aucassin's greeting to the rustic is no less courtly than is his greeting to Nicolette. He has a rather undefined sense of propriety and behaves somewhat like a novice who tries very hard not to make mistakes yet errs through his over-caution.

Calogrenant inquires of the cowherd what he is doing in the woods, and the rustic answers immediately,

> . . . Ge m'i estois,
> et gart les bestes de cest bois.

> (331-32)

Aucassin asks the same question: "que fais tu ilec?" (XXIV,26), but the rustic is not so accommodating. He asks suspiciously, "A vos que monte?" (XXIV, 28). The rustic of the *Yvain* is a herdsman who guards the wild cattle of the woods and who controls them utterly. They tremble, he says, to see him punish one among them by wrenching its horns, and they stand still, seeming to beg for mercy. The story of the rustic Aucassin encounters is

less fanciful. He has been hired to drive a plough with a yoke of four oxen, but he has lost one and is out seeking it. The herdsman of the *Yvain* is the sort of creature one would expect to find in a courtly romance. He is superhuman, monstrously ugly, and placed within the story only for the hero's benefit, for he serves to direct Calogrenant to the marvelous fountain. The only vestige of the original herdsman left in the "demythologized" rustic of *Aucassin et Nicolette* is his ugliness. He seems incompetent since he cannot even keep up with his domesticated ox. And the melodramatic story he tells of not having eaten for three days, of the prison that awaits him if he cannot pay for the ox, of his poor old mother whose very mattress has been taken from under her and who must lie on straw, is just a bit too familiar for us to accept it entirely at face value. In any case, whether the story is true or not, the rustic succeeds in relieving Aucassin of twenty sous.

The herdsmen ask in turn the purpose of the knights' presence in the woods. Calogrenant answers truthfully that he seeks adventure whereby to test his prowess and courage, but Aucassin replies with a lie (or perhaps the truth garbed in symbolic language) as though the naked truth were insufficient for such a world. "Je vig hui matin cacier en ceste forest, s'avoie un blanc levrer, le plus bel del siecle, si l'ai perdu: por ce pleur jou" (XXIV, 39-41). The peasant snorts, "Os! . . . por le cuer que cil Sires eut en sen ventre! que vos plorastes por un cien puant?" (XXIV, 43-44). Once the twenty sous has changed hands the encounter is ended; the rustic has served no useful purpose to Aucassin. Earlier in the story, however, Aucassin does receive directions from some younger herdsmen to whom Nicolette has paid five sous to deliver a message to him. Instead of delivering the message as soon as they see Aucassin, they tease him with a song:

> . . . Bel conpaignet,
> Dix aït Aucasinet,
> voire a foi! le bel vellet;
> et le mescine au corset
> qui avoit le poil blondet,
> cler le vis et l'oeul vairet,
> ki nos dona denerés
> dont acatrons gastelés,
> gaïnes et coutelés,
> flaüsteles et cornés,
> maçëles et pipés!
> Dix le garisse!

> (XXI, 5-16)

Aucassin, hearing their words, rides joyfully forward and asks them to repeat their song, but they coyly refuse until Aucassin offers them ten sous, whereupon one of the boys tells the tale in prose. It is significant that in both encounters some reference is made early in the conversation to Aucassin's wealth. On this occasion, one of the young herdsmen remarks, ". . . il n'a si rice home en cest païs sans le cors le Conte Garin" (XXII, 16-17), a statement which is echoed by the hideous rustic, ". . . se j'estoie ausi rices hom que vos estes, tos li mons ne me feroit mie plorer" (XXIV, 32-33). In each case Aucassin asks immediately if they know who he is, and the answer is a rapid "Oïl, nos savions bien que vos estes Aucassins nos damoisiax" (XXII, 11-12) or "Oie, je sai bien que vos estes Aucassins, li fix le conte" (XXIV, 35). Aucassin's reputation is apparently widespread, and he seems to be considered quite gullible.

A world like Beaucaire in which men are not always honorable and do not live by the rules of chivalry, where even herdsmen take advantage of a simple heart, is a difficult world for the courtly lover to operate in. But perhaps even these obstacles would not be insurmountable for Aucassin if only Nicolette behaved like a courtly lady. Physically she is perfect for the role:

> Ele avoit les caviaus blons et menus recercelés, et les ex vairs et rians, et le face traitice, et le nes haut et bien assis, et lé levretes vremelletes plus que n'est cerisse ne rose el tans d'esté, et les dens blancs et menus; et avoit les mameletes dures qui li souslevoient sa vesteure ausi con ce fuissent deus nois gauges; et estoit graille par mi les flans qu'en vox dex mains le peusciés enclorre; et les flors des margerites . . . estoient droites noires avers ses piés et ses ganbes, tant par estoit blance la mescinete.

(XII, 19-28)

This portrait of Nicolette, as Barbara Sargent points out, "could hardly be more conventional: an enumeration from head to foot of the qualities essential to feminine beauty".[9] And one can scarcely fail to notice the physical characteristics she shares with Aucassin—"caviaus blons et menus recercelés . . . ex vairs et rians . . . face traitice . . . nes haut et bien assis". But in spite of her physical qualifications for her role as Aucassin's "douce amie", she seems to know little more about a proper sort of courtly romance than does Aucassin's father, and she repeatedly shows Aucassin up in comic perspective by acting as a contrast to him. Throughout the work, the author plays with the inherent reversal of male-female roles in the courtly love relationship. For example, when they are both imprisoned, it is Nicolette, not Aucassin, who escapes. It is *she* who comes to *his* tower where they engage in a love debate before dawn. In his article "The *Aube* in *Aucassin et Nicolette*", William S. Woods contends that the separation of Aucassin and Nicolette in sections XII-XVI of the *chantefable* parodies the themes of the usual *aube* pattern. Here again, the parody is aimed not at the genre, but at the male protagonist. Woods notes, significantly, that the "usual roles are reversed here and it is the woman who is leaving the man".[10] The psychological roles are also reversed. "The man is passive, helpless, tearful, devoid of practical solution to the problem and full of idle threats. It is the woman, on the other hand, who is practical, sensible, active, stoical, and she doesn't shed a tear" (pp. 213-14). Warned by the watchman, Nicolette slips into the forest where she builds a bower for Aucassin and hides to wait for him. When Aucassin is finally released from his tower and goes off in search of Nicolette, he stumbles across the *loge* she has made. The discovery in the forest of evidence of the lady's presence recalls Lancelot's finding Guenevere's comb with some of the Queen's golden hairs still caught in its teeth. Lancelot, pale from love and grief, becomes suddenly weak and nearly falls from his horse. Aucassin, dreaming of Nicolette, *does* fall, hits a rock, and dislocates his shoulder. Traditional courtly-love imagery pictures the beloved as a physician, curing the love-malady by returning the love. In this scene by the bower, Nicolette becomes the literal physician of Aucassin, working his shoulder back into place and binding it up with a piece of cloth torn from her petticoat. ". . . et il fu tox garis" (XXVI, 14). The humor of the scene is derived, not from the transformation of a love image into literal reality *per se,* but rather from Aucassin's comical ineptness which forces the lady to become literally what she is intended to be only symbolically.

The scene echoes even more strongly, perhaps, the *loge* scene of the Tristan and Yseut story, thereby emphasizing once more the exaggerated reversal of male-female roles. For it is Tristan who builds the *loge* for Yseut:

> Sa loge fait; au branc qu'il tient
> Les rains tranche, fait la fullie;
> Yseut l'a bien espes jonchie.[11]

This building of the *loge* is by no means the only echo from the Tristan and Yseut legend. The fact that the bower is built at a point where seven roads converge, a place where Aucassin was sure to pass by, the fact that Nicolette hides, leaving the bower as a sort of lover's test, recalls Marie de France's *Lai du chevrefeuille* in which Tristan leaves a sign, a branch of hazel enlaced with honeysuckle, as a sort of test for Yseut, and withdraws to wait for her in the forest. Wayne Conner has pointed out that just as the honeysuckle was Tristan's identifying flower, so are the lilies entwined in Nicolette's bower her special sign, one which Aucassin, who calls her "flor de lis", recognizes immediately.[12] Nicolette's return to Beaucaire disguised as a *jongleur* is an unmistakable echo, as Jodogne has pointed out,[13] of a similar disguise of Tristan returning from exile to see Yseut. In each instance it is significant that Nicolette assumes the role of Tristan, not that of Yseut. She is not the typical swooning courtly lady of twelfth-century romances. Rather, she is a clever, active young woman who is, at one point, even described in virile terms as "Nicole li preus, li sage" (XXXVII, 1). Nicolette is practical; Aucassin is a dreamer. She is active; he is passive. It is not difficult to see how such a reversal suggests the extreme courtly love situation which makes a virtual *seigneur* of the lady and tends to emasculate the man who must always bow in obeisance to her will. Carried to its logical conclusions such a situation could well result in the total inversion of roles that exists in Torelore.

Gaston Paris has claimed that the Torelore episode is boring and absurd.[14] But, as Pauphilet has said, "on a commis, jadis et naguère, le contre-sens de ne pas reconnaître dans toute l'oeuvre la veine parodique de l'épisode de Torelore et de supprimer cet épisode comme une dissonante interpolation".[15] Those who have judged the visit to Torelore a poorly integrated episode, in some cases the same critics who have called Chrétien's romances badly constructed, have apparently not attempted to see the episode in terms of the entire work. First of all, it provides a traditional, almost essential, motif from the courtly romance—that of the visit to an otherworldly kingdom. Lancelot's visit to the Kingdom of Gorre, Yvain's adventures in the land of the marvelous fountain, even Erec's search in the strange garden for the "Joie de la cour" serve to affirm the knight's prowess. His deeds in the otherworld are often a sort of culmination of his deeds of everyday. But Torelore is an upside-down world, where the king lies in childbed while the queen leads the army against the enemy, a more extreme situation of inversion, but one that is certainly not unrelated to the reversed roles of Aucassin and Nicolette. The Torelore incident also recalls the visit to the magic castle which transforms all qualities into their opposites in the *Lanzelet* of Ulrich von Zatzikhoven, written sometime after 1194 and supposedly based on a French original by one Hugh de Morville. During his captivity at the magic castle of Schâtel le Mort, the hero, the best of knights in the outside world, is transformed into a cowardly wretch.[16] Torelore is apparently the same sort of world and provides for the reader a sort of parody within a parody. Within this world *à rebours*, Aucassin and Nicolette seem to exchange roles. He who is described as "li biax, li blons, / li gentix, li amorous" (XXVII, 1-2) only moments before setting foot on the shore of Torelore becomes within that land "li prex, li ber" (XXXI, 11). And she who, upon leaving Torelore and arriving in Carthage is immediately described as "Nicole li preus, li sage" (XXXVII, 1-2) was in Torelore "a gentle, retiring lady from the moment of their arrival".[17] Sister M. Faith McKean has claimed, and quite rightly so, that the Torelore episode "is deliberately cut off from the fictional real world not because it is an interruption but because it is the key passage, a necessary interlude highlighting the prime target of the poet's irony" (p. 68). Explaining her reasons for considering the Torelore episode a key passage, she comments: "Catching the fundamental reversal implicit in courtly love, he [the author] created the perfect parody by creating the perfect courtly lover, and climaxed his work in the much maligned Torelore episode by making the reversal of roles so obvious that even the courtly lover had to recognize its foolishness" (p. 64). Aucassin does, indeed, recognize the foolishness of Torelore. He is even offended by the king's lying in childbed, while the queen fights with the army, but there is no indication whatsoever that he understands the implications of the episode as they relate to himself. Nor does he carry away from Torelore any of his indignation. Whatever situation he is in, Aucassin is still fundamentally a misfit. His new virility and energy are just as much out of place in Torelore as were his weeping and inertia in Beaucaire. Torelore provides a sort of culmination for the everyday deeds of Aucassin as an otherworld adventure should, for his thrashing about in this gentle land brings him to the maximum point of foolishness. He nearly beats to death the poor king who has just given birth to a son; he cheerfully enters into battle killing the enemy who have only eggs, cheeses, apples, and mushrooms with which to defend themselves.

In short, the episode shows Aucassin to be hopelessly out of step with the rest of the world; and moreover, it reveals to the reader, if not to Aucassin, the potential humor inherent in the fundamental reversal of roles in the courtly love relationship when carried to its logical extremes.

Harden concurs with the notion that there is a reversal of roles in the *Aucassin*. Indeed, he sees inversion as the essential technique of the author:

> Inversion, especially in character, has always been an effective device for parody, one in which the great are made small and the small great, in which the solemn are made absurd and the absurd solemn, in which the ideal are made ridiculous and the ridiculous ideal. . . .
> It is, we believe, the very method and intention of the author of *Aucassin et Nicolette* as he mocks the vapid plots and equally vapid personages of the idyllic novel
>
> (p. 3).

Despite the fact that Harden's study is one of the best that has been done on *Aucassin et Nicolette,* I believe that he has, to some extent, oversimplified the question of parody by seeing inversion as "the very method and intention of the author". Clearly, inversion plays a key role in the author's technique, but one is hard put to find it extensively used in situations outside of the Aucassin-Nicolette relationship. And within this love relationship it is perhaps not so much that the author reverses their roles, but rather that he exaggerates a reversal already implicit. One may point out the Torelore episode as an exception, but I have attempted to suggest its essential relationship with the roles of the lovers. Harden points out several details that bear clear markings of this inversion technique. The names are a good example. Aucassin is a French hero with an Arabic name; Nicolette, a North African heroine with a French name.[18] Aucassin muses about life after death, finding pleasure in Hell rather than in Heaven. But even these details are in some way related to the lovers or the love relationship, the latter suggesting in a comparatively mild way the essential conflict between courtly love and Christianity. To see the technique of parody as limited to inversion alone, however, is to miss the fun of a hero who, when he behaves according to the code, as Aucassin attempts to do, meets continually with situations which are not quite what one expects them to be, although they may bear all the hallmarks of tradition. They are not necessarily inverted in any way. In fact, I believe that inversion, rather than being *the* technique of the parodist-author of *Aucassin et Nicolette,* falls under the more comprehensive category of incongruity, which is an essentially comic device. It may be incongruity between the character and the situation, between the words and their meaning, between style and content, between lover and lady. And to this technique one must add, for any good parody, a greater or lesser degree of exaggeration. In the *Aucassin* exaggeration is strong, so strong, in fact, that it leads logically to the inversion that is already hinted at within the convention itself.

Grace Frank has stated that "If parody alone were the author's motive then his sense of reality and his delight in his own playfulness got the better of him. And mere parody of forgotten chivalric romances would hardly charm us to-day, as this unpretentious trifle continues to do".[19] I am not quite sure what Mrs. Frank means by the author's "sense of reality"; certainly there is nothing markedly "realistic" about the **Aucassin.** Nor are the chivalric romances quite so forgotten as she suggests. The courtly love triangle of Arthur, Guenevere, and Lancelot has even succeeded as a Broadway musical, albeit in a rather spurious form. But most difficult of all to understand is why the author's "delight in his own playfulness" carries him so far beyond parody. Such delight and playfulness are part and parcel of the makeup of the parodist. It is unlikely, in view of her statement about "mere parody", that Mrs. Frank is using the term as I have used it here. She seems to consider parody as a debased art form. Surely it is no more so than satire when used in connection with the writings of Swift. Nor is it simply a mockery. While there is always a barb in parody, there may also be affection for the thing parodied. Robert P. Falk, in fact, claims that successful parody "holds in equilibrium two opposing attitudes towards its subject—satire and sympathy".[20] If this is so, then one may well claim that **Aucassin et Nicolette** is successful as parody. The juxtaposition of the exaggerated courtly lover with a world of practical considerations, suspicious rustics, and unreliable fathers, renders not only Aucassin, but also the people of Beaucaire, somewhat ridiculous. But the mockery is light, the criticism gentle. It is quite possible that, in parody, the didactic instinct of the author is in inverse proportion to his sense of humor. If so, one may conclude that, while **Aucassin** is, to some extent, didactic in that it inevitably points up the weaknesses of the courtly lover in conflict with a less romantically inclined society, its essential quality is humor. We laugh at Aucassin; we enjoy him. And while we have no desire to emulate him, we also have no desire to see him changed.

Notes

1. Albert Pauphilet, *Le Legs du moyen âge* (Melun, 1950), pp. 239-48; Omer Jodogne, "La Parodie et le pastiche dans *Aucassin et Nicolette*", *CAIEF*, 12 (1959), 53-65. Robert Harden, "*Aucassin et Nicolette* as Parody", *SP*, 63 (1966), 1-9.

2. See Erich Auerbach, "The Knight Sets Forth", *Mimesis*, trans. Willard Trask (Princeton, 1953; reprinted Garden City, N. Y., 1957), pp. 120-21.

3. For a delightful discussion of the Torelore episode see Sister M. Faith McKean, "Torelore and Courtoisie", *RomN*, 3, ii (Spring, 1962), 64-68.

4. Auerbach, p. 120.

5. *Aucassin et Nicolette,* ed. Mario Roques, 2e ed. (Paris, 1963), I, 1-7. All subsequent references are to this edition and will be given within the text.

6. Chrétien de Troyes, *Le Chevalier de la charrette,* ed. Mario Roques (Paris, 1958), 11, 714-24.

7. U. T. Holmes, Jr., in his preface to *Aucassin and Nicolette,* translated by Edward Francis Moyer and Carey DeWitt Eldridge (Chapel Hill, 1937), p. vii, first called attention to the similarity between these two rustics. Both of them undoubtedly owe much to the wild man lore of the Middle Ages. For a thorough discussion, see Richard Bernheimer, *Wild Men in the Middle Ages: A Study in Art, Sentiment and Demonology* (Cambridge, Mass., 1952). See also Alice M. Colby, *The Portrait,* pp. 72-88 for a discussion of what she calls "ideal ugliness".

8. Chrétien de Troyes, *Le Chevalier au lion (Yvain),* ed. Mario Roques (Paris, 1960), 11. 326-27. All subsequent references are to this edition and will be given within the text.

9. Barbara Sargent, "Parody in *Aucassin et Nicolette:* Some Further Considerations", *FR,* 43 (1969-70), 597-605. See also Edmond Faral, *Les Arts poétiques du XIIe et du XIIIe siècle* (Paris, 1924), pp. 75-81, 214-15.

10. William S. Woods, "The *Aube* in *Aucassin et Nicolette*", in *Mediaeval Studies in Honor of Urban Tigner Holmes, Jr.,* UNCSRLL, 56 (Chapel Hill, 1965), p. 213.

11. Béroul, *Le Roman de Tristan,* ed. Ernest Muret (Paris, 1903), 11. 1290-92.

12. Wayne Conner, "The *Loge* in *Aucassin et Nicolette*", *RR,* 46 (1955), 85.

13. Jodogne has noted that this motif appears in the *Folie Tristan* of Oxford as well as that of Berne, 61.

14. Gaston Paris, Review of *Aucassin et Nicolette,* trans. A. Bida and *Aucassin und Nicolette,* ed. Hermann Suchier, *Romania,* 8 (1897), 291.

15. *Le Legs,* p. 248.

16. See Ulrich von Zatzikhoven, *Lanzelet,* ed. K. A. Hahn (Frankfurt, 1845; reprinted Berlin, 1965), 11. 3536-3825. English prose translation by Kenneth G. T. Webster, revised by R. S. Loomis (New York, 1951), pp. 73-77. A land that automatically transforms qualities into their opposites would also account for an inconsistency of description pointed out by Barbara Sargent (p. 603) and earlier by Kaspar Rogger, "Etude déscriptive de la chantefable 'Aucassin et Nicolette'", *ZRP,* 67 (1951), 421. Nicolette is described while in Beaucaire as extremely slender, yet in Torelore she describes herself as "grasse et mole" (XXXIII, 5).

17. McKean, 67.

18. Harden, 8. Jodogne has also pointed this out in his earlier article, 56.

19. Grace Frank, *Medieval French Drama* (Oxford, 1954), pp. 238-39.

20. *The Antic Muse,* p. 10.

List of Abbreviations

AnM Annuale Medievale

ANQ American Notes and Queries

BHS Bulletin of Hispanic Studies

CA Cuadernos Americanos

CAIEF Cahiers de l'Association Internationale des Etudes Françaises

CCM Cahiers de Civilisation Médiévale

CEJ California English Journal

ChauR Chaucer Review

CL Comparative Literature

DA Dissertation Abstracts

ECr L'Esprit Créateur

ELH Journal of English Literary History

ELN English Language Notes

EUPLL Edinburgh University Publications Language and Literature

ES English Studies

FilR Filologia Romanza

FR French Review

FS French Studies

HSCL Harvard Studies in Comparative Literature

HSE Harvard Studies in English

HR Hispanic Review

ISLL Illinois Studies in Language and Literature

JAF Journal of American Folklore

JEGP Journal of English and Germanic Philology

LP Literature and Psychology

MA Le Moyen Age

MAe Medium Aevum

MH Medievalia et Humanistica

MLN Modern Language Notes

MLQ Modern Language Quarterly

MLR Modern Language Review

MP Modern Philology

MR Massachusetts Review

MS Mediaeval Studies

NQ Notes and Queries

NRFH Nueva Revista de Filología Hispánica

PL Patrologia Latina

PLL Papers on Language and Literature

PMLA Publications of the Modern Language Association of America

PQ Philological Quarterly

RDM Revue des Deux Mondes

RF Romanische Forschungen

RFE Revista de Filología Española

RFH Revista de Filología Hispánica

RL Revista de Literatura

RomN Romance Notes

RP Romance Philology

RR Romanic Review

SATF Société des Anciens Textes Français

SP Studies in Philology

SUS Susquehanna University Studies

TLS Times Literary Supplement

UColSSLL University of Colorado Studies Series in Language and Literature

UCPMP University of California Publications in Modern Philology

UCSSLL University of California Studies Series in Language and Literature

UNCSCL University of North Carolina Studies in Comparative Literature

UNCSGLL University of North Carolina Studies in the Germanic Languages and Literatures

UNCSRLL University of North Carolina Studies in the Romance Languages and Literatures

YRS Yale Romanic Studies

ZFSL Zeitschrift für Französische sprache und Literatur

ZRP Zeitschrift für romanische Philologie

Joan B. Williamson (essay date 1973)

SOURCE: "Naming as a Source of Irony in *Aucassin et Nicolette*," in *Studi Francesi*, No. 51, Sept.-Dec., 1973, pp. 401-09.

[*In the essay below, Williamson assesses the comic effect of the author's use of reversal in the naming of the lovers in* Aucassin et Nicolette. *Williamson also demonstrates that the "misnaming" of the characters makes the tale an "anti-idyll."*]

It was not the custom for medieval authors to ascribe titles to their works. But it was inevitable that, when the thirteenth century French *chantefable* acquired a title, it should be based on the names of the two principle protagonists. Thus the caption in the only extant manuscript reads: *C'est d'Aucasin et de Nicolete.*[1] Not only does the author name his two lovers in both his opening and closing verses, but he also emphasizes them throughou his work.

The hero's name, Aucassin, is Arabic, while that of the heroine, Nicolette, is Christian. The fact that the heroine, baptized and reared by the Viscount, bears a Christian name is not striking by itself, since it might have been her name only since her baptism. The Arabic name for the hero, however, is incongruous; and the two names in conjunction seem to require explanation. Much has been written about the Arabic origin of the name of the hero. But this writing has been concerned mainly with identifyng the real person or mythic hero from whence the name Aucassin derives, and with ascribing an Arabic origin to the whole tale on the basis of the name.[2] These considerations, however, are all extraneous to discovering why the author used the name in the *chantefable* **Aucassin et Nicolette.**

In searching for the reasons underlying the author's choice of names, it is pertinent to recall his intention in composing the *chantefable.* He tells us in the introduction that his verses will cure a sick man and make a man overwhelmed with grief rejoice:

> Nus hom n'est si esbahis,
> tant dolans ni entrepris,
> de grant mal amaladis,
> se il l'oit, ne soit garis
> et de joie resbaudis,
> tant par est douce.

(I, vv. 10-15).[3]

As O. Jodogne has pointed out, these initial verses reveal that the author intended to amuse his audience.[4] We are naturally led to investigate whether we may apply the author's stated purpose to the naming of his two lovers. O. Jodogne rightly sees a comic effect in their names.[5] The Christian hero bears an Arab name, while the heroine of Saracen origin has a Christian name. The two lovers are, in fact, inversely named, and to comic effect. The hero's name is an indication that he may be expected to do the unexpected.[6] This nomenclature, however, also has broader significance. It is basic to the humour of the tale, and the reasons for the author's choice of names become clear upon analysis of the comic within the story.

Recently, O. Jodogne and B. Nelson Sargent have provided insights into comic elements within **Aucassin et Nicolette.**[7] It is now clear that one of the basic mechanisms underlying the composition of the *chantefable* is the literary exploitation of the principle of reversal. It is the scope of this paper to analyse the use the author makes of the names Aucassin and Nicolette; to evaluate the comic effect of the application of the principle of reversal to the names and characters of the two lovers; and to show how the misnaming makes the idyll an anti-idyll by presenting, in the very telling, the story as absurd.

The author, having chosen his protagonists' names deliberately, made conscious use of them throughout his work. No comment upon, nor explanation of, the names of Au-

cassin and Nicolette appear in the work, but the author laid considerable stress upon them by using them with exaggerated frequency. The names appear repeatedly throughout each of the forty one sections into which the work is divided except in one. This is section XV, the *laisse* where the night-watchman calls out to the heroine to warn her of the approach of the guard addressing her as *Mescinete.* Using her name would have destroyed the logic of the story, for the guards were making their rounds with express instructions from Count Garin de Beaucaire to kill Nicolette should they apprehend her. Of the remaining forty sections, only three feature Nicolette's name but not Aucassin's; and only seven name Aucassin but not Nicolette. Thirty sections then mention both names several times.

Analysis of the circumstances in which these names occurs reveals why the author chose to be so repetitive. A critic has counted that Aucassin repeated twenty times the phrase *la tres douce amie qu'il aime tant.*[8] Significantly, the name of Nicolette precedes each of these iterations. The constant presence of the loved one's name on the lips of the lover conveys the sense of Aucassin's absorption in Nicolette. Such repetitions evoke a sense of the overwhelming incantatory power that the pronouncing of the loved one's name can produce, as the name Melibea does in *La Celestina* where Calixto reveals his entrancement thus:

¿Yo? Melibeo soy y a Melibea adoro y en Melibea creo y a Melibea amo.[9] In the *chantefable,* however, the incantatory force of the pronouncement of Nicolette's name by her lover is somewhat diminished by the even more frequent occurrences of her name in other circumstances.

The narrator uses the protagonists' names with greater frequency than do the protagonists themselves. The author's intercalations to identify the speaker in direct speech illustrate this fact. Significantly, the name of Aucassin occurs more frequently than does the name of Nicolette, who is often identified by the personal pronoun, *ele.* There are only two other female speakers besides Nicolette; Aucassin's mother, introduced before her speech as *sa mere,* (III. v. 6); and the Viscountess, referred to, also prior to her speech, as *la dame,* (XL, 1.41). When the identification of Nicolette as speaker is intercalated, she is named twice: *fait Nicholete,* (XVI, 1.1); and *ce dist la bele Nichole,* (XXXIII, v. 2). In the eleven other instances of this figure of speech, we find Nicolette identified by *ele,* as in *fait ele,* (XIV, 1.15).

The situation is different when Aucassin is the speaker. The use of the personal pronoun in the intercalation is almost always reserved for a speaker other than Aucassin. We find *fait il* twice only to indicate Aucassin, (XIV, 1.3; and XXII, 1. 7). Elsewhere the intercalations always contain Aucassins, proper name, as in *fait* **Aucassins,** (XXII, 1. 10). The author could have referred to Aucassin by common nouns had he wished to avoid repetition. For example, he might have identified his hero as *li ber,* a term he uses for him in:

> Aucassins les prist, li ber,
>
>   (XIII, v. 17).

But the author intentionally repeated time and again his hero's given name. This becomes clear upon close analysis of short conversations, as in the following extract:

> . . . et li quens Garins de Biacaire vint en la canbre u Aucassins faisoit deul et regretoit Nicolete da tresdouce amie que tant amoit.
>
> "Ha! fix, fait il, . . .
> —Pere, fait Aucassins, . . .
> —Fix, dist li pere, . . .
> "Peres, fait Aucassins, . . .
> —Et quex, biax fix? . . .

(Aucassin here offers to fight if allowed one kiss and two or three words with Nicolette).

> —Je l'otroi", fait li peres.
> Il li creante et Aucassins fu lié.

The distribution of proper names, common nouns and pronouns is a happy arrangement. No ambiguity as to who is speaking is possible. But particularly the position and relative importance of the protagonists in the story are defined. The relationship of the secondary figure to the hero is made clear. For Count Garin de Beaucaire, here identified as *li peres* is of interest only in that he is Aucassin's father. The constant recourse to the hero's proper name places the principle protagonist fully in the centre of the stage. This procedure, which repeatedly confronts us with the name Aucassin, emphasizes the principle role played by the young lover in the story.

The author seems to have let pass no occasion to bring before his audience his lovers' names, particularly that of his hero. The constant occurrences are comic through a sense of an exaggerated use of a formula; exaggerated even for the Middle Ages, which exploited *formulae* as devices for literary creation. They particularly serve to bring the names of the hero and heroine to the foreground. The insistence on the name of Aucassin over that of Nicolette also defines the relative positions of the two young lovers; while the narration of the story reveals that Nicolette is the more perfect creature, it is clear that Aucassin is the central figure of that narration.

Repetitions also emphasize the basic problem confronting the two lovers. The author outlines in bold relief both the names of his lovers and their predicament, thus ensuring that his audience would relate the names to the problem.

The difficulty the lovers face is that of parental opposition. The story is a simple one of star-crossed lovers, illustrating a universal theme. The boy and the girl love each other, but the boy's parents oppose the idea of marriage. Our concern is not with the solution of the problem, but with the reasons given for the parental opposition. The author lists these reasons at the beginning of the narration:

> —Fix, fait li peres, ce ne poroit estre. Nicolete laise ester, que ce est une caitive qui fu amenee d'estrange terre, si l'acata li visquens de ceste vile as Sarasins, si l'amena en ceste vile, si l'a levee et bautisie et faite sa fillole, si li donra un de ces jors un baceler qui du pain li gaaignera par honor: de ce n'as tu que faire. Et se tu fenme vix avoir, je te donrai le file a un roi u a un conte: il n'a si rice home en France, se tu vix sa fille avoir, que tu ne l'aies.
>
>   (I, II. 28-35).

The parents' objections are based on their opinion that Nicolette is not good enough for Aucassin. She is not suitable since she is a slave girl of Saracen origin. Listeners in the Middle Ages could accept the plausibility of a girl finding herself in Nicolette's situation, for History proves that slave girls of Saracen origin might well have found themselves in France. The action of the *chantefable* takes place at the town of Beaucaire. If this was the historical Beaucaire it was situated on the Rhone. The river would have provided easy access to the town, and Arab slave girls might have been sold at the yearly fairs by Viking slave-traders.[10] Nicolette's situation would have struck the audience of the *chantefable* as possible, even probable. The names of the hero and heroine, ensured, however, that the audience would reject the validity of the parents' objections. Nicolette's name confirms that she is Christian. Her Saracen origin might have been accepted as a valid social impediment had her lover not borne the Arab name of Aucassin. The comic point would be driven home each time the audience heard the names of the hero and heroine.

The author stressed the grounds for the opposition to the marriage of the young lovers by repeated enumeration of the objections (III, V, and VI). The arguments assume a litany-like quality in that each time they occur they are presented in full, in the same order and in almost the same words. The result is comical. The fact of repetition conveys also a humorous illusion of the mechanical. But the main result of the repetitions is to focus attention on the family opposition and to relate it to the repetitions of the significant names of the hero and heroine.

A second reason for the rejection of Nicolette as a suitable spouse for Aucassin was her supposedly inferior social rank. Aucassin's parents wished him to marry a count or a king's daughter. His mother insisted that he take as a wife a woman of noble birth:

> puis qu'a moulié te vix traire,
> pren femme de haut parage.
>
>   (III, vv. 11-12).

This command is later revealed as ironical, for Nicolette is really the very bride Aucassin's parents seek for their son. When Nicolette is captured by Saracens in the castle of

Torelore, they treat her with honour. For they have noticed her beauty. They have also noticed that she looked as if she were a lady and of gentle brth:

> . . . et molt li demanderent qui ele estoit, car molt san-bloit bien gentix fenme et de haut lignage.
>
> (XXXVI, II. 5-6).

What was immediately clear to the Saracens hand gone unmarked by Aucassin's parents. The parental opposition is completely and finally invalidated by what followed. As the Saracens approached the city of *Cartage,* (XXXVI, 1.8), the walls of the city acted as a visual catalyst upon Nicolette's memory. The sight of the previously seen masonry recalled her past, and she remembered that she was the daughter of the king of *Cartage.*

Although the author revealed his heroine's true identity towards the end of the narration, his audience knew almost from the beginning that Nicolette would prove to be a king's daughter. Jodogne recognised, in the inverse naming of the two chief protagonists, an indication that Aucassin's character would be the contrary of what one would expect.[11] In the same way, we believe that the medieval audience interpreted this same signal to mean that things throughout the story would be the reverse of what one would normally expect. The medieval mind was more keenly tuned than is the modern, confused by much migration, to the ethnic connotations of names. The repetitions of the names recalled these connotations, and each pronouncement of the hero and heroine's names produced in the medieval audience the pleasure of recognition of the author's ironic purpose. It was not just Torelore which constituted the domain of the absurd, but the whole of the *chantefable.*

Not content with tearing down the parental objections, the author completely vindicates his heroine. Nicolette finally appears as a paragon of virtue. She is proven to be the lady of high-born rank, the daughter of a king. She is furthermore, thoroughly Christian. The name of Nicolette had become both French and Christian by the time of the writing of the *chantefable.* H. Brunner affirms that the heroine's name had become French: "Aus dem letzteren Namen hat man gefolgert, dass die Heimat unserer Cantefable auch wie die des Romans von Floire der griechische Osten sei. Doch was dieser Name, wie G. Paris treffend bemerkt, 'Dant dem heil. Nicolas, der di Mädchen unter die Haube bringt,' auch in Frankreich früzeitig im Gebrauch.[12]" Similarly, although purportedly an Eastern saint, Saint Nicholas enjoyed such popularity in medieval Western Europe that anyone bearing a derivative of his name would have been immediately recognised as a Christian.[13] There is a clear indication that we are to so understand the heroine's name in the story. Nicolette is not only a Christian, she is accorded one of the attributes of a saint when she performs a miracle. Aucassin, meditating upon his love, recalls how he witnessed the event:

> L'autr'ier vi un pelerin,
> nes estoit de Limosin,
> malades de l'esvertin,

> si gisoit ens en un lit,
> mout par estoit entrepris,
> de grant mal amaladis;
> tu passas devant son lit,
> si soulevas ton train
> et ton peliçon ermin,
> la cemisse de blanc lin,
> tant que ta ganbete vit:
> garis fu li pelerins
> et tos sains, ainc ne fu si:
> si se leva de son lit,
> si rala en son pa ïs
> sains et saus et tos garis.
>
> (XI, vv. 16-31).

This incident has a comic effect. It is the ironic contrary of what one would expect, the sight of a girl's ankle in an age when skirts were worn long would tend to make a man mad rather than cure him of a mental disturbance.[14] Amusing though it may be, this incident imbues Nicolette with attributes of sanctity and thereby clearly establishes her as Christian. For the ability to perform miracles which were beneficial in their effects was almost always reserved for Christians in medieval literature. We have, therefore, in this incident, a further characterisation of the heroine in keeping with the implications of her name.

The characters of both the hero and the heroine are in keeping with their names. From the point of view of Christian morality, Nicolette was a desirable bride for a Christian youth. And yet the youth for whom she was not good enough not only was named Aucassin, but also professed a theology entirely consistent with a figure bearing an Arab name.

It is in this framework that we place Aucassin's tirade on Heaven and Hell. In an attempt to persuade Aucassin to cease his attentions to Nicolette, the Viscount had tried to reason with the young lover. He posited the social impossibility of a marriage between Aucassin and Nicolette, and the disadvantages to Aucassin's having sexual relations with the girl he loved outside the marriage bond:

> Enseurquetot, que cuideriés vous avoir gaegnié, se vous l'aviés asognentee ne mise a vo lit? Mout i ariés peu conquis, car tos les jors du siecle en seroit vo arme en infer, qu'en paradis n'enterriés vos ja.
>
> (VI, II.19-23).

But Aucassin was a young man in love. His sole concern was with winning Nicolette, with or without benefit of marriage. He replied that he cared nothing for Heaven, all he cared about was having Nicolette:

> —En paradis qu'ai je a faire? Je n'i quier entrer, mais que j'aie Nicolette ma tresdouce amie que j'aim tant;
>
> (VI, II. 24-25).

This interpretation, based on the fact that the punctuation is the modern editor's, not the author nor the scribe's, renders *mais* as *but,* and the phrase *mais que j'aie Nicolete* as elliptic:

Je n'i quier enter, mais [je n'i quier] que j'aie Nicolete . . .][15]

In marked contrast to Nicolette's sanctity, Aucassin's character is wholly of this earth. Careless of the sacrament of
matrimony, his over-riding desire was physical possession
of Nicolette, for so we understand the use of the verb
avoir in the hero's reply to the Viscount's rhetorical question.

Aucassin then went on to explain his views on Heaven
and Hell:

> c'en paradis ne vont fors tex gens con je vous dirai. Il i
> vont ci viel prestre et cil viel clop et cil manke qui tote
> jor et tote nuit cropent devant ces autex et en ces viés
> creutes, et cil a ces viés capes ereses et a ces viés tater-
> eles vestues, qui sont nu et decauc et estrumelé, qui
> moeurent de faim et de soi et de froit et de mesaises;
> icil vont en paradis: aveuc ciax n'ai jou que faire. Mais
> en infer voil jou aler, car en infer vont li bel clerc, et li
> bel cevalier qui sont mort as tornois et as rices gueres,
> et li buen sergant et li franc home: aveuc ciax voil jou
> aler; et s'i vont les beles dames cortoises que eles ont
> deus amis ou trois avoc leur barons, et s'i va li ors et li
> argens et li gris, et si i vont herpeor et jogleor et li roi
> del siecle: avoc ciax voil jou aler, mais que j'aie Nico-
> lete ma tresdouce amie aveuc mi
>
> (VI, II. 25-39).

This passage has deservedly received a great deal of attention. But the question still remains unanswered as to why
Aucassin conceived of Heaven as so drab and of Hell as
so attractive. Dramatic though the hero's preference for
Hell over Heaven is, this rejection of the regular order of
things was not an invention of the author of the *chantefable*. Several years ago, D. Scheludko presented evidence
for the existence of a fairly wide-spread folk anecdote in
which the protagonist preferred to go to Hell because
Heaven was such a dull place.[16] Once he had decided to
confer upon Aucassin the habit of doing the opposite of
what was expected, the author perhaps drew upon an existing folk motif to put a witty tirade in his hero's mouth.
If the motif were well-known, the audience would have
enjoyed an original treatment of a familiar theme. What is
most strikingly unusual about Aucassin's views is the fact
that the condition in the herafter continues to be exactly
the same as in this life.[17] The unhappy still continue to suffer and the joyous to celebrate. This unorthodox view is
juxtaposed along-side the quite orthodox categories of
those who go to Hell and those who go to Heaven. Aucassin's description of the inhabitants of Paradise reads
like a listing from the Sermon on the Mount. Heaven is
peopled by those to whom the promise of paradise was
made in the Eight Beatitudes. Similarly, Hell is filled with
those castigated by the Church: knights killed in wars
(except in crusades presumably) and jousts; ladies who
have two or three lovers in addition to their lords—adulterers; fair clerics, presumably those who vied with the
knights in debates as to which group made the better lovers; worldly kings and wealthy barons, whose wealth made

entry into Heaven so difficult; and those who loved luxury
and the soft things in life, who, serving Mammon, could
not also serve God.

Aucassin knew the teachings of the Church. The inferences he drew from that instruction led him in a direction
diametrically opposed to that in which he was supposed to
go. His literal-mindedness thus led him into a comic dichotomy. His beliefs about the life after death stemmed
from an acceptance of the literal meanings of words in total ignorance of the deeper concepts they symbolized. This
simplistic understanding of only the face value of words is
part of Aucassin's character, and a basic reason why it is
comical. The audience saw beyond what Aucassin did at
the same time that they were aware of his blindness; and
they derived amusement from the double vision.

The application of literal-mindedness to an understanding
of the Church evokes similar literary figures who conceived of aspects of the Christian faith only in terms of
the material world: Saracens of the Old French epics. The
most striking among them is the giant Corsolt in *Le Couronnement de Louis,* who speaks of the Cristian God in
human terms as a feudal lord striking down his father then
retreating to Heaven as into an impregnable fortress:

> "Niés pas bien enseigniez,
> Qui devant mei oses de Deu plaidier;
> C'est l'om el mont qui plus m'a fait irier;
> Mon pere ocist une foldre del ciel;
> Toz i fu ars, ne li pot on aidier.
> Quant Deus l'ot mort, si fist que enseigniez;
> El ciel monta, ea ne volt repairier;
> Je nel poeie sivre ne enchalcier,
> Mais de ses omes me sui je pois vengiez;
>
> (vv. 522-32).[18]

A comic effect is sought, and obtained, by a Christian author conferring upon his Saracen protagonist an understanding of the letter, but not the spirit, of the Christian religion. The author of the *Chantefable* and the author of the
epic, *Le Couronnement de Louis,* have both used the same
technique to similar effect. We should not, therefore, expect a hero with an Arab name to hold the standard view
of Heaven and Hell; for the Saracen, denied Faith, lacked
the comprehension to see beneath the surface. So Aucassin
believed the lame, the poor and the sad went to Heaven
where they continued to be lame, poor and said, because
he comprehended only a part, and not the whole, of the
Christian Faith. Such a presentation does not indicate a latent paganism on the part of the author. The resulting incongruities are comic and intentionally so. The application
of a limited view is productive of humour in that it juxtaposes an upside-down optic (Aucassin's) beside a right-
side view of reality (the Christian audience's). Aucassin's
literal-mindedness is consistent with his Arab name. His
religious attitude, the result of his literal-mindedness, is
ironical when seen in relation to the name and qualities of
the girl he is not permitted to marry.

Aucassin et Nicolette is a complex work with many humorous facets. It is undeniable that the misnaming of the
hero and heroine, and the consequent undermining of the

idyll each time they are named, contribute in large measure to the comedy. If one were to ask question, concerning the *chantefable Aucassin et Nicolette,* "What's in a name?" The answer would be, "Irony".

Notes

1. Manuscript Bibliothèque Nationale, Paris, fonds français, 2168, folio 70, column b.

2. H. Brunner, *Uber Aucassin und Nicolete,* Diss. Hall-Wittenberg, 1880 (Halle, 1880); L. Jordan, *Die Quelle des Aucassin und die Methode des Urteils in der Philologie,* "Zeitschrift für romanische Philologie", 44 (1924), pp. 291-307; D. Scheludko, *Orientalisches in der altfranzösischen erzählenden Dichtung,* "Zeitschrift für französische Sprache und Literatur", 51 (1928), pp. 255-93; and W. Suchier, *Weiteres zu Aucassin und Nicolette,* "Voretzsch Festgabe" (Halle, 1927), pp. 155-72.

3. *Aucassin et Nicolette,* éd. Mario Roques, 2ᵉ éd., (Paris, Champion, 1954). All quotations from the text are taken from this edition.

4. O. Jodogne, *La Parodie et le pastiche dans Aucassin et Nicolette"* in Cahiers de l'Association Internationale des Etudes Françaises: no. 12 (1959), p. 56. "Dès lors, comme il annonce une œuvre divertissante, notre attention est éveillé et nous devons saisir, dans le récit, du comique".

5. O. Jodogne, *op. cit.* p. 56: "Et, de fait, des traits plaisants apparaissent bientôt, sans qu'ils soient soulignés. Nicolette était sarrasine; elle porte un nom chrétien, peutêtre depuis son baptême. Mais Aucassin est un chrétien français, né de parents chrétiens: il porte un nom arabe! Et, m'attachant au procédé cocasse qui a inspiré cette attribution de nom, je le conçois comme un premier signalement du personnage. Son caractère sera inattendu, lui aussi".

6. Jodogne, *op. cit.,* p. 56.

7. O. Jodogne, and Barbara Nelson Sargent, "Parody in *Aucassin et Nicolette:* Some Further Considerations", "The French Review", 43, 4 (March, 1970), pp. 597-605.

8. Jodogne, *op. cit.,* p. 58.

9. Fernando de Rojas, *La Celestina,* (Spain: Espasa Calpe, 1957), p. 22.

10. D. Scheludko, *Zur Entstehungsgeschichte von Aucassin und Nicolete,* "Zeitschrift für romanische Philologie", 42 (1922), p. 476.

11. O. Jodogne, *op. cit.,* p. 56.

12. H. Brunner, *op. cit.,* p. 12.

13. For example, after examining the evidence for the intensity of the cult of Saint Nicholas during the 11th and 12th centuries, Patrick R. Vincent concludes: "It is scarcely within the power of the twentieth century mind to imagine the deep devotion of the medieval man to St. Nicholas and the great and widespread reputation of the saint as a miracle worker, equalling that of the greatest saints". *The Jeu de Saint Nicholas of Jean Bodel of Arras: A Literary Analysis,* Johns Hopkins Studies in Romance Literatures and Languages, 49 (Baltimore: The Johns Hopkins Press, 1954), p. 30.

14. O. Jodogne, *op. cit.,* p. 60.

15. This rendering is supported by Eugene Mason's English translation (*Aucassin et Nicolette,* England, Dutton, 1958, p. 6) of the passage which reads: "In Paradise what have I do do? I care not to enter, but only to have Nicolete . . .".

16. D. Scheludko, *Zur Entstehungsgeschichte . . .* pp. 464-64 et suiv.

17. B. N. Sargent, *op. cit.,* p. 600.

18. *Le Couronnement de Louis,* éd. E. Langlois, 2ᵐᵉ éd., Paris, Champion, 1965, p. 17.

Eugene Dorfman (essay date 1974)

SOURCE: "The Lamp of the Commandment in *Aucassin et Nicolette,*" in *Hebrew University Studies in Literature,* Vol. 2, Spring, 1974, pp. 30-72.

[*In the following essay, Dorfman traces the way in which Aucassin is presented, with his temptations outlined in the Ten Commandments, and argues that Aucassin's adventures in the fantastic land of Torelore constitute his education as a hero—an education necessary for Aucassin to become the "ruler in Israel," who restores his people to their homeland.*]

Aucassin, one of the unlikeliest of heroes in the annals of medieval romance, whose stated objection to having his head cut off by his enemies is that he would thereby be prevented from speaking[1] to his beloved, and whose expertise in the art of knightsmanship is exemplified by his toppling from the saddle because he was seated on such a 'high horse,'[2] boldly challenges the established religious order by declaring his unequivocal preference for the luxurious pleasures of Hell over the joyless aridities of Heaven.

> 'En paradis qu'ai je a faire? [. . .] Mais en infer voil jou aler [. . .]'
>
> (VI, 24-39).

This defiance of his Father in Heaven, as well as of his earthly parents whose opposition to his desired marriage to Nicolette he refuses to honor, highlights the fact that, like his beloved, he is still a child,[3] as the romance begins. Before it ends, he must climb down from his 'high horse' with due regard always to the consequences of his actions, and learn to use his head as it was intended he should, devoting himself to the acquisition of the basic education which will make a man of him, capable and worthy of fulfilling the strange and glorious role for which he is secretly[4] destined. Aucassin, the rebellious son and apathetic lover, who refuses to defend his people and has to be prodded to start off in pursuit of his beloved in exile, is to be nothing less than the long-awaited 'ruler in Israel,'[5] who will restors his people to their ancient Homeland.[6]

The nature of the education designed to prepare Aucassin for his awesome task is summed up in the name *Torelore*, the fabulous land whose king lies in childbed and whose queen leads its army fighting with baked apples, fresh cheeses, eggs and mushrooms as weapons; *Torelore*, read as *Tora* [. . .] *le'ra*,[7] capsulates the basic theme of the romance and the fundamental lesson that Aucassin must learn, based on a passage in Proverbs: Ki ner mitzva ve'*Tora or ve'derech chayim toch'chos musar: Li'shmarcha me'eshes ra* me'chelkas lashon nachriyya: . . .

> For the commandment is a lamp, and *the teaching is light, And the reproofs of instruction are the way of life; To keep thee from the evil woman;* From the smoothness of the alien tongue
>
> (6:23-24) (emphasis added).

The lesson is thematically relevant on both the overt and the covert levels. In the surface story, this is the basis for the opposition of Aucassin's parents to Nicolette; she is an alien slave girl whose smooth tongue—evil influence— prevents him from assuming his responsibilities in defence of his community. Interpreted parastructurally, the term 'evil woman' refers not to Nicolette herself but to the pagan seductress Ashtoreth, the goddess of Love of her native Carthage, the real culprit[8] diverting Aucassin into idolatrous neglect of 'the teaching' (Tora), closing his ears to the 'reproofs of instruction,' and keeping him from the 'way of life' which is his inheritance. Our hero will encounter[9] severe trials and perform prodigious feats in mastering the course of instruction necessary to furnish the 'light' which will guide his people back to the Promised Land.

Aucassin does not have far to go, does he but wish it, to find the 'light' he needs for his course of study. It is there in the three Hebrew words, *ki ner mitzva* ('for the commandment is a lamp,') which just precede the thematic *Tora* [. . .] *le'ra* capsulation. Similar in connotation to *mitzva* are the associated words *davar*, . . . pl. *d'varim* . . . 'word, saying; thing,' and *diber*, . . . pl. *dibros* . . . 'speech; commandment,' occurring in *aseres ha'd'varim* . . . and *aseres ha'dibros* . . . 'the Ten Commandments.' In the phrase 'for the commandment is a lamp,' *mitzva* is in the singular, implying that the 'lamp' of revelation lights up the Tora as a whole (*Tora or*). This may be interpreted to mean, as Leo Baeck informs us, that all the commandments are to be considered as one.

> The revelation was first documented in the Ten Commandments written on the two tablets, 'the tables of the testimony' (Ex. 32:15), the 'tables of the covenant' (Deut. 9:19). They are words of law and freedom, the constitution of this people and manifesto to all humanity in one. The introduction points to the foundation which alone can carry all of this. It says: (Ex. 20:1)

'God spoke all these words' ('these whole words'). These words have meaning only in their oneness, in their totality. They have not been brought together and counted, but each one is an essential part of the whole, and this whole proves itself in each of them. The whole comes before the parts, it is the life which lives in all.[10]

The future 'ruler in Israel' must know at first hand the pragmatic meaning of the commandments, 'the constitution of this people,' and understand the manner in which they are inseparably intertwined with each other and with the lives of the people in their daily acts. His education, to be complete in the sense of 'all these words,' the Ten Commandments of the Tora, depends on his coming into collision with each of them in one form or other in the various incidents of the romance which, in their oblique way, exemplify and illustrate them. In direct—if undercover—confrontation with them, he will come to understand their essence and their application, demonstrating in practice through painful efforts and acts of prowess that he has learned to benefit from the 'reproofs of instruction' that are the 'way of life.'

The parastructural lesson that Aucassin is required to derive from his experiences is based on the meaning of *mitzva* 'command, commandment; act of charity, pious action.' The keynote is *action*: 'command' implies One who commands; all His commandments are manifestations of a single, universal 'commandment'; every act of charity fulfils this commandment; the good life is realized not just in knowledge of the commandments—though study of them is essential—but in 'pious action,' the performance of *mitzvas*. Small wonder then that fortune fails to smile on Aucassin, who refuses to 'do what he should,' until he himself begins to invite success by performing his first *mitzva*, alleviating the distress of the poor oxherd whom he saves from debtor's prison by enabling him to replace his lost ox. This 'pious action,' which he accompanies with a blessing in response to the oxherd's curse, is a sign that the 'child' has come of age, ready at last to assume the duties and responsibilities of a man; he is now truly a *bar mitzva*,[11] a 'son of the commandment,' who has earned the right to his reunion with his beloved at the bower in the forest. One good deed, however, does not preclude recidivism; victory is not won at a single stroke but demands constant and repeated efforts. The challenge of idolatry in the form of Ashtoreth, goddess of Love, preying on the weakness of suffering humanity, as Aucassin, with his dislocated shoulder, prays to the evening star and the moon to reunite him with his beloved, does not relax its illusory attraction without a struggle.

The sweet fleshpots of Hell entice with greater force than the less visible and more austere delights of Heaven, particularly in youth, when the blood flows more vigorously and the appetites are stronger. As the romance begins, Aucassin is a self-centered child, blind to everything but the powerful drive of his love, stubbornly rejecting tthe wisdom and the teaching of his parents; alienated by the strains of the generation gap, he does not shrink from outright betrayal of his land and people. This cold anger,[12] responsible for the incredible oath he demands of Bougars, the enemy war-chief—that the latter harass his father in body and possessions for the rest of his life—must be curbed and channelled properly. In the process of fitting himself for his appointed task as the coming 'ruler in Israel,' Aucassin must learn to look beyond himself, to deal firmly and justly with all, rich and poor alike, and, not least, to create the conditions which will restore his people to their ancient homeland in peace. Presented on the surface as an amusing romance for the entertainment of a general public, *Aucassin et Nicolette* addresses itself in secret to a special audience in distress;[13] the promise to the latter is explicit: no matter how 'perplexed, sorrowful, dejected, or sickened by a great evil' they may be, if they but 'listen' they will be 'cured and comforted with joy.' The therapeutic lesson is a parable in which their destined leader confronts the forces of light and darkness, religion and idolatry, pointing out the 'way of life' as the road out of Exile, while he painfully struggles with the temptations involved in each of the Ten Commandments.

THE FIRST COMMANDMENT

And God spoke all these words, saying:

> I am the Lord thy God, who brought thee out of the land of Egypt, out of the house of bondage
>
> (Exodus 20:1-2).

This declarative statement, considered by some a prologue[14] to the Ten Commandments, expresses an imperative force, whose implied command is commented on by Baeck.

> This sentence is the first of the commandments, not just the first of the words. For when the eternal 'I' directs its world to men, there speaks at the same time the enduring commandment, this foundation and meaning of all freedom. Essentially and primarily, revelation is the revelation of the commandment, of man's freedom. Only when man has heard the 'I am He-Who-Is' is he aware of the commandment of his self; is he conscious of the origin of his freedom
>
> (p. 74.)

The call to freedom, symbolized by the release from Egyptian bondage, is a command to choose, and to take a permanent stand with the Lord. It is a call to action, with a condition, noted by Anderson.

> [. . .] Yahweh's initiative demanded that the people respond. It placed them in a situation of decision, summoned them to a task within the divine purpose. What Moses had experienced earlier at Sinai—the call to take his part in Yahweh's historical plan—was experienced by all the people [. . .] and with far-reaching implications for the future. Whether in fact these people would be the people of Yahweh depended upon a condition: 'If you will obey my voice and keep my covenant'
>
> (p. 53).

Aucassin comes into conflict[15] with both parts of the First Commandment, which constitute a single entity; he is required to recognize the Lord and, like all Jews born at whatever period, consider that it was he who was 'brought out of Egypt, out of the house of bondage.' This symbolic tie unites all Israel in brotherhood[16] and binds them in mutual responsibility to each other and to God. "His people," as Anderson observes, "were not intended to be a crowd but a *community,* bound to Him and to one another by a covenant bond" *(loc. cit.).* A failure to assume this responsibility toward his fellows is thus nothing less than a denial of God.

The terrible twenty-year war which Bougars[17] of Valence wages against Garin ('the strangers') of Beaucaire (Canaan) confronts Aucassin with a choice: to stand aside, or support his people. His stubborn refusal to fight in their defence, except at a price—a kiss and a few words with Nicolette—wears thin the bond which links him with his community. He breaks this covenant bond—fortunately the rupture is neither permanent nor irreparable—when he angrily betrays his people in the oath he forces upon Bougars, to perpetuate the war against them. He thus cuts himself off from the brotherhood of the community. The prison into which he is cast for his deed symbolizes his loss of freedom of action as a 'son of the commandment.' Locked in a self-imposed darkness which finds Hell preferable over Heaven, he has in prison a prophetic vision of himself as the messianic pilgrim of Limosin,[18] 'born of the people,' who is cured of his follies[19] *(esvertin)* and his many ills by the mere sight of a limb of Nicolette (the land of Israel, 'beautiful as Tirzah, comely as Jerusalem'), returning to 'his own land'[20] in perfect health.

The journey that Aucassin undertakes in pursuit of his beloved, after his release from prison, will present him with opportunities to prove his acceptance of responsibility for the unity of Israel. Before he is truly and permanently reunited with her, he will have to show that he is 'ready to obey His voice and keep His covenant.' Educated through trial and effort in the network of commandments which are all based on the First, he will have to demonstrate, as at Torelore, that he has finally seen the 'light' *(Tora ora)* and heard the 'I am He-Who-Is' in awareness of the 'commandment of his self.'

THE SECOND COMMANDMENT

> Thou shalt have no other gods before Me. Thou shalt not make unto thee a graven image, nor any manner of likeness, of anything that is in heaven above, or that is in the earth beneath, or that is in the water under the earth; thou shalt not bow down onto them, nor serve them [. . .]
>
> (20:3-5).

Aucassin recognizes the existence of God, sufficiently at least to render Him a certain amount of lip-service[21] under stress; even so, he prefers Hell with Nicolette to Heaven without her. Overwhelmed by *Amor,* the Carthaginian Astarte (Ashtoreth) of his beloved Nicolette, he takes her pagan deity for his own, making a 'graven image' of her in his heart, 'bowing down and serving her.' In glorifying love beyond its due, as Love, Aucassin is guilty of a grave fault, sinning in the manner described by Goldman:

> The sin against this commandment of which we are most in danger is giving to any creature the glory and honor which are due to God only. Pride makes a god of self, covetousness makes a god of money, sensuality makes a god of the belly; whatever is esteemed or loved, feared or served, delighted in or depended on, more than God, of that (whatever it is) we do in effect make a god. This prohibition contains a precept which is the foundation of the whole law, that we take the Lord for our God [. . .]
>
> (pp. 135-136).

The fall from his 'high horse,' which dislocates his shoulder, after he has seen a first glimmer of 'light' in his *mitzva* toward the oxherd, jars Aucassin back temporarily into the path of idolatry. Crawling painfully into the bower in prostrate position, he 'bows down' unto the evening star and the moon, invoking[22] them to restore his beloved to him.

> 'Estoilete, je te voi,
>   que la lune trait a soi;
>   Nicolete est aveuc toi [. . .]'
>
> (XXV, 1-3).

This appeal to Astarte-Ashtoreth and Tanit, the favorite deities of Carthage, reveals that Nicolette—before the revelation at Torelore which will affect them both—is still exerting the pagan influence of her 'alien tongue' on Aucassin, inducing this future *moshel be'Yisrael* to follow in the misguided footsteps of his prototype, Solomon, and for the same reason, as recounted in First Kings:

> For it came to pass, when Solomon was old, that his wives turned away his heart after other gods; and his heart was not whole with the Lord his God, as was the heart of David his father. For Solomon went after Ashtoreth the goddess of the Zidonians [. . .]
>
> (11:4-5).

Aucassin, however, is still young enough—though it is never too late—to learn from his errors and rejoin the fold in the course of his voyage of discovery in the 'way of life' and the way of truth.

THE THIRD COMMANDMENT

> Thou shalt not take the name of the Lord thy God in vain; for the Lord will not hold him guiltless that taketh his name in vain
>
> (20:7)

The meaning of this injunction, of capital importance in the education of Aucassin, who violates it flagrantly on more than one occasion, is examined by Goldman.

> The third commandment has been variously interpreted as prohibiting perjury, vow-making, certain magical practices, or applying the name of God to anything false or any idle purpose. Beer spoke for many sober-minded scholars when he asserted that this was the dawn of the awareness that the holy and lying and cheating must not be brought together, which signifies a great advance in religious thought. Homiletically, the commandment has been a veritable fountain, bubbling with ever fresh ideas. Taking, as all ancients did, a serious view of an oath, the rabbis fancied that the wohle earth trembled when there blazed forth from Sinai: 'You shall not take the name of the LORD your God [. . .] the LORD will not hold him guiltless who takes His name.' The 'will not hold him guiltless' terrified them. It suggested that penitence would procure no atonement, even though it did in the case of the violation of all other negative commandments. It suggested further that [. . .] punishment would be immediate and not after three generations; that a deceiver deserves no mercy at the hands of his fellow-men; that a false oath can destroy things which neither fire nor water can; and that this commandment was placed next to the one against idolatry because the habitual perjurer was to be viewed as an idolator
>
> (pp. 152-153).

The lip-service Aucassin offers to God in a vow demanding a bribe for services he is obliged to render (above, n. 21), thus 'cheating' those who have a natural right to his strength, brings together the holy with the profane, and takes the name of the Lord in vain, implying the lie that He supports this unworthy rejection of duty. Aucassin compounds the sin, bringing himself close to becoming an 'habitual perjurer' and an 'idolator' in violation of this commandment, when he repeats the vow in almost the exact words (VIII, 20-24). He descends even lower, plumbing the nadir in this sphere, when he extorts the impious oath from Bougars, threatening to cut off his head unless he swears to a permanent vendetta against his own people; this ungodly demand is introduced by the 'pious' phrase: "Ja Dix ne m'aït [. . .]" (X, 73-74), using the name of God in connection with the basest kind of treachery.

Before the end of his journey, Aucassin will again press an oath upon an adversary, the king of Torelore, compelling him to swear to outlaw 'male child-bearing' in his country. Few vows could appear, on the surface, to be addressed to a more 'idle purpose,' and thus also in violation of the commandment; yet it is here, as we shall see, that he finally demonstrates that he has mastered the lesson of *Tora* [. . .] *le'ra,* in full recognition of its import, and it is here that he will learn the full power of penitence, whatever his misdeeds. Until that happy time, and until he has come to terms with the meaning of his name in the capsulation *al-* [. . .] *kaas* [. . .]*-im* (above, n. 12), his feet will stumble more than once, as he learns to distinguish between that which is profane and that which is holy.

THE FOURTH COMMANDMENT

> Remember the sabbath day, to keep it holy. Six days shalt thou labour, and do all thy work; but the seventh day is a sabbath unto the Lord thy God, in it thou shalt not do any manner of work, thou, nor thy son, nor thy

daughter, nor thy man-servant, nor thy maid-servant, nor thy cattle, nor thy stranger that is within thy gates; for in six days the Lord made heaven and earth, the sea and all that in them is, and rested on the seventh day; wherefore the Lord blessed the sabbath day, and hallowed it

(20:8-11).

The Sabbath differs from the ordinary days of the week, enjoining 'rest' as a matter of religion. The commandment which sets it forth differs from the others in the same manner; concerning its uniqueness, Goldman writes:

The fourth commandment is the longest and most elaborate, the first that is explicitly positive, and the only one that is concerned with a positive religious institution. Respecting circumcision, for example, the festivals, prayer, or a house of worship, the Decalogue says nothing. Instead, it devotes nearly a third of its space to order the observance of a day of rest. Little further is required to indicate that something unique is proposed and contemplated here

(p. 160).

Not surprisingly, Aucassin's confrontation with this commandment will differ from the others in the difficulty it presents for documentation, since he, a Christian by implication[23] in the surface story, can hardly engage, negatively or positively, in any activity likely to hint at so visibly[24] Jewish a practice as Sabbath observance.

The poet neatly resolves this almost insuperable dilemma, which calls for the hero to 'rest' as a sign that he 'takes his membership in the community seriously,' without divulging that this is a religious test, by disguising it— except to the special audience with the key—as a secular 'love test'[25] to determine whether or not Aucassin truly loves Nicolette and will do everything necessary to be reunited with her:

Jure Diu qui ne menti,
se par la vient Aucasins
et il por l'amor de li
ne s'i repose un petit,
ja ne sera ses amis,
n'ele s'amie

(XIX, 17-22).

The key word is *repose* 'rest,' that is, observe the Sabbath. If he fails to do this, she—the land of Israel (Tirzah and Jerusalem)—will never be his. The uniqueness and importance of the commandment could hardly be more awesomely illustrated.

Aucassin's problem in connection with the Fourth Commandment is that he has not yet properly mastered the lessons of the first three, demanding respectively that he understand the meaning of 'I am the Lord'; that he shall not bow down unto other gods; that he shall not take the name of the Lord in vain through magical practices. This is why, though as a Jew he rises magnificently to the test and 'rests' at the bower, as one who is confused (*esbahis*) and

attracted to non-Jewish practices, he falls off his 'high horse.' His appeal to the evening star and the moon to restore Nicolette to him on this Sabbath day violates all four at one time; its relevance to the Sabbath is seen in this negative description by Goldman:

No stratum of the Bible knows of the Sabbath as a day of evil or misfortune, as in any way allied to the phases of the moon[26] or connected with its worship or implicated, be it astrologically or astronomically, with any planet or a planetary week

(p. 165).

The rabbis were concerned with apparent vestiges of primitive religious practices; in the Bible, as Goldman himself observes, "there are several passages [. . .] where *hodesh* and *shabbat* are coupled together and *hodesh* means 'new moon'" (pp. 160-61). Aucassin will have another opportunity to confront the Sabbath, linked by the poet to *hodesh,* which also means 'month,' when the king of Torelore explains to him why he is lying in bed:

Dist li rois: 'Je gis d'un fil;
quant mes mois sera conplis
et je serai bien garis [. . .]'

(XXIX, 8-10).

The king appears to be saying: "I am giving birth to a child; when my month is completed and I am cured [. . .]"; to his Jewish[27] audience, however, his words mean: "I am a sinner in pain as a woman in travail; when my new moon is proclaimed and I am itchy with excitement [. . .]." The oblique reference is to orgiastic rites in worship of Ashtoreth, goddess of fertility, and in profanation of the Sabbath. Seeing himself[28] in the king lying prostrate before him, Aucassin finally learns the true meaning of *Tora* [. . .] *le'ra* and the identity of the 'evil woman' who stands between him and the Lord. But if he understands at last his duty to God, he still has to come to terms with his responsibilities and obligations to the family of man, beginning with his community and, first of all, with his parents.

The Fifth Commandment

Honour thy father and thy mother, that thy days may be long upon the land which the Lord thy God giveth thee

(20:12).

The family quarrel between Aucassin and his parents, in which both sides fail lamentably to show the respect due each other, is the point of departure which launches[29] all the successive events in the narrative as a whole, providing the initial impetus both for the narremic core of the substructure in the surface story and for the linked chain of ethical concepts in the core instruction of the parastructure. The Fifth Commandment, first in the series specifying the conduct expected of man in relation to his fellow men, underscores the priority, established in the natural[30] order of things through birth, of the social obligation to parents. The duty to 'honor thy father and thy mother' in order to assure and prolong possession of the Promised Land thus holds a commanding and central position in the organic structure of the romance; it is instructive to compare this with its place in the Decalogue, as described by Goldman:

> At times the rabbis went so far as to regard this commandment as the most important of all, having, in fact, attributed its position in the Decalogue to the role and mission of parents in life. Parents, they said—and many commentators repeated and enlarged upon their views—were the bearers of the tradition that attested both the existence of God and Revelation; they were the link between Heaven and human society; they were comprehended in the Deity and embraced in *re'acha*, . . . 'your neighbor.' And what was the present commandment? It was the link between the laws directing men how to live with their Maker and the laws instructing them how to live among themselves. It marked the transition from the first tablet—the Godward tablet—to the second—the manward tablet. Thus the rabbis esteemed and revered parents, and thus they understood the commandment to enjoin. Beyond this their sober judgment would not let them go. They would brook neither ancestor worship nor ancestor tyranny
>
> (p. 177).

The conflict between Aucassin and his parents is complex. On the surface, he wishes to marry a Carthaginian slave girl, whom they consider unsuitable; they deem it proper to teach him that there are other considerations in marriage beyond physical attraction. So determined is he to have his way that he absolutely refuses to defend them or his land against their enemies, except for a reward involving Nicolette. Garin accepts the condition, but then refuses to keep the agreement with his son, charging him, as does his mother, with being a fool. Aucassin, with complete disrespect, calls his father a liar:

> 'Certes,' fait Aucassins, 'je sui molt dolans quant hom de vostre eage ment'
>
> (X, 57-58).

In retaliation for his father's broken promise, he betrays his parents and his land, in the oath of perpetual harassment he extorts from Bougars. The consequences for not understanding the implications of the commandment, and for not acting in accordance with them, may be terrible indeed for all concerned.

It is first of all incumbent upon Aucassin to honor and respect his parents, to defend them in their need, and—above all—to pay heed to their teaching. The latter requirement receives the strongest possible stress by appearing (parastructurally) in the verses immediately preceding the *Tora* [. . .] *le'ra* capsulation, in Proverbs:

> My son, keep the commandment of thy father,
> And forsake not the teaching of thy mother;
> Bind them continually upon thy heart,
> Tie them about thy neck.

> When thou walkest, it shall lead thee,
> When thou liest down, it shall watch over thee;
> And when thou awakest, it shall talk with thee
>
> (6:20-22).

The Fifth Commandment, however, according to rabbinical interpretation,[31] implies a reciprocal obligation between parents and children. Garin, for all his good intentions, misused his parental prerogatives by lying, and delayed rather than hastened his son's understanding of the 'way of life.'

The parastructural interpretation of events involves similar considerations. The opposition of Aucassin's parents to his union with Nicolette is based on excellent intentions; the lesson they wish to impart to him is precisely the one embodied in the *Tora* [. . .] *le'ra* capsulation:

> [. . .] the teaching is light,
> And the reproofs of instruction are the way of life;
> To keep thee from the evil woman [. . .]
>
> (6: 23-24).

Their desire is to safeguard him from the clutches of Amor and idolatry, from the Canaan devoted to the pagan rites of Ashtoreth. So determined is Garin to have his way that he descends to lying and breaking his solemn word. Parents, however, are not necessarily infallible, and may themselves sometimes need a lesson in behavior toward their grown children, their 'copartners' with God; the story of Samson, another prototype[32] of Aucassin, is instructive in this regard:

> And Samson went down to Timnah, and saw a woman in Timnah of the daughters of the Philistines.[33] And he came up, and told his father and his mother, and said: 'I have seen a woman in Timnah of the daughters of the Philistines; now therefore get her for me to wife.' Then his father and his mother said unto him: 'Is there never a woman among the daughters of thy brethren, or among all thy people, that thou goest to take a wife of the uncircumcised Philistines?' And Samson said unto his father: 'Get her for me; for she pleaseth me well.' But his father and his mother knew not that it was of the Lord [. . .]
>
> (Judges 14:1-4).

Aucassin's story directly parallels that of Samson; he has a first quarrel with both father and mother, and a second quarrel with his father, stubbornly insisting on his desire for an alien bride. Both sets of parents 'knew not that it was of the Lord.' Aucassin has good reason to resist the 'tyranny' of his parents, who are unaware of the deeper purpose he is intended to serve. Once he learns the real meaning of the lesson they are trying to teach him, and identifies the 'evil woman' at Torelore as Ashtoreth, he can truly honor his parents by exorcising the pagan goddess, which he accomplishes[34] through the heroic beating he administers to the king, forcing him to eliminate male childbearing from the country, and through the 'slaughter' of the strange warriors whose weapons are such tempting tidbits as baked apples, fresh cheeses, eggs, and mushrooms. Little wonder that Nicolette undergoes a complete change of character at Torelore, allowing Aucassin to dominate the scene in a wild melee which cleanses her—the land of Israel—of paganism. A battlefield can be murder, figuratively.

THE SIXTH COMMANDMENT

Thou shalt not murder

(20:13).

Aucassin tilts squarely with the starkly simple commandment against murder, and its various aspects, on at least three separate occasions. His first brush with it occurs early in the story; when he declines to fight for his people unless he is given Nicolette—or even just a kiss—in recompense, he is admitting his readiness to shed the blood of others not in the reluctantly permitted[35] act of self-defense but for a price. True, he is not motivated by a crude appetite for booty[36] and material gain, but he is still willing, out of self-interest unrelated to the necessity, to kill ten fellow men and wound seven others without a second thought.

[. . .] il comence a ferir a destre et a senestre et caupe hiaumes et naseus et puins et bras et fait un caple entor lui, autresi con li senglers quant li cien l'asalent [. . .]

(X, 24-27).

Not for nothing does the poet designate his deed a *caple* 'massacre,' and compare the killer with the *senglers* 'wild boar.' Even when most nobly motivated, killing infringes the sanctity of life and entails awesome consequences, as Cohon observes:

Human life, like personality, forms an end in itself and is sacred. Life is an attribute of God, who is visioned as 'the source of life' and as 'delighting in life.' Coming from God, it is man's highest good, which he must cherish as a trust. Life is identified with the good, and death with evil (Deut. 30:15, 19). Shedding of blood, say the rabbis, defiles the land and causes the Shechinah[37] to depart from Israel. Preservation of life has recommended itself to the Jew as the supreme duty of man. The laws of Sabbath observance, of fasting on Yom Kippur, of *kashrut*, etc., are set aside when life is at stake. Even where it is not certain that life can be saved, these laws may be set aside. 'There is naught that stands in the way of saving life, except apostasy, incest and murder,' i.e., life obtained at the cost of the desecration of its supreme values is not warth having

(pp. 157-158).

It is neither for the purpose of avoiding apostasy,[38] nor incest, nor murder, the only three causes superior to the preservation of life, that Aucassin comes into conflict with a second aspect of the commandment, relating to self-murder.[39] During the comic debate of the lovers' quarrel,[40] when Nicolette insults him by declaring that he does not love her as much as he says he does, and he insults her even more by contrasting the fickleness and carnality of woman's love against the stead-fastness and purity of man's, she announces her intention of crossing the sea to escape Garin's wrath and at the same time protect Aucassin from it. He angrily conjures up an imaginary scene in which she is raped and he in consequence dashes out his brains in hopeless fury:

[. . .] li premiers qui vos verroit ne qui vous porroit, il vos prenderoit lués et vos meteroit a son lit, si vos asoignenteroit. Et puis que vos ariiés jut en lit a home, s'el mien non, or ne quidiés mie que j'atendisse tant que je trovasse coutel dont je me peusce ferir el cuer et ocirre. Naie voir, tant n'atenderoie je mie; ains m'esquelderoie de si lonc que je verroie une maisiere u une bisse pierre, s'i hurteroie si durement me teste que j'en feroie les ex voler et que je m'escerveleroie tos [. . .]

(XIV, 4-12).

Rape in real life is not inherently funny, but the ability to laugh at trouble is a gift, and sign, of life. The hero who is ready to kill himself if his beloved lies in the arms of another is the same lad who said he prefers Hell because:

[. . .] s'i vont les beles dames cortoises que eles ont deus amis ou trois avoc leur barons [. . .]

(VI, 35-36).

This liberality presumably extends to all other wives but his own. There is additional humor in the inversion of roles; it is not the angry lover who has the justification for suicide, but the threatened heroine, and Aucassin would do well not to be too hasty, as his name advises in *al*-[. . .] *kaas* [. . .]-*im*. The same advice against haste to be angry appears on the serious, or parastructural level. Aucassin, as the people of Israel, threatens to kill himself if Nicolette, as the land of Israel, comes into the possession of others rather than himself; in doing so, he shows his readiness to violate the commandment against murder because he places his love for the land above his love of God. The land has been promised to him; the promise will be kept when he demonstrates that he has learned to place first things first.[41]

Aucassin's third involvement with the complexities of murder hinges on self-defense, and furnishes an excellent example of the author's subtle homiletic technique in the contrast between the slaughter of the forces of Valence and those engaged on the battlefied of Torelore. In the former case, as we have seen, Aucassin seems to be killing in defense of his land and people whereas he is actually committing murder out of self-interest; at Torelore, he seems to be commtting murder[42] without cause, whereas he is actually acting in self-defense, pitting himself against the overwhelming forces of *Amor* (Ashtoreth), who stir up love before the young, untutored mind is capable of coping with them. Our hero, firmly seated in the saddle this time,[43] studies the *estor canpel*, the 'battle in the field,' and takes the measure of his opponents.

Aucassins est arestés,
sor son arçon acoutés,

si coumence a regarder
ce plenier estor canpel [. . .]

(XXXI, 1-4).

The parastructural singal is *estor,* a pun compounded of
Heb. *es-*, the untranslatable morpheme introducing a common noun as a specific direct object, and *tor* 'turtle,' that
is, a capsulation, *es-*[. . .] *tor,* is indicated, pointing to a
relevant passage, enclosed between these forms, in the
Song of Songs.

'I adjure you, O daughters of Jerusalem,
By the gazelles, and by the hinds of the field,
That ye awaken not, nor stir up *love* [*es-ha'ahava,*
. . .]
Until it please.'
Hark! my beloved! behold, he cometh,
Leaping upon the mountains, skipping upon the hills.
My beloved is like a gazelle or a young hart;
Behold, he standeth behind our wall,
He looketh in through the windows,
He peereth through the lattice.[44]
My beloved spoke, and said unto me:
'Rise up, my love, my fair one, and come away.
For, 1o, the winter is past,
The rain is over and gone;
The flowers appear on the earth;
The time of singing is come,
And the voice of the *turtle* [ha'*tor;* . . .] is heard in
our land [. . .]'

(2:7-12).

The passage signifies Aucassin's awareness that the
'daughters of Jerusalem' are 'awakening and stirring up
love' for which he and Nicolette are not yet ready; that
they both have much to learn and to live through before 'it
please,' and is sanctified. The immediate task is to eliminate forever Nicolette's goddess, Ashtoreth, and her min-
ions, who are fighting their 'battle in the field' in pagan
feasting on baked apples, fresh cheeses, and oversized
mushrooms, ending in a drunken orgy whose champion is
well described in an ingenious pun:

cil qui mix torble les gués
est li plus sire clamés

(XXXI, 9-10).

Fr. *gués* is a pun on Heb. *gas* (. . .) 'wine-press, wine
vat'; no wonder that Aucassin breaks into laughter ("s'en
prist a rire," XXXI, 13) at the Rabelaisian scene, while
proceeding in all seriousness to dispatch the gluttons and
guzzlers unceremoniously (see "The Ashkenazic *sof*").

Whatever else Aucassin's cavalier treatment of the intrepid
warriors may be called, with regard to his own and to
Nicolette's moral regeneration through education[45] it can
hardly be associated with murder; parastructurally, the
people of Israel have the right and the duty to cleanse the
land of defilement[46] in self-defense. Now that Aucassin has
learned to distinguish among murder in self-interest, suicide, and killing in self-defense—with stress on the ter-

rible consequences of any actual shedding of blood—he is
prepared to examine another infraction traditionally associated with death, the sin of adultery.

THE SEVENTH COMMANDMENT

Thou shalt not commit adultery

(20:13).

The poet draws a modest curtain over any conceivable
sexual activities which might have occured during the joyful night of reunion shared by Aucassin and Nicolette at
the bower, during their three halcyon years at Torelore,
and during their last night together preceding their wedding. The question arises whether, even if they had been
so engaged, the act would involve adultery, since Nicolette
is not 'another man's wife,' the condition specified in Leviticus 20:10. Goldman's commentary, exploring the ramifications of the commandment, suggests this might be a
possibility:

'My people of the house of Israel, do not be adulterers,
nor companions nor accomplices of adulterers; nor shall
there be seen in the congregation of Israel an adulterous people, so that your sons may not arise after you to
teach one another to be the accomplices of adulterers;
for because of the sin of adultery, death comes upon
the world' *(Targum Jonathan)*. A warning against adultery, the penalty being stipulated in Leviticus, XX, 10.
Technically, adultery is sexual intercourse of a married
woman with any other man than her husband (Leviticus,
XX, 10, *et al.*). Forbids intercourse also with unmarried
women; so ibn Ezra, who quotes Saadia to the effect
that there are grades in adultery, the gravity of the sin
depending on whether the one with whom it is committed is unmarried, in her menstrual period, married, a
heathen, male, or beast. The rabbis applied the commandment also to masturbation. The references to adultery are limited in the Pentateuch to the two Deca-
logues and Leviticus, XX, 10; there are frequent
references throughout the remainder of the Bible

(pp. 182-183).

The commandment thus extends to the Nicolette portrayed
in the surface story, even though she is unmarried. Since
the poet gives Aucassin the opportunity to express himself
on the subject, without involving him in the act itself, it
may be assumed that he is directing the attention of his
hero to a more abstract conception of adultery, in which
the issue is his general attitude. Nicolette's godfather, the
viscount, upholds the traditional view balancing momen-
tary pleasure against eternal torment, when he demands to
know what Aucassin expects to gain from making Nicolette his mistress:

'Enseurquetot, que cuideriés vous avoir gaegnié, se
vous l'aviés asognentee ne mise a vo lit? Mout i ariés
peu conquis, car tos les jors du siecle en seroit vo arme
en infer [. . .]'

(VI, 19-22).

The same Aucassin who admires the *beles dames cortoises*
with their several lovers besides their husbands—but

would dash his brains out if Nicolette joined their company—would gladly accompany them on the road to Hell, provided only that he can have his sweet beloved with him:

> '[. . .] avoc ciax voil jou aler, mais que j'aie Nicolete ma tresdouce amie aveuc mi'
>
> (VI, 38-39).

Aucassin must learn to guard himself against the treacherous onset of evil-doing, which may begin long before it is visible to the beholder. Adultery can take place in the eye and in the mind, as well as in the deed, according to Solomon Schechter.

> "[. . .] we have heard that it is written, 'Thou shalt not commit adultery' [. . .]. But the phrase in Job (24:15), 'The *eye* also of the adulterer waiteth for twilight,' teaches us that an unchaste look is also to be considered as adultery; and the verse, 'And that ye seek not after your own heart and your own eyes, after which ye used to go awhoring' (Num. 15:19), teaches us that an unchaste look or even an unchaste thought are also to be regarded as adultery."[47]

For expository purposes, Schechter has cast the reflexions expressed in the old rabbinic style; his design is to show how in Jewish lore a corrective is applied to the Law. This is effected, as he declares, "not by something antagonistic or outside of it, but by its own proper interpretation and expansion" (p. 213).

It is not with the physical act of adultery that Aucassin faces his challenge but with an expanded interpretation of it, relating to his attraction to the idolatrous 'evil woman' of *Tora* [. . .] *le'ra*. In his celebrated commentary[48] on Proverbs 7:6-26, Maimonides teaches:

The general principle expounded in all these verses is to abstain from excessive indulgence in bodily pleasures. The author compares the body, which is the source of all sensual pleasures, to a married woman who is at the same time a harlot.[49]

The passage which Maimonides is expounding is directly relevant to the situation of Aucassin, 'a young man void of understanding,' as he 'looks forth through the lattice' at the bower, and as he nonchalantly prefers the 'netherworld' in his conversation on adultery with the viscount.

> For at the window of my house
> I looked forth through my lattice;
> And I beheld among the thoughtless ones,
> I discerned among the youths,
> A young man void of understanding,
> Passing through the street near her corner,
> And he went the way to her house [. . .].
> . . . . .
> Her house is the way to the nether-world,
> Going down to the chambers of death
>
> (7:6-26)

The strictures of Maimonides are not directed against bodily pleasures but against 'excessive indulgence' in them. The fundamental lesson Aucassin and the perplexed people of Israel are expected to draw from the key message exemplified by adultery is neatly summed up by Milton Steinberg: "All depends, with the passions, on the controls to which they are subjected and the ends to which they are turned."[50] The love of Aucassin for Nicolette as a woman, or in symbolic expansion as the land of Israel, is good in itself when under control; it becomes 'adultery' when it leads to idolatrous worship of person, place, or thing. Concomitantly, 'excessive indulgence' may increase the appetite beyond the capacity to feed it, and unwittingly give rise rise to stealing.

THE EIGHTH COMMANDMENT

> Thou shalt not steal
>
> (20:13).

Aucassin demands Nicolette as the price of his services to defend his people and his homeland; in refusing him, Garin indicates that she belongs to the viscount, who has purchased her from the Saracens:

> 'si l'acata li visquens de ceste vile as Serasins [. . .]'
>
> (II, 30).

When Garin insists that the viscount exile Nicolette to remove her influence over Aucassin, he agrees, but reminds the former, who has treatened to burn her, that she is his property, bought with cash:

> 'Je l'avoie acatee de mes deniers [. . .]'
>
> (IV, 11).

The poet stresses Nicolette's status as property a third time; when Aucassin asks the viscount what he has done with her, the latter bluntly bids him drop the matter:

> 'car laisciés ester. [. . .] si l'acatai de mon avoir [. . .]'
>
> (VI, 14-16).

His determination to have her, against the will of the parents who literally 'own' her, means that he must 'steal' her from them; the stealing of a human being,[51] like anything else that belongs to another, is forbidden by the commandment.

The fact that Aucassin reduces his price to a kiss and a few words with Nicolette in no way lessens his guilt. Anything that he extorts in payment for carrying out obligations that he owes by right is a theft, whose actual value has nothing to do with the case; in the view of the rabbis, according to Schechter:

> [. . .] he who robs his neighbor, even if the goods robbed do not amount to more than the value of a Perutah, is as much as if he murdered him
>
> (p. 227).

The hero himself sees the kiss as worth a good deal more than a 'Perutah'; he would not take a hundred thousand marks of pure gold in place of it (IX, 1-4).

Aucassin, son of a ruler, is himself destined to rule; his rank, however, does not give him the right to infringe the rights of others, subverting public order. The commandment, Goldman states:

> Establishes the right to property, thus excluding aggressions, reprisals, and consequent chaos and disorganization [. . .]. He who gapes after what belongs to others is the common enemy of the state, willing to rob all [. . .]. So all thieves who have acquired the strength rob whole cities, careless of punishment because their high distinction seems to set them above the laws. These are allegorically minded persons, ambitious for despotism or domination, who perpetrate thefts on a great scale, disguising the real fact of robbery under the grandsounding names of 'government' and 'leadership.' Let a man, then, learn from his earliest years to filch nothing by stealth that belongs to another, however small it may be, because habit in the course of time is stronger than nature and little things, if not checked, grow and thrive until they attain to great dimensions [. . .]
>
> (pp. 183-184).

The future *moshel be'Yisrael* is required to take notice; the Promised Land will be his—the romance ends with a wedding and a permanent reunion of the lovers—but he must employ none but honorable methods, with due regard for the rights of his neighbor.

THE NINTH COMMANDMENT

Thou shalt not bear false witness against thy neighbour

(20:13).

The intent of this commandment is to regulate the daily acts of the individual in relation to his fellows, going far beyond the obvious prohibitions against perjury, scandalmongering, tale-bearing, verbal injuries which announce themselves. The command, 'thou shalt love thy neighbor as thyself' (Leviticus 19:18), entails specific obligations, as described by Steinberg:

> [. . .] when I inquire as to my duties to my fellow, I can accept only one answer: I may not withold from him [. . .] any of the reverence, solicitude, and freedom I claim for myself.
>
> To this obligation there are no exceptions. Since all men partake of God with me, I may exclude none from my deference, not by reason of race, creed, color, social position, economic class, or any other consideration [. . .].
>
> [. . .] this means that I may not use him as a mere tool for my purposes [. . .]. I may not injure him in any fashion, oppress, exploit, humiliate him, or deprive him of anything to which he is entitled. Nor may I deceive him or withhold the truth from him, since, as the rabbis

pointed out long ago, oppression may be through words as well as deeds

(pp. 75-76).

The first infraction of the commandment is committed against, not by, Aucassin; Garin, whose word should be his bond, deliberately deceives him with a false promise to allow him a kiss from Nicolette in reward for his services:

'Je l'otroi,' fait li peres

(VIII, 37).

The blame, however, still rests on Aucassin, since it is he who provokes his aged father to 'bear false witness' by exploiting his need and 'stealing' a promise to which he is not entitled. The vicious chain is forged link by progressive link: a 'small' theft promotes a lie in a 'good'[52] cause; the lie diminishes the 'deference' a son owes his father and makes it more difficult to honor him; the withholding of deference to the father ends in betrayal of his people and in the darkness of a prison cell. The lesson for Aucassin is salutary, if not immediately absorbed; a ruler must respond to provocation in ways designed to increase, not decrease, the public order; as the 'first among equals,' he must accord his subjects the respect that their equality[53] entitles them to expect.

Aucassin fails to apply this lesson in his encounter with the shepherds. In his pursuit of Nicolette, he overhears the shepherds singing a song about her. When they refuse to repeat it at his request, he attempts to overawe them through superior[54] rank, demanding haughtily:

'Bel enfant,' fait Aucassin, 'enne me conissiés vos?'

(XXII, 10).

They do indeed know who he is, and properly rebuke him; no one but the reigning count is privileged to give them orders. This use of social status as a tool to force those more humble into unwilling obedience is a flagrant violation of their human rights, implying their inferiority, and thus 'bearing false witness' against them. Little acts verge into greater ones, and a ruler may easily become a tyrant.

The shepherds, on their part, are not guiltless either. One sin begets another; if Aucassin tries to exert undue pressure, it is they who provoke him by their gratuitous refusal to help a fellow being in distress, at no trouble to themselves. Their complete lack of 'solicitude' for the plight of their neighbor is perfectly expressed in their casual reply[55] to Nicolette, after accepting her money to pass on a message to Aucassin. Technically, they now 'owe' him the information in a double sense, as a natural obligation and as a purchased item. Their failure to hand it over, except after badgering and a second payment from him, exploits his need just as much as his bargaining with his father exploited the latter. The command to 'love thy neighbor as thyself,' which means help him when he needs it, does not include the proviso, 'if the price is right.'

Aucassin's grasp of the nuances of the commandment is soon put to the test. Given Nicolette's message finally, that he should hunt in the forest for a 'beast' possessing a limb[56] for which he would not take five hundred gold marks or any wealth in exchange and which has the medicine to 'cure' his illness, he continues his pursuit, tearfully. His path is suddenly obstructed by a formidable oxherd with a massive club, whose appearance frightens him. Asked why he is weeping, he replies with a lie:

> 'je vig hui matin cacier en ceste forest, s'avoie un blanc levrer, le plus bel del siecle, si l'ai perdu: por ce pleur jou'

> (XXIV, 39-41).

Perhaps he fears that if the ugly giant knew the truth, he might find Nicolette first and rape her, with the dire consequences to himself that he has already predicted. In any event, he trusts in a lie more than he does in God, and affronts his neighbor without sufficient cause.

There is a positive side to Aucassin's encounter with the oxherd. When the latter informs him of his own problem—he has somehow misplaced an ox, cannot replace it, and faces debtor's prison—our hero immediately gives him the money to relieve his distress. This is a *mitzva*, in compliance with an important obligation, commanded in Proverbs:

> Withhold not good from him to whom it is due,
> When it is in the power of thy hand to do it.
> Say not unto thy neighbour: 'Go, and come again,
> And to-morrow I will give'; when thou hast it by thee

> (3:27-28).

Before Aucassin asks the value of the ox and hands over the cash to pay for it, he listens attentively to the oxherd's fulminations, damning him for weeping over a 'stinking hound' when others have real problems. The lesson is not lost upon him, and he replies:

> 'Certes, tu es de bon confort, biax frere [. . .]'

> (XXIV, 63).

He has it in his power now to do a good deed; will this wash out his evil one? Schechter gives the answer to this typical rabbinical question.

> Here is a man who committed an immoral action [. . .] but he hardly left the place when a poor man met him and addressed him for alms. This man thinks that God put this poor man in his way with the purpose of making him find pardon through the alms he gave, but the Holy One, blessed be He, says: Wicked man, think not so. The hand which gives alms will not cleanse the other from the evil which it did by paying the wages of sin.[57]

The oxherd is grateful for the help and prays that Aucassin will find what he seeks; in the next incident, Aucassin is reunited with Nicolette at the bower, but only temporarily. Before the reunion can become permanent, he still has to learn of his subjection to covetousness.

THE TENTH COMMANDMENT

> Thou shalt not covet thy neighbor's house; thou shalt not covet thy neighbor's wife, nor his man-servant, nor his maid-servant, nor his ox, nor his ass, nor any thing that is thy neighbor's

> (20:14).

'Love thy neighbor as thyself' includes a sacred obligation to respect the sanctity of his household and the inviolability of everything that belongs to him. Wanting what is his, and determining to get it, no matter how despicable the means necessary, is not only to break the commandment but to smash it to fragments. The love of Aucassin for Nicolette, established right from the beginning, is so overwhelming that it leaves no room in his heart or mind for the rights of others. Love is good and desire, its handmaiden, is productive of life; but inordinate desire, covetousness, 'Amor, qui tout vaint' (II, 15-16) which sweeps away all in its path, leads to the 'chambers of death.' The poet lays great stress on the fact, three times repeated, that the object of Aucassin's love was 'purchased' by the viscount from the Saracens, baptized and raised by him with love, and destined by him for someone else. She thus 'belongs' to the viscount, and in wanting her against all remonstrance:

> nuis hom ne l'en puet retraire [. . .]

> (III, 4)

he covets that which is his neighbor's, in violation of the commandment.

The silken web, which holds him ensnared and paralyzes his ability to aid his people against the warring forces arrayed against them, begins here, in the tender embrace of Ashtoreth and in the 'smoothness of her alien tongue.' Woven as with a single thread, it bounds the limits of his dark odyssey, in a linked chain of broken commandments. Mesmerized by covetous desire, he rejects the Lord in favor of Hell, bows down to the graven image of Ashtoreth, takes the name of the Lord in vain in a despicable oath of treachery against his people, violates the hallowed Sabbath with a magical appeal to the heavenly bodies for help, dishonors his father and mother, murders for a price, commits adultery in his eye and heart through uncontrolled passion, steals that which belongs to his neighbors by natural right, bears false witness against them through deception and assumed airs of superiority, and finally, closes his ears to the 'reproofs of instruction' designed to eliminate the poison of covetousness at its source.

The way out of the web, the 'way of life' and true love, is revealed to Aucassin at Torelore. Seeing himself as the sinner he is, in the guise of the wretched king, he picks up a handy club to beat his worst foe—himself into correction. His strongets weapon, however, in his language. Bluntly, he opens his instructive tirade to the sinner with the arresting words:

> 'Par le cuer Diu!' fait Aucassins, 'malvais fix a putain [. . .]'

> (XXX, 7).

The message, delivered overtly in profanity, carries a para-structural hope of redemption. The *par* [. . .] *le* [. . .] *cuer* capsulation,[58] *al-* [. . .] to [. . .] *lev,* is found in First Samuel:

> 'Fear not [*al-*tira"u; . . .] ye have indeed done all this evil; yet turn not aside from following the Lord, but serve the Lord with all your heart [be'chol-*leva*vechem; . . .] [. . .]'

(12:20).

Our hero now understands the lesson of *Tora* [. . .] *le'ra* (p. 7), that he cannot yield to the blandishments of the 'evil woman' and at the same time 'serve the Lord with all his heart.' The light of Tora, and not the darkness of Ashtoreth, is the way to genuine and permanent union with his beloved Nicolette.

The desire of Aucassin, representing the people of Israel, to be reunited with Nicolette, as the Promised Land, no less than in his relationship to her as man to woman, is equally engaged in the violation of the commandments. Nicolette, first described as a Carthaginian, or Saracen, has been baptized as a Christian by the viscount; she reverts to the Saracens when they capture her at Torelore. The analogy is with Canaan, or Palestine. A possession of the Saracens, it is 'purchased' by the Crusaders at great expenditure of blood and treasure; the Saracens, under Saladin, capture Jerusalem and reclaim ownership. It is not for the putative owners to determine possession, however, but for Nicolette herself, guided by the lesson of *Tora* [. . .] *le'ra,* meant equally for her as well as Aucassin. When the latter returns to Beaucaire (Canaan) after his capture by the Saracens at Torelore, it is as king in his own land. Nicolette, for her part, breaks away—against their will—from her own people and returns voluntarily to her lover, free of the 'evil' influence. Together again, Aucassin and Nicolette can share their joy with all troubled readers in the happy vision—since realized—of an exiled people reunited with their Promised Land; a land whose schools facilitate the study of Tora to all who yearn for light, 'for the commandment is a lamp [. . .].'

Notes

1. "Et puis que j'arai la teste caupee, ja mais ne parlerai a Nicolete me douce amie que je tant aim" (X, 18-20). Text citations are from: *Aucassin et Nicolette: Chantefable du XIIIe siècle,* ed. Mario Roques, 2nd rev. ed. Paris: H. Champion, 1969.

2. "Il mist le pié fors de l'estrier por descendre, et li cevaus fu grans et haus [. . .]" (XXIV, 82-85).

3.   "Qui vauroit bons vers oïr
del deport du viel antif
de deus biax enfans petis [. . .]"

(I, 1-3).

4. The romance is secretly coded with signals of various kinds, referring to passages in the Hebrew Bible, which add a covert—or parastructural—dimension to the tale; this aspect was restricted—around the time

of the Albigensian Crusade when unauthorized study of the Bible was dangerous—to readers familiar with the Bible and its commentaries in Hebrew. See Dorfman, "Tora Lore in Torelore: A Parastructural Analysis," *Memorial Volume for Ruth Hirsch Weir* (Mouton, in press); "The Flower in the Bower: *Garris* in *Aucassin et Nicolette,*" pp. 77-87 in *Studies in Honor of Mario A. Pei,* Chapel Hill (University of North Carolina Press, 1972); "Aucassin and the Pilgrim of 'Limosin': A Bilingual Pun," *Festschrift for Archibald A. Hill* (in press); "The Sacred and the Profane in *Aucassin et Nicolette,*" *Festschrift for Robert A. Hall, Jr.* (in press); "The Ashkenazic *Sof* in *Aucassin et Nicolette: Torble les gués,*" *Far-Western Forum* (in press); *Parody and Parable in Aucassin et Nicolette: A Narremic and Parastructural Analysis* (in preparation).

5. The poet specifies in his exordium that his subject matter is "del deport du viel antif" (above, n. 3). The form *du viel antif,* which has been criticized for redundancy because of the reduplication, is in fact a loan translation of the Hebrew *mi'kedem mi'ymey olam* . . . 'from of old, from ancient days,' and thus serves to signal the celebrated prophecy of Micah, in which the reduplication is associated with the Messiah:

> But thou, Beth-lehem Ephrathah,
> Which art little to be among the thousands of Judah,
> Out of thee shall one come forth unto Me that is to be ruler in
>   Israel;
> Whose goings forth are from of old, from ancient days

(5:1).

Biblical citations are from: *The Holy Scriptures, according to the Masoretic Text* (Philadelphia: Jewish Publication Society, 1965), and *Sefer Tora Neviyim ve'Ktuvim,* ed. Norman Henry Snaith (London: British and Foreign Bible Society, 1965).

Deport in Judeo-French signifies 'action d'élever' (Raphael Levy, *Trésor de la langue des Juifs français au moyen âge,* Austin: University of Texas Press, 1964); in a thirteenth century Jewish community the 'raising' of children would involve instruction in the Tora, or the teaching of the Law. The verse as a whole therefore indicates the poet's intention of describing the education of a Jewish prince, the long-promised 'ruler in Israel,' whose coming will deliver his people from their miseries in Exile; see "Tora Lore in Torelore," and *Parody and Parable.* Significantly, the coming Deliverer will not be of supernatural origin, but a man 'born of the people'—*nes estoit de Limosin;* the bilingual pun *Limosin* combines O.Fr. *li* 'the' and Hebrew *mas* . . . 'person,' pl. *mosim* . . . 'people'; see Aucassin and the Pilgrim of 'Limosin.'" See also below, no. 18.

6. When Aucassin returns to Beaucaire, after his adventures in Torelore and his deliverance from the Sa-

racen pirates, he finds that his parents have died and he has inherited the 'kingdom,' which he manages to hold in peace, against all claimants (XXXIV, 10-16, XXXV, 1-4). His Beaucaire is not the well-known French city but a land to be identified through a pun based on a passage in which Hosea adjures Ephraim and Judah, the Northern and the Southern kingdoms, that is, the whole Land of Israel:

> O Ephraim, what shall I do unto thee?
> O Judah, what shall I do unto thee?
> For your goodness is a morning could [*ka'anan-boker* . . .]
> And as the dew that early passeth away

> (6:4).

Heb. *ka-* 'like' plus *anan* 'cloud' yields *Ka'anan* . . . a readily visible pun on *kena'an* 'Canaan' . . . in combination with *boker* 'morning,' as *kena'an-boker* . . . forming Canaan-Beaucaire, the identification of Beaucaire is established as the Promised Land.

7. The poet employs the Hebrew preposition *le-* 'to' as a device to signal a capsulated Biblical message standing between the word which precedes and the one which follows; thus, *Tora* [. . .] *le* [. . .] *ra* signifies: read from *Tora* [. . .] *to* [. . .] *ra*, that is, *Tora or ve'derech chayim toch'chos musar: li'shmarcha me'eshes ra* (the letter *sof* . . . is transliterated as Ashkenazic *s* rather than Sephardic *t*, in view of Franco-Hebrew puns in the text which require the sibilant). The French word *le* 'the, it, him' (and in this text also 'her') serves this same purpose in the romance; the French words which precede and follow it—wherever it occurs in the text—yield similar capsulations when translated into Hebrew. For the discovery of this key and the variety of devices used, see *Parody and Parable,* and "Tora Lore in Torelore."

8. [. . .] mais si estoit soupris d'Amor, qui tout vaint, qu'il ne voloit [. . .] fare point de quanque il deust" (II, 15-18).

9. The poet explicitly declares in the exordium his intention to relate the great pains Aucassin will endure and the prowesses he will perform for the sake of his beloved:

> des grans paines qu'il soufri
> et des proueces qu'il fist
> por s'amie o le cler vis [. . .]

> (I, 5-7).

This is amusing in the surface story, since Nicolette, in contrast to the passive Aucassin, appears to be the active hero everywhere, except in Torelore. On the parastructural level, the verses mean what they say.

It may be remarked that the *amie*, the 'beloved,' for whose sake the hero suffers and strives, is characterized by the apparently formulaic description *o le cler vis* 'with the bright face.' The *le* signals a capsulation

o [. . .] *le* [. . .] *cler*, reading from *o*, Heb. *be-, ba-* 'in, with, among' to *cler*, Heb. *bar*, f. *bara* 'clean,, clear, pure'; the relevant passage, found in the Song of Songs, is a beautiful description of Solomon's beloved, the Shulamite:

> '[. . .] among the lilies [*ba'shoshanim* . . .],
> Thou art beautiful, O my love, as Tirzah,
> Comely as Jerusalem [. . .].

> . . . . .

> Who is she that looketh forth as the dawn,
> Fair as the moon,
> Clear as the sun [*bara* ka'chama; . . .] [. . .]?

> (6:3-10)

Nicolette is thus identified with the Shulamite, as Aucassin, the 'ruler in Israel' [*Moshel* be-Yisrael . . .], is associated with the author of the *Mishley Shlomo* (The Proverbs of Solomon), in which the *Tora* [. . .] *le'ra* capsulation occurs. Aucassin and Nicolette each play several roles in the parastructural part of the romance; among these, Aucassin represents the Jewish people and Nicolette the Promised Land, first as a pagan Canaan and later as the Land of Israel ('beautiful as Tirzah, comely as Jerusalem'). The essential purpose of the romance is to bring the two lovers together, after being twice separated involuntarily, into a third and—hopefully—permanent reunion. For additional details on the various roles of the protagonists, see *Parody and Parable,* and "Tora Lore in Torelore"; on Nicolette as the Land of Israel, see "Aucassin and the Pilgrim"; on the lilies as identification tag for Nicolette, see "The Flower in the Bower."

10. Leo Baeck, *This People Israel: The Meaning of Jewish Existence* (Philadelphia: Jewish Publication Society, 1965), pp. 73-74; see also Solomon Goldman, *The Ten Commandments* (Chicago and London, University of Chicago Press, 1956), pp. 79, 124-189.

11. In recent times, the ceremony of *bar mitzva* often includes a speech by the thirteen-year old celebrant, proclaiming: "Today I am a man!" Realization of its meaning, as with Aucassin, is usually deferred until the youth, in collision with the concrete problems of life, demonstrates his capacity to balance against his egocentric needs and desires a voluntary acceptance of responsibility toward others.

12. The name *Aucassin* is itself an ingenious warning against unrestrained anger. As Al-Kâsim, which takes on its French form by normal phonetic change (see Robert Griffin, "*Aucassin et Nicolette* and the Albigensian Crusade," *Modern Language Quarterly,* 26 (1965), 243-256, p. 247), the general public may accept it as part of an amusing inversion in which the "Christian" hero bears a "Saracen" name while the "Saracen" heroine has a "Christian" name (see Omer Jodogne, "La Parodie et le pastiche dans *Aucassin et Nicolette,*" *Cahiers de l'Association Internationale des Etudes Françaises,* 12 (1960), 53-65, p. 56). A *je* [. . .] *le* [. . .] *puis* capsulation, however, reveals it

ass an acronym, based on a relevant passage in Kohelet (Ecclesiastes), in the form of *al* [. . .] *kaas* [. . .] *im:*

> *al*-t'vahel b'ruchacha li'chos ki *kaas* be'acheik k'sil*im* yanuach . . .
> *Be not* hasty in thy spirit to be angry;
> For *anger* resteth in the bosom of fools

(7:9).

For supplementary details, including the Hebrew meanings of the names *Nicolette,* given in the text also as *Nicole* (*nikele:* 'of low esteem'), and *Garin* (*gerim:* 'strangers'—traditional sobriquet of the Jews), and of the manner in which these names link together Garin, Aucassin and Nicolette in a family relationship tied to that of King David, Solomon and the Shulamite, see *Parody and Parable.*

13. Nus hom n'est si esbahis,

> tant dolans ni entrepris,
> de grant mal amaladis,
> se il l'oit, ne soit garis,
> et de joie resbaudis,
> > tant par est douce

(I, 10-15).

The Book of Esther records an earlier occasion when the Jewish community in distress was saved from extermination; as a result la'Yehudim hayesa ora ve'simcha ve'sason v'ikar . . .

> The Jews had light and gladness, and joy and honour

(8:16).

Addressing himself to those whom it concerns, the poet promises light for the 'perplexed,' gladness for the 'sorrowful,' joy for the 'dejected,' and honor for the degraded, 'sickened by the great evil' which pursues them, threatening them with conversion, expulsion, or death. The order of the nouns, *ora, simcha, sason,* and *ikar,* is matched precisely by that of the adjectives, *esbahis, dolans, entrepris,* and *amaladis.* Equally significant is the rabbinical interpretation of *ora* as *Tora ora* 'teaching is light'; the synonomous expression, *Tora or,* is the lead phrase in the *Tora* [. . .] *le'ra* capsulation, cited above, serving as the thematic foundation for the education of Aucassin.

14. See Bernhard W. Anderson, *Understanding the Old Testament* (Englewood Cliffs, N.J.; Prentice-Hall 1957), p. 56. Baeck defends the traditional view, p. 74: "It would be misunderstood, and its loftiness and power would be impaired, were one to assume [. . .] that it became a commandment through the connection with the following sentence [. . .]." See also Goldman, op. cit., p. 133.

15. The poet must be congratulated for his extraordinary ability to treat such obviously Jewish matter *in extenso* without once arousing the suspicion of anyone not provided with the key. The multitude of capsulations leading to relevant Biblical passages, however, leaves no doubt concerning the parastructural import of Aucassin's adventures.

16. The popular expression of this, heard whenever anyone is in need, is: *kol Yisrael chaverim . . .* 'all Israel are brothers.' Aucassin respects this requirement for the first time in the romance when he replaces the lost ox of the oxherd; he is immediately rewarded by finding Nicolette's bower in the forest.

17. The name *Bougars,* unlike those of Aucassin, Nicolette, and Garin, is not Hebrew but French; as a twelfth-century development of Lat. *Bulgarus* 'heretic' (see Bloch and Wartburg, *Dictionnaire étymologique de la langue française,* 3rd ed., Paris: P.U.F., 1960), it typifies Aucassin's youthful pull toward assimilation, underscoring the real meaning of his betrayal in demanding that the 'heretic' wage everlasting war against his people. For the explanation of Bougars' alternate name in the text, *Borgars* 'the bud,' and of Valence (Judeo-French *balenç*) as the land of the idolatrous 'balances of deceit,' see *Parody and Parable.*

18. See above, n. 5. Aucassin is *dolans* as he conjures up the vision of the pilgrim, *malades de l'esvertin, entrepris,* and *de grant mal amaladis* (XI, 8-21); together, that is, as one, they share all the ills which the poet, in the exordium, promises to cure (above, n. 13).

19. 'Folly' is precisely the accusation Garin levels against Aucassin, in denying him the reward for which he has finally agreed to defend his land:

> 'Biax fix,' fait li pere, 'tes enfances devés vos faire, nient baer a folie'

(X, 40-41).

20. si rala en son païs
> sains et saus et tos garis

(XI, 29-30).

21. Our hero, for example, exclaims: "Ja Dix ne me doinst riens que je li demand [. . .]" (II, p3-24). The words call upon the Lord, but their content denies Him, since their intent is to obtain a reward—union with Nicolette—as the price of doing 'what he should.'

22. See William Foxwell Albright, *Archaeology and the Religion of Israel* (Garden City, N.Y.: Doubleday, 1969), p. 73: "Astarte was goddess of the evening star [. . .]"; Salomon Reinach, *Orpheus: A History of Religions,* rev. ed. (New York: Horacle Liveright, 1930), p. 42: "The Aphrodite Urania (celestial) of the Greeks was no other than the Phoenician celestial goddess, or Astarte, held in special reverence at Carthage [. . .]. The lunar Tanit of Carthage [. . .] was assimilated to to the Greek Artemis [. . .]."

23. It is to be noted, however, that unlike Nicolette, specifically declared to be baptized, Aucassin never mentions the name of Jesus, or Mary, or makes the sign of the cross.

24. See Max Weber, *Ancient Judaism* (New York: Free Press and London: Collier-MacMillan, 1967), p. 354: "In Exile times the strict observance of the Sabbath came to the fore as one of the most important 'differentiating commandments,' for, in contrast to mere circumcision, it furnished a sure and generally visible sign that the respective person actually took his membership in the community seriously [. . .]."

25. The key to the love test, with its identification of Nicolette as the land of Israel, is found in the verses:

> je ne sera ses amis,
>   n'ele s'amie
>
> (XIX, 21-22).

Transformed into the negative and future, the lines are taken directly from the Song of Songs:

> *ani le'dodi ve'dodi li ha'ro'e ba'shashonim*
> '*I am my beloved's and my beloved is mine,*
> *That feedeth among the lilies*"
>
> (6:3).

This sentence introduces the *o* [. . .] *le* [. . .] *cler* capsulation, describing the Shulamite, beloved of Solomon, 'beautiful as Tirzah, comely as Jerusalem'; see above, n. 9, and "The Flower in the Bower."

26. See Weber, op. cit., pp. 149-50: "The Yahweh cult had to accommodate to the fact that in the agricultural territory of Palestine the usual sidereal and vegetation deities continued to exist [. . .]. However, these strange gods did not have decisive significance for the formation of Yahweh religion [. . .]. There is one exception to this. Clearly, the highly important institution of the Sabbath is related to the *shabattu* of the moon cult [. . .]." See also W.F. Albright, *Yahweh and the Gods of Canaan: Historical Analysis of the Contrasting Faiths* (Garden City, N.Y.: Doubleday, 1968), *passim.*

27. For the Judeo-French connection between *conplir* 'achever, remplir' ('to complete') and Heb. *milel* 'to speak, utter, proclaim,' see Levy, *Trésor.* For the interpretation of 'male child-bearing' through Isaiah's simile of the 'sinner in pain as a woman in travail,' the meaning of Heb. *gari* 'itchy with excitement,' and the rest of the king's explanation, see "Tora Lore in Torelore," and *Parody and Parable.*

28. When Aucassin's mother expostulates with him on the impropriety of his unworthy love for Nicolette (in the pagan state), she demands:

> 'Di va! faus, que vex tu faire?'
>
> (III, 7)

He finally understands why she called him a fool when he sees the king lying in "childbed,' a sinner 'itchy' and avoid for the kind of excitement Ashtoreth has to offer, allowing himself to be *soupris d'Amor* instead of placing God above all; it is to himself he is speaking, as he berates the king with almost the identical words:

> 'Di va! fau, que fais tu ci?'
>
> (XXIX, 7)

29. For the methodology of narremic (functional and structural) analysis, and the role of the family quarrel and other narremes in medieval narratives, see Dorfman, *The Narreme in the Medieval Romance Epic* (Toronto: University Press), 1969.

30. See Goldman, op. cit., p. 175: "The fifth commandment requires no preliminary statement. It is self-evident. The ancients knew enough of animal life to recognize that men could learn from the lowest creature in the animal kingdom to be grateful to parents. The Greeks knew it, so did the rabbis, so did many others. Having learned from both Greeks and Jews, Philo wrote: 'Among the storks the old birds stay in the nests when they are unable to fly, while their children fly [. . .] gathering from every quarter provision for the needs of their parents; [. . .] thus without any teacher but their natural instinct they gladly give to age the nurture which fostered their youth' (Decalogue xxiii, 116-17)."

Aucassin's father, under prolonged attack by Bougars, is 'vix et frales, si avoit son tans trespassé' (II, 7-8). Unlike the young storks, Aucassin needs a teacher before rendering his parents their due.

31. See Goldman op. cit., p. 176: "It is the merit of the rabbis to have maintained the golden mean here, as they did with respect to other phases of human behavior, and to have read into this verse the parent's obligation to respect their grown children. Their sober judgment is the more remarkable when we recall that they said of parents that they were copartners in their children with God and that honoring the parents was tantamount to honoring God. Philo was only echoing these teachings when he taught that 'parents [were] the servants of God for the task of begetting children and he who dishonored the servant dishonored the Lord.'"

32. The description of Aucassin could well be that of Samson: "Biax estoit et gens et grans et bien tailliés de ganbes et de piés et de cors et de bras" (II, 10-12). Our hero relives many of the major events in Jewish history, as he represents the Jewish people; see above, n. 9.

33. Nicolette may be linked to the story of Samson through the fact that the triliteral root of Carthage, her birth place, is Heb. *k-r-t;* in Hebrew, the name *Kreti* . . . may apply to Philistines (Marchand-Ennery, *Lexique Hébreu-Français,* 6th ed., Paris: Durlacher, 1947).

34. For the capsulations and other linguistic signals which clarify the nature of the idolatrous practices on the 'battlefield' of Torelore, see *Parody and Parable.*

35. See Samuel S. Cohon, *Judaism: A Way of Life* (New York: Schocken Books, 1962), p. 158: "An exception was made in the case of self-defense. Philo writes: 'Though the slaughter of enemies is lawful, yet one who kills a man, even if he does so in self-defense

and under compulsion, has something to answer for, in view of the primal common kinship of mankind'."

36. "Or ne quidiés vous qu'il pensast n'a bués n'a vaces n'a civres prendre, ne qu'il ferist cevalier ne autres lui. Nenil nient! *onques ne l'en sovint;* ains pensa [. . .] a Nicolete sa douce amie [. . .]" (X, 7-10). (emphasis added).

Love is indeed a better motive for action than greed, but does not excuse killing; it is even worse when the deed is done in forgetfulness of the human toll, the *cevalier* who must strike and be struck.

37. See Isidore Epstein, *Judaism: A Historical Presentation* (Harmondsworth, Middlesex: Penguin Books 1966), p. 137: "Judaism [. . .] emphasizes God's omnipresence, and the Talmud has coined a special term to describe this divine attribute. God is *Shechinah* ('The Indwelling'), immanent and omnipresent, not necessarily in the sense that God is co-extensive with creation, but that His providence extends over all creation."

As a future 'ruler in Israel,' Aucassin's responsibility is to keep the Shechinah in Israel, not cause it to depart through thoughtless and irresponsible behavior.

38. In joining forces with Bougars, the 'heretic,' through the oath he forces upon him, Aucassin comes perilously close to apostasy; only the fact that, after escorting the enemy to safety, he returns—even if unrepentant—to face his punishment prevents his being completely cut off from his community.

39. See Cohon, op. cit., p. 158: "In the history of Jewish martyrdom, pious women preferred death to defilement. Suicide under any other circumstances is condemned as a form of murder."

40. See above, n. 29.

41. On his return to Beaucaire, after his capture by the Saracen pirates, Aucassin discovers that his parents are dead and he is king. Instead of dashing off in pursuit of Nicolette, who had been captured with and then separated from him, he finally renders God his due and accepts as a ruler's first responsibility the need to serve his people and bring them peace. Nicolette comes to him, and his reward is final and permanent reunion with his beloved.

42. Aucassin appears to have no personal stake in the war at Torelore, except an interloper's concern for other people's affairs, as he asks:

'Et vouriiés vos que je vos venjasse?'

(XXXII, 5).

When the king consents, he launches into a furious slaughter of the enemy.

[. . .] si se lance en mi ax, si conmence a ferir a destre et a senestre, et s'en ocit molt

(XXXII, 7-8).

The king hastens to stop him on the plea that this is the kind of war in which it is not the custom for the participants to kill each other.

'Sire,' dist li rois, 'trop en avés vos fait: il n'est mie costume que nos entroncions li uns l'autre'

(XXXII, 14-15).

In turning a Utopian war of banquet edibles into a butchery, Aucassin seems to be taking a cowardly and undue advantage of defenseless foes; see Robert Harden, "*Aucassin et Nicolette* as Parody," *Studies in Philology,* 63 (1966), 1-9, pp. 6-7.

43. This is in stark contrast with his ridiculous fall from his 'high horse' the last time at the bower.

44. The reference is again to the bower but, in inverted fashion, the hero does the opposite of his prototype, peering out rather than in (XXIV, 87-89).

45. The double exposure, which superposes a parastructure on the surface story, showing Nicolette as the overt and Aucassin, the future 'ruler in Israel' as the covert hero, provides an 'education' for both handsome young children, in accordance with the *deport* promised in the exordium; see above, ns. 3, 5, 9.

46. The pagan rites demanding eradication, signalled by other capsulations in the text (see *Parody and Parable*), include that ultimate horror in the form of murder, child sacrifice; see Albright, op. cit. pp. 236-242, and Adolphe Lods, *Israel: From Its Beginnings to the Middle of the Eighth Century* (London: Routledge and Kegan Paul, 1962), pp. 89, 99.

47. Solomon Schechter, *Aspects of Rabbinic Theology* (New York: Schocken Books, 1961), p. 214.

48. The verses immediately preceding the relevant passage of the commentary paraphrase the *Tora* [. . .] *le'ra* capsulation:

"My son, keep my words,
And lay up my commandments with thee.
Keep my commandments and live,
And my teaching as the apple of thine eye.
. . . . .
Say unto wisdom: 'Thou art my sister',
And call understanding thy kinswoman;
That they may keep thee from the strange woman,
From the alien woman that maketh smooth her words"

(7:1-5).

There is reason to suspect that, though the romance uses the thematic verses of Proverbs 6:23-24—with the convenient *Tora . . . (le) . . . ra* key to the author's unique method of homiletical interpretation— one of the original sources of inspiration may be precisely the verses of 7:1-5 and the commentary by Maimonides; see following note.

49. Maimonides, *The Guide for the Perplexed,* transl. Mr. Friedländer, rev. ed., New York: Dover Publications, 1956, p. 7.

The *deport* 'education' promised in the exordium is directed toward the *esbahis* 'perplexed,' and will presumably funnel through the actors and actions— properly interpreted—in the romance. The first name, after the exordium, to appear in the story, and thus the initial teacher, is Bougars, the 'heretic' (II, 1), who 'wages war' against the people of Beaucaire (Canaan). Maimonides' work was burned as 'heretical' in the public square of Monpellier in 1234, in all probability just before the writing of *Aucassin et Nicolette*. Aucassin, the *moshel be'Yisrael* from Bethlehem-Ephrathah (above, n. 5), is thus, like Maimonides, a 'descendant of David'; see Henri Sérouya, *Maïmonide: Sa vie, son oeuvre* (Paris: P.U.F., 1964), p. 9, n. 1. Since Bougars represents the rebellious, 'heretical' aspect of Aucassin's character (above, p. 7 and n. 17), the 'war' is an internal one; it is as Maimonides, the teacher, that Aucassin 'at the window of his house looks forth through his lattice' and beholds himself as Maimonides, 'a young man devoid of understanding.' Given the author's mischievous sense of humor, in which everything is inverted to its opposite, it appears that he calls Maimonides a 'heretic" in the very act of employing his mentor's technique of theological instruction 'by means of metaphors and allegories' (*The Guide,* p. 4), with particular regard to the latter's famous illustration of Proverbs 7:5; see Louis Ginzberg, *On Jewish Law and Lore* (Cleveland and New York: World Publishing; Philadelphia: Jewish Publication Society, 1962), p. 140. Perhaps our author was trying in his kindly way to moderate the terrible scandal which was turning the Jewish community into a 'battlefield' of controversy over 'assimilationist' tendencies toward Greek categories of thought; see Daniel Jeremy Silver, *Maimonidean Criticism and the Maimonidean Controversy,* 1180-1240, Leiden: E.J. Brill, 1965), pp. 1, 4-5, 11, 16-17, 48. For other early attempts to moderate the struggle among French Jews, see Fred Gladstone Bratton, *Maimonides: Medieval Modernist,* Boston: Beacon Press), 1967, pp. 100-105, 127-232. For a summary of contemporary scholarship, see Marvin Fox, "Prolegomenon," pp. xv-xliv, in Abraham Cohen, *The Teachings of Maimonides,* (New York: Ktav Publishing House, 1968); for Maimonides' 'secret doctrine,' see especially p. xvii.

50. Milton Steinberg, *Basic Judaism,* (New York: Harcourt, Brace, 1947), p. 74.

51. See Goldman, op. cit., p. 184; also Rashi, *Commentaries on the Pentateuch,* New York: W.W. Norton, 1970, pp. 93-94.

52. See above, pp. 64-65.

53. The living force of this concept over the centuries is described by Robert St. John, *Jews, Justice and Judaism: A Narrative of the Role Played by the Bible People in Shaping American History,* (Garden City, N.Y.: Doubleday, 1969), p. 194. For the practice of equality in the armed forces under conditions of modern warfare, see S. L. A. Marshall, *Sinai Victory,* (New York: William Morrow 1967), pp. 19-21. The most firmly entrenched tradition needs guarding against encroachment.

54. The most outspoken of the shepherds firmly rejects any notion of Aucassin's superiority with a simple question, twice repeated:

'Et por quoi canteroie je por vos, s'il ne me seoit?'

(XXII, 15-16, 19-20).

55. The shepherds do not understand how important it is that Aucassin And Nicolette be reunited, could not care less whether or not they ever are, and will not lift a finger to help:

"Par foi," fait il, "les deniers prenderons nos, et s'il vient ci, nos li dirons mais nos ne l'irons ja quere"

(XVIII, 35-36).

They appear to be the same ones to whom Isaiah refers:

"And these are shepherds
That cannot understand;
They all turn to their own way,
Each one to his gain, one and all"

(56:11).

The shepherds, numbering six, are personalized as: Esmerés, Martinés, Früelins, Jehanés, Robeçons, and Aubriés. It is possible that, with Aucassin, they represent the 'Seven Shepherds of Israel,' but the names, unlike every other in the text, do not seem to have a Jewish significance.

56. Nicolette (XI, 26) which restores the 'pilgrim of Limosin' to health and homeland and the 'white hound' Aucassin tells the oxherd he has lost is also the same 'beast.' The parastructural reason for his lie appears to be his fear that the stranger, knowing his goal, may try to prevent his attaining it.

57. Schechter, op. cit., p. 228.

58. Fr. *par* is Heb. *al* . . . 'on, by, with'; this preposition, spelled with *ayin, i*s a homonym of *al*— . . . , the morpheme introducing a negative command (see also above, n. 12), spelled with *alef*. The pun is part of the fun.

S. L. Clark and Julian Wasserman (essay date 1976)

SOURCE: "Wisdom Buildeth a Hut: *Aucassin et Nicolette* as Christian Comedy," in *Allegorica,* Vol. 1, No. 1, Spring, 1976, pp. 250-68.

[*In the following essay, Clark and Wasserman contend that* Aucassin et Nicolette *is better described as an instructional allegory than a parody, in that it uses inversion to highlight the absurdity of human sin.*]

As a result of the growing critical awareness that irony was not an art mislaid by medieval writers until it was "rediscovered" by the Renaissance,[1] many romances, such as those of Chrétien de Troyes, are now recognized as parodies of a form which they were at first thought to trace out so mindlessly.[2] Yet in compensating for the previously ill-conceived charges of naivete, there may be the danger of reducing many a fine romance to little more than a belly laugh at the expense of the traditional genre. Such has been the case with *Aucassin et Nicolette,* which has begun to be treated as a rollicking parody of romance conventions.[3] However, despite the fact that this tale can indeed be demonstrated to provide a plethora of inversions of the motifs most commonly associated with the genre, the narrative, like Chrétien's Erec et Enide, may best be thought of as an instructional allegory, rather than a parody, which uses inversion to point out the folly of human error instead of praising it.

Like its twelfth-century counterpart Erec et Enide,[4] *Aucassin et Nicolette* proves to be an allegory for the pursuance and attainment of wisdom and its attendant virtue of moderation.[5] Therefore, if Aucassin does not always seem to be the very flower of knighthood—and one may certainly cite as evidence his reluctance to fight, his passivity and his occasional obtuseness—it is because the poet wishes to show the hero's evolving journey to a point at which he can embrace the wise and reject the foolish. The poet effects this growth within his hero by repeatedly placing him in decision-making situations and through trial and error training him to make the correct responses. For example, it is fitting that the tale begin with Aucassin being forced to choose between the luxury of pining for his beloved and the necessity of fulfilling his knightly duties and responsibilities—in other words, between love and honor.[6]

Aucassin chooses love and, hence, dishonor in societal terms. After bargaining for love with his father and in the process adopting a role associated with the Devil, who buys souls,[7] Aucassin rides rashly and unthinkingly into battle and almost loses his head. Subsequently, having to exact a ransom for his captured enemy, he chooses to have his captive swear an oath against his father. All of these choices and actions are marked by rashness that demonstrates lack of proper thought and are justifiably labelled foolish; indeed, Aucassin's mother brands him as a fool ("Di va, faus! Que vex tu faire!"—3, 7[8]) and Aucassin's father calls his aspirations nothing more than foolish dreams ("Biax fix! fait li pere, tes enfanćes devés vos faire, nient baer a folie!"—10, 41-42[9]).

Aucassin's next decision consists in listening to and following the wise counsel of a fellow knight:

> Montés sor un ceval, fait il, s'alés selonc ćele forest esbanoiier, si verrés ćes flors et ćes herbes s'orrés ćes oisellons canter. Par aventure orrés tel parole dont mix vos iert.
>
> (20, 22-25)[10]

He rides to the woods where Nicolette waits and is promptly given a choice by the shepherds who tell him of the miraculous beast, i.e., Nicolette, which can cure his lovesickness:

> Or le ćaciés, se vos volés, et se vos volés, si le laisçié; car je m'en sui bien acuités vers li.
>
> (22, 40-42)[11]

Aucassin correctly chooses to hunt for Nicolette. Yet while searching for his beloved, he encounters a grotesque and giant "yokel"[12] and, when the relative value of a greyhound or an ox comes into question, does not give the correct answer to the man in whom wisdom is clearly placed.[13] However, berated by the yokel, Aucassin quickly repents, so that following this unfortunate mistake in judgment, he responds correctly to the crucial test of the hut[14] which Nicolette describes as the proof of her lover's intentions:

> A porpenser or se prist
> qu'esprovera son ami,
> s'i' l'aime si com'il dist.
>
> (19, 9-11)[15]

His next adventure takes him to the land of Torelore, where he again misjudges the situation, albeit an unusual one, to the chagrin of the king and the outright anger of the citizenry, who are, as they put it, not accustomed to fight to the death. Finally, separated from Nicolette once more, when the lovers are placed in separate ships and borne to the lands of their origin, he accepts the responsibilities of his birth, a great turnabout from his original behaviour, and correctly places himself in Nicolette's wise hands. When Aucassin's progress is evaluated, it soon becomes apparent that he keeps alternating between correct and incorrect responses: siege (wrong), shepherds (right), yokel (wrong), hut (right), Torelore (wrong), kingship (right), so that by trial and error he is brought from ignorance to wisdom and to the ability to make correct choices. Although he continues to make mistakes, they become progressively less severe and, more importantly, although he begins by making a wrong decision, he concludes by making the right one.[16]

Nicolette, in contrast, always chooses the right alternative and, hence, becomes the model for correct decision-making within the romance. She confronts distinct dilemmas three times, the exact number of times that Aucassin chooses correctly, and as will be shown later the heroine becomes identified with that same number. Her first dilemma comes as she stands on the walls of the castle, assesses her prospects, and states:

> Se je me lais caïr, je briserai le col, et se je remain ći, on me prendera demain, si m'ardera on en un fu. Encor ainme je mix que je muire ći, que tos li pules me regardast demain a merveilles.
>
> (16, 12-16)[17]

She makes the correct decision and flees to the woods where she is faced with yet another set of alternatives:

> Or estoit li forés pres a deus arbalestees, qui bien duoit trente liues de lonc et de le, si i avoit beste sauváges et serpentine. Ele ot paor que, s'ele i entroit, qu'eles ne

l'oćesisçent, si se repensa que, s'on le trovoit ileuc,
c'on le remenroit en le vile por ardoir.

(16, 28-32)[18]

The whole of the seventeenth section of the romance consists of Nicolette's poetic lament of the dilemma and her choice of flight. Her decision to flee once again is clearly the right one, for her life is spared. Thus, Nicolette twice rejects death by fire, yet in her third dilemma, she wisely reverses herself when her father wishes to arrange a marriage for her:

Si li veut on doner cascun jor baron un des plus haus
rois de tote Espaigne. Mais ele se lairoit anćois pendre
u ardoir, qu'ele en presist nul, tant fust rices.

(40, 10-12)[19]

What emerges appears not to be the foolish consistency of always avoiding death by fire, but rather the wisdom to recognize when such a fate, regardless of her personal feelings, would be the appropriate choice; in effect, she rejects fire, except as an instrument of martyrdom, in order to save her from an "unholy" marriage which would lead doctrinally to consumption in the fires of Hell.[20]

Nicolette's preference of martyrdom above unholy marriage must be contrasted directly with Aucassin's oft repeated threats and desires for suicide. While Nicolette rightly avoids consumption in flames, Aucassin, already aflame with love, actively embraces conscription into Hell, for, as he states, he wants no part of Heaven with its martyrs, "qui sont nu et decauć et estrumelé, qui moeurent de faim et de soi et de froit et de mesaises" (6, 30-31),[21] and instead accepts a Hell populated with "li bel clerc, et li bel cevalier qui sont mort as tornois et as rices gueres, et li boin serġant et li franc home. Aveuc ćiax voil jou aler. Et s'i vont les beles dames cortoises, que eles ont deus amis ou trois avoc leur barons . . ." (6, 33-37).[22] Finally Aucassin decides "Avoc ćiax voil jou aler, mais que j'aie Nicolete, ma tresdouće amie, aveuc mi" (6, 39-40).[23] However, the last statement provides the turning point of the argument for it becomes suddenly clear that Nicolette will not reside in Hell with him. This is shown in iconographical terms alone by the fact that Nicolette's foster father places her in a vaulted tower in order to keep her from the flames, while Aucassin is hidden away in a dungeon, significantly located below the surface of the ground, in a hellish dungeon, dark, cracked and imperfect. Nicolette's tower possesses one window which not only gives upon a pleasant garden but also indicates illumination, since the light shines into her chamber, and spiritual awareness, since the senses are to the man in much the same way as windows are to the tower.[24] It should also be noted that Nicolette's foster father places her in the tower to prevent her being cast into the flames, which metaphorically indicates an attempt to save her from Hell.

Not only is the fact that Nicolette will not reside with Aucassin in Hell demonstrated by the lovers' respective physical confines, but also Nicolette does not fit the description of those placed in Hell; in addition, Aucassin can be shown not really to adhere to what he has stated concerning Heaven and Hell. For one thing, Nicolette is not portrayed as a lady with several lovers; she is, in fact, faithful to the point of martyrdom. Aucassin as well gives ample testament to belief in fidelity when he is brought to the idea of suicide by Nicolette's hypothetical infidelity:

Et puis que vos ariiés jut en lit a home s'el mien non,
or ne quidiés mie que j'atendisse tant que je trovasse
coutel dont je me peüsçe ferir el cuer et oćirre! Naie
voir, tant n'atenderoie je mie, ains m'esquelderoie de si
lonc que je verroie une maisiere u une bisse pierre, s'i
hurteroie si durement me teste, que j'en feroie les ex
voler, et que je m'esćerveleroie tos. Encor ameroie je
mix a morir de si faite mort, que je seüsçe que vos
eüsçiés jut en lit a home s'el mien non.

(14, 6-14)[25]

This is to say that, despite Aucassin's protestations to the contrary, he does not want to spend eternity in the Hell which he has described to Nicolette's father, if women there have more than one lover, any more than he wants to spend the rest of his earthly life in the dungeon in which his actions and preferences have placed him. In fact, even the knighthood which Aucassin says leads to Hell is not embraced by Aucassin, since he refuses to fight to defend his own inheritance. Once he begins his search for Nicolette and wisdom, however, he even comes to resemble the Christ-like holy martyrs whom he previously derided as inhabitants of Heaven, since, as the narrator takes pains to note:

Ne quidiés mie que les ronćes et les espines
l'esparnaisçent! Nenil niént! Ains li desronpent ses
dras, qu'a painnes peüst on nouer desu el plus entier, et
que li sans li isçi des bras et des costés et des ganbes
en quarante lius u en trente, qu'après le vallet peüst on
suïr le traće du sanc qui caiot sor l'erbe.

(24, 2-7)[26]

Thus, the problem of proper decision-making has much greater implications than the winning of the individual's heart's desire, and becomes an issue of eschatological importance, for at the core of this pleasant romance lies the problem of the central character's embracing either Heaven or Hell. In the beginning Aucassin accepts Hell as the appropriate consequence of the life he desires to lead, yet Nicolette, who is consistently portrayed as the wisdom which recognizes and wishes to flee from danger,[27] saves him from his own foolish ambitions. It can be no coincidence that she repeatedly insists that Aucassin find her in three days (18, 34; 22, 39)[28] thereby symbolizing the harrowing of his soul from its self-inflicted Hell.[29]

But the question remains, who is Nicolette that she can, like Beatrice, guide the soul from Hell to Paradise? She is, perhaps, best described in her own words, spoken while disguised as a jongleur, one of the people Aucassin thought resided in Hell:

. . . j'en sai con de le plus france creature et de la plus
ġentil et de le plus saġe qui onques fust nee . . .

(40, 5-6)[30]

Nobleness and gentleness are general, abstract qualities, but wisdom is distinct and a virtue not often found in romance heroines. In the same vein, Nicolette is an unknown entity, a typical romance heroine, until she is at last revealed to be the daughter of a king and is proclaimed to be high-born and wise. Again, since it is revealed that her father is a king, it is natural that she be described as high-born,[31] yet at this strategic moment of revelation she is also named wise and, indeed, the reader does not learn Nicolette's true identity until the hero has become wise, so that the artistic accomplishment of the relaying of this information parallels the epistemology whereby Aucassin comes to know wisdom.

Of all Nicolette's myriad good qualities, her wisdom proves to be the one which comes most naturally and most often to the fore. Whereas Aucassin is rebuked for his foolishness in spurning his knightly responsibilities, and then ironically goes on to upbraid the king of Torelore for being a fool for abandoning his kingly and husbandly duties, Nicolette informs that same king:

> 'Sire rois de Torelore,'
> ćе dist la bele Nichole,
> 'vostre ǵens me tient por fole!'
>
> (33, 1-3)[32]

Shortly after, she is named wise ("Nicole li preus, li saǵe"—37, 1) and Aucassin is made a king. Thus, one sees Aucassin following wisdom, learning to apply it, and slowly casting off the well-earned name of "fool."

However, before Aucassin can apply wisdom, he must learn what wisdom is. From the beginning it is clear that he neither understands what he seeks nor how to obtain it. This ignorance has already been seen in his descriptions of Heaven and Hell. Similarly, he believes wisdom to lie in superficialities of form as revealed in the love debate, so that when Nicolette escapes and comes to see him, he insists on initiating a rather pointless argument over whether men are more faithful than women. Nicolette simply ignores the whole question as being unimportant if not silly. Instead, throughout the story, she poses a series of problems and riddles for Aucassin to solve. First, she insists upon the rather transparent conundrum of the miraculous beast and later presents Aucassin with the test of the hut. As Aucassin develops his gamesmanship, he understands more about knowledge and how it is applied. To illustrate, one might consider the scene in the first part of the tale, when Aucassin describes the healing of a sick pilgrim, such as those with whom he populated Heaven, by means of Nicolette's raising her skirt to expose her leg. Upon first consideration, the recounting of the event with its obvious sexual overtones seems worthy enough of the man who is preoccupied with the love debate, but when Aucassin himself is wounded and cured by Nicolette, the healing process seems quite different, so that the reader can conclude that Aucassin has been mistaken in his interpretation of the anecdote of Nicolette and the pilgrim, since his primary interest in the little story is sexual and

he misses the real thrust of the story, which is that of Nicolette's healing power; he finds fascination in the tale because it describes Nicolette's advantages as a beautiful lover rather than as a miracle-working martyr-saint whose actions with the sick pilgrim emulate those of Christ. In this regard the anecdote itself proves a unique representation of the allegorizing process and the problem of how to read a romance, for if it is proper to couch healing powers in the flesh of a naked limb, then it is certainly possible, and even probable, that the story which contains this incident couches the message of wisdom in the fleshly characters of a romance.[33] Thus, one sees here the carrot-on-a-stick theory of learning, in which God sends messages not only in their most appropriate but also their most palatable form, in order to lead men to wisdom. Thus, it is with an exposed limb that Nicolette first catches Aucassin's fancy, much in the tradition of the seductive spiritual healer of the Canticum Canticorum, and later she will use the same imagery in her riddle. For this reason, Nicolette's insistence that Aucassin will not give five hundred pieces of gold for one of the limbs of the miraculous beast in the forest becomes explicable, since indeed he, too, now has become a pilgrim and is seeking to be healed. Accordingly, Nicolette binds Aucassin's injured limb, and since this action occurs within the three-day period already associated with the Harrowing of Hell, she is in a sense binding the wound, the evil and disjointed part of Aucassin, thereby metaphorically binding Satan as well.

Just as Aucassin has failed to grasp the sententia of the anecdote involving Nicolette's bared limb, so has he again been guilty of gross misunderstanding of the nature of things, as is readily apparent upon re-examination of his acceptance of Hell. He was told:

> Enseurquetot que cuideriés vous avoir gaegnié, se vous l'aviés asognentee ne mise a vo lit? Mout i ariés peu conquis, car tos les jors du siecle en seroit vo arme en enfer; qu'en paradis n'enterriés vos ja.
>
> (6, 20-24)[34]

Aucassin's acceptance of Hell, then, is based on the premise that Nicolette will be his mistress, which, given the nature of Nicolette, is false. It is not until the end of the tale that Aucassin learns the proper relationship between man and wisdom and, abandoning the idea of the necessity of having Nicolette as a mistress, takes her to wife, as is proper.[35]

It has already been pointed out that Aucassin is not much of a knight, but one finds in the romance a serious rather than an entirely humorous cast to the portrayal where inversion evokes more overtones of damnation than laughter. The faults which characterize Aucassin the knight are rashness, overindulgence and despair, all of which betoken the immoderation of thought and deed which arises from lack of wisdom and the inability to make correct judgments. Nowhere is this more graphically displayed than in Aucassin's first charge into battle. This passage must be examined at length since it provides the audience with the first real glimpse of Aucassin in action and therefore also establishes much of the key imagery which recurs throughout the romance.

The poet goes to great lengths to present the mental state of his protagonist as he rides into the fray:

> Or ne quidiés vous qu'il pensast n'a bués n'a naces n'a civrès prendre, ne qu'il ferist cevalier n autres lui! Nenil niênt!
>
> (10, 6-8)[36]

It proves curious that the poet notes that Aucassin has no thought of oxen, since oxen will reappear in the tale of the giant yokel when Aucassin will be shamed for thinking only of his greyhound[37] while the wise giant tells of the lost oxen of which Aucassin was unaware. Significantly, medieval emblems show the ox as a symbol of submissiveness, patience, and a spirit of self-sacrifice,[38] the very qualities of which Aucassin is indeed unmindful.

After such a reckless entrance into battle, Aucassin is subsequently captured and makes some rather remarkable conclusions about the imminent fate of his head:

> Ha! Dix, fait il, doucé creature! Sont ćou mi anemi mortel qui ći me mainent, et qui ja me cauperont le teste? Et puis que j'arai la teste caupee, ja mais ne parlerai a Nicolete, me douće amie, que je tant aim.
>
> (10, 17-20)[39]

Rather than being simply an outlandish tribute to silliness intended to provide a parody of knightly sentiments,[40] this exclamation presents an important iconographical addition to the presentation of Aucassin as a foolish man. The source of the knight's foolishness, a foolishness which makes him mistake Hell for Heaven, is made immediately clear. He is plainly guilty of excessive love to the point of idolatry,[41] for the language of his lament makes God a "douce creature," a term for a lover rather than for a deity. And this idolatry of his beloved is seen overtly in Aucassin's treatment of the lock of Nicolette's hair as a holy relic.[42] Since Aucassin's problem both here and in the case of the yokel's oxen seems to be largely a matter of perception, the poet chooses to express the knight's loss of judgment as a loss of his head, the proverbial seat of wisdom. In fact, Aucassin himself appears to be preoccupied with his own misconceptions concerning the head. At the thought of losing his own head, Aucassin revives in battle and promptly pummels his enemy over the head (10, 33-34)[43] and later threatens to behead that same captive if he will not swear an oath against Count Garin (10, 76-77)[44]. The Knight's problem, as in the case of confusing his love of God for the fleshly love of a woman,[45] is one of judgment and perception, since he does not understand that the impulses of the heart and the head are contrary, and not co-incidental:

> Par mon cief! qui que les [his father's promises to let him see Nicolette] oblit, je nes voil mie obliër, ains me tient mout au cuer.
>
> (10, 46-48)[46]

In this passage he clearly equates the two. He has lost his heart and as a result of this false equation proceeds to put his head in jeopardy. Finally, in a fit of jealousy—indeed, madness—Aucassin declares:

> Et puis que vos ariiés jut en lit a home s'el mien non, or ne quidiés mie que j'atendisse tant que je trovasse coutel dont je me peüsçe ferir el cuer et ocirre! Naie voir, tant n'atenderoie je mie, ains m'esquelderoie de si lonc que je verroie une maisiere u une bisse pierre, s'i hurteroie si durement me teste, que j'en feroie les ex voler, et que je m'esćerveleroie tos.
>
> (14, 6-12)[47]

Returning to the battle in which Aucassin first voices his concern for his head, one notes that Aucassin immediately upon recognizing his perilous situation lashes out with the immoderation of a wild animal, "con li senglers quant li cien l'asalent en le forest" (10, 27)[48], and promptly slays ten men and wounds seven. However, if Aucassin is like the boar, that animal, with its murderous lack of restraint, is one of the very beasts which Nicolette fears before entering the forest. Furthermore, when Aucassin in his boarlike frenzy kills first ten knights and then wounds seven, he demonstrates through use of symbolic numbers[49] a disregard for the moderation which order and law provide and which is symbolized by the number ten, associated with perfection, completeness and law through the Ten Commandments.[50] Indeed, Aucassin, who has already embraced Hell, will be seen to be guilty of breaking most of the Ten Commandments either in thought or in deed, as he worships an idol in Nicolette, refuses to honour his father and mother, wishes to be guilty of adultery, covets Nicolette, proves guilty of murder in Torelore, and lies concerning the greyhound, to name but a few of his misdeeds. Similarly, when this berserker-like knight strikes out in his immoderation and subsequently wounds seven more men ("foes") he in effect renounces the seven cardinal virtues or, more likely, the seven sacraments, or any other of the positive groupings of seven which are common in medieval thought,[51] and in Samson-like blindness topples over the seven pillars which support the House of Wisdom. Accordingly, the first real proof that Aucassin is beginning to renounce his previous immoderate behaviour is his decision to reside at the hut which Nicolette has built at the intersection of seven paths in the forest.

However, the most striking and most important aspect of Aucassin's immoderation and rejection of wisdom appears in the initial charge into battle which has already been seen to prove so much of the iconographical foundation of the poem:

> Onques ne l'en sovint, ains pensa tant a Nicolete, sa douće amie, qu'il oublia ses resnes et quanques il dut faire. Et li cevax, qui ot senti les esperons, l'en porta parmi le presse, se se lanće tres entremi ses anemis.
>
> (10, 9-12)[52]

In interpreting this curious passage, one should keep in mind the negative connotations of the horse, which was often associated with the flesh and man's libidinous self in medieval iconography. As D. W. Robertson points out in his study of this motif,[53] one can with right reason bridle one's horse. In fact, reins were often considered symbolic of the restraints which wisdom exerted over the flesh when the two were brought into the proper hierarchical relationship. Certainly Aucassin has lost all restraint and here appropriately drops the reins and allows his horse to take him whither it will. However, the poet makes repeated and striking use of this widely known medieval metaphor, which finds one of its most famous applications in the prologue to Andreas' treatise, in order to bind together various segments of his own romance, since bridles are found in almost every adventure in *Aucassin et Nicolette.* What Aucassin does with his bridle is often the barometer of his wisdom in a given situation. For example, when he follows the wise advice of a fellow knight and decides to ride off into the woods in order to cheer himself, he places a bridle upon his horse. As he is riding, he hears the song of the shepherds and, assuming that it concerns Nicolette, begins to prick his horse; this sign of immoderation is almost immediately followed by his rather sharp questions which incite a brief argument between himself and the shepherds. It is not until he reins himself in that he is told that much-desired riddle, which he promptly solves. After once again being remonstrated with for his lack of wisdom and taking the lesson to heart, Aucassin immediately reins in his horse when he sees wisdom's hut, yet in a sudden reverie for Nicolette which parallels the language of his first dropping of the reins, falls from his horse and once again learns the painful lesson of the need for self-control and thus humbled, crawls to the hut and ties his horse to a neighboring thorn. The thorn itself proves significant as a symbol for tribulation,[54] which hearkens back to the purifying forty wounds received by Aucassin, and as a symbol of patient endurance, which likewise is reminiscent of the lost oxen of which Aucassin was previously unmindful.

Having internalized the experience of the hut and gained wisdom in the person of Nicolette, Aucassin yields himself to the proper relationship between himself and his wise councillor and accordingly places Nicolette on the horse before him, so that she may theoretically be the pilot or guide of his future actions. At this point the poet shows himself to be a subtle master of language, since the phrase "metre a raison" (27, 8)[55] means "to address," yet the word "raison" itself gives testimony to the reason which Nicolette represents. Again the attainment of reason and the iconography of reins coincide, for having followed Nicolette's advice to flee, the pair arrives at the sea, where Aucassin dismounts and appropriately has his damsel in one hand and his horse's reins in the other, so that the attainment of wisdom goes hand in hand with the reining in of one's lower self. Thus, when Aucassin goes to upbraid the king of Torelore for forsaking his social responsibilities, a lesson which Aucassin has just learned of late, the hero leaves Nicolette holding his horse, as the poet takes pains to note. However, Aucassin slips one final time on his tortuous path to reason, and this, too, finds its expression within the metaphor of horses and reins. Upon being shown the mock battle of apples and cheeses, the hero

asks the king if he would like him to avenge him on them, to which the king replies in the affirmative. The result is that Aucassin briefly mirrors his previous boar-like propensity for killing, which forces the king to take him by the bridle and say to him:

> Sire, dist li rois, trop en avés vos fait. Il n'est mie costume que nos entroćions li uns l'autre.
>
> (32, 14-15)[56]

What has happened here is that Aucassin is indeed guilty of wrong action, in that he is guilty of too much action, that is, of lack of moderation.

Thus, when one considers the iconography of the romance and the progression of the hero through his many decision-making adventures, the observations of the many critics who have discussed the tale do not serve as well as those of a fellow countryman who wrote a similar tale of wisdom thirty years before. As Chrétien de Troyes points out concerning his tale of Erec et Enide:

> Li vilains dit an son respit
> Que tel chose a l'an an despit,
> Qui mout vaut miauz que l'an ne cuide.
> Por ce fet bien qui son estuide
> Atorne a bien, quel que il l'et;
> Car qui son estuide antrelet,
> Tost i puet tel chose teisir,
> Qui mout vandroit puis a pleisir.
> Por ce dit Crestiiens de Troies
> Que reisons est que totes voies
> Doit chascuns panser et antandre
> A bien dire et a bien aprandre,
> Et tret d'un conte d'avanture
> Une mout bele conjointure,
> Par qu'an puet prover et savoir
> Que cil ne fet mie savoir,
> Qui sa sciance n'abandone
> Tant con Deus la grace l'an done.
>
> (1-18)[57]

In this light, *Aucassin et Nicolette* is neither an improbable love story aimed at the swooning hearts of thirteenth-century courtiers, nor a light-hearted romp through courtly conventions, but a parable which instructs by demonstrating the absurdity of sin and is thus better labelled a Christian comedy.

Notes

1. See D. W. Robertson, A Preface to Chaucer: Studies in Medieval Perspectives (Princeton: Princeton University Press, 1962), p. 83.

2. See, for example, W. T. H. Jackson, "Problems of Communication in the Romances of Chrétien de Troyes," in Medieval Literature and Folklore Studies: Essays in Honor of Francis Lee Utley, ed. Jerome Mandel and Bruce A. Rosenberg (New Brunswick, New Jersey: Rutgers University Press, 1970), pp. 50ff.

3. See in particular Robert Harden, "Aucassin et Nicolette as Parody," Studies in Philology 63 (1966), 1-9, and Jessie Crossland, Medieval French Literature (Oxford: Basil S. Blackwell, 1956), p. 86ff.

4. For an allegorical reading of Chrétien, see Tom Artin, The Allegory of Adventure: Reading Erec and Yvain (Lewisburg, Pa.: Bucknell University Press, 1974), p. 32ff.

5. Wisdom is an active virtue, in that its purpose is to solve mysteries (see Robertson, pp. 33 and 53ff.) so that one derives pleasure from the solutions of such divine puzzles, since their solutions invariably lead to God. Furthermore, there is a distinct danger in the inactive mind, because this indicates delight in the surface, which leads to an acceptance of the "chaf" rather than of the "fruyt" (Robertson, p. 61). Thus, active reason is reason used, while passive reason which dwells on the surface is reason abused (Robertson, p. 65).

6. This proves to be a very common choice in medieval romance, a choice which both Erec and Tristan make as well, with varying results.

7. The Devil traditionally purchases souls with the flesh. See Chaucer's "Parson's Tale," line 850.

8. Line numbers in parentheses refer to Aucassin und Nicolette: Kritischer Text mit Paradigmen und Glossar, ed. Hermann Suchier, 10th ed. (Paderborn: Ferdinand Schöningh, 1932). The following translation, "'Fool, to weep the livelong day'" is from Aucassin and Nicolette and Other Medieval Romances and Legends, trans. Eugene Mason (New York: E. P. Dutton & Co., Inc., 1958), p. 3. Subsequent translations of the Old French will appear in the notes and will refer to page numbers in the Mason edition, unless otherwise indicated.

9. "'Fair son,' replied his father, 'better are such deeds as these than foolish dreams.'" (p. 11)

10. "'Get to horse,' said he, 'take your pleasure in the woodland, amongst flowers and bracken, and the songs of the birds. Perchance, who knows? you may hear some word of which you will be glad.'" (pp. 22-23)

11. "'Now go to your hunting if you will, and if you will not, let it go, for truly have I carried out my bargain with her.'" (p. 25)

12. Crossland, p. 170, calls the yokel "appealing."

13. The yokel is wise, insofar as he knows who Aucassin is and whom he seeks.

14. Proverbs 9:1 "Wisdom hath builded her house, she hath hewn out her seven pillars." In addition, see Roberta D. Cornelius, The Figurative Castle: A Study in the Mediaeval Allegory of the Edifice with Special Reference to Religious Writings (Bryn Mawr, Pa.: Bryn Mawr Press, 1930).

15. "There she called to heart her love, / There bethought her she would prove / Whether true her lover's vows." (p. 21)

16. Northrop Frye, Anatomy of Criticism (Princeton: Princeton University Press, 1957), pp. 186ff. points out the episodic and the relation between the episodic and the progressional nature of romance, so that each single episode is a microcosm of the greater dialectical movement of the work as well as acting as a stairstep in the achievement of that dialectic. Thus, when he faces the problems of judgment within each individual adventure, Aucassin learns a little more and comes a little bit closer to perfect attainment of wisdom, which is the theme of the romance as a whole.

17. "'. . . should I fall, my neck must be broken; and if I stay, tomorrow shall I be taken, and men will burn my body in a fire. Yet were it better to die, now, in this place, than to be made a show tomorrow in the market.'" (p. 18)

18. "Now the forest lay but the distance of two bolts from a crossbow, and ran some thirty leagues in length and breadth; moreover, within were many wild beasts and serpents. She feared these greatly, lest they should do her a mischief; but presently she remembered that should men lay hands upon her, they would lead her back to the city to burn her at the fire." (p. 19)

19. "Any day he would give her for husband one of the highest kings in all Spain; but rather would she be hanged or burned than take him, however rich he be." (p. 40)

20. This relates to Constance's marriage in Chaucer's "Man of Law's Tale"; there the heroine refuses to marry a heathen until he is baptized.

21. "'. . . those who are naked, and barefoot, and full of sores; who are dying of hunger and of thirst, of cold and of wretchedness.'" (p. 6)

22. "'. . . the fair clerks and the fair knights who are slain in the tourney and the great wars, and the stout archer and the loyal man. With them will I go. And there go the fair and courteous ladies, who have friends, two or three, together with their wedded lords.'" (pp. 6-7)

23. "'With these will I go, so only that I have Nicolette, my very sweet friend, by my side.'" (p. 7)

24. J. E. Cirlot, A Dictionary of Symbols, trans. Jack Sage (New York: Philosophical Library, 1962), pp. 326-327, points out "the analogy between the tower and man: for just as the tree is closer to the human figure than are the horizontal forms of animals, so, too, is the tower the only structural form distinguished by verticality: windows at the topmost level, almost always large in size, correspond to the eyes and the mind of man."

25. "'Be sure that if thou wert found in any man's bed, save it be mine, I should not need a dagger to pierce my heart and slay me. Certes, no; wait would I not for a knife; but on the first wall or the nearest stone would I cast myself, and beat out my brains alto-

gether. Better to die so foul a death as this, than know thee to be in any man's bed, save mine.'"

26. "Do not think that the spines and thorns were pitiful to him. Truly it was not so; for his raiment was so torn that the least tattered of his garments could scarcely hold to his body, and the blood ran from his arms and legs and flanks in forty places, or at least in thirty, so that you could have followed after him by the blood which he left upon the grass." (p. 26)

27. One should note that she advises herself to flee often but advises Aucassin to flee only after they have met by the hut.

28. Mason, pp. 21 and 25.

29. Chrétien alludes to the imagery of the Harrowing of Hell in Erec et Enide and in Lancelot; the time between Christ's entombment and his rising on the third day is, apocryphally speaking, the time when Christ descended into Hell and freed souls from Satan's domination.

30. "'. . . well I know her for the most loyal of creatures and as the most winning and modest of maidens born.'" (p. 39) A better reading would be "wise" for the Old French sage, as opposed to Mason's "modest."

31. Since Nicolette has twelve brothers, her linkage to Christ is strengthened, since the sum 12 + 1 (disciples and Christ) proves to be a manifestation of typical numbers.

32. "'Simple folk, and simple King, / Deeming maid so slight a thing.'" (p. 34) A better reading would be the more literal "Sir King of Torelore," said the beautiful Nicolette, "your people consider me a fool . . ."

33. Consider one of the statements in the prologue to Erec et Enide:

> Por ce dit Crestiiens de Troies
> Que reisons est que totes voies
> Doit chascuns panser et antandre
> A bien dire et a bien aprandre,
> Et tret d'un conte d'avanture
> Une mout bele conjointure . . .

(ll. 9-14)

The text is from Erec und Enide von Christian von Troyes, ed. Wendelin Foerster (Amsterdam: Rodopi, 1965). The following translation is from Chrétien de Troyes, Arthurian Romances, trans. W. W. Comfort (New York: E. P. Dutton, 1914), p. 1: "So Chrétien de Troyes maintains that one ought always to study and strive to speak well and teach the right; and he derives from a story of adventure a pleasing argument . . ."

34. "'Beyond this, what profit would you have, had you become her lover, and taken her to your bed? Little enough would be your gain therefrom, for your soul would lie tormented in Hell all the days of all time, so that to Paradise never should you win.'" (p. 6)

35. See Robertson, pp. 393-448.

36. "Now think not that he sought spoil of oxen and cattle, nor to smite others and himself escape. Nay, but of all this he took no heed." (p. 10)

37. See George Ferguson, Signs and Symbols in Christian Art (New York: Oxford University Press, 1961), p. 15; the dog serves as a symbol of fidelity and as such well represents Aucassin's faithfulness to Nicolette.

38. Ibid., p. 22.

39. "'Ha, God,' cried he, 'sweet Creature, these are my mortal foes who lead me captive, and who soon will strike off my head; and when my head is smitten, never again may I have fair speech with Nicolette, my sweet friend, whom I hold so dear.'" (p. 10)

40. Harden's article (note 3) explores this approach; see as well Barbara N. Sargent, "Parody in Aucassin et Nicolette: Some Further Considerations," French Review 43 (1970), 597-605.

41. See Robertson, pp. 450ff.

42. Lancelot and Alexander (Cliges) react in much the same fashion concerning locks from their respective beloveds' heads.

43. Mason, p. 11.

44. Mason, p. 12.

45. In effect, it proves to be a case of cultivation of cupiditas rather than caritas.

46. "'By my head, I will remember, whosoever may forget; so close is it to my heart.'" (p. 11)

47. "'Be sure that if thou wert found in any man's bed, save it be mine, I should not need a dagger to pierce my heart and slay me. Certes, no; wait would I not for a knife; but on the first wall or the nearest stone would I cast myself, and beat out my brains altogether." (p. 16)

48. ". . . as the wild boar deals when brought to bay by hounds in the wood . . ." (p. 11)

49. V. F. Hopper, Medieval Number Symbolism (New York: Columbia University Press, 1938), pp. 3-11 gives a good background on symbolic numbers.

50. See Hopper, p. 114 for the division of the Ten Commandments into groups of three and seven.

51. Ibid., pp. 113-115 for positive Christian groupings of seven.

52. "Another was with him, and he thought so dearly upon Nicolette, his fair friend, that the reins fell from his hand, and he struck never a blow. Then the charger, yet smarting from the spur, bore him into the battle, amidst the thickest of the foe." (p. 10)

53. Robertson, pp. 253-254.

54. Due to its linkage with the crown of thorns, the thorn becomes a symbol of tribulation. See Ferguson, p. 38.

55. "But she spake to him, sweetly wise. . . ." (p. 30)

56. "'Sire,' replied the King, 'too ready is such payment as yours. It is not our custom, nor theirs, to fight a quarrel to the death.'" (p. 34)

57. The text is from the Foerster edition cited above. The Comfort translation, p. 1, follows:

> "The rustic's proverb says that many a thing is despised that is worth much more than is supposed. Therefore, he does well who makes the most of whatever intelligence he may possess. For he who neglects this concern may likely omit to say something which would subsequently give great pleasure. So Chrétien de Troyes maintains that one ought always to study and strive to speak well and teach the right; and he derives from a story of adventure a pleasing argument whereby it may be proved and known that he is not wise who does not make liberal use of his knowledge so long as God may give him grace."

Tony Hunt (essay date 1977)

SOURCE: "Precursors and Progenitors of *Aucassin et Nicolette*," in *Studies in Philology*, Vol. 74, No. 1, January, 1977, pp. 1-19.

[*In the essay that follows, Hunt studies the form of* Aucassin et Nicolette *and maintains that its author drew on literary precedents in which prose and verse are combined. The originality of* Aucassin et Nicolette, *argues Hunt, arises from the regularity and consistency of the work's structure.*]

Critics of the celebrated *chantefable* have long puzzled over its originality of form. Hermann Suchier wrote "La forme de la nouvelle—l'auteur l'appelle *cantefable*—est unique en son genre en France: des morceaux en vers alternant avec des morceaux en prose."[1] Yet it is precisely the poem's originality of form which has been deemed to account for its apparent lack of success, its greatest devotee F. W. Bourdillon frankly declaring,

> One may reasonably conjecture that it is to the unattractiveness of its mingling of prose and verse to its contemporary hearers and readers that is due the fact, so strange in our eyes, of its survival in a single manuscript only. That it was, in fact, in its own day a failure.[2]

In complete contrast to the putative verdict of medieval audiences, however, stand the judgments of several modern students of the poem. Signor Monsonégo sees in the alternation of prose and verse the interpretative heart of the work, a contrasting of lyrical references to courtly conventions with a bathetic and trivializing treatment of them in the narrative.[3] Professor Vance, in an evidently strained interpretation of the poem as a "comedy of language," sees the action of the work as a conflict of incompatible literary styles, the noble poetic style of the lyrics being "tested" (it is unclear what is meant) by the trials of the world of prose narrative.[4] Different from both these approaches is the view of Kurt Rogger that the author of *Aucassin et Nicolette* has made a virtue out of what was once a mere expedient, namely the prose résumés which he claims *jongleurs* furnished for the less interesting parts of their narrative.[5] Most recently of all, Mariantonia Liboro has detected certain genetic implications in the way in which verse and prose are exploited:

> Alle origini poema narrativo del tipo dei testi citati [*Pyramus et Tisbé*, etc.], preso e messo grossolanamente in scena da un gruppo di clerici (studenti) desiderosi di sfruttare tutti i talenti a loro disposizione, l'originale è diventato un semplice canovaccio. Quello che bisogna fare è allora rendere esplicite e moltiplicare le possibilità parodiche del testo e esagerarne il latto spettacolo. Non è forse per caso che degli episodi più grotteschi (la battaglia, la lite col padre, l'incontro col bovaro) non ci sia traccia nelle parte in versi, che tenderei a considerare le più vicine all' originale.[6]

It is clear, therefore, that the alternation of prose and verse is one of the poem's most interesting and controversial features. It has, however, never been satisfactorily accounted for. A general model has been discerned, by some in Arabian romances,[7] by others in Celtic literature.[8] Neither of these suggestions is firmly established, but both are characteristic of an older, "romantic" trend in the study of the genesis of Old French literature which, as Professor Ullman has remarked, appeared to find Latin evidence unappealing.[9]

The possibility of Latin influences certainly deserves examination. The treatment of the same material in different forms is already recommended as a school exercise by Quintilian (*Inst. orat.* X.v, 9-11) and from its beginning in Antiquity the *prosimetrum* enjoyed considerable fortune. It first achieved popularity in the field of satire,[10] beginning so far as we can tell with Mennipus of Gadara, described by Strabo as *spoudogeloios,* whose works have not survived and for whom we must rely on the testimony of Lucian of Samosata (180-102 B.C.). From Mennipus Varo of Reate seems to have derived his mixture of prose and verse (employed in a variety of meters), but his work survives only in fragments, representing *c.* 600 lines from the original 150 books of the *Menippean Satires.* The *Apocolocyntosis* of Seneca, though drawing on the *Saturae Menippeae,* represents the first consistent exemplar of the technique to survive. It is a savage and bitter satire on the deification of Claudius after his death.[11] The initial link, however, of the *prosimetrum* with Menippean satire is of little importance for the future development of the technique in the Middle Ages, few of these works being known in the medieval period. It is oversimplifying to say of Menippean satire that "Boethius in his *Philosophiae Consolatio* insured its continuous popularity down to Bernard Silvestris, Alain de Lille, and the authors of such chantefables [*sic*] as *Aucassin et Nicolette* in the vernaculars."[12] Praiseworthy, but equally simplistic, is the essay published half a century ago by J. R. Reinhard, who neglects the musical aspects of *Aucassin et Nicolette* and the more specific characteristics of Menippean satire such as the mixture of amusement and instruction.[13] Moreover, in charting the tradition of the *prosimetrum* he adduces little material between Boethius and Brunetto Latini. In a part of what follows, we may attempt to refine and amplify Reinhard's cursory view of the tradition.

Proponents of the increasingly influential view that *Aucassin et Nicolette* is a parody[14] will find much material for reflection in the mixture of prose and verse in Petronius's celebrated satirical novel, the *Satyricon*, a work which consistently parodies literary themes and which Macrobius described as *argumentum fictis casibus amatorum refertum* (*Somn. Scip.* I.2, 8). Courtney has shown how pervasive literary allusion and parody are in Petronius.[15] Heinze has already shown how the *Satyricon* parodies the Greek love-romances[16] and Cèbe sees in it a parody of both the epic and the romance, the prose or verse registers often being used in ironic contrast to the material treated.[17] There are some interesting parallels here with recent interpretations of *Aucassin et Nicolette,* especially that of Monsonégo. Preston even called the *Satyricon* a "literary mime," a term which has, of course, been more than once applied to the *chantefable,*[18] whilst Stubbe prefers "Revueroman."[19] Courtney's description of Petronius's handling of the verse is not unsuited to the French poem: "Though he sometimes employs verse for incongruous effects . . . his most frequent use is to round off a situation with a gnomic treatment, an epigrammatic summary of its essence, sometimes slightly ironically in view of the contrast between the serious tone of the poem and the sordid context; but in most cases his motive seems to me to be mere epideictic pleasure in his literary versatility" (*art. cit.,* p. 100). Fascinating though a comparison of such judgments is, it should not blind us to the fact that the *Satyricon* had no literary progeny, that its author was little known in the Middle Ages,[20] and that the interpretation of *Aucassin et Nicolette* as a parody is unconvincing in some respects. For my own part, I do not think that the initial link of the *prosimetrum* with Menippean satire is of significance for its future development or for the mixed form of the *chantefable.*

If we leave the world of parody for one of extreme seriousness, we come to the influential *De Nuptiis Mercurii et Philologiae* of Martianus Capella, the medieval transmission of which has been well documented by Cora E. Lutz.[21] Probably written between 410 and 429, it contains a systematic exposition of the trivium and quadrivium, preceded by a rambling allegorical depiction of the marriage of Philology and Mercury which treats the *sapientia-eloquentia* theme. It would be difficult to overestimate the celebrity of this work in the Middle Ages. As a *prosimetrum* it is scarcely distinguished, the polymetric verse (fifteen varieties) having little essential connection with the prose text, and in its bizarreness it is quite inimitable. As a unity it all but defies analysis, though its structure has recently been explained along numerological lines.[22]

The relation of the verse sections to the prose is complex and conforms to no simple pattern, as Dr. LeMoine makes clear.[23] The otherwise somewhat indigestible learning is leavened by the Menippean style and the allegorical framework in place of the formerly favored sympotic device, last represented by Macrobius's incomplete *Saturnalia.* Martianus is ambitious but clumsy, lacking the skill displayed by Varro, Seneca, and Petronius in handling the prosimetric form. Nevertheless, the *De Nuptiis* remained a popular and influential textbook throughout the Middle Ages.[24]

It is likely, for example, to have influenced the sixth-century *Mythologiae* of Fabius Planciades Fulgentius, possibly to be identified with the Christian saint Fulgentius of Ruspe (d. 532/3), but more probably a contemporary who was active in North Africa as a *grammaticus* or *rhetor.* The three books of the *Mythologiae* are written in prose, but the elaborate prologue to Book One is obviously indebted to Martianus for its insertion of verses and the method of establishing the fabulous narrative setting. Fulgentius in turn enjoyed considerable influence in the Middle Ages.[25]

Most important of all, of course, is the example of Boethius, whose *Consolatio Philosophiae* remains one of the great books of the medieval period and the influence of which has been carefully charted in the masterly study of Pierre Courcelle.[26] Dr. Susan Ford has studied the nature and function of the thirty-nine poems interspersed throughout the prose and has emphasized Boethius's poetic artistry in exploiting the poems for scenesetting, effecting narrative transitions, elaborating important imagery, introducing new elements, providing summaries, and so on.[27] Boethius shares with other writers of *prosimetra,* to be mentioned later, the belief that verse will delight and relieve the reader who is tired by argument. Thus he frames the sixth prose of Book IV with these remarks of Philosophia:

> Quod si te musici carminis oblectamenta delectant, hanc oportet paulisper differas voluptatem, dum nexas sibi ordine contexo rationes.
>
> Sed video te iam dudum et pondere quaestionis oneratum et rationis prolixitate fatigatum aliquam carminis exspectare dulcedinem. Accipe igitur haustum quo refectus firmior in ulteriora contendas.

By the twelfth century, therefore, writers in the new renaissance of learning had models for the mixture of prose and verse in two of the most celebrated text-books of the age, Martianus and Boethius.[28] The influence is obvious, for example, in Bernard Silvester's *Cosmographia,* composed in the 1140's, which includes nine poems in different meters.[29] In another work which unites the new scientific learning with the old, Adelard of Bath's *De eodem et diverso,* there are two short sections in verse and in the depiction of Philocosmia and Philosophia clear echoes of Boethius who doubtless inspired the inclusion of the verses.[30] Another well-known case is the *De Planctu*

Naturae of Alan of Lille, a youthful work (*c.* 1160-70) of outstanding originality. The dream-vision, which so influenced later vernacular poets, is certainly derived from Boethius but details of style clearly recall Martianus and account, no doubt, for the scribal note "Alani minimi Capellae" found in several manuscripts.[31] The function of the poems contained in the work seems to be essentially epideictic. After analyzing many of them, G. Raynaud de Lage concludes "presque tous ces poèmes sont des hors d'oeuvre, et l'on a même l'impression que l'auteur a ouvert des 'tiroirs' pour y loger telle ou telle pièce antérieure à laquelle il ne voulait pas renoncer."[32]

We may conclude this summary of the influence on prosimetric writing of Martianus and Boethius by pointing to the particularly significant instance of the Old French translations of the *Consolatio,* which exist in a variety of versions. They number over a dozen and survive in over 100 manuscripts. The relations of the different versions are puzzling and for a long time there was disagreement on questions of chronology and authorship. It is now established that the version by Jean de Meung is a prose version only[33] but there are other versions, some in verse only, others in a mixture of prose and verse.[34] There are two distinct translations which retain the *prosimetrum* form, both undated and anonymous. The first contains a prologue as follows:

> Quar ceulx qui sont en grans tristeces
> Conforte doucement Boeces
> C'on dit *De Consolacion,*
> Propos ay et entencion
> De lui translater en françois,
> Si que chevaliers et bourgois
> Y praingnent confort, et les dames,
> S'ilz ont triboul de corps et d'ames.
> Ou livre a vers et s'i a prose:
> Si vueil si ordonner la chose
> Que li vers soient mis en rime
> Ou consonant ou leolime;
> La prose est mise plainnement
> Or oez le commencement.

> (Thomas and Roques, *art. cit.,* p. 450)

It was used by Renaud de Louhans in 1336 for his versified version, but it has never been dated with certainty; it may well date from soon after the middle of the thirteenth century.[35] If Dr. Blakey is right in suggesting a late date (*c.* 1270) for **Aucassin et Nicolette,**[36] it is not impossible that these two works are very close to each other in time. The second translation into prose and verse, also anonymous, was for a long time attributed to Jean de Meung. It survives in over 40 manuscripts,[37] and the author seems to have made use of the first verse-and-prose rendering. It, too, might be contemporary with the composition of **Aucassin et Nicolette.** It is possible, therefore, that the author of the *chantefable* may not only have been influenced by the existence of two celebrated schoolbooks which mixed prose and verse but also by the knowledge that the prosimetric form had already been attempted in vernacular French. As will become clear, this is not, in my opinion, the most likely hypothesis.

It would be wrong to give the impression that medieval writers of the *prosimetrum* were all copying Boethius. Some degree of spontaneity must be conceded in those writers who made less than systematic use of the procedure and who were principally concerned to display their literary virtuosity. Such a case is Ermenrich of Ellwangen (814-74) who, in a long encyclopaedic letter to Abbot Grimaldus of St. Gall, includes four moderately long dactylic poems and one "metro tetrametro aceatalecto."[38] The *Liber de rectoribus Christianis* (*c.* 831) of Sedulius Scottus is unique in representing the *miroir de prince* genre in prosimetric form. In this case the function of the polymetric poems is clear. They are used to provide a concluding summary to each chapter dealing with a virtue which the Christian prince should possess and at the same time are designed to provide pleasing variety: "Sed haec quae breviter stylo prosali diximus, aliqua versuum dulcedine concludamus."[39] A similar desire to delight and refresh the audience is found in Hildebert of Lavardin's *Liber de querimonia et conflictu carnis et spiritus seu animae,* a short work which represents a unique conflation of *altercatio* and *consolatio,* containing five longish verse sections.[40] It is a debate poem rather than a conflict and the debt to Boethius is obvious with the initial entry of the allegorical lady (the soul) in the manner of Philosophia. The verse sections are polymetric and are designed for the *delectatio* of the reader and to alleviate tedium: "Ac ne male deliciosus prosam fastidias longiorem, promissa mea metrico persolvam compendio."[41] We also find a mixture of prose and verse in letters. In the second half of the twelfth century Guido of Basoches (d. 1203) ends his letters (in prose) with poems of moderate length to show off his learning and literary skill.[42] Hagiography also produces some examples. It is believed that Notker of St. Gall composed a prosimetric *Vita S. Galli.* There are a few ornamental verses (rhymed hexameters) in Hucbald of St. Amand's *Vita Sanctae Aldegundis Virginis* but it is hardly a *prosimetrum.* On the other hand, the *Vita Deoderici ep. Mettensis* of Sigebert of Gembloux contains a poem of 100 hexameters on the city of Metz together with some smaller verse insertions, whilst the *Vita Gerardi abbatis Bromensis* comes nearest to the prosimetric genre with frequent if modest hexametric insertions.

Despite such continuing experiments in the genre the hagiographers produced no pure *prosimetrum.* They did, however, create an interesting innovation which is of considerable significance for the history of prose-and-verse composition, namely the so-called *opus geminum.* In his study of this double genre Ernst Walter has shown how Sedulius came to be regarded as the founder of the form with his *Carmen paschale* and *Opus paschale.*[43] In reality Sedulius wrote the prose *Opus* at the request of the dedicatee of the *Carmen,* Macedonius, who wished for a simpler, less poetic representation of the Gospel miracles, closer to the Biblical narrative, but Sedulius was later assumed to have written the two works together, as complementary to each other, the one in prose, the other in verse. Other authors of *opera gemina* include Aldhelm of Malmesbury, Bede, Alcuin, Hrabanus Maurus, Candidus of

Fulda, and, according to a slightly looser definition than that given by Hrabanus, Walther of Speyer, Rodulfus Tortarius, Alexander Nequam.[44] For Hrabanus the essence of the *opus geminum* resided in the fact that the prose and the verse narratives were regarded as belonging together in complementary fashion by their authors. Subsequently, however, writers composed such double forms separately, for differing reasons, and they came to constitute independent or alternative rather than complementary versions. For Hrabanus the double form had an aesthetic and a didactic purpose, relieving tedium by variety and aiding intelligibility by repetition:

> Mos apud veteres fuit, ut gemino stilo propria conderent opera, quo iocundiora simul et utiliora sua legentibus forent ingenia. Unde et apud saeculares et apud ecclesiasticos plurimi inveniuntur qui metro simul et prosa unam eandemque rem descripserunt. Ut de ceteris taceam, quid aliud beatus Prosper ac venerandus vir Sedulius fecisse cernuntur? Nonne ob id gemino stili caractere duplex opus suum edunt, ut varietas ipsa et fastidium legentibus auferat et si quid forte in alio minus quis intellegat, in alio mox plenius edissertum agnoscat?[45]

Although by 1100 the *opus geminum* was no longer a living form, the function of the double form could be taken over by the *prosimetrum,* as is clear from certain historical narratives. Verses are included in Liutprand of Cremona's *Antapodosis.*[46] A taste for the ornamental value of verses which Liutprand displays in several other works is here guided by the desire to give poetic expression to important elements of the narrative. Many chronicles, of course, include short verse quotations from the *auctores* and some writers, like Ordericus Vitalis, include historical testimonies in verse such as epitaphs, eulogies of famous figures, and so on. Other examples are Henry of Huntingdon and Roger of Hoveden. The two most notable cases, however, are Guibert of Nogent's *Gesta Dei per Francos* and Godfrey of Viterbo's *Pantheon.*

The Benedictine Guibert of Nogent began his admirably critical history of the First Crusade, the *Gesta Dei per Francos,*[47] *c.* 1106, and it reveals only too clearly his concern for style, derived no doubt from his early reading in the Scriptures and in exegesis and also from his fondness for the classics, especially Ovid and Virgil. In the course of the seven books of the *Gesta* there are twelve verse inserts of more than four lines and three of over forty lines. More important is the *Pantheon* of Godfrey of Viterbo.[48] Godfrey, of German origin and schooled in Bamberg, was much less discriminating than Guibert and his learning is showy but unreliable. His *Memoria seculorum* or *Liber memorialis,* composed in 1185, might loosely be termed an *opus geminum,* for the first part is written in prose, the second in verse. Godfrey later utilized it for the historical part of his compendium *Pantheon,* inserting into the second part in verse a number of prose passages. The *Pantheon* is divided into thirty-three *Particulae* and alternates prose and verse in roughly equal proportions. Godfrey explains that the verse sections, which frequently repeat the

material of the prose, are designed to please and refresh the reader who easily masters the narrative, whereas the less intelligent reader can resort simply to the prose sections:

> Hoc autem opus non tantum in prosis, set versibus adnotavi, ut lectores eius, si aliquando legendo prosas fuerint fatigati, cum versus sequentes inspexerint, consonantia et delectatione metrorum ad legendum ulterius provocentur; illi autem, qui versus forte non intelligunt, prosarum saltem lectionibus delectentur.
>
> (*ed. cit.,* p. 132)

From these examples it can thus be seen that prosimetric compositions were produced not only under the inspiration of Boethius but also spontaneously as demonstrations of authorial skill and virtuosity and as aids to readers' digestion. It is therefore most unlikely that the author of *Aucassin et Nicolette* thought that he was breaking new ground by mixing prose and verse. Rather, his originality might seem to lie in the fact that he mixes sung lyrics with recited narrative. It is concerning this feature of his work that I may, perhaps, make some new suggestions which will encourage us to accept a late date, such as that proposed by Dr. Blakey, for *Aucassin et Nicolette.*

It has perhaps not been remembered, in this connection, that there was a considerable vogue in North-eastern France in the thirteenth century for the insertion of lyric strophes in narratives, albeit verse narratives. This vogue appears to have been started by Jean Renart's Romance of the Rose, usually known as *Guillaume de Dôle.* Like *Aucassin et Nicolette* it takes its plot from the popular tale or *Märchen,* exploiting several widely attested themes. Composed *c.* 1228 according to M. Lecoy (Mme Lejeune prefers 1212), it is dedicated to Milo of Nanteuil, who was bishop of Beauvais (1222-34). The work gives a somewhat idealizing picture of the life of the times, though not without an ironic humor which sometimes resembles that of the author of the *chantefable.* The most striking feature of the work is the inclusion of forty-six chansons (or fragments) which are performed by the characters of the action. Some of them are the attested works of lyric poets, others are anonymous popular pieces. The effect is new and striking. Jean Renart proudly announces in the prologue that his *Romans de la rose*

> . . . est une novele chose
> et s'est des autres si divers
> et brodez, par lieus, de biaus vers
> que vilains nel porroit savoir.
> Ce sachiez de fi et de voir,
> bien a cist les autres passez.
> Ja nuls n'iert de l'oïr lassez,
> car, s'en vieult, l'en i chante et lit,
> et s'est fez par si grant delit
> que tuit cil s'en esjoïront
> qui chanter et lire l'orront,
> qu'il lor sera nouviaus toz jors.
> Il conte d'armes et d'amors
> et chante d'ambedeus ensamble,
> s'est avis a chascun et samble

que cil qui a fet le romans
qu'il trovast toz les moz des chans,
si afierent a ceuls del conte.[49]

The reference to "biaus vers" reminds us of the "bons vers" of *Aucassin et Nicolette*'s prologue. The division of *chanter* and *lire* clearly suggests the concept of the *chantefable*. One is bound to consider the possibility that *Aucassin et Nicolette* was influenced by the vogue for which Jean Renart seems to have been responsible. Clearly related in both theme and form is the *Roman de la Violette* of Gerbert de Montreuil, the composition of which would appear to be contemporaneous with *Guillaume de Dôle*—if we accept M. Lecoy's dating of the latter. Gerbert does not stress the novelty of his manner, but rather the matter, which is not Arthurian:

    . . . s'est li contes biaus et gens,
    que je vous voel dire et conter,
    car on i puet lire et chanter;
    et si est si biens acordans
    li cans au dit, les entendans
    en trai a garant que di voir . . .

      . . . . .

    mainte courtoise chançonnette
    orrois, ains que li contes fine.[50]

In this work there are over forty chansons of various types. Indeed, so great was the vogue for the inclusion of chansons in literary productions of the period that Friedrich Ludwig has listed over fifty such sources.[51] Some writers, like Jean Renart and Gerbert de Montreuil, included existing pieces; others, like the author of the *Perceforest*, composed their own. Adenet's chansons in *Cleomadés* (completed 1285) are his own and are carefully adapted to the narrative situation; they number only seven.[52] A similar state of affairs exists in the *Meliacin* of Girart d'Amiens, which, though independent of *Cleomadés*, treats the same subject.[53] From the *Tournoi de Chauvency*, which includes popular refrains of the day,[54] Jakemes took material for his *Roman du Castelain de Couci et de la Dame de Fayel*, composed at the end of the thirteenth century in the northeast of the Picard region, which includes seven lyric pieces attributed to the hero of the romance, four of which are authentic poems by the Castellan, as well as rondeaux performed by ladies at festivities.[55] Soon after *Guillaume de Dôle* Henri d'Andeli had included the full text of four chansons in his *Lai d'Aristote*. In view of the mounting evidence for the vogue in the northeast of works with lyric insertions it is not surprising that the most recent editor of *La Chastelaine de Vergi* has suggested that the author, who included a strophe of a chanson by the *Castelain de Couci*, was a Picard, composing *c.* 1240.[56] The vogue affected very different types of work. Adam de la Bassée, a canon of Lille who died in 1286, composed a modified summary of Alain's *Anticlaudianus* which he called *Ludus super Anticlaudianum* and which was evidently intended as recreation during a difficult period of illness. It is written in monorhyme quatrains of thirteen syllables, interspersed with nearly forty songs which make up almost a fifth of the *Ludus*. These songs cover a wide range of con-

temporary genres from hymns and sequences to popular airs and dances and even religious parodies. The melodies contained in the manuscript are frequently well-known and include celebrated hymns like *Veni Creator*, trouvère melodies such as those of Gace Brulé and Thibaut de Champagne, and popular tunes of the day.[57] Too little studied is *Li romanz de la poire*, composed in the middle of the 13th century by one Thibaut. The poem exploits a number of meters and is interspersed with songs or the beginnings of songs and in the fragmentary MS BN fr. 24431 they are provided with musical notation.[58] Similarly varied is the long allegorical poem *Renart le Nouvel*, produced *c.* 1289 by Jacquemart Gielée of Lille. The verse narrative is interlarded with a number of parodic letters in prose and by fashionable refrains. Another work, *Sone de Nausay*, by a Picard author, has a prose introduction followed by a verse narrative which includes a long strophic lay sung by Papegai (ll. 15983-16142).[59]

Alongside these examples of the vogue, especially in Picardy, for verse insertions we must also mention an earlier, outstanding work which mixed prose and verse, namely the prose *Tristan*, which not only contains lyric pieces designed to be sung, but also verse sections. In the complicated state of the manuscript relations it is not always easy to tell how many of these lyrics are later interpolations, but Mlle J. Lods writes "il est hors de doute que l'initiative de mêler des vers à la prose appartient au premier auteur."[60] According to Dr. Curtis, the work dates from *c.* 1215-35, being begun by "Luce del Gat" and completed, after a labor of five years, by "Hélie de Boron." The prose *Tristan* was extremely popular and Dr. Curtis has listed 77 manuscripts.[61]

Thus the originality of *Aucassin et Nicolette* resides in the regularity and consistency of its structure rather than in the fact of its mixture of prose and verse (attested outside the Latin *prosimetrum* by the prose *Tristan*, two Old French translations of Boethius and a satirical piece[62]) or of sung lyric and recited narrative (fashionable from *Guillaume de Dôle* onwards), though the choice of seven-syllable lines in *laisses* remains individual and unaccounted for. In sum, we may offer the following conclusions concerning the poem's inspiration.

In the first place, there is a fortuitous coincidence of the *prosimetrum*'s origins in Menippean satire and the use of the *chantefable* by a writer with allegedly parodic intentions. There is no evidence to suggest any genetic link between these two phenomena, interesting though the parallels may be, and it is likely that recent critics have exaggerated the satirical aspects of the French poem.

There is no doubt, however, that anyone who had been near the schools would be aware that two of the most important schoolbooks of the twelfth and thirteenth centuries, Martianus and Boethius, were in prosimetric form and that they had inspired a number of similar productions during the "renaissance" of learning. The *ambiance* of the schools furnished further precedents. The *artes poeticae*, beginning with Matthew of Vendôme's *Ars versificatoria* of *c.* 1175, set verse illustrations within a prose commentary. As a teacher at Orleans, impregnated with the spirit of twelfth-century humanism, Matthew shows a particular fondness for verse quotations from the classical poets, as does Konrad of Mure, a century later, in his *Summa de arte prosandi.* The glosses and paraphrases of scriptural exegetes might also produce a mixture of prose and verse, as in the case of William of Ebersberg's *Expositio in Cantica Canticorum* (*c.* 1059-65) which paraphrases and explains the verses of the Song of Songs in internally rhyming Latin hexameters and translates them into German prose.[63] In addition, as we have already pointed out, it is possible that a late date for *Aucassin et Nicolette,* such as that proposed by Dr. Blakey, would mean that the author already had the examples of the prose *Tristan* and the French translations of Boethius behind him, and the contrast of prose and verse would be more natural with the establishment of prose as a vernacular medium.[64]

Finally, instrumental in the inspiration of the *chantefable,* in my opinion, were Jean Renart and his imitators, who imported sung lyrics into their narratives and created a fashion which continued to flourish through the fourteenth century. Manuscripts survive, for example, of the prose *Tristan* and the *Roman de la poire,* in which the music is transmitted with the text. It may therefore be said that the author of *Aucassin et Nicolette,* rather than inventing *ex nihilo* a new literary form, exploited the possibilities of two literary precedents and by a systematic combination of the two produced a uniquely proportioned entertainment.

Notes

1. *Aucassin et Nicolette. Texte critique . . . par Hermann Suchier,* 8th ed. (Paderborn, 1913), p. vi.

2. *Aucassin et Nicolette,* ed. F. W. Bourdillon (Manchester, 1919), p. xii.

3. S. Monsonégo, *Etude stylo-statistique du vocabulaire des vers et de la prose dans la chantefable Aucassin et Nicolette* (Paris, 1966), p. 100. See the summary of his conclusions on the function of the prose and verse passages on p. 97 and cf. Geoffrey of Vinsauf, *Poetria Nova,* ll. 1858-70.

4. E. Vance, "The Word at Heart: *Aucassin et Nicolette* as a Medieval Comedy of Language," *YFS,* XLV (1970), 33-51.

5. K. Rogger, "Etude descriptive de la chantefable *Aucassin et Nicolette,* I," *ZRP,* LXVII (1951), esp. 437. More recently, John A. Rea, "The Form of *Aucassin et Nicolette,*" *RomN,* XV (1973-4), 504-8, has sought the formal inspiration of the *chantefable* in the Provençal lyrics with their *razos* and *vidas.*

6. M. Liboro, "*Aucassin et Nicolette:* limiti di una parodia," *Cultura Neolatina,* XXX (1970), 160, n. 19.

7. Bourdillon, *op. cit.,* p. xiii. Cf. the objections of Scheludko, *ZRP,* XLII (1922), esp. 487-90, to Suchier's theory of Arabic origins.

8. Cf. more recently G. Goetinck, "*Aucassin et Nicolette* and Celtic Literature," *ZCP,* XXXI (1970), 224-9.

9. B. L. Ullman, "Medieval Latin and Comparative Literature," in *Comparative Literature. Proceedings of the Second Congress of the International Comparative Literature Association* (Chapel Hill, N.C., 1959), I, 16. An exception to the critical trend noted by Ullman is now G. B. Gybbon-Monypenny, "Guillaume de Machaut's erotic 'autobiography': precedents for the form of the *Voir-Dit,*" in *Studies in Medieval Literature and Languages in Memory of Frederick Whitehead* (Manchester, 1973), p.p 133-52.

10. O. Immisch, "Über eine volkstümliche Darstellungsform in der antiken Literatur," *Neue Jahrbücher für das klassische Altertum,* XLVII (1921), 409-21, tried to prove the existence of a primitive, popular *prosimetrum* form.

11. Cf. H. M. Currie, "The Purpose of the *Apocolocyntosis,*" *L'Antiquité Classique,* XXXI (1962), 91-7.

12. C. Witke, *Latin Satire: The Structure of Persuasion* (Leiden, 1970), p. 157.

13. J. R. Reinhard, "The Literary Background of the *Chantefable,*" *Speculum,* I (1926), 157-69.

14. I argue against this view in a forthcoming study "Medieval Parody: The Case of *Aucassin et Nicolette,*" but it would be willful to restrict the discussion here in accordance with a view concerning which I may be proved wrong.

15. E. Courtney, "Parody and Literary Allusion in Menippean Satire," *Philologus,* CVI (1962), 86-100. Cf. J.-P. Cèbe, *La Caricature et la parodie dans le monde romain antique des origines à Juvénal* (Paris, 1966), *passim.*

16. R. Heinze, "Petron und der griechische Roman," *Hermes,* XXXIV (1899), 494-519.

17. *Op. cit.,* p. 313.

18. K. Preston, "Some Sources of Comic Effect in Petronius," *Classical Philology,* X (1915), 263.

19. H. Stubbe, *Die Verseinlagen im Petron, Philologus* Supplementband XXV, Heft 2 (Leipzig, 1933), p. 19: "Die 'Revue', das neuere Bühnen-Ausstattungsstück, hat mit Petrons literarischem Erzeugnis ausser der losen Kompositionsform die Tendenz, durch mannigfache Stoffe nebeneinander, die phantastisch, realistisch, komisch-burlesk, endlich satirisch sein können, unterhalten zu wollen gemeinsam. Die handelnden Personen sind in beiden Fällen nur Vehikel des Stoffes."

20. Cf. V. Pioletti, "Giovanni di Salisbury e la 'Cena Trimalchionis,'" *Giornale Italiano di Filologia,* XVII (1964), 350-58; for an author of a 12th C. miscellany in Trinity College, Dublin MS 602 (E.4.26), who mixes prose and verse and shows first-hand knowledge of Petronius, see M. L. Colker, *Analecta Dublinensia* (Cambridge, Mass., 1975), p. 184.

21. In P. O. Kristeller, ed., *Catalogus Translationum et Commentariorum. Medieval and Renaissance Latin Translations and Commentaries*, II (Washington, D.C., 1971), 367-81. This article gives full bibliographical references which it is unnecessary to rehearse here.

22. Fanny LeMoine, *Martianus Capella. A Literary Reevaluation*, Münchener Beiträge zur Mediävistik und Renaissance-Forschung 10 (München, 1972).

23. *Ibid.*

24. The best guide to the work is W. H. Stahl, "To a Better Understanding of Martianus Capella," *Speculum*, XL (1965), 102-15, and *id. et al., Martianus Capella and the Seven Liberal Arts*, I (New York, 1971).

25. For full details on all questions concerning Fulgentius, see *Fulgentius the Mythographer*, translated from the Latin, with introduction, by L. G. Whitbread (Columbus, Ohio, 1971).

26. P. Courcelle, *La Consolation de Philosophie dans la tradition littéraire* (Paris, 1967). Cf. K. Reichenberger, *Untersuchungen zur literarischen Stellung der Consolatio Philosophiae* (Köln, 1954).

27. Susan Chappell Ford, Poetry in Boethius' Consolation of Philosophy (Diss. Columbia, 1967). Cf. H. Scheible, *Die Gedichte in der Consolatio Philosophiae des Boethius* (Heidelberg, 1972).

28. Cf. Rather of Verona who writes in the prooemium of the *Phrenesis,* the first book alone of which survives, "Quidam vero sex linearum per sententias ideo est divisione discretus, quod auctor ejusdem versibus eum disposuerat, ut in Martiano, Fulgentio atque Boetio cernitur . . . eadem ex materia sumptis pangere sententiis." *PL* 136, col. 373.

29. *The* Cosmographia *of Bernardus Silvestris*, translated with introduction and notes by Winthrop Wetherbee (New York, 1973). Cf. B. Stock, *Myth and Science in the Twelfth Century. A Study of Bernard Silvester* (Princeton, 1972), pp. 70 f. and W. Wetherbee, *Platonism and Poetry in the Twelfth Century. The Literary Influence of the School of Chartres* (Princeton, 1972).

30. Cf. P. Courcelle, "Adelard de Bath et la 'Consolation' de Boèce," in *Kyriakon. Festschrift für Johannes Quasten* (Münster, Westf., 1970), pp. 572-5.

31. See M.-T. d'Alverny, *Alain de Lille. Textes inédits* (Paris, 1965), p. 33. Another prosimetric dreamvision is the *De Consolatione rationis* of Peter of Compostella, ed. P. B. Soto (Münster i. W., 1912).

32. G. Raynaud de Lage, *Alain de Lille, poète du XIIe siècle* (Montreal and Paris, 1951), p. 109.

33. See R. Crespo, "Jean de Meun traduttore della Con-solatio Philosophiae di Boezio," *Atti della Accademia delle scienze di Torino, classe di scienze morali, storiche e filologiche*, CIII (1969), 71-170.

34. For a conspectus of these versions, see A. Thomas and M. Roques, "Traductions françaises de la Conso-latio Philosophiae de Boèce," *Histoire Littéraire de la France*, XXXVII (Paris, 1938), 419-88. For the most recent bibliography, see R. A. Dwyer, "The Old French Boethius: Addendum," *MÆ*, XLIII (1974), 265-6.

35. Cf. A. van de Vyver, "Les traductions du *De Consolatione Philosophiae* de Boèce en littérature comparée," *Humanisme et Renaissance,* VI (1939), 253. If a 13th C. dating is correct, it would make the work chronologically the second translation into Old French, a prose version by a Burgundian clerk (MS Vienna 2642) being earlier.

36. B. Blakey, "*Aucassin et Nicolette* XXIX, 4," *French Studies*, XXII (1968), 97-8.

37. See L. W. Stone, "Old French Translations of the *De Consolatione Philosophiae* of Boethius: some unnoticed manuscripts," *Mæ,* VI (1937), esp. 22-5, and G. M. Cropp, "La traduction française de la *Consolatio Philosophiae* de Boèce: encore un manuscrit," *Romania*, XC (1969), 258-70. See also R. A. Dwyer, "The Appreciation of Handmade Literature," *ChauR,* VIII (1974), esp. 230 ff., who mentions two later versions employing the mixed form, one in the National Library of Wales, the other represented in a print of 1477.

38. Ed. E. Dümmler, *MGH, Ep.* V (Berlin, 1899), pp. 534-80.

39. *PL* 103, col. 295. According to R. Düchting, *Sedulius Scottus: Seine Dichtungen* (München, 1968), p. 12, a new edition is being considered by M. Duggan.

40. Cf. P. von Moos, *Hildebert von Lavardin 1056-1133* (Stuttgart, 1965), pp. 118 ff.

41. *PL* 171, col. 1000.

42. *Liber Epistularum Guidonis de Basochis,* ed. H. Adolfsson (Stockholm, 1969). Cf. p. vi. See also B. Munk Olsen in *Revue des Etudes Latines*, XLIX (1971), 66-77.

43. E. Walter, Opus geminum. Untersuchungen zu einem Formtyp in der mittellateinischen Literatur (Diss. Erlangen-Nürnberg, 1973). "Opus geminum" is the term used by Aldhelm; "geminatum opus" is preferred by Bede.

44. Cf. Walter, *op. cit.*, and P. Vossen, *Der Libellus Scolasticus des Walther von Speyer* (Berlin, 1962), pp. 208-12.

45. *Epistolae,* ed. E. Dümmler, *MGH, Ep.* V (Berlin, 1899), p. 384.

46. Third ed. by J. Becker, *MGH, Scriptores rer. Germ. in us. Schol.* (Hannover, 1915).

47. See *Recueil des historiens des croisades. Historiens occidentaux*, IV (Paris, 1879), 113-263.

48. Ed. G. Waitz, *MGH, Script.* XXII (Hannover, 1872), 107-307.

49. *Le Roman de la Rose ou de Guillaume de Dôle*, ed. F. Lecoy, *CFMA,* XCI (Paris, 1962), ll. 12-29. On

the dating of the work, see C. Mattioli, "Sulla datazione del *Guillaume de Dôle*," *Cultura Neolatina,* XXV (1965), 91-112 and, most recently, R. Lejeune, "Le Roman de *Guillaume de Dôle* et la principauté de Liège," *CCM,* XVII (1974), 1-24, who defends a date 1208-10.

50. *Le Roman de la Violette ou de Gerart de Nevers,* ed. D. L. Buffum, *SATF* (Paris, 1928), ll. 36-41, 46-7.

51. "Die Quellen der Motetten ältesten Stils," *Archiv für Musikwissenschaft,* V (1923), esp. 216-8. I have not seen Anne Preston Ladd, Lyric Insertions in Thirteenth-Century French Narrative (Diss. Yale, 1973).

52. *Les Oeuvres d'Adenet le roi,* ed. A. Henry, V, *Cleomadés* (Bruxelles, 1971).

53. See the partial edition of P. Aebischer, *Le Roman du Cheval de Fust ou de Meliacin, TLF* (Genève, 1974).

54. Ed. M. Delbouille (Liège and Paris, 1932). Refrains of *chansons* are also included by the Picard trouvère Mahiu le Poriier in his long allegorical poem, *Le Court d'amours.*

55. Ed. M. Delbouille, *SATF* (Paris, 1936).

56. Ed. R. E. V. Stuip (The Hague and Paris, 1970), p. 63. P. Zumthor, "De la chanson au récit: *La Chastelaine de Vergi*," *Vox Romanica,* XXVII, (1968), 77-95, offers an analysis of the poem which provides some interesting parallels with *Aucassin et Nicolette.*

57. See Adam de La Bassee, *Ludus super Anticlaudianum . . . par M. L'Abbé Paul Bayart* (Tourcoing, 1930).

58. Messire Thibaut, *Li Romanz de la poire,* ed. F. Stehlich (Halle, 1881).

59. Ed. M. Goldschmidt (Tübingen, 1899).

60. J. Lods, "Les parties lyriques du *Tristan* en prose," *BBSIA,* VII (1955), 78. See also J. Maillard, "Lais avec notation dans le *Tristan* en prose," *Mélanges Lejeune* (Gembloux, 1969), II, 1347-64; and E. Baumgartner, "Sur les pièces lyriques du *Tristan* en prose," *Mélanges Lecoy* (Paris, 1973), 19-25.

61. *Le Roman de Tristan en prose,* ed. R. L. Curtis, I (München, 1963).

62. The thirteenth-century satire, *Des XXII Manières de Vilains,* composed by a Picard author, begins with a satirical description of *vilains* in prose which is then followed by a long verse section which parodies well-known prayers; see E. Faral, *Romania,* XLVIII (1922), 243-64. A lost chronicle of the life of Philippe-Auguste had a verse prologue, which survives, while the rest was in prose; see P. Meyer, *Romania,* VI (1877), 494 ff.

63. Cf. M.-L. Dittrich, "Die literarische Form von William's *Expositio in Cantica Canticorum*," *ZDA,* LXXXIV (1953), 179-97.

64. Cf. H. G. Jantzen, Untersuchungen zur Entstehung des altfranzösischen Prosaromans (Diss. Hamburg, 1966).

Eugene Dorfman (essay date 1977)

SOURCE: "The Sacred and the Profane in *Aucassin et Nicolette,*" in *Homenaje a Robert A. Hall, Jr.,* edited by David Feldman, Playor, S. A., 1977, pp. 117-31.

[*In the following essay, Dorfman asserts that the contradictions, inversions, and absurdities in* Aucassin et Nicolette, *including examples of profanity, all serve to disguise an even greater inversion: the transformation of the passive Aucassin into the "active deliverer of his people." Elements in the poem, explains Dorfman, parallel the Hebrew Bible, and such allusions point to Aucassin as the coming Messiah.*]

The Lord is a gracefully hovering Presence in *Aucassin et Nicolette*[1], mentioned more than forty times in as many pages of text, where he is usually called upon respectfully[2] to observe, support, or intecede in the affairs of the protagonists. On three occasions, however, there is recourse to profanity; the shepherds of Beaucaire, who have been paid by Nicolette to transmit a message to Aucassin, the ugly oxherd, whom she meets in the forest, and finally Aucassin himself all swear 'by the heart of God': *por le cuerbé* (XXII, 15), *por le cuer que cil Sires eut en sen ventre* (XXIV, 42), and *par le cuer Dieu* (XXX, 7).

In none of these instances, as Philippe Ménard[3] recognizes for medieval literature in general, is there any intention to blaspheme, offend, or deride the Lord, the speaker's purpose being merely to emphasize his determination in the matter at hand. The use of profanity, moreover, by the shepherds and the oxherd, members of the common folk, occasions no surprise; its utterance, on the other hand, by a youth of noble rank, compounded by the vulgarity of *fix a putain*, with which Aucassin addresses the king of Torelore, not unnaturally causes a reflex lifting of the eyebrows. Ménard attributes it—rightly, with regard to the surface story (or superstructure)—to a 'trait comique' (p. 714); it is harmoniously in consonance with all the other elements in that wildly burlesque[4] scene of rough and tumble in which Aucassin, acting out a comic parody[5] of contemporary epics and romances, neglects the sword at his side for a common club as a weapon of combat. No less startling than the unreasonable motive for the unmerciful drubbing administered by Aucassin to the king of Torelore is the impossible result it seeks to achieve; our hero is repelled by the fact that the king is lying in childbed, and demands—could anything be more absurd?—that all male childbearing in the country be outlawed.

The unreasonableness of this request is the link uniting all three expressions of profanity, which vary in phraseology though not in content; although in the first two instances the profanity is addressed *to* Aucassin and in the last instance *by* him, it is always he whose conduct is beyond the pale. The spokesman for the shepherds reacts as he does, because he resents the crude attempt on the part of Aucassin, who is not his master, to compel him to repeat against his will a song he has just sung; the oxherd, burdened by practical problems of poverty and social injustice, is equally resentful of Aucassin's facile weeping for a lost hound, which his father's wealth could replace with fifteen or twenty without a second thought. There is nothing to suggest, on the surface, that the profanity may, in each case, serve a secret function.

The story of *Aucassin et Nicolette* is, on the face of it, a treasure trove of contradictions, inversions, and absurdities. The passive hero, who allows his lady love to play the active role, thinks of nothing but her as he rides ineptly into battle and allows himself to be captured without a struggle; not until he is threatened with decapitation, which would prevent him from speaking with her again, does he begin to fight in earnest, and then, in a few moments of concentrated effort, brings to heel an army of ten thousand foes, thus ending a war of twenty years duration. Later, still concentrating his thoughts on his beloved, he dislocates his shoulder in the act of dismounting from his horse, by tumbling upside down onto a rock. When Aucassin and Nicolette are incarcerated in their separate prisons, it is not he who escapes to visit his beloved at any price, but she who does so, coming to him at peril of her life; and in these dangerous circumstances, he wastes their precious moments together disparaging the carnality of women and their incapacity to love like men. Obsessed with Love to the degree that he prefers Hell over Heaven, provided that he has his beloved with him, he has to be characteristically urged, pushed, and proded into every step he takes in her direction. Tongue in cheek, the poet sums him up as the epitome of kinighthood, except for a minor flaw; he merely refuses to do anything a good knight should. It would be difficult to imagine a less likely candidate for the role to which God, with the help of our poet, has destined him.

The superstructural contradictions, inversions, and absurdities, including the examples of profanity, are a well disguised cover for the greatest inversion of all: the transformation of the apparently passive hero, in the eyes of the world a comic *schlemiel* of the Charlie Chaplin[6] type, into an active deliverer of his people, whose awesome role in a secret, or parastructural, scenario, concealed by signals which point to relevant passages in the Hebrew Bible, is that of the coming Messiah. This is announced in the controversial[7] opening lines:

> Qui vauroit bons vers oïr
> del deport du viel antif . . .
>
> (I, 1-2).

The deceptively innocent and apparently unnecessarily redundant phrase *du viel antif* (*du viel* 'from of old', *antif* 'from ancient days'), which has puzzled the critics because of its unusual Old French syntax, is a loan translation from the Hebrew, directing the alerted[8] reader unerringly to Micah's celebrated prophecy of a future 'ruler in Israel'.

> But thou, Beth-lehem Ephrathah,
> Which art little to be among the thousands of Judah,

> Out of three shall one come forth unto Me that is to be ruler in Israel [*moshel be'Yisrael*];
> Whose goings forth are *from of old, from ancient days* [*mi'kedem mi'ymey olam* (*du viel antif*)]
>
> (5: 1).

This human[9] 'ruler in Israel', the Messiah, is subject to the frailties of men, and has to be educated to his task.

The key to the parastructural meaning of the profanity, as well as to the kind of education envisaged to fit Aucassin for his destined role, is signalled, first of all, by *del deport . . . de deus biax enfans petis* (I, 2-3). The alerted reader, if familiar with the Judeo-French sense of *deport* 'action d'élever, action de favoriser',[10] is also aware that in a Judeo-French (or Jewish) community the 'raising of children' centers on instruction in the *Tora* 'the teaching', and on 'encouraging' its study. The name *Torelore* therefore hints—to a searching eye—at a place of instruction, through its resemblance to the well known Hebrew phrase *Tora ora* 'teaching is light'. This phrase, recognized as a homiletic interpretation of a verse in Esther, takes the reader, in a second step, to the relevant passage.

> La'Yehudim hayesa *ora* ve'simcha ve'sason vi'ykar:
> The Jews had *light* and gladness, and joy and honour
>
> (8:16).

These blessings, which resulted when the Jews were saved by the intercession of Esther—one of Nicolette's prototypes—from the annihilation threatened by Haman, show a direct correlation with the healing of the reader's ills, promised by the poet in the exordium (I, 10-15). There is *ora* 'light' for the *esbahis* 'confused', *simcha* 'gladness' for the *dolans* 'sorrowful', *sason* 'joy' for the *entrepris* 'dejected in spirit', and *ikar* 'honor' for the *de grant mal amaladis* 'sickened by some great evil', such as the degradation that accompanies helplessness in the face of massacre, expulsion, forced conversion, and the general libels to which a homeless and wandering nation may be subjected.

A third[11] step reveals the function of the -*l*-, present in *Tore-l-ore,* though missing from *Tora ora,* and furnishes the essential key to the poet's ingenious coding system. The Rabbinical interpretation of *ora* in Esther 8: 16 as *Tora ora* calls to mind the synonomous phrase *Tora or,* which occurs in the Proverbs of Solomon.

> kir ner mitzva ve'*Tora* or
> ve'derech chayim toch'chos musar:
> li'shmarcha me'eshes *ra*
> me'chelkas lashon nachriyya:
> For the commandment is a lamp, and the *teaching* is light,
> And the reproofs of instruction are the way of life;
> To keep three from the *evil* woman,
> From the smoothness of the alien tongue
>
> (6: 23-34).

Embedded between the Hebrew words *Tora* and *ra* is summed up the core of Aucassin's education, and the lesson his parents have been trying to teach him; they wish, through 'the reproofs of instruction', to draw him to the Tora as a 'way of life', and away from his obsessive love of the alien Nicolette, a form of idolatry which inclines him to the worship of the 'evil woman', the goddess Ashtoreth. When the Hebrew morpheme *le-* 'to' is inserted between *Tora* and *ra,* the resulting *Tora . . . le . . . ra,* or *Tora . . . le'ra* (as in *Torelore*) informs the reader that a Biblical passage may be found which, read from *Tora . . .* to *. . . ra,* provides a parastructural Jewish dimension to the ongoing parable.

Tora, le-, and *ra* are all Hebrew forms; conveniently, however, *le* is also a French morpheme, meaning 'him, it, the', and in this text often 'her'. It has the advantage moreover of extremely frequent occurrence, and thus lends itself easily as a camouflaged signalling device. Wherever *le* occurs, standing between two French forms, it is necessary to translate the latter into Hebrew and read the *le-*[12] itself as Hebrew 'to', signalling the (sometimes approximate) starting and ending points of a relevant capsulated message in the Bible. This applies to the profanity of the shepherds, the oxherd, and Aucassin, which in each case, contrary to appearances, expresses a prophetic revelation.

AUTHORITY AND THE SHEPHERDS OF BEAUCAIRE

Aucassin, the son of Garin, Count of Beaucaire, has been released from prison by his father, after his act of treachery in support of Bougars, Count of Valence, the enemy war chief. Rumor has it that his beloved Nicolette has either been slain by Garin, or has fled the country. Spurred on by a compassionate knight, a servant of the king, Aucassin is aroused from his inaction to set off on a journey in her pursuit, not knowing which direction to take. Outside the castle, he encounters six shepherds of Beaucaire in the act of eating, and overhears one of them chanting a song about Aucassin and a lovely blond maiden. He demands a repetition of the song, but is refused; to his question whether the shepherd knows him, the reply is that he does, but that Aucassin has no authority over him and his fellows, 'mais nos ne somes mie a vos, ains somes au conte' (XXII, 12-13). When Aucassin repeats his request, the outspoken one responds with profanity.

> 'Os, *por le cuerbé!'*[13] fait cil; 'por quoi canteroie je por vos, s'il ne me seoit . . .?'
>
> (XXII, 1-16).

By what authority does Aucassin indeed speak?

The parastructural counterpart scene, in First Samuel, describes the celebrated incident in which the prophet selects Saul as the first king of Israel, in response to the misguided demand of the people: '. . . now make us a king to judge us like all the nations' (8: 5). Saul, the son of Kish, is off on a journey to hunt for the asses which his father has lost. Seeking everywhere without success, he is about to return home—inverting the situation where Aucassin is about to begin the hunt—when his servant, like Aucassin's knight, makes a fruitful suggestion; he urges Saul to seek out the prophet Samuel in order to learn which direction to take to find the lost animals.

And he said unto him: 'Behold now, there is *in* this city [*ba'ir ha'zos*] a man of God, and he is a man that is held in honour; all that he saith cometh surely to pass; now let us go thither; peradventure he can tell us concerning our journey whereon we go'

> (9: 6).

Aucassin is here reliving a modified version of the beginnings of the kingdom of Israel, whose starting point is Saul's pursuit of some lost asses; our hero is hunting a single 'beast', the one which, as the shepherds have been paid by Nicolette to inform him, has the medicine to heal his ills (XXII, 36-37), and which he himself later identifies to the oxherd as an irreplaceable, lost 'white hound' (XXIV, 39-40). Both Aucassin and Saul require a prophetic voice to give direction to their journeys in search of the lost beasts; and both are set on the road to the prophet by a compassionate servant. Significantly, for both, the prophet is to be found 'in this city', that is, in Beaucaire,[14] the Land of Canaan.

Saul has nothing with which to pay the prophet, but the servant is prepared to make good the deficiency.

> Then said Saul to his servant: 'But, behold, if we go, what shall we bring the man? for the bread is spent in our vessels, and there is not a present to bring to the man of God; what have we?' And the servant answered Saul again, and said: 'Behold, I have in my hand the fourth of a shekel of silver, that will I give to the man of God, to tell us our way'
>
> (9: 7-8).

Saul's lack of funds is inverted by Aucassin's apparently unlimited supply; moreover, the shepherds themselves seem to have plenty of bread, *si mangoient lor pain et faisoient mout tresgrant joie* (XX, 30-31). Both Aucassin and Saul understand, however, that they must pay for the information.

Saul and his servant set out to find Samuel and are aided by some young maidens who are, going out to draw water.

> So they went unto the city where the man of God was. As they went up the ascent to the city, they found young maidens going out to draw water, and said unto them: 'Is the seer here?' And they answered them, and said: 'He is; behold, he is before thee; make haste now, for he is come to-day into the city; for the people have a sacrifice to-day in the high place. As soon as ye are come into the city, ye shall straightway find him, before he go up to the high place to eat; for the people will not eat until he come, because he doth bless the sacrifice; and afterwards they eat that are bidden. Now therefore get you up; for at this time ye shall find him'. And they went up to the city; and as they came within the city, behold, Samuel came out toward them, to go up to the high place
>
> (9: 10-14).

There are several striking similarities, as well as inversions. Aucassin encounters his shepherds at a *fontaine,* or well; Saul and his servant meet the young maidens as they are going to a well for water. Aucassin seeks help from some prophetic shepherds to find a maiden; Saul seeks help from some maidens to find a prophet. Aucassin's shepherds are already eating as he comes upon them; Saul's prophet is getting ready to eat, while the people wait for him to give the word to begin. Aucassin approaches the shepherds; Samuel comes toward Saul and his servant. Aucassin is going away from the city for his encounter; Saul is coming into the city. In both incidents, the central figures seek a message of great importance.

Samuel, forewarned of Saul's coming by the Lord, has been delegated by Him to deliver the message that Saul has been chosen to rule and have authority over God's people, in order to save them in their distress.

> Now the Lord had revealed unto Samuel a day before Saul came, saying: 'To-morrow about this time I will send thee a man out of the land of Benjamin, and thou shalt anoint him [*u'meshachto*] to be prince over My people Israel, and he shall save [*ve'hoshi'a*] My people out of the hand of the Philistines; for I have looked upon My people, because their cry is come unto Me.' And when Samuel saw Saul, the Lord spoke unto him: 'Behold the man [*hine ha'ish*] of whom I said unto thee: This same shall have authority over My people'
>
> (9: 15-17).

The shepherds are likewise forewarned of Aucassin's coming by Nicolette, as surrogate of the Lord, and are thus delegated to transmit to him the equivalent of Samuel's message of *ecce homo,* 'behold the man' who is to be the *meshiach,* the 'anointed one', the savior of his people. The spokesman for the shepherds is as reluctant[15] as Samuel to perform his assigned task; God, however, has heard the cry of His people, represented by Aucassin (Ephraim and Judah), and Nicolette's message of the 'beast' that can heal him—enabling him to save his people in helpless Exile—is passed on.

Saul encounters Samuel, but does not recognize him. The prophet informs him that his father's asses have been found, and, at the same time, that he is the fulfillment of Israel's desire [for a king]; to the latter announcement, Saul interposes a modest demurrer.

> Then Saul drew near to Samuel in the gate, and said: 'Tell me, I pray thee, where the seer's house is.' And Samuel answered Saul, and said: 'I am the seer; go up before me unto the high place, for ye shall eat with me to-day; and in the morning I will let thee go, and tell thee all that is *in thy heart* [*bi'levavecha*].[16] And as for thine asses that were lost three days ago, set not thy mind on them; for they are found. And on whom is all the desire of Israel? Is it not on thee, and on all thy father's house?' And Saul answered and said: 'Am not I a Benjamite, of the smallest of the tribes of Israel? and my family the least of all the families of the tribe of Benjamin? wherefore then speakest thou to me after this manner?'
>
> (9: 18-21).

There is here a complex inversion of the source materials: while Saul, the petitioner, does *not* recognize the prophet Samuel, the shepherd-seer *does* recognize Aucassin, the

petitioner. Conversely, there is a fundamental identity in the two scenes: while Samuel and the shepherd recognize their petitioners, Saul and Aucassin are unaware that they are accosting prophets. Samuel informs Saul that his asses were found within three days; the shepherd-seer inverts the past into the future and informs Aucassin, in accordance with Nicolette's specification, that he will have to find the 'beast' within three days, if he is to be healed (XVIII, 32-34; XXII, 36-39). Aucassin's arrogance in attempting to impose his will on the shepherd because of his superiority of rank contrasts strongly with Saul's diffidence in regard to his modest family background; both men are alike, however, in having to be prodded into acceptance of their destined roles.

Saul and his servant, in the place of honor, dine with Samuel and about thirty guests. Later Samuel and Saul converse, and the next morning the prophet prepares to send Saul away with 'the word of God' (9: 22-27). Samuel then anoints Saul, and reveals to him the signs which will confirm that the offer of kingship is from God.

> Then Samuel took the vial of oil, and poured it upon his head, and kissed him, and said: 'Is it not that the Lord *hath anointed thee* [ki-*meshachacha*] to be prince over His inheritance? When thou art departed from me to-day, then thou shalt find two men by the tomb of Rachel, in the border of Benjamin at Zelzah; and they will say unto thee: The asses which thou wentest to seek are found; and, lo, thy father hath left off caring for the asses, and is anxious concerning you, saying: What shall I do for my son? Then shalt thou go on forward from thence, and thou shalt come to the terebinth of Tabor, and there shall meet thee there three men going up to God to Beth-el, one carrying three kids, and another carrying three loaves of bread, and another carrying a bottle of wine. And they will salute thee, and give thee two cakes of bread; which thou shalt receive of their hand. After that thou shalt come to the hill of God, where is the garrison of the Philistines; and it shall come to pass, when thou art come thither to the city, that thou shalt meet a band of prophets coming down from the high place with a psaltery, and a timbrel, and a pipe, and a harp, before them; and they will be prophesying. And the spirit of the Lord will come mightily upon thee, and thou shalt prophesy with them, and shalt be turned into another man [*le'ish acher*]. And let it be, when these signs are come unto thee, that thou do as thy hand shall find; for God is with thee. And thou shalt go down before me to Gilgal; and, behold, I will come down unto thee, to offer burnt-offerings, and to sacrifice sacrifices of peace-offerings; seven days shalt thou tarry, till I come unto thee, and tell thee what thou shalt do'
>
> (10: 1-8).

The cool indifference, even rudeness, with which the shepherds treat Aucassin, not even inviting him to share their simple meal, inverts the honor shown to Saul and his servant by Samuel in a banquet-hall among many guests. Who would suspect that the intent of the scene is to anoint Aucassin, investing him, like Saul, with royal power? Yet the first sign mentioned by Samuel applies equally to both;

they are told that the lost beasts they are hunting have been, or can be, found. It must comfort Aucassin too, to learn that his father, like Saul's, has stopped worrying about the 'beast' Nicolette, the equivalent of the asses—or will stop when she is found—and is now anxious concerning him. The second sign is obliquely inverted: Saul is to meet three men who will give him two 'cakes of bread'[17]; it is Aucassin who gives money to the shepherds, with which—if they use it in the same way as the money given them by Nicolette—they will purchase *gastelés* 'cakes' (XXI, 12) among other things, including some musical instruments. Substituting *flaüsteles* 'flutes', *cornés* 'cornets', and *pipés* 'pipes', for the psaltery, timbrel, pipe, and harp, the shepherds can as readily prophesy to the accompaniment of music appropriate to their time, as Samuel's 'band of prophets' in their period, thus accounting for Samuel's third sign.

The poet has compressed the three signs for Aucassin into a single time, place, and group of participants, concentrating attention on the major import of the scene: when the spirit of the Lord does come upon him, as a result of the shepherd-seer's, or Samuel's prophecy, he will become 'another man' [*ish acher*]. This is summed up in the conclusion of the capsulation.

> And it was so, that when he had turned his back to go from Samuel, God gave him another *heart* [*lev* acher]; and all those signs came to pass that day
>
> (10:9).

Saul, Aucassin's prototype, is given 'another heart' [*lev acher*], and rises to royal stature, attended by victories over Israel's enemies. In the aftermath, however, he fails to measure up to his responsibilities as man, king, and servant of God. The consequences for Israel and for the house of Saul son of Kish are disastrous. Samuel reports that because Saul has rejected the word of the Lord, the Lord rejects him (15: 23) and repents having made him king over Israel (15: 35). The people of Israel, in the person of Aucassin, have need of 'another heart' and a new ruling house; meanwhile they have grave cause to fear the appearance of dark shadows looming on their horizon.

APPEARANCE AND THE OXHERD IN THE FOREST

Aucassin has understood Nicolette's message, transmitted by the shepherds, and pursues his way through the forest in search of the 'beast' that can heal him, amusingly[18] aware of its identity as his beloved. The abrupt appearance, looming on his horizon, of a tall, dark, and ugly stranger, whose repulsive features are crowned by a huge mop of coal-black hair and whose menace is increased by the enormous club upon which he leans, fills our hero with fear, *s'eut grant paor* (XXIV, 23). The two tensely exchange greetings and then begin to question each other. Aucassin wants to know what the ugly giant is doing here, and is asked in turn[19] what business it is of his. The stranger then wants to know why Aucassin is weeping and grieving, and is asked in turn whether he knows who Au-

cassin is. The fearsome giant, who shows that he does know him, indicates his readiness to strike a bargain: if Aucassin will reveal why he is weeping, he will tell what he is doing here. Aucassin agrees, but—as Garin did to him in the bargain of a kiss from Nicolette as reward for his services in the war against Bougars (X, 40-58)—breaks his word by telling a lie. He explains that he is weeping because he has lost a white hound, with which he was hunting this morning. Hearing this, the stranger becomes truly angry; he is a man with real troubles. He is an oxherd, in charge of a drove of four oxen, one of which he somehow misplaced three days ago (XXIV, 50)—the time period is the same for Saul's lost asses and for Aucassin's lost 'beast'—and now faces not only debtor's prison for himself but, much worse, the loss of his poor old mother's last possession, the very mattress under her back. Small wonder that he bursts into profanity.

> '. . . *por le cuer*[20] que cil Sires eut en sen ventre! que vos plorastes por un cien puant?'
>
> (XXIV, 42-43)

Aucassin's statement about the 'white[21] hound' is apparently a lie, but can one judge by appearances?

The parastructural counterpart scene, again in First Samuel, continues the story of Israel's quest for a king, and describes Samuel's selection of David[22] as the successor to Saul, in response to a command of the Lord.

> And the Lord said unto Samuel: 'How long wilt thou mourn for Saul, seeing I have rejected him from being king? fill thy horn with oil, and go, I will send thee to Jesse the Beth-lehemite; for I have provided Me a king *among* his sons [*be*-vanav]'
>
> (16: 1).

Aucassin, in his encounter with the oxherd (a prophet in disguise and in the role of Samuel), is reliving the founding of the house of David, the line from which the Messiah will issue. But while it is the prophet who mourns in the Biblical account, by normal inversion it is Aucassin, not the oxherd, who expresses such grief, *si fait duel* (XXIV, 31) in the *chantefable*.

Samuel, the messenger of the Lord, hesitates to do as told, for fear of what Saul may do to him.

> And Samuel said: 'How can I go?[23] if Saul hear it, he will kill me'
>
> (16:2)

In the continuing pattern of inversion, it is Aucassin, no the oxherd-prophet, who displays fear. Like Samuel, however, his true fear is not of death but of his possible failure to be able to carry out his designated mission, given the powerful and threatening obstacle in his path. Since Aucassin feels the same fear as Samuel, at the same time that the oxherd represents Samuel, Aucassin and the oxherd may be considered one combined personality, the oxherd being that part of it which hears the voice of the Lord, knows what has to be done, yet hesitates through lack of sufficient confidence.

The Lord instructs Samuel in how to proceed to avoid the discovery which might wreck his true mission.

> And the Lord said: 'Take a heifer with thee, and say: I am come to sacrifice to the Lord. And call Jesse to the sacrifice, and I will tell thee what thou shalt do; and thou shalt anoint [*u'mashachta*] unto Me him whom I name unto thee'
>
> (16: 2-3).

Aucassin again inverts the model; he is the one who prevaricates, rather than the oxherd-prophet. But if, like Samuel, he equivocates for fear of discovery, unlike him, he fails to take an important precaution. Samuel's heifer, as well as the oxherd's ox, are concrete realities, giving substance to the appearance[24] of truth in their stories; Aucassin's reference to the 'white hound', on the other hand, though figuratively meaningful, is concretely a lie, and thus not only potentially dangerous where subterfuge is needed but also a direct violation of the commandment to be truthful.

Upon arrival at his destination, Samuel is greatly impressed by Jesse's eldest son, and believes he has found the right man to succeed Saul.

> And Samuel did that which the Lord spoke, and came to Beth-lehem. (. . .) And he sanctified Jesse and his sons, and called them to the sacrifice. And it came to pass, when they were come, that he beheld Eliab, and said: 'Surely the Lord's anointed [*meshiycho*] is before Him'
>
> (16: 4-6).

Eliab's noble stature and extremely handsome features give rise to Samuel's hasty assumption that this man, whom God will reject for this purpose, is to be the *meshiach*, the human[25] Messiah, destined to rule Israel as the Lord's anointed. Conversely, at first sight, Aucassin equally hastily assumes from the oxherd's monstrous stature and extremely hideous features that this man, who is a messenger of the Lord, intends to harm him. Aucassin and Samuel commit the same fundamental error: they judge from outward appearances.

The capsulation concludes with the lesson which Samuel—and Aucassin after him—should draw from this illustrative incident.

> But the Lord said unto Samuel: 'Look not on his countenance, or on the height of his stature; because I have rejected him; for it is not as man seeth: for man looketh on the outward appearance, but the Lord looketh on the heart [la'*levav*]'
>
> (16: 7).

The *meshiach* is not to be Eliab, for all his imposing appearance, but David, Jesse's youngest son, whose greatness, concealed from the eyes of men though not of God,

is in his heart. Aucassin, representative of the Jewish people in Exile and a *schlemiel*[26] in the eyes of the world—including himself in times of despair (as when he first meets the oxherd)—is as unlikely a choice for the role of the Messiah, or *moshel be'Yisrael,* as David himself at the beginning of his career; fortunately, God can look in his heart.

The oxherd incident is a major turning point for Aucassin. For the first time, he ceases to brood in self—pity and opens his heart to another's tale of woe. When the oxherd ends by cursing Aucassin, the latter—astonishingly in the surface story—responds with a blessing.

> 'Certes, tu es de bon confort, biax frere; que benois soies tu!'
>
> (XXIV, 63-64).

The parastructural comfort derives from the fact that Aucassin has understood the prophetic message: the oxherd's predicament is not, as it may seem, a random event, but rather a symbol of the injustice suffered by the poor, who desperately need a *moshel be' Yisrael* to relieve their distress; and it is a task which he can—and must—fulfill. Aucassin gives the oxherd money to pay for the lost ox. He has also given money to the shepherds, but the two acts, similar in appearance, are different in quality. One was a bribe, to induce the shepherds to give up something (information) against their will; a ruler who does this exceeds his authority and oppresses his people. The other is an act of justice, relieving oppression and showing a ruler's obedience to God. Aucassin's parting from the shepherds and from the oxherd reflects this difference; the former could not care less whether Aucassin and Nicolette were reunited or not; the latter prays that Aucassin may find what he seeks (XXIV, 69-70). Our hero is on the way to redemption.

REDEMPTION AND THE KING OF TORELORE

Aucassin's initiative in relieving the oxherd's misery is soon rewarded when he comes upon Nicolette's bower in the forest. Life, however, is full of ups and downs for fallible man; although Aucassin should have learned—from the oxherd incident—to moderate his obsession, once again, as in his capture by Bougars' men, he is thinking of nothing but Nicolette, and falls from his 'high horse' (XXIV, 82-85). As if in retribution for this act of idolatry and other sins[27], he dislocates his shoulder. The joyful first reunion takes place and, after Nicolette heals his wound, the two board a merchant-ship which transports them, in a storm, to the fabulous land of Torelore. They learn there that the king of this strange country is lying in childbed. The sight of the king in this condition[28] finally unmasks Aucassin to himself; while Nicolette, for the first time, plays the secondary role, he moves masterfully into the lead. The question he addresses to the 'pregnant' king is one which the poet wishes his readers to examine attentively.

> . . . si parla; oés que dist:
> 'Di va! fau, que fais tu ci?'
>
> (XXIX, 6-7).

This is the same question his mother has asked him, in trying to turn him away from his obsession with Nicolette, that is, to keep him from the *eshes ra*, the 'evil woman' of idolatry, in the lesson of *Tora . . . le'ra* (above, p. 6).

> 'Di va! faus, que vex tu faire?'
>
> (III, 7).

Aucassin can finally see himself, through his mother's eyes, as the king of Torelore, the 'unwise son'[29] [*hu-ben lo chacham*], the man in the 'throes of a travailing woman', carrying a heavy burden of sin. Since Aucassin is Solomon and his father Garin is David, his mother is Bathsheba[30]; and since Aucassin is temporarily reliving the role of David, the second king of Israel, who better than she knows the terrible burden of guilt he bears, a guilt—the premeditated murder of Uriah the Hittite—attributable above all to the *eshes ra*. Aucassin stands greatly in need of the Lord's redeeming forgiveness.

The forgiveness is provided in the wild melee which follows, when the king of Torelore explains[31] that he is giving birth to a son, 'Je gis d'un fil' (XXIX, 8), and is beaten almost to death by a seemingly enraged Aucassin, wielding a providential rod that happens to be lying about. The elucidation of this strange behavior requires a preliminary[32] explanation of the Hebrew meaning of Aucassin's name, which is an acronym—homophonous with the Arabic name Al-Kâsim—taken from a verse of Ecclesiastes.

> *al-*tvahel bruchacha li'chos ki *kaas* be'cheik ksil*im* yanuach:
> *Be not* hasty in thy spirit to be angry;
> For *anger* resteth in the bosom of fool*s*
>
> (7: 9).

The combination of *al-* 'not', *kaas* 'anger', and *-im* (the morpheme of plurality) yields *al-* . . . *kaas* . . . *-im,* that is, *Al-kaas-im,* capsulating its own message (the pronunciation would normally be transformed into *Aucassin* in Old French). This hasty anger, which betrays itself when Aucassin, in his foolish period, commits his inexcusable act of treachery against Garin in alliance with Bougars, is present in the Torelore incident only in appearance.

The providential rod with which Aucassin 'beats' the king of Torelore is the profane expression—outwardly surprising in one of his rank—that he uses to flay his 'victim'.

> 'Par[33] le cuer Diu!' fait Aucassins, 'malvais fix a putain,
> je vos ocirai, se vos ne m'afiés que ja mais hom en vo
> tere d'enfant ne gerra'
>
> (XXX, 7-9).

The expression *fix a putain* denotes that the king of Torelore, who represents the sinful portion of Aucassin's character given to idolatrous adultery or adulterous idolatry, is subject to the *eshes ra,* the 'evil woman. Our hero, whom the poet has described as *soupris d'Amor* (II, 15), so obsessed with Love that he places it above God and refuses

to do anything he should, now redeems himself completely through *par . . . le . . . cuer,* a capsulation which, like the two other expressions of profanity, directs the reader to First Samuel. The prophet this time is addressing all the people of Israel.

> And Samuel said *unto* the people [*el*-ha'am]: 'Fear *not* [*al*-tira'u]; ye have indeed done all this evil; yet turn not aside from following the Lord, but serve the Lord with all *your heart* [be'chol *levavechem*] . . .'
>
> (12: 20).

Aucassin, taking Samuel as witness, renounces the evil he has done and pronounces the redemption of Israel. Henceforth, he will not love Nicolette less, since God loves lovers too (*Dix . . . qui les amans ainme,* XXVI, 12), but he will place God first, loving Him with all his heart, and not turn aside from following him. In reward, Nicolette, the beloved Homeland, will come to him in final and permanent reunion, once he has satisfied the Lord that he can truly distinguish between the sacred and the profane.

Notes

1. *Aucassin et Nicolette: Chantefable du moyen âge,* ed. Mario Roques, 2nd. rev. (Paris, 1969). For additional analyses of the *chantefable,* see Dorfman, *Parody and parable in Aucassin et Nicolette: A Narremic and Parastructural Analysis* (in preparation); "Tora Lore in Torelore: A Parastructural Analysis", in *Papers in Linguistics* and *Child Language: Memorial Volume for Ruth Hirsch Weir* (Mouton, forthocoming); "The Flower in the Bower: *Garris* in *Aucassin et Nicolette*", pp. 77-87 in *Studies in Honor of Mario A. Pei,* eds. John Fisher and Paul A. Gaeng (Chapel Hill, North Carolina, 1972); "Aucassin and the Pilgrim of 'Limosin': A Bilingual Pun", *Festschrift for Archibald A. Hill* (forthcoming); and "The Lamp of the Commandment in *Aucassin et Nicolette*", *Hebrew University Studies in Literature* (forthcoming).

2. In the scene where Aucassin declares a possible preference for Hell ever Heaven (VI, 24-39), it is not God who is mentioned but the kind of people who seem destined for the one place or the other.

3. *Le Rire et le sourire dans le roman courtois en France au moyen âge, 1150-1250* (Genève, 1969), pp. 713-14.

4. See A. Micha, "En relisant *Aucassin et Nicolette*", MA 14 (1959), 279-92, p. 284.

5. For instances of parody, taken individually, see Omer Jodogne, "La Parodie et le pastiche dans *Aucassin et Nicolette*", CAIF 12 (1960), 53-65; Robert Harden, "*Aucassin et Nicolette* as Parody", 63 (1966), 1-9.

The parody goes beyond content, that is, the superstructural incidents as they occur in the story, to the form itself, the narremic core, or substructure, as an organic whole. Surprisingly in so brief a narrative, and uniquely in medieval literature (so far as this author is aware), all four types of narremic substructure described in Dorfman. *The Narreme in the Medieval Romance Epic: An Introduction to Narrative Structure* (Toronto, 1969) are represented: the Epic of Prowess, the Epic of Treachery, the Romance of the Lovers' Quarrel, and the Romance of the Lovers'— Triangle Quarrel; see pp. 19-21, 50, 58, 64, 72-75.

See also *Parody and Parable,* and "Tora Lore in Torelore".

6. See Micha, pp. 286; Harden, p. 4.

7. For a treatment of the controversy, see Leo Spitzer, "Le Vers 2 d'Aucassin et Nicolette et le sens de la chantefable", MP 45 (1947-1948), 8-14, and "*Aucassin et Nicolette,* Line 2, Again", MP 48 (1950-1951), 154-56. For the Hebraic aspect, see *Parody and Parable,* and "Tora Lore in Torelore".

8. Unless the reader is given advance notice—which may have been the situation for a special cicle in the anonymous poet's day—it is not likely that the phrase by itself would create suspicion of a reference to a Hebrew source. A key, based on the secret meaning of the name *Torelore,* is needed to prompt a rereading of the text from the beginning.

Biblical citations are from: *The Holy Scriptures, according to the Masoretic Text* (Philadelphia, 1965), and *Sefer Tora Neviyim u'Ketuvim,* ed. N. H. Snaith (London, 1965). Hebrew consonants are transliterated according to Ashkenazic pronunciation, since internal linguistic evidence, based un several Franco-Hebrew puns, requires the articulation of the letter *sof* as [s] rather than the Sephardic [t]. For the one exception, and its Sephardic justification, see below, n. 22.

9. In view of competing aspirants for the role of Messiah, who may be credited with the atribute of divinity, the poet stresses, in his oblique way, that the future *moshel be'Yisrael* is human. Lying in prison for his act of treachery against his father. Aucassin one day has a prophetic vision of a pilgrim, ill with *esvertin*—a malady of the spirit identical with the *folie* with which Aucassin's father challenges him (X, 40-41)—who is completely healed when Nicolette lifts her skirt and displays to him her leg, that limb of the 'beast' which, as she has informed the shepherds of Beaucaire, is the medicine needed to cure Aucassin of his illness (XVIII, 30-31). The pilgrim is thus Aucassin himself, the *moshel be'Yisrael* in exile, and Nicolette is the goal for which he yearns, the beloved Land of Israel (this identification is reinforced again and again), the mere sight of whose limb is sufficient to get him off his sickbed and back to his own land:

> si se leva de son lit,
> si rala en son pais
> sains et saus et tos garis

> (XI, 29-31).

Once it is established that the pilgrim is Aucassin, the apparently gratuitous information that he was born in Limosin, *nes estoit de Limosin* (XI, 17), becomes parastructurally functional through a hybrid Franco-Hebrew pun, combining *li* 'the' (Old French definite article, masculine plural) and *mosim* 'people' (< heb. *mas* 'man, person', pl. *mosin* [*mosim*] 'people'); the *sof* must here be read as [s]. The messianic pilgrim, who will cease his wandering and, in the person of Aucassin, will lead his nation back to their own land, 'was born of the people'. See "Aucassin and the Pilgrim of 'Limosin'."

The form *mosin,* or *mosey* [mosey] in the construct case, evokes a passage in Psalms singularly relevant to the distress of the pilgrim, ill with *esvertin* through persecution.

> When they were but a few *men* in number [*mosey* mispar].
> Yea, very few, and sojourners in it [Canaan],
> And when they went about from nation to nation,
> From one kingdom to another people,
> He suffered no man to do them wrong,
> Yea, for their sake He reproved kings:
> 'Touch not *Mine annointed ones* [al-tiggu vi'*meshichay*],
> And do My prophets no harm'

> (105: 12-15).

Aucassin, a man 'in prison' through his own fault (placing earthly Love above God), can change, if he wills it, and become the *mashiach,* one of the Lord's annointed, chosen in his case to relieve his people of their homelessness.

10. See Raphael Levy, *Contribution à la lexicographie française selon d'anciens textes d'origine juive* (Syracuse, 1960); and *Trésor de la langue des Juifs français au moyen âge* (Austin, 1964).

11. The writer, who was not alerted and had no suspicion of a Hebraic content in the *chantefable,* proceeded in reverse order. The need to explain the narremic relationship between the insult which motivated the acts of prowess and the peculiar doings in Torelore where the hero should theoretically demonstrate that he has mastered the lesson implied in the insult led to the conclusion that something occult was taking place in Torelore, possibly bound up with the name. Its resemblance to *Tora ora* suggested the passages in Esther and Proverbs, and led back to *deport* and the coda of the exordium.

12. A similar use is made of the French morpheme *me* 'me, myself', homophonous with Heb. *me-* 'from', which stands before two French forms, and signals: 'read a capsulation *from* the word directly following to the word after that'.

13. Since *cuerbé* is a form of *cuer Diu,* the capsulation begins with *por,* Heb. *be-* 'in, at, on, among, within, into, with, by; of, through, when, while; because of, as' (with appropriate morphological variation as required, e.g. *ba-, bi-,* etc.), and continues on to *cuer,* Heb. *lev* 'heart' (with whatever affixes may be

necessary). See Reuben Alcalay, *Complete Hebrew-English Dictionary* (Tel Aviv, Jerusalem, 1965).

14. Beaucaire is identified as the Land of Canaan, or Israel, symbolically represented by a Nicolette given to idolatry, through a capsulation in Hosea based on the innocently formulaic description of the object of Aucassin's love, *s'amie o le vis cler* (VII, 3). The *le* in *o . . . le . . . vis* signals a passage capsulated between *o*, Heb. *be-*, and *vis*, Heb. *panim*, descriptive of Nicolette, in which Hosea excoriates his people.

For the spirit of harlotry is *within* them [*be'kirbam*], . . .

And the pride of Israel testifieth *to his face* [*be'fanav*];
But they have not returned unto the Lord their God,
Nor sought Him, for all this

(5: 4-7: 10).

Midway between these verses is Hosea's apostrophe to wicked Ephraim and Judah, the northern and southern kingdoms.

O Ephraim, what shall I do unto thee?
O Judah, what shall I do unto thee?
For your goodness is as a *morning cloud* [*ka'anan-boker*],
And as the dew that early passeth away

(6: 4).

The phrase *ka'anan-boker* (composed of the preposition *ka-* 'like', *anan* 'cloud', and *boker* 'morning') is a pun on the names 'Canaan', Heb. *Kena'an,* and 'Beaucaire', Hebrew pronunciation *Boker;* the juxtaposition of *Kena'an-Boker,* that is, Canaan-Beaucaire, reveals that Beaucaire is actually the Land of Canaan, the Promised Land, the *amie o le vis cler,* without which Aucassin cannot live.

The poet repeats this identification of Beaucaire with Canaan and with an idolatrous Nicolette through a second capsulation in Hosea, based on Nicolette's prison lament, in which she apostrophizes her lover:

'ja sui jo li vostre amie
et vos ne *me haés mie . . .*'

(V, 18-19).

The *me* in *me . . . haés . . . mie* signals a relevant passage starting from (that is, Heb. *me-*) a form of the verb *haés,* Heb. *sana* 'hate', and ending with a morpheme of negation, *mie,* Heb. *lo* or *eyn* 'not' (*ne . . . mie* is the standard form of negation in the text, with thirty-four occurrences, compared with only one of *ne . . . pas*). Once again, as the capsulation begins, Hosea flays his people; this time, for their pagan practices at the sanctuary of Gilgal.

All their wickedness is in Gilgal,
For there *I hated them* [*s'nesim*];
Because of the wickedness of their doings

I will drive them out of My house;
I will love them *no* [*lo*] more,
All their princes are rebellious

(9: 15).

Nicolette's declaration in the negative, that Aucassin, her future lord, does not hate her, inverts the Lord's affirmative statement; in her later test of Aucassin's love, at the bower, she will likewise invert the Shulamite's affirmative 'I am my beloved's, and my beloved is mine' into its negative (see "The Flower in the Bower", pp. 84-85).

The capsulation concludes with a description of the 'rebellious prince', directly relevant to the situation at Torelore.

The iniquity of Ephraim is bound up;
His sin is laid up in store.
The throes of a travailing woman shall come upon him;
He is an *un*wise son [*hu-ben lo chacham*];
For it is time he should *not* [*lo*] tarry
In the place of the breaking forth of children

(13: 12-13).

Aucassin is the 'unwise son' who rejects the instruction of his parents concerning *Tora or* and 'the way of life', and must consequently expiate his sin in the guise of the king of Torelore, that is, 'in the throes of a travailing woman'. Hosea spells out the sin which has reduced Israel from its former glory to its present plight.

When Ephraim spoke, there was trembling,
He exalted himself in Israel;
But when he became guilty through Ball, he died . . .

Therefore they shall be as the *morning cloud* [*ka'anan-boker*] . . .

(13: 3).

The *amie* whom Aucassin 'does not hate', whom he loves, in fact, above God Himself, is thus again identified, through *ka'anan-boker*, as *Kena'an-Boker,* Canaan-Beaucaire.

Nicolette's identification with the Land of Canaan, or Israel, is prefigured from the beginning, when the poet announces that his hero will suffer great pains and perform deeds of prowess *por s'amie o le cler vis* (I, 7). The *le* in *o . . . le . . . cler* signals a capsulation in the Song of Songs, beginning with *be-* and ending with *cler,* Heb. *bar,* f. *bara* 'clear'.

'I am my beloved's, and my beloved is mine,
That feedeth *among* the lilies [*ba*-shoshanim].'
Thou art beautiful, O my love, as Tirzah,
Comely as Jerusalem . . .

Who is she that looketh forth as the dawn,
Fair as the moon,
Clear [*bara*] as the sun. . . ?

(6; 3-10).

In part, Nicolette represents the Shulamite, recognizable by the lilies with which she adorns her bower; but she also symbolizes Tirzah and Jerusalem, the beautiful capitals of the northern and southern kingdoms. The apposition of *amie* with *o le cler vis* and *o le vis cler*, supplemented by *me haés mie*, leaves no room for doubt that Aucassin's *amie* is the Promised Land.

For the use of the name 'Canaan' by the Jews in reference to Israel, see Abba Eban, *My People* (New York, 1968), p. 19; in reference to a land in the Exile, see Roman Jakobson and Morris Halle. "The Term 'Canaan' in Medieval Hebrew', in *For Max Weinreich on His Seventieth Birthday: Studies in Jewish Languages, Literature, and Society* (The Hague, 1964), p. 148.

15. Samuel's hesitation to accede to the people's request for a king, with all its implications of assimilation to the vices of the neighboring nations, including idolatry, is well founded; but the Lord, who is equally displeased, orders him to 'hearken unto their voice' (see 8: 6-9). (For a description of the evils of monarchical rule, see 8: 11-18.) The surface indifference of the shepherd-seer to the fate of Aucassin and Nicolette—'hunt the beast if you wish, or let it alone, as you please' (XXII, 39-40)—may be considered a reflection of Saul's eventual inadequacy and failure as king.

16. The capsulation could theoretically end here, but succeeding verses, leading to another instance of 'heart', contain additional materials directly relevant to the story.

17. The word *lechem*, in *shtey-lechem* 'two cakes of bread', may be translated as 'bread' or 'cake'.

18. His mind on Nicolette, he muses thoughtfully:

> '. . . por vos sui venus en bos;
> je ne cac ne cerf ne porc . . .'
>
> (XXIII, 10-11).

The readers who have been following the signals in Hebrew can smilingly agree the 'beast' he seeks is neither stag nor pig, but one of the kosher variety.

19. One of the characteristic traits of Jewish conversation is the repeated use of questions as the response to questions.

20. See above, n. 13.

21. The whiteness of the 'hound' is that of Nicolette, *tant par estoit blance la mescinete* (XII, 28), and of her healing hands, *ses blances mains* (XXVI, 11) which easily straightened Aucassin's dislocated shoulder.

22. David, whose role is being filled for the moment by Aucassin, is symbolized in the *chantefable* by Garin, pronounced [gari]. He identifies himself as such in a capsulation from First Chronicles (28: 1-29: 19), based on *vers . . . le . . . palais* (VII, 6), that is,

from '*unto* Jerusalem [*el*-Yerushalayim] . . . to . . . the *palace* [ha'*bira*]', which describes his handing over to his son Solomon the task of building the Temple. Embedded in the passage is the well known verse:

> 'For we are *strangers* [*gerim*] before Thee, and sojourners, as all our fathers were . . .'
>
> (29: 15).

Garin, pronounced as the poet would, thus stands for David, representing the *gerim* (plural of Heb. *ger*); and these would be the Jews, 'strangers' in France and in the world of the Diaspora.

David likewise reveals the meaning of Nicolette's surprisingly Hebrew name. Aucassin has refused to defend his land or his people, except at a price:

> '. . . se vos ne *me donés Nicholete* . . .'
>
> (II, 26).

The capsulation in First Samuel (18: 17-26), based on *me . . . donés . . . Nicholete,* that is, 'from . . . (a form of) Heb. *nasan* 'give' . . . (to) *Nicholete* [*nikel-et*]', recounts Saul's offer of his daughter Merab in marriage to David, and David's modest disclaimer of merit.

> And David said: 'Seemeth it to you a light thing to be the king's son-in-law, seeing that I am a poor man, and *lightly esteemed* [ve'*nikele*]?'
>
> (18: 23).

Nicolette, also called Nichole (XXXIII, 2; XXXVII, 1; XXXIX, 11) and Nicole (V, 1) in the text, is a poor girl and, like David, she is *nikele,* that is, 'lightly esteemed' by Garin (David), her prospective father-in-law. Saul has made the offer, which involves a hundred foreskins of the Philistines as bride-price, only as bait to get David killed by the enemy; but it is a challenge David accepts gladly, as the capsulation closes.

> And when his [Saul's] servants told David these words [*et-ha'dvarim ha'ele*], it pleased David well to be the king's son-in-law
>
> (18: 26).

There is a stroke of genius in the communal humor of the *et-*, the untranslatable Hebrew morpheme signifying a specific, direct object. It is written with *sof,* and therefore the morpheme would normally be read as *es-* in an Ashkenazic community (see above, n. 8); since it connects with *nikele* (18: 23) to form *nikel-et* (Nicolette), it must here be read with the Sephardic [t]—the only such occurrence in the text—and thus marks the heroine as a 'foreigner' from the Eastern community (she is from Carthage). The verses in the capsulation between *donés* and *nikele* concern the *giving* of the bride (Merab-Nicolette); those between *nikele* and *et-* (Nicolette as *nekel-et*) set the bride price; the *et-* itself, however, points to the phrase *these words,* which introduces the notion of David's pleasure in becoming the king's son-in-law, a sentiment Nicolette hopes to share in becoming the king's daughter-in-law through marriage with Aucassin. Since Garin is David, father of Solomon, and Nicolette has been previously identified (above, n. 14) with the Shulamite, beloved of Solomon, her desire to become Garin's (David's) daughter-in-law is consistent both superstructurally and parastructurally.

23. See S. Goldman, *Samuel: Hebrew Text with English Translation with an Introduction and Commentary* (London, 1967), p. 93, n. 2: "*how can I go? Samuel does not fear death at the hand of Saul; but if that were to happen to him, the mission on which he was being sent would not be fulfilled.*"

24. The example may have furnished the poet's readers the occasion to discuss the thorny problem of truth, and how it may be stretched for the preservation of life, especially with regard to such pressures as forced conversion, the incrimination of others in interrogations by persecuting authorities, etc.

25. See above, n. 9.

26. For *schlemiel* and *moshel be 'Yisrael,* see above, p. 4.

27. Parastructurally, Aucassin violates every one of the Ten Commandments as he tries to master the art of becoming a righteous 'ruler in Israel', capable of restoring his dispersed people to their ancient Homeland; see "The Lamp of the Commandment".

28. For the figure of the 'travailing woman' as the symbol of sin, see above, n. 14. For frequent use of the same simile or metaphor, see Isaiah, 13: 8, 21: 3, 26: 17, 42: 14; Jeremiah, 4: 31, 6: 24; 13: 21, 22: 23, 30: 6, 31: 8, 48: 41, 49: 22, 49: 24, 50: 43; Micah, 4: 9, 4: 10; Psalms, 48: 7.

29. The 'son' is in the singular, but represents Ephraim, that is, the people of Israel, collectively; see above, n. 14. In the same way, Aucassin represents Solomon, but also David and all the others whose histories he relieves, through Bourgars, the shepherds, the oxherd, the king of Torelore, etc., as a kind of Everyman.

30. The story of David and Bathsheba is introduced quite early, in connection with the war against Beaucaire, as a capsulation from Second Samuel, based on *de le vile* (II, 3-4), that is, 'from Heb. *me-* 'from' . . . to . . . Heb. *ir* 'city', see 11:2 - 12:30.

31. For a line by line interpretation of the king's parastructural message, rich in unexpected wit, see *Parody and Parable,* and "Tora Lore in Torelore".

32. The meaning of Aucassin's name is signalled through an angry outburst of Garin's, directed at the viscount; it is based on *je . . . le . . . puis* (IV, 7), that is, 'from Heb. *ani* 'I' . . . to . . . a form of Heb. *yochal* 'can, be able', taken from Ecclesiastes, 1: 12 - 7: 13; the long, enveloping capsulation is broken up into several, smaller ones, in the last of which is found the acronym.

For the Arabic name Al-Kâasim, see Robert Griffin, "*Aucassin et Nicolette* and the Albigensian Crusade", *Modern Language Quarterly,* 26 (1965), 243-56, p. 247.

33. See above, n. 13; the shepherds' and the oxherd's oaths begin with *por,* Aucassin's with *par.* The capsulation for the letter may therefore begin with a different, though related, preposition. *Par* may be Heb. *el-* 'to, unto, at, by', or *al-* (with *ayin*) 'on, upon, above, over; by, near; to, unto, towards, against', etc.; or it may, through a pun on the latter, be *al-* 'no, not; do not' (as in *al-tira'u*).

It is difficult to determine whether the poet expected his readers to select the one best passage from the Bible when several might be seen to be somehow relevant, or to combine a few in each case (where possible) in order to produce a protean parastructure. It is probably safe to assume, however, that the central purpose was not the linear organization of the relevant passage—true though this must have been for the narremic structure (see above, n. 5)—but the opportunity to study the Bible for content. In any event, a second *par . . . le . . . cuer* capsulation, quite relevant, but not treated here for lack of space, may be found in Jeremiah, 30: 1-21.

Anne Elizabeth Cobby (essay date 1995)

SOURCE: "*Aucassin et Nicolette,*" in *Ambivalent Conventions: Formula and Parody in Old French,* Rodopi, 1995, pp. 55-81.

[*In the following essay, Cobby argues that analyzing the manner in which the author manipulates his readers' expectations reveals the essentially parodic nature of Au-cassin et Nicolette.*]

Much has been written on ***Aucassin et Nicolette*** in the last hundred years, but alone among our texts it is at present not a very active field.[1] Work on parody in the text was surveyed thoroughly and critically by Tony Hunt in 1979, in an article which argues against its being a parodic work and calls attention most usefully to the dangers which beset parody scholarship in general; a more recent but brief survey is by Imre Szabics.[2] The presence of parody is now taken for granted by most critics, though the extent and significance attributed to it vary: from 'allusion pleine d'humour' to a parody of virtually every form of contemporary literature, or a specific exploitation of both Chrétien de Troyes and the romance of *Fergus.*[3] Particularly relevant to this chapter, since the author's implicit view of parody resembles mine, is an article by Reinhold Grimm on the use and parody of courtly norms.[4]

A few critics have analysed formulae and repetitions in the text. Renate Baader believes they prove the work was orally composed and summarily refuses to see parody in them.[5] Jean Trotin discusses the use of formulae to structure the narrative, Joan B. Williamson the repetition of naming formulae.[6] Repetitions and patterns of recurrence are a basic theme of Simone Monsonégo's book on the vocabulary of the text, and are important in two articles by Nathaniel B. Smith.[7] Smith links repetition with parody, seeing *Aucassin et Nicolete* as a 'burlesque directed against both the content and style of traditional literary genres'.[8]

The Establishment of Expectations

Whereas the parodic fabliaux, broadly speaking, use the language of courtly literature to establish their literary background, the author of *Aucassin et Nicolette* exploits above all its conceptual formulae. The work's use of the romance tradition is subtle, so that we need to bring to it sensitivity to its content, its literary context and the values of reality alike. On these three levels it is also comic, and its humour is not only an aim but also an aid to the direction of our judgement.

The essential part played by parody in this work is evident when we analyse the ways in which the author manipulates our expectations. He sets up a clear and repeated reference to the literary traditions of his day, to their conventions and, most importantly, to their assumptions; but he treats them in such a way as continually to thwart our expectations and to lead us to review the preconceptions we have as we deal with those traditions.[9] Here, as in the fabliaux, the audience's initial impressions are crucial; and the opening sections both establish relations and disorientate us by revealing that our expectations are not to be respected.

The text begins with a prologue which seems to give us a basis for prediction but which in fact sets up contradictory expectations:[10]

> Qui vauroit bons vers oïr
> Del deport du viel antif,
> De deus biax enfans petis,
> Nicholete et Aucassins,
> Des grans paines qu'il soufri
> Et des proueces qu'il fist
> Por s'amie o le cler vis,
> Dox est li cans, biax li dis
> Et cortois et bien asis.
> Nus hom n'est si esbahis,
> Tant dolans ni entrepris,
> De grant mal amaladis,
> Se il l'oit, ne soit garis
> Et de joie resbaudis,
> Tant par est douce.
>
> (I.1-15)

If we hope for deeds of prowess we are doomed to disappointment, but more significant than the announcement of the work's content are the wider expectations which are established indirectly; for the prologue sets the work in several literary traditions at once.[11] It affiliates it to the courtly romance (by announcing a tale of love and by characterising it as 'dox', 'biax', 'cortois'), to the *chanson*

de geste (by the use of assonance, the *laisse* form, the *vers orphelins* and the opening address to the audience) and to lyric verse (the seven-syllable line). The brevity of the lines undermines both the dignity of the epic reference and the elegance of the romance style, for the odd number of syllables and the frequently recurring assonance result in a limping metre and a playful effect.

In the second section we learn that the work combines prose and verse, which further distances the text from any one genre. The prose style is prolix, with adjectives and clauses being heaped up; whilst such prolixity is far from unusual in early Old French prose, there is a striking effect of contrast as the staccato verse is punctuated by the trailing prose sections. The first sections thus give a misleading summary of the tale to come and disorientate us stylistically and generically; and conceptual disorientation follows quickly. Indeed, the whole of the first part of the work (up to the first reunion of the lovers in section XXVI) is devoted to showing that our assumptions are not to be respected; the author continually evokes formulaic expectations based on our previous literary experience and then destroys them.

The Formula as the Mark of the External: Aucassin

Immediately after the prologue we are given a description of Aucassin. He is presented as the typical courtly lover, though already in the introductory portrait it is indicated that he falls short of the ideal, for a burlesque note runs through it:

> Aucasins avoit a non li damoisiax. Biax estoit et gens
> et grans et bien tailliés de ganbes et de piés et de cors
> et de bras. Il avoit les caviax blons et menus recercelés
> et les ex vairs et rians et le face clere et traitice et le
> nes haut et bien assis.
>
> (II.8-11)

The terms used are utterly standard, but there is a fundamental abnormality in the portrait.[12] For after the abstract and general opening we expect and are given a more detailed description; but the order of the elements is both unconventional and in visual terms jerky: legs, feet, body, arms, finally head. The description of the head is very traditional, and is repeated almost verbatim much later, for Nicolette: 'Ele avoit les caviaus blons et menus recercelés, et les ex vairs et rians, et le face traitice, et le nes haut et bien assis' (XII.14-15). The similarity of the two portraits—the only full-length descriptions of beauty in the work—makes clear that the author is inserting a set piece. The style of the passage enhances this impression. The feeling of breathless oversimplification, conveyed by the density of formulae strung together by repeated 'et', suggests on a stylistic level that reference is being made to a pre-existing standard portrait familiar to author and audience;[13] so too does the incoherent arrangement of the description of Aucassin, which gives the impression of elements being borrowed in random order. The implication is that there is no need to delay on a well-known stereotype;

this is always true, but unlike most authors of courtly portraits, the author of *Aucassin* does not even seek the illusion of originality that a leisurely description would give.[14]

Outwardly Aucassin is thus the incarnation of the stereotype, and to an exaggerated degree. His moral portrait, on the other hand, which (as tradition prescribes) follows the physical one, shows how he conforms to the letter of the stereotype but not to its spirit. This important aspect of the character of Aucassin is expressed here on a verbal, formulaic level: 'Mais si estoit soupris d'Amor, qui tout vaint, qu'il ne voloit estre cevalers, ne les armes prendre, n'aler au tornoi, ne fare point de quanque il deust' (II.12-14). On first hearing the formula 'Amor, qui tout vaint' we hardly notice it, except as an example of a tag which is so usual as to be virtually obligatory. Then, as the description of love's effects progresses, we realise that the label is being applied there in a way different from its normal use. Love is overcoming not obstacles, but the lover himself, so that far from being fired by it to do great things, he is led to shun his knightly duties.[15] It is true that this effect of love is both exemplified and recognised in the courtly romance;[16] but what is unusual and significant is that love is described in the most formulaic, courtly terms in a sentence which goes on to show its potential for negativity, and thus brings out an inherent contradiction. The formula 'Amor, qui tout vaint' is used without change in a context which causes us to see it semantically, and thus to realise that its formulaic meaning is only one of its possible senses, and very different from the one we have to give it here. As in many of our fabliau examples, the effect is to show how selective and unjustified our assumptions are. The courtly ideal of love is subjected to a similar process. Neither needs material alteration to bring out its negative aspects, which are within it but which our acceptance of the limited, conventional interpretation causes us to overlook. The reappraisal to which we are led reflects on us (we readily accept limited and preconceived expectations), on Aucassin (he is measured against the literary ideal called up by the use of the formula, and found wanting), and on the literary ideal (it is dismantled by having its lack of cogency made clear).

The basis of the character of Aucassin is his total conformity to the externals of the ideal hero, combined with his lack of the inner qualities usually associated with them. His description demolishes the assumption underlying all such portraits, namely that physical beauty coincides with and indicates moral worth. Aucassin is handsome according to the courtly rules, but he lacks one of the two fundamental courtly virtues, that of valour. The conventional association between this and the other fundamental virtue, love, is destroyed at the same time, for the latter is depicted as leading to the absence of the former.

It is the hallmark of Aucassin's behaviour that he adheres to externals only. This trait manifests itself in many forms, and notably in an incident which again describes Aucassin and which is a well-developed instance of deflation: his arming. The handsome, enamoured youth agrees to fight only when bribed by the promise that he will be allowed to see Nicolette if he does so (VIII). At this he is full of a formulaic joy: 'Por.c^m. mars d'or mier / Ne le fesist on si lié' (IX.3-4). The arming scene which follows is totally faithful to the literary convention:

> Garnemens demanda ciers,
> On li a aparelliés.
> Il vest un auberc dublier
> Et laça l'iaume en son cief,
> çainst l'espee au poin d'or mier,
> Si monta sor son destrier
> Et prent l'escu et l'espiel.
>
> (IX.5-11)

His hauberk and sword are characterised in typical epic formulae, and the whole traditional picture causes us to expect a warlike scene. But the tone is deflated at a blow, when Aucassin 'Regarda andex ses piés: / Bien si sissent es estriers. / A mervelle si tint ciers' (IX.12-14). Not only is self-satisfaction destructive of all the dignity which the scene has built up, but the contemplation of his feet is bathetic. As soon as the individual Aucassin plays a rôle, as soon as the general arming motif is superseded by the specific, the stereotype is shattered.

It is, however, rebuilt, to allow the story and the humour to continue. Aucassin exemplifies the courtly knight, externally at least:

> De s'amie li sovient,
> S'esperona li destrier.
> Il li cort mout volentiers,
> Tot droit a le porte en vient
> A la bataille.
>
> (IX.15-19)

To make the ensuing fight more ridiculous, the author stresses Aucassin's conformity to the stereotype:

> Aucassins fu armés sor son ceval, si con vos avés oï et entendu. Dix, con li sist li escus au col et li hiaumes u cief et li renge de s'espee sor le senestre hance! Et li vallés fu grans et fors et biax et gens et bien fornis, et li cevaus sor quoi il sist rades et corans, et li vallés l'ot bien adrecié par mi la porte.
>
> (X.1-5)

Yet one senses a touch of irony in the narrator's repetition, in his own voice, of Aucassin's admiration for his external appearance. The legitimate admiration of the narrator recalls the vainglorious self-admiration of Aucassin, and in this way it is itself undermined. Noble expectations are thus set up and destroyed, then re-formed only to have the destruction ironically recalled.

The beginning of Aucassin's military action, which follows, shows further examples of expectations—both linguistic and conceptual—being first established and then exploited, and it illustrates clearly how the author manipulates the reactions of his audience. Immediately after Aucassin is described, the register changes abruptly from the world and vocabulary of chivalry to those of agriculture: 'Or ne quidiés vous qu'il pensast n'a bués n'a vaces n'a civres prendre . . .' (X.6). The author plays a game with his audience, causing a series of jolting reappraisals. 'Or ne quidiés vous', he begins, to involve the audience and to stress by contrast what is to come. Aucassin the knight is not about to catch beasts; the differing style levels express the difference in worlds, for the animals mentioned are mundane, domestic ones, which, moreover, typify the middle and low styles according to Virgil's wheel and thereby affirm Aucassin's courtly superiority.[17] Our reaction to this exhortation is two-fold. On the one hand we expect an assurance that Aucassin has come to catch not beasts but the opposite, namely men. On the other, having just witnessed his arming, why should we be likely to think he was thus dressed to catch animals, and tame ones at that? The appeal seems gratuitous. But the game is not over. We are next thwarted in our expectations of a tale of great deeds: 'Or ne quidiés vous qu'il pensast n'a bués n'a vaces n'a civres prendre, ne qu'il ferist cevalier ne autres lui. Nenil nient! onques ne l'en sovint' (X.6-7). The author directs sarcasm both at an outlandish expectation, which we expect to hear denied, and at a normally legitimate one. The combination at first sight seems ridiculous, and so it would be with a true hero; but with Aucassin it is justified, for to expect valour from him is as ludicrous as to expect an armed knight to catch cattle and goats. Yet once more the conventional hero surfaces; when, having deduced that decapitation would prevent his speaking to Nicolette, he begins to fight, he does so in traditional style: 'Aucassins ne le mescoisi mie: il tint l'espee en la main, se le fiert par mi le hiaume si qu'i li enbare el cief' (X.26-27).

Aucassin, then, is presented as a character forever at odds with conventions to which he is yet closely linked; and through him we are kept in constant touch with our literary experience and expectations, whilst being shown that they are far from reliable. The author thus evokes the literary background necessary for his parody whilst distancing us from it sufficiently to appreciate his irony; the initial prominence of Aucassin, together with incongruities of detail, ensure that we are prepared from the start for his unconventional approach.

Aucassin's adherence to mere externals continues throughout the work. It is expressed, for example, in his choice of the conventional reaction over the appropriate one, when he finds the bower Nicolette has made (XXIV-XXV). On happening upon it and knowing it was of her making, anyone other than he would have set about looking to see if she were near. But he prefers to make a romantic address to a star, ignoring the reality before him in order to live out a literary response; he reacts to the convention of night as a subject for poetry rather than to the facts of his situation which demand that he search for Nicolette. Since the conventional response and the demands of reality in this instance are in direct opposition to each other, Aucassin's preference for the former is particularly striking, and his reaction particularly misguided.

Throughout the work he is found lamenting, so that we come to see him as one whom we expect to find weeping, and who would rather lament than help himself or be comforted; he chooses a superficial response rather than one requiring action. The predictability of his tears is stressed by the monotony of their expression:[18]

> Si comença a plorer
> Et grant dol a demener
> Et s'amie a regreter
>
> (VII.9-11)
>
> S'oï Aucassin plourer
> Et s'amie regreter
>
> (XIII.3-4)
>
> Si comença a plorer
>
> (XXIV.8)
>
> Il regretoit Nicolete s'amie
>
> (VIII.1)
>
> Aucassins faisoit deul et regretoit Nicolete sa tres douce
> amie que tant amoit
>
> (VIII.7-8)
>
> Si oï Aucassin qui la dedens plouroit et faisoit mot grant
> dol et regretoit se douce amie que tant amoit
>
> (XII.26-27)
>
> Si trova Aucassin qui ploroit et regretoit Nicolete s'amie.
>
> (XL.31-32)

And finally, in a typically courtly setting he has a typical courtly reaction:

> A Biaucaire sous la tor
> Estoit Aucassins un jor;
> La se sist sor un perron,
> Entor lui si franc baron.
> Voit les herbes et les flors,
> S'oit canter les oisellons;
> Menbre li de ses amors,
> De Nicholete le prox,
> Qu'il ot amee tans jors;
> Dont jete souspirs et plors.
>
> (XXXIX.1-10)

The monotony makes a point both within the work and externally. Aucassin's unwillingness to emerge from his grieving state both expresses his preference for inaction and exemplifies another formulaic aspect of his nature: his character and reactions hardly change throughout the work. This is because he incarnates a type, and types are constant. So, as we saw, the author expresses the standardness of the type of the hero by calling it up in detail not once but repeatedly. Indeed, Aucassin is described in similar terms twice in one battle: 'Li vallés fu grans et fors et biax et gens et bien fornis, et li cevaus sor quoi il sist rades et corans' (X.3-4), and 'Li vallés fu grans et fors, et li cevax so quoi il sist fu remuans' (X.19).[19] The repetitious depiction of Aucassin thus both conveys his repetitive and inactive character, and reflects on the literary stereotype and its conventionality within the tradition. For the author takes the convention to its logical conclusion. Since the courtly lover laments if crossed in love and Aucassin is permanently crossed in love, the author introduces lamentation wherever it is at all apposite, and that is most of the time; and since the action is stereotyped he does not vary the wording. The frequency and the lack of variety draw attention to the repetition and to what he is doing, and stress by intensification how standard the subject is. Through Aucassin, the external courtly hero, the author exemplifies, exaggerates and shows up a static and repetitious aspect of the tradition which is the hero's background.

Aucassin, then, lives in formulae, both by living out conceptual ones and by fulfilling the external, asemantic aspect of verbal ones without fulfilling their substance or presuppositions. He also speaks in formulae. He almost never speaks Nicolette's name without a qualifying phrase, and when the narrator is speaking from Aucassin's point of view the same tendency is evident. There are two standard formulations; in verse 'o le cler vis' and in prose variations on 'Nicolete ma (tres)douce amie que je tant aim'. It is this longer formula which is Aucassin's especial preserve; and its length leads to its appearing more and more clumsy on repetition, to the point of comedy. It is comic because the author has transplanted into prose a technique essentially of verse. In the *chanson de geste* and the romance the tag is a device for qualification in passing; it may become a label and may be monotonous, but it is too short to be intrusive or turgid. Here however the tag is expanded to produce a tedious and patently repetitious catch-phrase. It is abstract and does not tell us anything about Nicolette herself, so it is not even a good label; unlike verse tags, it lasts long enough for us to become very aware of its presence; and freed from the constraints of metre, assonance or rhyme, it shows minimal variation:[20]

'Nicolete me douce amie que je tant aim'

(II.20-21, VIII.17-18, X.16)

'Nicolete ma tres douce amie que j'aim tant'

(VI.18-19)

Nicolete sa tres douce amie que tant amoit

(VIII.8)

Nicolete se tres douce amie qu'il tant amoit

(XXII.1-2)

Se douce amie que tant amoit

(XII.27)

Nicolete sa douce amie que tant amoit.

(XXXIV.2)

The author has adopted a standard device of all Old French narrative verse but has exaggerated both the length of the formula and its invariability, thus highlighting the habit of labelling. At the same time he shows his hero as one who espouses and exemplifies all the repetitiousness, conventionality and automatism which the author is showing up. It is noteworthy that Aucassin's own words in the table above show even less variation than the narrator's.[21]

Aucassin is thus shown as a shallow character; he is further portrayed as striving to fulfil the literary rôle of the courtly lover in which he casts himself, but as failing to go beyond its stock reactions and phraseology; and on a third level he is a channel and a focus for the author's parody of the tradition to which his hero aspires. In his conventional responses, his living and speaking in formulae, Aucassin exemplifies the nature of the formula at the same time as he establishes a parodic relation to the tradition from which the formulae are drawn. For his actions are governed by convention, by what is long established and therefore expected, by outward form and not by inner aptness or adaptation.[22] Through him the author plays upon the relation between traditional literary conventions and their implications, and makes us aware of our readiness to accept literary stereotypes without analysis; their emptiness and the conventionalism of the traditions which Aucassin represents are thus made clear. This function of the character of Aucassin is but one example of the author's purpose. He uses many formulae of serious literature, ranging from phrases to the very plot of his work, in such a way as to show up their conventionality.

THE TRANSPARENCY OF CONVENTIONS: NICOLETTE

In his repeated formulaic characterisation of Nicolette, Aucassin uses the clumsier of the two formulae which label her. The other is produced usually in the narrator's own voice and always in verse. Its use is typical of that of formulae in the *chanson de geste,* showing variation for the needs of assonance and metre: 'o le cler vis' (I.7, XI.13, XIX.1, XLI.2), 'o le vis cler' (VII.3, XIII.1, XVII.1, XXXV.10), 'au cler vis' (XI.4), 'au vis cler' (XXXV.7). The form and frequency of the formula exaggerate by excessive repetition the labelling habit found in romances and later epics; for of all the other formulae on the same pattern—that is, an adjective or adjectival phrase following Nicolette's name or a noun signifying her—there are only eight other occurrences: 'le bien faite' (III.3), 'o le cuer franc' (XV.5), 'o le gent cors' (XXIII.9), 'o le blont poil' (XXV.4), 'li preus, li sage' (XXXVII.1), 'le prox / la prous' (XXXIX.8, 18, 24). As for their content, the verse formulae for Nicolette present her by implication as the typical courtly heroine, whereas in fact she is a highly unconventional one, and this contrast further makes plain the emptiness of labels.

Larger-scale conventions are similarly, and more subtly, shown for what they are. The author uses some of the standard narrative motifs of romance in such a way as to direct critical attention at them, so that the implausibility or selectivity which are inherent in them, but usually glossed over, are thrown into relief. Conventions both of plot and of character undergo this treatment in the passage depicting Nicolette's imprisonment (IV-V). In this scene several literary stereotypes are evoked in sketch form; selected formulae call up the wider conventions with which they are associated in our experience, and which are then manipulated.

> En une canbre la fist metre Nicolete en un haut estage,
> et une vielle aveuc li por conpagnie et por soisté tenir;
> et s'i fist metre pain et car et vin et quanque mestiers
> lor fu. Puis si fist l'uis seeler, c'on n'i peust de nule
> part entrer ne iscir, fors tant qu'il i avoit une fenestre
> par devers le gardin assés petite, dont il lor venoit un
> peu d'essor.
>
> (IV.15-19)

This brief scenario is sufficient to prepare us for a splendid prison, an inept guardian and subsequent escape. And so it proves. The old woman by whom Nicolette is guarded, a stock character in such scenes, also features in some fabliaux.[23] Ineffectual there, where she intervenes too late, she is here even more colourless; she is mentioned again only as being asleep when Nicolette escapes (XII.8). Her total lack of narrative function stresses the gratuitousness of her inclusion; her only rôle is to conform to the conventions which govern the depiction of the literary imprisonment of young girls.

The place of Nicolette's imprisonment is conventionally magnificent; it has frescoes, a vaulted roof, and a marble window on which Nicolette leans, displaying physical attributes taken from the standard portrait of the courtly heroine:

> Ele avoit blonde la crigne
> Et bien faite la sorcille,
> La face clere et traitice:
> Ainc plus bele ne veïstes.
>
> (V.7-10)

By virtue of their close association with the standard portrait of courtly beauty, these few elements suffice to call up the conventions and thus to characterise Nicolette as the typical courtly lady.[24] Looking out of the window she sees flowers and birds, a traditional introduction to thoughts of love. But her thoughts are far from traditional, though love is part of them; this typical courtly girl in a typical courtly setting has quite untypical plans: 'Longement n'i serai mie, / Se jel puis fare' (V.24-25). The bluntness of these lines contrasts sharply with the lyricism of the earlier part of the *laisse*. We had been lulled by the familiarity of the standard elements into expecting an ordinary courtly heroine, but our expectations are disappointed: Nicolette does, as she said, act to free herself and engineers her reunion with Aucassin. The sudden contrast makes us reappraise both the convention we had expected (why should beauty imply passivity?) and the ease of our assumptions; it makes us see how uncritical our expectations are.

All the depictions of Nicolette give the impression of alluding openly to an existing stereotype, familiar and therefore in no need of elaboration. We saw that both the narrator and Aucassin label her; and she is described as formulaically as she is labelled. When Aucassin first depicts her it is in vague laudatory terms: 'Tant est france et cortoise et debonaire et entecie de toutes bones teces' (II.31-32), and

> 'Nicolete est cointe et gaie . . .
> Nicolete est deboinaire;
> Ses gens cors et son viaire,
> Sa biautés le cuer m'esclaire.'
>
> (III.8-13)

The full portrait of Nicolette (XII) is very obviously a set piece, and makes clear its conventionality in a way which complements that of the brief allusions to the stereotype. Its content is utterly standard:

> Ele avoit les caviaus blons et menus recercelés, et les
> ex vairs et rians, et le face traitice, et le nes haut et
> bien assis, et lé levretes vremelletes plus que n'est
> cerisse ne rose el tans d'esté, et les dens blans et menus,
> et avoit les mameletes dures qui li souslevoient sa ves-
> teure ausi con ce fuissent.ii. nois gauges; et estoit graille
> par mi les flans qu'en vos dex mains le peusciés enclo-
> rre, et les flors des margerites qu'ele ronpoit as ortex
> de ses piés, qui li gissoient sor le menuisse du pié par
> deseure, estoient droites noires avers ses piés et ses
> ganbes, tant par estoit blance la mescinete.
>
> (XII.14-21)

This portrait falls into two halves separated by a discordant element. As we saw, the first part closely parallels that of Aucassin. This is an effective means of advertising the author's obedience to the portrait convention; since stereotypes are by definition standard, two allusions to the stereotype should logically be identical. Normally the illusion of individuality is produced precisely by variation in the combination of details which are taken from the stereotype; but not so here, for it is the lack of individuality that the author wishes to make clear. That the same physical appearance should be assigned to each of the two lovers both expresses on the physical level the romance convention of the marriage of like beauties, and prepares for their parity on a moral level.[25] Instead of being, complementarily, a well-built, active man and a beautiful, delicate woman, the two are equivalent. The 'femininity' of Aucassin's inaction, and Nicolette's 'masculine' positiveness, are reflected by Aucassin's feminine 'face clere' and Nicolette's tight curls.[26]

At the end of the stereotyped first section of Nicolette's portrait, an unusual and concrete simile produces a sudden change of register. The traditional 'avoit les mameletes dures qui li souslevoient sa vesteure' is followed by an image based upon the homely walnut and an unusual element for women, namely feet.[27] The elevated tone returns, however, for the second half of the portrait, with the hyperbole concerning the whiteness of Nicolette's skin. The intruding walnut simile has the effect of breaking the illusion of the stereotype, which is in all other respects so extreme. The interruption makes us aware how extreme it is: the author places the courtly stereotype before us by conforming to it, and by diverging from it he causes us to view it critically.

Nicolette is the subject of a further convention whose effect is very complex. We have seen how the first part of the work disorientates us by thwarting our formulaic expectations. Accordingly, by the time the pair are reunited in the forest we have become used to being surprised, and we expect our existing literary assumptions to be contradicted and conventions to be denied. But in the second part of the text we are presented with a second reversal: whereas we have come to expect that expectations will be disappointed, they are now—some of them—fulfilled. The development is exemplified by the revelation and treatment of Nicolette's background.

Her history as first presented is utterly conventional. It is given in sections II, IV and VI and is in no case particularly apt. The first instance is in the mouth of Aucassin's father:

> 'Nicolete laise ester, que ce est une caitive qui fu amenee d'estrange terre, si l'acata li visquens de ceste vile as Sarasins, si l'amena en ceste vile, si l'a levee et bautisie et faite sa fillole, si li donra un de ces jors un baceler qui du pain li gaaignera par honor; de ce n'as tu que faire.'

(II.22-26)

This is doubly forced. On a dramatic level it is quite unnecessary, for its content is well known to Aucassin to whom it is addressed. It is, moreover, highly stereotyped: a Saracen girl adopted, baptised and loved.[28] The speech further gives the impression, in its breathless haste, of being an obligatory set piece, an exposition to the audience which is traditionally necessary but largely lacking in internal motivation. We are used to such set pieces in Old French narrative, but in dialogue they remain implausible.

Subsequently the paragraph is twice repeated by the viscount, when in its long-windedness it has the comedy of the predictable. In each case it is, psychologically, a substitute for thought; it is his standard reaction to the topic of marriage between Nicolette and Aucassin. Its second occurrence, addressed to Aucassin's father, shows particularly well the unthinking, runon formulaic nature of the speech, since the inclusion of 'de ce n'eust Aucassins vos fix que faire' (IV.9-10) is quite irrelevant: both speakers are agreed on it, the more clearly since it was the listener who originally expressed the sentiment.

Nicolette's background thus is not only utterly conventional, but is shown to be so by the manner in which it is presented. So typical is it, and its narration so excessively repeated, that its function is patently to establish the convention of the captive Saracen heroine against which the individualistic Nicolette is set. We know, moreover, that

the conventional character is normally of royal birth, an implication which will become important. After its overuse in these early sections, the stereotype is not mentioned for some time, but it reappears after her escape, her reunion with Aucassin, and the journey to Torelore. Now, when we no longer expect it, it returns not as a simple formulaic description but as part of the action, and as the literal truth. Henceforth it is now of importance to the plot that the conventional Saracen princess in fact has a tangible background, a homeland and a family: she is nearly separated from Aucassin for good as a result. The stereotype is proved to be the truth and is lived out by the Nicolette whom we have come to see as conventional only in description but not in deed.

Smaller-scale conventions are proved true in the process. The revelation of Nicolette's true background depends on and enacts conventions which are laid bare by it. First, by an exaggerated coincidence, Nicolette, who has been captured by Saracens, is in the very boat of her father's sailors, who are on their way to none other than her homeland (XXXVI). (The storm which separates Aucassin and Nicolette equally obligingly takes Aucassin home to Beaucaire.) They recognise her rank not by any family resemblance—as they might reasonably have done—but by her beauty: the literary commonplace that rank reveals itself. The convention is used in preference to plausibility in the specific circumstances, and is made transparent by the implausibility of the coincidence.

Even less believable is Nicolette's sudden realisation of who she is. Here implausibility is flaunted. Within six lines we read first, 'Ele ne lor sot a dire qui ele estoit, car ele fu pree petis enfes' (XXXVI.5-6), and then, 'Ele ne fu mie si petis enfes que ne seust bien qu'ele avoit esté fille au roi de Cartage' (XXXVI.9-10). The contrast is too blatant to be unintentional, and mocks by its gratuitousness and coincidence the recognition of a person lost as a child by a physical mark or by a piece of clothing or jewellery. Here, Nicolette is 'recognised' first on account of her apparent nobility, then by a flash of intuition, and finally on her word. The standard device of recognition by some unlikely object here becomes recognition on no evidence at all, and the convention, far from being denied as we have come to expect, is affirmed, and that in an extreme form.

This flaunting serves to draw attention to the origin of which she so suddenly becomes aware. The proverbial formula 'fille au roi de Cartage', indicating great wealth, has here to be taken literally: she is in truth his daughter, and this fulfilment of the formula is at once comic in its literalism and very confusing.[29] For we have learnt that the text undermines formulae; and here it is vindicating one. In fact, of course, the vindication undermines, for the formula (like any metaphor) is not normally tested by reality; here it is so tested, and is proved true in both its metaphorical and its literal senses. Our surprise shows us that we do not expect formulae to be thus fulfilled, and this deprives the formula of validity; for why should we accept something which is by common consent inherently unreal?

Through this development the understanding which we had of Nicolette's background on her initial presentation is replaced by a very different one. No longer does her Saracen origin make her a benighted captive and unworthy of Aucassin; as daughter of the king of Carthagena she is much more noble than he, and rich both proverbially and actually. As such she is precisely the kind of bride Aucassin's parents destined for him when opposing his marriage to Nicolette (II), and a match worthy of approval both in literary and in social terms. As she demonstrates through literal fulfilment the potential of the convention of the Saracen captive, Nicolette fulfils the formulae of the romance type to the letter, but adds new dimensions and puts flesh onto the stereotype.

This is, indeed, the fundamental characteristic of the figure of Nicolette; but before discussing it further let us look at the Torelore episode, for, like Nicolette's origins, it causes us to revise our already revised expectations. In this fairy-tale land Aucassin and Nicolette behave as we would have expected them to do, had we not by now been trained otherwise; that is, they act in accordance with the stereotypes of the hero and heroine. This can be explained in terms of the relation of both Torelore and the protagonists to the tradition of the world upside down.[30] Since Aucassin and Nicolette fail to fit the standards of the 'real' world (Beaucaire), in an inverted world they, being inverted, conform to those standards. But more importantly, it is made clear that we are not justified in accepting the literary conventions by the fact that only in a fantasy world are these fulfilled, whereas in the 'real' world they are shown to be unfounded.

Torelore is a nonsense land, where kings lie in childbed and battles are fought with cheese and fruit. Here Aucassin and Nicolette conform to their literary types, but they are out of step in so doing, and thus show the types up once more. Whilst Nicolette holds Aucassin's horse and stays in the queen's chambers, as one might expect a girl to do, Aucassin comes nearer to what we think of as a typical courtly knight.[31] He enters Torelore in chivalric style, 's'espee çainte, s'amie devant lui' (XXVIII.12), and he is called 'li cortois et li gentis' (XXIX.2). And indeed, he shows some of the moral and active qualities of the knight: he exhorts the king and he fights. But both actions are misplaced, so that once more we see Aucassin making the conventional response rather than the appropriate one.[32]

In battle Aucassin imitates the epic knight, but inappropriately. His conformity to this stereotype is stressed by the formula used of him: 'Aucassins, li prex, li ber' (XXXI.11), but his conventionality turns against him, for the circumstances are not epic. The contrast between this and true warfare is expressed neatly in a pun which brings formulaically to mind the epic norm: 'ce plenier estor canpel' (XXXI.4). For 'canpel' here means literally 'of the fields', using agricultural produce for weapons; whereas 'estor canpel' and 'estor plenier' are both epic formulae, the first meaning 'pitched battle', and the second being a standard intensification.[33] Since in this battle the opponents do not

seek to kill each other, Aucassin's valour is both inappropriate and devalued, for he has no effective enemies. An important element of the chivalric ethic—fighting prowess—is thus presented as unfounded and destructive.[34]

NICOLETTE, AUCASSIN AND THE STANDARDS OF REALITY

The presentation of the work's protagonists is thus highly ambivalent, not to say contradictory. We have seen how Aucassin represents the external aspects of the courtly hero, without the stereotype's essentials or moral qualities—except when these are inapt, in Torelore. Nicolette on the other hand is altogether more complicated.[35] In her appearance and many of her functions she fully conforms to the external characteristics of the courtly heroine. But she goes beyond this; though she fulfils the stereotype's positive externals she does not demonstrate its negative implications. She is, as tradition demands, beautiful, beloved, noble and the rest; indeed in her origin as a Saracen princess she fulfils in action what elsewhere exists merely as part of the stereotype, but which here is fundamental to the plot. Yet she is not, as our literary experience would lead us to infer, helpless, passive and weak. On the contrary: it is she who escapes when both she and Aucassin are imprisoned, she who acts whilst he laments, she who engineers their reunion in the forest, and she who seeks Aucassin until she finds him at the end of the story. She does not belie the conventional courtly attributes given her—the formulaic denotation of the type of the heroine; but she does belie its connotations, the moral qualities we expect to find accompanying the external aspects of the stereotype. In a similar way to certain fabliaux, Nicolette makes us see that our interpretation based on connotations is not necessarily warranted by the denotation of the type she represents; for she combines adherence to the denotation with contradiction of the connotations. Accordingly, the author's treatment of her shows how much potential the reality contains which the conventions do not fulfil. To be a courtly heroine need not—but elsewhere usually does—entail having the passive qualities conventionally associated with the rôle. Rather, once disencumbered of its negative connotations, the figure of the courtly heroine implies many positive qualities: inspiration and encouragement of the lover, control of the love relationship, decision-making and the taking of responsibility.

So Nicolette has the external qualities of the courtly heroine, but not the inner qualities usually associated with the type; and for Aucassin it is the same. For, as we have seen, he attempts to conform to the convention of the hero, and indeed he expresses to the extreme the external qualities of the courtly lover, in his handsome appearance, his admiration of Nicolette, his use of courtly formulae to characterise her, and his absorption in her to the exclusion of all else; but he does not combine with these effective love or active valour. Rather, he demonstrates the negative potential of the type of the hero, as Nicolette shows the positive potential of that of the heroine. It is because he is so totally the romantic lover that he is ineffectual. If it is the lover's duty to think always of his lady, it is logical that the courtly knight who is a perfect lover should forget, for love, to fight, as Aucassin does (X). Most lovers are in this sense less perfect than Aucassin.[36] The ideal is inherently self-contradictory.

If, then, Aucassin fulfils the accidentals but not the essentials of the stereotype, and Nicolette does the same thing, why do we laugh at Aucassin but not at Nicolette? For that is surely our reaction. We see Nicolette as appealing because she diverges from the courtly convention, but we laugh at Aucassin, the failed hero. The answer is twofold. Part of it depends on the nature of the courtly stereotypes. That of the man is essentially based on character and action: the externals are expressive of the internal qualities (thus the brave are conventionally handsome). The figure of the heroine, on the other hand, is first and foremost external: she is beautiful, elegant and inspires love, and any internal qualities are additional. This being so, we see that Nicolette fulfils the prime area of the convention, diverging in the secondary aspect by her forceful character. Aucassin fulfils the secondary area but does not have the character of a hero, which is all-important to the type.

The second part of the answer is that the values of reality condemn Aucassin and commend Nicolette. We are led to see this through our laughter itself: the comic episodes are the ones in which Aucassin is involved and in which he acquits himself ill, for example his two fights, his accident at the bower, his overreactions. If we abstract the relation of the two heroes to the courtly convention, they present themselves as a pretty girl full of good qualities (fidelity, devotion, generosity, courage, resourcefulness, energy) and a buffoon who tries to impress but gets the important things wrong, and who is conspicuously lacking in the self-same courage, energy and resourcefulness. She is better than her type, he worse.[37]

To make this abstraction, however, is greatly to impoverish our appreciation; for even as we judge with the standards of reality, our criticism is closely dependent on the relation of *Aucassin et Nicolette* to contemporary literature. Indeed, without the presence of parody, Aucassin would not gain our sympathy at all, so great is his stupidity and so potentially dangerous his fecklessness; we should either find him odious or see in him a failure on the author's part. At most we might derive amusement from his failures, his exaggerations and his accidents. It is by comparison with the literary background from which he derives and which he recalls that he is deeply comic, and ironic, and parodic. For his flaws of character, superficially amusing in themselves (absent-mindedness, overreaction and so forth), are given a deeper humour by being related to a literary convention which implies them but does not elsewhere demonstrate them so openly; by establishing such relations, the author leads us to judge the conventions themselves. So as a parodic figure Aucassin regains our sympathy, since he is not merely a butt of mockery or a disastrous mistake; he is rather a focus for, and an instrument of, effective parody.

The author uses him for parody by manipulating in two ways the formulae he represents. On the one hand they are exaggerated and thus rendered obvious; on the other they are brought into sharp contrast with reality and with realism. The exaggeration has been discussed: in Aucassin the external courtly qualities are shown in extreme form and deprived of a basis in internal character, and their weaknesses are thus shown up. He demonstrates the convention pushed to its conclusion, and his poor showing condemns it. We see the emptiness of his character and reject both him and what he stands for; in the one example we judge the type, for we recognise that he is both faithful to it and inane. We therefore see the literary ideal's potential for ridicule when, as here, it is untempered by human qualities and pushed to its extreme; we are thus made aware of our own uncritical acceptance of the stereotype in our broader literary experience.

In order for Aucassin's emptiness to be made apparent, the values of reality are again relied upon. Since convention is in essence opposed to realism, anything which shows that the values of reality call into question the validity of a convention poses a threat to the very foundation of conventional literature. Accordingly, a fruitful means of parodying such literature is to show that it unrealistic. An example is the insensitivity to pain which both Aucassin and Nicolette experience. When escaping from Beaucaire, Nicolette 'ne santi ne mal ne dolor por le grant paor qu'ele avoit' (XVI.14-15). Aucassin on the other hand, as he rides through the brambles looking for her, 'pensa tant a Nicolete sa douce amie qu'i ne sentoit ne mal ne dolor' (XXIV.6). The contrast shows well the difference between the two characters, and how the author wishes to present them; their plights are similar and in both cases to be taken as real, but whereas a realistic reason is given for Nicolette's insensitivity to pain (fear), Aucassin's is explained conventionally (a lover's rêverie) and in formulaic language ('Nicolete sa douce amie'). The conventionality seems the more misplaced because we know from experience of real life that his situation is indeed unpleasant and therefore he should feel pain. The contrast between the two frames of reference—the realistic and the literary—thus works to the detriment of the conventional expression.

A second example is Aucassin's finding the bower built by Nicolette.[38]

> Aucassins si cevauce. La nuis fu bele et quoie, et il erra tant qu'il vin[t pres de la u li set cemin aforkent] si [vit devant lui le loge que vos savés que] Nicolete [avoit fete, et le loge estoit forree] defors et dedens et par deseure et devant de flors, et estoit si bele que plus ne . . . estre. Quant Aucassins le perçut, si s'aresta tot a un fais, et li rais de le lune feroit ens.
>
> (XXIV.54-58)

The whole scene mocks the unlikely coincidences and recognitions of the romance tradition; for Nicolette relies on his finding it, and he does, and moreover he knows it is of her making. Reality intrudes, however, as in dismounting he falls from his horse: 'Il pensa tant a Nicolete se tres douce amie qu'il caï si durement sor une piere que l'espaulle li vola hors du liu' (XXIV.63-64). If it is traditional that the lover thinking of his lady should notice no pain, it is grotesque that in his distraction he should fall from his horse, and not even in a noble circumstance like Lancelot, but whilst dismounting. It is a mundane injury and an ungraceful accident, and one which reflects poorly on Aucassin's horsemanship as well as making his love comic—thus deflating two prime qualities of the courtly knight. His love is so exaggerated and ethereal that it destroys the horsemanship which should serve it. Though the effect of his absorption here is more realistic than the conventional insensitivity to pain, the explanation given is still the fully conventional one, so that the discrepancy between reality and literary ideal is again, and more strikingly, shown up.

Aucassin continues by showing a ludicrously inappropriate reaction: though his shoulder is injured and not his legs, he drags himself along the ground and 'vint tos souvins en le loge' (XXIV.66): a preposterous motion, the more so when it is unnecessary. Nicolette, by contrast, concludes the incident by adapting a courtly convention to practical needs: the healing power of love, far from clashing with the reality of the circumstances as in the case of Aucassin, is expressed by her actually resetting his shoulder. The critical reflection on the convention of the courtly hero as contrasted with realistic events is set off and enhanced by the differing treatment of Nicolette, through whom positive and practical sides of the stereotype are developed. In this incident where the stereotypes of hero and heroine are brought into contact with the demands of reality, the author shows in microcosm the message of his work as a whole: he demonstrates the negative potential of the figure of the courtly hero and the positive potential of that of the courtly heroine.

CONCLUSION

In *Aucassin et Nicolette,* then, parodic references to the romance, and to a lesser extent to the *chanson de geste,* are fundamental. In those fabliaux which make use of parody we saw how it adds a further dimension to a simply humorous story. In *Aucassin et Nicolette* it is parody which makes the story humorous; such comedy as it would otherwise have is very slight, and would be such as to direct laughter at the author for producing poorly motivated events and a ridiculous hero. In fact, however, its comedy is deeply ironic, for it depends on the establishment of a subtle relation between the work and contemporary literature. The character of Nicolette shows us the convention of the courtly heroine redeemed by the addition to the stereotype of qualities which are laudable in real terms; whilst that of Aucassin shows the depths to which the convention of the courtly hero can sink if it is presented in pure and extreme form without the inner qualities normally associated with it. Both conventions are thus shown up as potentially empty: Aucassin's by demonstration, Nicolette's by contrast with the fulness she gives it. Good courtly authors

use the traditional elements with discretion, whilst second-rate ones, by relying on them, reveal their negative potential. The author of *Aucassin et Nicolette* highlights this negative potential by making the conventions transparent. Depictions are so formulaic, and so standardised on repetition within the work, as to make plain how standard they are elsewhere; the coincidences on which romances depend are laid bare by having no veil cast over their implausibility; and the vacuity of courtly sentiments is revealed by the expression in a very prosaic prose of what would pass notice cloaked in poetic verse. Our author thus exposes the faults of the courtly tradition in order to undermine that tradition; he makes fundamental to his work a point some fabliaux make in passing. His parody is critical of its model; in this it contrasts with *Le Pèlerinage de Charlemagne,* to which I shall now turn.

Notes

1. Barbara Nelson Sargent-Baur and Robert Francis Cook, *'Aucassin et Nicolete': A Critical Bibliography* (London, 1982) surveys work to 1979.

2. Hunt, pp. 341-53, 376-80; Imre Szabics, 'Amour et prouesse dans *Aucassin et Nicolette*', in *Et c'est la fin pour quoy sommes ensemble: hommage à Jean Dufournet. Littérature, histoire et langue du moyen âge,* ed. by Jean-Claude Aubailly and others (Paris, 1993), III, 1341-49 (pp. 1341-43).

3. See respectively F. Carmona Fernandez, 'Parodie et humour dans le roman en vers de la première moitié du XIIIᵉ siècle: allusion et tradition littéraire dans *Aucassin et Nicolette*', in *Le Rire au moyen âge,* pp. 97-106 (p. 104); Charles Méla, *Blanchefleur et le saint homme; ou, la semblance des reliques: étude comparée de littérature médiévale* (Paris, 1979), p. 58; D.D.R. Owen, 'Chrétien, *Fergus, Aucassin et Nicolette* and the Comedy of Reversal', in *Chrétien de Troyes and the Troubadours: Essays in Memory of the late Leslie Topsfield,* ed. by Peter Noble and Linda M. Paterson (Cambridge, 1984), pp. 186-94.

4. 'Kritik und Rettung der höfischen Welt in der Chantefable', in *Höfische Literatur, Hofgesellschaft, höfische Lebensformen um 1200: Kolloquium am Zentrum für interdisziplinäre Forschung der Universität Bielefeld (3. bis 5. November 1983),* ed. by Gert Kaiser and Jan-Dirk Müller (Düsseldorf, 1986), pp. 363-86.

5. 'Ein Beispiel mündlicher Dichtung: *Aucassin et Nicolette*', *Fabula,* 15 (1974), 1-26.

6. Jean Trotin, 'Vers et prose dans *Aucassin et Nicolette*', *Romania,* 97 (1976), 481-508; Joan B. Williamson, 'Naming as a Source of Irony in *Aucassin et Nicolette*', *SFr,* 17 (1973), 401-09.

7. Simone Monsonégo, *Etude stylo-statistique du vocabulaire des vers et de la prose dans la chantefable 'Aucassin et Nicolette',* (Paris, 1966); Nathaniel B. Smith, 'The Uncourtliness of Nicolette', in *Voices of Conscience: Essays on Medieval and Modern French Literature in Memory of James D. Powell and Rose-*

mary Hodgins, ed. by Raymond J. Cormier (Philadelphia, 1977), pp. 169-82; idem, 'Aucassin et Nicolette as Stylistic Comedy', *Kentucky Romance Quarterly,* 26 (1979), 479-90.

8. 'Aucassin et Nicolette', p. 487. To Hunt's and Szabics's surveys should also be added: Vladimir R. Rossman, *Perspectives of Irony in Medieval French Literature* (The Hague, 1975), pp. 96-106; Norris J. Lacy, 'Courtliness and Comedy in *Aucassin et Nicolette*', in *Essays in Early French Literature presented to Barbara M. Craig,* ed. by Norris J. Lacy and Jerry C. Nash (York, S. Carolina, 1982); Fernando Carmona, *El Roman lírico medieval* (Barcelona, 1988), pp. 227-95.

9. Cf. Grimm, especially pp. 368, 373-74.

10. Quotations are from my own edition in Glyn S. Burgess and Anne Elizabeth Cobby, *The Pilgrimage of Charlemagne (Le Pèlerinage de Charlemagne), Aucassin and Nicolette (Aucassin et Nicolette)* (New York and London, 1988). Roman numerals indicate sections, arabic lines.

11. Grimm, pp. 370-74, studies the mix of genres in the text as a whole.

12. Cf. Colby, pp. 14-16, 29-50.

13. As does the predictability of the clichéd pairs of adjectives; cf. Smith, 'Aucassin et Nicolette', p. 486.

14. Carmona points out the comic and ironic potential of the text's concision, abbreviation and skeletal quality (*El Roman lírico,* e.g. p. 250).

15. On this use of the topos cf. for example Omer Jodogne, 'La Parodie et le pastiche dans *Aucassin et Nicolette*', *CAIEF,* 12 (1960), 53-65 (pp. 57-58); June Hall Martin, *Love's Fools: Aucassin, Troilus, Calisto and the Parody of the Courtly Lover* (London, 1972), pp. 25-36; Lachet, *La 'Prise d'Orange',* pp. 174-76.

16. e.g. *Erec, Yvain;* cf. Erich Köhler, *L'Aventure chevaleresque: idéal et réalité dans le roman courtois. Etudes sur la forme des plus anciens poèmes d'Arthur et du Graal,* trans. by Eliane Kaufholz (Paris, 1974), especially p. 202.

17. Cf. Edmond Faral, *Les Arts poétiques du XIIe et du XIIIe siècle: recherches et documents sur la technique littéraire du moyen âge* (Paris, 1924), p. 87.

18. Cf. Smith, 'Aucassin et Nicolette', p. 484.

19. A further example is the almost identical passages (II.15-21 and VIII.11-18) in which he is exhorted, and refuses, to fight. Smith, 'Aucassin et Nicolette', pp. 482-83, shows how these and other repetitions stress themes and contrasts and make 'comic exploitation of rhetorical *variatio* and *amplificatio*' (p. 483).

20. To this list could be added as many more occurrences of 'Nicolete ma / sa (tres)douce amie'.

21. This is the most striking instance of Aucassin's formulaic and repetitious references to Nicolette, but there are others in the verse sections, e.g. 'flors de

lis' (XI.12, 32), 'gens cors' (III.15, XXIII.9, 13), and the vocative 'douce amie' (VII.20, XI.13, 32, XXIII.18, XXV.15, XXVII.11, XXXV.10). On such formulae, cf. Trotin, pp. 481-99, and Williamson, pp. 402-04.

22. Cf. Rudy S. Spraycar, 'Genre and Convention in *Aucassin et Nicolette*', *RR,* 76 (1985), 94-115. Significantly Aucassin chooses externals over essentials when he prefers hell in the company of courtly types with their social graces to heaven with beggars (VI). Similarly in his conversation with Nicolette at the tower (XIV), he says he would kill himself rather than know her to be in another man's bed, proposing not to prevent the fact but to avoid the knowledge, to spare his feelings but not to help her.

23. e.g. *Le Chevalier à la Corbeille* (MR, II, 183, *NRCF,* vol. IX), *Cele qui fu foutue et desfoutue* (*NRCF,* IV, 151).

24. Cf. Colby, pp. 27-29, 33, 38, 43-47.

25. Cf. e.g. *Floire et Blancheflor, Piramus et Tisbé.*

26. Men's hair is usually curled, women's long and fine; cf. Colby, pp. 34-35. On a 'face clere' as a female characteristic, cf. Colby, p. 47. The exchange of rôles between the sexes is a commonplace of *Aucassin* criticism; see note 35 below.

27. Cf. Hermann Sauter, *Wortgut und Dichtung: eine lexikographisch-literargeschichtliche Studie über den Verfasser der altfranzösischen Cantefable 'Aucassin et Nicolette'* (Münster and Paris, 1934), pp. 37-38, 136, and Colby, p. 96.

28. Cf. Hunt, p. 359.

29. Cf. Albert Pauphilet, *Le Legs du moyen âge: études de littérature médiévale* (Melun, 1950), p. 241; the proverb is used by Conon de Béthune in 'Il avint ja en un autre païs'.

30. This has often been discussed; e.g. by Darnell H. Clevenger, 'Torelore in *Aucassin et Nicolette*', *RomN,* 11 (1969-70), 656-65; J.H. Martin, pp. 32-35; Hunt, pp. 370-73; Moses Musonda, 'Le Thème du "monde à l'envers" dans *Aucassin et Nicolette*', *MedR,* 7 (1980), 22-36; Paule Le Rider, 'La Parodie d'un thème épique: le combat sur le gué dans *Aucassin et Nicolette*', in *La Chanson de geste et le mythe carolingien: mélanges René Louis publiés par ses collègues, ses amis et ses élèves à l'occasion de son 75e anniversaire* (Saint-Père-sous-Vézelay, 1982), II, 1225-33. Grimm, pp. 377-82, discusses at length its parodic and carnival nature, with particular reference to courtly norms.

31. Not that Nicolette is so self-effacing that she cannot express independent and unconventional thought when faced with an unwelcome marriage (XXXIII).

32. Cf. Grimm, p. 380.

33. See Tobler-Lommatzsch s.vv. 'champel' (II, 201-02) and 'plenier' (VII, 1139-40). Le Rider, p. 1231, discusses the parodic effect of this pun.

34. Cf. Clevenger, p. 663.

35. As witness the disagreement between critics as to whether or not she is an anti-courtly heroine, and whether or not her positiveness is unusual; e.g. Hunt, p. 374, Carmona Fernandez, 'Parodie et humour', p. 101: she is not atypical; M. Faith McKean, 'Torelore and Courtoisie', *RomN*, 3 (1961-62), 64-68 (p. 66), Robert Harden, '*Aucassin et Nicolette* as Parody', *SP*, 63 (1966), 1-9 (p. 7): she inverts the type of the heroine. It is not how unusual her positiveness is that is important, but the use to which it is put, and it is certainly made to contrast with Aucassin's inaction. Cf. J.H. Martin, pp. 30-31: though the perfect courtly lady, Nicolette shows Aucassin up by not acting according to the rules of courtly romance.

36. Though Lancelot shows the same absorption; cf. D.D.R. Owen, 'Profanity and its Purpose in Chrétien's *Cligés* and *Lancelot*', *FMLS*, 6 (1970), 37-48 (p. 47); J.H. Martin, pp. 26-27.

37. On the rôle played by various aspects of reality, cf. Jill Tattersall, 'Shifting Perspectives and the Illusion of Reality in *Aucassin et Nicolette*', *French Studies*, 38 (1984), 257-67; idem, 'Social Observation and Comment in *Aucassin et Nicolette*', *NM*, 86 (1985), 551-65.

38. Lacunae filled from Suchier's reconstruction (reproduced in Burgess and Cobby, p. 180). On this episode and its literary background see Wayne Conner, 'The *Loge* in *Aucassin et Nicolette*', *RR*, 46 (1955), 81-89.

Roger Pensom (essay date 1999)

SOURCE: "Lost and Found," in *"Aucassin et Nicolette": The Poetry of Gender and Growing up in the French Middle Ages*, Peter Lang, 1999, pp. 129-33.

[*In the following essay, Pensom maintains that the poem emphasizes the concept of "recognition" as a unifying theme in the adventures of the perpetually-separated Aucassin and Nicolette.*]

> Aucassin has now returned
> To his city of Biaucaire,
> Holding the lands of his domain
> As uncontested sovereign.
> He swears by God's almighty power
> That Nicolete is more to him
> Than all his kith and all his kin,
> If he were suddenly to die.
> 'My dear sweetheart of the bright face,
> I don't know where to look for you.
> Never was kingdom made by God,
> Whether on land or upon sea,
> That, had I hope of finding you,
> I would not search!'

> *Now we will leave off talking of Aucassin and return to Nicolete.*

The ship in which Nicolete found herself belonged to the King of Carthage who was indeed her father. Also she had twelve brothers who were all either princes or kings. When her captors saw how beautiful Nicolete was, they treated her with great respect and entertained her royally, pressing her with questions about her origins, for she seemed to them to be a well-born woman of high lineage. But she was unable to answer their enquiries because she had been carried off by pirates as a tiny child. So on they sailed until they found themselves under the walls of Carthage, and when Nicolete saw the stronghold and the countryside, she suddenly remembered who she was, that she had been brought up in this place and carried off as a tiny child, but not so tiny as not to know quite well that she was the daughter of the King of Carthage and that she had been brought up in this very city.

. . . . .

VERSE:

Aucassin's dilemma has been transformed by his new-found status as lord of Biaucaire. Now political responsibility has replaced Chivalry as the antagonist of love. He has received the oath of homage from his vassals and is thus bound to them in a compact of mutual support and responsibility. Although he reigns as lord of Biaucaire, his inner thoughts are still of his sweetheart. He is no longer a rebel against parental authority, since he has now literally become the man his father was, Lord of Biaucaire. But he wears his power with a difference. Love is part of him as it was never part of his father. Although it is suppressed in his life as a political magnate, in his speech to himself, he makes it clear that it is still the most important thing in life to him. In the life of his father, love had been not suppressed but repressed, that is, lost to conscious awareness in a way that forced it to re-emerge unbidden as a destructive force. The suppression of powerful desires is the price the mature adult pays for the security of himself and those who depend on him. What is desired is everpresent to his mind, and his life is a search for a way between the opposing claims of his desire and his duty. So it is that Aucassin has become his father yet not his father. He has found in his experience the strength to confront the contradiction in his being without banishing from consciousness that part of himself which causes him pain. Because business of state and feudal responsibilities have the first claim on his time and energy, love is banished to a remote conditional tense:

> Never was kingdom made by God,
> Whether on land or upon sea,
> That, had I hope of finding you,
> I would not search!

The emergence of the theme of heterosexual love in the literature of twelfth-century France created a language for the articulation of the concept of the individual in social life. The world of the Old French epic was dominated by mainly homosocial family ties and feudal allegiances. The affective bonds which count outside family ties are between peers fostered together (as was the custom) in the same aristocratic household, Roland and Oliver, Gerin and Gerers and so on. We have already seen in the case of the nightwatchman in Chapter Eight how the words denoting the concrete qualities of the feudal vassal were progressively attached to moral and psychological qualities as the twelfth century advanced. It is just as interesting to see how words denoting kinbonds and feudal bonds were expropriated to describe partners in an essentially illicit heterosexual love relationship.[1] Here are the knight and the niece of the Duke of Burgundy (from the *Chastelaine de Vergi*) meeting secretly at the niece's house:

> *And he returns her kiss and hug*
> *And says,' Lady, my friend (m'amie),*
> *My love, my heart, companion, (druerie) . . .*
> *And she replied, 'My sweetest lord (seignor),*
> *My sweetest friend (amis), my most sweet love. . . .*[2]

Here the words *amie* and *amis* were in their earliest use applied to kinsmen and kinswomen, while *druerie* and *seignor* originally described homosocial feudal relations:[3] *druz* is used to describe a close companion and vassal of a feudal lord and *seignor* the lord of that vassal. It seems that cultural and social changes as they appear in the literature led to the transformation of areas of Old French vocabulary in a way which assimilated this new heterosexual mode to the models provided by the existing social and political institutions of the family and feudality.

Thus when Aucassin, as an *uncontested sovereign* swears *by God's almighty power* that he loves his sweetheart, his *douce amie*, more than all his kin, we see someone who is seeking to draw together domains of human allegiance which are opposed. But now he has the strength to endure the paradox, to discharge his duties as Lord and to keep his own wishes to himself.

PROSE:

Now that the lovers are separated, the narrative proceeds in the mode known as *interlace*. This is the dominant mode of construction for the vast and complex prose-romances of the thirteenth century. Its polar opposite is the single plot-stand structure of the classical seventeenth-century French tragedy. *Interlace* gives us two or more strands of narrative woven together in such a way that episodes from different stories alternate. This is the nearest narrative can come to what in music is called polyphony, that is two or more melodies played simultaneously. Since narrative exists only in time, simultaneity is impossible for it; simultaneity presupposes articulation in *space*, which of course, is what music has in common with the visual arts.

Interlace probably began as a way of introducing variety into story-telling, but its poetic and constructional potential soon became clear to the professionals. Readers of Malory will be familiar with the formula in such cases as *Now leave we Sir Tristram and turne we to Kynge Marke*. This is derived from the French prose romances in which interlace was put to work to produce unexpected and unparaphrasable poetic meaning. Let us take a hypothetical

example for brevity's sake. Let's imagine a romance which juxtaposes two episodes from different stories: one is the tale of lovers, one of whom eventually deserts and hence indirectly causes the death of his former beloved. The second tale is of a King and a vassal who breaks his oaths of fealty to the King and betrays him to an enemy, thus causing his death. In this overly obvious example, our imagined romance is creating thematic structures in the succeeding episodes which, despite the discontinuity of plot-material, are perceived by the reader as metaphorically related. Although the characters are different and the nature of their relationship is different, clear similarities emerge which perhaps suggest to the readers a relationship between a love affair and a feudal bond.

It clear that something of the kind is happening in our own story at this point. It is more than possible that the interlace formula:

> *Now we will leave off talking about Aucassin and turn to Nicolete.*

would have triggered interpretative activity in the listener's mind, stimulating him to scan subliminally the following prose episode for parallel structures. Nicolete, although far away in Carthage, is also the object of *anagnorisis,* the universal dramatic device (labelled by Aristotle in his *Poetics*) according to which a lost person is recovered through recognition and restored to his rightful place. While Aucassin is recognised literally by people who knew him, Nicolete is at first only recognised, as she was in Torelore, as a person possessing innately aristocratic qualities. But the text also subtly carries us into a more secret manifestation of the principle of *anagnorisis*. This is closer to the literal meaning of the Greek word which mean something like 'bringing up into awareness', which of course is exactly what Nicolete is slowly doing here. So 'the return of something lost' in *anagnorisis,* does not have to be a person; it can also be the true recollection of something forgotten.

We see in this that the text reiterates the idea of 'recognition' as a common theme in interlacing of the adventures of the separated lovers. While recognition for Aucassin is a single and uncomplicated process of being re-known by people who had known him years before, the process of *anagnorisis* operates for Nicolete at a double level; first, she is 'recognised' by others for what she really is, an aristocrat, but more importantly she recovers from forgetfulness in herself her own real social identity.

Incurable readers of mythology and folk stories will certainly have spotted the theme which culminates in Nicolete's rediscovery of her royal identity. This is a theme whose significance is explored by Freud in his essay called 'Family Romances', and it is that of the child who believes that his parents are not his real parents but that he is in reality the child of someone far more important. This idea that one's parents are, as it were, 'illegitimate' is the symmetrical obverse, from the child's viewpoint, of the fear of the illegitimacy of male offspring suffered by feudal patriarchs. Stories in which this theme figures are many and important: Oedipus was abandoned by his royal father and brought up by humble people, Jesus Christ, brought up by a carpenter as his own child, turns out to be the Son of God, Arthur, also the illegitimate offspring of a King, lives as the son of Pellinor and the brother of Kay before drawing the sword from the stone and becoming King of the Britons. Readers can take a Freudian line on these stories, seeing in them the child's desire for revenge on parents who have not lived up to a desired ideal, or they may prefer the Jungian approach which sees in the child's fantasies of lost grandeur a remembrance or an anticipation of his spiritual vocation. Whichever view they take, the story remains powerfully suggestive and its magic is used by the storyteller in a characteristic way. As we will see, it doesn't end the story, but shows rather a further phase in the evolution of Nicolete's self-awareness.

Notes

1. The love affairs which attracted most attention in the literature were adulterous, (the love poems of the troubadours and trouvères, Tristan and Isolt, Lancelot and Guinevere). The love of Aucassin, though not adulterous, is illicit in the sense that it goes against feudal custom.

2. Frederick Whitehead's edition, lines 405-13.

3. As defeat approaches, Roland, at the Battle of Roncevalles, calls upon the absent Charlemagne, his mother's brother:

    1697 *E! reis amis, que vos ici nen estes!*

FURTHER READING

Bibliography

Sargent-Baur, Barbara Nelson and Robert Francis Cook. "*Aucassin et Nicolette*": *A Critical Bibliography.* London: Grant & Cutler Ltd., 1981, 83p.
    Critical discussion of significant editions and translations, followed by a detailed bibliography.

Criticism

Dorfman, Eugene. "The Flower in the Bower: Garris in *Aucassin et Nicolette.*" *Studies in Honor of Mario A. Pei,* edited by John Fisher and Paul A. Gaeng, pp. 77-87. Chapel Hill, N.C.: University of North Carolina Press, 1972.
    Identifies parallels between the details of the bower episode and the Biblical *Song of Songs.*

Frank, Grace. "The Cues in *Aucassin et Nicolette.*" *Modern Language Notes* XLVII, No. 1 (January 1932): 14-16.
    Maintains that certain passages in the text of *Aucassin et Nicolette* serve as signals exchanged by the singer and reciter who originally performed the *chantefable.*

————. "*Aucassin et Nicolette.*" *The Medieval French Drama,* pp. 237-42. Oxford: Clarendon Press, 1954.
    Examines *Aucassin et Nicolette* as an example of a work of the Middle Ages in which narrative recitation and dramatization are co-mingled.

Griffin, Robert. "*Aucassin et Nicolette* and the Albigensian Crusade." *Modern Language Quarterly* 26, No. 2 (June 1965): 243-56.
    Investigates the possibility of the influence of Cathar dogma and of troubadour style on *Aucassin et Nicolette,* cautioning that readers should not view the work as allegory.

McKean, M. Faith. "Torelore and Courtoisie." *Romance Notes.* 3, No. 2 (Spring 1962): 64-8.
    Argues that the Torelore episode represents the climax of the author's parody of the courtly lovers.

Rea, John A. "The Form of *Aucassin et Nicolette.*" *Romance Notes* 15, No. 3 (Spring 1974): 504-08.
    Suggests that the form of the material performed by the Provençal troubadours might have been adapted by the author of *Aucassin et Nicolette* to suit his comic purposes.

Urwin, Kenneth. "The Setting of *Aucassin et Nicolette.*" *Modern Language Review* 31, No. 3 (July 1936): 403-05.
    Contends that despite some critical opinion to the contrary, the author of *Aucassin et Nicolette* may have had personal knowledge of the town in which he set his story.

Woods, William S. "The *Aube* in *Aucassin et Nicolette.*"
    Examines the differences between the traditional *aube* poem and the way the *aube* is dramatized in *Aucassin et Nicolette.* Woods suggests that the author used stock elements so that the audience would recognize the *aube* pattern, and then manipulated their expectations by undermining those patterns.

Chu Hsi
1130-1200

Chinese philosopher.

INTRODUCTION

Often referred to as the "Great Synthesizer," Chu Hsi, was the principal exponent of Neo-Confucianism in his day. He brought together and systematized the various threads of Neo-Confucian thought professed by other philosophers, who tended to focus on individual principles of philosophy rather than a more unified system. Chu Hsi's teachings in later centuries became the orthodox views of the state and also influenced thinkers in other parts of East Asia.

BIOGRAPHICAL INFORMATION

Born in Anhui, China, Chu Hsi studied for a number of years under his father, who headed various departments of the government. Chu Hsi's opposition to official state policies, such as accepting peace terms from invaders, compelled him to leave the capital, and for years resulted in his declining of offered official positions, or his removal or demotion from the government positions in which he served. Although he spent nine years in public service, his philosophical positions were viewed as too radical by his superiors. In 1196, a censor accused Chu Hsi of several crimes, including the refusal to serve and spreading false learning. He was officially removed from his posts and died several years after, in 1200.

MAJOR WORKS

Chu Hsi's most recognized achievement is *Chin-ssu lu*, or *Reflections on Things at Hand*, written in 1175. The work is viewed as the classic statement of Neo-Confucianism and is an anthology of the views of the Sung dynasty philosophers who conceptualized and formulated a new Confucian metaphysical system. Compiled by Chu Hsi and Lü Tsu-ch'ien, with the preface written by Chu Hsi, the work reflects, through both its selections and editing, Chu Hsi's personal philosophy. The *Chin-ssu lu* emphasizes the concept of *li*, or principle, as the basis for all truth. The prominence of *li* in Neo-Confucianism is one of the primary contrasts between the new philosophy and Confucianism, in which the *li* is less significant. Other doctrines of the Neo-Confucianism espoused by Chu Hsi in the *Chin-ssu lu* include the advocating of investigation and the "exercise of seriousness" in order to know *li* and live in accordance with it. The work also re-evaluates classic Confu-

cian texts, such as the *Book of Changes*, using a rationalist approach as opposed to the spiritual approach typical of the Taoists. Chu Hsi also collected various commentaries on Confucian texts and wrote the "Jen-shuo" (c. 1171), or "Treatise on Humanity." In this work, revised over a number of years, Chu Hsi analyzes the concept of *jen*, roughly translated as "humanity" or "humaneness." Chu Hsi discusses *jen* as "the character of the mind" and as "the principle of love." Scholars have also learned more about the essence of Chu Hsi's philosophy by studying his correspondence with other philosophers.

CRITICAL RECEPTION

Chu Hsi's approach to such aspects of Neo-Confucianist thought as the concepts of *li*, *Tao*, and *jen*, have been analyzed by modern critics who seek to explain Chu Hsi's views and to contrast Chu Hsi's philosophy with Buddhist and Taoist doctrines. Other critics have studied Chu Hsi's philosophy in comparison with Western philosophical principles. J. Percy Bruce studies Chu Hsi's beliefs regarding *Tao*, translated as the "Way," and understood as universal moral law. Bruce examines the difference between moral principle, or *li*, and *Tao*, in Chu Hsi's system. In addition, Bruce compares Chu Hsi's conception of *Tao* with that of his contemporary Taoists of his time, arguing that while Chu Hsi accepted the transcendental nature of *Tao*, he rejected the "ultra-transcendentalism" preached by the Taoists of his time. Russell Hatton focuses his analysis on the role of *li* in Chu Hsi's philosophy. Hatton compares the concept of *li* to that of Western philosophy's "substantial form." While some critics have maintained the equivalency of *li* and substantial form, Hatton challenges such conclusions. Allen Wittenborn, on the other hand, offers a different approach to the study of *li* in Chu Hsi's philosophy. In analyzing what he views as the problematic relationship between *li* and *ch'i*, Wittenborn states that to Chu Hsi, *li* is the determinant of the nature or essence of every individual thing and *ch'i* is the "constitutive energy" that brings about the thing in question through interaction with *li*. Wittenborn praises Chu Hsi for developing a theory of knowledge founded on psychological principles and for presenting a forceful argument for the existence of *li*, rather than merely presupposing it. Tomoeda Ryūtarō assesses the influence of Zen Buddhism on Chu Hsi's thought on *Tao* and *li*, contending that Chu Hsi demonstrated an early interest in Buddhism but later rejected its principles. For example, Zen emphasizes intuitive enlightenment, whereas Chu Hsi stressed reflection and inquiry into the principles of things. Chu Hsi's notion of *jen* has also been the subject of critical examination. Wing-tsit

Chan reviews Chu Hsi's motivation for writing the "Jen-shuo," arguing that the philosopher sought to dispel the confusion among his contemporary scholars regarding *jen*. Chan further discusses the originality of Chu Hsi's conception of *jen* as the "correct principle" or "character" of the mind, and also reviews Chu Hsi's thoughts on *jen* as the "principle of love." Additionally, Chan discusses the correspondence between Chu Hsi and another philosopher, Chang Shih, on the subject of *jen,* and notes that Chu Hsi made some revisions to the "Jen-shuo" due to his discussions with Chang Shih. John Borthrong, taking another critical avenue, investigates Chu Hsi's ethics as revealed in his discussions of the concepts of *jen* and *ch'eng*. Finding genius in an ethics often viewed as derivative, Borthrong explains that to Chu Hsi, *jen* represents "humaneness," or the unforced element of the principle of love, and that *ch'eng* is the process of self-realization by which *jen* is achieved. Like Chan, Hoyt Cleveland Tillman investigates Chu Hsi's correspondence with Chang Shih, and maintains that Chang Shih had a significant impacto on the development of Chu Hsi's philosophy, particularly in the areas of self-cultivation and the understanding of the mind. Tillman summarizes their relationship by quoting that while Chu Hsi's focus was on theory, Chang Shih emphasized the practice of the principles the two philosophers discussed.

PRINCIPAL WORKS

"Jen-shuo" ["Treatise on Humanity"] (treatise) c. 1171
Chin-ssu lu [*Reflections on Things at Hand*] (editor, with Lü Tsu-ch'ien) (anthology) 1175

Principal English Translations

Reflections on Things at Hand (translated by Wing-tsit Chan) 1967
Learning to Be a Sage: Selections from the Conversations of Master Chu, Arranged Topically (translated by Daniel K. Gardner) 1990
Chu Hsi's "Family Rituals" (translated by Patricia Buckley Ebey) 1991

CRITICISM

Herbert A. Giles (essay date 1901)

SOURCE: "History—Classical and General Literature," in *A History of Chinese Literature,* D. Appleton and Company, 1931, pp. 212-31.

[*In the excerpt below, Giles offers a brief overview of Chu Hsi's life and his major contributions to Chinese philosophy.*]

. . . The name of Chu Hsi (1130-1200) is a household word throughout the length and breadth of literary China. He graduated at nineteen, and entered upon a highly suc-

cessful official career. He apparently had a strong leaning towards Buddhism—some say that he actually became a Buddhist priest; at any rate, he soon saw the error of his ways, and gave himself up completely to a study of the orthodox doctrine. He was a most voluminous writer. In addition to his revision of the history of Ssŭ-ma Kuang, which, under the title of *T'ung Chien Kang Mu,* is still regarded as the standard history of China, he placed himself first in the first rank of all commentators on the Confucian Canon. He introduced interpretations either wholly or partly at variance with those which had been put forth by the scholars of the Han dynasty and hitherto received as infallible, thus modifying to a certain extent the prevailing standard of political and social morality. His principle was simply one of consistency. He refused to interpret words in a given passage in one sense, and the same words occurring elsewhere in another sense. The result, as a whole, was undoubtedly to quicken with intelligibility many paragraphs the meaning of which had been obscured rather than elucidated by the earlier scholars of the Han dynasty. Occasionally, however, the great commentator o'erleapt himself. Here are two versions of one passage in the Analects, as interpreted by the rival schools, of which the older seems unquestionably to be preferred:—

> *Han.*
>
> Mêng Wu asked Confucius concerning filial piety. The Master said, "It consists in giving your parents no cause for anxiety save from your natural ailments."
>
> *Chu Hsi.*
>
> Mêng Wu asked Confucius concerning filial piety. The Master said, "Parents have the sorrow of thinking anxiously about their children's ailments."

The latter of these interpretations being obviously incomplete, Chu Hsi adds a gloss to the effect that children are therefore in duty bound to take great care of themselves.

In the preface to his work on the Four Books as explained by Chu Hsi, published in 1745, Wang Puch'ing (born 1671) has the following passage:—"Shao Yung tried to explain the Canon of Changes by numbers, and Ch'êng I by the eternal fitness of things; but Chu Hsi alone was able to pierce through the meaning, and appropriate the thought of the prophets who composed it." The other best known works of Chu Hsi are a metaphysical treatise containing the essence of his later speculations, and the Little Learning, a handbook for the young. It has been contended by some that the word "little" in the last title refers not to youthful learners, but to the lower plane on which the book is written, as compared with the Great Learning. The following extract, however, seems to point more towards Learning for the Young as the correct rendering of the title:—

> "When mounting the wall of a city, do not point with the finger; when on the top, do not call out.
>
> "When at a friend's house, do not persist in asking for anything you may wish to have. When going upstairs,

utter a loud 'Ahem!' If you see two pairs of shoes outside and hear voices, you may go in; but if you hear nothing, remain outside. Do not trample on the shoes of other guests, nor step on the mat spread for food; but pick up your skirts and pass quickly to your allotted place. Do not be in a hurry to arrive, nor in haste to get away.

"Do not bother the gods with too many prayers. Do not make allowances for your own shortcomings. Do not seek to know what has not yet come to pass."

Chu Hsi was lucky enough to fall in with a clever portrait painter, a *rara avis* in China at the present day according to Mr. J. B. Coughtrie, late of Hongkong, who declares that "the style and taste peculiar to the Chinese combine to render a lifelike resemblance impossible, and the completed picture unattractive. The artist lays upon his paper a flat wash of colour to match the complexion of his sitter, and upon this draws a mere map of the features, making no attempt to obtain roundness or relief by depicting light and shadows, and never by any chance conveying the slightest suggestion of animation or expression." Chu Hsi gave the artist a glowing testimonial, in which he states that the latter not merely portrays the features, but "catches the very expression, and reproduces, as it were, the inmost mind of his model." He then adds the following personal tid-bit:—

"I myself sat for two portraits, one large and the other small; and it was quite a joke to see how accurately he reproduced my coarse ugly face and my vulgar rustic turn of mind, so that even those who had only heard of, but had never seen me, knew at once for whom the portraits were intended." It would be interesting to know if either of these pictures still survives among the Chu family heirlooms.

At the death of Chu Hsi, his coffin is said to have taken up a position, suspended in the air, about three feet from the ground. Whereupon his son-in-law, falling on his knees beside the bier, reminded the departed spirit of the great principles of which he had been such a brilliant exponent in life,—and the coffin descended gently to the ground.

J. Percy Bruce (essay date 1923)

SOURCE: "The Moral Order," in *Chu Hsi and His Masters: An Introduction to Chu Hsi and the Sung School of Chinese Philosophy,* Probsthain & Co., 1923, pp. 161-83.

[*In the essay below, Bruce analyzes the concept of* Tao *and examines how Chu Hsi's interpretation of it differed from that of contemporary Taoists. Bruce emphasizes that Chu Hsi opposed the "ultra-transcendental" view of* Tao *held by the Taoists of his day.*]

. . . [The] fundamental meaning of the word *Li* is Law; that it is essentially ethical; and that, while it derives its name from the fact that every single thing has its own rule

of existence, it also has a universal application. There is another word, *Tao,* which specially expresses both the universal and the ethical aspect of *Li.*

TAO OR MORAL LAW

The term *Tao* . . . fills a large place in Chinese philosophy of all schools. It has given its name to one of the three religions of China, it is a general term for philosophy itself, and it is the word most used as the term for religion. Its primary meaning, which must not be lost sight of in the study of its deeper meanings, is a "road" or "way".[1] It is called a "road" from the fact that it is a universal law common to all the ages as distinguished from *li,* the law of individual existence;[2] it is a highway "so level that it can be travelled upon for countless myriads of years, and all men find their way to it".[3] But it is an invisible road; the evidence of its existence is to be found in men's actions. In other words, it is the hidden moral principle from which proceed the common virtues of every day life, the Moral Law followed by all men in all ages.

This is the fundamental meaning of the term *Tao,* and formed the starting-point or line of approach for Chu Hsi in his exposition of its more comprehensive meanings. Shao Tzŭ said: "The Nature is the concrete expression of the Moral Order (*Tao*)." "This," says Chu Hsi, "is what is taught by all the Masters, but by none is it expressed so exactly as by Shao Tzŭ."[4] It is also in accord with the teaching of Mencius. "Love is the distinguishing characteristic of man," said the Sage; "as embodied in man's conduct it is termed *Tao.*"[5] *Tao* is seen in the relations of father and son, sovereign and minister, husband and wife, elder and younger brother, friend and friend. "*Tao* is near," said he, "and men seek it in what is distant. The work of duty lies in what is easy, and men seek for it in what is difficult. If each man would love his parents, and show due respect to his elders, the whole empire would enjoy tranquillity."[6] Chu Hsi's own interpretation of *Tao* was fully in accord with the teaching of the Sage. "Though *Tao* is present everywhere," he said, "how are we to find it? The answer is: simply by turning and looking within."[7] "We need not talk about empty and far-away things; if we would know the reality of *Tao* we must seek it within our own nature."[8]

But while this was the line of approach, the Philosopher did not stop there. Looking out from his own heart into the hearts of men in all ages, and beyond the domain of man into the wider world of phenomena in general, the Philosopher saw the very same principles pervading the universe as those which constituted the law of his own being. They are manifested in the moral excellence of the sages, they are written in the consciences of the most wicked of men. Heaven, earth, and all things follow along the same ethical highway as man himself. The essential meaning, then, of the word *Tao* is that the moral principles which we find engraved upon our own hearts are common to all our fellow-creatures. "From the fact that we ourselves possess the principles of Love, Righteousness, Reverence, and Wisdom, we infer that others possess them also; that, indeed, of the thousands and tens of thousands of human beings, and of all things in the universe, there are none without these principles. Extend our investigations as far as we will, we still find that there is nothing which does not possess them."[9]

There is thus a co-ordination of the principles underlying all phenomena in what is called "The Moral Order". Probably no one English word can be found consistently to represent the meaning of the word *Tao,* but of all possible renderings, such as Way, Path, Truth, Reason, or Logos, that perhaps which best expresses its meaning is this term "The Moral Order". Moral Order, however, is simply Moral Law as pervading the Universe, and it is often more convenient to use the latter form of expression. The essential thing to note is the twofold idea conveyed by either term. It is Law, but it is moral Law; it is Order, but it is an ethical Order. Dr. Faber speaks of *Tao* as "The Universal Reign of Law". He says: "According to the Chinese, there is only one universal law that makes itself known in all the unities throughout the course of the universe. Physical nature or spirit life makes no difference. Each follows in its way a fixed ordered course."[10] That is true, but it is from the ethical aspect of Law and its co-ordination in a universal moral standard for man and the universe that *Tao* derives its name. "According to my view," says Chu Hsi, "*Tao* obtains its name simply from the principle of inherent right present in all phenomena."[11] Speaking of the varied species of the myriad phenomena, he says, "Each one has within it the principle of right, what we call *Tao,* the road along which we ought to walk."[12] That is, not only is there a principle of right in everything, but it is the same "right" for all men and all things. This is *Tao.* "There must be some reason why, when the hawk and the fish come into existence they are hawk and fish. The cause is in the presence of the substance of *Tao.* The hawk flies and the fish leaps, not by the individual choice of the hawk and fish, but because of the Divine Law imparted to them in unceasing flow."[13] "The sun sets and the moon rises, the cold passes and the heat returns, the four seasons pursue their course, and all things are continually being produced." This is the pervading and manifested operation of *Tao,* while the immovable and abiding element in all this procession of phenomena is the substance of *Tao.*[14]

It is this wide and comprehensive meaning attached to the term *Tao* which differentiates it from *Li* (Law). It must not be forgotten that both terms refer to the same entity. The unity and universality of *Li* are clearly asserted more than once. The two terms, however, represent different aspects of this unity. The term *Tao* calls attention to the vast and comprehensive; the term Li calls attention to the minute and infinitesimal,[15] and refers to the innumerable vein-like principles inherent in every individual thing, like the grain in wood, or the lines vertical and horizontal in bamboo, or the strands of a piece of thread, or the bamboo splints of a basket.[16] *Li* derives its name from the fact that everything has each its own rule of existence; *Tao* expresses the fact that everything conforms to one Moral Law, and is part of

one Moral Order. Thus *Li* may be compared to the innumerable trees in a dense forest, whilst *Tao* is compared to a vast, trackless desert with its vision of the illimitable.[17] It is here that we reach the full transcendental meaning of the word *Tao.* Shao K'ang Chieh said: "Moral Law is the Supreme Ultimate," and Chu Hsi confirms his statement as referring to *Tao* as the self-existent law of the universe.[18] *Tao,* as we saw in the preceding chapter, existed before all things, and is the true source of all things.[19]

It was in his doctrine of *Tao* from the transcendental point of view that Chu Hsi came into conflict with Taoism, although at the same time there were marked affinities between the two systems. Lao Tzǔ, the reputed founder of this sect, in the classic work entitled *Tao Tê Ching* says: "There is an Infinite Being which was before Heaven and Earth. How calm it is, how free! It lives alone and changes not. It moves everywhere, but is not affected. We may regard it as the universal Mother. I know not its name. I call it *Tao.*"[20] Here is the same idea as that which we have found in Chu Hsi's teaching. Moreover, Lao Tzǔ's *Tao* was also the principle of which *Tê* . . . , or Virtue, is the manifestation; which is closely akin to Chu Hsi's doctrine of *Tao* as the comprehensive term for the four cardinal virtues, the principles which become *Tê* . . . when appropriated by man. What, therefore, Mr. Gorn Old says of Lao Tzǔ and Confucius is true: "At most they were not far divided on essential points."[21]

Where, then, was the point of divergence which resulted in the controversy between the two systems? We must bear in mind that Chu Hsi in his attacks on Taoism and the teachings of Lao Tzǔ was attacking them as interpreted by the representatives of that sect centuries after its founder had uttered his mystical teachings. Chu Hsi's charge against Taoism as interpreted by the scholars of his own day was what he regarded as its ultra-transcendentalism, which, he maintained, tended to destroy all moral distinctions. The chief points of controversy gathered round two passages, or sets of passages, in the *Tao Tê Ching,* which touch on the two aspects of *Tao* referred to above, the ethical and the transcendental. In Chapter XVIII Lao Tzǔ said, "When the great *Tao* is lost, men follow after Love and Righteousness,"[22] and in the chapter following he gives utterance to the bold paradox that "if men would forsake Love and Righteousness they might revert to their natural relationships."[23] Of the chapter in which the first of these passages occurs, Mr. W. Gorn Old gives the following explanation: "In this chapter Laotze (Lao Tzǔ) refers to the doctrines of Confucius as a system of 'patching up' that which is already worn out. The so-called virtue of Charity and Duty to one's neighbour (translated above as Love and Righteousness), the recognition of wisdom and learning by marks of merit, filial duty, and parental indulgence, are all regarded by the Old Philosopher as so many marks of degeneracy in the people. Against them he sets the natural virtue of integrity, and to this he would have us revert."[24] That is, Lao Tzǔ maintained that when Confucius inculcated Love and Righteousness he in that very fact confessed that *Tao* was lost, and therefore the only true remedy is to seek, and revert to, the lost *Tao*. To which Chu Hsi retorts: "If we separate *Tao* from Love and Righteousness we have no ethical principle at all, in which case how can *Tao* be *Tao?*[25] You have nothing left but an empty abstraction. What is *Tao* but Love and Righteousness? If you forsake Love and Righteousness you have forsaken *Tao* itself. You cannot destroy them without destroying virtue, for the simple reason that they *are* virtue. You cannot weaken the bonds of the Five Relationships without injuring the moral sanction itself, because they are the embodiment of it." It may perhaps be questioned whether Chu Hsi did not misconceive the Old Philosopher's meaning. It is hardly likely that when rightly understood the latter would lay himself open to so obvious a retort. The gloss by C. Spurgeon Medhurst suggests what is possibly a truer interpretation: "Virtues and duties are separative, subtle forms of self-assertion, something lower than that Ideal of ideals which identifies itself with the All, and in the joy of service annihilates self. Benevolence, righteousness, filiality, paternalism, loyalty, devotion, is each in its own way a degenerate, when the Tao, the Great Ideal, the One Life, recedes from view. Woe to that captain who, when navigating his vessel into port, allows the various lights and sounds of the harbour to turn his attention from the flashing signals of the lighthouse."[26]

Chu Hsi's point, however, remains. It is just here, indeed, that he joins issue with what he regards as a false mysticism. *Tao* itself *is* Love and Righteousness. It is not some far away, vague, and incomprehensible ideal. It has to do with everyday life and its relationships. This he makes clear in his answer to the other group of classic statements referred to above, in which the great Mystic's love of paradox is still more manifest. "The *Tao* which can be expressed in words," says Lao Tzŭ, "is not the eternal *Tao*. The name which can be named is not its eternal name. Nameless, it is the Beginning of heaven and earth; with a name it is the Mother of all things."[27] "All things in the universe are born of the Existent; and the Existent is born of the Non-Existent."[28] To quote again from Mr. W. Gorn Old, "The Causal Principle of all effects Laotze calls the Non-Existent. The well-known philosophical gamut of Principles, Causes, Effects, and Ultimates is reduced by the Sage to Non-Existent and the Existent, for seeing only One Cause (*Tao*) he regards all else as a single Effect (Nature)."[29] And in another passage the Sage speaks of *Tao* as the intangible and inscrutable. "Inscrutable, intangible," he says, "yet within are Forms. Intangible, inscrutable, yet within there is substance."[30] Chu Hsi's answer to this doctrine was that *Tao* has a real existence and is not transcendental to such a degree that it has no connexion with men. "The Nature is what men receive substantively; *Tao* is the natural Law of Right which we find in the phenomena of the universe. The law which we find in phenomena is really inherent in the Nature; but when we speak of it specifically as *Tao*, our idea is of something which is boundless as a vast desert and diffused in infinite variety so that its substance is invisible, and it is only when we seek it in our own Nature that we see what constitutes its reality—here and nowhere else!"[31] Chu Hsi therefore did not ex-

clude the transcendental aspect of *Tao*, but he held that the transcendental *Tao* is identical with the *Tao* which we find in our own hearts. "Is it maintained," he says again, "that *Tao* is lofty and distant, inscrutable and mysterious, and beyond the possibility of human study? Then I answer that *Tao* derives its very name from the fact that it is the principle of right conduct in every day life for all men, that it is like a road which should be travelled upon by the countless myriads of people within the four seas and nine continents; it is not what the Taoist and Buddhist describe as *Tao*: empty, formless, still, non-existent, and having no connexion with men. Is it maintained that *Tao* is far removed from us, so vast as to be out of touch with our needs, and that we are not called upon to study it? Then I say that *Tao*, present as it is in all the world in the relation between sovereign and minister, and between father and son, in down-sitting and up-rising, and in activity and rest, has everywhere its unchangeable clear law, which cannot fail for a single instant."[32]

> O world invisible, we view thee;
> O world intangible, we touch thee;
> O world unknowable, we know thee;
> Inapprehensible, we clutch thee.

The antithesis of the Non-Existent and the Existent . . . suggests the famous dictum of Chou Tzŭ: "Infinite! And also the Supreme Ultimate!" Those who entered into controversy with Chu Hsi frequently referred to this as teaching Lao Tzŭ's doctrine of the Non-Existent, contending that it was so implied in the word "not" . . . , which enters into the term "Infinite". . . . Chu Hsi, however, as was seen in the preceding chapter, was careful to explain that Chou Tzŭ in his doctrine asserted the invisibility and infinity of the Supreme Ultimate, and not that it was a separate entity paradoxically named the Non-Ens.

To sum up: *Tao* is the all-comprehensive Moral Law pervading the universe. It is identical with *Li* the ultimate element in the dualism of the cosmos. It is before all things, in all things, and the source of all things. Illimitable, it nevertheless has a real substantive existence; and—not least in the emphasis which the Philosopher places upon it—though transcending all things, it is identical with the Moral Law written upon the heart of man. For there is only one Moral Law. Any other hypothesis would conflict with the fundamental thesis of Chu Hsi's philosophy—the unity of the Nature.

THE FOUR ULTIMATA

The opening sentence of the *Yi Ching* contains four words of exceptional interest to the student of the Sung philosophy. They are *Yüan, Hêng, Li, Chêng* . . . , or the principles of Origin, Beauty, Utility, and Potentiality.

In Section I of the First Appendix of that classic the writer sets forth, somewhat vaguely it must be confessed, the relation of these principles to physical phenomena and to the virtues of the Sage. To quote Dr. Legge's note: "In paragraphs 1, 2, 4 the four attributes in Wên's Text are illustrated by the phenomena taking place in the physical world. In paragraphs 3 and 5, the subject is the sage."[33] In the Fourth Appendix the relation of these attributes to man's nature, with special reference to the Noble Man, is enlarged upon. The whole passage is as follows:—

> 1. What is called *Yüan* is in man the first and chief quality of goodness; what is called *Hêng* is the assemblage of all excellences; what is called *Li* is the harmony of all that is right; and what is called *Chêng* is the faculty of action.

> 2. The Noble Man, embodying love is able to preside over men; presenting the assemblage of all excellences he is able to show in himself the union of all forms of reverence; benefiting all creatures he is able to exhibit the harmony of all that is right; correct and firm, he is able to manage all affairs.

> 3. The fact that the Noble Man practises these four virtues justifies the application to him, of the words: "*Ch'ien*[34] represents the Principle of Origin (*Yüan*), the Principle of Beauty (*Hêng*), the Principle of Utility (*Li*), and the Principle of Potentiality (*Chêng*)."[35]

In this and the other passage referred to we have two ideas set forth. The first is that pervading the whole cosmos are four principles; they are ethical in character, they enter into all physical phenomena, and may be termed the Ultimata of the Universe. The second is that these ethical principles which pervade the universe enter into the nature of man; they are exemplified in the character of the Noble Man, and find their highest expression in the Sage or Saint. These two ideas constitute the germ from which the Sung School doctrine of the Four Ultima was developed.

In the preceding pages it has been pointed out that, according to our philosopher, *Li* (Law) consists of the four principles Love, Righteousness, Reverence, and Wisdom, while *Tao* represents the transcendental and universal aspect of *Li*. We have also seen that Chu Hsi, in criticizing what he regarded as the ultra-transcendentalism of Taoist philosophy, maintained that the transcendental *Tao* is identical with the moral principles to be found in our own hearts. What it is now desired to make clear is that just as the term *Tao* represents this transcendental and universal aspect of *Li* (Law), so the four terms *Yüan, Hêng, Li, Chêng,* translated in this work as the principles of Origin, Beauty, Utility, and Potentiality, represent the transcendental and universal aspect of the ethical principles of man's nature—Love, Righteousness, Reverence, and Wisdom. In other words, *Yüan, Hêng, Li, Chêng* are the ethical principles which constitute that Moral Order which was the subject of the preceding section.

Further, in a passage cited in the "Symposium" Ch'ên Ch'un, one of Chu Hsi's most noted pupils, quoting his Master, says: "*Yüan, Hêng, Li, Chêng* are the eternal constants of Heaven's Moral Order; Love, Righteousness, Reverence, and Wisdom are the governing principles of man's nature. . . . The Decree of Heaven is the diffusion of the Moral Law of Heaven throughout the universe and its impartation to the creature. Regarded as *Yüan, Hêng,*

Li, Chêng it is called the Moral Order of Heaven; regarded as diffused throughout the universe and imparted to the creature it is called the Decree of Heaven."[36] From this passage it will be seen that these Ultimata have both a transcendental and an immanent aspect. As transcendental, they constitute the *Tao,* or Moral Order; as immanent they are the Decree of Heaven, which is implanted in the creature and becomes the law of his being.

In their relation to the physical universe, the most conspicuous manifestation of these Four Ultimata is in the Four Seasons. "The first budding forth of things into life is the manifestation of the Principle of Origin, and among the seasons is Spring. The growth and development of things is the manifestation of the Principle of Beauty (or Development), and among the seasons is summer. The attainment to full fruition of things is the manifestation of the Principle of Utility, and among the seasons is Autumn. The storing up of nature's resources is the manifestation of the Principle of Potentiality, and among the seasons is Winter."[37]

The relation of the Four Ultimata, thus manifested in the Four Seasons, to the Four Cardinal Virtues which constitute man's moral nature is also set forth by Ch'ên Ch'un in the passage alluded to above. "Of the principles of which the Decree of Heaven is composed the Principle of Origin when received by me is termed Love; the Principle of Beauty when received by me is termed Reverence; the Principle of Utility when received by me is termed Righteousness; and the Principle of Potentiality when received by me is termed Wisdom."[38]

It will be noted that the Four Ultimata are always named in the same order, namely, Origin, Beauty, Utility, and Potentiality, corresponding to the order of the Seasons. But this order differs from that in which the Cardinal Virtues are almost invariably named, thus:—

Seasons:	Spring	Summer	Autumn	Winter
Ultimata:	Origin	Beauty	Utility	Potentiality
Virtues:	Love	Righteousness	Reverence	Wisdom.

The reason is that the order of the Cardinal Virtues arose from the historical development of their doctrine. In the early period Love alone, and later Love and Righteousness, coupled together, were emphasized as comprising all the virtues. Later still, these were further analysed with the result that Reverence and Wisdom were added; Reverence having a special relation to Love, and Wisdom to Righteousness. In considering, therefore, the anology between the Ultimata and the Cardinal Virtues, it must be borne in mind that there is this difference in the order in which they are named, so that the Principle of Beauty in the universe corresponds to Reverence in man, and the Principle of Utility to Righteousness, while the principles of Origin and Potentiality correspond respectively to Love and Wisdom.

The first of the Four Ultimata is *Yüan,* the Principle of Origin. Chu Hsi thus explains the relation of this principle to Love . . . : "The Principle of Origin is the beginning of the production of things by Heaven and Earth. The *Yi* says, 'Great is the Principle of Origin indicated by Ch'ien! All things owe to it their beginning.' 'Perfect is the Principle of Origin indicated by *K'un*! All things owe to it their birth.' From this we learn that the Principle of Origin is the thread running through all stages in the production of things by Heaven and Earth. *Yüan,* the Principle of Origin, is the vital impulse itself; in *Hêng,* the Principle of Beauty, it becomes the development of the vital impulse; in *Li,* the Principle of Utility, it becomes the fruiting, and in *Chêng,* the Principle of Potentiality, the completion of the vital impulse. It is the same with Love. Love in its essence is the vital impulse, the feeling of solicitude. If this vital impulse is wounded, then the feeling of solicitude is called forth. Conscientiousness also is Love manifesting itself in Righteousness; courtesy is Love manifesting itself in Reverence; and moral insight is Love manifesting itself in Wisdom."[39] Elsewhere he endorses the statement, "Love is the creative mind of Heaven and Earth, which is received by all men as their mind. . . . It is what is called the Principle of Origin of *Ch'ien* and *K'un*."[40]

The passage here referred to teaches that *Yüan,* the Principle of Origin pervading the physical universe, and Love, the premier virtue in man, are identical; and that it is to this Principle of Origin, or Love, that all things owe their beginning. But that is not all. Not only do all things physical owe their beginning to this principle, but all four principles are wrapped up in this one. We see it in the case of the Cardinal Virtues in man, and we see it in the material universe as exemplified in the progress of the seasons, which, though they differ one from another, all proceed from the Spring: Spring is the birth of Spring, Summer is its growth, Autumn is its consummation, and Winter is the storing up of Spring.[41]

The second of the Four Ultimata is *Hêng,* the Principle of Beauty. The word *Hêng* is explained by two Chinese words—*t'ung* . . . , which has the double significance of "permeating" and "continuing"; and *chia* . . . , which means "beautiful" or "excellent". In the gloss on the original text of the *Yi Ching,* which appears in the passage already quoted from the Fourth Appendix, the meaning of *Hêng* is given as "the assemblage of all excellencies"[42] But the idea of *t'ung* . . . , "permeating" or "continuing", is also present to the mind of the Chinese student when considering this word. It is the latter meaning which is most emphasized in explaining the relation of the Ultimata to the seasons. *Hêng* finds its manifestation in the Summer season, which is the "continuance" or "development" of the vital impulse of Spring. "Spring is characterized by the vital impulse; in the Summer we see its persistent and permeating principle."[43] But the meaning "excellence" also in this connexion is obviously appropriate; Summer is the Beauty season just as Spring is the Love season. In fact, the underlying thought in the use of this word seems to be a combination of both ideas—"permeating" or "continuing", and "excellent". Pervading all physical phenomena is a peculiar appropriateness and harmony, a surpassing excellence which produces in us the sense of Beauty. A mod-

ern writer on Theistic Philosophy says, "If Beauty be an ultimate element in the Universe—not analysable into anything else, but an essence or characteristic quality which defies the disintegrating effort of the analyst—it may perhaps supply us with one means of escape from that 'slough of despond' into which materialism plunges us. Beauty is as ultimate as anything that is known in the spheres of the true and the good; and while the discussion of its 'ultimate' is as interesting as the problem of metaphysical and ethical philosophy, it may be found to cast much light upon the latter." One of the special characteristics of Beauty, the same writer says, is its prodigality, "and its being diffused in quarters where it is not at first recognized. There is, in truth, 'no speech or language where its voice is not heard.' It is not only in external aspects of form and colour, however, that it is to be seen as an adornment of the world. It exists in the very heart of its laws, as these hold sway over the realm of the organic and the inorganic world. . . . Nature everywhere ornaments herself. There is a process at work which is a real effort of Nature to realize the Beautiful by the production of harmony. That is much the same thing as saying that the inmost spirit of Nature is itself beautiful, and that it strives to disclose itself through this channel. It is not the world of matter, or dull inert substance, however, that is beautiful, or that ornaments itself. It is the spirit of the cosmos that shines through, and irradiates, or transfigures material substance. It thus becomes a genuine apocalypse. . . . So far as, and so long as, it is discerned, our apprehension of it is a knowledge of the very essence of things, and therefore of that which transcends Nature."[44] In this passage Professor Knight admirably expresses in modern phrase the underlying thought which this word *Hêng* represents to the Chinese philosopher. The "assemblage of all excellencies" manifest in physical phenomena, or the prodigality of beauty diffused throughout the cosmos, is due to an ethical principle behind and beneath it all which ranks among the ultimata of the universe, and this principle is termed *Hêng,* or the principle of Beauty.

This meaning of the term best explains its relation to its corresponding virtue Reverence. "The Principle of Beauty (*Hêng*) inherent in the Decree of Heaven when received by me is termed Reverence."[45] The connexion is sufficiently apparent. Poet and artist alike will tell us how near akin are Beauty in the universe and Reverence in man, and there is no need to enlarge upon it here. But this is not the only connexion between the two terms. Reverence is itself beautiful, it is "Love in graceful expression".[46] It is the spirit of worship, the essence of ceremony. Worship and ceremony are perhaps the most common meanings of *Li* . . . , the word which in this work is translated Reverence; and worship and ceremony, though they include much more, are, or are intended to be, forms of Beauty. While "Beauty" . . . best explains the relation of *Hêng* to Reverence, the other meaning of the word *Hêng,* namely "continuance" or "development" . . . , is not excluded. Reverence is the development of Love just as Summer is the development of Spring. Love seeks expression. It cannot stop at the subjective, it must find its continuance in objective manifestation. Love seeks to express itself in _deferring_ to the object of its solicitude, and deference or courtesy is Reverence in operation.

The third of the Ultimata is _Li_ . . ., the Principle of Utility. The use of the word "utility" to express that ultimate principle in the Moral Order which answers to Righteousness in man is at least arresting, if not startling. A little reflection, however, will show its peculiar appropriateness. At the very root of the idea of Righteousness is that of order; and order in the philosophical sense implies not only regularity but, what is another name for the same thing, adaptation or useful collocation also. These two ideas are coupled together in one of the "Proofs" so familiar to the student of Theism. The late Professor Flint in his Baird Lecture said, "In what may be called general order, that which strikes us chiefly is regularity; in what may be called special order, that which chiefly strikes us is adaptation or adjustment. . . . While we may readily admit the distinction to be so far valid, it is certainly not absolute. Regularity and adjustment are rather different aspects of order than different kinds of order, and so far from excluding each other, they will be found implying each other. . . . Wherever regularity can be found adjustment will also be found, if the search be carried far enough."[47] It is the aspect of adaptation or useful collocation which is most suggested by the term _Li_. . . . A phrase which has been much used in connexion with the doctrine of Evolution is "the survival of the fittest". Chinese philosophy sees something deeper, namely, mutual service. All things are made to serve. Everything has stamped upon it as the law of its being the creative purpose that it should be of service to its neighbour.

> Oh, we live! Oh, we live!
> And this life which we conceive
> Is a great thing, and a grave,
> Which for others' use we have.

This principle of Utility is manifested in the Autumn season. The vitality which is born in the Spring and of which the Summer is the growth and development, finds its consummation and full fruition in Autumn, the harvest or fruit season. Western science teaches us that fruit in contrast to the leaf is self-giving.

In fruiting, the tree expends its life for the enrichment of others, so that Autumn may be characterized as the service season. The fulfilment of such service for all, says the Chinese philosopher, is what constitutes Order in the universe and Righteousness in the individual. Righteousness, then, is the fulfilment by each individual of the purpose of his existence in serving and benefiting his fellow creatures. "Benefiting all creatures he is able to exhibit the harmony of all that is right."[48] This principle pervading the universe is termed _Li_ . . ., the Principle of Utility.

The last of the Four Ultimata is _Chêng_ . . ., the Principle of Potentiality. Its physical manifestation is in the Winter season. In man it becomes Wisdom. Like the word for the Principle of Beauty, _Chêng_ has a double interpretation,

chêng . . . and _ku_. . . . Legge translates it "correct and firm". Its meaning is: "strong to do, and to do rightly." In the gloss given in the Fourth Appendix this principle is defined as the "faculty of action" and is said to confer on the noble man ability to "manage all affairs".[49] It is, however, a reserve faculty; and this is the special characteristic of Wisdom: a reserve of knowledge and ability adequate to all emergencies.

But this sense of reserve is not the characteristic of man alone; it is everywhere, in all the phenomena of the universe. Its typical manifestation is in the season of Winter. Life's powers to all outward seeming have died down. The fruit has passed, the leaves have fallen, the tree itself is dry and hard. But we are not deceived. We know that there are hidden resources reserved within it; the forces of its vitality are stored up for future need, and when the need emerges they will be called forth to the new task, strong and unerring in their efficiency. "Of the Four Attributes of _Ch'ien_, Origin is the chief and next to it is Potentiality as revealing the meaning of the end and beginning. Apart from the Principle of Origin there could be no birth; apart from the Principle of Potentiality there could be no end; apart from an ending there would be no means of making a beginning; and without a beginning the end could never be consummated; and so on in endless rotation."[50] In other words, Spring is the Mother of the Seasons, but Winter is the Mother of Spring. The hidden reserves of Winter are the guarantee of the permanence of the cosmos. This is _Chêng,_ the Principle of Potentiality. And what Winter is among the seasons, that is Wisdom among the virtues. Love as Love is creative; as Reverence it finds its development and expression in humility and self-repression, as Righteousness it finds its consummation in sacrifice and service, and as Wisdom it is fathering up its energies for new creations of love and humility, of service and sacrifice.

These then are the Four Ultimata, the Attributes of Heaven. We see the creative principle at work throughout the universe; we see its development in all-pervading beauty and harmony; we see its consummation in a universal perfection of adjustment the secret of which is mutual service; and we see everywhere, not less in the tiniest insect than in the mightiest physical forces, a reserve of efficiency which ensures the permanence of all things. These principles find their expression in the typical characteristics of the Four Seasons—in the Love season of Spring, in the Beauty season of Summer, in the Service season of Autumn, and in the Reserve season of Winter; their highest manifestation is in Man—in his Love, in his Righteousness, in his Reverence, and in his Wisdom; and among these Love is pre-eminent as the source and sum of all the rest.

Notes

1. . . . bk. xlvi, f. 1. (_P.H.N.,_ p. 269).

2. Ibid.

3. Ibid.

4. Ibid., f. 4 (*P.H.N.*, p. 275).

5. *Mencius*, p. 361.

6. Ibid., p. 178; cf. Faber's *Mind of Mencius*, p. 76.

7. . . . bk. xlii, f. 13 (*P.H.N.*, p. 32).

8. Ibid., bk. xlvi, f. 5 (*P.H.N.*, p. 276).

9. Ibid., bk. xlii, f. 13 (*P.H.N.*, p. 32).

10. *Mind of Mencius*, by E. Faber, p. 75

11. . . . bk. xlvi, f. 10 (*P.H.N.*, pp. 285-6).

12. Ibid.

13. Ibid., f. 9 (*P.H.N.*, pp. 283-4).

14. Ibid., f. 1 (*P.H.N.*, p. 270).

15. Ibid.

16. Ibid., ff. 1, 12 (*P.H.N.*, pp. 269, 290, 291).

17. Ibid., f. 16 (*P.H.N.*, p. 298).

18. Ibid., bk. xlix, f. 14.

19. . . . pt. i, f. 4.

20. Chap. XXV; cf. *The Simple Way*, by W. Gorn Old, p. 9.

21. *The Simple Way*, p. 6.

22. Chap. XVIII.

23. Chap. XIX.

24. *The Simple Way*, p. 53.

25. . . . bk. xlvi, f. 3 (*P.H.N.*, pp. 273-4).

26. *The Tao Teh King*, by C. Spurgeon Medhurst, p. 32.

27. See Chap. I; cf. Lionel Giles, *The Sayings of Lao-Tzŭ*, p. 19. Mr. C. Spurgeon Medhurst explains this passage thus: "That aspect of God which is hidden in eternity, without bounds, without limits, without beginning, must be distinguished from that side of God which is expressed in nature and in man. The one, apparently, subjective, certainly unknowable; the other, a self-manifestation, or a going forth, the commencement of our knowledge, as of our being." *The Tao Teh King*, by C. Spurgeon Medhurst, p. 1.

28. Chap. XL.

29. See *The Simple Way*, p. 26.

30. Chap. XXI; see ibid., pp. 57-8.

31. . . . bk. xlii, f. 22 (*P.H.N.*, p. 48).

32. Ibid., bk. xlvi, f. 6 (*P.H.N.*, pp. 278).

33. *Yi Ching*, pp. 213-4.

34. For the meaning of *Ch'ien* see p. 157.

35. *Yi Ching*, p. 408.

36. . . . , bk. xxix, f. 3.

37. Ibid., f. 4.

38. Ibid., f. 3.

39. . . . , bk. xlvii, f. 14 (*P.H.N.*, p. 336).

40. Ibid., f. 39 (*P.H.N.*, p. 382).

41. Ibid., bk. xlviii, f. 12 (*P.H.N.*, p. 407).

42. *Yi Ching*, p. 408.

43. . . . , bk. xlviii, f. 13 (*P.H.N.*, p. 410).

44. *Aspects of Theism*, by William Knight, pp. 191-3.

45. . . . , bk. i, f. 2.

46. . . . , bk. xlviii, f. 17 (*P.H.N.*, p. 417).

47. *Theism*, by Robert Flint, pp. 132-4.

48. *Yi Ching*, p. 408.

49. Ibid.

50. . . . , bk. xlviii, f. 14 (*P.H.N.*, p. 411).

Wing-tsit Chan (essay date 1963)

SOURCE: "The Great Synthesis in Chu Hsi," in *A Sourcebook in Chinese Philosophy*, translated and compiled by Wing-tsit Chan, Princeton University Press, 1963, pp. 588-604.

[*In the essay below, Chan discusses Chu Hsi's contribution to Neo-Confucianism, arguing that Chu Hsi eliminated the remnants of Buddhist and Taoist traditions in Neo-Confucianism, as well as refined and synthesized the six major concepts advocated by various Neo-Confucian philosophers. Chan also introduces several brief essays by Chu Hsi, included here.*]

No one has exercised greater influence on Chinese thought than Chu Hsi (Chu Yüan-hui, 1130-1200), except Confucius, Mencius, Lao Tzu, and Chuang Tzu. He gave Confucianism new meaning and for centuries dominated not only Chinese thought but the thought of Korea and Japan as well.

Our philosopher early distinguished himself as a patriot-scholar, having repeatedly petitioned the emperor to practice the Confucian principles of "the investigation of things" and "the extension of knowledge," to impeach inefficient officials, and not to make peace with the invading enemy. But he preferred a life of peace and poverty. From 1163 to 1178, he declined official positions and devoted his time to scholarship. Eventually he spent nine years in public service, and gave an excellent account of himself in promoting education and agriculture. He revived the intellectual center at the White Deer Grotto in present Kiangsi Province, and his lectures there attracted all prominent scholars of the time. But his philosophical views were too radical for the rulers to accept. He was repeatedly dismissed from office. In 1196, his teachings were prohibited, and someone even demanded his execution. He continued to write after his dismissal from government service, and in so doing made tremendous contributions.[1]

His contributions were by no means confined to philosophy, although that is the most important. He synthesized Confucius' concept of *jen* (humanity), Mencius' doctrines of humanity and righteousness, the idea of the investigation of things in the *Great Learning,* the teaching of sincerity in the *Doctrine of the Mean,* the yin yang (passive and active cosmic forces) and the Five Agents (Water, Fire, Wood, Metal, Earth) doctrines of Han times (206 B.C.-A.D. 220), and practically all the important ideas of the Neo-Confucianists of early Sung (960-1279), as we shall point out later on. His breadth of insight and his scholarship are equalled by few men in Chinese history. Rightly or wrongly, he was the one who established the orthodox line of transmission of the Confucian School from Confucius through Mencius, Chou Tun-i (Chou Lien-hsi, 1017-1073), Chang Tsai (Chang Heng-ch'ü, 1020-1077), Ch'eng Hao (Ch'eng Ming-tao, 1032-1085), and his brother Ch'eng I (Ch'eng I-ch'uan, 1033-1107).[2] He inaugurated new tendencies in textual criticisms. Among other things, he considered the *Book of Changes* as a book primarily for divination, thus radically differing from other Neo-Confucianists who depended on it for much of their philosophical inspiration. His most radical innovation was to select and group the *Analects,* the *Book of Mencius,* the *Great Learning,* and the *Doctrine of the Mean* (both of which are chapters of the *Book of Rites*), as the Four Books, wrote commentaries on them, interpreted them in new lights, and made them the foundation of his social and ethical philosophy. From 1313 to 1905 the Four Books were the basis of the civil service examinations. As a result, they have exercised far greater influence on Chinese life and thought in the last six hundred years than any other Classic. Through his interpretations of the Four Books, he made Neo-Confucianism truly Confucian, stripped of the Buddhist and Taoist influence which had been conspicuous in previous Neo-Confucianists.

Generally speaking, while he reaffirmed the basic doctrines of Confucianism, he brought its development over the centuries, especially during the Sung period, into a harmonious whole and gave it a new complexion.

Up to this time, Neo-Confucianism was characterized by six major concepts advocated by the different philosophers, namely, the Great Ultimate, principle (*li*), material force (*ch'i*),[3] the nature, the investigation of things, and humanity. All of these were developed, systematized, and synthesized in the greatest of Neo-Confucianists, Master Chu.

Assimilating the concepts of the Great Ultimate advocated by Chou Tun-i and combining it with the concept of principle of Ch'eng Hao and his brother Ch'eng I, Chu Hsi held that the Great Ultimate has no physical form but consists of principle in its totality. All actual and potential principles are contained in the Great Ultimate, which is complete in all things as a whole and in each thing individually. The relationship between the Great Ultimate in the universe and the Great Ultimate in each individual thing is not one of whole and part, but one similar to moonlight shining on objects. Each object has its own moonlight but this moonlight is moonlight as a whole.

It is the principle of things to be actualized, and actualization requires principle as its substance and material force

as its actuality. Thus the Great Ultimate involves both principle and material force. The former is necessary to explain the reality and universality of things. It is incorporeal, one, eternal and unchanging, uniform, constituting the essence of things, always good, but it does not contain a dichotomy of good and evil, does not create things. The latter is necessary to explain physical form, individuality, and the transformation of things. It is physical, many, transitory and changeable, unequal in things, constituting their physical substance, involving both good and evil (depending on whether its endowment in things is balanced or partial), and is the agent of creation.

While seemingly dualistic, principle and material force are never separate. Principle needs material force in order to have something to adhere to, and material force needs principle as its own law of being. The fact that they always work together is due to the direction of the mind of the universe, which is the universe itself. In man this mind becomes, on the one hand, the moral mind, which is the principle of his original nature, and on the other, the human mind, which is the principle of original nature mixed with physical endowment and human desires. The principle of a thing or man is his very nature, real and concrete, unlike the nature in Buddhism, which is Emptiness. Original mind is principle in itself, unmoved, and perfectly good, while physical nature, on the other hand, is principle mixed with material force; it is the aroused state, involving both good and evil. The two natures, however, are always interfused, one the substance and the other, function. As substance, it is the nature, and as function, it is the feelings. That which unites and commands both human nature and feelings, according to Chang Tsai, is the mind. By unifying and commanding is meant the mind unifying itself by harmonizing man's nature and his feelings and by transforming the human mind into the moral mind. Hence the possibility of morality. Moreover, all human beings and things have a mind, and this mind is in essence identical with the mind of the universe. Therefore there is the possibility of knowledge and the mutual influence and response among things and human beings, whether living or dead. Hence the investigation of things and religious sacrificial rites.

In his doctrine of the investigation of things, Chu Hsi follows closely Ch'eng I, as he does in the doctrine of principle. Indeed he was a fourth-generation pupil of the two Ch'eng brothers; and of the two, Ch'eng I was his main source of ideas. But he did not merely follow him or elaborate on him. He differs from him at many points. For example, while to Ch'eng I physical nature is outside principle, to Chu Hsi they are intermingled. Like Ch'eng, he taught seriousness (*ching*)[4] as the psychological prerequisite for true knowledge and exhaustive investigation as the method. But he was careful to emphasize equally both the deductive and inductive methods and both objective observation and intuitive understanding.

The greatest understanding to be achieved is that of *jen,*[5] an idea close to the hearts of all Confucianists. It was one of the most persistent subjects in the history of Chinese philosophy, and its long evaluation finally culminated in Chu Hsi's famous description that it is "the character of man's mind and the principle of love." The significance and implications of this idea as well as of other ideas of his will be elaborated in the comments. Suffice it to say here that virtually every cardinal Confucian concept was brought to a higher peak by Chu Hsi.

Such a well organized and freshly envigorated philosophy could not but overwhelm the Chinese. Although not without opposition from such outstanding Neo-Confucianists as Lu Hsiang-shan (Lu Chiu-yüan, 1139-1192), his philosophy and that of Ch'eng I, that is, the Ch'eng-Chu School of Principle, dominated the intellectual life of the Southern Sung period (1127-1279). In the Yüan dynasty (1271-1368) that followed, the supremacy of the Ch'eng-Chu School remained unchallenged. With a few exceptions, great scholars were all exponents of Chu Hsi's rationalism. Even those who attempted to reconcile the conflicts between him and Lu Hsiang-shan were essentially faithful disciples of his. In the Ming period (1318-1644), before the idealism of Wang Yang-ming (Wang Shou-jen, 1472-1529) emerged as the leading philosophy, his rationalism was the strongest intellectual current. Even during the fifteenth and sixteenth centuries when Wang overshadowed him, it did not entirely disappear. There were philosophers like members of the Tung-lin School who defended it and others like Liu Tsung-chou (1578-1645) who tried to synthesize it with the idealism of Wang. Consequently as opposition against idealism grew in the seventeenth century, Chu's philosophy was revived in strength. This period was one of independent and critical thinking, but some of the most outstanding scholars of the time, notably Ku Yen-wu (1613-1682) and Wang Fu-chih (1619-1692) were greatly influenced by and strongly inclined toward Chu Hsi. While eventually the critical spirit overthrew the speculative philosophies of both Wang and Chu, the latter had left a permanent imprint on the philosophical life of China. From the beginning of the fourteenth century on, his and Ch'eng I's interpretation of the Confucian Classics were officially held as the orthodox doctrines, and as already mentioned they formed the basis of civil service examinations and were therefore the intellectual standards for the Chinese literati until 1905 when the examination system was abolished. His philosophy survived the Intellectual Revolution of 1917 and became in the thirties the foundation of Professor Fung Yu-lan's new rationalism. His influence was not limited to China. It became an orthodoxy in Korea and the outstanding school of thought in the history of Japan.

The following selections include three short essays and a letter from the ***Chu Tzu wen-chi (Collection of Literary Works by Chu Hsi)***,[6] and a number of sayings from the ***Chu Tzu ch'üan-shu (Complete Works of Chu Hsi)***.[7] . . .

A. TREATISES

1. A TREATISE ON JEN

Original note: In the Chekiang edition, the "Treatise on Jen" by Chang Shih (Chang Nan-hsien, 1133-1180) is erroneously considered to be by Master Chu and Master Chu's treatise is considered to be a preface to Chang's essay. There is also a note saying that this treatise is perhaps a preface to Chang's essay. This is a mistake and is here corrected.

"The mind of Heaven and Earth is to produce things."[8] In the production of man and things, they receive the mind of Heaven and Earth as their mind. Therefore, with reference to the character of the mind, although it embraces and penetrates all and leaves nothing to be desired, nevertheless, one word will cover all of it, namely, *jen* (humanity). Let me try to explain fully.

The moral qualities of the mind of Heaven and Earth are four: origination, flourish, advantages, and firmness.[9] And the principle of origination unites and controls them all. In their operation they constitute the course of the four seasons, and the vital force of spring permeates all. Therefore in the mind of man there are also four moral qualities—namely, *jen*, righteousness, propriety, and wisdom—and *jen* embraces them all. In their emanation and function, they constitute the feeling of love, respect, being right, and discrimination between right and wrong—and the feeling of commiseration pervades them all. Therefore in discussing the mind of Heaven and Earth, it is said, "Great is *ch'ien* (Heaven), the originator!" and "Great is *k'un* (Earth), the originator."[10] Both substance and function of the four moral qualities are thus fully implied without enumerating them. In discussing the excellence of man's mind, it is said, "*Jen* is man's mind."[11] Both substance and function of the four moral qualities are thus fully presented without mentioning them. For *jen* as constituting the Way (Tao) consists of the fact that the mind of Heaven and Earth to produce things is present in everything. Before feelings are aroused this substance is already existent in its completeness. After feelings are aroused, its function is infinite. If we can truly practice love and preserve it, then we have in it the spring of all virtues and the root of all good deeds. This is why in the teachings of the Confucian school, the student is always urged to exert anxious and unceasing effort in the pursuit of *jen*. In the teachings (of Confucius, it is said), "Master oneself and return to propriety."[12] This means that if we can overcome and eliminate selfishness and return to the Principle of Nature, (*T'ien-li*, Principle of Heaven), then the substance of this mind (that is, *jen*) will be present everywhere and its function will always be operative. It is also said, "Be respectful in private life, be serious in handling affairs, and be loyal in dealing with others."[13] These are also ways to preserve this mind. Again, it is said, "Be filial in serving parents," "Be respectful in serving elder brothers."[14] and "Be loving in dealing with all things."[15] These are ways to put this mind into practice. It is again said, "They sought *jen* and found it,"[16] for (Po-i) declined a kingdom and left the country (in favor of his younger brother, Shu-ch'i) and they both remonstrated their superior against a punitive expedition and chose retirement and hunger,[17] and in doing so, they prevented losing this mind. Again it is said, "Sacrifice life in order to realize *jen*."[18] This means that we desire something more than life and hate something more than death, so as not to injure this mind. What mind is this? In Heaven and Earth it is the mind to produce things infinitely. In man it is the mind to love people gently and to benefit things. It includes the four virtues (of humanity, righteousness, propriety, and wisdom) and penetrates the Four Beginnings (of the sense of commiseration, the sense of shame, the sense of deference and compliance, and the sense of right and wrong).

Someone said: According to our explanation, is it not wrong for Master Ch'eng[19] to say that love is feeling while *jen* is nature and that love should not be regarded as *jen*?[20]

Answer: Not so. What Master Ch'eng criticized was the application of the term to the expression of love. What I maintain is that the term should be applied to the principle of love. For although the spheres of man's nature and feelings are different, their mutual penetration is like the blood system in which each part has its own relationship. When have they become sharply separated and been made to have nothing to do with each other? I was just now worrying about students' reciting Master Ch'eng's words without inquiring into their meaning, and thereby coming to talk about *jen* as clearly apart from love. I have therefore purposely talked about this to reveal the hidden meaning of Master Ch'eng's words, and you regard my ideas as different from his. Are you not mistaken?

Someone said: The followers of Master Ch'eng have given many explanations of *jen*. Some say that love is not *jen,* and regard the unity of all things and the self as the substance of *jen*. Others maintain that love is not *jen* but explain *jen* in terms of the possession of consciousness by the mind. If what you say is correct, are they all wrong?

Answer: From what they call the unity of all things and the self,[21] it can be seen that *jen* involves love for all, but unity is not the reality which makes *jen* a substance. From what they call the mind's possession of consciousness,[22] it can be seen that *jen* includes wisdom, but that is not the real reason why *jen* is so called. If you look up Confucius' answer to (his pupil) Tzu-kung's question whether conferring extensive benefit on the people and bringing salvation to all (will constitute *jen*)[23] and also Master Ch'eng's statement that *jen* is not to be explained in terms of consciousness,[24] you will see the point. How can you still explain *jen* in these terms?

Furthermore, to talk about *jen* in general terms of the unity of things and the self will lead people to be vague, confused, neglectful, and make no effort to be alert. The bad effect—and there has been—may be to consider other things as oneself. To talk about love in specific terms of consciousness will lead people to be nervous, irascible, and devoid of any quality of depth. The bad effect—and there has been—may be to consider desire as principle. In one case, (the mind) forgets (its objective). In the other (there is artificial effort to) help (it grow).[25] Both are wrong. Furthermore, the explanation in terms of consciousness does not in any way approach the manner of (a man of *jen*

who) "delights in mountains" (while a man of wisdom delights in water)[26] or the idea that (*jen* alone) "can preserve" (what knowledge has attained),[27] as taught his pupil by Confucius. How then can you still explain love in those terms? I hereby record what they said and write this treatise on *jen*. (***Chu Tzu wen-chi,*** or ***Collection of Literary Works of Chu Hsi,*** CTTC, 67:20a-21b)

Comment. This short treatise is both a criticism of certain theories and the incorporation of others into a harmonious whole. In addition, as Sun Ch'i-feng (1584-1675) has said, it expresses what the Ch'eng brothers had not expressed.[28] As can readily be seen, the central point is the synthesis of substance and function. In a way Chang Heng-ch'ü had implied it,[29] but the relationship between substance and function of *jen* was not clear until Chu.

In ignoring the nature of *jen* and confining his teachings only to its practice, Confucius taught only the function of *jen*. In a sense Mencius was the first to stress both substance and function when he laid equal emphasis on *jen* and righteousness. In interpreting *jen* as love, Han Confucians viewed it almost exclusively from the point of view of function. Early Neo-Confucianists, on the other hand, whether in their doctrines of *jen* as impartiality, as forming one body with Heaven and Earth, or as consciousness, viewed *jen* almost exclusively from the point of view of substance. Here Chu Hsi gives substance and function equal importance, as they are synthesized neatly in the saying that *jen* is "the character of the mind" and "the principle of love."[30] This has become a Neo-Confucian idiom. It means that, as substance, *jen* is the character of man's mind, and, as function, it is the principle of love.

Since *jen* is the character of the mind, it is the nature of every man, and as such, universal nature. Thus it includes wisdom, propriety, and righteousness. The reason for this is the generative character of *jen*, which he got from the Ch'eng brothers.[31]

2. A TREATISE ON CH'ENG MING-TAO'S DISCOURSE ON THE NATURE

[Master Ch'eng Hao also said,] "What is inborn is called nature. . . . They (nature and material force, *ch'i*) are both inborn."[32] [His meaning is this]: What is imparted by Heaven (Nature) to all things is called destiny (*ming,* mandate, fate). What is received by them from Heaven is called nature. But in the carrying out of the Mandate of Heaven, there must first be the interaction, mutual influence, consolidation, and integration of the two material forces (yin and yang) and the Five Agents (of Metal, Wood, Water, Fire, and Earth) before things can be produced. Man's nature and destiny exist before physical form [and are without it], while material force exists after physical form [and is with it]. What exists before physical form is the one principle harmonious and undifferentiated, and is invariably good. What exists after physical form, however, is confused and mixed, and good and evil are thereby differentiated. Therefore when man and things are produced, they have in them this material force, with the endowment of which they are produced. But the nature endowed by Heaven is therein preserved. This is how Master Ch'eng elucidated the doctrine of Kao Tzu that what is inborn is called nature, and expressed his own thought by saying that "One's nature is the same as material force and material force is the same as nature."[33]

[Master Ch'eng also said,] "[According to principle, there are both good and evil] in the material force with which man is endowed at birth. . . . [Nature is of course good], but it cannot be said that evil is not nature."[34] It is the principle of nature that the material force with which man is endowed necessarily has the difference of good and evil. For in the operation of material force, nature is the controlling factor. In accordance with its purity or impurity, material force is differentiated into good and evil. Therefore there are not two distinct things in nature opposing each other. Even the nature of evil material force is good, and therefore evil may not be said to be not a part of nature. The Master further said, "Good and evil in the world are both the Principle of Nature. What is called evil is not original evil. It becomes evil only because of deviation from the mean."[35] For there is nothing in the world which is outside of one's nature. All things are originally good but degenerated into evil, that is all.

[The Master further said,] "For what is inborn is called one's nature. . . . [The fact that whatever issues from the Way is good may be compared to] water always flowing downward."[36] Nature is simply nature. How can it be described in words? Therefore those who excel in talking about nature only do so in terms of the beginning of its emanation and manifestation, and what is involved in the concept of nature may then be understood in silence, as when Mencius spoke of the Four Beginnings (of humanity, righteousness, propriety, and wisdom).[37] By observing the fact that water necessarily flows downward, we know the nature of water is to go downward. Similarly, by observing the fact that the emanation of nature is always good, we know that nature involves goodness.

[The Master further said,] "Water as such is the same in all cases. . . . [Although they differ in being turbid or clear, we cannot say that the turbid water ceases to be water. . . . The original goodness of human nature is like the original clearness of water. Therefore it is not true that two distinct and opposing elements of good and evil exist in human nature and that] each issues from it." This is again using the clearness and turbidity of water as an analogy. The clearness of water is comparable to the goodness of nature. Water flowing to the sea without getting dirty is similar to one whose material force with which he is endowed is pure and clear and who is good from childhood. In the case of a sage it is his nature to be so and he preserves his Heavenly endowment complete. Water that flows only a short distance and is already turbid is like one whose material endowment is extremely unbalanced and impure and is evil from childhood. Water that flows a long distance before becoming turbid is like one who, as

he grows up, changes his character as he sees something novel and attractive to him, and loses his child's heart. That water may be turbid to a greater or smaller extent is similar to the fact that one's material force may be dark or clear and pure or impure in varying degrees. "We cannot say that the turbid water ceases to be water" means that it cannot be said that evil is not nature. Thus although man is darkened by material force and degenerates into evil, nature does not cease to be inherent in him. Only, if you call it nature, it is not the original nature, and if you say it is not nature, yet from the beginning it has never departed from it. Because of this, man must increase his effort at purification. If one can overcome material force through learning, he will know that this nature is harmonious and unified and from the beginning has never been destroyed. It is like the original water. Although the water is turbid, the clear water is nevertheless there, and therefore it is not that clear water has been substituted by turbid water. When it is clear, it is originally not turbid, and therefore it is not that turbid water has been taken out and laid in a corner. This being the case, the nature is originally good. How can there be two distinct, opposing, and parallel things existing in nature?

[Master Ch'eng finally said,] "This principle is the Mandate of Heaven. [To obey and follow it is the Way. . . . One can neither augment nor diminish this function which corresponds to the Way.] Such is the case of Shun[38] who, [obeying and following the Way], possessed the empire as if it were nothing to him.[39] The sentence "This principle is the Mandate of Heaven" includes the beginning and ending, and the fundament and the secondary. Although the cultivation of the Way is spoken of with reference to human affairs, what is cultivated is after all nothing but the Mandate of Heaven as it originally is and is nothing man's selfishness or cunning can do about it. However, only the sage can completely fulfill it. Therefore the example of Shun is used to make the meaning clear. (*Chu Tzu wen-chi,* 67:16b-18a)

Comment. In this essay, Chu Hsi not only removes the ambiguity in Ch'eng Hao's original treatise, which uses the same term, "nature," for basic nature—which is perfectly good—in the first part, and for physical nature—which involves both good and evil—in the second part. He also harmonizes all theories of human nature before him, whether Mencius' theory of original goodness, Hsün Tzu's (fl. 298-238 B.C.) theory of original evil, or Cheng Tsai's theory of physical nature.[40] Evil can now be explained, while the key Confucian teaching that evil can be overcome is reaffirmed. In addition, the ambiguity in Ch'eng Hao's statement that there are both good and evil in man's nature, which led to severe criticism of him, is now removed.[41]

3. FIRST LETTER TO THE GENTLEMEN OF HUNAN ON EQUILIBRIUM AND HARMONY[42]

Concerning the meaning in the *Doctrine of the Mean* that equilibrium (*chung,* centrality, the Mean) is the state before the feelings of pleasure, anger, sorrow, and joy are aroused and that harmony is that state after they are aroused,[43] because formerly I realized the substance of the operation of the mind, and, furthermore, because Master Ch'eng I had said that "whenever we talk about the mind, we refer to the state after the feelings are aroused,"[44] I looked upon the mind as the state after the feelings are aroused and upon nature as the state before the feelings are aroused. However, I have observed that there are many incorrect points in Master Ch'eng's works. I have therefore thought the matter over, and consequently realized that in my previous theory not only are the [contrasting] terms "mind" and "nature" improper but the efforts in my daily task also completely lack a great foundation. Therefore the loss has not been confined to the meanings of words.

The various theories in Master Ch'eng's *Wen-chi* (Collection of Literary Works) and *I-shu* (Surviving Works) seem to hold that before there is any sign of thought or deliberation and prior to the arrival of [stimulus] of external things, there is the state before the feelings of pleasure, anger, sorrow, and joy are aroused. At this time, the state is identical with the substance of the mind, which is absolutely quiet and inactive, and the nature endowed by Heaven should be completely embodied in it. Because it is neither excessive nor insufficient, and is neither unbalanced nor one-sided, it is called equilibrium. When it is acted upon and immediately penetrates all things, the feelings are then aroused.[45] In this state the functioning of the mind can be seen. Because it never fails to attain the proper measure and degree and has nowhere deviated from the right, it is called harmony. This is true because of the correctness of the human mind and the moral character of the feelings and nature.

However, the state before the feelings are aroused cannot be sought and the state after they are aroused permits no manipulation. So long as in one's daily life the effort at seriousness and cultivation is fully extended and there are no selfish human desires to disturb it, then before the feelings are aroused it will be as clear as a mirror and as calm as still water, and after the feelings are aroused it will attain due measure and degree without exception. This is the essential task in everyday life. As to self-examination when things occur and seeking understanding through inference when we come into contact with things, this must also serve as the foundation. If we observe the state after the feelings are aroused, what is contained in the state before the feelings are aroused can surely be understood in silence. This is why in his answers to Su Chi-ming, Master Ch'eng discussed and argued back and forth in the greatest detail and with extreme care, but in the final analysis what he said was no more than the word "seriousness" (*ching*).[46] This is the reason why he said, "Seriousness without fail is the way to attain equilibrium,"[47] and "For entering the Way there is nothing better than seriousness. No one can[48] ever extend knowledge to the utmost without depending on seriousness,"[49] and again, "Self-cultivation requires seriousness; the pursuit of learning depends on the extension of knowledge."[50]

Right along, in my discussions and thinking, I have simply considered the mind to be the state after the feelings are aroused, and in my daily efforts I have also merely considered examining and recognizing the clues [of activities of feelings] as the starting points. Consequently I have neglected the effort of daily self-cultivation, so that the mind is disturbed in many ways and lacks the quality of depth or purity. Also, when it is expressed in speech or action, it is always characterized by a sense of urgency and an absence of reserve, and there is no longer any disposition of ease or profoundness. For a single mistake in one's viewpoint can lead to as much harm as this. This is something we must not overlook.

When Master Ch'eng said that "whenever we talk about the mind, we refer to the state after the feelings are aroused," he referred [only] to the mind of an infant [whose feelings have already been aroused]. When he said "whenever we talk about the mind," he was mistaken in the way he expressed it and therefore admitted the incorrectness and corrected himself [by saying, "This is of course incorrect, for the mind is one. Sometimes we refer to its substance (namely, the state of absolute quietness and inactivity) and sometimes we refer to its function (namely, its being acted on and immediately penetrating all things). It depends on one's point of view"].[51] We should not hold on to his saying which he had already corrected and on that basis doubt the correctness of his various theories, or simply dismiss it as incorrect without examining the fact that he was referring to something else. What do you gentlemen think about this? (*Chu Tzu wen-chi*, 64:28b-29b)

Comment. As Liu Tsung-chou (Liu Ch'i-shan, 1578-1645) has pointed out, this letter represents Chu Hsi's final doctrine on moral efforts.[52] Chou Lien-hsi had taught tranquillity. Chu Hsi's own teacher, Li T'ung (Li yen-p'ing, 1088-1158) had taught sitting in meditation. Chu Hsi was at first much convinced. But after he learned the doctrine of seriousness from the Ch'eng brothers, he felt, as the Ch'engs did, that tranquillity was an extreme, and in seriousness one maintains the balance of internal and external life. In this letter, Chu Hsi emphasizes the point that the key to moral cultivation is to have a great foundation. Once the foundation is firm, tranquillity, sitting in meditation, and seriousness are all helpful. This is not only a synthesis of the teachings of his predecessors but a new approach.

4. A Treatise on the Examination of the Mind

Someone asked whether it is true that the Buddhists have a doctrine of the examination of the mind.

Answer: The mind is that with which man rules his body. It is one and not a duality, is subject and not object, and controls the external world instead of being controlled by it. Therefore, if we examine external objects with the mind, their principles will be apprehended. Now (in the Buddhist view), there is another thing to examine the mind. If this is true, then outside this mind there is another one which is capable of controlling it. But is what we call the mind a unity or a duality? Is it subject or object? Does it control the external world or is it controlled by the external world? We do not need to be taught to see the fallacy of the Buddhist doctrine.

Someone may say: In the light of what you have said, how are we to understand such expressions by sages and worthies as "absolute refinement and singleness (of mind),"[53] "Hold it fast and you preserve it. Let it go and you lose it,"[54] "Exert the mind to the utmost and know one's nature. . . . Preserve one's mind and nourish one's nature,"[55] and "(Standing) let a man see (truthful words and serious action) in front of him, and (riding in a carriage), let him see them attached to the yoke."[56]

Answer: These expressions and (the Buddhist doctrine) sound similar but are different, just like the difference between seedlings and weed, or between vermilion and purple, and the student should clearly distinguish them. What is meant by the precariousness of the human mind is the budding of human selfish desires, and what is meant by the subtlety of the moral mind is the all-embracing death of the Principle of Heaven (Nature).[57] The mind is one; it is called differently depending on whether or not it is rectified. The meaning of the saying, "Have absolute refinement and singleness (of mind)" is to abide by what is right and discern what is wrong, as well as to discard the wrong and restore the right. If we can do this, we shall indeed "hold fast the Mean,"[58] and avoid the partiality of too much or too little. The saying does not mean that the moral mind is one mind, the human mind another, and then still a third one to make them absolutely refined and single. By "holding it fast and preserving it" is not meant that one mind holds fast to another and so preserves it. Neither does "letting it go and losing it" mean that one mind lets go another and so loses it. It merely means that if the mind holds fast to itself, what might be lost will be saved, and if the mind does not hold fast but lets itself go, then what is preserved will be lost. "Holding it fast" is another way of saying that we should not allow our conduct during the day to fetter and destroy our innate mind characterized by humanity and righteousness.[59] It does not mean that we should sit in a rigid position to preserve the obviously idle consciousness and declare that "This is holding it fast and preserving it!" As to the exerting of the mind to the utmost, it is to investigate things and study their principles to the utmost, to arrive at broad penetration, and thus to be able fully to realize the principle (*li*) embodied in the mind. By preserving the mind is meant "seriousness (*ching*) to straighten the internal life and righteousness to square the external life,"[60] a way of cultivation similar to what has just been called absolute refinement, singleness, holding fast, and preserving. Therefore one who has fully developed his mind can know his nature and know Heaven,[61] because the substance of the mind is unbeclouded and he is equipped to search into principle in its natural state, and one who has preserved the mind can nourish his nature and serve Heaven,[62] because the substance of the mind is not lost and he is equipped to follow

principle in its natural state. Is this the same as using one mind fully to develop another, or one mind to preserve another, like two things holdings on to each other and refusing to let go?

The expressions "in front of him" and "attached to the yoke" are intended to teach loyalty, faithfulness, earnestness, and seriousness,[63] as if saying that if these moral qualities are always borne in mind, we will see them no matter where we may go. But it does not mean that we observe the mind. Furthermore, suppose the body is here while the mind is in the front beholding it, and the body is in the carriage while the mind is attached to its yoke. Is that not absurd? Generally speaking, the doctrine of the sage is to base on one's mind on investigating principle to the utmost and to respond to things by following it. It is like the body using the arm and the arm using the finger. The road will be level and open, the abiding place will be broad and easy, and the principle concrete and its operation natural.

According to the doctrine of the Buddhists, one seeks the mind with the mind, one employs the mind with the mind, like the mouth gnawing the mouth or the eye seeing the eye. Such an operation is precarious and oppressive, the road dangerous and obstructed, and the principle empty and running against its own course. If their doctrine seems to have something similar (to the Confucian), in reality it is different like this. But unless one is a superior man who thinks accurately and sifts clearly, how can be avoid being deluded in this matter? (*Chu Tzu wen-chi,* 67:18b-20a).

Notes

1. Chu Hsi was a native of Anhui. For several years he studied under his father who was head of various departments but eventually left the capital because he opposed accepting humiliating peace terms from the northern invaders. In 1151, Chu Hsi was a district keeper of records. But he preferred quiet study. From 1160 he studied under Li T'ung (Li Yen-p'ing, 1088-1158) who continued the tradition of the Neo-Confucianism of Ch'eng Hao and Ch'eng I. Most of his life, Chu Hsi was off and on a guardian of some temple, utilizing the peace and quiet to study, write, and talk with the most prominent scholars of the day. His official life, other than the guardianship, was intermittent and turbulent, for he strongly opposed concluding peace and repeatedly memorialized the throne to criticize officials and policies. Time and again he declined official positions. In 1178 he was appointed a magistrate. A year later he was demoted to a minor post because he incurred the anger of the emperor by attacking the incompetency of officials on all levels. In 1188 he was appointed vice minister of the army department, but the minister himself petitioned for his impeachment and he was shifted to a small position. Later in the year he was appointed a junior expositor in waiting to expound the Classics to the emperor, but he declined. In 1189 he became a prefect in Fukien and in 1194 a governor in Hunan

for several months. Later that year he became expositor in waiting but because he memorialized to attack the wicked prime minister and other officials he was demoted to the rank of a temple guardian. Two years later a censor accused him of ten crimes, including refusing to serve and spreading false learning, and an official even petitioned for his execution. All his posts were taken away. An imperial order came in 1199, the year before he died, for him to serve again, but he declined. For greater details, see Wang Mou-hung (1668-1741), *Chu Tzu nien-p'u* (Chronological Biography of Chu Hsi), *Kuo-hsüeh chi-pen ts'ung-shu* (Basic Sinological Series), ed., *Sung shih* (History of the Sung Dynasty, 960-1279), ch. 429, and Bruce, *Chu Hsi and His Masters,* pp. 56-96.

2. In his *I-Lo yüan-yüan lu* (Record of the Origin of the School of the Two Ch'engs), he placed Chou Tun-i ahead of the two Ch'engs, thus asserting that Chou was the founder of Neo-Confucianism and the two Ch'engs more or less transmitted his doctrines. For comments on this matter, see above, pp. 482, 520.

3. See Appendix for a discussion of these two terms.

4. For comment on this term, see *ibid.*

5. See *ibid.* for a discussion of the term.

6. This work, dated 1532, consists of letters, official documents, short essays, poems, and the like in 121 chapters (36 vols.). The SPPY edition of 1930, entitled *Chu Tzu ta-ch'üan* (Complete Literary Works of Chu Hsi), is used.

7. The 1714 edition is used. The title "Complete Works" is misleading, for actually it consists of selected passages from the *Chu Tzu wen-chi* and sayings from the *Chu Tzu yü-lu* (Classified Conversations of Chu Hsi) of 1270 which is in 140 chapters (40 vols.). It was compiled by imperial command in 1713 in a topical arrangement in 66 chapters (25 vols.) and published in 1714. It is worth noting that in the arrangement, moral cultivation comes first and metaphysics comes very much later. In practically all anthologies of Chu Hsi's works in Chinese, this characteristic dominates. The best example is the *Hsü Chin-ssu-lu* (Supplement to the *Reflections on Things at Hand*) by Chang Po-hsing (1651-1725). Even sayings on metaphysics are selected with moral cultivation in mind, as can be seen by his annotations. In our selections, the original topical arrangement is followed simply to keep the original order.

Chapters 42-49 of this work have been translated by Bruce into English, called *The Philosophy of Human Nature,* and ch. 49 has been rendered in European languages several times, the most recent in French by Pang Ching-Jen, in his *L'idée de Dieu chez Malebranche et l'idée de Li chez Tchou Hi,* pp. 73-119.

8. *Wai-shu* (Additional Works), 3:1a, in ECCS. There is no indication which of the two brothers said this. It is considered to be Ch'eng Hao's in the *Ming-tao*

ch'üan-shu (Complete Works of Ch'eng Hao) by Shen Kuei (of Ming, 1368-1644).

9. *Changes,* commentary on hexagram no. 1, *ch'ien* (Heaven). Cf. translation by Legge, *Yi King,* p. 57.

10. *ibid.,* commenting on hexagram nos. 1 and 2, *k'un* (Earth). See Legge, pp. 213-214.

11. *Mencius,* 6A:11.

12. *Analects,* 12:1.

13. *ibid.,* 13:19.

14. Both quotations from *Book of Filial Piety,* ch. 14. See Makre, trans., *Hsiao Ching* p. 31.

15. This is not a quotation from early Confucian texts but Ch'eng I's interpretation of the Confucian concept of altruism. See *I-shu* (Surviving Works), 11:5b, in ECCS.

16. *Analects,* 7:14.

17. When their father left the throne to Shu-ch'i, he declined in deference to his elder brother Po-i, but Po-i would not violate the order of his father and therefore chose to flee. Later, when King Wu (r. 1121-1116 B.C.) overthrew the Shang dynasty in spite of their remonstration, and founded the Chou dynasty, they would not eat the grains of Chou and starved to death.

18. *Analects,* 15:8.

19. Presumably Ch'eng I.

20. *I-shu,* 18:1a.

21. Referring to Yang Kuei-shan (Yang Shih, 1053-1135), in the *Kuei-shan yü-lu* (Recorded Conversations of Yang Shih), SPTK, 2:28a.

22. This is a reference to Hsieh Shang-ts'ai (Hsieh Liang-tso, 1050-1103), who described *jen* as consciousness. See *Shang-ts'ai yü-lu* (Recorded Conversations of Hsieh Liang-tso), *Cheng-i-t'ang ch'üan-shu* (Complete Library of the Hall of Rectifying the Way) ed., pt. 1, 2a-b. See also Forke, *Geschichte der neueren chinesischen Philosophie,* pp. 110-116.

23. For the answer to Tzu-kung (520-c. 450 B.C.), see *Analects,* 6:28 (in ch. 2, above).

24. *I-shu,* 24:3a.

25. Quoting *Mencius,* 2A:2.

26. *Analects,* 6:21.

27. *ibid.,* 15:32.

28. *Li-hsüeh tsung-ch'uan* (Orthodox Transmission of Neo-Confucianism), 1880 ed., 6:17a-b.

29. See above, ch. 30, comment on sec. A.

30. These phrases appear separately in the treatise. However, they form one sentence in his *Lun-yü chi-chu* (Collected Commentaries on the *Analects*), ch. 1, commentary on *Analects,* 1:2. For a refutation of the theory that these phrases were borrowed from a Bud-

dhist, see Yamaguchi Satsujō, *Jin no kenkyū* (An Investigation on *Jên*), 1936, pp. 370-372.

31. On *jen,* see above, ch. 30, sec. 1, ch. 31, comment on secs. 1 and 11, and ch. 32, comment on sec. 42.

32. *I-shu,* 1:7b. In the beginning sentence, Ch'eng is quoting Kao Tzu (c.420-c.350 B.C.) See *Mencius,* 6A:3.

33. *I-shu,* 1:7b.

34. *ibid.*

35. *ibid.,* 2A:1b.

36. *ibid.,* 1:7b. The same for all the following quotations from Ch'eng Hao.

37. *Mencius,* 2A:6.

38. Legendary sage-emperor (3rd millennium B.C.)

39. Paraphrasing *Analects,* 8:18.

40. See above, ch. 30, sec. 41.

41. See above, ch. 31, comments on secs. 7-8.

42. According to Wang Mou-hung, *Chu Tzu nien-p'u,* p. 37, this letter was written in 1169 when Chu Hsi was forty. The Hunan friends included Chang Nanhsien (Chang Shih, also called Chang Ching-fu and Chang Ch'ien-fu, 1133-1180), with whom Chu Hsi carried on extensive correspondence on equilibrium and harmony and other subjects. (*Chu Tzu wen-chi,* chs. 31-33). For an account of him, see Forke, *Geschichte der neueren chinesischen Philosophie,* pp. 260-264 or *Sung-Yüan hsüen-an,* ch. 50. Chang was a resident of Hunan. According to the *Chu Tzu nien-p'u,* in 1167 when Chu Hsi was thirty-eight, he and Chang visited Mount Heng in Hunan. The group also included Lin Tse-chih with whom Chu Hsi once visited Chang in Ch'ang-sha, Hunan, and with whom he also corresponded extensively, chiefly on equilibrium and harmony (*Chu Tzu wen-chi,* 43-17a-32b). In a letter to Lin, Chu Hsi mentioned "Human friends" and also Chang (*ibid.,* 43:30b), who is also mentioned in other letters to Lin.

43. *The Mean,* ch. 1.

44. *I-ch'uan wen-chi* (Collection of Literary Works by Ch'eng I), 5:12a, in ECCS.

45. Generally stating the ideas in *Changes,* "Appended Remarks," pt. 1, ch. 10. Cf. Legge, *Yi King,* p. 370.

46. The discussions are found in *I-shu,* 18:14b-16a.

47. *ibid.,* 2A:23b.

48. This word is added according to the *I-shu.*

49. *I-shu,* 3:5b.

50. *ibid.,* 18:5b.

51. *I-ch'uan wen-chi,* 5:12a. The insertions in parentheses are Ch'eng's own.

52. See Liu's comment on this letter in the *Sung-Yüan hsüeh-an,* (Anthology and Critical Accounts of the Neo-Confucianists of the Sung and Yüan Dynasties,

960-1368), ed. by Huang Tsung-hsi (1610-1695) *et al.,* SPPY, 48:9a.

53. *History,* "Counsels of Great Yü." Cf. translation by Legge, *Shoo King,* p. 62.

54. *Mencius,* 6A:8.

55. *ibid.,* 7A:1.

56. *Analects,* 15:5.

57. *History, ibid.* Cf. Legge, p. 62.

58. *ibid.*

59. Paraphrasing *Mencius,* 6A:8.

60. *Changes,* commentary on hexagram no. 2. *k'un* (Earth). Cf. Legge, *Yi King,* p. 420.

61. *Mencius,* 7A:1.

62. *ibid.*

63. *Analects,* 15:5.

Abbreviations and Abridgments

CTTC *Chu Tzu ta-ch'üan* (Complete Literary Works of Chu Hsi), SPPY

ECCS *Erh-Ch'eng ch'üan-shu* (Complete Works of the Two Ch'engs), SPPY

NHCC *Nan-hua chen-ching* (Pure Classic of Nan-hua, another name for the *Chuang Tzu*), SPTK

PNP *Po-na pen* (Choice Works Edition)

SPPY *Ssu-pu pei-yao* (Essentials of the *Four Libraries*) edition

SPTK *Ssu-pu ts'ung-k'an* (*Four Libraries* Series) edition

TSD *Taishō shinshū daizōkyō* (Taishō Edition of the Buddhist Canon)

Changes The Book of Changes

History The Book of History

Mencius The Book of Mencius

Odes The Book of Odes

The Mean The Doctrine of the Mean . . .

Wing-tsit Chan (essay date 1967)

SOURCE: An introduction to *Reflections on Things at Hand: The Neo-Confucian Anthology,* compiled by Chu Hsi and Lu Tsu-Ch'ien, translated by Wing-tsit Chan, Columbia University Press, 1967, pp. xvii-xli.

[*In the essay that follows, Chan examines the way in which Chu Hsi's anthology,* Reflections on Things at Hand, *treats three major doctrines of Neo-Confucianism. Chan also maintains that Chu Hsi was objective in selecting and editing the sayings of the Confucian masters included in the text.*]

Reflections on Things at Hand is the classic statement of Neo-Confucian philosophy by its leading exponent, Chu Hsi. It brings together the views of the Sung dynasty philosophers who met the challenge of Buddhism and formulated a new Confucian metaphysics. Stimulated by the Hua-yen philosophy of Perfect Harmony and by the psychology of Ch'an (Zen) Buddhism,[1] the Neo-Confucianists went on, under the leadership of Chou Tun-i (1017-73), Ch'eng Hao (1032-85), his brother Ch'eng I (1033-1107), Chang Tsai (1020-77), and Shao Yung (1011-77), who were called the Five Masters of the earlier period of the Sung dynasty (960-1279), to revitalize the teachings of Confucius and Mencius, give their doctrines a more rational theoretical foundation, and develop new methods of moral cultivation and study.

Broadly speaking, there are at least three major doctrines in Neo-Confucianism that are new. The most important is that principle (*li*) is the foundation of all truth and values. The concept of principle was not prominent in ancient Confucianism. The word *li* is not mentioned in the *Analects*.[2] It appears several times in the commentaries on the *Book of Changes* where we find "general principle," "the principle of the world," "following the principle of nature and destiny," and "investigating the principle to the utmost and fully developing one's nature until destiny is fulfilled."[3] But few modern scholars accept Confucius as the author of these commentaries. One of the two greatest Confucianists in ancient times, Mencius, did speak of *li* in the sense of moral principles, it is true,[4] but not in the sense of the law of being, and not as a major concept. Although the other great Confucianist, Hsün Tzu (313-238 B.C.?), spoke more often of principle,[5] the concept still does not occupy a key position in his philosophy. During the first millennium Confucianists hardly spoke of it at all. It was instead the Neo-Taoists in the third and fourth centuries who conceived of principle as governing all existence. The Buddhists in the next several centuries followed suit by formulating their famous thesis of the harmony of principle and facts. Challenged by the Buddhists, the Neo-Confucianists seized upon the sayings in the *Book of Changes* and the *Book of Mencius* and made principle a basic concept in their philosophy. For the first time in Chinese history an entire system was built on it: that of Ch'eng I. How the Neo-Confucianists understood principle will be taken up later. The important thing to note now is that they put the whole Confucian system on a metaphysical foundation and a rational basis.[6]

To know principle and to live according to it, the Neo-Confucianists advocated the methods of the investigation of things and the exercise of seriousness. When things are investigated, one's knowledge will be extended, and when seriousness is attained, one's emotional and moral life will be correct. This methodology is utterly new in the Confucian tradition. There is no question that the dual emphasis on the extension of knowledge and the cultivation of seriousness reflects the influence of the twofold formula of wisdom and calmness in the Ch'an school.

The third innovation was the new evaluation of the Confucian Classics. The Taoists also regarded the *Book of Changes* as their classic, but they used it primarily for divination and similar occult practices, and thus it became associated with superstition and fantasy. Change was believed to be mysterious and controlled by spiritual beings. But since the Classic was extremely influential and popular, with a strong hold on scholars as well as on the ignorant masses, the Neo-Confucianists could not very well ignore it. Instead, they interpreted it in the spirit of rationalism and, like Chou Tun-i, used it as an intelligent explanation of the evolution of the universe, or, like Ch'eng I, as an explanation of the principles of daily human affairs. In addition, they raised the *Analects*, the *Book of Mencius*, the *Great Learning*, and the *Doctrine of the Mean*,[7] later called the Four Books, to the level of the Classics. For a thousand years the Five Classics, namely, the *Book of History*, the *Book of Odes*, the *Book of Changes*, the *Book of Rites*, and the *Spring and Autumn Annals*,[8] rather than the Four Books, were accepted and even officially sanctioned as "standards" for thought and action. But the Neo-Confucianists, especially Ch'eng Hao, Ch'eng I, and Chang Tsai, resorted more often to the Four Books than to the Five Classics for explanation and support of their views, because the Four Books dealt more directly, clearly, and simply with daily affairs and concrete situations. The Ch'eng brothers attached so much importance to the *Great Learning* and the *Doctrine of the Mean* that they took them out of the *Book of Rites*, in which they are chapters, and treated them as separate works. Each of them rearranged the text of the former and Ch'eng I also wrote a commentary on the latter. The new attitude implied a challenge to the traditional acceptance of the Five Classics as the only standards. More significantly, it brought Confucianism back to a vital concern with daily life.

These innovations gave Confucianism a new complexion. It has dominated Chinese life and thought from the eleventh through the nineteenth century. Even today, in spite of the onslaught by Western thought and Marxian ideology, it still has its spokesmen and may well be renewed once more.

Although this philosophy was by no means systematically formulated or presented, it was carefully thought out by Neo-Confucianists and closely followed in their own lives. Many of them wrote extensively. Others wrote little but taught through conversations with their pupils. These conversations were recorded in many volumes. The literature of Neo-Confucianism is therefore very large. But there was no single volume that could serve as a summary, introduction, or framework. An anthology was clearly needed. Chu Hsi (1130-1200) and his collaborator, Lü Tsu-ch'ien (1137-81) supplied this need by compiling the **Chin-ssu lu**. This is the work here translated as **Reflections on Things at Hand**.[9]

The story of the role each man played in the compilation, the order and contents of the work, and the sources of its selections will be taken up later.[10] It is, however, necessary to note here the significance of the title. The Chinese title literally means "records of thoughts about what is near." The term *chin-ssu* comes from the *Analects,* 19:6, where Confucius' pupil, Tzu-hsia (507-420 B.C.), says that what one thinks about should be matters near at hand. In his commentary on the saying, Chu Hsi quotes[11] Ch'eng Hao's statement that one should "reflect on things at hand, that is, what is in oneself," and Ch'eng I's words: "reflecting on things at hand means to extend on the basis of similarity in kind."[12] When asked about "extension on the basis of similarity in kind," Chu Hsi replied that the utterance was "well said."

> One should not skip over steps or look too far [he said]. Nor should one drift in all directions or go or stop abruptly. One should start only with what one understands in things nearby and then keep on. . . . For example, after having gone the first step, one can, on the basis of this step, advance to the second, and so on to the third and the fourth. . . . When one has understood how to be affectionate to one's own parents, one will, by extension on the basis of similarity in kind, be humane to all people, for being humane to all people is of the same kind or class as being affectionate to parents. When one has understood how to be humane to people, one will feel love for all creatures, for loving all creatures is of the same kind as being humane to people.[13]

Chu Hsi believes that if one starts with one's immediate concern such as duty toward one's parents, one will eventually encompass the whole moral life as prescribed in the Confucian Classics. This is why he said that the Four Books are the ladders to the Five Classics and that the *Chin-ssu lu* is the ladder to the Four Books.[14]

The *Chin-ssu lu,* consisting of the works and sayings of Chou Tun-i, the Ch'eng brothers, and Chang Tsai, is not only an excellent outline of their teachings but also presents the whole Neo-Confucian philosophy in a short, yet comprehensive, survey. It brings their scattered sayings into bold relief and gives their variegated philosophy a structured whole. After a chapter on basic philosophy, the chapters proceed from personal cultivation to the regulation of the family, to national order, and then to an observation of heterodoxical systems and the dispositions of Confucian sages and worthies. Underlying all this is the basic idea of principle. Neo-Confucianism, because this idea is so fundamental to its thought, is called the School of Principle *(li-hsüeh).*

According to the Neo-Confucianists, for everything that exists there must be the law of being. The law is principle, according to which a thing comes into existence and has its being through the interaction of the two material forces, yin, the cosmic force of tranquillity, and yang, the cosmic force of activity. As the law of the existence of things, principle is self-evident, self-sufficient, eternal, concrete, definite, unalterable, and correct.[15] It is in all things. "Every blade of grass and every tree have it," said Ch'eng I.[16] All things possess it sufficiently.[17] It is the principle of the production and reproduction of things.[18] And it is public, shared by all men.[19]

Such are the universal characteristics of principle. The Neo-Confucianists explained virtually everything in its light. Action and response between things, for example, are no longer understood as the influence of mysterious beings but as natural operations according to principle. *Kuei-shen* are no longer taken to be spiritual beings who control human life at their whim but are now understood, especially by Ch'eng I and Chang Tsai, as "forces of creation" and the "spontaneous activities of the material force."[20] All phenomena of rising and falling, going and returning, whether in natural events or in human affairs, are to be explained in this light.[21] Moreover, principle is the source of goodness and the standard of right and wrong. As such it is the Principle of Nature. If one obeys it and preserves it, everything will be right. The Neo-Confucianists sharply contrasted it with selfish human desires, which violate and disturb it.[22]

If one understands principle clearly, one will be happy to follow it.[23] One's first task, then, is to investigate principle to the utmost. It does not matter whether one does it through study, reading books, investigating history, or handling human affairs, and does not matter whether one studies one thing deductively or many things inductively. When enough effort has been made, one will achieve a thorough understanding. When that is done, one will see the distinction between right and wrong and abandon all superstitious beliefs in spiritual beings and immortals.[24]

Since principle is good, one's nature is good.[25] Evil arises because of material force, for the endowment of material force in man may be impure or unbalanced. But nature and material force are not to be diametrically opposed. Actually one involves the other. There are not two things, good and evil, opposed to each other in one's nature.[26] When sufficient effort has been made to remove impurities, goodness will reveal itself. One must endeavor to transform one's physical nature.[27] When nature is cultivated to the fullest, one's nature and destiny will be in accord with principle.[28]

The foundation of goodness is humanity *(jen).*[29] It is one of the Five Constant Virtues, namely, humanity, righteousness, propriety, wisdom, and faithfulness, but actually it embraces all the rest because it is also virtue in the general sense.[30] It is essential to understand its substance, as Ch'eng Hao has strongly insisted.[31] In essence, *jen* involves love for all and at the same time specific virtues in one's various social relations. In other words, in its oneness it is universal love for all, while in its multiplicity it operates as filial piety, brotherly respect, and so forth in various human relations. This is the theme of Chang Tsai's celebrated essay, the "Western Inscription."[32] *Jen* has two facets: self-perfection and the perfection of others. A man of *jen* is altruistic; he makes no distinction between himself and others.[33] Ultimately, his feeling of *jen* will grow so extensive as to enable him to "form one body with Heaven, Earth, and all things."[34] This doctrine of the unity with all, propagated most strongly by the Ch'eng brothers and supported by all Neo-Confucianists, has become a cardinal one in the Chinese tradition.

The idea of extension is closely connected with another meaning of the word *jen,* namely, "seeds." No one before the Neo-Confucianists had used the word in this sense in connection with virtue. *Jen* thus understood becomes the virtue of creation. As seeds produce flowers and plants, so *jen* produces all virtues. It is out of this creative quality that the virtues of love, compassion, and the like have come, ultimately, embracing all things. *Jen* is the spirit of life in all things.[35] It should be the spirit of man.

For the cultivation of virtue, the Neo-Confucianists were careful to strike the balance between the internal and the external. They repeatedly quoted the *Book of Changes:* "Seriousness to straighten the internal life and righteousness to square the external life."[36] Seriousness[37] means concentration on one thing.[38] One will then be calm, obtain a sense of equilibrium and harmony, and be at ease with himself.[39] One will no longer worry, harbor selfish desires, be manipulative, or make deliberate and artificial efforts.[40] One can then "face the Lord on High," overcome all evil, and preserve one's sincerity.[41] The quality of sincerity is of special value to the Neo-Confucianists, and especially to Chou Tun-i, for whom the foundation of family harmony and national order rests on the correctness of the heart, and thus on sincerity.[42]

Seriousness alone, however, will be useless unless it is supported by righteousness. Righteousness means the sense of right and wrong and the understanding of the correct way to do things. In short, righteousness is acting according to principle. It is not enough to be serious in one's mind about filial piety, for example. In addition, one must act correctly in the actual service of one's parents. Both seriousness and righteousness must be established and they must support each other.[43]

As seriousness must be coupled with righteousness, so must it be coupled with knowledge. Ch'eng I's saying, "Self-cultivation requires seriousness; the pursuit of learning depends on extension of knowledge," has become an axiom in the Neo-Confucian school.[44] The Neo-Confucianists were emphatic in urging one to study, for otherwise, they said, one will decline.[45]

In the matter of extension of knowledge, the Neo-Confucianists were extremely critical of the prevalent habits of memorization, recitation of texts, and devotion to literary studies and flowery compositions. It seemed to them that these habits destroy one's purpose in life.[46] Instead, one must look for and understand principle in the written word. One must probe and examine the principles of things.[47] One must think, for thought is the source of learning, and one must reflect repeatedly over one thing after another, until one's understanding is penetrating and profound.[48] One must also know how to doubt.[49] Most important, one must get at the essentials, explore them, and get a real appreciation of them, so that one will achieve something new every day and advance every day.[50] There is no harm in differing from others in the interpretation of the Classics. The main thing is to acquire something in a natural way.[51]

The achievement of knowledge is, of course, for the purpose of application. In Neo-Confucianism, as in Confucianism throughout the ages, knowledge and action are of equal importance. The achievement of knowledge is the beginning of learning, while practicing knowledge with effort is its end.[52]

The practice of moral virtue begins with filial piety and brotherly respect, for they are the foundation on which one's nature will be developed and one's destiny fulfilled. In fact, this development and fulfillment can be accomplished in the very acts of filial piety and brotherly respect.[53] One should obey one's parents. However, one's chief objective is to help them and lead them so that they will not go astray from righteousness.[54] Between husband and wife, the lines of superiority and inferiority are to be strictly drawn. Widows are not to remarry, for by doing so they would lose their integrity. In the opinion of Ch'eng I, if a widow is poor, it is better for her to starve to death than to remarry. "To starve to death is a very small matter," he said. "To lose one's integrity, however, is a very serious matter."[55] This is perhaps the most extreme statement in the ***Chin-ssu lu,*** the most controversial, and, in the twentieth century, the most condemned.[56] However, if Ch'eng's attitude toward the widow is too strict, we must not forget that his primary concern was integrity.

As to the family as a whole, there should be personal affection among members of the family, and there should be monthly banquets to strengthen the bond of the clan, but personal affection must be in accord with righteousness.[57] The genealogy of the clan should be clarified, family property should be kept together under one head, and the ancient system of heads of descent should be restored so the head of each branch of the clan can be clearly identified. The people will then be held together, will have a sense of community, and will not forget their source. In this sense the system of heads of descent is based on the Principle of Nature. For everything must be traced to its source.[58]

Integrity is also the keynote in the Neo-Confucianists' attitude toward government service. To them, whether or not to serve in the government was a matter of the most serious consideration. In their opinion there was nothing wrong in taking the civil service examinations or accepting government positions, but these must not be allowed to destroy one's moral purpose.[59] One should go forward to serve only when the time is right. In any case, whether one advances or retires, one should be in accord with the correct principle. Righteousness should be the only standard of action, regardless of what one's fate may be.[60]

Righteousness and profit are to be sharply distinguished, for the former leads to impartiality and the latter to selfishness.[61] One should not be motivated by profit. In all activities in the government one should be guided only by moral principles.[62]

The government, too, must be guided by these principles. The best government is one in which "the correctness of the Principle of Nature is achieved and the ultimate of human relations is fulfilled."[63] This can be accomplished only by practicing moral principles instead of resorting to political technique.[64] But this does not mean that there should be no governmental measures. Rather, it means that the measures must be governed by righteousness and humanity; otherwise they would be no better than the methods or tricks of despots.[65] In sharp contrast to despots, whose works are primarily for their own success and profit, the true king will institute ceremonies and promote moral education. He will establish schools to teach not only practical duties but also filial piety, brotherly respect, faithfulness, and loyalty.[66] His laws will be few and his punishments will be light. He will be devoted to the social and economic welfare of his people.[67]

This comprehensive philosophy is embraced in 622 passages which Chu Hsi, with the help of Lü Tsu-ch'ien, selected from the works and recorded sayings of the four Masters. Chu Hsi listed in the **Chin-ssu lu** fourteen works from which the selections were made. They are:

Master Chou's "T'ai-chi t'ung-shu" (The diagram of the Great Ultimate and the book penetrating the *Book of Changes* by Chou Tun-i)

Master Ming-tao's *Wen-chi* (Collection of literary works by Master Ch'eng Hao)

Master I-ch'uan's *Wen-chi* (Collection of literary works by Master Ch'eng I)

Ch'eng's *I chuan* (Ch'eng I's commentary on the *Book of Changes*)

Ch'eng's *Ching shuo* (Ch'eng I's explanations of the Classics)

Ch'engs' *I-shu* (Surviving works of the two Ch'engs)

Ch'engs' *Wai-shu* (Additional works of the two Ch'engs)

Master Heng-ch'ü's *Cheng-meng* (Master Chang Tsai's Correcting Youthful Ignorance)

Master Heng-ch'ü's *Wen-chi* (Collection of literary works by Master Chang Tsai)

Master Heng-ch'ü's *I shuo* (Master Chang Tsai's explanations of the *Book of Changes*)

Master Heng-ch'ü's *Li-yüeh shuo* (Master Chang Tsai's explanations of ceremonies and music)

Master Heng-ch'ü's *Lun-yü shuo* (Master Chang Tsai's explanations of the *Analects*)

Master Heng-ch'ü's *Meng Tzu shuo* (Master Chang Tsai's explanations of the *Book of Mencius*)

Master Heng-ch'ü's *Yü-lu* (Recorded conversations of Master Chang Tsai)[68]

Many things have happened to these works since Chu Hsi's time. Some have been altered and others have disappeared.[69] The selections are now found in the following works:

CHOU TUN-I:

T'ai-chi-t'u shuo (Explanation of the diagram of the Great Ultimate)[70]

T'ung-shu (Penetrating the *Book of Changes*)[71]

Both are included in the *Chou Tzu ch'üan-shu* (Complete works of Master Chou).

THE TWO CH'ENGS:

Ming-tao wen-chi (Collection of literary works by Ch'eng Hao)[72]

I-ch'uan wen-chi (Collection of literary works by Ch'eng I)[73]

I-shu (Surviving works)[74]

Wai-shu (Additional works)[75]

I chuan (Commentary on the *Book of Changes*)[76]

Ching shuo (Explanations of the Classics)[77]

The above works of the Ch'eng brothers, plus the *Ts'ui-yen* (Pure words), which contains additional conversations, make up the *Erh-Ch'eng ch'üan-shu* (Complete works of the two Ch'engs).

CHANG TSAI:

Cheng-meng (Correcting youthful ignorance)[78]

I shuo (Commentary on the *Book of Changes*)[79]

Yü-lu (Recorded conversations)[80]

All the above are included in the *Chang Tzu ch'üan-shu* (Complete works of Master Chang).[81]

The collections of conversations supplied the majority of the 622 selections. Most of the selections, probably more than half, have come from Ch'eng I, between 67 and 162 from Ch'eng Hao, 110 from Chang Tsai, and 12 from Chou Tun-i.[82] Many of the works listed above are very short.

The four philosophers dedicated their lives to elucidating and spreading the Confucian doctrine. They accepted governmental positions with the greatest reluctance, prefering to remain poor and teach. Compared with other Confucianists, they wrote little. Chou wrote only a short work, and Ch'eng Hao did not write any book at all.

Chou was a native of Tao-chou (present Tao County, Honan Province). His personal name was Tun-i and his courtesy name Mao-shu. He named his study after the stream Lien-hsi, also pronounced Lien-ch'i (Stream of waterfalls), which he loved, and posterity has honored him by calling him Master Lien-hsi. He also loved lotus flowers ardently, evidently because of their purity and tranquillity. His love for life was so strong that he would not cut the grass outside his window.[83] The two Ch'eng brothers, who studied under him in 1046-47, were influenced by him in every way, including their decision not to take the civil service examinations or engage in hunting.[84] Because Chou was a great admirer of Buddhism, Ch'eng I called him the "poor Zen fellow."[85] But actually Buddhist influence on Chou was negligible. In fact, he may be said to have set the course for Neo-Confucianism in such a way that neither Buddhist nor Taoist influence could change its fundamentally Confucian character.

In official life Chou was, among other things, district keeper of records, or assistant magistrate (1040), magistrate in various counties (1046-54), prefectural staff supervisor (1056-59), and professor of the directorate of education and assistant prefect (1061-64). It was when he was prefect in Nan-k'ang in Modern Kiangsi Province in 1071 that he built his study, "Stream of Waterfalls." He resigned from his governmental position in 1071, eighteen months before he died.[86] It was said of him that his mind "was free, pure and unobstructed, like the breeze on a sunny day and the clear moon," and that "in his governmental administration, he was careful and strict, and treated others like himself. He saw to it that he was in complete accord with moral principles."[87]

The Ch'eng brothers were sons of a chief officer. When they were fourteen of fifteen, they made up their minds to learn to be sages,[88] studying not only under Chou Tun-i, but also under Chang Tsai, their uncle.

Ch'eng Hao's courtesy name was Po-ch'un. When he was fifteen or sixteen, he heard Chou Tun-i lecture on the Way and gave up the idea of taking civil service examinations. He went in and out of the Taoist and Buddhist schools for almost ten years before he returned to Confucianism.[89] After he obtained the "presented scholar" degree in 1057 he was successively a keeper of records in two counties and scored great success in averting a famine by saving the dikes, in equalizing taxes, and in rehabilitating prisoners. Later he was magistrate for three years (1065-67), during which he established schools, organized community societies, brought about peace and order, and gained the great affection of the populace. In 1070 he became undersecretary of the heir apparent. Emperor Shen-tsung (r. 1068-85) gave him a number of audiences and was much impressed with his recommendations. But Ch'eng Hao strongly opposed Wang An-shih (1021-86) in his radical reforms. In his conversations with the emperor, he stressed the Confucian doctrines of sincerity and humanity and would not even refer to profit or success. This was an indirect way of attacking the utilitarianism of Wang's reforms. Their conflict gradually became more open and bitter. As a result, in 1071, Ch'eng was demoted to the position of assistant prefect. In 1078-80 he was once more a magistrate but his political enemies finally had him dismissed. The new emperor, Che-tsung (r. 1086-93), appointed him a bureau assistant executive, but before he could take office he died.

Ch'eng Hao was warm and peaceful in disposition.[90] A pupil who followed him for thirty years never saw him show anger or even a harsh expression.[91] His elucidation of the Confucian doctrine was thought so profound and his influence so great that he was called Master Ming-tao (Illumination of the Way). His brother believed that, in the centuries since Confucius and Mencius, Ming-tao was the first to represent the authentic transmission of the Way of the Sages.[92]

Ch'eng I's courtesy name was Cheng-shu. Because he and his brother lived in the I River area in Honan, he was called Master I-ch'uan (I River). In 1056 he and his brother entered the national university where he was so outstanding that a schoolmate treated him as a teacher. At the age of twenty-five (1057) he entreated the emperor in a memorial to practice the Confucian kingly way. Two years later he obtained the "presented scholar" degree. He lived and taught in Lo-yang in Honan, and repeatedly declined high offices, including a professorship at the directorate of education in 1085. Thus, even at the age of fifty-three, he did not care to be an official. Finally, in 1086, he became junior expositor in waiting. For twenty months he lectured the emperor on Confucian principles and attracted many followers. Although he had to borrow money to live at this time, he neither sent in his application for salary, nor requested for his wife the honor to which she was entitled, for he felt the initiative should not come from him.[93] His sense of moral integrity was uncompromising, but his firm attitude, his critical opinions, and his outspokenness created bitter enemies, one of the most important of whom was Su Shih (Su Tung-p'o, 1036-1101), leader of the Szechuan group. This led to the bitter factional struggle between that group and the Lo-yang group led by Ch'eng I. In 1087 Ch'eng I was appointed head of the directorate of education in the western capital Lo-yang but resigned a few months later. When he was again head of the directorate in 1092, censors repeatedly petitioned for his impeachment. At last he resigned. In 1097 his teachings were prohibited, his land was confiscated, and he was banished to Fu-chou Prefecture (modern Fu-ling County in Szechuan). He was pardoned three years later and resumed his position at the directorate. By that time, government persecution of factions had become severe. Both he and Su Shih, along with several hundred other scholars, were blacklisted. His followers left him. In 1103 his books were destroyed and his teachings were once more prohibited. He was pardoned in 1106, a year before he died, but the ban on his teachings remained until 1155. By that time, however, Chu Hsi was twenty-five years old. Before long he began to promote Cheng I's doctrines, and their teaching soon became the basis of a concerted philosophical movement.[94]

The two brothers were as widely different in temperament as can be imagined. Ch'eng Hao was warm, always at ease, tolerant, agreeable, understanding, and amiable. Ch'eng I, on the other hand, was stern, grave, strict, forthright, and so self-controlled that when a boat he was riding in seemed about to sink, he kept his composure.[95] Such was the difference between the dispositions of the brothers[96]. Perhaps the most dramatic illustration of the effect they had on people is that once, when they entered a hall, everybody followed Ch'eng Hao to one side, while no one followed Ch'eng I to the other.[97]

Chang Tsai's courtesy name was Tzu-hou. He was a native of the town of Heng-ch'ü in modern Mei County, Shensi Province, and was therefore also called Master Heng-ch'ü. In his youth he loved military arts. At twenty-one he wrote to the outstanding scholar official, Fan Chung-yen (969-1052), whom he later visited and who told him to study the *Doctrine of the Mean*. Still not satisfied with Confucian learning, he turned to Buddhism and Taoism for years, but finally returned to the Confucian Classics, especially the *Book of Changes* and the *Doctrine of the Mean,* which eventually formed the basis of his philosophy. In 1056, when he lectured on the *Book of Changes* in the capital, his students included the prominent Neo-Confucianist and statesman, Ssu-ma Kuang (1019-86), and two of his own nephews, the Ch'eng brothers. He obtained a "presented scholar" degree in 1057 and was appointed a magistrate. In 1069 he pleased the emperor with his orthodox Confucian answers to questions on government and was appointed a collator in the imperial library. In his political views, however, he was at odds with the reformer Wang An-shih, for he insisted on reviving ancient Confucian economic systems, including the "well-field" system. Under this system a field was divided into nine squares and assigned to eight families each of which cultivated one square separately for its own support and joined in cultivating the ninth square for governmental revenues. Chang retired from minor governmental positions to farm and attempted to persuade other scholars to join him in practicing the "well-field" system. Although he was extremely poor, he would sit calmly all day, thinking, reading, or having discussions with his students. He was greatly loved by his pupils and the community alike. In 1077 he was a director of the board of imperial sacrifices but, because his proposal for restoring ancient rites was not accepted, he resigned. He became ill and died on his way home.[98] A contemporary said of him, "The Master was firm and resolute in nature. His virtue was eminent and his appearance dignified. But in his association with people, he became more intimate with them as time went on. In regulating his family and in dealing with others, his basic principle was to correct himself in order to influence others. If people did not believe in him, he would examine himself and set himself right but would say nothing about the matter. Although some people might not understand his ideas, he would conduct himself naturally and equally without regret. Therefore, whether people knew him or not, they all submitted to him when they heard of his disposition, and dared not do him the slightest wrong."[99] This is perhaps an idealization, but no one doubts the essential soundness of the characterization, for Chang Tsai was a most respected scholar and teacher of his time.

Shao Yung supported himself by farming and called himself "Mr. Happiness" and his home "Happy Nest." He was so well liked that, when he went around Lo-yang in a small cart, people both rich and poor, hearing the sound of his cart, would come out and say, "Our Master is coming!" And he was so much respected that many prominent scholars and officials, including the eminent Ssu-ma Kuang, often visited him. The Ch'eng brothers too were his great friends. About 1060 he was keeper of records in the board of public works and about a decade later he was a militia judge. In both functions his rank was that of an assistant executive.[100]

Chang was senior to the Ch'eng brothers, but in the ***Chinssu lu,*** both in the list of books from which the selections were made and in the order of the selections themselves, Chang always follows the Ch'engs. In Chu Hsi's belief, Neo-Confucianism was founded by Chou Tun-i and developed by the Ch'eng brothers, particularly by Ch'eng I. To him, Chang Tsai comes after the Ch'engs, so far as the transmission of the Confucian tradition is concerned. Whether it is correct or not, this is the line of transmission fixed by Chu Hsi.

Another direct result of Chu Hsi's personal views is the omission of Shao Yung from the anthology.[101] One reason for this is that Shao Yung did not devote much discussion to the central Confucian problems of humanity and righteousness. In other words, he had nothing to add to what the Four Masters had to say. But a more important reason is that Shao Yung's philosophy is too similar to Taoist occultism to suit Chu Hsi. In Shao's cosmology, change is due to spirit, which gives rise to number, number to form, and form to concrete things. Since the Great Ultimate engenders the four forms of major and minor yin and yang, Shao used the number four to classify all phenomena, so that there are the four seasons, the four heavenly bodies, the four kinds of rulers, the four periods of history, and so forth. Because elements of the universe are calculable, the best knowledge is objective, that is, "viewing things as things." This mechanistic philosophy is of Taoist origin and is clearly out of harmony with Neo-Confucianism as developed by the Four Masters. According to the records,[102] Shao Yung learned indirectly from a Taoist priest certain diagrams connected with the *Book of Changes,* out of which his theory of diagrams and numbers evolved.

Chu Hsi's dislike for Taoism is shown not only in his omission of Shao Yung but also in his editing of one of Ch'eng I's essays.[103] In the original there are these two sentences, "This is called turning the original nature into the feeling" and "This is called turning the feeling into nature," which Chu Hsi deleted. The first sentence comes from the commentary on the *Book of Changes* by Wang Pi (226-49), the Neo-Taoist. There is no doubt that Chu Hsi omitted the sentences because they express the Taoistic idea that while nature is good, feelings are evil, a position Neo-Confucianists would not accept. In doing so, Chu Hsi was also loyal to Ch'eng I, for Ch'eng I would not contrast the two.

This is the only place where Chu Hsi's editing affects the sense of any passage, if only by implication. Otherwise he was quite objective both in his selection and in his editing.

Ch'eng I often interpreted the sayings of Confucius and Mencius in his own way. Chu Hsi did not substitute the original meaning for Ch'eng I's versions. Instead, he presented Ch'eng I's interpretations and then pointed out the ways in which they modified the original. For example, although in the *Analects* the term *chih-ming* means giving up one's life, Ch'eng I gave it the meaning of investigating fate to the utmost. This fact is pointed out in Chu Hsi's commentary.[104] Nevertheless Chu Hsi did not hesitate to criticize Ch'eng I when he disagreed with him. For example, Ch'eng I felt one should be free from contact with external things, but Chu Hsi said that this was not possible.[105] In one case, Ch'eng understood "order" to mean correct principles, but Chu Hsi preferred to understand it as governmental order.[106] He also questioned Ch'eng I's contention that feelings should not be called the mind.[107]

Perhaps the best illustration of Chu Hsi's objectivity is his liberal quotation from Ch'eng I's commentary on the *Book of Changes*. There are more selections from this than from any other single work, although the largest group of extracts comes from collections of the two Ch'engs' sayings.[108] Chu Hsi and Ch'eng I differed fundamentally on the nature of the *Book of Changes*. Chu Hsi regarded it as primarily a book for divination whereas Ch'eng I took it to be an explanation of principle.[109] Again and again Ch'eng I drew from it lessons on the Mean and correctness.[110] Chu Hsi thought that Ch'eng I's interpretation of the book was not in accordance with its original meaning, and that consequently his comments and the text on which he commented often did not agree. Besides, Chu Hsi said, Ch'eng I's comments were often too general and abstract and therefore very difficult to understand.[111] In spite of all this, however, Chu Hsi drew heavily on the commentaries because, as he said, every paragraph is necessary for our practical effort and the book is therefore of great benefit to the student.[112] Chu Hsi's whole purpose was an anthology that should present Neo-Confucianism as comprehensively and yet as concisely as possible and at the same time should contribute in a concrete way to the improvement of the reader's daily life.

The *Chin-ssu lu* became one of the most important books in Chinese thought. It is the first of the Neo-Confucian collections, some of which became classics in their own right and served for centuries as official tests in civil service examinations. It has inspired and set the pattern for anthologies of Chu Hsi's sayings and those of other Neo-Confucianists from Chu Hsi's own time to the nineteenth century.[113] Scholars have treated the *Chin-ssu lu* as a source book in Neo-Confucianism, in spite of the fact that it is only an anthology. Commentaries on it were written over the centuries by leading Confucianists in Korea as well as in China. In Japan it was widely commented on and exercised considerable influence during the Tokugawa period (1603-1867). This was due to the efforts of Yamazaki Ansai (1618-82), a towering Confucianist in Japanese history, whose followers totaled six thousand. Because he was not satisfied with the commentary of Yeh Ts'ai (*fl.* 1248),[114] he published the *Chin-ssu lu* without it,

provided his own commentary, and required his pupils to read the anthology. As a result, many of his followers wrote on the *Chin-ssu lu* which became indispensable to an understanding of the thought of the Tokugawa period.[115]

The influence of the *Chin-ssu lu* was due not only to the importance of the Four Masters' philosophy but also to Chu Hsi himself for, outside of Confucius and Mencius, he has had a greater impact on Chinese, Korean, and Japanese thought than any other Confucianist.

Chu Hsi was born in Yu-hsi County, Fukien, in 1130, son of a former district sheriff who later became assistant department director of the ministry of personnel. He obtained the "presented scholar" degree in 1148. From 1153 to 1158 he was district keeper of records (assistant magistrate) of T'ung-an County in Fukien, where he promoted education, founded a library, and regulated civil ceremonies. In 1179 he became prefect of Nan-k'ang Prefecture in present Kiangsi. While there, he alleviated economic suffering, built a temple for Chou Tun-i, and reestablished the White Deer Grotto Academy, an important institution that was to play a great role in Neo-Confucianism. When his term expired in 1181, he was appointed superintendent designate of "ever-normal graneries, tea, and salt" in charge of finance and taxation in Chiang-nan West, and later appointed to the same position in Chekiang East[116] where there was a famine. He established community granaries and impeached many officials and big families in the stricken area.[117] Six years later, in 1187, he was judicial intendant of Chiang-nan West. From 1190 to 1191 he was prefect of Chang-chou Prefecture in Fukien where he promoted moral education but failed in his attempts at land and tax reforms. In 1194 he was prefect of T'an-chou Prefecture[118] in Human for one month, just long enough to persuade the rebellious aboriginals to surrender. When Emperor Ning-tsung (r. 1194-1224) ascended the throne later that year, Chu Hsi became lecturer in waiting for forty-six days expounding the *Great Learning*. Because he repeatedly attacked a powerful official before the emperor, he was relieved and went home.[119]

Thus for almost fifty years after he received his degree he was in the government for only nine years and in court for merely forty-six days. He presented three sealed memorials to Emperor Hsiao-tsung (r. 1162-89): in 1162 when he urged him to practice the teachings of the *Great Learning*, not to make peace with the Chin invaders, and to put worthy men in office;[120] in 1180 when he insisted that economic distress, military weakness, and political corruption can be removed only if the ruler rectifies his mind, and thus made the emperor furious;[121] and in 1188 when he advocated fundamental reforms.[122] He also had three audiences with the emperor: in 1163 when he reiterated the points of his memorial of 1162;[123] in 1181 when he took the emperor to task for allowing wicked officials to rule;[124] and in 1188 when he emphasized that only when the Principle of Nature overcomes human selfish desires, the mind is rectified, and the will becomes sincere can economic difficulties be removed, the government be reformed, and the enemy be repulsed.[125]

In between these political activities, he declined many positions.[126] Often he pleaded a foot ailment but actually he was unwilling to support appeasers and corrupt officials whose hatred of him was considerable. In 1188, for example, when he declined a directorship in the army department, a vice minister of the department itself, who disagreed with him in the interpretations of the *Book of Changes* and Chang Tsai's "Western Inscription," attacked him as an ignoramus plagiarizing Ch'eng I and Chang Tsai.[127]

During most of his life he was granted a temple guardianship,[128] often at his request, a sinecure which did not remove his poverty but enabled him to stay home with leisure to write, teach, and talk with the most outstanding scholars of the day. Thus he devoted his life to the development of Neo-Confucianism which he inherited from Li T'ung (Li Yen-p'ing, 1093-1163), whom he visited in 1158, 1160, and 1162, and from whom he received instructions during each of the several-months-long visits. But the Neo-Confucian philosophy was a dangerous doctrine to corrupt officialdom. By 1196 government attacks on Neo-Confucianism as "false learning" had become intense. The teachings of Ch'eng I and others were proscribed. A powerful censor impeached Chu Hsi for ten crimes, including "false learning," and an official candidate even petitioned for his execution.[129] He was dismissed from a new appointment and from his temple guardianship. The attack on "false learning" became more severe in 1197 and 1198. But he had his loyal followers. When he died in 1200 several thousand people attended his funeral. When the political climate improved, nine years later, he was honored with the posthumous title of Wen (Culture).[130] In 1230 he was given the title of State Duke of Hui, and in 1241 he was accorded sacrifice in the Confucian temple.[131]

He wrote almost a hundred works in the fields of philosophy, history, religion, literature, and biography. Many of these are no longer extant. It was he who grouped the *Great Learning*, the *Doctrine of the Mean*, the *Analects*, and the *Book of Mancius* as the Four Books. He wrote commentaries on many Confucian Classics but paid special attention to the Four Books, on which he wrote not only commentaries but also books to explain these commentaries. Three days before he died he was still working on the commentary on the *Great Learning*. In 1313 an imperial decree ordered that his and Ch'eng I's commentaries on the Four Books and the Five Classics be the standard official interpretations and the basis for the civil service examinations. They remained the authorities until the examinations were abolished in 1905. Thus for almost six hundred years they were the political Bible of the Chinese, so to speak.

Lü Tsu-ch'ien, whose courtesy name was Po-kung, was a native of Chin-hua County in modern Chekiang Province. Because his ancestral home was Tung-lai[132] in modern Shantung, he was also called Master Tung-lai.

He obtained the "presented scholar" degree in 1163 and became a professor at the national university and also a compiler in the bureau of national history. In his audiences with the emperor, he always urged the ruler to pay attention to Confucian teachings. Later he was appointed an examiner of top level civil service personnel and served until he resigned to mourn his father's death. When the three-year mourning period was over, he was appointed director of the imperial library and a compiler in the bureau of national history. After his task was completed he was transferred to the position of staff author but he declined the post and returned home. Subsequently he became a guardian of two temples, one after the other.

He wrote extensively, though not so extensively as Chu Hsi. While Chu Hsi was an authority on philosophy, Lü Tsu-ch'ien was original and expert in the discussion of history. He and Chang Shih (Chang Nan-hsien, 1133-80) were constant companions to Chu Hsi in conversation and correspondence, and the three were called the Three Worthies of the Southeast.[133]

Lü studied under a pupil of the Ch'eng brothers, but while Chu Hsi perpetuated and developed their doctrines, Lü traveled in a different direction. At that time there were within Neo-Confucianism three rival schools of thought, namely, the rationalistic school of Chu Hsi, the idealistic school of Lu Hsiang-shan (Lu Chiu-yüan, 1139-93), and the East Chekiang school, of which Lü was a leader. Lu Hsiang-shan, instead of stressing the investigation of principles in things, as did Chu Hsi, taught the investigation of the mind, for he believed that principles are identical with the mind. Lü Tsu-ch'ien did not go to either extreme but attempted a compromise. The importance of the Chekiang school lies in the fact that it aimed at practical results and the concrete application of Confucian thought to social, economic, and political life. In many respects he was a greater rival of Chu Hsi than Lu Hsiang-shan was. But they were also good friends. They joined their efforts in compiling the *Chin-ssu lu* in the belief that Neo-Confucianism was a sound philosophy of life and that the anthology would be a useful guide to the essentials of that philosophy.

It is interesting and instructive to see what Chu Hsi himself thought of the book. The following quotations express his opinions on this subject:

> The fundamentals of self-cultivation are completely covered in the *Hsiao-hsüeh* [Elementary education],[134] while refined and subtle principles are fully treated in the *Chin-ssu lu.*[135]

> The *Chin-ssu lu* is worth reading. The Four Books are the ladders to the Six Classics.[136] The *Chin-ssu lu* is the ladder to the Four Books.

> Everything in the *Chin-ssu lu* is intimately connected with man's life and can save him from defects.

> Chang[137] was commenting on how practical and close to human life the sayings in the *Chin-ssu lu* are. Chu Hsi said, "The Sage and the worthies[138] put things plainly. For example, the *Doctrine of the Mean*, the *Great Learning*, the *Analects*, and the *Book of Mencius* are all plain and simple. The *Chin-ssu lu*, however, are

words of men of recent times. They are more intimately connected with our lives."

Someone asked about the **Chin-ssu lu.** Chu Hsi said, "Suppose you read the _Great Learning_ thoroughly, and then go right on to the _Analects_ and the _Book of Mencius._ The **Chin-ssu lu** is difficult to read."

The first chapter of the **Chin-ssu lu** is difficult to read. This is the reason I talked the matter over with Po-kung and asked him to write a few words as post-script.[139] If one reads this chapter only, he will be unable to relate to life the principles he finds in it. Stopping there would be like halting one's troops outside the strong defenses of a city. It would be far better to read the _Analects_ and the _Book of Mencius,_ which are plain and straightforward and can be enjoyed.

In reading the **Chin-ssu lu,** if the student does not understand the first chapter, he should begin with the second and the third. In time he will gradually understand the first chapter.

When Fei-ch'ing[140] was asked how he was getting along with the **Chin-ssu lu,** he said that there were many doubtful points. Chu Hsi said, "If one hurriedly reads it for the first time, it is difficult, that is true. Sometimes it says something first this way but later that way, or says one thing here and a different thing there. However, if one reads it carefully again and again, one will find in it a certain direction. When a searching effort has been made to understand forty or fifty sections, one will find that there is only one principle running through all. I-ch'uan said that principle cannot be investigated to the utmost in one day and that when one has investigated a great deal, one will thoroughly understand it."[141]

The **Chin-ssu lu** discusses very keenly the defects of the patterns of learning in recent times. It will be fine if one can read it along with [the Four Books].[142]

The **Chin-ssu lu** is fundamentally for the student who cannot read all the works of the several Masters. For this reason the most important passages and those of immediate concern have been selected so the student can gradually enter into the Way. If he thoroughly understands these, he will extend on the basis of similarity in kind, to understand the rest and thus achieve an extensive learning. If he does not read it thoroughly, he cannot understand even this book of several chapters. How can he have the energy or time to read all the works listed in the beginning of the book?[143]

In the **Chin-ssu lu** what Master Heng-ch'ü [Chang Tsai] has to say about the order of reading books is excellent. Try to think about it and you will get the idea.[144]

Notes

1. See Wing-tsit Chan, _A Source Book in Chinese Philosophy,_ chaps. 25, 26.

2. For this book, see below, ch. 3, n. 59.

3. _Book of Changes,_ commentary on hexagram no. 2, _k'un_ (Earth) (_Yi King,_ tr. by James Legge, p. 420); "Appended Remarks," pt. 1, ch. 1 (Legge, p. 349); "Remarks on Certain Trigrams," ch. 2 (Legge, p. 423); _ibid.,_ ch. 1 (Legge, p. 422), respectively. For this Classic, see below, ch. 1, n. 12.

4. _Book of Mencius,_ 6A:7. The word also appears in 7B:19 and 5B:1, but there it means "to depend" and "to order," respectively. For the _Book of Mencius,_ see below, ch. 3, n. 68.

5. In the _Hsün Tzu,_ chs. 1, 2, 5, 7-9, 11, 15, 17-23, 26-28. For an English translation, see Homer H. Dubs, _The Works of Hsüntze._ Chs. 1, 2, 15, 17, and 19-23 have been translated by Burton Watson in _Hsün Tzu: Basic Writings._

6. For a discussion of Chinese philosophers' concepts of principle, see Wingtsit Chan, "The Evolution of the Neo-Confucian Concept _Li_ as Principle," _Tsing Hua Journal of Chinese Studies,_ IV (No. 2, 1964), 123-49.

7. For the _Great Learning_ and the _Doctrine of the Mean,_ see below, ch. 2, n. 182.

8. See below, ch. 1, n. 12, for the _Book of Changes;_ ch. 3, n. 47, for the _Book of Odes;_ ch. 3, n. 90, for the _Book of History;_ and ch. 3, n. 128, for the _Spring and Autumn Annals._ The fifth Classic, the ancient classic on rites, is no longer extant but has been replaced by the _Li chi,_ or _Book of Rites,_ a collection of treatises on rituals and detailed prescriptions for social ceremonies, religious rites, and governmental and diplomatic etiquette, and the principles underlying them, traditionally ascribed to pupils of Confucius but probably compiled many centuries later. For an English translation of the _Li chî,_ see _The Li Ki,_ tr. by James Legge.

   These Five Classics and the _Book of Music_ constituted the ancient Six Classics, but the latter, if it ever existed, was lost before the third century B.C. and since the Sung dynasty (960-1279) has been replaced by the _Chou-li._ For the _Chou-li,_ see below, ch. 3, n. 154.

   Tradition ascribed the original Six Classics to Confucius. Most modern scholars, however, believe that they were compiled later.

9. For other translations of the title, see below, "On Translating Certain Chinese Philosophical Terms," pp. 360-61.

10. See below, pp. 309 ff., 323 ff.

11. See Chu Hsi, _Lun-yü chi-chu,_ ch. 10, commenting on the _Analects,_ 19:6.

12. _Wai-shu,_ 6:9a and _I-shu,_ 22A:5a, respectively. For the latter saying, see below, ch. 3, sec. 14.

13. _Chu Tzu yü-lei,_ 49:5a-b. The three steps of affection to parents, being humane to all people, and love for all creatures are taught in the _Book of Mencius,_ 7A:45.

14. _Chu Tzu yü-lei,_ 105:4b. His famous pupil, Huang Kan (1152-1221), claimed that Chu Hsi did not say so (see _Huang Mien-chai chi,_ 2:2a), but since the statement is recorded by Chu Hsi's equally famous pupil, Ch'en Ch'un (1153-1217), there is no reason

to doubt its authenticity, especially in view of the importance Chu Hsi attached to the work. It is possible that Huang never heard the statement.

15. See below, ch. 2, secs. 8, 29; ch. 7, sec. 25; ch. 12, sec. 12.

16. Ch. 1, sec. 15; ch. 3, sec. 12.

17. Ch. 1, sec. 18.

18. Ch. 1, sec. 33.

19. Ch. 12, sec. 9.

20. Ch. 1, secs. 5, 8, 19, 46.

21. Ch. 1, sec. 13; ch. 8, sec. 10.

22. Ch. 2, secs. 8, 85; ch. 4, sec. 26; ch. 8, secs. 2, 12; ch. 12, sec. 21.

23. Ch. 3, sec. 8.

24. Ch. 3, secs. 5, 9; ch. 7, sec. 25; ch. 13, sec. 10.

25. Ch. 1, secs. 38-41.

26. Ch. 1, sec. 21; ch. 2, sec. 30.

27. Ch. 1, sec. 21; ch. 2, secs. 80, 100.

28. Ch. 1, sec. 38; ch. 2, sec. 81.

29. For the translation of this word, see below, "On Translating Certain Chinese Philosophical Terms," pp. 365-66.

30. Ch. 1, secs. 6, 11, 23.

31. Ch. 2, sec. 20.

32. Ch. 2, sec. 89.

33. Ch. 2, sec. 52.

34. Ch. 1, sec. 20.

35. Ch. 1, secs. 23, 36.

36. Ch. 2, secs. 7, 16, 44; ch. 4, sec. 44; ch. 13, sec. 3.

37. *Ching* is often translated as "reverence." For the translation "seriousness," see below, "On Translating Certain Chinese Philosophical Terms," pp. 361-62.

38. Ch. 4, secs. 44, 45, 48.

39. Ch. 4, secs. 16, 25, 27, 47.

40. Ch. 2, secs. 54, 78; ch. 4, secs. 24, 25, 27, 28.

41. Ch. 4, secs. 37, 38, 44.

42. Ch. 8, sec. 1. For other ideas on sincerity, see ch. 1, secs. 2, 31; ch. 2, secs. 16, 17, 19; ch. 4, sec. 28.

43. Ch. 2, secs. 7, 34, 60, 61.

44. Ch. 2, sec. 58.

45. Ch. 2, sec. 35.

46. Ch. 2, secs. 27, 56, 57.

47. Ch. 3, secs. 19, 25.

48. Ch. 3, secs. 6, 10, 22.

49. Ch. 2, sec. 102; ch. 3, sec. 15.

50. Ch. 2, sec. 67; ch. 3, secs. 33, 35, 36.

51. Ch. 2, sec. 41; ch. 3, sec. 33.

52. Ch. 2, sec. 6.

53. Ch. 6, sec. 11.

54. Ch. 6, sec. 3.

55. Ch. 6, sec. 13.

56. For Chang Po-hsing's deletion of Ch'eng I's saying from his commentary, see below, ch. 6, n. 21.

57. Ch. 6, sec. 5; ch. 9, sec. 14.

58. Ch. 9, secs. 12, 13, 18.

59. Ch. 7, secs. 33, 35; ch. 12, sec. 27.

60. Ch. 7, secs. 22, 38.

61. Ch. 2, sec. 40; ch. 7, sec. 26.

62. Ch. 7, secs. 3, 8, 12, 14, 21.

63. Ch. 8, sec. 2.

64. Ch. 8, sec. 16.

65. Ch. 8, sec. 25.

66. Ch. 9, secs. 1, 2, 5, 6.

67. Ch. 7, sec. 14; ch. 8, secs. 9, 14, 23; ch. 9, secs. 1, 3, 23, 26, 27.

68. This list appears in the beginning of the *Chin-ssu lu* but is omitted from the translation. For a detailed list of selections from these works, see below, "On the *Chin-ssu lu* and Its Commentaries," pp. 330-35.

69. See below, p. 334.

70. Originally this was at the end of the *T'ung-shu* but Chu Hsi shifted it to the beginning. Now it is no longer part of the *T'ung-shu* but an independent work. It constitutes the first section of the *Chin-ssu lu.* For an English translation, see Wing-tsit Chan, *A Source Book in Chinese Philosophy,* pp. 463-64.

71. This short work in 40 chapters, each of which is only a paragraph, deals with various subjects. The book is so called because Chou Tun-i felt that its principles penetrate and are harmonious with those in the *Chou-i* (*Book of Changes*). For an English translation, see Chan, *Source Book,* ch. 28. See also French translation by Chow Yih-Ching, *La Philosophie Morale dans le Neo-Confucianisme (Tcheou Touen-Yi).*

72. This work consists of five chapters, including poems, memorials to the emperor, a letter, and some essays.

73. This work contains eight chapters. It is similar to the *Ming-tao wen-chi,* but is twice as long. For an English translation of several letters and essays by the Ch'engs, see Chan, *Source Book,* chs. 31-32.

74. The *I-shu* of the two Ch'engs is a collection of conversations recorded by their pupils. It has 25 chapters and a supplement. Chs. 1-10 are conversations of the two brothers, most of which are not identified with either master. Chs. 11-14 contain Ch'eng Hao's conversations; chs. 15-25, Ch'eng I's. There is a supplement, containing their biographies and similar mate-

rials. For English translations of selections from these conversations, see Chan, *Source Book*, chs. 31-32. Ts'ai Yung-ch'un has selected and translated many of Ch'eng I's sayings in his *The Philosophy of Ch'eng I*. Many of the two brothers' sayings are also translated in A. C. Graham, *Two Chinese Philosophers: Ch'eng Ming-tao and Ch'eng I-ch'uan*.

75. The *Wai-shu* of the two Ch'engs, in twelve short chapters, consists of additional sayings of the two brothers. In most cases the speaker is not identified, and many of the passages repeat ideas discussed in the *I-shu*.

76. This is Ch'eng I's commentary on the *Book of Changes (Chou-i)*. It is a lengthy four-chapter work commenting on the texts and commentaries of the *Book of Changes*, often sentence by sentence.

77. This work by Ch'eng I is in eight chapters. Much of the work has been lost. For example, in ch. 6 it has comments on only nine of the 20 chapters of the *Analects*, and of ch. 7, the explanation of the *Book of Mencius*, nothing remains.

78. This work in 17 sections is Chang Tsai's most important work, setting forth his philosophy in short passages rather than lengthy treatises. English translations of chs. 1 and 6 are given in Chan, *Source Book*, ch. 30. For an incomplete French translation of the work, see Ch. de Harlez, "L'École philosophique moderne de la Chine ou Système de la Nature (Sing-li)," *Mémoire de L'Académie Royale des Sciences des Lettres et des Beaux-Arts de Belgique*, XLIX (1890), 36-76.

79. This is in three chapters. Some parts are missing.

80. The present work is not the original compilation but contains authentic sayings.

81. There is a separate *Chang Tzu yü-lu* (Recorded conversations of Master Chang), which contains more sayings, many of which duplicate those in the *Chang Tzu ch'üan-shu*. The *Wen-chi* is no longer extant, although excerpts from it are preserved in the *Chang Tzu ch'üan-shu*. The *Li-yüeh shuo, Lun-yü shuo* and *Meng Tzu shuo* are lost.

82. For statistics, see below, p. 331 ff.

83. *I-shu*, 3:2a.

84. *Ibid.*, 2A:2b, 7:1a, 3:1b; *Ts'ui-yen*, 2:13b.

85. *I-shu*, 6:4a.

86. For further details of his life, see the *Sung shih*, 427:2b-5b, and Bruce, *Chu Hsi and His Masters*, pp. 18-24.

87. See below, ch. 14, sec. 16.

88. See below, ch. 14, sec. 26.

89. See below, ch. 14, sec. 17.

90. See below, ch. 14, sec. 21.

91. See below, ch. 14, sec. 23.

92. *I-ch'uan wen-chi*, 7:1a-7b. See also *Sung shih*, 247:5a-10a, and Bruce, *Chu Hsi and His Masters*, pp. 41-45.

93. See below, ch. 12, sec. 31.

94. For fuller accounts, see the *Sung shih*, 427:10a-15b; Yao Ming-ta, *Ch'eng I-ch'uan nien-p'u;* and Bruce, *Chu Hsi and His Masters*, pp. 45-47.

95. *Wai-shu*, 11:5b; 12:3b, 6b.

96. See below, ch. 14, sec. 22.

97. Chu Hsi, comp., *I-Lo yüan-yüan lu*, 4:15a.

98. For more details, see the *Sung shih*, 427:15a-17b; *Chang Tzu ch'üan-shu*, 15:10b-14a; and Bruce, *Chu Hsi and His Masters*, pp. 50-52.

99. See below, ch. 14, sec. 25.

100. See the *Sung shih*, 427:18b-21a; and Bruce, *Chu Hsi and His Masters*, pp. 31-35.

101. Except for a quotation from him by Ch'eng Hao in ch. 5, sec. 15.

102. See the *Sung shih*, 427:19a.

103. In ch. 2, sec. 3. In ch. 1, sec. 38, Chu Hsi omitted the phrase "That is, the so-called nature of principle," probably a Buddhist term, originally. But this clearly repeats the idea of the opening sentence.

104. See below, ch. 7, sec. 13. See also Chu's commentary on ch. 4, sec. 6. For other instances of Ch'eng I's alteration of the meanings of Confucian Classics, see below, ch. 1, secs. 14, 40; ch. 7, sec. 3.

105. See below, his comments on ch. 4, sec. 6, and also the *Chu Tzu yü-lei*, 73:15b.

106. See below, Chu Hsi's comment on ch. 12, sec. 14.

107. See below, comment on ch. 1, sec. 39. For other criticisms of Ch'eng I, see his comments on ch. 1, secs. 5, 10, 17, 21; ch. 10, sec. 31; ch. 11, sec. 15, etc. See also his comments on ch. 1, secs. 3, 20, 22, 23.

108. See below, tables, pp. 332-36.

109. See below, ch. 1, secs. 10, 12, 13, 15.

110. For lessons on the Mean, see below, ch. 3, sec. 53; ch. 5, sec. 6; ch. 6, sec. 4; ch. 7, secs. 11, 15, 19. For lessons on correctness, see below, ch. 6, sec. 8; ch. 7, secs. 3, 6, 12, 14, 21; ch. 12, secs. 7-9. For lessons on both the Mean and correctness, see below, ch. 5, secs. 7, 9; ch. 7, sec. 16; ch. 10, sec. 10; ch. 12, sec. 3.

111. *Chu Tzu yü-lei*, 67:6a, 8b; 117:7b-8b.

112. *Ibid.*, 119:10a. For Lü Tsu-ch'ien's prodding him into using this book, see below, p. 325.

113. The most outstanding example of the Neo-Confucian collections is the *Hsing-li ta-ch'üan* (Great collection of Neo-Confucianism), comp. by Hu Kuang (1370-1418) and others. As the *Ssu-k'u ch'üan-shu tsung-mu t'i-yao* (p. 1918) has pointed out, the collection of

the Neo-Confucian sayings in the *Hsing-li ta-ch'üan* is an enlargement of the *Chin-ssu lu*. The anthologies inspired by the *Chin-ssu lu*, which, with slight variations, have all followed its fourteen-chapter division, are: Liu Ch'ing-chih (Chu Hsi's pupil, 1139-95), comp., *Chin-ssu hsü-lu* (Supplement to the *Reflections on Things at Hand*), containing sayings of pupils of the Ch'eng brothers, an anthology of which Chu Hsi did not entirely approve because he thought the pupils did not match their masters (see *Chu Tzu yü-lei*, 101:1a); Ts'ai Mu (Chu Hsi's pupil, *fl.* 1220), comp., *Chin-ssu hsü-lu* (Supplement to the *Reflections on Things at Hand*); Kao P'an-lung (1562-1626), comp., *Chu Tzu chieh-yao* (The essentials of Master Chu's teachings); Liu Yüan-lu (1619-1700), comp., *Chin-ssu hsü-lu* (Supplement to the *Reflections on Things at Hand*); Chu Hsien-tsu (*fl.* 1684), comp., *Chu Tzu chin-ssu lu* (Master Chu's *Reflections on Things at Hand*); Chang Po-hsing (1651-1725), comp., *Hsü chin-ssu lu* (Supplement to the *Reflections on Things at Hand*); Chu Ch'üan (1702-59), comp., *Hsia-hsüeh pien* (Anthology on studying things on the lower level), all seven containing sayings by Chu Hsi; and Wang Yu (1827-60), comp., *Wu-tzu chin-ssu lu* (The reflections on things at hand of the five philosophers), which adds Chu Hsi's sayings to those of the Four Masters. Also Ts'ai Mu, comp., *Chin-ssu pieh-lu* (Separate records of reflections on things at hand), a collection of sayings by Lü Tsu-ch'ien and Chang Shih; Chiang Ch'i-p'eng (*fl.* 1604), comp., *Chin-ssu pu-lu* (The *Reflections on Things at Hand* supplemented), an anthology of Sung (960-1279) and Ming (1368-1644) Neo-Confucianists, including Chu Hsi; Chang Po-hsing, comp., *Kuang chin-ssu lu* (Further records of reflections on things at hand), containing sayings of Lü Tsu-ch'ien, Chu Hsi's pupil Huang Kan, and later Neo-Confucianists; Sun Ch'eng-tse (1592-1676), comp., *Hsüeh-yüeh hsü-pien* (Supplement to the *Essentials of Learning*), an anthology of four Ming Neo-Confucianists; Cheng Kuang-hsi (*fl.* 1700?), *Hsü chin-ssu lu* (Supplement to the *Reflections on Things at Hand*), a collection of sayings by Ming thinkers including Wang Yang-ming; and Chu Ch'üan, comp., *Shu-ai lu* (Records of self-cultivation and self-discipline), a selection of sayings from his teacher Chang Lü-hsing's (1611-74) *Pi-wang lu* (Records as a reminder).

114. For this commentary, see below, pp. 338-39.

115. See below, pp. 337-58, nos. 1-62, for Chinese, Korean, and Japanese commentaries and nos. 29-31, 33-35, 39-40, 49-50, and 52 for commentaries by the followers of Yamazaki.

116. "Circuits" of 11 prefectures in present Anhui and Kiangsi and of six prefectures in Chekiang, respectively.

117. See Wang Mou-hung, *Chu Tzu nien p'u,* pp. 109-15.

118. Modern Ch'ang-sha County, Hunan Province.

119. For this episode, see *ibid.,* pp. 212-13, *Sung shih,* 429:17a, and Huang Kan's "Biographical Account" in his *Huang Mien-chai chi,* 8:27a-b.

120. *Chu Tzu wen-chi,* 11:1a-10a.

121. *Ibid.,* 11:10a-16b.

122. *Ibid.,* 11:17a-37b.

123. *Ibid.,* 13:1a-6a. The audience took place in the capital Lin-an (modern Hangchow).

124. *Ibid.,* 13:6a-20a. The audience took place in the capital.

125. *Ibid.,* 14:1a-8b. The audience took place in the capital.

126. Notably professor designate of the military academy in 1163, compiler designate of the bureau of military affairs in 1169, librarian of the imperial library in 1176, a post in the imperial archives in 1181, judicial intendancy of Chiang-nan West in 1182, judicial intendancy in Kiangsi, and junior expositor in waiting in 1188, assistant regional governor (see below, ch. 10, n. 75.) of Chiang-nan East in 1189, assistant commissioner of Hunan in 1191, and pacification commissioner of Kwangsi in 1192. Once he declined a post seven times over a period of several years.

127. For this episode, see Huang Kan, *Huang Mien-chai chi,* 8:14b, and Wang Mou-hung, *Chu Tzu nien-p'u,* p. 143.

128. In 1158-79, 1183-89, and 1191-96, he was guardian of six different temples in various parts of China, holding nine different appointments.

129. See the *Sung shih,* 429:18b, and Wang Mou-hung, *Chu Tzu nien-p'u,* pp. 218-20.

130. According to Huang Kan, 8:29a-b, the year was 1209.

131. For Hui, see below, p. 2, n. 11. For fuller details on Chu Hsi's life, see the *Sung shih,* ch. 429; Wang Mou-hung, *Chu Tzu nien-p'u;* Bruce, *Chu Hsi and His Masters,* pp. 56-96; Conrad M. Schirokauer, "Chu Hsi's Political Career: A Study of Ambivalence," in Wright and Twitchett, eds., *Confucian Personalities,* pp. 162-88, 353-59; Gotō Shunzui, *Shushi,* pp. 1-198.

132. Present Yeh County.

133. For fuller information on Lü, see the *Sung shih,* 434:2a-5a.

134. Chu Hsi's collection of sayings on daily conduct and human relations, and exemplary deeds of sages and worthies from ancient times to his own. For a French translation, see Chu Hsi, *La Siao Hio ou morale de la jeunesse avec le commentaire de Tschen-siuen,* tr. by Ch. de Harlez.

135. This and the following seven passages are from the *Chu Tzu yü-lei,* 105:4b-5a. For two additional passages from the same place, see below, "The *Chin-ssu lu* and Its Commentaries," p. 324, n. 7.

136. See above, nn. 2, 4, 7, and 14.

137. Chu Hsi had several pupils by this name. There is no further identification.

138. Confucius, Mencius, Tzu-ssu (492-431 B.C.), and Tseng Tzu (505-*c.* 436 B.C.).

139. This is Lü Tsu-ch'ien's Preface.

140. Courtesy name of T'ung Po-yü, Chu Hsi's pupil.

141. Paraphrasing the *I-shu,* 18:5b.

142. *Chu Tzu wen-chi,* 59:12b.

143. *Ibid.,* 64:37a. The list is that referred to above, n.72. For Chu Hsi's additional sayings exhorting people to read the *Chin-ssu lu,* see the *Chu Tzu wen-chi,* 46:29b and 63:19a; and for his intention to include certain sayings, see below, "On the *Chin-ssu lu* and Its Commentaries", n. 7.

144. *Chu Tzu wen-chi,* 63:19a. For the "order" referred to, see below, ch. 3, secs. 70-78.

Tomoeda Ryūtarō (essay date 1971)

SOURCE: "The Characteristics of Chu Hsi's Thought," in *Acta Asiatica,* Vol. 21, 1971, pp. 52-72.

[*In the following essay, Ryūtarō examines the way in which Chu Hsi criticized his predecessors and developed his own philosophical system. In particular, Ryūtarō traces the influence of Zen Buddhism on Chu Hsi's thought and discusses the differences between the Zen and Neo-Confucian treatment of various philosophical principles. Chinese characters have been deleted from this essay.*]

INTRODUCTION

What are the characteristics of Chu Hsi's philosophy? I shall try to elucidate its outline in this article by re-examining my past studies which I have pursued for over fifteen years.

The general trend of the Japanese world of thought today is to reject not only the achievements of the founders of Confucianism such as Confucius and Mencius, but also of the leaders of Neo-Confucianism who developed them into metaphysics such as Ch'êng Yi and Chu Hsi, regarding them as philosophical thoughts representing feudal society. It seems that the characteristics of these ideas are not duly appreciated. It is easy to reject a thought of the past by bringing it to a court imbued with modern materialistic philosophy and by pointing out its defects without trying to listen to what it has to say.

Outstanding ideas of the past, however, have characteristics of their own. By re-examining them, it is possible to rejuvenate modern philosophical thought. Philosophy would not have existed without the history of philosophy. True and genuine philosophy is always rejuvenated by feedback from the history of thought.

In this article, the present writer intends to see how Chu Hsi in the twelfth century criticized his predecessors, and how he established his own philosophical system by adopting earlier thoughts. We shall also see the characteristics of his thought and how they were received by philosophers of later ages. Thus, by clarifying the characteristics of Chu Hsi's ideas in both positive and negative aspects, we shall naturally be able to find an answer to the problem of how his thought can be resuscitated in the modern trend of thought.

I. FORMATION OF CHU HSI'S PHILOSOPHY

1. INCLINATION TO ZEN BUDDHISM

Chu Hsi (1130-1200) spent his early years, reading Confucian works such as *Ssu-shu* (the Four Books) and *Hsiao-ching* under his father. After his father died when Chu Hsi was fourteen years old, he studied under Liu Pai-shui (1091-1149), Liu Ping-shan (1101-1147), and Hu Chi-ch'i (1086-1162). Around the age of fifteen or sixteen, he met Ch'ien K'ai-shan, disciple of Ta Hui (1089-1163), and was attracted to Zen.

However, since Chu Hsi at this stage was still inexperienced in politics, he did not seem to appreciate Ch'ien K'ai-shan's dynamic teaching of K'an-hua-ch'an (*Kōan-zen,* a kind of Zen training that seeks enlightenment through the *kōan*). He was more influenced by the static Mo-hua-ch'an (silent meditation without thinking), which had been acquired by Liu Ping-shan.

It may be said that the decade following this period up to the year he reached the age of twenty-four was the period in which Chu Hsi inclined toward Buddhism. As an example, let us quote one of his poems which he wrote at the age of twenty-three:

> Staying at home alone, and having nothing else to do,
> I leafed through a book on Sakya.
> Emancipated for a while from earthly distractions,
> Transcending (this world), I came in unison with the Way.
> The garden gate covered with a bamboo bush,
> Birds chirping around the hills after rain,
> Apprehending this law of non-activity,
> Both body and mind attained peace.
>
> (*Chu-tzu wen-chi* I)

The world sought by Chu Hsi in this poem is static, the aim being unity with the Way amidst secluded quiet and apprehension of *wu-wei-fa* (the principle of non-activity). Since zen espoused by Ch'ien K'ai-shan and Ta Hui was experience and appreciation of the Way through daily activities, it was diversely different from the world indicated in this poem. There are also many other poems reading the world of of tranquility in *Chu-tzu wen-chi* I.

2. STUDYING UNDER LI YEN-P'ING

Having been appointed Chu-po (Chief Accountant) of T'ung-an hsien, Ch'uan-chou, Chu Hsi left his home in Wu-fu-li, Ch'ung-an hsien for his new post. On his way, he stopped over at Yen-p'ing to receive instructions from Li Yen-p'ing (1093-1163). When Chu Hsi expressed his views on the basis of Zen as he understood it, Yen-p'ing told him "to go through the words of the sages" (**Chu-tzu yü-lei** 104), and further advised, "You seem to have ample knowledge of many principles in their abstract but not of the reality lying before you. You will be able to appreciate it if you try to apprehend what you encounter in your daily life by faithful observation." (*Yen-p'ing ta-wen pu-lu*)

After meeting Yen-p'ing, Chu Hsi said, "When I reviewed Sakya's teaching after having relished the words of the sages, my image of Buddha began to crumble, noticing many inconsistencies in his teaching." (**Yü-lei** 104).

The relationship of Chu Hsi with Yen-p'ing continued for approximately ten years from the age of twenty-four to thirty-four. The details of the intercourse between the two are given in *Yen-p'ing ta-wen* edited by Chu Hsi himself.

Yen-p'ing impressed upon Chu Hsi the significance of *ts'un-hsin* (preservation of a true mind) and *han-yang* (self-cultivation) and emphasized cultivating *yeh-ch'i* (a mind free from earthly thoughts) based on *Meng-tzu* and acquiring *Hsi-nu-ai-le-wei-fa-chih-chung* (one's emotion in the inmost state of potency) through meditation. Once this mental state is attained, Yen-p'ing taught, all matters pertaining to daily life will be carried out smoothly, since the principle is already grasped. (See *Yen-p'ing ta-wen*) Chu Hsi consequently exerted all efforts in concentrating his mind upon attainment of that mental state.

Attainment of *Hsi-nu-ai-le-wei-fa-chih-chung* through meditation exposed by Yen-p'ing and that of the aforementioned *wu-wei-fa* or non-activity of Mo-huo-ch'an share something in common in the sense that both are experience and attainment of the Way in a state of tranquility. However, whereas comprehension of *wu-wei-fa* is but remotely connected with daily human life, Yen-p'ing's theory, which teaches that comprehension of 'one's feelings in the inmost state of potency' facilitates his daily activities, is inexorably linked with daily human life. As a matter of fact, the method of experiencing and comprehending the inmost of the potential state of human feelings through meditation is found also in the thoughts of Lo Yü-chang (1072-1135), Yen-p'ing's master, as well as with other scholars such as Yang Kuei-shan (1052-1135), Ch'êng Ming-tao (1032-1085) and Ch'êng I-ch'uan (1033-1107).

The theories of these Confucian scholars are closely related with the method of the Zen school. Zen, however, presupposed renunciation of or exodus from the human world, and therefore in the attainment of the Way through such exodus there was always the danger of estranging oneself from human life. The Confucian scholars, on the other hand, wholly denied such an exodus. Therefore, although they espoused attainment of the Way through meditation like the Zen scholars, the fundamentals of human being conceived thereby were naturally to lead one back to the world of daily human life.

It is doubtful as mentioned later, whether Chu Hsi actually attained enlightenment by fully appreciating 'feelings in the inmost state of potency.' It is clear, however, that Yen-p'ing's method helped Chu Hsi push forward his static thought which he had formed on the basis of Mo-hua-ch'an in his early years before the age of twenty-four.

Why, then, was Chu Hsi attracted to Yen-p'ing's teachings? It was because all his duties as Chu-pu for four years since the age of twenty-four had been concerned with matters pertaining to daily human affairs. During this period, he devoted himself to the life of a bureaucrat. He checked taxation documents daily to prevent embezzlement by low officials, and thereby to maintain fairness in taxation. Seeing that government officials, plutocrats and merchants were suppressing farmers, taking advantage of their wealth, he worked to protect the rights of the farmers. Chu Hsi further founded a library, established rituals for matrimony, and trained a militia corps.

Chu Hsi probably sought establishment of a purely spiritual state, namely experience of *wei-fa* (state of potency) as the ground for fair and unbiased execution of his governmental duties. This was precisely the reason why he was attracted to Yen-p'ing's teachings.

3. ACQUAINTANCE WITH CHANG NAN-HSÜAN

Soon after the death of Yen-p'ing, Chu Hsi gained acquaintance with Chang Nan-hsüan and was greatly infatuated with his thoughts. He had felt that Yen-p'ing's thought of 'experience and comprehension of the inmost world of potency' was, because of its static nature, difficult to make it compatible with ever-changing daily life despite Yen-p'ing's stress on the close relationship between the two worlds. Yen-p'ing himself often complained of the difficulty of attaining enlightenment on this very point. It was all the more so with Chu Hsi.

Nan-hsüan's father Chün was an sympathetic friend of Ta Hui, leader of the dynamic K'an-hua-ch'an. Nan-hsüan was also of a dynamic type, having been influenced by the teachings of Hu Wu-feng (?-1161) and having participated in military actions in his youth under his father. Although both set a value on daily human deeds, Yen-p'ing's thought was static, while Nan-hsüan's was dynamic. The latter took a stand divergently different from that of Yen-p'ing, attaching less importance to experience and comprehension of the Way through *ching-tso*. Nan-hsüan taught that since the essence of *t'ien-li* (Heaven's Principles) are always revealed in daily human deeds, it is sufficient if one grasps the signs of the truth of the Heavenly Principles in the passage of daily life such as serving one's parents, obeying one's elders or dealing with daily matters (*Nan-hsüan-chi* 10). According to Nan-hsüan this was Ch'a-shih-tuan-ni-shuo (theory of discernment and conjecture), which meant to discern and firmly grasp even the slightest signs of *t'ien-li* or the Heavenly Principles.

Deeply impressed by Nan-hsüan's thought, Chu Hsi decided to attain enlightenment by perceiving the signs of the Heavenly Principles and Truth, setting aside for a while experience and comprehension of the inmost of the world of potency, which is insensible.

He therefore wrote to Nan-hsüan that human life as such, from birth to death, is a world of consciousness and perception which changes every minute, animated through constant contact with matters of this world. It is therefore useless, Chu Hsi wrote, to try to set one's mind of the inmost world of potency in which consciousness does not function, and try to apprehend it, disregarding the dynamic daily life. Rather, the truth of *t'ien-li,* which is in the state of potency and silently immovable, is manifested in this real world of *i-fa* (the world in action), which is constantly drifting. It is therefore important to discern its signs and to grasp them firmly. (***Chu-tzu wen-chi*** 30)

Since human life, to Chu Hsi at that time, seemed like the flow of a river or the movements of heavenly bodies, what was important for him was to grasp the truth of the Heavenly Principles as manifested in the flux of human life, rather than experience in the inmost world of potency, which is static. First, influenced by Yen-p'ing, he tried to grasp the essence of *wei-fa* and thereby to descend to *i-fa* or the activated world of daily life, whereas after accepting Nan-hsüan's theory, he made an effort first to grasp the signs of the essence of the unactivated world as reflected on activated daily life, and subsequently to work up from *yung* (external functioning) to *t'i* (internal substance). Here we can see that Chu Hsi's standpoint is reversed from quiescence into movement. The poems he composed around this time are also more vivid, depicting landscapes suggestive of enlightenment.

> Yesterday evening when the riverside was brimming with spring water,
> Even the warship Meng-ch'uang looked as light as a feather;
> Although a great power was needed to move it in the past,
> Today, it can be drifted freely with the flow.
>
> (***Chu-tzu wen-chi*** II)

Chu Hsi met Nan-hsüan for the first time at the age of thirty-four, when he went to the capital to memorialize the throne in connection with the Chin problems. He insisted that the government should initiate great reforms in its administrative policies and repel the barbarians. At the age of thirty-eight or nine, he took an active role, although having retired, in fighting against the flood and famine which affected his native village Ch'ung-an. This experience served as a motive for him to establish shê-ts'ang (community granary to store rice for emergencies). Chu Hsi, amidst the calamity, wondered why even the slightest sign of *jên* (benevolence) which pertains to Heavenly Principles is not manifested in times of calamity such as flood and famine. He denounced the well-fed and well-clad, saying that it is proper for a man, under such circumstances, to devote himself to relief activities, getting good hold of the situation and following the direction of the Heavenly Principle of *jên.* (***Chu-tzu wen-chi*** 43, 40).

His acceptance of Nan-hsän's theory of discernment of signs, which seemed to him most dynamic, was closely associated with his political activities. For Chu Hsi, a scholar-bureaucrat who shouldered the destiny of the Sung Empire, pursuit of learning and practice were inseparable. This is precisely one of the characteristics of Chu Hsi's philosophy.

4. FORMING OF HIS THEORY OF I-FA AND WEI-FA AT THE AGE OF FORTY

Chu Hsi, while supporting Nan-hsüan's theory, deepened his understanding of the teachings of Ch'eng Yi by continuing his work of revising *Ch'êng-shih wên-chi* and editing *Ch'êng-shih i-shu.* As a consequence, what has to be questioned is the relationship between Ch'êng I-ch'uan's concepts of *wei-fa* (potency or unactivated state) and *i-fa* (activated state) and *chü-ching ch'iung-li* (earnest rectification of one's mind and investigation of principles) and the teachings of Nan-hsüan and Yen-p'ing. Further, we have to see how these thoughts are related with *T'ai-chi t'u shou* of Chou Lien-ch'i (1017-1073).

One day in spring at the age of forty, when Chu Hsi was having discussions with his friend Ts'ai Hsi-shan (1135-1198), he incidentally noticed a weakpoint in Nan-hsüan's theory. If one were to repeat observing matters that occur in every-drifting daily life, Chu queried, would he not come to lose stability and profundity of mind, lacking *ts'un-yang* (cultivation) and *han-yang* (education)? Thus, on an assumption that there are two aspects in I-ch'uan's thought, namely cultivation and education of mind in the state of *wei-fa* or potency and *ch'a-shih* (observation) and *chih-chih* (extension of knowledge) in the state of *i-fa* or act, Chu Hsi, by quoting passages from *Ch'êng-shih wen-chi* and *Ch'êng-shih i-shu,* reached the following conclusions: "The inmost state of *wei-fa* means that in which the mind is not yet activated for discernment and cognition and in which objects therefore are not brought forth to the mind. It is a state in which the ever-drifting mind converges into a 'silently immovable' state whose essence is a heaven-endowed nature. This inmost state of *wei-fa* is said to be *chung* (middle) since it is neither excessive nor deficient in quantity and free from propensity. . . . Since the inmost state of *wei-fa* represents substance in its natural state, one should not pursue it consciously by means of judgement. If one grasps the essence of the inmost state of *wei-fa* through *ching* (earnestness), and if he tried to retain its state of mind he will, when activated, invariably reach harmony by conforming to the rule . . . When Ch'eng I-ch'uan said, "I observe matters and reflect on them in the immost state of *i-fa,*" he is referring to the means to discern the signs of the movements of the substance and to help develop them in a proper way." (***Chu-tzu wen-chi*** 67, 'I-fa wei-fa shuo'). Here, by combining Yen-ping's theory of discernment of the inmost state of *wei-fa* with the theory of *han-yan* and *ts'un-yan* through *ching* or earnestness originally propounded by I-ch'uan, Chu Hsi teaches cultivation and comprehension of one's nature in the inmost state of *wei-fa,* and further by blending Nan-hsüan's theory of *ch'a-shih tuan-ni* with I-ch'uan's *kuan-hsing-chih-chih*, expatiates that one widens the scope of observation by discerning and becoming conscious of the signs of the nature of things which are activated.

Further, in order to comprehend the signs of nature, it is necessary to have a thorough knowledge of what is benevolent nature. Thus, his *kuan-hsing chih-chih* is developed into *ko-wu ch'iung-li*, which means to clarify the reasons of things and matters. Here we can see that the static aspect of Chu Hsi's standpoint, which arrived at Yen-p'ing after inclining toward Zen, and his dynamic standpoint which led him to devote himself to Nan-hsüan's teachings, are sublated with Ch'êng I-ch'uan's thought as a pivot.

With the theory of *i-fa wei-fa* as the point of departure, Chu Hsi came to form his own theory which expounded the method of controlling one's mind by analysing both its conscious and unconscious aspects through application of *ts'un-yang* (cultivation) and *han-yang* (education) to the mind in the state of *wei-fa* and *ch'a-shih ch'iung-li* (*chih-chih*) to that in the state of *i-fa*. Although the mind is considered in two different aspects, *i-fa* and *wei-fa*, it is but the same mind simply conceived in two different modes: that of convergence and of diffusion. What was characteristic of the theory of *i-fa* and *wei-fa* is that it supplied a clue for acquiring both the converged and diffused states of the mind.

Following this theory of *i-fa wei-fa*, Chu Hsi, at around the age of forty-three or four, advanced the theory of *hsing-ch'ing*, in which he explained man from the relationship between *hsing* (nature) and *ch'ing* (emotion) as well as the so-called the theory of *jên* (love). Further, the theory of *i-fa wei-fa* is also reflected on his commentary on *Ta-hsüeh* and *Chung-yung*. *Ts'un-yan* in the state of *i-fa* is applied to the concept of *chieh-shên k'ung-chü* (self-denial in the state of unconsciousness without seeing or hearing) in *Chung-yung* and *ch'a-shih, hsing-ch'a* in the state of *i-fa* to *shên-tu* (self-restraint) in *Ta-hsüeh* and *Chung-yung*.

Further, as for *ko-wu chih-chih* (investigation of things and extension of knowledge) in *Ta-hsüeh* Chu Hsi regarded it as inquiry into the principles of things through reflection and discernment, and thereby established his theory of *ko-wu ch'iung-li*. It was diametrically opposed to Zen, which preaches intuitive enlightenment.

What we have seen above is how the theory of *i-fa wei-fa* developed in connection with the problems of the human mind and consciousness. The dichotomy applied in the theory of *i-fa wei-fa* concerning the human mind was further applied in analysing heaven, earth and nature. Just as the human mind and consciousness converge on, diffuse into, or circulate between *i-fa* and *wei-fa*, so do heaven, earth and nature converge upon, diffuse into and circulate between *yin-ching* (*yin*-quiescence) and *yang-tung* (*yang*-movement), spring-summer and autumn-winter, and day and night. As for the reason why the order and harmony of man and nature are maintained through convergence and

diffusion between *wei-fa yin-ching* and *i-fa yang-tung*, he attributed it to *t'ai-chi* (Supreme Ultimate) which is the ground-providing principle of man and nature.

Thus, Chu Hsi's theory of the Supreme Ultimate was formed when he was between forty and forty-four. From the above, we may say that Chu Hsi, after wandering about in the world of thought, was able to establish his philosophical system during a decade of secluded life on the basis of the theory of *i-fa wei-fa* which he had discovered at the age of forty. While serving such posts as 'Chih-nan-k'ang-chün' (50 years 3 months~53 years 9 months old), 'Liang-chê-tung-lu ch'a-yen-kung-shih' (52 years 8 months~53 years 9 months old), 'Chih-chang-chou' (61 years 4 months old~62 years 2 months old), 'Chih-t'an-chou' (65 years 5~7 months old) and 'Shih-ts'ung shih-chiang' (40 days since August), he could practice his academic ideas in politics, and secluded life in the intervals of civil service which helped him elaborate on his theory. Promulgation of the law of community granary, demonstration of the technique of growing paddy rice, arbitration between tennants and landlords, land survey and reform; all these political measures taken by Chu Hsi were closely related with his philosophical thought, manifesting the practical character of his philosophy.

II. THE SYSTEM OF CHU HSI'S PHILOSOPHY

1. THE GROUND-PROVIDING PRINCIPLE (*WU-CHI-ERH-T'AI-CHI*)

As mentioned afore, Chu Hsi started writing a commentary on *T'ai-chi-t'u* (Diagram of the Supreme Ultimate) after establishing his theory of *i-fa wei-fa* and completed it at the age of forty-four. Tracing back the process of his theoretical development, he first asserted identity of man and nature, and later came to recognize that they are both governed by the same principle, *wu-chi-erh-t'ai-chi* (The Ultimateless! And yet also the Supreme Ultimate!). In a letter to Wu Hui-shu, he states: "The principle of *i* (change) is that of *pien-i* (transformation), denoting movement and quiescence or *i-fa* and *wei-fa*. *T'ai-chi* is the principle of movement and quiescence and *i-fa wei-fa*. (**Chu-tzu wen-chi** 42)

Further, he indites:

> *Yin* and *yang* never cease to function
> Chill and heat replace each other . . .
>
> One principle harmoniously governs
> A principle not obscure but clear.

>   (**Chu-tzu wen-chi** 4)

In the above poem, *t'ai-chi* is postulated as the ground-providing principle of this world. Elucidating Chou Lien-ch'i's concept of *wu-chi-erh-t'ai-chi*, Chu Hsi states, "Things pertaining to Heaven are devoid of voice or smell. They are indeed the very pivot of creation and the root of everything." The term *wu-sheng-wu-ch'ou* (no voice, no smell) indicates the infinity of the principle *wu-chi* (the Ultimateless) and the phrase *tsao-hua-chih-shu-niu pin-*

hui-chih-ken-ti shows that the principle of *t'ai-chi* is neither nil nor non-being, but rather the pivot of creation of Heaven and Earth and the ground of different species in the world of man and other creatures. The intention of Chu Hsi here is not to distinguish the principle that governs man as *Sollen* and the principles governing Heaven, Earth and nature as *Sein*. According to Chu Hsi, both man and other creatures maintain order and harmony according to *li-fa t'iao-li* (principles and laws) =*so-tang-jan-chih-tse* (the principle that makes things precisely what they should be). The ultimate principle underlying them is nothing but *wu-chi-erh-t'ai-chi=so-i-jan-chih-ku* (The basic principle of all things and their laws).

The principle of *wu-chi-erh-t'ai-chi* itself is not a fixed entity but rather an indefinite being. It is therefore referred to as *wu-chi* or the Ultimateless. It is, on the other hand, far from nil or non-being. It is therefore said to be *t'ai-chi* or the Supreme Ultimate. In his letter to Lu So-shan (elder brother of the celebrated scholar Lu Hsiang-shan, who died earlier than his brother), Chu Hsi elucidates this point in detail:

> Unless the term *wu-chi* is used, *t'ai-chi* will lose its qualification as the basic principle of myriad beings, and become merely one of them. If the expression *t'ai-chi* is not used, *wu-chi* will be reduced to nought and will not be able to serve as the basic principle of all beings.

> (**Chu-tzu wen-chi** 36)

What is said here is that if one uses only the expression *t'ai-chi* without referring to *wu-chi* in defining the basic principle of myriad beings, such a definition would be insufficient, since the Principle would be unqualified to transcend and sublate the world of *hsing-erh-hsia* (what is within shapes) which cultivates myriad beings of both *yin* and *yang,* as the Principle itself would be brought to the same level as beings in the world 'within shapes.' On the contrary, if one uses only the expression *wu-chi* without referring to *t'ai-chi,* the definition would again be insufficient, since the principle would become empty and non-existent or nil in its negative sense, being unqualified to serve as a principle of the world 'within shapes' in which myriad beings are generated and nurtured.

Wu-chi represents the all-embracing and transcendent aspect of the ground-providing principle, while *t'ai-chi* shows its ground-providing aspect. Since the Principle is indefinite and nil, it is able to embrace all beings and to provide a firm ground for them. Thus Chu Hsi understood the expression *wu-chi-erh-t'ai-chi.*

Satō Naokata (1650-1719), disciple of Yamazaki Ansai (1618-1682), a Japanese Confucian scholar, elucidated this point pertinently. When Naokata says *"Taikyoku (t'ai-chi)* is presumably non-being," he means that *t'ai-chi,* unlike myriad beings 'within shapes' caused by *yin* and *yang,* cannot be regarded as a substance in the sense of a being. Further, by the words "When you once assume that it (the Principle) is nil, it works sometimes as *yin* and at other

times as *yang,"* he means that precisely because the Supreme Ultimate is indefinite and non-existent, it facilitates generating and nurturing of myriad beings through circulation between *yin*-quiescence and *yang*-movement.

Finally, when he says, "Precisely by defining the Supreme Ultimate as nil, one will come to recognize that it has to exist," it is meant that just because the Supreme Ultimate, which is non-existent in character, has to be postulated as the ground for myriad beings or the world 'within shapes.'

In short, it was necessary for Chu Hsi, in defining the character of the ground-providing Principle, to use the expression *wu-chi-erh-t'ai-chi,* whereas for Lu So-shan and Lu Hsiang-shan, it was sufficient to use only the term *t'ai-chi, wu-chi* being regarded as unnecessary. This was because the Lu brothers disregarded the all-embracing and ground-providing character of the Principle. The Principle of *t'ai-chi,* according to the Lu brothers, was contained in the world 'within shapes,' devoid of the power to transcend the real world 'within shapes.' Chu Hsi, on the other hand, postulated the ground-providing Principle as an entity pertaining to the metaphysical world (world above shapes), which provides ground for the world 'within shapes.' When compared with the concept of *t'ai-chi* of the Lu brothers, the character of Chu Hsi's *wu-chi-erh-t'ai-chi* becomes clear.

2. Heaven, Earth and Nature

How are heaven, earth and nature formed? Further, how is the aforementioned non-existent ground-providing Principle manifested in them? Chu Hsi regarded the original state of heaven, earth and nature as a flux of *ch'i* (Ether), which is an endless action of Ether characterized by the positive and negative *yin* and *yang* and cold and heat. To him, the generation of heaven, earth and nature was entirely due to the movement and condensation of such Ether, while *li* or the Principle, on the other hand, was devoid of such a material function. Namely, whereas *ch'i* or the Ether has a function of *ning-chieh tsao-tso* (condensation and production), *li* or the Principle is *wu-ch'ing-i, wu-chi-tu, wu-tsao-tso* (devoid of volition, plan or creative power), being *ching-chieh-k'ung-kuo-ti-shih-chien* (a pure, empty, and vast world) (*Chu-tzu yü-lei* 1).

Li manifests itself by holding itself on the operations of *ch'i* as the latter sinks, flows and conglomerates. When expressed in terms of the cycle of the four seasons of the year, the Ether pertaining to the four seasons are *ch'un-ch'i, hsia-ch'i, ch'iu-ch'i* and *tung-ch'i,* their principles being *yüan* (originating growth), *hêng* (prosperous development), (advantageous gain) and *chên* (correct fairness) respectively. The indefinite ground-providing Principle displays itself in the physical world of four seasons subdivided as *yüan, hêng, li* and *chên.*

Let us see Chu Hsi's own view according to the descriptions in **Chu-tzu yü-lei,** Volumes I and II. "In the beginning of Heaven and Earth, there existed only the *yin* ether and *yang* ether. This Ether underwent rotary movements. As its speed increased, a great deal of sediment was sealed inside, and having no place to go, the sediment came to form the Earth at the center. The clearer part of the Ether, on the other hand, came to form the sky, sun, moon and stars. Staying outside of the earth, they perpetually go round it. The Earth, lying at the center, does not move. Nevertheless, it does not lie under Heaven." Although this view of Chu Hsi was greatly influenced by Chang Heng-ch'ü (1020-1077), it is characteristic in that he propounds a kind of a nebular hypothesis by maintaining the rotation of the Ether and centripital force. He further states, "In the beginning of Heaven and Earth, when they were still indifferentiated and in a state of chaos, there were only water and fire. Presumably the part where the sediments from water piled up came to form the earth. If one climbs to a high spot and views the mountains, they invariably represent the form of waves, which undoubtedly suggest that the water had drifted in this way. However, we do not know how and when solidification of earth took place. At first it was exceedingly soft whereas later it came to be solidified."

The image of the beginning of Heaven and Earth conceived by Chu Hsi was exceedingly vivid. He thought that the Earth drifted in the center while water surrounded all around and beneath, and its outskirts conjoined with Heaven. According to him, the only reason why the Earth stays in the center without falling is that the whole sky surrounding it is constantly rotating. Chu Hsi further compared heaven to a bowl, calling the joint *ch'ih-tao* (equator) and the path of the sun *huang-tao* (Yellow Way). Moreover, heaven was thought to rotate with both the south and north poles as the axis.

Furthermore, Chu Hsi calculated in detail the movements of the sun, moon and fixed stars, and supported the theory of seven in intercalary months in nineteen years. . . .

Chu Hsi also made detailed observation on the waxing and waning of the moon by adopting Shen Huo's (1031-1095) theory, touching also on the problem of solar and lunar eclipses.

In a letter to Ts'ai Po-ching (1148-1236), Chu Hsi states:

"Open holes on a large globe as to make them look like stars and cut the part of the globe which hides those stars (the portion inside a circle drawn with a radius at 36° from the south pole) like the mouth of an earthen pot. Then attach a short axis to the north pole to make the globe rotate and a short rod on the north side of the south pole to sustain the mouth of the pot. Finally place a four-legged ladder at the mouth, and entering inside the globe, lay a board at the end of the ladder horizontally to the north and look up at the holes on the wall of the globe opened in a way resembling the actual stars." (**Chu-tzu hsü-chi**)

This was virtually a planetarium devised by Chu Hsi. As it is evident from the above, Chu Hsi clearly perceived that the movements of the celestial body maintained order and harmony according to *ch'ang-li ch'ang-tu* (perpetual principles and laws), which are nothing but the manifestation of the ground-providing principle of *t'ai-chi*. Precisely because of its non-existent character, it manifests itself as a principle that gives order to the physical world. Chu Hsi defined the ground-providing principle of *t'ai-chi* as *so-i-jan-chih-ku* (the basic principle of all things and their laws) and *ch'ang-li ch'ang-t'u* as *so-tan-jan-chih-tse* (the principle that makes things what they should be). The latter, according to Chu Hsi, is manifested in the human as well as physical world.

3. MAN

How did man come to exist, and what form of existence does he assume? Chu Hsi maintained that man was first formed by *ch'i-hua* (evolutions of the Ether), but once formed, he propagates generation after generation through *hsing-hua* (propagation in the same image) by means of germs. (*T'ai-chi-t'u-shuo-chieh*) Man is endowed with the ground-providing principle of *t'ai-chi* at the time he is born into this world. This principle becomes his *hsing* or nature such as *chien* (vigour), *shun* (obedience), *jên* (love), *i* (righteousness), *li* (propriety) and *chih* (wisdom). The Ether of man conglomerates into his body equipped with organs, with the distinction of male and female, and possessing various emotions such as *t'sê-yin* (commiseration), *hsin-ê* (shame and dislike), *t'zu-jang* (modesty and yielding), *shih-fei* (sense of right and wrong), *hsi-nu-ai-le* (joy, anger, sorrow and happiness). Man becomes a sage or mediocre depending on whether the Ether he receives at the time of his birth is pure or impure. (*Ta-hsüeh-huo-wen Ta-hsüeh-chang-chü-hsü*). Metaphorically speaking, just as a gem stone in clear water glitters, whereas that in contaminated water is invisible, man's nature, although the same when endowed, differs according to the disposition of those who receive it. The virtues of love, righteousness, propriety and wisdom, for instance, are properly manifested in some people and not directly in others. This is what causes man either to be a sage or mediocre. (**Chu-tzu yü-lei** 4) As we have seen before, the movements of the celestial bodies are exceedingly regular, conforming to perpetual principles and laws. Even natural phenomena of Heaven and Earth, however, are not always reliable, occasionally violating "the principle that makes things what they should be" in minute points as exemplified by casualities and damages caused by natural disasters such as an unusual change of weather (*Chung-yung chang-chü*). This being the case, although saints and sages may fully master and practise "the principles that make man what he should be," mediocrities are always exposed to the danger of violating that principle. That is, however, by no means the proper state in which man should be.

Chu Hsi thereupon seeks "the principle that makes man what he should be," and concludes that *so-tang-jan-chih-tse* manifested in the natural world is also applicable to the human world. For instance, just as the principles of *yüan, heng, li* and *chen* corresponded to the Ether of four reasons in nature, so do love, righteousness, propriety, and wisdom correspond to the feelings of commiseration, shame and dislike, modesty and yielding, and the sense of right and wrong. "*Jên* is the principle governing the feelings of benevolence and gentleness, *i* moral judgement, *li* reverence and humility, and *chih* discrimination between good and evil." (**Chu-tzu wen-chi** 67, "Jên-shuo" *ibid* 74, "Yü-shan chiang-i"). Here, too, we discover that nature and man are grasped according to the same pattern.

Thus, *jên, i, li,* and *chih* are the fundamentals of *so-tang-jan-chih-tse.* Besides these, however, there are certain subsidiary principles such as *ming* (clear observation), *ts'ung* (acuteness), *kung* (obeisance), and *shun* (compliance) in seeing, hearing, appearance and language of man, respectively, or *i* (loyalty) between master and servant, *ch'in* (affection) between parent and child, *pieh* (distinction) between husband and wife, *hsü* (order) among seniors and juniors, and *hsin* (faith) among friends. These are all regarded as '*so-tang-jan-chih-tse.*' There are of course subsidiary principles also for daily conduct such as dressing, eating, acting and resting. (*Ta-hsüeh-huo-wen; Chung-yung-huo-wen*)

Man, beings a compound of Ether, has a body, and shows various forms of existence according to the status he assumes. It is precisely this form of existence that manifests *so-tang-jan-chih-tse* or the principles that makes man what he should be." If man acts willfully following his desires, the human world will fall into a state of chaos, lacking affection between father and son, loyalty between master and servant, and distinction between husband and wife.

So-tang-jan-chih-tse, which include love, righteousness, propriety, wisdom, affection, loyalty, distinction, order and faith are the key to maintain order and harmony in the human world. If so, "the principles that makes man what he should be" must have a basis which transcends human nature, feelings and desires. That is *hsing* (nature) of man, which unifies all the principles that make man what he should be, and this *hsing* when grasped metaphysically, is *ch'êng* (sincerity) or *t'ai-chi.* It may be said that the foundation of human beings is *hsing* or *ch'êng,* whilst that of natural beings is *t'ai-chi.* (*T'ai-chi-t'u-shou-chieh,* "T'ung-shu-chieh"). However, since Chu Hsi as a conclusion equates *hsing* with *li* and *ch'êng* with *t'ai-chi,* the logical consequence in *T'ai-chi-t'u-shuo-chieh, T'ung-shu-chieh* and *Yü-shan-chiang-i* would be that the basis of man and nature is nothing else but the principle of *Wu-chih-erh-t'ai-chi.* In other words, the indefinite, ground-providing principle of *t'ai-chi* is manifested in the human as *so-tang-jang-chih-tse* such as love, righteousness, propriety, wisdom, affection, loyalty, distinction, order and faith.

If man's nature and emotion were always in harmony, cultivation of mind is unnecessary for man. In reality, however, they frequently contradict each other. Thus, the method of cultivating the human mind is to restore harmony between human nature and emotion by overcoming all the contradictions between them.

What is to be noted here, however, is that the consciousness of original sin as seen in Christianity is missing in Chu Hsi's theory or Chinese thought in general. Furthermore, there is no gap between man and the ground-providing principle of *t'ai-chi* as is in the case between man and God. It is not that a divine being called *t'ai-chi* creates man and myriad beings.

Since the ground-providing principle of *t'ai-chi,* when the emotions of joy, anger, sorrow, and delight are not activated, is inherent in human mind as *hsing* or nature, it is sufficient, in cultivating one's mind, just to grasp and develop this nature without exercising the senses. Furthermore, when the emotions are about to be activated, it is necessary to consider consciously and discern whether such emotional movement complies with *so-tang-jan-chih-tse.* Although man's nature and emotions might conflict with each other at this stage, man can ultimately obtain harmony through cultivation of his mind.

Is it then sufficient with only cultivation and discernment? In order to make the emotions conform with one's nature, it is necessary to grasp first the criteria for discerning good from evil. Hence, Chu Hsi, interpreting *ko-wu* (investigation of things) appearing in *Ta-hsüeh* (Great Learning) as *ch'iung-li* (investigation of principles), proposed the learning of *ch'iung-li* as a science to study the principles of things or *so-tan-jan-chih-tse. Ch'iung-li* means to investigate the moral and natural principles referred to as *so-tang-jan-chih-tse,* objectively by reviewing the knowledge thereof. Such pursuit of the principles of things through reflection and discernment, which has a scientific character, was a powerful weapon against the Zen school since it was unknown by them.

For Chu Hsi as a bureaucrat, it was probably impossible for him to carry out his official duties without this method of *ch'iung-li* through reflection and discernment; construction of warehouses, setting a pattern for cultivating paddy rice, organizing measures againt famine, forming plans for land reform, proposing measures for domestic and foreign affairs. All these were closely related with the science of *ch'iung-li.* Also as a scholar, the spirit of *ch'iung-li* was essential for studying the classics.

If the method of Zen is primarily 'moving in' to the world of the absolute by means of *chih-chieh-chih* (direct cognizance) and *wu-chiao-chih* (cognizance attained through enlightenment), Chu Hsi's philosophy living in the problem of knowledge as an intermediary stage by maintaining three stages: *chih-chieh-chih=ts'un-yang, fan-hsing-chih=ch'iung-li hsing-ch'a* and *wu-chiao-chih=huo-jan-kuan-t'ung* (sudden enlightenment). The fact that a scientific method in the modern sense was proposed with awakening of the trend to prize knowledge obtained through reflexive thought indicates the progressive character of Chu Hsi's philosophy.

Some might criticize his thought as lacking a clear distinction between *Sein* and *Sollen* or the spirit of endless pursuit characteristic of natural science. We should, however, bear in mind that he was a person who lived in the twelfth century. Had natural science reached that stage in Europe in those times? The answer will evidently have to be in the negative.

III. Characteristics of Chu Hsi's Philosophy

The characteristics of Chu Hsi's philosophy, whose process of formation and system we have reviewed in the above two chapters, may be summarized as follows:

1) The principle of *wu-chi-erh-t'ai-chi* is postulated as the foundation of nature and man. This ground-providing principle, although indefinite by itself, is manifested in man and nature as *so-tang-jan-chih-tse* or "the principles that make man (nature) what he (it) should be" precisely because of its non-existent character. In short, *li* or the Principle possesses a dual character of *so-i-jan* (foundation) and *so-tang-jan* (principle and law).

2) While Chu Hsi's theory resembles Zen on one hand in that it teaches cultivation of mind in potency (*wei-fa*) and enlightenment through sudden penetration, it has, on the other hand, a progressive and intellectual character in that it proposes a scientific method by maintaining the investigation of *so-tang-jan-chih-tse*.

3) Although Chu Hsi employs elaborate logic due to his long secluded life, his philosophy after all is practical in nature because of his position as a bureaucrat of the Sung dynasty.

1) and 2) show that his philosophy fulfilled the shortcomings of the Buddhist philosophy of the preceding ages, whereas 2) and 3) are relevant to the fact that Chu Hsi himself was a scholar and government official.

Regarding 1) and 2), let us first review the preceding ages and then see various criticism on Chu Hsi's thought in the later ages. In the T'ang period, Tsung-mi (770-841), one of 'Wu-tse' (five patriachs) of Hua-yen sect, refuting the theory in *Chou-i-cheng-i* that *t'ai-chi* is "one of the Ether existed when heaven and earth were still undifferentiated and were in the state of chaos," contended that the world of *i-yüan-ch'i*—(one original Ether) in the Book of Changes was an objective world formed when *chên-i-ling-hsin* (true, single spirit) splits into the subjective and objective world through consciousness of ālaya-vijñāna. Regarding *chên-i-ling-hsin* as something like the absolute Spirit, Tsung-mi asserted that *i-yüan-ch'i* is merely a product of tenacity and delusion. Although Tsung-mi's thought, when examined closely, maintains the ultimate state of the mind in which subjectivity or consciousness is totally discarded, it overlooks the problems of Heaven and Earth.

Since the Chinese, ever since antiquity, regarded Heaven and Earth as the most certain of entities, Chu Hsi could not evade the problem of Heaven and Earth versus subjectivity and consciousness. In this, however, he had to find some other principle surpassing *i-yüan-ch'i*, since Tsung-mi had already ascribed it as the foundation of Heaven and Earth. Thus, Chu Hsi postulated the Principle of the Ultimateless and the Supreme Ultimate as the ground for man and nature by combining Chou Lien-ch'i's *wu-chi-erh-t'ai-chi* and *hsing* (sincerity) with Ch'êng I-ch'uan's (the basic principle that causes *yin* and *yang* to interact alternately). Thus, a metaphysical ground was provided for the existence of both man and nature.

As for Chu Hsi's intellectualism in stressing reflexive thought, we have already seen that it was missing in Zen or Buddhism in general, and we may say that it was one of the characteristics of Chu Hsi's philosophy when viewed against the general trend of Buddhist thought in the preceding ages.

Let us next take up various criticism against Chu Hsi's thought in later ages. First, Wang Yang-ming (1472-1528), who belonged to the Lu school, maintained that both the ground-providing principle as a metaphysical foundation and 'the principle that makes things precisely what they should be,' which should be investigated objectively, can duly be considered as belonging to the mind. He asserted that it would be sufficient if one gives full play to *liang-chih* (intuitive knowledge) of the mind which works in the actual world (*chih-liang-chih* = full display of intuitive knowledge), since *liang-chih* of the mind itself, which is the flux of life, is at once the Principle (*hsin-chi-li*). The systematical philosophy of reason completed by Chu Hsi is changed into a subjective philosophy of life by Wang Yang-ming. Yang-ming flatly denied the features of Chu Hsi's philosophy, and the very points he denied represented the characteristics of Chu Hsi's thought.

Furthermore, Lo Chêng-an (1465-1547) and Wang Ting-hsing (1474-1544), contemporaries of Wang Yang-ming, setting aside the problem of *ko-wu ch'iung-li* (investigation of things and principles) attacked Chu Hsi's theory of the ground-providing principle of *t'ai-chi* by maintaining that the origin of the world is nothing but *i-yüan-chi* (one original Ether). Although there were slight differences between the two, they completely reject Chu Hsi's concept of the ground-providing principle of *t'ai-chi* by postulating the substantive *i-yüan-ch'i* as an objective principle. This means objectification of Chu Hsi's theory. Approving the standpoint of reflexive thought, they accept *ch'iung-li* which is to investigate the "principles that make things what they should be," since they are understood as the principles and laws of the Ether.

Moreover, later in the Ch'ing period, Tai Tung-yüan (1723 (Jan. 1724)-1777), taking the position of Ch'i Hsüeh or the School of Ether, equated *li* with *t'iao-li* (principles and laws) and elevated the study of '*so-tang-jan-chih-tse*' to the scientific level by stressing investigation of the principles that necessitate things in daily human life to be what they are, and hence regarding the study of '*so-i-jan-chih-ku*' as unnecessary. Here again, Chu Hsi's theory of the ground-providing principle of *t'ai-chi* is rejected, while that of *ch'iung-li* which represents his intellectualist aspect is pushed forward.

The first Japanese scholar who questioned Chu Hsi's theory of the ground-providing principle of *t'ai-chi* was

Hayashi Razan (1583-1651), who, referring to Wang Yang-ming's *Ch'uan-hsi-lu* (Record of Instructions), held that *li* (Principle) and *ch'i* (Ether) are but one. Kumazawa Banzan (1619-1691), modifying Chang Hêng-ch'u's thought, asserted that *t'ai-hsü* comprised only *li* and *ch'i*. Yamaga Sokō (1622-1685) laid emphasis merely on investigation of Chu Hsi's '*so-tang-jan-chih-tse*," intentionally discarding '*so-i-jan-chih-ku*' or the ground-providing principle of *t'ai-chi*. Further, Itō Jinsai (1627-1705), from his own standpoint of text criticism, maintained *i-yüan-ch'i*, rejecting the ground-providing principle of *t'ai-chi,* and propounded an original philosophy of life by giving emphasis to *jên-tao* (way of man), love, righteousness, propriety and wisdom, disregarding *t'ien-tao* (the way of Heaven). Finally, Kaibara Ekiken (1630-1714) advanced his own theory of *i-yüan-chi,* supporting Lo Chêng-an's teachings, although blending it with botany which he had mastered.

Although these Japanese scholars appeared later than Wang Yang-ming, Lo Chêng-an, and Wang Ting-hsiang, they preceded Tai Tung-yüan by approximately a century. Especially, the text criticism and method of Itō Jinsai is to be noted in that they not only resemble those of Tai Tung-yüan but also in that they preceded them.

Both in China and Japan, those who maintained *i-yüan-ch'i* understood Chu Hsi's ground-providing principle of *t'ai-chi* as the substantial entity preceding Ether, and refuted his theory on the ground that *ch'i* cannot generate from *li*. This, however, is merely a criticism made only from the standpoint of the theory of generation, indicating a lack of understanding toward the dialectic relationship between *li* and *ch'i* which is *pu-li-pu-tsa pu-i-pu-erh* (neither separate nor mixed; neither one nor two) or the dual character of *li,* as expressed by the 'transcendent-immanent,' 'absolute-relative' notions of the ground-providing principle of *t'ai-chi* or by '*so-i-jan-chih-ku*' and '*so-tang-jan-chih-tse*.' In this sense, we should revaluate the orthodox interpretation of Satō Naokata.

In short, the characteristics of Chu Hsi's philosophy are that it confirmed through investigation of man and nature that they are governed by the same principles and laws, and that it established an elaborate system by postulating a metaphysical principle of *wu-chi; t'ai-chi* or the Ultimate-less and yet the Supreme Ultimate. Whereas the early Confucian thoughts of Confucius and Mencius centered on practical ethics, the Sung philosophy completed by Chu Hsi may be said to have provided a philosophical ground to practical ethics by adopting even Buddhist and Taoist thoughts.

To establish a philosophical system tends to obstruct the flow of internal life. For Chu Hsi, However, to grasp '*so-tang-jan-chih-tse*' intellectually and to comprehend the foundation-providing principle of '*so-i-jan-chih-ku*' gave him firm confidence in political activities in practical life. Postulation of the ground-providing Principle of *t'ai-chi* enabled him to overcome personal desires and transcend the arbitrariness of governmental affairs. His severeness in admonishing the Emperor and accusing those in authority stemmed in his firm belief in the Basic Principle which he had attained through *ko-wu ch'iung-li* or investigation of things and principles. Judging from the fact that Chu Hsi was purged on the charge that he was a propounder of false teachings, was of low social standing, and seduced the world by acquiring great influence over people, we may say that Chu Hsi lived up to his theory throughout his life,

One may insist that his philosophy was inadequate, pointing out that his theory of identity of man and nature lacks distinction between *Sollen* and *Sein*. However, is it not the time to consider introducing the principles of *Sollen* in cultivating the principles of *Sein,* especially in an age when the atomic bomb threatens to destory mankind and pollution caused by industrial development menaces man's health and life. We should not discard Chu Hsi's '*so-tang-jan-chih-tse*' but rather revalue it as something that gives harmony to the progress of modern civilization.

Notes

Note: For further details, see the author's work *Shushi no Shisō-keisei (Study on the Formation of Chu Tzu's Thought),* Shunjū-sha, Tokyo, 1969.

Allen Wittenborn (essay date 1982)

SOURCE: "Some Aspects of Mind and the Problem of Knowledge in Chu Hsi's Philosophy," in *Journal of Chinese Philosophy,* Vol. 9, No. 1, March, 1982, pp. 11-43.

[*In the essay below, Wittenborn studies Chu Hsi's theory of the mind, maintaining that although the theory represents the least successful facet of Chu Hsi's philosophical synthesis, his investigation of this issue resulted in a theory of knowledge rooted in a "firm psychological foundation." Wittenborn further contends that Chu Hsi argues convincingly for the existence of* li, *or constitutive principle, rather than simply presupposing its existence, as did many of his predecessors and contemporaries.*]

There is a great deal of difficulty in understanding such basic Neo-Confucian concepts as *jen, tao,* and *li* largely because of their fundamental simplicity in the sense that they are vast, sweeping and comprehensive, and hence very vague and not easily defined or precisely delineated. In contrast, mind (or "the" mind)—*hsin*—is difficult to understand because of its utter complexity; these are so many ramifications involved in discussing the mind that trying to cover them all only serves to further confuse other aspects of Chu Hsi's thinking that have been neatly dealt with and fitted into his system of philosophy. Even when one does approach some semblance of success in being able to tie together all the loose strands one ultimately finds that many simply do not fit.

Chu Hsi's theory of mind is clearly one of the least successful elements of his otherwise masterly synthesis. I suspect that this is due both to the fact that he was unwittingly but necessarily treading new paths, and that he was trying to do too much with too little.[1] By this I mean that Chu was trying to make the mind perform too many functions: he was attempting to adhere to the notion of mind that he believed Mencius had held, to account for a theory of knowledge expounded by the *Great Learning,* to deal with features of the mind found in the *Doctrine of the Mean,* to include elements from the *Classic of Change* that were further modified by Chou Tun-yi, to account for the emphasis put on constitutive energy (*ch'i*) by Chang Tsai, to try to escape the somewhat mystical approach of the mind by Ch'eng Hao without jettisoning it altogether, and to use the mind itself to oppose the Buddhists—but all of this was simply too much for any one concept to include. Mind, therefore, in the philosophy of Chu Hsi, became overextended. The result, nevertheless, is a mixed blessing: in one sense, mind is a tangled web of often conflicting and even contradictory statements that serve to make Chu appear a very inconsistent thinker and to that extent ineffectual; on the other hand, the very inclusion of so many divergent strands of thought make it all the richer, and in fact this very reservoir of charged and viable ideas far outweighs the limitations of its inconsistencies.

However, that Chu Hsi was treading a new path in the theory of mind is, in my opinion, his greatest contribution to Chinese thought. Unfortunately, this is one aspect that was often ignored by subsequent Chinese thinkers and has been recognized by only a few contemporary observers.[2] What Chu Hsi appears to have tried to do, and in a certain way he may not even have been aware of just what he was doing, was to develop a theory of knowledge based on a firm psychological foundation. Hence, Chu Hsi's theory of mind is one step in the advancement of Chinese philosophical psychology.

In addition to the difficulty of trying to trace a consistent argument in Chu's discussions on the mind, there is another more explicit problem that arises from Chu's psychological musings which should be noted. This is the question of how we come to know about constitutive principle (*li*).

Chu clearly asserts that for everything there must first be *li*[3] and then it interacts with some form of *ch'i* to bring about the thing in question to which it accords in its makeup and function. Everything has its own particular *li*[4] which determines its nature or essence or quality or constitution, and which fixes it in a certain class or category of being. Everything, whether it is animate or inanimate, natural or artificial, has *li*. Without *li* there can be no thing. Thus, the *li* of a ship is that it is of a certain design which best enables it to glide through the water, and the *li* of a cart provides it with wheels so that it can better move on land.

The necessity of *li* is so strong that not only can we infallibly deduce that where there is something there is a *li* of it and for it, but in fact, we must make such a deduction if we are to know *li,* for this is the only means open to us for knowing about *li*. In order to assert that there is a certain *li* of something and that it operates in some particular fashion, we must first understand its *ch'i* manifestation or actualization.

This, however, leads to a dilemma, for *li* is (or are) imperceptible and inexperiential; we can know *li* only by deduction from observing *ch'i*. But how do we really know *li* until we completely know *ch'i?* How do we know that there are any *li* at all? Just as we may always be in error about the makeup or function of some *ch'i,* so we may also be in error about its *li,* and so we may be in error about the entire concept of *li*.

Suppose for a moment that this manifestation of *li* and/or its function, or at least our understanding of it, changes. For instance, the cart may actually be able to move on water and to function just as well there as it does on land, just as well as does the boat which supposedly has a different *li*.[5] Since the *li* of a thing does not appear to change, then we can only conclude that we were mistaken in the first place. This leads us inevitably into the quagmire of Cartesian doubt, for if we were mistaken in the beginning we can never be completely certain that we will not be mistaken again. The logical conclusion is that we can always be mistaken, and thus it will be impossible for us to be perfectly correct all the time about our understanding of a thing and its *li*. Or if we are correct, we can never be certain that we are, and the whole notion of *li* is thrown into doubt.

This may be Chu Hsi's greatest single flaw in his entire synthetic philosophy: How do we account for error? If we can be wrong about one thing, and there is no doubt that we can and are, then we can be wrong about anything. The standard explanation of error among the Neo-Confucian thinkers is that it stems basically from cloudiness in our *ch'i,* in the *ch'i* which forms our body and mind, the same *ch'i* which also accounts for bad and evil in the world. Since this is the very manifestation of *li,* then our knowledge of *li* must always be uncertain. That is, the very medium by which we perceive or apprehend *li* is also that very medium which is the sole cause of error. And so the notion of *ch'i* takes on the role of Descartes' "evil demon": how can we ever know that we are not being tricked in absolutely everything that we think? How can we ever be certain that our understanding of *ch'i* is correct? Perhaps *ch'i,* all *ch'i* is always cloudy, perhaps not. But how do we know?

Descartes extricated himself from the quagmire by standing on a firm bed of an indubitable thought: the fact that he was thinking at all, even though all his other thoughts may have been fallible, was completely certain. And from this one certain and infallible fact, Descartes built his entire epistemological edifice.

But Chu Hsi was not open to such a theory of knowledge. The most rock-solid assumption or presupposition in Chu's entire philosophy appears to be the very *li* which has been drawn into question. In his eyes, there could be no doubt that such principles, or concepts, existed, and that they were exactly as he believed them to be. In this, Chu was very close to the "common sense" philosophy of G. E. Moore, who believed that the "good" is directly apprehensible, and Moore became known as an "ethical intuitionist," a moniker that might very well fit Chu Hsi.[6] How true this is largely problematical, but the point to be made here is that both philosophers said that there is Good (or the Goodness of *li*) because I can use my own common sense to see that this is so and no amount of speculation is going to change that. In this sense, they were just as unshakeable as the clergyman who will not be denied in his belief in God.

But I believe that by analyzing certain aspects of Chu's philosophy of mind we can shed light on this problem of knowledge and come to see that Chu Hsi, in fact, offers a compelling argument for the existence of constitutive principle in contrast simply to presupposing it.

I. MIND, CONSTITUTIVE ENERGY (*CH'I*) AND CONSTITUTIVE PRINCIPLE (*LI*)

Constitutive principle and constitutive energy are the two fundamental ontological principles. These two principles interact with each other to bring about all that we know as the world order. Generally speaking, constitutive principle is the logical patterning system and constitutive energy is the substantiating actualizable element.

> Throughout the world there is constitutive principle and constitutive energy. Constitutive principle is the transcendent *tao* and is the root which produces all things; constitutive energy is the experiential material and is the instrument by which all things are produced. This is why when man and things are produced they must be endowed with constitutive principle before they have their nature, and why they must be endowed with constitutive energy before they have form.[7]

In regard to the mind, constitutive energy plays a dual role. In terms of the substance of the mind, mind is composed of the most refined (*ching*) portion of constitutive energy.[8] Second, associated as it is with human-heartedness (*jen*), constitutive energy, as the function of the mind, is the actualizing agent of all that is potential, imparting to the mind a creative or generative function. As such, the mind is the source of the emotions and feelings.[9] Hence, constitutive energy not only serves as the actualizing agent in the process of creation and transformation, but it also leads to evil and badness in a person. Mind itself, composed of the most refined constitutive energy, harbors no innate badness; as we shall see further on in the discussion on concentration, it is only when the psychological processes of the mind interact with constitutive principle that this energy has the ability to contaminate what eventually issues forth as feelings.

The relation between the mind and constitutive principle is more germane to a discussion of Chu Hsi's psychological epistemology. The mind is like a receptacle or enceinte for the constitutive principles. That is, the mind embraces or possesses all principles and all principles are complete within the mind[10] and therein known as the Great Ultimate[11] (*t'ai-chi*). Chu at one point even states that the mind and constitutive principle are one.[12] But this should not be mistakenly understood that mind *is* principle and therefore in agreement with Lu Hsiang-shan's assertion that the mind is the universe. For Chu goes on to qualify his statement by explaining that principle is not next to (literally, in front of, *tsai ch'ien-mien*) but lies *within* the mind (*tsai hsin-chih-chung*). Liu Shu-hsien reminds us that "the mind and principle do have a very close relation between them, even though it falls short of identity. Chu Hsi maintains that the mind embraces all principles. He says, 'Without the mind, principle would have nothing in which to inhere.'[13] Thus, mind and principle are two, but the relation between them is that of inherence. It is in this sense that from the very start they pervade each other."[14]

We may also say that mind has a relation to constitutive principle similar to that which constitutive energy does. The diffusion of principle permeates constitutive energy just as it permeates the mind, only its diffusion and permeation of constitutive energy is an occurrence in nature while its diffusion and permeation of mind occurs within the human world. Just as in cosmology Chu Hsi said that constitutive principle cannot be separated from and is dependent on constitutive energy, so in human affairs it cannot be separated from and is dependent on the mind. Therefore, both constitutive energy and mind are what give meaning to constitutive principle in that they act as agents for the expression of principle. What is important to note, however, is that in regard to the mind, constitutive principle is known as nature (*hsing*).

II. MIND, NATURE, AND FEELINGS

When principle is embraced by the mind it becomes man's nature. "In relation to the mind, [constitutive principle] is called nature. In relation to events, [mind] is called constitutive principle."[15] It is in this way that Chu Hsi often quoted Ch'eng Yi in saying that nature is principle (*hsing-chi-li*). If this is the case, then we cannot say that mind is principle as Lu Hsiang-shan did since mind and nature are clearly not equivalent,[16] with mind *enclosing* principle. Furthermore, principle as the substance of heaven[17] becomes embraced by the mind. It seems that when a person is born, he is born of heaven as well as of his parents, for heaven imparts to him the constitutive principle.[18] Another way of saying this is that heaven endows the mind with constitutive principles and once endowed it becomes that individual's nature by virtue of being the "humanized" aspect of heaven. To clarify this, Chu Hsi agreed with the following assessment:

> About the distinction between heaven, endowment, nature, and constitutive principle: Heaven refers to what is self-existent; endowment refers to that which operates and is endowed in all things; nature refers to the total substance and that by which all things attain their being; and constitutive principle refers to the laws un-

derlying all things and events. Taken together, heaven is constitutive principle, endowment is nature, and nature is constitutive principle.[19]

Endowment (*ming*) is what is imparted by heaven to man and which becomes his nature. We may liken nature and endowment to two sides of the same coin. Endowment is what heaven imparts to man and things, and nature is what man and things receive from heaven.[20] Nevertheless, endowment is really a passive phase of heaven while nature is active and commensurate with the moral virtues of humanheartedness, rightmindedness, decorum, and wisdom (*jen yi li chih*) which in turn become manifest as compassion, conscientiousness, deference, and knowledge.[21] In another development which brings the entire cycle around full circle, the virtues are reflections of the natural seasons[22] as well as of the cosmic virtues of origin, growth, perfection, and fulfillment[23] (*yuan heng li chen*).

It is also important to note that "endowment" is different for different people: "The word 'endowment' is the same one we use when we say that 'what is endowed by heaven is nature,' which is to say, the constitutive principle of all that something innately receives. Nature also has this 'endowment' of that which is endowed in something, which is to say the portion of that which is so endowed, having the differences of many and few, and thick and thin."[24] Chu emphasizes this in another section and stresses the point that there is nothing we can do about the particular nature we have been endowed with:

> Man's nature is like a ray of sunlight: that which people and things receive is different. It is like the ray of sunlight shining through an opening which can be either large or small. So form and matter of people and things are fixed and once they are it is difficult to change them. It is like the cricket and the ant being so tiny— simply know the difference between the primary and the secondary [i.e., between what is important and what is not].[25]

But just as the potential of constitutive principle is made manifest or actual by constitutive energy, nature, too, in its unstimulated phase is something different after it has been aroused. When nature becomes manifest it is known as the feelings (*ch'ing*). "Nature is the constitutive principle of the mind, and feelings are the movements of the mind."[26] In fact, it is only because of the feelings that we even know about nature.[27] When the feelings are good then they will appear as compassion, conscientiousness, deference, and right knowledge, and from these manifest feelings we can infer the four innate virtues.[28] If we do not base our observations first on the feelings then we simply cannot correctly know our nature. "It is like discussing whether the nature of medicine is hot or cold. It is only after administering the medicine that it will become hot or cold and this is its nature."[29]

However, the opposite is not strictly the case. That is, if we see some manifest evil feelings, we cannot infer that one's nature is bad, for nature is always good. "The feel-

ings are not necessarily good. However, in their origin they can be considered good and not evil. It is only when they have been overturned (*fan*) that the feelings are bad."[30] In such a case we will know that that person did not successfully keep his mind concentrated on purifying his innate virtue as it became contaminated through interaction with constitutive energy.

The concept of *ch'ing* itself, commonly translated "feelings," or occasionally (and incorrectly in the philosophy of Chu Hsi) as "passions" or "emotions," should not be confused with the emotive feelings usually ascribed to desires (*yü*). In particular, in the philosophy of Chu Hsi, *ch'ing* refers to the state or condition of the mind which is manifest after the mind has been stimulated and issued forth. In this sense, it is a complement to *hsing*, a person's basic human nature as it is endowed by heaven. Thus, a major Confucian theme is the interconnectedness of feelings (*ch'ing*), constitutive principle (*li*), and human nature (*hsing*).[31]

Of course, it is correct to say that it is proper to want to attain a position of sageliness, and in this way it can be argued that we have a "desire" to be a sage. But such a noble feeling for moral purification, revolving as it does around *ch'ing*, was inextricably connected to a cognitive process. In other words, the four virtues which issue forth as feelings after the mind is stimulated out of its latent phase of nature involves a spontaneous yet determined reaction, not the uncontrollable and often violent response totally independent of any rational control which "feelings" often connotes. Feelings for Chu Hsi are a controlled reaction, more empathetic than emotive.

Finally, we may note that not only is the mind the seat of nature and feelings, but it is the bridge between them. The mind unites or links together (*t'ung*) nature and feelings[32] and in this way the mind controls (*t'ung*) our feelings. This is also why the mind is called the "ruler"[33] whether during periods of movement (i.e., when feelings are dominant) or during periods of rest (when nature is dominant). "The mind unites and regulates our nature and feelings. It is not the case that it is united with nature and feelings into one thing with no differentiation between them."[34] Mind also acts in a manner similar to humanheartedness (*jen*) in that it is likened to a grain with the same generative properties as the kernel (also *jen*).[35] Because the mind is ruler and controls or links together nature and feelings, and because the mind is all-pervading and without any peers,[36] we may conclude that mind is on a level with *tao* itself since *tao*, too, is the only all-pervading entity that is without match.[37] In this sense, then, we may think of the mind as being absolute or nonpareil.[38] However, the functioning of the mind is an even more important aspect than its essence, and this leads us to consider a notion that has already been alluded to, that of the phases of the mind.

III. THE PHASES OF THE MIND

By dealing with the phases of the mind I hope to bring attention to a topic which is crucial to the philosophy of Chu Hsi but one which has been almost totally ignored by

Western Sinologists and, with rare exceptions, dealt with summarily even by Chinese and Japanese scholars.[39] This dearth of attention seems strange, especially since two of the phases (imminent issuance and accomplished issuance,[40] *wei-fa* and *yi-fa*) are found originally in the Neo-Confucian handbook, the *Doctrine of the Mean*. Even Tu Wei-ming, in his excellent and otherwise thorough discussion of this classic, merely throws quotes around the two phrases and then continues on to further matters.[41] Moreover, the somewhat authoritative *Encyclopedic Dictionary of the Chinese Language*[42] (*Chung-wen ta tz'u-tien*) notes only their appearance in the *Doctrine of the Mean* as the first instance of their use and then jumps ahead to Wang Yang-ming's *Instructions for Practical Living* (*Ch'uan-hsi lu*). Clearly, the idea of these phases or states of the mind had to await the heyday of speculative psychological philosophy which eventually emerged in the Sung. This having been said, we must ask what bearing this has on Chu Hsi's concept of mind.

In order to pass from a state of pre-consciousness to the activity of consciousness, that is, from unconsciousness through awareness to thinking, the mind moves through a series of phases. The first phase is that of total stillness (*ching*) when the mind is in a state of pure consciousness (i.e., with no thinking or reasoning involved), a state not unlike a condition of "unconsciousness," which is not to say no consciousness or a lack of consciousness; it is simply that the potential of awareness is not yet realized. This stage cannot be said to have any inclinations toward good or evil, nor any capacity for sensation or cognition. Chu often characterized it as a place of total stillness (*chi-ch'u*) or as total stillness without movement[43] (*chi-jan pu-tung*).

Assuming that something occurs to stimulate the mind at rest in its abeyant state, the mind acquires a new attitude after stimulation, that of imminent issuance (*wei-fa*), wherein the mind's potential consciousness becomes "poised for take-off." (Whether the mind has the capacity to stimulate itself is a question I am still not able to answer. Chu at times seems to lean in this direction, but possibly from his fear that this could result in a theory of "two minds" or a "dual mind," he desisted from pursuing the matter.[44]) *Wei-fa* literally means that time when the mind, or more properly, when the operations or processes of the mind have not yet issued forth. But because this step immediately precedes the activation of these processes they implicitly are imminent, ready for expression.

Imminent issuance is the phase where the potential functions of sensation have not yet become activated and remain in a latent state. It is the time when the subliminal states of feeling of joy, anger, sorrow and happiness (*hsi nu ai le*) are still dormant, when the virtues of human-heartedness, rightmindedness, propriety and wisdom (*jen yi li chih*) have not appeared as virtues but remain only potential. That is, they point to those states when they are still only in the stage of pure nature (*hsing*). Or, to put it another way, the phase of imminent issuance is that state when the mind has just been stimulated out of its state of

perfect rest and which, because it is simply a condition of pure nature, or where there is nothing other than constitutive principle, it cannot but accord with the inner equilibrium (*chung*) of the principle of heaven.

Moreover, because the phase of imminent issuance is a state of pure nature, it follows that it is wholly good. And according to Chu, it is analogous to the substance or essence (*t'i*) of the mind. This is the true nature of a person's being, that aspect of essential characteristics which determines what an individual's personal attributes will be.[45] But in order to fully appreciate *wei-fa* it is necessary to contrast it with its mental correlate, *yi-fa* (accomplished issuance), of which more in a moment.

First, however, we consider the third phase of "incipient issuance" (*chi*). Aside from its numerous instances in the *Classic of Change* and the occasional interest shown by Hsun-tzu,[bd] the earliest use of *chi* as a mental phenomenon seems to be that of Chou Tun-yi in his *T'ung-shu*, a treatise on the *Classic of Change*. Fortunately, Chu Hsi wrote fairly copious notes to Chou's work and it is to these that we turn. Chu explains *chi* as the most subtle of movements and that point at which good and evil separate or become distinct. "As soon as incipient issuance appears there is awareness of good and evil."[46] As such, it is also the juncture where constitutive principle initially appears and where human desire begins to grow.[47] Elsewhere Chu notes that this phase lies between no movement and the movement of desire.[48] *Chi* illustrates the essence of imminent issuance (*wei-fa*) as well as indicates the very beginnings of accomplished issuance (*yi-fa*).[49]

Nevertheless, being the beginning of movement, *chi* is also the initial stage of conscious awareness. Incipient issuance is not only the point where sensation (*kan*) begins[50] but it is also the departure point for consciousness.[51]

In order to remain consistent with Chou's remarks Chu Hsi here posits an interesting notion. He writes that *chi* (incipient issuance) lies between what is normally termed "sincerity" (*ch'eng*) and, for want of a better word, "sensibility."[52] As used in these particular passages by both Chou and Chu, *ch'eng* seems to be a pure state of unadulterated and unstimulated unconsciousness; perhaps it may be likened to a subconscious level of awareness. What I have translated as "sensibility," however, is far from the normal rendering of *shen* as soul or spirit. But my use of "sensibility" is based on Chu's own explanation that consciousness (*chih-chüeh*) is *shen*. "When we hit our hand or foot, then our hand or foot hurts. This is *shen*."[53] This is clearly one more instance where Chu's insights outrace his vocabulary; he is forced once again to draw on conventional words to describe new concepts. It is also possible that Chou's use of *ch'eng* and *shen* were meant to convey similar ideas represented by *wei-fa* and *yi-fa* according to Ch'eng Yi and Chu Hsi.

Chi, then, is that subtle yet potential incipient state in the mind which is the hub where good and evil diverge. It is at this point in the mind's functioning that the mind is "uncommitted," that instant when the mind could go either the way of good or of eivl. It is also that moment linking the very important span between imminent and accomplished issuance, when the mental faculties reach from being unconscious and insensate to the beginnings of conscious and rational awareness. As such, it is the moment when the phenomena of things are first investigated and when knowledge begins to be perfected, that is, when concepts begin to be formed and ideas formulated.

Finally, the movement passes on to the phase of "accomplished issuance" (yi-fa), mentioned earlier, where the mind becomes fully conscious of the active phase of the mind. This phase of the mind's operation indicates that time when the subliminal states of awareness and the innate virtues have become actual or manifest, the expressions which are visible to others as our feelings (ch'ing). Accomplished issuance is that stage when the mind is moving (tung) and active. And while imminent issuance, as noted earlier on, accords with the inner equilibrium of heaven, accomplished issuance accords with the harmony (ho) of the universal order.

This phase is also where the mind has become conscious of the senses: the ear and the eye hear and see, the hand and the foot move and feel.[54] And whereas the phase of imminent issuance is morally good only, accomplished issuance may realize good or evil feelings. In further contrast to wei-fa as the essence of the mind, yi-fa is the mind's function, the carrying out or exercising of the innate natural characteristics. In short, the feelings (ch'ing) are the manifestations of our nature (hsing). We may think of nature, then, as a sort of blueprint for the exercise of feelings which are completely visible. And once we have become conscious of the feelings we can then infer our nature. This is the only way a person can know his nature, for when one's mind is still in the phase of hsing, of imminent issuance, they do not yet command a sufficient state of consciousness to enable them to "know" anything.

Chu Hsi did not always subscribe to this interpretation of the mind's states or phases. In a letter written to some Hunan friends in 1169[55] Chu admits that in following Ch'eng Yi's early views that he himself had been mistaken in considering nature as the state of imminent issuance and the mind itself as the state of accomplished issuance. It was only later that he came to see that because the mind includes both of these states that the mind cannot, therefore, be equated with one of them. Instead the state of accomplished issuance is what we call the feelings, that is, the expression of the mind, in contrast to nature, the essence of the mind. Moreover, Ch'eng and Chu both came to acknowledge that the mind is one and cannot then be viewed in contrast or in opposition (tui) to any state or phase as it would be if it were taken as complementary to nature. Rather, feelings and nature are part of and within the mind.[56]

Lest it appear that this writer is ascribing to Chu Hsi a theory or view of the mind never explicitly argued by Chu, it should be noted that the comments concerning the "phases" are pieced together from various remarks in his entire corpus of writings. It is a truism that Chinese philosophers were seldom given to the deductive step-by-step reasoning characterizing Western thinking. Perhaps it is an overstatement to agree with those observers who see the Chinese as intuitive thinkers shunning the postulate for instantaneous enlightenment or spontaneous insight, but it does seem fair to admit that whole theories are rarely laid out from beginning to end in a single comprehensive treatise; rather, synoptic theories are scattered piecemeal throughout many different writings and one must sift through essays, letters, eulogies, commentaries and other tracts to fit these pieces into a comprehensive whole.

With Chu Hsi the problem is particularly acute because of the especially voluminous and copious writings left behind. But the task is compounded since, as pointed out before, it appears, as is the case with so many great thinkers delving into speculations never before encountered, that Chu Hsi was breaking new ground with a relatively limited vocabulary at hand for expressing his ideas. Furthermore, Chu himself may not have been entirely consciously aware of his pathfinding ideas. Fortunately, with the aid of later thinkers and with the benefit of our own hindsight, we are able to see from a new vantage point many perspectives that Chu was bound to miss. Even if Chu Hsi did not theorize exactly as I have shown in this paper, it seems reasonable to say that such ideas were never far from his mind and that he can take credit for sowing the seeds of a new dimension in Chinese intellectual thought.

One final note: If "phases of the mind" does not go down very well, then perhaps something like "states of consciousness" is more acceptable. However, by referring to the various stages or states of consciousness this presupposes the whole attitude of consciousness itself, which is exactly what I hoped to avoid. It has also been suggested that seeing in Chu Hsi's philosophy any hint of phases or states or quantum jumps at all is at least begging the question if not actually spurious. Admittedly, part of the reason for positing these phases was to magnify their status for explanatory purposes; certainly they move from first through last instantaneously, or as Chu says, "There is not a hair's difference between them."[57] We do not yet really know the exact nature of the phases or precisely the conditions of transition between them. They may in fact be extremes of one state of consciousness rather than discrete states, and the movement throughout similar to William James's stream of consciousness. But because the study of the mind is still in its infancy, I am forced to emphasize these aspects, although it is also clear that Chu Hsi did discuss such phases. While it may not be wholly correct to say that Chu developed a complete theory of mind, it is legitimate to note his insights into the mind's makeup and functions, including the phases.

IV. Evil and Concentration

Before going on to discuss Chu Hsi's views on consciousness we may at this point ask that if the feelings and our awareness of them originate with a state of the mind that has been endowed by heaven, then where does evil or bad thinking come from? Metzger,[58] following Ch'ien Mu,[59] makes an interesting case that for Chu Hsi evil and good are found in both the transcendental as well as in the experiential worlds. That is, the common view of *tao* or *li* as being solely good and evil as arising only through contact with *ch'i* is a mistaken view that has unfortunately been perpetuated by such influential thinkers as Fung Yu-lan, whose strict interpretation underscored the *li-ch'i* duality in Chu Hsi.

It is true that on occasion Chu alluded to the idea that human desire (a source of evil if allowed to go unchecked) flowed out from the principle of heaven.[60] And we have seen that Chu, in supporting Chou Tun-yi, apparently accepted Chou's contention that the state of incipient issuance (*chi*), itself seemingly "pure," was the point where good and evil separate and become distinct. It is tempting to follow up on this view if for no other reason than that it gives the volitional aspects of mind a greater role in a person's life.

If we follow the conventional theory that *ch'i* was the cause of evil then it is the mind, made up of constitutive energy—albeit not the "dregs" (*cha-tzu*) but the pure or refined (*ching*) portion—that is responsible for evil. But we can no longer think of the mind in such a generally indivisible way. Instead, we may think of the mind not as that which brings about evil, but rather that place or process wherein evil *may* first arise.

Evil, for Chu Hsi and other Neo-Confucians, seems to come about in the following manner. When the original state of nature (the time of the Great Void, *t'ai-hsü*) assumes its form, it necessarily becomes differentiated. In this state of differentiatedness there is bound to be opposition, discrimination and conflict, for it is this very contrasting nature between *li* and *ch'i* that gives rise to different things. But it is also this contrasting nature which is the potential for evil. In the process of differentiation, our "heavenly endowment" (*t'ien-ming*) may lack balance and harmony (*chung-ho*), and this lack causes us to deviate from the mean (*chung*).

Constitutive energy, whose unrefined portions can give rise to evil, is not in itself bad, and it is certainly necessary to life. It is in the *interaction* of *li* and *ch'i* where evil may arise. In other words, the Neo-Confucians did not say that differentiation resulting from physical nature as such is evil. To assert such an idea would be to fall into the Buddhist doctrine that the world is an illusion. What the Sung Confucians meant was that differentiation was the occasion for evil, not a necessary concomitant.

In order to understand this more fully, we must first determine just what the interaction between *li* and *ch'i* is. In the first place, one's nature is a combination of emptiness or void (*hsü*) and constitutive energy (*ch'i*).[61] Moreover, we already know that the mind is made up of *li* and *ch'i*, and because *li* is analogous with consciousness[62], Chu says

that mind is a combination of nature and consciousness.[63] In other words, as we begin to differentiate and distinguish the various aspects of the mind more and more precisely, rather than being simply a result of the dichotomy of *li* and *ch'i*, the mind passes through a variety of phases, one which is one's nature and another which is a phase of movement, that is, the feelings (*ch'ing*). We may say that the mind is a result of the combining of, or the interaction between constitutive principle and constitutive energy, but this is not where evil comes from except in the sense that the interplay produces the mind wherefrom evil arises, although it is not strictly equivalent to evil.

Instead, we have the feelings, which is the movement phase of the mind. In addition, the feelings released is what we consider as desire. But desire itself is not necessarily bad; there are also good desires:

> The mind is like water: nature resembles still water, and feelings are the water's flow. Desire is turbulent waves, but waves which can be both good and bad. The good sort of desire is the kind like my desire for humanheartedness, while the bad just rushes out like seething breakers. In general, a bad desire will destroy the constitutive principle of heaven, just as with pent up waters, [when suddenly released], there is nothing they do not harm. Mencius said that the feelings can be good. This is to speak of the uprightness of the feelings, for the feelings that flow out from our nature are originally all good. So in asking, what about the desire of "what is desired is called good," I say that this is not the desire of passion but rather the desire of love.[64]

Therefore, for reasons still unexplained, evil is the result of the state of the mind that has developed into desire which for some reason, beginning in the phase of incipient issuance, becomes an undesirable or a bad desire.

Such a Neo-Confucian attempt to find an explanation of evil had a two-fold thrust. In the first place, it provided an answer to the question about evil itself, and in the second place, it attempted to preserve Mencius' doctrine of original goodness. Even so, the Neo-Confucians did not wholeheartedly agree with Mencius that evil originated with man. To them, evil originated with physical nature. But his should not be taken to mean that they held evil to be a natural phenomenon and not a moral one. Although at times they seemed to confuse nature and moral evil, there is little doubt that they believed that moral good and evil arise only in society.

That is, the problem of good and evil becomes real only when one's moral life has begun, when in a one-on-one relationship one has to deal with a physical nature which is unbalanced, and which therefore causes one to deviate from the mean and which puts one in the position of isolation, discrimination and opposition, thus setting oneself against another individual. While evil, or evil desires or thoughts, may be seated in the mind, it only becomes an issue to contend with in a social situation. The moral problem is not so much why there is evil or where it comes from, although this aspect is important and certainly was not ignored, but rather how to keep from having evil thoughts and especially how to rectify them once they become emergent.[65] This is dealt with largely through the practice of concentration.

"Concentration"[66] (ching) is another concept, along with imminent issuance and accomplished issuance, which I believe has not received the attention it warrants, especially in its regard to the problem of evil. How to overcome evil was a continual dispute among Neo-Confucians, and Chu Hsi took great pains to exhort the unwary to root it out and to realize tao. One method he so strenuously encouraged was the pursuit of learning and the investigation of the phenomena of things.[67] But how does one go about this? One way was to "study below and reach above"[68] (hsia-hsüeh shang-ta). A more specific approach is to follow the ways of the ancients by learning the classics.[69] Other methods of study are through inquiry and thought,[70] establishing oneself,[71] putting the mind in order,[72] and through discriminating between right and wrong.[73]

Invariably, all of these pursuits, and others as well, lay in preserving the originally good mind (ts'un liang-hsin) and not letting it go (pu-fang). This was seen originally by Mencius, and Chu held to it steadily and believed in it implicitly. Preserving one's mind is a prerequisite for gaining knowledge: "The mind embraces all principles and all principles are complete in this one mind. If you are not able to preserve the mind, you will not be able to investigate thoroughly the constitutive principle. If you are unable to investigate thoroughly constitutive principle, then you will not be able to exert your mind to the utmost."[74]

Underlying all of these methods for attaining a right mind and for preserving it was the practice of concentration: "If there is no concentration then we will never preserve it."[75] Concentration is the fundamental method both for keeping evil thoughts away and then for being able to extend our knowledge in the investigation of principles.[76] Concentration, in fact, is the essence of the mind.[77] To concentrate is to maintain equilibrium, harmony, and balance, and to allow no discord in our thoughts,[78] to keep from being remiss or dissolute,[79] straightening our inner character,[80] making the mind upright and keeping the thoughts sincere,[81] having no outward desires,[82] and remaining attentive.[83] But primarily, concentration was for Chu Hsi, just as it was for Ch'eng Yi, to focus on one thing and not to let the mind wander from it. In short, to maintain singularity of mind or purposes is the essence of concentration.[84]

Concentration was the cardinal precept of Chu Hsi's epistemological pursuit and not even for a moment could it be interrupted.[85] Concentration is also another way of making the mind the ruler,[86] for once we have brought our attention to the problem at hand and made our inner character accord with the universal order through sheer will power, then there is nothing that can command it or make it waver. If we can but be our own master, it follows that any evil thoughts which may arise will be turned aside and our mind will remain tranquil and clear and hence well-prepared for investigating principles in the pursuit of knowledge.[87]

V. CONSCIOUSNESS

The most important point to be made concerning Chu Hsi's account of the phases of the mind is that they seem to be a formative theory of consciousness and of how consciousness arises. A significant development from this concerns knowledge, that is, how we come to have knowledge, how we know something or realize that something is the case. Clearly, consciousness and knowledge are closely linked together and cannot be considered apart from each other, and it is to Chu's insight that he understood this.

The whole problem of consciousness (chüeh, or more often, chih-chüeh) is tricky because Chu spoke so little about it. Still, he did address the issue at one point in dealing with the concept of humanheartedness. It may be recalled that Ch'eng Yi and Chu Hsi, in one sense, viewed jen as a kernel or seed and therefore that it possessed or was capable of a generative power. Chu was questioned a number of times whether jen could be considered as being conscious,[88] and he consistently denied any attempt to equate jen with consciousness (as Hsieh Liang-tso did),[89] not only because this would be too confining to jen, but also because consciousness is too cold, like intellect, whereas jen is warm, like love.[90] What Chu did not deny, however, was that mind possessed consciousness.[91] In accepting this, consciousness becomes an inherent state in the mind, an innate faculty of the mind. But it is necessary to distinguish between the state of consciousness and actively being conscious of something. Being conscious of a sense is a second-level awareness.[92] Although Chu does not address this specifically, we are forced to conclude that our consciousness of something comes from the faculty of consciousness.

Now, this faculty of consciousness, being an innate faculty of the mind, itself comes from or is an instance of the generative quality of jen, and this in turn is endowed in us, in our mind as our nature, by heaven. So the faculty of consciousness is a characteristic of heaven or the universe. Since the capacity to have awareness and to think intelligently was itself not the product of human intelligence, it existed as a cosmic given.[93] Neo-Confucians also assumed that this purely natural consciousness was indivisible throughout the cosmos. This idea was a correlate of their belief in the organic oneness of the cosmos and in the mind's transnatural power to control the cosmos.[94] Chu explicitly states that consciousness has power[95] (chüeh-yu-li).

Consciousness is a state of the mind but it is also awareness of being a state of the mind. Consciousness is, so to speak, aware of itself, and being a state of the mind as well as being aware that it is so, we can say that consciousness is a mental act or a mental state. Consciousness is the awareness or perception of what passes in a person's own mind. It is by means of consciousness that we acquire the notion of thinking and knowing. Furthermore, as awareness of itself through perception of the mind, consciousness can also be equated with "self-reflection" (fan-hsing) or introspection. In addition, there is the further distinction between the act of observing something for the purpose of acquiring knowledge about it and the awareness that we have come to possess such knowledge, i.e., the difference between simply knowing that X, and knowing that we know that X.[96] For instance, we may be aware of a sensation even though we may not distinguish what the sensation is. In other words, we have consciousness of a sensation in general without having knowledge of any particular sensation.

Let us think, for a moment, of the two major phases of the mind's operation, imminent issuance and accomplished issuance, as some kind of basic awareness and, in the case of the latter, an awareness of being aware, a self-awareness. The basic awareness is a potential ability to "know" or "sense" or "cognize" or "recognize" that something is happening. It is a basic theoretical and experiential given. We are not certain what its ultimate nature is, but it is the essence, the "total body"[97] (*ch'uan-t'i*), of the mind. In contrast is the phase of self-awareness, i.e., accomplished issuance, which is not limited to being conscious simply of one's existence, but where the mind is capable of being cognizant that it is in operation, where the mind is aware that it is formulating and applying (*miao-yung*) concepts.[98] And, it is consciousness which transverses the experiential continuum between mere awareness and the awareness of being aware (self-awareness). So, it is the function of the mind to reach from being conscious of something to having awareness of what this is, i.e., to having knowledge of it.

VI. THE PROBLEM OF KNOWLEDGE

The general view of Westerners writing on Chinese philosophy is that its main interest lies in human relations and ethical problems. Most such writers either do not see or do not want to see that in Chinese philosophy there is any epistemological consideration in examining the mind in regard to knowledge.[99] But ever since the Sung, even though ethical questions have certainly been dealt with and occupy a central position, it is also fair to say that Chinese thought has become very intellectual in nature and based on a rational process. If the ends are not entirely intellectual, the means certainly are. We should note, however, that knowledge and ethics are in no way exclusive, for just as "knowledge" (*chih*) is one of the four innate virtues or categories of the mind, so can we infer that knowledge itself is an ethical concept in that knowledge that a certain proposition is true, whether ethical or not, presupposes acceptance or belief of the proposition. Hence, the function of knowledge is present in any moral issue.

I have noted above that Chu Hsi's idea of the phases of the mind led to the notion of consciousness. Once there is consciousness then there can be knowledge of the object of our awareness. The reason for this is that consciousness is the essence of the mind, or of a person's mental state. That is, the essence of our mental process consists of phases of consciousness taken as a state of subjective awareness. Another way of saying this is that conscious-

ness seems to be understanding arrived at intuitively, while knowledge is understanding attained through a process of learning. The mind on the natural level functions as consciousness, but in its functioning as knowledge or learning, which consists primarily of distinguishing differences and then making judgments about them, the mind is operating at an extended or transnatural level.

We have already determined that all principles inhere in the mind, that the mind in some way houses the principles. In addition, it is axiomatic in the philosophy of Chu Hsi that all things are a combination of constitutive principle and constitutive energy. Therefore, we have the condition that principles are in the mind, and principles also and at the same time inhere in constitutive energy to form "things" and "events." This may lead one to imagine that there are two kinds of principles, or two sets of principles, something which no one has ever been willing to admit. But if these principles in the mind are the same as, are identical to those in objects in the real world, then we are on the verge of admitting that Lu Hsiang-shan was right in stating that mind is principle. As we have seen, Chu Hsi did come close to this when he mentioned that mind and constitutive principle are one. But what he may have discovered in saying this is that the principles in the mind and the principles in things and events are one phenomenon, not that the mind itself is one with principle.

In a way, these principles may be considered as being of two kinds: those inhering in constitutive energy are "pattern formations" or "forms of pattern," while those in the mind are "forms of thought" or "forms of understanding." In fact, this seems a necessary step to take for if we think of these "forms of thought" as "mental categories" or as "innate ideas" then we have the basic and essential ingredients with which to have knowledge. Chu Hsi, like so many thinkers, believed that the mind could not be a "blank slate," a *tabula rasa*. The mind had to have some innate properties with which it could order the perceptions of outside phenomena in forming concepts. In doing this, principle took a step away from being the principle in things to being a principle in the mind to being a principle of the mind's functioning process, hence reason. In this respect, Chu Hsi is a good example of being a synthesis of both Rationalism and Empiricism.

Now, once a concept of something is formed through manipulating the "forms of thought" (principles) in our mind through a conscious process, the mind directs the application of this concept to the object whose constitutive energy has impinged on our mind and caused us to have a perception of that object. By applying a concept is meant making a judgment by means of this concept through a process of comparison and discrimination in an attempt to penetrate the *ch'i* and get behind it (*t'ung*) in order to reach or extend our understanding (*chih-chih*) in apprehending its principle.

More precisely, the mind engages in a process of "testing" and "inference." The process of testing (*yen*) is an exercise in contrasting the thing with its opposite or its analog or relation[100] or correlate[101] which, for Chu Hsi, must occur for there ever to be knowledge of a thing. The process of inference (*t'ui*) is the proceeding from our realization of our own innate principles (in the mind) and what is "close at hand" (*chin-ssu*) and pushing out in ever broader spheres[102] in mentally grasping the essence of the nature of the phenomenon in question.[103]

Once the mind has apprehended and identified the principle or "form of pattern" in the object, that object then becomes intelligible to us, and in becoming intelligible to the mind, to the principles or "forms of thought" in the mind, these forms or principles may be said to have been objectified.[104] Furthermore, in the forms of the mind being objectified, we can know our own mind. Rather than the mind turning in on itself with empty concepts that have not been "filled" by outside perceptions, we examine our knowledge of experience that comes through objectifying the mind by apprehending the principle in things.[105]

In other words, the principles in the mind, limited as they are only to empty, or potential forms of knowledge, are stimulated by the *ch'i* of an object. This stimulation gives rise to an ever-increasingly broader range of comparisons between the principles in the mind and the principle in the thing, which we might well even think of as its primary qualities. Eventually, the mental principles become "objectified" by being filled with impressions of the object, at which point they reflect (*ying*) the nature of the object in that combining self-awareness or consciousness with the now filled neutral principles brings about our knowledge of the thing in question. Thus, Chu Hsi was able to avoid the rather bedevilling conundrum that so plagued the Kantian school which insisted that humans can have knowledge only of the "appearance" of things, never of the things-in-themselves.

In this way, Chu not only gave both meaning and existence to things as well as substantiality, but he also emphasized that pure introspection has no place in the process of knowledge. These were firm grounds for opposing the Buddhists as well as for countering such philosophical foes as Lu Hsiang-shan who believed that the concepts with which we know our mind and hence the world about us need not have been "filled" by any outside perceptions. The mind, thought Lu, can know itself without being objectified and so there is no meaning given to things.

VII. Conclusion

Although Chu Hsi did not explicitly theorize in this way, he does allude to such an intellectual process if we are willing to accept new interpretations of certain terms. For instance, in his comments to the *Great Learning* Chu writes, "Everything that people receive from heaven is free and spontaneous and thus *contains* all principles and responds in accordance with all affairs."[106] The key word here is *chü*, "to contain completely," although there is some equivocation on this word and exactly what it means here is open to interpretation.[107] In the **Chu-tzu yu-lei** are

several instances where *chü* can be interpreted as "thoroughly" or "completely" (*chü-tsai*) in the sense that all principles are contained within the mind.[108] While it is true that the mind is seen as housing all principles, this passive sense offers no help in trying to explain an active mind in the conscious process of knowing.

Instead, I suggest that Chu Hsi, perhaps unconsciously or perhaps forced to explain a new concept with old terminology, took a step forward, away from *chü* as meaning completion or possession, to the notion of being substantial or even solid, as it is used to stand for "concrete" (*chü-t'i*), in contrast to "abstract" (*ch'ou-hsiang*). Hence, *chü* would indicate an "object" and in a verbal position, "make an object of" or *objectify*.[109]

In addition, the concept of *ch'eng-yi;* which is usually taken to mean "sincere thoughts" or to make the thoughts sincere or genuine, could be taken, in this instance, in the sense of "solidifying" one's thoughts. Chu Hsi himself glosses *ch'eng* as *shih which is* generally interpreted, especially in its relation to *ch'eng,* as genuine or true. But since *shih* can also mean what is real, or actual, or substantial, I am tempted to conjecture that Chu is explaining, in his comments on the *Great Learning,* that by making our ideas, those ideas in our mind as principles, real through the process of objectifying them in external things and events, of making them objectively certain, we are, in effect, also rendering them genuine and true.[110]

Another instance of the coalescence of mental with phenomenal principles is Chu Hsi's notion of *chi-wu,* "to approach and contact a thing," found in Chu's supplement to the *Great Learning*. Chu asserts that if we indeed wish to perfect our knowledge we must do this by thoroughly examining those things with which we come into contact. It is possible that by coming into contact with a thing Chu has in mind one's body touching or making some such union with an object. However, it seems much more in line with Chu's general outlook, and with the context in which the phrase *chi-wu* appears, that he understands a moral mental connecting with the internal properties of a thing in order to understand it rather than merely to gain a tactile experience of it. It would seem, as has been suggested,[111] that *chi-wu* is similar to Whitehead's notion of "prehension," a mental comprehension or sensual apprehension.

One final example. Chu Hsi often spoke about the operation of the mind and that when acted upon the mind immediately penetrates all phenomena.[112] Being made up of the finer portions of constitutive energy, the mind is a purely spiritual entity (*ling*). It is so fine that it can penetrate the most minute thing, and when it does there is knowledge. This happens when the mind goes out to the world by *embodying* the things in the universe.[113] Chu Hsi here uses *t'i* as a verb ("to embody") in the sense of coming together with a thing and physically becoming one with it, becoming, at least figuratively, part of the thing itself.[114] *T'i* was explained specifically by Chu as placing the mind in a thing so as to investigate its principle, and it differs here from the use of *t'i* meaning substance as a complement to function.[115] Once our mind embodies a thing it exercises a form of reflection, or "returning" (*fan-fu*) When the mind is imparted in a thing, it reflects that which stimulated it and then turning in upon itself, upon the principles inherent in it, the combination of consciousness and reflection of the external object brings about knowledge of that object.[116]

In summary, Chu Hsi was not, after all, trapped into a position of simply presupposing the concept of principle. Rather, he may have reasoned, at least indirectly or intuitively, that because we humans have knowledge about things (and this may be the one basic assumption that he did make, analogous to Descartes' final indubitable certainty that he was at least thinking), because there is the "fact" of knowing, this implies knowledge, or knowing, about something. Once we understand that there is something to have knowledge about (and the idea of an object is implicit in the concept of knowledge), then it is obvious that there must be something which has this knowledge. This leads to the idea of the knowing subject in contrast to the known object. Finally, Chu posited the concept of constitutive principle as that factor which is common to both subject and object, and reasoned that principle must inhere in our mind as well as in the object as the fundamental property of intelligence, linked together through the process of consciousness.

Chu Hsi, in the final analysis, raised to a new level in Chinese philosophy the concept of mind by adding a further dimension to our understanding of philosophical psychology, thus providing an ironclad argument for the profundity and the circumspection of Chinese reasoning.

Notes

* Part of this article developed from my paper delivered at the 1980 Association for Asian Studies Conference in Washington, D.C., "The Problem of Li in Chu Hsi (Zhu Xi)." My appreciation to the numerous comments made at that time, and especially to the suggestions from Professor Cheng Chung-ying, although any and all inaccuracies are certainly my own.

1. Both Liu Shu-hsien, "The Function of the Mind in Chu Hsi's Philosophy," *Journal of Chinese Philosophy,* 5:2 (June 1978), 206; and Thomas Metzger, *Escape from Predicament: Neo-Confucianism and China's Evolving Political Culture,* New York: Columbia University Press, 1977, 85, agree that Chu's concept of mind is especially difficult and that a thoroughgoing account is most tricky.

2. The only sources I have found which address themselves directly, at least in part, to Chu Hsi's philosophy of mind are the following: (in English): Metzger, *Escape From Predicament;* Liu Shu-hsien, "The Function of the Mind in Chu Hsi's Philosophy" Vincent Y. C. Shih, "The Mind and the Moral Order," *Melanges Chinois et Bouddhiques,* 10, 1959, 347-

364; W. E. Hocking, "Chu Hsi's Theory of Knowledge," *Harvard Journal of Asiatic Studies,* 1, 109-127; Carsun Chang, "Is There No Epistemological Background for the Chinese Philosophy of Reason?", *Oriens Extremis,* 1:2, 1954, 129-138; (in Chinese): Vincent Yu-chung Shih, "Hsin yü yü-chou chih chih-hsü" (The Mind and the Cosmological Order), in *Chung-kuo hsüeh-shu shih lun-chi*[cd] (Collected Essays on the History of Chinese Scholarship), ed. by Ch'ien Mu, 4:2, Taipei: Chung-hua wen-hua ch'u-pan shih-yeh she, n.d., n.p. (actually a Chinese version of the above article by Shih in English); Ch'ien Mu, "Chu-tzu fan-lun hsin-ti kung-fu" (Chu Hsi's General Discussion of the Cultivation of the Mind), *Chung-hua wen-hua fu-hsing yueh-k'an*[ce] (Chinese Cultural Renaissance Monthly), 2:12, February 1969, 11-15; and Ch'ien, *Chu-tzu hsin-hsüeh-an*[cf] (A New Scholarly Record on Chu Hsi), 5 vols., Taipei: San-min shu-chu, 1971, the section dealing with the imminent issuance and accomplished issuance phases of the mind, 2:123-182; T'ang Chun-yi, *Chung-kuo che-hsüeh yuan-lun*[cg] (Studies on the Foundations of Chinese Philosophy), Hong Kong: Hsin-Ya shu-yuan yen-chiu-so, 1973, v. 2; Mou Tsung-san, *Hsin-t'i yü hsing-t'i*[ch] (Mind and Nature), 3 vols., Taipei: Cheng-chung shu-chü, 1973, especially v. 3; (in Japanese): Araki Kengo, "Shu-shi no jissen ron" (Chu Hsi's Practical Philosophy), *Nihon Chugoku gakkai ho*[ci] (Journal of Japanese Sinology), 1 (1950), 37-48, especially section 5, 42-44; Tomoeda Ryutaro, "Shushi no jinsho" (Chu Hsi's Theory of Humanheartedness), *Tokyo Shina gakuho*[cj] (Tokyo Journal of Sinology), 12 (1966), 55-74; and Tomoeda, "Shushi taikiron no seiritsu katei—ihatsu mihatsu sho no taikigaku ni oyoboseru eikyo" (The Formative Process of Chu Hsi's Theory of the Supreme Ultimate—Its Influence on the Explanation of the Supreme Ultimate in the Theory of Accomplished Issuance and Immanent Issuance), *Tetsugaku*[ck] (Philosophy), Hiroshima, 37 (1959), 25-37; Yamane Mitsuyoshi, "Shushi ronri shiso no kenkyu—ki no igi ni tsuite' (A study of Chu Hsi's Ethical Thought—On the Significance of Incipient Issuance), *Hiroshima Daigaku bungakubu kiyo*[cl] (Bulletin of the Department of Literature of Hiroshima University), 19, April 1961, 104-130, Goto Shunzui, *Shushi no ronri niso*[cm] (Chu Hsi's Ethical Ideas), Nishinomiya: Goto Shunzui hakase iko kankokai, 1964, especially 126-132; and Goto, "Shushi no ishiki shutai no mondai" (The Problem of Chu Hsi's Epistemological Subjectivism), *Tetsugaku zasshi*[cn] (Philosophy Journal), 34:394 (1919), 1081-1089; Kinami Takuichi, "Moshi shinseisho to Shushi-gaku" (Mencius' Theory of Mind and Nature and the Philosophy of Chu Hsi), *Tetsugaku* (Philosophy), 6, 1956, 118-133.

3. "There is nothing under heaven which does not have *li*." See *Hsü chin-ssu lu* [Supplement (or Sequel) to Reflections on Things at Hand], comp. by Chang Po-hsing, Taipei: Shih-chieh shu-chu, 1974, 24. Hereafter cited as *HCSL*.

4. Chu Hsi, *Ssu-shu chi-chu*[cu] (Collected Commentaries on the *Four Books*), in the *Ta-hsueh chang-chü*[cv] (Commentary on the *Great Learning*), Taipei: Shih-chieh chu-chu, 1971, 3.

5. It has been suggested, only partly in jest, that it then becomes a square boat with wheels.

6. See, however, the interesting article by Huang Siu-chi, "Chu Hsi's Ethical Rationalism," *Journal of Chinese Philosophy*, 5:2, June 1978, 175-193.

7. Chu Hsi, *Chu-tzu ch'üan-shu*[co] (Complete Works of Master Chu), ed. by Li Kuang-ti, Kuang-hsüeh ts'ung-k'an ed., 2 vols., Taipei: Kuang-hsüeh she-yin shu-kuan, 1977, 49/5b. Hereafter cited as *CTCS*.

8. *CTCS*, 44/2a.

9. *CTCS*, 44/3a.

10. *CTCS*, 2/4b, 44/2b.

11. *T'ai-chi*, the Supreme Ultimate, is the primary source of all reality and the final cause which controls the alternating forces of *yin* and *yang*[cp] and through them the operations of the Five Agents (*wu-hsing*)[cq] Specifically for Chu Hsi, *t'ai-chi* is the sum total of all principles as well as Principle in its oneness, which means that there is only one *T'ai-chi*, yet each individual thing has *t'ai-chi* complete in it; that is, every thing is a complete system in itself—*t'ai-chi* is all things and is in all things. However, at times Chu says that the Supreme Ultimate is not itself something but is simply the name for all that there is.

12. *CTCS, ibid.*

13. *CTCS*, 44/2a.

14. "The Function of the Mind in Chu Hsi's Philosophy," 197.

15. *CTCS*, 42/6a.

16. Liu Shu-hsien, "The Function of the Mind in Chu Hsi's Philosophy," 199.

17. *CTCS*, 42/1b.

18. *CTCS*, 42/5a.

19. Wing-tsit Chan, *A Source Book in Chinese Philosophy*, Princeton: Princeton University Press, 1963, 612. Hereafter cited as *Source Book*.

20. This from the opening sentence of the *Doctrine of the Mean*.

21. *HCSL*. 9.

22. *HCSL*, 13.

23. *HCSL*, 13; *CTCS*, 45/8a; Metzger, 88-89. For a discussion of the cosmic virtues, or cosmic cyclical points, see my "*Tao* and *Jen*: The Moral Dimension of Chu Hsi's Philosophy," in *Asian Culture Quarterly*, 7:4 (Winter 1979), 11, n. 46.

24. *HCSL*, 10.

25. *HCSL*, 8.

26. *HCSL*, 11.

27. *HCSL*, 20.

28. *CTCS*, 45/5a.

29. *HCSL*, 9.

30. *CTCS*, 45/9a.

31. Metzger, *Escape From Predicament*, 31.

32. *CTCS*, 45/4a.

33. *HCSL*, 20. The idea of "ruler" (*chu-tsai*)[cw] implies some sense of controlling or directing or governing. In fact, all of these words might just as well suffice, as could "lord" which Metzger employs, although its verbal form is misleading. However, since rule is not so active or forceful as are the other words, being closer to the sense of *prescribing* a way of conduct rather than actually controlling through power or authority, i.e., closer in spirit to *wu-wei*,[cx] I have decided to use it.

34. *CTCS*, 45/4a-b; *HCSL*, 20.

35. *HCSL*, 20.

36. *HCSL*, 12.

37. *HCSL*, 27.

38. *HCSL*, 12.

39. Except for a spare note, the only genuine treatment I know of in English is by Metzger in *Escape Form Predicament*, 85-88, where he discusses them under the heading "The Naturally Given Phases of the Mind." Metzger translates these two phases (he mentions three others) as "not yet issued; imminent issuance," and "already issued; accomplished issuance."

40. My use of the word "issuance" for *fa* is tentative and might also be rendered as "emerged," "aroused," "released," "stimulated," or even "manifest." I have, admittedly, been influenced by Metzger's choice of words. The phrases refer to the two phases of the mind before and after they have been stimulated or provoked or actuated. It is probably too early still in the development of our observations of Chinese psychological theories to have at hand perfectly acceptable translations. Western psychologists might very well opt for "conscious" and "unconscious," "sensible" and "insensible," or "cognitive" and "noncognitive." These of course are extended and implied meanings and I try to retain the flavor of the original by using "issuance." For other examples, see, for instance, the table, Examples of the Various Modes of Human Consciousness, in "Intuitive Thinking" by H. R. Pollio in *Aspects of Consciousness*, v. 1, ed. by Geoffrey Underwood and Robin Stevens, London: Academic Press, 1979, 33.

41. Tu Wei-ming, *Centrality and Commonality: An Essay on Chung-yung*, Monograph No. 3 of the Society for Asian and Comparative Philosophy, Honolulu: University of Hawaii Press, 1976, 27.

42. See 4:1587/70.

43. Ch'ien Mu, 2:148.

44. "The mind is like a stretch of road; it certainly cannot be taken as two things or events," Chu Hsi, *Chu-tzu yü-lei* (Classified Conversations of Master Chu), comp. by Li Ching-te, 1473 ed., 8 vols., Taipei: Cheng-chung shu-chu, 1962, 1/9b. Hereafter cited as *CTYL.*

45. *CTYL,* 5/7b.

46. *Chou-tzu ch'üan-shu* (Complete Works of Master Chou), Kuang-hsüeh ts'ung-k'an ed., Taipei: Kuang-hsüeh she-yin shu-kuan, 1975, 129. Hereafter cited as *Chou-tzu.*

47. *Chou-tzu,* 126.

48. *Ibid.,* 129.

49. *Ibid.,* 130

50. *Ibid.,* 136. "Although the phase of incipient issuance is already given to sensation, it is only the very beginning of sensation."

51. *Ibid.,* 129.

52. *Ibid.,* 136.

53. *Ibid.,* 133.

54. *CTYL,* 5/4a.

55. This letter is included in the *HCSL,* 30-32, and has been translated by Chan in *Source Book,* 600-602.

56. *HCSL,* 7.

57. *HCSL,* 29-30.

58. *Escape From Predicament,* 110-111.

59. *Chu-tzu hsin-hsüeh-an,* 1:406, 2:36; also cf. Metzger, 261, n. 210.

60. *Chu-tzu hsin-hsüeh-an,* 1:406.

61. *CTYL,* 5/11a.

62. *CTYL,* 5/3b.

63. *CTYL,* 5/11a.

64. *HCSL,* 7-8.

65. Anyone holding to the view that *ch'i* is the sole cause of evil should consult Metzger's account which argues against this traditional interpretation. Metzger admits to being strongly influenced by Ch'ien Mu. See the section on "The Given Force of Evil," in *Escape From Predicament,* 108-113.

66. Wing-tsit Chan translates *ching* as "seriousness." Chan writes in his *Source Book,* p. 785, that *ching* is a state of mind, that this seems to be similar to the Buddhist calmness of mind and has probably led Carsun Chang to translate it as "attentiveness" and "concentration," and Graham to render it as "composure." Chan goes on to explain that the Neo-Confucianists emphasized making an effort in human affairs, and therefore, that "seriousness" is the best choice.

Certainly "seriousness" has its grounds, but Chan's arguments do not seem convincing. Seriousness is every bit as much a state of mind as is concentration. In fact, concentration implies a greater mental effort than does simply being serious. Some short comments from Chu Hsi himself can show this.

Focusing on one thing is an explanation of the word *ching.*

> (Ch'ien Mu, *Chu-tzu hsin-hsüeh-an,* 2:299.)

Not letting go is *ching.*

> (Ch'ien Mu, 2:299.)

Ching is to manage something with singleminded emphasis.

> (Ch'ien Mu, 2:307.)

Ching is a through-and-through effort.

> (*CTCS,* 1/21a.)

In addition, the most common definition of the Sung concept of *ching,* at least as the Neo-Confucian philosophers used it, includes that found in both the *Dai Kanwa Jiten*[da] (Great Sino-Japanese Encyclopedia), ed. by Morohashi Tetsuji, and the *Chung-wen ta tz'u-tien* (Encyclopedic Dictionary of the Chinese Language), the meaning stated by Ch'eng Yi and quoted on numerous occasions by Chu Hsi: "*Ching* is the mind concentrated on one thing and never allowed to wander," or "*Ching* is emphasizing one thing without distraction" (*ching-che chu-yi wu-shih*).[db]

Furthermore, a well-known commentator on Confucian terminology, Liu Shih-p'ei, writes that "to the Sung Confucians *ching* was to preserve the mind (*ts'un-hsing*)[dc] to the point of being unconscious of outside abstractions." Liu Shih-p'ei, "Li-hsüeh ting-yi t'ung-shih" (A Survey of the Meanings of Words ir Neo-Confucian Philosophy), in *Liu Shen-shu hsien-sheng yi-shu*[dd] (The Post humous Works of Liu Shih-p'ei), 1936, 1:22a. Also, "*Ching* indicates a person's perseverance," Liu, 1:21a. Moreover, Cheng Chung-ying disagrees with Chan's "seriousness" by arguing that "in the usage of Cheng Yi-chuan and Chu Hsi, '*ching*' signifies a state of mind characterized by self-control and self-concentration," and concluded that "the term "seriousness' is [not] sufficient for indicating the main conceptual content of the term '*ching*' . . . On the other hand, Carsun Chang's 'attentiveness' or 'concentration' is a closer translation. "Review of Chan's translation of *Reflection on Things at Hand,*" in *Philosophy East and West,* 20, 4 (October 1970), 425.

However, after all is said and done, I admit to being in basic agreement with Prof. Chan's view that rather than engage in endless discussion of terms, which seldom convinces anyone anyway, it is far better to read more of the Chinese works. (Personal communication, September 18, 1978).

67. My addition of the word "phenomena" to the standard translation of *ko-wu*[de] is largely for purposes of clarity. "Investigation of things," though closer in the

literal sense, exhibits an uncomfortable imprecision. "Things" is so sweeping and vague, and "investigation" is open to so many methods and forms of examination, that it seems proper to bring a greater focus to bear on this knotty concept. Even so, it remains comprehensive which, no doubt, Chu Hsi intended.

68. *HCSL,* 41.

69. *HCSL,* 41-42; see also 75–80 for specific works.

70. *HCSL,* 41.

71. *HCSL,* 46.

72. *HCSL,* 44.

73. *HCSL,* 49.

74. *CTYL,* 2/4b.

75. *HCSL,* 87.

76. *HCSL,* 81.

77. *Ibid.*

78. *HCSL,* 95-96.

79. *HCSL,* 86.

80. *HCSL,* 82.

81. *HCSL,* 87.

82. *HCSL,* 92.

83. *HCSL,* 88.

84. *HCSL,* 91-92.

85. *CTYL,* 2/21b.

86. *CTYL,* 2/22a.

87. *HCSL,* 81.

88. *CTCS,* 47/7a-9a.

89. Cf. Chan, *Source Book,* 596.

90. *CTCS,* 47/8b.

91. While it is true that Chu was hesitant to speak of *jen* in terms of consciousness, the fact that both were incorporated by the mind inferentially makes them commensurate.

92. *CTCS,* 47/12b. The state, or innate attribute or faculty of consciousness would be a first-level awareness.

93. *CTCS,* 30/19a.

94. Metzger, *Escape From Predicament,* 67.

95. *CTYL,* 12/13a.

96. Cf. *HCSL,* 16.

97. *CTYL,* 5/11a.

98. *Ibid.*

99. In contrast, Japanese scholars delve deeply into questions concerning knowledge and intelligence and the supramoral aspects of the mind and man's knowing processes.

100. *CTCS,* 1021D, Cf. also *The Philosophy of Human Nature* by Chu Hsi, translated by J. Percy Bruce, London: Probsthain and Co., 1922, 291.

101. *CTCS,* 1022c; cf. Bruce, 294.

102. *CTCS,* 957b; cf. Bruce, 32.

103. *CTCS,* 1022a; cf. Bruce 292-293.

104. Cf. "*Li* is the nature which a person's mind becomes aware of in the process of his learning. Learning therefore ultimately serves the purpose of achieving self-awakening in a person." in Cheng Chung-ying, "Practical Learning in Yen Yuan, Chu Hsi and Wang Yang-ming," in *Principle and Practicality: Essays in Neo-Confucianism and Practical Learning,* Ed. by William Theodore de Bary and Irene Bloom, New York: Columbia University Press, 1979, 49.

105. I believe this is essentially what Cheng Chung-ying is indicating when he explains that it is only when mind apprehends the principles in things that mind can establish the truth and avoid selfish desires.

Because of the ontological difference between mind and nature, mind must be exercised in a rational manner before it can reach a state of illumination of knowledge and insights into supreme goodness. Instead of holding that mind by its own power however could reveal its true identity, Chu Hsi, following the suggestion of Cheng Yi, holds that the true identity of mind is only established in a process of investigation of things and extension of knowledge of principles of things.

Prof. Cheng goes on to clarify that mind may have some knowledge of principle to begin with, and that the ultimate aim of the mind is to realize total illumination of mind by knowledge. If I understand him correctly, what Prof. Cheng refers to as having some innate knowledge of principle is what I mean by pointing to the innate principles-cum-nature in the mind which act as the faculty for awareness or consciousness. The "illumination by knowledge" then would be the process of the principle of a thing becoming objectified in the mind.

Finally, Cheng draws his own conclusion for the objective reality of the mind, as I have tried to show also, by arguing that when mind engages in the investigation of principles, it is this way in which the mind gains certainty about things. This is so because this form of knowing or reasoning, which Cheng calls intuitive induction, assumes that the nature from which mind receives its rational ability contains all the truth that there is to find. As a result, the mind is assured against "losing itself in a maze of unrelated bits of information and broken ideas." See Cheng Chung-ying, "Conscience, Mind and Individual in Chinese Philosophy," *Journal of Chinese Philosophy,* 2,1, December 1974, 3-40, esp. 20-22.

106. See Chu's comments to section 1.2.

107. Metzger translates *chü* as "(fully) put forth" and suggests that Chu adopted this view in order to keep

from identifying mind as an equivalent with principle as did Lu Hsiang-shan. That is, Chu used *chü* to escape such copulas as *chi*[df] or *pien-shih*[dg]. See Metzger, *Escape From Predicament,* 143-144.

108. Cf. *CTYL,* 5/8b, 12/10a.

109. Mou Tsung-san[cy] has shown how *chü* may mean something like, "reality." See hi discussion on T'ien-t'ai Buddhism in *Chih-te chih chüeh yü Chung-kuo che-hsüeh*[cz] (Intellectual Intuition and Chinese Philosophy), Taiwan: Commercial Press, 1971, 309-310. Thanks to Prof. John Berthrong for pointing this out to me.

110. See Cheng Chung-ying's excellent discussion of Chu's theory of learning, "Practical Learning in Yen Yuan, Chu Hsi and Wang Yang-ming": "[Chu] generally meant by *shih* the truthful principle or the real principle of things. *Shih* in this sense is clearly tied up with his doctrine of *li,*" 50.

111. See David C. Yu, "Chu Hsi's Approach to Knowledge," *Chinese Culture,* 10,4, December 1969, 8.

112. *CTCS,* 990b; cf. Bruce, 168.

113. *CTCS,* 992d; cf. Bruce 178.

114. *CTCS,* 1036d; cf. Bruce, 350-351.

115. *CTCS,* 993b-c; cf. Bruce, 180-181.

116. Any uncomfortable feeling that "know" and "knowing" is being used in several different senses here may be assuaged by noting that for Chu Hsi, just as for G. E. Moore and other serious thinkers, there was more than just one kind of knowledge. For Chu there are at least six kinds, or levels: (1) consciousness as knowledge—natural knowledge; (2) knowledge of acquaintence or apprehension—sensory knowledge; (3) knowledge of the self—subjective knowledge; (4) knowledge that X is the case—objective knowledge; (5) knowledge of right and wrong, or good and evil—moral knowledge; and (6) comprehension of the oneness or totality of the universe—sagehood, or sagely knowledge.

Russell Hatton (essay date 1982)

SOURCE: "A Comparison of *Li* and Substantial Form," in *Journal of Chinese Philosophy,* Vol. 9, No. 1, March, 1982, pp. 45-71.

[*In the essay that follows, Hatton compares Chu Hsi's conception of* li *with the Western notion of "substantial form." Hatton traces the origins of this debate, and challenges those critics who have suggested that* li *and substantial form are equivalent.*]

I. INTRODUCTION

The concept of *li*[a] is central in the philosophy of the Sung Dynasty Neo-Confucian philosopher Chu Hsi[b] (1130-1200). In discussions of his philosophy by Western or Westernized interpreters, *li* has often been compared with substantial form. Indeed, it might be said that there has been a simmering conflict for the last fifty years as to whether *li* is equivalent to substantial form. The first skirmish, as it were, occurred in 1923, the year of the publication of the 2nd edition of Stanislas Le Gall's *Tchou Hi: Sa Doctrine, Son Influence* and J. Percy Bruce's *Chu Hsi and His Masters.* In Le Gall's work, which contains a French translation of Chapter 49 of Chu Hsi's **Chu-Tzu Ch'üan-Shu** (**Complete Works of Master Chu**), "*li*" is left untranslated. However, he refers parenthetically to *li* several times as "forme".[2] Bruce notes this in his own work and cautions that "*Li* . . . however suggestive of Aristotle's 'form', is not identical with it."[3] It is, in fact, "essentially different" from it.[4]

However, in 1934 Fung Yu-lan's *Chung-kuo Che-Hsueh Shih*[c] appeared in China. Here he suggests that," *Li* is just like what Greek philosophy called form."[ds] His work was written in Chinese and aimed at a Chinese audience, but in 1942 the first step was taken to make it available to a wider audience. In this year the chapter dealing with Chu Hsi appeared in an English translation of Derk Bodde in which the statement cited above is translated as "*Li* is equivalent to what Greek philosophy called form."[6] In 1952, a translation of the entire *Che-hsüeh Shih* appeared, and in it, a second translation of the Chapter on Chu Hsi. This time *li* is now "similar to" form.[7]

Then, in 1956 the 2nd volume of Joseph Needham's *Science and Civilization in China* appeared. According to Needham, with respect to the translation of *li* as "form," "this reads into the thought of the Sung Neo-Confucians an Aristotelianism which was not there."[8] The equation of *li* and *ch'i*[f] with "The form and matter of Platonic-Aristotelian philosophy," he says later, "is entirely unacceptable."[9]

But in 1957 the first volume of Carsun Chang's *A History of Neo-Confucian Thought* appeared. According to Chang "The universal notions combine in one whole all the essential attributes of objects. They represent what Aristotle calls 'form' and what Chu Hsi calls '*li*'."[10]

In 1963 Wing-tsit Chan entered the fray. After briefly reviewing the debate about *li* and substantial form (referring specifically to Fung, Bruce, Chang, and Needham), he concludes with a word of caution: "These comparisons show that in any comparative study similarities are usually accompanied by dissimilarities. The important point to note is that Chu Hsi is neither Platonic nor Aristotelian. The usual Western polarities "do not apply in Chinese philosophy."[11] Be that as it may, Chan suggests later that "The closest parallel to the concept of *li* in Western philosophy is a Platonic Idea."[12]

The latest voice in the controversy is that of Stanislaus Sun, whose article entitled "The Doctrine of the *Li* in the Philosophy of Chu Hsi," appeared in 1966. His position is essentially that while *li* is indeed the essence or nature of a thing, and thus equivalent to substantial form in this respect, it is more than form for it is also the moral principles which all things follow. As he says, "the term *li* in Chu Hsi is not only law, or ethical standard but also the essence or nature of a thing."[13] Sun reviews the literature on the controversy in the course of his discussion of *li,* and indeed, it has remained dormant since the appearance of his article. However, it is the contention of this article that not only is his conclusion wrong, but his discussion is so flawed that it is evident from a careful reading of the article itself that his conclusion is wrong. Thus, it is the purpose of this article to resurrect the controversy once again and settle the matter once and for all.

Thus the discussion of *li* that follows is not intended to be complete and is best viewed as an extended argument for the denial of the equivalence of *li* and substantial form. This argument has three parts. It is argued first that according to Chu Hsi all things (*wu4*[g]) contain *li.* It is then pointed out that according to Chu Hsi all things which contain *li* contain essentially the same *li.* This is the key part of the argument with respect to the conclusion to be drawn about li. For finally it is argued that if *li* is essentially the same in all things, it cannot be responsible for any of the essential differences between things, and thus it cannot be equivalent to substantial form. As a preliminary to the third part of the argument, the scholastic conception of substantial form is briefly reviewed.

After this discussion of *li* in which the arguments for rejecting the equation of *li* and substantial form are presented, there will be a consideration of the previous discussions of this question noted above.

However, before we begin a discussion of "*li,*" we must briefly discuss two other terms, "*hsing*[h]"[14] and "*t'ai-chi*[i]".[15] This is because passages about the *hsing* and the *t'ai-chi* will be quoted in the course of discussion of *li,* and it is necessary to establish beforehand that these passages are relevant to such a discussion.

II. *Li, Hsing* AND *T'ai-Chi*

Chu Hsi inherited the terms "*li,*" "*hsing,*" and "*t'ai-chi*" from his predecessors, and in his synthesis of the materials which they provided him Chu Hsi treats these terms as essentially synonymous. Chu Hsi sometimes uses one term rather than another when he wishes to emphasize a particular aspect, as it were, of the one reality to which they all refer, the *li.*

It will be argued that all things contain essentially the same *li* and that *li* is the source of certain tendencies which all things have. Thus, if it were not for their *ch'i,* all beings would exhibit these tendencies to the same extent. *Ch'i,* however, obstructs these tendencies so that some beings manifest them less than others. Therefore, we can look at *li* either as "universal" or as "individualized." When we think of it as universal, we think of it as that which is essentially the same in all beings and as the po-

tentiality for certain behavior which all beings have. When, on the other hand, we consider *li* as individualized, we consider it insofar as it is able to manifest itself or insofar as the behavioral potential for which it is responsible is actualized.

Chu Hsi often uses "*hsing*" to refer to *li* as individualized and *t'ai-chi* to refer to *li* as universal in the senses which have just been explained. This distinction between "*li*" and "*hsing*" is well known and unproblematic.[16] However, the relationship of "*li*" and "*t'ai-chi*" is problematic. On the one hand, there is the contention of this article that Chu Hsi uses the term "*t'ai-chi*" to refer to the *li* as universal in the previously explained sense.[17]

Fung Yu-lan, however, interprets the relation of *li* and *t'ai4-chi2* in an essentially different way. This is because his interpretation of *li* itself differs essentially from that of this article. As has already been pointed out, he interprets *li* as substantial form. Since Fung interprets *li* in this way, he holds that there are different kinds of *li* corresponding to the different kinds of things, both natural and manmade. According to Bodde's translation Fung says, for example, that,

> Before the boat or cart yet exists, the *li* or concept of that boat or cart is already there. In other words, what we call the invention of a boat or cart is nothing more than the discovery by man of the Principle [*li*] that pertains to boats or carts, and the conforming to this Principle in order to create an actual boat or cart. The latter is thus only the physical embodiment of the already subsisting concept. For every potentially existent object, therefore, whether natural or manmade, there must first be a Principle—a Principal lying within a world "above shapes" that consists entirely of such Principle, and is in itself all-perfect and all-complete.[18]

As for the *t'ai-chi,* it "consists of the Principles or *li* of all the things in the universe, brought together into a single whole".[19] Thus, the relation of a thing's *li* to its *t'ai-chi* is the relation of an element in a collection to the collection.

If each thing contains the *t'ai chi* and therefore every possible kind of *li,* why is it a thing of one kind rather than another? According to Fung,

> It has been stated earlier that every individual object contains the Supreme Ultimate [*t'ai-chi*] in its entirety. It should be noted, however, that, for any individual thing, it is only that thing's own particular Principle that is able to manifest itself. As to the Supreme Ultimate as a whole, this, though also present, remains concealed. The reason lies in the fact that it is obscured by the physical Ether or *ch'i,* with which the object in question is also endowed.[20]

Thus, according to Fung, out of all the various kinds of *li* which a thing contains, the *ch'i* allows only one *li* to manifest itself. But if the *t'ai-chi* is a collection of all *li,* then the terms "*t'ai-chi*" and "*li*" cannot have the same referent nor can the two terms be thought of as distinguishing different ways of looking at the same thing. For example, a philosophy class is a collection of students, but we cannot say that "student" and "philosophy class" have the same referent and simply represent two different ways of looking at the same thing.

Fung cites various passages from the works of Chu Hsi as textual support of his contention that the *t'ai-chi* is a collection of *li*.[21] However, the question of the relationship of *li* and *t'ai chi* is not to be settled on the basis of textual references to this relationship alone. It cannot be decided until the more basic question of the nature of the *li* is settled. If, as this article contends, *li* is essentially the same in all things, then it is impossible to make sense of the conception of the *t'ai-chi* as a collection of *li*. Only if, as Fung contends, *li* is responsible for differences in kind, and different kinds of things contain different kinds of *li*, is it possible to make sense of the conception of the *t'ai-chi* as a collection of *li*. Since it is argued at length here that Chu Hsi does not conceive of *li* as differing in any way, and conceives of it as essentially the same in all things, it is concluded on this basis that "*li*" and "*t'ai chi*" are synonymous insofar as by "*t'ai-chi*" Chu Hsi most often means *li* as universal in the previously explained sense of the term.

Keeping the relationship of the terms "*li*," "*hsing*," and "*t'ai-chi*" in mind, we now turn our attention to their common referent, which will usually be referred to as "the *li*" in the following discussion. To repeat what was said earlier, this discussion is not intended to be complete. The function of the *li* will be outlined only to the extent necessary to show that it cannot be equivalent to substantial form.

III. ALL THINGS CONTAIN *LI*

According to Chu Hsi, "If there is the *ch'i*, then there is the *li*. If there is no ch'i, then there is no *li*."[22] While Chu Hsi has no expression for "if and only if," this assertion is equivalent to saying that there is *ch'i* if and only if there is *li*. Thus the two are in some sense inseparable.

In addition to general assertions such as the above about the relationship of *li* and *ch'i* (the "components," as it were, of things) which imply that all things contain *li*, Chu Hsi also explicitly affirms that all things have *li*. From the records of Chu Hsi's conversations, it is clear that some of his students were surprised to learn that certain kinds of things contain *li*. The assertions of the inseparability of *li* and things vary in generality. The most general are exemplified by Chu Hsi's agreement with a student that, "All things contain the same *t'ai-chi*",[23] and Chu Hsi's own statements that, "Everybody has the *t'ai-chi*; everything has the *t'ai-chi*",[24] and "As for the production of men and things, they must obtain the *li*".[25]

Chu Hsi also enumerates various classes of the "ten thousand things" and affirms that all the members of each class contain the *li*. He speaks most often of natural beings, as opposed to man-made things. For example,

As for the things which heaven produces, there are those which have blood—*ch'i* and consciousness. These are men and beasts. There are those which do not have blood—*ch'i* and consciousness, but have only life-*ch'i*. These are grass and trees. There are those in which the life—*ch'i* has been cut off and which have only shape, tactile qualities, smell, and taste.

These are decayed and withered things. Although there are all these differences between these types of beings, the *li* are never different.[26]

Although decayed and withered things are without life, they are not without existence and thus we must conclude that they too have *li*.[27] Birds and beasts also have the same *hsing* as that which men have, Chu Hsi affirms in another place.[28]

Not only do natural beings, whether animate or formerly so, have *li*, but man-made objects have *li* as well. Such things as bricks, bamboo chairs, pens, boats, and carts have the *li*. For as soon as there is a thing, there is *li*.[29]

In light of all of Chu Hsi's statements on the matter, both general and specific, it seems reasonable to conclude that all things in some sense have or contain the *li*, and that Chu Hsi does not recognize the existence of "simple" beings, i.e., beings consisting only of *li* or only of *ch'i*.

IV. ALL THINGS CONTAIN ESSENTIALLY THE SAME *LI*

Everything has or contains the *li*. Do *li* differ specifically, i.e., are there different kinds of *li* for different kinds of things Again and again Chu Hsi says that although things have their differences, their *li* are the same. In a typical passage he says that "As for the *hsing* of men and things, basically they are without dissimilarity. But as for the endowment of *ch'i*, it cannot be without differences".[30]

The fact that all things possess the same *li* is indicated, Chu Hsi says, by the fact that they all exhibit, to some extent, virtuous behavior.[31] Tigers and wolves, he points out, exhibit humanity (*jen*[n]) insofar as they exhibit the bond of love between father and son. Jackals and otters offer sacrifice to their ancestors. This reference is to the Chinese belief that these animals spread out their prey before them in order to offer sacrifice.[32] Bees and ants exhibit righteousness insofar as they are aware of the relationship of ruler and minister. This is evident from the orderliness of their societies. Ducks and pigeons make distinctions.[33] These species mate for life and thus the Chinese felt that they too observed the principles of morality between the sexes.[34] These four examples are Chu Hsi's standard examples of the virtuous behavior of lower animals, and should not be taken as an exhaustive list of the ways in which animals were felt to be capable of virtuous behavior. Some express an awareness of the obvious similarities in behavior between man and other animals, while others are more uniquely Chinese folk beliefs which Chu Hsi apparently took quite seriously. Such beliefs about animal behavior are universal. For example, in rural West Virginia, it was (and probably still is) believed that a snake would try to avenge the killing of its mate. With some thought, the reader can probably come up with many examples of his/her own.

Chu Hsi resorts to analogies to explain how the *li* can be the same in different things, but there can still be such diversity in their moral behavior. The *li* in things, he says at one point, is like the sun or moon. If one is in an open place, he sees their light most completely. If one is under a roof in need of repair, it cuts off the light. Some is seen through the holes in the roof, most, however, is not. The *ch'i* is like the roof which obscures the light of the sun or moon. Non-humans have the *li*, but it is obscured by the *ch'i*. Their virtuous behavior is like the light shining through a chink.[35]

In another place Chu Hsi likens the *li* to a valuable pearl. If it is placed in clear water it is completely visible. If it is dropped into muddy water, it can be seen only with difficulty. In the virtuous behavior of the best of men they manifest their *li* just as crystal clear water allows the pearl to be completely visible. The virtuous behavior of birds and beasts is like the faint glimmering of a pearl in muddy water.[36]

In these analogies there is no suggestion that there are different kinds of *li*. The same sun is obscured to a greater or lesser extent by all roofs; there are no differences in the pearls dropped into water of varying degrees of clarity. What differs is the ease with which the light and the pearls can be seen.

At one point Chu Hsi speaks to someone who has suggested that humanity, the highest virtue, is distinct from the *hsing*.[37] If this were true it would explain why men exhibit it but other creatures do not. All beings would have the *hsing*, but men alone would have humanity. Chu Hsi had said that the *hsing* differs only in the degree of completeness (*ch'üan*[o]) and this would be one interpretation of such a statement. It would also account for some of the obvious differences in behavior exhibited by men and animals. If a dog's *hsing* were incomplete, for example, while that of a man were complete, this would be because man's *hsing* contains all that the dog's *hsing* contains and more. The person to whom Chu Hsi is speaking might have envisioned the relationship of the various *hsing* in a way similar to the way in which Aristotle envisioned the relationship of the three types of soul. Each type includes the functions and capabilities of all the lower types, but not conversely. Each type of soul also includes functions and capabilities which the lower ones do not have.

Whatever view Chu Hsi's interlocutor had in mind when he suggested that humanity is distinct from the *hsing*, Chu Hsi rejects the suggestion. Humanity is included in the *hsing*, all *hsing*. The human mind, however, is the most spiritual (*ling*[p]) because human *ch'i* is the clearest and purest. Therefore, men can completely manifest the virtues which their *hsing4* contains potentially. The *ch'i* of nonhu-

mans is impure and unclear and thus their minds are dull. Thus they cannot be expected to manifest completely the virtues. But on the other hand, they are not without traces of virtuous behavior.

And so the notions of completeness (*ch'üan*[o]) and incompleteness (*pu-ch'üan*[q]) Chu Hsi has in mind are completeness of actualization and incompleteness of actualization. A man's *hsing* is said to be complete while a dog's is not, not because the man's *hsing* contains something that the dog's does not. Rather, the potentialities of the man's *hsing* can be more completely actualized than those of the dog. Nor does the man's *hsing4* have potentialities which the dog's *hsing* lacks. The *hsing* of man and dog are the same and so their potentialities are the same. However, the man's *ch'i* allows these potentialities to be more completely actualized than does the dog's *ch'i*. As Chu Hsi puts it,

> Although their *ch'i* has inequalities, still they must obtain it in order to be produced, and among men and things every single one has it. Although *li* is the same, and things must obtain it in order to constitute the *hsing4*, men differ in one way from things. Therefore, as for that which constitutes humanity, righteousness, propriety, and wisdom, this is *li*. As for consciousness and movement, men can have them and things can have them. As for humanity, righteousness, propriety, and wisdom, things certainly have them but how can they be complete?[38]

It might still be doubted that Chu Hsi did indeed claim that all things contain essentially the same *li*, but two interesting passages indicate that his students interpreted him as saying this and were well aware of the consequences of such a claim.

> 1. Question: Do decayed and withered things have *li* or not Answer: As soon as there is a thing, then there is *li*. Heaven cannot produce a pen. Men take rabbit hairs and make pens. As soon as there is a pen, then there is *li*. Another question: As for the pens mentioned before, how can we discern righteousness and humanity? Answer: In the case of very small things, it is not necessary to discern humanity and righteousness in this way.[39]

> 2. Ts'ai Ch'ing says that very minute things all have the *hsing* too; but we cannot speak of them in terms of humanity, righteousness, propriety, and wisdom because it is certain that there is nothing which we can see in them which can be considered to be humanity, righteousness, propriety, and wisdom? But how can we see that they do not have humanity, righteousness, propriety, and wisdom? These kinds of things have not yet been carefully examined. We should think about them even more.[40]

The point raised in these passages is well taken. Chu Hsi has repeatedly said that the fact that a thing contains *li* or the *hsing* is indicated by its manifestation of virtuous behavior. Since all things possess the *li*, all would be expected to exhibit, to some extent, the four virtues. But how can we make sense of the suggestion that a pen should also exhibit, for example, humanity and righteousness?

When Chu Hsi replies in (1) that it is not necessary to be able always to discern humanity and righteousness, he could be seen as simply avoiding the issue by denying that it is necessary to discern humananity and righteousness even in pens before accepting the general premiss that all things contain the *li*. The implication would be that the example is irrelevant, but it is not made clear why it is irrelevant. Or Chu Hsi might have in mind the principle with which he answered the original question, "Do decayed and withered things have *li* or not"? As he replied, "As soon as there is a thing, then there is *li*". Such a general statement would imply that even man-made things have *li*. And so if this principle is accepted, then it must be concluded that a pen also has *li,* even if it is not apparent that it has humanity, etc. But it is not explained how the general principle was established. If we have some way of knowing that *li* is in all things independent of our observing that all things exhibit virtuous behavior, then the lack of virtuous behavior in pens can be safely dismissed. But if the principle that all things contain the same *li* is a generalization from observation of virtuous behavior in men, beasts, birds, etc., then the pen is an obvious counter-example and thus quite important.

Perhaps because he was aware of such problems, in (2) Chu Hsi is not as quick to admit that the humanity, etc. of certain things was completely non-apparent. These kinds of things, he says, have not yet been carefully examined, so we cannot be sure that there is absolutely no manifestation of the four virtues in them.

Thus, although there might be some question as to how obvious it is that pens and such are on the same behavioral continuum as man, Chu Hsi seems not to have questioned the fact that they are. His replies are as important for what he does not say as for what he does say. In particular, he does not suggest that he has been misinterpreted. He does not suggest that he never meant to say that all things contain essentially the same *li*.

V. SUBSTANTIAL FORM

Before arguing that *li* is not equivalent to substantial form, a short review of the Aristotelian-scholastic conception of substantial form is in order.[41]

The substantial form (also called the essence or nature) of a thing determines its specific nature, i.e., the "kind" of thing it is. For example, Russ Hatton's substantial form, humanity, makes him the kind of thing he is, a man. Therefore, it is that which makes him the same as all other things of the same kind, men. The substantial form or essence is expressed by the definition. For example, Russ Hatton's definition would be "rational animal." Aristotle and his interpreters believed that things divided naturally into kinds or species, each different species having a different substantial form.

A thing's substantial form is imperceptible in itself. However, it does have sensibly perceptible manifestations through which we can come to know it. In particular, we can acquire knowledge of substantial forms through properties and natural operations.

As for properties, because of the substantial form certain characteristics are always found in the things which have a given type of substantial form. These are called properties. Although properties are not included in the substantial form, they "follow" or "flow from" it, and so they are logically implied by the definition. Therefore, the lack of a given property is a sign that the thing lacks the substantial form which is the source or foundation of the property. For example, the capacities for speech and true laughter, and the ability to reason are generally considered by Aristotelians to be properties which flow from the substantial form of humanity. Thus, all things which contain this substantial form, i.e., all men, will be able to speak, laugh, and reason. And from the lack of one of these in a thing it can be concluded that there is also the lack of rationality, and thus that the thing is not a man.

The substantial form is also the source or foundation of a thing's natural operations (also called "proper," "specific," or "essential" operations). These are capabilities which are proper to and characteristic of things of a given kind. That is, if X is a natural operation of things of a given kind, then they always have X, while other things never have them. They too are said to "flow from" or "be determined by" the things's substantial form, and are the reason it tends towards its natural end. For example, the natural operations of man include intellect and will. Since intellect is also often given as a property of man, "property" and "natural operation" do not denote mutually exclusive categories.

VI. *LI* AND SUBSTANTIAL FORM

It could be argued that *li* is not equivalent to substantial form because it does not have precisely the same functions as form. There is some overlapping of functions to be sure. For example, both the *li* of man and the substantial form of humanity could be said to be responsible for intellectual ability. But there are also differences in function. For example, it is *ch'i* rather than *li* which is the source of life.[42] Substantial form, on the other hand, communicates being to the thing in which it is found, and in particular communicates life to living beings. Thus it is the source of life in living things.

But such comparisons would be essentially beside the point, for the non-equivalence of *li* and substantial form is more basic than this. If it were simply pointed out that *li* and substantial form do not share all functions, this might be misinterpreted in two ways. According to the first misinterpretation, it might still be thought that both *li* and substantial form make a thing the kind of thing it is. For example, the *li* of a man is what makes him a man. And it might be thought that if the *li* of a man is not the same as his substantial form—i.e., if they do not have exactly the same functions—this is because the Western and Chinese views of man are not equivalent. The differences between the *li* and substantial form are due to differences of emphasis within the two traditions.

According to the second misinterpretation, it might be thought that both *li* and substantial form serve the same basic role within their respective philosophies, i.e., both are responsible for making things the kinds of things they are. However, the Chinese categorization of the ten thousand things is not the same as the Aristotelian division of natural beings into natural species. Thus, any dissimilarity between a thing's substantial form and its *li* is due to the fact that each tradition sees it as a different kind of thing.

But both of these are misinterpretations. For I do not wish to deny simply that a man's *li* is the same as his substantial form in the sense that the kinds of things determined by *li* are not exactly equivalent to the kinds of things determined by substantial form. What I wish to deny is that *li* is responsible for a thing's being the kind of thing it is in any sense. But this is the basic function of substantial form. For example, Russ Hatton is the kind of thing he is, a man, because of his substantial form. The same is true of a horse. It is the kind of thing it is because of its substantial form. Further, Russ Hatton and a horse are different kinds of things. But this difference in kind is due to the fact that their substantial forms are essentially different. *Li,* however, cannot be responsible for such differences in kind simply because it is, as has just been argued, essentially the same in all things. As Chu Hsi himself says in a key passage, among the ten thousand things, their similarity is due to *li* and their differences are due to *ch'i.* That which is the same in things or which makes them the same cannot make them different, nor can that which is different in things or which makes them different make them the same.[43]

It must be admitted that substantial form is also responsible for similarities. It is, of course, responsible for all of the essential similarities among thhings of the same species, i.e., of the same kind. But more important for this discussion, it is also responsible for certain similarities among things of different species. For example, the substantial form of a man is the source of his life, as is the substantial form of a dog. This is because a substantial form is the foundation of both generic and specific properties. But all substantial forms also include the specific difference, i.e., that which makes one species different from all others, that which is unique to a single species. For example, the definition of a man is "rational animal." "Animal" in this case is the genus, "rational" is the specific difference. Because a man is an animal (a member of the genus "animal") he shares certain properties and natural operations with all other animals—growth, nutrition, reproduction, instinct, habit, sensation, imagination—and these similarities with other, different kinds of things are due to the substantial form. Thus the substantial form is to some extent responsible for similarities among different kinds of things, as is *li.* But the specific difference of man's substantial form is unique to men, i.e., rationality. And it is this which ultimately makes a man the kind of thing he is and different from all other kinds of things. *Li,* however, contains nothing which is unique to any species. *Li,* as was argued above, is essentially the same in everything. The *li* of a man contains nothing that is not found in the *li* of a horse, a tree, or a pen. For example, man is not unique in that he possesses the four virtues. It should be

remembered that Chu Hsi supports his contention that all things contain *li* by pointing out that they all manifest, to some extent, the four virtues. Man is unique, rather, because he alone is capable of fully manifesting them. But it is his *ch'i,* not his *li,* which makes this possible. All other things also possess the four virtues in potency, but because of their *ch'i* this is not always obvious. Therefore, *li* cannot be responsible for "kinds" in the way in which substantial form is responsible. Therefore, *li* cannot be equivalent to substantial form. If Chu Hsi can be said to recognize the existence of "kinds" (i.e., species) in the Aristotelian sense, then they must be said to be due to *ch'i.* It can, in fact, be argued that for Chu Hsi all differences are differences in degree among things which are composed of *li,* which is essentially the same in all, and *ch'i,* which is continuously variable in various aspects. Thus it might be siad, that the only differences Chu Hsi recognizes are accidental differences and that there is no place for substantial differences in the Aristotelian sense within his system. Therefore, there is no place for substantial form. Thus, *li* cannot be substantial form.

VII. Previous Comparisons of *Li* and Substantial Form

Having presented arguments for the non-equivalence of *li* and substantial form, I turn now to a consideration of some of the discussions of the question of the relation of *li* and substantial form mentioned earlier.

Of those mentioned, only Fung, Sun, Needham and Bruce can be said to argue for their respective positions. Fung, on the one hand, argues that *li* is essentially the same as substantial form. Sun agrees but insists that *li* is more than this. Both cite passages from the works of Chu Hsi in support of their contentions. However, Sun cites the same passages as Fung. In addition, his discussion is inconsistent. Thus, only Fung will be considered in detail. On the other hand, Needham and Bruce agree that *li* and substantial form are not equivalent, although they argue along different lines. Thus each will be discussed separately.

As for the discussions of Carsun Chang and Stanislaus Sun, both can be dealt which quickly. Both hold that *li* is equivalent to substantial form while correctly pointing out that *ch'i* is responsible for all differences. As Chang says, "In the natural world different kinds of things exist,—men, animals, plants, inanimate bodies. For Chu Hsi, these dissimilarities are the result of the endowment of *ch'i*".[44] According to Sun, "Things are many and different. These differences are not due to *li,* but [are] due to *ch'i*".[45] Thus both disagree with this article's basic contention—that *li* is not equivalent to substantial form—while accepting the foundation of that contention—that according to Chu Hsi *ch'i* is responsible for all the differences among things, including specific differences. What neither seems to realize is that such an interpretation of the function of *ch'i* rules out the possibility that *li* can be equivalent to substantial form, since substantial form is responsible for certain differences, specific differences.

In support of his contention that "*Li* is just like what Greek philosophy called form^d",[46] Fung Yu-lan cites various passages from the works of Chu Hsi which, as he interprets them seem to suggest that *li* is responsible for the differences which are attributed to substantial form. The most significant of these passages will be considered in the following.

The first such passage, as translated by Bodde, runs,

> *Question:* How is it that dried up withered things also possess the nature (*hsing*)?"
>
> *Answer:* "For them there has been from the beginning such a Principle (*li*). Therefore it is said that in the universe there is no single thing that lies beyond the nature (*hsing*)." As he walked on the steps, (the Master then) said: "*The bricks of these steps have within them the Principle (li) that pertains to bricks.*" And sitting down he said: "*This bamboo chair has within it the Principle pertaining to bamboo chairs*".[47]

How problematic this passage is for this chapter's contention that *li* is not equivalent to substantial form—i.e., that there is not a different kind of *li* for each different kind of thing—depends upon how the underlined sentences are translated. The first thing to notice that Chu Hsi is asked if "dried up withered things"—i.e., dead things—have *li*. The interlocutor apparently thinks of *li* as a principle of life and so he cannot see how dead things could have it. Chu Hsi affirms that even dead things have *li,* for all things have *li.* Thus, the question which initiates Chu Hsi's remarks about bricks and chairs is not whether different kinds of things have different kinds of *li,* but whether certain kinds of things have *li* at all. Therefore, Chu Hsi's reply should be read, not as making reference to different kinds of *li,* but as pointing out that not only do "dried up withered things" have *li* but even such things as bricks and chairs—things which are not only not alive but have never been alive—have *li.* The Chinese sentences themselves are ambiguous. The ambiguity is due to the facts that *yu*^t means both "to have" and "there is/are" and, that they include no definite article. The omission or inclusion of the definite article is quite significant. For we can read the sentences either as referring to "the *li* of bricks" or "the *li* of the bricks." The latter is much less suggestive that bricks have a specific kind of *li* than the former. Therefore, if we translate *yu* as "have" and omit any definite article, we will get Bodde's translation: "The bricks of [these] steps have [within them] the Principle (*li*) that pertains to bricks." If we translate *yu* as "there are" and add a definite article, we get a more literal translation: "As for the bricks of [these] steps, there is the *li* of the bricks." Both translations are possible and neither is a forced reading. However, given the context, the latter is to be preferred because it is more suggestive of the idea that the statements about bricks and chairs are simply specific instances of the general assertion that all things have *li.*

> *Question:* "Principle [*li*] is received from Heaven by both men and other creatures alike. But do inanimate things also possess Principle?"

> *Answer:* "Certainly they possess Principle. For example, (the Principle of) a boat is that it can move only on water; of a cart, that it can move only on land."[48]

Although man-made objects are not generally considered to have substantial forms, this passage suggests that *li* is in some sense responsible for differences in kind, and Fung takes it as indicating that *li* is comparable to substantial form. The passage, however, is quoted out of context, and there is an interesting passage following it in the *Ch'üan-shu* which Fung does not quote.

> Chi-T'ung said, "The ones on dry land cannot enter the water. The ones in the water cannot dwell on dry land. The ones on dry land have more *yang* and less *yin.* The ones in the water have more *yin* and less *yang.* As for the ones which can come out of the water and dwell on the dry land, the tortoise and otter are such.[49]

In this passage, given the former passage about boats and carts, one would expect that the differences between land and waterdwelling creatures would also be attributed to *li.* However, here they are attributed to *yin* and *yang*—i.e., *ch'i.* Admittedly, these are the words of Chi T'ung, a pupil of Chu Hsi rather than the master himself, but they are neither qualified nor commented upon. This can be taken to indicate that Chu Hsi agreed with what was said. Therefore, this passage makes problematic the conclusion which Fung draws from the passage about boats and carts which immediately precedes it.

Finally, Fung quotes Chu Hsi and Bodde translates the passage as,

> *Question:* "I have seen how in your reply-letter to Yu Fang-shu you maintain that even a dried up withered thing has Principle [*li*]. But I do not understand how such dried up things as a tile or a pebble should have this Principle."
>
> *Answer:* "(There is Principle) even for rhubarb or aconite. These too are dried up things, and yet rhubarb cannot act as aconite, nor can aconite act as rhubarb."[50]

Bodde suggests in a footnote that,

> I.e., each can follow only its own specialized function. The dried leaves and stems of these plants are used in China for medicine.[51]

Thus, Bodde at least, interprets this passage as suggesting that differences in the effects of certain drugs are due to differences in their *li;* therefore, specific differences are due to *li.*

Bodde's translation is reasonable, but this passage must be compared with another:

> *Question:* "Men, birds, and beasts certainly have consciousness. But consciousness has penetration and obstruction. Do grass and trees also have consciousness or not?"

Answer: "They also have it. For example, consider a potted flower. If we pour a little water upon it, then it blossoms. If we break it off, then it withers. Can we say that it is without consciousness? Chou Mao Shu did not cut the grass in front of his window. He said, 'Its thoughts are exactly like my own thoughts.' This then is having consciousness. It is just that the consciousness of birds and beasts is not like men's. As for the consciousness of grass and trees, it is not like that of birds and beasts. For example, consider rhubarb. If we consume it, then in a little while we will be purged. If we consume aconite, then in a little while we will become hot. This is just because their consciousness is only manifested in a single way (literally, 'only follows this one road')."[52]

In these two different passages Chu Hsi attributes the differences in the effects of rhubarb and aconite to both *li* and consciousness. But for Chu Hsi, *li* and consciousness are not equivalent. This is clear from such passages as,

Question: "As for consciousness, is the mind's spirit certainly like this or is it the action of *ch'i*?"

Answer: "It is not solely *ch'i*. First there is the *li* of consciousness, but *li* is not conscious. *Ch'i* condenses and takes shape; *li* and *ch'i* are united; and then there can be consciousness."[53]

Thus, when asked about consciousness, Chu Hsi says that *li* is not conscious, and consciousness is not due solely to the *ch'i*. Consciousness is not the result of a conscious *li* coming to rest in unconscious *ch'i*. But if consciousness is a characteristic of the composite as a whole rather than one of the other of the components, then differences in consciousness will be among those differences between things which must be explained, rather than an explanation of the differences between things. Thus, if, with Fung, we hold that generic and specific differences are due to *li*, then we will hold that differences in consciousness are also due to *li*. Whereas, if we hold that generic and specific differences are due to *ch'i*, we will hold that differences in consciousness are also due to *ch'i*. Therefore, in these two passages in which Chu Hsi is not consistent in pointing out the source of certain important differences between things, the way in which these passages are interpreted and reconciled will depend upon our interpretation of Chu Hsi. The interpretation of these passages presupposes an interpretation of Chu Hsi rather than offering evidence in support of one or another interpretation. To cite one passage in support of the contention that *li* is the source of generic and specific differences without mentioning the other is misleading.

In this consideration of the most important textual evidence for Fung's thesis that *li* is equivalent to substantial form, all I have attempted to do is cast aspersions upon this textual support. It certainly cannot be denied that some passages seem to suggest that differences in kind are due to *li*. However, such passages are not common, and as I have tried to show, all are to some extent problematic. Admittedly, the passages Fung cites are problematic for the interpretation of *li* given in this paper, but they are all

too vague to be sufficient textual support of the contention that *li* is equivalent to substantial form. The best Fung can do is present a handful of vague passages as compared to large numbers of clear passages which can be offered in support of the contention that *li* is not equivalent to substantial form. It would be significant if the passages which Fung cites were simply a sampling of a much larger number of such passages; but as far as I have been able to determine, these are literally almost all of the textual evidence Fung can offer. And these are so vague that they can be seen as supporting Fung's position only if one is already convinced of the truth of his interpretation of *li* as substantial form.

As for Needham's assertion that the equation of *li* and *ch'i* with "the form and matter of Platonic-Aristotelian philosophy . . . is entirely unacceptable", he gives various reasons for it which prove to be a rather mixed lot.[55] Some of his comparisons and contrasts are potentially good but some of his statements are quite inaccurate.

One basic problem is that there is a certain amount of confusion in Needham's discussion which complicates any attempt to deal with it. For example, at one point he speaks of the relation of substantial form to things, and compares it to the relation of *li* to *ch'i*. To be consistent, Needham should compare either substantial form's relation to things with *li's* relation to things, or substantial form's relation to prime matter with *li's* relation to *ch'i*. The two relations are quite different.

A more serious problem is that the discussion betrays some fundamental misunderstandings of prime matter and substantial form. For example, he implies at one point that they are illusory or subjective and says at another that "matter is potentially form." However, I am unaware of any interpretation of Aristotelian hylomorphism which viewed prime matter or substantial form as "illusory" or "subjective". Further, the suggestion that matter is potentially form can only be based upon a misunderstanding of the relation of form as act and matter as potency. Matter is not potentially form in the sense that matter has the potential to become form. Matter is potentiality *to* form in the sense that it has the potentiality to become informed. But in this sense, *ch'i* could be said to be potentiality to *li* in that it has the potentiality to unite with *li* (become in-*li*-ed, as it were).

Thus, some of Needham's comparisons are potentially relevant, but some indicate a lack of real understanding of the notion of substantial form and its relationship to prime matter. However, even his correct contrasts between substantial form and *li* are beside the point since he misses the most essential contrast: substantial form is responsible for generic and specific differences while *li* is not. Chu Hsi does not use *li* to account for difference at all. Thus, Needham correctly rejects the equation of *li* and substantial form, but for the wrong reasons.

Bruce discussed at length the question, "Whether we have not here a system similar to that of the Greek philosophers, and whether *Li* does not constitute the type of each individual thing or class of things, the norm to which it conforms, in such a way as to make it practically identical with Aristotle's 'form'."[56] The answer, he continues, "cannot . . . be wholly in the affirmative,"[57] for *Li*, while suggestive of form, is essentially different from that conception.[58]

In his discussion of the relationship between *li* and substantial form, Bruce comes quite close to self-contradiction. He says at one point that "the differences of form and function in the infinite variety of species are due in the ultimate to *li* as the controlling and directing principle."[59] Later he says that "the differences between species and the differing degrees in which the ethical principles of which *Li* is composed are embodied in different individuals, are attributed to *Ch'i* rather than to *Li*."[60] Bruce apparently feels that there is no problem in saying that the differences of form and function of species are ultimately due to *li* and also saying that the differences between species are attributable to *ch'i*.

Bruce gives two reasons why *li* is not identical with substantial form. The first is that *li* is an "ethical norm" while substantial form is not. However, according to Aristotle all beings have natural inclinations or operations—e.g., self-preservation, reproduction, etc. An act is good insofar as it is in accordance with these natural inclinations and evil insofar as it is not. The source of these natural inclinations is the substantial form. Thus, the substantial form determines not only what a being is, but what a being should be. Men, for example, are rational animals. This is because of their substantial form. Thus, they have a natural inclination to act rationally. Therefore, acts in accordance with this tendency are good, and acts contrary to it are evil. Thus, the substantial form determines not only the kind of being a man is, but the type of behavior proper to him. In light of this conception of substantial form, if it does not satisfy Bruce's criteria for being an "ethical norm" (whatever they might be) then it is difficult to conceive what would satisfy the criteria.

Bruce's second reason why *li* is not identical with substantial form is that *li* is not responsible for the differences between species, while substantial form is. This is, of course, the basic contention of this article.

VIII. Comments and Conclusions

Fung's interpretation of Chu Hsi might be viewed as exemplifying the wishful thingking common to so many interpreters of Chinese philosophy. Like many of his generation he was, perhaps, disillusioned with his own tradition, but rather than rejecting it outright as did some of his contemporaries, he made a valiant attempt to reinterpret it. His work is perhaps best seen as an attempt to render Chinese philosophy palatable to Westerners by presenting it as essentially indistinguishable from Western philosophy.

Fung's philosophical sophistication is evident throughout his magnificent two-volume history as well as in his discussion of Chu Hsi. As a result he chooses his textual references very carefully. Significantly, he knows which texts to ignore as well as which texts to cite. He presents a carefully thought out, well-integrated interpretation which, however, is basically a conscious attempt to bring Chu Hsi into line with Aristotle rather than an accurate and objective presentation of Chu Hsi. In the final analysis it is simply not true to Chu Hsi's vision of reality.

Chang and Sun can be seen as taking their cue from Fung, although their presentations are more accurate than his insofar as they admit that Chu Hsi attributes all differences to *ch'i*. What they apparently did not realize was that one cannot have things both ways. One cannot equate *li* with substantial form and still attribute specific differences to *ch'i*.

While Needham and Bruce cannot be faulted in their interpretation of *li* insofar as their conclusions are concerned, both leave something to be desired as far as their approach to answering the question "Is *li* equivalent to substantial form?" is concerned. It would seem to be obvious that before one tries to answer the question, one should have a clear understanding, not only of *li*, but also of substantial form. But it is here that both Needham and Bruce can be said to fall short.

Needham's lack of understanding of substantial form is the more extreme. He dispenses sophisticated and rather technical characterizations of substantial form quite freely—"factor of individuation," "that which gives rise to the unity of any organism," "that which confers substantiality"—but his discussion is so confusing and the mistakes he makes are so elementary that his grasp of the function of substantial form is open to question. Given such misunderstandings, his correct conclusion with respect to the relation of substantial form and *li* is somewhat surprising.

As for Bruce, although he comes close to contradicting himself and his denial that substantial form is an ethical norm is wrong, it must be admitted that he has a good grasp of substantial form and its functions within a hylomorphic metaphysics. This, coupled with a sound understanding of *li* and its function within Chu Hsi's system, enables him, eventually, to put his finger precisely upon the essential difference between *li* and substantial form. However, his discussion and comparison of the two does leave something to be desired. It lacks focus and tends to ramble, and he devotes too much time to a presentation of poor evidence that *li* is "suggestive" of substantial form. Thus, his final conclusion that *li* and substantial form are not the same tends to be lost among the qualifications and so lose its impact.

In sum, it would seem that the most basic reason why the discussion of the relation of *li* and substantial form has dragged on for so long is, on the part of some, an out-and-out misunderstanding of substantial form and, on the part of others, an inadequate understanding of substantial form. A basic problem has been a consistent lack of appreciation of the fact that that which makes a thing the kind of thing it is, i.e., the substantial form, is also that which makes it different from *other* kinds of beings. If, for example, men are different from dogs and a man's substantial form is what makes him a man while a dog's substantial form is what makes it a dog, then in some way a man's substantial form must be different from a dog's. It has been a lack of understanding of this that has apparently prevented the parties in the dispute from realizing that Bruce had more or less settled the matter definitively fifty years ago.

The lesson for comparativists is obvious: we must really understand bot both terms the comparison. A superficial knowledge will not generally suffice to avoid serious mistakes. Most would agree that it is dangerous to assume that one's audience will know what one is talking about. But it can be just as dangerous to assume that one knows what one is talking about. Taking the time to state carefully and systematically the "obvious" can make one aware of one's own confusions and uncertainties, which can then hopefully be remedied before proceeding further. It is significant that not one of the scholars dealt with took the time to explicate, even minimally, substantial form. If they had done so, it would probably not have been necessary to write this article.

Notes

1. This article is based upon the fourth chapter of my dissertation entitled *A Comparison of the Role of Prime Matter in the System of Francis Suarez (1548-1617) with that of Ch'i in the System of Chu Hsi (1130-1200).* I wish to thank the directors of the dissertation, Profs. Jorge E. Gracia and Kenneth K. Inada of the State University of New York at Buffalo, for their patience and the invaluable suggestions and criticisms which they gave me while I was writing the dissertation. I wish also to thank Prof. Christina Madajewicz, formerly of the University of Warsaw. Most of the original research for this chapter was done under her direction and the most important ideas in it were first explored in the course of discussions of the philosophy of Chu Hsi with her.

2. Stanislas Le Gall, *Tchou Hi: Sa Doctrine, Son Influence,* 2nd. ed., Variétes Sinologique, No. 6, Shanghai, La Mission Catholique à l'Orphelinant de T'ousè-wè, p. 81.

3. J. Percy Bruce, *Chu Hsi and Hsi Masters,* London, Probsthain & Co., 1923, p. 113.

4. Bruce, p. 109.

5. Fung Yu-lan[e], *Chung-kuo Che-hsüeh Shih[c], A History of Chinese Philosophy,* 1934, rpt. Taiping, Taiping Foreign Publishing House, 1975, p. 903.

6. Fung Yu-lan, "The Philosophy of Chu Hsi," trans. Derk Bodde, *Harvard Journal of Asiatic Studies,* 7, 1942, 1-51.

7. Fung Yu-lan, *A History of Chinese Philosophy,* trans. Derk Bodde, 2 vols., Princeton, Princeton University Press, 1952, II, p. 542.

8. Joseph Needham, *Science and Civilization in China, Vol. 2: History of Scientific Thought,* Cambridge, Cambridge University Press, 1956, p. 472.

9. Needham, p. 475.

10. Carsun Chang, *The Development of Neo-Confucian Thought,* 2 vols, New York, Bookman Associates, 1957, 1962, I, p. 244.

11. Wing-tsit Chan, *A Sourcebook in Chinese Philosophy,* Princeton, Princeton University Press, 1963, p. 641.

12. Wing-tsit Chan, "Chu Hsi," *The Encyclopedia of Philosophy,* ed. Paul Edwards, 8 vols, New York, Macmillan & The Free Press, 1967, II, p. 111.

13. Stanislaus Sun, S. J., "The Doctrine of the "LI" in the Philosophy of Chu Hsi," *International Philosophical Quarterly,* 6, 1966, 155-88.

14. *"Hsing"* has been universally translated as "nature" or "the nature." However, it has been left untranslated because within the Aristotelian-Scholastic tradition "nature" refers to the substantial form as the internal principle of change. Since it is argued in this paper that *li* is not substantial form, it seems inconsistent to continue to translate *"hsing"*a as "nature."

15. *"T'ai4-chi2"* has been variously translated as "supreme ultimate" (Fung, Bruce, Chang), "great ultimate" (Chan), and "great extreme" (M'Clatchie). It has been left untranslated here because neither *"li"* nor *"hsing4"* are translated.

16. See, for example: Fung, *History,* p. 551; Bruce, p. 193; Le Gall, p. 52, etc.

17. This is essentially the view of Bruce. See, e.g., pp. 109 and 136-7.

18. Fung, *History,* p. 536.

19. Fung, *History,* p. 537.

20. Fung, *History,* p. 552.

21. See, e.g., *History,* pp. 537-8.

22. Chu Hsi, *Chu-Tzu Ch'üan-shu[j]* (*Complete Works of Master Chu*), 1714 ed. 66 bks. in 25 vols., bk. 49, p. 7b. Hereafter all references to this work will be abbreviated. This one would be abbreviated: *CS* 49, 7b. All translations are my own unless otherwise noted. For alternative translations see: Le Gall 94, #31; Thomas M'Clatchie, *Confucian Cosmogony,* London, Trübner and Co., 1874, p. 21, #31; Pang Ching-jen, *L'idée de Dieu chez Malebranche et l'idée de li chez Tchou Hi,* Paris, Librairie Philosophique J. Vrin, 1942, p. 79, #31. This passage has apparently been a source of problems for editors and/or typesetters. Le Gall includes the Chinese whith his translation and his edition reverses the order of *ch'i* and *li* in the second hypothetical proposition. Thus it reads, "If there is no *li*, then there is no *ch'i.*" Pang does not include the Chinese, but he translates the second hypothetical as, "s'il n'y a pas tel *li*, tel *k'i* n'existe pas non plus." M'Clatchie also includes the Chinese with

his translation, but in the second hypothetical he has the character for *li* in both antecedent and conclusion. Thus it would read, "If there is no *li*, then there is no *li*." However, he translates it as, "Where the Air [*ch'i*] does not exist, there, Fate [*li*] does not exist." The translation given here is of the sentence as it appears in the copy of the *Ch'üan-shu* to which I had access.

23. *CS* 42, 27a. For an alternative translation see Chu Hsi, *The Philosophy of Human Nature,* trans. J. Percy Bruce, London, Probsthain & Co., 1922, p. 60, #5. Hereafter all references to this work will be abbreviated. This reference would be abbreviated: *HN* 60, #5. See also Chan 620, #56.

24. *CS* 49, 14b. Chan 641, #121; Le Gall 103, #16; M'Clatchie 33, #16; Pang 84, #16.

25. Chu Hsi, *Ta-Hsüeh Huo-Wen*[k] (*Questions about the Great Learning*), p. 3a. Quoted in Toshimizu Goto, *Index to Chu-tsu's Philosophy,* 3 vols., Hiroshima, Hiroshima Univ., 1955, II, p. 37.

26. Chu Hsi, *Chu-Tzu Ta-Ch'üan*[l] (*Complete Literary Works of Master Chu*), 121 bks. in 12 vols., *Sz Pu Pei Yao*[m] ed., 1927; rpt. Taipei, Taiwan Book Co., 1967, *bk* 59, pp 35a-b. Hereafter all references to this work will be abbreviated. This reference would be abbreviated: *TC* 59, 35a-b. All translations from this work were made with the help of Professors Kenneth K. Inada and Christina Madajewicz.

27. *CS* 42, 30a. Chan 623, #59; *HN* 65, #10.

28. *CS* 42, 27b. Chan 621, #57; *HN* 61, #6.

29. *CS* 42, 29b-30a. Chan 623, #59 and #60; *HN* 64-5, #'s 10, 11, and 12.

30. *CS* 42, 35a. *HN* 74, #5.

31. *CS* 42, 27b; 43, 7b. *HN* 61, #6; 91, #11.

32. Chan 621, note 111; Fung, *History,* 553, note 1; *HN* 91, note 2.

33. *CS* 43, 8a. *HN* 91, #11.

34. *HN* 91, note 2.

35. *CS* 42, 27a-b. Chan 621, #57; *HN* 60-1, #6.

36. *CS* 43, 7b-8a. *HN* 91, #11.

37. *CS* 42, 32b-33a. *HN* 69-70, #1.

38. *CS* 42, 28b. Chan, 622; *HN* 62-3, #8.

39. *CS* 42, 30a. *HN* 65.

40. *CS* 42, 34b. *HN* 73.

41. For this discussion of substantial form, the following were consulted: Thomas Harper, S. J., *The Metaphysics of the School,* 3 vols., 1879, rpt. New York, Peter Smith, 1940; Cardinal Mercier and Professors of the Higher Institute of Philosophy, Louvain, *A Manual of Modern Scholastic Philosophy,* trans. T. L. and S. A. Parker, 3rd. ed., 2 vols., St. Louis, B. Herder Book Co., 1950; Bernard Wuellner, S. J., *Dictionary of Scholastic Philosophy,* Milwaukee,

Bruce Pub. Co., 1956. Of particular help was the discussion of substantial form and related terms in the Glossary to Professor Jorge Gracia's translation of Disputation 5 ("Individual Unity and Its Principle") of Francis Suarez's *Metaphysical Disputations.* I wish to thank Prof. Gracia for graciously allowing me to use the manuscript.

42. *CS* 42, 28b. *HN* 63.

43. *CS* 42, 28a. Chan 621-2, #58; *HN* 62.

44. Chang, p. 261.

45. Sun, p. 175.

46. Fung, *Che-hsüeh Shih,* p. 903.

47. Fung, *History,* pp. 536-7. He quotes Chu Hsi, *Chu-Tzu Yü-lei*[s] (*Classified Conversations of Master Chu*), bk. 4, p. 6. Hereafter, all references to this work will be abbreviated. This would be abbreviated *YL* 4, 6. See also *CS* 42, 29b. For alternative translations see: Chan 623, #59; *HN* 64-5, #10.

48. Fung, *History,* p. 536. He quotes *YL* 4, 6. The passage is also found in *CS* 42, 30a. See Chan 623, #60; *HN* 65, #12.

49. *CS* 42, 30a-b. *HN* 65-6, #13.

50. Fung, *History,* pp. 551-2. The passage is taken from *YL* 4, 6.

51. Fung, *History,* p. 552, note 1.

52. *CS* 42, 31b-32a. Chan 623, #61; *HN* 68, #17.

53. *CS* 44, 1a. *HN* 159, #5. Fung also quotes this passage, History, p. 556. He takes it from *YL* 5, 3.

54. Needham, p. 475.

55. See Needham, p. 475.

56. Bruce, p. 108.

57. Bruce, p. 108.

58. Bruce, p. 109.

59. Bruce, p. 112.

60. Bruce, p. 113.

Daniel K. Gardner (essay date 1983)

SOURCE: "Chu Hsi's Reading of the *Ta-hsueh*: A Neo-Confucian's Quest for Truth," in *Journal of Chinese Philosophy,* Vol. 10, No. 3, 1983, pp. 183-204.

[*In the following essay, Gardner investigates Chu Hsi's fascination with the shortest text in Confucian canon, the* Ta-hsueh, *reviewing the evidence of Chu Hsi's "endless" revision of his commentary on it. He argues that Chu Hsi's intensive study of the text resulted in an understanding of it that challenged the traditional reading of the* Ta-hsueh.]

The *Ta-hsüeh*[a] is the shortest text in the Confucian canon. With its scant 1747 characters it can be read, even memorized, in a matter of days. Yet Chu Hsi[b] spent more than forty years engaged in the study of the text, producing by the end of his life a commentary on it that would soon become authoritative.

Prior to the Sung dynasty (960-1279) classical studies tended to be principally exegetical. The aim of the classical scholar was to gloss, phonetically and philologically, characters and phrases whose sound or meaning was in need of elucidation. The assumption of the scholar was that once the characters and phrases had become intelligible the text itself would be immediately clear and meaningful to him. Understanding of the words equalled an understanding of the text.

Neo-Confucian scholars of the Sung did not align themselves with the exegetical tradition. Believing fervently that the sages of the past had manifested truth in the Confucian classics, they regarded the canon as revelatory and felt a religious commitment to it. Yet the truth contained in the texts was not easy to get at, for no words could ever fully express the profound intentions of the sages. In reading a classic, the individual had to do more than run his eyes over the characters, apprehending their superficial meaning. As Chu Hsi was fond of saying, the reader should not simply read the text, he should "experience" it.[1] He had to carry on a dialogue with the text, struggling to reach an understanding with it. Without the active participation of the reader, the text had little meaning; by rediscovering the truth through serious dialogue with the text, the reader gave significance to the text. Repeated encounters of this sort with the work led the reader over time to an ever-deepening appreciation of the imbedded truth.

The devotion of the Sung Neo-Confucians to the classical texts resulted in a flurry of studies on them. There was hardly a Neo-Confucian thinker of any significance who did not write commentary or interpretive essays on the canon. But of all the work done on the Confucian texts Chu Hsi's was surely the most influential, raising crucial philosophical issues that would continue to preoccupy the Chinese intellectual tradition until the present century. Particularly important were his commentaries on the Four Books, which in the early fourteenth century became the officially-sanctioned interpretations of the texts. Chu spent many years of his life writing and rewriting these commentaries and in them developed much of his Neo-Confucian vision.

Two years before his death Chu Hsi casually remarked that of the Four Books the text that most exhausted him was the *Ta-hsüeh*.[2] Indeed, a reading of his memorials, letters, and recorded conversations with friends and disciples reveals his profound commitment to the brief text; from 1162, when he discusses it in a memorial to the throne, until the end of his life nearly forty years later it never seems to have been far from his thoughts. His painstaking work on his commentary to the *Ta-hsüeh* most clearly demonstrates his dedication to the text. Having written a draft of the commentary no later than 1174, Chu was forever revising it, as we shall see in the first part of this article; for as he read and reread the text, its meaning became clearer and clearer to him. Chu Hsi's endless struggle to come to an understanding of the *Ta-hsüeh* was a Neo-Confucian's quest for truth. Not surprisingly, his intense search for the truth led him to an understanding of the text that differed dramatically from pre-Sung interpretations of it. The second part of this article will suggest what in particular was new in Chu Hsi's interpretation of the *Ta-hsüeh*.

I.

In 1189, at the age of sixty,[3] Chu Hsi completed prefaces to the *Ta-hsüeh chang-chü*[c] and the *Chung-yung chang-chü*[d]. We know from his *nien-p'u*[e], written by Wang Mou-hung[f] (1668-1741) in the early Ch'ing period,[4] that Chu Hsi had labored long over both of these works before finally appending the prefaces:

> He had done the drafts for these two books long ago but kept altering them from time to time. Being satisfied now in his own mind he wrote prefaces to them for the first time. For each he also wrote a *Huo-wen*[g].[5]

Evidence of a deep interest in the *Ta-hsüeh* goes back at least twenty-seven years, to 1162, when Hsiao-tsung succeeded to the throne and invited memorials from scholars and officials.[6] In response the thirty-three year-old Chu Hsi submitted a sealed memorial (*feng-shih*[h]),[7] his first memorial ever, in which he emphasized the importance of ideas found in the *Ta-hsüeh* for cultivating the ruler's person and for bringing order to the empire:

> In the learning of the sage emperors and wise kings of antiquity one apprehended the principle in things and extended knowledge in order to probe the transformation of affairs and things. If the meaning and principle of affairs and things that one encounters are illumined in every detail and are clear to one's mind without the slightest obscurity then naturally one's thoughts will become true and the mind will become set in the right;[8] hence, dealing with the affairs of the empire will be as [simple as] counting one and two and discriminating between black and white. . . . It would seem that 'apprehending the principle in things' and 'extension of knowledge' is what Yao and Shun called 'be discriminating and undivided,' and that 'setting the mind in the right' and 'making the thoughts true' is what Yao and Shun called 'holding fast the Mean.'[9] From antiquity on, what was transmitted by the sages and what was manifested in their conduct was nothing more than these things. As for Confucius, he gathered together all that was good but in advancing did not acquire the right position and thus did not practice it [i.e., all that was good] in the empire. Therefore, he withdrew and wrote it down in the form of the Six Classics in order to make it known to those of later generations who would rule the empire, the state, and the household. In these [works] he discussed the order of the roots and branches, the beginning and the end, the first and the last. The portion that is particularly detailed and clear may now be found in the book of Tai [Sheng], in the so-called 'Ta-hsüeh' chapter. Therefore, the Ch'eng-i dignitary (*Ch'eng-i lang*[i]) Ch'eng Hao[j] (1032-1085) to-

gether with his younger brother the Lecturer of the Ch'ung-cheng Pavilion (*Ch'ung-cheng tien shuo-shuk*) Ch'eng I[l] (1033-1107), great Confucians of recent times who truly got at that learning that had not been transmitted since Confucius and Mencius, both considered this chapter to be a work handed down from Confucius and a text that scholars should devote themselves to first; indeed, this is an examplary view. I humbly hope that your majesty will renounce old practices, and useless and frivolous writings; put aside those ideas that seem right but are wrong and those that are heterodox; and give your attention to this classic which has been handed down, search for a true Confucian who profoundly understands its meaning, and place him beside you at court in order to provide advice.[10]

This is the first historical account given by Chu Hsi of the *Ta-hsüeh* text; the esteem in which he already holds the work at this early age is quite apparent.

In the following year at the age of thirty-four Chu Hsi was summoned to the temporary capital, Lin-an (modern Hangchow), for an audience with the emperor. At that time he presented three memorials, one of which continues the theme introduced in the sealed memorial:[11]

I have heard that in the way of greater learning 'the Son of Heaven on down to the commoners, all without exception regard the cultivation of the person as the root.'[12] The way in which harmony is established in the household, the way in which the state becomes well-governed, and the way in which the empire becomes tranquil all derive from this root.[13] Thus one's person cannot be cultivated aimlessly; thorough inquiry into the root depends simply upon apprehending the principle in things in order that one's knowledge may be extended to the utmost.[14] 'Apprehending the principle in things' is a term meaning 'probing principle' (*ch'iung li*[m]).[15] If there is a thing there must be its particular manifestation of principle. But principle is without physical form and difficult to understand; things have physical traces and so are easy to observe. Therefore, follow a thing in seeking its manifestation of principle; if the manifestation of principle becomes perfectly clear to one's mind then naturally in dealing with affairs there will not be the slightest mistake. Hence, the thoughts being true and the mind being set in the right one's person becomes cultivated; and as for establishing harmony in the household, governing the state well, and bringing tranquility to the empire, they too rely upon this [process of apprehending the principle in things and extending knowledge]. This is the so-called 'way of greater learning.' Although the great sages of antiquity were born knowing it, there is not a case of one who did not [continue to] study it. Yao and Shun handed it down—such is the so-called 'be discriminating, be undivided, that you may sincerely hold fast the Mean.'[16] From that time on sage passed it on to sage, and each thereby got possession of the empire. When Confucius did not acquire the right position he committed it to writing in order to make it known to those of later generations who would govern the empire, the state, and the house-hold. Moreover, his disciples together transmitted it and elucidated it further; the way of greater learning indeed can be said to have been

well-studied. However, since the Ch'in and Han dynasties this learning has ceased.[17]

As in the earlier memorial Chu briefly outlines the history of the *Ta-hsüeh* text. He argues that the "way of greater learning" described there by Confucius had been the foundation of the sage-emperor's learning in the golden age of antiquity. Since the days of the Ch'in dynasty, however, the "way" had been neglected. Chu Hsi's message in these memorials to the emperor is clear: the ruler who once again follows that "way" and makes it the basis of his learning will become a true sage-king and bring complete tranquility to the empire.

In a lecture given in Yü-shan[n] district in the province of Chiang-nan in 1194,[18] thirty-one years later, Chu Hsi continues to stress the central importance of the "way of greater learning" in the education of the ancients:

I have heard that in antiquity scholars followed their own standards; contemporary scholars follow the standards of others. Therefore, sages and worthies in teaching others did not have them link together phrases or write literary compositions simply that they might be successful in the examination or acquire rank and emolument.[19] Rather it was necessary that they apprehend the principle in things, extend their knowledge, make their thoughts true, set their minds in the right, cultivate their persons, and then by extension establish harmony in their households and govern their states well in order to bring tranquility to the empire. Only then was their learning what it should be.[20]

Here, it is the scholar, not the emperor, who is admonished to follow the "way of greater learning." In olden times scholars, together with sage-rulers, had followed the "way" and thereby brought about the golden age; implied here, of course, is the idea that by following the principles set forth in the *Ta-hsüeh,* scholars as well as rulers of the Sung could help to bring about another golden age in Chinese history.

Clearly, Chu Hsi had already done much thinking about the *Ta-hsüeh* as early as 1162. But it is not clear when exactly he began to commit his reading and interpretation of the text to writing. In a letter from 1167[21] to Hsü Shun-chih[o] (12th c.),[22] a young follower of his, Chu Hsi declares:

Recently my explanation of the *Ta-hsüeh* has been revised in a number of places. There were many extremely vulgar points in my earlier work. In general my ability was not up to it; I just wrote without care. I myself was confused and so confused others—how terribly dreadful![23]

This remark indicates that Chu Hsi had been writing down his thoughts on the *Ta-hsüeh* for some time prior to 1167. It seems likely that these writings had circulated, although it is possible that they were simply Chu's notes on the text for use in lecturing. Whether these writings might have constituted a manuscript, in very preliminary form, of the *Chang-chü* remains a question.

We do know definitely, however, that by 1174, at the age of forty-five, he had completed or nearly completed a draft of the *Ta-hsüeh chang-chü;* and this he circulated among trusted friends, seeking suggestions for its improvement. In a letter to Lü Tsu-ch'ien[P] (1137-1181)[24] from 1174[25] he writes:

> I am forwarding to you a copy of the *Chung-yung chang-chü.* (This is a draft so I trust that you will show it to no one.) There is also a *Hsiang-shuo*[q];[26] it is lengthy so I have not had the time [to complete it]. I will send it to you later. If you see questionable passages I would be grateful if you would point them out to me. I am also sending the *Ta-hsüeh chang-chü;* it too has a *Hsiang-shuo,* which I will send later.[27]

Fifteen years passed from the writing of this letter to the completion of the preface of the *Ta-hsüeh chang-chü* in 1189. It is conceivable too, as already noted, that the manuscript mentioned here had been begun much earlier than the year of the letter, possibly earlier than 1167. Thus, prior to 1189 Chu Hsi had already worked on the *Ta-hsüeh chang-chü* a minimum of fifteen years.

In 1176 we find Chu already engaged in a revision of his *Chang-chü* manuscript. In a letter[28] to Chang Nan-hsüan[r] (1133-1180)[29] he comments:

> As for the *Chung-yung chang-chü* and the *Ta-hsüeh chang-chü* I have . . . revised both of them once through; I will make copies and forward them to you. I am aware, however, that they still contain passages that should be deleted.[30]

There can be little doubt that during the fifteen-year period from the first mention of a draft to the prefacing of the *Ta-hsüeh chang-chü* in 1189 Chu Hsi devoted much of his time and mental energy to improving his understanding of the *Ta-hsüeh* text; during this period it would appear that he made numerous revisions of his *Chang-chü* and solicited suggestions for improvements from his most respected colleagues.

The completion of the preface in 1189, however, by no means marked the end of Chu Hsi's work on the *Chang-chü.* Indeed it is recorded in his *nien-p'u* that he was still revising chapter six on "making the thoughts true" three days before his death on April 23, 1200.[31] Comments in the *Chu-tzu yü-lei*[S32] and letters in the *Hui-an hsien-sheng Chu Wen-kung wen-chi*[t], many datable to years after 1189, allow us to observe Chu Hsi's continued openness to revision and doubts about his own interpretation of the *Ta-hsüeh.*[33] When asked, for example, just a year after writing the preface to the *Chang-chü,* whether his explanation of the *Ta-hsüeh* was final or not, Chu responded:

> At the moment I myself would say that it is reliable. I only fear that in a few years I might again deem it unreliable. This is something out of my control.[34]

According to such comments it would seem that Chu Hsi was not as "satisfied in his own mind" about his interpretation of the *Ta-hsüeh* in the *Chang-chü* as the *nien-p'u* statement cited above might suggest.[35]

In fact, even years after he wrote the preface, Chu's interest in the *Ta-hsüeh* never ceased, and doubts about his own understanding of the text never completely disappeared. In a remark made sometime after his sixty-fifth year:

> When I read through my explanation of the *Chung-yung* I have no serios doubts. But when I read the *Ta-hsüeh* I do have doubts; I am not very satisfied with it and therefore continue to revise it.[36]

And even on those few occasions when he does show some degree of satisfaction with his understanding of the text he is quick to admit that with reconsideration and the passing of time satisfaction may easily turn to dissatisfaction. In a letter to P'an Tuan-shu[u37] he writes:

> This year I have revised various texts of mine once through; the revisions in the *Ta-hsüeh* have been particularly numerous. Compared to my earlier work on the *Ta-hsüeh* the revised work is extremely detailed and comprehensive, yet I do not know how I will view it in the future.[38]

Such comments reveal Chu Hsi's commitment to further inquiry on the text and his lack of inhibition about revising earlier held opinions. That the truth is in the text, he seems never to doubt; he doubts only his ability to appreciate the truth fully and thus always is willing to reconsider his understanding of the text. In a letter to his most prominent disciple Huang Kan[v] (1152-1221)[39] sometime after the prefacing in 1189, Chu argues that only a sage or an idiot is unwilling to revise:

> I myself believed that the *Ta-hsüeh* I had previously written was the final edition. Recently, I have discussed it with several people and feel that the section on 'having the proper measure in one's own mind to measure the minds of others'[40] still contains unrefined passages. The writing basically is extremely difficult to understand—one who arrives at an interpretation and sticks to it for one's whole life, if not a sage is an idiot.[41]

It is apparent then that even after writing the preface for the *Ta-hsüeh chang-chü* in 1189, which would seem to signal the completion of his work on the text, Chu Hsi never left the *Ta-hsüeh* for long. In a comment made near the end of his life at the age of sixty-nine Chu speaks poignantly of his untiring devotion to the brief work:[42]

> I have expended tremendous effort on the *Ta-hsüeh.* [Ssu-ma] Wen-kung[w] wrote the [*Tzu-chih*] *t'ung-chien*[x] and said that the strength and spirit of his whole life were exhausted on that work. The same may be said of my work on the *Ta-hsüeh;* I did not expend the same strength on the *Lun-yu,* the *Meng-tzu,* or the *Chung-yung*[y].[43]

II.

In his life-long quest for the truth then, Chu Hsi demonstrated an 'openness' to the *Ta-hsüeh* text, a willingness to modify or abandon earlier views as the truth imbedded in the text became increasingly apparent to him. Chu felt keenly that he had to discover for himself—no matter how much time it took—the truth manifested in the work. As might be expected, this sort of personal, religious approach to the *Ta-hsüeh* led to an understanding of the text that was quite new, an understanding that broke significantly with the traditional Han through T'ang readings of the text in at least three important respects.

First, the general orientation of Chu's interpretation of the *Ta-hsüeh* is fundamentally different from that of the standard pre-Sung interpretations of Cheng Hsüan[z] (127-200) and K'ung Ying-ta[aa] (574-648) found in the *Li chi chu*[ab] and the *Li chi cheng-i*[ac]. Cheng and K'ung viewed the text primarily as a political handbook for the use of the ruler alone. According to them, the book was entitled "*Ta-hsüeh*," "because it recorded extensive learning which could be used in the administration of government."[44] Chu, in rather sharp contrast, sees the *Ta-hsüeh* as a guide for self-cultivation and the ordering of society, for the use of all men, not only the ruler; he interprets the title to mean "learning for adults." Chu briefly proposes this gloss for the title in his *Chang-chü* commentary and *Ta-hsüeh huo-wen*[ad], but in his lecture on the *Ta-hsüeh* to Emperor Ning-tsung in 1194[45] he explains the significance of the book's title in some detail:

> '*Ta-hsüeh*[a], refers to *ta-jen chih hsüeh*[ae]. In the education of antiquity there was learning for children (*hsiao-tzu chih hsüeh*[af]) and learning for adults. Learning for children consisted in the chores of cleaning and sweeping, in the formalities of polite conversation and good manners, and in the refinements of ritual, music, archery, charioteering, calligraphy, and mathematics. Learning for adults consisted in the Way of probing principle, of cultivating the person, of establishing harmony in the household, of governing the state well, and of bringing tranquility to the empire. What this work treats is the learning for adults; hence it is named '*Ta-hsüeh*.'[46]

Chu Hsi thus greatly enlarges the *Ta-hsüeh's* readership, for he finds in the text a Way of cultivating the self and governing others that is to be studied by everyone, not just by political leaders. According to Chu, the *Ta-hsüeh's* message begins with the premise that all men are capable of perfecting themselves morally and, indeed, must perfect themselves morally.

Second, Chu finds in the *Ta-hsüeh* a declaration of the ontological assumption and aim behind the self-cultivation process. The opening line of the text reads: "*Ta-hsüeh chih tao tsai ming ming-te*[ag]" and is understood by Chu to mean: "The way of greater learning lies in keeping the inborn luminous Virtue unobscured."[47] This reading of the line differs dramatically from the pre-Sung interpretation. "The way of great learning lies in manifesting luminous virtue."[48] This earlier interpretation of the phrase *ming ming-te*—"to manifest luminous virtue"—is addressed primarily to the ruler: he is to teach his subjects morality by manifesting outwardly his own virtue throughout the land;

following his example, the people too will act virtuously. By contrast, Chu Hsi takes *ming ming-te*—"to keep the inborn luminous Virtue unobscured"—to be a process of inner self-perfection applicable to every man, not only to the ruler. Just as he believes the term *ta-hsüeh* to refer to learning for all, so too he sees *ming ming-te* as a process relevant to all.

For Chu Hsi, *ming-te* is not outwardly-expressed virtue or virtuous conduct, but rather the originally virtuous mind and nature with which every man is endowed at birth, and which may become obscured by material endowment or human desires. "To keep unobscured" or to *ming* the *ming-te* is the goal of the self-cultivation process; each individual is to strive to maintain or to regain contact with his originally good mind and nature. And by keeping his *ming-te* unobscured he may then cause others, through his grace and good example, to renew their *ming-te*; this is what is meant by "renewing the people" (*hsin min*[ah]).[49] In his commentary on the *Ta-hsüeh* passage Chu explains *ming-te* in some detail:

> '*Ming-te*[ai], is what man acquires from heaven; it is unprejudiced, spiritual, and completely unmuddled and thereby embodies the multitudinous manifestations of principle and responds to the myriad affairs. But it may be restrained by the endowment of *ch'i* or concealed by human desire, so at times it will become obscured. Never, however, does its original luminosity cease. Therefore the student should look to the light that emanates from it and seek to keep it unobscured, thereby restoring its original condition.[50]

This explanation caused considerable controversy among Chu Hsi's disciples[51] and later Confucians of the Sung and Yüan periods.[52] They were anxious to determine whether Chu identified *ming-te* with the mind or with the nature. In fact, the explanation here seems to refer to an entity that includes both the mind and the nature. Terms such as "unprejudiced" (*hsü*[aj]) and "spiritual" (*ling*[ak]) clearly refer to the mind. For example, in chapter five of the *Yü-lei*, Chu says, "The unprejudiced and the spiritual are by nature the original essence of the mind."[53] Furthermore, it is the mind, not the nature, that embodies the multitudinous manifestations of principle according to Chu Hsi's teachings.[54] On the other hand, his discussion of human nature in chapter twelve of the *Yü-lei* is remarkably similar in terminology and spirit to parts of his explanation of *ming-te*. This similarity leads one to believe that *ming-te* is to be identified with the nature:

> Man's nature is originally luminous, but it is like a precious pearl immersed in dirty water where its luminosity cannot be seen. Remove the dirty water and the precious pearl is luminous of itself as before. If the individual could appreciate that it is human desire that conceals [the luminosity] this would bring enlightenment.[55]

Also, Chu implies in the *Yü-lei* that the nature and *ming-te* are the same by identifying each with the virtues of benevolence, righteousness, propriety, and wisdom.[56]

It would appear, then, that Chu Hsi does not understand *ming-te* in terms of either mind or nature exclusively. To appreciate his understanding of the term we must remember that for him the mind embraces both the nature and the emotions, as it had earlier in Chang Tsai's[al] (1020-1077) philosophy.[57] For Chu, the heaven-given Virtue (*ming-te*) refers to an entity including both the original mind, that is, the mind that shares in the mind of heaven and is thus unprejudiced, spiritual, and unobscured, and the perfectible luminous nature within the mind. From his point of view to keep the *ming-te* unobscured is to preserve the integrity of the original mind, a process that naturally implies the realization of the luminous nature.[58]

According to Chu, the *Ta-hsüeh* prescribes the precise means of cultivating oneself: *ko wu*[am]. This is the third respect in which Chu's understaning of the text differs from earlier interpretations. In the opening lines of the work we read:

> Those [of antiquity] who wished to cultivate themselves first set their minds in the right; wishing to set their minds in the right, they first made their thoughts true; wishing to make their thoughts true, they first extended their knowledge to the utmost
>
>   (*chih ch'i chih*[an]).[59]

The line that immediately follows is: "*chih chih tsai tsai ko wu*[ao]." *Ko wu*, the final two characters of the line, is a philologically ambiguous term which has been interpreted in a variety of ways since the Han. Cheng Hsuan glossed it in this way:

> '*Ko*' means *lai*[ap], 'to come.' '*Wu*' is the same as *shih*[aq], 'affair.'

And he explained the line:

> When one's knowledge of the good is profound, one attracts (*lai*) good things. When one's knowledge of evil is profound, one attracts evil things. In other words, things come to a man according to what he is fond of.[60]

In this explanation, *ko wu*—the sort of thing attracted—is a consequence of *chih chih*—the sort of knowledge that is extended. K'ung Ying-ta, in his *Li chi cheng-i,* concurred in Cheng's reading of the line. Chu Hsi, however, following his spiritual master, Ch'eng I, understands *ko wu* differently:

> '*Ko*' means *chih*[ar], 'to arrive at,' 'to reach.' '*Wu*' is the same as *shih,* 'affair.' '*ko wu*' is 'to reach to the utmost the principle in affairs and things.'[61]

And his explanation of the line "*chih chih tsai ko wu*" is startlingly different from the explanations of Cheng and K'ung, because he takes *ko wu* to be the means of *chih chih* rather than its consequence:

> we wish to extend our knowledge to the utmost we must probe thoroughly the principle in those things that we encounter.[62]

In Chu's reading of the text then, *ko wu* becomes the first step, the foundation of the self-cultivation process. That is to to say, only through the apprehension of the principle in things may an individual gradually perfect himself, thereby "keeping his inborn luminous Virtue unobscured." Implicit in this method of self-cultivation is the belief that all things in the universe share a common principle.[63] Thus understanding of the priniciple in external things leads ultimately to an understanding of the principle within oneself. And since principal in man is identical to his nature,[64] understanding of that principle leads to complete self-realization.

Chu's most eloquent statement of *ko wu* and *chih chih* is found in the so-called "supplementary chapter" that he inserted into the *Ta-hsüeh* text. According to Chu, originally there had been a chapter in the *Ta-hsüeh* elucidating these two critical terms, but it has been lost. He therefore "reconstructed" the chapter in 134 characters, drawing on ideas previously suggested by Ch'eng I. He introduces the chapter:

> It would appear that the . . . fifth chapter of commentary [by Tseng Tzu] elucidated the meaning of 'fully apprehending the principle in things' and 'the extension of knowledge,' but it is now lost. Recently, I made bold to use the ideas of Ch'eng-tzu to supplement it as follows.

The chapter reads:

> What is meant by the 'extension of knowledge lies in fully apprehending the principle in things' is, that if we wish to extend out knowledge to the utmost we must probe thoroughly the principle in those things that we encounter. It would seem that every man's intellect is possessed of the capacity for knowing and that everything in the world is possessed of principle. But, to the extent that principle is not yet thoroughly probed, man's knowledge is not yet fully realized. Hence, the first step of instruction in greater learning must teach the student, whenever he encounters anything at all in the world, to build upon what is already known to him about principle and to probe still further, so that he seeks to reach the limit. After exerting himself in this way for a long time, he will one day become enlightened and thoroughly understand [principle]; then, the manifest and the hidden, the subtle and the obvious qualities of all things will all be known, and the mind, in its whole sbstance and vast operations, will be completely illuminated. This is called 'fully apprehending the principle in things.' This is called 'the completion of knowledge.'[65]

As might be expected, from the moment the *Ta-hsüeh chang-chü* began to circulate until the present day serious questions have been raised about the authority of the supplementary chapter. But the authority of the chapter is not an issue here. What must be asked is why Chu Hsi, to use his own words, "took the liberty . . . of filling in the lacunae"[66] in the *Ta-hsüeh* text. After all, the *Ta-hsüeh* was a canonical texrt. How could he, a mere scholar, meddle with it?

Chu must have been convinced that after years of struggling with the text he had come to an appreciaiation of its profound meaning. He had grasped the truth manifested there by the ancient sages. But, the truth had been difficult to understand since some of the sages' words had been lost. He dared to "fill the lacunae" only because doing so, he thought, would help to make the truth as evident as it once had been. He was not violating tthe text; he carefully noted what were his additions. Chu composed the supplementary chapter in his own words and those of Ch'eng I, but the truth he exressed was that of the sages of the past.

Notes

1. For example, see Chu-tzu yü-lei[s] Ch'uan-ching t'ang[as] ed., 1880, (hereafter *Yü-lei*), 10.4b.

2. *Yü-lei* 14.10a.

3. Throughout this article ages are given in Chinese *sui*; the Western equivalent may be obtained by subtracting one from the number of *sui*.

4. On the *Chu-tzu nien-p'u*[at] ("Chronological Record of Master Chu's Life") see Conrad Schirokauer, "Chu Hsi's Political Career: A Study in Ambivalence," in Arthur F. Wright and Denis Twitchett, eds., *Confucian Personalities*, Stanford, Stanford University Press, 1962, pp. 354–355, footnote 8.

5. *Chu-tzu nien-p'u, Ts'ung-shu chi-ch'eng* ed., (hereafter *Nien-p'u*), p. 168. For each of the Four Books Chu wrote a *Huo-wen;* together they are known as the *Ssu-shu huo-wen*[au].

6. Actually there is evidence indicating that Chu was familiar with the text much earlier. According to the *Nien-p'u* (p. 3) Chu was first instructed in the *Ta-hsüeh* by his father Chu Sung[av] (1097-1143) in 1140 at the age of eleven. (See Chu Sung's short biographical notice together with a listing of relevant biographical material in Ch'ang Pi-te[aw] et al., comps., *Sung-jen chuan-chi'tzu-liao so-yin*[ax], Taipei, Ting wen shu-chü, 1974-1976—as . . . SJCC-pp. 569-570.)

And in 1156, as a subprefectural registrar in T'ung-an[ay], Fukien, Chu Hsi wrote:

Learning begins with knowledge. Only the apprehension of the principle in things is sufficient to extend that knowledge, and when knowledge is extended the thoughts become true and the mind set in the right; in this way the order described in the *Ta-hsüeh* is carried out thoroughly and without difficulty.

(*Hui-an hsien-sheng Chu Wen-kung wen-chi*[t], *Ssu-pu ts'ung-k'an* ed.—hereafter *Wen-chi*—77.4b-5a.

But neither the *Nien-p'u* entry nor the *Wen-chi* comment reveals a particularly strong commitment to the text yet.

7. *Nien-p'u*, pp. 18-19. Schirokauer, "Chu Hsi's Political Career," p. 166, mentions this memorial.

8. The terms that appear here, "the apprehension of the principle in things," "the extension of knowledge,"

"the thoughts will become true," and "the mind will become set in the right" are all concepts important to the *Ta-hsüeh*.

9. "Be discriminating and undivided" and "holding fast the Mean" are allusions to *Shang shu*[az], *Shih-san ching chu-shu*[ba], 1815, 4.8b. I follow James Legge's translation, *The Chinese Classics,* 5 vols., 3rd ed., Hong Kong, Hong Kong University Press, 1960, vol. III, 61-62 (3.61-62). Here Chu Hsi paraphrases the *Shang shu;* I have modified Legge's translation to accord with Chu's changes.

10. *Wen-chi* 11.3a-4a.

11. *Nien-p'u*, pp. 19-20. These three memorials of 1163 are briefly described in Schirokauer, "Chu Hsi's Political Career," pp. 166-167.

12. *Ta-hsüeh,* "The Classic of Confucius," par. 6.

13. "Harmony is established in the household," "the state becomes well-governed," and "the empire becomes tranquil" are all important terms from the *Ta-hsüeh*.

14. The idea expressed in the memorial up to this point is straight from *Ta-hsüeh,* "The Classic of Confucius," pars. 4-5.

15. This is a definition of *ko wu*[am] suggested first by Ch'eng I; see, for example, *Ho-nan Ch'eng-shih i-shu*[bb], *Kuo-hsüeh chi-pen ts'ung-shu* ed., p. 347 and p. 209.

16. A direct quote from *Shang shu* 4.8b; Legge 3.61-62.

17. *Wen-chi* 13.1a-b.

18. In *Nien-p'u*, p. 218, it is recorded that in December of 1194 Chu Hsi went to Yu-shan to give a lecture at the district school; the district magistrate, a certain Ssu-ma Mai[bc], then published the lecture notes (*chiang-i*[bd]) to make them known to all. Po Shou-i[be], *Ts'ung-cheng chi chiang-hsüeh chung te Chu Hsi*[bf], Peking, Kuo-li Pei-'ing yen-chiu yuan, 1931, p. 37, cites this *Nien-p'u* entry.

19. This is criticism of the circumstances prevailing during Chu Hsi's lifetime.

20. "Yü-shan chiang-i[bg]" in *Wen-chi* 74. 19b.

21. This letter is cited in *Nien-p'u*, p. 169.

22. See a short biographical notice in SJCC, pp. 2152-2153.

23. *Wen-chi* 39.17b.

24. A biographical notice may be found in SJCC, pp. 1212-1215.

25. This letter is cited in *Nien-p'u*, p. 169.

26. Nothing of this title survives. However, in *Nien-p'u*, p. 169, Wang Mou-hung suggests that the *Hsiang-shuo* is a draft version of the *Huo-wen*.

27. *Wen-chi* 33.26a.

28. This letter appears in *Nien-p'u*, p. 169.

29. See his biography in SJCC, pp. 2268-2271.

30. *Wen-chi* 31. 16b.

31. *Nien-p'u*, p. 226.

32. The *Yü-lei* in one hundred and forty *chüan* was compiled in 1270 by Li Ching-te[bh] (fl. 1263) from five already existing collections of conversations between Chu and his disciples; these collections were based on the notes recorded by the disciples. Ichikawa Yasuji's[bi] "Shushi gorui zakki[bj]," *Jinbun kagakuka kiyo*[bk], 21 (1959), 137-184, discusses the background of the *Yü-lei* and its compilation and provides a chart (based on the preface to the *Yü-lei*) for dating the conversations recorded in the text.

33. Comments about revision of the *Ta-hsüeh* appear, for example, in letters dating from 1190 and 1196 (*Wen-chi* 62.1a and 63.23a); these letters are referred to in *Nien-p'u*, p. 66.

34. *Yü-lei* 14.9a. This comment is recorded by Chu's pupil, Ch'en Ch'un[bl] (1159-1223) (SJCC, pp. 2471-2472), whose notes according to the *Yü-lei* preface date from the years 1190 and 1199. Given the tone of the question, I would say that this comment was made rather soon after the completion of the *Chang-chü* in 1189. Ch'ien Mu[bm], in his *Chu-tzu hsin hsüeh-an*[bn], 5 vols., Taipei, San-min shu-chu, 1971, vol. IV, 214-215, also dates it to 1190 rather than 1199.

35. In a letter to Ying Jen-chung[bo] (SJCC, p. 4092) Chu Hsi comments:

> I have repeatedly revised the *Ta-hsüeh* and the *Chung-yung;* still they are not perfect. And only now does the *Ta-hsüeh* seem to have somewhat fewer defects. The principles of the work are explained best when discussed orally; when I put them on paper I am able to get at only a very small percentage of them
>
> (*Wen-chi* 54.11a-b).

There is no way to date this letter precisely, for it is extremely brief and provides absolutely no internal evidence. Ch'ien Mu, however, on completely unconvincing grounds, argues that it must have been written sometime after Chu left his prefectural post in Chang-chou[bp] in Fukien in 1191; see *Chu-tzu hsin hsüen-an*, vol. IV, 216. Although I do not agree with Ch'ien's line of reasoning in the *Hsin hsüeh-an*, because of the reference to repeated revisions, I too would date the letter rather imprecisely to Chu's later years.

36. *Yü-lei* 19.9b. This comment is from the record of Wang Kuo[bq] (SJCC, pp. 194-195); according to the *Yü-lei* preface his record contains remarks made during the period from 1194 until Chu's death.

37. SJCC, p. 3636.

38. *Wen-chi* 50.4a. This letter cannot be dated precisely; the only clue we have to its date is in *Nien-p'u*, p. 67, where Wang Mou-hung states that it was written sometime after 1183.

39. His biography may be found in SJCC, pp. 2865-2866.

40. *Ta-hsüeh*, "The Commentary of Tseng Tzu," X. 2.

41. *Hui-an hsien-sheng Chu Wen-kung hsü-chi*[br], *Ssu-pu ts'ung-k'an* ed., 1.3b. This last line derives from *Lun-yü* 17/3; Legge, 1.318.

42. From the notes taken in 1198 by Kuo Yu-jen[bs].

43. *Yü-lei* 14.10a. Cf. also *Yü-lei* 14.9b-10a.

44. *Li chi chu-shu*[bt], *Shih-san ching chu-shu*, 1815, 60.1a; this is a modification of a translation found in the notes on the "Title of the Work" in Legge, 1.355.

45. When Kuang-tsung abdicated and Ning-tsung became emperor, Chu received an imperial decree requesting that he present a lecture on the *Ta-hsüeh* to the new ruler. For a brief account of Chu's forty-day lectureship at court see Schirokauer, "Chu Hsi's Political Career," pp. 182-183. The complete record of this lecture on the *Ta-hsüeh* is preserved in *Wen-chi* 15.1a-20b.

46. *Wen-chi* 15.1a. In setting down his views on the educational system of the ancients in his eloquent preface to the *Ta-hsüeh chang-chü*, Chu again explains *ta-hsüeh* as learning for adults. Thus I choose to render *hsiao-hsüeh*[bu] as "lesser learning," that is, the more basic curriculum for children and *ta-hsüeh* as "greater learning," the more advanced curriculum for adults.

47. *Ta-hsüeh*, "The Classic of Confucius," par. 1.

48. *Li chi chu-shu* 60.1a.

49. See *Ta-hsüeh*, "The Classic of Confucius," par. 1 and Chu Hsi's commentary on it.

50. This is from the *Chang-chü* commentary to *Ta-hsüeh*, "The Classic of Confucius," par. 1.

51. See, for example, questions put to Chu Hsi in *Yü-lei* 14.11b-18a.

52. See their discussions about the nature of *ming-te* in *Ssu-shu ta-ch'üan*[bv], Japanese ed. of 1626 (based on Yung-lo ed. of 1415), 1.1b-3a.

53. *Yü-lei* 5.5b. Also, in *Yü-lei* 5.3b, when asked whether the seat of the spiritual is the mind or the nature, Chu responds: "The seat of the spiritual is the mind alone; it is not the nature. Nature is simply principle." Again in *Yü-lei* 5.6b we read: "Although the mind is a distinct entity, it is unprejudiced and therefore able to embody the multitudinous manifestations of principle."

54. For example, see *Yü-lei* 5.6b (cited in the previous footnote).

55. *Yü-lei* 12.8a; Fung Yu-lan, *History of Chinese Philosophy* (tr. by Derk Bodde), 2 vols., Princeton, Princeton University Press, 1953, vol. II, 560 (with modification). And in *Yü-lei* 4.17b we encounter a similar passage:

> Once there is such-and-such a manifestation of principle there is such-and-such a *ch'i*[bw]. Once there is such-and-such a *ch'i* there is necessarily

such-and-such a manifestation of principle. It's just that he who receives clear *ch'i* is a sage or worthy—he is like a precious pearl lying in crystal clear water. And he who receives turbid *ch'i* is an idiot or a degenerate—he is like a pearl lying in turbid water. What is called 'keeping the inborn luminous Virtue unobscured' is the process of reaching into the turbid water and wiping clean this pearl.

In this way, the principle or the nature becomes luminous as before.

56. The Sung Neo-Confucians, in accord with the Mencian view of the original goodness of human nature, believed that human nature is comprised of the four virtues (e.g., *Yü-lei* 5.2a and 6.9a). In 14.13b *ming-te* too is said to be comprised of these four virtues:

Men all originally embody *ming-te*. Within the *te* there exist the four virtues, benevolence, righteousness, propriety, and wisdom. It is only that they are confused by external things and thus become obscured, and so they all decay. Therefore, in the way of greater learning it is necessary first to keep the *ming-te* unobscured.

And again, in 14.12a, Chu Hsi is asked whether *ming-te* is the nature of benevolence, righteousness, propriety and wisdom (*jen i li chih chih hsing*[bx]), to which he responds, "Yes, it is." See also *Yü-lei* 14.22a-b.

57. See *Chang-tzu ch'üan-shu*[by], *Kuo-hsüeh chi-pen ts'ung-shu* ed., p. 290.

58. The hitherto ignored importance of the mind in Chu Hsi's thought is discussed at great length in Ch'ien Mu's *Chu-tzu hsin hsüeh-an* and in Tu Wei-ming's review of Ch'ien's book in *The Journal of Asian Studies,* vol. XXXIII, no. 3 (May, 1974), 441-454. Tu, in commenting upon Chu's understanding of the mind, says (p. 446).

In his discussion of the human mind (*jen-hsin*[bz]) and ontological mind (*tao-hsin*[ca]), he signified that the human mind, conditioned by the 'self-centeredness of the material being' (*hsing-ch'i chih ssu*[cb]), can be transformed through moral cultivation to become identified with the ontological mind. Such an identification enables the ontological mind, which is the true basis of humanity, to manifest the 'heavenly principle' in human affairs. It is therefore important for one to cultivate the mind so that, despite the inherent limitation of the physical self, it can 'embody' principle, which is the ultimate ground of human nature.

This explanation of the mind is helpful in understanding Chu's interpretation of *ming-te*.

59. *Ta-hsüeh,* "The Classic of Confucius," par. 4.

60. *Li chi chu-shu* 60.1b; cf. D. C. Lau, "A Note on Ke Wu," *Bulletin of the School of Oriental and African Studies,* 30 (1967), 353.

61. From the *Chang-chü* commentary on *Ta-hsüeh,* "The Classic of Confucius," par. 4.

62. *Ta-hsüeh,* "The Commentary of Tseng Tzu," V (the supplementary chapter of Chu Hsi).

63. Indeed, such a belief was central to the Ch'eng-Chu philosophical system. See, for example, Ch'eng I's comments in *Ho-nan Ch'eng-shih i-shu,* p. 214 and p. 3, and in *I-ch'uan I-chuan*[cc], *Ssu-pu pei-yao* ed., 3.3b. In *Yü-lei* 1.2a Chu praises Ch'eng I's view.

64. Man's nature as principle is discussed in *Yü-lei* chapters 4 and 5, *passim.*

65. *Ta-hsüeh,* "The Commentary of Tseng Tzu," V.

66. "*Ta-hsüeh chang-chü hsü*[cd]" in *Ssu-shu chi-chu*[ce], *Ssu-pu pei-yao* ed., 2b-3a.

John Borthrong (essay date 1987)

SOURCE: "Chu Hsi's Ethics: *Jen* and *Ch'eng,*" in *Journal of Chinese Philosophy,* Vol. 14, No. 2, June, 1987, pp. 161-178.

[*In the following essay, Borthrong contends that although Chu Hsi's views on ethics have been criticized as unoriginal and derivative, they display an ingenious approach based on the concept of humanity. Borthrong goes on to explore how Chu Hsi's conception of* jen *and* ch'eng *contribute to his views on the development of one's full humanity.*]

INTRODUCTION

For over a decade Chu Hsi's thought has fascinated me—in a positive sense. I further think that Master Chu deserves to be considered second only to Master K'ung in the entire history of Chinese thought. Yet Chu remains remarkably unknown and understudied in the West—and even until recently relatively unstudied in modern China. That trend is now reversing itself slowly. It would, in itself, be a fascinating study to examine the historical causes for the comparative lack of interest in Chu in the 20th century, both in the East and in the West. The case of China is comparatively clear: Chu is often seen as reparesenting all the negative qualities of China's early modern past. In short, he is the paradigmatic feudal, conservative oppressor of creativity and freedom. Western reactions are perplexing and probably have more to do with the spotty development of Chinese studies in the West than with any intrinsic revulsion to Chu Hsi in particular and to the neo-Confucians in general. One only has to note the veritable renaissance of excellent studies of Wang Yang-ming (and other Ming thinkers) to prove that point. But intellectually no one can today deny the crying need to revisit and re-evaluate Chu Hsi and his monumental intellectual achievement.

Yet there are neglected puzzles within puzzles in the study of Chu Hsi. For instance, why has so little emphasis been placed or research devoted to what Chu himself would have considered the heart of his system: ethical reflection, conduct and its theoretical elaboration? Surely Chu Hsi was an ethicist first and foremost. He was also a subtle cosmologist, classical scholar and a talented bureaucrat. No one would deny these facts for a minute. Perhaps the reason for the undue neglect of Chu's ethical theories can be ascribed to the often heard comments that his ethics were unoriginal, derivitive, stereotyped, in a word, rather dull when compared to his theories of li^a and $ch'i^b$. On that reading what is interesting in Chu Hsi is not what he would have considered important. Rather Chu is interesting for his metaphysics and cosmology, not for his development of the Confucian ethical notions of jen^c and $ch'eng^d$.

I have difficulty with this line of reasoning for a number of reasons. The first major objection is actually rather mundane. Given the fact, and we will let it stand for a moment for the sake of argument, that there are no major modern studies of Chu Hsi's ethics, how then can we accept this common criticism that his ethics are derivitive or of secondary intellectual importance? And beyond the lack of studies of Chu Hsi's ethics, we know even less about his Sung predecessors. For instance, and it is another minor scandal, we do not yet have a decent monographic study of Shao Yung or Chang Tsai. And even the literature on Chou Tun-i and the Ch'eng brothers is hardly what one would call voluminous. How we can say Chu Hsi is derivitive when we do not know much about what he is purported to have borrowed? I for one would like to see the evidence prior to accepting the theory.

The second major objection is no doubt related to the first. Would it make one bit of difference if Chu Hsi derived all his ethical theories from earlier Sung thinkers? People have long recognized that Chu's genius in thought came from his re-arrangement and novel modification of previous Confucian conceptuality and sensibilities. His theory of $ch'i^b$, for instance, clearly owes a huge debt to Chang Tsai; yet the genius of Chu is what he did with an inherited intellectual vocabulary and sensibility. Novelty comes in many forms—not all of them related to the creation of novel intellectual vocabulary. And further, what else could we reasonably expect from a Confucian thinker, someone devoted to a profound veneration of the past? One ought to remember the Confucian burden was often to be creative transmitters rather than solipistic creators of culture. In short, it seems what we really have in Chu Hsi is a case of stunning 'creative fidelity' to the Confucian tradition in general and to the Sung era of that tradition in particular. And this 'creative fidelity' most certainly includes his ethical reflections as well as his cosmological speculation.

Frankly, as in so many aspects of Chu Hsi's thought, I feel that his ethics is interesting for its re-arrangement and refinement of traditional material. He surely did not invent jen^c and $ch'eng^d$. Yet his nuanced consideration of these terms is novel and stimulating. We should not let the antiquity of these terms obscure the careful elaboration of jen and $ch'eng$ in his thought. Nor should we forget what

Mou Tsung-san has taught us. The genius of Chu's thought depends on a careful analysis of what it means to be human and how to develop this full humanity in an ethical sense. It is indeed a moral cosmology. Mou's massive reinterpretation of the development of Chu's thought focuses our attention yet again on the ethical, moral core of his system. Other areas are important, and here again Mou has instructed a whole generation of scholars, *but,* to echo St. Paul, without jen^c and $ch'eng^d$ the whole symphony would be empty, vain and dissonant.

The closely linked virtues of jen^c and $ch'eng^d$ represent the apex of Chu Hsi's plan for self-cultivation, and, in a sense, are the twin foci of his whole philosophic enterprise. As symbols of a perfected life, jen and $ch'eng$ represent the hoped-for outcome of life. Structurally, they are more difficult to place. It is clear that they are not specific parts of Chu Hsi's moral anthropology of mind, nature, and feeling or of his meta-system (which resembles most closely the Western notion of cosmology) of li^a, $ch'i^b$, $t'ai$-chi^e and $ming^f$. However, these ethical notions inform all parts of Chu Hsi's system. No notions better express the kind of inner life and outer behavior the Neo-Confucians sought to cultivate. Jen and $ch'eng$ both express most forcefully Chu Hsi's organic vision of the world. Jen, as a supreme ethical goal, demands that a person live a life of deepened intersubjectivity: a person must learn to understand and empathize with his world. But a student on the road to sagehood must do even more, and for this reason, $ch'eng$ is an important notion for Chu Hsi. A person must actively realize jen, which is one way of defining Chu Hsi's understanding of $ch'eng$.

But why does Chu Hsi seem to employ *two* terms for supreme exemplification? One is tempted to offer two suggestions. The first is that Chu Hsi was always interested in demonstrating the processive quality of life. By stating that $ch'eng$ is the process by which jen is realized, jen is protected from being interpreted in a static, substantialistic manner. In his own way, Chu Hsi was quite worried about the problem of false reification or substantialization: jen is never a completed thing—it is always a subtly shifting response to the inexhaustible fecundity of tao^g as unceasing creativity. Second, and closely related to the first, was Chu Hsi's desire to highlight the relational traits of the universe. Jen might well be considered the principle of principles that links all the others together in an organic unity. It is a principle of spontaneous mutual empathy that reaches out of itself to another, and Chu Hsi seeks to capture this expansive quality of relationality through his exposition of $ch'eng$ as self-actualization. A person who is fully cultivated realizes that the thrust of being, his or her very essence, is jen, which literally forces respect for others. The essence of self-actualization through self-cultivation issues in the virtue of shared humanity. Metaphorically at least, jen and $ch'eng$ serve to mediate all the various elements of Chu Hsi's system. In doing so, they express his deepest conviction that the world is a process of creativity in which human beings are necessarily related through their common humanity: whether or not he was successful in articulating this vision, Chu Hsi evokes a sense of a moral metaphysics.

Jen and *ch'eng* can therefore provide a valuable bridge between Chu Hsi's moral anthropology and the other segments of his philosophy. When the student has undergone the arduous process of self-cultivation, from first choosing to establish reverence to the practice of *ko-wu*[h], certain virtues become manifest. For Chu Hsi, there are two cardinal virtues. We will first discuss *jen* and then conclude with a discussion of *ch'eng*.

JEN

Jen is the most famous of the Confucian and Neo-Confucian virtues. As with so many other key terms there have been numerous English translations of *jen*.[1] But as with the Christian term *agape*, there is no perfect English equivalent. The word "love" suffers from the problem that the Neo-Confucians were not anxious to identify their favorite ethical norm with the more emotional forms of love. Love is clearly a component of *jen*, as *eros* is of *agape*, but it is not all of what is meant in either case. The most promising translations have been those those that suggest the relationship of *jen* with humaneness, co-humanity, or humanity itself. These English translations illustrate the Neo-Confucian emphasis on the social nature of *jen*: virtue is always social and relates to how people choose to live together.[2]

Ch'en Ch'un, one of Chu Hsi's foremost disciples, in his *Pei-hsi tzu-i* provides us with an overview of Chu Hsi's understanding of *jen*. Ch'en's discussion of *jen* is part of his larger section on the virtues of *i*[i]("justice"), *li*[j] ("ritual"), *chih*[k] ("wisdom"), and *hsin*[l] ("faithfulness"). He is emphatic in stating that these five constants (*wu-ch'ang*[m]) infuse the creative process of the universe and give it ultimate meaning. Each of the virtues corresponds to one of the five phases (*wu-hsing*[n]). Among these, *jen* is the spirit or essense of wood and comes first on Ch'en's list.[3] From the point of view of principle, "*Jen* is the principle of love".[4] But this love must be manifested externally, and this is the function of *jen*. It is the virtue that holds the other four virtues together.[5] The means by which the human mind sets forth all the heavenly principles is *jen*. These heavenly principles are always active, constantly productive without cessation, and when we give them a collective title we call them *jen*. All the other virtues are contained in this "one thread" of *jen*. If there is a single selfish thought, the heavenly principles are hopelessly separated. Only acting in a *jen* manner is sufficient to hold all these virtues together.[6]

Ch'en Ch'un points out that, because of its essence as unceasing concern for others, *jen* must issue forth from the heart in compassionate action. When these seeds of concern are carefully nurtured, they become an expression of the completion of love. *Jen* is the root of love and compassion is the seed of this root: love in its totality is the exuberant completion of this seed of compassion.[7] This

principle of creativity is lifted up as the one prime characteristic of *jen*: "*Jen* is the complete virtue of the mind."[8] If the person is not *jen*, then none of the other virtues will have any meaning. *Jen* is the principle of constant and unceasing creativity in the mind, which, if it ceased for a moment, would mean the end of true humanity.[9]

Ch'en Ch'un states that one of the great teachings of the Confucian school is to seek *jen* (*ch'iu-jen*[o]), and that *jen* encompasses all the good of the world. A person who acts in a *jen* fashion has *jen* within him or her. This clear teaching, Ch'en showed, had been lost after Mencius and had not been revived until the two Ch'eng brothers. But even with the teaching of the Ch'engs, the possibility for error was still great, as was graphically illustrated by the mistaken understanding of *jen* propounded by the students of the Ch'engs. Hsieh Liang-tso (d. c. 1121), for example, spoke of *jen* in terms of consciousness and fell into the Buddhist interpretation of human nature as pure consciousness. Likewise, Yang Shih's (1053-1135) suggestion that the unity of the myriad things in oneself is the essence of *jen* was rejected by Ch'en. For Ch'en *jen*, is prior even to the mystic sense of unity with the world and represents the creativity of the cosmos, not pure non-differentiation.[10]

An examination of Chu Hsi's comments on *jen* in *chuan* 6 of the dialogues only serves to strengthen the interpretation of *jen* set forth in Ch'en's treatise.[11] Chu Hsi also makes the point that *jen* is a mediating concept that involves both a normative standard of judgment and the spontaneity of creativity. He says, "*Jen* has two sides: an aspect of determined action and an aspect of spontaneity."[12] Any analysis of *jen* must be predicated on the union or fusion of these two aspects. All natural events and things are shot through and through with patterns that imply ethical judgments. All things have their own standpoints on the world, and hence fit into the larger cosmic pattern which we call the universe.[13]

On balance, Chu Hsi prefers to talk of *jen* as the unforced aspect of the principle of love. It lacks the element of conscious choice that we would find in *shu*[p] ("reciprocity").[14] But since all things have their proper correlates, if we have *jen* we must also have *i*[i] (justice). This keeps *jen* from becoming too subjective, a merely private emotion.[15] Chu Hsi states that *k'o-chi fu-li*[q] ("to discipline the self and return to ritual") is *jen*: to like the good and hate the bad is just action.[16] In terms of self-cultivation, *jen* must be achieved in conjunction with action and self-conscious deliberation.[17] *Jen* is the quality of being well-versed or totally immersed in the effort of self-cultivation.[18] It is the fusion of experiential activity and knowledge. Chu Hsi often uses the term *t'i-jen*[r] ("experiential knowledge") to express the depth and profundity of the process of *jen*.[19]

CH'ENG

The second important ethical concept expressing perfection for Chu Hsi is *ch'eng*.[d] This is not surprising given the fact that the *Chung-yung,* which Chu Hsi accepted as the most profound of the Four Books, stresses *ch'eng* as one of its central messages.[20] *Ch'eng* had been a favorite theme of Chu Hsi's Northern Sung predecessors, the most important in this respect being Chang Tsai and Chou Tun-i.[21] Chu Hsi preserves the old meaning of *ch'eng* as "sincerity", but adds new meanings to this important Neo-Confucian concept. For this reason, which will be defended in detail in a moment, *ch'eng* will usually be translated as "self-realization".[22]

As noted above, the interpretation of *ch'eng* has a long history in Confucian philosophy, and is found in many texts of the pre-Han period. One text, the *Chung-yung*, provides Chu Hsi with the beginning point for his reflections on *ch'eng*. Chu Hsi thought that the *Chung-yung* was the most important cosmological text of the Confucian canon, and it was on the basis of this text that he developed his mature definition of *ch'eng*.[23] Not only does the *Chung-yung* emphasize *ch'eng*, but it does so in a fashion that situates *ch'eng* precisely where it would be most useful for Chu Hsi in his complicated system.

Chu Hsi's own commentary on the *Chung-yung* devotes a great deal of time and space to *ch'eng*. His discussion of *ch'eng* is even more intense in his *huo-wen*[u] ("subcommentary") and in the first six *chüan* of the dialogues. Furthermore, even though a great deal of his *ch'eng* theory is connected with his work on the *Chung-yung*, the concept appears in many other places, too.[24]

Generally speaking, Chu Hsi defines *ch'eng* in two ways. The importance of these definitions reverses their historical origins. Chu Hsi concedes that the old meaning of *ch'eng* as "sincere" is still valid, even though he is more interested in the Neo-Confucian understanding of *ch'eng* as "self-realization". The first and older meaning of *ch'eng* is more specifically ethical: the sincere, the genuine, the true. In short, just the kinds of meanings which would justify the traditional translation of *ch'eng* as "sincerity". Chu Hsi holds that this meaning of "sincere" (*ch'eng-ch'üeh*[v]) is a perfectly good one.[25] He alludes to the fact that from Han times on the meaning of "sincere" was uppermost in the minds of scholars. While this is a perfectly good meaning in some cases, it hides the real import of *ch'eng* for the Confucian scholar.

The new emphasis on *ch'eng* as the realization of the unity of being in perfection is attributed to Ch'eng I. If the post-Han scholars adhered too closely to the old interpretation of *ch'eng* as "sincere", there was a danger of overreacting to this in the Sung. Chu Hsi claimed that *ch'eng* carries the dual meaning of "sincere" and "self-realization" equally well. According to him, neither is a completely accurate rendering of *ch'eng* in all cases.[26] There can be no self-realization without sincerity, and *vice versa*.

But there seems to be little doubt that for Chu Hsi the most important meaning of *ch'eng* has to do with its mediating role in the process of self-cultivation. In his first section on *ch'eng* in *chüan* 6 of the dialogues he affirms,

"*Ch'eng* is that which really has principle."[27] Or, as the next section has it, "*Ch'eng* is solid and real."[28] Or finally, "*Ch'eng* is principle".[29] The comment on being "solid" or "real" is particularly interesting. As A. C. Graham points out, when Chu Hsi uses this kind of language, he is saying that "solid" subjects are substances or essential parts of an event, while "empty" subjects are the contrasting functional terms. What Chu Hsi is driving at is that in its most essential mode *ch'eng* provides us with a criterion for knowing when we are in a state of proper ethical harmony.

How can we distinguish *ch'eng* as a virtue from *li* as principle? Chu Hsi answers by pointing to the difference between *ch'eng* and *hsing*[t] ("nature"), which he identifies with principle. Reversing his first definition, he points out that *ch'eng* is empty or void.

> "Nature is real while *ch'eng* is void. Nature refers to principle; *ch'eng* refers to perfection. If nature is like this fan, then *ch'eng* may be compared to this fan being well made."[30]

He later maintains that *ch'eng* is the concept of complete perfection without a flaw.[31] Chu Hsi *is* willing to say that the solid is empty and *vice versa* if the situation demands. This is analogous to his point that *jen* has both an essential and a functional aspect. Much the same can be said about *ch'eng,* even though the terminology is different in both cases. If *jen* is the core of Chu Hsi's ethical thinking, *ch'eng* is the element which gives it a certain solidity and depth of meaning.

This is clear again when Chu Hsi distinguishes *ch'eng* from reverence. The distinction is made during a discussion of the point with a group of his disciples. The disciples respond to his question about the difference between *ch'eng* and reverence by quoting Ch'eng I's statement that *ch'eng* means to will one thing without error or improper deviation. Chu agrees, but goes on to say that reverence means not being disrespectful, while *ch'eng* is the action of not disregarding one's conscience.[32] Even later, he paraphrases Ch'eng I to the effect that to be firmly established in a unitary fashion is reverence while "the unity itself is *ch'eng*."[33] Here, Chu Hsi obviously means to equate reverence systematically with *kung*[w] ("respectfulness") and *ch'eng* with the normative state of being a sage. *Ch'eng* represents not just the manifestation of virtue, but also symbolizes the principle informing perfected ethical action.

When the sage is surely an exemplary person, the model is one that we can all theoretically realize. The distinction is made clear when Chu Hsi discusses the difference between *ch'eng* and *hsin*[l] ("faithfulness"). *Ch'eng* is the self-determinate realization of *jen* in perfection, while *hsin* is the realization of virtue in a partial manner. By this Chu means that *hsin* is the activity that makes complete the effort of self-cultivation in *jen*.[34]

He further states that *ch'eng* is the way of Heaven and hence the sage's true faithfulness towards the creative mind of Heaven. In the sage, *hsin* becomes *ch'eng*. The sage is therefore the actual connective link between Heaven and Earth. The faithfulness of common men and women can only be called *hsin* in a partial sense, and cannot be univocally equated with *ch'eng* in the full sense of *jen* as an all-encompassing sagely virtue.[35]

This sense of *ch'eng* as a full or complete state is emphasized by Chu Hsi's comment on its relation to *chung* ("steadfastness"). He says that "*Ch'eng* refers to the complete essence of the mind, while *chung* refers to its responding to events and coming into contact with things."[36] Chu Hsi indicates that *ch'eng* points to a fullness or perfection of the process of self-determination. The natural and spontaneous achievement of *ch'eng* is the preserve of the profound person. But there is an effort that can lead ordinary people to *ch'eng*. Chu Hsi holds that those who do not innately realize the perfection of the sage must select the good in order to comprehend the perfection of *li*[a]. This is the concerned effort of *ch'eng* which is possible for the normal person seeking sagehood.[37]

Ch'en Ch'un's treatise adds a few points to Chu Hsi's view. *Ch'eng* as an ethical term most closely resembles *chung*[x] and *hsin*[l].[38] But the special characteristic of *ch'eng* is that it points to its own self-determinate realization. *Ch'eng* is securely part of the fundamental activity of the way of Heaven. Ch'en notes that Chu Hsi makes an important addition to one of Ch'eng I's definitions of *ch'eng*. While Ch'eng defined *ch'eng* as the "non-false", Chu Hsi added the following phrase: "The true and the non-false is what is called *ch'eng*."[39] What is true is ethically good and what is non-false will not mislead us in our dealings with other people. The content of what we discover in wisdom reflects back on the method of discovery and the actions we take in light of this self-consciousness.

Ch'en Ch'un goes on to emphasize another aspect of *ch'eng* which had not yet been adequately covered. How does *ch'eng* relate to the becoming or growth of any object or event? Ch'en writes that while *ch'eng* is part of the normative side of Chu Hsi's system, it also carries a dynamic quality. *Ch'eng* is the decree of the Way.[40] It is a mandate to action as well as a description of that action.

Ch'en Ch'un does not forget, however, the purely ethical dimension of *ch'eng*. *Ch'eng* manifests itself in a person through activity seeking the good as its goal.[41] He concludes the last part of his discussion of *ch'eng* by quoting the term *ch'eng-chih*[y] ("to have the disposition to *Ch'eng*") in the *Chung-yung*. *Ch'eng-chih* is the effort men make to live according to moral principle. "The myriad principles all achieve their complete genuineness without one iota of vacuous deceit. Only that can they deserve [to be called *ch'eng*]."[42]

The last set of meanings for *ch'eng* deals with it as the beginning and end of a thing, a metaphor taken from section 25 of the *Chung-yung*.[43] The self-creation of humanity is like the organic unity of a tree. The perfection of the whole is related to the interaction of the various limbs, branches,

roots, and leaves. Just as in a tree there is an organic unity, a human being is also a whole, a living unity of the various senses and bodily limbs.

All proceed from the natural self-determination of that particular object, the actualization of its own nature. Here again, the spontaneous order of the universe is involved along with the normative pattern of human relations that this pattern implies. *Tzu-jan*[z] ("the spontaneous") and *tang-jan*[aa] ("the normative") find their essential unity in *ch'eng*.[44]

But *ch'eng* is not just a term for the unitary state of self-realization, it is also one element in the process of selection. It is the explanation of why there is a certain particularity to any object or event. As Chu Hsi puts it: "When a man is alive, he embodies this principle, and at the time of death, this principle is scattered."[45] Using Mencius at this point, he shows how the way of Heaven and the way of Man are related in *ch'eng*.

> *Ch'eng* is the way of Heaven. *Ch'eng* is principle which is self-determination without being falsely ordered. How to realize *ch'eng* is the way of Man. It is to carry out this real principle and therefore to make an effort to realize it. Mencius said: 'All things are complete in us'—this is *ch'eng*. [There is no greater delight] than to be conscious of *ch'eng* upon self-examination—this is how to realize *ch'eng*. Self-examination is merely to seek in oneself. *Ch'eng* refers to the fact that all things are complete.[46]

A certain triadic structure is clear. There is the way of Heaven, the way of humanity and their mediation through the process of *ch'eng* ending in *jen*. As in so many other cases, Chu Hsi frames his philosophy in a triadic structure.

Fan Shou-k'ang, in his study of Chu Hsi's philosophy, points out that a person is modeled on the creative order of the Way as expressed ideally by *ch'eng*. The essence of the Way includes the principle of *jen*.[47] As Chu Hsi says in his commentary on Chou Tun-i's *Diagram of the Supreme Ultimate*: "*Ch'eng* is the foundation of the profound person, the beginning and end of things, and the Way of the Decree."[48] As with all of Chu Hsi's key concepts, none can be understood without reference to their context with the whole of his thought. *Ch'eng*, as the last quotation indicates, directs our attention to the profound person in action, the things of the world, and to the normative order that decrees these interrelated components to be the way they are. Chu Hsi never varies his triadic formulation of his key principles. The actual manifestation of virtue in the sage is no exception to the general rule.

CONCLUSION

In the necessarily broad ambit of comparative ethics, what can we say about Chu Hsi's contribution? I would suggest three short, and yet hopefully, proleptic comments. First, it seems that Chu Hsi clearly stands firmly within the Confucian mainline. Both his ideas and lifestyle indicate a location more towards the conservative than the radical end of the spectrum. For instance, Chu is certainly more 'conservative' than Ho Hsin-yin or Li Chih, just to mention two 'radical' late Ming thinkers. He is also less daring than Wang Yang-ming. But we should also keep in mind that the relative lack of an exciting personal life does not mean a concomitant lack of intellectual creativity. The term 'creative fidelity' probably quite accurately describes Chu Hsi's life and thought. Balance and integrity are other tags which easily also come to mind. Chu was no martyr but he likewise was no coward either.

Second, in that perennial pan-Asian debate between the 'gradual' and the 'sudden,' Chu Hsi is definitely identified with the 'gradual' approach to ethics. Nor is this at all surprising given his preference for the Confucian image of sagehood as a human ideal of conduct. Other religious sensibilities suggest other models, for instance that of the saint, who might well be inclined toward a more dramatic, 'sudden' vision of the culmination of life. Be that as it may, Chu himself opted for achieving the arduous, difficult and lengthy process of Confucian sagehood. His *Tao*[g] was, whatever else, long and strenuous, but not impossible. Chu's 'gradual' ethics are positive and directed towards the evocation of a harmonious, balanced and ultimately sagely pattern (*li*[a]) of human life.

Third, and this is probably the most difficult characterization, Chu Hsi, in a global context, represents axiological and 'processive' sensibilities. His thought is resolutely axiological because all of its aspects are based on a profound concern for values—normative, harmonious and demanding. The decree of heaven (*t'ien-ming*[ab]) both commands us to be something definite and also leaves open the future for our own choice as how to achieve some definite form of the *tao*[g]. Chu's vision is 'processive' in that it is open ended, never static, never completed. History taught Chu that there are always new questions to be answered. The Confucian cumulative tradition provides resources and guidelines for approaching these questions, yet the person must creatively respond to the process in order to achieve the human good.

This third characterization is truly difficult. We are just beginning to develop a golobal vocabulary for discussing adequately comparative issues. Given Chu Hsi's pre-eminent place in the Chinese and entire East Asian tradition he certainly merits our careful attention in this new and vital undertaking. And finally we would be remiss if Chu's ethics were omitted from our broader comparative efforts.

Notes

1. For a historical study of *jen* see Wing-tsit Chan. 'The Evolution of the Confucian Concept of *Jen,"* *Philosophy East and West* (January 1955): 295-319.

2. One of the more interesting treatments of the religious nature of the Confucian tradition has been suggested by Herbert Fingarette. For his interpretation of *jen* see Herbert Fingarette, *Confucius: The Secular as Sacred* (New York: Harper & Row, Publishers, 1972), pp. 37-56.

3. PHTI 1:22a.

4. PHTI 1:22b.

5. *Hsin*l ("faithfulness") also has a synthetic quality for Chu Hsi. CTYLTC 1:351 (6:5a).

6. PHTI 1:22b-23a.

7. PHTI 1:23b.

8. PHTI 1:26B.

9. Of course Ch'en also draws all sorts of analogies between *jen* and the other virtues and to various-phenomena and to the process of *yin* and *yang*. *Jan* and *i* are equated with the spring and summer months, and by extension, to the *yang* powers of those seasons. PHTI 1:26a-27A.

10. PHTI 1:31a-32a.

11. CTYLTC 1:356-93 (6:7b-26a).

12. CTYLTC 1:372 (6:15b).

13. CTYLTC 1:372-73 (6:15b-16a).

14. CTYLTC 1:379 (6:19a).

15. CTYLTC 1:390-91 (6:24b-25a).

16. CTYLTC 1:388 (6:23b).

17. CTYLTC 1:379 (6:19a).

18. CTYLTC 1:376 (5:17b).

19. CTYLTC 1:376-77 (6:17b-18a). Mou Tsung-san devotes the whole central section of volume 3 of *Mind and Nature* to the problem of *jen* in Chu Hsi's *Jen-shuo* (*Treatise on Jen*), HTHT 3:229-447. The text of the *Jen-shuo* is on pages 234-246. As Tu Wei-ming has pointed out, Mou provides us with a character by character reading of this crucial text. According to Mou, this text represents Chu Hsi's thought and debates with the Hu Hung school sometime during his forty-third year (3:229). From age forty to forty-three Chu Hsi was struggling with the problem of *chung-ho*[s] and moving on to a critique of the Hu school's concept of *jen*. Mou outlines this position on pages 231-232, and goes on to demonstrate that Chu Hsi followed Ch'eng I in all important details.

Mou hammers away at his main contention that Chu Hsi really does not have a Mencian theory of the morally transcendent mind, but merely relies on the cognitive powers of the mind to define it (p. 243). After defining Chu Hsi's usages, (pp. 244-245), Mou goes on to prove that whereas Chu Hsi may use language similar to the Mencian mainline, he actually has a different set of values in mind (pp. 245ff). On page 270 he assents that *jen* for Chu Hsi is just principle which he takes to be an abstraction, and not a mode of determination of true being. On page 277 he argues that Chu Hsi was, by implication, an epistemologist and not a moral metaphysician in the orthodox sense of Ch'eng Ming-tao and Hu Hung. By page 279, after defining in English what he takes to be sound Confucian doctrine, he points out that Chu Hsi had an external view of reality that effectively blocked him from the ontological transcendent powers of the mind. All kinds of evils spring form these initial errors. On page 322, Mou shows that Chu Hsi has a passive concept of knowledge and consciousness befitting his reliance on the external world for principle (see also page 352). The objective viewpoint is ontological while the subjective makes for a defintion of *t'ai-chi*[e] ("the Supreme Ultimate") which lacks any reference to true "active reason." While this is not the end of the critique, on pages 383-384 Mou even points out the similarities of Chu Hsi's position with that of Hsun-tzu. This is truly a case of guilt by association.

Suffice it to say that one can agree with Mou that Chu Hsi was trying to do certain things which indicate an interest in epistemology, but it is another thing entirely to then say that this interest keeps Chu Hsi from developing a sound moral metaphysics.

20. This point is amply documented in Wu I, *Chung-yung ch'eng tzu te yen-chiu* [*The Concept of Ch'eng in the Chung-yung*] (Taipei: n.p., 1972), pp. 27-39. For further support of this interpretation see Tu Wei-ming, *Centrality and Commonality: An Essay On Chung-yung* (Honolulu: University of Hawaii Press, 1976), pp. 106-141.

21. For a study of Chou Tun-i's use of *ch'eng* see Chow Yih-ching, *La Philosophie Morale dans le Néo-confucianisme* (Paris: Presses Universitaires de France, 1954), pp. 104-126. See also T'ang Chun-i, *Chung-kuo che-hsueh yuan lun: Yuan Chiao P'ien* [*Fundamental exposition of Chinese Philosophy: Education*] (Knowloon, Hong Kong: New Asia Research Institute, 1968), pp. 70-75, where he points out the importance of *ch'eng* in the philosophy of Chang Tsai.

22. See *infra* p. 139, n. 3.

23. Mou Tsung-san, *Chung-kuo che-hsueh te t'e-chih* [*Special Characteristios of Chinese Philosophy*] (Taipei: Student Book Co, 1974), p. 52, states that the *Chung-yung,* along with the *I-Ching,* represents the cosmological approach in early Confucian philosophy. Mou argues that the *Chung-yung* uses the concept of *ch'eng* to define *hsing*[f] ("human nature"). *Ch'eng* is the nature as the "flowing decree of Heaven," which is the creative principle of the way (p. 53). See also HTHT 1:19-42.

24. CTYLTC 1:353 (6:6a).

25. CTYLTC 1:350 (6:4b).

26. CTYLTC 1:350 (6:4b).

27. CTYLTC 1:349 (6:4b).

28. CTYLTC 1:349 (6:4b).

29. CTYLTC 1:350 (6:4b).

30. CTYLTC 1:350 (6:4b); A.C. Graham, *Two Chinese Philosophers: Ch'eng Ming-tao and Ch'eng Yi-ch'uan* (London: Lond Humphries, 1958), p. 67,

points out that the "solid" words often indicate substances while "empty" words indicate qualities or states of being.

31. CTYLTC 4:3311 (64:17a); CTHHA 2:414.

32. CTYLTC 1:350 (6:4b).

33. CTYLTC 1:352 (6:5a).

34. Cf Tu Wei-ming, "Confucian Perception of Adulthood," *Daedalus* (Spring 1976), pp. 109-123.

35. CTYLTC 1:351 (6:5a).

36. CTYLTC 1:352 (6:5b).

37. CTHHA 2:410 CTYLTC 4:3288-89 (64:5b-6a).

38. PHTI 1:34b.

39. PHTI 1:40b.

40. PHTI 1:41a-b.

41. PHTI 1:41b-42a.

42. PHTI 1:42b.

43. *Chung-yung,* p. 17b. SPPY ed.

44. CTYLTC 4:3313 (64:18a).

45. CTYLTC 4:3315 (64:19a).

46. CTYLTC 4:3287-88 (64:5a-b); James Legge, trans., *The Chinese Classics,* 5 vols. (Hong Kong University Press, 1970), 2:450-451.

47. Fan Shou-K'ang, *Chu-tzu chi ch'i che-hsueh* [*Chu Hsi and His Philosophy*] (Taiwan: K'ai-min shu-chu, 1964), p. 128.

48. Chow, *La Philosophic Morale,* pp. 155, 210.

Abbreviations

CTHHA Ch'ien Mu. *Chu-tzu hsin hsueh-an* [A New Study of Chu Hsi]. 5 vols. Taiwan: San Min Shu-chu, 1971.

CTYLTC Li Ching-te (Fl.1263), ed. *Chu-tzu yu-lei ta-ch'uan* [The Dialogues of Chu Hsi]. 8 vols. Tokyo: n.p., 1973.

HTHT Mou Tsung-San. *Hsin-t'i yu hsing-t'i* [Mind and Nature]. 3 vols. Taiwan: Chen-Chung Shu-Chu, 1968-1969.

PHTI Ch'en Ch'un (1159-1227). *Pei-hsi tzu-i* [Pei-hsi's Glossary]. Hsi Yin Hsuan Ts'ung-shu ed., 1840.

SPPY ed. Su-pu pei-yao ed.

Wing-tsit Chan (essaydate 1989)

SOURCE: "Chu Hsi's *Jen-shuo*" (Treatise on Humanity)," in *Chu Hsi: New Studies,* University of Hawaii Press, 1989, pp. 151-83.

[*In the essay below, Chan studies Chu Hsi's* Jen-shuo ("Treatise on Humanity"), *examining the reasons Chu Hsi wrote the treatise, discussing the likely period of composi-*

tion, and reviewing the major concepts—the character of the mind and the principle of love—explored by Chu Hsi within the treatise.]

Chu Hsi's philosophical thought centered on the basic concepts of the Great Ultimate *(T'ai-chi)*, principle *(li)*, material force *(ch'i)*, humanity *(jen)*, righteousness *(i)*, equilibrium *(chung)*, and harmony *(ho)*. In these he perpetuated the doctrines of the Ch'eng brothers (Ch'eng Hao, 1032-1085, and Ch'eng I, 1033-1107) and added his own innovative views to compete with the prevailing philosophical schools of Hunan, Kiangsi, and Chekiang. To this end he carried on debates with Lu Hsiang-shan (1139-1193) of Kiangsi on the problem of the Great Ultimate,[1] with Change Shih (1133-1180) of Hunan on the issue of equilibrium and harmony,[2] and with Ch'en Liang (1143-1194) of Chekiang on the questions of righteousness versus profit and the way of the sagely king versus the way of the powerful despot.[3] But there was no debate on the central concept of *jen* (humanity), as if Chu Hsi were not much concerned with it. In reality, however, after he compiled the *Lun-yü yao-i* (Essential meanings of the *Analects*) in 1163 at the age of thirty-four, Chu Hsi hardly passed a day without thinking and talking about *jen*. His ideas on it are found in his commentaries, letters, and conversations. The number of people with whom he discussed *jen*, both in person and in his correspondence, far exceeded the number with whom he discussed other topics. His correspondence on *jen*, now preserved in the **Wen-chi,** includes letters to Chang Ching-fu (Chang Shih), Lü Po-kung (Lü Tsu-ch'ien), Ho Shu-ching (Ho Hao), Hu Kuang-chung (Hu Shih), Wu Hui-shu (Wu I), Shih Tzu-chung (Shih Tun), Lin Hsi-chih (Lin Ta-ch'un), Lin Tse-chih (Lin Yung-chung), Hu Po-feng (Hu Ta-yüan), Lü Tzu-yüeh (Lü Tsu-chien), "Venerable Sir," Yü Chan-chih (Yü Yü), Chou Shun-pi (Chou Mu), Chou Shu-chin (Chou Chieh), Fang Pin-wang (Fang I), Li Yao-ch'ing (Li T'ang-tzu), Ch'en An-ching (Ch'en Ch'un), Yang Chung-ssu (Yang Tao-fu), Ch'en Ch'i-chih (Ch'en Chih), and Hsü Chü-fu (Hsü Yü). The degree of fervent discussion can readily be seen.[4]

Besides his correspondence, Chu Hsi wrote the **Jen-shuo,** a 824-character treatise now preserved in chapter 67 of the **Wen-chi.** It is divided into two sections, the first on *jen* as "the character of the mind" *(hsin chih te)*, and the second on *jen* as "the principle of love" *(ai chih li)*. He also criticized the theories of *jen* forming one body with all things and *jen* as consciousness of pain. In addition, he drew the "Jen-shuo-t'u" (Diagram of the **Treatise on Humanity**) which appears at the end of chapter 105 of the *Yü-lei*—and in chapter 18 below (p. 281). The diagram was drawn after many years of discussion on *jen* and numerous revisions of the treatise. To Chu Hsi, the concept of *jen* was clearly far more important than those of the Great Ultimate and other philosophical categories. Why was this? As Chu Hsi himself confided, he simply could not help it.

THE MOTIVE

In a letter to Lü Tsu-ch'ien (1137-1181), Chu Hsi wrote,

Of course this treatise is superficial and lacks reserve. But in my humble opinion, in the teaching of the an-

cients there was already a clear explanation of terms like this beginning with elementary education, unlike the superficial, abstract, and artificial interpretations of later generations. In their learning, they understood the term clearly, but a principle like this must be put into actual practice. Therefore, in the School of the Sage [Confucius] the important task has been to search for humanity. The reason is that having understood the term to some extent, one has to strive to arrive at that state. People today have completely failed to understand. This being the case, what they are seeking eagerly is something of which they are ignorant throughout life. How can they be expected to love to discuss it and to know where to devote their effort? Therefore, although my words today are simple and plain compared to those of the ancients, I cannot help uttering them.[5]

Two points should be noted in this letter, namely, Chu Hsi's explanation of the term *jen* and his emphasis on the necessity of putting it into concrete practice. But one must first comprehend the principle of *jen* before one can practice it. In a letter to Lü Tsu-ch'ien's brother, Lü Tsu-chien (d. 1196), Chu Hsi said,

Jen, of course, cannot be interpreted purely from the point of view of function, but one must understand the principle that *jen* has the ability to function. Only then will it do. Otherwise, the term will be meaningless and cannot be explained. Take the sentence, "Origination is the leading quality of goodness."[6] It means the original substance which is the starting point of the origination of all things and which can function. One should not regard the original substance of *jen* as one thing and its function as another. . . . Generally speaking, the meaning of *jen* must be found in one idea and one principle. Only then can we talk on a high level about a principle that penetrates everything. Otherwise, it will be the so-called vague Thusness and stupid Buddha-nature,[7] and the word *jen* will be left dangling. I have written my humble treatise precisely for this reason.[8]

The idea in this passage is similar to that in the letter to Lü Tsu-ch'ien—namely, that the concept of *jen* must be understood before its substance and function can be distinguished.

In his letter to Wu I, Chu Hsi said,

Generally speaking, in recent years scholars do not like to talk about *jen* in terms of love. Therefore, when they see that the Master Gentleman [Ch'eng I] talked about the mind of Heaven and Earth in terms of one yang [positive cosmic force] element producing things,[9] they are certain to be sadly dissatisfied, and furthermore, to ascribe ideas over and above what is originally intended and make abstract inferences without realizing that the way Heaven and Earth exercise their mind is none other than this. If we talk about *jen* beyond this sense, we will degenerate into emptiness and fall into quiescence, and substance and function, and the fundamental and the secondary, will have no relation to each other.[10]

This letter puts special emphasis on the interpretation of *jen* as love, which is rooted in the mind of Heaven and

Earth to produce things. The purpose is still to clarify the concept of *jen.*

From the above, we can see that Chu Hsi had three reasons for writing the **Jen-shuo.** First, scholars of his time wrote on the subject of *jen* in great confusion. Chang Shih, Lin Ta-ch'un, Chou Chieh, Yang Tao-fu, and "Venerable Sir" each wrote a treatise on *jen.* Strange doctrines sprang up, with no agreement among them. Especially mistaken were the theories that *jen* meant forming one body with all things and of *jen* as consciousness. Thus Chu Hsi wrote his treatise to clarify the meaning of the term. Second, he wanted to show that the concept *jen* as love is based on the notion that the mind of Heaven and Earth is to produce things, and thereby prevent scholars from falling into the errors of emptiness and quiescence. The **Jen-shuo** says, "I fear scholars talk about *jen* without reference to love. I have therefore propounded this particular doctrine of *jen* to make the idea clear." Third, Chu Hsi wanted to correct the erroneous theory that substance and function are two different things.

Main Ideas of the "Jen-shuo"

Although the **Jen-shuo** is short, its ideas are well thought out. It starts with the sentences, "The mind of Heaven and Earth is to produce things. In the production of man and things, they receive the mind of Heaven and Earth as their mind." The first sentence is a quotation from Ch'eng I;[11] the second was added by Chu Hsi himself. Chu Hsi continues, "The moral qualities of the mind of Heaven and Earth are four: origination, flourishing, advantage and firmness,[12] and origination unites and controls all their operations." In the human mind, "There are also Four Virtues, namely: humanity, righteousness, propriety, and wisdom,[13] and humanity embraces all their functions." "Therefore, with reference to the character of the mind . . . we can only say that it is *jen.*" "For *jen* as constituting the Way consists of the fact that the mind of Heaven and Earth to produce things is present in everything. Before the feelings are aroused, this substance is already existent in its entirety. After feelings are aroused, its function is infinite. Thus if we can truly realize *jen* and preserve it, we have in it the spring of all virtues and the root of all good deeds. This is why the Confucian School always urged students to exert anxious and unceasing effort in the pursuit of *jen.*" Self-mastery, respect and reverence, conscientiousness and altruism, filial piety and brotherly respect—all are ways to preserve this mind and put it into practice. Before the feelings are aroused, it is nature, which is identical with *jen.* As feelings are aroused, it becomes love. That is why Chu Hsi defined *jen* as "the principle of love." Though nature and feelings seem to belong to different spheres, their interpenetration make them one system, like arteries and veins. But among followers of the Ch'eng brothers,

> Some [notably Yang Shih, 1053-1135] say that love is not *jen* and regard the unity of all things and the self as *jen,* while others [notably Hsieh Liang-tso, 1050-c. 1120] maintain that love is not *jen* but explain *jen* in

terms of the possession of consciousness by the mind.[14] . . . From what they call the unity of all things and the self, it can be seen that *jen* involves love for all, but unity is not the reality that makes *jen* a substance. From the way they regard the mind as the possession of consciousness, it can be seen that *jen* includes wisdom, but that is not the real reason why *jen* is so called. . . . To talk about *jen* in general terms of the unity of things and the self will lead people to be vague, confused, neglectful, and make no effort to be alert. The bad effect—and there has been one—may be to consider other things as oneself. To talk about *jen* in specific terms of consciousness will lead people to be nervous, irascible, and devoid of any quality of depth. The bad effect—and there has been one—may be to consider [selfish] desire as principle. In one case, [the mind] forgets [its objective]. In the other, [there is artificial effort to] help [it grow].[15] Both are wrong.

This is the gist of the "Jen-shuo."

When Was the Treatise Written?

We do not know exactly when the **Jen-shuo** was written. Liao Te-ming (1169 *cs*) asked, "Sir, in the **Jen-shuo** that you wrote some time ago, you generally consider the mind to embrace the principle of love, and that is why it is called *jen.* But now in your [*Meng Tzu*] *chi-chu* [Collected commentaries on the *Book of Mencius*], commenting on the sentence '*Jen* is the human mind,'[16] you take it to mean 'the master of dealing with all changes.' How about it?"[17] This was recorded by Liao after 1173, suggesting that the **Jen-shuo** was written before the compilation of the [*Meng Tzu*] *chi-chu* in 1177. However, Chu Hsi said, "For more than forty years I have thought over the **Lun-Meng** [*chi-chu*] [Commentaries on the *Analects* and the *Book of Mencius*],"[18] and several days before he died he was still revising his commentary on the *Great Learning.* Thus what is found in the **Lun-Meng chi-chu** may very well have been written after the **Jen-shuo.**

In any case, the writing of the treatise must have taken a long time, although it also must not have been completed too late. In his letter to Lü Tsu-ch'ien on *jen,* Chu Hsi said that Ch'in-fu (Chang Shih) had written that he had no more doubts about the "Jen-shuo." He added that he "wanted to write the **[I-Lo] yüan-yüan lu** [Records of the origin of the school of the Ch'engs] to include all the deeds and writings of the various gentlemen, from Chou [Chou Tun-i, 1017-1073] and the Ch'engs on. I am troubled not to have the material or the complete accounts of various scholars of the Yung-chia School. I have, therefore, written Shih-lung [Hsüeh Chi-hsüan, 1134-1173] to ask him to search and send them to me."[19] The fact that Chang Shih had no more doubts about the **Jen-shuo** indicates that the treatise had assumed its final form. Only then did Chu Hsi conceive the idea of compiling the **I-Lo yüan-yüan lu** and find that the material needed to do so was not yet available. The **Yüan-yüan lu** was completed in the sixth month of 1173. Assuming it took a year or two to write, the idea of compiling it must have occurred around 1171, by which time the final draft of the **Jen-shuo** must also have been written. Professor Tomoeda Ryūtarō believes that the treatise was completed about 1173, when Chu Hsi was forty-four.[20] My opinion is that it was finished before, not after, that year.]

We do not know how many years Chu Hsi debated with Chang Shih on the *Jen-shuo*. There are four letters to Chang Shih in the *Wen-chi* devoted to discussions on the treatise.[21] In his funeral address for Chang Shih, Ch Hsi said that for almost ten years they had debated back and forth, finally coming to an agreement.[22] Although this is a general statement, it must include their discussions on the *Jen-shuo,* and indeed, the four letters are clear evidence of this fact. When Chu Hsi visited Chang Shih at Changsha in 1167, one of the topics for discussion was *jen.*[23] Although Chang Shih said he had no more doubts, that did not necessarily mean the two men were in complete agreement. As Chu Hsi said, in their former discussion he and Chang Shih "still had one or two points of disagreement."[24] Thus the final draft of the treatise must have been preceded by years of discussion with Chang Shih. We may say that the *Jen-shuo* was largely finished by 1171, but it must have been started many years earlier.

Because one of the letters in which Chu Hsi discussed the *Jen-shuo* with Chang Shih contains the sentence, "In your letter you consider what I say in the *K'e-chai [chi]* [Account of the studio of self-mastery] to be better,"[25] and the *K'e-chai chi* was written in 1172, Professor Mou Tsung-san has determined that the first draft of the *Jen-shuo* was written before that date.[26] His theory is correct. However, he also maintains that Chu Hsi wrote the *Jen-shuo* two or three years after he had established the new doctrine of equilibrium and harmony in 1169; that his debates with scholars on the subject generally took place after he was forty-three years old (1172); and that the final draft was also written after this date. I am afraid he puts the matter too late, for we know that in 1172 Chang Shih had no more doubts. It may be argued that Chu Hsi said in his letter, "I wanted to make some revisions but have had no time to do so," indicating that when the "K'e-chai chi" was written, the *Jen-shuo* was not yet completed. However, I am convinced this is not the case, because the letter also says, "Formerly, I presented the *Jen-shuo* to you." "Formerly" may refer either to the first draft of a numbers of years before, to the final draft of only a year or two earlier, or even to some intermediate version. We do not know what it was that Chu Hsi had wanted to revise. He went on to say that Chang Shih "did not understand this completely." The entire emphasis in the *K'e-chai chi* is on self-mastery, which is not a key idea in the *Jen-shuo*. Perhaps Chu Hsi did not make the revision, whatever it was, but even after he finished the treatise, he continued to discuss it with scholars. As late as 1185 he discussed it in a letter to Lü Tsu-chien,[27] in which he also referred to his debate with Ch'en Liang during the same year.[28] If Chu Hsi had wanted to make revisions even at this late date, there ought to have been no problem in doing so, just as after the *Lun-Meng chi-chu* was finished, he continued to make changes in it.

Based on the dates mentioned above, we may conclude that Chu Hsi's discussions on the *Jen-shuo* took place for many years after 1165 or 1166, when Chu Hsi was thirty-six or thirty-seven, and culminated in about 1171, when he was forty-two. In any case, the completion of the *Jen-shuo* preceded not only that of the *Yüan-yüan lu* but also that of the *Chin-ssu lu* (Reflections on things at hand) in 1175; the *Ssu-shu chi-chu* (Collected commentaries on the Four Books)[29] and the *Ssu-shu huo-wen* (Questions and answers on the Four Books) in 1177; his publication of the Four Books in 1190; and the *Yü-shan chiang-i* (Yü-shan lecture) in 1194.[30] Although the Four Books are the foundation of Chu Hsi's doctrines and the Yü-shan lecture their outline, Chu Hsi's thoughts had come to maturation in the *Jen-shuo* twenty years earlier.

IMPORTANT PHRASES

The *Jen-shuo* contains two key phrases, "the character of the mind" and "the principle of love." These two refrains occur in more than ten places in the *Lun-yü chi-chu* (Collected commentaries on the *Analects*) and the *Meng Tzu chi-chu* (Collected commentaries on the *Book of Mencius*). In the former, it is said in the comments on *Analects* 1:2 that "*Jen* is the principle of love and the character of the mind," and on 18:1 that "*Jen* does not violate the principle of love and has a way of preserving the character of the mind." In the latter, in a comment on 1A:1, it is said that "*Jen* is the character of the mind and the principle of love." In the *Lun-yü huo-wen* (Questions and answers on the *Analects*), it is also said that "The principle of love is the reason for the character of the mind."[31] In other places, the phrases "the character of the mind" and "the complete character of the mind" often occur, as do "the mind of *jen* is the mind to love people," "the foundation of *jen* is love," and "to love people is the application of *jen*."[32] Thus the use of "the character of the mind" and "the principle of love" is not incidental but the result of decades of careful deliberation. As Chu Hsi said, "In my *Yü-Meng chi-chu* [Collected commentaries on the *Analects* and the *Book of Mencius*], not a single word may be added and not a single word deleted."[33] He also said, "For more than forty years I have thought over the *Lun Meng* [*chi-chu*]. I have weighed every word in them and would not allow myself to be offtrack."[34]

ORIGIN OF THE PHRASES

In his *Kairoku* (Records of the sea), Yamazaki Bisei (1797-1863) noted that in the *Ryūgan tekagami* (Paragon of the dragon niche) *jen* is explained thus: "Pronounced *jen*. It is the character of the mind and the principle of love." Since the *Ryūgan tekagami* was written in 997 and the *Lun-Meng chi-chu* was completed 180 years later, in 1177, he concluded that the two phrases were originally Buddhist and were borrowed by Chu Hsi.[35] But as Yamaguchi Satsujō (1882-1948) pointed out, the preface of the *Ryūgan tekagami* says the book consists of some 26,430 words, whereas the edition that Yamazaki used contains 39,428 words. In the notes to this longer edition are notations such as "present addition," and in the case of *jen* the enlarged edition has added, "It means affectionate love." Yamaguchi therefore decided that the phrases "the character of the mind" and "the principle of love" were obviously later additions.[36] Accordingly, Fujitsuka Chikashi (1879-1948) said, "These phrases are found in the Korean enlarged edition of the *Ryūgan tekagami*. Both the *Kairoku* of Yamazaki Bisei and the *Kobun kyūshō kō* (Investigation of ancient texts) of Shimada Kan (1879-1915) are based on this reprint for their conclusions. How can they be relied on?"[37]

Yamaguchi did not believe that Chu Hsi borrowed his key phrases from Buddhism, but he did assert that he borrowed from Chang Shih. According to Yamaguchi, Chang Shih's comment on *Analects* 12:22 says, "As we investigate human nature, its principle of love is *jen* and its principle of knowledge is wisdom." Chang's *Lun-yü chieh* (Explanation of the *Analects*) was written in 1173, while Chu Hsi's **Chi chu** was completed after his **Lun-Meng ching-i** (Essential meaning of the *Analects* and the *Book of Mencius*) and **Lun-Meng huo-wen**. The **Ching-i** was compiled in 1172, a year earlier than Chang's *Lun-yü chieh*, but the **Huo-wen** was completed in 1177, four years after the *Lun-yü chieh*. For the sake of argument, Yamaguchi concluded that had the phrases "the character of the mind" and "the principle of love" not been used in the **Ching-i,** Chang Shih might have been the first to use them in his *Lun-yü chieh*.[38] We do not know in what month of 1173 the *Lun-yü chieh* was completed, but Chu Hsi's **Yüan-yüan lu** was finished in the sixth month of that year, at which time the "Jen-shuo" had assumed its final form. Even if Chang Shih finished the *Lun-yü chieh* in the first month of 1173, did Chu Hsi see it, immediately borrow the phrase "the principle of love," and insert it in his **Jen-shuo?** Would this have been typical of Chu Hsi, who did not add or delete a word without a long period of thinking? Did his many discussions with Chang Shih on the **Jen-shuo** take place only during these several months of 1173? And even supposing that "the principle of love" did come from Chang Shih, where would "the character of the mind" have come from? In his reply to Chu Hsi, Chang Shih said, "I have read your letter several times and have been greatly benefited. What you called the principle of love has certainly opened me up."[39] Thus we can see that it was Chu Hsi who inspired Chang Shih, not vice versa. It is therefore more convincing to say that Chang Shih borrowed from Chu Hsi, rather than the other way around. ōtsuki Nobuyoshi regarded "the principle of love" and "the character of the mind" as new meanings contributed by Chu Hsi.[40] This is not his own opinion but the consensus of scholars over the centuries.

THE CHARACTER OF THE MIND

The central concepts of the **Jen-shuo** are "the character of the mind" and "the principle of love." What do these mean? "The character of mind" is sometimes rendered as "the Way of the mind"[41] and "the character of nature."[42] Hu Hung (1106-1161) had said in his *Hu Tzu chih-yen* (Master Hu's understanding of words) that "*Jen* is the way

of the mind,"[43] which could have inspired Chu Hsi. The words *tao* (way) and *te* (character) are interchangeable. Nevertheless, *tao* refers to function, whereas *te* refers to substance. There was a special reason for Chu Hsi to use the term "character." He said, "It is like saying that being moist is the character of water and being dry and hot is the character of fire."[44] The chief character of *jen* is *sheng*, to produce or to give life. In commenting on the *Book of Mencius* 5A:11, he said, "*Jen* is the character of the mind. As Master Ch'eng [Ch'eng I] has said, 'The mind is comparable to seeds of grain. The nature of growth is *jen*.'"[45] Chu Hsi's idea was derived from Ch'eng I's doctrine of *sheng-sheng* (production and reproduction, perpetual renewal of life). Ch'eng I's novel interpretation of *jen* as seeds was a breakthrough in the philosophy of *jen*. And just as *jen* is comparable to seeds, Ch'eng I said, so "the mind is the principle of production."[46] He also said, "The mind of Heaven and Earth is to produce things."[47] Chu Hsi agreed with this. The first sentences of the **Jen-shuo** are "The mind of Heaven and Earth is to produce things. In the production of man and things, they receive the mind of Heaven and Earth as their mind." This is the basic point of the **Jen-shuo,** a point that provoked a great deal of discussion among scholars. We shall deal with it in more detail below.

Because *jen* has the connotation of growth, it can include the Four Virtues of humanity, righteousness, propriety, and wisdom. Ch'eng I said, "Spoken of separately, it is one of the several, but spoken of collectively, it embraces all four."[48] Chu Hsi also agreed with this. His pupil Ch'en Ch'un (1159-1223) once asked, "*Jen* is the character of the mind. Are righteousness, propriety, and wisdom also characters of the mind?" Chu Hsi answered, "They are all characters of the mind, but *jen* alone embraces all of them."[49] And in answering a similar question from Huang Kan (1152-1221), he said, "They all are, but *jen* is the greatest."[50] What he meant by "embraces all of them" and "is the greatest" is that "spoken of together, all four are characters of the mind, but *jen* is the master."[51] In other words, "*Jen* being the character of the mind, it possesses all the other three. . . . What is called the character of the mind here is similar to what Master Ch'eng meant by 'collectively, it embraces all four.'"[52]

Although Chu Hsi agreed with Ch'eng I, his **Jen-shuo** is original in many respects. Ch'eng I had said, "*Jen* is the correct principle of the world."[53] Chu Hsi did not adopt this definition but coined his own—namely, "the character of the mind." Many of his pupils were skeptical about this and questioned him repeatedly, either in person or by letter. Chu Hsi thought Ch'eng I's definition too broad or too vague,[54] for righteousness, propriety, and wisdom can also be correct principles of the world.[55] To Chu Hsi, Ch'eng I was speaking only in general terms, not about the substance of *jen*.[56] If correct principle is applied to *jen*, it would be the character of the mind.[57] That is to say, *jen* is not a general principle of the world but the correct principle of the mind; it "is merely the correct principle of my mind."[58] Hence, in answering his pupil Ch'eng Hsün's letter, in which Ch'eng had equated *jen* with the Principle of Heaven, Chu Hsi said, "This statement should be fully explained and not dismissed like this."[59] Elsewhere he noted, "It is necessary to say that *jen* is the complete character of the original mind, and there is thus the Principle of Heaven,"[60] and because "*jen* is the complete character of the original mind, if the innate mind of the Principle of Heaven as it naturally is has been preserved and not lost, whatever one does will be orderly and harmonious."[61]

Thus the character of the mind is of course the substance of *jen*,[62] and is of course internal, not external.[63] As Chu Hsi said, "One must see what the feeling is if one loses or preserves the character of the mind, and then one can see what *jen* really is."[64] The *Jen-shuo* says,

> "Be respectful in private life, be serious (*ching*) in handling affairs, and be loyal in dealing with others."[65] This is the way to preserve the mind. "Be filial in serving parents, be respectful in serving the elder brother,[66] and be altruistic in dealing with others."[67] These are the ways to practice this mind. [The *Analects* also say,] "One obtains *jen* if one seeks it."[68] The fact that [Po-i and Shu-ch'i] yielded the throne to each other, filed, and later appealed [to King Wu (*r*. 1121-1104 B.C.)] not to send a military expedition [against the Shang dynasty (c. 1751-1112 B.C.)], choosing to starve to death [after the Shang fell],[69] was because of their ability not to lose the mind.

Preserving, practicing, and not losing all refer to the character of the mind. There are only two questions on the *Jen-shuo* in the *Yü-lei*. One was asked by Shen Hsien, who inquired about the mind of Heaven and Earth to produce things, a point discussed below. The other was asked by Kan Chieh, who inquired about preserving and not losing the character of the mind. Kan Chieh asked, "Sir, in your *Jen-shuo* you say this is to preserve [*jen*] and this is not to lose [*jen*], but at the same time you say that when one practices this, *jen* is in it, but practicing is not *jen*." Chu Hsi answered, "Of course it is not all right to call it *jen*, but to say that it is not *jen* is simple to deny it is *jen* in so many words. Mencius went on to explain *jen*, but Confucius did not do this."[70] What Kan Chieh meant was that practice belongs to worldly affairs, whereas *jen* is character. At bottom, *jen* is man's mind, while righteousness is man's path.[71] Chu Hsi himself also said, "*Jen* is the character of the mind. As soon as one preserves this mind, there will be nothing but *jen*. Take the saying, 'To master oneself and return to propriety [is *jen*].'[72] What the saying calls for is that after selfish desires have been eliminated, the mind is forever preserved. It does not cover practice."[73]

There is clearly a difference between principle and worldly affairs. However, since Chu Hsi interpreted *jen* as the character of the mind, and since this character means the spirit of life, ideas must be expressed in practice. Here Chu Hsi seems to contradict himself. As Ch'en Ch'un explained, "*Jen* is the complete character of the mind. It includes and controls all the other four virtues. Righteousness, propriety, and wisdom are impossible without *jen*.

This is so because *jen* is the principle of production in the mind, always operating in the process of production and reproduction without cease, and remaining from the beginning to the end without interruption."[74] This means that *jen* is the principle of production and reproduction, operating everywhere in actual practice.

THE PRINCIPLE OF LOVE

As Chu Hsi explained it, "*Jen* is the principle of love. Principle is the root, while love is the sprout. The love of *jen* is comparable to the sweetness of sugar and the sourness of vinegar. Love is the taste."[75] The principle of love is also "comparable to the root of a plant and the spring of water."[76] Love is active while principle is tranquil.[77] Here the word "principle" should be emphasized. Lü Tsu-ch'ien interpreted "the principle of love" as "the beginning of activity and the way of growth," but Chu Hsi considered that the word "beginning" was too weak.[78]

By love, Chu Hsi meant the principle of *jen* in the mind. This mind is expressed in filial piety and brotherly respect. Before these feelings are aroused, what is preserved in the mind is only the principle of love.[79] Chang Shih had explained the passage "Filial piety and brotherly respect are the root of *jen*"[80] by saying that "beginning with filial piety and brotherly respect, the way of *jen* will grow indefinitely." Commenting on this, Chu Hsi said, "Here the word *jen* refers precisely to the principle of love."[81] Because it is this principle, it has the spirit of life of *jen*, which has to be expressed. Liao Te-ming asked about *jen* as the principle of love, saying, "Sir, in the 'Jen-shuo' that you wrote some time ago, you generally consider the mind to embrace the principle of love, and that is why it is called *jen*. But now in your [*Meng Tzu*] *chi-chu* [Collected commentaries on the *Book of Mencius*], commenting on the sentence '*Jen* is the human mind,'[82] you take it to mean 'the master of dealing with all changes.' How about it?" Chu Hsi answered:

> You don't have to look at it this way. Nowadays, when people talk about *jen* they mostly look upon it as something abstract. That won't do. At the time [of the presence of mind], the sprouts of humanity, righteousness, propriety, and wisdom are already there, but have not yet been activated. . . . Propriety is basically the principle of culture. As it is activated, it becomes deference and humility. Wisdom is basically the principle of discrimination. As it is activated, there are the right and wrong.[83]

If the mind is merely considered the master of dealing with the tens of thousands of transformations, *jen* as the spirit of growth will be lost.

The principle of love is the same as the original substance of *jen*. In a letter in reply to Hu Shih, Chu Hsi said,

> Of course it is wrong simply to equate *jen* with love, but the principle of love is the substance of *jen*. Since Heaven, Earth, and the ten thousand things form one body with the self, of course love should cover every-

thing, but that is not the reason that *jen* is the principle of love. We must realize that humanity, righteousness, propriety, and wisdom are all characters of nature, the principle that originally exists by itself without any artificial manipulation. But *jen* is the principle of love and the way of growth. Because of this, it can include the Four Virtues and is the essential of learning.[84]

To say that *jen* is the principle of love means that "*jen* is nature while love is feeling." In other words, "Love is the feeling of *jen* and *jen* is the nature of love,"[85] but the two cannot be separated.[86] Questioned about *jen* as the principle of love, Chu Hsi said,

> The term will become clear if you look at the mind, nature, and feeling separately. Undifferentiated within one's person is the master, which is the mind. There are humanity, righteousness, propriety, and wisdom, which are one's nature. When these are expressed, they become commiseration, shame and dislike, deference and humility, and the sense of right and wrong. These are feelings. Commiseration is love, the beginning of *jen*. *Jen* is substance, while love is function.[87]

Someone asked, "Why is *jen* the principle of love?" Chu Hsi answered,

> Man is endowed with the best of the Five Agents[88] at birth. Therefore, his mind is constituted so that before it is activated it possesses the nature of humanity, righteousness, propriety, wisdom, and faithfulness as its substance, and after it is activated it has the nature of commiseration, shame and dislike, respect and reverence, the sense of right and wrong, and truthfulness as its function. For the spirit of Wood is *jen*,[89] which is the principle of love. . . . All this is the Principle of Heaven as it surely is, and why the human mind is wonderful. From this we can infer that *jen* is the principle of love.[90]

He also said,

> *Jen* is the principle of love, while love is the function of *jen*. It is simply called *jen* before it is activated, when it has neither shape nor shade. It is called love only after it is activated, when it has shape and shadow. Before it is activated and called *jen,* it can include righteousness, propriety, and wisdom. After it is activated and called commiseration, it can include respect and reverence, deference and humility, and the sense of right and wrong. We call these the Four Beginnings,[91] "beginning" being comparable to sprouts or buds. Commiseration is the beginning that issues from *jen*.[92]

In his explanation of the principle of love, Ch'en Ch'un said,

> *Jen* is the totality of the mind's principle of production. It is always producing and reproducing without cease. Its clue becomes active in the mind. When it sets forth, naturally there is the feeling of commiseration. As the feeling of commiseration grows in abundance to reach a thing, it becomes love. Therefore, *jen* is the root of love, commiseration the sprout from the root, and love the sprout reaching its maturity and completion. Look-ing at it this way, we can easily see the vital connection between *jen* as the principle of love and love as the function of *jen*.[93]

Ch'en Ch'un understood his teacher's ideas quite well.

From this we know that Chu Hsi regarded love as active and as the force of production. Before it is activated, love is nature, is the substance of *jen,* and includes the Four Virtues. When it is aroused and expressed as feeling because of its activity and growth, it includes the Four Beginnings. However, nature and feeling are not to be separated, for substance and function are not bifurcated. The principle of love is original with one's nature, and does not become so because of impartiality. Since one's nature is pure, one can penetrate Heaven, Earth, and the ten thousand things, yet one does not become *jen* after such penetration.

THE CHARACTER OF THE MIND AND THE PRINCIPLE OF LOVE

Thus far the character of the mind and the principle of love have been treated separately, but this does not mean that they are two different things. In his elucidation of *jen,* Chu Hsi combined the two, a point that should not be overlooked. However, *jen* is neither love nor the mind, nor love and mind combined. Chu Hsi said, "Love is not *jen;* the principle of love is *jen*. The mind is not *jen;* the character of the mind is *jen*."[94] Therefore *jen* combines the character of the mind and the principle of love. Moreover, Chu Hsi explained *jen* not only in terms of the mind but also in terms of principle. He said, "*Jen* is the principle of love. That is why it is the character of the mind. Because it is principle, it is therefore character. The relation between the two is a necessary one and neither can be lacking."[95] In other words, principle is the cause and character is the effect. In the final analysis, Chu Hsi's explanation of *jen* is in terms of principle. Therefore Ch'en Ch'un said, "*Jen* may be spoken of in terms of principle or in terms of mind. . . . When Wen Kung [Chu Hsi] said that *jen* is the character of the mind and the principle of love, he was speaking in terms of principle."[96]

According to Chu Hsi, in the *Analects* and the *Book of Mencius* there are cases where *jen* is spoken of purely from the point of view of the character of the mind, such as "Master oneself and return to propriety,"[97] "Be respectful in private life,"[98] and "Humanity is man's mind."[99] There are also cases where *jen* is spoken of purely from the point of view of the principle of love, such as "Filial piety and brotherly respect are the root of *jen*,"[100] "The man of *jen* loves others,"[101] "The mind of commiseration [is *jen*],"[102] and so forth.[103] But this does not mean that the two aspects are two different things. The difference between them is only that between substance and function, and between being spoken of collectively or separately. When Chu Hsi said that *jen* is the principle of love, he meant what Ch'eng I intended in saying that "spoken of separately, it is one of the four"[104]—that is, humanity, righteousness, propriety, and wisdom spoken of separately;

when he said that *jen* is the character of the mind, he meant what Ch'eng I intended in saying that "spoken of collectively, it embraces all four"[105]—that is, the Four Virtues spoken of together.[106] Chu Hsi said, "The character of the mind is spoken of from the combination of the Four Beginnings, while the principle of love is spoken of merely from the whole and part of *jen* itself, the issuing forth of which is love, while its principle is *jen*. *Jen* includes the Four Beginnings because of the operation of its spirit of life."[107] He also said, "Righteousness, propriety, and wisdom are all present in the mind, but humanity is merged as one. Separately speaking, *jen* is the master of love. Collectively speaking, it includes the other three virtues."[108] In other words,

> The principle of love is spoken of separately as one thing, while the character of the mind is spoken of collectively as including the four. Therefore, when spoken of together, all the four are characters of the mind and *jen* is the master. Spoken of separately, *jen* is the principle of love; righteousness, the principle of appropriateness; propriety, the principle of respect and reverence, deference and humility; and wisdom, the principle of discriminating what is right and wrong.[109]

The character of the mind and the principle of love can also be spoken of as substance and function. Chu Hsi said, "To speak of the character of the mind collectively, before it is activated it is substance, and after it is activated it is function. To speak of the principle of love separately, *jen* is substance and commiseration is function."[110] Ch'en Ch'un said, "The character of the mind refers, collectively, to substance, while the principle of love refers, separately, to function."[111] But regardless of whether one is speaking collectively or separately, of substance or of function, *jen* cannot be divided in two. It is not the case that aside from the character of the mind there is a separate principle of love.[112] That is why Chu Hsi said, "The character of the mind is the same as the principle of love. They are not two different things."[113] The character of the mind as the substance of *jen* is the mind of Heaven and Earth to produce things, and the principle of love as the function of *jen* is "the warm and rich air of spring in which the mind of Heaven and Earth is revealed. By summer the force of life grows, by autumn the force of life is collected, and by winter the force of life is stored."[114] The central point here is that the character of the mind and the principle of love are both forces of life. A pupil asked, "To be completely merged without any selfishness is the principle of love. Is the practice of *jen* with realization in the self the character of the mind?" Chu Hsi answered, "It is all right to explain the terms this way, but I am afraid it is not thorough enough as far as the fundamental is concerned."[115] By "the fundamental," Chu Hsi meant Ch'eng I's doctrine of *jen* as comparable to seeds.[116]

There is a long passage by Chu Hsi that summarizes the ideas brought forth above:

> The [*Lun-meng*] *chi-chu* explains *jen* as the principle of love and the character of the mind. Love is commisera-

tion, which is feeling. Its principle is called *jen*. With reference to the character of the mind, character is merely love. When it is called the character of the mind, it means the controlling power of love. In the way man is made up, his principle is the principle of Heaven and Earth and his material force is the material force of Heaven and Earth. Principle has no trace and cannot be seen; it can be seen in material force. One must realize that the idea of *jen* means a warm and harmonious force without differentiation. Its material force is the material force of the positive cosmic element (yang) and spring of Heaven and Earth, and its principle is the mind of Heaven and Earth to produce things. . . . Disciples in the Confucian School generally only asked about the task of practicing *jen*. As to the whole and part of *jen*, each of them had understood the idea. . . . There is only one *jen*. Although spoken of separately, numerous principles are embraced in it, and although spoken of collectively, numerous principles are embraced in it.[117]

We have here the cardinal ideas of the **Jen-shuo**.

Scholars understood the principle of love and the character of the mind differently. Perhaps the most sophisticated among them were Chu Hsi's pupils Li T'ang-tzu and Hsü Yü. Li T'ang-tzu said,

> "Comforting the old, being faithful to friends, and cherishing the young"[118] are of course *jen*, but they are also love. . . . The reason for comforting, being faithful, and cherishing is principle, not love. . . . Therefore love belongs to feeling and is one of the items of *jen*. Principle belongs to nature and the totality of the way of *jen*. Hence love is not *jen* but the principle of love is *jen*. . . . The mind is the master of nature and feeling. Since it is the master of nature, all principles of why a thing is so are present in the mind, and since it is the master of feeling, all principles of why a thing should be so issue forth from the mind. In this process principle is fully realized and love operates, because the mind is the master. This being the case, isn't *jen* the character of the mind?

Commenting on this, Chu Hsi said, "Your explanation of the principle of love is close to the truth, but with regard to the character of the mind you should think of Master Ch'eng's analogy of seeds."[119] Li's interpretation in terms of what is and what should be, and of the mind as the master of nature and feeling, is truly refined, but he overlooked the mind of Heaven and Earth to produce things and *jen* as seeds, and thus overlooked the opening passage of the **Jen-shuo**.

Hsü Yü said,

> The character of the mind is the way to produce. This is so because the mind of Heaven and Earth is to produce things, and man receives it as his mind, which is called *jen*. Its substance is identical with Heaven and Earth and penetrates all things. Its principle unites all goodness and includes the Four Beginnings. . . . Spoken of collectively, it is the character of the mind. Spoken of separately, it is the principle of love. The foun-

dation of what is spoken of collectively issues forth to become the function of what is spoken of separately, and the function of what is spoken of separately is combined to become the foundation of what is spoken of collectively. They should not be bifurcated as two different things that are big and small, fundamental and secondary. Because the principle of *jen* has not been clearly understood, people have been misled by material endowment and beclouded with selfish desires, causing the way of growth to stop and the Principle of Heaven to cease operation. . . . If man can personally realize *jen,* he will make sure that not the slightest selfishness can be injected into the substance of production and reproduction, so that it will operate and penetrate, reaching everywhere and covering everything. Only then can the character of the mind and the principle of love be fully realized.

Commenting on this, Chu Hsi said, "The general idea of this passage is correct, but the principle of love should not be understood [purely] as function. You should ponder this. In time, things will become smooth and harmonious, and what is right and what is wrong will naturally be seen.[120]

Hsü's interpretation is superior to Li's because Hsü emphasized the way of production. But his idea of identification with Heaven and Earth was a notion that Chu Hsi did not easily accept. In his reply to Chou Mu (1141-1202), the Master said,

What is called the character of the mind is the same as what Master Ch'eng called seeds of grain, and what is called the principle of love is precisely *jen* as love before it is activated and love as *jen* that has been activated. You should only think along these lines and need not introduce extraneous conceptions that will only confuse the issue. If one understands *jen* at this point, it is all right to be identified with Heaven and Earth and the ten thousand things. If one does not understand this and forthwith considers forming one body with Heaven and Earth and the ten thousand things as *jen,* there will be no solution.[121]

As to the task of practicing *jen,* Chu Hsi repeatedly said that if one personally realizes and thinks about the character of the mind and the principle of love, one will understand *jen.*[122] Personal realization means effort. A pupil said, "When one compares the love that has been activated, one knows that it is the character of the mind. And when one points to *jen* that has not been activated, one knows that it is the principle of love." Chu Hsi commented,

One must clearly see the principle in places where one applies oneself to the concrete task. Then the particular meaning will emerge. Take "Mastering oneself and returning to the propriety."[123] How should these be done to become *jen?* "Be respectful in private life and be serious in handling affairs,"[124] and "When you go abroad, behave to everyone as if you were receiving a great guest."[125] Mastering oneself and returning to propriety is basically not *jen,* but one must find out from mastering oneself and returning to propriety wherein *jen* lies, personally realize it in the way relevant to oneself, and not seek it outside.[126]

Professor Mou Tsung-san vigorously opposes Chu Hsi's doctrine of the principle of love and the character of the mind. He regards Chu Hsi as following Ch'eng I's theory of *jen* as nature and love as feeling; dividing the substance of *jen* into the three portions of mind, nature, and feeling; splitting principle and material force into two categories; and explaining *jen* according to the formula of "the character of the mind and the principle of love." In this way, he says, Chu Hsi made *jen* static and dead. The *jen* Chu Hsi talked about is "merely the existing principle of existentialism, quietly lying there," according to Professor Mou. Therefore it is not concrete, vital, or alive. The character of the mind is merely the character of the operation of the material force, for the Four Virtues are rooted in origination, flourishing, advantage, and firmness,[127] which are but the four stages of the transformation of the two material forces of yin and yang (passive and active cosmic forces).[128]

Professor Mou agrees with Ch'eng Hao and Lu Hsiang-shan's theory that mind is principle. To him, the mind is the original mind, not the mind that commands and unites nature and feeling; likewise, nature is the original nature, not the nature different from feeling that involves material force. Hence Professor Mou thinks that Chu Hsi rigidly adhered to Ch'eng I's line of thought and that his theoretical construction was based on the idea that *jen* is the character of the mind and the principle of love—a formula decidedly different from the linear, direct system of Confucius and Mencius as understood by other Sung dynasty (960-1279) Confucians.[129] Since Mou's standpoint is that "mind is principle," whereas Chu Hsi's was that "nature is principle," naturally they cannot be expected to agree. To Ch'eng I and Chu Hsi, *jen* was a force of growth and the mind was the principle of growth. To say that their idea of *jen* was a static one is hardly fair. According to Professor Ch'ien Mu, Chu Hsi's "doctrine that *jen* is the character of the mind and the principle of love is a synthesis of the ideas of Ch'eng I and Lu Hsiang-shan. Later scholars who arbitrarily put Chu Hsi on the side of Ch'eng I and declare him different from Lu really have failed to examine the matter clearly."[130]

JEN AS FORMING ONE BODY WITH THINGS AND JEN AS CONSCIOUSNESS

The **Jen-shuo** puts forth the theory that *jen* is the character of the mind and the principle of love. On this basis Chu Hsi criticized two doctrines. One is that *jen* means forming one body with things. Its chief representative was Yang Shih. Chu Hsi held that forming one body with things does not really make *jen* a substance. The other is the doctrine that *jen* is consciousness, as advocated by Hsieh Liang-tso. To Chu Hsi, this theory does not explain what *jen* itself is. But in neither case did Chu Hsi go into detail. Having made these main points in the **Jen-shuo,** he proceeded to say that, generally speaking, those who advocate the theory of forming one body will cause people to be vague, confused, and perhaps to treat things as the self, while those who advocate the theory of *jen* as consciousness will cause people to get excited and perhaps confuse selfish desires with principle. He did not explain further.

There has been a great deal of discussion on these two theories, but it is not necessary to go into them here except to quote Professor T'ang Chün-i. According to him, Chu Hsi regarded impartiality as what precedes *jen* and forming one body as what follows *jen,* and therefore regarded neither as being its substance. As to consciousness, T'ang holds that it refers to *jen* as including wisdom, for the mind can be conscious of principle and does possess the character of wisdom. Thus consciousness is the last expression of *jen* but is not *jen* itself. This explanation by T'ang is simple and perfectly clear. He goes on to say that Chu Hsi was different from previous thinkers, who only discussed *jen* in one respect:

> Chu Hsi views *jen* from what precedes it, namely impartiality; from what follows it, namely, forming one body with things; from the inside, namely, the nature of consciousness of the mind; and from the outside, namely, the feeling resulting from the consciousness of things. Above, it penetrates Heaven. Below, it permeates man. As the root, it exists in the one principle in the self. As branches, it scatters to become the ten thousand things—from love, respect, appropriateness, and the discrimination of right and wrong, to loving people and benefiting things. All these are delineated. In this discussion of *jen* from what is before and what is after, from the inside and the outside, from above and below, and from the root and branches, there is, of course, a refined and careful idea.[131]

This amounts to a eulogy for the *Jen-shuo.*

Professor Mou looks at the matter differently. To him, forming one body with things is the manifestation of the true mind, which is precisely substance in the true sense. He also says that the consciousness of people's pain is precisely that which explains what *jen* itself is. In his view, Chu Hsi's assertion that the doctrine of *jen* as forming one body is inadequate and the doctrine of *jen* as consciousness goes too far is absolutely absurd.[132] Mou's analysis of the *Jen-shuo* is extremely sophisticated.[133] His refutation is also in sharp contrast to T'ang's standpoint. Chu Hsi rejected the two doctrines because *jen* as forming one body with things deals with only one aspect of *jen,* and *jen* as consciousness does not distinguish between substance and function. In other words, the former fails to understand substance and the latter attends exclusively to function. For Chu Hsi, *jen* is a complete virtue with both substance and function, which come from the same source and are not two different things.

DISCUSSIONS ON THE "JEN-SHUO"

Both before and after the *Jen-shuo* was finalized, it must have circulated extensively among pupils and friends, for the response to it was great. The *Jen-shuo* was the focus of many of the discussions about the mind of Heaven and Earth to produce things, the character of the mind, the principle of love, forming one body with things, and the theory of *jen* as consciousness. Chu Hsi's replies to Wu I on the mind of Heaven and Earth to produce things, the character of nature, the principle of love, and conscious-

ness[134] do not explicitly refer to the *Jen-shuo,* but the fact that the order of topics is the same as that in the *Jen-shuo* makes it plausible that the questions pertained to the treatise. His discussions with Chang Shih on the *Jen-shuo* consist of four letters in the *Wen-chi* and two in Chang's literary collections on the *Jen-shuo.*[135]

The first letter to Chang Shih explains every sentence of the *Jen-shuo.*[136] Chu Hsi's treatise begins with the statement that "the mind of Heaven and Earth is to produce things." Chang Shih found fault with this, but Chu Hsi insisted that the aim of Heaven and Earth is to give life and that the sentence is not wrong. In reply, Chang Shih said, "The sentence that 'the mind of Heaven and Earth is to produce things' is all right as ordinarily understood, but I am afraid it makes better sense merely to say that there is the mind of Heaven and Earth to produce things and that man receives this mind as his mind."[137]

What Chang Shih was saying is that Heaven and Earth do not consciously produce things, but that man receives from them the mind to produce things. This suggestion was not accepted. Chang Shih also questioned whether "the mind that cannot bear to see the suffering of others can embrace [or encompass] the Four Beginnings [of the feelings of commiseration, shame and dislike, deference and compliance, and right and wrong]." To Chu Hsi, however, "That the mind that cannot bear to see the suffering of others can embrace the Four Beginnings is comparable to the fact that humanity can embrace the Four Virtues of humanity, righteousness, propriety and wisdom." Later, Chang Shih wrote to say that although the mind that cannot bear to see the suffering of others can embrace the Four Beginnings, it is better to generalize and call it humanity.[138] To Chang Shih, the substance of the man of *jen* is always good, but Chu Hsi felt that Chang Shih did not understand that *jen* is the source of all virtues. Chang Shih thought that "when spoken of along with righteousness, propriety, and wisdom, the manifestation of humanity becomes the mind that cannot bear the suffering of others." Chu Hsi felt this was unsatisfactory, because humanity, righteousness, propriety, and wisdom "are all rooted in the mind. They are principles before manifestation." Chang Shih held that "the way of the man of *jen* embraces everything," but Chu Hsi wanted to know why it embodies everything.

Chang Shih also considered that "what Master Ch'eng [Ch'eng I] criticized was defining *jen* as love." This is a criticism of Chu Hsi's statement in the *Jen-shuo* that "what Master Ch'eng criticized was defining the expression of love as *jen.*" Chu Hsi countered, "Master Ch'eng said, 'Humanity is nature while love is feeling. How can one regard love as humanity?' This saying explicitly disapproves of treating feeling as nature, but does not say that the nature of humanity is not expressed in the feeling of love, or that humanity in love is not based on the nature of humanity."

Moreover, Chang Shih took the meaning of *yüan* (origination) as going beyond producing things. Chu Hsi thought it was a great defect to say this, for he believed that *yüan* is the source not only of things but of all virtues.[139] Chang Shih replied, "When I said the other day that the meaning of *yüan* goes beyond the production of things, it leads to the suspicion that I was only talking about producing things and thus did not fully bring out the idea of *yüan* as production and reproduction [in all spheres of life]. Now you have fully explained the concept of production."[140]

Finally, Chang Shih believed that the man of *jen* loves everything but that there is a distinction in the application of *jen*, whereas Chu Hsi regarded making the distinction as the task of righteousness. "Although humanity and righteousness are not separated, in their function they each have their own sphere and should not be confused."

Chu Hsi's second letter on the *Jen-shuo*[141] is his reply to Chang Shih's response to his first letter.[142] Chang Shih had contended that the substance of *jen* is impartiality *(kung)*. When one is impartial, he said, there will not be the selfishness that divides the self and others, and thus love will prevail everywhere. To Chu Hsi, however, "*Jen* is the character of nature and the foundation of love. . . . If impartiality, which is extended to the whole world and which eliminates the selfishness that divides the self and others, is considered the substance of *jen*, I am afraid that that impartiality is totally devoid of feeling, like the emptiness of wood and stone."

Chu Hsi's third letter is concerned with the theory of *jen* as consciousness.[143] Chang Shih had written Chu Hsi on the theory, but his letter is no longer extant. In his reply Chu Hsi said, "The man of *jen* has consciousness, it is true, but consciousness itself is not *jen*. Who is going to make the mind know, or make it conscious? . . . However, consciousness is merely the functioning of wisdom. Only the man of *jen* can have both *jen* and wisdom. Therefore it is all right to say that a man of *jen* certainly has consciousness, but is not all right to say that the mind's consciousness is *jen*."

Chu Hsi's fourth letter stresses the point that neither impartiality nor forming one body with things is the substance of *jen*. Chang Shih had written that "one forms one body with Heaven and Earth because man and things share the secret of production and reproduction inherent in the mind of Heaven and Earth, and this is the principle of love."[144] In response, Chu Hsi said that when one is impartial one looks upon Heaven and Earth and things as one body and loves all, but added that "the principle of love is an original principle that exists by itself and is not the result of forming one body with Heaven and Earth and all things."[145]

In this debate, Chu Hsi won most of the arguments, although sometimes he went too far in criticizing his friend. For example, Chang Shih merely said that the man of *jen* is always good, but Chu Hsi criticized him for not knowing that *jen* is the highest good; also, Chang Shih only said that love is prevalent everywhere, but Chu Hsi cen-

sured him for not recognizing the substance of *jen*. Moreover, Chu Hsi's understanding of consciousness left something to be desired. As Professor Mou Tsung-san has pointed out, "Chu Hsi mistakenly considers the consciousness of *jen* as the consciousness of wisdom. Because of this misunderstanding, he has confined consciousness to wisdom."[146] Mou's analysis of Chu Hsi's four letters is extremely refined.[147] He does not completely agree with Chang Shih, but in every case considers Chu Hsi to be wrong.

In the **Wen-chi** there are also two letters to Ho Hao (1128-1175) on the **Jen-shuo**.[148] A survey of the **Yü-lei** and the **Wen-chi** shows that the opening sentence of the **Jen-shuo**, about the mind of Heaven and Earth, generated the most controversy. To Ho Hao, the mind of Heaven and Earth is *jen* because when the yang element grows, the spirit of unceasing production and reproduction is revealed; however, Chu Hsi thought that to wait for the yang element to grow would divide the process into two sections, because that theory leaves the yang element before its return unaccounted for.[149] Chu Hsi's student Shen Hsien did not understand the idea that the mind of Heaven and Earth is to produce things. The Teacher explained it to him, saying, "The mind of Heaven and Earth is simply to produce. Everything has to be produced before there can be a thing. . . . This is a general discussion on the substance of *jen*. Within it are items and specifications."[150] We do not know whether this clarified matters for Shen, but Chu Hsi's discussions with Chang Shih, reported above, in all likelihood satisfied him. As Chu Hsi told Hu Shih, "I recently received two letters from Ch'infu [Chang Shih] on the 'Jen-shuo' in which he raised many critical questions. I have answered them all. Lately he has written to say that he no longer has any doubts."[151]

Due to these discussions, the **Jen-shuo** was modified in some respects. As Chu Hsi wrote Lü Tsu-ch'ien, "The **Jen-shuo** has recently been revised further, becoming clearer and more refined than before."[152] Comparing the treatise with Chang Shih's questions and objections, we can see that the passage about the Four Beginnings being encompassed by the mind that cannot bear to see others' suffering is no longer found in the treatise. Nor does the final treatise refer to Mencius' idea that the man of *jen* loves all, an omission obviously due to Chang Shih's argument. But Chu Hsi held firmly to the doctrine that the mind of Heaven and Earth is to produce things. In his letter to Ho Hao, he said,

> I have maintained that *jen* is the mind of Heaven and Earth, and that man and things receive this mind as their mind. Although this idea is the product of my personal opinion of the moment, I humbly believe that it opens up precisely the point that there is no separation between Heaven and man. In this respect, the treatise seems to be refined and thorough. If one follows this matter through, one will see that in the undifferentiated unity between *jen* and the mind is naturally a distinction.[153]

For Chu Hsi to say that he had opened up the point that there is no separation between Heaven and man seems a bold statement, but it does not mean that he was completely satisfied with the *Jen-shuo.* On the contrary, he himself said that only the earlier section of the treatise is satisfactory.[154] Probably he meant that the latter section dealing with the theories of *jen* as consciousness and as forming one body with all things does not clearly explain why they are not *jen.* Be that as it may, in Chu Hsi's *Jen-shuo,* the doctrine of *jen* reaches its highest point of development in the history of Chinese thought. As Ch'en Ch'un put it, scholars from the Han dynasty (206 B.C.–A.D. 220) on "have lost the fundamental idea of the law of the mind traditionally transmitted in the Confucian School. Wen Kung [Chu Hsi] was the first to describe *jen* as the character of the mind and the principle of love. For the first time the explanation of *jen* is to the point."[155]

THE DIAGRAM OF THE "JEN-SHUO"

The "Jen-shuo-t'u" (Diagram of the *Treatise on Humanity*) is reproduced below in chapter 18 (p. 281). The important points are given in the comment following the diagram and need not be repeated here. Suffice it to say that the diagram's general emphasis on practice and its inclusion of impartiality twice both suggest Chang Shih's influence on Chu Hsi.

CHANG SHIH'S "JEN-SHUO"

Chang Shih also wrote a "Jen-shuo," which has sometimes been confused with Chu Hsi's treatise. Under the title of Chu Hsi's treatise there is a note which says, "The Chekiang edition erroneously considers Master Nan-hsüan's [Chang Shih's] 'Jen-shuo' as the Master's 'Jen-shuo' and considers the Master's 'Jen-shuo' as its preface."[156] Even Chu Hsi's pupil Ch'en Ch'un thought that Chu Hsi had written both of the "Jen-shuo," one of which had gotten into Chang Shih's literary collection by mistake.[157] Another pupil, Hsiung Chieh (1199 *cs*), took Chang's treatise to be Chu Hsi's.[158] In reality, each man wrote his own treatise, and there is no basis for believing that one is the preface to the other. Chang Shih's "Jen-shuo" is preserved in chapter 18 of the *Nan-hsüan Hsien-sheng wen-chi* (Collection of literary works of Master Chang Shih). The whole treatise consists of 477 characters, plus notes totaling 33 characters, so it is not quite half the length of Chu Hsi's *Jen-shuo.* It says, in brief,

> In man's nature the Four Virtues of humanity, righteousness, propriety, and wisdom are present. Humanity is the principle of love, righteousness the principle of appropriateness, propriety the principle of deference, and wisdom the principle of knowledge. . . . In man's nature there are only these four, and they control the ten thousand goodness. What is called the principle of love is the mind of Heaven and Earth to produce things, from which *jen* is born. Thus *jen* is the leader of the Four Virtues and can embrace all of them. Because in man's nature there are these Four Virtues, when they are expressed in feelings the feeling of commiseration penetrates all of them. That is why nature and feeling are respectively substance and function, and the way of the mind is the master of nature and

> feeling. Because man is beclouded by selfish desires, he loses the principle of nature and becomes devoid of *jen.* . . . The essential point in the practice of *jen* lies in self-mastery. . . . Nothing can becloud the principle of love, which penetrates Heaven and Earth and all things like arteries and veins, and which functions everywhere. Therefore, to designate love as *jen* is to be blind to its substance, for *jen* is the principle of love, and to designate impartiality as *jen* is to lose its reality, for impartiality is what enables man to be *jen.* . . . Only the man of *jen* can extend it and be appropriate; that is what is preserved by righteousness. . . . This being the case, the student must consider searching for *jen* as essential, and in the practice of *jen* consider self-mastery as the way.[159]

Readers may well be amazed at the similarity between this treatise and that of Chu Hsi. Practically all its major ideas are found in both treatises, except that Chang's treatise puts more emphasis on the ideas of self-mastery, eliminating becloudedness, and knowing what to preserve. Chang's treatise also stresses how the man of *jen* can preserve righteousness, propriety, and wisdom. Chu Hsi rejected Yang Shih's doctrine that forming one body with things is *jen,* while Chang Shih rejected impartiality, which means practically the same thing. Chu Hsi criticized Hsieh Liang-tso's theory that consciousness is *jen,* while Chang Shih merely said that the man of *jen* can be conscious and cannot be darkened. Their major difference is that Chu Hsi talked about the two aspects of the character of the mind and the principle of love, whereas Chang Shih spoke only about the principle of love.

It may be argued that Chang's treatise came first and that that is why Chu Hsi's is fuller. However, in his letter to Lü Tsu-ch'ien, Chu Hsi mentioned that Chang Shih had written him to say that Chang's own "Jen-shuo" had been revised, and in the same letter, Chu Hsi also mentioned Lü's promise to write a preface for the *I-Lo yüan-yüan lu* [Records of the origin of the school of the Ch'engs].[160] Since the *Yüan-yüan lu* was completed in 1173, two years after Chu Hsi's *Jen-shuo,* Chang Shih's "Jen-shuo" must have been written later. As to why Chang Shih chose to write a "Jen-shuo" after Chu Hsi had written one, there is a possible explanation: he accepted the concept of *jen* as produced by the mind of Heaven and Earth, but did not accept the idea that the mind of Heaven and Earth is to produce things. Hence Chang Shih refrained from talking about the character of the mind. Chu Hsi's *Jen-shuo* tends to be theoretical. Although it says that the student should eagerly search for *jen,* it does not prescribe any method for doing so. In contrast, Chang Shih elaborated on the ability of the man of *jen* to extend to the point of preserving righteousness, propriety, and wisdom. Most importantly, he emphasizes the point that to practice *jen,* one must master oneself.

Chu Hsi's *Jen-shuo* quotes the *Analects* on self-mastery once, but only in passing. We know that Chang Shih considered Chu Hsi's "K'echai chi" [Account of the studio of self-mastery] to be superior to Chu Hsi's *Jen-shuo,* thus implying that the latter was deficient on self-mastery. Chang Shih may have written his "Jen-shuo" to make up for Chu Hsi's deficiency, since for Chang Shih, self-mastery was a key virtue. This can be seen in Huang Tsung-hsi's *Sung-Yüan hsüeh-an* (Anthology and critical accounts of the Neo-Confucians of the Sung and Yüan dynasties), whose only quote from Chang Shih's "Jen-shuo" is the shortest sentence on self-mastery in it.[161] Yet it is not true that Chu Hsi neglected self-mastery. In a letter to Lü Tsu-ch'ien he maintained that learning and self-mastery must be pursued equally, and added that in a letter to Chang Shih he had written one or two paragraphs on the defect of ignoring self-mastery.[162] (The letter referred to is lost, so Chu Hsi must have written more than four letters to Chang Shih on the *Jen-shuo.*)

Chu Hsi also wrote a letter to Chang Shih specifically on the latter's "Jen-shuo," taking exception to a number of points in Chang's draft.[163] He said that his friend "only talks about nature but not feeling, and furthermore, does not say that the mind penetrates both nature and feeling, thus seeming to oppose nature to mind." In the final text of Chang Shih's "Jen-shuo," there are sentences expressing the ideas that nature and feeling are mutually penetrated as substance and function, and that the mind is the master of nature and feeling—undoubtedly additions due to Chu Hsi's criticism. Chu Hsi had also objected to Chang Shih's statement that "when one is broad and extremely impartial and interpenetrates, like arteries and veins, with Heaven and Earth and things, the principle of love will be obtained internally and the function of love will be expressed externally." To Chu Hsi, "The principle of love is native to one's nature. It prevails because of broadness and extreme impartiality, but it is not the product of broadness and extreme impartiality." The final draft of Chang's "Jen-shuo" says, "If one is broad and extremely impartial, the principle of love originally present in nature will not be beclouded . . . and, like arteries and veins, will penetrate Heaven and Earth and all things and function everywhere." This shows that Chang Shih adopted Chu Hsi's theory that the principle of love exists before forming one body with things. Moreover, Chang's statement that "to designate impartiality as *jen* is to lose its reality," together with its note, which quotes Ch'eng I's saying that "one should not forthwith point to impartiality as *jen,*"[164] is obviously a revision made because of Chu Hsi's criticism.

However, Chang Shih strongly adhered to the idea of impartiality. Therefore, in the final text there is the sentence, "Impartiality is why a person can be *jen.*" In the original draft, Chang Shih had said "Everything in the world is part of my humanity," to which Chu Hsi objected, "Things are things and *jen* is my mind. Why do you take things to be my mind?" The original sentence does not appear in the final draft, another indication of Chang's respect for Chu Hsi's opinion. Actually, as Professor Mou Tsung-san has pointed out, Chang Shih did not equate things with the mind but merely meant that everything is penetrated by the operation of the substance of *jen.*[165] Comparing the earlier draft to the final draft, we must conclude that Chang

Shih modified his "Jen-shuo" in accordance with Chu Hsi's opinions. This is further evidence that Chang Shih's "Jen-shuo" is later than Chu Hsi's.

DID CHU HSI WRITE CHANG SHIH'S "JEN-SHUO"?

At the International Conference on Chu Hsi held in Honolulu, Hawaii in 1982, Professor Satō Hitoshi presented a paper on Chu Hsi's *Jen-shuo*[166] in which he stated that both Ch'en Ch'un and Hsiung Chieh failed to realize that Chu Hsi had nothing to do with Chang Shih's *Jen-shuo.* In 1981, I had published an essay in Chinese on Chu Hsi's *Jen-shuo,* of which the material here is a translation. It was reprinted in my *Chu-hsüeh lun-chi* (Studies on Chu Hsi),[167] but appeared too late for the conference. After the conference, Dr. Liu Shu-hsien published his reflections, which read in part:

> The *Nan-hsüan wen-chi* [Collection of literary works of Master Chang Shih] was completely compiled by Chu Hsi. He deleted all letters and essays that did not conform to his own line of thought and regarded them as Chang Shih's immature work of early years. Is it possible that Nan-hsüan never revised his early draft into the final form after it had met with Chu Hsi's criticism? After Nan-hsüan's death, Chu Hsi wrote another *Jen-shuo* based on his agreement with Nan-hsüan, included it in the *Nan-hsüan wen-chi* as Nan-hsüan's own work, and published it as such. That is why some pupils such as Ch'en Ch'un and Hsiung Chieh regarded this *Jen-shuo* as the work of Chu Hsi. In my understanding, unless this was the situation, it is fundamentally impossible to imagine that Chu Hsi's personal pupils got confused in such a manner. Of course, probably because of his limited ability to express himself in English, Professor Satō basically did not give any answer to the question I raised. Mr. [Wing-tsit] Chan answered for him and said that Ch'en Ch'un was not with Chu Hsi at the time and that Hsiung Chieh's understanding was greatly deficient, and that that was why such a confusion resulted. But I consider such an answer to be unsatisfactory. Ch'en Ch'un was Chu Hsi's favorite pupil in his late years and "defended the Teacher with great energy" [quote from Ch'üan Tsu-wang, 1705-1755].[168] Since he decidedly said that Chu Hsi wrote two versions of the "Jen-shuo," he must have had some basis [for this]. Probably Chu Hsi wrote another *Jen-shuo,* accepted Nan-hsüan's criticism, put in an essay the concept of self-mastery, and adopted Nan-hsüan's sayings such as "Heaven, Earth, and the ten thousand things penetrate one another like blood and arteries." To commemorate his deceased friend, he took this essay as Nan-hsüan's final conclusion and included it in the *Nan-hsüan wen-chi.* Such a scenerio is certainly not beyond the imagination.[169]

Professor Liu's theory is both original and bold, but I hold to my opinion and agree with Professor Satō that Chu Hsi and Chang Shih each wrote a "Jen-shuo." As the *Ssu-k'u ch'üan-shu tsung-mu t'i-yao* (Essentials of the contents of the *Complete Collection of the Four Libraries*) states, Hsiung Chieh "was extremely superficial and there is nothing to recommend him."[170] But Ch'en Ch'un did not become a pupil of Chu Hsi until 1190. By that time, Chu Hsi's **Jen-shuo** had been finished for twenty years. Since several writers had written a "Jen-shuo" and each one had been copied and passed around, it was natural for Ch'en Ch'un, living in an isolated village, to believe that his Teacher had written two treatises on *jen*. The "Jen-shuo" issue was no longer alive, and Ch'en was not familiar with Chu Hsi's **Jen-shuo**. As he told a pupil, "Wen Kung has two treatises on *jen*. Have you seen them? One treatise got into the *Nan-hsüan wen-chi* by mistake, and the other recently reached me from Wen-ling."[171] Thus Ch'en was simply not well informed. As to putting Chang Shih's name on a treatise of his own, this would have been entirely out of character for Chu Hsi. He was never known to employ such devious means, and he could easily have commemorated his friend in a straightforward way.

Notes

1. *Wen-chi,* 36:7a-16b, fourth, fifth, and sixth letters in reply to Lu Tzu-ching (Lu Hsiang-shan).

2. *Ibid.,* 30:19a-20b; 32:4a-6a, 24a-26b; 64:28b-29b, third, thirty-third, thirty-fourth, and forty-eighth letters in reply to Chang Ch'in-fu (Chang Shih), and letter to the gentlemen of Hunan.

3. *Ibid.,* 36:19a-28b, fourth through ninth letters in reply to Ch'en T'ung-fu (Ch'en Liang).

4. *Ibid.,* 31:4b-8a, 32:16b-24b, 35:6b (Chang Ching-fu); 33:15a-16a (Lü Po-kung); 40:29a-30e (Ho Shu-ching); 42:8a (Hu Kuang-chung); 42:17b-19b (Wu Hui-shu); 42:35a-36a (Shih Tzu-chung); 5:13a (Lin Hsi-chih); 43:28a (Lin Tse-chih); 46:26a-29a (Hu Po-feng); 47:7b-8a, 26b-28a (Lü Tzu-yüeh); 47:7b (Venerable Sir); 50:25a (Yü Chan-chih); 50:34a (Chou Shun-pi); 54:14b (Chou Shu-chin); 56:12b-13b (Fang Pin-wang); 57:2b-3a (Li Yao-ch'ing); 57:10a-11a (Ch'en An-ch'ing); 58:2b-3b (Yang Chung-ssu); 58:21a (Ch'en Ch'i-chih); and 58:28b-29b (Hsü Chu-fu).

5. *Ibid.,* 33:15b, twenty-fourth letter in reply to Lü Po-kung (Lü Tsu-ch'ien).

6. This is from the commentary on the first hexagram, *ch'ien* (Heaven, male), in the *Book of Changes.*

7. *Yün-men Wen-yen Ch'an-shih yü-lu* [Recorded sayings of the Ch'an Patriarch Wen-yen of Yün-men Mountain], in the *Hsü-tsang-ching* [Supplementary Buddhist canon], first collection, B, *Ku-tsun-su yü-lu* [Recorded sayings of ancient elders], 17:189a.

8. *Wen-chi,* 47:26b-27a, twenty-fifth letter in reply to Lü Tzu-yüeh (Lü Tsu-chien).

9. *I chuan* [Commentary on the *Book of Changes*], 2:33a, in the *Erh-Ch'eng ch'üan-shu* [Complete works of the two Ch'engs] (*SPPY* ed.).

10. *Wen-chi,* 42:18a, tenth letter in reply to Wu Hui-shu (Wu I).

11. *Wai-shu* [Additional works], 3:1a, in the *Erh-ch'eng ch'üan-shu.* The *Wai-shu* does not specify whether

this saying was uttered by Ch'eng I or Ch'eng Hao, but it is generally accepted as Ch'eng I's saying. In his *Ming-tao ch'üan-shu* [Complete works of Ch'eng Hao], Shen Kuei of the Ming dynasty (1368-1644) ascribed it to Ch'eng Hao.

12. These are the Four Qualities of the *ch'ien* hexagram in the *Book of Changes.*

13. *Book of Mencius,* 2A:6.

14. Yang Shih's doctrine may be found in the *Kuei-shan wen-chi* [Collection of literary writings of Yang Shih] (1590 ed.), 11:1b; 26:3a; and the *Kuei-shan yü-lu* [Recorded sayings of Yang Shih] (*SPTK* ed.), 2:10b. Hsieh Liang-tso's doctrine may be found in the *Shang-ts'ai yü-lu* [Recorded sayings of Hsieh Liang-tso] (*Chin-shih han-chi ts'ung-k'an* [Chinese works of the recent period] ed.), pt. 1, p. 2b, 13a-b; pt. 2, p. 1a.

15. *Book of Mencius,* 2A:2.

16. *Ibid.,* 6A:11.

17. *Yü-lei,* ch. 59, sec. 155 (p. 2239).

18. *Ibid.,* ch. 19, sec. 61 (p. 704).

19. *Wen-chi,* 33:12a-b. The "scholars of the Yung-chia school" refers to the historians and utilitarians active in the area of Yung-chia County in southeastern Chekiang Province.

20. Tomoeda Ryūtarō, *Shushi no shisō keisei* [Formation of Master Chu's thought] (Tokyo: Shunjūsha, 1979), p. 114.

21. *Wen-chi,* 32:16b-26b, forty-second through forty-seventh letters in reply to Chang Ch'in-fu (Chang Shih).

22. *Ibid.,* 87:9b, funeral address for Chang Shih.

23. *Yü-lei,* ch. 103, sec. 41 (p. 4142).

24. *Ibid.*

25. *Wen-chi,* 32:21a, "Further Discussion on the 'Jen-shuo.'" The "K'e-chai chi" [Account of the studio of self-mastery] is found in the *Wen-chi,* 77:15a-16b.

26. Mou Tsung-san, *Hsin-t'i yü hsing-t'i* [Substance of the mind and substance of nature] (Taipei: Cheng-chung Book Co., 1969), vol. 3, p. 229.

27. *Wen-chi,* 47:27a, twenty-fifth letter in reply to Lü Tzu-yüeh (Lü Tsu-chien).

28. *Ibid.,* 36:27a, ninth letter in reply to Ch'en T'ung-fu (Ch'en Liang).

29. The Four Books are the *Great Learning,* the *Analects,* the *Book of Mencius,* and the *Doctrine of the Mean.*

30. The "Yü-shan chiang-i" [Yü-shan lecture] is found in the *Wen-chi,* 74:17b-22a. Yü-shan is a county in Kiangsi. See also ch. 23 below.

31. Chu Hsi, *Lun-yü huo-wen* [Questions and answers on the *Analects*] (*Chin-shih han-chi ts'ung-k'an* ed.), 1:12a (p. 27), comment on 1:3.

32. Chu Hsi used the phrase "the character of the mind" in comments on the *Analects* 1:3, 6:5, 7:29, 15:8; and on the *Book of Mencius* 6A:11. He used "the complete character of the mind" in comments on the *Analects* 7:6, 33; 8:7; 12:1 and 2. "The mind of *jen* is the mind to love people" occurs in a comment on the *Book of Mencius* 4A:1; and "the foundation of *jen* is love" on 4A:27. "To love people is the application of *jen*" is used in reference to the *Analects* 12:22. "The principle of love" appears in the *Lun-yü huo-wen* 1:7b (p. 18); "the character of the mind" is found in *ibid.*, 6:5b (p. 260), 12:1a-b (pp. 423-424), and 18:2a (p. 625).

33. *Yü-lei,* ch. 19, sec. 57 (p. 703).

34. *Ibid.,* sec. 61 (p. 704).

35. Yamazaki Bisei, *Kairoku* [Records of the sea], ch. 20.

36. Yamaguchi Satsujō, *Jin no kenkyū* [Study of *jen*] (Tokyo: Iwanami Book Co., 1936), pp. 370-371.

37. Quoted in Ōtsuki Nobuyoshi, *Chu Tzu ssu-shu chi-chu tien-chü k'ao* [Investigation into the textual evidence of Master Chu's *Collected Commentaries on the Four Books*] (Taipei: Student Book Co., 1976), p. 5.

38. Yamaguchi, *Jin no Kenkyū,* pp. 376-377.

39. *Nan-hsüan Hsien-sheng wen-chi* [Collection of literary works of Master Chang Shih] (*Chin-shih han-chi ts'ung-shu* ed.), 20:12a (p. 661), thirteenth letter in reply to Chu Yüan-hui (Chu Hsi).

40. Ōtsuki, *Chu Tzu ssu-shu chi-chu tien-chü k'ao,* p. 5.

41. *Wen-chi,* 30:28b, ninth letter in reply to Chang Ch'in-fu; 32:25b, forty-seventh letter.

42. *Ibid.,* 42:19a, tenth letter in reply to Wu Hsi-shu.

43. *Hu Tzu chih-yen* [Master Hu's understanding of words] (*Yüeh-ya-t'ang ts'ung-shu* [Hall of Kwang-tung elegance series] ed.), 1:1a.

44. *Wen-chi,* 60:18a, second letter in reply to Tseng Tse-chih.

45. *I-shu* [Surviving works], 18:2a, in the *Erh-Ch'eng ch'üan-shu.*

46. *Ibid.,* 21B:2a.

47. *Wai-shu,* 3:1a.

48. *I chuan,* 1:2b.

49. *Yü-lei,* ch. 20, sec. 95 (p. 751).

50. *Ibid.,* ch. 25, sec. 27 (p. 979).

51. *Ibid.,* ch. 20, sec. 103 (p. 752).

52. *Ibid.,* sec. 102 (p. 752).

53. *I-ch'uan ching-shuo* [Ch'eng I's explanations of the classics], 6:2b, in the *Erh-Ch'eng ch'üan-shu.*

54. *Yü-lei,* ch. 25, sec. 21, 22 (pp. 976-977).

55. *Ibid.,* sec. 23 (p. 977).

56. *Ibid.,* sec. 20 (p. 976).

57. *Ibid.,* sec. 24 (p. 978).

58. *Ibid.,* ch. 45, sec. 19 (p. 1830).

59. *Wen-chi,* 41:12b, fourth letter in reply to Ch'eng Yün-fu (Ch'eng Hsün).

60. *Yü-lei,* ch. 25, sec. 21 (p. 976).

61. *Ibid.,* sec. 22, (pp. 976-977).

62. *Ibid.,* ch. 95, sec. 12 (p. 3839).

63. Chu Hsi, *Lun-yü chi-chu* [Collected commentaries on the *Analects*], comment on 7:29.

64. *Wen-chi,* supplementary collection, 9:1a, letter in reply to Liu Tao-chung (Liu Ping).

65. *Analects,* 13:19.

66. *Classic of Filial Piety,* ch. 14.

67. *I-shu,* 11:5b.

68. *Analects,* 7:14.

69. According to tradition, the lord of Ku-chu had wanted to transmit the throne to Shu-ch'i, his younger son. When he died, Shu-ch'i yielded to his elder brother Po-i, but Po-i declined and they both fled rather than take the throne. Later, when King Wu launched a military expedition against the Shang dynasty, out of loyalty the brothers tried to prevent it, but failed. Thereupon they retired to live on berries on a mountain and eventually starved to death.

70. *Yü-lei,* ch. 105, sec. 45 (p. 4186).

71. *Book of Mencius,* 6A:11.

72. *Analects,* 12:1.

73. *Wen-chi,* 59:8a, letter in reply to Li Yüan-han.

74. *Pei-hsi tzu-i* [Ch'en Ch'un's explanation of terms], sec. 59 (*Hsi-yin-hsüan ts'ung-shu* [Studio where time is highly valued series] ed., 1:26a-b). See my translation entitled *Neo-Confucian Terms Explained* (New York: Columbia University Press, 1986), pp. 75-76.

75. *Yü-lei,* ch. 20, sec. 87 (p. 748).

76. *Wen-chi,* 60:18a, second letter in reply to Tseng Tse-chih.

77. *Yü-lei,* ch. 20, sec. 98 (p. 751).

78. *Wen-chi,* 33:12a-b, eighteenth letter in reply to Lü Po-kung (Lü Tsu-ch'ien).

79. *Yü-lei,* ch. 20, sec. 127 (p. 767).

80. *Analects,* 1:2.

81. *Wen-chi,* 31:21b, thirtieth letter in reply to Chang Ching-fu (Chang Shih). The same idea is expressed in the *Yü-lei,* ch. 20, sec. 94 (p. 750).

82. *Book of Mencius,* 6A:11.

83. *Yü-lei,* ch. 59, sec. 155 (p. 2239).

84. *Wen-chi,* 42:8b, fifth letter in reply to Hu Kuang-chung (Hu Shih).

85. *Yü-lei,* ch. 6, sec. 117 (p. 191).

86. *Ibid.,* ch. 20, sec. 90 (pp. 748-749).

87. *Ibid.*

88. The Five Agents (or Five Elements) are Metal, Wood, Wood, Water, Fire, and Earth.

89. In Cheng Hsüan's (127-200) commentary on the first chapter of the *Doctrine of the Mean,* the Five Agents are equated with the Five Constant Virtues of humanity, righteousness, propriety, wisdom, and faithfulness.

90. *Lun-yü huo-wen* 1:7b (p. 18), comment on 1:2.

91. In the *Book of Mencius,* 2A:6, the Four Beginnings are the starting points of the Four Virtues of humanity, righteousness, propriety, and wisdom.

92. *Yü-lei,* ch. 20, sec. 93 (p. 750).

93. *Pei-hsi tzu-i,* sec. 50 (pt. 1, p. 24b); *Neo-Confucian Terms Explained,* p. 71.

94. *Yü-lei,* ch. 20, sec. 124 (p. 765).

95. *Ibid.,* sec. 97 (p. 751).

96. *Pei-hsi tzu-i,* sec. 73 (pt. 1, p. 32a); *Neo-Confucian Terms Explained,* p. 84.

97. *Analects,* 12:1.

98. *Ibid.,* 13:19.

99. *Book of Mencius,* 7B:16.

100. *Analects,* 1:2.

101. *Ibid.,* 4:2.

102. *Book of Mencius,* 2A:6.

103. *Yü-lei,* ch. 20, sec. 113 (p. 760). See also sec. 106 (p. 753).

104. *I chuan,* 1:2b.

105. *Ibid.*

106. *Ibid.,* sec. 101 (pp. 751-752).

107. *Ibid.*

108. *Ibid.,* sec. 109 (p. 755).

109. *Ibid.,* sec. 103 (p. 752).

110. *Ibid.,* sec. 104 (p. 750).

111. *Pei-hsi tzu-i,* sec. 73 (pt. 1, p. 32a); *Neo-Confucian Terms Explained,* p. 84.

112. *Yü-lei,* ch. 20, sec. 101 (p. 753).

113. *Wen-chi,* 51:38b, letter in reply to Wan Cheng-ch'ou (Wan Jen-chieh).

114. *Yü-lei,* ch. 20, sec. 103 (p. 754).

115. *Ibid.,* sec. 111 (p. 757).

116. *Ibid.,* sec. 111 (p. 758).

117. *Ibid.,* ch. 6, sec. 78 (pp. 179-180).

118. *Analects,* 5:25.

119. *Wen-chi,* 57:2b-3a, letter in reply to Li Yao-ch'ing (Li T'ang-tzu).

120. *Ibid.,* 58:29a-b, first letter in reply to Hsü Chu-fu (Hsü Yü).

121. *Ibid.,* 50:34b, fifth letter in reply to Chou Shun-pi (Chou Mu). Also in the *Yü-lei,* ch. 20, sec. 111 (pp. 758-759).

122. *Yü-lei,* ch. 6, sec. 87 (p. 185).

123. *Analects,* 12:1.

124. *Ibid.,* 13:19.

125. *Ibid.,* 12:2.

126. *Yü-lei,* ch. 20, sec. 112 (pp. 759-760).

127. These are the Four Qualities of the first hexagram, *ch'ien* (Heaven, male), in the *Book of Changes.*

128. Mou Tsung-san, *Hsin-t'i yü hsing-t'i,* vol. 3, pp. 232, 242, 245-246.

129. *Ibid.,* p. 243.

130. Ch'ien Mu, *Chu Tzu hsin-hsüeh-an* [New anthology and critical accounts of Master Chu] (Taipei: San-min Book Co., 1971), vol. 2, pp. 54-55.

131. T'ang Chün-i, *Chung-kuo che-hsüeh yüan-lun: Yüan-hsing-pien* [Origin and development of Chinese philosophical ideas: Volume on nature] (Hong Kong: New Asia Research Institute, 1968), pp. 390-399.

132. Mou Tsung-san, *Hsin-ti yü hsing-t'i,* vol. 3, pp. 249-252.

133. *Ibid.,* pp. 234-252.

134. *Wen-chi,* 42:17b-19a, tenth letter in reply to Wu Hui-shu (Wu I).

135. *Ibid.,* 32:16b-21b; *Nan-hsüan Hsien-sheng wen-chi,* 20:7b (p. 652), ninth letter in reply to Chu Yüan-hui (Chu Hsi); 21:5b (p. 674), twenty-first letter.

136. *Ibid.,* 32:16a-18b, letter in reply to Chang Ching-fu (Chang Shih) on the "Jen-shuo."

137. *Nan-hsüan Hsien-sheng wen-chi,* 21:5b (p. 674), twenty-first letter in reply to Chu Yüan-hui.

138. *Ibid.,* 20:7b (p. 652), ninth letter.

139. *Wen-chi,* 32:17b-18a. *Yüan* is the first of the Four Qualities of origination, flourishing, advantage, and firmness in the process of change, according to the commentary on the first hexagram, *ch'ien,* in the *Book of Changes.*

140. *Nan-hsüan Hsien-sheng wen-chi,* 20:7b (p. 652), ninth letter in reply to Chu Yüan-hui.

141. *Wen-chi,* 32:19a-b, "Further discussion on the 'Jen-shuo.'"

142. *Nan-hsüan Hsien-sheng wen-chi,* 21:5b-6a (pp. 674-675), twenty-first letter to Chu Yüan-hui.

143. *Wen-chi,* 32:20a-b, "Further discussion on the 'Jen-shuo.'"

144. *Nan-hsüan Hsien-sheng wen-chi,* 20:7a (p. 651), ninth letter to Chu Yüan-hui.

145. *Wen-chi,* 32:20a-b, "Further discussion on the 'Jen-shuo.'"

146. Mou Tsung-san, *Hsin-t'i yü hsing-t'i,* vol. 3, p. 280.

147. *Ibid.,* pp. 259-281.

148. *Wen-chi,* 40:29a-30a, sixteenth and seventeenth letters in reply to Ho Shu-ching (Ho Hao).

149. *Ibid.,* p. 29a.

150. *Yü-lei,* ch. 105, sec. 44 (p. 4186).

151. *Wen-chi,* 42:8a, fifth letter in reply to Hu Kuang-chung (Hu Shih).

152. *Ibid.,* 33:15a, twenty-fourth letter in reply to Lü Po-kung (Lü Tsu-ch'ien).

153. *Ibid.,* 40:29b, seventeenth letter in reply to Ho Shu-ching.

154. *Yü-lei,* ch. 105, sec. 42 (p. 4184).

155. *Pei-hsi tzu-i,* sec. 71 (pt. 1, 31a-32a). See my translation, *Neo-Confucian Terms Explained,* pp. 81-83. Also *Sung-Yüan hsüeh-an* [Anthology and critical accounts of the Neo-Confucians of the Sung and Yüan dynasties] (*SPPY* ed.), 68:2a-b.

156. *Wen-chi,* 67:20a, "Treatise on *Jen.*"

157. *Pei-hsi ta-ch'üan-chi* [Complete collected works of Ch'en Ch'un] (*Ssu-k'u ch'üan-shu chen-pen* [Precious works of the *Complete Collection of the Four Libraries*] ed.) 26:5b, fifth letter in reply to Ch'en Po-tsao (Ch'en I).

158. Hsiung Chieh, *Hsing-li ch'ün-shu chü-chieh* [Punctuation and explanation of books on nature and principle] (*Chin-shih han-chi ts'ung-k'an* ed.), 8:8a-10b (p. 367-372).

159. *Nan-hsüan Hsien-sheng wen-chi,* 18:1a-b.

160. *Wen-chi,* 33:18a-b, twenty-seventh letter in reply to Lü Po-kung (Lü Tsu-ch'ien). See also above, p. 155.

161. *Sung-Yüan hsüeh-an* [Anthology and critical accounts of the Neo-Confucians of the Sung and Yüan dynasties] (*SPPY* ed.), 50:11a, chapter on Chang Shih.

162. *Wen-chi,* 33:20a-b, thirtieth letter in reply to Lü Po-kung.

163. *Ibid.,* 32:23a-24b, forty-seventh letter in reply to Ch'in-fu on his "Jen-shuo."

164. *I-shu,* 3:3a.

165. Mou Tsung-san, *Hsien-t'i yü hsing-t'i,* vol. 3, p. 295.

166. Professor Satō's paper is published in Wing-tsit Chan, ed., *Chu Hsi and Neo-Confucianism* (Honolulu: University of Hawaii Press, 1986), pp. 212-227.

167. Wing-tsit Chan, *Chu-hsüeh lun-chi* [Studies on Chu Hsi] (Taipei: Student Book Co., 1982), pp. 37-68.

168. In the *Sung-Yüan hsüeh-an,* introduction to ch. 68 on Ch'en Ch'un.

169. Liu Shu-hsien, "Further examination of Chu Hsi's 'Treatise on *Jen,*' the concept of the Great Ultimate, and orthodox tradition of the Way—Reflections on participating at the International Conference on Chu Hsi [in Chinese]," in *Shih-hsüeh p'ing-lun* [Historical tribune], no. 5 (January, 1983), p. 173-188.

170. *Ssu-k'u ch'üan-shu tsung-mu t'i-yao* [Essentials of the contents of the *Complete Collection of the Four Libraries*] (Shanghai: Commercial Press, 1933), p. 1919.

171. *Pei-hsi ta-ch'üan chi,* 26:5b, fifth letter in reply to Ch'en Po-tsao. Wen-ling is an elegant name for Ch'üan-chou Prefecture in southern Fukien.

William Theodore De Bary (essay date 1989)

SOURCE: "The Learning of the Mind-and-Heart in the Early Chu Hsi School," in *The Message of the Mind in Neo-Confucianism,* Columbia University Press, 1989, pp. 24-52.

[*In the essay below, De Bary examines the way in which the interpretation of Chu Hsi's teachings concerning the learning of the mind has resulted in confusion regarding the role of the "mind-and-heart" in his philosophy.*]

In *Neo-Confucian Orthodoxy and the Learning of the Mind-and-Heart*[1] I reported on developments in the thirteenth through fifteenth centuries which saw the rise of the new Learning of the Mind-and-Heart as an accompaniment to Neo-Confucianism's establishment as an official orthodoxy—a development which had been largely ignored in earlier histories both of ideas and institutions. By the mid-Ming, however, with the more intensive development of Neo-Confucian thought that followed from its dominance of the educational and scholarly scene, important philosophical issues surfaced which had not been so fully addressed in the phase of rapid early growth. My earlier study stopped short of this later development, recognizing it to constitute a new chapter in the history of Neo-Confucian thought. Yet as long as this later phase remained unexamined, we would be left without an adequate explanation of how such a radical change could have come about in the later way of perceiving the earlier development. This is especially true of the modern identification of the Learning of the Mind-and-Heart (*hsin-hsüeh*) with the so-called "Lu-Wang School," reserving it to that branch of Neo-Confucianism alone, while the Learning of Principle (*li-hsüeh*), originally almost coextensive with *hsin-hsüeh,* became designated as a separate Ch'eng-Chu reservation.

By now the association of "*hsin-hsüeh* with "Lu-Wang" has become such a fixture of modern scholarly thinking that one encounters it almost everywhere in histories, text-books, encyclopedias, and dictionaries.² Two brief quotations from Fung Yu-lan's *History of Chinese Philosophy* will serve to illustrate the point:

> Contemporary with Chu Hsi, the greatest figure in the Rationalistic *(Li-hsüeh)* school of Neo-Confucianism, there lived another thinker who is important as the real founder of the rival idealistic *(Hsin Hsüeh)* school. This is Lu Chiu-yüan (1139-93), better known under his literary name as Lu Hsiang-shan . . . If we wish to sum up the difference between the two schools in a word, we may say that Chu's school emphasizes the "Learning of Principle" *(li-hsüeh)* . . . whereas that of Lu emphasizes the "Learning of the Mind *(Hsin-hsüeh)*.³

A concomitant of this oversimplification has been the tendency to view principle *(li)* as opposed to mind *(hsin)*, and thus arrive at a neat dichotomy of the orthodox Ch'eng Chu school, representing the "school of principle," versus the unorthodox "Lu-Wang School of the Mind." Further confusion has arisen from the breadth of the concept of "mind-and-heart" *(hsin)* itself, as also from the inherent generality and multiple uses of the Chinese term for learning, *hsüeh*, which serves equally as a form of learning, a school of thought, or some institutionalization of it.

Some of this confusion underlies the issue raised by Ch'ien Mu in his monumental study of Chu Hsi's teaching, the *Chu Tzu hsin hsüeh-an*. After presenting his overview of Chu's "learning," Ch'ien devotes a major portion of his five-volume work to Chu's view of the mind-and-heart, and comments on the Ch'eng-Chu/Lu-Wang dichotomy as follows:

> In later times men have said that Ch'eng-Chu emphasized the nature as principle, while Lu-Wang stressed the mind as principle. Accordingly they differentiated Ch'eng-Chu as the learning of principle *(li-hsüeh)* and Lu-Wang as the learning of the mind-and-heart *(hsin-hsüeh)*. This distinction has something to be said for it, but actually there was no one to match Master Chu in his ability to elucidate the similarities and differences, divergences and convergences, in the matter of mind and principle, as well as the precise connections and interactions between them. Therefore in general to say that the learning of Chu Hsi was most thoroughly, from beginning to end, a vast and fully-defined learning of the mind is not at all inappropriate.⁴

Lest this be taken as a mere passing comment of Ch'ien's rather than one truly representative of his work as a whole, it should be said that these lines introduce a major segment of Ch'ien's study (vol. 2), and the view they express is reinforced frequently elsewhere in the work. For instance:

> To say that the learning of principle is the learning of the mind may be allowable, but to say that Ch'eng-Chu and Lu-Wang can be divided into two separate lineages, is something for which I find no warrant. . . .

> (2:106)

Men of later times have spoken of the learning of principle as the learning of human nature and principle. As one can see from the preceding quotations [by Chu Hsi on the mind and nature], the learning of the nature and principle *(hsing-li hsüeh)* is truly the learning of the mind. All understanding and effort with respect to the nature and principle depends completely on the mind, so that if you leave out the mind, there is nothing left of the learning of the nature and principle to speak of.

> (1:49)

> When recent scholars have discussed the similarities and differences between Chu and Lu, they have generally identified Chu with the Learning of Principle and Lu with the Learning of Mind, the error of which I have discussed above. Actually the difference between the two lies squarely in [their different views of] the learning of the mind.

> (1:139; see also 1:49, 59, and 2:5)

When Ch'ien Mu says, as in the first quotation above, that "the learning of Chu Hsi was most thoroughly, from beginning to end, a vast and fully-defined learning of the mind-and-heart . . . ," he speaks in terms almost exactly like those used by early followers of Chu Hsi;⁵ but not in the terms of Chu himself, who referred to the new teaching most often as the Sage Learning *(sheng-hsüeh)* or Learning of the Way *(tao-hsüeh)*. "Sage Learning" meant the learning which had come down from the sages, but also the "learning of sagehood," i.e., how one can achieve sagehood, as the overarching conception of the new movement and as the alternative to the ideal of attaining Buddhahood. Although Chu talked a great deal about human nature, principle, and mind, it was only after Chu Hsi's time that the terms "learning of principle" *(li-hsüeh)*, "learning of human nature and principle" *(hsing-li hsüeh)*, and "learning of the mind" *(hsin-hsüeh)* came into wide use to describe the essential content of the sage learning. As Ch'ien Mu has said, discussing Chu Hsi's learning of the mind as one that leads to sagehood:

> Those who have not yet reached the stage where the mind is completely identified with principle, must have a gate and a path, through which, by degrees and stages, they come to understand the substance of the mind and make judgments in practice, and through which they can hope to attain their goal—this is the essence of the learning of the mind as discussed by Chu Hsi.

> (2:5)

If a proper understanding of the mind-and-heart was essential to the attainment of sagehood, it was no less intimately bound up with Chu's philosophy of human nature as grounded in his cosmology of principle and material force *(ch'i)*. Of this Ch'ien Mu says:

> In this Master Chu made every effort to point out the importance of the mind. . . . Therefore when it is said that Lu-Wang represents the learning of the mind and Ch'eng-Chu the learning of principle, this distinction is not appropriate. If one said the Lu-Wang school was exclusively oriented toward the human order, while

Ch'eng-Chu equally emphasized the human and cosmic orders, that might be closer to the truth."[6]

Chu Hsi apparently did not use the term *"hsin-hsüeh"* himself, but then neither did Lu Hsiang-shan, the reported progenitor of the School of the Mind, although their contemporary Yang Wan-li (1127-1206), known for his devotion to the teaching of the *Great Learning*, gave the title "Essays on the Learning of the Mind-and-Heart *(Hsin-hsüeh lun)* to a series of discussions on themes central to the developing Neo-Confucian *hsin-hsüeh:* the Confucian classics and rites as manifestations of the Way; the word in speech, writing and book-learning as means of communicating the Way of the Sages; the holistic unity of the Way joining inner self and outer world; and the roles of Yen Hui, Tseng Tzu, Tsu Ssu, Mencius and Han Yü as the transmitters of the Way and defenders of it against heterodoxy.[7] Yet, notwithstanding Yang's title, he too makes no use of the term *hsin-hsüeh* in the essays themselves.

The terms Chu Hsi himself used, which became most important in the later discussion of the learning of the mind, were the transmission of the mind *(ch'uan-hsin),* the method of the mind *(hsin-fa),* and by contextual association the Tradition of, or Succession to, the Way *(tao-t'ung).* All three concepts involve a similar conception of the Way, how it is communicated, and practiced, and how these relate to the mind. First I shall deal with the concept of *tao-t'ung.*

1. SUCCESSION TO, OR TRADITION OF, THE WAY
(TAO-T'UNG)

This concept is used to represent both the process by which the Way is perpetuated ("Succession to the Way") and its content ("Tradition of the Way"). It came down to Chu through the school of Ch'eng I but was first formulated in these terms by Chu in his preface to the *Mean (Chung-yung).*[8]

"Why was the *Mean* written? Master Tzu-ssu wrote it because he was worried lest the transmission of the Learning of the Way *(tao-hsüeh)* be lost.[9] When the divine sages of highest antiquity had succeeded to the work of Heaven and established the Supreme Norm, the transmission of the Tradition of the Way *(tao-t'ung)* had its inception. As may be discovered from the classics, "Hold fast the Mean" is what Yao transmitted to Shun.[10] That "the mind of man is precarious" and the "mind of the Way is subtle and barely perceptible"; that one should "have refined discrimination and singleness of mind" and should "hold fast the Mean,"[11] is what Shun transmitted to Yü. Yao's one utterance is complete and perfect in itself, but Shun added three more in order to show that Yao's one utterance could only be carried out in this way. . . .

Subsequently sage upon sage succeeded one another: T'ang the Completer, Wen and Wu as rulers, Kao Yao, I Yin, Fu Yüeh, the Duke of Chou, and Duke Shao as ministers, received and passed on this tradition of the Way. As for our master Confucius, though he did not attain a position of authority, nevertheless his resuming

the tradition of the past sages and imparting it to later scholars was a contribution even more worthy than that of Yao and Shun. Still, in his own time those who recognized him were only [his disciples] Yen Hui and Tseng Ts'an, who grasped and passed on his essential meaning. Then in the next generation after Tseng, with Confucius' grandson Tzu-ssu [reputed author of the *Mean*], it was far removed in time from the sages and heterodoxies had already arisen. . . .

Thereafter the transmission was resumed by Mencius, who was able to interpret and clarify the meaning of this text [the *Mean*] and succeed to the tradition of the early sages; but upon his demise the transmission was finally lost. . . . Fortunately, however, this text was not lost, and when the Masters Ch'eng, two brothers, appeared [in the Sung] they had something to study in order to pick up the threads of what had not been transmitted for a thousand years, and something to rely on in exposing the speciousness of the seeming truths of Buddhism and Taoism. Though the contribution of Tzu-ssu was great, had it not been for the Ch'engs we would not have grasped his meaning from his words alone. But alas, their explanations also became lost.[12]

Chu goes on to explain with what difficulty he pieced together and pondered for himself the essential message of the *Mean* from the fragmentary material available to him. He reiterates not only the theme of the precariousness of the Way as transmitted by human hands, but also the successive struggles of inspired individuals to recover its true meaning. Thus, *tao-t'ung* almost literally has the sense of "linking or stitching the Way together."

A few key points should be noted in this passage. One is that the *tao-t'ung* involves the transmission of a teaching which comes down from the sages but is discontinuous after the age of the sage-kings.[13] Then there is the tribute to individuals like Confucius, Mencius, and the Ch'eng brothers for reviving the Way after it had fallen into disuse. Another point is the importance to these individuals of the surviving fragmentary texts as a clue to the sage's teaching; in the case of the Ch'engs "they had something to study in order to pick up the threads of what had not been transmitted for a thousand years." Finally, there is the statement "had it not been for the Ch'engs, we would not have gotten the mind [of the sages] from the words of Tzu-ssu alone."[14]

Taken together these statements characterize a tradition which depends on both text and interpretation for its transmission. One cannot have a "worldless transmission" as in Ch'an Buddhism, nor on the other hand can one depend simply on the preservation of texts and their literal reading. Only a few inspired individuals are capable of grasping the inner meaning of the text, and their contribution is indispensable. Without it, texts like the *Mean* and *Great Learning* are as lifeless (according to this Neo-Confucian view) as they had been for over a millennium since the passing of Mencius. On the other hand, without the texts there is no objective, public record, only subjective imagination and private experience, incommunicable in words (as in Ch'an Buddhism)—which cannot serve to reestablish the Way of the sage-kings as the solid basis for a humane polity and community.

In *Neo-Confucian Orthodoxy and the Learning of the Mind-and-Heart*, I have distinguished two aspects of the *tao-t'ung*, as prophetic and scholastic, depending on whether one emphasizes the inner inspiration or solitary perception which Chu so highlights in this passage, or whether one appeals to received authority by continuous transmission either of texts or instruction from teacher to student.

This ambiguous legacy is the product of Chu's own intellectual situation as heir first to the Ch'eng brothers, and then to other Sung masters. He affirms at once the Ch'eng brothers' independent access to the essential meaning, or heart *(hsin)*, of the Way, along with the collective contributions which other Sung thinkers, starting with Chou Tun-i, made to his own philosophical synthesis. The constructing of this synthesis was itself a creative process, depending on both inner inspiration and Chu's unique "linking-up" of elements drawn from diverse sources. Chu's *Reflections on Things at Hand (Chin-ssu lu)* is a good example of the latter. In it, he pulled together, in a way not done before, disparate elements from predecessors not themselves linked by any master-disciple relation or Ch'an-like succession. Moreover, his own experience in trying to piece together the philosophy of the Ch'eng brothers from the discrepant and conflicting versions of their disciples and successors, is another example of the need actively to repossess the Way rather than just passively to receive it.[15] Yet it was equally important that this synthesis be grounded in classical texts, which is why Chu devoted so much of his time in later years to editing or commenting on the classics as the documentary foundation of his synthesis. Chu's commentary on and preface to the *Mean* was recognized as one of the most important statements of this mature scholarship. Every word of Chu's in it was chosen with extreme care.[16]

Both versions of the *tao-t'ung*, prophetic and scholastic, appear frequently in later Neo-Confucian writings. It is rare indeed that a scholar in the later tradition does not orient himself or his scholarly lineage, in one way or another, to the tradition of the Way as set forth in this preface to the *Mean*. Like Chu's preface to the *Great Learning*, it was among the first things read by students almost anywhere in East Asia as part of their basic education in the Four Books.

T'ung (here translated as "tradition" or "succession") conveys the senses both of a chain or link and of overall control or coordination. The term *cheng-t'ung*, in its Neo-Confucian guise, appeared at about the same time as *tao-t'ung* to express the idea of legitimate succession by virtue of reestablishing control over the empire (and not necessarily in direct succession to the previous dynasty).[17] For Chu Hsi *tao-t'ung* represented the active repossession or reconstituting of the Way in a manner akin to regaining or reconstituting the Empire as the basis for legitimate dynastic succession.

In 1172, some seventeen years before Chu wrote his preface to the *Mean*, a work entitled *Sheng-men shih-yeh t'u* (Diagrams of the Proper Business of the Sages' School) was produced by Li Yüan-kang, a follower of the Ch'eng brothers and Chang Tsai.[18] The first of Li's *Diagrams* is entitled "Ch'uan-tao cheng-t'ung" (The Legitimate Succession in the Transmission of the Way; see figure 1). Its account of this succession is similar to that in Chu's preface, showing the Ch'eng brothers to be the direct successors to Mencius, and including no mention of Chou Tun-i or Chang Tsai.[19] The great eighteenth-century scholar Ch'ien Ta-hsin (1728-1804) drew attention to this, saying, "The two characters *tao-t'ung* first appear in Li Yüan-kang's *Sheng-men shih-yeh t'u*. The first diagram speaks of 'The legitimate succession to the transmission of the Way' in explanation of the Ch'engs' inheriting it from Mencius. This work was completed in 1172, contemporaneous with Chu Hsi."[20]

In this very brief note Ch'ien Ta-hsin is quite precise in stating only what he knew—that Li's work represents the first appearance of these two characters in an extant text (though not abbreviated to the compound *tao-t'ung)*, and that this appearance was contemporaneous with Chu Hsi. He does not say that it was the first *use* of the term *tao-t'ung*, or that Chu got the compound term from this source. He leaves open the possibility that it had been current in the Ch'eng brothers school and might have come to Chu by another route.

The only reason this minor point was worth noting at all by Ch'ien was that his readers would be familiar with Chu Hsi's reference to *tao-t'ung* in the preface to his commentary on the *Mean*, a reference repeatedly cited by generations of Neo-Confucian scholars, whereas hardly anyone would have seen or known about Li's charts. Ch'ien was reporting an out-of-the-way fact about the Succession to the Way everyone had come to know through Chu Hsi, as the dominant authority in the later tradition.

In Chu Hsi's preface the active agency of the individual mind in grasping the meaning of fragmentary texts and discerning the original intent of the sages was indicated. In Li Yüan-kang's charts the role of the mind is also greatly emphasized (see figures 2, 3, or original diagrams 4, 5, 8, 9, and 11). But, aside from this, it was the immediate juxtaposition of the Succession to the Way (*tao-t'ung*) with the Method of the Mind (*hsin-fa*) that led to the association of the two in the Learning of the Mind (*hsin-hsüeh*).

2. THE METHOD OF THE MIND (*HSIN-FA*).

At the beginning of Chu Hsi's commentary on the *Mean* and immediately following his preface in most early editions, he quoted some comments of Ch'eng I on the general nature of the Mean:

> This work (the *Chung-yung*) represents the method of the mind-and-heart as transmitted in the Confucian school. Tzu-ssu feared that in time it would become misunderstood, and so he wrote it down in this work so

as to pass it on to Mencius. This book was the first to explain that the unitary principle, from its position of centrality, is dispersed to become the myriad things and from its outer reaches returns to become one principle; release it and it fills the universe; roll it up and it is retracted into the most hidden recesses. Its savor is limitless. It is all solid learning. The careful reader, having searched its depths and savored its meaning until he has truly gotten it, can use it throughout his life without ever exhausting it.[21]

This quotation, which is a concatenation of several different phrases appearing in the extant writings of Ch'eng I[22] became the primary reference to the method of the mind among later Neo-Confucians. Here too, however, we have it prefigured by one of the diagrams by Li Yüan-kang, entitled "The Essential Method for the Preservation of the Mind" (Tsun-hsin yao-fa) (see figure 3). The contents of the diagram come largely from the Mean, as interpreted in the light of Mencius and Ch'eng I; they concern the preservation of the equilibrium of the mind in the unaroused and unexpressed state, and the attainment of harmony in one's expressed thoughts and desires through such disciplines as self-watchfulness, caution and apprehension, holding to reverence. Thus both Li and Chu Hsi associate the method of the mind with the Mean and with a transmission from the sages. Chu confirms this later in a subsequent preface to the Mean which also cites Ch'eng I and the method of the mind handed down from the sages.[23]

The message from Ch'eng I as quoted by Chu, however, is more metaphysical than Li's and has a more oracular tone. It speaks of the mysterious process by which principle manifests both its unity and diversity, and thus can serve as the ground for a practical learning based on solid principle. From this it is evident that hsin-fa could cover a range of meanings from the most abstruse to the very practical. Later writers took full advantage of this flexibility to make hsin-fa serve their own purposes.

One use to which it should not have been put, however, was the earlier Buddhist use of the term to represent a nonverbal communication of enlightenment from mind-to-mind, as from master to disciple, or patriarch to patriarch.[24] Earlier I have discussed preexisting Buddhist and Neo-Confucian use of hsin-fa and need not repeat that here.[25] Chu Hsi made plain in his preface that the transmission from the sages differed fundamentally from that of the Buddhas, and he did so further in his commentary on the important passage in the Analects (12:1) dealing with Confucius' disciple Yen Yüan and "subduing the self and restoring riteness." There Chu specifically identifies hsin-fa with this key concept of sustained moral discipline:

This chapter, with its questions and answers, represents a most cogent and important statement concerning the method of the mind-and-heart as handed down to us [from the sages]. If one is not altogether clear in his mind about this, he will not be able to discern its subtle points, and if one is not altogether firm about it, one cannot carry out one's decisions. Thus what Yen Yüan alone had been able to hear and understand [by virtue of his determined effort] no scholar should fail to apply himself to. Master Ch'eng's admonitions [cited in the commentary] too are most revealing. The scholar should savor and ponder them deeply.[26]

Elsewhere, in the Classified Conversations, Chu emphasized the point that the Buddhists might have a method of self-control but they do not have the method of "restoring riteness" (fu-li), as a way of defining the norms of practical action. Here in his commentary Chu points out that rites are not to be equated simply with principle in the abstract; rites are the measured expression of Heaven's principle (t'ien-li chih chieh-wen) and thus are the "the means whereby the virtue of the mind-and-heart may be perfected."[27] Without the latter the Buddhists and Taoists have no means of determining what specific standards should guide one's actions in the conduct of daily life. Thus principle remains for them something vague, amorphous, and subject only to the rule of expedient adaptation.[28]

Further in the Classified Conversations of Master Chu (Chu Tzu yü-lei) there is a reference to Ch'eng I and the hsin-fa which clearly identifies the latter with the key elements in Chu Hsi's presentation of the tao-t'ung in his preface to the Mean: with the distinction between the human mind and the mind of the Way, with the method of refined discrimination and singleness of mind, with the transmission of the Way from Yao and Shun which lapsed after Mencius, and even with the essentials of mind-cultivation in the eightfold method of the Great Learning:

Master Ch'eng says "The human mind is human desires; hence it is precarious. The mind of the Way is Heaven's principle; hence it is refined and subtle. 'Refined discrimination' is that whereby [the method] is carried out; singleness of mind is for preserving [the mind of the Way]. With this one is able to hold fast the Mean!" These words say it all! Refinement is to have refined discrimination and not let [the mind] become mixed and confused. Singleness is to concentrate on unity from beginning to end. Never since this was transmitted from Yao and Shun has there been any other theory. First of all there were these words, and ever since there has been no change in the sages' method of the mind-and-heart.

In the classic [of the Mean] one finds many expressions of this idea. In what is referred to [in the Mean] as "choosing the good and firmly holding to it," "Choosing the good" is "having refined discrimination." "Firmly holding to it" is "singleness of mind." "Broad learning, judicious inquiry, careful thought, and clear differentiation" (in the Mean 20) are all "refined discrimination," and "earnest, resolute practice" is "singleness of mind." "Understanding the good" in the Mean (also ch. 20) is "refined discrimination" and [in the same chapter] "achieving personal integrity" is "singleness." In the Great Learning the extension of knowledge and investigation of things cannot be accomplished without "refined discrimination," and achieving integrity of intention (ch'eng-i) is singleness of mind. He who pursues learning only has this principle to learn. When the transmission was lost after Mencius' time, it is just this that was lost.[29]

This was not, however, the first time that the method of the mind had been identified with the ruler's method of self-cultivation as taught in the *Great Learning*. As I pointed out in *Neo-Confucian Orthodoxy and the Learning of the Mind-and-Heart*, Ch'en Ch'ang-fang (1108-1148), in his "Essay on the Learning of the Emperors *(Ti-hsüeh lun)*," spoke of it as the essential message passed down from Yao and Shun to Confucius and Mencius. "Its content is identified both as 'the learning of the sage emperors and kings' and as 'the ruler's method of the mind' *(jen-chu hsin-fa)*. No other knowledge, no other capability, is so important for the ruler as being able to examine his own motives and conduct to insure that he is not misled into making errors of catastrophic consequence for the people."[30] Thus the method of the mind was already understood as a political doctrine before Chu Hsi's time, and it was so understood by followers of Chu Hsi like Ts'ai Shen and Huang Chen, whose views will be discussed presently.

3. TRANSMISSION OF THE MIND (*CH'UAN-HSIN*).

We have already noted in discussing the "Succession to the Way" *(tao-t'ung)* how important it was for Chu Hsi that this succession should be achieved by grasping the mind of the sages, or their true intention, based on a correct reading of the classic texts. In fact, for Chu Hsi, the "transmission of the [sage's] mind" was something that evolved from the earlier concepts of the "transmission of the Way *(ch'uan-tao)*." Ch'ien Mu has already shown, at some length and in detail, how this development took place from Chu's earlier writings to his articulation of the concept in his later works.[31] Chu's personal development is reflected in the regrets he expressed in 1163-64 over his own failure to appreciate fully the instruction he had received earlier from Li T'ung, because he had not yet grasped the significance of the "transmission of the mind [of the sages]."[32] Also, in a postface for the *Written Legacy of the Ch'eng Brothers (Ch'eng shih i-shu)* Chu speaks of the errors of "scholars who have not yet learned the essentials of the transmission of the [sages'] mind and get stuck in the literal meaning of words." From this paraphrase of Ch'eng I and much other evidence Ch'ien concludes that for Chu "the transmission of the Way lay in the transmission of the mind [of the sages]," and that Chu had discussed this long before Lu Hsiang-shan.[33]

> Later scholars who call Lu-Wang the learning of the mind and Ch'eng-Chu the learning of principle do not realize what [Chu] had said about the "transmission of the [sages'] mind." . . . Impressed by Hsiang-shan's fondness for talking about the mind, they fail to take note of all that Chu had said about the learning of the mind.[34]

Given this genetic connection between the "transmission of the Way" and "transmission of the mind," we can more readily understand why Chu closely associated the succession to the Way *(tao-t'ung)* with what Ch'eng I had said about the "method of the mind transmitted from the sages." We note however that there is a shift in the content of

what is considered essential in these transmissions. Li Yüan-kang's version of the "Essential Method for Preserving the Mind" had featured the concepts appearing in the *Mean*: the unexpressed and expressed states of the mind, self-watchfulness, etc., but these are not found in the message Chu conveys in his preface to the *Mean*. In the latter the keys to the Way and the essentials of the transmission are identified in what became famous as the "Sixteen Words" concerning the "human mind being precarious, the mind of the Way being subtle," "having utmost refinement and singleness of mind," and "holding fast to the Mean." This view, centering on the distinction between the human mind and the mind of the Way, predominates in Chu's later thought and in his commentaries on the Four books. His preface to the *Mean* (1189) may be taken as a definitive statement of this central concept.[35]

If however we refer back to Li Yüan-kang's charts again, we find that this same cluster of ideas is represented in the eighth chart, entitled "Secret Purport of the Transmission of the Mind" *(Ch'uan-hsin mi-chih),* wherein the mind is seen to combine two aspects (the human mind and mind of the Way); where one is instructed to follow Heaven's Principle while overcoming human desires; where refinement and subtlety are counterposed to the danger and insecurity of the human mind; and wherein singleness of mind is spoken of as appropriate to the mind of the Way, while refined discrimination is proper to the human mind. Thus Li identifies with the Transmission of the Mind what Chu identifies with the Succession to the Way, while both associate the Method of the Mind *(hsin-fa)* with the *Mean* but in different ways. From this it would appear that these concepts were closely related in the thinking of late twelfth-century representatives of the Ch'eng brothers school, and that this cluster of associations clung to Chu Hsi's use of the terms when he incorporated them into his widely used prefaces and commentaries on the Four Books. Since each of them stood as an alternative to Buddhist understandings of the same term—of the Way and its transmission, of the mind and its cultivation—it was only natural for early followers of Chu Hsi to think of this ensemble as representing the Confucian alternative to the Buddhist Learning of the Mind, and for a much later scholar like Ch'ien Mu to think of them as the Ch'eng-Chu Learning of the Mind in contrast to that which became identified with "Lu-Wang." Neo-Confucians did not think of these Chinese expressions as having become the exclusive property of Buddhism, any more than did Han Yü, who, in his celebrated essay "On the Way *(Yüan tao),*" was unwilling to concede to Buddhists an exclusive right to interpret the Way in their own terms.[36]

There is one other concept concerning the mind which has an important place in Chu Hsi's teachings on the mind. This is *hsin-shu*, representing basic attitudes, dispositions, or habits of mind. It is a major category of self-cultivation in Chu Hsi's *Elementary Learning,* and because of the latter work's wide use as a Neo-Confucian textbook was a term much employed by thinkers who also discussed the learning of the mind-and-heart.[37] It is not, however, encountered frequently in discussions of *hsin-hsüeh* itself, and does not appear to have had such a direct connection with it as did the sixteen-word message concerning the human mind and mind of the Way, the tradition of the Way, or the transmission of the mind of the sages. While, therefore, it may be taken as evidence of the basic orientation of Neo-Confucian thought toward a discipline of mind, *hsin-shu* is not part of the cluster of terms—*tao-t'ung, hsin-fa,* and *hsin-ch'uan*—that constitute the essential core of the *hsin-hsüeh* in early Neo-Confucian discussions of the learning of the mind-and-heart.

The view of the orthodox tradition presented above is reiterated by Chu Hsi's premier disciple, Huang Kan (1152-1221),[38] in his "General Account of the Transmission of the Succession to the Way Among the Sages and Worthies" (*Sheng-hsien tao-t'ung ch'uan-shou tsung-hsü shuo*), wherein he explains the content of the "sixteen-word" teaching concerning the human mind and mind of the Way as the essential message handed down from Yao and Shun in the Succession to the Way (*tao-t'ung*).[39] Elsewhere, commenting on the work of his colleague Huang Shih-i,[40] entitled "Two Diagrams on the Transmission of the [Sages'] Mind from Shun and Yü, and the views of Chou and Ch'eng on Human Nature" (*Shun Yü ch'uan-hsin Chou Ch'eng yen hsing erh t'u*), Huang Kan confirms that the teaching concerning the human mind and mind of the Way is the authentic "transmission of the mind" from Shun and Yü as interpreted by Chu Hsi in the preface to the *Mean,* but he criticizes the interpretations of Huang Shih-i which would blur the distinction between these two aspects of the mind.[41] From this we can see that Huang Kan equated the Transmission of the [Sages'] Mind (*ch'uan-hsin*) with the Succession to the Way (*tao-t'ung*) as imparted by the Sages, on the basis of their common content in the doctrine of the mind set forth in Chu Hsi's preface to the *Mean.*

From another major disciple of Chu Hsi, Ch'en Ch'un (1159-1223), often considered one of the most reliable interpreters of Chu Hsi, we get a similar picture.[42] In his important Yen-ling lectures Ch'en gave a concise summary of Chu's mature teachings, how they were to be studied and practiced, and how the Confucian Way has been transmitted through many vicissitudes. In the second lecture, entitled "The Source of Teachers and Friends (*Shih-yu yüan-yüan*)," Ch'en gives a fuller and more systematized account of the orthodox tradition than is found in Chu's preface to the *Mean.* Having described the lapse in the tradition after Mencius, he speaks of its resumption in the Sung by Chou Tun-i, who "did not receive it from any teacher but got it directly from heaven,"[43] and then passed it on to the Ch'engs and Chu. Of Chu himself Ch'en Ch'un says, "He got at the subtle words and ideas the Ch'engs had left to posterity, and refined and clarified them. Looking back he penetrated the mind of the sages; looking to the present he drew together the many schools and assembled them as one."[44] As a result of these efforts, says Ch'en, those who would seek to attain sagehood have a sure guide in Chu. "But should anyone refuse this guid-

ance and seek to enter upon the path to sagehood by some other gate, there would be no reason to believe that he could attain the true transmission of the mind of the sages."[45]

Further, in the Fourth Lecture concerning the order in which the Four Books should be read, Ch'en reaffirms the sequence Chu Hsi had recommended, starting with the *Great Learning,* going on to the *Analects* and *Mencius,* and ending with the *Mean.*[46] Of the latter he says:

> Coming to the Book of the Mean (*Chung yung*), it represents the method of the mind handed down in the Sages' School.[47] Master Ch'eng I said: "Its savor is limitless. The careful reader, having searched its depths and savored its meaning until he has truly gotten it can use it throughout his life without ever exhausting it."[48] But what it speaks of refers mostly to the higher level and there is relatively little that refers to the lower level. This is not something the beginner can start talking about all at once. He must familiarize himself with the *Great Learning,* the *Analects,* and *Mencius* before he can expect to reach this level, for only so can he appreciate that it is all, without any doubt, solid, practical learning.[49]

Ch'en Ch'un, as an able student closely acquainted with Chu Hsi's thought in his later years, has long been recognized as an authoritative interpreter of Chu's teaching. In the preceding passages he confirms the following points relevant to our inquiry:

1. In the repossession of the Way after Mencius, the penetrating insights of the Sung masters and the great intellectual powers of Chu Hsi—both analytic and synthetic—play a key role in the reinterpretation of classic texts. Among the Sung masters Chou Tun-i, unmentioned in Chu Hsi's account in the preface to the *Mean,* assumes the path-breaking role Chu had previously assigned to the Ch'eng brothers, but this role is still a "prophetic" one in that Chou was said to have had no teacher and received his inspiration from Heaven.

2. If the mind of Chou Tun-i was directly illumined by Heaven, Chu Hsi's contribution was made through the depth and subtlety of his insight into the thought of the Ch'engs and his penetration of the mind of the sages. As a result Chu became the true heir and supreme authority on the "transmission of the Sage Mind."

3. Ch'en Ch'un sees the *Mean* as the culminating expression of this mind in the Four Books, but acknowledges that much of it is metaphysical. He repeats, however, Chu's quotation from Ch'eng I about the *Mean* representing the method of the mind transmitted from the sages, and tries to explain, like Ch'eng, how this teaching, while seemingly abstruse, can serve as the solid basis for a truly practical learning.

Thus, in this succinct presentation of Chu's legacy, Ch'en Ch'un closely associated the sages' method of the mind (*hsin-fa*), the transmission of the mind of the sages, and the sixteen-word teaching concerning the human mind and mind of the Way, with the succession to the Way (tao-t'ung). If both Huang Kan and Ch'en Ch'un agree on these points in their summation of the essential teachings of Chu Hsi, it is not reasonable to suppose that these were inadvertent, ill-considered, or gratuitous appendages to the system.

In fact this conclusion is confirmed by prefaces to Ch'en's work written by scholars in the thirteenth, fifteenth, and eighteenth centuries successively: in a preface of 1247 the *Pei-hsi tzu-i* is described as containing the Message or Method of the Mind (hsin-fa); another preface of 1490 speaks of Ch'en Ch'un as the successor to Chou, the Ch'engs, Chang, and Chu as perpetuators of the Learning of the Mind-and-Heart; while still another of 1714 speaks of Ch'en's work as an integral synthesis of the Learning of the Mind;[50] thus over a span of five centuries the same characterization of Ch'en's (and Chu's) thought was acknowledged.

Another disciple of Chu Hsi was Ts'ai Shen (1167-1230), whose father Ts'ai Yüan-ting (1135-98),[51] also considered a student and colleague of Chu Hsi, had had a special interest in the Great Plan (Hung-fan) section of the *Book of Documents* (Shu-ching). After the elder Ts'ai's death, Chu, in failing health himself, sensed that he would be unable to fulfill his own ambition of compiling a commentary on the *Documents* and, in the winter of 1199, asked Ts'ai Shen to carry out this task. In his preface to the *Collected Commentaries on the Book of Documents* (Shu-ching chi-chuan), Ts'ai modestly disclaims any qualifications for the task but says he felt compelled to undertake it, not only out of filial obligation to parent and teacher, but also because of the great importance of the *Book of Documents*, which held the key to good government:

> The orderly rule of the Two Emperors and Three Kings was rooted in the Way, and the Way of the Two Emperors was rooted in the mind-and-heart. If one could grasp (lit. "get") this mind, then the Way and orderly rule could be expressed in words. What then were these words? "Be refined and single-minded. Hold fast the Mean." This was the method of the mind handed down from Yao, Shun, and Yü. Establishing the Mean and setting up the Supreme Norm was the method of the mind as passed on by King T'ang of Shang and King Wu of Chou. Call it "virtue," call it "humaneness," call it "reverence," call it "sincerity"—the expressions may differ but the principle is one and the same. They are all without exception means of explaining the wondrousness of this mind. As expressed in terms of Heaven, it conveys the majesty whence this mind derives. As expressed in terms of the people, it conveys the care with which this mind is to be exercised. The rites, music, and transforming power of education issue from this mind. All institutions and cultures are products of this mind. The regulation of the family, ordering of the state, and bringing of peace to all-under-Heaven are extensions of this mind. Thus indeed does the virtuous power of this mind flourish abundantly. . . .

> Preserve this mind and order prevails; lose it and there is disorder. The difference between order and disorder

is determined by whether or not this mind is preserved. How so? Rulers in these later ages, if they aspire to the orderly rule of the Two Emperors and Three Kings, cannot but seek their Way; if they aspire to this Way, they cannot but seek this mind; and if they seek the essentials of this mind, how can it be done except through this book?[52]

Here the message of the mind transmitted from Yao and Shun is identified with the sixteen-(here abbreviated to four) word formula which Chu Hsi had spoken of in the preface to the *Mean* as the orthodox tradition (tao-t'ung). Its central importance is further underscored by Ts'ai's description of it as embracing the central Confucian virtues that should constitute the basis of the ruler's self-cultivation.

The same point is reiterated by Ts'ai in commenting on the apocryphal text of the sixteen-word formula itself as it appeared in the "Counsels of the Great Yü" in the *Book of Shang* (Shang-shu). After explaining the distinction between the human mind and the mind of the Way, and the need to be discriminating and single-minded, he concluded:

> The ancient sages, at the point of handing over the empire to others, never failed to pass on with it the method for its orderly rule.[53] Seeing it like this in the classic, rulers today cannot but ponder it deeply and reverently take it to heart.[54]

Later in the next generation of Chu Hsi's school, the distinguished historian, classicist, and official, Huang Chen (1213-1280), a student of one of Chu Hsi's principal disciples, Fu Kuang (n.d.),[55] had occasion, when commenting on the "human mind/way mind" formula in the *Book of Shang*, to complain of how this had been misconstrued. He noted that in the original context of the passage, it had a hortatory and admonitory significance in the handing on of the mandate to rule. This is ignored, he says, by those who make much of the passage for purposes other than those originally intended:

> Nowadays those who delight in talking about the Learning of the Mind-and-Heart disregard the original context and concentrate only on the mind of man and the mind of the Way. The worst of them just seize upon the two words "Way mind" and proceed to speak of the mind as the Way. This is to fall into Ch'an Buddhism and not realize that one is departing far from the basic mandate transmitted by Yao, Shun, and Yü.

> Ts'ai Chiu-feng [Ts'ai Shen], when he wrote his commentary on the *Book of Documents*,[56] cited Master Chu's words as follows: "The ancient sage-kings, at the point of passing on the empire to others, never failed to pass on with it the method for governing it." We can say that this truly conveys the basic meaning of this passage. Although by this Chiu-feng meant to set forth clearly the "mind of the emperors and kings," for him it was the mind-and-heart for governing the state and pacifying the world. This view is solidly grounded in principle.

> Although Chiu-feng himself took this as setting forth the mind of the sage emperors and kings, in his expla-

nation of this mind as the root and basis of ordering the state and bringing peace to the world, he certainly affirmed the correct principle. Later, those who presented his commentary at court spoke of it as the "transmission of the mind" of the three sages, whereupon scholars of the time pointed to the sixteen-word formula as the essence of the "transmission of the mind" and Ch'an Buddhists borrowed this as support for their own view [of the transmission].[57]

In my humble opinion the mind does not need to be transmitted. What pervades heaven-and-earth, links past and present, and is common to all things, is principle. Principle inheres in the mind and is experienced in things and affairs. The mind is what coordinates these principles [within and without] and makes distinctions of right and wrong. Worthiness or unworthiness among men, success or failure in human affairs, order and disorder in the world, are all determined in this way.[58]

In contrast to this, says Huang, Ch'an Buddhism sees the principles articulated by the sages as handicapping self-realization and impeding enlightenment, so they simply point directly to the mind and seek to transmit hints without the use of words. The mind of the sages, however, was common to all men and the principles which should govern affairs were clearly known to all without the need for any special transmission of mind. It was only necessary for men to act on these principles and for their minds to make the necessary judgments in dealing with human affairs.

If Huang Chen found the "transmission of the mind" an unfortunate choice of words susceptible of misappropriation by Ch'an Buddhists, he did not disagree with Ts'ai Shen's basic view of moral self-cultivation and its importance for the mind of the ruler, or with Ts'ai's view, as Huang put it, that "this mind is the root of ordering the state and bringing peace to the world." Such a view of the nature and nurture of the morally responsible, socially conscious mind, was what the true learning of the mind-and-heart was about, in contrast to the wordless transmission of the Ch'an Buddhists.

Huang made this still clearer in his discussion of the orthodox tradition in the Sung. Tracing the "correct teaching" as it came down from Chou Tun-i to Chu Hsi, and thence to Huang Kan, he acknowledges that in the course of its transmission two followers of the Ch'eng brothers, Yang Shih (1053-1135) and Hsieh Liang-tso (?-1120), became somewhat tainted by Ch'an. Nevertheless enough of the original teaching was conveyed to Lo Ts'ung-yen (1072-1135) and Li T'ung (1093-1163) so that the latter "could save Chu Hsi from falling into Ch'an," and Chu, with his brilliant powers of analysis could shed great light on the teachings of the Ch'engs and regain the main road of the orthodox way. This was possible only because Li T'ung, "through this clarifying of the learning of the mind, could, despite the proclivity to become diverted toward Ch'an, himself hold onto the correct learning of the mind (*hsin-hsüeh*)."[59]

From this one can say that despite his reservations concerning the use of the expression "transmission of the mind," Huang Chen saw the "learning of the mind" itself, not as a deviant form of Confucianism contaminated by Buddhism, but precisely as the authentic orthodoxy holding fast against such occasional lapses.

At about the same time Ch'en Ta-yü (c.s. 1259),[60] a Ch'eng-Chu scholar in the line of Huang Kan, in his commentary on the *Book of Shang* asserted that the passage on the human mind and mind of the Way "presented the tradition of the Way (*tao-t'ung*) as transmitted in the method of the mind (*hsin-fa*)," while the immediately following passage in the same text, having to do with the love and respect which the ruler should command, represented the succession to rulership (*chih-fa*).[61] Thus he makes the same connection as Ts'ai Shen between the tradition of the Way, the method of the mind, and the succession to rulership.

Ch'en Ta-yü's views on the point are reiterated by another commentator on the *Book of Shang*, Ch'en Li (1252-1334),[62] known for his devotion to Chu Hsi, who cites the latter's *Recorded Conversations (Yü-lu)* as confirmation of the view that the formula of "refinement and singleness of mind" was the method or practice (*kung-fu*) handed down from Shun to Yü as the Sages' method of the mind (*hsin-fa*).[63] Thereafter the practice (*tzu-ti*) in the Confucian school followed this formula. Though the methods of self-cultivation set forth in the *Mean* and *Great Learning* were expressed in different terms, the meaning was the same as the method of refinement and singleness. "What one needed to study was only this principle, and when, after Mencius, the transmission was lost, it was this that was lost."[64] In other words, the practice of "refinement and singleness" was the "method of the mind" and the latter was the heart of the "tradition of the Way" passed down from the sages but lost after Mencius.

This view is also found in other writings of Ch'en Li. In his preface to the Collected Commentaries, he says: "The *Book of Shang* records the orderly rule of the early emperors and kings. One seeks the Way through the cultivation of reverence in the mind-and-heart, and one seeks orderly rule through the practice of the Mean in government.[65] The teaching concerning the human mind and mind of the Way, he says, is the essence of the Tradition of the Way (*tao-t'ung*),[66] while the teachings of "refinement and singleness" and "holding fast to the Mean," as found in Chu Hsi's preface to the *Mean,* are indispensable ingredients of the Tradition of the Way (*tao-t'ung*). They represent as well the practice of the real principles and real learning spoken of in Ch'eng I's characterization of the message of the mind placed by Chu Hsi at the beginning of his commentary on the *Mean.*[67] Moreover, since this message is concerned with "real principles," it is in no way incompatible with the "learning of the Way" (*tao-hsüeh*) and "learning of principle" (*li-hsüeh*) which comes down from Chou Tun-i, the Ch'engs, Chang Tsai, and Chu Hsi.[68] Finally, Ch'en sums it all up in his comment on the *Analects'* passage in which Confucius speaks of setting his heart on learning at age fifteen (a comment of Ch'en's preserved in the Ming *Great Compendium on the Analects (Lun-yü ta-ch'üan),* though Ch'en's own commentary on the Four Books *(Ssu-shu fa-ming)* has been lost):

> The learning of the sage [Confucius] began with his heart set on learning [at the age of fifteen] and ended (at age seventy) with his being able to follow his heart's desire without transgressing the norm. From beginning to end it was all learning of the mind-and-heart
>
> (hsin-hsüeh).[69]

For another view of the matter among the early followers of Chu Hsi, we may cite the testimony of Wei Liao-weng (1178-1237) and Lo Ta-ching (n.d.). Wei is often cited with Chen Te-hsiu as a principal leader of the learning of the Way in the early thirteenth century. Together Wei and Chen were responsible for the Sung courts' reversal of the ban on Chu Hsi. Lo Ta-ching, active in the mid-thirteenth century,[70] had a great admiration for Chu Hsi, Chen Te-hsiu, and Wei Liao-weng, and in a miscellany of reading notes included the following quotation from a letter by Wei to a friend concerning the role of the mind in studying the classics:

> "One should study the classics, reflecting on each word so as to get it oneself. One cannot just employ the method of simply following what has been said by former scholars." He also said, "In employing the method of fathoming principles through the investigation of things, one should always bear in mind and keep in one's heart the model of the Three Dynasties. If one just follows in the tracks of the Han and Chin scholars, one will not have done the job." Wei also said: "Just reading a great deal in the recent interpretations and reflections of former scholars is not as good as reading the sages' classics one by one for oneself. . . ."

> These comments of Wei Ho-shan are something students should cherish and respect. I have compiled a work entitled "*Classics and Commentaries on the Learning of the Mind-and-Heart*"[71] in ten fascicles, and have said in the preface: "It will not do if one does not seek to learn from Chou [Tun-i], the Ch'engs, Chang [Tsai], and Chu [Hsi], but [on the other hand] only to learn from them and not base it all in the Classics would be like neglecting one's father's memory and venerating one's elder brother. One must certainly not fail to read the Six Classics, but only to study them and not reflect upon them in one's own mind would be like buying a jewel box and throwing away the pearl.[72]

If one considers this passage in the light of what was said earlier about Chu Hsi's insistence on the equal need for reading the original texts, studying the commentaries and reflecting oneself on the meaning of texts, as combined in Chu Hsi's conception of the "transmission of the mind [of the sages]" *(ch'uan-hsin],* we can recognize another component of the learning of the mind-and-heart referred to earlier by Ch'ien Mu (see above, pp. 24-27). Since Wei Liao-weng and Lo Ta-ching were both from Kiangsi, one might suspect some lingering influence on them of Lu

Hsiang-shan, but in fact the kind of classical textual study recommended here and practiced by Wei Liao-weng was quite in contrast to the teaching of Lu, as was the emphasis above on the fathoming of principles through the investigation of things. Moreover Wei Liao-weng was associated with Fu Kuang, a leading disciple of Chu Hsi, and though like Chen Te-hsiu, disposed to minimize the differences between Chu and Lu, had no comparable association with the latter's limited following in the early thirteenth century.[73]

It was at about this time that Chen Te-hsiu compiled his *Classic of the Mind-and-Heart (Hsin-ching,* abbreviated here as "Heart Classic"), based on passages in the Confucian classics and the interpretations of the Sung masters, which, as anthologized in concise form, became a "classic statement" of the Learning of the Mind-and-Heart. That this "Learning" was clearly identified with the well-known sixteen-word passage from the *Book of Documents,* as quoted by Chu Hsi in his preface to the *Chung-yung chang-chü,* is shown by Chen's choice of it as the opening passage of the *Heart Classic,* together with Chu's comment on it.[74] Moreover, that Ts'ai Shen had served as an intermediary in linking this "message of the mind" and "transmission of the mind" is suggested by a eulogy Chen had written for Ts'ai Shen in which he praised his commentary on the *Book of Documents* and cited it particularly for its account of the transmission of the Sages' and Kings' doctrine of the mind and its practice in rulership.[75] To his own "classic" Chen Te-hsiu appended a paean of praise for this "Learning," which begins with the lines:

> *Transmitted from Shun to Yü*
> *Were these sixteen words,*
> *The Learning of the Mind-and-Heart for all ages*
> *Had its inception here.*[76]

These words were quoted by the late Sung scholar Hsiung Chieh (c.s. 1199), a Chu schoolman who studied under Huang Kan, when he compiled his *Anthology on Human Nature and Principle,* showing that this use of the term *hsin-hsüeh* was in no way incompatible with the view of Chu Hsi's teaching as centrally concerned with human nature and principle *(hsing-li).*[77] In the anthology it is included in the matter prefatory to selections from Chu Hsi, as if to sound a keynote.

Elsewhere Chen made it clear that *hsin-fa* represented not only the essential message handed down from the sages, but also the essential method to be practiced and attitude to be cultivated by all those committed to the Way of the Sages:

> When one has committed himself to this Way, to what should he then devote his practice of it? If we look to remote antiquity, we can see that in the one word 'reverence,' as passed down through a hundred sages, is represented their real method of the mind-and-heart *(hsin-fa).*[78]

Chen's *Heart Classic* had an especially deep influence on the great champion of Ch'eng-Chu orthodoxy in Korea, Yi T'oegye (1501-1570), for whom Lu Hsiang-shan was completely anathema. Yi wrote his own summation of the essentials of the tradition in *Ten Diagrams of the Sages' Learning (Song-hak sip-do),*[79] the seventh diagram of which was entitled "The Learning of the Mind-and-Heart" (see figure 7). Yi incorporated therein most of the concepts discussed above, and acknowledged that his chart was based on that of Ch'eng Min-cheng (c.s. 1466) (see figure 6), which was in turn devised from an earlier Yüan dynasty prototype by Ch'eng Fu-hsin (1257-1340)[80] appearing in the latter's *Diagrams and Explanations of the Four Books (Ssu-shu t'u-shuo)* of 1313[81] (see figures 4, 5).

Ch'eng Fu-hsin was from Chu Hsi's ancestral hometown of Hsin-an in An-hui. Early accounts speak of him as having studied the words of Huang Kan and Fu Kuang and having become thoroughly "devoted to Chu Hsi's teaching, through which he was able to grasp (lit. 'get') the mind of Confucius, Mencius, Tseng Tzu and Tzu-ssu (i.e., as revealed in the Four Books)."[82] He believed that the *Great Learning* particularly featured the doctrine of the mind, while the *Mean* featured the teaching concerning the nature *(hsing),* which was equated with principle *(li).* The two texts together thus expounded the combination of mind and principle so central to the tradition of the Way and to the early learning of the mind in the Ch'eng-Chu school, a combination emphasized in Ch'eng's diagrams.[83]

Besides citing Ch'eng's views on the Learning and Method of the Mind in the text accompanying his own diagram, T'oegye, in his *I-hak t'ong-nok* (Comprehensive Record of the Learning of Principle),[84] identified this source of his Learning of the Mind with the Learning of Principle (to which he said Ch'eng made signal contributions) and also with the orthodox succession.[85] This orthodox tradition of the Learning of the Mind-and-Heart T'oegye clearly identified with the message and method of the mind *(hsin-fa)* coming down from the sages to the Sung masters as is indicated in his commentary on Chu's "Precepts of the White Deer Grotto," summarized by Yiu as "the essentials of the Method of the Mind."[86] Ch'eng presented his own *Diagrams and Explanations of the Four Books* to the Yüan court in 1313, at precisely the moment in Chinese history when the Four Books were first being adopted for use as the standard texts in the resumed civil service examinations. Prime among Ch'eng's sponsors in this presentation was Ch'eng Chü-fu (1249-1318), the chief architect of the system that would remain the official orthodoxy of China and Korea down into modern times.[87] (For illustration of above, see T'oegye's diagram in the Japanese edition of *Ri Taikei Zenshū,* 2:260.)

From the foregoing discussion of the Neo-Confucian Learning of the Mind-and-Heart in its initial phase, we may draw the following conclusions as to its essential characteristics:

1. Although the expression *hsin-hsüeh* was not used by either Chu Hsi or Lu Hsiang-shan, Chu had much to say about the nature and nurture of the mind which warranted his immediate followers' use of the term of differentiate Chu Hsi's view of the mind from the Buddhists' or Taoists'.

2. Chu's early followers identified this Learning of the Mind with three concepts appearing in key writings of Chu—key in the sense that they dealt with central issues and also, having wide dissemination, played an important role in shaping the new Learning of the Way as it left the hands of Chu Hsi. These concepts were the "Tradition of the Way" *(tao-t'ung),* the Method of the Mind *(hsin-fa),* and the Transmission of the [Sages'] Mind *(ch'uan-hsin).* Early writers of the Chu Hsi school spoke of these as inseparably related aspects of a core tradition handed down from the sages.

3. The passage most often cited as expressing the kernel of this teaching was the sixteen-word formula identified by Chu Hsi with the "tradition of the Way" *(tao-t'ung)* in his preface to the Mean. Elsewhere Chu, and others after him, also referred to it as the Message or Method of the Mind *(hsin-fa),* thus establishing a close correlation between this method and the tradition of the Way.

4. Though the "sixteen words" were obscure in themselves and drawn from an apocryphal version of the *Book of Shang,* they were taken by Chu Hsi as scriptural authority for the distinction between the human mind and the Mind of the Way—a crucial distinction in Ch'eng-Chu philosophy between the fallible mind of the ordinary man and the Sages' mind of pure principle (the mind of the Way). As moral injunctions these dicta comprised a method of self-cultivation including constant self-examination; making fine moral and cognitive distinctions (corresponding to the manifold particularizations of the Way in practice); concentrating the mind on the oneness of principle as constituting the essential unity of the human order with the creative process in Heaven, Earth, and all things; and holding to the Mean in the conduct of human affairs. Thus principal Neo-Confucian doctrines, especially as based on the *Mean,* were seen as implicated in these sixteen words.

5. Further, this kind of correlation was extended to include the methodical steps of intellectual and moral cultivation found in the *Great Learning.* From this the sixteen-word formula came to be seen as a concise, though cryptic, encapsulation of the Confucian teachings found in the *Great Learning* and the *Mean,* now coordinated by Chu Hsi's commentary with the interpretation of the Four Books as a whole, and most particularly with the important passage in the *Analects* on the discipline of "subduing the self and restoring riteness." Given the almost mystical language in which Ch'eng I, as quoted by Chu, spoke of the "method of the mind," it took on the aspect of an oracular message from the primordial age confirming not only the perennial truths of Confucian self-cultivation but also the fully articulated speculations of the Sung philosophers.

The cryptic character of this message is not to be confused with the kind of secret transmission spoken of in Ch'an (Zen) or Esoteric Buddhism. It involves no passing on of a truth which goes beyond all formulation in words, nor is there any implied distrust of language such as one finds in the Ch'an "nondependence" on words and phrases *(pu-li wen-tzu).* When Chu Hsi speaks of the "secret purport" of the sixteen-character message he means only that the words alone do not convey the full-meaning and significance of the sages' teaching. It is a teaching, however, written by Heaven, so to speak, on the mind-and-heart of everyman, by its endowment of the luminous rational and moral nature replete with all principles. All that is needed for the comprehension of this truth is clarity of perception—the kind of unobstructed vision possessed by the sages and the Sung masters, vouchsafed, in terms of their psycho-physical dispositions, by a specially clairvoyant ethereal endowment, brought to its full realization by a corresponding effort at self-cultivation of their individual natures.

Thus the Sages' teaching remains in the domain of rational discourse, and the orthodox tradition, far from claiming to be a private or exclusive transmission, is something open to all. Indeed it is this open and public character of the Way, so vital to its educational propagation in the late Sung and Yüan periods, to which appeal is made by later Neo-Confucians who protest the tendency to make of the orthodox tradition a private or exclusive possession in a single line of transmission.

6. Since this Tradition of the Way had come down from Sage-kings who had presided over a social order fully consonant with that Way, the injunctions discussed in no. 4 above were thought to have a special relevance to rulership. Here was the crucial link between the Neo-Confucian philosophy of mind and its political philosophy: the method of self-discipline and intellectual cultivation that was key to the governance of men *(hsiu-chi chih-jen)*—a point emphasized by early commentators on the sixteen-word passage in the *Book of Shang.*

7. The process by which this message was communicated—a combination of careful textual study and inspired interpretation by the Sung masters—was expressed in the term "transmission of the mind [of the sages]" *(ch'uan-hsin).* For Chu Hsi the significance of this transmission lay in the balance of cognitive learning, critical reflection, deep insight, and lofty vision as the Way was reconstructed in the mind of the dedicated scholar seeking to realize the ideals of the sages. There was no established process, no automatic transmission by which the tradition of the Way *(tao-t'ung)* could be assured of perpetuation in a given age. In this view the routine scholarship of the Han and T'ang had failed to appreciate the inner dynamic of the classics that had come into their possession, a dynamic which could be perceived by reading between the lines, bridging the gaps in the texts, piecing together the fragments, and entering body and soul—indeed, heart and mind—into both the spacious halls and secret recesses of the sagely mind.

8. Each of these Neo-Confucian terms and concepts had parallels in Buddhism and Taoism for which they might be mistaken, but Chu Hsi and his followers saw this as no reason for surrendering the use of such terms as the method

of the mind *(hsin-fa)* or transmission of the mind *(ch'uan-hsin)* to Buddhism. Instead they spoke of the former as a systematic moral and intellectual discipline in the service of the latter as an explicit, publicly transmitted and documented discourse, open to reexamination and rational discussion.

9. From the foregoing a further conclusion can be drawn of the greatest importance for the later development of Neo-Confucianism: this learning of the mind-and-heart was also understood to be a learning of principle. There could be no opposition between *hsin-hsüeh* and *li-hsüeh* for these Neo-Confucians because their whole view of the mind, in contrast to the Buddhist, was that this mind was fundamentally imbued with the rational, moral principles implanted in it by Heaven. There might be some—but few enough in the thirteenth century—who questioned the distinction between the human mind and the mind of the Way, but none among the Neo-Confucians who doubted that the whole point of this mind was to understand and express Heaven's principles.

The Learning of the Mind-and-Heart, as a term or concept in itself, was not a major focus of discussion in the early Ch'eng-Chu school, but it was a way of characterizing disciplines and doctrines considered essential to the learning of the Way. When Chen Te-hsiu promoted that learning in the early thirteenth century, acclaiming it as the Learning of the Mind-and-Heart, he was also recognized as the great champion of the Learning of the Way and the Learning of Principle in his time, not as someone propounding an idiosyncratic or deviant doctrine.

Nevertheless, as we have seen, it was a doctrine, for all its exoteric professions, not free of its own enigmatic and ambiguous formulations. As the sixteen-word formula had it, the mind of the Way was subtle and difficult to perceive, while the human mind was unstable and liable to err in its judgments. Whatever the Neo-Confucians might say about the palpability of the word or constancy of the Way, the endurance of the teaching—even on Chu Hsi's terms—was contingent upon its critical reexamination and creative reinterpretation. As the teaching spread, and became deeply rooted, one could expect to see new buds bursting from the old wood and new branches reaching out—which also means contending with each other—for a place in the sun.

Notes

1. *Neo-Confucian Orthodoxy,* Parts I, II.

2. Typical examples are *Tz'u-hai,* 3b; *Tz'u-yüan,* p. 1096; Wei Cheng-t'ung, *Chung-kuo che-hsüeh tz'u-tien ta-ch'üan,* pp. 112-15. Morohashi Testsuji, *Dai kanwa jiten,* 1960 No. 10295-45; Hihara Toshikuni, ed., *Chūgoku tetsu-gaku jiten,* p. 225. Fung Yu-lan, *History of Chinese Philosophy,* Derk Bodde, tr., 2:500, 572, 586, 623; de Bary, Chan, and Watson, eds., *Sources of Chinese Tradition,* pp. 510, 559; Wing-tsit Chan, *Source Book in Chinese Philosophy,* p. 573. Chan's comments in this earlier work should be viewed in light of his later article in Wei Cheng-t'ung above.

3. Fung, *History,* Bodde, tr., 2:572, 586, see also pp. 500, 623. The corresponding passages in the original Chinese edition of 1934 remain unaltered in the latest edition, *Chung-kuo che-hsüeh shih,* 2:928-29, 938-39.

4. Ch'ien Mu, *Chu Tzu hsin hsüeh-an,* 2:1.

5. See reference to Ch'en Li (T'ing-yu)'s commentary on *Analects* 2; Shih yu wu chang.

6. Araki Kengo, citing the *Hsin hsüeh-an* 1:418, differs with Ch'ien on this. Although I do not find the language Araki cites on 1:418, similar statements are made here and on 2:106. Araki's view is presented in the aforementioned preface to his *Minmatsu shūkyō shisō kenkyū,* 27, 48.

7. *Hsin hsüeh-an,* 1:55.

8. Yang Wan-li, "Hsin Hsüeh lun," in *Ch'eng-chai chi,* SPTK, ch. 84-86, esp. 85:10b-12b. On Yang Wan-li see *Sung-shih* 433:12863-66; MJHA 44:74-81; *Sung-jen so-yin* 3186-88; Hervouet, *Sung Bibliography,* pp. 417-18. See also Wing-tsit Chan, "Hsin-hsüeh," in Wei Cheng-tung, ed., *Chung-kuo che-hsüeh tz'u-tien ta-ch'üan,* p. 113.

9. de Bary, *Neo-Confucian Orthodoxy and Learning of the Mind-and-Heart,* pp. 5-6.

10. As recounted in *Analects* 20:1.

11. *Book of History,* "Counsels of Great Yü," in James Legge, *The Chinese Classics,* 3:61.

12. Chu Hsi, Preface to *Chung-yung chang-chü,* in *Ssu-shu chi chu,* also in *Shushigaku taikei* (Tokyo: Meitoku Shuppansha, 1974), 8:451-52 (11-14). In references to this edition the Chinese text is cited first, the Japanese second. My translation has benefited from consulting, in addition to the Japanese translation of Tanaka Masaru and notes of Kurihara Keisuke, the draft translation by Wing-tsit Chan prepared for the *Sources of Neo-Confucianism* project.

13. An idea advanced by Han Yü and reiterated by Ch'eng I. See *Neo-Confucian Orthodoxy,* pp. 3-5.

14. Chu Hsi, *Chung-yung chang-chü hsü,* p. 3 (42).

15. Ch'ien, *Hsin hsüeh-an,* 1:186-96; 4:184.

16. *Ibid.,* 1:28-35, 143, 160-61, 169-70; 4:184-87, 197; and, 2:113, 4:218.

17. See de Bary, Chan, and Watson, eds., *Sources of Chinese Tradition,* pp. 503-9; Richard L. Davis, "Historiography as Politics in Yang Wei-chen's 'Polemic on Legitimate Succession'"; and Hok-lam Chan, *Legitimation in Imperial China,* pp. 38-40.

18. Li Yüan-kang, *Sheng-men shih-yeh t'u,* in *Pai-ch'uan hsüeh-hai,* 1927 photolithographic ed. of original Sung ed. of T'ao Hsiang as supplemented by the Ming Hung-chih (1488-1505) ed. of Hua Ch'eng; prefaces of Li dated 1170, 1173. See Hervouet, *Sung Bibliography,* p. 490.

The extant edition of the Diagrams also carries a post-preface dated 1172 by one Wang Chieh of San-shan. In paying tribute to Li, Wang expresses views common to Ch'eng I and Chu Hsi. Given Chu's great reputation and the wide influence of his writings, as well as mutual scholarly associations such as this, it is as possible that Li was familiar with some of Chu's ideas as vice versa. However, given the date of this preface, the Wang Chieh here could hardly be the Wang Chieh (1158-1213) identified as a follower of Chu Hsi from Chinhua. See Ch'ang Pi-te *Sung-jen chuan-chi tzu-liao so-yin,* p. 106; Chan Wingtsit, *Chu Tzu men-jen,* pp. 60-61; *Sung shih,* 400:12152-55; SYHA, 73:30-31; Pu-i, 73:6b.

Li Yüan-kang (n.d.); T. Kuo-chi, H. Pai-lien chen-yin. A reclusive scholar of Ch'ien-t'ang, Chekiang, known for his devotion to learning. He is linked by the *Sung-yüan hsüeh-an pu-i* with the school of Chang Tsai, but his diagram identifies the Ch'engs as the successors to the Way and makes no mention of Chang. *Sung-jen so-yin,* p. 951; SYHA, Pu-i, 17:18b.

19. Both Davis (p. 48) and H. L. Chan (p. 41) include Chou Tun-i in the transmission, but Li's chart is quite clear in representing the Ch'eng brothers as direct successors to Mencius, and has no mention of Chou Tun-i. Both Li and Chu Hsi bespeak a view apparently prevalent in the Ch'eng brothers' school. The other view, including Chou Tun-i, is found in Chu Hsi's "Memoir for the Altar to the Three Masters at the Yüan-chou Prefectural School," *Yüan-chou chou-hsüeh san hsien-sheng tz'u-chi,* in Chu, *Wen-chi,* 78:76a-77b (pp. 5709-12), which also describes Chou's reception of it in terms of a direct unmediated inspiration from Heaven, rather than a teaching acquired by some lineal transmission. So far as I know Chu never completely reconciled the two accounts, and later Neo-Confucians invoked both.

20. Ch'ien Ta-hsin, *Shih-chia chai yang-hsin lu,* 18:10a.

21. *Ssu-shu chi-chu, Chung-yung chang-chü,* 1:1 (p. 45).

22. *Neo-Confucian Orthodoxy,* p. 129 and n. 157.

23. Chu, *Wen-chi,* 81:10a; Shu *Chung-yung* hou, p. 5845.

24. Ch'ien, *Hsin hsüeh-an,* 1:112.

25. *Neo-Confucian Orthodoxy,* pp. 128-30. See also Wing-tsit Chan's article on *hsin-fa* in *Chung-kuo che-hsüeh tz'u-tien ta-ch'üan* (Taipei: Shui-niu ch'u-pan-she, 1983), pp. 111-12.

26. *Ssu-shu chi-chu, Lun-yü,* 6:12; Comm. on *Lun yü,* 12:1 (p. 307).

27. *Ssu-shu chi-chu, Lun yü,* 6:10b-11a; Comm. on *Lun yü,* 12:1 (p. 304).

28. Ch'ien Mu, *Hsin hsüeh-an,* pp. 121-22.

29. *Chu Tzu yü-lei,* 78:30ab No. 212 (Ta Yü Mo Item 37) (pp. 3199-3200). Here and in subsequent reference to the *Yü-lei* the first citation will be to the *chüan* and page number of the original edition, and the "p" number will refer to the overall pagination of the Cheng-chung reprint.

30. *Neo-Confucian Orthodoxy and the Learning of the Mind-and-Heart*, pp. 30-31.

31. *Hsin hsüeh-an*, pp. 104-105.

32. Chu, *Wen-chi*, 2:26a. Wan Yen-p'ing Li hsien-sheng san-shou (p. 349); 87:3a, Chi Yen-p'ing Li hsien-sheng wen (p. 6175).

33. *Hsin hsüeh-an*, pp. 104-5. See also Julia Ching, *To Acquire Wisdom: The Way of Wang Yang-ming*, pp. 18-19.

34. *Ch'eng shih i-shu*, 19:7a; Chu, *Wen-chi*, 75:16-17a (p. 5521); Cheng-shih i-shu hou hsü; *Hsin hsüeh-an*, 2:105-6.

35. *Hsin hsüeh-an*, 2:113.

36. *Ch'ang-li hsien-sheng wen-chi*, SPTK 11:1a-3b; de Bary, Chan, and Watson, eds., *Sources of Chinese Tradition*, p. 431 (Pb I, 376).

37. See Chu Hsi, *Hsiao-hsüeh chi-chu*, 3:1a-2b; 5:16a; 6:19b; Uno Seiichi, *Shōgaku*, pp. 139-49, 320, 469.

38. Huang Kan; T. Chih-ch'ing, H. Mien-chai. *Sung-jen so-yin*, p. 2865; Chan, *Men-jen*, pp. 261-62; *Sung-shih*, 430:1; SYHA, 63:5.

39. Huang Kan, *Mien-chai hsien-sheng Huang Wen-shu kung wen-chi*, 26:18a-20a.

40. Huang Shih-i (fl. c. 1170); T. Tzu-hung. A student of Chu Hsi from Fukien. See *Sung-jen so-yin*, p. 2884; Chan, *Men-jen*, p. 254; SYHA, 69:514-15.

41. Huang Kan, *Mien-chai hsien-sheng wen-chi*, 26:26b-28a. Shun Yü ch'uanhsin . . . Huang Tzu-hung.

42. Ch'en Ch'un; T. An-ch'ing, H. Pei-hsi. *Sung-jen so-yin*, p. 2471; Chan, *Men-jen*, pp. 220-21; *Sung shih*, 430:12789; SYHA, 68:1.

    Ssu-k'u ch'üan-shu tsung-mu t'i-yao, 91:1916-17 (see also Ch'en Ch'un, *Pei-hsi tzu-i*, pp. 95-96); Chan, *Men-jen*, pp. 220-21; also his introduction to translation of *Pei-hsi tzu-i*, published as *Neo-Confucian Terms Explained: The Pei-hsi tzu-i*, pp. 1-32.

43. Ch'en Ch'un, *Pei-hsi tzu-i* (The Meaning of Terms [in the Four Books] according to Ch'en Ch'un), p. 76.

44. *Ibid.*, p. 77. *Shih-yu yüan-yüan*.

45. *Ibid.*, p. 7.

46. Chu, *Wen-chi*, 82:26ab (5939-40); Shu Min-ch'ang so kan ssu-tzu hou.

47. Ch'en uses the same language as Chu Hsi, quoting Ch'eng I; I have translated it in the same way in both cases. Professor Chan renders *hsin-fa* as "the central tradition," an interpretation which confirms its importance for both Ch'en and the Ch'eng-Chu school.

48. A close approximation of Chu's quotation. See p. 32 above.

49. Ch'en, *Pei-hsi tzu-i*, pp. 78-79 Tu-shu tzu-ti.

50. *Pei-hsi tzu-i*, pp. 89, 95; Chan, *Neo-Confucian Terms*, pp. 211, 213, 233.

51. Ts'ai Shen; T. Chung-mo, H. Chiu-feng, *Sung-jen so-yin*, p. 3783; Chan, *Men-jen*, p. 333; *Sung shih*, 434:1287; SYHA, 67:1.

    Ts'ai Yuan-ting; T. Chi-t'ung, H. Mu-an, Hsi-shan. *Sung-jen so-yin*, p. 3809; Chan, *Men-jen*, pp. 331-32; *Sung shih*, 434:12875; SYHA, 62:1.

52. Ts'ai Shen, *Shu-ching chi-chuan*, preface, pp. 1b-2a. Hervouet, *Sung Bibliography*, pp. 22-23.

53. Chu Hsi, *Chung-yung chang-chü*, hsü, 2a (p. 39).

54. *Ibid.*, 1:28b-29a.

55. Huang Chen; T. Tung-fa, H. Yü-yüeh. From T'zu-ch'i, Çhekiang. *Sung-jen so-yin*, p. 2870, *Sung shih*, 438:12991; SYHA, 86:1.

    Fu Kuang; T. Han-ch'ing, H. Ch'ien-an, Ch'uan-t'ai. From Chekiang, Chia-hsing fu, Ch'ung-te hsien. *Sung-jen so-yin*, p. 3606; Chan, *Men-jen*, pp. 302-3, SYHA, 64:1.

56. Ts'ai Shen, *Shu-ching chi-chuan*, 1:18b-29a.

57. Cf. Benjamin Elman, "Philosophy *(I-li)* versus Philology *(K'ao-cheng):* The *Jen-hsin Tao-hsin* Debate," p. 182. Elman takes this passage as referring to certain others who presented Ts'ai's commentary to the throne in such a way as to put undue emphasis on the "transmission of the mind." The editors of the *Ssu-k'u t'i-yao* (1:228-29) indicate that the presentation was made by Ts'ai's own son, Ts'ai Hang (c.s. 1229) during the Ch'un-yu period (1241-52) and Chan Hing-ho in Hervouet, *Sung Bibliography*, p. 23, says it took place about 1245. This timing is significant in regard to Elman's suggestion (p. 181) that in this passage Huang expressed the fear of the "consequences of an overemphasis on doctrines centering on studies of the mind *(hsin-hsüeh)* by court scholars such as Chen Te-hsiu." Chen had died in 1235, ten years before. Moreover there is strong countervailing evidence in both Chen's *Hsin-ching* and *Ta-hsüeh yen-i* that his understanding of the *hsin-fa* and *hsin-hsüeh* is the same as Ts'ai Shen's and Huang Chen's, i.e., that it is a method of world-ordering and nothing resembling the Ch'an transmission of the mind. Further, Huang identifies those who are at fault here with concentrating on the Mind of the Way, and equating the Mind with the Way. This would suggest a view similar to Lu Hsiang-shan and not Chen, who, if he differed at all from Chu Hsi, would have to be said to have overemphasized the *dangers* of the human mind rather than the equation of the mind with the Way. See my *Neo-Confucian Orthodoxy*, pp. 80-82, 99, 116. Huang Chen, *Huang shih jih-ch'ao*, in *Ssu-k'u ch'üan-shu chen-pen, erh chi*, 5:2a-3b Ta yü mo: Jen-hsin wei-wei.

58. *Huang shih jih-ch'ao*, 5:3b-4a.

59. *Huang shih jih-ch'ao*, 43:5b-6b, Yen-p'ing ta-wen.

60. Ch'en Ta-yü; T. Wen-hsien, H. Tung-chai. From Tu-ch'ang in modern Shantung province. He studied under Jao Lu, a follower of Huang Kan, and wrote the *Shang-shu chi-chuan hui-t'ung* (Comprehensive Explanation of the Collected Commentaries on the *Book of Shang*, which is no longer extant). *Sung jen so-yin*, p. 2541; SYHA, 83:2; Pu-i, 83:12. There were two scholars named Ch'en Ta-yü; the other, a follower of Yang Chien, received the *chin-shih* degree in 1229. See SYHA, Pu-i, 74:66ab, and the comment of the Ssu-k'u editors in *Ssu-k'u ch'üan-shu tsung-mu t'i-yao*, 11:63, on the surviving work of the earlier Ch'en Ta-yü: *Shang-shu chi-chuan huo-wen*.

61. Cited in Ch'en Li, (Shang)-*Shu chi-chuan tsuan-shu*, 1:59a (v. 61, p. 231). Ch'en drew extensively on the writings of Chu Hsi, especially the *Yü-lü*, to supplement Ts'ai Shen's commentary. The comment of the *Ssu-k'u* editors, which prefaces this edition, emphasizes Ch'en's fidelity to Chu Hsi (v. 61 p. 202).

Since both the earlier and later Ch'en Ta-yü are said to have compiled collected commentaries on the *Shang-shu*, neither of which is extant, one cannot be sure which might have been quoted by Ch'en Li. However the passage in question does not appear in the extent *Shang-shu chi-chuan huo-wen* (Wen-yüan ko Ssu-k'u ed., A:38ab) of the earlier Ch'en Ta-yü. Here it is accepted by Ch'en Li as in essential harmony with the commentary he has drawn from "orthodox" sources. Thus if the question of authorship is not actually moot, it would seem that the later Ch'en Ta-yü, identified with the Jao Lu line of the Chu Hsi school, is the more likely source. This would also be consistent with the practice of the near contemporary of Ch'en Li, Tung Ting, who is in the same line of Huang Kan as the later Ch'en Ta-yü and whose collected commentary *Shang-shu chi-lu tsuan-chu*, cited the earlier Ch'en Ta-yü by his *hao* Fu-chai and the later by his *ming*, i.e., Ch'en shih Ta-yü, as is the case here. See *Ssu-k'u t'i-yao*, 11:63, *Shang-shu chi-chuan huo-wen*, and 11:67-68, *Shang-shu chi-lu tsuan-chu*. On Tung Ting (n.d.) see *Yüan-jen chuan-chi tzu-liao*, 1596; SYHA, 89:2b; SYHA, Pu-i, 89:9.

62. Ch'en Li; T. Shou Weng, H. Ting-yu from Hsiu-ning (modern Anhwei province). A classicist and devoted follower of Chu Hsi, who wrote commentaries on the ritual texts and Four Books as well as on the *Book of Documents*. *Yüan-jen so-yin*, p. 1301; *Yüan shih*, 189/4321; SYHA, 70:97; SYHA *Pu-i* 70:79a-92a.

63. Ch'en Li, *Shu-chi-chuan tsuan-shu*, 1:57a (61-230).

64. *Ibid*.

65. SYHA, 70:98, Shu-chuan tsuan-shu hsü.

66. SYHA *Pu-i* 70:86b, Jen-hsin wei-wei ssu-chü k'ou-i.

67. *Ibid.*, 70:81b, *Chung-yung* k'ou-i.

68. *Ibid.*, 70:82a, Preface to *T'ai-chi-t'u shuo*.

69. Hu Kuang et al., editors, *Lun-yü chi-chu ta-ch'üan*, 2:10b (p. 118), *Shih yu wu erh chih yü hsüeh chang*. In Genroku 4 (1691) ed., 2:14b-15a.

70. Lo Ta-ching (n.d.); T. Ching-lun, from Lu-ling in Kiangsi. *Sung-jen so-yin*, p. 4277; Hervouet, *Sung Bibliography*, pp. 314-15.

71. *Hsin-hsüeh ching-chuan*, a work no longer extant.

72. Lo Ta-ching, *Ho-lin yü-lu*, 18:3b-5b, Wen-chang hsing-li. See Hervouet, *Sung Bibliography*, pp. 314-15, where the entry for the *Ho-lin yü-lu* by Araki Toshikazu mentions only the less complete 16 ch. ed. available in China, and omits this more complete edition preserved in the Naikaku bunko.

73. See my *Neo-Confucian Orthodoxy*, pp. 17, 81, 150, 156; *Shushigaku taikei*, 10:8-11, article by Itō Tomoatsu.

74. *Neo-Confucian Orthodoxy*, pp. 67-69, 73-83, 177-80.

75. *Hsi-shan hsien-sheng Chen Wen-chung kung wen-chi* (Taipei: Commercial Press, KHCPTS ed., 1968), 42:750-51, Chiu-feng hsien-sheng Ts'ai chün mu-piao.

76. Chen Te-hsiu, *Hsin ching*, early Ming edition in the National Central Library, Taipei, p. 21b. The National Central Library also has the original Sung edition of 1242, with the same text, but the print is much less legible.

77. Hsiung Chieh, *Hsing-li ch'ün-shu, chü-chieh*, with commentary by Hsiung Kang, 1:16a (p. 54). On Hsiung Chieh see *Sung-jen so-yin*, p. 3622, and Chan, *Men-jen*, p. 289.

78. *Chen Hsi-shan wen-chi* (KHCPTS ed.), p. 448 (also SSGTK, 10:96), "Nan hsiung chou-hsüeh ssu hsien-sheng ssu-t'ang chi."

79. See Ri Taikei kenkyūkai, *Ri Taikei zenshū* (Tokyo, 1975), 2:260, for chart of the Learning of the Mind and for the views of Ch'eng Fu-hsin as cited by Yi T'oegye.

80. Ch'eng Fu-hsin, T. Tzu-chien, H. Lin-yin. *Yüan-jen so-yin*, p. 1429.

81. Also known as *Ssu-shu chang-t'u*. There are two extant versions known to me: 1) *Ssu-shu chang-t'u yin-k'uo tsung-yao*, 1337 ed. in two ts'e preserved in the National Central Library, Taipei; 1b) a hand-copied version of the same in the Shōheikō collection of the Naikaku bunko, Tokyo; and 2) *Ssu-shu chang-t'u tsuan-shih*, Te-hsin t'ang ed. of 1337 in 21 chüan with *Ssu-shu chang-t'u yin-k'uo tsung-yao* in 3 ch. in the Naikaku bunko. Unless otherwise noted, references herein are to this edition.

82. Ch'eng T'ung, ed., *Hsin-an hsüeh tzu-lu*, in *An-hui ts'ung shu*, 12:7a-10b.

83. *Ssu-shu chang-t'u*, 6a Fan li, Chung yung tao-t'ung chih ch'uan; chang-t'u shang 12b Lun hsin t'ung hsing-ching; Tsung yao chung 1b Sheng-hsien lun hsin chih yao; 7b Lun hsin t'ung hsing-ching.

84. Wing-tsit Chan appraises this work favorably for its careful scholarship in his "How T'oegye Understood Chu Hsi."

85. Yi T'oegye *I-hak t'ongnok*, 10:21b-22a (2:519).

86. For a fuller discussion of T'oegye's views of the Learning of the Mind and method of the mind as based on the Ch'eng-Chu concept and practice of reverence, see Sin Kuihyon, Sosan Chin Toksu ui Sinkyong kua T'oegye Yi Huang ui Sinhak [Chen Te-hsiu's *Hsin ching* and Yi Huang (T'oegye's) Learning of the Mind-and-Heart] in *T'oegye hakpo* (Seoul: T'oegye Study Institute, 1987), no. 53.

87. See my *Neo-Confucian Orthodoxy*, pp. 55, 59, 65, 148-49.

Abbreviations

The following standard sinological abbreviations are used:

CKTHMCCC Chung-kuo tzu hsüeh ming-chu chi-ch'eng

MJHA Ming-ju hsüeh-an

SKCSCP Ssu-k'u ch'üan-shu chen-pen

SPPY Ssu-pu pei-yao

SPTK Ssu-pu ts'ung-k'an

SSGTK Shushigaku taikei

SYHA Sung-Yüan hsüeh-an

TSCC Ts'ung-shu chi-ch'eng

Hoyt Cleveland Tillman (essay date 1992)

SOURCE: "Chu Hsi and Chang Shih," in *Confucian Discourse and Chu Hsi's Ascendancy,* University of Hawaii Press, 1992, pp. 59-82.

[In the essay that follows, Tillman states that much of Chu Hsi's philosophical development resulted from his relationship with Chang Shih and the correspondence exchanged between the two philosophers. Tillman reviews the issues they discussed, including self-cultivation and the understanding of the mind; Hu Hung's text on the relationship between goodness and one's actions and original inner nature; and humaneness and how it is achieved. Overall, Tillman notes, Chu Hsi's focus was on theory, whereas Chang Shih's emphasis was on practice.]

During the second period of the *Tao-hsüeh* fellowship in the Southern Sung, much of Chu Hsi's development occurred in friendly intellectual exchange with Chang Shih. Chu regarded Chang as exceeding his own quickness and intuitiveness of mind, as evident in the speed and ease with which Chang comprehended ideas and expressed them in writing. Chu Hsi also claimed that whereas he had to work hard to learn, Chang obtained the *Tao* earlier and more easily. Although he was senior to Chang by about

three years, Chu acknowledged: "[Chang Shih's] knowledge is so outstanding as to be unreachable, and having been in his company for a long time, I've repeatedly gotten a lot from him."[1] After the triumph of Chu's school, Chu's originality and profundity have generally been emphasized at the expense of Chang's contributions. Benefits of their interaction were actually mutual. Chu and Chang discussed a wide range of philosophical issues, on which they generally agreed. In addition to exploring terms and concepts, they also exchanged views on differences regarding specific passages in their commentaries on the *Analects* and the *Mencius*.[2] Instead of cataloging their differences here, we will focus on three issues of importance for the *Tao-hsüeh* fellowship itself.

On Self-Cultivation, Equilibrium, and Harmony

The first major issue involved two different traditions of self-cultivation and the understanding of the mind. Self-cultivation involved developing an internalized discipline. Although Chu Hsi's progression from one tradition through the other toward his own synthesis represented probably the most crucial watershed in his development as a Confucian theorist, it is important to realize that Chu's overall evolution was a gradual and cumulative one without sudden, radical breaks. His exchange with Chang Shih over the meaning of centrality or inner equilibrium (*chung*) and harmony (*ho*) in relation to the inner nature and the cultivation of the mind has been exhaustively investigated by modern scholars.[3] Hence I will provide only an overview and highlight its relevance.

The primary locus classicus of the issue was the opening section of the *Doctrine of the Mean* that identified centrality or equilibrium as the state before the feelings were aroused and harmony as the state after the feelings were aroused—if the feelings were appropriately expressed. According to the *Mean*, attaining equilibrium and harmony was the key to achieving oneness with Heaven and the myriad things; hence, it was a person's utmost ethical imperative. Chou Tun-i and Shao Yung had emphasized concentrating on tranquility in one's ethical discipline and had spoken of the mind as the Supreme Ultimate or source of all things. Chou had further equated tranquility and oneness with a state without desires. Chang Tsai had made a distinction between knowledge gained through the senses and the mind's innate knowledge arising from the inner nature. Ch'eng Hao had advocated dispelling selfish feelings as the way to settle the nature. Ch'eng I sought to enhance the rigor of cultivation with reverent composure and by concentrating the mind on one essential thing. Compared with earlier Confucians, the Northern Sung *Tao-hsüeh* Confucians had more sharply defined concepts of the mind and inner nature. Therefore, they placed greater emphasis on the task of cultivation to reach the centrality of the nature and/or mind. Their goal was to know the *Tao* and to attain oneness with the proper order of Heaven and the myriad things. They had not developed a systematic position, however. For example, Ch'eng I had advocated preserving and nourishing the feelings before they were aroused as well as examining these feelings after they had been expressed.

During the first half of the twelfth century, two distinct approaches developed within the *Tao-hsüeh* fellowship to the methodological task of cultivating the mind to know its ultimate oneness with all things. One approach was developed in Fukien and the other in Hunan. In Fukien, one line of Ch'eng I's disciples, led by Yang Shih and Lo Ts'ung-yen (1072-1135), introduced quiet sitting in meditation as the way to experience the essence of the mind and settle the nature. In silent meditation, one was to clarify the mind by expelling all selfish desires. Lo taught this method to Li T'ung, who in turn passed it down to Chu Hsi. Li had Chu concentrate on attaining this state of clarity of mind in tranquil stillness but also focus on his tasks in daily life. Chu regarded Li's instructions about self-cultivation in tranquility and activity as two distinct teachings. Although Li considered this state of mind to be the foundation for praxis in daily activities, Chu felt uncomfortable with the contradictory tension between these two intuitive teachings that could be rationally deduced. The crux of the problem was how the active mind could perceive its own tranquil state before action. After wrestling with Li's teachings for about eight years, Chu declared in 1166 that they were essentially correct as long as one understood that the state of intuitive oneness could not be realized quickly. Perhaps in an attempt to persuade Chang Shih, he traveled in 1177 to Hunan, where he visited for two months with Chang—whose alternative views had encouraged his doubts about Li's teachings.

The Human school represented the other major line of development from the Ch'eng brothers' teachings about the mind. Expanding on Ch'eng I's identification of the mind with the already-expressed state and Hu Hung's view of mind as the function of the inner nature, Chang wanted to focus exclusively on the mind's actual experience in daily affairs. Only by experiencing tranquility in activity or motion could one find the centrality of the mind. Instead of quiet sitting in meditation, one should use the mind's potential—arising from its essential oneness with the inner nature—for observing the subtle first stirrings of the virtues. Thus one could grasp Heaven's principles through their functioning in daily activities. One should apprehend these principles before attempting to preserve and nourish them in personal cultivation. Compared with Li T'ung's approach, Chang had one that was more dynamically oriented toward action.

Chu Hsi abandoned Li T'ung's view and almost fully embraced the Hunan approach during the two-month visit in 1167 and in four letters written in the subsequent year. Following the Hunan school, he identified human nature as essence and mind as nature's function. The incipient state before the feelings were aroused was now associated with the nature, and the expressed state of the feelings with the mind.

Soon questions flourished in Chu Hsi's mind about the Hunan approach. Trying to explain to one of his students why he had abandoned Li's method, Chu was apparently uncomfortable about rejecting his own teacher. He further confessed a feeling of declining ethical vigor after he had stopped following Li's prescribed concentration on the state of tranquility and had begun focusing exclusively on apprehending incipient principles in activity. Intellectually, Chang's position seemed now to have only partially resolved the issue by finding tranquility in the midst of activity. Since tranquility and activity were always in a dialectical relationship in the Supreme Ultimate, why could one not also discover motion in tranquility? Could one not preserve and nourish the essence of the mind before apprehending it in activity? Such questions drove him beyond both his immediate teacher and his friend to the Ch'eng brothers' writings.

As Chu declared in an 1169 letter to his friends in Hunan, studying Ch'eng I's writings provided the answer to his perplexity about inner equilibrium and harmony in tranquility and activity. He told his Hunan friends that his earlier views, which had been based on their teachings, lacked a great foundation. He thereupon selected passages from Ch'eng I's writings to resolve apparent inconsistencies from other passages to which they had all been attentive. The passages to which Chu drew attention now were in the *Surviving Works of the Two Ch'engs*, which he had just completed editing the year before. Chu now claimed that his friends had been wrong to follow Ch'eng I's apparent identification of the mind only with the state after the feelings were aroused. Master Ch'eng had corrected himself when he proclaimed the oneness of mind with both essence, the state of quietness and inactivity, and function, the state of active penetration of all things.

If one resided in reverent seriousness, as Ch'eng had advocated, one's mind would be properly poised in both tranquility and activity to apprehend and nourish principles. It was best to follow Master Ch'eng's twofold path of reverent seriousness and study: "Self-cultivation requires seriousness; the pursuit of learning depends on the extension of knowledge."[4] With this concept, Chu now had a complete view of equilibrium and harmony; moreover, he did not need to await activity before engaging in the cultivation process of examining and then nourishing. Even in the tranquil state before the feelings were aroused, the mind was consciously present. Although tranquil, this was a state of the mind, rather than the nature. Hence this state of mind within one's conscious experience was also a proper object of cultivation. Only after reaching this understanding was Chu able to attend to both traditions of cultivation. When around 1172 Chu wrote a preface to an earlier essay on equilibrium, he further surveyed his evolution from Li's view of cultivation through Chang's to his own. Thus he fully realized that his position had now matured, and he never again made substantial changes on this issue. Much later in his life, however, Chu tended to speak only in terms of preserving the mind, as his dual approach to cultivation of the mind gradually shifted farther away from the component that the Hunan scholars had emphasized.[5]

Chu's evolution on this issue was of major significance for several reasons, and we will elaborate on three. First, he had synthesized his predecessors into a new approach. By adopting Ch'eng I's emphasis on reverent seriousness, he moved beyond both Chou Tun-i's theme of tranquility, in which one emptied one's mind of passions, and Ch'eng Hao's slightly less passive view of calming or settling the inner nature. Besides seeking to restore a state of calm within the inner nature, Ch'eng Hao had sanctioned responding to things as they were encountered. Thus Ch'eng had already embraced a more active stance than Chou's. Having incorporated the Hunan approach to apprehending principles in daily activity and the Fukien preference for meditating in tranquility, Chu enhanced the role of book-learning. Earlier *Tao-hsüeh* thinkers in Fukien had a more reflective and intuitive understanding of the mind and less enthusiasm for reading books. From Chu's new standpoint, the mind was *comparatively* more oriented outward toward the study of books and the empirical observation of things, although he used empirical observations as an ethical philosopher rather than as a scientist.[6] Hence Chu became far more dedicated to a life of scholarship and far more prolific as a writer than earlier *Tao-hsüeh* Confucians from Fukien.

Second, in abandoning and later altering his own teacher's position, Chu Hsi apparently passed through a crucial phase of inner tension toward a maturation that provided a sense of liberation or transcendence. It must have been at once liberating and comforting to discover that he could approach the teachings of Ch'eng I directly through critical and painful evaluation of the ideas of his own teacher as well as those of one of his closest friends. In this experience, he was convinced that he had corrected conventional understanding of Ch'eng I's doctrines through critical textual study of Ch'eng's surviving works. Because of his experience of maturation on this issue, he would certainly have become more self-confident about his own authority. Henceforth, his critical evaluation and restructuring of the Confucian tradition markedly progressed.

Third, Chang Shih was significant as a catalyst in Chu's evolution on this issue. Chang's Hunan school method of cultivation encouraged Chu to doubt his own Fukien approach. Chang's emphasis on experiencing tranquility in activity also served as a transitional stage from which Chu sought motion in tranquility. Thus Chang further contributed to Chu's quest for a solution to the tension between the two *Tao-hsüeh* traditions on cultivation and inner equilibrium. One might even suggest that the Hunan conception of nature as essence and mind as its function had prompted Chu to seek a resolution specifically in terms of essence and function.

Based on our earlier discussion of Chang's attention to Ch'eng I's doctrines of the investigation of things and reverent seriousness, we could entertain the possibility that Chang might well have interjected these themes into his discussions with Chu on the mind and inner equilibrium. We have very little record of what was discussed during their meetings in 1163, 1164, and 1167; moreover, some of Chang's early letters and writings were not included by Chu in Chang's collected works. Even extant material is often hard to date precisely. Because of such factors, it is extraordinarily difficult to speculate on the specifics of the direction of influence between these two friends. We do know from Chu's 1172 reflections that Chang readily agreed with his last formulation. Chang's only continuing point of disagreement reportedly was his idea that one first needed to apprehend principles before preserving or nourishing them.[7] The apparent ease of this agreement suggests that Chu had struck a responsive cord with Chang's own emphasis on reverent composure and the investigation of things. Even if Chang had been the first to interject some of these ideas or to prompt Chu to consider them, such considerations still do not detract from the importance of Chu's articulation of a synthesis or his role as a theoretician. We might, however, be observing the beginnings of a pattern of Chu and later scholars of ignoring or downplaying his debts to his contemporaries.

In another set of exchanges from 1170 to 1172, it was Lü Tsu-ch'ien who had to admonish Chu about this dual approach to cultivating the mind. Chu had made what Lü regarded as an unfair criticism of a passage from Hu's *Understanding of Words*. According to Lü's analysis, Chu's objection was made from the perspective of the effort of holding fast and nourishing amidst tranquility, whereas Hu's comments were made in reference to the discipline of examining and scrutinizing amidst the flow of activities. Lü Tsu-ch'ien also noted that both modes of cultivation were important, and one could not be engaged without the other. Chu's criticism of Hu for having no place to seek the true mind was excessive, for Hu had specifically cited Mencius' example of an expression of the true mind in the case of the King of Ch'i: Mencius (1A/7 and 2A/6) had advised King Hsüan (r. 342-324 B.C.) to extend to others the feelings that the monarch himself had experienced when unwilling to see an ox suffer. So articulate was Lü in expressing the view of a balanced approach to cultivation that he must have been either immediately and totally converted to it or already oriented in that direction himself. As we will see in later discussions of Lü's personality and thought, it is quite likely that he was already oriented toward a balanced approach. In any event, Chu appeared less even-handed than Lü. Chu responded: "Certainly neither of the two modes of cultivation should be emphasized at the expense of the other, but the teachings of the sages emphasize holding fast and preserving far more than apprehending and examining, which is the opposite of the meaning in this section from Hu's text."[8] To Chu Hsi, apprehending and examining principles was directed toward the outer realm; hence, it had to come only after preserving and nourishing.

DISCOURSE WITH HU'S TEXT

The second major exchange centered on the text of Hu Hung's *Understanding of Words*. In the process of coming to his new understanding of equilibrium and harmony as states of the mind, Chu Hsi became dissatisfied with Hu's work. Beginning about 1170, he engaged Chang Shih and Lü Tsu-ch'ien in critically evaluating the text. The three had, according to Chu, reached basic agreement by 1172 on which passages were problematic.[9] Chu compiled the account of this exchange, "Misgivings about Master Hu's *Understanding of Words*" (*Hu-tzu chih-yen i-i*). Chang Shih expressed basic agreement with this record.[10]

Chu's account of the discourse with Hu's text reveals Confucians of the day in the process of rectifying a text. Quoting a passage from Hu's text, Chu expressed his preference for Chang Tsai's language for describing the function of the mind. Chang Shih expressed uneasiness about both wordings and offered a substitute. Chu Hsi praised Chang Shih's substitute wording as apt. Then he quickly added: "However, whatever revisions we discuss should only be our own private deliberations about how we think it ought to read, but we won't alter the original manuscript."[11] At the beginning of the exchange, Chu Hsi thus disavowed any actual intent to alter Hu's text itself.

In another case, it was Chang Shih who objected to Chu's expunging part of one sentence and inserting substitute words that changed the meaning of Hu's text. Chang Shih cautioned Chu that the previous generation's ideas should be respected and preserved. Yet in the case of two other passages, Chang himself suggested that one "ought to be omitted" and that the other was "not necessary to preserve."[12] Only Lü Tsu-ch'ien, in the three statements attributed to him, spoke consistently in defense of Hu and in opposition to altering the text. Indeed Lü had a very high regard for Hu's *Understanding of Words*.[13] During the last exchange, Chu spoke quite candidly about altering Hu's original text: "Although this passage truly does not need to be preserved. . . . Now, I would like to preserve this passage but slightly change the wording."[14] It would appear that Chu had convinced himself of the need to modify Hu's text.

Chu's criticisms prevailed: the passages to which Chu objected are not found within the six chapters of Hu's *Understanding of Words* in extant editions.[15] Although it is difficult to ascertain whether it was Chu or Chang who actually expunged Hu's text, the impetus clearly came from Chu. As an indication of the relative importance of this project to the three friends, Chu provided the only account of the exchange, and statements attributed to Chang and Lü therein are not found in their own collected works. More important, however, "Misgivings" is a retrievable record that reveals members of the *Tao-hsüeh* fellowship wrestling with a recent text and restructuring their tradition.

Chu Hsi took aim at eight problematic passages in Hu's text, and these have been summarily grouped under three themes.[16] Chu objected, first of all, to Hu's having placed human nature beyond good and evil. Second, having identified the mind as the already expressed state of the inner nature and humaneness as the mind, Hu necessarily dis-

cussed both mind and humaneness from the perspective of function rather than essence. Third, only after examining the mind in its state of incipient action, Hu claimed, could one hold fast and preserve it. Whereas self-cultivation and humaneness are discussed respectively in the preceding and succeeding sections of this chapter, let us now focus on the inner nature and the mind.

Hu Hung had proclaimed that human nature was the great foundation of all under Heaven, but the mind ordered the myriad things and brought the nature to completion of fulfillment. Chu Hsi objected to Hu's saying that the mind fulfilled the nature. Citing Ch'eng I's elucidation of Mencius' (7A/1) phrase, "exerting or fathoming mind to the utmost" (*chin hsin*) to know the nature, Chu argued that Ch'eng had been referring to the first principles (i.e., the nature) within the mind. Consequently, Ch'eng I had not limited the discussion to mere functions or products of the mind, as Hu had done. Hu had envisioned human nature and the mind as two parts of the same reality and related them to one another as essence and its function. To break this polarity, Chu proposed substituting a phrase taken from Chang Tsai, "the mind directs and unites (*t'ung*) the nature and the feelings."[17]

Another passage explored a similar theme. Chu cited the following comment from Hu: "To clarify its [the *Tao*'s] essence, the sages refer to it as the inner nature, and to clarify its function, they refer to it as the mind. The nature cannot but be active, and when active it is mind." Tracing such alleged confusion to the Ch'engs' disciple Hsieh Liang-tso, Chu again drew upon Chang Tsai's view of the feelings to substitute the following: "The nature cannot but be active, and when active it is the feelings. The mind directs the nature and the feelings." Responding to Chu's substitute wording, Chang Shih attempted to go back to Ch'eng I instead of Chang Tsai. He quoted Ch'eng I: "When the nature has form, it's called the mind; and when the nature moves, it's called the feelings." But in this case, Chu rejected Ch'eng's wording on the grounds that the words "having form" were unclear.[18] Hence Chu could not be persuaded simply by calling on the authority of Ch'eng I.

Even though they differed on whether the mind fulfilled the nature or simply directed it, both Hu and Chu gave prominence to the mind. Both viewed the mind as somewhat transcendent, and made distinctions between the mind of Heaven and Earth, which penetrated everywhere, and the mind within individual persons, which depended upon the body's vital energy for life. Hu Hung, playing on one occasion with a student's question, had suggested that the mind itself was not subject to life and death. Seizing upon the apparent bewilderment of the student, Chu denounced Hu for seeming to have embraced Buddhist notions of reincarnation. Hu should simply have spoken in terms of the principle being one but having many manifestations. In other words, it was the principle within the mind, rather than the mind per se, that was transcendent.[19] That principle within the mind was, to Chu, the same as the inner nature.

Hu Hung had written that Heaven's principles and human desires shared the same essence but differed in function; moreover, they engaged in the same action but differed in feelings. Although Hu's expressed intent was to have people distinguish between principles and desires in the process of ethical cultivation, Chu Hsi condemned Hu's assumptions about what was innate within human nature. Chu argued that even though the beginnings of Heaven's principle were unknown, they were present at the birth of a person; hence, principle was innate. Desires arose only when people were bound by bodily form, indulged in habits, and were confused by feelings; hence, desires were not innate. If one thought that the two had the same innate essence, how could one ever distinguish between them? Instead of realizing that the original essence was completely pure and without human desires, Hu had aimed—Chu alleged—to find principle and desires within each other.[20]

A passage in the same vein was Hu's statement that one could understand the difference between Heaven's principle and human desires by scrutinizing how people liked or disliked things and other people. Likes and dislikes were human nature. The petty person simply liked or disliked in reference to the ego, but the superior person did so in terms of the *Tao*. Chu charged that Hu had thus "implied the *Tao* was outside of human nature" so that there was no priority between Heaven's principle and human desire. As such, Chu suggested that Hu would be wrongly negating the proclamation in the *Book of Poetry*:

> Heaven in giving birth to the multitudes of the people,
> To every faculty and relationship annexed its law.
> The people possess this normal nature,
> Thus they love its normal, beautiful virtue.[21]

Mencius (5A/6) had set a precedent for citing this ode to support the claim that human nature possessed virtue innately. Chu sought to extend its scope to segregate desires and Heaven's law, for he associated Heaven's law with principle and human nature.

Although Chu conceded that liking and disliking were inherent in the nature, he insisted that they could not be directly referred to as the nature. Attempting to substantiate this distinction, Chu referred to likes and dislikes as "things" in order to summon further classical sanction. The *Book of Poetry* had recorded, "There are things, there must be their laws." This distinction must have been what Mencius (7A/38) was referring to when he said, "Our body and complexion are the manifestations of Heaven's nature within us." Chu concluded: "Now, if in discussing human nature we want to bring up things but omit the laws inherent therein, I'm afraid flaws will be unavoidable."[22] Making liking and disliking into "things" seems needlessly cumbersome, for Chu could have been more consistent with his overall philosophy if he had described them as feelings. Feelings were the function of human nature, as distinct from the nature itself. But Chu Hsi was driven here to strike as authoritative a blow as possible against Hu's assumption. Chu wanted a nature equivalent to ethical principles rather than accepting Hu's view of inner nature as transcending good and evil.

If human nature were neither good nor evil as Hu believed, from where would good (behavior) arise? That Hu also adhered to the Confucian goal of good behavior was evident to Chu, who lauded Hu's statement "Doing the *Tao* is the most great and utmost good." Chu quickly added that this goal appeared impossible without a foundation of goodness in human nature itself.[23]

In a later section, Chu dealt with part of Hu's answer to the question regarding good behavior. Speaking of how even sages had feelings, desires, anxieties, and resentments, Hu had said differences in the ethical quality of persons were observable in the appropriateness of their responses and actions: "What is in accord with the Mean is right, and what is not in accord with the Mean is wrong. Holding to the right while taking action is correct, but holding to the wrong while taking action is perverse. One who is correct does good, and one who is perverse does evil. But conventional Confucians discussed human nature itself in terms of good and evil; aren't they far from the mark!" Chu judged this logic to be quite inadequate: "Yet we might question whether the norm of the Mean arises from something done by the sages themselves or something possessed by the inner nature. There is certainly no reason for saying that it arises from what the sages did. If we acknowledge that the nature certainly possesses this Mean, the original goodness of human nature is clear."[24] The connection between the sages and the Mean made sense, Chu forcefully argued, only if the appropriateness of the Mean was the goodness of the inner nature. As evident in our exposition of Chang's view of human nature, Chang had already abandoned Hu's tenet that the nature was beyond good and evil; hence, he readily agreed that Hu was wrong on this point.

Still, Chang held to Ch'eng Hao's view that although the nature was good, one could not deny that evil was also the nature. Building on Ch'eng Hao's analogy with water, Chang compared the goodness of the nature to its original purity and the evil to the turbidity resulting from its fluidity. Good actions were in accord with the inner nature, and evil arose from improper movement upset by things and desires. The goal in learning was to transform the turbidity to regain the purity of the origins. In this instance, Chu merely added that Ch'eng Hao's statement about evil referred only to the physical nature.[25]

This passage by Ch'eng Hao was so problematic to Chu Hsi that more should be said about it. Chu discussed this passage more than any other one from the Ch'engs. It is possible to set aside the apparent difficulties arising from Ch'eng Hao's statement by reference to the context—in which Ch'eng Hao compared the goodness of the nature to water's original purity.[26] Nonetheless, in over thirty passages in the *Classified Conversations of Chu Hsi* (*Chu-tzu yü-lei*), Chu complained about how difficult this particular theory was; moreover, he said that Ch'eng Hao's view of the nature was not complete. He seized upon Ch'eng I's statement "nature is principle" as an insight that no one since Confucius had realized. Thus Chu was implicitly criticizing Ch'eng Hao. At the same time, Chu proceeded to use this lone statement by Ch'eng I to rationalize all of the views of both Ch'eng brothers on human nature, but Ch'eng Hao's view was actually different.[27] From Ch'eng Hao's idea that the nature has good and evil, Hu Hung advanced to say that the nature had neither good nor evil.

Another gap in understanding between Chu Hsi and Hu Hung involved the question of the substance or essence of things. The Ch'eng brothers had spoken of essence in relation to the state after the existence of things but not of an essence that preceded the coming of things into existence. For instance, they were fond of Chang Tsai's "Western Inscription" but not of his *Correcting Youthful Ignorance (Cheng-meng)*. The former concentrated on the essence of actual entities, but the latter was more abstract. Late in his life, Ch'eng I had become more receptive to Chang Tsai; moreover, Chu seized upon his saying "nature is principle" to link Chang, Chou, and the Ch'eng brothers into a more unified philosophy. Hu Hung's comments were grounded more directly in the proclivity of the Ch'eng brothers for speaking of essence only after the existence of things. But Chu Hsi insisted on interpreting essence in an abstract sense of first principles before the existence of actual things.[28]

Hu and Chu spoke of essence from very different levels of discourse. It had been from the perspective after things came into existence that Hu had spoken of Heaven's principle and human desires as sharing the same essence and the mind as the function of the nature. Chu chose to analyze the implications of Hu's statements in light of his own speculative philosophy. Hu's point that the nature was perfection beyond the characterization of good was acceptable to Chu only if spoken in reference to a hypothetical state before activity. Once activity began, there was a contrast between good and evil; moreover, action in accord with the Mean was good. Chu postulated that Hu's position would require two goodnesses or even two natures: the original state of the nature in itself and the nature expressed in activity through the function of the feelings. Although Chu was the one who actually spoke of both an ethical, original nature and a physical nature, he did not really think in terms of two separate natures; furthermore, he regarded positing two actual natures as an untenable position.[29] In fact, he believed that he had rendered Hu's position untenable, even though Hu had not spoken in terms of two natures as Chu himself sometimes did.

The only solution, in Chu's mind, to this problem was to hold that the goodness attainable through one's actions was one and the same as the goodness of the original inner nature. Along these lines, Chu wrote to Hu Hung's cousin in 1171:

> We can say that what Heaven imparts is not confined to things, but if we consider it as not confined to goodness, we will not understand what makes Heaven Heaven. We can say that we cannot speak of human nature as evil; however, if we consider goodness as in-

adequate to characterize the nature, we will not understand where goodness comes from. Between such theories and other points, which are good, in *Understanding of Words*, there are numerous mutual contradictions.[30]

The essence of goodness was a primary principle, for knowing that ultimate essence was to know what made Heaven Heaven and the source of goodness.

It was from the level of speculative philosophy and in the defense of fundamental principles that Chu objected so vigorously to Hu's view of human nature. Writing in an 1171 letter to Hu's son, Chu acknowledged that Hu Hung had intended to exalt the mysterious nature. Hu's praise of the nature as being beyond the distinction between good and evil had, Chu argued, unintentionally demeaned the nature. If the nature were not absolutely good but rather of the same essence as human desires, it was rendered less than pure. Hu's interpretation would mean that the nature was "an empty object"; moreover, Chu warned his students that Hu's view of the nature was similar to the heterodoxy of the Su brothers and Buddhism.[31]

ON HUMANENESS

How to characterize humaneness was the third major issue between Chu Hsi and Chang Shih. This discussion began as early as their first meeting in 1163 and continued for over a decade. Although it was one topic discussed during Chu's two-month visit in 1167, it did not emerge as the central question until the issue of equilibrium and harmony had been settled. Chu Hsi drafted a treatise on humaneness and exchanged letters in 1172 and 1173 with Chang and Lü Tsu-ch'ien about humaneness. During 1173, Chu and Chang reached general agreement on most points and, after consultation with Lü Tsu-ch'ien, made final revisions to their treatises.

Chu Hsi's final treatise on humaneness had as its foundation the mind of Heaven and Earth. The *Book of Changes* had stated: "The great virtue of Heaven and Earth is to produce [things]."[32] Having been influenced by this idea of identifying Heaven and Earth with the production of things, the Ch'eng brothers equated this great virtue with the mind of Heaven and Earth: "The mind of Heaven and Earth is to produce things."[33] After quoting this statement, Chu reasoned:

> When people and things are produced, they receive the mind of Heaven and Earth as their mind. Therefore, with reference to the virtue or character of the mind, although it embraces and penetrates all and leaves nothing to be desired, nevertheless, one word will cover all of it, namely, humaneness. . . . The moral qualities of the mind of Heaven and Earth are four: origination, growth, benefit, and firmness. And the principle of origination unites and controls them all. In their operation they constitute the course of the four seasons, and the vital energy of spring permeates all. Therefore, in the mind of people there are also four moral qualities—namely, humaneness, rightness, propriety, and wisdom—and humaneness embraces them all. In their

emanation and function, they constitute the feeling of love, respect, being right, and discrimination between right and wrong—and the feeling of commiseration pervades them all. . . . What mind is this? In Heaven and Earth, it is the mind to produce things infinitely. In people, it is the mind to love people gently and to benefit things. It includes the four virtues of humaneness, rightness, propriety, and wisdom, and it penetrates the four beginnings of the sense of commiseration, the sense of shame, the sense of deference and compliance, and the sense of right and wrong.[34]

Contrary to conventional translations, "virtue of the mind" is probably more apt than "character of the mind" to convey Chu's philosophical context. Although this virtue resides in and in a sense belongs to the mind, as virtue and principle it is actually the character of the nature rather than a characteristic of the mind per se.

Chu next elucidated humaneness in reference to essence and function. Essence and function were characteristic of Heaven and Earth as well as the mind of people. Because of this relation of essence and function, all of the qualities of Heaven and Earth were implied when origination was mentioned; moreover, all of the virtues in the mind of people were implied with the mention of humaneness. Chu proclaimed:

> Humaneness constituting the *Tao* refers to the fact that the mind of Heaven and Earth to produce things is present in everything. Before feelings are aroused, this essence is already existent in its completeness. After feelings are aroused, its function is infinite. If we can truly practice love and preserve it, then we have in it the spring of all virtues and the root of all good deeds. This is why in the teachings of the Confucian school, the student is always urged to exert anxious and unceasing effort in the pursuit of humaneness. In the teachings of Confucius, it is said [in *Analects,* 12/1], "Master yourself and return to propriety." This means that if we can overcome and eliminate self-centeredness and return to the principle of Heaven, then the essence of this mind [i.e., humaneness] will be present everywhere and its function will always be operative.

Chu then cited passages from the classics as examples of what one should actually do in order to put the universal essence of humaneness into operation in one's own life.

In the following part of his treatise, Chu Hsi sought to correct what he regarded as mistakes made by earlier *Taohsüeh* Confucians. He also sought to resolve an apparent contradiction with Ch'eng I, who had said that love should not be regarded as humaneness. Chu pointed out that he was claiming that humaneness was the "principle of love" rather than love itself; hence, there was no conflict with Ch'eng I's true but hidden meaning.

Coupling "the principle of love" and "the virtue of the mind" soon became for Confucians the standard way to characterize humaneness. Together covering both essence and function, the phrases clarified the character of humaneness more than anyone had been able to do earlier.

Chang Tsai had explicitly addressed the essence of humaneness and implicitly its function in his famous "Western Inscription." In addition to clarifying Chang's essay, Ch'eng I had established the doctrine that humaneness was the nature, but love was a feeling. Chu built upon Ch'eng's doctrine but heightened the component of love and synthesized important components of the Confuncian tradition into a balanced essay.

Chinese and Japanese scholars have extensively studied Chu Hsi's essay and his letters to Chang Shih; moreover, they have generally emphasized Chu's creative synthesis and Chang's eventual acceptance of it. For instance, Satō Hitoshi speaks of "the unqualified defeat of Chang's Hunan scholarship as well as his total submission to Chu's views," and Liu Shu-hsien laments the lack of any sign of Hu Hung's legacy in Chang's extant writings.[35] In addition to surveying these findings, I will make an effort to balance them with more attention to Chang's side and how he might have enriched Chu's synthesis. Chang had been diligently studying the concept of humaneness ever since his 1161 draft of the "Record of Admiring Yen-tzu." Furthermore, he had repeatedly revised it over the years until his final colophon in 1173. The timing of the final form of that essay coincided with the revised version of Chang's own "Treatise on Humaneness" (which was translated in Chapter 2). That revised treatise is so similar to Chu's in tone and content that some scholars, beginning with Chu's own disciple Ch'en Ch'un (1159-1223), have wrongly concluded that it was written by Master Chu himself.[36]

Because of the similarities between the two treatises, it has been important to some scholars to argue that Chu's essay was prior and thus the locus of originality. But the evidence is problematic. The primary articles of evidence offered by others are two of Chu's letters to Lü Tsu-ch'ien. In the first, Chu reported to Lü early in 1173 that Chang Shih had written that he had no more doubts about the "Treatise on Humaneness."[37] One might conclude from this that Chu's own treatise "had assumed its final form."[38] But by the late autumn or early winter—after he reported receiving Chang's "Treatise on Humaneness"—Chu told Lü that he had "recently revised [his own] 'Treatise on Humaneness' *again*" (emphasis mine). Hence Chu's treatise continued to be revised during 1173.[39] In the second letter to Lü, Chu reported at the end of 1173 that Chang had recently sent a letter and also a certain "Record of Comments on Humaneness" *(Yen jen lu),* which Chu said was superior to previous draft(s). Moreover, the "Treatise on Humaneness" had also been revised as a result of the exchange of views.[40] Even if this unspecified treatise was Chang's, it was merely the last version of his treatise. In short, linking the series of letters together shows that both Chang's and Chu's treatises had continued to evolve— even after Chang had reportedly said that he had no more doubts.

Since the writings of both men on humaneness had been undergoing revisions and because Chang Shih's key writings on humaneness are no longer extant, it is difficult to prove that Chu Hsi's treatise was prior. As editor of Chang's literary corpus, Chu did not include "Record of Comments on Humaneness," "The Record of Admiring Yen-tzu," and some of Chang's letters to Chu about humaneness. Because Chang had been writing on humaneness since 1161, his writings must have been a focus of discussions between the two on humaneness—especially during Chu's 1167 visit, years before Chu drafted his own treatise—as well as a catalyst for Chu's treatise. Although we cannot compare the language in Chang's earlier writings on humaneness to that in Chu's treatise, from what does remain in their writings, as we will see, Chang appears to have made contributions to Chu's evolving synthesis on humaneness.

In his letters to Chang about humaneness, Chu Hsi criticized earlier Confucians' views for being partial and incomplete. Prior to the Ch'eng brothers, Confucians had reduced humaneness to the feeling of love; hence they failed to see its importance. Ch'eng I clearly differentiated between humaneness as the nature and love as a feeling, so the importance of humaneness was reasserted. His disciples, however, became so preoccupied with the exposition of humaneness as the nature that they overlooked love. Their forgetting about love resulted in a condition inferior even to earlier Confucians who recognized humaneness only as the feeling of love. Losing their grasp of essentials, the disciples of the Ch'engs failed to accomplish anything in their personal cultivation and soared into empty speculation about the principle of humaneness. In their ignorance, they were like those whom Confucius (in *Analects*, 17/8) criticized for being fond of humaneness but not of learning. Such a stinging indictment against major figures within the *Tao-hsüeh* tradition is a graphic pronouncement of Chu's emerging confidence by the early 1170s that he had the authority to define the tradition.

Chu Hsi proceeded to declare early in 1171 what had to be done. To counter the misconceptions prevalent because of the disciples of the Ch'eng brothers, a clearer perception of humaneness was requisite:

> In my opinion, when one really focuses one's mind on the pursuit of humaneness, the most effective way is of course to put it into practice. But unless one establishes a definite idea on the meaning and content of humaneness through learning, one encounters the danger of being mired in aimless confusion. The defect of the lack of learning is ignorance. If one can exert the effort of abiding in reverence and extending knowledge, and make them complement each other, then this defect will be eliminated. When one wants to gain a clear understanding of the meaning and content of humaneness, one will do well if one uses the concept of love as aid. When one realizes that humaneness is the source of love and that love can never exhaust humaneness, then one has gained a definite comprehension of humaneness. Thus it is absolutely not necessary to search for humaneness in obscure places.[41]

In short, one had first to have a sharper understanding of the meaning and content of humaneness before self-cultivation and Confucian discussion could return to the proper path.

Among the most significant points of contention that developed in the correspondence between Chang and Chu on humaneness, one centered on the mind of Heaven and Earth. In his treatise, Chu Hsi incorporated a statement by one of the Ch'engs: "The mind of Heaven and Earth is to produce things." The statement originally was an explanation of one of Ch'eng I's comments on the *Book of Changes*. Chang objected to Ch'eng's statement and recommended a similar one from Ch'eng I's commentary, "the mind of Heaven and Earth that produces things." From Chang Shih's perspective, there was a fundamental difference between the two statements.[42] He shared Hu Hung's conception of the mind as wondrously transcendent, as comprehending all under Heaven, and as commanding all things. "The mind of Heaven and Earth that produces things" was language that reflected their conception of an active and inexhaustible mind. As Chang read the phrases, the mind of Heaven and Earth that produces things was not restricted to the production of things, but the phrase Chu had adopted denoted such a restriction upon the mind.

Chu replied that both of the statements from the Ch'engs had the same meaning. Although he readily quoted Chang's preferred phrase in another essay he was currently writing, Chu asserted that both statements should be understood as identifying the mind of Heaven and Earth with the function of producing things. In an 1172 letter to another friend, he attacked with exceptional force the Hunan position:

> Scholars of late do not use love to define humaneness. They therefore feel dissatisfied when they see that our late Master Gentleman [Ch'eng I] interpreted the mind of Heaven and Earth through the workings of the single yang life-force producing the myriad things. They establish theories different from those of the ancients and portray the mind of Heaven and Earth as something transcendental and lofty. They do not understand that what Heaven and Earth focus on as their mind is none other than the production of things, and that if one interprets this mind any other way, one will invariably be drowned in emptiness and submerged in quietude and will fail to attain the proper connection between essence and function, root and branches.[43]

Chu was here warning that the Hunan notion of a transcendent mind would lead to the emptiness and quietude of Taoism and Buddhism. Compared with his own record to this point in the early 1170s, however, the Hu family and Chang Shih had been far more engaged in government service and cultivating the mind in daily activities. Thus Chu's criticism was overdrawn. But Chu was attempting to focus attention on the mind in people rather than the one in the cosmic realm.

In spite of their disagreement over the mind of Heaven and Earth, there was an *apparent* agreement over the following sentence, which connected that mind to the mind in people. Chu proposed: "When Heaven and Earth endow human beings and things with the mind of productiveness, this becomes the mind of human beings and things as well." Each thinker understood the sentence differently, however. To Chu, the emphasis was on the warm and gentle feelings of commiseration with which people were endowed so they could love and benefit others. Chang Shih followed other leads from the Ch'engs to emphasize being related, as if members of one body, to all things through all-encompassing humaneness. Although Chu acknowledged that the universality of humaneness made possible the extension of love to all things, he was also mindful that Ch'eng I had warned against the dangers of an indiscriminating universality. Identifying other things as the self could result in self-negation as absurd as sacrificing oneself to feed a hungry tiger. Compassion was more practical. Furthermore, compassion and love for other things were the effects rather than the essence of humaneness.[44] In ethics, some who emphasize love and oneness with others fail to realize that love alone is not enough; love does not itself inform us of what we should do for others. Despite Chu's caricature of Chang's position, Chang was not in any real danger of falling into such empty relativism and sentimentality. Confucians linked love with specific behavioral virtues, such as justness or rightness and filial piety, which gave guidelines for action and bonding among persons.

A similar apparent agreement centered on the use in both men's essays of the phrase "the principle of love" to describe the essence of humaneness. Even though the phrase might well have been coined by Chu, Chang readily used it in his treatise and in his 1173 *Commentary on the Analects.* Chang used the phrase in the context of his emphasis on the oneness of all things and extending love universally toward all things. Thus Chang interpreted the principle of love as impartiality and being at one with all others. Nonetheless Chu denied that the phrase was predicated upon assuming oneness with all things. To Chu, all things had this same principle, so there was no need to await being one body with all things to achieve the principle of humaneness. Although impartiality was close to humaneness, Chu reiterated Ch'eng I's point that impartiality itself was "inadequate to denote the essence of humaneness." From the perspective of Hunan scholars, Chu was limiting the mind and the essence of humaneness. But from Chu's vantage, Hunan scholars restricted humaneness by emphasizing its character as impartiality and having no desires. Even though in his treatise he did not use the term "impartiality" and scarcely addressed expelling desires, Chu was of course still interested in achieving impartiality and controlling desires. In his correspondence, however, he strove to differentiate such characteristics from humaneness itself and to link humaneness more absolutely with principle. Instead of highlighting only love's universal extension, Chu's "principle of love" encompassed all cardinal Confucian virtues as values in and of themselves. These virtues were *a priori* principles, which did not depend on anything else for their existence or justification.[45] To Chu, humaneness was an *a priori* principle because it was the inner nature rather than either a feeling or the mind.

Chu Hsi also objected to the Human scholars' association of humaneness with the consciousness of the mind. Chang and other Hunan scholars had been led by Hsieh Liang-tso and also by Ch'eng Hao to identify humaneness with the mind's incipient and active functioning. This conception of the mind was the basis upon which their view of spiritual cultivation was grounded. Chang's reassertion of this theme in one of his letters discussing humaneness would suggest that the debate over equilibrium and harmony had not convinced him to abandon as much of his Hunan tradition as conventionally assumed. What Chang referred to as consciousness *(chüeh)* was conscience arising from being conscious of others' suffering. Mencius (2A/6) had drawn attention to the mind-and-heart that could not bear to see others suffer and would spontaneously respond, as though saving a child about to fall into a well. Hence consciousness denoted spontaneous ethical feelings arising from the mind and inner nature. Our use of the word "consciousness" to discuss this point of contention with Chu is apt because it also denotes a cognitive state of mind; indeed, the weight of this denotation in English privileges Chu's interpretation of this issue. Chu chose to focus on this denotation to interpret what Chang and other Hunan scholars were saying. Referring to the broad meaning of humaneness as encompassing the other Confucian virtues, Chu suggested that it was because humaneness encompassed wisdom that Hunan scholars mistook wisdom for humaneness. A person having humaneness was of course conscious, but humaneness itself could not be reduced to consciousness. In an effort to maintain a focus on humaneness as the nature or principle instead of the mind, Chu designated humaneness as "the virtue of the mind."[46]

According to Chu Hsi, regarding consciousness as humaneness would presuppose using a mind to pursue the mind. As in the debate over cultivating equilibrium and harmony, he meant that examining the incipient feelings in the mind would require both the observing mind and the mind observed. He had difficulty understanding that Hu Hung, Chang Shih, and other followers of Ch'eng Hao were talking about intuitive reflection of the mind rather than using one mind to seek another mind. Similarly, he criticized the Hunan interpretation of Confucius' comment (in *Analects,* 4/7) "By observing faults, humaneness may be made known." Ch'eng I had glossed the passage: through observing the faults of others, one would know if they were humane. Hunan scholars interpreted the passage as an admonition about one's own spiritual cultivation. Although Chu lauded such concern for self-cultivation, he argued that the Hunan interpretation required the mind instantaneously to make a mistake, observe the mistake, and be cognizant that humaneness was observing the mistake. Such an approach, Chu charged, resulted in unnecessary levels of mental stress.[47] The incisiveness of this attack is nevertheless confounded, it seems to me, by Chu's earlier charge that the Hunan scholars' assumption of oneness with all things led to laxness in self-cultivation.

Chang Shih's recorded replies to questions from his students reveal how far he went in accepting Chu's criticisms. Such passages are particularly important because

Chang's letter replying to Chu about humaneness as consciousness is not extant. When a student asked about Chu's critique of Hsieh Liang-tso, Chang agreed that humaneness could not be reduced merely to consciousness but asserted that Chu's criticism was excessive. Chang added that what the mind knows is simply humaneness. Another student cited Chu's criticism of having one mind pursue another mind as the probable impetus for Chang's apparent change in recent comments about the passage in *Analects, 4/7.* The student asked Chang to clarify earlier statements about knowing humaneness from reflecting on failures to attain the Mean. How could examining extreme behavior, such as the man who cut a piece of flesh from his leg to make a medical potion for his parent, teach anything about the humaneness in filial piety?[48]

In reply, Chang Shih credited his pondering Ch'eng I's teachings with enabling him to correct his previous flaws, which had inclined him toward Buddhism. He then revealed that he had accepted Chu Hsi's distinction between generosity and humaneness, but he still believed that examining faults was useful. Although acknowledging the importance of study, he still upheld the Hunan view of the superiority of an intuitive perception of humaneness:

> One must carefully study; then one can see the meaning of the words that sages established at that time. It's improper to say that excessive generosity is humaneness, but one can know that the generous person's mind was not far from humaneness. If compared with excessive pettiness or even with being merciless, isn't the difference great? Please use this to perceive intuitively *(t'i-jen);* then you will recognize the meaning of the reason why humaneness is humaneness and won't end up with insignificant details and lack of clarity.[49]

Commenting on this passage, Huang Tsung-hsi, in the *Records of Sung and Yüan Confucians,* approvingly likened Chang's observing faults to know humaneness to one's daily self-discipline. In recognizing a break in discipline, one resumed the discipline. Huang suggested that Chu Hsi had not given Chang Shih enough credit for knowing where to start; for "if one observed faults to know humaneness and softened one's temperament, that was the very way to begin." After all, Ch'eng Hao's similar admonition about "perceiving humaneness" did not merely mean knowing.[50]

Huang's judgment is comparable to some twentieth-century critiques of the exchange between Chang Shih and Chu Hsi over the character of humaneness. Most critical of Chu is Mou Tsung-san, who finds Chu culpable for perverting what Chang meant by the mind and the essence of humaneness. Mou identifies Chang as being within the mainstream of Confucianism that can be traced back through Hu Hung and Ch'eng Hao to Mencius. The mainstream view of the mind emphasized innate and spontaneous ethical feelings; moreover, the essence of humaneness had no limits. Mou identifies Chu Hsi with Ch'eng I and ultimately even Hsün-tzu (298-238 B.C.), especially in their reduction of the mind to its cognitive function at the expense of its innately ethical and active qualities. Instead of appreciating the unity of the mind, feelings, and nature, Chu Hsi allegedly rendered these asunder in his overly intellectualized analysis. According to Mou, Chu's reduced perception resulted in a passive conception of consciousness: one was dependent on external things to know even the principles inherent within the mind. Mou faults Chang for an inadequate defense of the mainline tradition. At times when Chu cited Master Ch'eng as an authority, Chang was too confused to realize that Ch'eng I's positions were being used to misrepresent Ch'eng Hao's.[51]

Ch'ien Mu (1895-1990) probably provided the best implicit answer to Mou. Attempting to counter Buddhist claims that the mind and principle were empty, Chu needed the mind to mesh with principle; therefore, he identified humaneness with the life-force and mind inherent in the cosmos. To establish a ground for the linkage, Chu said, for instance: "The mind of the myriad things is like the mind of Heaven and Earth. The mind of all under Heaven is like the mind of the sages. With Heaven and Earth's giving life to the myriad things, there is a mind of Heaven and Earth in each thing. With the sages in the world, every person has a mind of the sages."[52] Assuming this kind of connection, he could proclaim: "For a person of humaneness, the mind is principle."[53] In a passage that tied self-cultivation to achieving the life-force of humaneness in Heaven and Earth, Chu remarked: "When a scholar disciplines himself in overcoming the ego and returning to propriety to the point of eliminating egocentric desires completely, then his mind is purely this mind of Heaven and Earth giving life to things."[54] Within such passages, according to Ch'ien, principle, humaneness, and mind were all presented as one.[55] Such passages demonstrate that Chu had a broader view of the mind and one closer to Mencius than Mou had claimed. Yet Chu was at the same time insistent that people know the difference between mind and humaneness as well as the ethical gaps generally operative between one's own mind and that of Heaven and Earth. It was Chu's attentiveness to such gaps and distinctions that made him object so strongly to views like those of the Hunan scholars.

During the exchange of views between Chu Hsi and Chang Shih, some agreement was actually reached that resulted in specific revisions in their treatises on humaneness. Chu, in one of his letters, criticized Chang for not having the nature and the feelings related as essence and function as well as for not having the mind presented as commanding the nature and the feelings. Chang's extant treatise includes such language, so he must have been persuaded. Chang also apparently accepted Chu's point that the principle of love had priority over oneness with all things. In his draft, Chang had commented that nothing within Heaven and Earth is not one's own humaneness. Chu objected that such comments would imply that humaneness was a thing and obliterate the distinction between things as things and humaneness as arising from the mind. Chang never actually intended to make humaneness or the mind into things but only pointed to the all-inclusiveness of humaneness. Even though Chu clearly misrepresented Chang's point, Chang omitted the comment in the final version.[56]

By comparing the final version of Chu's treatise with statements in the letters of both men, we can observe that some minor alterations in Chu's treatise were also made because of Chang's objections.[57] In the "Diagram of the Discourse on Humaneness" *(Jen-shuo t'u)*, which was charted after the treatise was revised, Chu incorporated the concept of impartiality twice. The practice of humaneness in daily activities also came more to the fore. These changes reflected Chang's preoccupations. According to Satō Hitoshi, Chang's contributions to Chu's evolution on the concept of humaneness were even more pervasive than these specific details: "Chu's discussions with Chang Nanhsien [Shih] on the nature of *jen* provide the finishing touch to his thinking on the subject. Furthermore, they also enable Chu to brush off an earlier influence exerted on him by the Hunan School through Chang."[58]

Differences remained in their treatises on humaneness. Chu focused more on theory, and Chang on practice. Chang had more emphasis on overcoming ego as well as on expelling ignorance and desires. Chu balanced overcoming ego and discussing learning. How far Chang would go to accommodate Chu also had limits. In his treatise, Chang did not renounce Hsieh Liang-tso's concept of humaneness as consciousness, but his statement (that a person of humaneness had consciousness without confusion) was expressed in such a way as not to confront Chu. Although he agreed that one could not reduce humaneness to impartiality, Chang did not drop the term altogether. Moreover, his final version of the treatise proclaimed: "Impartiality is the reason people can be humane."[59]

Most significant, Chang's treatise did not mention Chu's characterization of humaneness as "the virtue of the mind." Modern scholars have speculated about why Chang apparently neither adopted nor made an issue out of this characterization. Chang might have seen this issue as subsumed under other differences.[60] Or perhaps there was no disagreement over this wording because of a common heritage from the Ch'engs, who had used the metaphor of seeds of grain for humaneness as the principle of life in all things.[61]

Actually, the phrase "virtue of the mind" was originally Chang Shih's. Although some might object that the evidence for this claim comes a dozen years after Chu Hsi had used the phrase in his treatise, Chu himself is the witness. Chang had been dead for five years when Chu made his statement, so he was not compelled to make his admission and give Chang this credit. Having recently edited Chang's collected writings, Chu apparently had refreshed his memory of the sequence and content of his correspondence with Chang. His admission came in an 1185 letter to Lü Tsu-ch'ien's brother, in which he recounted how Chang had responded to his draft on humaneness. Chang "had wanted to change the words—the virtue of the nature

and the foundation of love—into the virtue of the mind and the foundation of the good as well as to say Heaven, Earth, and the myriad things all share my essence."[62] Clearly, Chu was admitting that the phrase "virtue of the mind" had initially been put forward by Chang as his own alternative to Chu's "virtue of the nature." In the context provided by Chu's statement, the phrase fits well with the Hunan concept of the mind. The linkage is even clearer if the phrase is translated as the "character of the mind," instead of the "virtue of the mind." One wonders if Chang was drawing it from the "Record of Admiring Yen-tzu" or the "Record of Comments on Humaneness," neither of which Chu preserved.

Chu thus reminisced in the 1185 letter that he had objected to Chang's suggestion of "the virtue of the mind" on the grounds that it was too vague and could be used by different people to point to different things. Yet this was the phrase that Chu settled on for his own treatise. Chu apparently felt satisfied that, by counterbalancing it with the principle of love, he had offset the danger of the phrase being understood from the perspective of the Hunan conception of the mind. Chu's 1185 statement was a rare acknowledgment of an intellectual debt to a contemporary, so later scholars have easily overlooked it and what it suggests about the evolution of his thought.

Although it is unfair to say that Chang Shih simply capitulated to Chu Hsi, Chu did triumph quite convincingly. Accepting Chu's characterization of Hunan ideas as having been inherited from Hsieh Liang-tso, Chang was unable to establish his roots in Ch'eng Hao's philosophy. Instead, he followed Chu in looking to Ch'eng I for textual authority. Chang has been criticized from the perspective of modern textual scholarship for not differentiating between the strains of thought of the Ch'eng brothers. His failure to make those distinctions clearly as well as Chu's skill in using one Ch'eng brother to supplement—and even to alter—the ideas of the other one demonstrate the broad and fluid nature of *Tao-hsüeh* Confucianism in the twelfth century.

Generally, Chu addressed issues of theory, but Chang focused more on practice. Chang preferred to discuss cultural values and actual policies, but he was compelled to address the more abstract level of fundamental principles. At times, Chu chose to ignore what Chang or Hu Hung had intended in order to press an argument forward to its implications for theory. For example, Chu interpreted some statements as dealing with the essence of fundamental principles even though Hu and Chang had spoken from the perspective of the essence and function of actual entities. Such differences in preferred level of discourse meant that on some occasions the agreement Chu won was more apparent than real. The exchanges with Chang demonstrate how much more given to speculative philosophy Chu was than other contemporary *Tao-hsüeh* Confucians.

The exchanges with Chang played a role in Chu's process of defining an integrated synthesis of Confucianism and taking the clarity and significance of ideas, particularly humaneness and self-cultivation, to a new zenith. Confucian scholars of later generations have been aware that Chang contributed to Chu's development. Often that awareness has been overshadowed by needs within two camps of scholars. Some have needed to authenticate Chu's and by extension their own orthodoxy. Others have needed to blame the eclipse of their own tradition on Chang's poor defense of the legacy from Ch'eng Hao and Hu Hung. In order to reconstruct the dynamics of twelfth-century Confucian thought, I have sought here to highlight Chang's contributions more than others have done. Such reconstructions have been complicated by the incompleteness of Chang's works.

Chu's omission of important materials when editing Chang's collected works along with his alteration of Hu Hung's text cannot but disturb our sense of historical honesty. When he decided not to preserve such materials, Chu was taking steps to excise some of the diversity of the *Tao-hsüeh* tradition and leave a far more homogeneous and certain legacy. His real concern was neither to uphold some objective standard of textual integrity nor to deny the contributions of his friend. To Chu, the ultimate issue was the transmission of the *Tao,* and he considered his actions most appropriate for ensuring—his view of—that transmission. Unfortunately, Chu's editing of Chang's works makes it difficult for us to reconstruct the struggle of either man to apprehend that *Tao* or the world of their thought. . . .

Notes

1. Quoted by Huang Tsung-hsi in *SYHA,* 50.1635. See also the passages quoted in *SS,* 427.12710 and 429.12775; *CTYL,* 103.4140, Chung-hua ed., 103-2605; Wing-tsit Chan, *Hsin t'an-so,* 525-529, or *New Studies,* 396-404.

2. *CTWC,* 31.10a, 17a-20b, 21a-37a. See also the discussion in Ch'ien Mu, *Chu-tzu hsin hsüeh-an,* 4:510-530; Takahata Tsunenobu, "Chō Nanken no *Rongo-kai* ni ataeta Shushi no eikyō," 110-123; Wing-tsit Chan, *Hsin t'an-so,* 530-537, or *New Studies,* 404-409.

3. Ch'ien Mu, *Chu-tzu* 1:105-112, 2:123-182; Ch'ien Mu, *Sung Ming li-hsüeh kai-shu,* 103-109; Mou Tsung-san, *Hsin-t'i* 3:71-228; Wang Mao-hung, *Chu-tzu nien-p'u,* 1A.23-27, 1B.35-42. Matthew Levey's dissertation elucidates differences between Wang, Ch'ien, and Mou on this issue. See also Wing-tsit Chan, *Hsin t'an-so,* 537-543, or *New Studies,* 409-416; Ch'en Lai, *Chu Hsi che-hsüeh yen-chiu,* 91-188; Chang Li-wen, *Chu Hsi ssu-hsiang ye-chiu,* 434-440; Ts'ai Jen-hou, *Sung Ming li-hsüeh,* 1:76-106; Tomoeda Ryūtarō, *Shushi no shisō keisei,* 38-102; Liu Shu-hsien, *Chu-tzu che-hsüeh ssu-hsiang te fa-chan yü wan-ch'eng,* 71-138; Shen Mei-tzu, *Chu-tzu shih chung te ssu-hsiang yen-chiu,* passim; Chung-ying Cheng, "Chu Hsi's Methodology and Theory of Understanding," 179-186; Thomas A. Metzger, *Escape from Predicament,* 85-99; and John Berthrong, "Glosses on Reality," 78-86.

4. Ch'eng Hao and Ch'eng I, *Erh-Ch'eng chi* 1:188; *CTWC,* 64.28b-29b. Translated in Chan, *Source Book,* 600-602.

5. Ch'ien Mu, *Chu-tzu* 3:219-223.

6. Yung Sik Kim, "The World-View of Chu Hsi," passim, and "Problems in the Study of the History of Chinese Science," 83-104.

7. *CTWC,* 75.22b-23b; Wing-tsit Chan, *Hsin t'an-so,* 543.

8. *CTWC,* 73.46b; *SYHA* 42.1375-1376.

9. Ch'ien Mu, *Chu-tzu* 3:198-228, especially 200.

10. *NHC,* 21.9b.

11. *CTWC,* 73.40b; *SYHA,* 42.1370.

12. *CTWC,* 73.44b, 45a, 47a; *SYHA,* 42.1374, 1375, 1377.

13. Lü regarded Hu's work as superior to Chang Tsai's *Correcting Youthful Ignorance (Cheng-meng);* see *SYHA* 42.1366.

14. *CTWC,* 73.47a; *SYHA,* 42.1377.

15. Wu Jen-hu in the introduction to his punctuated edition of the *Hu Hung chi,* p. 3, made this observation. Wing-tsit Chan, in *Hsin t'an-so,* p. 544, n. 165 (or *New Studies,* p. 423, n. 165), made the same observation as well as the observation that the statements attributed to Chang and Lü are not in their collected works. Despite his observation that statements to which Chu objected are not in existing editions, Professor Chan informed me that he believes "no one changed Hu's text." Rather, "In the discussion of the text, Chu, Chang, and Lü proposed changing certain words." These comments from his June 1990 letter would appear to conflict with his published observation. Surely Chu was quoting Hu's statements from Hu's original text. Since these statements are not in existing editions of Hu's text, it seems safe to conclude that his text was changed to omit these passages to which Chu had objected in his "Misgivings."

16. Listed in *CTYL,* Cheng-chung ed., 101.4104, Chung-hua ed., 101.2582; and categorized by the editor in *SYHA,* 42.1377.

17. *CTWC,* 73.40b-41a; *SYHA,* 42.1370; Chang Tsai, *Chang Tsai chi,* 374; see also T'ang Chün-i, "Chang Tsai's Theory of Mind and Its Metaphysical Basis," 113-136; and Ira Kasoff, *The Thought of Chang Tsai,* 28-33, 86-90.

18. *CTWC,* 73.47a-47b; *SYHA,* 42.1377.

19. *CTWC,* 73.43a-43b; *SYHA,* 42.1374; Schirokauer, "Chu and Hu," 490, 493.

20. *CTWC,* 73.41b-42a; *SYHA,* 42.1371.

21. *CTWC,* 73.42a. *Book of Poetry* translation adapted from James Legge, *The Chinese Classics* 4:541. For Chu's reading of this poem see his *Shih chi chuan,* 214.

22. *CTWC,* 73.42b-43a; *SYHA* 42.1372, and editors' criticism of Chu's taking likes and dislikes to be things; also cf. the translations in Legge, *Classics* 4:541, and D. C. Lau, *Mencius,* 191.

23. *CTWC,* 73.43a; *SYHA,* 42.1372.

24. *CTWC,* 73.44b-45a; *SYHA,* 42.1374-1375.

25. *CTWC,* 73.43ab; *SYHA,* 42.1373. Ch'eng Hao's statement appears in *Erh-Ch'eng chi* 1:10, translated in Chan, *Source Book,* 528.

26. This is done by Wing-tsit Chan in *Source Book,* 529. Chan translated the phrase *li yu shan e* ("principle possesses good and evil") to read "according to principle, there is both good and evil." For my translation, see Chapter 2. Ch'ien Mu apparently reads the phrase more literally and regards it as quite troublesome for Chu (see below).

27. I am here following the case made by Ch'ien Mu in *Chu-tzu* 3:209-215. See also Chiu Hansheng, "Zhu Xi's [Chu Hsi's] Doctrine of Principle," 116-137; and A. C. Graham, "What Was New in the Ch'eng-Chu Theory of Human Nature?" 138-157.

28. Ch'ien Mu, *Chu-tzu* 3:215-216.

29. *CTYL,* 101.4109-4110, Chung-hua ed., 101.2585-2586; translated in Chan, *Source Book,* 616-617; another view is presented in Schirokauer, "Chu and Hu," 494. Chu made the comment in reference to the reiteration of Hu Hung's position by one of his sons.

30. *CTWC,* 42.4b, third letter to Hu Shih (1136-1173), cf. the translation in Schirokauer, "Chu and Hu," 494.

31. *CTWC,* 46:27b-28a; Schirokauer, "Chu and Hu," 494; e.g., *CTYL* 101.4117 and 4119, Chung-hua ed., 101.2590 and 2591.

32. *Hsi-tz'u* (Appended Remarks, second section) in *Chou I cheng-i,* 8.3a, in *Shih-san ching chu-shu* 1:86; translated in Chan, *Source Book,* 268.

33. *Wai-shu,* 3, in Ch'eng and Ch'eng, *Erh-Ch'eng chi* 2:366.

34. *CTWC,* 67.20a-21b; translation adapted from Chan, *Source Book,* 593-596. Chan also identifies references to earlier sources. See especially *Book of Changes,* commentary on hexagram no. 1, *ch'ien* (Heaven).

35. Satō Hitoshi, "Chu Hsi's 'Treatise on Jen,'" 218; Liu Shu-hsien, *Chu-tzu che-hsüeh,* 172; also Ch'ien Mu, *Chu-tzu* 1:55-60, 73-81, 345-366, 2:39-81; Mou Tsung-san, *Hsin-t'i* 3:229-234, 234-258, 258-300; Tomoeda Ryūtarō, *Shushi no shisō keisei,* 102-122; Liu Shu-hsien, "Chu-tzu te jen-shuo, t'ai-chi kuan-nien yü tao-t'ung wen-t'i te tsai sheng-ch'a," 173-188; Olaf Graf, *Tao und Jen,* passim; Wing-tsit Chan, "Lun Chu-tzu chih jen-shuo," 37-68, and *Hsin t'an-so,* 371-381, 521-548.

36. Liu Shu-hsien, "Chu-tzu tsai sheng-ch'a," 177-181, uses Ch'en's view to argue that Chu used some of

Chang's draft to write the final treatise when editing Chang's works. Wing-tsit Chan's rebuttal is in *Hsin t'an-so,* 376-381, or *New Studies,* 176-177.

37. *CTWC,* 33.12a, 16th letter to Lü.

38. Wing-tsit Chan, in *New Studies,* 155-157, draws this conclusion. In this letter, Chu mentions wanting to compile the *I-Lo yüan-yüan lu* and needing some materials from Che-tung about the Yung-chia school. Chan seems to assume that the final draft of the treatise must have been completed before Chu began compiling the *I-Lo yüan-yüan lu.* Chu was, however, certainly capable of working on both at the same time. (The *I-Lo yüan-yüan lu* will be discussed in chapters 4 and 5.)

39. *CTWC,* 33.15a, 23d and 24th letters to Lü.

40. *CTWC* 33.18b, 27th letter to Lü. The *Yen jen lu* is an alternate title of *Chu Ssu yen jen* [Comments on Humaneness from the Chu and Ssu Rivers (the Confucian heartland of Shantung)]; preface in *NHC,* 14.4a-5b. Chu had referred to it earlier; see his 16th letter from 1171 in *CTWC,* 31.4b-5b. See also Wing-tsit Chan, "Lun jen-shuo," 56, 58-59, and *Hsin t'an-so,* 547.

41. *CTWC,* 31.4b-5b, 16th letter to Chang, translation adapted from Satō Hitoshi, "Treatise," 216-217.

42. *NHC,* 21.4a-5b. Satō Hitoshi, "Treatise," 218-219; Mou Tsung-san, *Hsin-t'i* 3:259-261.

43. *CTWC,* 42.18a, 10th letter to Wu I (Hui-shu) from Hunan, translation adapted from Satō Hitoshi, "Treatise," 219; Ch'ien Mu, *Chu-tzu* 1:55-60. Ch'eng I's statement is from his comments on the Return hexagram of the *Book of Changes;* see *Erh-Ch'eng chi,* 3:819.

44. *CTWC,* 32.16b-17a, 33b-34b; also *NHC,* 21.5ab. See the discussion in Ch'ien Mu, *Chu-tzu* 2:57-66; Mou Tsung-san, *Hsin-t'i* 3:259-261; and Satō Hitoshi, "Treatise," 220-221.

45. *CTWC,* 32.18a-18b, 19a-19b, 21a-21b, 23b-24b, 33b-34b; *NHC,* 21.5b, 22.5b-6a. See the discussion in Wing-tsit Chan, "Lun jen-shuo," 40-50; Ch'ien Mu, *Chu-tzu* 1:73-81, 2:66-68; Mou Tsung-san, *Hsin-t'i* 3:267-272, 285-296; Satō Hitoshi, "Treatise," 221-222.

46. *CTWC,* 31.6a, 32.17a-18a, and 20a-20b. See also the discussion in Ch'ien Mu, *Chu-tzu* 2:70-72; Mou Tsung-san, *Hsin-t'i* 3:273-284; Satō Hitoshi, "Treatise," 222.

47. *CTWC,* 31.5b-6a; *NHC,* 21.2b. See also the discussion in Mou Tsung-san, *Hsin-t'i* 3:298; Satō Hitoshi, "Treatise," 222-223.

48. *NHC,* 31.5b-6a; *SYHA,* 50.1620-1621.

49. *NHC,* 31.6b.

50. *SYHA,* 50.1621.

51. Mou Tsung-san, *Hsin-t'i,* especially 3:234-300. Liu Shu-hsien's and Ts'ai Jen-hou's evaluations follow Mou's.

52. *CTYL,* 27.1107; Chung-hua ed., 27.689-690.

53. *CTYL,* 37.1570; Chung-hua ed., 37.985.

54. *CTYL,* 20.754; Chung-hua ed., 20.467.

55. Ch'ien Mu, *Chu-tzu* 1:357-358, 362-363, 2:56. Although he implicitly answers some points in Mou's critique, Wing-tsit Chan ("Lun jen-shuo," 44, 49-51) sets it aside on the grounds that it arose from another school of Confucianism.

56. Wing-tsit Chan, "Lun jen-shuo," 55-58, agrees with Mou Tsung-san that Chu misread Chang on this point.

57. Chu omitted wording about "none who do not love," the relationship between the heart/mind unwilling to allow suffering, and the four cardinal virtues; see Wing-tsit Chan, "Lun jen-shuo," 54-55. For Chu's "Diagram," see *CYTL,* 105.4185, Chung-hua ed., 105.2633; Chan, *Hsin t'an-so,* 371-374, or *New Studies,* 280-282.

58. Satō Hitoshi, "Treatise," 217.

59. *NHC,* 8.1a-2a. For points of difference, see *CTWC,* 32.21a-33b, 33.15a, 18a-18b, 20a-20b; these differences are very clearly delineated in Wing-tsit Chan, "Lun jen-shuo," 56-58.

60. Wing-tsit Chan, "Lun jen-shuo," 57.

61. Satō Hitoshi, "Treatise," 224.

62. *CTWC,* 47.27a, 25th letter, dated 1185, to Lü Tsu-chien; Liu Shu-hsien, *Chu-tzu che-hsüeh,* 145, 189-190, and "Chu-tzu tsai sheng-ch'a," 180.

Abbreviations Used in the Notes

CLC Ch'en Liang, *Ch'en Liang chi*

CTWC Chu Hsi, *Hui-an hsien-sheng Chu Wen-kung wen-chi (Chu-tzu wen-chi)*

CTYL Chu Hsi, *Chu-tzu yü-lei*

HNYL Li Hsin-ch'uan, *Chien-yen i-lai hsi-nien yao-lu*

LCYC Lu Chiu-yüan, *Lu Chiu-yüan chi*

LTLWC Lü Tsu-ch'ien, *Lü Tung-lai wen-chi*

NHC Chang Shih, *Nan-hsien chi*

SB Herbert Franke, ed., *Sung Biographies*

SCWCL Yeh Shao-weng, *Ssu-ch'ao wen-chien lu*

SMLHS Ch'iu Han-sheng et al., eds., *Sung Ming li-hsüeh shih*

SS T'o-t'o et al., eds., *Sung shih*

SSCSPM Ch'en Pang-chan and Feng Ch'i, eds., *Sung shih chi-shih pen-mo*

SYHA Huang Tsung-hsi, Ch'üan Tsu-wang, et al., eds., *Sung Yüan hsüeh-an*

TML Li Hsin-ch'uan, *Tao ming lu*

FURTHER READING

Criticism

Birge, Bettine. "Chu Hsi and Women's Education." *Neo-Confucian Education: The Formative Stage,* edited by Wm. Theodore de Bary and John W. Chaffee, pp. 325-67. Berkeley: University of California Press, 1989.
  Examines Chu Hsi's writings about women's education and the role of women in society, contrasting the severe standard of behavior Chu Hsi proscribed with the accounts of the virtuous activity of women in the philosopher's other writings.

Chan, Wing-tsit. "Chu Hsi and Yüan Neo-Confucianism." *Yüan Thought: Chinese Thought and Religion under the Mongols,* pp. 197-228. New York: Columbia University Press, 1982.
  Traces the development and spread of Chu Hsi's Neo-Confucianism throughout the years of the Yüan period.

————. *Chu Hsi: Life and Thought.* Hong Kong: The Chinese University Press, 1987, 212 p.
  Studies Chu Hsi's life, religion, philosophy, and his dominance and influence in China.

Chang, Carsun. "Chu Hsi: The Great Synthesizer." *The Development of Neo-Confucian Thought,* pp. 243-83. New York: Bookman Associates, 1957.
  Examines the dominance of Chu Hsi's Neo-Confucianism in China and maintains that his works were favored by government officials because his reinterpretation of the sacred texts supported Confucian orthodoxy.

De Bary, William Theodore. "Chu Hsi and Liberal Education." *The Liberal Tradition in China,* pp. 21-66. Hong Kong: The Chinese University Press, 1983.
  Analyzes the way in which Chu Hsi's goal of "learning for the sake of one's self" shaped his views on liberal education.

Ebrey, Patricia Buckley. Introduction to *Chu Hsi's "Family Rituals,"* pp. xiii-xxxv. Princeton, N.J.: Princeton University Press, 1991.
  Offers an overview of the content, reception, and influence of the manual, compiled by Chu Hsi to aid the performance of such standard Chinese family rituals as initiations, weddings, funerals, and sacrifices to ancestral spirits.

Fung, Yu-Lan. "Chu Hsi." *A History of Chinese Philosophy,* Vol. II, translated by Derk Bodde, pp. 533-71. London: George Allen & Unwin, 1953.
  Survey of Chu Hsi's philosophical views.

Tong, Lik Kuen. "Nature and Feeling: The Meaning of Mentality in the Philosophy of Chu Hsi." *Journal of Chinese Philosophy* 9 (1982): 1-10.
  Investigates Chu Hsi's doctrine of the mind, including the role of *li, ch'i* and *jen* in Chu Hsi's theories. Tong concludes that according to Chu Hsi, the limits of the human mind and knowledge are related to *ch'i* rather than *li.*

St. Irenaeus
c. 130-c. 200-02

Greek theologian.

INTRODUCTION

Described as the "founder of Christian theology," St. Irenaeus composed a detailed statement of second-century orthodox Christian thought in his *Adversius Haereses,* or
Against Heresies. The five-volume work was intended as a
refutation of the Gnostics, whose beliefs were thought to
be threatening to the early Christian Church. Through the
course of his argumentation, Irenaeus offers the first systematic discussion of orthodox Christian theology.

BIOGRAPHICAL INFORMATION

Little is known for certain about Irenaeus's life. He was
probably born around the year 130 in Smyrna, in Ionia.
After traveling to Gaul as a missionary and becoming a
priest, he was sent as an envoy to Eleutherius, Bishop of
Rome, in order to convey to him news of the conflicts suffered by the church in Gaul. Serving as a presbyter in
Lyon during the reign of Marcus Aurelius, Irenaeus was
elected to the bishopric of Lyon, or Lugdunum, around
177-78. He is believed to have died around 200-02.

MAJOR WORKS

Irenaeus's primary work is *Adversus Haereses.* In it, he
outlines the beliefs of the Gnostics and then presents rebuttals to their arguments. The major disputes addressed
by Irenaeus include the Gnostic doctrine of election, according to which only those who possess knowledge of
the "unknown Father" hidden in the Scriptures will be
saved. The Gnostics also take an allegorical approach to
the Scriptures, and view Jesus as one of many "cosmic intermediaries" between God and the world. The Gnostics
further contended that since the world contains evil, it
could not be God's creation. In *The Proof of the Apostolic
Preaching,* Irenaeus focuses on the significance of the doctrine of the Trinity and emphasizes that the truth revealed
in the four Gospels was foretold in the Old Testament.

TEXTUAL HISTORY

Only portions of *Adversus Haereses* have survived in the
original Greek, through quotations by other writers. A
complete version of the text is extant in Latin; the oldest
of these manuscripts dates from the ninth century, although

S. IRENÆUS

BISHOP of LYONS.

S. IRENÆUS.

the first Latin translation was most likely made in the
early third century. It is estimated that Irenaeus completed
the original text of books one and two of *Adversus Haereses* before 180, and that the fifth book was finished by 188
or 189. The text of *The Proof of the Apostolic Preaching*
was discovered in 1904 in an Armenian church. Scholars
date its original Greek composition to the late second or
early third century.

CRITICAL RECEPTION

Criticism of Irenaeus's thought focuses on his two written
treatises and on particular aspects of his biblical theology.
Scholars such as Hamilton Baird Timothy and Dominic J.
Unger examine in detail the arguments Irenaeus makes in
Adversus Haereses. Timothy discusses Irenaeus's dissec-

tion of the Gnostic beliefs and studies Irenaeus's rebuttals to the arguments of the Gnostics, noting in particular that Irenaeus objected to the Gnostic doctrine of election based on knowledge, Gnostic allegorization of Scripture, and the Gnostic view of Jesus as one among many intermediaries between God and the world. Timothy also stresses that Irenaeus did concede that knowledge, or reason, served to supplement revelation and enlighten faith. Unger observes that by writing *Adversus Haereses* Irenaeus became the first Christian writer to provide a systematic treatise on theology, a treatise which includes discussion of the doctrine of the Trinity, creation, Christ as savior, the Church, salvation, and resurrection. According to Unger, a study of Irenaeus's style reveals such flaws as repetition, prolixity, and overly involved constructions. Unger does, however, praise Irenaeus's use of figurative language, his precision in word choice, and his calm, modest tone.

Despite the relatively recent discovery of the treatise *The Proof of the Apostolic Teaching,* there is much criticism about the text. Scholars have examined the Armenian translation and the German translation made soon after the discovery of the Armenian text. English translations shortly followed. J. Rendel Harris finds that the treatise does not deviate substantially from the conventional teachings of the second-century Christian Church, despite the fact that Irenaeus places less emphasis on the sacraments and on ritual than one might expect. Additionally, Harris finds that the work contains a strongly anti-Judaic tone. In his examination of *The Proof,* Joseph P. Smith explains that the form of the work is that of a letter, although it is obvious, Smith states, that the treatise was planned as a composition for the general public. Smith finds that the construction is clear and logical, although the style is sometimes confused and repetitive. The intention of the treatise, contends Smith, is to prove that the preaching of the apostles was true; it is not an exposition of their preaching, as the title seems to suggest.

While some critics have focused their analyses on particular texts, others have studied specific elements of Irenaeus's theology as a whole. Gustaf Wingren examines Irenaeus's emphasis on the absolute power of God as creator, and on the role of the Son and his relationship with God's creation—man. Wingren observes that according to Irenaeus, the Son *is* the image and the likeness of God, whereas man is created in God's image and likeness. John Lawson provides a detailed investigation of certain aspects of Irenaeus's exegesis on the Old and New Testaments in order to demonstrate that Irenaeus's exegesis was subjective and allegorical, despite the fact that some critics maintain Irenaeus's stood firmly against allegorization of Scripture. Terrance L. Tiessen centers his study on Irenaeus's doctrine of divine revelation as it concerns the non-Christian. A key point in Irenaeus's thinking, Tiessen states, is the fact that Irenaeus assumed that the Church's teachings were spread across the world and that the faith was preached uniformly. Therefore, non-Christians were justly condemned, for they had personally rejected the Gospel. Tiessen seeks in Irenaeus's theory the possibility

of exemption for the non-Christian and questions whether Irenaeus would have been more optimistic regarding the salvation of non-Christians if the saint had been aware of people who had not been exposed to Christ.

PRINCIPAL WORKS

Adversus Haereses [*Against Heresies*] (treatise) c. 180-89
Proof of the Apostolic Preaching [also referred to as *Demonstration of the Apostolic Preaching, Epidexis,* and *On the Apostolic Preaching*] (treatise) c. late 2nd - c. early 3rd century

Principal English Translations

The Writings of Irenaeus (translated by A. Robert, and W. H. Rambant) 1868-69; reprinted 1979
Five Books of S. Irenaeus, Bishop of Lyons, against Heresies (translated by J. Keble) 1872
The Demonstration of the Apostolic Preaching (translated by J. A. Robinson) 1920
Proof of Apostolic Teaching (translated by J. P. Smith) 1952
St. Irenaeus of Lyons, against the Heresies (translated by Dominic J. Unger) 1992

CRITICISM

J. Rendel Harris (essay date 1907)

SOURCE: "Irenaeus on the Apostolical Preaching," in *Expositor,* Vol. 3, 1907, pp. 246-58.

[*In the essay that follows, Harris analyzes Irenaeus's* On the Apostolic Teaching *and observes that the treatise is in many ways conventional, marred by historical inaccuracies, and unexpectedly focused on spiritual enlightenment.*]

We have now before us the text of the newly-found treatise of Irenaeus **On the Apostolical Preaching,** which forms the first part of the thirty-first volume of Harnack's *Texte und Untersuchungen.* More exactly we should have put, instead of Harnack, the joint names of Harnack and Schmidt, and that collocation would have at once reminded us that another of the great patristic lights has gone out, and that the long-continued co-operation of von Gebhardt and Harnack has been ended in the way in which the best-established of partnerships must be broken up at the last. The record of von Gebhardt's literary work remains, and it will not be easy, even for a well-trained and capable scholar, to succeed him.

But here is Irenaeus, fresh from the press, and full of interest and surprises. To begin with, a discovery of second-century literature can never be anything but interesting, in view of the fact that it was in this century that the organization and doctrine of the Church were really established, and the interest is unusual in the case of a writer like Irenaeus, who claims to be in touch with the Apostolical tradition through Papias and Polycarp and the elders who had known the Apostle John. As is well known, we have the already extant works of Irenaeus only through translation or by quotation; his great work, the five books against Heresies, is only known from the Latin translation, with the supplement of a few Greek, Syriac, and Armenian quotations; the original Greek is supposed by Zahn to have been extant in the sixteenth century; and, although doubt has been cast on his argument, we are not without hope that a complete copy of the original Greek may yet be lurking somewhere. But beside the five books against Heresies, there are traces of a number of other writings which have either wholly, or in great part, perished. Fragments are extant of certain letters to Florinus, in which he warns him against the erroneous nature of the beliefs which he was embracing, and holds Polycarp up to him *in terrorem.* He wrote also certain other tracts relating to controversial matters of the time, such as the date of the Easter festival; and we learn from Eusebius that he dedicated a treatise to one Marcianus **On the Apostolical Preaching,** and it is this treatise which has suddenly come to light from as unexpected a quarter as could have been conceived, the library of the Armenian Church at Erivan, in Russian Armenia, where it was unearthed in 1904 by one of the most able of the younger Armenian ecclesiastics, Karabet ter-Mekerttschian. He has now edited the text in collaboration with his friend, ter-Minassiantz, accompanied by a German translation of such fidelity and excellence that it needed very little emendation at the hand of Harnack and his editorial office. I was in Erivan in 1903, and had the pleasure of visiting these learned Armenians at the great convent of Etschmiadzin; little suspecting, as we examined the treasures of their great library, that a patristic document of the first magnitude was lying only a few miles away and waiting to be discovered. We may at least take heart in two directions: first, in the belief that it is still reasonable to expect the recovery of the lost documents of the early Church; and second, that the Armenian people have given us one more proof that they are not the dying race which they are, in many quarters, assumed to be; but that in the region of religion, as well as in that of science, they are, as I have often maintained publicly, the brain of Asia.

The first reading of the new book will, I think, cause something of a sense of disappointment; it appears to be wanting in originality. This is partly due to the fact that it is a catechetical treatise, following the conventional lines of the teaching of the Church of the second century, and using the same arguments and proof-texts as are found elsewhere in that period and the time immediately subsequent. The Gospels are *not* the foundation of the argument, the whole weight of which is thrown upon the Old Testament,

that is to say, upon the prophecies, together with the allegorical and mystical explanation of the histories. At first sight this is both surprising and disappointing, for Irenaeus is instructing his friend Marcianus in the very foundations of the Faith, and he hardly uses the Gospel at all; everything is prophecy and gnosis, just as it is with Justin Martyr; and the Gospels, which Irenaeus speaks of elsewhere, in a well-known passage, as comparable to the four pillars of the world and the four winds of heaven, take relatively less place than they do in Justin Martyr. The fault is in the method of teaching, which Irenaeus has clearly inherited. His real gospel is the Book of Testimonies, concerning which we wrote something in this magazine last November. We will return to this point presently. But the fault, as it seems to us, is the more patent when we remember that the book before us is probably one of the last things that Irenaeus ever wrote. He refers to his great work on Heresies, which can hardly have been completed much before 190 A.D., so that the new tract must belong to the last decade of the second century. One would have supposed that, by this date, the Gospels would have taken their right place in the education of a catechumen, and that the person of Christ would have been presented historically, and not by the method of obscure and often impossible reflections from the Prophets or the Psalms.

So far is Irenaeus from using the historical foundations of Christianity, that he does not even know how old Christ was when He died, nor what emperor He died under. There is a well-known passage in the **Adv. Haereses,** ii. 22, which has caused grave searchings of heart, because it implied a belief (based, perhaps, in the first instance, on a misunderstood passage of St. John's Gospel) that our Lord must have been nearly fifty years of age, in opposition to the common belief that He was little more than thirty years when He finished His public ministry. And here, in the Apostolical Preaching, we are quietly informed that He suffered under Pontius Pilate (so far we are following the Apostolical Symbol), but that Pontius Pilate was the procurator *under the emperor Claudius.* It will be very difficult, in view of the known procuratorship of Pontius Pilate under Tiberius, and his subsequent recall, to trust Irenaeus in any matter that requires the exercise of the historical sense; for if chronology is one of the eyes of history, he has deliberately put that eye out. We must not look to the new tract (nor to the old author) for historical details. Its value, and his, lie in another direction.

The argument of the book is as follows. One attains truth through purity of soul and body: through right thinking and right acting, through right belief and right love. Right belief consists in knowing the things that really are . . . : it is a doctrine of God the Father, God the Son, and God the Holy Ghost. The Holy Ghost brings us to the knowledge of the Son, the Son to the knowledge of the Father. The world was created by the Word of God, and was made for a habitation of men, to whom is given lordship over the angels. Irenaeus then proceeds to summarize the whole of the history of the world, from the Creation, Fall, Flood, Call of Abraham, and so on, down to the building of the

Temple and the rise of the Prophets. (In writing the history of the flood, he borrows freely from the Book of Enoch.) The Prophets declare the Incarnation of Christ and the redemption of men. The Virgin Birth is proved by the prophecies and by an Old-Testament gnosis which makes Mary the second Eve. A few lines are given to the preaching of John the Baptist and to the works and sufferings of Christ recorded in the Gospels. After which the writer returns to the Old Testament and the theology supposed to be latent in it, with regard to the Deity and Pre-existence of Christ. A casual reference is made to John the disciple of the Lord and the opening sentence of his Gospel. The order and method of the Book of Testimonies are closely followed, and after establishing all the main points of the Gospel account from the Old Testament, he concludes that "*these testimonies* show his Davidic descent, according to the flesh, and His birth in the city of David"; we are not to look for His birth among the heathen *or anywhere else but in Bethlehem.* His works and sufferings were also foretold. It is surprising that the teaching of Christ is almost entirely absent; His sayings are not quoted, and, more disappointing still, there are no apocryphal sayings or new words of Jesus. The writer concludes with a little warning against the heresies of the time, which are classified as heresies concerning the Father, the Son, and the Holy Spirit. We must not divide the Father from the Creator, we must not depreciate or deny the Incarnation, and we must not undervalue the gifts of the Holy Spirit, especially the prophetic gift, for it is through these gifts that life becomes fruitful.

Such being the structure of the book, we repeat that the first reading is somewhat disappointing, even when we agree with Harnack that there are directions in which it makes a great impression upon us: as, for example, in the complete absence of hierarchical and ceremonial elements, and in the relatively small position given to the Sacraments. Church authority and tradition are not appealed to; they are latent, but not directly affirmed. The sum of the doctrine of Irenaeus is that a life of faith in God is a life of love to man. We wish he had divided his subject a little more evenly, and given more place to the human relations of the Christian man. In this respect he does not come near to the ethical elevation of Aristides, for example. But now, having done with preliminary disappointments, let us turn to the text and see what light we can throw on some of the passages.

In the first place, we have the important evidence of a quotation from Polycarp's Epistle to the Philippians. Up to the present we had no early quotation from Polycarp, and the external evidence for his Epistle was limited (as far as the first two centuries after its composition are concerned) to a statement of Irenaeus (**Haer.** iii. 3, 4), in which he declares that—

"There is a very adequate letter of Polycarp written to the Philippians, from which those who desire it, and who care for their own salvation, can learn both the character of his faith and the message of the truth."

Now let us turn to the **Apostolical Preaching,** c. 95:—

"Through faith in the Son of God, we learn to love God with all our heart and our neighbour as ourselves. But *love* to God *is far from all sins,* and love to the neighbour causes no evil to the neighbour."

Compare with this the following from Polycarp, *ad Phil.* 3:—

"Faith is the mother of us all, followed by hope, in front of whom goes love to God and to Christ and to the neighbour. For if one be within these, he has fulfilled the law of righteousness; *for he that hath love is far from all sin.*"

The coincidence in words is reinforced by the coincidence of the whole argument, and there cannot be any doubt that Irenaeus is using Polycarp, with whose writings he shows himself in another passage to be acquainted. It is curious that Harnack does not seem to have noticed the quotation, any more than the Armenian editors; but it is of some importance critically.

Another interesting case of an unidentified quotation will be found in c. 77. Here we are told, amongst the prophecies of the Passion, to reckon the following:—

"It is said in the book of the Twelve Prophets: they chained him and brought him there to the king as a present. For Pontius Pilate was the procurator of Judaea, and was at that time at enmity with Herod, the king of the Jews. But after, when Christ was brought to him in chains, Pilate sent Him to Herod, leaving him to examine Him, in order to know exactly what he would do with Him, using Christ as an excuse for reconciliation with the king."

Here the editors are at fault, and Harnack adds that to the best of his knowledge there is no such passage in the Minor Prophets, and that it is significant that Irenaeus, in this instance, does not give the name of the prophet whom he is quoting.

The passage is Hosea x. 6. . . .

It is not easy to see how this Greek was made out of the Hebrew, as we know it; and it is well known that the passages relating to King Jarib are to this day a *crux interpretum.* But that the passage was taken as a prophetic testimony to Christ and His trial, is certain. Suppose we turn to Justin, *Dialogue with Trypho,* c. 103. . . .

Justin makes the same connexion as Irenaeus between the passage in Hosea and the account of what passed between Pilate and Herod.

The same connexion is made in Tertullian against Marcion (iv. 42):—

"Nam et Herodi velut munus a Pilato missus, Osee vocibus fidem reddidit: de Christo enim prophetaverat: et vinctum eum ducent xeniam regi."

Tertullian, as is well known, used the prophetic testimonies in slaying Marcion; and I think it is quite likely that both he and Justin are using a formal collection of such testimonies; for the connexion between Hosea and the Gospel is by no means obvious, even to a person whose mind was set on finding Christ in the Old Testament. In any case, there can be no doubt where Irenaeus' quotation comes from. We shall find the same connexion made in Cyril of Jerusalem (*Cat.* xiii. 14) . . . And also in Ruffinus on the Symbol.

And this brings us to the interesting question of the relation of the composition, and of the catechetical teaching which underlies it, to the collection of prophetic passages which I have shown to be current in the early Church, whose original title seems to have been *Testimonies against the Jews.* Does the new treatise involve Irenaeus in the use of that early book in the way that I have suggested in the too brief article which I wrote on the subject in the Expositor for last November? For example, we are to ask whether it quotes the same proof-texts as the Book of Testimonies, whether it quotes them with similar sequences, with the same misunderstandings, like combinations, similar displacements of the names of authors quoted, and so on.

Perhaps it will be sufficient if I present a few striking cases of coincidence in the matter quoted from the Old Testament and in the manner in which it is quoted.

It will be remembered that I drew attention to the way in which Bar Salibi, in his *Testimonies against the Jews,* quotes as follows:—

"David said: Before the day-star I begat thee. And before the sun is his name and before the moon. Now explain to us, when was Israel born before the day-star, etc."

The combination of passages from the 110th Psalm and the 71st Psalm was noted, and it was shown that the same two passages were combined in Justin, *Dialogue,* 76, and in the collection of prophetic extracts ascribed to Gregory of Nyssa.

Now turn to the new treatise, c. 43, and you will find Irenaeus establishing the pre-existence of Christ from the first verse of the book of Genesis, after which he goes on:—

"And Jeremiah the prophet also testifies this as follows: Before the morning-star have I begotten thee, and before the sun is his name."

Here the very same sequence occurs, in exact agreement with Bar Salibi; and we have, over and above that coincidence, an error of ascription such as frequently occurs in these collections, by which Jeremiah is made responsible for the Psalms! Probably, though I have not been able to verify this, a proof-text from Jeremiah lay adjacent. A similar case exists in our Gospel of Matthew with reference to the potter's field, and the parallel is particularly interesting because Irenaeus quotes it in the newly-found treatise, and evidently *not* from the Gospel. His language is as follows:—

c. 81, "And again Jeremiah the prophet said: 'And they took the thirty pieces of silver, the price of the one that was sold, whom they of the children of Israel had bought, and gave them for the potter's field, as the Lord commanded me.' For Judas, who was of Christ's disciples," etc.

A comparison of the other passages which are similarly treated will show that Irenaeus means to quote the prophet, and does not mean to quote the Gospel. From which again we infer that the famous reading stood in a book of Testimonies.

Another famous passage to which I referred was the prophecy of Jacob concerning Judah ("the sceptre shall not fail from Judah," etc), which I showed to have been current in the book of Testimonies as a prophecy of Moses (see Iren., *adv. Haer.* iv. 10, and Justin, 1 *Ap.* 32). In c. 57 of the new treatise we get the same matter brought forward, with the preface, "And Moses says in Genesis," the change in the manner of introducing the passage being made so as to avoid the error of the ascription of the prophecy to Moses. Then, after explaining the meaning of the blessing of Judah, and how he washes his garments in wine, which is a symbol of eternal joy, he goes on, "And on this account he is also the hope of the heathen, *who hope in him.*" . . . And if we read on in Irenaeus, we shall find the words actually extant which he has proleptically treated at the end of c. 57. The order of the passages in the original book can be clearly made out. And the same thing can be shown elsewhere in the new treatise, but for brevity I forbear further reference to this matter.

Here is one other curious and interesting passage in which the treatment of prophecies by Irenaeus is closely parallel to that which we find in Justin, but apparently without any direct dependence of the former upon the latter.

In c. 70, in dealing with Christ's sufferings, Irenaeus quotes from Isaiah liii. 8 ("Who shall declare His generation?"). He then goes on (c. 71) to quote Lamentations iv. 20 under the name of Jeremiah; and then (c. 72) to point out from the same prophet (it should have been Isaiah) "how the righteous perish and no man layeth it to heart; and pious men are taken away" (Isa. lvii. 1); and proceeds to prove from it (i.) the death of Christ, (ii.) the sufferings of those who are His followers; and neither of these points would have been made by a rational exegete; and he concludes thus: "'Who,' says the prophet, 'is perfectly righteous except the Son of God, who leads on those who believe in him to perfect righteousness, *who are persecuted and killed like himself?*'"

Here the parallel in Justin Martyr, 1 *Ap.* 48, is very striking: "And as to the way he pointed out in advance by the prophetic spirit, that he should be done to death *along with those who hope in him,* listen to the things that were spoken by Isaiah," etc.

I do not think that the coincidence, which we here observe in the treatment of the passage in Isaiah at the hands of Irenaeus and Justin, is due to the fact that Irenaeus has been reading Justin; it is more natural to suppose that the treatment of the passage is conventional and is invited by a headline in the Testimony book. But enough has probably been said on this point. The inference which we draw is something more than our previous conclusions: we not only confirm our argument as to the existence of written collections of prophecies used for controversial purposes against the Jews, but since the treatise we have before us is almost the equivalent of a Church Catechism, we see that the Book of Testimonies became a regular book of Church teaching, and that it passed out of controversial use with Jews into doctrinal use for the instruction of Greeks, and that, being so used, it is, as we have said above, the equivalent of a Gospel for the instruction of the catechumens; a little later and it will be displaced by the Gospels themselves, and will rapidly disappear.

Now, in conclusion, we may point out that the anti-Judaic character of the early Apostolical Preaching which Irenaeus is commending to Marcianus is reflected in the ethics of the book, which, although meagre in quantity, are lofty in tone and anti-Judaic in temper. The writer has no further use for the Mosaic Law! Why should we tell a man not to kill, who does not even hate? or not to covet his neighbour's goods when he loves his neighbour as himself? or why tell him to keep an idle day of rest every week, when he keeps every day a Sabbath rest in himself? Is not the true temple the human body, where God is constantly served in righteousness? As for sacrifices, read what Isaiah says about the sacrifice of an ox being the equivalent of the offering of a dog.

Could anything be more characteristically anti-Judaic, or more definitely Christian? And this is the teaching which professes to present the Apostolical tradition; it has none of the natural machinery of religion, and very little supernatural machinery; the terrors of the world to come are as little in evidence as the offerings of bulls and goats. The proportion of the doctrines presented is certainly significant. We should have expected more in this direction and less in that, more in the direction of ritual and less in the direction of ethics unqualified by eschatology. But it would clearly be going too far to assume an argument from silence, and say that Irenaeus had no ritual conceptions, and taught no eschatology. For we have the five books against Heresies to reckon with, as well as a number of preserved fragments from lost books.[1]

It seems clear, however, that the tradition which he presents made much of the interior change and of the spiritual enlightenment. And it is in reference to this spiritual vision and experience that we come nearest to the actual teaching of the New Testament. In c. 93 Irenaeus quotes the famous passage from Hosea (ii. 25), where the Not-Beloved becomes Beloved, and the not-people the children of the living God. For, says he, this is what John the Baptist meant when he said, "God can raise up children to Abraham from the stones." *For after our hearts have been torn away from their stony service and made free, then we behold God by faith and become the children of Abraham, those, namely, who are justified by faith.*

Notes

1. It should be noticed that the parallels between the *adv. Haer.* and the *Apostolic Preaching* are constant and often very illuminating. For instance, in c. 14 Irenaeus explains the innocence of Adam and Eve in the garden by the fact that they were created as boy and girl: and, as Harnack notes, this was already implied in *adv. Haer.* iii. 22. 3 (Erant enim utrique nudi in Paradiso et non confundebantur, quoniam paulo ante facti, non intellectum habebant filiorum generationis: oportebat enim illos primos adolescere, dehinc sic multiplicari). See also the curious argument for the Virgin Birth in c. 36, based on the promise to David, "Of the fruit of thy body, etc.," and the same argument in *adv. Haer.* iii. 21. 5.

Gustaf Wingren (essay date 1947)

SOURCE: "Creation," in *Man and the Incarnation: A Study in the Biblical Theology of Irenaeus,* translated by Ross Mackenzie, Muhlenberg Press, 1947, pp. 3-38.

[*In the following essay, Wingren studies the significance of God's absolute power as Creator and of the relationship between Christ and man in Irenaeus's theology.*]

GOD THE CREATOR

Our best starting-point for a full understanding of the concept of God in Irenaeus is the sovereignty of God—the absolute power of the Creator. The Gnostics' pessimism in regard to the world forced them into assuming a God who had nothing to do with the world, and they kept large parts of reality separate from God's sphere of influence. Against this, Irenaeus maintained that if God is held to be powerless in any respect, then that before which He is powerless is in point of fact *God*. We make certain deductions about the universe, deducing one proposition from another, but there is some point at which we have to stop, an already existing reality which cannot conceivably have originated from anything else, and it is this which we designate as "God." But if we conceive of some substance, or matter, that is independent of God, then this independent substance is sovereign, and God is not, and it makes no difference however actively God may work and "create" with this substance as the basic stuff of His Creation, He is still not *Creator,* and what we ought consistently to call God is really matter, because the point at which we have stopped is that which does not require to depend upon any prior cause. But it is precisely this which characterises God, and which cannot be expressed about anything else except God, namely, that He cannot be deduced from anything.[1]

By this it is implied that all things and all forms of life have originated from God. Whatever exists in heaven or on earth has had its origin in something else, but the matter from which everything has originated must in its turn have originated somewhere; but God has created the whole world from *nothing* out of His own unlimited power. The matter from which everything in Creation was to be formed must itself have been made from nothing, because it is only from God that Creation can originate, and because there is nothing greater than God and nothing equal to Him. It is only God who has a scheme for Creation and the will to create, and there is none to assist Him in His Creation other than His own "hands," in other words God Himself. The hands of God are His Spirit and His Son, who are thus uncreated; they belong to the Creator, and are active in all Creation.[2] It is as impossible for us to state how the Son and the Spirit originated as it is to penetrate into the mystery of God's existence at all. God and his "hands" are inseparable.[3]

It may be stated at this point that the Son—and also, as we shall see, the Spirit—is revealed to us in Jesus Christ. Now since the Son appears to us in Christ, it would be plausible to argue that belief in Him could only come with the Incarnation. But Irenaeus strenuously opposes such an interpretation, and in the **Epideixis** his opposition to this interpretation becomes almost tediously monotonous. Irenaeus frequently connects this with the statement in the Johannine Prologue about the Word which was in the beginning with God, and which became flesh in the birth of Jesus. "Because, for God, the Son was (as) the beginning before the creation of the world; but for us (He was) then, when He appeared; and before that He was not for us, who knew Him not."[4] The fact that we had not seen the Son or known about Him does not, therefore, mean that the Son did not exist. Irenaeus avoids the idea of a world which existed before the Son as studiously as he does speaking about matter which exists independently of God, for to maintain either of these propositions is to diminish the sovereignty of God, and to make as incredible the idea that God can work miracles upon the earth as that Christ will one day rule over the whole world.[5] For a complete understanding of the theology of Irenaeus we must keep firmly in our minds from the very first the belief that God and His Son *are* before everything that has been created, and before any matter or any world they *are*.[6]

In the section that follows I propose to examine in particular the creation of *man*. Man is created in the likeness of God—God says to His Son and the Spirit, His own hands, "Let us make man in our image, after our likeness" (faciamus hominem ad imaginem et similitudinem nostram). In the present section, where we are dealing with God as Creator in general, my purpose is to lay stress on the following proposition, namely, that the Son of God, who was made man in Jesus, exists *before* man, and, indeed, when man is created he is created through the Son and *for* the Son, so as to reach his destiny in the Son, his Saviour. Man's coming into being is something which occurs after the Son, and since the Saviour existed before man came into being, it was proper that something to be saved should come into being, lest the Saviour should exist by Himself alone.[7] This point requires to be emphasised

quite strongly, since the concept in primitive Christianity and in the early Church of the world as having been created in the Son has disappeared in modern theology. Oscar Cullmann holds, not without some justification, that the celebrated controversy between Karl Barth and Emil Brunner rests on the false alternative of *the work of Creation* (without Christ altogether) or *the work of salvation* (in Christ).[8] Irenaeus holds, on the contrary, that everything is created in the Son, or the *Verbum,* the same *Verbum* which becomes flesh in Christ. In this fundamental premise he continues an early Christian line of thought.[9]

In point of fact the concept of pre-existence is often established on very inadequate Biblical foundations, creating only a variation of the un-Biblical separation of Spirit and matter. Matter as such is then held to be disclosed in reality and value—matter has an ideal pattern and is only a shadow of this eternal idea. The concept of pre-existence in early Christianity proceeds from God's sovereignty, that is, from God the Creator, who controls what is in existence, and who cannot be confounded by anything that originates from outside Himself, for nothing outside God has any existence. God does not, as it were, discover that there is something in existence farther forward in history, but rather, if anything new comes into existence, then it has come from the Creator, and therefore existed previously in Him. It follows that the question whether in its pre-existence it existed in a spiritual or a material way is irrelevant, and does not even need to be asked.[10] There is a clear understanding of this concept of pre-existence, which is linked together with the idea of Creation, in Eph. II.10, in which the writer speaks of "good works, which God prepared beforehand, that we should walk in them." For Irenaeus the whole of the history of salvation is a series of "works" done by God with the Son and the Spirit as his "hands," and God has done them all in order that in them man might partake of Life. The power of God is, therefore, impeded neither by the Devil, God's adversary, nor sin, nor death, and the victory over these enemies of God, which is won through Christ, and which extends to their utter destruction in the Consummation, has been ordained by God from the very beginning, and exists in God as Creator. The existence of the Devil and his conflict with God in men does not involve for Irenaeus the same intolerable encroachment upon God's sovereignty as the existence of matter before God's creation of the whole universe. The Devil, too, has been created by God and has no life in himself, but has his existence by the power of God, and only for so long as the Creator and Father wills: his time is fixed by the decree of God.[11]

Hence, if it is a characteristic of God to create, it is characteristic of man that he is created, i.e. that he is made, not that he is, but that he becomes, or increases.[12] And these two facts, God's creation and man's continual becoming, are identical—the same reality seen from two different aspects. At times the description in Irenaeus of man's increase has been represented as an instance of an almost modern theory of evolution, but Karl Prümm has justifiably insisted that this aspect of Irenaeus's thought has also first to be seen against its Gnostic background. The Gnostics proceeded from beneath, in differences, for instance, between certain aspects of the Old Testament and contradictory passages in the New Testament, and classified "God" in the categories of an Old Testament God and a New Testament God. It is against this disintegration in the idea of God that Irenaeus contends.[13] God is one, but man becomes, and for him there are many stages of development.[14] In both Testaments we encounter the same God, and it is only to be expected that, in spite of this fact, they contain differences, for God is the creating One, i.e. man is continually in process of becoming.[15]

Because of this relationship it is impossible for man to obtrude on God's existence. Any knowledge which man possesses of God is dependent on the active revelation of God, and where God has not revealed the mystery of His own person, man knows nothing. Irenaeus is decidedly averse to speculation, and frequently observes that Scripture does not tell us everything, but only what we need to know, in order that we may be able to have faith and obedience. There are blanks in our knowledge at several points, e.g. no one knows what God did before the creation of the world, and so no one can say how the Son proceeded from the Father; the period before the Last Day is and remains unknown, and the reason why certain created beings (man and the Devil) fell into sin is likewise hidden.[16] Where there are blanks of this kind in our knowledge it is because they have to be, and it is futile for us to attempt to amplify our limited knowledge of God by our own thinking. Man may properly study what lies "before his eyes," and what is clearly written in Scripture: both these ways lead to incontrovertible knowledge, although, of course, it is limited knowledge.[17] However persistently we may try, we cannot reach any knowledge of what God is like in His majesty, in his *magnitudo,* despite the fact that God is so close to us, and that He never ceases to know everything that is in every man.[18] When van den Eynde speaks about the simple "theology of faith" in the early Church as an expression of the common life of faith within the local congregations, and holds that the theology of Irenaeus, but not the theology of Alexandria, belongs to this less intellectualised theology of the early Church, we should note that the unwillingness of Irenaeus to employ *la théologie savante* is founded on principle,[19] for Irenaeus could not have admitted either Gnostic or Alexandrian speculation without destroying the basis of his theology.

As we have just seen, our inquiry has to be directed not only at the unequivocal affirmations of Scripture, but at everything "before our eyes," and the Gnostics proved deficient in both of these respects, for they had no interest either in a balanced exegesis of Scripture, or in the visible, external world. It is at this point that another aspect of Irenaeus's belief in the Creator presents itself. The Gnostics held (and here I am referring to sensual *gnosis*) that it was a necessity to experience everything, even what was evil; yet they were never known to take part in anything that required resilience or adaptability, but, being the sensualists they were, either devoted themselves to every kind of

excess, or kept ascetically remote from the world. Irenaeus held that we ought by rights to be finding the Gnostics occupied on occasion with medicine, botany, painting, sculpture, or different types of handwork, agriculture, seafaring, and also gymnastics, hunting, the art of warfare, and politics—but in every one of these pursuits we look for the Gnostics in vain.[20] And yet it is the corruptible things, too, which have been made by God, and the whole earth is the Lord's, despite the fact that it is transitory and destined to pass away[21]—God the Creator is at work even in the least of His creatures which reproduce, and by so doing continue His Creation.[22]

In this present connexion particular attention should be given to the statements in Irenaeus about the Roman Empire, and what God is doing for the benefit of mankind and the preservation of His world by using a pagan power such as this as His instrument. These statements of Irenaeus are given in great detail and lucidity, although they are infrequently mentioned in theological literature. His interpretation of Mt. xxii.7 is quite characteristic. The verse, "The king was angry: and he sent his troops and destroyed those murderers and burned their city," is an allusion to the destruction of Jerusalem by the Roman army. The Roman armies are called God's armies—the king (God) sent *his* armies. And the Lord may speak thus "since all men belong to God." Some lines farther on this theme is expanded: "Every man, as a man, is His creation, even though he may be ignorant of his God."[23] Irenaeus puts the theme in question into its proper context by quoting in full three passages from Scripture, and his selection of passages is highly significant. The first is from Psalm xxiv: "The earth is the Lord's, and the fulness thereof" (Ps. xxiv.1). The second is Paul's statement about the powers that be as the servants of God (Rom. xiii. 1-6), and the third is Mt. v.45, the passage about the sun and the rain on the just and the unjust.[24]

Also of interest is the defence which Irenaeus attempts to make of the passages Ex. iii.21 f. and xii.35 f., the description of how, before the Exodus, the Israelites took jewels of gold and silver from the Egyptians. As Christians, he maintains, we act in a similar kind of way towards non-Christians around us, and make free use of what they produce for us by their efforts in giving the world peace, and creating the possibility of unimpeded intercourse and secure sea-communications.[25] It belongs to God's nature to give us such worldly gifts as these, although they come to us from the Creator through other men, and although these others have no knowledge of God.[26] The belief in Creation, which underlies passages such as this, sees man as being on the earth for God to make use of in the same way as he makes use of the fig-tree to give us figs—it is not necessary that it should first be converted or received into the congregation!

Of very great importance, however, is the extended analysis in Irenaeus of Lk. iv.6, the declaration of the Devil at the temptation of Jesus that he, the Devil, can give away all the kingdoms of the world, since he has power over them (*A.h.* v.24).[27] The whole of the exegesis of this passage forms part of a larger systematic context dealing with the Devil as Falsehood and the Lord as Truth (from v.21 onwards). When the Devil claims that he possesses the kingdoms of the world he is lying, because "the hearts of kings are in the hand of God." It is not Satan who administers the kingdoms of this world, but God.[28] When Christ contradicts the Devil at every temptation with a word from the Old Testament, the word of the Law, He speaks the truth and declares *which* God His Father is, viz. the God of Creation and the Law.[29] The Devil is continually active, and never gives up his desire to embroil the whole of mankind in warfare and strife, but all that he is able to do by this is to *disturb* God's government of the world; it is an impossibility for him to get the whole of the created order into his control, for *God rules*.[30] When men sinned and began to destroy one another, God put a "fear of man" into mankind, because men no longer knew how to fear God. In subjection to the mastery of their fellowmen, and bound by their laws, men were to learn to be righteous at least in some measure. So men are forced into curbing one another and treating with respect the repressive control which confronts them. The laws of authority are "a garment of righteousness." Severity checks sin,[31] and new rulers continually gain power as new generations of men are born. In both of these the continuing work of Creation is discerned: "The One by whose command men are born commands also rulers to be appointed who are fit to govern those over whom they rule at the time."[32]

But the demand for obedience to authority is only one aspect of the fundamental view of kings as the servants of God. The other side is that all rulers, independently of whether or not they are Christian, are to be judged in the Last Judgement by the God who appointed them. The Judgement will be upon all without exception. And if the rulers have done anything contrary to the law, as tyrants do, it will inevitably bring upon them destruction and ruin.[33] The sun rises on the evil and the good now, but it will not always be so, and the God who is so long-suffering now to His Creation will some day cause His Judgement to come upon mankind.[34]

There is a further point in the teaching of Irenaeus where his belief in Creation emerges in a precise definition in a comparable way, and that is his interpretation of Holy Communion. In more recent theology, and especially in Anglican quarters, the Holy Communion is regarded as "an extension of the Incarnation," and in this definition there is something which was part of the theology of the early Church. But it is, in fact, an Anglican theologian who has pointed out that Irenaeus tended rather to connect Holy Communion with the belief in *Creation*: God has created the world through His Word, His Son, and in the Eucharist there is "an extension of His creative energy."[35] Christ took the bread from Creation and said of it: "This is my body." The wine too had been produced by the earth, and of it He said: "This is my blood."[36] When the Gnostics took these gifts of Creation, they treated them as having been created by the Demiurge, a lower Creator-God, and

not by the God and Father of Jesus Christ. It was a matter of astonishment to Irenaeus that the Gnostics could celebrate Holy Communion at all, using bread and wine as food and nourishment, and he could not see how they were able to relate the elements to Christ. A precondition for such a connexion as this is that in Christ we see the Son of the Creator of the world. Christ is the Word made flesh, He is the *Verbum* through which the vine bears its fruit, the springs flow, and the earth has strength to produce the stalk, the ear of corn, and the grain of wheat for bread.[37] The Creator has power to give life to the grain which is cast into the earth and is changed, and it is the same Creator who has power to nourish and feed us with Christ in the Eucharist, so that when we die and are buried in the earth we may await the resurrection from the dead. The bread and wine of the Holy Communion both testify that the Creator of the world is in Christ, and that our earthly bodies share in the life which the Creator wills to bestow upon mankind through the incarnate Son.[38] Farther on in our study we shall have cause to return frequently to this profound relationship between Creation, the Incarnation, the Church, and the resurrection of the body.[39]

God is life; the Devil is death. Irenaeus regards all life as being in the hand of God, and death as a lost connexion with God, a lost contact with the source of life, and captivity to the enemy of God. He therefore held together in his understanding natural life and the Spirit, Creation and the Sacraments, and man's body and his communion with God. By the very fact of our being in the presence of *life* in all its countless forms we are confronted by a wholly divine activity in which God is directly at work in His Creation.[40] Whatever affects life adversely is wrong and contrary to the will of the Creator, but at the same time too it is *death,* something which destroys life like poison in the body. It is from God that man has proceeded, and so the only life he has is the one which he has received from God. But at this point let us leave the idea of Creation in general and turn our attention to the man whom God has put into His created world.

IMAGO AND SIMILITUDO

In Gen. 1.26 both *image* . . . and *likeness* . . . are mentioned together. These two substantives are rendered in Greek as ειχων and ομοίωσις respectively, and in Latin as *imago* and *similitudo*. This combination of words occurs in a very large number of places in Irenaeus, mostly as a hendiadys. There are, however, passages where Irenaeus uses only one of the words, and there are other places where he makes a distinction in meaning between the two. The majority of the interpreters of Irenaeus's anthropology have concentrated on these latter passages, with some loss in the total understanding of their meaning. We shall have to examine the whole of this discussion when we come to deal with man and his faith in Christ, man in the Church, for by then we shall have drawn together all the necessary material for discussion. There are other problems too which we are unable to study at this particular point—the question of free will and of immortality, for example—and so we limit ourselves here solely to the relationship between the Son on the one hand (or, rather, the Son and the Spirit), and man on the other, as this relationship existed when man was created. This relation between the Son and man, having been established by God from the beginning of Creation, is an expression of the same truth as the statement that man is created in the *imago* and *similitudo* of God.

Prümm states that there is hardly any verse in the Old Testament which is more frequently quoted "in der alten Christenheit" than Gen. 1.26. The statement is true enough of Irenaeus, but otherwise it is somewhat of an exaggeration.[41] It cannot be said that this quotation abounds in theological literature before *Adversus haereses.*[42] In Irenaeus, on the other hand, repeated allusions are made to the verse in question, sometimes in reference to the Creation of man, at other times with allusion to Christ Himself, or again to Christ's dealings with men in the present, or even in connexion with some futurist or eschatological expectation, which man awaits in faith.[43] In regard to the points of contact in Irenaeus with contemporary thought it is of very great interest to note that the Gnostics—at least the Valentinian *gnosis*—also built on Gen. 1.26 f.[44] The Valentinians, it is true, were Irenaeus's chief opponents, but for this very reason we may well assume that they had a real influence on him, as indeed several scholars maintain.[45] It was a characteristic of this Gnosticism that, in accordance with the division into *higher* and *lower* which was applied to the whole of the Gnostic world-view, it made a sharp distinction between *imago and similitudo.* The exaggerated influence of Valentinian Gnosticism on Irenaeus is, however, closely bound up with the tendency which has been found recently of putting into the centre of discussion the relatively few passages in which Irenaeus appears to distinguish between *imago* and *similitudo,* in a manner which is reminiscent of the scholastic scheme of nature and supernature. But even among those who for reasons such as these over-emphasise the Gnostic influence there is nonetheless general agreement that the Valentinian interpretation of Gen. 1.26 f. exercised at the most a subsidiary influence, and was important only in that it impelled Irenaeus to take up the interpretation of the passage in earnest, but was not his basic reason for doing so. His interest in the passage was Biblical and Pauline.[46]

At the same time, however, there is an obvious difference between the theology of Irenaeus and the Pauline theology in their general interpretation. In Rom. v.12-21 Paul compares Adam and Christ. Through Adam sin and death have come into the world, but through Christ has come righteousness and life. Paul focuses his attention on the *defeat,* the "fall," of Adam.[47] By so doing he is not denying that Adam was created by God, but it is not this which, as an Apostle, he has to proclaim. The Gospel is about what Christ has done. And so in Paul's theology Adam and Christ are set over against one another. Irenaeus found himself involved in controversy with Gnostics who denied what was self-evident to Paul, namely that Adam was created in the image of God, as it is written in Gen. 1.26 f.,

and created by the God who sent Christ into the world.[48] The Gnostics likewise rejected the Law and the Old Testament which God the most high had given, and so Irenaeus was forced not only to try to demonstrate how both the Old and the New Testaments were derived from God, and how both the Law and the Gospel were addressed to men by the same God, but also to make it clear to his own period that Adam was created by God to live, body and soul, in accordance with His will. For this very reason it is important to speak of Adam's sin as a *fall.* Irenaeus also lays strong emphasis on the fact that Adam's defeat and Christ's victory are the extreme opposites of one another.[49] If, however, we examine what Adam was created *for,* what appears is not the contrast between Adam and Christ, Irenaeus maintained, but, on the contrary, the connexion between them.[50] And it is this connexion which we must first of all now define.

There is a suitable starting-point for our discussion in Loofs's analysis of a line of thought which appears in Irenaeus. Loofs isolates a special line of thought in *Adversus haereses,* according to which the historical Christ who lived on earth was the pattern which God had in His mind when he fashioned the first man. Christ was the man about to be, *homo futurus,* and the Creator, as it were, foresaw Christ. While the earth was being formed, Christ was in the mind of God, and matter took shape in the hands of God in accordance with this future pattern. In particular, Loofs links up this line of thought with a much-debated passage in Tertullian's *De resurrectione carnis,* where the Christological and anthropological concepts which I have just mentioned are quite prominent.[51] In Tertullian, however, these ideas have no systematic significance, and the idea of Christ as *homo futurus* is one which comes up only for a time and then disappears.[52] There is, however, one dominant idea in the main writing of Irenaeus, which Loofs was continually trying to split up into several parts, in which the line of thought of which I have just spoken would be fundamental.[53] It is characteristic of Loofs's interpretation of Irenaeus that this line of thought—the Christ yet to be—is set in sharp contrast to the idea of Christ as the pre-existent Son. The idea of pre-existence belongs to a quite different part of *Adversus haereses,* and it was solely on account of his general theological lack of depth, Loofs held, that Irenaeus as a compiler was able to attempt the task of joining together two such unrelated elements to form a unity which had to be forced.[54]

It is easier to see the significance of Loofs's reasoning if we take a parallel from the history of dogma. On the question of election it is sometimes suggested that God elects, but that He does so on the basis of His foreknowledge of what course man is going to take. But if this foreknowledge is allowed to become the principal thing, then obviously the decisive factor will be man's free will—whatever takes place does so independently of God and in isolation from Him, while God is added on later as the One who foresees, but in an essentially passive way. The view which underlies Loofs's dichotomy between the idea of pre-existence and the idea of the future is just the same.

Christ is a reality in the future; the Son is not with God from eternity, but rather the future, historic Christ is foreseen by God. In the preceding section, however, it was made clear that a deistic concept of God such as this was altogether alien to Irenaeus. Irenaeus maintained not only that God has foreknowledge of everything, but also that His foreknowledge is an element in His creation of all things, and before we see them emerging in history these things are already real in God.[55] It is an artificial contrast that Loofs makes between what is pre-existent and what is of the future. The affinity between these two ideas is natural and primary. Mankind's prototype is the Son, the *Logos,* the *Verbum,* who, in His future aspect as Saviour, existed in God. It is perhaps a matter of some doubt whether Tertullian looks at the matter in the same way, for his references to the subject are scattered, but as far as Irenaeus is concerned this inner connexion is certain.[56]

"Man is created in the image of God, and the image of God is the Son, in whose image man was created. For this reason the Son also appeared in the fulness of time to show how the copy resembles Him."[57] The Son was first, before Creation. Man, like every other thing, is created in the Son and the Spirit, i.e. he has been formed by God's own hands, but he is different from the rest of Creation in that in addition he was created in order to become like God—to become the very image of God. This is his destiny. Irenaeus does not say that he *is* this image, nor was this destiny wholly realised in Creation before sin entered into the world, because man was a *child.* This means, in part, that man has not arrived at his appointed destiny in Creation, because he is not the son of God in that sense, but it also means that, if he grew up to maturity without being confused by his adversary, he would reach the end which has been ordained for him by God. In our next section we shall look at the statements in Irenaeus about man as a *child* in Creation, and we shall postpone making references and offering a more detailed analysis till then, but this, at any rate, may be said in the meantime: a healthy, newborn child is unable to talk, for example, but it has every likelihood of being able to do so in the future, and provided only that the child grows, it will reach the stage of being able to talk. An injury to the child, however, may prevent it from ever beginning to talk. This is the situation of the first man. He is a child, created in the image of God, but he is not the image of God. That he lacks something, however, is not due to sin. No injury has yet happened to the child. He is uninjured, but he is just a child—he does not yet realise what he is to be. All the while, however, there is already in Creation one who *is* the image of God, the only-begotten Son.[58] There is nothing lacking in Him; He is more than man, and man, by being created "in the image of God," is created and established in Him, who was at a future point in history to become incarnate.

And yet at the same time there is an absolute distance between God and man. The Son is God, and therefore Creator; but man is created in the image of God, and is and remains created.[59] This distinction between the Son and man is such that it may never be abolished, however man may become like the Son who is man's prototype. There is a passage in Irenaeus, in which he is emphasising this difference between Christ and man, where his very choice of words is significantly changed. Dealing with man, he states that having succumbed to his adversary man has become a captive of the Devil, and the question is, How shall anyone be able to overcome this adversary of mankind unless he is different from the man who has suffered defeat? But only the Son of God is stronger than man who has been created in the image of God, the Son in whose image man was created. The Son, therefore, was made man in the Incarnation in order to defeat man's adversary and to reveal the *similitudo.*[60] It is the Son's superiority to man which Irenaeus is emphasising here, and he demonstrates this distance by his statement that man was created in the likeness of the Son. The affinity between the Son and man and the distinction between them are part of the same reality, and both the distance between them and the bond which unites them are expressed by saying that man is created in the *imago* and *similitudo* of the Son; but it is a better definition simply to say that the Son *is* the *imago* and *similitudo* of God, and that man is *created in* God's *imago* and *similitudo.*

Man is created by God's hands, the Son and the Spirit, so as to become the very image of God.[61] The fulfilment of the purpose of Creation implies accordingly that man should grow in conformity with the Son, and since the Son is Christ, this coalescence with Christ in the Church, which is the Body of Christ, means that Creation is moving towards its consummation. We shall have more to say about this farther on, but it should be stressed at this point that, since the Spirit is given in the Incarnation and is inseparably bound with the Body of Christ, the Spirit too is active in Creation as well as the Son. Irenaeus will refer to the Son or the *Logos,* the *Verbum,* as "God's hand," but even more frequently he connects the Son with the Spirit and speaks of them together as "God's hands."[62] It is not only the Son, it is also the Spirit, who represents God's likeness. When man is formed after the image and likeness of God the Spirit too is active in that formation. This may be an appropriate point at which to mention some references to the Spirit as taking part in the formation of man, in spite of the fact that in so doing we are anticipating part of what is to follow.

There is a passage in the *Epideixis* which speaks of God as being triune in the following terms: "He is over all things as Father, He is with all things as the Word, since all things proceeded from the Father through the Word, but He is in us all as the Spirit who cries 'Abba, Father,' and forms man in the image of God."[63] Immediately before this Irenaeus had made the traditional identification of the Son with the Word and the Spirit with Wisdom—the Spirit forms the flesh, and "the flesh forgets its own property and assumes that of the Spirit by becoming conformable to the Word of God," i.e. to the Son.[64] In this last quotation the Spirit forms man in the likeness of the Son. There is a further related fact, which is that Christ's work of salvation consists in His bestowal of the Spirit: it is the Spirit which unites man with Christ.[65] Man's identity with the Son is not finally achieved until the resurrection from the dead, and in Irenaeus as well as in early Christianity the resurrection is connected with the Spirit which forms the body, and in forming the body takes possession of it, making it a *soma pneumatikon*. In faith man already possesses the Spirit as an earnest, but the full dominion of the Spirit in the resurrection will perfect man in accordance with the Father's purpose in Creation, and conform him to God's *imago* and *similitudo*.[66] The Son and the Spirit are one in the Church and the resurrection, but not only there: they are already one at the beginning in the work of Creation.[67] From them, as the hands of God, man proceeds.

There are certain statements in Irenaeus about Christ's work of salvation which are put in such a way that we may at the same time deduce from them something about man as he was destined to be in Creation. Among these are all his statements of how Christ re-established man through the Spirit and restores him to his original status, and annuls the harm wrought by the Fall. The point is frequently made in **Adversus haereses** that what man lost in Adam, namely his conformity to the image and likeness of God, is restored again in Christ, and it was for this very reason that the Son, who was always with the Father, was made flesh.[68] The divine decree at man's creation comes to fulfilment through what is realised by Christ in His Incarnation: God's Word emerges as an effective reality.[69] There is hardly any passage in Irenaeus of greater importance than the one in which he describes in detail how it is only the man who receives the Spirit that is truly man.[70] If a man rejects the Spirit he remains in the power of his adversary, and by being so held he remains in a state that is contrary to his nature. The man, however, who receives God's Word returns to his original state: "Those who are created after God's *imago* and *similitudo* gain man's original state.[71] Accordingly, what is given in salvation is not a supernatural addition to what is purely human, as Roman Catholic theologians in particular frequently interpret Irenaeus to mean, but rather, the typical condition of mankind is his state of not being human—and what perverts man is his captivity to a power over himself—and Christ, by what He has done, frees man from his inhumanity and lets him become truly man.

The passage in Col. iii.10 about the new man who "is being renewed in knowledge after the image of its creator" is an affirmation which Irenaeus finds of profound and particular significance. It implies that man, by faith in Christ, becomes a new man, becomes like Christ. And yet it was in the likeness of Christ, the Son, that man was created. The first creation, which was corrupted by sin, is begun again when man by faith is united with Christ who is the image of God.[72] In the "new man" Christ is active, and in Christ the Creator is active. God has not given up the work which He began when He said, "Let us make man in our own image," but in fact is active in creating man by His "hand," that is, by Christ; and when Christ, God's "hand" and "mouth," is accomplishing His work among

men, the first creation is being brought to its fulfilment. These references in Irenaeus to the recreating power of Christ in the Incarnation are confirmed by similar statements about his view of Creation "in the beginning," which bear out what we have already discovered: from the very beginning the Son *is* the *imago* and *similitudo* of God, while man *is created* in the *imago* and *similitudo* of God.

To reach an understanding of the concept of man in Irenaeus we shall have to avoid making distinctions between his various statements about Adam, the descendants of Adam, or man after Christ, etc.,[73] for Irenaeus would never have defined these different periods separately. In speaking of Adam he speaks of man, and in speaking of what Christ does for men he speaks of what Christ does for Adam; or again, in using the word *Adam* or the word *man* he is always in some way referring either to himself, or to those to whom he was preaching, to all men everywhere, that is, the dead as well as those yet to be born. There is a real difficulty, certainly, for us today in understanding such a view as this, only the difficulty is of a religious nature. As soon as we assume a view of man in himself as a creation of God, possessing nothing which has not come from God, and destined by the Creator for eternal life, we find that there are no insoluble difficulties connected with the concept of man which was held in the early Church. Certainly, we shall have to take time and trouble to understand it, but our whole understanding of man and everything connected with him is itself bound up with our belief in Creation. If we find that we are conceiving of man instinctively as being an isolated individual among other isolated individuals, we are proceeding on the assumption that the ground of his existence is something other than God. In this kind of individualistic view there is a difficulty in making any reference to Christ as Saviour.[74] The universal application of the work of Christ and its alteration of the status of the whole of humanity is a quite incomprehensible idea apart from the view of mankind as a unity, and the idea of man as having been created and destined for eternity. This understanding of man does not add any new difficulty to those which already exist in our comprehension of man, but is simply one of the assumptions which the Christian faith makes.

There is a helpful metaphor in Wilhelm Hunger where he says that Irenaeus regards mankind as a river—seen, however, not from the bank at a certain point in its course, and later seen again at another point from the bank, but seen at a glance from the source right down to the river-mouth, the same river all the way, and the same water with the same name.[75] The history of Adam is fulfilled only at the Consummation.[76] This aspect of the Irenaean anthropology will become a little clearer when we examine the statements in which he refers to a man as a *child*.

"A Child"

Both in the **Adversus haereses** and the **Epideixis** Irenaeus declares that man, as God created him, is a *child*. . . . His statements have frequently been noted, without any great importance being attached to them. These passages, however, are directly connected with a concept which is fundamental in Irenaeus, the concept of man "growing," of man as one who is constantly developing, or who ought to be so. By trying to discover what it means to speak of man as a child in Creation we shall succeed in avoiding a hard-and-fast attitude in the analysis of the term *recapitulatio*. It is clear from what we have already seen above that Irenaeus conceives of recapitulation, or Christ's work of salvation, as a restoration of Creation, a return to man's original state. Against this, however, a number of different statements have been adduced from Irenaeus in which he maintains that Christ completes Creation, making it into something better and richer than it had ever been from the beginning. There would appear, then, to be an inconsistency between this perfectionist view, and the kind of statement which is frequently repeated in Irenaeus, that what we lost in Adam we recover in Christ.[77] It is difficult to reconcile the pattern of *loss and recovery* with that of *imperfect beginning to perfection,* and it is only too clear that one cannot lose what one has never possessed. It was at this particular point, the double aspect in the concept of recapitulation, that H. H. Wendt put a wedge into the theology of Irenaeus, a wedge which was intended to prove to Irenaean scholars conclusively that the theology of Irenaeus consisted of at least two disconnected parts.[78] Perhaps the assumption must be that it was only in the nineteenth century that this dichotomy was revealed! Two distinguishable parts there are indeed in the Irenaean concept of recapitulation, but the unity which unites the two parts consists of the concept of *child* and the concept of *growth.*

If we take as an example a child's power of speech, it is not in the least illogical to argue that one may lose what one has never had. An accident may deprive a child of the power of speech before it has reached the age when it occasionally spoke a few words. If, however, the child which suffered from such a defect were cured by medical skill, the recovery of its health would be evidenced by the fact that it spoke, by doing something, that is, which it had never done before the accident occurred. The child recovers its power of speech which it never had. In this phrase "power of speech" there is a certain variation of meaning, but it is exactly this kind of variation which is characteristic of Irenaeus, and which is a quite different thing from maintaining that Irenaeus's thought proceeds on two different lines.[79] The same thing happens when Irenaeus deals with the concept of *growth,* and attempts to demonstrate that the full-grown man is exactly the same being as the undeveloped man, and yet is something completely different, because he has *grown* and become something different. In Irenaeus the thought vacillates between identity and change, and is continually fluctuating between the two.[80] The historian of dogma who, in dealing with this kind of problem, merely states that there is a general confusion, is justified in saying so provided that he himself clearly demonstrates how man's *growth* is to be interpreted, for what Irenaeus was attempting to undertake was nothing less than the interpretation of words such as *grow, growth,* and

so on, terms which, for an interpretation of man, are central to the New Testament.[81]

Bonwetsch points out that Irenaeus never speaks of man as being "perfect" in his "original state,"[82] and while he is quite correct in what he says, I think it would be better to give up this rigid scheme with its three or four "states" which was so characteristic of later Scholasticism, both on the Roman Catholic and the Protestant side.[83] A theology of man's "original state" does not emerge before the controversy between Augustine and Pelagianism, and before that time we find hardly any account of the first paradisiacal world and its perfect man.[84] When Irenaeus refrains from saying that the man whom God created was perfect, he has no intention of repudiating any elaborate theory of perfection, and consequently no suggestion that there was any weakness, want, or mortality in Adam.[85] The line is clear: death came through *sin*—every hurt in the life of man has its source in mankind's primal adversary, in evil, and disobedience. But on the other hand the yielding to temptation and defeat is so intimately associated with Adam that the only remaining contribution of the first man to the human race is his Fall, and his introduction of death into the world of men. Mortality thus is characteristic of original man, without itself having been created by God. Mortality is not of itself involved in the concept of *son,* but is a work of sin and the Serpent against the Commandment of God.[86]

This point is made clear in the **Epideixis,** in which it is maintained that the first two human beings were sinless and child-like, and were so because they had been created by God.[87] But having said this, Irenaeus goes on immediately to stress that there is a gulf which separates man from God, a gulf which has been made by the Creator Himself; and that in contrast to God man has a Lord over him, and a Will imposed upon his own. One expression for the dominion which the Creator has over His created child is the *Commandments* of God. At once, therefore, the ethical factor comes into the foreground at this point, in the sense of a regulated conduct of life from man's side, namely the Law.[88] From the very first Irenaeus connects life, that is, the physical factor, with the Commandments, the ethical, and continues to do so throughout his thinking. If man were to live in accordance with the Commandments he would continue in the state in which he once was, *that is, he would be immortal,* for obedience and life belong together.[89] Had he violated God's Commandment *he would become subject to death and be resolved into dust,* for sin and death belong together. Man is free, and can acquire any power at all, life as well as death. If "mortality" means that the possibility of death as well (through sin) remains open, then man is mortal from the time he leaves God's hand, since Irenaeus is always firm in maintaining that man is free and created free through the power of God.[90] Irenaeus, however, does not usually refer to this as mortality, but, on the contrary, man plunges into mortality when he yields to the temptation of disobedience. The man who chooses evil, says Irenaeus, or who gives up the struggle between good and evil, destroys himself in his inner man—"latenter semetipsum occidit hominem."[91]

We may now note here in parenthesis that just as the physical and the ethical are connected in relation to life or death for mankind in Creation, the same combination recurs in recapitulation. Christ defeats death by resisting temptation in the wilderness and on the Cross. The "physical" resurrection proceeds from the "ethical" death on the Cross. But Christ's ethical purity is consequent also on the fact that God dwells in Him. Christ's ethical works have their source in the physical Incarnation. And the man who receives the Spirit gains thereby an attitude to his neighbour which is induced by God, and which corresponds to the Commandment, *and* he gains everlasting life in the resurrection from the dead. The Church is to be understood as a creative ethical force in the non-Christian society simply because it is Christ's martyred Body which awaits the resurrection of the dead, the physical miracle. The Christian believer's participation in Christ consists as much in the willingness of the mind to obey Christ's commandment of love, as in the enjoyment which the body has in the bread and wine of the Eucharist. If the sharp distinction between physical and ethical, which was at one time customary in the history of dogma, is applied to Irenaeus, the result does not tend to clarify, but rather to confuse. All this, of course, is by the way,[92] and we may now return to what Irenaeus has to say about man as a child.

It is significant that in his description of the Fall of Adam Irenaeus can co-ordinate two separate expressions: one, that the first man lost through sin his natural character and his child-like mind, and the other, that he lost the garment of holiness which he possessed by the Spirit.[93] The same thing is expressed in both of these statements. The gift of the Spirit is *child-likeness.* When Irenaeus deals later with the concept of the Church there is, therefore, an indissoluble connexion between the Spirit and sonship. The Spirit, bestowed by Christ, makes us anew the children of God. It is, therefore, hardly correct to speak, as Brunner does, of man, in the view of Irenaeus, as being sealed by his condition as a "child" in such a way that his distinctive mark is *innocence, not righteousness.*[94] If we set innocence and righteousness over against one another, then we must necessarily think of righteousness as being the sum of a series of righteous works. But righteousness is rather the unbroken receiving of life from the "hands" of the Creator; it is man's acquiescence in his own creation and not his self-willed resistance to God. Righteousness is involved in man's status as a child, for righteousness can scarcely be anything other than the "garment of righteousness," which the child possesses "by the Spirit."[95] God's act of creation and His continuing activity among men are implied in the concept of νμπιος.

We have just seen that for Irenaeus man's growth is an immediate consequence of God's act of creation. The cessation of man's growth would be the same as the cessation of God's creativity, and we should be left with a powerless, passive and unmoved God. A direct corollary of the concept of sonship is the concept of *growth.* It is a distinctive characteristic of the child that he grows and becomes. This is exactly the same idea as the one which we saw above: man is created in the *imago* and *similitudo* of God, but he is not God's *imago* and *similitudo*—only the eternal Son is that, and only He possesses the whole of God's fulness in Himself. Man is created for the Son, and he attains to his perfection in the Son. His destiny was realised only when the image of God took human life in the Incarnation and took up into Himself the man who had been created in the image of God. The Incarnation and its benefits had no reality when man was first created: man, therefore, is a child, a son, whose goal and objective is full growth. In this idea of growth, however, we are not to discern any trace of the suggestion that man's initial condition, his life as a child, was in any way inherently sinful; it was characterised simply by the fact that man is *created,* and being created he lacks the divinity and perfection of the Son.[96]

Since Irenaeus sees man's goal lying in his conformity to the image of God, that is, to Christ, a conformity to which man attains only in the eternal Kingdom, the whole of the Christian life becomes a pilgrimage towards this goal. That which God presents to man through Christ is perfect in itself, but the man who receives it and incorporates it into himself is imperfect and in the process of growth. Whatever man may be given, and however high and holy may be everything that the Church bestows on him, yet, anything that man takes into himself is *eo ipso* limited and finite—man is "on the way," not at his destined goal. It has to be clearly remembered throughout that in the Irenaean concept of growth there is first and foremost an emphasis on the smallness of man and the greatness of God—but on the greatness of God as Creator, that is, the bestower of inexhaustible gifts. Man's growth has its source in the power of God. There is a gulf fixed between God and man, but this gulf is transformed into an increasingly close relationship, not because man is what he is, capable of increase and growth, but because God is what He is, good and powerful. The modern concept of a growth that is entirely from within the growing self, while benefits are bestowed from outside, is alien to Irenaeus. His concept of growth is well conveyed by the words which Paul uses of the grain: "But God gives it a body as he has chosen" (1 Cor. xv.38). Any growth from the grain is the *creation of God,* the gift of God. The power to bestow growth lies beyond man and beyond the grain of wheat, in "God who gives the growth" (1 Cor. III.7).

Man's growth is thus not simply a work, a consequence of God's act of creation, but actually *is* God's act of creation, exactly the same reality as God's creation, though seen from a different angle.[97] When theologians of a later period speak of man's spiritual growth, his inward progression is generally understood as a development of the latent powers of the personality, and the consequence of this particular view is the conception of old age and death as being, by their own evidence, the cessation of this growth. Irenaeus speaks of death in this simple and natural kind of way as standing somewhere in the middle of man's growth, in his exposition of the adoption as sons which is given to us through Christ. There is nothing of an idealistic development of personality in this expression of Irenaeus: the personality *dies,* man dies, just as the grain in the earth dies in order to "grow," to rise, to be created by God, and as Christ was crucified and put to death in order that He might rise from the dead as the Prince of Life. Irenaeus conceives of man's growth, that is, as a growing together with Christ, who is the image of God. By this he does not imply that there is any imitation of the life which Christ led and His development of the life He lived within the compass of the years He spent on earth. Rather, Irenaeus would have us keep our attention fixed on the two quite definite points of Christ's *death* and His *Resurrection,* the two points which have shattered the modern immanent and romantic idea of Jesus, and which transfer man's goal from the development of his personality to the resurrection of the dead. For this reason, therefore, growth takes place at the time of martyrdom, when Christians are torn in pieces by wild animals or burned to ashes. It is at the point of martyrdom that man is formed in the *imago* and *similitudo* of God, brought into communnion with the dead Christ, and his participation in the Body of Christ becomes a reality.[98]

In the view of growth which we have here put forward there are several conceptions, the examination of which we must put off till later, since there is involved in them the idea of the growth which sinful and fallen man resumes again because of the sustenance he derives from Christ, the Incarnate one. It would, however, be appropriate even at this point to say a few words about this whole idea, since only so will the significance of the concept of "child" become perfectly clear. But the point at issue is that as long as man had not yielded to the Serpent's temptation to disobey God, there was no sin in the world, and therefore no death. In this section, however, we are dealing only with the starting-point of growth in God's Creation, with man as an innocent, though at this initial stage living, child.

In order that we may have some understanding of what follows later, there is one other subject which we must at least mention, and that is one aspect of Irenaeus's doctrine of freewill. The essential principle in the concept of freedom appears first in Christ's status as the sovereign Lord, because for Irenaeus man's freedom is, strangely enough, a direct expression of God's omnipotence, so direct, in fact, that a diminution of man's freedom automatically involves a corresponding diminution of God's omnipotence. This fundamental emphasis in Irenaeus's doctrine of freedom is bound up with his attack on the Gnostic classification of men, according to which the "pneumatics" are saved, while the "hylics" are destroyed, on the basis of their respective substances—God is powerless before this predestination from below, and can only watch passively while man's substance divides itself according to its own inherent quality into worldly and unworldly, spirit and matter. This Gnostic heresy provides us with the background of Irenaeus's characteristic statements about freedom, by which he makes man's freedom a direct expression of God's saving power, God's power of using man's freedom to break through all classifications of men and in

Christ to free every man who believes. But this main aspect of freedom must not occupy our attention here, for it is another side of freedom with which we are concerned at this point, namely freedom as a condition for temptation and defeat.

Man is free because he has been created by the power of God to be free. He cannot be driven to take one course of action or another by some external, mechanical force or compulsion, as though he were simply an object or a creature, but has rather to will what he does from inside himself; in so far as he does so he resembles God, his Creator, whose nature is freedom. This human freedom corresponds closely to God's dealings with men both through the Commandment which was given at the very beginning of Creation, and through the Gospel which was given at the Incarnation, and which, before Christ, existed in the form of the promise. The intent of the Law is free obedience, while the intent of the Gospel or the promise is free faith, and also obedience to God's will. But man's freedom is also expressed in the possibility that he may reject both the Commandment and the promise in his disbelief or disobedience.[99] Time and time again we find the stress in Irenaeus on the fact that whole of God's revelation has this open and unconditional character. It is a revelation to *all* Creation, and on the day of Judgement, when the whole world, in spite of the fact that God's revelation has been disclosed to all, is divided and assigned to blessing or to curse, those who have rejected His revelation will be held responsible. In this regard there are consequently two related ideas involved in Irenaeus's concept of freedom, first, the idea of revelation for all in the time of grace— whether it is in Creation, in Moses, or in Christ, God's revelation is everywhere open and has been universally proclaimed—and second, the Last Judgement, in which every man will be judged by the clear revelation which God granted to him, whether that revelation was complete or limited. God's judgement is just because man is free, and man's disobedience involves guilt. His ultimate destiny is not determined from within himself by his inalienable substance.

We might well look at the comparisons and problems which Irenaeus avoided, such as, for instance, the contrast between free will and grace, and his attempt to detail their respective contributions in the deliverance of man from the power of his superior enemy. Man is held captive by the Serpent, and Christ alone bruises the Serpent's head. Besides this, Irenaeus has also refrained from putting the speculative question of how the Fall might have originated, and then solving the problem with the help of free will. As we saw earlier on in describing the omnipotence and inscrutability of God, Irenaeus quite clearly and expressly avoids putting the problem in this way. He proceeds from man's actual temptation and establishes as a fact man's actual defeat, and farther on proceeds from man's actual bondage to Satan and establishes his actual deliverance through Christ. Man who falls and is delivered has been created by God. He is a free man. He was not forced, mechanically, into sin, but rather allowed himself to be dragged into sin; nor is he forced, mechanically, out of his imprisonment by the victory of Christ, but rather is freed from his bonds and can now go anywhere he wants—out into freedom in Christ, or back into bondage to the Devil. But since through all that happens to him, from Creation to the Last Judgement, he remains *man*, he has the responsibility for everything that he does from first to last. However he may deprive himself, God retains His power. God alone possesses power, and this is demonstrated by the fact that at the moment man turns from being the child of God to being the captive of the Devil he moves from life to death. Man's new lord is stronger than himself, but he is not strong enough to be able to create. He has only one thing to offer—death.

Notes

1. See the whole discussion in *A.h.* from II. i. 1 to II. xxii. 5 (Stier. II. i. 1-xvii. 11). The passage II. x. 2 (Stier. II. x. 4) deals with matter: "Attribuere enim substantiam eorum quae facta sunt virtuti et voluntati ejus qui est omnium Deus, et credibile et acceptabile et constans et in hoc bene diceretur: quoniam quae impossibilia sunt apud homines, possibilia sunt apud Deum; quoniam homines quidem de nihilo non possunt aliquid facere, sed de materia subjacenti: Deus autem quam homines hoc primo melior, eo quod materiam fabricationis suae cum ante non esset ipse adinvenit." Cf. II. xlvi. 1-4 (Stier. II. xxx. 1-5) and the important argument for the resurrection of the body in v. iv (Stier. v. iv. 2). The proposition that God is the source of all things occurs also in the *Epideixis*, e.g. in *Epid.* 4. There are two monographs on the concept of God, one by Johannes Kunze, *Die Gotteslehre des Irenaeus*, Leipzig 1891, which has a commendable emphasis on God's creative power, but which decidedly overestimates the philosophical aspect in Irenaeus. The other book is the longer *God in Patristic Thought*, London 1936, a textbook of liturgical study by G. L. Prestige, which also deals with Irenaeus. See, e.g., the discussion in this work on p. 46 f. of God as *agennetos* and *agenetos* in Irenaeus, and cf. on the whole discussion Bonwetsch, *Theologie des Irenäus*, pp. 53-5.

2. "Nec enim indigebat horum Deus ad faciendum quae ipse apud se praefinierat fieri, quasi ipse suas non haberet manus. Adest enim ei semper Verbum et Sapientia, Filius et Spiritus, per quos, et in quibus omnia libere et sponte fecit," *A.h.* IV. xxxiv. 1 (Stier. IV. xx. 1). See also IV. xiv (Stier. IV. vii. 4), and cf. Joseph Barbel, "Christos Angelos," in *Theophaneia*, VOL. III, Bonn 1941, p. 64.

3. In Loofs, *Theophilus von Antiochen*, pp. 16 ff. this "pre-temporal Trinity" is treated as a concept unknown to Irenaeus himself, but see Montgomery Hitchcock in *J.T.S.*, 1937, pp. 131-4.

4. *Epid.* 43, *St Irenaeus, The Apostolic Preaching*, ed. J. Armitage Robinson, pp. 108 ff. Cf. *Epid.* 52, and several other references from 40 to 52. Another important New Testament reference to this is Col. I.15 f.

5. The thought of the Son as being the first-born before the whole of Creation, and the One in whom everything has been created, is inseparably linked with the idea that everything is to be judged by the Son. See *Epid.* 48.

6. Cf. E. Scharl in *Orientalia*, 1940, p. 387, and Adolf Harnack, *Lehrbuch der Dogmengeschichte*, 4th edn., Tübingen 1909, VOL. I, p. 584, Eng. trans. of 2nd German edn., *History of Dogma*, London 1899, VOL. II, p. 263.

7. "Cum enim praeexisteret salvans, oportebat et quod salvaretur fieri, uti non vacuum sit salvans," *A.h.* III. xxii. 1 (Stier. III. xxii. 3). This passage has been the cause of a lively discussion which I propose to deal with in a different connexion. Cf. III. xix. 1 (Stier. III. xviii. 1), IV. xi. 5 (Stier. IV. vi. 7), and the important passage on Christ as *in universa conditione infixus* in v. xviii. 2 (Stier. v. xviii. 3).

8. Cullmann, *Earliest Christian Confessions*, p. 51.

9. Loofs, *Theophilus von Antiochien*, pp. 347 f., 393, holds that the idea of the pre-existent Logos-Son, belongs to "Irenaeus selbst" and is not characteristic (p. 444) of early Christianity. Ernst Barnikol makes a determined attempt to eliminate the concept of pre-existence from the New Testament in his *Apostolische und neutestamentliche Dogmengeschichte als Vor-Dogmengeschichte*, 4th edn. Halle 1938, pp. 57 ff. The relevant passages in Irenaeus are carefully scrutinised and stated by Bonwetsch, *Theologie des Irenäus*, pp. 62-6.

10. Cf. Harnack, *History of Dogma*, VOL. I, pp. 797-806; R. Liechtenhan, *Die göttliche Vorherbestimmung bei Paulus und in der posidonianischen Philosophie*, henceforth cited as *Göttliche Vorherbestimmung*, Göttingen 1922, pp. 17-24, 122-4; and Cullmann, *Christ and Time*, e.g. pp. 70, 91. See *Epid.* 67 (beginning).

11. "Nihil enim in totum diabolus invenitur fecisse, videlicet cum et ipse creatura sit Dei, quemadmodum et reliqui angeli. Omnia enim fecit Deus," *A.h.* IV. lxvi. 2 (Stier. IV. xli. 1). There is a general reference to the power of God in comparison with the power of the creature . . . *A.h.* v. v. 3 (Stier. v. v. 2). On the idea of the risen Christ as still awaiting the hour appointed by the Father, cf. *Epid.* 85.

12. "Facere enim proprium est benignitatis Dei: fieri autem proprium est hominis naturae," *A.h.* IV. lxiv. 2 (Stier. IV. xxxix. 2). Cf. Louis Escoula, "Le verbe sauveur et illuminateur chez Saint Irénée," in *Nouvelle revue théologique*, henceforth cited as *N.R.T.*, 1939, pp. 393 ff.; see further *A.h.* IV. xxv. 1-2 (Stier. IV. xiv. 1-2) and esp. IV. xxi. 2 (Stier. IV. xi. 2).

13. K. Prümm, "Göttliche Planung und menschliche Entwicklung nach Irenäus *Adversus haereses*, in *Scholastik*, 1938, p. 208; cf. p. 350.

14. *A.h.* IV. xix. 2 (Stier. IV. ix. 3) and IV. xxxiv. 6-7 (Stier. IV. xx. 6-7).

15. *A.h.* IV. xliv. 2 (Stier. IV. xxviii. 2).

16. *A.h.* II. xli. 4 (Stier. II. xxviii. 3) and II. xlii. 3-xliii. 2 (Stier. II. xxviii. 6-7).

17. . . . *A.h.* II. xl. 1 (Stier. II. xxvii. 1); cf. II. xli. 4 (Stier. II. xxviii. 3).

18. *A.h.* IV. xxxiii (Stier. IV. xix. 2-3). This fundamental "hiddenness" is not given a clear enough emphasis in Friedrich Böhringer's analysis of the doctrine of the Devil in Irenaeus, *Die Kirche Christi und ihre Zeugen,* henceforth cited as *Kirche Christi,* 2nd edn. Stuttgart 1873, VOL. II, pp. 476-8. Cf. in this connexion Herrera, *S. Irénée de Lyon exégète,* pp. 139-46.

19. For the distinction between these two types of theology, see Damien van den Eynde, *Les Normes de l'enseignement chrétien dans la litérature patristique des trois premiers siècles,* henceforth cited as *Normes de l'enseignement,* Gembloux and Paris 1933, pp. 132-41. Cf. Lietzmann, *Church Universal,* p. 214 f.

20. *A.h.* II. xlix. 1 (Stier. II. xxxii. 2). Cf. Andreas Bigelmair, *Die Beteiligung der Christen am öffentlichen Leben in vorconstantinischer Zeit,* Munich 1902, pp. 296-8, 327. Note too the original illustration of the unpractised wrestler who is booed by the audience. *A.h.* v. xiii. 2 (Stier. ibid.).

21. *A.h.* IV. vi-vii (Stier. IV. iv. 2-3).

22. *A.h.* II. xlvii. 2 (Stier. II. xxx. 8). Creation is not finished but still continues. There is a more exhaustive treatment of the belief in Creation in my essay "Skapelsen, lagen, och inkarnationen enlight Irenaeus" ("Creation, the Law, and the Incarnation according to Irenaeus"), in *S.T.K.,* 1940, pp. 133 ff.

23. ". . . et propter hoc ait: Mittens exercitus suos: quoniam omnis homo, secundum quod est homo, plasma ipsius est, licet ignoret Deum suum", *A.h.* IV. lviii. 8 (Stier. IV. xxxvi. 6).

24. *A.h.* III. xxxix, God as the One who directs all men and gives His counsel to the leaders of the heathen (Stier. III. xxv. 1). The destruction of Jerusalem took place according to the will of God, and the fall of Jerusalem and the beginning of the Church are two stages in the same process, the supersession of the old Covenant by the new.

25. *A.h.* IV. xlvi (Stier. IV. xxx). This does not prevent Irenaeus from applying the principles of the Apocalypse to the State, but in negative statements of this sort he is not concerned with what the heathen State produces from the *good of the earth.* Jahveh gave His own people jewels of silver through the Egyptians who were evil, and from whose power His people were on the point of being liberated. The Church now is Israel. Linked up with this is a double view of the surrounding heathen State.

26. ". . . non quasi mundus alienus sit a Deo, sed quoniam hujusmodi dationes ab aliis accipientes habemus, similiter velut illi ab Aegyptiis qui non sciebant Deum," *A.h.* IV. xlvi. 3 (Stier. IV. xxx. 3). The attack on the narrative in Exodus came from the Gnostics who were looking for signs of the discreditable nature of the Old Testament demiurge.

27. The figures in Harvey and Stieren coincide in this chap.

28. *A.h.* v. xxiv. 1. He cites passages from Prov. and Rom. XIII.

29. *A.h.* v. xxi. 2-v. xxiii. 2. This important combination of ideas is unfortunately neglected by Jean Rivière in *Le dogme de la rédemption, Études critiques et documents,* henceforth cited as *Dogme de la rédemption,* Louvain 1931, in which he attempts to establish what Irenaeus means by saying that the Devil is defeated *juste,* pp. 137-41. See III. xxxii. 2 (Stier. III. xxiii. 1).

30. *A.h.* v. xxiv. 3.

31. *A.h.* v. xxiv. 2. It is continually stressed that God and the Devil are the two protagonists, and mankind lies between these two.

32. *A.h.* v. xxiv. 3.

33. "Et propter hoc etiam ipsi magistratus indumentum justitiae leges habentes, quaecumque juste et legitime fecerint, de his non interrogabuntur, neque poenas dabunt. Quaecumque autem ad eversionem justi, inique et impie et contra legem, et more tyrannico exercuerint, in his et peribunt; justo judicio Dei ad omnes aequaliter perveniente, et in nullo deficiente," *A.h.* v. xxiv. 2; cf. v. xxiv. 3 and also *Epid.* 8.

34. *A.h.* III. xl. 3 (Stier. III. xxv. 4).

35. Montgomery Hitchcock in his above-named work, *Irenaeus of Lugdunum,* p. 278, and the same author's forthright article "The Doctrine of the Holy Communion in Irenaeus," in the *Church Quarterly Review,* henceforth cited as *C.Q.R.,* 1939-40, p. 213, in which he represents Irenaeus as a good Anglican receptionist, pp. 220 f., 225. See the criticism even in J. Werner, *Der Paulinismus des Irenaeus,* p. III f.

36. *A.h.* IV. xxix. 5 (Stier. IV. xvii. 5).

37. Cf. *A.h.* IV. xxxi. 3 (Stier. IV. xviii. 4), and see also the unusual passage in *Epid.* 57 with its exuberant imagery.

38. See *A.h.* v. ii (Stier. v. ii. 2-3) and cf. H.-D. Simonin, "A propos d'un texte eucharistique de S. Irénée," in *Revue des sciences philosophique et théologique,* henceforth cited as *Rev. des sciences,* 1934, pp. 286 f., and *A.h.* III. xi. 9 (Stier. III. xi. 5) and IV. li. 1 (Stier. IV. xxxii. 2).

39. See Anders Nygren, *Den kristna Kärlekstanken genom tiderna,* Stockholm 1936, VOL. II, pp. 190-205, Eng. trans. *Agape and Eros,* London 1953, VOL. II, pp. 276-88.

40. Cf. *A.h.* v. iii. 3 (Stier. ibid.).

41. Karl Prümm, *Christentum als Neuheitserlebnis,* Freiburg-im-Breisgau 1939, p. 64.

42. Gen. 1.26 is not often quoted in the Apostolic Fathers; for other literature of the early Church see the

commentary on *Die apostolischen Vater*, ed. K. Bihlmeyer, VOL. III, Hans Windisch, *Der Barnabasbrief*, Tübingen 1920, p. 328 (Barn. v. 5), and Montgomery Hitchcock in *Z.NT.W.*, 1937, p. 56. Later on we shall have the opportunity of mentioning a passage in Tertullian and two in the Apostolic Fathers.

43. Cf. F. Vernet's article "Irénée" in *Dictionnaire de théologie catholique*, VOL. VII, PT. II, Paris 1923, p. 2452 f. and the excellent discussion by Wilhelm Hunger, "Der Gedanke der Weltplaneinheit und Adameinheit in der Theologie des hl. Irenäus," in *Scholastik*, 1942, pp. 167-76.

44. *A.h.* I. i. 10 (Stier. I. v. 5); cf. I. xi. 2 (Stier, I xviii. 2).

45. Prümm in *Scholastik*, 1938, p. 213 and Emil Brunner, *Der Mensch im Widerspruch*, 3rd edn. Zürich 1941, p. 523, Eng. trans. *Man in Revolt*, London 1939, p. 503 f. (a description of A. Struker's book which I do not have available, *Die Gottebenbildlichkeit des Menschen in der urchristlichen Literatur der esrten zwei Jahrhunderte*, 1913). Cf. Klebba, *Anthropologie des hl. Irenaeus*, p. 23 f.

46. So also, for example, Bousset, *Kyrios Christos*, p. 437; see however p. 443 with its interpretation of Paul that was characteristic of that period. More recently E. Käsemann, *Leib und Leib Christi*, Tübingen 1933—see pp. 81 ff, 147 ff., 163 ff.—admittedly has maintained that in his use of the term *eikon* and related words Paul came under the Gnostic influence. On the question of speculation in general within Gnosticism on primitive man see W. Bousset, *Hauptprobleme der Gnosis*, Göttingen 1907, pp. 160-203; and C. H. Kraeling, *Anthropos and Son of Man*, New York 1927, pp. 17 ff; and also Jonas, *Gnosis*, pp. 344-51. With regard to Paul cf. Ernst Lohmeyer, *Die Briefe an die Philipper, an die Kolosser und an Philemon*, henceforth cited as *Briefe*, Göttingen 1930, pp. 55, 140 (On Col. I. 15 and III. 10).

47. See Nygren, *Pauli brev till Romarna*, Stockholm 1944, pp. 214-19, Eng. trans. *Commentary on Romans*, Philadelphia 1949, pp. 218-24, 232 f. Against this background the individuality of Irenaeus stands out with the greatest clarity. He takes up for discussion a subject which in the N.T. is a subsidiary one. Cf. Franz Stoll, *Lehre des hl. Irenäus*, pp. 40, 51.

48. See Heinrich Schlier, "Vom Menschenbild des Neuen Testaments" in the volume of essays entitled *Der alte und der neue Mensch*, Munich 1942, p. 25, and Edmund Schlink, "Gottes Ebenbild als Gesetz und Evangelium" *op cit.*, pp. 79 ff.; cf. p. 83 where Irenaeus is mentioned with others as one who laid a theological foundation in his doctrine of *imago* and *similitudo*. Brunner's massive work of Christian anthropology, *Man in Revolt*, London 1939, which first appeared (in German) in 1937, had probably both a positive and a negative influence on this compilation referred to—in both books the idea of *imago* occupies a prominent place. It is remarkable that this important Pauline concept is left completely unexam-

ined in a volume which appeared three years before Brunner's, Walter Gutbrod's *Die Paulinische Anthropologie*, Stuttgart 1934.

49. E.g. *A.h.* v. xxi. 1-2 (Stier. ibid.).

50. Ibid. See also *A.h.* III. 30 (Stier. III. xxi. 10).

51. Tertullian, *Opera*, ed. E. Kroymann, PT. III, *De resurrectione carnis*, Bonn 1906, p. 33. Loofs has a detailed exegesis of the text, "Das altkirchliche Zeugnis gegen die herrschende Auffassung der Kenosisstelle," in *Theol. Stud. u. Krit.*, 1927-8, pp. 44 ff.; note that Loofs punctuates the text differently from Kroymann, which is also of importance for the theological explanation of the passage in question. Tertullian is here expounding Gen. I. 26 f., among other passages. The same passage was referred to for illustration by Irenaeus in Klebba, *Anthropologie des hl. Irenaeus*, p. 25. Similar passages are found in Hippolytus and in two other places in the writings of Tertullian.

52. Cf. Harnack, *History of Dogma*, VOL. II, p. 283, n. 2, where the passage referred to in Tertullian is similarly touched on.

53. Loofs, *Theophilus von Antiochien*, pp. 135, 253 f.

54. *Op. cit.*, pp. 288, 446 f. On "*Irenaeus selbst*" as the mechanically operating co-writer, see p. 355. Loofs's view of pre-existence in the N.T. appears on p. 444 f., n. 2. Cf. too his lengthy article mentioned above in *Theol. Stud. u. Krit.*, 1927-8, pp. 3 ff. on Phil. II. 5-11.

55. On this idea in general cf. Liechtenhan, *Göttliche Vorherbestimmung*, pp. 114-16, and with ref. to Irenaeus see Escoula in *Nouvelle revue théologique*, 1939, where, however, he accentuates the idea of predestination with all the emphasis on one side, pp. 387 ff., 395. If we are to represent Irenaeus correctly, the characteristic of sin as disobedience to God must not be obscured. The Irenaean view cannot be satisfactorily described if we do not bear in mind that according to Irenaeus there are certain matters of which we do not have any knowledge. Among these is the reason for the Fall. It can be demonstrated pragmatically that sin is a positive reality, an act of resistance which is defeated by God in Christ.

56. Scharl makes this clear in *Orientalia*, 1940, pp. 390-2; cf. Hugo Koch in *Theol. Stud. u. Krit.*, 1925, p. 211.

57. *Epid.* 22. Cf. *Epid.* 11 and 55.

58. See *A.h.* III. xxxi. 1 (Stier. III. xxi. 1) and III. xxxii. 1 (Stier. III. xxii. 3), and also IV. xi. 5 (Stier. IV. vi. 7), where Irenaeus lays stress on the fact that from the very beginning of Creation it is through the Son that God acts and reveals Himself. On the textual variants of the last-quoted passage see Loofs, *Theophilus von Antiochien*, p. 381, n. 1.

59. Cf. *A.h.* II. xlii. 2 (Stier. II. xxviii. 4) and—even more pronouncedly—v. iii. 1 (Stier. ibid.). See Bonwetsch, *Theologie des Irenänus*, pp. 104-7.

60. "Quomodo autem eum qui adversus homines fortis erat, qui non solum vicit hominem, sed et detinebat eum sub sua potestate, devicit, et eum quidem qui vicerat vicit, eum vero qui victus fuerat hominem dimisit, nisi superior fuisset eo homine qui fuerat victus? Melior autem eo homine qui secundum similitudinem Dei factus est, et praecellentior quisnam sit alius nisi Filius Dei, ad cujus similitudinem factus est homo? Et propter hoc in fine ipse ostendit similitudinem, Filius Dei factus est homo, antiquam plasmationem in semetipsum suscipiens," *A.h.* IV. lii. 1 (Stier. IV. xxxiii. 4). Cf. *A.h.* IV. xxii. 1 (Stier. ibid.). In the quotation given here the simple *similitudo* is quite typically used as being synonymous with *imago et similitudo*.

61. *A.h.* IV. Pref. iii (Stier. IV. Pref. iv) and IV. xxxiv. 1 (Stier. IV. xx. 1) Cf. v. xv. 2-xvi. 1 (Stier. v. xv. 2-xvi. 2) and v. xxviii. 3 (Stier. v. xxviii. 4) where he also speak of the *manus Dei*, but where it is God's acts through the Son or the Spirit in the Incarnation and the Church which are referred to.

62. Of the passages referred to in the previous note, v. xv. 2 ff., e.g., refers to God's *hand* (the Son) whereas the other passages speak of God's *hands* (the Son and the Spirit).

63. *Epid.* 5. Cf. on the whole of this question Bonwetsch, *Theologie des Irenäus,* pp. 66 ff., and Scharl in *Orientalia,* 1940, p. 389; but see too p. 407: the subject of the verb *recapitulare* is always the Son, not the Spirit or the Father.

64. ". . . caro a Spiritu possessa oblita quidem sui, qualitatem autem Spiritus assumens, conformis facta Verbo Dei," *A.h.* v. ix. 2 (Stier. v. ix. 3); cf. v. ix. 1 (Stier. ibid.).

65. See Paul Gächter, "Unsere Einheit mit Christus nach dem hl. Irenäus," in *Zeitschrift für katholische Theologie,* henceforth cited as *Z.K.T.,* 1934, p. 526.

66. *A.h.* v. viii. 1 (Stier. ibid.). Note how Irenaeus consistently avoids saying that man *is* the image of God. The resurrection is also the perfection of the *body,* which reaches its fulfillment only then.

67. See lastly in this connexion *A.h.* IV. xiv. (Stier. IV. vii. 4); and cf. on this much debated passage Léon Froidevaux, "Une difficulté du texte de S. Irénée," in *Revue de l'orient chrétien,* 1931-2, pp. 441-3. In this passage the Spirit is called God's *figuratio,* by which is meant God's creative power. Loofs, *Theophilus von Antiochien,* p. 14, n. 2, provides the most reliable interpretation of the text.

68. ". . . ut quod perideramus in Adam, id est, secundum imaginem et similitudinem esse Dei, hoc in Christo reciperemus," *A.h.* III. xix. 1 (Stier. III. xviii. 1). Cf. III. xxxii. 2 (Stier. III. xxiii. 1) and v. i. 1 (Stier. ibid.), and the last lines of v. xiv. 1 (Stier. ibid.).

69. ". . . neque vere nos redemit sanguine suo, si non vere homo factus est, restaurans suo plasmati quod

dictum est in principio, factum esse hominem secundum imaginem et similitudinem Dei," *A.h.* v. ii. 1 (Stier. ibid.).

70. *A.h.* v. ix. 1 (Stier. v. ix. 2). Only from this can v. vi. 1 (Stier. ibid.) be understood. Those who make a distinction in Irenaeus between the natural and the supernatural always fail to interpret these passages satisfactorily.

71. *A.h.* v. x. 1-2 (Stier. v. x. 1).

72. "Et in eo quod dicit, *Secundum imaginem conditoris,* recapitulationem manifestavit ejusdem hominis, qui in initio secundum imaginem factus est Dei," *A.h.* v. xii. 4 (Stier. ibid.).

73. Klebba, *Anthropologie des hl. Irenaeus,* approaches Irenaeus with this fundamental misunderstanding, which explains his frequent complaints that Irenaeus "mixes up" various things—see e.g.p. 22 f., 34. In referring to Irenaeus we should not even use the term "original state," since it tends to suggest a static scheme.

74. Cf. Nygren in *Corpus Christi* (En bok om kyrkan), Stockholm 1942, p. 18 f., on Adam and Christ as the two by whom the destiny of mankind is determined.

75. *Scholastik,* 1942, p. 170.

76. Hunger, *op. cit.,* pp. 171, 173, 176. The solidarity of all mankind in every age resides in men's common origin in God (Creation), and their common destiny (the Last Judgement), and therefore in both origin and destiny. Modern individualism is a direct consequence of the conception of man as a creature who exists for a certain length of time between birth and death, and no more. Individualism therefore concentrates on this period of time alone, this "life" which is held to have had a purely accidental origin and which comes to nothing at its end, but in doing so, individualism makes man into a creature existing wholly for himself.

77. Cf. above, note 68.

78. H. H. Wendt, *Die christliche Lehre von der menschlichen Vollkommenheit,* henceforth cited as *Christliche Lehre,* Göttingen 1882, pp. 26 ff. This is the source of all subsequent division of the theology of Irenaeus and his writings. Harnack, *History of Dogma,* VOL. II. p. 272 f., follows Wendt, and many more follow in Harnack's footsteps.

79. Irenaeus himself does not use the metaphor of power of speech, but it casts light on the Irenaean terminology as a whole. One might have chosen any of the abilities which a child possesses or does not possess. The full meaning of the language used by Irenaeus will not be seen until we have brought man's Fall into the discussion—the blow which strikes the child and injures it. We shall return to the point in the later chapter on Satan and man's defeat.

80. The dominion of sin is the interruption of man's growth, a contravention of nature, and death.

81. E.g. Eph. II. 21, III. 16, IV. 15 f., Col. II. 19; these passages should be connected with the idea of "growing together with Christ" in Rom. VI and the other related passages; and also I Jn. III. 2, which proceeds from the concept of *son,* and II Cor. IV. 16-18, and also II Cor. III. 18. The growing likeness to Christ in death and resurrection of Phil. III. 10 f., and III. 21 is an integral part of the same complex of New Testament ideas upon which Irenaeus worked vigorously.

82. Bonwetsch, *Theologie des Irenäus,* p. 74.

83. Klebba, *Anthropologie des hl. Irenaeus,* pp. 27 ff. takes this approach. Seven Silén, *Den kristna människouppfattningen intill Schleiermacher,* Stockholm 1938, pp. 70-3, adopts the theories of division propounded by Wendt and Harnack in his view of Irenaeus.

84. Cf. Antoine Slomkowski, *L'État primitif de l'homme dans la tradition de l'église avant Saint Augustin,* henceforth cited as *État primitif,* Paris 1928, in his summary on p. 143. This book does not go very deeply in its details, but is right in its main thesis. Cf. also O. Zöckler's more apologetic work, *Die Lehre vom Urstand des Menschen,* Gütersloh 1879, p. 41, an exposition which otherwise has as its dogmatic basis an unconcealed belief in evolution. See also Brunner, *Man in Revolt,* p. 84, n. 1; broadly speaking, Brunner's picture of Irenaeus is built on Klebba's book published in 1894.

85. Neither in *A.h.* IV. lxii-lxiii (Stier. IV. xxxviii) nor in *Epid.* 12 does Irenaeus think of death as being a part of God's Creation. When he says that man lacks perfection he is simply giving expression to the fact that man is *created,* and therefore he "grows," he "becomes," but he does not create like God. We must also take into account the fact that when Irenaeus speaks about Adam he is sometimes referring to fallen Adam, Adam who was conquered by the Devil, since there was nothing much that could be said about what Adam had done before the Fall: his first significant act was sin. See Reinhold Niebuhr, *The Nature and Destiny of Man,* London 1944, VOL. I, p. 296, and *A.h.* IV. xxiii. 2 (Stier. ibid.). But in so far as man's destiny is fixed by sin, passages like these say nothing about Creation—Creation, that is, which is intact, and which has its source in God.

86. This is obscured in Hugo Koch's description of Irenaeus's view in *Theol. Stud. u. Krit.,* 1925, pp. 209 ff. (cf. p. 201, n. 1), which in other respects contains some of the best material ever written on Irenaeus.

87. *Epid.* 14. On the term *child* cf. *Epid.* 46 and the beginning of 96.

88. *Epid.* 15.

89. Cf. Hermann Jordan, *Armenische Irenaeusfragmente,* Leipzig 1913, p. 129 f.: life and death are thought of as being in continual conflict. Jordan's compilation of fragments consists of a series of hypotheses with some useful observations interspersed among assumptions which he does not substantiate. On the continued discussion on his book cf. W. Ludtke, "Bemerkungen zu Irenäus," in *Z.NT.W.,* 1914, pp. 268 ff. and W. Durks, "Eine fälschlich dem Irenäus zugeschriebene Predigt des Bischofs Severian von Gabala," in *Z.NT.W.,* 1922, pp. 64 ff., which continues without very much evidence an idea suggested by Jordan, *op. cit.,* pp. 190 ff.

90. *Epid.* 11.

91. This passage comes into the context of *A.h.* IV. lxiv.1 (Stier. IV. xxxix. 1) abruptly, and is somewhat obscure; cf. v. i. 1 (Stier. ibid.) with its assertion that God, in His dealings with man, must also preserve his freedom, and v. viii. 1-2 (Stier. v. viii. 2) on the resemblance of the wicked man to the animal. Strangely enough this passage on self-destruction is seldom expounded; cf., however, J. A. Robinson's suggestions, "Notes on the Armenian Version of Irenaeus' *Adversus haereses,*" in *F.T.S.,* 1931, p. 377.

92. On the problem of *physical* and *ethical* in the early period in general see Brunner, *Der Mittler,* 2nd edn. Tübingen 1930, pp. 219-33, Eng. trans. *The Mediator,* London 1934, pp. 249-64, in which Irenaeus is specially dealt with, Folke Boström, *Studier till den grekiska teologins frälsningslära,* pp. 1-97, and in particular Ragnar Bring, "Till kritiken av Harnacks syn på den gammalkyrkliga frälsningsuppfattningen," in *S.T.K.,* 1933, pp. 232 ff., in which a penetrating criticism of both Brunner and Boström appears.

93. ". . . quoniam indolem et puerilem amiserat sensum, et in cogitationem pejorum venerat . . . Quoniam, inquit, eam quam habui a Spiritu sanctitatis stolam amisi per inobedientiam," *A.h.* III. xxxv. 1 (Stier, III. xxiii. 5). On the struggle against the flesh see the parallel in v. ix. 2 (Stier. ibid.).

94. Brunner, *Man in Revolt,* p. 84, n. 1. Compare, however, the meaning of *child* in *Epid.* 96.

95. The statements in *A.h.* III. xxxv. 1 are sometimes understood as an extenuation of the Fall, as though Adam were not wholly responsible. Irenaeus does not attempt to diminish Adam's guilt, but what he tries to show is that Adam is not unrepentant. The final destruction will fall on the Serpent, but not on Adam. Cf. Stoll, *Lehr e des hl. Irenäus,* pp. 11 ff., 25.

96. . . . *A.h.* IV. lxii (Stier. IV. xxxviii. 1). On the text, however, see Karl Holl, *Fragmente vornicänischer Kirchenväter,* Leipzig 1899, pp. 64 ff. The concept of νωπιος is introduced here from the contrasting ideas of Creator and created, a concept which later on in this chapter of *A.h.* is of primary importance. Irenaeus passes at once to growth and to Christ. Cf., however, Hugo Koch in *Theol. Stud. u. Krit.* 1925, p. 201, where the contrast between natural and supernatural somewhat obscures the line of thought, and also Karl Prümm in *Scholastik,* 1938, p. 221, where the term *plasma* in Irenaeus and the idea of growth

are investigated (see too p. 222); Prümm shows how closely held together these concepts are in the New Testament. Cf. also *A.h.* II. xxxvii. 3-xxxviii (Stier, II. xxv. 2-4) and II. xli. 1 (Stier. II. xxviii. 1) on man as created and continually coming into being.

97. "Et hoc Deus ab homine differt, quoniam Deus quidem facit, homo autem fit: et quidem qui facit, semper idem est: quod autem fit, et initium, et medietatem, et adjectionem, et augmentum accipere debet. Et Deus quidem bene facit, bene autem fit homini. Et Deus quidem perfectus in omnibus, ipse sibi aequalis et similis; totus cum sit lumen, et totus mens, et totus substantia, et fons omnium bonorum; homo vero profectum percipiens et augmentum ad Deum. Quemadmodum enim Deus semper proficiet ad Deum. Neque enim Deus cessat aliquando in benefaciendo, et locupletando hominem: neque homo cessat beneficium accipere, et ditari a Deo," *A.h.* IV. xxi. 2 (Stier. IV. xi. 2, wrongly numbered in Stier.). In the passage immediately before this Irenaeus based the idea of growth on Gen. I. 28: *Crescite et multiplicamini.* We find the same relation between God and man in *Epid.;* cf. L. T. Wieten, *Irenaeus' geschrift 'Ten bewiize der apostolische prediking,'* henceforth cited as *Irenaeus' geschrift,* Utrecht 1909, p. 184 f. On the idea of continued growth and "training" in the Son's Kingdom after the resurrection of the just, see *A.h.* v. xxxv. 1 (Stier. ibid.). Cremers in *Bijdragen,* 1938, pp. 60 ff., tries to maintain that this "millenarian" idea is incompatible with what Irenaeus says elsewhere. See, however, Hugo Koch's comparison (which he made as early as 1925) of Irenaean passages on the "training" in *Theol. Stud. u. Krit.* 1925, p. 199 f., n. 1. In *Theophilus von Antiochen,* published in 1930, Loofs can occasionally reveal great understanding of how the idea of growth unites different aspects of Irenaeus's thought which are otherwise difficult to harmonise (see, e.g., p. 59 f., n. 3, where Loofs is fairly positive in his criticism of Koch's interpretation), while at other times he directly opposes such an understanding of Irenaeus (see e.g. p. 284, n. 2, and p. 372). It may be that these and similar discrepancies are found in Loofs because of the fact that his work was published posthumously.

98. Cf. *A.h.* IV. lxiii. 3 (Stier. IV. xxxviii. 4), in which Irenaeus interprets Ps. LXXXII. 6-7, with *A.h.* v. xxviii. 3 (Stier. v. xxviii. 4), which deals with the significance of martyrdom, and with III. xx. 3 (Stier. III. xix. 3) on man's death and resurrection in the Body of Christ as His body in the resurrection. We must bear these passages in mind when we are evaluating the statement in v. xxix. 1 (Stier. ibid.): *Creation is made for man's sake, not man for Creation's*—a passage which is otherwise easily misinterpreted. Man has been created for eternal life: this is his distinctive characteristic in Creation. This is the primary concept, and from it we may also understand quite readily *A.h.* IV. viii

(Stier, IV. v. 1) and IV. xxv. 3 (Stier. IV. xiv. 3), passages into which we might otherwise be inclined to read the later doctrine of a special "supernature"—a doctrine which is not to be found in Irenaeus; cf. what Irenaeus says about the destruction of Jerusalem in a parallel passage in *A.h.* IV. v (Stier. IV. iv. 1) which helps to clarify the point at issue. There has been a lengthy discussion on the question of the place of man in the theology of Irenaeus, and whether he was given a place in the centre of Creation that competed with God. It is better to start from *A.h.* IV. xxxiv. 6-7 (Stier. IV. xx. 6-7). I hope to be able to take up the examination of this discussion later on. For the present all we need do is to emphasise the fact that man's growth is not a development of his personality within this world, but that his essential moments in time are death and resurrection (cf. Rom. VI and Phil. III). The superficial and optimistic description of growth which we find, e.g. in Montgomery Hitchcock, *Irenaeus of Lugdunum,* pp. 52-64, is in any case wrong.

99. Many historians of dogma have held that the Irenaean doctrine of freedom is a deviation from Paul, and they have unfavourably criticised it. See, e.g., Ernst Luthardt, *Die Lehre vom freien Willen,* Leipzig 1863, pp. 15 f.; Klebba, *Anthropologie des hl. Irenaeus,* pp. 137 ff.; Dufourcq, *Saint Irénée,* p. 167; and Aleith in *Z.NT.W.,* 1937, p. 72 f. The following passages in *A.h.* are important for a proper treatment of this question: IV. vii (Stier. IV. iv. 3), IV. xi. 2-5 (Stier. IV. vi. 3-7), IV. xxvi. 2 (Stier. IV. xv. 2), in which Irenaeus maintains that freedom is the ground of justice in God's judgement; and IV. xlv (Stier. IV. xxix), a passage on Pharaoh's hardness of heart, with Irenaeus's insistence that nonetheless God is not the author of evil; IV. lx-lxi (Stier. IV. xxxvii. 2-7), in which he denies emphatically God's use of force, and of which the most important passage is IV. lxi. 1 (Stier. IV. xxxvii. 6) with its striking introduction: "Qui autem his contraria dicunt, ipsi *impotentem introducunt Dominum . . .*"; and also IV. lxiii. 3 (Stier. IV. xxxviii. 4) on free will as the basis of growth and therefore as being synonymous with the status as *child;* IV. lxiv. 3 (Stier. IV. xxxix. 3-4) and v. xxvii. I-xxviii. 1 (Stier. ibid.) with its echo of the passage on judgement and faith in Jn. III. 18 f., but also v. xxviii. 2 (Stier. ibid.) on Antichrist as one who acts by his own free will, *and yet who has been sent by God who has foreknowledge of all things and who governs all things.* Cf. *Epid.* 11 and 55. On this main problem see Nygren, *Commentary on Romans,* pp. 368-70, and especially what is said on p. 369 on "predestination from below." Lastly in this connexion, cf. Wolfgang Schmidt, *Die Kirche bei Irenäus,* Helsingfors 1934, p. 159.

John Lawson (essay date 1948)

SOURCE: "On the Exegesis of the *Bible*," in *The Biblical Theology of Saint Irenaeus*, The Epworth Press, 1948, pp. 55-86.

[*In the following essay, Lawson contends that in Irenaeus's writings on both the Old and the New Testament, exegesis is subjective and allegorical. Superscript numbers next to biblical references throughout this essay refer to verse numbers.*]

The manner in which S. Irenaeus expounded the Bible and the justice he did to it are studies of the most far-reaching consequence for the understanding of a Christian Father who was so largely a Biblical theologian. It is unfortunate, therefore, that this aspect of his work has been so commonly dismissed in a perfunctory way with the rather obvious remark that he was an exponent of 'mystical' or 'allegoristic' exegesis. It remains to investigate this matter more carefully.

So numerous are his citations of Scripture that to examine in detail the use made by Irenaeus of every book of the Bible would be a vast task. The crucial points are, however, his evaluation of Old Testament prophecy and his relation to Pauline thought. Therefore the field of study may with advantage be narrowed by considering only the most important item of each category. Of all the prophetical books, Christian theology has used Isaiah more than any other. S. Irenaeus foreshadows this historic development, for this was his favourite Old Testament writing. Quotations from Isaiah will be found to be four times as numerous in proportion to the length of the book as from the Psalms and Jeremiah, which come next in order of frequent use. There is one citation for every five verses in the whole. In his use of Isaiah, if nowhere else, Irenaeus will show his ability to explore 'the dark wood of prophecy'.

S. IRENAEUS ON ISAIAH

We may first notice that S. Irenaeus did not show himself interested in the prophet as a man, or as an author. Only a scanty glance is given at the nature of the prophetic call. No comment is made upon the literary style of the work. The first element to receive a measure of attention is Isaiah's conception of God.

In some eight passages Irenaeus cited the Book of Isaiah as witness that God is an all-glorious and all-powerful transcendent Being, the Creator and the Lord of all, great nations being but His tools. All but one example come from Deutero-Isaiah, where the theme of the majesty of God receives perhaps its most sublime expression. Irenaeus here shows himself inspired by his source. Isaiah 40_{12}, 'Who hath measured the waters? . . .' is quoted to prove that there is no God superior to the One known to us.[1] In *Dem.* 45 the same text is used to distinguish between the God of Creation and the Logos: 'It was not He that came and stood in a very small space, and spake with Abraham, but the Word of God.'[2] Irenaeus interprets Isaiah

43_7, 'Every one that is called by my name, and whom I have created for my glory,' to show that God calls man not at all because his service is needed to enhance His glory, but that the service may glorify man.[3] Isaiah 45_7, 'I make peace, and create evil', speaks to Irenaeus of God 'making peace and friendship with those who repent and turn to Him . . . but preparing for the impenitent . . . eternal fire and outer darkness'.[4] The use made of Isaiah 51_6 is particularly interesting. The Gnostics argued that the Christian teaching that the Supreme Being was the Creator was absurd, because He would undergo change when the heavens which are His throne and the earth which is His footstool should vanish away. In answer S. Irenaeus cites: 'and the earth shall wax old like a garment, and they that dwell therein shall die in like manner. But my salvation shall be for ever . . .'[5] The appeal from Hellenistic pantheism is made with perfect rightness to Hebrew transcendentalism. In marked contrast to this usage is the treatment of Isaiah 55_8, 'for my thoughts are not your thoughts'. The comment runs: 'For the Father of all is at a vast distance from those affections and passions which operate among men. He is a simple uncompounded Being, without diverse members, and altogether like, and equal to Himself, since He is wholly understanding, and wholly spirit, and wholly thought, and wholly intelligence . . .'[6] The Latin is difficult, the Greek of this important passage being lost. *Multum enim distat omnium Pater ab his quae proveniunt hominibus affectionibus et passionibus: et simplex, et non compositus, et similimembrius,[7] et totus ipse sibimetipsi similis, et aequalis est, totus cum sit sensus, . . . et totus spiritus, et totus sensuabilitas, . . . et totus ennoea . . .*[8] Here is a substantial departure from the original, for though the conception of the awful chasm which separates the Being of God from that of man is preserved, that conception is completely transported out of the Hebraic into the Hellenistic idiom. In general we may say that one inclines to the view that S. Irenaeus was not without some real grasp of the Hebrew conception of the Living God.

Upon the doctrine of the Sovereign God of the nations Isaiah built a Gospel and a practical policy. National safety and honour, he insisted, lay neither in alliance with the Gentiles nor in building the walls of Jerusalem. The nation was to live by faith in God. This theme provides a number of texts of which the Christian preacher can make ready use, but S. Irenaeus hardly shines here. The exposition of Isaiah 7_9 is most interesting, yet a little disappointing.[9] The text is read from the Septuagint: . . . 'But if ye believe not, neither shall ye understand.' The quotation is part of an argument which certainly displays the first two stages of faith, namely, conviction of the truth and committal of one's life to that truth, but which does not rise to the full idea of faith as personal trust in a God of power and love.[10] Thus so far as this particular piece of exegesis is concerned Irenaeus falls short of the faith of which the prophet spoke to King Ahaz. However, as a counterpart to this is the evidence of the exposition of the post-exilic text Isaiah 35_{3-4} (LXX): 'Be ye strengthened, ye hands that hang down: . . . behold, our God has given judgement with retribution. . . . He will come Himself, and save us.'

S. Irenaeus is surely right in his comment: 'Here we see that not by ourselves, but by the help of God, we must be saved.'[11] It is noteworthy that Irenaeus has just given a clear witness to the fact that, owing to human infirmity, man's salvation is to be by the grace of God, on the basis of Romans $7_{18, 24}$. 'In me . . . dwelleth no good thing . . . Who shall deliver me out of the body of this death?' Here is a token that when he speaks of faith, on the basis of the prophets, S. Irenaeus can rise to an adequate conception of saving faith.

The next element to be considered in this composite prophetic book is the prophet's zeal for righteousness. This strain makes a certain appeal to Irenaeus. Several times he turns to Isaiah when he is casting about for telling words of exhortation or rebuke. In connexion with several texts he strikes the genuine prophetic ethical note: God is righteous; sin is awful in its guilt, ruinous in its consequences; repentance is therefore demanded, and is possible. An example of this usage may be given: 'And those who do not believe, and do not obey His will, are sons and angels of the devil . . . And that such is the case He has declared in Isaiah: "I have begotten and brought up children, but they have rebelled against me." . . . According to nature, then, they are children, because they have been so created; but with regard to their works, they are not His children.'[12] In enforcing the unity of the religion of the Old and of the New Covenants, S. Irenaeus seeks to show that Christ treated the genuine Mosaic commandments as of perpetual obligation. To this end Isaiah 29_{13}, 'this people honoureth me with their lips, but their heart is far from me, . . . teaching the commandments of men', is quoted with the explanation: 'he does not call the Law given by Moses commandments of men, but the traditions of the elders themselves, which they had invented.'[13] S. Irenaeus is at one with the prophet here, in asserting that true religion is essentially ethical, and in the proposition that Law is the eternal principle of true morality, the only proviso being that the Law must be authentic, God-given, and ethical. Springing from this idea of the perpetual obligation of true ethical commandments is the exposition of Christianity as the 'New Law'. We notice that Isaiah 2_{3-4}, 'for out of Zion shall go forth the law etc.,' is interpreted as a prophecy of 'the new covenant which brings back peace, and the law which gives life', *vivificatrix lex*.[14] This is certainly an applied meaning read into the text, yet also certainly true to the spirit of the original. The prophet was looking to the day when a reformed and truly ethical Judaism should become the universal religion. If Christianity be viewed as a religion of ethical Law, this expectation has been fulfilled in its spread.

The Book of Isaiah, particularly 'Deutero-Isaiah', is a missionary book. It might have been expected that this would have appealed to Irenaeus, for he was very much a missionary bishop himself. There is, however, but one missionary message cited with the prophet's missionary zeal in view, though several others are quoted in other connexions. The main interest of S. Irenaeus in Isaiah $49_{5f.}$ is indeed to draw from it the Christian doctrine of the Person

of Christ, but the original intention of the text is not lost, for he does mention that Christ came for all, both Jew and Gentile. 'So then right fitly Christ says through David that He converses with the Father . . . as in other instances, so also after this manner by Isaiah: "And now thus saith the Lord, who formed me as His servant from the womb . . . A great thing shall it be to thee to be called my servant, to stablish and confirm the tribe of Jacob: . . . and I have set thee for a light of the Gentiles, that thou shouldst be for salvation unto the end of the earth." Here, first of all, is seen that the Son of God pre-existed, from the fact that the Father spake with Him; . . . and that He is the Lord of all men, and Saviour of them that believe on Him, both Jews and others.'[15] Two of the main missionary outbursts of Irenaeus are curiously centred round passages which in the original refer not to the Gentiles, but to the Jews. 'And that these promises the Calling from among the Gentiles should inherit . . . Isaiah says thus: "These things saith the God of Israel: In that day a man shall trust in his Maker: . . . and they shall not trust in altars, nor in the work of their own hands."'[16] We conclude, therefore, that the strong sense of the Church's universal mission treasured by S. Irenaeus was not vitally connected with his reading of Isaiah.

Another great prophetic theme was the coming restoration of Israel. Many texts with this reference were used by Irenaeus, but always with a secondary Christian application. In some cases the prophecy was regarded as already fulfilled in the coming of Christ or of the Holy Spirit, or in the historic Church as the New Israel.[17] In others the prophecy was read as of the future Advent and the Millennial Kingdom.[18]

The last element of importance in the Book of Isaiah is 'Trito-Isaiah's' emphasis on correct religious observance. One might have expected that this would have appealed to an eminent advocate of episcopal discipline. This is not so, however. The only text of this type used is cited as part of an argument that he who has righteousness written on the heart has no need of external commandments. 'Wherefore also we need not the Law as a tutor . . . And there will be no command to remain idle for one day of rest, to him who perpetually keeps sabbath, that is to say, who in the temple of God, which is man's body, does service to God, and in every hour works righteousness. "For I desire mercy", He saith, "and not sacrifice; and the knowledge of God more than burnt offerings" (Hosea 6_6). "But the wicked that sacrificeth to me a calf is as if he should kill a dog; and that offereth fine flour, as though he offered swine's blood."'[19] By this exegesis S. Irenaeus goes far toward reversing the writer's original intention.

There yet remains a consideration of the main interest which drew the attention of Irenaeus to Isaiah, as to the other prophets. He saw the book as a mysterious oracle, to which one could turn to provide divine sanction for what one had to say. This attitude is not the scientific and historical, which approaches an ancient author with the question: 'How may I understand what this writer has to say?'

It is the polemic attitude which argues: 'Here is a venerable book of acknowledged authority. How may I best use it to establish my position?' It is not that there is anything wilfully unscientific or unhistorical in so arguing. This attitude was so much part of the traditional mental background of S. Irenaeus that he was quite clearly unconscious that he was so arguing, and was of the opinion that all he was able to find in Isaiah came straight from the Prophet himself. This usage presupposes, and is indeed one aspect of, that tradition of subjective or allegorical exegesis which is so important an element in the work of Irenaeus.[20]

The citations already investigated are those which display a measure of appreciation for the historic message of the Prophet. These are the cases where the allegorical exegesis is more or less in the background. It is, however, much otherwise with the great bulk of the quotations from Isaiah. Constantly one finds the severing of texts from contexts, and the artificial union of such severed texts. With this goes the seeking of 'types', and the extraction of meanings from the accidents of composition. It goes without saying that results are frequently produced fantastically removed from the intention of the original. There is little to be gained by making a collection of extreme examples, and a single one will stand for very many. 'They shall beat their swords into ploughshares, and their spears into pruninghooks' is rendered as follows: the plough and the pruninghook represent 'the creation exhibited in Adam', while the plough shows the salvation of the world: 'for this reason, since He joined the beginning to the end, and is Lord of both (i.e. the Adamic creation and the fruit of the Gospel), He has finally been displayed in the plough, in that the wood has been joined on to the iron, and has thus cleansed His land; because the Word, having been firmly united to flesh, and in its mechanism fixed with pins, has reclaimed the savage earth'; *quoniam firmum Verbum adunitum carni, et habitu taleis[21] confixus emundavit sylvestrem terram.*[22]

We may rather turn to some happier and less astonishing results. 'For out of Zion shall go forth the Law' refers to the fact that the Apostles were to start the preaching of the New Law in the land of Judea.[23] There is real insight in forcing a connexion between the prophet's 'they shall beat their swords into ploughshares' and the Lord's command to turn the other cheek.[24] There is also a quaint but profound comment on Isaiah 10_{23} (LXX), . . . : 'A word brief and short in righteousness: for a short word will God make in the whole world.' This indicates that men are to be saved 'not by the much speaking of the law, but by the brevity of faith and love'.[25] Again, upon 'Behold I make new (things) which shall now spring up . . . And I will make in the wilderness a way, and in the waterless place streams:' we have the following: the promise of a 'new thing' is a prophecy that Christ will not call all men back to the legislation of Moses, but will bring a new Covenant of faith. The 'wilderness' and the 'desert' are the Gentiles, 'for the Word had not passed through them'; the 'streams' are the Holy Spirit, who is to be poured out over the earth by the Logos.[26]

So also the second 'Servant Song' provided the details of a doctrine of the Person of Christ. That the Father spoke indicates that the Son was pre-existent. That the Lord 'formed Him from the womb' shows that He must become incarnate by a special action of God through the Holy Spirit. Furthermore, 'the Son of the Father' calls Himself 'Servant' on account of 'His subjection to the Father'.[27] As was but natural, the fourth 'Servant Song' was also given a most extended allegorical exegesis by S. Irenaeus. Quotations are very frequent, and in every case the reference is to Christ. It is important to notice that Irenaeus did not find here any notion of a Penal Substitution theory of the Atonement.[28] This is obviously no mere accident of omission, for he takes Isaiah 53_{5-6} so far as to assert that the tortures of Christ came upon Him by the will of the Father, and that this was for our salvation. Significantly he does not take the last step.[29] An interesting confirmation of this is that both citations of 'Surely He hath borne our griefs and carried our sorrows' are made to refer to our Lord's miracles of healing.[30] On three occasions Irenaeus finds a prophecy of the divine begetting of the Son in 'who shall declare His generation?' (Isaiah 53_8, LXX.) The first is notable as an approach to the doctrine of eternal generation. 'But ye (Gnostics) pretend to set forth His generation from the Father, and ye transfer the production of the word of man which takes place by means of a tongue to the Word of God, and thus are righteously exposed by your own selves as knowing neither things human nor divine.' Actually God's Word is native to Him. *Deus autem totus exsistens Mens, et totus exsistens Logos* there is no separation between God and Original Mind.[31] The significance of this argument is that S. Irenaeus disowns as Gnostic emanationism the familiar Stoic distinction of In the second case Irenaeus connects the phrase both with Christ's Godhead, as begotten of the Father, and with His manhood, as born of the Virgin.[32] Thirdly, 'This was said to warn us, lest on account of His enemies and the outrage of His sufferings we should despise Him as a mean and contemptible man. For He who endured all this has a generation which cannot be declared . . . for He who is His Father cannot be declared'.[33] It is of interest to notice that in *Dem.* 68 Irenaeus begins 'The Song of the Suffering Servant' at Isaiah 52_{13}, and continues straight through to the following chapter. This certainly shows a better sense for the construction of the text than that exhibited by those responsible for the unfortunate chapter-division familiar today.

Two passages of Isaiah are interpreted as prophecies of the Virgin Birth. On Isaiah 66_7, 'before she that travailed (gave birth . . .) she escaped and was delivered of a man child', the comment runs: 'Thus He showed that His birth from the Virgin was unforeseen and unexpected.'[34] There is also the inevitable use of Isaiah 7_{14-16} in a number of passages, of which the chief may be noted. 'The Lord Himself shall give you a sign' refers to 'a sign . . . which man did not ask for, because he never expected that a virgin could conceive'.[35] In antithesis to the views of modern scholarship is: 'For what great thing or what sign should have been in this, that a young woman conceiving by a man should bring forth—a thing that happens to all women that produce offspring.'[36] There are two signs of Christ's divinity, the name Immanuel,[37] and the Septuagint rendering of vv. 15b-16a: . . . 'For before the child shall know good or evil, he refuses evil, to choose the good.'[38] Likewise appear two signs of Christ's real manhood: 'Butter and curds shall He eat', and the use of the phrase 'child' in verse 16a.[39]

There remain four notices of Isaiah 61_1, 'the Spirit of the Lord is upon me'. In the first S. Irenaeus is at pains to make it plain that the reference is to Christ's manhood, and not to His divine nature.[40] This appears to be an effort to avoid an Adoptionist reading. It is certainly noteworthy that this text is associated in the writer's mind with the baptism of Jesus. In another place the point is made that the Holy Spirit descended upon One who was the incarnate Son of God.[41] This is aimed against the Gnostic theory of the descent of the heavenly Christ upon the man Jesus. A third reference is of general application,[42] while for the fourth Irenaeus has a most interesting statement which serves as a kind of key to his appreciation of Scripture. The fact that Jesus was able to apply this ancient Scripture to Himself made faith easier for His hearers. In the same way, the circumstance that the Apostles had ancient prophecy which 'even prefigured our faith' to which to appeal, so worked that the world 'might easily accept the advent of Christ'.[43] This is a significant witness to the mentality of the age. Experience showed that the plea that ancient prophecies were literally fulfilled in the life of Christ served effectually to convince many that the Christian preaching was true. It was natural to attempt to make the most of this appeal. This was the incentive behind much working out of ingenious examples of 'prophecy fulfilled'. It was this that demanded the allegoristic exegesis. The argument was doubtless reciprocal and cumulative. That the prophets were able wonderfully to forecast events of future centuries proved the fact of their inspiration by an all-knowing God. The inspiration of Scripture having thus been confirmed, one could use Scripture as a mine of authoritative proof-texts to enforce the Church's contentions about Christ. This method of argument has had a most providential result in preserving the Old Testament for the Church. Beneath there is a deeper gain. The prophetic movement did indeed educate the People to which God could send His Son. S. Irenaeus spoke wisely when he said that 'posterity, possessing the fear of God', did 'easily accept the advent of Christ, having been instructed by the prophets'.[44]

In turning from the exegesis of the Old Testament to that of the New we find that the first Gospel is the favourite book. S. Irenaeus has one quotation for every three verses. Next in order of frequent use come Romans, 1 Corinthians, Galatians, and Ephesians, each with about two citations to nine verses. A long debate has raged regarding the question whether or no Irenaeus was faithful to the Pauline Gospel, and in particular, whether he had a competent understanding of the conception of saving faith. This is one of the most important issues affecting our estimate of him

as a Biblical Christian. In seeking an example of New Testament exegesis it will therefore be as well to pass over the first Gospel in favour of the Epistle to the Romans, that weighty and considered letter of S. Paul.

Once again a survey may be made of the various theological elements which S. Irenaeus might have extracted from the Epistle. In the first place we find that one of the largest groups of quotations occurs in contexts where he is engaged in establishing the doctrine of God. In all but three of these cases S. Paul is used to overturn the Marcionite antithesis between the grudging God of bare legal justice of the Old Testament, and the generous Father of mercy of the New. This heresy was a perversion of the strong contrast Paul had made between the religion of Law and the religion of Grace. It is therefore natural that in countering the Marcionites Irenaeus should largely use those same portions of Scripture of which they had made such ill-use. In one place this polemic interest is made explicit. 'How beautiful are the feet of them that bring glad tidings of good things' is wrested to show that 'it was not merely one, but that there were very many who used to preach the truth'. This shows S. Paul himself disowning the Marcionite proposition that Paul alone had the genuine tradition.[45] Akin to this is the use made of Romans 4_3, 'Abraham believed God'. The witness of Paul, who was accepted by the Marcionites as an inspired Apostle, overthrows the doctrine of another God of the Old Testament, by speaking of the salvation of Abraham by faith in the true God.[46] Several other passages are quoted with the simple observation that they prove the unity of the God of the Old Testament with the God of the New.[47]

One or two interesting extensions of this theme remain to be noted. There is the citation of Romans 1_{18}: 'For the wrath of God shall be revealed', to dispose of Marcion's assertion that only the God of the Jews visited with Wrath, the Christian God visiting only with mercy.[48] This is legitimate exegesis, reproducing the sense of the original, in so far as S. Paul certainly taught that the Wrath was still at work in the world, even in the period when God had manifested His saving Grace. Furthermore, the heretic had fastened upon God's 'hardening the heart of Pharaoh' as evidence that that God was the reverse of good. The difficulty is curiously avoided by joining Romans 1_{28}: 'God gave them up to a reprobate mind', to the quotation of Isaiah 6_{10}: 'make the heart of this people gross', in Matthew 13_{11-16}, and also to 2 Thessalonians 2_{11}: 'God shall send them the working of error', with the comment: 'If, therefore, in the present time also, God knowing the number of those who will not believe, since He foreknows all things, has given them over to unbelief, . . . leaving them in the darkness which they have chosen for themselves, what is there wonderful if He did also at that time give over to unbelief Pharaoh, who never would have believed?'[49] Thus the disharmony is resolved by a bold importation of the apparent difficulty of Exodus into Romans also. Hereby S. Irenaeus shows that he did not understand that Hebrew manner of thought which had no room for the conception of indirect divine causation, as it comes to expression in Romans 1_{28}, Exodus 9_{35}, and the other passages referred to.

At the close of the section, Romans 9-11, there is a passage whence Irenaeus draws a doctrine of God much more in accordance with S. Paul's intention. He commands our confidence as an exegete in picking upon Romans 11_{32}, 'For God hath concluded all in unbelief that He may have mercy on all' as the occasion for a statement that the purpose of God in showing mercy is that man might love Him the more.[50] Paul himself would surely have answered in this spirit had he been questioned concerning these chapters, which have proved so great a stumbling-block to many. Romans 11_{33} is also most appropriately used as the climax of all the deep mysteries of the Faith, which the Church alone understands: 'Oh! the depth of the riches both of the wisdom and knowledge of God'.[51] The rhetoric of Romans 11_{34}, 'For who hath known the mind of the Lord?', draws the response that 'no other being had the power of revealing to us the things of the Father, except His own proper Word'.[52] God is in fact the transcendent One, who is to be known through the Son. The conception of divine transcendence is most properly derived from the utterance of the Apostle when his mind flies back from soaring speculation upon the secret purposes of God to the simple numinous approach of religious worship. In conclusion we may observe that, so far as the doctrine of God is concerned, S. Irenaeus made worthy use of the Epistle to the Romans.

A further considerable group of citations deals with the doctrine of the world and of man, and of the origin of evil. Romans 13_{1-7}, with its exhortation of loyalty to the Imperial Government, was manifestly a favourite passage with Irenaeus. This is for an interesting reason. If 'the powers that be are ordained of God' the implication is that this world does not belong to the devil. Thus a useful proof-text is provided to give answer to the dualism of the Gnostic.[53] It is further observed that this text is not to be explained away as referring to the angelical rulers, for taxes are to be paid to them.[54] In another place Romans 13_{1-6} comes in for an involved exposition.[55] The forces referred to are identified by Irenaeus with 'the armies' sent out in retribution in the Parable of the Marriage Feast. Thus 'the King' is symbolical of God, but 'the armies' literal, being those of Rome. These Roman armies are of God, 'because all men are the property of God'. S. Irenaeus is of course far from S. Paul's sense here, but his exegesis is legitimate to a certain extent. The patriotic Apostle is by anticipation repudiating the later apocalyptical identification of the Roman Empire with the Antichrist. Irenaeus is on not dissimilar ground in his assertion that the civil order of this world is not the domain of the devil.

Other texts in Romans deal with the nature of man as a moral agent. Romans $2_{4-5,10}$: 'Or despisest thou the riches of his goodness . . . not knowing that the goodness of God leadeth thee to repentance?' is incorporated in an ar-

gument that men are morally responsible, seeing that they are possessed of a free will.[56] This application is justified in so far as S. Paul's chapter assumes moral responsibility, but one is disappointed that S. Irenaeus passes over the deepest truth here present, namely, that God's forbearance is aimed at winning man to penitence. He proceeds with a deduction that reflects the optimistic view that man's power of moral choice remains substantially intact. 'Those who do it [good] not shall receive the just judgement of God, because they did not work good when they had it in their power so to do.' Romans 3_{23} is given an interesting treatment in a passage dealing with the sins recounted of Old Testament worthies.[57] The Christian should not be puffed up with pride, and lay undue blame upon sins committed in less happy ages, before the coming of Christ, 'for "all men come short of the glory of God", and are not justified of themselves, but by the advent of the Lord'. There is, however, another side. The sins af the Patriarchs 'have been committed to writing that we might know, in the first place, that our God and theirs is one, and that sins do not please Him although committed by men of renown'. This is surely Pauline ground. S. Paul is arguing that, 'as there is no distinction' between the more and the less favoured parts of the human race, for none can keep himself from sin, so there is no room for recrimination and odious comparison. S. Irenaeus is on similar ground in teaching that evil deeds of old time were indeed wrong, but are not to be judged by full Christian standards.

Another legitimate use made of Romans is in countering dualist Gnostic heresy, even though anti-dualist polemic forms no part of S. Paul's direct purpose in this Epistle. For example, to avoid the Gnostic reading of 'flesh and blood cannot inherit the Kingdom of God', and to prove the salvation of the body as well as of the soul, S. Irenaeus refers to 'Let not sin therefore reign in your mortal body', with the remark: 'It has not been declared that flesh and blood, in the literal meaning of the terms, cannot inherit the Kingdom of God; but [these words apply] to those carnal deeds already mentioned.[58] This is apt, in that Paul is attacking Anti-nomianism, which is a dualism of practical life, while Irenaeus adapts his words to oppose a system of speculative dualism. It is worthy of note that in general an exact understanding is displayed of the Pauline term 'the flesh',[59],[60] though S. Irenaeus does not notice the special usage in the text in question.

Under the heading of the doctrine of the Person of Christ there are also a number of citations. All save one of these are in passages where S. Irenaeus is rebutting the Gnostic distinction between Jesus and the Christ. As S. Paul does not treat of this subject the exegesis is in each case a drawing out of implications. The short Christological introduction to Romans comes in for two notices. Romans 1_{1-4}, 'Who was born of the seed of David according to the flesh, who was declared to be the Son of God with power', is quoted to prove that the One who was born was the Son of God made man, and not merely the man Jesus.[61] Romans 1_{3-4} is likewise cited in another place as evidence that Christ assumed actual flesh of the Virgin.[62] Romans

$5_{6,8-10}$ proves 'that the same being who was laid hold of, and underwent suffering, and shed His blood for us, was both Christ and the Son of God, who did rise again, and was taken up to heaven'. The Apostle knew nothing of the Gnostic Christ 'who flew away from Jesus'.[63] One would have been more satisfied had Irenaeus made some recognition of the circumstance that the text in question is essentially a noble utterance on the love of the redeeming God. However, this content is not altogether lost, for the true antithesis to the utterly remote and unknown Supreme Being of the Gnostic systems is the God who loves, and who will therefore suffer. There are other passages cited as evidence for the unity of Christ, but the theme of the original is largely lost.[64]

There remains the place where mention is made of Romans 5_{14}. 'Hence also was Adam himself termed by Paul "the figure of Him that was to come" . . . God having predestined that the first man should be of an animal nature, with this view, that he might be saved by the spiritual one. For inasmuch as He had a pre-existence as a saving being, it was necessary that that which might be saved should also be called into existence, in order that the being who saves should not exist in vain.'[65] This is a speculation quite foreign to S. Paul, but the idea underlying it, that the dispensation of salvation through Christ is not a mere contingency, but a part of God's eternal purpose, is certainly one that is pre-supposed by what Paul says in this text.

Relating to the doctrine of Christ as derived from S. Paul, there is at first sight some force in Werner's objection that S. Irenaeus makes a strikingly external use of the text.[66] For example, upon Romans 14_{14-15} the comment runs: 'And everywhere when [referring to] the passion of Our Lord, and to His human nature and His subjection to death, he employs the name of Christ, as in that passage: "Destroy not him with thy meat for whom Christ died".'[67] It is obvious that it is by way of an accident that the word 'Christ' is here used, for the Apostle could as well have written 'for whom Jesus died'. On the surface, therefore, this is a typical example of unsound exposition, for a distinction is read into the text where none is. In answer it may be claimed that the circumstance that this usage can be accidental is itself not without significance. Had S. Paul known anything of a Gnostic distinction between Jesus and the Christ he would certainly not have written as he did, for the Gnostic doctrine is definitely precluded by his system. Had he been faced with Gnostic error S. Paul would surely have made it plain that the use of the word 'Christ' for the suffering One was no mere accident of composition. The text in question does speak of the suffering of a divine Being, so S. Irenaeus is not without some justification in his exegesis. Werner clearly errs by overstatement.

Most of the quotations from Romans are accounted for when these three foundation doctrines of speculative theology have been dealt with. However, S. Irenaeus takes up various elements in the evangelical message of the Epistle. First among these is the doctrine of the universal moral impotence of humanity, apart from the grace of God. Irenaeus does not show a very positive appreciation of this. Against the Gnostics he had to be very firm that moral failure in man is a matter of wrong personal choice, and not merely of inherent constitution. He is so dominated by this interest that his statements on free will sometimes sound almost Pelagian. Allowance must consequently be made for this. The assertion of some[68] that Irenaeus was a Pelagian is to be rejected. For example, Romans $2_{4-5,10}$, 'But dost thou despise the riches of His goodness?' etc. is thus expounded: 'God therefore has given us that which is good, as the apostle tells us in this epistle, and they who work it shall receive glory and honour, because they have done that which is good when they had it in their power not to do it; but those who do it not shall receive the just judgement of God, because they did not work good when they had it in their power so to do.'[69] At first sight the last phrase of this, taken out of the context, would certainly appear to give a non-Pauline exegesis. A more careful reading, however, gives at least some good ground for supposing that this is not so. The general intention of the chapter is to safeguard the freedom of the human will. The earlier part of this paragraph indicates that what is here called 'the good' is the grace of God. It is God's goodwill, which is the antithesis of coercion. This is described as 'good counsel'. It must be confessed that this latter, taken alone, is quite inadequate as a definition of grace. However, in general Irenaeus rises well above this in his teaching regarding the saving grace of God.[70] Free will has been given 'so that those who had yielded obedience might justly possess that which is good, given indeed of God, but preserved by themselves'. That 'working of good' which is in man's power would therefore appear to be nothing other than a steadfast holding on to the grace of God. If this supposition be well founded S. Irenaeus rises above mere moralism if anything more clearly than does S. Paul himself in this particular chapter.

Irenaeus continues with a comment upon Romans 13_{13}, 'Let us walk honestly, as in the day', which here forms part of a chain of ethical exhortations drawn from Pauline sources. 'If then it were not in our power to do or not to do these things, what reason had the apostle . . . to give us counsel to do some things, and to abstain from others? But because man is possessed of free will . . . advice is always given to him to keep fast the good, which thing is done by means of obedience to God.'[71] It may be agreed that one who was unfailing in scrupulous care to safeguard the doctrine of Grace might have expressed himself with some necessary added proviso, but Irenaeus is not more at fault than this. He has also the excuse that he wrote long before controversy taught the Church the necessity of careful utterance. For all his emphasis upon man's need of grace, S. Paul, like all other prophets, does inevitably and rightly exhort to good works. The deduction that moral responsibility is pre-supposed is entirely legitimate, and the pre-supposition of a real measure of free will is not far from this.

S. Paul gave the great historic witness to the futility of religion based upon the hope of man earning forgiveness and righteousness in the sight of God by his own efforts. It is disappointing to find that S. Irenaeus made so little of this vital element in Romans. Romans 10_{3-4}, 'For Christ is the end of the law' is indeed noticed once, but is used in a sense directly opposite to that probably intended by Paul.[72] At this point, at least, Werner has raised an objection which may be upheld in his efforts to demonstrate that the thought of Irenaeus was un-Pauline.[73] S. Irenaeus is here arguing that there is one God of the Old and of the New Covenant from the fact that Christ condemned the traditions of men, when they were contrary to the Law of Moses, and that He established its main precepts. He asks: 'And how is Christ the end of the law, if He is not also the final cause of it? For He who has brought in the end has Himself also wrought in the beginning.' From the context it appears that S. Paul's . . .: 'Christ is the culmination of the Law.'[74] This is very far from what must be assumed to be Paul's intention: 'Christ is the termination of Law (as a principle of religion).' That Christianity is identical with Judaism in that it is founded upon the principle of Justification by the works of the Law, differing only in that the Gospel is a correct and pure Law, is clearly an un-Pauline position. This is what would appear to be involved by the present exegesis of Irenaeus, and he is here in error. In venturing upon this unsound ground, drawn by zeal to establish the unity of the Old and New Covenants, S. Irenaeus has this excuse. He shows that he was led on by the authority of the Matthaean 'the Scribes and Pharisees sit in Moses' seat, etc.'.

The counterpart of man's impotence is the assurance of divine help. S. Paul taught that God would show His righteousness, that is, would come to vindicate the distressed cause of the right. This is His act of grace, a gift of helping power which man has done nothing to earn or deserve. S. Irenaeus thrice takes up this theme. Upon Romans 7_{18}, 'for I know that there dwelleth in my flesh no good thing', he comments: 'our salvation is not from us, but from God.' Owing to human infirmity man can do nothing to save himself. He must depend upon the grace of God in Jesus Christ.[75] The response to the outburst of Romans 7_{24}, 'Who shall deliver me from the body of this death?', likewise rings true to the spirit of S. Paul. 'Here we see, that not by ourselves, but by the help of God, must we be saved.'[76] To this is to be joined the comment on Romans $10_{6-7,9}$: 'as it was also impossible that he could attain to salvation who had fallen under the power of sin,—the Son of God effected both these things, . . . descending from the Father, etc., upon whom [Paul] exhorting us unhesitatingly to believe, again says . . . "If thou shalt believe in thine heart that God hath raised Him from the dead, thou shalt be saved".'[77] Here is an evangelical note which goes far to counter-balance the tendency noticed above.

The 'righteousness of God' is also for S. Paul partly eschatological. The present triumph of the Saints over evil, through the power of God, is something which is to culminate in 'the Day of the Lord'. This note is not prominent in Romans, but the millenarian Irenaeus not unnaturally fixes upon such mention as is made of it. When speaking of the earthly millennial Kingdom he says of Romans 8_{19-21}: 'the creation itself also shall be delivered from the bondage of corruption' etc.: 'It is fitting, therefore, that the creation itself, being restored to its primeval condition, should without restraint be under the dominion of the righteous.'[78] S. Irenaeus has, however, not got the whole sense of this text. The transformation of the Creation is not merely the preparation of conditions under which the righteous may 'receive the reward of their suffering' in that same world in which they toiled. S. Paul has something deeper than this. His faith is that God's loving purpose extends to all His works, and that His redemptive activity will in the future work outward from mankind to every creature.

The consideration of statements about the saving work of Christ made as expositions of texts from Romans is a study of special interest and importance. It is at this point that the treatment given by S. Irenaeus is most nearly adequate to the thought of S. Paul. The latter part of Romans 5 comes in for ample notice. There is a passing allusion to Romans 5_{14} 'death reigned from Adam to Moses, etc.', in the course of an argument, quite in accord with Pauline thought, that those who deny that Christ became man are 'holding out patronage to sin: for, by their showing, death has not been vanquished'.[79] Romans 5_{19}, 'through the one man's disobedience the many were made sinners', is twice quoted. It is asserted that it was necessary for Christ to become man, because man's bondage to sin had to be destroyed by a man for men.[80] In relation to the doctrine of Recapitulation it is also cited as one of several parallels between Adam and Christ.[81] Romans 5_{20} appears on behalf of a belief in the salvation of Adam. Irenaeus identified Adam with the human race. He was the sheep that was lost. Therefore, 'if it has not been found, the whole human race is still held in a state of perdition'. Against the salvation of Adam, Tatian had quoted 'In Adam all die'. The answer is: 'But where sin abounded, grace did abound more exceedingly.'[82] A kindred reference is that upon Romans 1_{1-4}: 'the Son of God being made Son of Man, that through Him we may receive the adoption.'[83]

In S. Paul's scheme this deliverance is appropriated by faith. S. Irenaeus once develops this idea in exposition of a text from this Epistle. Upon Romans 4_3, 'Abraham believed God', he writes: 'In like manner we also are justified by faith in God . . . not by the Law, but by faith, which is witnessed to in the Law.'[84] The best definition of this faith is contained in another comment on the same text. The faith of Abraham was 'the undoubting and unwavering certainty of his spirit', when confronted with the promise that his seed should be as the stars in number.[85] The idealized Abraham of Scripture tradition is a good example of a life lived by that which the Christian knows as saving faith. He responded to the divine call by committing his whole life and future to God, in the steadfast conviction that despite all appearance to the contrary God was altogether sufficient. He was prepared to accept the offer of grace, and God's promises of good-will toward him, and to live as if they were valid. In a powerful chapter S.

Irenaeus draws from Romans 4_3 an important part, though perhaps not the whole, of this conception of faith.[85] Werner goes too far in maintaining that Irenaeus had little conception of the faith of Abraham.[86] Certainly, 'to believe in things future, as if they were already accomplished, because of the promise of God' is by itself inadequate as a definition of faith. However, it is not necessary, in the light of the above, to assume that S. Irenaeus by 'the faith of Abraham' meant nothing more than this, any more than it is to deduce from the same passage that the content of the Christian faith is exhausted in 'beholding the future kingdom'.[87]

Other references are less hopeful. Another note on Romans 4_3 savours of the idea of faith as no more than intellectual assent to a proposition.[88] This is clearer still in an exposition of Romans 4_{12}, 'who also walk in the steps of that faith of our father Abraham', where Irenaeus writes of 'Jesus . . . bringing us over from hard and fruitless cogitations, and establishing in us a faith like to Abraham'.[89] An allusion to Romans 3_3 is worthy of careful note. 'Yet the scepticism of men of this stamp shall not render the faithfulness of God of none effect.'[90] The 'scepticism' is that of those who 'oppose their own salvation, deeming it impossible for God, who raises up the dead, to have power to confer upon them eternal duration'. Such are sceptical because they do not receive the signs of God's power to preserve life, the tokens of which are the miraculous longevity of the Patriarchs, the translation of Elijah, and the preservation of Jonah. One would be inclined to infer that 'saving faith' is here built upon the foundation of acceptance of these stories. Furthermore, it is not without significance that in one of those passages where S. Irenaeus strikes a clear evangelical note he should fall back, rather inappropriately, upon Romans 10_{6-9}, 'If thou shalt confess with thy mouth the Lord Jesus, etc.', the one passage in Romans where faith at all approximates to 'acceptation of a proposition'.[91] In conclusion, the witness to the conception of saving faith in S. Paul's Epistle is of unequal adequacy. If this were characteristic of all that S. Irenaeus has to say upon this subject there would be some ground for the doubts that have been expressed under this head.

Another major theme of Romans is the nature of the Christian Church. This is represented as the legitimate spiritual successor of the Hebrew nation, the new and true Israel of God. Considering the importance of the idea of the Church in S. Irenaeus it is a little surprising that his treatment of the relevant texts is so inadequate. He follows S. Paul in his application of Hosea 2_{23}, 'I will call that my people which was not my people', to the call of the Gentiles into the Church, with the interesting difference that he is conscious that the words apply to himself, as a Gentile Christian. 'God . . . by His Son Jesus Christ has called *us* to the knowledge of Himself, from the worship of stones.'[92] He also follows Paul in the claim that the Christians are the true children of Abraham.[93] Two other passages are quoted against Marcion. Romans 3_{21}, 'the righteousness of God has been manifested, being witnessed by the Law and the prophets', is used to prove that the prophets made reference to the coming Christ.[94] Here only the secondary thought of the original is reproduced. Still less apposite is the use of Romans 11_{26} to prove that the Father preached by Jesus was one with the God of the Old Testament. In arguing that the Law is good Irenaeus writes: 'And Paul likewise declares, "And so all Israel shall be saved" . . . Let them not therefore ascribe to the Law the unbelief of certain of them. For the Law never hindered them from believing in the Son of God; nay, but it even exhorted them so to do.'[95] This argument is not really sustained by the text, though it would be by the accompanying Galatians 3_{24}, 'the Law has been our tutor to bring us unto Christ'. There is, however, a certain propriety in resisting Marcion's effort to sever the Church from its Jewish root by an appeal to this text. The verse is the climax of S. Paul's protestation of affection for the Jewish people, and of his certainty that they yet have a special part to play in God's purposes.

Regarding the problems of Christian ethics, S. Irenaeus seems to pass over one of the great arguments of this Epistle, namely, that the sufficient foundation for all Christian morality is love in the heart, worked by the gift of the Holy Spirit. Ethical exhortations are, however, cited in warning against spiritual and worldly pride,[96] and to show that believers ought to obey the government.[97]

A final use of the Epistle to the Romans is one similar to that observed to be dominant in the case of Isaiah. S. Irenaeus could regard it as a mysterious oracle of proof-texts. The New Testament is not used in this way to anything like the same extent as the Old. In most cases a quotation from Romans is given a meaning with at least some approach to the original. Irenaeus had therefore a much firmer grasp of the real meaning of the Epistle than he had of the Prophecy. The reason for this is not far to seek. In the case of S. Paul he had some solid background of knowledge for his understanding of the writing, for it originally went out into a world mentally similar to his own. In the case of the Prophets no such knowledge was available at the time.

Of the nine texts from Romans rendered allegorically there is only one example of a passage interpreted in disparate senses in different places. Romans 11_{17b}, from the allegory of the Grafted Olive Tree, is on one occasion further allegorized to refer to the salvation of the body. The wild branch is the body; the grafting on to the good stock is the joining to the Spirit of God.[98] However, in another place this same text, united with Romans 11_{21}, is taken in the original sense of S. Paul's allegory.[99] The lesson here drawn is that the Christian must not be puffed up with pride when he reads of the failings of Old Testament worthies. One of the more interesting examples of a significance read into words the form of which is a mere accident of style is the rendering of Romans 10_{15}. 'And again, when Paul says, "How beautiful are the feet of those bringing glad tidings of good things and preaching the gospel of peace", he shows that it was not merely one, but that there were many who used to preach the truth.'[100] This disproves Marcion's thesis that S. Paul was the only true Apostle.

In summing up the value of the work of S. Irenaeus as an exegete, on the basis of the examples taken, tribute must first be paid to his powers. Irenaeus shows that he appreciated aright the vision of the transcendent God in Hebrew prophecy. He echoed the prophetic zeal for ethical religion and righteous conduct. The conviction that Israel must trust only in God for salvation received some notice, though only in a secondary and applied sense as referring to Christian salvation. Likewise, large justice is seen to have been done to the hope of the coming restoration of Israel, but only as applied to the glorified Church of the Millennial Kingdom. This represents a substantial measure of comprehension for the message of the prophets.

S. Irenaeus fared better with S. Paul. This is indeed a matter of the first importance. He found the Hebrew Living and Righteous God in Romans. This God is the Creator. His providence and His possession extend to this created world, and to the bodies as to the souls of men. Irenaeus, furthermore, was able to demonstrate his doctrine of the divine Son, who for love's sake became incarnate and suffered, as something firmly grounded upon S. Paul. To some extent, however, this aspect of the work is spoiled by the polemical interest of establishing the identity of Jesus with the Christ. A somewhat more optimistic view of human nature is perhaps taken than that characteristic of S. Paul, though Irenaeus was not a Pelagian. Justice was done to man's need of grace. Here again the exegesis suffers by an incautious attempt to demonstrate the identity of the divine Source of the religions of the Old and New Covenants by means of the doctrine of the New Law. The Apostle's eschatological hope was fully reproduced. Upon the saving work of Christ the exposition is satisfactory, though Irenaeus was not altogether clear-sighted in drawing from the Epistle the conception of that faith by which are appropriated the fruits of this saving work. He did not fall back as much as might have been expected upon Romans for the conception of the Church as the New Israel. Hence it is not too much to claim that in general S. Irenaeus was a fairly sound expositor of S. Paul. Werner has given a detailed discussion of this exegesis, with the damaging conclusion that the crucial passages of Paul are either ignored or interpreted contrary to the writer's intention, and that the Pauline Epistles are not used as a source for thought, but as mere external props.[101] This is to be rejected as a serious overstatement. Individual unfortunate examples can certainly be produced, but this is very far indeed from being the general rule.

We now pass to the consideration of the so-called 'allegorizing' or 'mystical' exegesis. In the proper sense allegorism consists in making the characters or scenery of a story 'stand for something'. A celebrated example occurs in Galatians 4_{21-31}, where S. Paul makes the sons of Hagar and of Sarah represent respectively the Jewish and Christian communities. A distinctive activity along these lines is the seeking of 'types of Christ', such as the Melchizedek of Hebrews. Other exegetical practices are very naturally associated with allegorism, by virtue of a common mental background. Like allegorism these spring from the axiom that Scripture is in every phrase and word an oracle packed with open or hidden divine revelation. Such practices are: seeking passages which may be construed as forecasts of the future (i.e. 'prophecies'), now fulfilled; detaching phrases from the context, and expounding them apart from the determinative effect of that context upon the meaning; connecting such detached phrases one to another in continuous narrative by the link of some common word or association, as, for example, the several texts mentioning 'a stone' in 1 Peter 2_{5-8}; and the reading of a significance into the accidents of grammar or composition, as exemplified by the distinction found by S. Paul between 'seed' and 'seeds' in Galatians 3_{16}. When, in the present discussion, 'allegorism' is spoken of, we have in mind also these allied practices in general.

Schmidt makes a rather surprising statement when he ventures to assert that in general S. Irenaeus avoids allegorism, that when he uses it the exegesis is mostly typology, and that allegoristic passages are not for him determinative for faith.[102] This is manifestly incorrect, for all the practices enumerated above are constantly used. There is, however, a kernel of truth in this statement. It has been demonstrated that allegorical exegesis is much less prominent in the case of the New Testament, and this is also the part of the Bible which provides the passages most significant for distinctive Christian doctrine. There is, however, no definite separation in usage as suggested by Schmidt.

There is perhaps more truth in Harnack's statement that S. Irenaeus was the first to apply the mystical interpretation to the New Testament.[103] Harnack gives as his examples a case of exposition of the Parable of the Good Samaritan, where the victim is the human race, and the two pence the gift of the Spirit;[104] and also the explanation that Christ administered food to the disciples at the Last Supper in a recumbent posture 'indicating that those who were lying in the earth were they to whom He came to impart life'.[105] So also the sleep of the disciples in Gethsemane is a type of the sleep of mankind. We have also observed allegorical exegesis of Romans.[106] However, Harnack probably goes too far. That Irenaeus appears as the first who practised this method upon the New Testament is probably due to the circumstance that he is the first from whom we have inherited any considerable exposition of this part of Scripture. The quotations from the Gospels in S. Justin Martyr are almost purely descriptive. Allegoristic exegesis was a part of the heritage of the original Christians from Judaism, and had already been practised upon the sayings of Jesus in the composition of the Four Gospels.[107]

We cannot agree with Beuzart, who in zeal to find Scripture as the supreme proof of doctrine in S. Irenaeus maintains that allegorism is an inconsequential accident of the times.[108] Plainly, allegoristic exegesis is almost purely subjective. He who uses it can find in the Holy Book anything he already has in mind, so that every conceivable system of doctrine may be substantiated from Scripture. Past and present Christian history clearly shows this. The acid test of the unhistorical and unscientific nature of this method is that a given writer can be found to interpret one and the same text in opposite senses in different parts of his work. This will be found the case with Irenaeus, within the scope of his quotations of Isaiah alone. For example, Isaiah $11_{6f.}$, 'And the wolf shall dwell with the lamb', is in *Dem.* 61 given a spiritualized rendering, as referring to righteous men. This view is in 5.33.4 (ii.147) noticed as one held by some, but is politely disowned by Irenaeus as being beside the point. Furthermore, Isaiah 26_{19} (LXX), 'the dead which are in the grave shall arise', is twice cited as referring to Christ's miracles of healing,[109] and twice as of the Millennial Resurrection.[110] Again, Isaiah 35_{3-6}, 'then the eyes of the blind shall be opened', can be read of these healing miracles,[111] yet in another place of the salvation of the soul.[112] An example from the Epistle to the Romans has been mentioned already.[113] As Vernet has to admit, S. Irenaeus is not a sure guide to the historic sense of the Old Testament.[114] An accident of the times this allegorism certainly is, but it is an accident of infinite consequence.

The more historical treatment of S. Paul's writings is a measure of greater knowledge and mental affinity. S. Irenaeus had some actual knowledge of Paul's life, and of its background. Above all, he lived in a community which still spoke the religious language of the Apostle. He therefore had no difficulty in 'making sense of' most parts of Paul's writings. With the old prophets it was quite otherwise. Irenaeus had not, and in his day could not have had, any adequate historical knowledge of the religious or social background of their lives, nor of the religious issues of their day. Neither had he such knowledge of Hebrew psychology or literary style as would allow the interpretation of one mode of expression into another. There was therefore chapter after chapter in the Old Testament which had no obvious religious sense, or which even contained that which was offensive to the piety of the Church. The more strongly it had to be maintained that every part of these writings was a plenary revelation from God the darker became the mystery. The only way to wrest crumbs of spiritual food from the sordid story of the incest of Lot's daughters, for example, was to turn the old legend into a parable of the Old and of the New Israel.[115] S. Irenaeus himself unconsciously confesses to the difficulty which was the mainspring of such exposition. To those who have not a knowledge that prophecy is fulfilled in Christ the Old Testament reads like a fable.[116] The mental process which is at work is perfectly exemplified by the instruction of a presbyter quoted by Irenaeus. The believer should not censure wicked actions recorded in Scripture without specific blame, but 'should *search for a type.* For not one of those things which have been set down in Scripture without being condemned is without significance.'[117] The Church therefore did as the Rabbis had done before

when in the same position, and carried on the allegoristic tradition. At the expense of launching into subjectivity she put to silence the Gnostic scoffer.

In closing we may observe that at one point S. Irenaeus makes a slight approach to the conception of progressive revelation, which scientific doctrine is the true resolution of the difficulties referred to above. He teaches that God, on account of their hardness of heart and idolatry, subjected the Hebrew People to the whole Mosaic Law.[118] This hard discipline was, however, temporary, and is done away in Christ.[119] In appearance Irenaeus is not far from the Gnostics here. He agrees with them in separating in the Scriptures precepts which were fulfilled in Christ, and precepts which were abolished. The former are the fundamental rules of moral life, the 'natural precepts'.[120] The latter are the added ritual commandments of the Law. In one important respect, however, he rises above the heretical systems, which saw the inferior commandments as the work of an inferior god. The precepts of merely temporary validity were just as certainly an authentic revelation of the Supreme God as were the eternal and absolute. The temporariness and imperfection of some of the commandments of the Mosaic Law was the provision of the true God in pursuit of an eternal and unchanging purpose, yet by methods temporarily adapted to the frailty of mankind. S. Irenaeus had here grasped the essential principle of progressive revelation. When he allowed himself to be inspired by Christ's words about divorce,[121] rather than by theories about 'Scripture Types', he was well in advance of the Gnostics, both in religious insight and in historical appreciation of the Old Testament.

Notes

1. IV.19.2, i.437.

2. cf. *Dem.* 45 on Isaiah 66_1.

3. IV.14.1, i.417.

4. IV.40.1, ii.49.

5. IV.3.1, i.383.

6. II.13.3, i.155.

7. . . . In this case Irenaeus would be using the term coined by Anaxagoras to express the identity of the molecules, of which any substance was formed, with the substance itself. . . .

8. Harvey, i.282.

9. *Dem.* 3.

10. See pp. 240-2 *infra.*

11. III.20.3, i.350.

12. Isaiah $1_{2,10,16}$, in IV.41.2, ii.51.

13. IV.12.4, i.411.

14. IV.34.4, ii.20; Harvey, ii.271.

15. *Dem.* 50,51.

16. Isaiah 17_{7-8} in *Dem.* 91; see also Isaiah 54_1 in *Dem.* 94.

17. The chief examples are: Isaiah 9_6 in III.19.2, i.346; 11_{1-4} in III.9.3, i.280; 11_{2a} in III.17.1, i.334; 11_{2b} in III.17.3, i.336; 11_{2-3a} in *Dem.* 9; 11_{1-10} in *Dem.* 59; 26_{19} in IV.33.11, ii.14, and in *Dem.* 67; 43_{19-21} in IV.33.14, ii.17, and in *Dem.* 89; 45_1 (LXX) in *Dem.* 49; 49_{5-6} in *Dem.* 50; 50_{5-6} in *Dem.* 34 and 68, and in IV.33.12, ii.15; 50_{8-9} in *Dem.* 88; 52_{13}-53_8 in many places; and 60_{17b} (LXX) in IV.26.5, i.464.

18. 13_9 in V.35.1, ii.151; 25_8 (LXX) in V.12.1, ii.83; 26_{19} in V.15.1, ii.95, and in V.34.1, ii.148; 30_{25-6} in V.34.2, ii.148-9; 32_1 in V.34.4, ii.150; 54_{11-14} in V.34.4, ii.150-1; 65_{17-18} in V.35.2, ii.154; 65_{18-22} in V.34.4, ii.151; and 66_{22} in V.36.1, ii.156.

19. Isaiah 66_3 in *Dem.* 96.

20. See pp. 82-5 *infra.*

21. Harvey restores this word for '*talis*'; see an interesting foot-note to this passage.

22. Isaiah 2_4 in IV.34.4, ii.21, Harvey, ii.272.

23. Isaiah 2_3 in *Dem.* 86.

24. Isaiah 2_4 in IV.34.4, ii.21.

25. *Dem.* 87.

26. Isaiah 43_{19} in *Dem.* 89.

27. Isaiah 49_{5-6} in *Dem.* 50,51.

28. See pp. 193-4 *infra.*

29. *Dem.* 69.

30. Isaiah 53_4 in IV.33.11, ii.14, and in *Dem.* 67.

31. II.28.5, i.224; Harvey, i.354.

32. III.19.2, i.345.

33. *Dem.* 70.

34. *Dem.* 54.

35. III.19.3, i.346.

36. III.21.6, i.356.

37. *Dem.* 54.

38. III.21.4, i.355.

39. III.21.4, i.355.

40. III.9.3, i.280.

41. III.17.1, i.334.

42. *Dem.* 53.

43. IV.23.1, i.455-6.

44. IV.23.1, i.455-6.

45. Romans 10_{15} in III.13.1, i.314.

46. IV.8.1, i.396.

47. Romans 3_{30} in III.10.2, i.283, and in V.22.1, ii.114-15; Romans 4_3 in IV.5.3, i.388; Romans 8_{15} in III.6.1, i.269-70.

48. IV.27.4, i.471.

49. IV.29.1-2, i.475.

50. III.20.2, i.348-9.

51. I.10.3, i.45.

52. V.1.1, ii.55.

53. Romans 13_1 in V.24.3, ii.120.

54. Romans $13_{1,4,6}$, in V.24.1, ii.119.

55. IV.36.6, ii.33-4.

56. IV.37.1, ii.37.

57. IV.27.2, i.468.

58. On Romans 6_{12-13} in V.14.4, ii.94.

59. See also on Romans 8_{8-11} in V.8.1, ii.73, and in V.10.2, ii.80.

60. See also pp. 231-2 *infra.*

61. III.16.3, i.325-6.

62. III.22.1, i.359-60.

63. III.16.9, i.333.

64. Romans $6_{3-4,9}$, in III.16.9, i.332-3; Romans 8_{34} in III.16.9, i.333; Romans 9_5 in III.16.3, i.326.

65. III.22.3, i.360.

66. *Paulinismus,* p. 87.

67. III.18.3, i.339.

68. See pp. 223-5 *infra.*

69. IV.37.1, ii.36-7.

70. See pp. 228-9 *infra.*

71. IV.37.4, ii.39.

72. IV.12.4, i.411.

73. *Paulinismus,* p. 101.

74. The Latin version runs: *finis enim Legis Christus;* Harvey, ii.179.

75. III.20.3, i.349-50.

76. III.20.3, i.350.

77. III.18.2, i.338.

78. V.32.1, ii.141-2.

79. III.18.7, i.343.

80. III.18.7, i.344.

81. III.21.10, i.358.

82. III.23.8, i.368.

83. III.16.3, i.326.

84. *Dem.* 35.

85. *Dem.* 24.

86. *Paulinismus,* p. 102.

87. On Galatians 3_{5-9} in IV.21.1, i.451.

88. IV.5.3, i.388.

89. IV.7.2, i.395.

90. V.5.2, ii.67.

91. III.18.2, i.338.

92. Romans 9_{25} in III.9.1, i.278.

93. Romans 4_{12} in IV.7.2, i.395.

94. IV.34.2, ii.19.

95. IV.2.7, i.382.

96. Romans 12_{16} in V.22.2, ii.115.

97. Romans $13_{1,4,6}$ in V.24.1, ii.119.

98. V.10.1, ii.78.

99. IV.27.2, i.468.

100. III.13.1, i.314.

101. *Paulinismus,* p. 98.

102. *Kirche b.I.* p. 43.

103. *H.D.* II.252.

104. III.17.3, i.336.

105. IV.22.1, i.454.

106. See pp. 80-1 *supra.*

107. The interpretation of the Parable of the Sower, Mark 4_{14-20}, is probably later allegorism. Many passages in the Fourth Gospel are also probably of a similar nature.

108. *Essai,* p. 31.

109. IV.33.11, ii.14-15; *Dem.* 67.

110. V.15.1, ii.95; V.34.1, ii.148.

111. IV.33.11, ii.14; *Dem.* 67.

112. III.20.3, i.350.

113. See p. 80 *supra.*

114. *Dictionnaire,* VII, col. 2422.

115. IV.31.1-2, ii.1-3.

116. IV.26.1, i.461.

117. IV.31.1, ii.1.

118. IV.15.1-2, i.419-20; IV.16.3, i.423-4; IV.16.5, i.425; *Dem.* 8.

119. III.2.2, i.260; III.12.14, i.313; IV.15.2, i.420; *Dem.* 35, 89, 95.

120. IV.13.4, i.415; IV.16.5, i.425. For this phrase see also IV.13.1: *Et quia Dominus naturalia Legis, per quae homo iustificatur, quae etiam ante legisdationem custodiebant qui fide iustificabantur et placebant Deo, non dissolvit, sed extendit et implevit, ex sermonibus eius ostenditur.* Harvey, ii.180-1.

121. IV.15.2, i.420-1.

Table Explanatory to References in Footnotes

I. Texts

Harvey, ii.50 represents Volume II, page 50 of W. W. Harvey's edition of the Greek, Latin, Syriac, and Armenian texts of *Adversus Haereses* (Cambridge, 1857).

II.30.6, i.235 represents *Adversus Haereses,* Book II, chapter 30, paragraph 6, trans. by Roberts and Rambaut: being found on page 235 of Volume I of the translation of S. Irenaeus in the *Ante-Nicene Christian Library* (T. & T. Clark, Edinburgh, 1868). N.B. *This translation follows the chapter divisions of Massuet and Migne,* to which the references given consequently correspond.

Dem. 54 represents *The Demonstration of the Apostolic Preaching,* Chapter 54, as translated from the Armenian and edited by Dr. J. Armitage Robinson, 'Translations of Christian Literature' (S.P.C.K., London, 1920).

II. Works Cited

Anthropologie d.H.I. Die Anthropologie des Hl. Irenaeus, Ernst Klebba (in *Kirchengeschichtliche Studien;* Knöpfler, Schrörs, Sdralek) (Münster, 1894).

Christus Victor Den kristna försoningstanken, Gustav Aulén (Stockholm, 1930), trans. under the title *Christus Victor* by A. G. Hebert (S.P.C.K., 1931).

Corps Mystique Le Corps Mystique du Christ, Émile Mersch, Second Edition (Paris, 1936). . . .

Der Mittler Der Mittler, Emil Brunner, Second Edition (Tübingen, 1930).

Dictionnaire Article 'Saint Irénée', by F. Vernet, in *Dictionnaire de Théologie Catholique,* Volume VII (Vacant, Mangenot, Amann) (Paris, 1923).

DG. Lehrbuch der Dogmengeschichte, Reinhold Seeberg, Volume I, Second Edition (Leipzig, 1908).

Entstehung d.a.K. Die Entstehung der altkatholischen Kirche, Albrecht Ritschl, Second Edition (Bonn, 1857).

Essai Essai sur la Théologie d'Irénée, Paul Beuzart (Paris, 1908).

H.D. II *History of Dogma,* A. von Harnack; translation of Third Edition by Neil Buchanan, Volume II (1896).

Idea of Faith The Idea of Faith in Christian Literature, W. H. P. Hatch (Strasbourg, 1925).

Irenaeus Irenaeus of Lugdunum, F. R. Montgomery Hitchcock (Cambridge, 1914).

Irenäus Christologie Des heiligen Irenäus Christologie in Zusammenhange mit dessen theologischen und anthropologischen Grundlehren, Ludwig Duncker (Göttingen, 1843).

Jesus and His Church R. Newton Flew (London, 1938).

Jesus and His Sacrifice Vincent Taylor (London, 1937).

Kirche b.I. Die Kirche bei Irenäus, Wolfgang Schmidt (Helsinki, 1934).

Kyr.Ch. Kyrios Christos, Bousset (Göttingen, 1921).

L'Église L'Église Naissante et le Catholicism, Pierre Battifol, Fifth Edition (Paris, 1911).

Logosidee Geschichte der Logosidee in der Christlichen Litteratur, Anathon Aall (Leipzig, 1899).

Marcellus Marcellus von Ancyra, Theodor Zahn (Gotha, 1867).

m.Vollkommenheit Die Christliche Lehre von der menschlichen Vollkommenheit, H. H. Wendt (Göttingen, 1882).

Paulinismus Der Paulinismus des Irenaeus, Johannes Werner (in *Texte und Untersuchungen,* Gebhardt & Harnack, Volume VI) (Leipzig, 1889).

Reich-Gottes Die Geschichte des Reich-Gottes-Gedankens in der alten Kirche bis zu Origenes und Augustin, Robert Frick (Giessen, 1928).

Romans Moffatt New Testament Commentary, C. H. Dodd (London, 1932).

St. Paul Christianity According to St. Paul, C. A. A. Scott, Second Edition (Cambridge, 1932).

Studium DG. Leitfaden zum Studium der Dogmengeschichte, Friedrich Loofs, Fourth Edition (Halle, 1906).

Theologie d.I. Die Theologie des Irenaeus, G. Nathaniel Bonwetsch (Gütersloh, 1925).

Theophilus Theophilus von Antiochen adversus Marcionem und die anderen theologischen Quellen bei Irenaeus, F. Loofs (in *Texte und Untersuchungen,* Harnack & Schmidt, fourth series, Volume I) (Leipzig, 1930).

Other works References given *in loco.*

Joseph P. Smith (essay date 1952)

SOURCE: An introduction to *St. Irenaeus: Proof of the Apostolic Teaching,* translated by Joseph P. Smith, The Newman Press, 1952, pp. 3–44.

[*In the essay below, Smith examines the history, form, style, and structure of Irenaeus's* Proof of the Apostolic Preaching. *Smith states that Irenaeus's motivation for writing the treatise was to prove that what the apostles preached was true, and that his intention was not to provide an exposition on apostolic preaching.*]

A. AUTHOR AND WORKS. PUBLICATIONS OF THE
PROOF.

1. THE AUTHOR

St. Irenaeus (end of second century) comes in the history of patrology after the "Apostolic Fathers," and the "Apologists," and in some ways constitutes a link between the latter and the Alexandrians. He may be said to belong to the third generation of Christian teachers, for in his youth in Asia Minor he had known the celebrated Polycarp, and the latter had himself known our Lord's own disciples, in particular the apostle St. John, who made him bishop of Smyrna.[1] In the reign of Marcus Aurelius, when persecution was raging at Lyons, Irenaeus was a presbyter in that city, and about the years 177-8 succeeded the martyr St. Pothinus as its bishop.[2] The year of Irenaeus's death is un-

known; it is commonly put at about 202, at the time of the renewed persecution under Septimius Severus, and he is venerated as a martyr; but the evidence for his martyrdom is unsatisfactory.[3]

2. HIS WORKS.

Eusebius of Caesarea, to whom we are ultimately indebted for all we know about Irenaeus (apart of course from what may be gathered of him from his own writings), mentions as his works a treatise against Marcion, various letters, of which the most celebrated is the one written to Victor of Rome on the Paschal controversy, sundry other treatises, including one "for the proof of the apostolic preaching" (the one here translated: hereafter referred to as "the *Proof*"), and—his principal work—the five books of his treatise against the Gnostics, commonly known under the title **Adversus haereses,** "Against the heresies."[4] This work, as we shall see later, is of especial importance for the understanding of several passages of the *Proof.* Irenaeus wrote in Greek, but his works have not come down to us, as such, in the original.[5] We have, however, in addition to numerous fragments in various languages, much of the original Greek as quoted by later writers, and the complete text, in an early Latin version, of **Adversus haereses,** and also an Armenian version of the last two of the five books of that work, and of the *Proof.* This last-named version is the one here translated into English; with the exception of a few fragments textually of little help and also in Armenian, it is our only source for the text of the *Proof.*

3. ARMENIAN TEXT.

The *Proof* was for long supposed to have been irretrievably lost, but in 1904 an Armenian version of it was found, in a manuscript belonging to the church of Our Lady at Erevan (now the capital of Soviet Armenia) by the Most Rev. Archimandrite (of Etschmiadzin) Karapet Ter Mekerttschian, who was at the time acting as Vicar to the Catholicos, and later became bishop of Azerbaidjan.[6] In addition to the *Proof,* the same manuscript contained several other items, including the Armenian version, referred to in the previous paragraph, of books 4 and 5 of **Adversus haereses,** which is in the same peculiarly distinctive Armenian style as that of the *Proof.* The Armenian text of the *Proof* was first published, by the finder of the manuscript, in 1907, along with a German translation, and with annotations by Adolf von Harnack, who also divided the text into a hundred "chapters."[7] It was republished in 1919 in Graffin and Nau's *Patrologia Orientalis.*[8]

4. TRANSLATIONS.

The German translation of the *editio princeps* appeared in a revised edition in 1908; meanwhile a Russian version had been published by Professor Sagarda.[9] In 1912 Professor Simon Weber published a new German translation, and in 1917, after a controversy as to the accuracy of the rival German versions, the same scholar published a Latin one whose aim was to reproduce the Armenian text, so far as possible, word for word.[10] In the meantime a French version, made by the Rev. J. Barthoulot, S. J., had been published by Professor Tixeront.[11] This was reprinted as an appendix to the *Patrologia Orientalis* republication of the text (1919), which was itself accompanied with an English version made by the finder and others. In 1920 another English version was published by J. Armitage Robinson, and a Dutch one by H. U. Meyboom; and in 1923 an Italian one, by Ubaldo Faldati.[12] The present translation was made from the text of the *editio princeps* (attention being paid to various emendations since suggested) and collated with the text as republished in the *Patrologia Orientalis*. All the other translations mentioned above, except the Dutch one and the second edition of the first German one, were glanced through, and are occasionally mentioned in the notes to this version, but no attempt was made to collate them exhaustively. The chapter-division of the *editio princeps,* though open to certain criticisms, has of course been retained.

B. TEXTUAL HISTORY.

5. AUTHENTICITY.

That the work here presented to us is really, as the manuscript describes it, the "Proof of the Apostolic Preaching" of Irenaeus, is certain on internal grounds. The title and the name (chapter 1) of the addressee agree with the information given us by Eusebius;[13] the work reflects the conditions of the end of the second century,[14] and its matter and manner and many of its turns of expression agree with Irenaeus's known writings, and with his views and preoccupations; the parallels with *Adversus haereses* are many and striking; in chapter 74, to mention a particular example, we have the erroneous statement that Pontius Pilate was procurator under Claudius, a peculiar error which agrees with what we know to have been Irenaeus's opinion;[15] and in chapter 99 the author refers to his work against heretics, using the longer title which is given by Eusebius as that of *Adversus haereses.*[16]

6. DATE AND PLACE OF COMPOSITION.

This reference in the *Proof* of the author's *Adversus haereses* enables us to date the former work approximately, since it must be posterior to at least the earlier part of *Adversus haereses.* In book three of this work there is a list of the bishops of Rome, which concludes with the mention of Eleutherus as then reigning.[17] Since Eleutherus became bishop of Rome about the year 174, and Irenaeus became bishop of Lyons about 177-8 and died early in the following century, we may say that he composed the *Proof* at Lyons, when bishop of that city, in the last two decades of the second century, or possibly in the early years of the third. Certain indications have been taken to favour a later rather than an earlier date within that period, and it has even been suggested that the work belongs to the last years of its author's life; but this is all pure conjecture.[18]

7. DATE OF THE MANUSCRIPT. TEXTUAL TRADITION.

Our manuscript bears, at the end of the *Proof,* a scribal postscript naming as its owner the "Lord Archbishop John . . . brother of the holy king." This can be none other

than the well-known "John Arkhayeghbayrn (= 'king's-brother')," for his learning also called "Rabbun," younger brother of King Hethum I of Cilicia (1226-1270). John, who died in 1289, was consecrated bishop in 1259 and only some years later is given the title "archbishop." Hence one may date the manuscript around the middle of the second half of the thirteenth century, say between the years 1265 and 1289. The translation itself was certainly made long before that date, and is in a style which lends itself to certain corruptions; exactly to what extent corruption has taken place we have no external means of judging; as has already been said, our only sources for the text of the *Proof* are this manuscript and a few Armenian fragments. The latter exhibit certain differences from the text of the manuscript, and these differences are most likely to be accounted for by "editing" of a text more faithfully copied in our manuscript.[19] Two questions, however, we are now able to answer with a certain degree of confidence: at what date was the Armenian translation made, and was it made directly from the Greek. As will be seen from the following paragraphs, it was almost certainly made in the sixth century, and most probably between the years 570 and 590, and was made directly from the Greek.

8. DATE OF TRANSLATION: EXTERNAL EVIDENCE.

In previous editions of the *Proof,* or of the Armenian version of *Adversus haereses 4-5,* the dating has been based on quotations from those works found in earlier manuscripts than ours. Both versions are in the same peculiar style, and were assumed to be the work of the same translator and so of the same approximate date. When the two versions were first published, earlier quotations were known from "Stephen the Philosopher," who was identified with the eighth-century Stephen of Siunikh, and from the "Catholicos Sahak," who was identified as Sahak (Isaac) III, who died about the end of the seventh century.[20] Hence the translations were said to be not later than the seventh century.[21] Later, however, quotations were found which were datable to the beginning of that century.[22] The quotations are but slight, and show certain differences from our text, so that one might suspect them to be the result of independent translation, and so far from proving that our translation already existed, rather to suggest the contrary. There is, however, sufficient evidence of the peculiar style of our version to allow us to account for the differences by supposing editorial revision and the corruption to which the style lends itself, and conclude, with Jordan, that our version must have been made before the year 600.[23]

9. DATE OF TRANSLATION: INTERNAL EVIDENCE.

As soon as the Armenian text of the two works in our manuscript was published, Conybeare pointed out its stylistic resemblance to the Armenian version of Philo, and maintained that it must be from the same pen, and hence of the early fifth century, since the version of Philo was then assigned to that period.[24] Subsequent research has established beyond a doubt that our text does in fact belong, if not necessarily to the same pen, at least to the same school and to the same short period as the Armenian Philo and certain other translations from the Greek; but the dating of this school has been matter of dispute.[25] The Armenian Philo was known to Moses of Khoren, who used to be assigned to the mid-fifth century. Considerable doubt has been thrown on this dating, most scholars now maintaining that Moses of Khoren must be assigned to the eighth or ninth century. Conybeare controverted this view, and so do other scholars.[26] Failing Moses of Khoren, the earliest witness to the Armenian Philo is the historian Elisaeus; he also used to be assigned—and by many still is assigned—to the mid-fifth century; but it has been maintained that he wrote subsequently to 570.[27] What may be regarded as certain is that the translation of the *Proof,* along with that of Philo and others, belongs to the earliest phase of the so-called "Hellenising" school of Armenian. It has been maintained that this school cannot be earlier than the sixth century: it has seemed necessary to allow for a considerable lapse of time between the "golden age" of Armenian (first half of fifth century) and this strange style; and the school seems to have been unknown to the philhellene historian Lazar of Pharp, who wrote at the beginning of the sixth century. If we accept the beginning of the sixth century as the earliest date, and the end of the same century as the latest, both because of the evidence mentioned in the previous paragraph and because of Elisaeus, we are left with the sixth century as the period within which our translation was made. The extraordinary style, however, of the versions in question can scarcely be accounted for except by supposing them to have been intended as "keys" to the Greek text, and the most probable dating of the rise of the Hellenising school is that of Akinean, who places it among the Armenian exiles at Byzantium after 570.[28] That was the period at which Armenian students had need of such keys. The early phase in question cannot have lasted long, and in any case many of the exiles returned after 590, so that one may say that our version was most probably made at Byzantium between the years 570 and 590. In deference, however, to the views of a number of scholars, it should be pointed out that this is the latest dating, that the reasons for denying that the Hellenising school can have existed before the sixth century are by no means cogent, and that if those scholars are right in maintaining the traditional date for Moses of Khoren or Elisaeus, our translation may be put into the first half of the fifth century. This, however, seems to the present writer unlikely.

10. TRANSLATION DIRECTLY FROM GREEK.

In the case of an Armenian translation of an early Greek work, one has to take into account the possibility that the translation was made not directly from the Greek, but from a Syriac version. In the *editio princeps* of the *Proof* attention was drawn to certain peculiarities in the text of the *Proof* and of *Adversus haereses* which seemed to indicate such a Syriac intermediary, but in view of the counter-indications the question was left open, and in republishing the text in *Patrologia Orientalis* Bishop Karapet mentions the general agreement that the version had been made directly from the Greek (though indeed in the meantime it

had even been suggested that the translation had been made from a Latin version).[29] In fact, the indications of Syriac transmission were with one exception utterly negligible, and even that exception is inconclusive, while the indications of translation directly from the Greek were very strong.[30] One may now assert with confidence that our version, like the other products of the Hellenising school, is based immediately on the Greek text; one may even go further and say that it seems to have been made with a view to providing those insufficiently acquainted with Greek with a key to a text they were studying in the original.

11. STATE OF TEXT.

From what has just been said, the reader will be able to form an idea of the style of Armenian in which the version is cast.[31] At its worst it approaches the type "The hand-shoes, which on the table were, have I in the pocket put." A particular feature of this early period of the Hellenising school is the use of doublets or expanded expressions to render Greek compound words or "bracket" the exact meaning of single Greek words.[32] This does not as a rule occasion any difficulty, as the resulting expressions, though often awkward, are fairly intelligible. The attempt, however, to reproduce the syntactical features of the original in a language which has its own different syntax results inevitably in passages whose meaning is most obscure, even when one known the language whose syntax is so reproduced, and which are not infrequently quite unintelligible to the average scribe and so give rise to corruptions in the text which increase the difficulty of reconstructing the original.[33] The text presented to us by our manuscript is no doubt fairly faithful, and is on the whole not unsatisfactory, but it is too often obscure, and in several places is manifestly corrupt.[34] It may however be said that there is no doubt in any matter of importance as to the general sense, and one can confidently accept the version as being on the whole a faithful rendering of Irenaeus's work.

12. PRINCIPLES OF THIS TRANSLATION.

In making the present version, the translator has aimed at producing a readable English text which should represent not the peculiarities of the text of our manuscript, but Irenaeus's work, while still remaining a translation of our manuscript, not a paraphrase. Accordingly, where the Armenian text seemed certainly at fault, the necessary emendation has been rendered in the text of this version, the meaning of the manuscript's text being relegated to the notes. Other emendations, while not so accepted into the text, have been mentioned in the notes. Where the exact sense of the Armenian was uncertain, the present version has sometimes aimed at reproducing in English the same ambiguity; at other times a likely version has been given in the text, and alternatives in the notes; in one or two places, where the general sense was clear enough, but the expression obscure or corrupt, a paraphrase has been given, representing what seemed most likely to have been the original expression. In all such cases the reading of the manuscript is given and briefly discussed in the notes, as also in cases in which it might be useful to readers to know the origin—and the degree of probability or possibility—of variant renderings in other versions. Such textual notes, however, have been kept as brief as might be, this series not being the place for philological discussions. The punctuation of the Armenian text is not invariably felicitous, and has been departed from without acknowledgement of such departure in the notes, except once or twice where the change of punctuation has induced a notable change of sense. In the Scriptural quotations the wording of the Douay version has been used as a rule wherever the Armenian seemed to rest on the same reading of the Scriptural original. In dealing with the peculiarities of the Armenian style (use of doublets and expansions) there is perhaps a certain inconsistency. Such doublets are not seldom desirable in English, and they have occasionally been retained for that reason; in general, however, expanded expressions have been reduced where English usage normally requires such a reduction (for example, the constantly recurring "it is right and necessary" is regularly rendered by use of the verb "must"); moreover, in several places a wordy expression of the text has been kept even though in all probability it represents an expansion of the original.

C. Title, Addressee, Form and Style.

13. Title.

Eusebius refers to the work as . . . "(a treatise) for the demonstration of the apostolic preaching."[35] The word here rendered "demonstration" is in Greek *epídeixis,* and the treatise is therefore sometimes referred to as "the Epideixis." This word means, more or less, "demonstration," since it connotes not only "proof" but also "display, exposition," and J. Armitage Robinson used for his English version the title "Demonstration of the Apostolic Preaching."[36] The present version retains the title "Proof . . . ," both because it has some claim to be regarded as the traditional English title, and because it goes better in English, and because it represents in fact the scope of the treatise. The academic question has been raised, whether Irenaeus's title was . . . "(A treatise) for the proof . . . ," as we read in Eusebius, or simply . . . "Proof . . . ," the rest being merely the turn of phrase used by Eusebius in order to work the title into his sentence. In any case, the Armenian manuscript bears the shorter form: "Proof of the Apostolic Preaching."

14. Addressee.

The treatise is addressed, in chapter 1, to "my dear Marcianus," and Eusebius tells us that Irenaeus wrote it . . . "to brother Marcianus."[37] The use of this expression does not necessarily mean that Marcianus was the writer's brother according to the flesh, though this is a natural interpretation of it, and there seems to be no reason why that should not be the meaning. If Marcianus was Irenaeus's brother, he was presumably some years his junior. A "brother Marcianus" is also named as author of the *Martyrium Polycarpi,* and some have sought to identify him

with the addressee of the *Proof;* but the reading "Marcion" is regarded as more likely than "Marcianus" in the *Martyrium.*[38] Others have thought our Marcianus must have been a recent convert from Judaism, in view of Irenaeus's repeated insistence, in the *Proof,* that the Old Law has been abrogated.[39] This insistence is indeed remarkable, and calls for an explanation, but as we shall see, it is not necessary to seek such an explanation in any judaising tendency of the addressee. He must have been a former companion of Irenaeus, for in chapter 1 we read: "Would that it were possible for us to be always together . . . As it is, as we are at the present time distant in body from each other . . ."; and he may perhaps have been a bishop, or at least a priest, for in the same chapter he is told that the treatise will help him to confound heretics and preach the truth, and it seems to be suggested—though the rendering here is uncertain—that he has the "care of souls."[40] It seems clear at least that he was not a mere catechumen.

15. Literary Form.

The *Proof,* then, is written in the form of a letter, as indeed all of Irenaeus's writings seem to have been, not only the "letters" more properly so called, but his other treatises also being cast in letter form; even *Adversus haereses* is addressed, in the prefaces to the individual books, to an unnamed "dearly beloved" (in the singular). It is, however, evident that the *Proof,* like *Adversus haereses,* is a planned composition, and destined for the general public, so that though it was doubtless addressed to a real Marcianus, we may regard the letter-form as being in effect a literary artifice; it was at that time a common one. The construction is on the whole clear and logical enough in the arrangement of the matter, though in this, as we shall see later, Irenaeus was probably simply following his source; and precisely in the earlier chapters, where he is himself responsible for the arrangement of the matter, there is a little of the confusion and repetitiveness which seems to have been characteristic of Irenaeus.[41] If one has at times the impression of a string of quotations introduced by nearly identical formulas, this is only to be expected in view of the nature of the work; and in other places the quotations are led up to or followed in a more artistic manner.

16. Style.

In the preface to the first book of *Adversus haereses* Irenaeus says that niceness of language is not to be expected of him, since he was living "among Celts" and speaking for most of his time a foreign tongue; nor artistic elegance, since he had never learnt it; but he adds that he writes with affection and expects to be read with affection. The style of the *Proof,* like that of *Adversus haereses,* is frequently confused—in fairness to the men who translated Irenaeus into often enigmatic Latin and Armenian, it should be remarked that not all of the obscurity is due to the fault of the translators—and at times repetitive and diffuse; and here, in fairness to Irenaeus, it may be said that the failure of his translators to see their author's point has led to not a little false phrasing and lost emphasis which have made the style seem even more repetitive. The very sentence, in the first chapter, in which the author promises to be brief, is itself a model of rhetorical prolixity. So indeed is the whole chapter, and the following section, and it seems clear that, as is normally the case, the introductory portion of the work was aiming deliberately at literary effect.

D. Division and Contents.

17. Division.

Harnack, as has already been said, divided the text into a hundred numbered "chapters," and this division is retained in the present translation. In addition, for convenience of reference, headings have been added, which do not always coincide with the chapter-division, and the treatise has been divided into four main sections. There is a fairly clear distinction of topic in the course of the treatise, which serves as a basis for this division, but it is not so easy to choose the exact spot at which to divide, and the division here adopted makes no claim to being better than others. The treatise may be first divided into two parts, corresponding to the "moments" before and after Christ, and each of these parts may be further divided into two sections. After a short introduction on the need of orthodox faith and good works, there follows a section on the Trinity, creation, and the fall of man. This constitutes the first section of the "pre-Christian" part; the second section recounts the development of God's plan for the undoing of the evil wrought by the fall, in the course of Old Testament history, culminating in the Incarnation. The first section of the "Christian" part deals with Christ as seen in the Old Testament; and the second section with the New Law. There is a short conclusion, warning once more against heretics. The thesis of each of the four sections may be summarised as follows.

18. God and the Creatures; the Fall.

(Chapters 1-16): the way of life is that of the orthodox faith and good works. Faith tells us we are baptised for the remission of sins in the name of one God almighty, Father, Son (who became man and died and was raised), and Holy Spirit (who spoke through the prophets and is poured out upon the faithful). God is supreme ruler over all things, for they are His own creation; with His Word (the Son) and Wisdom (the Holy Spirit) He made all things. The Father is invisible and incomprehensible, the Son appears as a link with man, the Holy Spirit is given by the Son to man, and leads him to the Son, who brings him to the Father, who gives incorruptibility; God has made us His sons. There are seven heavens in which dwell angels. God is glorified by His Word and Spirit and by their angels. He made man as His own image, from earth and His own Spirit, free and lord of the world, including its angels, and set him in Paradise, giving him a help like himself. Adam and Eve were children, innocent and guileless, and were deceived by the jealous angel into disobeying God's prohibition of the tree of knowledge, imposed on them as a sign of subjection and a condition of immortality; so man was cast out of Paradise and became subject to death, the angel and the serpent being cursed for their part in his fall.

19. History of Redemption.

(Chapters 17-mid. 42): The devil brought about the first death through Cain, and man went from bad to worse, especially through marriage with angels, who corrupted him with wicked knowledge, until man was destroyed by the Flood. God saved Noe and his sons; of the latter, Cham was cursed and the curse worked itself out in his descendants, while first Sem and then Japheth were blessed, the blessings being inherited in the same order by their descendants. That of Sem came to Abraham, who found God and was justified by faith, and to his seed, whom God rescued from Egypt through Moses, and to whom He gave the Old Law. Through Jesus son of Nun (to whom He had given that holy name) He brought them into the promised land, which they took from the descendants of Cham, and where they had a kingdom and were taught by the prophets, until God's promises were fulfilled in the virgin birth of Christ of the seed of Abraham and of David; so man was brought into contact with God, by a repetition of creation and by obedience which restored man to the likeness of God and undid the primal disobedience. Christ's birth, death, and resurrection are real, so we are really saved. His apostles founded the Church and gave the Holy Spirit to the faithful, and in the calling of the Gentiles through the Church the blessing of Japheth is inherited by his descendants.

20. Christ in the Old Law.

(Chapters mid. 42-85): All this is foretold in the Old Testament. Christ is there as the "Son in the beginning" in creation; He appeared to Abraham and to Jacob, and spoke with Moses, and spoke through the prophets. The prophets foretold His eternal kingdom, His incarnation, the virgin birth, and told where and of what stock He would be born, and foretold His kingdom of peace in the Church. They prophesied His entry into Jerusalem, His miracles, His sufferings and crucifixion, His descent into hell, His resurrection and His ascension into glory, where He now reigns at the right hand of the Father, till He judge in triumph. (This section, though it may so be resumed in brief space, is the largest of the four.)

21. Christ in the New Law.

(Chapters 86-100): The fulfilment of the prophecies confirms our faith, showing the truth of the mission of the apostles. The abrogation of the Old Law was foretold; it is superseded by the Law of Charity. Christ's exaltation was foretold, and the establishment of the New Covenant, as the inheritance of the Gentiles, who were to become a holy people. So is brought about a change of heart in man, and the Church is more fruitful than the Synagogue; the old chosen people has given place to the new, and we have no need of the Law. Man is restored to his lost innocence and is virtuous without the Law. He is saved by the invocation of the name of Christ; God accomplishes what is impossible to man. This is the preaching of the truth, which is that of the Church and must be sincerely accepted. Heretics sin against Father or Son or Holy Spirit; we must avoid their ways if we hope to be saved.

22. PROBLEMS PRESENTED.

Certain problems cannot fail to present themselves to the reader of the *Proof.* In the first place, the title suggests that the work is an exposition of the preaching of Christianity; but though the theology is of course Christian, the argument is drawn practically entirely from the Old Testament, and there is no mention for instance of the Eucharist, or of several other points essential to Christianity. On the other hand, there are certain curious emphases, and in particular the repeated insistence on the abolition of the Old Law. These and similar problems find an answer in the following sections in this Introduction.[42]

E. SCOPE AND IMPORTANCE.

23. APPARENT AIM: CATECHETIC.

The aim of the treatise is stated in its first chapter: to give Marcianus "in brief the proof (*or* exposition) of the things of God," or, as we would put it nowadays, "a compendium of theology," which should serve both to guide him to salvation and to enable him to refute heretics and expound the faith with confidence "in its integrity and purity." This description suffices to show the importance, as a Christian document, of the *Proof;* it seems to correspond to the title understood in the sense "exposition of the apostolic preaching," and to promise to be the earliest summary of Christian doctrine we have, and at that, from the pen of a bishop separated by only one intervening generation of teachers from the apostles themselves. It has in fact been called a catechetical work, representing Christianity as then expounded by the bishops to the faithful.[43] Nevertheless, this estimate must be accepted with reserve. Beyond a doubt, we have here in fact an exposition of much of what was preached by the apostles; but a persual of the *Proof* suffices to show that it cannot be regarded as a complete exposition of their preaching, or of what Irenaeus regarded as "Christianity."

24. REAL AIM: APOLOGETIC.

Though Marcianus is told that by means of the treatise he may "comprehend all the members of the body of truth," this is to be "in a few details"; the treatise is "in the form of notes on the main points," and its aim is to confirm the faith of Marcianus and enable him to confound heretics.[44] The real thesis of the work is seen from the passage in chapter 42 in which we are told that God caused our redemption to be prophesied in order that when it came we might believe, and from the passage in chapter 86 in which we are told that the realisation in Christ of the prophecies is the proof that the witness of the apostles is the truth, and from the author's preoccupation especially at the beginning and end of the work to insist on the need for or-

thodoxy and the avoidance of heresy.[45] The author wishes to prove that what the apostles preached was true rather than to give an exposition of their preaching, and is concerned for the "integrity" of the faith not so much in the sense of its "exhaustiveness" as in the sense of its "soundness."[46] The points on which he repeatedly insists are those which were denied by the heretics. Hence the work has been said to be apologetic rather than catechetical;[47] and while its catechetical aspect cannot be denied, it is certainly apologetic in aim, though not in quite the same sense as the works of the earlier "apologists." It is rather "apologetics" in the modern sense, aiming not so much at the defence of Christianity against paganism or Judaism, as at the positive establishment of the credentials of the orthodox Church. It is, in fact, a "proof of the apostolic preaching," that is, a proof of the divine mission of the Church founded by the apostles. It may indeed be called a "compendium of theology," but, as Weber puts it, it is "fundamental theology."[48] It has the practical aim of establishing the truths whose acceptance means acceptance of the orthodox Church—the rest will follow from that.

25. METHOD. EXEGESIS.

This proof is drawn mainly from the Old Testament, and the treatise is important for its use of Scripture; indeed it has been called a Biblical manual.[49] It passes in review practically the whole of the Old Testament, showing how it prepares the way for the New. Irenaeus's exegesis is characterised by that development of "typical" senses which was so much in accord with the spirit of the times, the method employed by the apologists, developed still further by Irenaeus and Clement of Alexandria, and carried to its greatest heights by the latter's successors. The exegesis of the *Proof,* as befits a work written not for edification alone, but to bring conviction, is comparatively sober. Inevitably it is at times arbitrary or based on mere associations, but it is free from the wilder flights of fancy found elsewhere, and there is no cabbalistic juggling with letters or numbers.[50]

26. IMPORTANCE.

The importance of the *Proof* as a "manual of theology," although not in the same sense as might have been hoped, is clear enough from what has been said in the preceding paragraphs; it should be pointed out, however, that the finding of this lost work has in fact added little to what was already known. The *Proof* contains little that was not already to be found in even earlier documents; in particular, little that is not in *Adversus haereses.* There are, it is true, one or two points which may be regarded as an advance on that work, but the real importance of the *Proof,* as compared with *Adversus haereses,* is due to its manner of presentation, its brevity and coherence. One may say that it is important not so much for its theology, as for being precisely a *manual* of theology.

F. THEOLOGY OF THE *PROOF.*

27. IRENAEUS'S PREOCCUPATIONS.

For an account of Irenaeus's theology in general, or of that of the *Proof* in particular, or of the systems of his

Gnostic adversaries, the reader must be referred to the existing treatises on those subjects. There are certain points, however, which should be touched on here, because some acquaintance with them is necessary to the proper understanding of the author's expressions in the *Proof.* Irenaeus has certain definite ideas to which he constantly returns, and his allusions are not seldom difficult to interpret without knowledge of the idea underlying them. Moreover there are in the *Proof* several statements of which one risks missing the point unless one knows what prompted the author to make them, namely his preoccupation with the errors—now long forgotten—of his opponents, the Gnostics in general, and Marcion in particular. It will not be out of place, therefore, to give here a brief account of such points of Irenaeus's theology, and of Gnosticism, as are relevant to the understanding of the *Proof.*

28. GNOSTICISM; MARCION.

The proper title of Irenaeus's principal work, commonly known as **Adversus haereses,** was "Exposure and Overthrowal of Knowledge falsely so called"; and the "knowledge falsely so called" was Gnosticism, which may be roughly described as belief in various systems of esoteric doctrine, whose knowledge was supposed to bring salvation to the initiate.[51] In the board sense Gnosticism is fairly universal both in time and in space, but in the strict sense the world is applied to certain forms current in the Greco-Roman world from some time before the birth of Christ until several centuries later. In Irenaeus's time such "fancy religions" were rife, and constituted an especial danger to Christian orthodoxy. Gnosticism is not, of course, a specifically Christian heresy, but then, as ever since, Gnostic sects drew largely from Biblical and Christian sources; several of their leaders, and many of their adherents, were ex-Christians, or regarded themselves as being Christians, as having the true interpretation of Christian revelation. Marcion, against whom Irenaeus wrote a special treatise, was the son of a bishop, and seems to have been a bishop himself, and was one of the most prominent of the pseudo-Christian leaders, numbered by Irenaeus and others along with the Gnostics, though his system differed considerably from the general run of Gnosticism.[52] Though all Gnosticism was distinguished by certain fundamental peculiarities, the various sects differed considerably in their views; not all sects held all the views attributed in the following paragraphs to "the Gnostics," as is clear enough from the fact that several of them are mutually exclusive.

29. GOD AND THE WORLD.

The perpetual problem of theology is to reconcile the transcendence and goodness of God with this world's dependence on Him and with the existence of evil. For the Gnostics, the supreme God was unknowable, entirely aloof from matter, and matter was the root of evil. The void between God and the world was filled by a number of spiritual beings produced by "emanation" from God and by multiplication among themselves, and called Aeons.[53] Matter was eternal, or the abortive product of a fallen Aeon; material things and the spiritual principle in the world

were not of like nature, matter being foreign to God and the root of corruption and beyond salvation, but spirit being (ultimately) from God, and immortal. This world was created, or formed from chaotic matter, by a being, who himself owed his origin to God or to the Aeons, known as the demiurge;[54] for some sects, the angels were creators. Though, as has been said, the origin of evil was seen in matter, an evil principle was commonly posited as a third member of a triad: God—demiurge—"devil." From this account there arise several particular points which have their repercussions on the *Proof,* and which will be considered in greater detail in the following paragraphs. Irenaeus's own outlook naturally resembles that of the Gnostics in certain respects; both were the product of the same intellectual milieu, and both were ultimately based on the same sound philosophy. For Irenaeus too, as we shall see, the gulf between God and the world had to be filled in; but it was filled in not by intermediate "emanated" beings, but by God's own Word and Spirit; matter was of itself incapable of salvation or incorruption, but was nevertheless good, created by God, and part of man, and so, by the redemption, brought into touch with incorruptibility; evil is due not to any essentially evil principle but to the misuse of godlike free will.

30. GOD THE FATHER.

The "God the Father" of the New Testament is the supreme God. In that, Irenaeus and the "Christian" Gnostics are in agreement. For Irenaeus, as for the Gnostics, He is invisible, incomprehensible, not to be circumscribed in space; yet it is He who "contains" all things; He is unknowable and unapprochable—save through His Son and the Holy Spirit.[55] The "God" of the Old Testament is, as He Himself says, the creator. Hence, for the Gnostics, He was *not* the supreme God, the Father-God of the New Testament, but the demiurge; some of them even represented Him as the enemy of God, and the source of evil. Marcion in particular elaborated the distinction between the God of the Old Testament and the God of the New; the former was the demiurge, the "God" of the Law, just but severe, jealous and violent, having for his favourite people the Jews, and intent on bringing about a Messianic Jewish empire, and the source of strife and evil; whereas the God of the New Testament is kind and merciful, a God of peace, and wishes to save men from evil, by making use of the demiurge's Messianic plans and turning them to His own ends. In all these views, God's intervention to save mankind could be described as the interference, by an "other God" with the creatures of the demiurge. Hence the importance for Irenaeus of the line of argument adopted in the *Proof,* showing the continuity between the Old Law and the New; and hence the special emphasis on the identity of God the Father with the creator, on the fact that He—the creator—is Lord of all men, Jews and Gentiles alike, both just judge and loving Father.[56]

31. GOD THE SON.

As "God the Father" is the supreme God, so Christ is His Son. Here too Irenaeus is at least in verbal agreement with the Gnostics. For Irenaeus, He is the Word of God; God created through Him, it is He who gives matter its solidity, and He is immanent in the universe as the Platonic world-soul.[57] He was ever with man, and is the link whereby we have access to the transcendent Father.[58] He is "the Son" because He is the "reproduction" of the Father, His image, expressed on the plane of possible contact with creation; He was always with the Father; the manner of His "generation" is inscrutable.[59] Because He is the visible image of the invisible Father, it was He who manifested Himself materially in the theophanies of the Old Testament (to Adam, to Abraham and Jacob and Moses).[60] So too man is made in His image;[61] and in His incarnation He reproduced the original creation of man in order to "recapitulate" all things.[62] It is He who confers the Holy Spirit. For the Gnostics, Christ the Saviour was an Aeon. In consequence of their view of matter as essentially evil, they maintained that he did not really assume a human body. According to Marcion and others he took only a "seeming" body, and that not through the Virgin, but by a special act; Marcion represented him as appearing for the first time in the synagogue at Capharnaum; according to others, he came "through" the Virgin, but "took nothing from her."[63] According to others, the child born of Mary was not Christ but only Jesus, the son of Joseph, or of the demiurge, or a man prepared to act as the "vehicle" of Christ; Christ descended upon him in the form of a dove at his baptism, and left him before his passion. In all these views "Christ" was not really born, nor did he really die or rise again. These errors also find their reactions in the *Proof.*[64]

32. THE HOLY SPIRIT.

The Holy Spirit, for Irenaeus, is the Wisdom of God; in creation, He is associated with the Word; it is He who speaks through the prophets, and in Scripture, but it is the Word who communicates Him to men.[65] At man's creation, God breathed into him His own Spirit, which is free from evil and so kept man innocent until man rejected Him by the fall.[66] Man's likeness to God was given by the Spirit, and restored by the pouring out of the Spirit on the faithful, which gives man back his lost innocence, rendering him virtuous without the law; it is the Spirit who leads man to Christ.[67] Irenaeus does not state explicitly the divinity or personality of the Holy Spirit, but that is no reason for speaking of his "binitarianism." He enumerates Father, Son, and Holy Spirit as the three "articles" of the faith; he says the Spirit is the Wisdom of God, and he constantly associates Him with the Word, whose divinity and personality he does expressly declare; so that his view is clearly perfectly orthodox: the Holy Spirit is a divine Person, proceeding from the Father (though Irenaeus does not of course use that expression), and conferred on creatures through the Son.[68] Marcion and others rejected the sending of the Holy Spirit, and His gifts, especially that of prophecy; for which they are taken to task, without being named, in the *Proof.*[69]

33. MAN.

God made man with His own hands, that is, with the Word and the Spirit; He made him from earth, giving him an outward form to His own "image" (that is, to that of the Son), and gave him "likeness" to God by breathing into him His own Spirit.[70] Man was created free like God, and lord of the world, including its angels, and immortal; he was intended to develop a more and more perfect likeness to God, but the very freedom of will which likened him to God proved his undoing, since he misused it and so lost his high estate and his "likeness" to God (though the "image" was in his outward form and not lost) and his immortality.[71] Man is composed of body, soul, and spirit; in *Adversus haereses* Irenaeus gives an account of this composition, with the soul drawn between the attractions of spirit and body, resembling the description of the charioteer in the *Phaedrus.*[72] All three elements are necessary to man as God made him and meant him to be, but whereas body and soul are the constituents of man as an animal forming part of creation as a whole, the spirit is a special "godlikeness."[73] For the Gnostics, matter was evil and incapable of salvation; only the soul and spirit could be saved. Irenaeus insists that the body too is part of man, and that everything is equally the creation of the one God, not only angels and the (spiritual) heavens, but also this world and man, body as well as soul and spirit.[74]

34. "SPIRITUAL MAN" AND GOOD WORKS.

For the Gnostics, all men were not alike; fundamental to Gnosticism was a special interpretation of the trinity body—soul—spirit. As has already been said, the body was for them beyond salvation. The soul might be saved, the spirit could not but be saved. A current characterisation of men (not peculiarly Gnostic; it is found for example in the New Testament) divided mankind into three classes; according to his "spiritual level" a man might be described as "material" (or "earthly" or "carnal"); or as "sensual" (to use the translation adopted in the Douay version); or as "spiritual."[75] For the Gnostics this represented a division of the human race into three classes with respect to salvation. The "material" man—the unbeliever—would not be saved in any case; the "sensual" man—the ordinary run of believers; for the "Christian" Gnostics, orthodox Christians—could attain a measure of salvation, by reason of his faith, but must supplement it by good works; the "spiritual" man—the Gnostic initiate—was saved as such, by virtue of his superior knowledge, quite apart from "good works."[76] Irenaeus interprets quite differently from the Gnostics the statement that *flesh and blood cannot possess the kingdom of God;*[77] and if he agrees with them not only that the "sensual man" needs good works as well as faith, but also that he who has the spirit is thereby saved and is superior to the law, which *is not made for the just man;*[78] this is because the spirit knows no evil, and he who has it is virtuous by reason of the "change of heart" which it produces, and abounds in good works without needing to be admonished by the formulated word of the law.[79] The Spirit is offered to all men and necessary to all men; the man who does evil loses the spirit and ceases to be a "spiritual man." Instead of being distributed between three classes, belonging as it were to the devil, to the demiurge, and to God, all men alike—believers, Jews, or Gentiles—are the creatures of the one God, though He does not stand in the same relation to all of them.[80]

35. THE TRINITY AND MAN.

Particularly clear and striking in Irenaeus is the account of the persons of the Trinity in their dealings with man. Reference has already been made to the distinction between the "image" of God (the Son) and the "likeness" (in the Spirit), and to the representation of the Son and the Spirit as the "hands" of God.[81] The rôles of the persons of the Trinity are expressed in the exegesis of Eph. 4. 6: here it is the transcendent Lord, the Father, who is *above all,* the creative Word, the "world-soul," who is *with all,* and the vivifying Spirit in man's constitution who is *in us all.*[82] The Father reveals Himself in His "reproduction," the Son, and the Son gives the Spirit to the prophets, who convey the revelation to man. In the process of redemption there are two chains of action, from God to man and from man to God. In the former, God the Father sends the Son, who becomes incarnate, and who confers the Spirit, who enables man to live as he should; in the latter, the Spirit leads man to the Son, who presents him to the Father, and the Father confers "rebirth" and incorruptibility.[83] "The Son is knowledge of the Father, and knowledge of the Son is through the Holy Spirit."[84]

36. RECAPITULATION; COMMUNION; INCORRUPTIBILITY.

Mention should also be made of certain other ideas to which Irenaeus often makes reference: the "recapitulation" of all things in Christ, man's "communion" with God, and his reception of "incorruptibility" as the fruit of the redemption. The idea of "recapitulation" ("summing up," "restoring") is a central theme in Irenaeus; the word is of course taken from St. Paul, but the idea has been worked out by Irenaeus in his own way.[85] For him the "recapitulation" is a "fresh start," accomplished in the manner of the incarnation; a taking up again and restitution of God's original plan for man by the reproduction in the incarnation of the features of the original creation, and the reversal of the features of the fall. The immediate effect of this "fresh start" is to bring about, or rather, to restore, a "communion" between God and man. The reference is not merely to the two natures in the person of Christ, for the "communion" is between the human race and God the Father. It is more than a mere "reconciliation" in the sense of the putting off of wrath; the expression implies friendly intercourse, a readmission in some degree to the privileged position held by Adam as the companion of God. By it we are enabled to be "adopted" by God, and to approach the Father and so receive the ultimate fruit of the redemption, "incorruptibility."[86] For the Gnostics, as has been said, incorruptibility, the immortality of the body, was a contradiction in terms, matter being essentially corruptible; only the soul or spirit could be immortal. For Irenaeus too, incorruptibility was bound up with the transcendence and unattainability of God, not "natural" to matter, but a special favour, granted originally under condition, and after the fall unattainable to man, had it not been for the visible coming of Christ. Soul or spirit, however, is part of man but not man; the whole man is saved, body included; thanks to the coming of Christ, to the "fresh start" or reca-

pitulation accomplished in His incarnation, and the restored communion with the Father, man is enabled to receive from the Father that incorruptibility which will finally restore him to the state to which the first, immortal, man was destined before the fall.[87]

G. LITERARY AFFINITIES OF THE *PROOF.*

37. IRENAEUS AND HIS SOURCES; CONTRA IUDAEOS.

It has been suggested that Irenaeus is rather a reporter or compiler than either an original thinker or even a systematiser; and it is true that investigation of his works reveals much that parallels or echoes the works of earlier writers, and that if one amplify the echoes, almost the whole of Christian literature up to his time might seem to have been drawn upon by him; he can hardly, however, be called an uncritical compiler, and his system, though often confusedly expressed, is—*pace* Loofs—coherent enough.[88] Moreover, many parallels between Irenaeus and earlier writers are doubtless to be explained not so much by direct borrowing as by a common source in the catechetical tradition, or by independent exploitation of a common work of reference. In the case of the *Proof,* it was suggested by J. Rendel Harris, as soon as the text was published, that the source of the main body of the work was probably a collection—since lost—of "Testimonies against the Jews," that is to say, of Scriptural texts grouped under argument-headings, intended to convince the Jews out of the Old Testament itself that the Old Law was abolished, that its abolition was foreseen in the Old Testament, and that its purpose had been to prepare and prefigure the New Law of Christ.[89] Such "testimonies" have come down to us from later times, and it seems not improbable that such a collection of Scriptural "ammunition" existed already before the time of the apologists, perhaps even before the New Testament was written. The "apostolic preaching" itself must have relied largely on such arguments (witness the examples in the New Testament), and that not only as addressed to the Jews. Such a hypothesis explains not only the almost exclusive use, in the *Proof,* of the Old Testament, and that in an ordered series of texts, and the insistence on the abolition of the Old Law, and such arguments as the greater fruitfulness of the Church as compared with the Synagogue, but also several points of detail, which will be mentioned briefly in the following paragraphs.

38. SCRIPTURE.

It would seem, from the *Proof,* that Irenaeus was not acquainted with the whole of the Old Testament—not that there is anything very remarkable in that. Both Harnack and Tixeront remark that he restricts his Old Testament history within the limits which are traditionally those of such a catechesis.[90] This is but natural; but in the course of his review of the historical books, Irenaeus has inserted, in the appropriate places, what seems to be intended as a description of the book of Leviticus, and what is expressly put forward as a description of the book of Deuteronomy, though neither of these books is of great use for the end in view; and both the descriptions leave one with the impression that Irenaeus knew little of the books in question, beyond their names, although he has quotations from both of them.[91] He must, of course, have been acquainted with such portions of the Old Testament as were in "liturgical" use, for reading at Christian assemblies; and no doubt for him, as for most other Christian writers and speakers, the liturgical text with which he was acquainted was often the immediate source of his quotations. For the *Proof,* however, he seems, as has been said, to have used a collection of texts grouped under argument-headings, rather than the original text or even such selections from it as were used liturgically. Certain of the texts cited by him as if they were continuous and taken *en bloc* from the book of the Old Testament which he names as their source are in fact formed out of the relevant portions of a longer continuous passage, or simply composite, consisting of phrases taken from quite different parts of the same book (though at other times he separates such phrases and says explicitly that they are from different places).[92] It would seem here that Irenaeus has simply transcribed what was grouped together in his source, rather than sought his matter in the text of the Scripture itself. The occasional false attribution of quotations is easily explained by supposing that Irenaeus has attributed a text to the author named in his source for a preceding text, but harder to explain if he looked up the original text; the same may perhaps apply to one or two apparently apocryphal quotations; Irenaeus may have mistaken a headline or gloss for a quotation.[93] Moreover, though he is as a rule careful to name the sources of his quotations, he leaves some of them attributed to an unnamed "prophet" or "the prophets," or "the book of the twelve prophets."[94] Had he taken the quotation directly from the source he could easily have ascertained who was the author; but perhaps his secondary source did not distinguish them; though it is of course possible that he was citing from memory or from his own notes and had simply forgotten or not noted the author. The quotation, in the *Proof,* of Isa. 5. 9 in two different forms, in close succession and apparently without realisation that the same passage was in question, shows that the passage was not simply taken from a copy of Isaias.[95] It may also be remarked here that where an Old Testament passage has been quoted in slightly different form in the New Testament, Irenaeus, while attributing the passage to its Old Testament source, and making no mention of the New, quotes nevertheless in the form used in the New Testament.[96] So too he quotes simply as "Jeremias" the passage attributed to that prophet in Matt. 27, 9-10, although it is not found in our Old Testament text.[97] Moreover, in one place he attributes to "the Law" not only the expression which is in fact from "the Law," namely *the God of Abraham and the God of Isaac and the God of Jacob,* but also the words *the God of the living,* which occur in the argument with which the New Testament follows up the quotation from the Law.[98] Apart from this circumstance, the actual text of the New Testament is little used in the *Proof,* though both St. Paul and St. John are quoted, and there are of course echoes of the New Testament and statements based on it, and a parallelism of argument—more likely due to Irenaeus's immediate source than to the New Testa-

ment itself—especially with the epistle to the Romans, and with the Acts. In *Adversus haereses* Irenaeus makes it clear that for him the Septuagint version represents the genuine Old Testament in Greek;[99] but his quotations occasionally depart from the standard "Septuagint," and that not only when they are in the form given in the New Testament. This may well be another indication of a collection of "Testimonies" as an immediate source; indeed the agreement with the New Testament forms seems to be accounted for in this manner rather than by use of the New Testament as the immediate source.[100]

39. APOCRYPHA.

Not only canonical Scripture, but also apocryphal books have evidently served, directly or indirectly, as sources. They are rarely, however, quoted as "Scripture." In addition to the quotation attributed to Jeremias in the New Testament, of which mention has already been made, there is in the *Proof* another quotation attributed to Jeremias, which is not to be found in our Old Testament text, and one attributed to David which is likewise not to be found.[101] There are several other statements or expressions, some of them apparently quotations, which may perhaps have an apocryphal source.[102] Under this heading it may be remarked here that the quotation from the *Shepherd* of Hermas which is found (unacknowledged) in the *Proof* is also found in *Adversus haereses,* and is there cited as "Scripture."[103] Apart however from direct quotation, there are several dependences upon apocryphal literature. The account of the corruption of humanity before the flood is evidently taken from an apocryphal source, almost certainly the book of Enoch.[104] The "seven heavens" are more likely to have been taken from such a source than from the Gnostics, whom Irenaeus would scarcely have copied; he may have taken them from the Testament of Levi, or from the *Ascensio Isaiae,* of which there seem to be some echoes in other places of the *Proof;* or he may have been influenced by the apologist Aristo.[105] The account of the behaviour of the star at Bethlehem, and of Abraham's search for God, are also doubtless of apocryphal origin.[106]

40. TRADITION; PLATO; THE "ELDERS."

As has already been remarked, much of what is common to Irenaeus and other writers may well represent not so much influence of one on another as the common stock. So too the influence of philosophical systems, especially Platonism, is to be accounted for not so much by direct influence of the authors of those systems, as by the intellectual common stock of educated men of the time. The influence of Platonism on Irenaeus's theology, as on that of his fellows, is evident; Christian theology was formulated against a background of Platonism, and the Platonic tradition passed into the Christian one. It is natural that Irenaeus, who was so proud of his connection, through Polycarp, with the apostles, should appeal to tradition in the form of the declarations of men of the apostolic age. He refers in several places (twice in the *Proof*) to the "elders," by which he means "the disciples of the Apostles," as evidence for what he says; but it is worthy of notice that one of the references in the *Proof* merely records as a tradition of the "elders" the chiliastic interpretation of Isa. II. 1-10 which Irenaeus defended in *Adversus haereses* against the one which he gives in the *Proof.*[107] The erroneous view, which reappears in the *Proof,* that Christ was crucified under Claudius, is said in *Adversus haereses* to have been the tradition of the "elders."[108] Irenaeus's source for what he attributes to the "elders" was no doubt, to a certain extent, Polycarp. For chiliasm in particular, however, though it is also found in Justin, and for other matters also, his source was that indefatigable and uncritical collector of "apostolic gossip," Papias.[109] Whether he had any other written source is doubtful. No doubt much of the Johannine and Pauline character of Irenaeus's thought is to be attributed to the influence of Polycarp, who had known St. John personally, and who repeatedly quotes St. Paul in his own epistle to the Philippians.

41. APOSTOLIC FATHERS.

In addition to Papias, whose chiliasm is represented in the *Proof* by the brief reference to the tradition of the "elders," and to Polycarp, who is quoted by name in *Adversus haereses,* and of whose epistle to the Philippians there may be an echo in the *Proof,* and to whom Irenaeus doubtless owed much that he had assimilated in youth and no longer consciously referred to any source, Irenaeus is indebted to others of the apostolic age.[110] Mention has already been made of the quotation in the *Proof* of the *Shepherd* of Hermas, and of the fact that in *Adversus haereses* the same quotation is attributed to "Scripture." There are also perhaps other echoes of the *Shepherd* in the *Proof,* and there is what may be a reminiscence of the *Didache,* though it is not likely that the expression "the teaching of the twelve apostles" in chapter 46 is an allusion to the title of that work; and there are echoes of the Epistle of Barnabas, and perhaps of Clement of Rome. All these "echoes" however are but echoes, some of them very faint, and do not prove any real dependence on those works.[111]

42. JUSTIN.

The most considerable of the apologists, and a man who enjoyed a great reputation for his learning, was St. Justin "philosopher and martyr." It seems not improbable that Irenaeus knew Justin personally at Rome, and it is certain that he knew his works and was influenced by them. The dependence of Irenaeus on Justin has commonly been regarded as evident and extensive. Whole passages of Irenaeus can be parallelled in the works of Justin; Irenaeus's Scriptural repertoire, and his readings of the text, agree to a large extent with Justin's; Irenaeus often repeats not merely the exegesis or argument of Justin, but even some of the actual wording used by Justin.[112] On the other hand, there are certain notable differences, and the community of Scriptural repertoire and exegesis may well be due to a common use of a source book rather than to dependence of Irenaeus on Justin.[113] The hypothesis put forward above, of a book of texts against the Jews, would account for the choice of texts and the order and nature of arguments of both writers, and would better account for the differences

of treatment, since such a source book would give simply the headings and the texts and glosses, not a detailed working out of the argument; while the occasional echoes of the wording used are, as Harris has pointed out, much better accounted for by supposing that both authors echo a gloss or a headline or an adjacent text of a source book, than by supposing that Irenaeus had gone to the works of Justin for his quotations and echoed some chance phrase in Justin's further argument.[114] In *Adversus haereses,* Irenaeus names Justin as the author of a treatise against Marcion; otherwise he does not refer to him, and Loofs, in his posthumously published article on the sources of Irenaeus, went so far as to say that there is no demonstrable borrowing on the part of Irenaeus from the extant works of Justin.[115] This statement, like several others in the same article, will scarcely meet with general approval; but it may well be admitted that direct dependence of Irenaeus on Justin cannot be shown to have been so extensive as it has been thought to be.

43. THEOPHILUS; OTHER APOLOGISTS.

In the work just referred to, Loofs endeavoured to show that one of Irenaeus's principal sources was the lost work of Theophilus of Antioch against Marcion. However that may be, it seems certain enough that Irenaeus owed something to Theophilus. There are not a few echoes in Irenaeus of Theophilus's extant work *Ad Autolycum.* The most striking of these to be found in the *Proof* is the representation of Adam and Eve as children, used to explain both their innocence and the ease with which they were misled into sin.[116] There are also in the *Proof* a couple of points of resemblance to Melito of Sardis, and perhaps an echo of the *Epistola ad Diognetum;* and in one or two points there may be dependence on Aristo: mention has already been made of the fact that belief in "seven heavens" is said to have been found in Aristo. The account given by Origen of Aristo's lost "Discussion between Jason and Papiscus" shows it to have been a sort of "Summa contra Iudaeos," but though such a work may well have influenced both Justin and Irenaeus, it is not likely that it is to be identified with the lost "Testimonies" supposed as a common source for the latter; more likely it too was an elaboration of that source.[117]

44. CLEMENT OF ALEXANDRIA?

That there are parallels between the works of Irenaeus and those of Clement of Alexandria is undeniable. It seems however more likely that such parallels are to be attributed to a common source, or that if there was any borrowing, it was Clement who borrowed from Irenaeus rather than vice versa. The literary activity of Irenaeus falls in the last quarter of the second century, until his death perhaps about 202; that of Clement extends from about the eighties of the second century until his death about 215. Hence the two were contemporaries, and influence in both directions is possible. Clement, however, probably started writing later than Irenaeus, and certainly continued after the latter's death. Moreover, book three of *Adversus haereses* can be dated by the reference to Eleutherus as the reigning pontiff to between the years 174 and 189.[118] Clement was already writing before the death of Eleutherus, but of his extant writings only the *Protrepticus* can be assigned with any likelihood to that early period; while both *Stromata* and *Paedagogus* were produced after the date commonly assigned for the death of Irenaeus.

H. Some Remarks on the Matter of the *Proof*.

45. Omissions and Inclusions.

What has been said in the preceding sections supplies an answer to some of the problems mentioned in § 21. The almost exclusive use of the Old Testament, the silence (apart from the mention of baptism) on ecclesiastical, liturgical, or sacramental discipline, and the insistence, on the contrary, on the abrogation of the Old Law, may be explained both by the scope of the work—to induce acceptance of the orthodox Church, which will ensure all the rest—and by the hypothesis that the source used was a book of "Testimonies against the Jews," a source suitable for a work with such a scope. The comparative silence on eschatological questions may be accounted for in the same way; this was not a point of importance for the question of orthodoxy, except in so far as Gnostic views on the possibility of bodily resurrection were concerned, and this point is dealt with. Various other emphases and repetitions are likewise due to the need to set orthodox theology against the views of the Gnostics. Thus in treating of the Trinity Irenaeus naturally does not concern himself with points that only later took on special importance, such as the divinity of the Holy Spirit or the Person and natures of Christ; but he does insist on the divinity of the Creator, and His identity with God the Father, and on the genuineness of Christ's birth, and on the charism of prophecy given by the Holy Spirit, because these points, little as it may now seem necessary to dwell on them, were the ones denied by the "trinitarian heretics" of the time. The curious insertion, as if it were fundamental to Christianity, of the "seven heavens" may perhaps be due to the desire to set this "orthodox Gnosticism" against the more extravagant Gnostic cosmologies.

46. Some Notable Points.

From what has been said of the contents of the *Proof* and of the theology of Irenaeus, it will be clear that the work contains much that is of interest to theologians: the theology of the Trinity, the Soteriology, and especially the development of the parallelism between creation—fall and incarnation—redemption; and the exposition of Old-Testament history as leading up to the Church. Among minor particular points may be mentioned the attribution of Scripture to the Holy Spirit, and of the fourth gospel to Christ's "disciple John," and the testimony to the use of the trinitarian formula in baptism.[119] The resemblance between the account of Christianity given at the end of the *Proof* and that given by the "Reformers" has been remarked on by several writers;[120] lest this resemblance be regarded as having any polemical value it should perhaps

be pointed out that it is purely negative and due to the scope of the work, which is clearly not the exposition of Christian institutions; and that Irenaeus does insist on the insufficiency of faith without good works, and that the faith which he demands is clearly "dogmatic faith," that is, orthodoxy; and that redeemed man undergoes a "change of heart," and by virtue of the Spirit is not "still a sinner."[121]

47. Some Peculiarities.

Mention may be made of several points in the *Proof* which are striking not because of their importance, but because of their comparative rarity, at least in an account of the fundamentals of Christianity. Thus the reading of Gen I. 1, whence Irenaeus derives his interpretation "a Son in the beginning . . . ," is not extant elsewhere than in the *Proof*, though similar interpretations are found elsewhere.[122] The other points are none of them uniquely Irenaean, and some of them are not very uncommon, but they may still be remarked upon; some of them are certainly erroneous. Thus he includes, as if it were essential to orthodoxy, the doctrine that there are seven concentric heavens; and he says Pontius Pilate was procurator of Claudius.[123] There is also a reference to the Millenarian tradition, so phrased however that it cannot be concluded with certainty that Irenaeus still upheld the truth of that tradition.[124] Other points more or less "peculiar" are the representation of Adam and Eve as children, and of man as lord of the world, including the angels in it; the attribution to the Word of God's walking with man in Paradise, and of the theophanies of the Old Testament, and of the punishment of Sodom and Gomorrha; and the statement that the decalogue was abolished along with the rest of the Old Law.[125] Remarkable also is the exegesis of the blessings of Sem and Japheth, the latter being realised in the calling of the Gentiles through the Church; and the detailed parallelism between the creation of Adam, from virgin soil and the Spirit of God, and the incarnation of Christ, from the Virgin and the Holy Spirit; and the identification of the Holy Spirit, instead of the Word, with divine Wisdom; and the distinction between the Persons of the Trinity founded on their activity *ad extra*.[126]

48. Leading Ideas.

It may be said that the main points of the doctrine of the *Proof* are, as Irenaeus says, the three "articles" of the baptismal "rule of faith": Father (Creator, transcendent but accessible giver of incorruptibility), Son (the Word with the Father from the beginning, immanent in the universe and always with man, linking him with the Father, and in His incarnation "recapitulating" the creation and reversing the fall), and the Holy Spirit (in man, giving him likeness to God and leading him to the Son, speaking through the prophets, making man sinless and superior to the Law, by abiding Charity). The framework of the various "Creeds" is here already clearly discernible.[127] The historical section is of course ruled by the Christian outlook on the history of the world as a history of redemption, with the incarnation as its culmination. In the working out of the argument one may perhaps, by a useful but not rigorously accurate generalisation, distinguish what may be called the "Johan-nine" and the "Pauline" trains of thought: the Johannine insistence on "the Word from the beginning" and His rôle as our link with the Father, and the primacy and sinless-ness of Charity in the Spirit; and the Pauline argument from the helplessness of fallen man and the reversal of the fall by Christ, and the abrogation of the Old Law, as the culmination of God's calling first of Israel and then of the Gentiles to be the heirs of Abraham's justification by faith. Regarded precisely as a "proof," the *Proof* has for its ba-sis the fact that the old dispensation was but the prepara-tion and prophecy of the new, and that the realisation of that prophecy is the proof of the genuineness of the mes-sage brought by the Gospel.

I. Conclusion (Summary).

49. Irenaeus and the Proof.

To resume, by way of conclusion, in the form of an appre-ciation of the work: it is certain that the thirteenth-century Armenian manuscript here translated is a version, made al-most certainly in the sixth century, and from the Greek original, of the "Proof of the Apostolic Preaching" written by St. Irenaeus, bishop of Lyons, in that city towards the end of the second century. Only one intervening genera-tion of tradition separated its author from the apostles themselves, and its value lies in the fact that, invested as it is with the authority of so early a successor to the apos-tolic ministry, it is the earliest document we have that pro-fesses to give an exposition of the basis on which the ap-ostolic preaching rests. It is important as a catechetic-apologetic document, and for its exegesis; though it adds little new matter to what we already knew from *Adversus haereses,* its value, as compared with that work, lies in its compendiousness.

50. The Message of the Proof.

The *Proof* must not be supposed to contain a full exposi-tion of what its author regarded as essential to Christian theology and behaviour; its scope is to prove the Church's credentials. It is addressed to a fellow-Christian, Mar-cianus, who may have been the author's brother, and who may have been a bishop. It expounds the "rule of faith" in the formula of baptism (the mysteries of the Trinity and of the Incarnation), and the history in the Old Testament of the creation and fall of man and the unfolding of God's design for his restoration, showing also how the details of the Incarnation, Ministry, Passion, Resurrection, Ascension and universal Kingdom of Christ were foretold, and thereby proves the truth of the mission of the apostles, and so of the Church which they founded. In the calling of all nations through the Church God's plan reaches its term; as was also foreseen and foretold, the Old Law is superseded by the Law of Charity; we are saved through the name of Christ, by good works and the faith of the orthodox Church.

Notes

1. For Irenaeus's friendship with Polycarp, and the lat-ter's with the first disciples, cf. Irenaeus's letter to Florinus, in Eusebius, *Hist. eccles.* 5. 20. 6-8. Re-garding Polycarp's appointment as bishop of Smyrna, cf. Irenaeus, A.H. 3. 3. 4 ("ab apostolis . . . consti-tutus episcopus"), and Tertullian, *De praescr. haer.* 32 (made bishop by St. John).

   "He may be said" to have belonged to the third gen-eration of Christian teachers; but as he himself says (letter to Florinus as above), he was only a boy when he knew the aged Polycarp; there is about half a cen-tury between their deaths (156?-202?).

2. Presbyter in Lyons (sent thence on embassy to Rome, to urge leniency towards Montanists), Eusebius, *Hist. eccles.* 5. 3. 4-4. 2. Succession to Pothinus, *ibid.* 5. 5. 8.

3. Irenaeus is venerated as a martyr by both Greeks (feast August 23) and Latins (feast June 28); but Eu-sebius does not say he was martyred. The first extant reference to him as a martyr seems to be in the fifth century (no. 115 of the *Responsa ad quaestiones ad orthodoxos* attributed to Justin; there is also a pass-ing reference in our text of Jerome's Commentary on Isaias 64. 4, but the word "martyr" is here probably an interpolation; Jerome makes no mention of mar-tyrdom in his life of Irenaeus, *De vir. ill.* 35). The statement—second half of sixth century—of Gregory of Tours (*Hist. Franc.* 1. 27; *In glor. mart.* [= *Mir.* 1] 50) that Irenaeus was martyred is rendered suspect by his placing the martyrdom under Marcus Aurelius (in former of *loc. cit.* above).

4. Eusebius, *Hist. eccles.* 4. 25 (treatise against Marcion); 5. 20 (letters to Blastus *On Schism,* to Florinus *On the Sole Sovereignty,* or *That God is not the Author of Evil;* book *On the Ogdoad,* also for Florinus); 5. 24 (letter to Victor of Rome, dissuading him from violence against the Asiatic Churches, who wished to keep to their own tradition in dating Eas-ter, instead of conforming to the Roman custom); 5. 26 (treatises *On Knowledge,* the *Proof,* and a collec-tion of what were probably sermons); 5. 7 and fre-quent references (*Adversus haereses*).

5. Zahn argued that the Greek text of Irenaeus was probably extant in the sixteenth or seventeenth cen-tury; cf. *Zeitschrift für Kirchengeschichte* 1878, p. 288-291 (Zahn); 1890, p. 155-158 (Ph. Meyer); *The-ologisches Literaturblatt* 1893, p. 495-497 (Zahn).

6. The following description of the manuscript is abridged from the full one given in PO* 657 f.: Bound codex, on paper, 245 x 165 mm., in the writ-ing called *boloragir* ("roundhand"), some titles in red ink. 383 sheets remain, but others are missing between nos. 7 and 8. Under the title "Proofs of the Apostolic Preaching" we have: 33ʳ-146ʳ the fourth book of *Adversus haereses,* 146ʳ-222ʳ the fifth book, and 222ʳ-262ʳ the *Proof.*

7. TU 31. 1 (1907): *Des heiligen Irenaeus Schrift zum Erweise der apostolischen Verkündigung . . . in ar-menischer Version entdeckt, herausgegeben und ins*

Deutsche übersetzt von D. Karapet Ter Mekertts-chian und Lic. D. Erwand Ter Minasseantz, mit einem Nachwort und Bemerkungen von Ad. Harnack.

Though this was the *editio princeps,* there was no description of the manuscript (this was supplied when the text was republished, cf. preceding note), and no *apparatus criticus,* though it is clear from the translation that several emendations were adopted (emendations were referred to in the margin of the republished translation, cf. next note but one). The German translation was in the circumstances a highly meritorious achievement, and not all the criticisms later directed against it (e.g. by Weber, cf. n. 10 to Introd. below) were justified; but inevitably it left much to be desired, and this fact hampered Harnack in his annotations.

The Armenian text (without version) of A.H. 4-5 was published by Ter Minasseantz in TU 35. 2 (1910).

8. Patrologia Orientalis 12. 5 (ed. R. Graffin—F. Nau, Paris 1919) 655-731: *S. Irenaeus . . . , The Proof of the Apostolic Preaching . . . , Armenian version edited and translated by His Lordship the Bishop Karapet Ter Měkěrttschian and the Rev. Dr. S. G. Wilson, with the co-operation of H.R.H. Prince Maxe of Saxony, D.D. and D.C.L.* For all that, the version is not infrequently at fault—though it presents several improvements on the original German one—and is further marred by strange misprints.

Tixeront-Barthoulot (cf. n. 11 to Introd. below) is reprinted (747-803) as an appendix to this edition.

9. The revised German version was published in Leipzig, 1908; I have not, however, seen it.

The Russian version of Professor N. I. Sagarda (the "Sagrada" of PO* 655 is an error): *Novo-otkrytoe proizvedenie sv. Irineä Lionskago: Dokazateljstvo apostoljskoj propovēdi,* published in *Hristianskoe čtenie* 87 (1907): 476-491 = foreword, 664-691 = c. 1-50, 853-881 = c. 51-100 and closing remarks. This version was made not from the Armenian, but from the German translation of EP*. Hence its independent value lies only in the competent introduction and notes.

10. German version: Bibliothek der Kirchenväter 4 (Kempten—Munich 1912): *Des hl. Irenaeus Schrift zum Erweis der apostolischen Verkündigung, aus dem Armenischen übersetzt von Dr. Simon Weber, o. Prof. an der Universität Freiburg i. Br.*

The German of this version is superior to that of the first German version, and the text had in the meantime been subjected to discussion; not all the changes so introduced, however, are correct (several were later abandoned by Weber himself).

Controversy: *Zeitschrift für neutestamentliche Wissenschaft* 14 (1913) 258-262 (Ter Minasseantz); *Der Katholik* 94. 1 (1914) 9-44 (Weber); *Zeitschrift für Kirchengeschichte* 35 (1914) 255-260, and 442 as note after the following (W. Lüdtke); *ibid.* 438-441 (Weber).

Latin version: *Sancti Irenaei Demonstratio Apostolicae Praedicationis . . . Ex armeno vertit, prolegomenis illustravit, notis locupletavit Simon Weber . . .* (Freiburg i. Br. 1917). The version is, apart from one or two slips, accurate, but in the nature of things often obscure, ambiguous, or even positively misleading. Though this version is the best means available whereby one who does not know Armenian can form an idea of how the text expressed itself, Latin is not a suitable medium for such a verbal transposition. A Greek version on the same lines would have been more useful. (Lüdtke, *loc. cit.* above, 256, did in fact reconstruct in Greek the second half of c. 34, as a means of judging the merits of the rival German versions).

11. *Recherches de science religieuse* 6 (1916) 361-432; version and annotations by Barthoulot, introduction and additional notes by Tixeront. Reprinted as appendix to PO*, from which it is cited in these notes. The version is very free, and in some places rather a paraphrase than a translation, and the translator has in several places been misled by lack of acquaintance with the peculiar Armenian style of the text.

A new French version is now being prepared, for the series "Sources chrétiennes."

12. English version: J. Armitage Robinson: *St. Irenaeus: The Demonstration of the Apostolic Preaching* (Society for Promoting Christian Knowledge: London and New York, 1920). A good version.

Dutch version: H. U. Meyboom (Leyden 1920). I have not seen this version, and take the reference from J. Quasten, *Patrology* 1 (Utrecht-Brussels 1950) 293.

Italian version: Ubaldo Faldati: *S. Ireneo, Esposizione della Predicazione Apostolica* (Roma 1923). A very accurate version, on the whole.

13. *Hist. eccles.* 5. 26 (cf. § 13 f. of Introd.).

14. This point is developed by Weber, BK* p.v.

15. Cf. n. 314.

16. Cf. § 28 of Introd., and n. 51 thereto.

17. A.H. 3. 3. 3.

18. Though O. Bardenhewer (*Geschichte der altkirchlichen Literatur* 1 [2nd ed. Freiburg i. Br. 1913] 409) and others admit the hypothesis that the *Proof* may have been written contemporaneously with the last two books of *Adversus haereses,* there are several points which have seemed to others to suggest that some time elapsed between the two works. Thus Faldati (F* 44) sees in the difference between the exegesis of Isa. 11. 6 f. in c. 60 of the *Proof* and that in A.H. 5. 32 f. a profound change in the author's views, which must have been the work of a considerable lapse of time; but I do not find this conclusion to be inevitable; cf. n. 270.

F. R. M. Hitchcock (*Journal of Theological Studies* 9 [1908] 286) sees in the statement of c. 48, that kings are Christ's enemies and persecutors of His name, a reference to the persecution under Septimius Severus, and so would put the composition of the *Proof* at the end of Irenaeus's life. But the bishop of Lyons did not have to wait for the persecution under Severus in order to make such a statement.

The reference to *Adversus haereses* in c. 99 of the *Proof* comes after the mention of the first of the three classes of heretics there mentioned. Now the other two classes also are dealt with in *Adversus haereses,* but whereas the first class is treated of in books 1 and 2 (though the principal refutation is in book 4), the other two are mentioned in books 3 and 4. Hence the reference to the earlier work does not necessarily imply that the whole work had been finished, indeed the restriction of the reference to the first class might be taken as a suggestion that only the first two books had been completed. It seems, however, on the whole more probable that *Adversus haereses* was completed some time before the *Proof;* but nothing can be affirmed with certainty in this respect.

19. The fragments are in H. Jordan: *Armenische Irenaeusfragmente,* TU 36. 3 (1913) Fr. 6, 13, 20, 25 (all from the same passage, the beginning of c. 31—cf. n. 156), and Fr. 7e (from c. 40—cf. n. 195). Cf. next paragraph of Introd., and the notes thereto.

20. "Stephen the Philosopher": Fr. 20-22 of Jordan, *op. cit.* in preceding note (20 is from the *Proof,* c. 31—cf. n. 156; 21 is from *Adversus haereses,* and 22 from some other work of Irenaeus).

"Catholicos Sahak": *ibid.,* Fr. 18 (= 22), 19 (= 21).

21. For this dating, cf. EP* p. iv-v. Ter Minasseantz, however, in the preface to the Armenian text of A.H. 4-5, in TU 35. 2 (1910) p. v, puts the period of translation at 650-750.

22. N. Akinean, *HAm.* 24 (1910) 205, puts 604 as the latest date, because of a quotation in a letter of Varthan Kherdogh, and even suggested that the latter was the translator, between 590 and 604.

In 1911 Ter Mekerttschian found yet another manuscript, bearing the title "Seal of the Faith," with a quotation from the *Proof,* distorted however into a Monophysite sense (Fr. 6 of Jordan, *op. cit.* in n. 19 above; from c. 31—cf. n. 156). This manuscript can be dated to the Catholicate of Comitas, which seems to have been about 611-628 (dating of Ter Minasseantz, TU, Neue Folge 11 [1904] 60-62).

Weber (L* 9-10) suggested that Eznik (early fifth century) knew both the *Proof* and *Adversus haereses;* but this would prove nothing, since Eznik used Greek sources directly.

23. Jordan, *op. cit.* 203; similarly Ter Mekerttschian in PO* 656.

In addition to the quotations from the *Proof* and from the last two books of *Adversus haereses,* of which we have the Armenian version, there are also Arme-nian quotations in the same distinctive style from the earlier books of *Adversus haereses,* so that it is clear that the whole work was translated at the same time. Cf. Jordan, *op. cit.* 204 f.

24. C. F. Conybeare, *American Journal of Theology* 16 (1911) 631 f.; more fully in *Huschardzan* (Vienna 1911) 193-203 (in English).

25. The classification of the periods of the "Hellenising" school of Armenian, the *Proof* etc. being assigned to the first period, was established by Manandean in his work *Yunaban dproc'ě ew nra zargac'man šrjannerě* = "The Hellenising school and the phases of its development" in Armenian (Vienna 1928), which had appeared by instalments in *HAm.* 39 (1925) 225-232, 347-354, 539-548, 40 (1926) 15-23, 121-129, 209-216, 305-313, 437-445, 525-533, 41 (1927) 16-23, 109-116, 289-301, 417-425, 559-569, 42 (1928) 25-30, 109-120, 205-213, 303-310, 401-407.

When Manandean wrote, it was still thought that the school must be dated in the fifth century; since that time, however, this view has been generally abandoned (cf. rest of this paragraph of Introd.). There is a concise account of the development of the Hellenising school, embodying the conclusions of the discussion on the dating, by Akinean, in *HAm.* 42 (1932) 271-292 (in Armenian; German résumé 376-380); and a brief account in English, concerned especially with the first group (to which the *Proof* belongs) in H. Lewy, *The Pseudo-Philonic* De Jona (Studies and Documents 7, London 1936) 9-16.

26. In the early period of the controversy over the dating of Moses of Khoren the principal opponent of the traditional date was A. Carrière, *Nouvelles sources de Moïse de Khoren: études critiques* (Vienne 1893); *Nouvelles sources de Moïse de Khoren: supplément* (Vienne 1894); or *HAm.* 6 (1892) 250; 7 (1893) 134, 178, 309; 8 1894) 53, 210. C. F. Conybeare: "The date of Moses of Khoren," *Byzantinische Zeitschrift* 10 (1901) 489-504, maintained the traditional dating; so also in *HAm.* 16 (1902) 1, 85, 129, 193, 236; 17 (1903) 30, 33, 152, 215, 317, 325.

For an account of the question in English, cf. H. Lewy, *op. cit.* and two articles in *Byzantion* 11 (1936) 81-96 and 593-596; in the former of these two articles are further references to earlier literature on the subject.

Other modern opponents of the traditional dating: Akinean, *Lewond Erec' ew Movses Xorenac'i* = "Leontius the Priest and Moses of Khoren" (Vienna 1930): suggests identification of "Moses" with eighth-century Leontius; and Manandean, *Xorenac'u aṙeǐcvaci lucumě* = "The solution of the problem of Khorenatzi" (Erevan 1934): puts Moses at beginning of second half of ninth century.

Against the two works mentioned in the preceding paragraph: S. Malkhasean: *Xorenac'u aṙeǐcvaci šurjě* = "Concerning the Problem of Khorenatzi" (Erevan 1940).

For the traditional dating, against Lewy's articles in *Byzantion,* cf. Adontz, after each of those articles (that is, *Byzantion* 11 [1936] 97-100, 597-599), and *Sur la date de l'Histoire de l'Arménie de Moïse de Chorène* (from *Byzantion,* Brussels 1936). Cf. also Abeghian (following note).

27. Akinean, *Eëlišē Vardapet ew iwr Patmut'iwnn hayoc' paterazmin* = "Elisaeus Vardapet and his History of the Armenian War," which appeared in instalments in *HAm.* 45 (1931) 21-49, 129-201, 321-340, 393-414, 449-473, 585-617, 677-690; 46 (1932) 293-298, 385-401, 545-576; 47 (1933) 33-56, 641-679; 48 (1934) 353-414.

A recent, highly authoritative, history of Armenian literature is that of Manuk Abeghian. I have not seen the Armenian original, but only the abridged Russian version, *Istoria drevnearmänskoj literatury* (Erevan 1948 [vol. 1]). He here maintains the traditional dating (mid-fifth century) for both Moses of Khoren (203-209) and Elisaeus (244 f.).

28. Akinean, *HAm.* 46 (1932) 271-292, referred to in n. 25 above; cf. also Lewy, *op. cit.* at end of same note.

29. EP* vi-vii; PO* 656.

Latin intermediary: Y. Awger, *Bazmavep* 67 (1909) 59-66, 145-160; and cf. Akinean, *HAm.* 24 (1910) 202 f.; 25 (1911) 305-310; also W. Lüdtke, *Theologische Literaturzeitung* 36 (1911) 541.

30. The indications of a Syriac intermediary were: (a) the occurrence in *Adversus haereses* of the name "Elisabeth" in the form *Elišabet'*, with the Syriac sound *š* instead of the Greek *s;* (b) the quotation of Zach. 9. 9, in c. 65 of the *Proof,* not according to the Septuagint but in a form agreeing rather with the Syriac version; (c) the rendering of the name of the prophet Malachy, on the two occasions in which it occurs in the *Adversus haereses* (4. 17. 5 and 4. 20. 2, corresponding to 4. 29. 5 and 4. 34. 2 respectively in the Armenian text as in TU 35. 2, which uses Harvey's numbering), as "angel," as if it were the Syriac common noun *mala'kâ,* "angel, messenger."

The first and second of these may be neglected, since (a) such forms as *Elišabet'* are common in Armenian, and are to be found even in works certainly translated directly from the Greek (cf. Akinean, *HAm.* 24 [1910] 201); and (b) the quotation is not taken from the Old Testament directly, but from Matt. 21. 5 or from a collection of texts (cf. § 38 of Introd. and n. 280).

The third point is more difficult to account for. It is true that "Malachy" is not a normal proper name, but a sort of pen name (cf. Mal. 3. 1: *Behold I send* my angel . . . etc.) and so might be rendered "Angel" or "Messenger" in much the same way as "Qoheleth" is rendered "Preacher" (Ecclesiastes); and that the prophet's name is in fact rendered αγγελος in the Septuagint (Mal. 1. 1); so that Irenaeus might well have used that word. The difficulty is, that he does

not in fact seem to have done so, since the Latin version of *Adversus haereses* has in both places "Malachias." Hence the rendering "angel" of the Armenian version presents a problem; but it does not force the conclusion that the version was made through a Syriac intermediary.

The principal indication of translation directly from the Greek is the style of the version. This is a point which cannot conveniently be documented here; let it suffice to say that the version clearly belongs to a class of servile renderings of Greek texts, so closely modelled on the Greek as to justify the conjecture that they were intended rather as "keys" to the original text than as "translations" in the normal sense. One peculiarity which tells especially against the possibility of a Syriac intermediary is the imitation of the Greek "genitive absolute," of which there are many examples in the version of the *Proof.* This construction is foreign to Armenian, but can be accounted for as a mechanical reproduction of the Greek in a "key"; it is however quite incredible that it can have been transmitted through the Syriac, in which such a construction is incapable of exact reproduction.

Against the use of the form *Elišabet'*, mentioned above, may be set the fact that proper names in general appear in a form which corresponds not to Syriac but to Greek—for example, Sem, Messias, Bethlehem. More telling still is the manner in which the corrupt text of Gen. 1. 1 is transcribed in c. 43: *baresit', sament'ares,* not *barešit', šament'ares.* A Syriac version would have transcribed back into *š* a Greek *s* standing for *š,* and an Armenian version from that Syriac would have reproduced this *š;* transcription in Armenian as *s* argues that the transcription is directly from the Greek transcription. (The corruption of the text in question has also been alleged as an argument against transmission through the Syriac; but corruption may have arisen in the transmission of the version as originally made to the manuscript in which we have it.)

Finally, in c. 25, we read, concerning the Passover, which is put forward as a type of the Passion, "the name of this mystery is *kirk'*." *Kirk'* is a hapax legomenon which seems, as Vardanian pointed out, *HAm.* 24 (1910) 303, to be an attempt to render Greek ασχα in the sense "Passion," as if it were related to πάσχειν "suffer" (Armenian *krel*). Now, any Armenian translator must surely have known that the word was a proper name "Pasch," Armenian *Pasek';* but one can understand how a translator from the Greek, meeting the word here, might have rendered it for the nonce *kirk',* either thinking that it was in origin a Greek word connected with πάσχειν, or at least thinking that Irenaeus was playing on the similarity of the two words (as indeed he almost certainly was: cf. A.H. 4. 10. 1: cuius et diem *passionis* non ignoravit [sc. Moyses] sed figuratim praenuntiavit eum, *Pascha* nominans; et in eadem ipsa, quae ante tantum temporis a Moyse praedicata est, *passus est Dominus adimplens Pascha*). A Syriac translator from the Greek would surely not have attempted any such rendering, even if he saw that there was a play on the similarity of the words in Greek, for *Pascha* is itself a Syriac word (the Greek having taken this word, like many others, not in the Hebrew form—*pesach*—but in the Aramaic = Syriac form); while an Armenian translating from the Syriac would surely not even have reflected that there had been such a play on words in the Greek original.

31. For a fuller, but brief, discussion in English of the style of the "Hellenising" school, cf. Lewy, *op. cit.* 16-24.

32. For examples, cf. Conybeare's articles, references in n. 24 above; this was the peculiarity on which he based his identification of the style of the Armenian Irenaeus with that of the Armenian Philo. Many such "doublets" are mentioned in the notes to the present version: cf. the following paragraph of the Introd., and the Index under "doublets."

33. It is often exceedingly difficult to determine the correct division and grouping of phrases. As an example of a particular difficulty may be mentioned the use of expressions imitating in various manners the Greek "genitive absolute." Such a construction is foreign to Armenian (cf. above, n. 30), and in several places, where normal Armenian usage would demand a certain interpretation of an expression, it is in fact probable, or at least possible, that the expression should be understood as an "absolute" construction, with a sense sometimes quite different from that which would be demanded by normal usage—a difficulty which is sometimes increased by the fact that in Armenian the genitive and dative of substantives are identical in form. For examples of such ambiguities, cf. n. 43, 195, 200, 201, 222, 249, 341; in the first three of these cases the difference of interpretation is considerable.

34. There is a list of textual defects in Weber, L* 11.

The *editio princeps* has no *apparatus criticus* (an omission for which the editors were taken to task by Weber, *Der Katholik* 94 [1914] 10), and there are few emendations mentioned in the republication in PO*. The revised edition of the German version of EP* referred to emendations proposed by Nestle and Conybeare; others are to be found in Akinean's article, "St. Irenaeus in Armenian Literature," *HAm.* (1910) 200-208, in Vardanian's articles on the new words in the Armenian Irenaeus, *ibid.* 281-284, 301-306, and on emendations to the *Proof, ibid.* 326-328, in Weber's articles in *Theologische Quartalschrift* 91 (1909) 560-573 and 93 (1911) 162 f., and his "Randglossen," *Der Katholik* 94 (1914) 9-44, and in Lüdtke's reply thereto, *Zeitschrift für Kirchengeschichte* 35 (1914) 255-260, and elsewhere. Weber's Latin version (L*) mentions most emendations made up to its publication. I think I have mentioned in the notes

to this version all the important emendations proposed; and I have suggested one or two new ones.

35. Eusebius, *Hist. eccles.* 5. 26.

36. So too Faldati has for title "Esposizione . . . ," though he remarks (F* 21 n. 1) that "dimostrazione" would be more accurate as a rendering of the word Επιδειξος. The Armenian title is *C'uyc' aṙak'elakán k'arozut'eann.*

37. Eusebius, *Hist. eccles.* 5. 26.

The name *Marcianus* ought doubtless to have been englished "Marcian," but that the latter form agrees in sound with "Marcion."

38. *Mart. Polycarpi* 20.

Identification of author of *Martyrium Polycarpi* with addressee of *Proof* was suggested by J. B. Lightfoot, *Apostolic Fathers* 2. 3 (London 1889) 398 f.; he was followed by, for example, T. Zahn (*Realenzyklopädie für protestantische Theologie und Kirche, s. v.* "Irenaeus"). Harnack remarks (EP* 54) that identification is unlikely, the reading "Marcion" being more probable for the name of the author of the *Martyrium.* F. X. Funk—K. Bihlmeyer, *Die Apostolischen Väter* (Tübingen 1924), also read "Marcion."

39. Insistence on abolition of Old Law: c. 35, 87, 89, 90, 94, 96. For a probable explanation, cf. § 37 of Introd. The suggestion that Marcianus was a recent convert from Judaism was made, to account for this insistence, by F. Diekamp in his review of EP*, *Theologische Revue* 6 (1907) 245, and is regarded as probable by O. Bardenhewer, *Geschichte der altkirchlichen Literatur* 1 (2nd ed. 1913) 411.

40. "care of souls": c. 1 (cf. n. 6).

J. Kunze, on the other hand, says it is clear from the whole tenor of the *Proof* that Marcianus was a layman (*Theologisches Literaturblatt* 28 [1907] 26). Similarly Sagarda, who adds however that there is insufficient ground for any certainty in the matter (S* 486).

41. The confusion and repetitiveness of Irenaeus's exposition is very noticeable in *Adversus haereses.*

42. Cf. § 45 of Introd. for résumé of probable solution to these "problems."

43. So Harnack in EP* 55, G. Rauschen in *Literarische Rundschau* 34 (1908) 468, and especially P. Drews in *Zeitschrift für neutestamentliche Wissenschaft* 8 (1907) 226-233, who compares the *Proof* with Augustine's *De catechizandis rudibus* and with the *Constitutiones apostolicae.* Similarly Sagarda says, "Irenaeus speaks not as a polemist, not even as a scholar, but as pastor and catechete" (S* 487).

44. c. 1.

45. c. 1 f. and 99 f.

46. The word rendered "in its integrity" in c. 1, and similarly rendered elsewhere, is *aṙolj*, meaning "en-

tire" in the sense "sound, healthy, lively"; cf. n. 4 and the parallel Tit. 2. 8 there quoted.

47. So Bardenhewer, *op. cit.* 1. 409, 411. So too Tixeront (PO* 752) and others.

48. BK* p. xiv.

49. G. Rauschen, *Literarische Rundschau* 34 (1908) 468.

50. For Irenaeus's poor opinion of fanciful exegesis and of "mystic numbers," cf. respectively A.H. 1. 8. 1 and 2. 24 f.

51. *Adversus haereses* (or *Contra haereses*), is given by Eusebius, *Hist. eccles.* 5. 7. 1 etc., its full title, which we find also in c. 99 of the *Proof:* α Ελεγχος καὶ ιναυροπ ινς ψευδοννμου γνωσεως, a title which may be variously rendered in English: for example, also "Critique and refutation . . ." The expression "knowledge falsely so called" is taken from 1 Tim. 6. 20. "Knowledge" (in this sense) is in Greek γνωσις, and from the related adjective γνωστικός are derived the words "Gnostic," "Gnosticism."

52. Marcion's system, though it agrees in many general points with those of Gnostics properly so called, is in detail and in spirit as different from them as is orthodox Christianity. Most Gnostic systems, so far as can be judged, were on the intellectual level of the various bogus -osophies which are their modern counterparts; Marcion's, on the other hand, was the work of a misguided genius. He founded a hierarchy, and his sect is said to have persisted into modern times, while other Gnostic systems have been artificially revived in modern times; cf. F. R. M. Hitchcock, *Irenaeus of Lugdunum* (Cambridge 1914) 332 f.; E. C. Blackman, *Marcion and his Influence* (London 1948).

53. On the word *aeon*, cf. n. 23 to the text.

54. δημιουργός in Greek means "craftsman, artisan" and was a normal term in Greek philosophy to denote the "creator" or rather "fashioner" of the ordered world. The word seems to have been used in the *Proof* (and in *Adversus haereses*) of the "creative" Word (c. 38, cf. n. 185); it is used of God in A. H. 4. 1. 2 and 4. 20. 4.

55. So in the *Proof,* c. 4-7, 45.

56. Identity of God the Father and Creator: c. 3-5, 11, 99; He is universal Lord, Judge and Father: c. 8.

57. So in the *Proof,* c. 5, 34, 39; for an echo of Plato on the world-soul, cf. n. 171.

58. So in the *Proof,* c. 7, 45.

59. "the Son," cf. c. 5 (and n. 32 f. thereto); "inscrutable generation," cf. c. 70 and n. 301 thereto; "always with the Father," cf. "His Son for ever" (c. 10), and His pre-existence, c. 51 f.; and for the question of the Word's eternity and of the Δόγος Ενδιάθετος and Δόγος προΦορικός, cf. c. 43 and n. 205 thereto.

60. *Proof,* c. 12 (in Paradise), 44 (Abraham), 45 (Jacob, and explicit statement that theophanies are of the Son), 46 (Moses).

61. Cf. § 33 of Introd. (and n. 70 thereto).

62. Cf. § 36 of Introd.

63. This belief in a "seeming" body is called "docetism," and its holders are called "docetes" (from Greek δοκειν, "seem").

64. Frequent reference to Christ's birth of the Virgin, of the seed of Abraham and of David; and cf. especially c. 33, 38 f.

65. So in the *Proof* c. 5-8, 49; for the identification Spirit = Wisdom, cf. n. 33 to c. 5; Scripture is the work of the Spirit: c. 49: "it is not a man who utters the prophecy; but the Spirit of God . . . spoke in the prophets"; c. 2: "the Holy Spirit says through the mouth of David"; c. 24: (God testified to Abraham) "saying through the Holy Spirit in the Scriptures"; c. 73: "the Spirit of Christ, who spoke in the other prophets about Him, now also through David says." If Irenaeus sometimes attributes the words of Scripture to the Word, this is not because "the Word articulates the Spirit, and . . . gives their message to the prophets" (c. 5), but because in the particular passages so attributed to the Word the Spirit is speaking "on the part of Christ" (c. 49), and using the first person in uttering words to be attributed to the Son (so c. 34 "the Word says through Isaias: *I refuse not . . .*"; similarly e. g. c. 50, 68); or because the Scripture is reporting the words of the Son in a theophany (so e. g. in c. 9).

66. Cf. c. 11, 14.

67. The Spirit in creation and in man, cf. § 33, 34 of Introd. He leads to the Son, cf. § 35 of Introd.

68. Divinity of the Son: *Proof* c. 47; cf. n. 223 thereto.

69. c. 99.

70. "hands": cf. account of creation in c. 11. In the parallel passage A.H. 4. *Praef.* 4 we have "with His own hands, that is, with the Son and the Spirit"; so too in A.H. 4. 20. 1, 5. 1. 3, 5. 6. 1, 5. 28. 4 the Son and the Holy Spirit are called the two hands of the Father. Similarly Theophilus of Antioch, *Ad Autol.* 2. 18. Cf. also *Proof* c. 26 (and n. 140 thereto) for a possible reference to the Spirit as the "finger" of God.

"Image" and "likeness" were commonly distinguished by the Greek fathers; the statement that the "image" is ineffaceable, but the "likeness" lost by the Fall was supported by the allegation that the latter word was never used of man in the Scripture after the account of the Fall; but this is a mere chance in the Septuagint version; the Hebrew word *dᵉmût,* to which it corresponds in Gen. 1. 26, occurs also in Gen. 5, 1, where however the Septuagint renders by εικων ("image") instead of ιμοίωσις ("likeness") as in Gen. 1. 26.

For this distinction in Irenaeus, cf. especially A.H. 5. 6. 1, where it is said that the "image" is in the frame (*plasma*) of man and the "likeness" in the spirit; with which cf. *Proof,* c. 11 (n. 65) for the original creation, and c. 97 (n. 397) for the restoration; for the "image" as that of the Son, c. 22: "the 'image' is the Son of God, in whose image man was made"; for the "likeness" as given by the Spirit, c. 5: "the Spirit, who . . . formed man to the likeness of God." (And for free will as especial point of resemblance of man to God, c. 11, n. 66.)

71. Man created free and lord of world and its angels: c. 11, 12; immortality, c. 15; "self-mastery" as especial resemblance to God, c. 11 (n. 66); man intended to develop, etc., c. 12 (n. 70); the Fall and its effects, c. 16 f.; loss of immortality, c. 15, 37 f.; "image and likeness," cf. n. 70 above; Incarnation as restoration, cf. § 36 of Introd.

72. A.H. 5. 9. 1 f.; Plato, *Phaedrus* 246a; 253c; cf. following note.

73. All three elements necessary, cf. A.H. 5. 9. 1 f.; 5. 6. 1, etc. Body and soul, cf. *Proof* c. 2 (n. 8); necessity of Spirit, c. 7, 14, 41 f., 89; Spirit a special "godlikeness," cf. n. 70 above, and A.H. 5. 9. 1-3, 5. 10. 1; 4. 6. 1; 4. 8. 1; cf. also c. 42 and n. 201.

74. Body also part of man, c. 2 (n. 8); and A.H. 5. 6. 1: "the soul and the spirit can be part of man, but by no means 'a man'"; cf. also insistence on "incorruption" (cf. § 36 of Introd.). All things created by the one God, c. 3 f., 10.

75. "Material": Greek ὑλικός < ὕλη, "matter"; ("earthly": χοικός, "carnal": σαρκικός); "sensual": ψυχικός < ψυχν, "soul"; Latin *homo animalis;* "spiritual": πνευματικός < πνευμα, "spirit."

Cf. 1 Cor. 2. 14 f.: *But the sensual man perceiveth not these things that are of the Spirit of God . . . But the spiritual man judgeth all things;* and 3. 1: *And I, breathren, could not speak to you as unto spiritual, but as unto carnal;* and Jude 19: *sensual men, having not the spirit.*

76. Not that the Gnostics were necessarily licentious; some of them were, if we are to believe Irenaeus; but others were ascetical. The Marcionites in particular affected an extreme asceticism.

77. 1 Cor. 15. 50, on which text in A.H. 5. 9. 1 f. Irenaeus explains the necessity of spirit *as well as* soul and body. For the Gnostics, "flesh and blood" did not participate in salvation.

78. 1 Tim. 1. 9, quoted in the *Proof,* c. 35.

79. *Proof,* c. 14 (spirit knows no evil), 89 f. (newness of spirit supersedes the law); 61, 95 f.

80. *Proof,* c. 8.

81. Cf. n. 70 above.

82. *Proof,* c. 5 (n. 34).

83. *Proof,* c. 5-7.

84. *Proof,* c. 7.

85. "Recapitulation" or "summing-up," Greek ἀνακεταλαίωσις. The corresponding verb is ren-

dered "re-establish" in Douay in Eph. 1. 10: *in the dispensation of the fulness of times, to re-establish all things in Christ.* In Irenaeus (cf. rest of this paragraph) the sense is rather "re-establish." Principal references in the *Proof:* c. 30 (end), 31-34, 37 f. (and cf. parallels cited in notes thereto).

86. "Communion": Armenian *hasarakut'iwn miabanut'ean,* literally "community of agreement," or more freely rendered, "terms of good fellowship," "friendly relations." In A. H. 4. 20. 4, however, (4. 34. 4 in Harvey's numbering, used in the edition of the Armenian text, TU 35. 2), the same expression corresponds to the Latin version's *communio.* Elsewhere (A.H. 4. 14. 2, Harvey's 4. 25. 2) twice the word *communio* has as its Armenian correspondence *hasarakut'iwn* alone (cf. n. 195, and variants in fragments of c. 31: n. 156). In the *Proof,* c. 6; and, with explicit reference to "incorruptibility," c. 31, 40.

87. Cf. *Proof,* c. 7, 31, 39, 40, 55; and the continuation of 1 Cor. 15. 50, cited above (n. 77); after stating that *flesh and blood cannot possess the kingdom of heaven,* the apostle goes on: *neither shall corruption possess incorruption.*

Not merely the spiritual principle, but the whole man to be saved, cf. A.H. 5. 6. 1, cited in n. 74 above.

88. F. Loofs, in his posthumously published work on the sources of Irenaeus, *Theophilus von Antiochien Adversus Marcionem und die anderen theologischen Quellen bei Irenaeus,* TU 46. 2 (1930), regards Irenaeus's reputation for original thought as exaggerated, and suggests that he reproduces incompatible views from his various sources. There is however much that is controvertible in the views expressed in that work (including, for example, the suggestion of "binitarianism" alluded to in § 32 of this Introd.

89. J. Rendel Harris, *Expositor* 7. 3 (1907) 246-358 (on the *Proof*) and 7. 2 (1906) 385-409 (on "Testimonies"); these articles are repeated, along with other matter, in the same author's book, *Testimonies,* 2 vols. (Cambridge 1916, 1920).

90. Harnack, EP* 58; Tixeront, PO* 771 n. 3.

91. Description of Leviticus, c. 26; of Deuteronomy, c. 28. Note the inaccuracy of the Deuteronomy quotations in c. 29 (n. 152, 153).

92. For composite quotations cf., in the *Proof,* c. 24 (n. 127), 29 (n. 152), 43 (n. 206), 79 (n. 324), 88 (n. 352).

93. For false attribution: c. 43 (n. 206), 65 (n. 280: here note parallel in Justin gives different false attribution), 72 (n. 307), 97 (n. 396).

Apocryphal quotations from rubrics or glosses: cf. c. 43 (n. 207), 68 (n. 289).

94. Cf. c. 5 (n. 31), 77 (n. 318); but the fact that the former is a commonplace and the latter inaccurately quoted lends support to the suggestion that Irenaeus may here be quoting from memory; c. 86 (n. 346),

but here the fact that the quotation echoes two different prophets might have accounted for the expression "the prophets"; cf. also c. 38 and 62 (Amos, cited also in Acts), 72 (Ps. 20), 86 (Isaias, cited also in Romans).

95. C. 54 (n. 247), 56 (n. 251); cf. also Isa. 53. 4 quoted c. 67 as in Matt. 8. 17, and (in longer citation) c. 68 as in LXX (n. 283, 288).

96. Cf. c. 35 (n. 176), 63 (n. 277), 65 (n. 280: note that the different false attribution in the Justin parallel suggests common source, not the gospel), 67 (n. 283), 93 (n. 365). In Rendel Harris's theory this agreement with the New Testament is due to the use by the latter also of the book of "Testimonies against the Jews."

97. C. 81 (n. 328).

98. C. 8 (n. 55). In A.H. 4. 5. 2 correct attribution to Christ of the gospel's addition.

99. A.H. 3. 21. 1-4. In the *Proof,* c. 69, there is a notable omission which is to be accounted for by use of the Septuagint (n. 295).

100. In c. 3 (n. 18) I have even ventured to emend a quotation into agreement with the Massoretic text.

The immediate source not the New Testament: cf. n. 96 above.

The style of the translation of the *Proof*—a key to the Greek original—makes it reasonable to suppose that the translator has simply translated Irenaeus's quotations as they stood in the Greek original, instead of substituting—as translators not uncommonly did—the (Armenian) version of the Scriptural passage quoted. In one or two places, it is clear that the translator has retained peculiarities of the original (cf. e. g. n. 324 to c. 79 of text).

It is interesting to note in the *Proof* a couple of striking agreements with the so-called "Western text" of the New Testament in the quotations of Mich. 5. 2 (= Matt. 2. 6; c. 63, n. 277) and Isa. 52. 7 (= Rom. 10. 15; c. 86, n. 346); and cf. n. 264, 329 (Codex Bezae).

101. Jeremias: c. 78 (n. 320); David: c. 68 (n. 289).

102. Cf. c. 9 (n. 60), 20 (n. 105), 43 (n. 207), 57 (n. 257).

103. C. 4 (n. 28); A.H. 4. 20. 2.

104. C. 18 (n. 100).

105. C. 9 (n. 57); other "echoes" of *Ascensio Isaiae* are c. 10 (n. 62) and 84 (n. 338).

106. Abraham: c. 24 (n. 124); star: c. 58 (n. 264).

107. The "elders": or "ancients" or "presbyters" (οι πρεσβντεροι, *presbyteri, seniores*), a word commonly so used, and regularly added by Irenaeus when he refers to the preceding generation of tradition, the "disciples of the apostles"; so in the *Proof,* c. 3 and (without the expression "disciples of the apostles") c. 61. In A. H., 2. 22. 5, 3. 2. 2, 5. 5. 1, 5. 33. 3, 5. 36.

1 and 2. For the word "elders," cf. Ancient Christian Writers 6 (*The Didache* etc.) 107 ff.

Chiliasm: c. 61; for an account of this doctrine, see n. 270. It has recently been called in doubt whether Irenaeus did in fact hold millenarian views; cf. the article of V. Cremers, "Het millenarisme van Irenaeus," *Bijdragen* 1 (1938) 28-80. Even on the millenarianism of Papias doubts have been expressed, by L. Gry, "Le Papias des belles promesses messianiques," *Vivre et Penser* 3 (1943-4) 112-124.

108. C. 74 (n. 314); A.H. 2. 22.5.

109. Chiliasm (in *Proof,* c. 61, n. 270) in Justin, cf. esp. *Dial.* 80 f.; Papias, cf. (Eusebius, *Hist. eccles.* 3. 39. 12 and) A.H. 5. 33. 4; but cf. end of n. 107 above.

110. Papias and chiliasm, cf. preceding paragraph of Introd.

Polycarp quoted by name: A.H. 3. 3. 4; echo in *Proof,* c. 95 (n. 376). In the last postscript to the *Martyrium Polycarpi* in the Moscow manuscript we are told that Irenaeus "wrote a solid refutation of every heresy, and, besides, handed down the ecclesiastical and Catholic rule of faith, just as he had received it from the saint," that is, from Polycarp. The "solid refutation of every heresy" refers obviously to *Adversus haereses;* it is possible that the "ecclesiastical and Catholic rule of faith" handed down by Irenaeus as he received it from Polycarp refers to the *Proof.*

111. Cf. Index.

112. Cf. Index. In his Introduction to the *Proof* (AR* 6-23) Robinson gives a detailed comparison between certain parts of the *Proof* and parallel passages in Justin (c. 57 and *Apol.* 1. 32; c. 44 f. and *Dial.* 56, etc.; and c. 53 as "cleared up" by *Apol.* 2. 6). So also F. R. M. Hitchcock, *Journal of Theological Studies* 9 (1908) 284-289, lists several parallels between the *Proof* and Justin.

It must be noted that there are many differences of Scriptural reading between Justin and Irenaeus; in the *Proof,* cf. n. 277, 302, 317, 318, 320, 322; cf. different attribution, n. 280.

113. Cf. § 38 above, and Harris (references in n. 89 above). Loofs, *op. cit.* (n. 88 above) 5 n. 1, thinks the parallels between Justin and Irenaeus may be attributed to what was already traditional.

A notable difference between the two lies in Irenaeus's frequent use of St. Paul, who Justin never mentions or quotes.

114. Two particular examples, taken from the *Proof,* given by Harris, *Expositor* 7. 3 (1907) 255-257, and *Testimonies* 1. 68 f.: in c. 57, after quoting Gen. 49. 10 f., Irenaeus continues, "He is also *the expectation of the nations,* of those who hope in Him . . ."; in *Apol.* 1. 32, after quoting Gen. 49. 10 f., Justin passes on to a composite quotation (Num. 34. 17, Isa. 11. 1, Isa. 11. 10; the whole attributed to "Isaias") ending *and in His arm shall the nations hope.* In c. 72, Irenaeus ap-

plies Isa. 57. 1 to the death of Christ and also of "those who believe in Him and like Him are persecuted and slain"; in *Apol.* 1. 48, Justin refers the same passage to Christ and "those who hope in Him." In both these cases it is more likely that the "echo" in Irenaeus is due to an adjacent text in the common source, than to a reminiscence of Justin.

115. Reference to treatise against Marcion, A.H. 4. 6. 2; Loofs, *op. cit.* (n. 88 above) 5.

116. *Proof,* c. 12, 14; Theophilus, *Ad Autol.* 2. 25.

117. Account of Aristo, Origen, *C. Cels.* 4. 52.

For references to echoes of apologists, cf. Index.

118. A.H. 3. 3. 3.

119. Holy Spirit and Scripture, cf. n. 65 above; fourth gospel, c. 43, 94; trinitarian formula, c. 3.

Interesting also is what seems to be an allusion to the formula of exorcism "in the name of Jesus Christ, crucified under Pontius Pilate" (c. 97 n. 393).

120. E. g. H. Jordan, *Theologischer Literaturbericht* 30 (1907) 78. (Weber, L* 13, refers to Krüger in the same sense, but as his reference, which is false, is to the same volume of the same periodical, it may well be a mistake for Jordan as above.)

121. Good works: c. 2, 98; dogmatic faith: c. 1-3, 100; redeemed man: c. 61, 93, 94, 96.

122. C. 43 (n. 205).

123. Seven heavens, c. 9; Pontius Pilate, c. 74 (n. 314).

124. C. 61 (n. 270).

125. Adam and Eve, c. 12, 14; man lord of world and its angels, c. 11, 12; theophanies, c. 12, 44-46 (Sodom and Gomorrha, c. 44); decalogue, c. 96.

126. Sem and Japheth, c. 21, 24, 42; Adam and Christ, c. 32; Spirit and Wisdom, c. 5; distinction between Persons, c. 47.

127. There is an "Irenaean" Creed, drawn up from his works, at the end of F. R. M. Hitchcock, *Irenaeus of Lugdunum* (Cambridge 1914). See also J. N. D. Kelly, *Early Christian Creeds* (London 1950) 76-82.

Abbreviations

A.H. = Irenaeus, *Adversus haereses* (cited according to the division in Massuet's edition, which is that printed in Migne's *Patrologia Graeca;* the numbering is the same in Stieren's also).

AR* = J. Armitage Robinson's English *Proof* (cf. n.12 to Introd.)

BK* = Weber's German *Proof* (in the Bibliothek der Kirchenväter; cf. n. 10 to Introd.)

c. = chapter (of *Proof*).

EP* = *editio princeps* of *Proof* (cf. n. 7 to Introd.)

F* = Faldati's Italian *Proof* (cf. n. 12 to Introd.)

HAm. = *Handes Amsorya* (monthly journal of the Mechitarists of Vienna: in Armenian).

L* = Weber's Latin *Proof* (cf. n. 10 to Introd.)

LXX = the Septuagint version of the Old Testament (references to Rahlfs' edition).

n. = note, the reference being to the notes to the text, unless otherwise indicated.

PO* = edition of *Proof* in Patrologia Orientalis 12. 5; unless the context refers to Barthoulot or Tixeront, the reference is to the main body of the edition (Ter Mekerttschian) (cf. n. 8 to Introd.)

S* = Sagarda's Russian *Proof* (cf. n. 9 to Introd.)

TU = Texte und Untersuchungen (Leipzig) . . .

H. B. Timothy (essay date 1973)

SOURCE: "Irenaeus of Lyons," in *The Early Christian Apologists and Greek Philosophy,* Van Gorcum & Comp., B.V., 1973, pp. 23-39.

[*In the essay below, Timothy examines the content and structure of Irenaeus's* Adversus haereses, *demonstrating Irenaeus's skill in refuting the arguments of the Gnostics.*]

In the manner of a surgeon performing a major operation, though not quite so methodically, Irenaeus, in the first book of the **Adversus haereses,** begins to lay bare the nerves and sinews and so take us to the very heart of the Gnostic heresy which he knew from all too close acquaintance with it in the valley of the Rhone and had, it seems probable, encountered before then when he was passing from youth to manhood in the province of Asia.

He describes it as "the many-headed Lernaean hydra" sprung from the Valentinian school[1] and likens it in respect of the rapidity of its self-proliferation to mushrooms growing from the ground,[2] alluding to the fact that its craftily constructed plausibilities draw away the minds of the inexperienced so as to take them captive[3] and have deluded many women.[4]

He gives us an insight into the Gnostic anthropology according to which there are three given types of men, the spiritual, the material, and the "psychical", represented by Cain, Abel and Seth[5] in the Old Testament. The good are those capable of receiving a seed of the divine nature into themselves. The bad, on the other hand, are by nature utterly and eternally devoid of this capacity.[6] The former are guaranteed salvation solely in virtue of their inherent spirituality,[7] and everything for them is considered lawful or permissible since they hold that it is incumbent on them to experience all things, however abdominable, so as to attain complete self-fulfilment in this life and thus evade reincarnation.[8]

The Gnostics boast of possessing a secret tradition revealed mystically to them in parables by Christ, because, on their submission, they alone are qualified to understand it.[9] They construe chapter XI, verses 25-27 of the first gospel as signifying that, whereas the creator of the world has always been known universally, the words uttered by Jesus in this passage refer to the Father of truth who has been unknown hitherto and whom they now consider themselves in a special position to proclaim.[10]

Knowledge of what they call the "unspeakable greatness",[11] they say, in and by itself constitutes perfect redemption,[12] and to know what they make out the truth to be is equivalent to the resurrection of the dead.[13] Whoever acquires the knowledge thus possessed by them has the power conferred on him of becoming invisible and incomprehensible to the angels and the powers,[14] so as to meet and pass through them with impunity when his soul, liberated from the evil environment that confines it in this world, takes its flight to the Beyond.

They also claim that the consummation of all things will come about when the spiritual or the elect attain finally to the perfect knowledge of God and have been initiated into the mysteries of their so-called soul-mother, Achamoth.[15]

According to the tenets of docetic Gnosticism, Jesus was simply Joseph's son and, as such, nowise different from other men, except for having kept his soul steadfast and pure and perfectly remembering the things seen by him within the sphere of the unbegotten God;[16] he is, in other words, simply the last of the Gnostic aeons or intermediaries between this world and the high spiritual realm, the pre-eminent revealer sent to lead men to the knowledge of the truth.

Jesus, in the drama of redemption, some of the Docetists make out, had a purely dispensational role. The Logos and the saviour, according to their views, never became incarnate, but descended on the dispensational Jesus at his baptism by John at the river Jordan, like a dove.[17] Jesus, so portrayed, was merely a receptacle for Christ who having declared the unnameable Father reascended into the Pleroma incomprehensibly and invisibly.[18] The baptism, moreover, which the visible Jesus instituted was for the remission of sins, whereas the redemption initiated by the Spirit that descended on him, as described, was for perfection.[19] The spirit of Christ, because of his being incomprehensible and invisible and, therefore, immune to suffering, was taken away from Jesus when he was delivered to Pontius Pilate,[20] while Simon of Cyrene was transformed by Jesus so as to pass for him and at the Crucifixion took his place.[21] The same applies to the post-resurrection appearances, since, as asserted by the heretics, it was the Gnostic Christ, not Jesus, who survived death on the cross.[22]

Those who know these things have, according to the teaching of Basilides been set free from the powers that formed the world and anyone confessing to belief in a crucified redeemer is to be looked on as a slave.[23]

Such is allegedly the basis of the position taken by the Gnostics and these are some of the arguments adduced by those who claim to speak for it. By way of stating the case for orthodoxy as plainly as possible. Irenaeus now proposes and proceeds to rebut these arguments.

Life in God being, on the Gnostic thesis, conditioned by the predetermined state or natural condition of the soul, producing this or that fixed type, faith is rendered meaningless. If nature or substance are the determinants of salvation and, on this principle, some are saved and some are not, righteousness will appear either impotent or unjust;[24] but, insists Irenaeus, it was for all mankind from the beginning that Christ came, not merely for the sake of those who believed in him in the days of Tiberius Caesar, nor was it for those only who are presently alive that the Father exercised his providence.[25]

There is—and this is the main thrust of Irenaeus' case against the heretics—the question of tradition of which they make so much, but, he reminds them, the tradition which is the only true, life-giving faith, received from the apostles by the Church and imparted to her sons,[26] and this the Church, though scattered throughout the world, as if occupying one house, carefully preserves.

The world's languages are all different, yet what is contained in and conveyed by the tradition is identical for them all. The churches in Germany do not believe or pass on anything different from those in Spain or Gaul or anywhere else on earth. Like God's own sun the light of which is the same wherever it shines on men, the proclamation of the truth handed down from the beginning of the Christian dispensation sheds its radiance on all those who are willing to come to a knowledge of the truth. The faith is always one and the same. Irrespective of how much or how little anyone has to say concerning it, no one can increase or diminish it.[27]

The Gnostics presuming, however, to improve on the apostles read into the scriptures their own interpretation and when challenged, or refuted from the scriptures, will retort that the latter cannot rightly be interpreted by anyone who is ignorant of the genuine tradition handed down, not in writing, but *viva voce* as a secret revelation to themselves, they having discovered the unadulterated truth. They will, besides, to justify themselves, assert that the apostles confused the Gospel and the Law drawing their inspiration from different sources, at one time from the Demiurge, at another from the middle sphere, at yet another from the Pleroma, and that the Lord occasionally even did the same himself.[28]

The apostles, Irenaeus answers, did not teach one set of doctrines privately and another publicly. Their testimony is open and stands sure. The reason why God caused so many testimonies to the Gospel to be pointed out by Luke may be that everyone, considering it essential to use all of them, might have access to the truly unadulterated rule of truth and so be saved.[29] The case made out by the Gnostics can be upheld by the authority of neither the prophets, nor the Lord, nor the apostles. This, then, is what they boast of having perfect knowledge of, surpassing anything that anyone else knows! They gather their views from sources other than the scriptures and adapt them, regardless of the order and connection of the scriptures, to the teaching of the prophets, the Lord and the apostles, so as to make their systems seem soundly Christian in character.[30]

The mere fact that the heretics differ so much among themselves affords *a priori* (ex extensione) proof of the falsity of the tales they fabricate and of the immovability of the truth the Church proclaims.[31] A sound mind which is pious and truth-loving will be ready to give thought to the things God has placed within our power, the things, that is to say, which are open to our view and have been set forth unambiguously in the scriptures, so that, if we progress therein by daily study, knowledge of them will be made easy. If, however, scripture is to be interpreted according to individual taste and elaborated by the application of expressions which are not clear or evident, nobody will possess the rule of truth. *Tot homines quot sententiae* will rather be the rule, and the outcome will be antagonistic doctrines, like the questions investigated by the pagan philosophers.[32]

Let right reason, Irenaeus pleads, be given its rightful place. Where in the bizarre mythologizing of the Gnostics is there any evidence of rationality?[33] God himself is Reason in one aspect of his being; therefore, it stands to reason that he has made all things rational and that those who live contrary to reason with which God endowed man at his creation and which the Logos and the Spirit have united to restore to men in Christ, live in effect opposed to God.[34] Irrational constructions placed upon a rationally constituted universe are faced with the charge even of repudiating reality. In their denial of the God who made all things the Gnostics, by being irrational in fact, deny themselves.

There is, emphasizes Irenaeus, pressing the point home, one and the same God and Father as announced in both the prophets and the Gospel.[35] Was it only in appearance that the Lord performed his wondrous works? The prophets foretold them and as part of God's unfolding history their predictions have come true.[36]

The birth of Christ is reported plainly enough in scripture. The Lord came in reality, not despising or evading any condition of human life,[37] nor dispensing in his own case with the law decreed by him for mankind, observing the law even of the dead, that he might become the first-begotten from the dead.[38]

The Gnostics aver that Jesus was born of Mary but that Christ descended from above. Matthew, however, in the first gospel[39] begins his narrative: "The book of the generation of Jesus Christ, the son of David, the son of Abraham", and also, "The birth of Jesus Christ was as follows".[40] For the received text[41] he might have written: "Now the birth of Jesus was as follows", but anticipating those who were to come as the corrupters of the truth the

Holy Ghost declared through him: ". . . the birth of Christ was as follows", that we should not perchance think he is only man or suppose Jesus to be one and Christ another, but should know they are one and the same.[42]

Because, says Irenaeus, elaborating on this point, our Lord Jesus Christ, one and the same, the Logos and Son of God, who always existed with the Father, by whom all things were made and who always was present with mankind,[43] who has power over all things from the Father . . . and is in rational communication (participans rationabiliter) with things invisible, while at the same time ruling over things visible and the affairs of men[44]—because this Lord Jesus Christ has for man's sake become incarnate, all the doctrines concocted concerning him by the heretics are proved false—their theories as to subdivisions in his personality, for instance.[45] He is in fact as God fashioned him, human in all respects and in order to provide man with a model and example passed through every stage of human life.[46] Administering all things for the Father he discharges them from the beginning to the end, and no man apart from him can attain to the knowledge of God.[47] He is the Son of the Creator of the world who, as Mind and Logos in their fulness, both speaks that which he thinks and thinks that which he speaks,[48] for the Logos is his thought and the Logos is his mind, and the Father himself is Mind embracing everything, through whom the wood fructifies and the fountains well forth and the earth gives "first the blade, then the ear, then the full corn in the ear".[49]

Since the Son is the Logos vested with power, and truly man, he redeemed men in a manner consonant with reason,[50] thus redeeming his own property, for, though he was not received by his own to whom he came, he came to what belonged to him,[51] the incarnation of the Logos being the union of himself with his own handiwork.[52]

The things of time have been divinely made for man that he might come to maturity in them and thus bring forth the fruit of immortality,[53] he is, as Irenaeus puts it, ripening for immortality that he may attain to the freedom that enables man to put himself in subjection to God.[54] All through the ages God kept drawing on his people by means of successive covenants, while they kept progressing by faith to complete salvation, the human race being in a variety of ways adjusted to agreement with the goal that God had set for it, and the whole process reaching its culmination through the Gospel which renews man and recapitulates all things in itself, raising up and winging men to the heavenly kingdom.[55]

Jesus poured out the spirit of the Father for the union and communion of God and man, whereby he imparted God to men. By his incarnation he attaches God to, and bestows immortality on, man.[56] He took up man into himself, the invisible being made visible, the incomprehensible being made comprehensible, the impassible being made capable of suffering, and the Logos becoming man, thus for all time summing up all things in himself, so that he might have the headship in things visible and invisible;[57] and bringing to its fulfilment the divine plan of salvation,[58] that by God's renewing knowledge man might repossess the divine image and likeness[59] and be promoted to receive a greater glory, namely, the expectation of being made like God Himself.[60] Jesus became the Son of Man that man might become a son of God.[61] This is how Irenaeus sums it up. "Wherefore", he wrote, "I do also call upon thee, Lord God of Abraham, and God of Isaac, and God of Jacob and Israel, who art the Father of our Lord Jesus Christ, the God who through the abundance of thy mercy hast had a favour toward us, that we should know thee, who hast made heaven and earth, who rulest over all, who art the only true God, above whom no other God exists, grant by our Lord Jesus Christ the governing power of the Holy Spirit. Give to every reader of this book to know thee, that thou art God alone, to be strengthened in thee, and to avoid every doctrine that is heretical and Godless and impious."[62]

He has been aptly styled "the great opponent of Gnosticism".[63] He had, it is evident, taken full stock of the situation and saw clearly where the vital issues lay. In the ensuing struggle there could be no compromise, for Gnosticism "in the second century, while it was yet living and agressive . . . constituted a danger greater . . . than any peril that has ever menaced the existence of the faith".[64] It attempted to overthrow "belief in the almighty God of creation and redemption".[65] It is, then, as the champion of that faith that Irenaeus steps forth into the arena to draw the teeth of the agressor and to take the many-headed hydra, as he calls it, by the tail.

The contest is fought out at two levels with weapons appropriate to each. First, with the weapons of an informed polemic for the most part within the confines of the Christian community; then with the weapons of a persuasive apologetic in a somewhat broader context where we find Irenaeus making effective use of certain concepts drawn from Greek philosophy.

The grounds of contention, already dealt with in some detail, may for convenience be more briefly presented here in terms of the following three chief areas of dispute:

First and perhaps foremost is the Gnostic doctrine of election and going along with it, the claim by the Gnostics to possession of an esoteric or exclusive type of knowledge in virtue of which, on the basis of their peculiar psychological or anthropological ideas, the heretics have created a sort of pre-determined class distinction in the spiritual life, with themselves as an élite minority at the upper end of the scale. They speak of the unknown Father whom they profess to have brought to light, unknown, not in the sense that he should not have been known at all, but unknown as he really is, because, from having lost or forgotten it, the majory of men are blind to the knowledge of his true nature and existence.[66] Faith is, in consequence, by-passed in favour of knowledge, as the Gnostics think of it, and coming to that knowledge is substituted for salvation, with pragmatic subjectivism set up as the norm in the sphere of moral conduct, as we should say.

Secondly, there is the tampering with tradition by the Gnostics in their allegorizing of the scriptures, wrested usually from the accepted reading or interpretation to accommodate their views and with the object of explaining away the content of the Christian revelation. Faith in the process becomes fiction and myth takes the place of history, the culprits having, as Irenaeus accuses them, substituted belief in unrealities for belief in what is real.

Thirdly, there is the Gnostic aeonology in which Jesus is represented as but one among the many cosmic intermediaries between God and the world. The Logos, consequently, on the Gnostic thesis, did not become flesh because he could not become flesh. It follows that the divinity of Jesus is not questioned but his humanity is denied. involved in this are the extravagances of Docetism which amounts to polytheism in a new and dangerous disguise.

The questions raised by such bold speculations would, at first glance, appear to pose more than one serious problem for the Church of the second century, but there is for Irenaeus, at least to begin with, a quite obvious solution and a perfectly straightforward, unequivocal reply.

On the claim to possession of a special gnosis and the doctrine of election which the Gnostics entertain, the Church makes no secret, Irenaeus points out, of the divine plan of salvation, because, handed down from the beginning and committed to the care and keeping of those rightfully regarded as successors of Christ's apostles, it is publicly proclaimed. It would not have been entrusted in the first place to those who transmitted it, had they not had requisite knowledge of what was entrusted to them to transmit. This is the only gnosis that exists or that ever has existed so far as true and truly informed Christians are concerned.

Neither is the plan of salvation in any way restrictive or limited. Its range in keeping with the faith obtaining everywhere from the first is universal in its scope. The Church has been entrusted with the light of God whose wisdom is the means whereby she saves all men. One and the same way of salvation is shown forth by the Church in all the world: she is the sevenbranched candlestick (. . . lucerna) that bears the light of Christ.[67] God's chosen or elect are those, and only those, who revere and love him, who give proof of their profession by the honesty of their dealings and their Godly attitude toward their fellow-men, and whose desire has been "to see Christ, and hear his voice".[68]

As to the counter-charge of inconsistency brought forward by the Gnostics when thrown back on the apostolic origin and nature of the teaching of the Church,[69] there is, retorts Irenaeus, in what has been given by God no inconsistency. It is per contra through the agency of the Gnostics that inconsistency has arisen. The Church's witness stands immovable and indisputable. There is but one testimony and the God by whom that testimony was given and to whom it testifies is the Creator of the world, the rule of truth being, so far as the Christian community is concerned, that there is one, almighty God who by his Logos established everything, who fashioned and formed from what had no existence all things that exist.[70]

As for manipulation of the scriptures by the Gnostics, nothing can take the place of the traditional interpretation that the Church has inherited on apostolic authority. Private interpretation in any shape or form accordingly is condemned and prohibited, the scriptures being appointed to be read in the churches in the presence of the presbyters with whom the apostolic doctrine has been duly deposited.

With respect to Gnostic aeonology, the crucial point is the Incarnation reported and recorded as one of the great, incontestably fundamental facts of Christian history. Invoking the sacramental principle in support of this basic fact, Irenaeus says of Jesus that "he took bread, that created thing (*eum qui ex creatura est panis*), and gave thanks and said: "This is my body". The cup which is "part of that creation to which we belong", Irenaeus comments, "he confessed to be his blood".[71] Because Jesus is the Logos of God almighty who pervades the whole creation in his invisible form, and because by God's Logos all things are disposed and administered, the Son of God was also crucified in these things, imprinted in the form of a cross on the universe,[72] his crucifixion consequently having cosmic significance.

Such is the sum and substance of the matter, as Irenaeus sees and expresses it, from the orthodox point of view. This is the true *fides credenda* whereby the churches live and they who believe or teach otherwise must regard themselves as *extra fidem* and, therefore, *extra ecclesiam.* That is the whole position in a nutshell and no more need be said, so far as concerns, at any rate, the Church's rule of faith and life.

The better, however, to dissuade any who may feel inclined to throw in their lot with the heretics, and, if possible, to save the latter from the error of their ways, Irenaeus shows his readiness to pass beyond the strictly orthodox position (on which, it must always be remembered, basically he refused to compromise) and to set the dialogue in a larger universe of discourse by invoking philosophic principles and arguing philosophically.

With reference to the apologies that abound in the early Christian centuries, Daniélou has drawn attention to the place occupied in them by affirmations concerning truths of a general nature where certain aspects of the content of the Christian message are concerned, and with regard to which he says:

> Elles tendent à montrer que le christianisme est conforme à ce qu'il y a de valable dans l'âme humaine . . . leur but est surtout de montrer l'accord du message chrétien et de la raison humaine. C'est là ce qui constitue leur ressort principal et qui établit en même

temps le contact entre le message chrétien et l'hellénisme.[73]

Irenaeus is no exception. He readily allows that reason complements or reinforces revelation and corroborates the faith. He "did not merely confine himself to describing the fact of redemption, its content and its consequences, but he also attempted to explain the peculiar nature of this redemption from the essence of God and the incapacity of man, thus solving the question *cur deus homo* in the highest sense," as Harnack says.[74]

Discussing the wholly otherness of God's thoughts as compared with the thoughts of men, Irenaeus states that God is both simple and uncompounded and that in his being there is no distinction between the whole and the parts of which it is composed—the evident meaning of the word, *similimembrius* which Irenaeus employs here—that . . . he is wholly mind or understanding, and wholly spirit, and wholly thought, and wholly intelligence, and wholly reason, and wholly hearing, and all eye and all light, and the sole source of everything that is good . . .".[75] Irenaeus is quoting Is. LV,8 as his proof text, but the idea itself recalls Xenophanes, fr. 24 Diels-Kranz (De Vogel, *Greek Phil.* I, nr. 72 b).

He says again: "What God had conceived in his mind was also brought about as soon as he mentally conceived it", and, with reference to the creation of the world that, if it was made such as it is, he himself also made it so who had as such indeed mentally conceived[76] it; which, if of Biblical origin, is rather the rationalization of the original than the original itself. The following which is only one among many similarly worded passages in the *Adversus haereses,* will serve to illustrate how philosophically-minded he can be:

> "Et utrum eiusdem substantiae exsistebant his qui se emiserunt, an ex altera quadam substantia, substantiam habentes? Et utrum in eodem emissi sunt, ut eiusdem temporis essent sibi; an secundum ordinem quendam, ita ut anti-quiores quidam ipsorum, alii vero iuveniores essent? Et utrum simplices quidam et uniformes, et undique sibi aequales et similes, quemadmodum spiritus et lumina emissa sunt; an compositi et differentes, dissimiles membris suis?"[77]

The Logos-concept which features so conspicuously in the early Christian apologists is given due prominence and employed by Irenaeus to full effect. Other concepts current in the philosophic circles of his day which he draws on to advantage for apologetic purposes are the notion of natural law, the doctrine of innate ideas[78] and the *consensus gentium* associated with the argument from design.

Certain of the Gentiles, he writes, less voluptuous and less misguided by idolatrous superstition were convinced, if only slightly, that the designation "father" should be attributed to the creator of the universe who providentially rules over all things and arranges this world's affairs.[79] Though "no one knows the Father, save the Son, nor the Son, save the Father and those to whom the Son will reveal him",[80] yet because reason is implanted in their minds, because it moves them and reveals the truth to them, all men know this one fact at least, that there is one God, the Lord of all,[81] acknowledged as the creator of the world even by those who speak in many ways against him.[82] All men in fact give assent to this persuasion which was preserved among the ancients as a legacy from the first-created man. Others coming after learned it from the prophets, and the heathen from creation. It is also part of the tradition passed down from the apostles to the universal church, for the established order of things reveals him who established it . . . and the world gives evidence of him who ordered it.[83]

God at first warned the Jews by means of natural precepts which he had implanted from the beginning in mankind.[84] Those righteous men who lived before Abraham were justified without the Mosaic Law because they had the meaning of the Decalogue inscribed in their hearts and souls and had within themselves the righteousness of the Law. God moreover has increased and widened those laws which are natural and noble and common to all.[85]

More pointedly, a propos of the determinism for which he takes the heretics to task, Irenaeus reiterates that man is a being imbued with reason which makes him godlike and endows him with free-will, compared with other forms of creation, such as *frumentum . . . et paleae, inanimalia et irrationabilia exsistentia, naturaliter talia facta...* This accounts for man's causing himself to become "sometimes wheat and sometimes chaff". He is responsible for his fall and deserving of judgment, since, despite his creation as a rational being, he lost the true rationality and lived irrationally in opposition to the righteousness of God.[86]

There appears, then, in the case of Irenaeus, one feels entitled to conclude, no great problem as regards the relation of the visible world to God or of the natural to the supernatural, and no insuperable obstacle to admitting reason or philosophy as footnotes to revelation, so to speak, or as means of enlightening faith. The latter must "to some extent include a knowledge of the reason and the aim of God's ways of salvation. Faith and theological knowledge are, therefore, after all, closely intertwined",[87] always provided, Irenaeus would have insisted that they do not become intertwined to the extent that as a consequence faith becomes obscured.

He asserts that the apostles "had nothing in common with the teaching of the Gentiles",[88] accusing the heretics of plagiarizing the comic poets, of bringing together the things that have been said by all those who are ignorant of God and who are called philosophers, and of sewing the rags and tatters they have picked up from such sources into a patchwork garment which they use as a cloak to cover their deceit.[89] He charges Basilides and his like with bringing into conformity with their own teaching matters "that lie outside the truth",[90] by which he means, in contrast to the Christian revelation the speculations of the contemporary pagan world. He seeks, however, on the

other hand to vindicate whatever the latter can be made to yield up as a means for facilitating the propagation of the faith. His attitude to such things, from this rather different point of view, is summed up forcefully and quite frankly in the following passage from *the Adversus haereses.*

With reference to the spoiling of the Egyptians by the children of Israel on the eve of their departure from the land of bondage, he first of all explains that God intended to provide this prototype in the history of the chosen people of what was one day to be the experience of the Church. He then goes on to say that, as the tabernacle in the wilderness was constructed out of the appropriated things, so Christians have every right to appropriate whatever will serve their purpose from the "mammon of unrighteousness", for he asks:

> From what source do we derive the houses in which we dwell, the garments in which we are clothed, the vessels that we use and all else ministering to our everyday existence, unless it be from those things which, when we were Gentiles, we acquired by avarice or received from our heathen parents, relations or friends who unrighteously obtained them, not to mention that even now we acquire such things? In what way are the heathen debtors to us from whom we receive both gain and profit? Whatever they amass with labour we make use of without labour, though we are in the faith.

Thus is using the goods bestowed on him by a society which is not Christian, the Christian redeems his own from the hand of the stranger. How can he say "stranger", as if the world did not belong to God? Whatever Christians, therefore, when they were heathen, acquired from unrighteousness, they, having become Christians, are proved righteous by applying it to the advantage of the Lord.[91]

Notwithstanding his vigorous critique of Gnostic irrationalism, Irenaeus might at times impress us as being himself irrational or at least anti-rationalist. He speaks, for example, of the Church as a garden planted in a world in which one may eat of every fruit except that which is forbidden, namely, the ubiquitous (universam) discord introduced by the heretics.[92] There are, he declares, certain matters about which we should not ask. Many things lying at our feet, such as the rising of the Nile, remain a mystery. How much more, then, of a mystery must be those things which are in heaven.[93] We know only in part and accordingly should leave all difficult questions in the hands of God who bestows in some measure grace on us whereby we are enabled to explain some things, though there are others we must simply leave to him.[94] Christians have the truth itself and the witness of God set clearly before them to go by in such things and, therefore, have no need to depart from the steadfast and true knowledge of God, by casting around for the various answers given to certain questions; and if Christians cannot find in scripture the explanation of the things with which human curiosity or investigation is concerned, the difficulty will not be lessened by their search for a divine being other than the God who really exists and to whom they owe their creation. Man is inferior to and lower in the scale of being than the Logos and spirit of God. To that extent the mysteries of God are beyond the limits of human knowledge and must be made known by revelation. That God should excel in knowledge is appropriate to his nature. Much may be said as to the causes of certain natural phenomena, but only God, their creator, can get at the truth regarding them. There are, then, certain questions which we must leave in his hands. The Christian, indeed, must leave them there, if he is to protect himself from danger and his faith from injury. The scriptures, given by God, can be relied on to be perfectly consistent. They speak with many voices but they all blend together into one harmony in praise of the Creator. Who but he can answer such questions as: "What was God doing before he made the world?"

Irenaeus quotes the scriptures testifying to the fact that evil exists but makes no effort to reflect on or account for its existence. God has, he notes, prepared eternal fire from the beginning for transgressors, but as regards the cause or origin of the latter, "neither has any scripture informed us, nor any apostle told us, nor the Lord instructed us".[95] It is sufficient to say of things the source of which we are unable to explain that God prearranged them so to be.[96] Such thornier problems would appear to fall into their proper, one might almost say, their appointed place, in what for Irenaeus is the harmonious perfection of the Creator's handiwork.

He lingers on the thought that it is "better and more profitable to belong to the unlettered class, better that one should have no knowledge whatsoever of why a single thing in creation has been made, but should believe in God and continue in his love, than that, puffed up through such knowledge, one should fall away from the love which is the life of man", but recollecting that he is writing with what the apostle Paul had said in mind, he hastens to add, "not that he meant to inveigh against a true knowledge of God, for in that case, he would have accused himself, but because he knew that some, puffed up by pretence of knowledge, fall away from the love of God . . ."[97]

Harnack said of Irenaeus that he "replaced the vanishing trust in the possibility of attaining the highest knowledge by the aid of reason with the sure hope of a supernatural transformation of human nature, enabling it to appropriate what is above reason",[98] which in the overall estimate holds substantially true.

Notes

1. *Adv. haer.,* I. xxviii. 8, 1-3.

2. ibid., I. xxvii. 1, 2-3.

3. ibid., I. Praefatio, 4-6.

4. ibid., I. vii. 6, 2-3.

5. ibid., I. i. 14, 1-2 *Hominum autem tria genera dicunt; spiritalem, psychicum, choicum, . . .*

6. ibid., I, i. 14, 12-15.

7. ibid., I. i. 11, 26-27.

8. ibid., II. xlviii. 4, 1-3; I. xx. 2, 15f.

9. ibid., I. i. 5, 8-10.

10. ibid., I. xiii. 2, 23-33.

11. ipsam agnitionem inenarrabilis magnitudinis.

12. *Adv. haer.,* I. xiv. 3, 9-11.

13. ibid., II. xlviii. 2, 18-19.

14. ibid., I. xix. 3, 15-17.

15. ibid., I. i. 11, 17-20 cf. *Adv. haer.,* I. xxviii. 7, 34-36, consumationem autem futuram, quando tota humectatio spiritus luminis colligatur, et abripiatur in Aeonem incorruptibilitatis.

16. ibid., I. xx. I, 3-7.

17. ibid., III. xi. 3, 7-10.

18. ibid., III. xvi. 1-4.

19. ibid., I. xiv. 1, 15-18.

20. ibid., I, i. 13, 16-19.

21. ibid., I. xix. 2, 13-16.

22. ibid., I. xxviii. 7, 1-16.

23. ibid., I. xix. 2, 26-29.

24. ibid., II. xliv. 1, 20-25.

25. ibid., IV. xxxvi. 2, 1-3.

26. ibid., III. Praefatio, 20-21.

27. ibid., I. iii. cf. III, i. 1, 7-13.

28. ibid., III. ii. 1, 1-5; 2, 5-8.

29. ibid, III. xv. 1, 18-22.

30. ibid., I, i. 15, 4-10.

31. ibid., I. i. 20, 60-62.

32. ibid., II. xl. 1, 1-16.

33. ibid., II. xxii. 3, 9-23; 4.

34. ibid., V. i. 3, 13-24.

35. ibid., III. xi. 6, 21-23.

36. ibid., II. xlix. 3, 1-3.

37. ibid., II. xxxiii. 2, 6-7.

38. ibid., V. xxxi. 2, 1-2.

39. ibid., III. xi. 11, 29-30 *Matthaeus vero eam quae est secundum hominem generationem ejus enarrat.* This gospel, explains Irenaeus, is *humanae formae, . . .*

40. ibid., III, xi. 11, 30-32.

41. Matt., I, 1-18.

42. *Adv. haer.,* III. xvii. 1, 26-29; 32-33.

43. ibid., III. xix. 1, 1-7; 2, 1-5, etc.

44. ibid., V. xviii. 2, 30-34.

45. ibid., III. xvii. 8, 1-9.

46. ibid., II. xxxiii. 2, 11-21.

47. ibid., IV, xi. 5, 17-23.

48. ibid., II. xlii. 2, 20-23.

49. ibid., IV. xxxi. 3, 22-24.

50. ibid., V. i. 1, 16-17.

51. ibid., III. xi. 7, 35-36 *in sua propria venit.*

52. ibid., III. xix. 1, 3-5.

53. ibid., IV. viii, 2-3.

54. ibid., V. xxix. 1, 4-6.

55. ibid., IV. xix. 2, 1-7, cf. IV. xxi, 1. 9-15 and III. xi. 11, 47-52.

The recapitulation idea occurs repeatedly. The Gospel, as here, recapitulates all things. Christ is the means of recapitulation; and God recapitulates (the creation of man) in humanity that by destroying death he may deprive it of its power and restore man to life.

56. *Adv. haer.,* V. i. 2, 1-7.

57. ibid., III. xvii. 6, 20-26.

58. ibid., III. xix. 2, 6-7.

59. ibid., V. xii. 4, 15-18.

60. ibid., III. xxi. 2, 23-24.

61. ibid., III. xi. 1, 38-39.

62. ibid., III, vi. 3.

63. F. Copleston, *A History of Philosophy,* London 1952, vol. II, p. 20.

64. C. Bigg, *The Christian Platonists of Alexandria,* Oxford 1886, p. 62.

65. Harnack, *History of Dogma,* vol. II, Boston 1903, p. 3. The essential character of the threat to orthodox Christianity is well brought out by E. F. Osborn, *The Philosophy of Clement of Alexandria,* Cambridge 1957, p. 176-177.

66. *The Jung Codex,* p. 105-106.

67. *Adv. haer.,* V. xx. 2, 1-4; 7.

68. ibid., IV. xxxvi. 2, 3-7.

69. See page 26, supra.

70. *Adv. haer.,* I. xv, 1-4.

71. ibid., IV. xxix. 5, 12-15.

72. *Epid.,* 34.

73. J. Daniélou, *Message Évangélique et Culture Hellénistique* aux IIe et IIIe Siècles, Tournai 1961, p. 34 cf. p. 39.

74. op cit., p. 289.

75. *Adv. haer.,* II. xv. 3, 15-19.

76. ibid., II, iii. 1, 17-18; 23-24; cf. II. iii. 2 and II. v. 2, 12-26, etc.

77. ibid., II, xxi. 2, 14-21.

78. See E. Bréhier, *Chrysippe et L'Ancien Stoïcisme,* Paris 1951, p. 65-67.

79. *Adv. haer.,* III. xxxix, 6-11.

80. Matt., XI, 27.

81. *Adv. haer.,* II. iv. 5, 11-15.

82. ibid., II. vii. 3, 5-6.

83. ibid., II. viii. 1, 7-9.

84. ibid., IV. xxv. 3, 21-22. The manna provided for the Hebrews in the wilderness is referred to by Irenaeus as *rationalem escam* (*Adv. haer.,* IV. xxvii. 3, 13).

85. ibid., IV. xxviii. 29-30. The Logos used to converse with the ante-Mosaic patriarchs (*Adv. haer.,* III. xi. 11, 39-41).

86. ibid., IV. vii. 7-13 *homo vero rationabilis, et secundum hoc similis Deo, liberin arbitrio factus et suae potestatis, ipse sibi causa est ut aliquando quidem frumentum aliquando autem palea fiat. Quapropter et iuste condemnabitur, quoniam rationabilis factus amisit veram rationem, et irrationabiliter vivens, adversatus est iustitiae Dei.*

87. Harnack., op cit., p. 246, footnote 1.

88. *Adv. haer.,* IV. lvii. 2, 3-4.

89. ibid., II. xviii. 2, 1-5.

90. ibid., II. xlviii. I, 28-29.

91. ibid., IV. xlvi, abridged.

92. ibid., V. xx. 2, 19-23.

93. ibid., II. xli. 2, 1-7.

94. ibid., II. xliii passim, cf. II. xlii. 4.

95. ibid., II. xliii. 2, 1-7.

96. ibid., II. ii. 3, 10-13.

97. ibid., II. xxxix. I, passim.

98. Harnack, *Dogmen.,* vol. II, pag. 240.

Dominic J. Unger (essay date 1992)

SOURCE: An introduction to *St. Irenaeus of Lyons: Against the Heresies,* Paulist Press, 1992, Vol. I, pp. 1-18.

[*In the following essay, Unger provides an overview of Irenaeus's* Adversus haereses *and argues that with the composition of this treatise, Irenaeus earned the right to be called the founder of Christian theology.*]

1. An earlier volume in this series presented a translation of the **Proof of the Apostolic Preaching,**[1] one of the two works of Irenaeus which have survived in their entirety. With this volume the series begins publication of Irenaeus's principal work, his **Exposé and Overthrow of What Is Falsely Called Knowledge.** It is this work, commonly called **Adversus haereses,** or, **Against the Heresies,** which

establishes Irenaeus as the most important of the theologians of the second century and merits for him the title of founder of Christian theology.[2]

2. The *Adversus haereses* is a detailed and effective refutation of Gnosticism, and it is a major source of information on the various Gnostic sects and doctrines.[3] In recent years this aspect of Irenaeus's writings has received increased attention, stimulated in part by the discovery in 1946 near Nag Hammadi in Upper Egypt of a large collection of ancient Gnostic texts in Coptic.[4] Included in this find were some previously lost works which Irenaeus and others used in their polemical anti-Gnostic writings, as well as some works not hitherto known even by title or description. The richness of this find has not yet been fully explored. Studies thus far, however, substantiate the centuries-old belief in the reliability of Irenaeus as a source.

3. The importance of Irenaeus as a writer of the early patristic era lies, of course, not so much in what he tells us of the Gnostics as in his clear and convincing descriptions of the doctrines of the Church, and in the fact that he is the first Christian writer to give a relatively complete and systematic treatise on theology.[5] Certainly, he does not have the systematic development of doctrines found in the scholastic or modern theologians; but in view of the early times in which he lived, he treats systematically what today we call the treatises on the One and Triune God, on Creation, on Christ the Savior, on the Church, on Salvation, and on the Resurrection. In many cases he has a rather coherent and unified treatment of individual doctrines; e.g., his treatise on the Church and on tradition in Book 3. Particularly noteworthy is that Irenaeus had a pivotal topic which unified all his other teachings—Jesus Christ as universal Recapitulator. He really placed Christ as the cornerstone of his theological edifice. This put a marvelous unity into all his theological thought.[6] Another source of unity is his constantly recurring theme of the salvation of men and women, which is a continuous and gradual process until it reaches the magnificent glory of the body. Of course, the truly basic and ruling idea levelled against the Gnostics in the total work of Irenaeus is the existence of only one, true, and all-perfect God. The *Adversus haereses,* composed in five books over a number of years, was written to show the errors of the Gnostics. At the same time, however, Irenaeus, who was a firm believer in the teaching authority of the Church, in the importance of apostolic succession, and in a primacy of Rome, followed the principle that a clear presentation of the truth is itself a forceful refutation of error. The fact that Irenaeus was a loyal follower of tradition did not make him stagnant; no, his was a creative genius. Some scholars write as if there were no development possible in theology according to Irenaeus.[7] But development is certainly possible and, actually, Irenaeus made great strides over his predecessors; for instance, in and because of his doctrine about recapitulation of all things in Christ. His is not merely a restatement pure and simple of Scripture and tradition. While he is not generally known as a great stylist, he accomplished his purpose remarkably well.

TITLE AND AUTHENTICITY

4. The short title for Irenaeus's main work, *Adversus haereses,* was known in Greek to Eusebius, Basil, Maximus, and Photius.[8] That short form, however, was not the original title, which Eusebius gives as *Elegkhos kai anatropē tĕs pseudōnumou gnōseōs.*[9] Irenaeus himself says in the prefaces to Books 2, 4, and 5 that this longer form is the title, and there are allusions to the longer form in his Books 1 and 2.[10] The *anatropĕ* in the title obviously refers to "overthrow" or "refutation" of the heresies by the use of arguments based on reason, Scripture, and tradition.[11] From Irenaeus's purpose and procedure in Book 1, it is equally clear that *elegkhos,* which can be translated either "exposé" or "refutation," here means a refutation by exposure of the errors. The final phrase of the title, *tĕs pseudōnumou gnōseōs,* "of the falsely called knowledge," or, "of what is falsely called knowledge," is found in 1 Timothy 6.20.

5. Irenaean authorship of the *Adversus haereses* is firmly established and universally accepted.[12] There are many citations of, and quotations from, the work in the writings of others, from Hippolytus and Tertullian, contemporaries of Irenaeus, to St. John of Damascus. The original Greek text has long been lost, but the work, as we have it, preserved in an early and quite literal Latin translation, is the complete work, and all parts of it are genuine.[13]

TIME OF COMPOSITION

6. The years in which Irenaeus wrote the *Adversus haereses* cannot be determined precisely, and at most some general indications may be noted of the periods in which at least some parts of the work were composed.

7. It is clear that Irenaeus did not write the work all at one time, and that the period of composition extended over a number of years. The reading of the heretical books which Irenaeus consulted entailed much labor. Each book of the *Adversus haereses* supposes a slow process of elaboration of many elements.[14] There are in the work some signs of interruption. Irenaeus sent the books singly to a friend of his as each was finished. From the preface to Book 3 it is certain that he had already sent Books 1 and 2 to his friend. Similarly, the preface to Book 4 indicates that Book 3 had already been sent, and the preface to Book 5 indicates that Book 4 had been forwarded. And since Irenaeus at the end of his Book 1 promises another book, it is probable that he dispatched Book 1 before doing Book 2.

8. Some parts of the work give the impression of having been written during a period when the Church was spared from external persecution. There seems to be an indication in 4.30.1 that Christians were at the Emperor's court; and in 4.30.3 the Christians were enjoying a peace that seems to be credited to the Romans. In fact, the composition of a work of such proportions would almost seem to require a period of cessation from political persecutions. There was such a period during the reign of Emperor Commodus (180-92), that is, in the latter half of Pope Eleutherius's

pontificate and the first part of Pope Victor's. In the famous catalogue of the Roman bishops given by Irenaeus in 3.3.3, Eleutherius is the last one mentioned. It is a safe assumption that Eleutherius was still reigning and that Book 3 was finished before the completion of Eleutherius's pontificate in 188 or 189.

9. Some historians believe that Book 2 was written during a persecution, that is, under Marcus Aurelius (161-80), because in 2.22.2 Irenaeus writes of persecutions of the just as if they are then going on. Books 1 and 2, then, may have been written before 180. The fact that in 3.21.1 Irenaeus speaks of the Greek version of the Old Testament done by Theodotion would not upset such a dating. Though authors have usually held that Theodotion's version appeared around 180,[15] modern scholars are sure that what goes by the name of Theodotion's version is not all from him at that late date. The revision of the Septuagint (hereinafter LXX) began already in the first century,[16] and so Irenaeus could have used Theodotion's version prior to 180.

Irenaeus's Readers

10. The friend to whom Irenaeus sent the books of *Adversus haereses* had asked him to write this work because he had for a long time desired to study Valentinianism.[17] This friend was most likely a bishop. Irenaeus admits that his friend is in many ways more competent than he, and he speaks of him as having the obligation of stemming the tide of error.[18] Irenaeus promised this work as a help to safeguard those who are with his friend, to whom his friend can explain the matters in more detail.[19] This supposes someone with a flock to care for. In the preface to his Book 5, Irenaeus writes of obeying the precept of his friend. This would seem to indicate that his friend was at least of equal rank. But it is clear that this friend was not the only one Irenaeus hoped would read his work. Near the end of Book 1 he writes: "You, too, and all those who are with you are now in a position to examine what has been said and to overthrow their wicked and unfounded doctrines . . ."[20] In the preface to Book 5 he speaks of his friend and "all who will read" the book.

11. Neither the name nor the region of the friend addressed by Irenaeus is known. The friend obviously knew Greek, for the *Adversus haereses* was written in Greek. Seemingly, he was also in a place where Greek was used generally, and where the Ptolemaean and Marcosian versions of Gnosticism were raging. Since Irenaeus wrote in Greek, some have suggested that his addressee was not in Gaul or in Rome, but somewhere in the East, perhaps in Alexandria or in Asia Minor. But if Irenaeus had been writing to someone in the East, he would scarcely have spent so much time on Western Gnosticism. Moreover, he often refers to the traditions of the presbyters of Asia Minor in language suggesting that these were not known to readers. In 1.13.5 he narrates an incident about "a certain deacon from among our people in Asia," by which he seems certainly to imply that his readers are not in Asia. In 1.26.1

he reports that Cerinthus taught in Asia; again, the implication is that his readers are not in Asia. For a similar reason, the references to Antioch and Alexandria in 1.24.1 would seem to exclude those places.

12. Gaul as well would hardly seem to be the locale of the readers—not because Irenaeus wrote in Greek, but because he probably would not have spoken of the people of Lyons as barbarians[21] if he had been writing to someone near there. He wrote at great length about the Marcosian heresy because it had become quite rampant in the Rhone valley, and he was able to study it in detail. But he seems to have written for people in some other area where that heresy had infiltrated.

13. That other area may well have been Italy, perhaps even Rome itself. Rome cannot be excluded because of the Greek language. Hippolytus wrote in Greek at Rome for the Romans. The fact that Hippolytus not very many years after the composition of the *Adversus haereses* used that work as a main source and quoted from it at length, could be an indication that Irenaeus sent his work to Rome or somewhere near there. It is a fact that Irenaeus wrote several letters to Rome. Also, his manner of referring in 1.25.6 to the heretic Marcellina and her influence in Rome may be another indication that Irenaeus's readers were there.

Purpose and Plan of *Adversus Haereses*

14. Irenaeus intended to offer his friend means for refuting the Gnostics. Since he believed that a clear exposition of error is in itself a refutation of that error,[22] he devoted Book 1 of the *Adversus haereses* entirely to exposing the heresies. In the other four books of his work, he advanced positive arguments against the heresies. Though the whole work is essentially a refutation of heresy, it contains much positive theology about divine revelation.

15. Some scholars seem to hold that Irenaeus initially had in mind only a short work, and that he changed his plans as he proceeded.[23] Irenaeus observes in 1.31.4 that his exposé of the heresies has been long, and he promises a "subsequent book." But there is no sign there of change in plans. He had intended from the start to give an exposé of the heresies and then to refute them positively. At the end of Book 2, he speaks of several other books that will follow.[24]

16. The basic plan of the *Adversus haereses* has already been noted. An exposé of the heresies is given in Book 1. In Book 2 there is a refutation of the heresies, chiefly the fundamental tenets of the Gnostics about two gods, by arguments drawn from reason. The next two books continue the refutation, Book 3 with arguments drawn mainly from the words of the apostles, Book 4 with arguments based mainly on the Lord's words. In Book 5 Irenaeus deals mostly with the salvation of the body, a doctrine which the Gnostics sharply denied.

17. This present volume contains only Book 1. The first eight chapters of the book give an account of Valentinianism as taught by Ptolemaeus. Chapter 9 is a short refuta-

tion of that heresy, and Chapter 10 presents a summary of the Catholic Rule of the Truth. Chapter 11 is an exposé of the errors of Valentinus and his disciples. Chapters 12-22 contain a long treatment of Marcosianism. Then, beginning with Simon Magus, the arch-heretic, there is a description of the heresiarchs of various branches of Gnosticism and their disciples in Chapters 23-27. Finally, Chapters 28-31 describe the errors of sects that do not seem to have had definite heresiarchs.[25]

STYLE

18. In the preface to Book 1, Irenaeus apologizes for his style: "From us who live among the Celts and are accustomed to transacting practically everything in a barbarous tongue, you cannot expect rhetorical art, which we have never learned, or the craft of writing, in which we have not had practice, or elegant style and persuasiveness, with which we are not familiar."

19. He underrates his abilities. It is true that his writing is frequently marred by prolixity, repetition, and involved constructions. Even so, his prose has a number of excellent qualities. In general his style is simple and forceful. He is precise in the choice of words, as can be seen, for example, in this series of clauses in 2.30.9: ". . . whom the Law announces, whom the prophets herald, whom Christ reveals, whom the apostles hand down, in whom the Church believes." He is noted also for his variety. He uses four different words to express the idea of preaching, and at least eight different verbs, with various shades of meaning, to express the fact that one thing is a copy of another. In Book 1, to make sure that the reader is aware that he is describing erroneous doctrines and not his own view, he uses phrases such as "they say" very often, but he employs at least fifteen different verbs for this. He is a master of figurative language and concrete illustrations, which are always apt and concise. Book 2 in particular abounds with examples. At times he rises to heights of genuine eloquence.[26] Scattered throughout the five books one finds many concise statements that have become classic, many of them jewels. Here are some examples: "He might indeed have been invisible to them because of His eminence, but He could by no means have been unknown to them because of His providence" (2.6.1); "God's friendship bestows imperishability on those who strive for it" (4.13.4); ". . . so that He might become the Son of man, in order that man in turn might become a son of God" (3.10.2); "Where the Church is, there is God's Spirit; and where God's Spirit is, there is the Church" (3.24.1). There are all shades of irony in Irenaeus, from light pleasantry to caustic thrusts,[27] as well as some very severe condemnations of heretics. Nevertheless, his general tone is one of calmness and modesty. As has already been indicated, the general plan of the work as a whole is clear and methodical. The same can be said of the plan of each book, despite the author's frequent digressions.

20. What Irenaeus lacks as a stylist, he makes up for in thought. He displays a broad knowledge of Catholic doctrine and a clear and sure grasp of it. Though he gives us a

disclaimer about writing ability, his work in fact merits the praise that St. Jerome gave when he referred to the *Adversus haereses* as a work of "most learned and eloquent style."[28]

SCRIPTURE AND TRADITION

21. For Irenaeus, the main witnesses to the Truth are Scripture and tradition.

22. The divine inspiration of the Scriptures is stressed time and again.[29] "The Scriptures are perfect, inasmuch as they were spoken by God's Word and Spirit" (2.28.2); "one and the same Spirit who heralded through the prophets . . . He Himself announced through the apostles" (3.21.4); "the Word . . . gave us the fourfold Gospel" (3.11.8); "the Scriptures are divine."[30] Not only the prophets, but the entire Old Testament is prophetic,[31] because the Holy Spirit spoke through all the writers just as He did through the prophets; the writers were His instruments. Moreover, the New Testament is as inspired and divine as the Old Testament, being equally the word of the Spirit.[32] The Scriptures are without error, "perfect," and "the mainstay and pillar of our faith."[33]

23. Though Irenaeus does not mention a list or canon of the books of the Bible, one can make a fairly complete list from his citations.[34] He cites all the Old Testament books except Judith, Esther, 1 and 2 Chronicles, Ecclesiastes, Canticle of Canticles, Job, Tobit, Obadiah, Nahum, Zephaniah, Haggai, and 1 and 2 Maccabees. But from a passage in Book 1 it is clear that he knew of Tobit, Nahum, and Haggai.[35] He also knew of the twelve minor prophets as a unit.[36] Of the New Testament, Irenaeus quotes or uses every book except Philemon and 3 John. Although some scholars have questioned whether he used James, Jude, and 2 Peter, in notes to the pertinent passages, I shall show that it is more than probable that he did.[37]

24. In Book 4, Irenaeus cites a sentence from Hermas (*Mandatum* 1), introducing it with the formula "the writing (*graphě*) says."[38] Because of the *graphě,* a word frequently used for Scripture, some scholars have concluded that Irenaeus considered the work of Hermas to be part of the Bible. The conclusion is not warranted. Irenaeus uses *graphě* also with reference to the letter of Pope Clement.[39]

25. Except perhaps for the use of Henoch in 4.16.2, Irenaeus did not use apocryphal books. But he actually quotes an apocryphal text on Christ's descent into "hell" six times, variously ascribing it to Jeremiah, to Isaiah, and to "the prophets."[40] He also quotes two sayings attributed to Jesus which are not in the canonical books.[41]

26. For Old Testament passages, Irenaeus generally used the Septuagint, though at times his text approximates the Hebrew more closely. For the New Testament, the Greek of the excerpts and the Latin version of Irenaeus have a Scripture text different from that of modern critical editions. Irenaeus's Bible text seems to have been substantially that of the Western family. Still, it is difficult here to

be certain of readings. In Book 1, in which we have long passages in Greek, when Irenaeus quotes Scripture he often is quoting the heretics, and hence these passages are not sure guides for the text of Irenaeus's Bible. Moreover, the Greek text is from excerpts of Irenaeus in the works of other authors, who may have adjusted the scriptural quotations to their scriptural texts. For Books 2 and 3 we have for the most part only the Latin version. The Latin translator, as Dom Chapman has proved, made his own translation from the Greek of Irenaeus, following the Greek slavishly even in word order.[42] Similarly, the Armenian translator of Books 4 and 5 translated the Greek of Irenaeus, though at times later scribes made some adjustments in the scriptural passages.[43]

27. Harvey strongly defended the theory that Irenaeus was acquainted with the Scriptures in the Syriac version and translated from that into Greek. There would seem to be no solid reason for that. The Western readings in the Old Syriac came by way of Tatian's *Diatessaron.* But Irenaeus appears to have used the Western text which was current in the West and which came to be used everywhere in the second and third centuries.[44] The difference in readings can at times be explained by the use of a harmonized version of the Gospels. Irenaeus probably made use of some kind of harmony in the Gospels, but whether he used Tatian's is disputed.

28. Irenaeus at times quotes the same scriptural passage in different ways; for instance, he cites Matt. 11.27 three different ways in Book 4.[45] Such variation could have been due to citation from memory; or it is possible he used various manuscripts of the Bible. He may also have had a kind of hexapla, as the Hebrew transcriptions of Gen. 1.1 in *Proof* 43 might indicate.[46] For the Messianic texts of the Old Testament, he need not have quoted the Bible directly, for there were collections of such texts for use by Christian writers.[47] Possibly Irenaeus took these texts from Justin's *Syntagma,* a work now lost. The use of *Testimonia* collections might account for false attributions by Irenaeus such as that of Numbers 24.17 to Isaiah in A.H. 3.9.2 and that of the *Magnificat* to Elizabeth in 4.7.1.[48]

29. Usually Irenaeus insists on the literal sense of Scripture. He holds that it is wrong to twist texts from their natural meaning by combining them with other texts that do not fit.[49] Truth itself must be the ultimate rule of interpretation.[50] One must have regard for the style of the Scriptures. Even the punctuation must be correct.[51] Obscure passages of the parables must not be interpreted by other obscure passages, but by such as are clear and certain.[52] The Gnostics indulged in exaggerated allegorical interpretations, and Irenaeus at times uses their weapon against them. But with him the allegorical interpretations are just ornaments added to the solid literal witnesses. The Scriptures are so vast in meaning that one should not be perturbed if he or she does not understand them all.[53]

30. Scripture, then, is an excellent source for the Rule of Faith. It is divine and must be believed. But the Scriptures are not always clear, nor did all of Scripture exist from the beginning. Hence it is not an absolute Rule of Faith.[54] Scripture is ultimately subject to the criterion of tradition, of the doctrine of the Church, of the Rule of Truth itself.

31. Irenaeus uses a variety of names to designate tradition, a variety based on the various aspects of the same reality: tradition, tradition of the apostles, tradition which derives from the apostles, tradition of the Truth, the preaching, the preaching of the Truth, the body of the Truth, the Rule of the Truth, or of the Faith, the doctrine, the doctrinal system.

32. Tradition must be derived from the apostles.[55] Any tradition outside this apostolic tradition must be resolutely rejected.[56] The condition and warranty for this is uninterrupted succession of bishops throughout the Church from the apostles and their disciples[57] so that every church throughout the world teaches one and the same unchangeable doctrine—tradition must really be catholic.[58] Moreover, the apostolic tradition must be verified in particular in the church at Rome, because that church has a preeminence over the others, and for that reason all the other churches, if truly apostolic, must agree with the Roman.[59]

33. Since tradition existed before the writings of the New Testament[60] it is an absolute source of revelation. It is the teaching of the living Church, which would have existed even if nothing had been committed to writing.[61]

Manuscript History

34. It is to be regretted that we do not have the original Greek for this important work. What of the original Greek we have today has been saved in the works of other writers who copied long passages from Irenaeus.[62] Much of Book 1 has been preserved by Epiphanius, who tells us that he copied verbatim and notes the fact when he merely condenses. Hippolytus used Irenaeus extensively and made sizable extracts from him. Eusebius has preserved some precious snatches, as has also Theodoret of Cyrus, who used Irenaeus copiously for his treatise on heresies. Some passages are extant in St. John of Damascus's *Sacra parallela,* and a few in the Catenae. There are several fragments in the Oxyrhynchus papyrus 405 and some longer but corrupted sections in the Jena papyrus. References to these various sources and to other minor sources are provided in the notes on the passages in question.

35. The loss of the complete text of Irenaeus's Greek is a mystery to scholars. The Greek text was available to the translators of the Armenian version in the sixth century, and in the eighth century when it was excerpted for the *Sacra parallela.* In the ninth century Photius read a copy at Baghdad; this copy could have disappeared in the sacking of Baghdad in 1258.[63]

36. For the *Adversus haereses,* then, we are for the most part dependent on the ancient Latin version, which provides for us the entire text. There are nine manuscripts, though not all are complete.[64] The manuscripts can be grouped into two distinct families. The oldest family is

represented by the Clermont, Voss, and Stockholm manuscripts. The second family is represented by the Arundel and other manuscripts.

37. The Clermont manuscript (C), which was found in the Jesuit college of Clermont, is now in the Preussische Staatsbibliothek in Berlin. It originated in the ninth century in the monastery of Corbie. Its Irish script is accounted for by the fact that St. Columbanus founded the monastery at Luxeuil around the year 590, and the monks of that monastery established the monastery of Corbie around the year 660. This monastery has all five books of the *Adversus haereses,* but ends at chapter 26 of Book 5. Thus it lacks the final ten chapters of the work. There is also a rather long lacuna from chapter 13.4 to chapter 14.1 in Book 5.

38. The Voss manuscript (V) is in the library of the University of Leiden. It was at one time owned by Sir Thomas Voss, an English humanist. Written in 1494 in England, it has the last ten chapters of Book 5, but it has the same lacuna as the Clermont manuscript in chapter 13 of Book 5.

39. The manuscript (H [Holmiensis A 140]) kept in Stockholm was bought by Queen Christina of Sweden in 1650. Written at the end of the fifteenth century, it is judged to be a copy of the Voss manuscript.

40. The Arundel manuscript (A) is in the British Museum. It was written in 1166 from a model in La Grande Chartreuse and for which a Florus of Lyons (d. 859/860) wrote a prologue, which is extant in this Arundel copy. The manuscript is incomplete, ending with chapter 31 of Book 5.

41. The Vatican Library has four manuscripts with the Latin version of the *Adversus haereses.* Vatican manuscript Latin 187 (Q) was written in 1429 or shortly before; it belongs to the second family of manuscripts. Vatican manuscript Latin 188 (R) depends on Latin 187 and was written during the pontificate of Nicholas V (1447-55). Another manuscript, Ottobonensis (Latin 752), normally designated O, which also depends on Latin 187, was copied between 1429 and 1440. The fourth manuscript at the Vatican, Ottobonensis (Latin 1154), normally designated P, was written around 1530.

42. The manuscript of Salamanca (Latin 202), normally designated S, was written before 1457, when John of Segovia gave it to the University of Salamanca.

43. The three manuscripts that Erasmus used are lost; they certainly belonged to the second family.[65] The humanist Passerat, who edited Book 1 and the beginning of Book 2 of the *Adversus haereses,* is said to have used a "very ancient manuscript." Loofs thought that this was simply the Voss manuscript, and that Passerat had not read it directly but through Feuardent, who, Loofs thought, had also used the Voss manuscript. M. L. Guillaumin has written that this is by no means certain. Rather, it seems to her that both Feuardent's vetus codex and Passerat's codex antiquissimus differed from each other and from the Voss manuscript. More recently L. Doutreleau has argued that Loofs's views should be upheld in this matter and that the codex Passeratii is nothing more than an illusion of the past.[66]

44. The relative value of these families and their manuscripts is somewhat in doubt today. The editors of Books 4 and 5 of the *Adversus haereses* in the *Sources chrétiennes* series made a careful study of the Armenian translation and compared it with the Latin manuscripts. They found that the Arundel manuscript is much more often in agreement with the Armenian version than are other Latin manuscripts. Since they thought the Armenian version was very faithful to the original, they preferred also the Arundel manuscript.[67] Prior to this, scholars quite generally, including F. Sagnard, who originally had edited Irenaeus's Book 3 for *Sources chrétiennes* in 1952, gave preference to the Clermont manuscript. And I am not so sure that this view should be altogether disregarded. I agree with B. Botte, who submits that the Clermont manuscript merits first place and can prevail even against both the Voss and Arundel manuscripts, but needs to be controlled in every case by, and at times corrected in favor of, the Armenian version and the Arundel manuscript.[68]

45. All in all the Latin text of the *Adversus haereses* is preserved as well as virtually any ancient document. There was no second Latin version, though some were misled on this point by a citation in Agobard's *De iudaicis superstitionibus,*[69] which differs from the normal translation. The quotation in Agobard is in fact a fragment that Rufinus had translated from the Greek of Eusebius.

46. The old Latin version of Irenaeus is noted for its slavish literalness. For this reason, though it is not without translator's errors and copyists' mistakes in the manuscripts, it is valuable for establishing the original text of Irenaeus. In many cases one can grasp the real sense of the Latin only by first translating it back into Greek.[70] The Latinity is of a corrupt kind, abounding in barbarisms and solecisms. It is clear that at times the translator did not understand the meaning of the Greek. Though scholars are not agreed on how well the translator knew Greek or Latin, it would seem on balance that he knew Greek but did not know Latin very well. The Latin text frequently retains the syntactical construction of the Greek, even to the point of attempting the Greek definite article with a demonstrative or relative pronoun construction. Had the translator known Latin well, he would scarcely have done that unless he was intent on preserving for posterity the language structure as well as the thought of Irenaeus. This does not seem likely.

47. Some scholars have suggested that Irenaeus himself made the Latin translation.[71] Irenaeus, however, would hardly have missed his own meaning, as the translator did in fact do at times. Some have also suggested that Tertullian made the translation. The language of the Latin ver-

sion, however, is simply not that of Tertullian, but rather of a barbaric type, Celtic in origin.[72] Tertullian seems to have used the translation, for there are passages from it, some of them verbatim, in his *Adversus Valentinianos*. When the ancient version has a faulty rendition, so does Tertullian, even in minute peculiarities, so that the agreement cannot be explained by mere accident.[73] The instances in which Tertullian agrees with the Greek against the Latin do not militate against this remark; rather, these instances would seem to indicate that Tertullian at times saw the errors in the Latin and corrected them, apparently with the aid of a Greek copy.

48. The Latin version seems to have been made not long after Irenaeus's time, that is, in the earlier decades of the third century, when Gnosticism was still a force to be reckoned with, since there would appear to have been little reason for making such a translation except as a weapon against Gnosticism. The majority of scholars have held to this early dating.[74] In more recent years it has been suggested that the translation was made in the latter half of the fourth century, probably in North Africa. The argument here is that Augustine quotes from the translation and is the first to do so.[75] Obviously, this involves contradiction of the evidence noted above regarding Tertullian's use of the translation. In any case, the translation could have existed, and have been used for some time, without having been quoted verbatim. Moreover, it seems almost incredible that a translator of the fourth century would have used so many archaic expressions, with which the Latin version abounds, and slavishly retained so many Greek constructions.

49. *Armenian version.* In the sixth century the entire *Adversus haereses* was translated, from the Greek, into Armenian. Only Books 4 and 5 of the work are extant.[76] We will discuss this version more at length in the Introduction to Book 4. There are also some important independent fragments in Armenian for other parts of the work. For a discussion of the Armenian fragments of Book 1 see SC 263.101-7.[77]

50. *Syriac version.* Some parts of the *Adversus haereses,* but not the entire work, were translated into Syriac.[78] Some fragments of this version are extant; in general the help they provide in establishing the text of Irenaeus is minimal. For a somewhat different evaluation of the Syriac fragments, at least for Book 1, see Doutreleau's remarks in SC 263.109-11.

Printed Editions

51. Erasmus was the first to put out a printed edition of the *Adversus haereses,* in 1526 at Basel. It is the *Editio princeps,* but it has only the Latin text, without any Greek fragments. In addition, it lacks the last five chapters of the work. A number of reprints were made of this edition during the next half century, till 1571. Nicolas Desgallards (Gallasius) published an edition in 1570 at Geneva in which he included the Greek excerpts found in Epipha-

nius. At Paris in 1575, F. Feuardent published a new edition; he used only the Latin but added the last five chapters from the Voss manuscript and supplied the text for a number of the lacunae in Erasmus's edition. For a later edition, in 1596 at Cologne, Feuardent added over forty Greek fragments found in various Greek writers. Meanwhile in 1575, J. de Billy (Billius) made a new translation of the first eighteen chapters of Book 1 as preserved by Epiphanius. His translation is printed in the seventh volume of Migne's *Patrologia graeca* below the older Latin version.

52. More than a century later, in 1702, J. E. Grabe, a learned Prussian who had settled in England and changed from Lutheranism to Anglicanism, put out an edition at Oxford, adding many Greek fragments. He introduced the use of the Arundel manuscript in printed editions.[79] A few years later, in 1710, the Benedictine R. Massuet put out an edition at Paris. He used the Clermont manuscript and preferred its readings. N. Le Nourry had already noted the existence of the Clermont manuscript in 1697.[80] Massuet used all the Greek fragments available and added a scholarly introduction. The Massuet edition became the popular edition, especially through its inclusion in Migne's *Patrologia graeca* 7.

53. Efforts were subsequently made to issue a more critical edition. First A. Stieren put out a two-volume edition between 1848 and 1853 at Leipzig. Then in 1857 W. W. Harvey put out one in Cambridge. Harvey had the advantage of the newly discovered Greek text of Hippolytus's *Refutation of All Heresies,* and a good number of Syriac fragments as well as a few Armenian fragments. He collated the three main manuscripts (Clermont, Voss, Arundel) of the Latin version. Though the Harvey edition has a number of defects, it was used quite generally by scholars.[81] In 1907 U. Mannucci began a still more critical edition at Rome, but only the first two books ever appeared. Another edition of the first book appeared when J. S. A. Cunningham submitted a doctoral dissertation in May 1967 at Princeton University entitled, *Irenaeus: Adversus haereses I: A New Edition of the Latin Text.* The excellent French series of patristic writings, Sources chrétiennes (hereinafter SC), has published a critical edition of the Latin text, together with all the excerpts and fragments extant, and with a French translation and ample scholarly notes. The series began with Book 3 which was published in 1952 by the Dominican F. Sagnard (SC 34). When Sagnard died, the work was taken over by a team of several scholars. Here is the publishing history of this acclaimed text and French translation:[82]

SC 100 *Irénée de Lyon: Contre les hérésies.* Book 4, edited and translated by A. Rousseau, B. Hemmerdinger, C. Mercier, and L. Doutreleau, 2 vols., 1965.

SC 151 *Irénée de Lyon: Contre les hérésies.* Book 5, edited and translated by A. Rousseau, L. Doutreleau, and C. Mercier, vol. 1: Introduction etc., 1969.

SC 152 *Irénée de Lyon: Contre les hérésies.* Book 5, edited and translated by A. Rousseau, L. Doutreleau, and C. Mercier, vol. 2: Text and translation, 1969.

SC 210 *Irénée de Lyon: Contre les hérésies*. Book 3, edited and translated by A. Rousseau and L. Doutreleau, vol. 1: Introduction etc., 1974.

SC 211 *Irénée de Lyon: Contre les hérésies*. Book 3, edited and translated by A. Rousseau and L. Doutreleau, vol. 2: Text and translation, 1974.

SC 263 *Irénée de Lyon: Contre les hérésies*. Book 1, edited and translated by A. Rousseau and L. Doutreleau, vol. 1: Introduction etc., 1979.

SC 264 *Irénée de Lyon: Contre les hérésies*. Book 1, edited and translated by A. Rousseau and L. Doutreleau, vol. 2: Text and translation, 1979.

SC 293 *Irénée de Lyon: Contre les hérésies*. Book 2, edited and translated by A. Rousseau and L. Doutreleau, vol. 1: Introduction etc., 1982.

SC 294 *Irénée de Lyon: Contre les hérésies*. Book 2, edited and translated by A. Rousseau and L. Doutreleau, vol. 2: Text and translation, 1982.

54. In preparing the present translation of Book 1, I have used the edition of Harvey, always comparing it where pertinent, however, with Holl's critical edition of Epiphanius.[83] In the notes to the text I have added the references to the various works in which the excerpts and fragments of the Greek can be found.

55. The divisions of chapters and paragraphs in this translation are based on those in the editions published by Massuet, Stieren, and Rousseau and Doutreleau. Although the chapter headings are for the most part my own, I have tried to fit the wording of the chapter headings to the contents of the chapter as far as possible. Past editors of the Latin text have kept the tables of contents and the chapter headings as found in the manuscripts for their historic value, even though they have little value for understanding Irenaeus. They do not come from Irenaeus himself. The tables of contents for the first four books were, however, already in the Greek manuscripts before the Latin and Armenian translations. The chapter headings were added later, possibly in the fifth or sixth century, and then not always correctly or exactly. The manuscripts for Book 5 do not have a table of contents or chapter headings. These were introduced for Book 5 in the edition of Desgallards in 1570, but later editors made various changes.[84]

56. Of the modern translations, the following were consulted: 1) the German by E. Klebba in *Bibliothek der Kirchenväter*[2] 3-4 (Munich 1912); 2) the following English translations: first, by A. Roberts and J. W. H. Rambaut, as revised and annotated by A. Cleveland Coxe, in *Ante-Nicene Fathers* 1 (Buffalo 1886)—this translation is quite faulty in places; and second, the translation of principal passages, with notes and arguments, published by F. R. Montgomery Hitchcock, *The Treatise of Irenaeus of Lugdunum against the Heresies* (2 vols., London 1916); 3) the Italian by Vittorino Dellagiacoma in *S. Ireneo di Lione. Contre Le Eresie* (I Classici Cristiani, 2 vols., Siena 1968[2]).[85]

Notes

1. Translated by J. Smith, this volume (ACW 16) was published in 1952. Hereinafter the *Proof of the Apostolic Preaching* will be referred to as *Proof*.

2. Tertullian, *Adv. Val.* 5 (CCL 2.756). See also H. B. Swete, *Patristic Study* (London 1902) 36. For recent scholarship on Irenaeus see the following: C. Kannengiesser, "Bulletin de théologie patristique: Ignace d'Antioche et Irénée de Lyon," RechSR 67, no. 4 (1979) 610-23; T. P. Halton and R. D. Sider, "A Decade of Patristic Scholarship: Volume 1," CW 76, no. 2 (November-December 1982) 96-101; M. A. Donovan, "Irenaeus in Recent Scholarship," SCent 4, no. 4 (Winter 1984) 219-41. Donovan mentions several Irenaean works published after this article in "Alive to the Glory of God: A Key Insight in St. Irenaeus," ThS 49 (1988) 283. For very recent surveys on Irenaeus see H.-J. Jaschke, "Irenäus von Lyon," TRE 16.258-68; A. Orbe, "Ireneo," DPAC 2.1804-16. In addition, see recent issues of *Bibliographia patristica*, ed. W. Schneemelcher (Berlin [and later Bonn and New York] 1959-) and *L'année philologique*.

3. The following works can be consulted on Gnosticism: W. Bousset, *Hauptprobleme der Gnosis* (Göttingen 1907); idem, "Gnosis," RE 7.2.1503-33; idem, "Gnostiker," RE 7.2.1537-47; H. Leclercq, "Gnosticisme," DACL 6.1.1327-67; G. Bareille, "Gnosticisme," DTC 6.2.1437-67; "Gnostizismus," LTK[2] 4.1021-31 has five articles by as many authors: K. Prümm, K. Schubert, R. Schnackenberg, H. Rahner, K. Algermissen; P. T. Camelot, "Gnose chrétienne," DSp 6.509-23; E. Cornelis, "Le Gnosticisme," DSp 6.523-41; G. Quispel, "Gnosticism," *Encyclopedia Brittanica* 10.505-7; K. Berger, "Gnosis/ Gnostizismus I," TRE 13.3-4. 519-35; R. McL. Wilson, "Gnosis/Gnostizismus II," TRE 13.3-4. 535-50; J. Lebreton, *Histoire du dogme de la Trinité* 2 (Paris 1928) 81-121, treats both pre-Christian and Christian Gnosticism; Lebreton-Zeiller 1.355-59, 2.617-53; L. Cerfaux, "Gnose pré-chrétienne et biblique," DBS 3.659-701 is particularly valuable for the origins of Gnosticism; C. Colpe, "Gnosis II (Gnostizismus)," RAC 11.537-659; G. Filoramo, "Gnosi/Gnosticismo," DPAC 2.1642-50; Sagnard *Gnose*, passim; Quasten *Patr.* 1.254-77, gives a handy classified bibliography; Sagnard, SC 34.44-70; H. A. Wolfson, *The Philosophy of the Church Fathers*, 2d ed., *Structure and Growth of Philosophic Systems from Plato to Spinoza* 3 (Cambridge, Mass. 1964) 1.495-574; H. Jonas, *The Gnostic Religion: The Message of the Alien God and the Beginnings of Christianity*, 2d ed. (Boston 1963); G. Van Groningen, *First-Century Gnosticism: Its Origins and Motifs* (Leiden 1967); J. Pelikan, *The Emergence of the Catholic Tradition (100-600)*, vol. 1 of *The Christian Tradition: A History of the Development of Doctrine* (Chicago 1971) 68-97; K. Rudolph, *Gnosis: The Nature and History of Gnosticism*, tr. P. W. Coxon, K. H. Kuhn, R. McL. Wilson (Edinburgh 1984; also in paperback edition, San

Francisco 1987; hereinafter Rudolph, *Gnosis*). H.-M. Schenke, "The Problem of Gnosis," SCent 3, no. 2 (Summer 1983) 73-87.

4. See the following items on Nag Hammadi: J. M. Robinson, "The Coptic Gnostic Library Today," NTS 14 (1968) 356-401; M. Krause, "Der Stand der Veröffentlichung der Nag Hammadi Texte" in Coll. Messina 61-89; G. Filoramo, "Nag Hammadi (scritti di)," DPAC 2.2329-32; J. Doresse, *The Secret Books of the Egyptian Gnostics: An Introduction to the Gnostic Manuscripts Discovered at Chenoboskion*, trans. P. Mairet (London 1960); J. Dart, *The Laughing Savior* (New York 1976); F. Wisse, "The Nag Hammadi Library and the Heresiologists," VC 25 (1971) 205-23; J. M. Robinson, "The Jung Codex: The Rise and Fall of a Monopoly," *Religious Studies Review* 3 (1977) 17-30. An English translation of the documents can be found in *The Nag Hammadi Library*, ed. J. M. Robinson et al. (3d rev. ed. with an afterword by R. Smith, San Francisco 1988). Important information is also available in D. M. Scholer, *Nag Hammadi Bibliography 1948-69*, Nag Hammadi Studies 1 (Leiden 1971), which is updated in annual supplements in *Novum Testamentum.*

5. See Quasten *Patr.* 1.294.

6. See D. J. Unger, "Christ's Rôle in the Universe according to St. Irenaeus," *Franciscan Studies* 5 (1945) 3-20, 114-37 (with bibliography); F. Beuzart, *Essai sur la théologie d'Irénée* (Paris 1908); A. M. Clerici, "Incontro tra la storia biblica e la storia profano in Ireneo," *Aevum* 43 (1969) 1-30. W. Widmann, "Irenaeus und seine theologischen Väter," ZTK 54 (1957) 156-73, examined what is proper to Irenaeus and not borrowed from predecessors, and correctly says it is his thought of a total economy of God for humankind, centered on Jesus Christ as the Beginning and the End, who recapitulates humankind's whole history and whole being. This same thought emerges from the study of G. Wingren, *Man and the Incarnation: A Study in the Biblical Theology of Irenaeus*, trans. R. MacKenzie (Edinburgh 1959) xiv, 26-27, 79-87, 122-28, 131, 170-75, 183, 191-202, 212, and J. Lawson, *The Biblical Theology of Saint Irenaeus* (London 1948) 140-98. Benoît 202-33 discusses the following as main themes in Irenaeus: the unity of God; the economy, which is universal and one; recapitulation; and gradual progress in salvation.

7. D. van den Eynde, *Les normes de l'enseignment chrétien dans la littérature patristique des trois premiers siècles* (Paris 1933) 163, writes as if there was no development in the doctrine of Irenaeus. A. Harnack was of the same mind; see his *History of Dogma,* trans. from the 3d German edition by N. Buchanan, 2 (Boston 1896) 312.

8. See Eusebius, *H.e.* 2.13.5; 3.28.6 (GCS 2.1.136, 258). St. Basil, *Spir.* 29.72 (SC 17².506). St. Jerome, *Vir. ill.* 35 (TU 14.1.a.25). St. Maximus Confessor, *Schol. e.h.* 7 (MG 4.176C). Photius, *Cod. 120* (MG

103.401), who placed this short title after the longer one. The definite article in the English translation is warranted by Eusebius and Basil and the contents. See Massuet, *Dissertatio* (hereinafter Diss.) 2.2.46 (MG 7.220-22).

9. Eusebius, *H.e.* 5.7.1 (GCS 2.1.440).

10. See A.H. 2 Prf. 2; 4 Prf. 1; 5 Prf. Irenaeus also alludes to it in A.H. 1.22.2; 1.31.3; and 2.24.4.

11. See *euersio huiusmodi aedificationis* (A.H. 2.27.3) with reference to doctrine.

12. Irenaean authorship is indicated particularly in view of the many citations and long quotations from this work, beginning with his contemporaries St. Hippolytus and Tertullian till St. John Damascene. J. S. Semler denied the Irenaean authorship in *Dissertatio I* from his edition of Tertullian (5 [Halle 1770-76; reprinted 1824-29] 245-90). He was amply refuted by G. F. Walch, *Commentatio de authentia librorum Irenaei adversus haereses* (cf. MG 7.381-404).

13. Grabe, *Prolegomena* 1.2.6 (MG 7.1358), held that the work is incomplete. Cf. Massuet, Diss. 2.2.54 (MG 7.235). W. Bousset, *Jüdischchristlicher Schulbetrieb in Alexandria und Rom: Literarische Untersuchungen zu Philo und Clemens von Alexandria, Justin, und Irenäus* (Göttingen 1915) 272-82, claimed the following sections are not genuine: 4.20.8-12, 21, 25.2, 33.10-14, 37-39; 5.21-36.

14. Sagnard *Gnose* 84, n. 4.

15. See A. Vaccari, S.J., *Institutiones Biblicae*, 6th ed. (Rome 1951) 1.283.

16. See R. E. Brown, D. W. Johnson, K. G. O'Connell, "Texts and Versions," NJBC #68, nn. 70-74, 82.

17. A.H. 1 Prf. 2; 1.9.1; 1.31.4; 3 Prf.; 4 Prf. 1; 5 Prf.

18. A.H. 1 Prf. 3; 4 Prf. 1.

19. A.H. 1 Prf. 2-3.

20. A.H. 1.31.4.

21. 1 Prf. 3.

22. A.H. 1.31.3.

23. See Dufourcq *Irénée* 74.

24. A.H. 2.31.2; 2.35.2. See also A.H. 3.12.12.

25. For a more detailed breakdown of Book 1 see SC 263.113-64.

26. See A.H. 1.15.4-5. Sagnard *Gnose* 72-74 rightly praises his rhetorical ability.

27. See A.H. 1.4.4; 2.6.3; 2.14.7.

28. Jerome, *Epist.* 75.3 (CSEL 55.33).

29. See Bonaventura ab Andermatt, O.M.Cap., "Sancti Irenaei doctrina de Sacrae Scripturae inspiratione atque inerrantia," (S.T.D. diss., Gregorian University, Rome 1937) passim; W. S. Reilly, "L'inspiration de l'Ancient Testament chez Saint Irénée," RBibl 14 (1917) 489-507; he does not always have a correct

evaluation of Irenaeus's thought. J. Hoh, *Die Lehre des hl. Irenäus über das Neue Testament* (NTAbhand 7.4-5 [1919] 62-75, 90-109).

30. A.H. 2.27.1; 2.35.4; 3.21.2.

31. A.H. 1.8.1; 2.2.5; 2.34.1; 5 Prf.; *Proof* 98.

32. A.H. 3.24.1.

33. A.H. 2.28.2; 3.1.1; also 3.5.1; 3.14.2-4.

34. A. Camerlynck, *St. Irénée et le canon du Nouveau Testament* (Louvain 1896) 26-27; T. Zahn, "Kanon des Neuen Testaments," RPT 9.768-96; idem, *Introduction to the New Testament,* 3d ed., trans. M. W. Jacobus and J. M. Trout (Edinburgh 1909) 2.295, 301, 310 n. 9, 387, 393-94, 433-34; 3.201 n. 14, 205 n. 27, 254 n. 6, 445, 448 n. 5.

35. A.H. 1.30.11.

36. A.H. 4.17.3; 4.17.5.

37. See Vernet 2416; Camerlynck, *Saint Irénée* 38-39; Benoît 103-47.

38. A.H. 4.20.2.

39. Irenaeus uses *graphĕ* in reference to the letter of Pope Clement at A.H. 3.3.3. Benoît 146 agrees that Irenaeus does not consider Hermas as strict Scripture. See also SC 100.248-50 on the question of whether or not Irenaeus considered Hermas as canonical Scripture as indicated by his use of *graphĕ*.

40. Twice he ascribes it to Jeremiah (A.H. 4.22.1; *Proof* 78); once to Isaiah (A.H. 3.20.4); three times to the prophets (A.H. 4.33.1; 4.33.12; 5.31.1). In *Proof* 4 he quotes this passage also, but he does not refer it to Hermas. There he adds "the Father" after "God," and changes "brought everything into being out of what was not," to "brought being out of nothing." See ACW 16.137 and n. 28. See SC 100.255, 687 n. 2 for a different view on A.H. 4.33.1; 4.33.12 and 5.31.1.

41. A.H. 5.33.3-4; 5.36.2. See E. Jacquier, "Les sentences du Seigneur extracanoniques (les Agrapha)," RBibl 15 (1918) 129-31.

42. See J. Chapman, "Did the Translator of St. Irenaeus Use a Latin N.T.?" RB 36 (1924) 34-51. See also K. T. Schäfer, "Die Zitate in der lateinischen Irenäusübersetzung und ihr Wert für die Textgeschichte des Neuen Testaments," *Von Wort des Lebens: Festschrift für Max Meinertz zur Vollendung des 70. Lebensjahres 19. Dezember 1950,* ed. N. Adler (Münster 1951) 50-59.

43. See SC 100.89-92.

44. See F. G. Kenyon, *The Text of the Greek Bible,* 3d ed. rev. A. W. Adams (London 1975) 169, 182; idem, *Our Bible and the Ancient Manuscripts,* 5th ed. rev. A. W. Adams (London 1958) 166-78.

45. A.H. 4.6.1; 4.6.3; 4.6.7 are texts where Matt. 11.27 is cited three different ways. See H. J. Vogels, "Der Evangelientext des hl. Irenaeus," RB 36 (1924) 25 and A. Merk, "Der Text des Neuen Testamentes beim hl. Irenaeus," ZKT 49 (1925) 307.

46. Such is the contention of B. Hemmerdinger, "Les Hexaples et Saint Irénée," VC 16 (1962) 19-20.

47. J. R. Harris and V. Burch, *Testimonies* (Cambridge 1920). P. Prigent, *Les Testimonia dans le christianisme primitif: L'épître de Barnabé I-XVI et ses sources* (Paris 1961), made a detailed literary study to discover patterns of citation that show up in pre-existing documents. J.-P. Audet, "L'hypothèse des Testimonia: Remarques autour d'un livre récent," RBibl 70 (1963) 381-405, disagrees with Prigent and sides with C. H. Dodd, *According to the Scriptures* (Welwyn 1952) 28-60, that the *Testimonia* were not collections of merely short proof texts but fairly extensive passages. R. A. Kraft, "Barnabas' Isaiah Text and the 'Testimony Book' Hypothesis," JBL 79 (1960) 336-50, argues that the matter is not as simple as Harris had presented it. In the late Jewish and early Christian period there was a *Schulbetrieb* which produced short and independent documents of a testimony page. Greek and Semitic communities handed down similar note pages which were eventually gathered into larger units that resulted in various recensions of the same testimony. A. Benoît, "Irénée *Adversus haereses* IV 17, 1-5 et les Testimonia," *Studia patristica* 4 (TU 79 [1961], 20-27), makes a good case that Irenaeus used *Testimonia* for this section of A.H.

48. Thus Hemmerdinger, "Les Hexaples," 19-20; see also idem, "Remarques sur l'ecdotique de Saint Irénée," *Studia patristica* 3 (TU 78 [1961] 70). Hemmerdinger incorrectly assigns the false attribution of Isaiah to A.H. 3.9.3; it should be 3.9.2.

49. A.H. 1.9.4.

50. A.H. 2.28.1.

51. A.H. 3.7.1-2.

52. A.H. 2.10.1; 2.27.

53. A.H. 2.28.3.

54. A.H. 3.1.1; 3.4.1-2; see A. J. Coan, "The Rule of Faith in the Ecclesiastical Writings of the First Two Centuries: An Historico-apologetical Investigation" (S.T.D. diss., The Catholic University of America, Washington, D.C. 1924) 69-93. N. Brox, in his careful introductory study of Irenaeus, *Offenbarung: Gnosis und gnostiker Mythos bei Irenäus von Lyon: Zur Charakteristik der Systeme* (Munich and Salzburg 1966) 69-103, holds that, according to Irenaeus, the Scriptures are perfect and complete, namely, as a source of revelation. But he must then modify somewhat his theory.

55. A.H. 3.1.1; 3.2.1-2; and passim.

56. See van den Eynde, *Normes de l'enseignment* 159-87.

57. A.H. 3.2.2; 3.3.1-3; and passim.

58. A.H. 1.9.4; 1.10.1-2; 3.1.1; 3.4.1-2; 3.24.1.

59. See Book 3 for a full discussion of A.H. 3.3.2., a justly famous passage.

60. A.H. 3.1.1.

61. A.H. 3.5.1; see van den Eynde, *Normes de l'enseignement* 261-80.

62. For a detailed study of the Greek for Books 1 to 5, see SC 263.61-100, SC 293.83-100, SC 210.49-132, SC 100.51-87, SC 152.64-157.

63. See SC 100.15 and L. Doutreleau, "Saint Irénée de Lyon," DSp 7.2.1934.

64. See SC 263.9-59, SC 293.17-82, SC 210.11-48, SC 100.15-50, SC 152.27-63. The following studies on the Latin text may be consulted: F. Loofs, *Die Handscriften des lateinischen Übersetzung des Irenäus und ihre Kapitelteilung,* Kirchengeschichtliche Studien H. Reuter gewidmet (Leipzig 1888) 1-93 (printed separately Leipzig 1890); O. Bardenhewer, *Geschichte der altkirchlichen Literatur* 1 (2d ed. Freiburg 1913) 500; *Nouum Testamentum Sancti Irenaei Episcopi Lugdunensis,* ed. W. Sanday, C. H. Turner, A. Souter et al., Old-Latin Biblical Texts 7 (Oxford 1923) xxv-xxxv; W. Sanday, "The MSS of Irenaeus," *Journal of Philology* 17 (1888) 81-94; F. C. Burkitt, "Dr. Sanday's New Testament, With a Note on Valentinian Terms in Irenaeus and Tertullian," JThS 25 (1923) 56-67; E. Köstermann, Neue Beiträge zur Geschichte der lateinischen Handschriften des Irenäus, ZNTW 36 (1937) 1-34; Sagnard *Gnose* 12-15; J. S. A. Cunningham, *Irenaeus: Adversus haereses I: A New Edition of the Latin Text* (Ann Arbor, Michigan 1968) xvii-xix (Microfilm).

65. For an attempt to discover the identity of one of Erasmus's MSS see J. Ruysschaert, "Le manuscrit '*Romae descriptum*' de l'édition Érasmienne de Irénée de Lyon," *Scrinium Erasmianum,* ed. J. Coppens, 1 (Leiden 1969) 263-76. Cunningham (*Irenaeus* xxi) believes that the *editio princeps* by Erasmus should have a claim on our attention as a witness to the tradition as his variants are just as valuable as those in the other *recentiores.*

66. See M. L. Guillaumin, *A la recherche des manuscrits d'Irénée* (Studia patristica 7.1 [TU 92, 1966] 65-70). For Doutreleau's views, see SC 263.319-27.

67. See SC 263.319-27 and SC 152.55-57 n. 1. I have not listed the Mercier MSS, because they are really not independent MSS.

68. See B. Botte, "Notes de critique textuelle sur l'*Adversus haereses* de saint Irénée," RTAM 21 (1954) 165-78. Cunningham (*Irenaeus* xxiv) also believes that C should be the MS against which the others should be compared.

69. Chap. 9 (ML 104.85). G. Mercati first held that there was a second translation, but later changed his mind. On this see G. Mercati, *Note di letteratura biblica e cristiana antica,* Studi e Testi 5 (Rome 1901) 241-

43. C. H. Turner, "Mercati on Cyprian and Irenaeus," JThS 2 (1901) 143-48, holds that there is no second translation.

70. Sagnard *Gnose* 18. Burkitt, "Sanday's New Testament of Irenaeus," 63: "The more I study the Latin Irenaeus the more I feel that its importance lies chiefly in what it tells us about the original Greek text of St. Irenaeus." The Armenian version of Books 4 and 5 prove that the Latin is in general a faithful translation of the Greek original. S. Lundström has made four helpful studies on the Latin version: *Studien zur lateinischen Irenäusübersetzung* (Lund 1943) (hereinafter Lundström *Studien*); "Textkritischen Beiträge zur lateinischen Irenäusübersetzung," *Eranos Löfstedianus: Opuscula philologica Einaro Löfstedt A.D. XVII Kal. Iul. Anno MCMXLV dedicata* (Uppsala 1945) 285-300; *Neue Studien zur lateinischen Irenäusübersetzung* (Lund 1948); *Übersetzungstechnische Untersuchungen auf dem Gebiete der christlichen Latinität,* (Lund 1955).

71. Feuardent, *Commonitio ad lectores de sua quinque librorum D. Irenaei editione* (MG 7.1340C-D).

72. See Massuet, Diss. 2.2.53 (MG 7.233-34).

73. A. Merk, "Der Text des Neuen Testamentes beim hl. Irenäus," 304, claims that the dependence of Tertullian on the Latin of Irenaeus is not proved, but that the end of the fourth century for the Latin translation is too late.

74. See Grabe, *Prolegomena,* 1.2.3 (MG 7.1356); Massuet, Diss. 2.2.53 (MG 7.234); W. Sanday, "The Date of the Latin Irenaeus: A Fragment," in *Nouum Testamentum Sancti Irenaei,* ed. W. Sanday et al., lvii-lxiv; Harvey l. clxiv. See also A. D. Alès, "La date de la version latine de saint Irénée," RechSR 6 (1916) 133-37; F. R. M. Hitchcock, *Irenaeus of Lugdunum: A Study of His Teaching* (Cambridge 1914) 44, 347-48; Sagnard *Gnose* 12. P. T. Camelot, "Eirenaios," LTK[2] 3.774, admits that it saw the light of day perhaps around the year 200, but certainly before 396. It is difficult to admit Henry Dodwell's idea that the Latin translator made use of Tertullian. See H. Dodwell, *Dissertationes in Irenaeum* (Oxford 1689) 397-400.

75. Augustine seems to have used Irenaeus, or at least was influenced by him, for a number of years. See B. Altaner, "Augustinus und Irenäus: Eine quellenkritische Untersuchung," ThQ 129 (1949) 162-72. This was published again in the author's *Kleine patristische Schriften,* TU 83 (1967) 194-203. Augustine quotes A.H. 4.2.7 and 5.19.1 in *C. Iul.* 1.3.5 (ML 44.644). He mentions Irenaeus by name when he sums this up again in 1.7.32 (ML 44.662). Augustine wrote this work in A.D. 422. So the Latin of Irenaeus had to exist then, at least. But Augustine might have used Irenaeus in earlier works. He might have used A.H. 1.23.1 in *Haer.* 1 (ML 42.25); and A.H. 4.33.10 in *Catech. rud.* 3.6 (CCL 46.125). But it is more certain that he used A.H. 4.30.1 in *Doctr. christ.*

2.40.60 (CCL 32.73-74). This last work was written for the greater part in 396-97 and so Altaner infers that the Latin translation of Irenaeus was made shortly before this, since it had not been quoted by anyone else. See Altaner, "Augustinus und Irenäus" 172, which is also reprinted in TU 83 (1967) 203. Dodwell, *Dissertationes in Irenaeum* 400-401, seems to have been the first to present this later date for Lat. Iren. It was accepted also by H. Jordan, "Das Alter und die Herkunft der lateinischen Übersetzung des Hauptwerkes des Irenäus," *Theologische Studien: Theodor Zahn zum 10. Oktober 1908 dargebracht,* ed. N. Bonwetsch et al. (Leipzig 1908) 133-92; also by F. J. A. Hort, in "Did Tertullian Use the Latin Irenaeus?" *Nouum Testamentum Sancti Irenaei,* ed. Sanday et al. xliv, and Burkitt, "Sanday's New Testament of Irenaeus" 56-67. Lundström (Lundström *Studien* 90-109) reexamined the data for both sides, and concluded that the arguments for the early date were scarcely convincing. Yet he rejects Souter's claim that the translator was the same person who made the Latin translation of Origen's commentary on Matthew, which was made between A.D. 370-420. Dodwell also suggested that the occasion for the translation was the refutation of Priscillianism. See Dodwell, *Dissertationes in Irenaeum* 405-7. B. Hemmerdinger (SC 100.16) is of the opinion that Dodwell's view has not received sufficient attention. He refers to his own review article, "Saint Irénée évêque en Gaule ou en Galatie?" REG 77 (1964) 291-92. In his translation with notes of Firmicus Maternus's *The Error of Pagan Religions* (ACW 37), C. A. Forbes calls attention to some parallels in Firmicus to Irenaeus and remarks: "The passages cited in this and the preceding notes argue for the probability that Firmicus knew the writings or at least the views of Irenaeus" (ACW 37.213, n. 470). He cited A.H. 3.18.1; 5.16.3; 5.17.4; 5.18.3 as parallels to *The Error* chap. 25.2 (ACW 37.101) and chap. 27.3 (ACW 37.105). He might have cited also A.H. 3.19.1; 3.19.3; 3.21.10; 3.22.3; 5.19.1; 5.21.1. Possibly there is a borrowing in chap. 21.2, where Firmicus speaks of the Lernean Hydra, from Irenaeus, A.H. 1.30.15. To be noted also is that, according to Forbes (ACW 37.31-32); "Vecchi sees a clear proof of Firmicus' discipleship to Irenaeus in his invariable attribution of the authorship of the Old Testament to the Holy Spirit.'" See A. Vecchi, "Guilio Firmico Materno e la 'Lettera agli Ebrei,'" *Convivium* 25 (1957) 641-51 (in particular, 650 n. 1). The ideas are certainly Irenaeus's; but the parallels in phrasing are not so strong that one can be certain that Firmicus used Lat. Iren. If his use of Lat. Iren. were proved, since Firmicus's work was written in A.D. 346-47, we would have an argument for a somewhat earlier date for Lat. Iren.

76. The text was discovered in 1904 by K. Ter-Mekerttschian and published by E. Ter-Minassiantz in TU 35.2 (1910) viii-264.

77. See also on this J. B. Pitra, *Analecta sacra* 4 (Paris 1883) 33, 304. H. Jordan, *Armenische Irenaeusfragmente mit deutscher Übersetzung nach Dr. W. Lüdtke zum Teil erstmalig herausgegeben und untersucht* (TU 36.3 [1913] viii-222), gives twenty-nine Armenian fragments with a German version.

78. See Vernet 2403. Harvey 1. clxiv, following Massuet (Diss. 2.2 [MG 7.237A]), believes that there was no complete Syrian version. The fragments referred to are in Harvey 2.431-53 and Pitra, *Analecta sacra* 17-25, 292-99. A. Houssiau, "Vers une édition critique de S. Irénée," RHE 48 (1953) 143, agrees that the Syriac fragments do not come from a full translation of A.H., but from Syriac works, such as Severus of Antioch and Timothy Aelurus.

79. Cf. SC 100.39-40.

80. Cf. SC 100.39.

81. Cunningham (*Irenaeus* xxvii) contends that Harvey's debt to Stieren is much greater than is generally realized.

82. The chronology of publication is set forth by A. Rousseau in SC 293.7-14, which is summarized in Donovan, "Irenaeus in Recent Scholarship" 220. M. Geerard, CPG 1.110, refers to the SC edition as an *"editionis laudatae."*

83. Before the Reverend Dominic J. Unger died in July, 1982, he asked me to update and complete the work that still remained before this translation could be published. He regretted that he had not able to compare his translation with the text published by A. Rousseau and L. Doutreleau in SC 263-64 in 1974. His translation has been checked against the SC text and modified where this was deemed necessary. I want to thank the Capuchin Province of Mid-America for the opportunity to work on this translation and also thank three of his confreres: the Reverend Blaine Burkey, O.F.M.Cap.; the Reverend Thomas Weinandy, O.F.M.Cap.; and the Reverend Ronald Lawler, O.F.M. Cap., for helping me on numerous occasions. Thanks are also owed to the Reverend Gerald O'Collins, S.J.; Doctor Margaret Schatkin; the Reverend Daniel Mindling, O.F.M. Cap.; and the Reverend Paul Watson for bibliographical assistance. Finally, I am grateful to the members of the Mother of God Community, Gaithersburg, Maryland, for their support and assistance (Ed. Note).

84. On this problem see SC 100.186-91 and SC 152.31-34. See also SC 210.47-48 where L. Doutreleau takes issue with what F. Sagnard had written in SC 34.77-78.

85. D. J. Unger was not able to review *Irenäus: Gott im Fleisch und Blut ausgewählt und übertragen von Hans Urs Von Balthasar* (Einsiedeln 1981). This work is a translation of selected passages of the *Adversus haereses* and the *Proof of the Apostolic Preaching* organized around six themes: the Sign of the Son of Man, the True God and the False God,

Faith and Gnosis, Salvation History, Incarnation as Recapitulation, and Fulfillment in God. Von Balthasar's introduction to this volume presents a perceptive and sympathetic overview of Irenaeus's theological concerns. This volume is now available in English: *The Scandal of the Incarnation: Irenaeus Against the Heresies,* introduced and selected by H. U. von Balthasar, trans. J. Saward (San Francisco 1990) (Ed. Note).

List of Abbreviations

ACW: Ancient Christian Writers (Westminster, Md.-London-New York-Paramus, N.J.-Mahwah, N.J. 1946-)

ANF: The Ante-Nicene Fathers (Buffalo, N.Y. 1885-96; repr. Grand Rapids, Mich. 1951-56)

Athanasius, *Ar.*: 1-3 Athanasius, *Orationes tres adversus Arianos*

Augustine, *C. Jul.*: Augustine, *Contra Julianum libri* 6

Augustine, *Catech. rud.*: Augustine, *De catechizandis rudibus*

Augustine, *Civ.*: Augustine, *De civitate Dei*

Augustine, *Doct. christ.*: Augustine, *De doctrina christiana*

Augustine, *Haer.*: Augustine, *De haeresibus ad Quodvultdeum*

Basil, *Spirit.*: Basil, *Liber de Spiritu sancto*

Benoît: A. Benoît, *Saint Irénée: Introduction à l'étude de sa théologie* (Paris 1960)

Bibl. Stud.: Biblische Studien

BKV: Bibliothek der Kirchenväter[2] (Kempten and Munich 1911-31)

BLE: Bulletin de littérature ecclésiastique

Caesar, *Gall.*: Caesar, *De bello Gallico*

CBQ: Catholic Biblical Quarterly

CCL: Corpus christianorum, series latina

CE: Catholic Encyclopedia (New York 1907-14)

Cicero, *De orat.*: Cicero, *De oratore*

Cicero, *Rab. Post.*: Cicero, *Pro C. Rabiro Postumo oratio*

Cicero, *Tusc.*: Cicero, *Tusculanarum disputationum liber*

Clement of Alexandria, *Ecl.*: Clement of Alexandria, *Eclogae ex scripturis propheticis*

Clement of Alexandria, *Exc. Thdot.*: Clement of Alexandria, *Excerpta Theodoti*

Clement of Alexandria, *Paed.*: Clement of Alexandria, *Paedagogus*

Clement of Alexandria, *Str.*: Clement of Alexandria, *Stromateis*

Coll. Messina: *The Origins of Gnosticism: Colloquium of Messina 13-18 April 1966,* ed. U. Bianchi (Leiden 1970)

CPG 1: *Clavis Patrum Graecorum,* vol. 1: *Patres Antenicaeni,* ed. M. Geerard (Turnhout 1983)

CSCO: Corpus scriptorum christianorum orientalium (Paris et alibi 1903-)

CSEL: Corpus scriptorum ecclesiasticorum latinorum (Vienna 1866-)

CW: The Classical World

Cyril of Jerusalem, *Procatech.*: Cyril of Jerusalem, *Procatechesis*

DACL: Dictionnaire d'archéologie chrétienne et de liturgie (Paris 1907-53)

DBS: Dictionnaire de la Bible, Supplément (Paris 1928-)

DCB: A Dictionary of Christian Biography, Literature, Sects, and Doctrines (London 1877-87)

DHGE: Dictionnaire d'histoire et de géographie ecclésiastiques (Paris 1912-)

DPAC: Dizionario patristico e di antichità cristiane (Casale Monferrato 1983-88)

DSp: Dictionnaire de spiritualité (Paris 1932-)

DTC: Dictionnaire de théologie catholique (Paris 1903-50)

Dufourcq *Irénée*: A. Dufourcq, *Saint Irénée,* Les Saints (Paris 1904)

Dufourcq *Pensée*: A. Dufourcq, *La pensée chrétienne* (Paris 1905)

Epiphanius, *Haer.*: Epiphanius, *Panarion* seu *Adversus lxxx haereses*

Eusebius, *H.e.*: Eusebius, *Historia ecclesiastica*

Eusebius, *P.e.*: Eusebius, *Praeparatio evangelica*

Filaster, *Haer.*: Filaster, *Diversarum haereseon liber*

GCS: Die griechischen christlichen Schriftsteller der ersten drei Jahrhunderte (Leipzig 1897-)

Gk. Epiph.: The Greek text of Irenaeus's *Adversus haereses* contained in Epiphanius (ed. K. Holl, GCS 25 [1915], 31 [1922], 37 [1933])

Goodspeed: *Die ältesten Apologeten: Texte mit kurzen Einleitungen,* ed. E. J. Goodspeed (Göttingen 1914)

Grabe: The edition of the *Adversus haereses* by J. E. Grabe (Oxford 1702)

Harvey: The edition of the *Adversus haereses* by W. W. Harvey (Cambridge 1857)

HERE: Encyclopedia of Religion and Ethics, ed. J. Hastings (New York and Edinburgh 1908-26)

Hermas, *Mand.*: Hermas, *Mandata pastoris*

Hippolytus, *Haer.*: Hippolytus, *Refutatio omnium haeresium sive philosophoumena*

Hippolytus, *Trad. ap.*: Hippolytus, *Traditio apostolica*

Homer, *Il.*: Homer, *Ilias*

Homer, *Od.*: Homer, *Odyssea*

HTR: Harvard Theological Review

Ignatius of Antioch, *Smyrn.*: Ignatius of Antioch, *Epistula ad Smyrnaeos*

JEH: Journal of Ecclesiastical History

Jerome, *Ad Jovin.*: Jerome, *Adversus Jovinianum libri 2*

Jerome, *Epist.*: Jerome, *Epistula*

Jerome, *In Tit.*: Jerome, *Commentarius in epistulam Pauli ad Titum*

Jerome, *Vir. ill.*: Jerome, *De viris illustribus*

JThS: Journal of Theological Studies

Justin, *Dial.*: Justin, *Dialogus cum Tryphone Judaeo*

Justin, 1, 2 *Apol.*: Justin, *Apologiae*

Klebba, BKV: *Des heiligen Irenäus Fünf Bücher gegen die Häresin,* trans. E. Klebba, BKV 3-4 (Kempten 1912)

Lampe, PGL: *A Patristic Greek Lexicon,* ed. G. W. H. Lampe (Oxford 1961)

Lat. Iren.: The Latin version of Irenaeus's *Adversus haereses*

Lebreton-Zeiller: J. Lebreton and J. Zeiller, *History of the Primitive Church,* trans. E. C. Messenger (New York 1942-47)

LSJ: *A Greek-English Lexicon* compiled by H. G. Liddell and R. Scott revised and augmented by H. Stuart Jones and R. McKenzie et al. (Oxford 1940)

LSJ Suppl.: H. G. Liddell, R. Scott, H. Stuart Jones, *Greek-English Lexicon: A Supplement,* ed. E. A. Barber et al. (Oxford 1968)

LTK: Lexikon für Theologie und Kirche (Freiburg 1930-38)

LTK^2: Lexikon für Theologie und Kirche, 2d ed. (Freiburg 1957-67)

Lundström *Studien*: S. Lundström, *Studien zur lateinische Irenäusübersetzung* (Lund 1943)

Mannucci: *Irenaei Lugdunensis Episcopi Adversus Haereses Libri Quinque* (Rome 1907)

Marius Victorinus, *Adv. Arrium*: Marius Victorinus, *Adversus Arrium libri 4*

Marius Victorinus, *Gen. div. verb.*: Marius Victorinus, *De generatione divini verbi*

Maximus Confessor, *Schol. e.h.*: Maximus Confessor, *Scholia* in Pseudo-Dionysius Areopagita, *De ecclesiastica hierarchia*

MG: Patrologia graeca, ed. J. P. Migne (Paris 1857-66)

ML: Patrologia latina, ed. J. P. Migne (Paris 1844-64)

M. Polyc.: Martyrium Polycarpi

NCE: New Catholic Encyclopedia (New York 1967)

Nilus the Ascetic, *Ep.*: Nilus the Ascetic, *Epistula*

NJBC: *The New Jerome Biblical Commentary,* ed. R. E. Brown, J. A. Fitzmyer, and R. A. Murphy (Englewood Cliffs, N.J. 1990)

NRT: Nouvelle revue théologique

NT Abhand.: Neutestamentliche Abhandlungen

OCD^2: The Oxford Classical Dictionary, 2d ed. (Oxford 1970)

ODCC^2: The Oxford Dictionary of the Christian Church, 2d ed. (Oxford 1983)

Origen, *Cels.*: Origen, *Contra Celsum*

Photius, *Cod.*: Photius, *Bibliothecae codices*

Plautus, *Most.*: Plautus, *Mostellaria*

Pliny, *Nat.*: Pliny, *Naturalis historia libri 37*

PO: Patrologia orientalis (Paris 1904-)

Proof Saint Irenaeus: Proof of the Apostolic Preaching, trans. J. Smith, ACW 16

Ps.-Tertullian, *Haer.*: Ps.-Tertullian, *Liber adversus omnes haereses*

Quasten *Patr.*: J. Quasten, *Patrology,* 3 vols. (Westminster, Md., Utrecht, and Antwerp 1950-60; repr. Westminster, Md. 1983)

RAC: Reallexikon für Antike und Christentum (Stuttgart 1950-)

RB: Revue bénédictine

RBibl: Revue biblique

RE: Real-Encyclopädie der classischen Altertumswissenschaft, ed. A. Pauly, G. Wissowa, W. Kroll (Stuttgart 1893-)

RGG: Die Religion in Geschichte und Gegenwart, 3d ed. (Tübingen 1957-65)

RHE: Revue d'histoire ecclésiastique

RPT: Realencyklopädie für protestantische Theologie und Kirche (Leipzig 1896-1913)

RSPT: Revue des sciences philosophiques et théologiques

RechSR: Recherches de science religieuse

RSRUS: Revue des sciences religieuses

RTAM: Recherches de théologie ancienne et médiévale

Rudolph *Gnosis*: K. Rudolph, *Gnosis: The Nature and History of Gnosticism*, tr. P. W. Coxon, K. H. Kuhn, R. McL. Wilson (Edinburgh 1984; also in paperback edition, San Francisco 1987)

Sagnard *Gnose*: F. Sagnard, *La gnose valentinienne et le témoinage de saint Irénée* (Paris 1947)

SC: Sources chrétiennes (Paris 1942-)

SCent: The Second Century

Stieren: The edition of the *Adversus haereses* by A. Stieren (Leipzig 1848-53)

Tacitus, *Ann.*: Tacitus, *Annales (ab excessu divi Augusti) libri 16*

TDNT: *Theological Dictionary of the New Testament*, ed. G. Kittel and G. Friedrich and trans. G. Bromiley (Grand Rapids, Mich. 1964-76)

Tertullian, *Adv. Marc.*: Tertullian, *Adversus Marcionem*

Tertullian, *Adv. Val.*: Tertullian, *Adversus Valentinianos*

Tertullian, *Anim.*: Tertullian, *De anima*

Tertullian, *Praescr.*: Tertullian, *De praescriptione haereticorum*

Tertullian, *Spec.*: Tertullian, *De spectaculis*

Theodoret, *Ep.*: Theodoret, *Epistula*

Theodoret, *Haer.*: Theodoret, *Haereticarum fabularum compendium*

Theophilus of Antioch, *Auto.*: Theophilus of Antioch, *Ad Autolycum*

ThRdschau: Theologische Rundschau

ThS: Theological Studies

TRE: Theologische Realenzyklopädie (Berlin 1976-)

TU: Texte und Untersuchungen zur Geschichte der altchristlichen Literatur (Leipzig-Berlin 1882-)

VC: Vigiliae christianae

VD: Verbum Domini

Vernet F.: Vernet, "Irénée (Saint)," in DTC 7.2.2394-2533

ZKT: Zeitschrift für katholische Theologie

ZNTW: Zeitschrift für die neutestamentliche Wissenschaft und die Kunde des Urchristentums

ZRGG: Zeitschrift für Religions- und Geistesgeschichte

ZTK: Zeitschrift für Theologie und Kirche

Abbreviations for books of the Old Testament and New Testament are those found in *The Chicago Manual of Style: The 13th Edition of A Manual of Style Revised and Expanded* (Chicago and London 1982) 388-89. Where a given book of the Bible is differently designated in the New American Bible (NAB) and in the LXX (and Vulgate), both forms are given. But the NAB designation is given first. For example, 2 Sam. (2 Kings), Sir. (Ecclus.), Rev. (Apoc.). When Psalms are cited, the Septuagint enumeration is given first. For example, Ps. 138(139).13.

Finally, a word about the citation of the justificative notes found in SC 263.167-316. There are often several justificative notes per page. To avoid confusion, the following system of citing these notes is used throughout this volume: SC 263.167 (SC 264.19 n. 1). This indicates which justificative note on p. 167 of SC 263 is meant (i.e., the first note on p. 19 of SC 264).

Terrance L. Tiessen (essay date 1993)

SOURCE: "Conclusion," in *Irenaeus on the Salvation of the Unevangelized*, ATLA Monograph Series, No. 31, The Scarecrow Press, Inc., 1993, pp. 250-82.

[*In the essay below, Tiessen investigates Irenaeus's doctrine of divine revelation as it pertains to the "non-Christian" and compares this doctrine with the modern notion of "anonymous Christianity."*]

It is possible now to draw together the results of the investigation that has been made of the salvation of the unevangelized, in the theology of Irenaeus. The question of the state of the non-Christian, particularly of the individual who has not had opportunity to learn of God as revealed in Christ, is of great importance. In the face of the apparent failure of Christian missions to reach larger groups of people with the Gospel, various theories have been developed to describe the situation of the non-Christian in relationship to divine revelation, and to divine grace in general. In the quest for a proper perspective on the non-Christian, and on non-Christian religions, there has been a considerable amount of interest in the writings of the early Church Fathers. Frequently, one encounters the suggestion that a more positive view is found in those early centuries than in more recent Christian theology.

One theory that has received a great deal of attention, and that still has many ardent proponents, is the concept of "anonymous Christianity," which has been most thoroughly expounded by Karl Rahner. There are writers who have claimed seeds of this idea in the second- and third-centuries, citing particularly Justin, Irenaeus, and Clement of Alexandria. It has been the purpose of this study, therefore, to examine the views of Irenaeus regarding divine revelation, particularly as it affects the unevangelized. Given the attempts to claim Irenaeus as an antecedent of the theology of "anonymous Christianity," special attention has been devoted to a comparison of Irenaeus's theology with that modern view of divine revelation and the non-Christian. However, the study made of Irenaeus could easily be compared with other theories now being proposed. This will be done only to a very limited extent in these final pages.

In this concluding chapter, a summary will be made of Irenaeus's doctrine of divine revelation and the non-Christian. Then a specific comparison will be made of Irenaeus's view with the theology of "anonymous Christianity" as one modern example of a perspective that has specifically been claimed by some writers (though not by Rahner himself) as having antecedence in Irenaeus.

A. A SUMMARY OF IRENAEUS'S DOCTRINE OF DIVINE REVELATION AND THE SALVATION OF THE UNEVANGELIZED

1. THE CONTEXT

In order to do justice to Irenaeus's theological formulation, it is important to understand the context within which Irenaeus was thinking and working. This will help to keep us from imposing upon Irenaeus a framework which was alien to his own context.

A. The Struggle with Gnosticism

The primary reference point of Irenaeus's theological work was his apologetic against the Gnostic heretics. Their doctrine of divine revelation and the non-Christian is the foil for Irenaeus's perspective. The Gnostic view against which Irenaeus contended was, as its very name indicates, a claim to special knowledge. They described themselves as a privileged class (the "spiritual") who possessed perfect knowledge of God and had been initiated into the mysteries by Achamoth. They appealed to the Scriptures to support their system of truth but also claimed secret traditions (a "living voice") handed down to them from Christ and the apostles. In this way, they represented themselves as having a knowledge of truth which was superior to that of Irenaeus and the Church which he represented.

The Gnostic doctrine of salvation was largely one of salvation by knowledge. In fact, knowledge was not only the major instrument of salvation; it was itself the form in which the goal of salvation is possessed. The situation was complicated, however, by an anthropology that distinguished between three kinds of people. Salvation was impossible for the lowest level—the hylic or material—by reason of their materiality. The metaphysical dualism of the Gnostics assumed the inherent evil of matter. The class in which Irenaeus, and most of the Church, was placed was the psychical. These are people whose destiny was not already determined. They do not have perfect knowledge but they may be saved through good works and faith. The spiritual are those who possess grace by virtue of their relationship to the Aeons, and whose salvation is ensured by their nature, apart from good works on their part, but on the assumption that they possess perfect knowledge.

The Gnostics had little to say about paganism, but they did not consider pagan religions to have attained the truth about God. The primary target of Gnosticism was not the pagan religions but the larger Christian community. It was probably assumed that the pagan was in the class of the material, and hence in a hopeless condition. Those in the Church were psychical and therefore worth the efforts made to bring them to knowledge of the truth.

B. The Success of the Christian Mission

It has been demonstrated that Irenaeus believed that in the time of the apostles, the world had been evangelized, in fulfillment of Old Testament prophecy and in obedience to the commission of Christ. Irenaeus viewed the Church in his own day as spread throughout the whole world with a unity of faith that was preached everywhere. This assumption on the part of Irenaeus is extremely important to this study. Because Irenaeus was wrong in this perception, the reader may be tempted to dismiss his statements on the extent of evangelization as hyperbole, and to suggest that this was not really the perspective from which Irenaeus viewed the unevangelized. However, it has been demonstrated that the assumption clearly underlay Irenaeus's understanding of the just judgment of the unbeliever. Those who are condemned are justly punished because they personally rejected the Gospel. Clearly, Irenaeus assumed that all people had salvific revelation. Yet he taught that salvation was restricted only to the Church in its institutional form. No one could be saved apart from the Church, but it was assumed that everyone had the opportunity to be saved, and those who did not believe were therefore culpable. Thus, his belief in the success of the Christian mission is evident, not only from his explicit statements regarding the spread of the Church, but even more significantly from his theology of salvation and judgment.

We have shown that Irenaeus's view was inaccurate, but what matters for this study is that he thought it was correct. Jean Daniélou therefore observes correctly that "Irenaeus's ecclesiastical frontiers are identical with those of the known world in his day."[1] The difference between Irenaeus's view of the success of the Christian mission and the situation as we see it in our own day is definitely a limiting factor in any comparison between Irenaeus's view of divine revelation and the non-Christian and modern theories on the subject.

2. THE GRACIOUS SELF-REVELATION OF THE TRANSCENDENT FATHER

Irenaeus stressed the transcendence of God no less than the Gnostics did, but he denied the Father's complete unknowability. Though God is incomprehensible in his essence and greatness, he has graciously made himself known to humankind in his love and great goodness. This is particularly important because the knowledge or vision of God is life-giving. It is, in fact, the ultimate goal of human life. To see God is to live, to have immortality and incorruptibility. This is why it is so important that God chose to reveal himself to human beings, and that he does so out of a continual good will toward humanity. Consequently, the Father has revealed himself, in some way, to *all* people.

Most basically, God has revealed himself through his creative work and through his continual providence over the affairs of the world which he created. In particular, God has demonstrated his power, wisdom and goodness by these means. It is possible for people, by their natural reasoning capacity, to attain knowledge of God the Creator by means of creation. However, Irenaeus distinguishes between the knowledge achieved in this way, and the saving knowledge, which is the experience only of those who are inwardly illumined by the Word.

3. THE EXCLUSIVE MEDIATION BY THE SON

To know the Father, in the full and salvific sense, the Son's work as mediator is essential. There is no way for people to know the Father except as the Son reveals him. So interrelated are the Father and the Son that any manifestation of the Son gives knowledge of both the Father and the Son. Thus, there has been a progressive self-manifestation of God to humanity, with the Son involved as exclusive mediator at every stage of that revelation. The Son was involved in the divine work of creation and continues active in providence. He is continually present with his creatures, revealing the Father to them from the beginning, and not only in his incarnation. Nowhere is this work of the Son more intriguingly described than in the passages that describe the "cosmic cross." The Word is invisibly imprinted upon the world, in the form of a cross, with his arms stretched out to gather the world together from one extreme to the other. He gives cohesion to all created things by his immanence in the creation. All beings participate in the cosmic cross. Furthermore, the cosmic cross has an orientation to the salvation of the dispersed elements. This activity of the Word leads to the knowledge of the Father, being the principle not only of a physical cohesion, but also of a moral and supernatural unity. The visible crucifixion of the incarnate Word thus has a particular appropriateness because it manifests that all things participate in the invisible cross.

In addition to the natural revelation of the Father by the Son, Irenaeus details the theophanic appearances of the Son to individuals of the Old Testament: Adam, Cain, Noah, Abraham, Jacob, Moses, and others. From the beginning, therefore, the Word had a certain visibility and was "seen" even by people of the Old Testament. He also spoke through the prophets, both in their preaching and in their writings. The Word was thus implanted or inseminated in the prophetic announcements of the Old Testament, and the Church reaps the fruit of that sowing. The great value of the Old Testament Scriptures in evangelism of the Jews is therefore obvious. The experiences of Peter, Cornelius and the Ethiopian eunuch all evidence the benefit of this knowledge of the Word through the Old Testament Scriptures, which fairly easily grew into recognition of Jesus as the fulfillment of those Old Testament prophecies. Evangelization of the Gentiles was more difficult precisely because of the lack of evangelistic preparation. The visit of Christ to the subterranean regions, after his death, was also a form of reaping the fruit which had been sown in his various modes of revelation in the Old Testament. There, He appeared to those who had anticipated his coming, and declared to them the good news of his coming, namely, the remission of sins for those who had believed in him.

The coming of the Word in the flesh brought an even more privileged revelation of the same Word who had been revealing himself and the Father from the beginning. This was an important stage in the economy of salvation, because by means of the Incarnation, the flesh is accustomed to see God and God is accustomed to live with human beings. Thus progress is made toward the eventual vision of God by humankind. The significance of the Incarnation is also demonstrated by means of the concept of recapitulation. Christ recapitulated the history of humanity in himself and thus procured salvation for humankind. Passing through all the ages of life, he restored "all people" to communion with God. He recapitulated in himself all the nations dispersed from Adam onwards, and all the languages and generations of humankind. The salvific importance of the Incarnation is thus immense. Notice was taken earlier of the tendency to universalism in Irenaeus's doctrine of recapitulation, a tendency which was followed to that conclusion by Origen. However, Irenaeus does not pursue the concept to that conclusion. It would appear that in the recapitulatory work of Christ, involving both the Incarnation and the Passion, the objective salvation of humankind is accomplished, but individuals' personal participation in the saving fruit of that work depends upon their own response to divine revelation. No one could be saved without the recapitulatory work of Christ, but it does not automatically ensure the salvation of anyone.

The final stage of the Son's preparation of humanity for vision of the Father will be his millennial reign, following his second coming. This period is an important stage in the Irenaean scheme. During that time, the resurrected righteous of both Testaments will reign on earth with Christ and prepare themselves, through the contemplation of the Son, for the immediate vision of the Father in heaven. Both those who lived before the Incarnation and desired to see Christ and those who have believed in Christ since he ascended to the Father will have the opportunity to know Christ in the flesh, and will be made ready to see the Father. Following the millennium, the saved will enter into an eternity with the Father, during which time they will continue to grow in their love and knowledge, even in its direct vision, through the mediation of the Son. Those who were called early in the economy of salvation will receive the same reward (incorruptibility) as those who were called later.

4. THE MINISTRY OF THE HOLY SPIRIT

Attention has been given to the role of the Spirit in preparing humanity for the knowledge of the Father through the Son. He was active with the Word in creation and providence, as Wisdom, one of the two hands of the Father. He spoke through the prophets as they declared the Son to their generation, empowered the Son for his ministry, and was later sent by the Son to empower the disciples for the evangelization of the nations. It is the work of the Spirit to lead people to the Son, who presents them to the Father. Thus, just as it is impossible to approach the Father apart from the Word, it is likewise impossible to see the Son without the Spirit. The Spirit continues to speak through the New Testament Scriptures, but especially works in and through the Church. Indeed, his saving work is restricted to the Church, so that where the Spirit is the Church is found, and where the Church exists the Spirit is present and active.[2]

5. THE FAITHFUL PROCLAMATION OF DIVINE REVELATION IN THE CHURCH

Faced with the threat of Gnostic heresy and its claim to a "living voice," Irenaeus took refuge in the Church as recipient of the apostolic tradition. The revelation that the Father has made of himself by means of the Son is now to be found in the Church, where the Holy Spirit has placed gifted people, whom he enables to understand the revelation and to faithfully proclaim it. The apostles had had a privileged position, being instructed personally by Christ and then inspired by the Holy Spirit for the recording of divine revelation, as well as empowered for its proclamation. They were instrumental in starting churches made up of those who believed in Christ and were baptized in the name of the Father, Son and Holy Spirit, and they handed those churches on to other people of their choosing. It was Irenaeus's conviction that these successors of the apostles—the presbyters or bishops of the churches—were the ones whose testimony to divine revelation was to be believed. When there was a question regarding the truth, it was to these people that one ought to listen, since they are the ones to whom the apostles handed on the truth. This objective truth that was handed down (*tradere*) was therefore designated the "tradition" or the "rule of truth." Its authenticity was recognizable by the consensus of the testimony of the churches all over the world to this core of truth. A particularly significant witness was to be found in the church at Rome, which had a normative role for Irenaeus, as a church whose presbyters could be traced back to Peter and Paul, and one which was a meeting point of Christians traveling from all over the world.

For those who lived in Irenaeus's day and afterwards, the divine revelation is therefore to be found in the Church. Not only is the testimony to truth clearly found there, but it is in and through the Church alone that the Holy Spirit carries out his saving operations. To be outside of the Church, as an institution led by the successors of the apostles, would be to be outside of the Holy Spirit and therefore separated from all his lifegiving work. *Since no one knows the Father except by means of revelation by the Son, and no one sees the Son except by the ministry of the Holy Spirit, and no one has the Holy Spirit except those who are a part of the Church, participation in the institutional Church (that is, the visible Church led by the apostolic successors) becomes the sine qua non for knowledge of the Father.*

6. THE NECESSITY OF HUMAN RESPONSE TO DIVINE REVELATION

Irenaeus foresaw two possible destinies for people: the vision of God, which is life, or separation from God's light, which is darkness and death. The choice between these destinies rests squarely with the individual. God has manifested himself to all people, and given to all the capacity to believe in him. Those who believe in the Father and the Son and who follow God, as Abraham (the father of the faithful) had done, will be saved. They receive the adoption as children and, provided they steadfastly maintain their faith, they will progress toward the vision of the Father. Those who respond to the revelation of God are given an increasing capacity to see the light of God. Those who do not respond, however, blind themselves and are eventually abandoned by God to the darkness which they have chosen for themselves. The justice of God in their judgment is therefore evident because it is the implementation of their freely chosen self-condemnation. There is no deficiency in divine revelation that causes the condemnation of any person. The fault lies in the individual.

7. THE NON-CHRISTIAN

Irenaeus never uses the term "non-Christian." He speaks of the unbeliever, the Gentile, the pagan, the ungodly, sinners, the unbelieving, and those who are outside the Church. The existence of non-Christians, designated by a variety of names, is thus perfectly clear. They are those who neither acknowledge the Creator nor recognize the providence of God from which they benefit; those who serve the creature and worship "idols of demons"; those who know God's commandments but do not do them; those who do not believe in the Father and the Son; those who not only personally reject the truth concerning the one God (Father, Son and Holy Spirit), but who lead others astray with them.

Irenaeus had a very negative view of other religions. The gods they served were idols of demons. However, he recognized that not all people are equally privileged in regard to divine revelation. The Gentiles or pagans did not have the words of God. However, God's punishment of the unbeliever is appropriate to the grace that he had experienced and is graded according to the opportunity of divine revelation that he had received. This is a conclusion drawn from the statement of Jesus concerning the more severe judgment of those who rejected the incarnate Christ, as compared to the people of Sodom, who had less revelation. The justice of God is evident in that distinction.

This study has concluded that Irenaeus viewed the world as evangelized to such an extent that no one was without specific revelation of Christ. This is a very important aspect of his view of the non-Christian. He therefore views non-Christians as those who had deliberately rejected Christ and preferred the darkness of their own way. He says nothing of unbelievers before Christ, who were without sufficient revelation to believe and be saved. He does not speculate about those who had neither Christophanies nor typical anticipations of Christ because of being out of contact with Israel. Although the ungodly of Psalm 1:1 are people who do not "know God," nothing is said to imply that their lack of knowledge was due to insufficiency of revelation. Irenaeus's focus is on those who have the Scriptures and have heard the proclamation of the faith by the Church, but who have chosen not to believe.

8. The Thesis of Irenaeus

In summary, the position of Irenaeus might be stated as follows:

1) God the Father has revealed himself to all people, from the beginning, by his two hands—the Word(Son) and Wisdom (Spirit)—in various modes. These included creation and providence, theophanic appearances of the pre-incarnate Logos; the preaching and writings of Moses and the prophets; the incarnate Word; the preaching and writings of the apostles, who handed on to their successors in the Church the truth taught by Christ, which they recollected and recorded with the help of the Holy Spirit; and the preaching of the Church all over the world, united in its testimony to the apostolic faith.

2) Jesus Christ, by his incarnation, obedient life, death and resurrection, has recapitulated the whole history of humankind and has, thereby, accomplished an objective reconciliation of all things to the Father. He will return to raise the righteous dead of all ages and will reign on earth with the resurrected righteous, who will become accustomed to the vision of God through their contact with the incarnate Word. At the close of that reign, the wicked will be judged, and the righteous will enter an eternity of ever-expanding knowledge of the Father.

3) Only those who believe in the Father and the Son, and do God's will, can be included among the righteous who will see the Father and live with him for eternity. People of all periods of history are saved on the same basis, and all will be prepared for eternity by the rule of Christ on earth, following his return.

4) The judgment of those who do not believe in order to be saved is a just act on God's part because of the universality of his self-revelation and because of the freedom which all people had either to believe and to obey or to disbelieve and disobey.

5) An unbeliever or "non-Christian" would therefore be someone who had known of Christ, but who had not believed in him or "desired to see him," as the case might be. The non-Christian religions are a false worship, their gods being idols of demons. Therefore, non-Christians are not saved, and non-Christian religions are not means of salvation. The same would be true of those outside of Israel, in the Old Testament, or those who lived before the patriarchs and who were outside of the one economy which was carried forward by the revelatory activity of the pre-incarnate Logos. "Unbelievers," in all stages of the economy, were not saved.

B. Irenaeus and "Anonymous Christianity"

1. "Anonymous Christianity" Restated

In order to determine to what extent Irenaeus may validly be cited as an early proponent of concepts that "anticipated" the theology of "anonymous Christianity," it will be helpful to summarize the main points of the theory as Karl Rahner has developed it.

Rahner's definition of the "anonymous Christian" is clear. He is "the pagan after the beginning of the Christian mission, who lives in the state of Christ's grace through faith, hope and love, yet who has no explicit knowledge of the fact that his life is oriented in grace-given salvation to Jesus Christ."[3] Basic to Rahner's theory are the following theses:

1) It is God's will that all people should be saved, a fact often described as the "universal salvific will of God."[4]

2) In spite of original and personal sin, God therefore offers all people a "genuine possibility of attaining to their own salvation." This offer of salvation exists before the practical proclamation of it and makes possible both the proclamation and the acceptance of it.

3) By the grace of God, all people have been given a "supernaturally elevated transcendence," a "transcendental experience of the absolute merciful closeness of God." Although people may not be distinctly conscious of this, it is a reality in the inmost core of their persons. In the "depth of his concrete nature," a human is a being who "looks for the presence of God himself." This is one side of the event of revelation.

4) One can say that people have faith if they "freely accept their own unlimited transcendence," which is graciously directed toward God. When people accept themselves in freedom as they are, in faithfulness to their own moral conscience, they are said to accept divine revelation (i.e., the *a priori* awareness of humanity) in faith.

5) The incarnation of the Word constituted a call to the human race to "share the life of God supernaturally." Because of the Incarnation, humanity has already "become ontologically the real sanctification of individual men by grace and also the people of the children of God." By virtue of this "consecration," they are already a "people of God which extends as far as humanity itself."

6) Because of this ontological reality brought into being by the Incarnation, the Church is a twofold reality. In addition to the established juridical organization, one can also describe the Church as "humanity consecrated by Incarnation." The institutional Church is thus the "concrete historical manifestation of the salvation which is achieved by the grace of God throughout humanity." It is the explicit expression of what is present as a hidden reality outside the visible Church.

7) Hence, people who "accept the concrete reality of their nature totally, in a free act of a supernatural justification by faith and love," are to be considered members of the Church. They have personally accepted (albeit unconsciously) the membership of the people of God which is already a fact on the historical plane. This is not merely membership in an "invisible" Church. It is an "invisible" belonging to the "visible" Church by grace, and it

has a "visible relation" to that Church even when it is not constituted by baptism, or by an "externally verifiable profession of the faith."

8) Non-Christian religions before Christ were, in principle, willed by God as legitimate ways of salvation. The coming of Christ, and his death and resurrection, made these religions obsolete. However, non-Christian religions may maintain some validity after the Incarnation, for individuals who have not been presented with the message of Christ so clearly that rejection of that message as the way of salvation offered by God would be a grave fault. Therefore, prior to that point at which the claims of Christ are clearly presented and understood, the non-Christian religion, as a way of salvation accepted from the genuine motives of conscience, does lead one to God.

2. ANTICIPATIONS IN IRENAEUS?

To what extent is it valid to speak of Irenaeus as anticipating the theology of "anonymous Christianity"?

A. Misleading Statement

It is clear from the careful study that has been made of Irenaeus's doctrine of revelation that such a statement could be very misleading. The reader of previously cited authors who point to Irenaeus as anticipating "anonymous Christianity" is likely to assume a much closer affinity between Irenaeus and the theology of "anonymous Christianity" than is actually the case. From the analysis that has been made of Irenaeus's position, as summarized above, it is clear that the conclusions which Irenaeus himself reached closely resemble the motivations that have traditionally stimulated missionary activity.[5] To cite as an antecedent of "anonymous Christianity" a man who believed that only those are saved who are members of the institutional Church, and who expressly confess its rule of truth, would seem a highly questionable appeal to history. In short, any reference to Irenaeus as an "antecedent," a "forerunner," or an "anticipator" of modern optimism concerning the state of the non-Christian (such as one finds in the theory of "anonymous Christianity") will have to be very cautiously worded.

There are, perhaps, two lines of approach which might be taken to the theology of Irenaeus in order to find legitimate "antecedence." Both of these will be examined.

1) Irenaeus did not address the situation which is addressed by the theology of "anonymous Christianity," because he was not conscious of significant groups of people without knowledge of Christ through the Church's witness. However, if the existence of unevangelized peoples is assumed, *inferences* could be drawn from the theological framework of Irenaeus which would point toward an optimism regarding the salvation of the "non-Christian."

2) Irenaeus was not himself a theologian of "anonymous Christianity." However, there are *aspects* of his theology which could be *developed in a different direction* from the one in which Irenaeus himself developed them, and which would then lead to different conclusions from the ones Irenaeus himself reached.

B. Inferences Drawn from Irenaeus's System

It has been the contention of this study that Irenaeus described divine revelation and the non-Christian in the context of the assumption that the world had been evangelized. Those who were unbelievers had chosen to be so, in explicit rejection of the Christ whom the Church had proclaimed as Savior of the world. There is always some danger in speculation about "what would have happened if . . . ?" However, the question still has some validity, provided that the answers reached are recognized as tentative. The question which the modern student of Irenaeus may ask is: "What would Irenaeus have concluded about the salvation or judgment of the unbeliever, if he had started from the recognition that there are large groups of people who have never had the message of Christ presented to them in an intelligible fashion?"

Irenaeus argued that God's judgment of the unbeliever (the "non-Christian") was just, because the unbeliever had had the revelation concerning Christ and had rejected it. But what if there were unbelievers who had not had the revelation of the incarnate Word as proclaimed by the Church?

1) A Reformed direction? Might Irenaeus have followed the direction taken by a large part of the Reformed tradition, with its focus on Romans 1, 2, and 5? This view proposes that, by virtue of the solidarity of the human race in Adam (because of a federal headship or because of corporate solidarity, not because of "substantial" or "realistic" unity), all human beings sinned in Adam (Romans 5). That original sin included original guilt, and not only a tendency to personal sin and guilt. God has revealed himself to all, in creation (Romans 1:19-20), and has written his law on their hearts, and given them an inner witness to it, in conscience (Romans 2:15). However, because of the natural depravity of fallen humanity, which affects every aspect of their being, they suppress God's revelation, and worship the creature rather than the Creator, and they disobey God's law written on their hearts. The revelation in nature results only in condemnation because 1) sinful people always distort it idolatrously, and 2) it does not reveal Christ, faith in whom is necessary for salvation. Consequently, the non-Christian who does not hear of Christ is justly judged. The justice of that judgment, however, is not based on an assumption that non-Christians had adequate revelation to believe unto salvation, but on the ground of their unbelief and disobedience at the level of natural revelation, for which they are culpable because of a self-incurred inability in Adam.[6]

This direction appears unlikely. Although it has been demonstrated that Irenaeus had an understanding of original sin, that was certainly not a major consideration for him, and would not likely be a starting point in defending the justice of divine judgment of the non-Christian. Irenaeus did not emphasize the insufficiency of natural revelation, as Reformed theology has done. Assuming that all people had more than natural revelation, he nonetheless gave it a positive importance, and spoke of the necessity of faith with regard to it. Furthermore, Irenaeus's emphasis on free will, and his reaction to Gnostic determinism, made him an unlikely "antecedent" of Reformed (predestinarian) theology.

An interesting attempt has been made to develop a more hopeful view of the salvation of "non-Christians" within the framework of traditional Reformed theology.[7] Neal Punt has suggested that the traditional Reformed manner of approaching the doctrine of election has been incorrect. The usual assumption has been that everyone is lost except those whom Scripture declares to be elect, namely, those who believe in Christ. Punt suggests that we ought rather to assume the election of everyone, unless Scripture specifically states otherwise. Rejection of Christ would thus be a clear sign of lostness (non-election or reprobation), but the position of those who do not know of Christ would be more hopeful than in the traditional formula as summarized above.

Faith in Christ is seen as the response of the elect who hear of Christ. It has, therefore, a conditional necessity (not unlike Rahner's conditional necessity of Church membership). The elect who do not hear the Gospel respond positively in regard to the revelation that they have received. The outcome is therefore similar to that discussed below, under B,2,b,2), but it begins from a Reformed concept of sovereign, divine election. Most of those who adopt the position described below would not work within the framework of unconditional election. They would be more likely to speak of an election based on God's foreknowledge. Irenaeus himself speaks of God's relationship to the unbelief of the non-Christian in terms of foreknowledge, and not of reprobation. A similarity to the work of Karl Barth is evident in regard to the concept of corporate, universal election in Christ.

Punt's work reminds one of the position of Ulrich Zwingli, in the sixteenth century. Zwingli also started with a strong doctrine of election and predestination as the cause of salvation. It is manifested in outward signs, and those signs differ according to one's situation. The pagans of antiquity, and those who have not had opportunity to hear the Gospel, may also be among the elect, because they will be judged on a different basis from those who have had Gospel revelation. Zwingli spoke hopefully, for instance, of the situation of Seneca or Socrates.[8] It is interesting to find this kind of optimism regarding the salvation of the non-Christian in a key Reformation figure.

2) Salvation on the basis of response to revelation at whatever level it is received? Irenaeus would not have surrendered his conviction of the justice of God's judgment of the unbeliever. The justice of God was too fundamental an aspect of the nature of God to be surrendered, and was viewed in coordination with his goodness. Irenaeus believed that people were judged according to their privilege or opportunity. This was a recognition that there are gradations within the modes of divine revelation. However, the assumption was that no one was below the level of salvific revelation. If Irenaeus had recognized people who have no more than natural revelation, would he have accepted that natural revelation as sufficient to the salvation of those who receive no more? We can only speculate. It is significant, however, that Irenaeus viewed the natural revelation as mediated by the Son. Although it was possible to come to knowledge of God as Creator by reason alone, it was only by a special illumination of the Word that faith was possible, in response to that revelation. Is it possible to conceive that (given a different context) Irenaeus might have accepted the possibility of salvation by a Word-illumined response to natural revelation? If one considers only Irenaeus's discussion of natural revelation, such a direction is not conceivable. He did regard the revelation in creation, at least germinally, as salvific, and he paralleled it to the greater privilege of revelation in the incarnate Word. Within the Irenaean framework, a person saved in such a case would no doubt be resurrected at the return of Christ and would have the millennium to become accustomed to the knowledge of the Son, and to be prepared thereby for the vision of the Father. However, this view would have called for considerable change in other areas of Irenaeus's theology. He would have had to modify considerably his concept of the Spirit's work in salvation, and of the role of the institutional Church. However, Irenaeus developed his strong emphasis on saving revelation within the scope of the institutional Church in response to the threat of Gnostic schismatics. In a different context, he might have taken a different turn.

This perspective has a theological simplicity that is still far from "anonymous Christianity." It sees no need to classify the saved as "anonymous Christians," accepting these people as saved on the ground of Christ's work, through a believing response to the light that they had. It does not describe this as a form of "implicit faith," or define it as an invisible form of membership in the visible Church. The assumption is simply made that explicit faith in Christ and membership in the Church are the means of salvation for those who know Christ and the Church, but that those who do not have that privilege are accepted on the basis of the response they make to the revelation that they do have. Among Protestant laypeople, this is a common view,[9] but it would call for considerable dislocation in Irenaeus's system to attribute the "seeds" of such a view to him.

3) Toward "anonymous Christianity"? Irenaeus did view God as willing the salvation of all people, and as offering to all people a possibility of salvation. From there on, Irenaeus and "anonymous Christianity" move in different directions, because of a difference in assumptions regarding the state of the evangelization of the world. Faith, for Irenaeus, has nothing to do with accepting one's own transcendence. It is recognition of the Creatorship of God, gratitude for his providence, confession of the one God

and Father of all, the one Son who is Lord and Savior of all, the one Holy Spirit, and the one economy of salvation. There is no need for a twofold reality of the Church, because all people have contact with the visible, institutional form. Membership is therefore defined in terms of that visibility. Non-Christian religions are not legitimate ways of salvation, because they all exist in conscious opposition to the Christian Church. If Irenaeus had known of non-Christian religions still without a hearing of the Gospel, he would more likely have postulated the salvation of individuals on account of a Word-illumined response to natural revelation, as under B,2,b,2) above, than because of revelational and salvific elements within the pagan religion. Irenaeus would not have called "Christian" any people who had no explicit knowledge of the fact that their life is "oriented in grace-given salvation to Jesus Christ."

In short, the differences of perspective are considerable, because of the difference of starting point. The "what if?" question is not, after all, a means by which one can demonstrate "antecedence" of "anonymous Christianity" with any degree of certainty.

4) Toward the even greater optimism of pluralistic soteriologies? Among those who have spoken approvingly of the Patristic period, for its perspective on revelation and salvation, is Raimundo Panikkar. He suggests that Christian theology has generally tried to "accentuate the differences between Christianity and the 'non-Christian' religions" but that "in the Patristic period things were different."[10] Panikkar himself goes beyond "anonymous Christianity" with regard to the salvific role that he attributes to Hinduism and, by extension, to other non-Christian religions. He makes occasional use of Rahner's theology in forming his own perspective, but his approach is not just an Asian model of "anonymous Christianity." Panikkar contends that "it is acceptable to Hindus to be 'anonymous Christians,' provided one also admits that Christians are 'anonymous Hindus.'"[11] Interestingly, Rahner himself was once asked by a well-known Japanese philosopher: "What would you say to my treating you as an anonymous Zen Buddhist?" Rahner replied:

> You may and should do so from your point of view; I feel myself honored by such an interpretation, even if I am obliged to regard you as being in error if I assume that, correctly understood, to be a genuine Zen Buddhist is identical with being a genuine Christian, in the sense directly and properly intended by such statements.[12]

The "proper sense" which Rahner intends is different from the sense in which Panikkar would use the term. For Rahner, there can come a point when the knowledge which non-Christians have of the message of Christ is such that it would be a "grave fault" for them to reject it any longer "as the way of salvation offered by God and as the fulfillment that goes beyond anything that" was offered by their former religion.[13] Rahner thus reserves an absoluteness to Christianity that transcends the relative value of non-

Christian religions which may nonetheless lead an individual to God, in the period prior to the coming of the message of Christ to that individual. For Panikkar, on the other hand, Christianity and Hinduism are both transcended by something absolute. Both are therefore of relative value.

From Hebrews 1:1-2, Panikkar surmises that "not only the prophets of Israel but also the sages of Hinduism" are inspired by the Son, who has been present "in all human endeavours."[14] The Logos himself is thus speaking in Hinduism. Furthermore, "there is in Hinduism a living Presence of that Mystery which Christians call Christ."[15] From the point of view of the Christian, Christ's grace is the force which is impelling Hinduism and he is its ontological goal.[16] However, that is only true from the point of view of the Christian. In fact, the Mystery which Christians call Christ cannot be completely identified with him. He is the Mystery in the sense that "to see Christ is to reach that Mystery,"[17] but "he is only one aspect of the Mystery as a whole."[18] "Even though he is *the* Way when we are on that way," when Christians actually reach the summit, they discover Christ "in all those who have reached the Mystery, even if their ways have not been the Christian one."[19] It is only for the Christian that the Mystery is indissolubly connected with Christ. What Christians need to realize therefore, is that "in believing and loving Christ as the central symbol of life and Ultimate Truth," they are being drawn towards the selfsame Mystery that attracts all other human beings who are seeking to overcome their own present condition.[20]

Panikkar grants that apart from Christ there is no redemption (Ephesians 1:3-14ff; Colossians 1:13-22). Therefore, anyone who is saved is saved by Christ, the only redeemer. Since "we know by reason and faith that God provides everybody with the necessary means of salvation," we must accept that "Christ is present in one form or another in every human being as he journeys towards God."[21] In some way, therefore, "Hinduism is incorporated into the universal economy of salvation by God through Christ."[22] Since there is no salvation outside the Church, the "'Church' should not be identified with a concrete organization, or even with adherence to Christianity."[23] The normal and ordinary means of salvation within the Christian Church are the sacraments. "Yet it remains true that Christ may be active and at work in the human being who receives any sacrament, whether Christian or any other."[24] Thus, the "good and *bona fide* Hindu" is saved by Christ, "not by Hinduism or Christianity *per se*, but through their sacraments, and ultimately, through the *Mysterion* active within the two religions."[25]

In this approach of Panikkar one can see clearly three of the aspects of Irenaeus's theology which might have developed in an optimistic direction. 1) God wills all people to be saved, 2) Christ is the Savior of all people, and 3) God provides everyone with the necessary means to salvation. However, Panikkar has moved on from those starting points to a position that is more distant from Irenaeus than is that of Rahner. It does not seem possible to stretch Irenaeus to the point at which Hindus could be confronted with the revelation of God in Christ, could reject Christ as the way of salvation, and the triune God as the one true God, and yet be saved (through Christ) by the sacraments and worship of their Hindu religion.

In comparing Irenaeus with "anonymous Christianity," we encountered a situation that Irenaeus did not specifically address. Panikkar, on the other hand, has described a situation that Irenaeus did confront. There seems to be no reason to assume that Irenaeus would have felt different about Hindu gods and idols from how he felt about the gods of the Gentile religions of his day, which he called "idols of demons." There is no reason to believe that he would treat the Hindu's rejection of Christ in a manner different from his treatment of the rejection by the Gnostic or the pagan of his own day. There is no reason to suggest that he would consider the "visible" Church dispensable for Hindus who have their own concrete manifestation of the Mystery, in Hinduism.

Irenaeus had no inclination to suggest that the Mystery toward which Valentinus moved by means of his doctrine of the Aeons was none other than the Mystery toward vision of whom Irenaeus was progressing. Nor was Irenaeus ready to accept that when he and Valentinus reached the summit they would find that they had arrived by different but equally valid ways. Even if Valentinus had been a very sincere Gnostic, with a clear conscience, unless he had given up his erroneous beliefs concerning the Aeons, had believed in Christ as the one Son of God, and had participated in the visible Church, he would have been doomed. In short, while we may discern some carefully qualified "antecedence" of "anonymous Christianity" in the theology of Irenaeus, there is a clear contrast between his thought and that of the pluralism represented in Panikkar's work.

C. Development of Aspects of Irenaeus's Theology

James Dupuis, Gerald O'Collins, and Eugene Hillman all indicated Logos-Christology as the point of greatest hopefulness in the second- and third-century Fathers, vis-à-vis the salvation of "non-Christians." Particularly the activity of the pre-incarnate Logos was cited. It appears that those statements have generally assumed too great a similarity between Irenaeus and Justin or Clement of Alexandria. This study has demonstrated that the pre-incarnate revelatory activity of the Logos was seen more in terms of theophanies, prophecies and types which were specifically Christological than in terms of an activity of the Logos outside of God's working within his covenant people. However, we have noticed the significance of the activity of the pre-incarnate Logos in creation and providence, and the universal cohesiveness provided by the immanence of the Word, as symbolized in the cosmic cross. The parallel which Irenaeus draws between revelation in creation and revelation in the Incarnation is very important, seen also in the relationship between the cosmic cross and the visible cross, even though Irenaeus himself did not conceive of

people who were limited to natural revelation. At that most basic level of revelation, faith or unbelief is critical. The economy of salvation moves in a straight line from Adam through Enoch, Noah, Abraham, his heirs, Moses and the Hebrew prophets, toward Jesus the Christ. From the beginning, this economy was characterized by a spirit of anticipation of his coming in the flesh.

Irenaeus does not speak of an activity of the Logos through pagan philosophers, as Justin does. The "seed of the Word" was not found in pagan philosophers, but in the Old Testament prophecies, whose fruit the Church reaped. Dupuis' comment that Irenaeus "made room for a salvific value of pre-biblical religions" is very doubtful, in view of this study.[26] Likewise, O'Collins' statement that Irenaeus saw the "Greek philosophers as 'Christians before Christ'" is incorrect, or at least greatly overstated (if one takes a maximally positive reading of Irenaeus's comment on Plato).[27] The statement is made out of a failure to distinguish adequately between the theologies of Justin and Irenaeus, and out of a conceptualization of the pre-incarnate saving activity of the Word that is different from Irenaeus's perspective. In view of the struggle that Irenaeus was having with the Gnostics, and the stress that he was forced to place on the Old Testament and apostolic Scriptures, it is very unlikely that he is the guide Vempeny is looking for with regard to the inspiration of non-biblical scriptures.[28]

The aspect of Irenaeus's theology which seems most likely to lead to an optimism regarding salvation is his doctrine of the Incarnation, including particularly the concept of recapitulation. Here one finds a fundamental and objective work of God in Christ that makes the salvation of all people possible. It is here that one finds some similarity to Rahner's concept of an ontologically real sanctification of humanity by the Incarnation. Irenaeus spoke of Christ's recapitulating the whole of humanity in order to sanctify it.

Mention was made in the previous chapter of the parallel drawn by Wingren between Irenaeus's doctrine of recapitulation and a Barthian doctrine of universal, corporate election in Christ, the elect One. Dai Sil Kim has compared this doctrine to Teilhard de Chardin's concept of "Omega."[29] Origen developed recapitulation into explicit universalism. It seems to this writer that this is a place from which one could begin, in Irenaeus's theology, to work toward an optimism concerning the salvation of the non-Christian. However, the system one would develop from this starting point would necessarily be very different from that of Irenaeus. It would hardly seem justified to call Irenaeus an "antecedent" of such a system. Even to say that the seed of such a system is found in Irenaeus would be somewhat misleading. One might say that this "seed" was not allowed to grow to maturity in Irenaeus, but that, too, is misleading. This was an integral part of Irenaeus's whole theological system. He grew the "seed" into fruit, within his own system. Others may feel, however, that this is a seed with different possibilities from those Irenaeus reaped from it.

C. A Final Statement

Irenaeus presents a theology of revelation and salvation that has an inner consistency. Beginning with his presuppositions, the system is coherent. Although unique in certain aspects, its overall perspective represents the view that has traditionally motivated Christian missions: the view that salvation requires explicit faith in Christ and that without the Church's missionary outreach, people in other religions are going to be lost. By changing the presuppositions of Irenaeus's system, we can speculate concerning other directions which he might have taken. By ignoring his own conclusions, but taking certain aspects of his theology as starting points, we can develop a position that reaches different conclusions. All of that, however, is modern speculation, and the conclusions reached by these means must be tentative. One would have to speak in very precise and carefully qualified terms in order to claim Irenaeus as an "antecedent" of such modern developments. However, taking all of these factors into account, one might make a statement such as this:

> *Irenaeus believed that those who were saved, who lived before the Incarnation of the Word, had responded in faith to the various modes of revelation by the pre-incarnate Logos. He believed that, after the ascension of Christ, only those are saved who are members of the institutional Church and who believe the "rule of truth" that capsulizes the apostolic faith of the Church. However, Irenaeus was not conscious of large groups of un-evangelized people. If he had known of such groups, and if he had responded to the Gnostic challenge with less emphasis on the institutional Church, he might have allowed of the salvation of individuals outside of the institutional Church.*

This statement, and its supposition, could be based on the following factors in Irenaeus's theology:

1) God wills the salvation of humankind.

2) The Word's immanence in creation, symbolized by a cosmic cross, has a cohesive and reconciliatory effect upon all of creation which is not only physical but also moral and supernatural. It is this invisible cosmic cross that stands behind the saving work of Jesus on the visible cross.

3) The revelation by the Word in creation is lifegiving and necessitates a human response of faith, which is made possible by an illumination by the Word.

4) In Christ's incarnation, obedient life, death and resurrection, a recapitulation of the history of fallen humanity was made which objectively accomplished the salvation of humankind.

5) Within the economy of salvation, the same reward (knowledge of the Son of God, or immortality) is eventually given to all whom God calls, regardless of the particular stage of the economy in which they lived and in which they were called.

6) The just judgment of sinful people, by God, assumes their voluntary rejection of divine saving revelation to *all* people.

7) Those who believe and follow God are given a greater illumination of the mind.

8) People will be judged according to the privilege of revelation that they have received.

9) During the millennium, those who have not known the incarnate Word, but who have had some form of "anticipation" of him, will become accustomed to living with him and will be prepared for the vision of the Father.

The tentativeness of the summary statement is markedly different from those that have been cited from other authors. However, it more accurately represents the limits placed upon such a statement by our ignorance of what Irenaeus himself would have said in a different context from the one in which he actually wrote.

In formulating a position that addresses our own context, we would do well to give careful attention to the witness that Irenaeus bears to the apostolic tradition, although we recognize the "time-boundness" of his own theological formation. We must proclaim divine truth in our own age, in the power of the Spirit, that the divine economy of salvation may progress yet closer to that day when all things shall finally be summed up in Christ.

Notes

1. Jean Daniélou, *Gospel Message and Hellenistic Culture: A History of Early Christian Doctrine Before the Council of Nicaea,* trans. and ed. John Austin Baker (Philadelphia: Westminster, 1973), 2:150.

2. The work of the Holy Spirit is given much attention in recent discussion of the state of the unevangelized. For this reason, the paucity of material in Irenaeus is somewhat disappointing. However, it is not surprising when one considers the time in which he wrote and the Gnostic context which he addressed.

3. "Observations on the Problem of the 'Anonymous Christian,'" in *TI,* (1979), 14:283.

4. A fuller exposition of this summary, with source documentation, is found in Chapter 1.

5. Cf. Walbert Bühlmann's description of the missionary seal which grew out of the motivation to save the souls of pagans who were going to hell unless they heard and believed the Gospel (*God's Chosen Peoples,* trans. Robert R. Barr [Maryknoll, New York: Orbis Books, 1982], 106-7).

6. Cf. Bruce Demarest's review of the positions of Luther, Calvin and the Puritans on general revelation and its value for salvation. *General Revelation: Historical Views and Contemporary Issues* (Grand Rapids: Zondervan, 1982), 43-73.

7. Neal Punt, *Unconditional Good News: Toward an Understanding of Biblical Universalism* (Grand Rapids: Eerdmans, 1980).

8. Cf. Justo L. González, *A History of Christian Thought*, vol. 3: *From the Protestant Reformation to the Twentieth Century* (New York: Abingdon, 1975), 69, citing G. W. Locher, "Die Praëdestinations-lehre Huldrych Zwinglis," [*Theologische Zeitschrift*] 12 [1956]:526-48).

9. Quite commonly, however, those who place a positive value on the response of the pagan to natural revelation deny the sufficiency of that response and contend that God will send them the Gospel in some way, to enable an explicit faith. Cf. Thomas Aquinas, who suggested that God could send an angel to those who have no contact with Gospel messengers (cited by Henry van Straelen, *Ouverture à l'autre laquelle? L'apostolat missionnaire et le monde non chrétien* [Paris: Beauchesne, 1982], 215). Stanley Ellisen has argued for the theory that God sends the light of the Gospel to those who follow the light of creation, providence and conscience. He cites the case of the Ethiopian eunuch, Saul of Tarsus, and Cornelius of Caesarea as examples of this principle, representing the three streams of humanity from Ham, Shem, and Japheth ("Are Pagans Without Christ Really Lost?" [*Conservative Baptist*] Spring 1983]:6-9). Likewise, Bruce Demarest argues for "the possibility that in exceptional circumstances God might choose to reveal himself in some extraordinary way, independently of Gospel proclamation" (*General Revelation*, 260-61).

10. *The Unknown Christ of Hinduism: Towards an Ecumenical Christophany*, revised and enlarged edition (Maryknoll, New York: Orbis Books, 1981), 164.

11. *The Unknown Christ*, 13.

12. "The One Christ and the Universality of Salvation," *TI*, vol. 16 (1979), 219.

13. "Church, Churches and Religions," *TI*, vol. 10 (1973), 48.

14. *The Unknown Christ*, 1.

15. Ibid., 2; cf. 169.

16. Ibid., 3.

17. Ibid., 24.

18. Ibid., 25; cf. 168.

19. Ibid., 25.

20. Ibid., 23.

21. Ibid., 67-68.

22. Ibid., 69.

23. Ibid., 82.

24. Ibid., 85.

25. Ibid., 85-86.

26. James Dupuis, "The Cosmic Christ in the Early Fathers," [Indian Journal of Theology] 15 (July-September 1966):111.

27. Gerald O'Collins, *Fundamental Theology* (New York: Paulist Press, 1981), 125.

28. Ishanand Vempeny, *Inspiration in Non-Biblical Scriptures* (Bangalore: Theological Publications in India, n.d.), 61.

29. "Irenaeus of Lyons and Teilhard de Chardin: A Comparative Study of 'Recapitulation' and 'Omega,'" [*Journal of Ecumenical Studies*] 13 (1976):69-93. José González-Faus makes a similar comparison (*Carne de Dios: significado salvador de la Encarnación en la teología de san Ireneo* [Barcelona: Herder, 1969], 52).

FURTHER READING

Criticism

Hitchcock, F. R. Montgomery. "The Creeds of SS. Irenaeus and Patrick." *Hermathena* 14 (1907): 168-82.
> Compares the contents of the creeds of the two saints and argues that Irenaeus belongs to the Greek school of thought and Patrick to the Latin school.

———. "The Apostolic Preaching of Irenaeus and Its Light on His Doctrine of the Trinity." *Hermathena* 14 (1907): 307-37.
> Studies the German translation of Irenaeus's Proof of the Apostolic Preaching and responds to the German editor's criticisms of the text, particularly those related to Irenaeus's conception of the relationship between God, the Son, and the Spirit.

———. "The *Apostolic Preaching* of Irenaeus." *Journal of Theological Studies* 9 (January 1908): 284-89.
> Summarizes the main points of Irenaeus's tract and reviews its literary influences and parallels.

———. *Irenaeus of Lugdunum: A Study of His Teaching.* Cambridge: at the University Press, 1914, 373 p.
> Comprehensive introduction to the ideas of Irenaeus as exhibited in his works.

Means, Stewart. "Irenaeus and the Catholic Church." In *Saint Paul and the Ante-Nicene Church: An Unwritten Chapter of Church History*, pp. 123-202. London: Adam and Charles Black, 1903.
> Examines the influences that shaped the Catholic Church during Irenaeus's day and analyzes the saint's own influence on the Church's development.

Minns, Dennis. "An Outstanding Christian Thinker?," in *Ireneus*, pp. 132–40. London: Geoffery Chapman, 1994.
> Assesses the significance of Irenaeus as a theologian and maintains that, while his thinking is not particularly original, Irenaeus successfully undertook an enormous endeavor in presenting a picture of second-century orthodox Christian thought. Minns characterizes the theologian's ideas as optimistic and confident.

Tristan and Isolde Legend

Legend with possible Celtic origins, dating from the twelfth century or earlier.

INTRODUCTION

The legend of Tristan and Isolde, a tragic tale of doomed romantic love, was one of the most popular romances of the Medieval era. It is extant in three twelfth-century versions: a fragment by Béroul, in the Norman dialect, dating from circa 1190, a French fragment by Thomas written circa 1170, and Eilhart von Oberge's German translation, also from circa 1170. These writings, and the legend itself, likely evolved from Celtic legends. Eventually, the tale was translated into several languages, and was incorporated into Arthurian legends, such as Thomas Malory's *Morte D'Arthur* (1485). Within the different versions of the Tristan and Isolde story, many variations in content and especially the poetic treatment of the lovers are found, yet the relationship between the two characters is unchanging. Tristan and Isolde are brought together travelling by ship to Cornwall. A love potion intended to be given to Isolde and her betrothed, King Mark of Cornwall, on their wedding night is mistakenly imbibed by Isolde and Tristan, binding them forever in love. Their passion for each other, despite Isolde's marriage to the King, is the center of each version of the story.

Much of the critical debate concerning Tristan and Isolde centers on the sources, origin, and development of the legend, as well as the relationship between the extant versions of the legend. Joseph Bedier acknowledges that while the legend sprung from Celtic thought, the origin of the extant versions of the legend is a single, French poem from the early twelfth century, composed by one author. Gertrude Schoepperle, on the other hand, rejects the notion that a single French source inspired each of the extant versions; she does suggest, however, that a French source— the *estoire*—accounts for the versions by Eilhart and was perhaps Thomas's source as well. Schoepperle also examines the courtly elements of the legend and concludes that since a portion of the poem embraces unlawful love, it may be dated from the second half of the twelfth century, when the cult of such immoral love was in vogue. Like Bedier, William Henry Schofield highlights the influence of Celtic material on the legend. Schofield then compares Thomas's version of the poem with the fragment by Béroul and the German translation by Eilhart, observing that Thomas's poem consists of simple and "flowing" octosyllabic couplets, typical of French romances. In tracing the development of the legend in Scandinavia, Henry Goddard Leach also comments on the characteristics of Thomas's

Thirteenth-century painting depicting Gottfried von Strassburg, in white robe and cap, author of the courtly epic "Tristan" (ca. 1210).

version, which was translated into Norwegian prose by a Brother Robert in 1226. Leach finds that the psychological motivations in the Thomas poem are more refined than in the Norwegian translation, as are the "brutal" elements of the story, and that the tale is characterized by the profound passion of the lovers. In his analysis of the transmission of the legend, Roger Sherman Loomis comments on the influence of the Irish legend of Diarmaid and Grainne on the Tristan romance, and traces the development of the legend from its Celtic origins, through its Welsh versions, and later to the French treatments of the legend. Loomis focuses particularly on the role of the Welshman, Bleheris, (who is referred to in some versions of the legend, including Thomas's) in the transmission of the legend. Summarizing the views of a number of critics, James Douglas

Bruce states that there is "substantial agreement among authorities on the subject" that the extant versions of the Tristan legend have their source in a "lost French romance" of a much earlier date than the extant versions. Bruce goes on to survey those extant versions and to review the plot of the legend. Additionally, Bruce stresses that the Celtic Aithed, or elopement story, of Diarmaid and Grainne (or a similar Aithed) served as the original inspiration for the Tristan legend. Also regarding the issue of the source poem from which the extant versions drew, Frederick Whitehead differentiates between the poems of Eilhart and Béroul on one hand and Thomas on the other, maintaining that the Eilhart and Béroul versions drew from a single source Whitehead refers to as the "archetype." Whitehead dates the archetype from 1150 or 1160 and discusses some of the qualities of the extant versions, noting that Eilhart's text is simple and lacks psychological motivation, while Béroul's is characterized by epic features.

Other critics examine specific episodes within the legend and compare how the episodes are treated in the extant versions of the legend. A. G. van Hamel studies the elements of the dragonslaying episode in the Tristan legend in which an imposter claims to have killed the dragon slain by Tristan, and in which Tristan, as the true dragon slayer, offers a suit for Isolde on behalf of King Mark of Cornwall. Van Hamel compares similar Celtic and Breton folk tales to the Tristan legend, noting that in the Tristan legend, some details were modified in order to highlight the "chivalresque" quality of the romance. Helaine Newstead traces the literary history of the episode in which the lovers meet secretly beneath a tree only to discover King Mark hidden in the branches above them. Through a series of deceptions, Tristan and Isolde escape the king's trap. Newstead finds that while the narrative framework of the story is constant in the different versions, variations nevertheless appear in the treatments by Béroul, Eilhart, Thomas, and in the Norse translation. Another element that appears repeatedly in the extant versions but with notable variation is that of the love potion motif. Eugene Vinaver examines the treatment of this motif in the extant versions of the legend, maintaining that the depiction of the role of the love potion in the Eilhart and Béroul versions represents the original Tristan romance. Vinaver argues that the romance presents the potion as symbolic of unchangeable love.

REPRESENTATIVE WORKS

Anonymous
Sir Tristrem (poem) c. 1300

Béroul
*Tristan (poem) c. 1190

Thomas
*Tristan (poem) c. 1170

Eilhart von Oberge
*Tristan (poem) c. 1170

Gottfried von Strassburg
*Tristan (poem) c. 1210

*These works exist in fragments and their exact titles are uncertain.

CRITICISM

Algernon Charles Swinburne (poem date 1882)

SOURCE: Prelude to *Tristram of Lyonesse* in *Selected Poems*, edited by L. M. Findlay, Carcanet New Press Limited, 1982 pp. 221-224.

[*The following is an excerpt from an 1882 edition of the prelude to* Tristram of Lyonesse.]

Love, that is first and last of all things made,
The light that has the living world for shade,
The spirit that for temporal veil has on
The souls of all men woven in unison,
One fiery raiment with all lives inwrought
And lights of sunny and starry deed and thought,
And alway through new act and passion new
Shines the divine same body and beauty through,
The body spiritual of fire and light
That is to worldly noon as noon to night;
Love, that is flesh upon the spirit of man
And spirit within the flesh whence breath began;
Love, that keeps all the choir of lives in chime;
Love, that is blood within the veins of time;
That wrought the whole world without stroke of hand,
Shaping the breadth of sea, the length of land,
And with the pulse and motion of his breath
Through the great heart of the earth strikes life and death,
The sweet twain chords that make the sweet tune live
Through day and night of things alternative,
Through silence and through sound of stress and strife,
And ebb and flow of dying death and life;
Love that sounds loud or light in all men's ears,
Whence all men's eyes take fire from sparks of tears,
That binds on all men's feet or chains or wings;
Love, that is root and fruit of terrene things;
Love, that the whole world's waters shall not drown,
The whole world's fiery forces not burn down;
Love, that what time his own hands guard his head
The whole world's wrath and strength shall not strike dead;
Love, that if once his own hands make his grave
The whole world's pity and sorrow shall not save;
Love, that for very life shall not be sold,
Nor brought nor bound with iron nor with gold;
So strong that heaven, could love bid heaven farewell,
Would turn to fruitless and unflowering hell;
So sweet that hell, to hell could love be given,
Would turn to splendid and sonorous heaven;
Love that is fire within thee and light above,

And lives by grace of nothing but of love;
Through many and lovely thoughts and much desire
Led these twain to the life of tears and fire;
Through many and lovely days and much delight
Led these twain to the lifeless life of night.

    So shine above dead chance and conquered change
The spherèd signs, and leave without their range
Doubt and desire, and hope with fear for wife,
Pale pains, and pleasures long worn out of life.
Yea, even the shadows of them spiritless,
Through the dim door of sleep that seem to press,
Forms without form, a piteous people and blind,
Men and no men, whose lamentable kind
The shadow of death and shadow of life compel
Through semblances of heaven and false-faced hell,
Through dreams of light and dreams of darkness tost
On waves innavigable, are these so lost?
Shapes that wax pale and shift in swift strange wise,
Void faces with unspeculative eyes,
Dim things that gaze and glare, dead mouths that move,
Featureless heads discrowned of hate and love,
Mockeries and masks of motion and mute breath,
Leavings of life, the superflux of death—
If these things and no more than these things be
Left when man ends or changes, who can see?
Or who can say with what more subtle sense
Their subtler natures taste in air less dense
A life less thick and palpable than ours,
Warmed with faint fires and sweetened with dead flowers
And measured by low music? how time fares
In that wan time-forgotten world of theirs,
Their pale poor world too deep for sun or star
To live in, where the eyes of Helen are,
And hers who made as God's own eyes to shine
The eyes that met them of the Florentine,
Wherein the godhead thence transfigured lit
All time for all men with the shadow of it?
Ah, and these too felt on them as God's grace
The pity and glory of this man's breathing face;
For these too, these my lovers, these my twain,
Saw Dante, saw God visible by pain,
With lips that thundered and with feet that trod
Before men's eyes incognisable God;
Saw love and wrath and light and night and fire
Live with one life and at one mouth respire,
And in one golden sound their whole soul heard
Sounding, one sweet immitigable word.
    They have the night, who had like us the day;
We, whom day binds, shall have the night as they.
We, from the fetters of the light unbound,
Healed of our wound of living, shall sleep sound.
All gifts but one the jealous God may keep
From our soul's longing, one he cannot—sleep.
This, though he grudge all other grace to prayer,
This grace his closed hand cannot choose but spare.
This, though his ear be sealed to all that live,
Be it lightly given or lothly, God must give.
We, as the men whose name on earth is none,
We too shall surely pass out of the sun;
Out of the sound and eyeless light of things,
Wide as the stretch of life's time-wandering wings,
Wide as the naked world and shadowless,
And long-lived as the world's own weariness.

Us too, when all the fires of time are cold,
The heights shall hide us and the depths shall hold.
Us too, when all the tears of time are dry,
The night shall lighten from her tearless eye.
Blind is the day and eyeless all its light,
But the large unbewildered eye of night
Hath sense and speculation; and the sheer
Limitless length of lifeless life and clear,
The timeless space wherein the brief worlds move
Clothed with light life and fruitful with light love,
With hopes that threaten, and with fears that cease,
Past fear and hope, hath in it only peace.
    Yet of these lives inlaid with hopes and fears,
Spun fine as fire and jewelled thick with tears,
These lives made out of loves that long since were,
Lives wrought as ours of earth and burning air,
Fugitive flame, and water of secret springs,
And clothed with joys and sorrows as with wings,
Some yet are good, if aught be good, to save
Some while from washing wreck and wrecking wave.
Was such not theirs, the twain I take and give
Out of my life to make their dead life live
Some days of mine, and blow my living breath
Between dead lips forgotten even of death?
So many and many of old have given my twain
Love and live song and honey-hearted pain,
Whose root is sweetness and whose fruit is sweet,
So many and with such joy have tracked their feet,
What should I do to follow? yet I too,
I have the heart to follow, many or few
Be the feet gone before me; for the way,
Rose-red with remnant roses of the day
Westward, and eastward white with stars that break,
Between the green and foam is fair to take
For any sail the sea-wind steers for me
From morning into morning, sea to sea.

Joseph Bédier (essay date 1904)

SOURCE: "The Legend of Tristan and Isolt," in *International Quarterly*, Vol. 9, 1904, pp. 103-28.

[*In the following essay, Bédier examines the origin and development of the Tristan and Isolde legend and maintains that there was one single source poem from which the extant versions proceeded.*]

In all the realm of legends, there is none more wonderful than the story of Tristan and Isolt. Long ago, a trouvère, dedicating it to posterity, wrote in gentle verse: "I have told this tale for those who love, and for none else. May it go down through the ages to those who are thoughtful, to those who are happy, to those who are dissatisfied, to those who are full of longings, to those who are joyful, to those who are troubled, to all lovers." More than seven centuries have passed and from the time of Gottfried von Strassburg to Wagner, the philtre of love and death has not lost its power to intoxicate the hearts of men. But, strong as is its hold upon men's hearts and dear as its theme is to the poets, the legend of Tristan is not less beautiful in the eyes of the philologist. In this rests its supreme dignity. Even as it has caused the birth of noble poems within our own times, so it has further inspired the admirable scholarly works of men like Gaston Paris, Zimmer, and Golther. Among all the problems that the legend of Tristan offers to the critic, I choose here to treat the one that is highest and most delicate: the problem of its origin and formation.

There is no lack of hypotheses and heated discussions which seek to explain in detail the mystery of its genesis and development. But there is one general opinion which all critics share indiscriminately and which dominates and overshadows their differences.

It is this: born of the "depths of Celtic thought," the legend of Tristan is not the sudden creation of one man, nor of a generation of men; centuries have collaborated in its formation. The day it crossed the confines of its own Celtic country, the type of Tristan had already passed through many avatars. Notwithstanding, what the Celts transmitted to the Germano-Roman world was not a wholly organized and determinate legend, it was simply this one central theme: Tristan and Isolt bound to one another by the power of love. There were a few *lays,* that is, short, episodical stories, independent of each other, gravitating around the principal theme as around a nucleus of crystallization. It was these lays, these short stories recited to the accompaniment of the harp, that the French jongleurs took up. At first they were content simply to repeat them, with a passive and delighted docility; soon, however, in their turn, they made bold to imagine analogous stories. These were the French lays, very similar to the Celtic lays, but more intricate, of varied motives, old epic or adventurous themes taken from the universal folk-lore, and according to the poet's caprice, united or disunited, bound together or separate. In the hands of these poets the legend was still a sort of indefinite and movable material whereon lay the dust of a hundred contradictory stories. Later, they sought to collect these incongruous lays, to bind them into consecutive narratives, but without success; it was at this time that they united the two oldest of these *romances,* those of Béroul and Eilhart, under the title of the "Version des Jongleurs,"—a name which in itself implies that the legend, given up to the nomadic poets, retained the alluring freedom and uncertainty of their life, and that their poems were only large aggregates of related pieces, or, to use the word universally adopted,—compilations. And when at length the more thoughtful poets of the court, Thomas and Gottfried von Strassburg, endeavored to introduce in them more order, their effort met with only a partial success; beneath their jointures and their paintings over, beneath the wholly superficial homogeneity of their works, there is still betrayed the incoherence of the amalgamated stories.

Every one recognizes this theory; it is a mere application of the one formulated to account for the Homeric poems. Scholars tried to apply it likewise to the Germanic epic poems and to the French "chansons de geste." But when they sought to apply this theory to the Spanish *cantares* their efforts met with a dismal failure. Just as the French "chansons de geste" are, as some still believe, "chapelets" or "bouquets de cantalinas," so the stories of Tristan must be mere collections of lays, French and Celtic. It is doubtful, however, whether this theory as to the formation of epics and legends by simple, mechanical juxtaposition, is a key that will fit all locks.

We wish to reduce the theory to its true value and determine exactly at what point it ceases to be true in the present case. We wish to show that in order to understand the history of the legend of Tristan, we must imagine one great workman instead of this anonymous and almost unconscious activity of several generations of jongleurs, acting by fragmentary inventions and unwittingly collaborating; instead of this indefinite development of the poem from generation to generation, we must picture one sovereign hour, one moment when the man, the individual, appeared, the conscious poet, the Homer who, taking possession of the vague, amorphous formations of earlier times, destined, but for him, to oblivion, laid his law upon them, breathed into them the life of his genius, and alone, the true creator, formed them for the coming ages. We wish to show that underlying all these poems of Tristan which have come down to us, there has been one great, single poem, from which all the others have proceeded. And if our theory prevails, our conclusions, exceeding the legend of Tristan, will themselves contain, perchance, some instruction.

I.

It has been proved that the Celts related stories of Tristan before the French. But, if we seek to discover what tales they related, we know how difficult the conditions of the problem are; it is the same with any legend whatever in the "Matière de Bretagne." Aside from a few rare allusions, in Welsh literature, to the lovers of Cornwall, the Celtic originals,—if, indeed, they were ever set down in writing,—have perished, and we have merely the French poems, or derivatives from the French poems, to go by, the oldest of which date back to the second half of the twelfth century. It is from these late texts that we must draw the archaic elements which they, perchance, may conceal. And first, something of the history of the characters in the drama may be revealed to the linguist by the different names they bear.

At the foundation of this onomastic research, and as its firm support, stands the beautiful discovery of M. Zimmer. In many Welsh texts, our hero is named *Drystan, son of Tallwch;* now, in the "Annals of Tigernach" and in the "Annals of Ulster," which contain lists of the kings who reigned from the sixth to the eighth centuries in the Pict marshlands of the present Scotland and Northumberland, figure the names of the kings *Drest, Drust,* or (the derivative form) *Drostán,* and these last named alternate with kings who are named *Talorc.* One king who reigned over the Picts from 780 to 785 was called *Drest filius Talorgen.* This name *Talorc* is found only among the Picts, just as the name of *Tallwch* is found only among the Welsh, and in those passages alone where the father of *Drystan* is referred to. Phonetically, *Drystan* is the derivative of

Drostán, Tallwch of *Talorc,* and the Welsh *Drystan, son of Tallwch* is identical with the *Drostán, son of Talorc* of the Picts. If we add, with M. Ferdinand Lot, that *Loonois,* the country of Tristan, and *Morois,* the forest in which part of the action of our stories takes place, are identical with the two ancient divisions of Scotland, *Loonia* and *Moravia,* formerly occupied by the Picts, we come to these surprising conclusions: the hero, whose life, according to the French stories, is passed almost entirely in Cornwall, Wales, and Brittany, was originally a stranger to these countries; without the knowledge of our trouvères, Tristan of Loonois was originally called Drostán, son of Talorc; he was a hero of the Picts and his legend was lived in Lothian, on the present confines of England and Scotland, and in Murray, on the plateau of the Scottish Highlands. And, as M. Gaston Paris writes, "there is something fascinating and almost touching in the thought that the soul of this vanished people, who have left us only their name and those of a few of their chiefs, with three or four words of their language, should survive even now in our souls, thanks to one of the most beautiful poetical creations of humanity."

There is nothing, however, to indicate that this Pict Tristan was already celebrated for love adventures; perhaps he was a purely epic hero and warrior. The Welsh, it seems, were the first to transfer him to their own country, to adopt him and make him the rival in love of King Marc of Cornwall, a semi-historical character of their literature. Whether the Pict Tristan was already a famous lover or whether the Welsh were the first to conceive the consummation of his heroic type through love, it was they who made him the lover of King Marc's wife and located his principal adventures in Tintagel, on the coast of Cornwall.

Many of the proper names in our stories bear witness to the activity of the Welsh; take, for instance, that minor character, the seneschal, Dinas of Lidan, whose name, misunderstood by the trouvères, means, in Welsh, the "lord of the great fortress." But there are other names which indicate that if the first stage of the legend was Pict and the second Welsh, still a third people collaborated with the Welsh: Perinis, Isolt's servant, Hoël de Carhaix, Duke of Brittany, Rivalin, the father of Tristan, Donoalen, the traitor, and many other characters in the stories, bear Breton rather than Welsh names, and we must admit that when the legend was received by the French poets, it was composed of Welsh and Armorican deposits.

Many hypotheses have been suggested to explain these facts but we shall limit ourselves here to pointing out the one that seems the most probable. From the tenth century on, the Norman and Breton aristocracy had become allied by frequent inter-marriage, till a Norman castle was more than half Breton. And from very ancient times, the Breton jongleurs had made the Armorican harp resound within these Norman castles, and by their lays, half sung and half recited, they had provoked the first awakening of the Romance imagination to the legends of Brittany. Then came the conquest of England by Duke William, and the whole

Romance civilization just as it was, found itself suddenly transplanted into the castles beyond the channel. The Armorican jongleurs, who were more than half romanticized, and who lived in the service of the Norman lords, followed their patrons into their new conquest; there they renewed their acquaintance with the Welsh tribes from whom they had been so long separated; they learned certain of their legends, recognized the relationship of these with the legends that they themselves had brought, and leavened the one with the other; it was they who acted as the agents of transmission between the Welsh and the Romance peoples.

Whatever may be the value of this hypothesis, the Celtic, Welsh, and Armorican names, which abound in our poems, prove by their very reiteration, that the Celts bequeathed to the Romance poets many legendary themes. But what were these? Are we authorized to conclude sweepingly, because of the many Celtic names, that the legend of Tristan was drawn entirely from "the Celtic soul"? In what measure, in its Welsh period, did it resemble the legend we now know? Is it not possible that the characters in our stories have only their names in common with their Celtic prototypes? Might we not imagine, for example, that, among the Welsh, Tristan, like Cuchulain, the hero of the Irish epic, may have had a legend with many variants among which his love for Isolt was merely an episode? What part did the French jongleurs play in their reception of the legend? Were they simply transposers and rhapsodists, or were they real creators?

To these questions it is scarcely necessary to say that all the researches of onomatechny cannot supply even the beginning of an answer, and we must now enter upon an entirely new field of inquiry; we must bring before us the whole tradition of mediæval poetry and sum up the Celtic elements which it has preserved, excerpting from the texts the features and the episodes which imply a civilization neither feudal nor French, and which send us back to very archaic conceptions, to the ways and customs of the Celts. This method has been applied often, and with a bold and deceitful rashness by certain critics; and, indeed, it is easy for any one, endowed with a little imagination, so to transform our French poems as to produce a Welsh romance of Tristan that will have all the coloring of the Eddas or of the Nibelungen. But the more difficult thing in trying to determine the ethnical elements of a narration is, on the contrary, to yield nothing to one's imagination. Nevertheless, when this research has once been conducted with the necessary critical scepticism, when we have eliminated many of those pretended mythical features that array Tristan sometimes as a solar god and sometimes as a Theseus, when we have set aside many bold combinations which seek to discover, on every page of the French romances, pre-Christian, pre-Romance, and Welsh survivals, there still remain a few ideas and a few episodes that are assuredly Celtic. If we group them together, we may form some idea of what the legend was at the time the Celts parted with it.

II.

At the outset, we note several features in the character of Tristan, so peculiar, so foreign, and so strangely in contrast with the knights of the "chansons de geste" or of the romances of chivalry, that we are forced to admit they were not drawn by French poets. There is, first, the fact that Tristan knows how to imitate perfectly the song of all the birds; what French poet would have imagined that of any knight? Further, he fashions and makes the bow, Arc-Qui-ne-faut, which always hits its object, man or beast, in the spot aimed at! Also, alone of all the epic heroes, he possesses, not a horse, but a favorite dog, loved equally with his dearest friends, and, doubtless, according to the older stories, enchanted like his bow. Let us add that King Marc (whose name, in many Celtic languages, means *horse*) hides fantastically the ears of a horse beneath his headdress, and these four features will suffice to relate Tristan and his rival with the times of barbarity, and to match them with heroes of the most authentic Welsh story, the *mabinogi* of *Kullwch and Olwen*.

There remains, also, the fact that the castle of Tintagel is a "chastel faé," which twice a year "loses itself" and disappears from mortal eyes; such is the castle of the Irish magician, Cúroi. There is also the hall of glass, suspended in the air, whither Tristan, in his feigned madness, tries to carry away Isolt; such, again, in the Irish epic, is the chamber of brilliant windows, to which Mac Oc carried Etain Echraide.

Finally, there are several scenes in the legend which we cannot explain if we attribute them to the French poets. First, there is the one in which Tristan, forbidden the sight of Isolt, hews down branches, carves them in marvelous fashion, and throws them into a stream, to warn his loved one that he is waiting for her beneath a tree that overhangs the brook; this stream flows through Isolt's very chamber and we must necessarily picture to ourselves, not a feudal castle, but a hut,—with floor of beaten earth.

There is also this scene: Tristan, separated from Isolt, takes refuge with King Arthur. To befriend his love, Arthur and Gawain and many followers, go out to hunt in a forest near Tintagel and, pretending to be lost, request King Marc to give them a night's hospitality. The latter admits them and bids all his guests lie down in the same hall where he and the queen sleep in two separate beds. But, the better to guard Isolt, the king has caused to be placed in the hall some wolf traps equipped with newly sharpened scythes. When every one is asleep, Tristan draws near in the darkness to the bed of the queen, and is cruelly cut by the scythes. He binds his wound with a bandage taken from his hempen shirt, comes to the edge of Isolt's couch, and, vexed, tells her his disaster. What shall he do? His blood is flowing and in the morning he will be discovered. He awakens his companions who take counsel with him and Kei invents a splendid stratagem. Upon his advice, all the knights rise from their beds and, pretending to quarrel, revile each other in the darkness and fight among themselves, pell-mell, and each is careful to throw himself upon the snares and receive wounds from the sharp steel. The good Kei, faithful to his heroi-comic character, and instigator of the plot, alone tries to escape the scythes, but Gawain pushes him upon them and Kei is wounded more cruelly than the others. Then, when all are wounded and the blood is flowing on every side, Kei cries, "Does he hunt wolves in his hall that such machines are placed here? Is this the hospitality of King Marc?" What is there left for King Marc but to quiet the quarrel and excuse himself for having caused such snares to be laid? All go to sleep again, while Tristan rejoins the queen, this time without peril. In the morning, since all the guests are equally wounded, no one dreams of molesting Tristan who passes unobserved among the crowd of limping hunters.

If we attribute this scene to the Celtic period of the legend, it is not merely on account of its magnificent, light hearted barbarity. It is because it is impossible to represent it as taking place in a feudal castle. Eilhart d'Oberg, who relates it, tells us of his surprise and his embarrassment. In the twelfth century, it may well have happened that guests of distinction were lodged in the lord's own bed-chamber, but not the thirty or forty strangers that were necessarily introduced in the scene of the scythes. It must have taken place originally in the same large royal hut through which the stream forced its passage.

Let us add, as the third Celtic episode, the one given us in a Welsh triad, the sixty-third of the "Livre Rouge," whose archaic character has been vainly suspected: Tristan sends the swine-herd of King Marc to demand an interview with Isolt. He, himself (disguised, doubtless, in the swine-herd's rags), watches the herd until the return of his messenger. Arthur, Kei, March, and Bedwyr come up unexpectedly and (knowing his disguise) amuse themselves by trying to rob him of his beasts, first by strategy, then by violence, and lastly by larceny; but they do not succeed in getting even a single sow away from him.

These are the scenes which we may safely call Celtic. We might, perhaps, by analogy and by making our way from point to point, add a few episodes closely related or bound to these; take, for example, the scene where Marc, clinging to the branches of a tree, his bow in his hand, spies upon the lovers who have made their tryst beneath him. Happily, by the rays of the moonlight, they see Marc's shadow reflected in the stream which flows at their feet and are careful; by clever words, they succeed in deceiving the jealous king and winning his pity. This episode follows almost necessarily that in which Tristan, in order to call Isolt, threw into this same stream the branches so wonderfully fashioned. Perhaps, since it is hard to represent it in the room of a castle, we might further retain the scene where a traitor, perched upon a window, watches an interview between the lovers. Isolt, who has seen the spy, tells Tristan in a low voice, to string his bow. He bends it, astonished, only half understanding. Isolt takes an arrow, notches it with her own hand, and looks to see if the cord be good: "Aim well, Tristan!" He takes his position, raises his head, and sees the traitor's shadow upon a curtain stretched across the room. The long arrow whistles through the air, pierces the traitor's eye, and goes through his brain.

Now, if we consider these several scenes as assuredly or very probably Celtic, what is their evident character? They are violent tales stained with blood. This swine-herd, Tristan, the wonderful archer, master of an enchanted dog and bow, this Tristan with the almost supernatural gift of being able, at his pleasure, to imitate the songs of all the birds, this Tristan of the marvelously cut branches, and among the wolf snares, this Tristan appears to us like the hero of a sort of barbaric "Decameron." It is a *romancero* of cynical love, at times sad, wherein we see simply a dissembling woman and her lover, famous for his mastery in all the primitive arts, duping a jealous and powerful husband. The trinity of the husband, the wife, and the lover, the lover possessing the woman by the sole supremacy of physical beauty, strength, and strategy, the tricks that they play at the risk of their life, this is what is brought before us in the several scenes which seem authentically Celtic.

Is it really this, is it these brutal, half barbaric stories, that make up what we call the legend of Tristan? What do we understand, we men of today, Romanticists, Celtists, or simple literary men, with our knowledge of the story gained either by critical, scholarly study or by simply hearing one of Wagner's operas, what do we understand when we repeat the names of the lovers of Cornwall or what did Béroul or Gottfried von Strassburg understand, when they told their story long ago for the men of earlier times and for the men of today? What are Tristan and Isolt? They are lovers who drank a philtre and, held captive by its power, suffered the fatality of this love against their will. The bitter conflict of love and law; this is the whole of the legend.

Now, are we authorized in believing that the Celts, beside their bloody tales, invented also this central conception without which the legend would not exist: two central figures, chained by love, but feeling upon them the pressure of the social law which subjects the vassal to his lord, and the wife to her husband, and suffering from this law in such a manner that every one of their pleasures is mingled with horror?

To begin with, we cannot feel at all certain that the invention of the love philtre is Celtic; we merely know that neither the ancient literature of Ireland, nor that of Wales, offers any example of such an enchantment. But even so, considering this negative statement to be of little value, if we admit that already in the Welsh story Tristan and Isolt had drunk a love philtre, can we believe that this enchantment had already had for the Celts the same value as for the French trouvères? that even among the Celts the two heroes endured their love as a fatality at once *delightful and bitter?* The following remarks would seem to contradict this.

That two rivals should contend passionately for a woman, is the most elementary of instincts. That others, spectators

of the fight, should be amused or moved by it, is also primitive, belonging specifically to neither the Cymri nor the French; the men of the stone age may already have possessed the rudiments of stories analogous to that of Tristan as swineherd. But that the woman and her lover should *suffer* from this struggle and *suffer* from their very triumphs, implies a state of culture far more complex. An "epic of adultery" can take place only among a people for whom marriage is an indissoluble and formidable bond. Only those who recognize a strongly imperative, rigid, and stern social law, can build a poem on this social law hostile to love.

But, as we read the Welsh "Mabinogion," or the Irish epics, or the pictures drawn by the historians of the old Celtic civilizations, as we read especially the *corpus* of the institutions of Wales, compiled from the tenth to the twelfth century, under the title of "Les Lois de Howel le Bon," we see that the most peculiar feature of Celtic life is the fragility of the conjugal bond. No legislation has ever been more significant. Marriage remained uninfluenced by either Roman or Christian ideals. It consisted simply, without any religious sanction ever being thought of, in the surrender, at a stipulated price, of the young girl by her father, surrounded by her relatives. The rupture of this contract was a peculiarly easy thing: if the husband and wife agreed to separate, they divorced each other with no further ceremony. If only one desired to separate, the husband could repudiate his wife; if he could produce a grievance against her, for example, that of her having given another man a single kiss, he was entitled, in putting her away, to retain her dowry; if he could produce any accusation, he might still send her away when he pleased but he must give back her dowry. In return the wife may leave her husband if she wishes, and in certain well defined cases she may retain her dowry, but only upon the condition that she gives it up, can she divorce herself without reason.

If Tristan and Isolt were purely Welsh conceptions, how, in the poems known to us, could they think and feel as their congeners had never thought or felt? By what unforeseen reversal of the natural order of things, at the very moment when passion was let loose in their hearts, overwhelming them, were they to rise to higher moral ideas, foreign to their wisest legislators? According to Welsh customs, King Marc had power over Isolt's dowry, but not over her life; she was free to leave him; why, with or without her dowry, did she not do so? Tristan did not even need to abduct her; the doors were open to her; she could go. Only, if she did, there would be no story left. King Marc might, out of tyrannic jealousy, keep possession of her and imprison her, but according to Welsh ideas her body alone would be captive; she would be bound only by an unjust physical constraint; in her heart she would feel free,—and the story as we have it would not exist. Tristan might abduct her, Marc, recapture her, Tristan carry her off again,—and in all this there would be room for bloody tales such as we have just been dealing with. Tristan might take her with him to the depths of the forest of Morois;

but, once they had entered there, once they had enjoyed there, even for an hour, within the hut of branches, that true life which alone is worthy of their barbaric love, then how could any power except the physical strength of their enemies ever drag them away from it? Or, in case they grew weary of living in the forest, why should not Tristan take Isolt to Ireland, where she is queen? or to his castles of Loonois, where he is king, and where he could defend her? Only, if he did so, the story would fall in pieces.

The very life of the story as we have it, lies in the fact that nowhere, in any of the known poems, does Isolt dream of leaving King Marc, nor Tristan of carrying her away. It is against their will, that, tracked and hunted, they submit to a common exile in the forest of Morois, but as soon as Tristan feels that the king's wrath is softened, his only thought is to give him back Isolt. Their love is not a restless lust, seeking to justify itself by the romantic argument of the sovereign rights of passion. Tristan is not in revolt against society, he does not repudiate the social institution, on the contrary, he respects it, he suffers on account of it, and this suffering alone imparts the beauty to his actions. He is the nephew and the adopted son of King Marc; he does not dispute the law of gratitude, he violates it and, in violating it, he suffers. He is King Marc's vassal; he does not dispute the law of a vassal's honor, he violates it and, in violating it, he suffers. The "idea" of the legend is not that the social law is bad; in all the extant poems of the Middle Ages, it is rather that love brings face to face with the law a world of rights, not superior to the social rights, but without common measure with them, and that it creates between law and nature a struggle which God Himself must judge. The legend is founded wholly upon a social law, recognized as good, necessary, and just. It is founded upon an indissoluble marriage bond. How, then, can it have been conceived by a people who looked upon marriage as the most easily broken of ties? If, however, this is the poetical foundation and framework of the story of Tristan, we may say that the legend is not Welsh,—I mean the tragic mood of the legend.

We may go further; we may set down this proposition as an axiom: the legend of Tristan had neither beauty nor even life until the day when a romance of Tristan existed. By *romance*, we do not mean necessarily a written, completed poem, but at least an epic subject somewhat richly developed. The subject of the "Chevalier au lion," of "Erec," or of "Perceval" may be contained in three or four little lays artificially brought together. But the fundamental theme of the legend of Tristan implies something more. It implies the two lovers bound together in life and death, a permanent and manifold conflict between love and the law. So long as this conflict finds expression only in one lay, in one short story, or in a series of little, similar stories (such as the narrations of the feminine strategies by which King Marc is deceived), we may say that the legend does not yet live. It comes to life only on the day when a poet, or a generation of men, represent the development of this conflict in a series of adventures, of struggles, and of obstacles, which attend the lovers from their birth until

their death; it exists only from the day when a biographical character is given to the love of Tristan and Isolt.

Now, it is contrary to all that we know of the stories of Brittany and of the modes of epic recitation among the Celts, to suppose that they ever possessed a great romance of love about Tristan. It is, however, conformable to all that we know of the poetry of either the Cymri or the Irish, to believe that they possessed and could have transmitted nothing else but lays concerning Tristan; and these were, doubtless, as we have seen, simple stories of adultery. The question, then, is this: what is there at the basis of the French poetical tradition? Lays, episodical narrations, vaguely related to one another? Or is there, indeed, a regular poem?

III.

When we approach the comparative study of the poems of Tristan, the first impressions that we receive confirm the pre-conceived theory that these *romances* are rhapsodies, or "compilations." What favors this theory is, first of all, the multiplicity of the versions: the English "Sir Tristrem," the Scandinavian Saga, the Tzech "Tristan," the poems of Gottfried von Strassburg, of Heinrich von Freyberg, of Ulrich von Türheim, the romances in French, German, Italian, and Spanish prose, and twenty other texts which cross and intertwine; secondly, there is the diversity of the different forms which these texts offer for every episode, the slowness of the critic to unravel the relations of these versions, the extreme complications in the method of classing them, all these points strengthening the opinion that we are face to face with an inextricable multitude of amalgamated stories, with a confused material, incompletely organized; and we are ready to believe that a vast "sea of stories" is spreading out before us. Nevertheless, according as we grow more intimate with the texts, and as we profit more and more by the philological works that have accumulated in the last thirty years, we perceive that the tradition is not nearly as rich and diverse as we had imagined, that the greater part of the versions must be eliminated entirely as translations or unimportant after products of preserved works, and we find that the whole legend of Tristan is contained in four, or perhaps five, primary versions, namely:—

1. The poem by Béroul, written in Normandy about 1160, of which we possess only a fragment of three thousand lines with a false sequel, added to it about 1200, by an unknown French jongleur.

2. The French poem, written in England about the same date, 1160, by Thomas, the trouvère, which has come down to us in a very mutilated condition, but whose tenor we are able to reconstruct from the various different versions of it in foreign languages.

3. The poem, composed about 1190, by Eilhart d'Oberg, vassal of Henry the Lion, Duke of Brunswick.

4. The romance in French prose, written about 1230, and later rewritten and added to indefinitely, in which, however, it is easy to find the *disjecta membra* of an archaic poem.

5. The episodical French poem of the "Folie Tristan," preserved in a manuscript at Berne, and composed in the second half of the twelfth century.

If we compare these primary versions, we see that they are made up of about sixty episodes, twenty of which appear separately, contained in one single romance, while the forty others figure in all five romances or in three or four among them. These sixty episodes, forty of which are preserved in three, four, or five copies, embrace the whole of the legend of Tristan. Beyond them there is nothing, and what impresses us now is not the richness and the multiplicity but the dearth of these legendary themes. In order to examine these, let us, for once, cease to confine our attention exclusively to the criticism of their differences; let us make up, on the contrary, the sum of the episodes common to all and presented in the same order by at least three of the versions. We may imagine as many lost intermediary versions between these primary ones as we wish; but in any case we must find, at the common foundation of these works, one intelligent and conscious thought which first united the common themes in the following order:—

In the olden times, when King Marc reigned in Cornwall, he received at his court a young man, a stranger; this was Tristan, the son of his sister Blanchefleur, whose birth had cost his mother her life and who had grown up, an orphan, in a distant land. King Marc, in whom dwelt all nobility and goodness, loved him from the day he saw him, even before he recognized in him the son of his sister Blanchefleur: Tristan owed to King Marc all that a son can owe to his father; to the king's infinite tenderness, he replied with an equal tenderness. On the very day that he is armed as a knight, Tristan is so happy as to be able to repay to Marc something of his many benefits: Morholt, a famous knight, comes to Cornwall to claim, in the name of the King of Ireland, a shameful tribute of young men and maidens. No one dared oppose him; Tristan alone engages him in battle; he kills Morholt, leaving a fragment of his sword buried in the skull of his adversary; he has freed King Marc's land from the tribute but he is himself wounded by Morholt's poisoned wooden spear. Feeling that he is about to die, he causes himself to be laid upon a barge, and the sea carries him to Dublin, to the hands of the Queen of Ireland and her daughter Isolt; this, above all others, is the country of danger, for Isolt is Morholt's niece, but no one recognizes the murderer in Tristan, for the venom in his wound has disfigured his features, and very soon the Queen of Ireland sends him back, cured, to Cornwall. No sooner has he reached there than, at Marc's command, he sets forth again for Dublin, at the peril of his life; Marc has commissioned him to bring back Isolt, his enemy's daughter, for he wishes to make her his bride. It happened that the King of Ireland has promised to give Isolt in marriage to whoever shall deliver his country from a terrible dragon, who is devastating it. Tristan kills the dragon, and cuts out his tongue, but, poisoned by the monster's venom, he falls senseless among the grasses in a swamp. An impostor cuts off the dragon's head and, pretending to have killed it, claims the promised reward. But Isolt has discovered Tristan in the swamp and transports him secretly to the castle where she restores him to his senses and makes him well again. One day, when he is in a bath which she has prepared for him, she notices that his sword is notched; she takes the bit of steel that she has formerly drawn from the head of Morholt and it fits exactly into the sword; she recognizes the murderer of her uncle, and grasping the huge weapon, wishes to kill Tristan while he is in the bath. He quiets her with skilful words and after confounding the impostor by producing the dragon's tongue, he reveals to the King of Ireland that he is a messenger from King Marc of Cornwall. He has won the girl both by strategy and by force and he swears upon the relics of the saints, before all the barons of Ireland and before a hundred knights of Cornwall, who are his companions, that he will conduct her loyally to her husband, King Marc.

We pass on from one scene to another; Tristan and Isolt, by mistake, drink a love philtre while at sea,—Marc weds Isolt and the latter substitutes her servant, Brangien, for herself in the king's bed, etc. * * * we may follow it in this way until the death of the lovers. And thus we obtain a *scenario* containing three quarters of all the known episodes of the legend,—all that are essential. Now, if we look carefully at this *scenario,* we are struck by its inward logic, by the harmony of its organic structure. It is not, as the theory of the "lays" and "compilations" sought to prove, a series of episodes whose order we may arrange and rearrange, at pleasure, as we may do without injury to the stories of the knightly deeds of Gawain or Lancelot in the romances of chivalry. Rather, it is a work of the conscious creative will, in which the unity of creation is superbly shown.

This unity of creation shows itself first in what constitutes the *scenario,* the harmonious series of combinations which lead the two central figures from one vicissitude to another, according to a law of logical progression.

All the incidents of the beginning, which we have just summed up, are put together in such a way that Tristan appears to us *dependent* upon his uncle Marc (by the ties of blood, of gratitude, and of a vassal's honor) and yet he appears to us quite *independent* of him, materially, for he may, if he pleases, go back to a kingdom which is his own. These incidents tend likewise to show Tristan as *independent* of Isolt, who hates in him the murderer of Morholt, and who remains for a long time indifferent to him, until the day when the love philtre makes him as *dependent* upon her as possible. And all these incidents are so ordered that Tristan's crime seems inexcusable in the eyes of the world and pardonable to those who know and understand.

It is a real uniformity of "preparations" which has brought into play a sort of obscure fatality weighing upon Tristan, and tending to set forth strongly the conflict of love and law. The lovers have drunk of the "vin herbé"; the action is begun. After that, many scenes are unrolled wherein the joys and torments of the two lovers are skilfully gradu-ated. The law of progression is this: the lovers pass through many phases in which they suffer trials constantly increas-ing in severity, each of these phases brings in a mode of suffering unknown to the preceding period of their life, and is made more intricate with the addition of the kinds of suffering endured in all the preceding periods.

1. *Remorse.* In the first phase, their love is not suspected by any one. As yet, they suffer only from the necessity of hiding their fault (the substitution of Brangien for Isolt) and from the fear which the agitation of their hearts arouses in them (Brangien delivered over to the serfs).

2. *Remorse and public shame.* In the second phase, be-sides the suffering caused by betraying the king, there is added the shame of feeling that they are watched by trai-tors, and suspected by Marc (Tristan's dismissal from the palace, the first lies, and the scene in which Marc spies upon them, hidden in the branches of the tree).

3. *Remorse, public shame, and exile.* The king, convinced at length, has driven them both away. They live, as out-laws, in the forest. This is the culminating point of the leg-end, where the greatest joys of their love and their worst social miseries meet. They suffer physical pain which is added to their increasing remorse and to their growing shame at being exiled from the life of men.

4. *Remorse, public shame, exile, and separation.* Until now, they have, at least, lived near one another. But now a worse trial arises: separation. Isolt is reinstated in her queenly dignity but henceforth she will always be watched and tormented by Marc's jealousy. Tristan, alone, contin-ues his life of exile. (Episodes of their exile, and those where Tristan, at the peril of his life, endeavors to see the queen secretly once more.)

5. *Remorse, public shame, exile, separation, and jealousy.* Tristan, tortured by the long silence of separation, ends by believing that Isolt no longer loves him. At this time, in a fit of despair, he marries another Isolt, the daughter of the Duke of Brittany. But scarcely has he wedded her when he realizes his offence and repents. Isolt the Golden-Haired learns of his marriage and now suspicion and jealousy separate them. Thus is completed, by the most cruel tor-ture of all, the progression of their sufferings. It is no longer their bodies merely, it is their hearts that are hence-forward distant from one another. With a ceaseless, obsti-nate persistency, in every vile disguise, as Tristan the mad-man, as Tristan the pilgrim, as Tristan the leper, he comes back to the queen, at the risk of being beaten by servants or killed as a common thief. Each of these meetings, the monotony of which is intentional and powerful, does noth-ing but increase the torments of the two wretched lovers. And what constitutes the grandeur of these episodes where the lover returns to his beloved, suspecting her even as she suspects him, exiled again and yet again returning, is the desolate feeling of the solitude of their souls. Then, the full cup of misery drunk to the very dregs, there is but one more trial, or rather refuge, and that is,

6. *Death.* In this plan, in this framework common to all the known versions, beautiful even in the schematic form to which we are here forced to reduce it, how can we doubt the unity of creation? It stands out clearly not only from the ingenious rigor of this *scenario,* but from the fact that the situations in it are always subordinate to the char-acters. Brief as is the summary we have just made, it is alone sufficient to give some idea of their consistency and strength: Tristan, knightly and loyal, bringing to his uncle the wife he might instead have robbed him of; disloyal, in spite of himself, and retaining until death his early tender-ness for Marc whom he betrays; Isolt, sorrowful and strong, loving in the midst of the blood that is shed for her; Marc, more beautiful than the lovers, living solely for the love that he bears to his adopted son and then to his queen, punishing them without being able to drive them from his heart, and ending, perchance, by the very strength of his compassion, in half divining the secret of the love philtre * * * truly, some one, at some time, must have combined this plan and these characters.

It is certain, as we have said before, that this some one did have Celtic stories to work on. Further than this, it is pos-sible, it is even infinitely probable, that he did not come directly in contact with the original Celtic stories but that he started from scattered French or English stories, more or less passive translations, more or less remodeled imita-tions, of the Celtic lays. But is it not possible, some one will ask, that among these varied stories he might have found one that was already enriched with moral ideas for-eign to the Celts, and that this privileged story may have provided him with the tone, the key note, and the color for his work? And further, is it not possible that the begin-nings of great romances in Roman or in Saxon lands may have preceded his romance and that his may be derived from them? It is possible, certainly. Every trick of logic is permissible here; since there is not one text that can hinder your hypotheses, all are possible, and as there is none to hinder so there is none to confirm them and all are vain. Our *scenario* reveals the activity of a man who feels his responsibility as the narrator of so tremendous a romance. Had he forerunners, you ask. What matter, if these fore-runners are condemned to remain purely people of our own creation? *Non sunt entia multiplicanda praeter neces-sitatem.* This one thing, indeed, is undisputed, that all the tradition known to us, implies this single *scenario:* there is not a poem preserved to us, that does not refer to it or adapt itself to it; not an episode nor a feature that differs from it or contradicts it. Suppose there did exist poems an-terior to this archetype, what do they matter, since they have all been absorbed into this one, and have no life ex-cept in and through it? if they are for us as if they never had been? and if all the stories known to us bring us back to this one poem?

IV.

It is, indeed, the name of *poem* that we must use hence-forth, rather than retain longer the ruder name of *scenario.* Let us venture to take up one of our romances, that by

Béroul. Many intermediaries, perhaps, separate him from the original trouvère. Observe, however, and see if, for a long series of adventures, we are not sure of finding herein the very sub-soil, the immediate invention of one single creator.

Through the treachery of a dwarf, Tristan is surprised by King Marc almost in flagrant fault. He is bound with ropes. The circumstances are such that there is nothing, it would seem, for him but to admit his crime. He should confess it; nevertheless, he denies: "King, if there be a man in thy house, brave enough to uphold this lie that I have loved the queen with a guilty love, let him stand before me in an enclosed field." He demands judgment: the judiciary combat; he calls upon God; he relies on God to fight with him. Is this a vulgar imposture? Perhaps; yet we see that the poet feels as he does, "Tristan put his faith in God, for he believed and knew that, if a regular judgment was instituted, no one would dare to wield a weapon against him." And we see further that, in the city of Tintagel, all the wealthy middle class and the humble people feel the same way. "The king commanded that a ditch should be dug in the earth and filled with vine branches and black and white thorns torn up by the roots. At the hour of prime, a ban is cried throughout the country in order to assemble immediately all the men of Cornwall. They come together with great noise, and there is not one who does not weep, except the dwarf of Tintagel. Then the king declares to all the people that he has had this pyre erected for his nephew and for the queen. But they all cry, 'King! this would be a crime. You must judge them first. Judgment first! and then, if so it be, punishment! But until judgment, mercy and pardon for them!'"

Is it a mere sentimental tenderness that thus makes the people of the crowd, the accomplices of the lovers? Again perhaps; but let us read further.

At the foot of the pyre, Dinas of Lidan, the king's seneschal, arises and declares, like the folk of Tintagel, that he cannot burn Tristan and Isolt without committing a crime. Dinas demands, not the pity of King Marc, but his justice; he claims the *plaid,* a remittance of hostages, the judiciary combat. The king refuses to listen to him; his anger blinds him. He orders that the fire be lighted and that some one seek the prisoners in the castle. The thorn branches blaze up, the people are silent, the king waits.

Then God Himself intervenes by miracles.

"Now listen how the Seigneur God was full of pity. He, who does not desire the death of the sinner, did not take amiss the tears and the supplications of the poor people who entreated Him for the tortured lovers. Near the road where Tristan passed, bound with cords and led by guards, on the summit of a rock stood a chapel, overlooking the sea. The wall of the apse was built close to a cliff, steep, rocky, and with pointed escarpments; in the apse, over the precipice, was a purple window, the work of a saint. Tristan says to those who are leading him: 'Sirs, see this chapel; permit me to enter it. My death is near; I will pray God that He have mercy upon me, who have so greatly sinned against Him. Sirs, the chapel has no other entrance than this * * * each one of you has his sword. You see clearly that I cannot pass out except by this door, and when I have prayed to God, I must needs give myself back into your hands.'

"The guards allow him to enter. He runs through the chapel, crosses the choir, reaches the saint's window in the apse, seizes its frame, opens it, and throws himself out. Rather this fall than death upon the pyre, before such an assembly!

"But know, seigneurs, that God gave him great mercy; the wind catches in his clothes, supports him, and sets him gently down on a large stone at the foot of the rock. The people of Cornwall still call this rock Tristan's Leap. And before the church, the guards still waited for him. But in vain. God gave him great mercy. He flees, the sand falls in behind his footsteps. In the distance he sees the pyre, the flames crackle, the smoke rises, he flees."

Thus Tristan is delivered by a miracle from God, but Isolt is left in the hands of those who seek to torture her.

"She is led, in her turn, to the pyre. She stands upright before the flames. The crowd shriek about her, cursing the king, cursing the traitor. The tears roll down her face. She is clothed in a strait grey tunic, wherein is woven a narrow thread of gold, and a golden thread is braided in her hair that falls even to her feet. He who could see her, standing there, so beautiful, without having compassion upon her, must have the heart of a scoundrel. Ah! God! how harshly her arms are bound! Now a hundred lepers, hastening thither upon their crutches, amid the clapping of their rattles, crowd before the pyre, and Yvain, their chief, cries to the king in a piercing voice:—

"'Sire, you wish to throw your wife upon this funeral pile; it is worthy justice, but too brief. This great fire will burn her quickly, this great wind will scatter her ashes too soon. And when the flames die down, her pain will be at an end. Do you wish me to teach you a worse punishment? so that she shall live, but in great dishonor, and ever seeking death? King, do you wish this?' The king replies: 'Yes, let her live, but in great dishonor, and worse than death. Whoever will teach me such punishment, I will love him the better for it.' 'Sire, I will tell you briefly then, my thought. See, I have here one hundred companions; give us Isolt and let her be common to us all! Our disease inflames our desires. Give her to your lepers, and never lady of high degree shall have come to so fearful an end. See, our rags are glued to our festering sores. She, who near thee, was pleased with richest stuffs furred with vair, with jewels, and with halls of marble, she, who enjoyed good wine, and honor, and joy, when she sees the court of thy lepers, when she must enter their hovels, then Isolt the Beautiful, Isolt the Golden-Haired will know her sin and will long for this fire of thorns.' The king listens to him, rises, and stands for a long time motionless. At length he moves towards the queen and takes her by the hand. She cries: 'In pity, Sire, burn me rather than that, burn me!' The king hands her to Yvain, who receives her, and the hundred lepers crowd about her. At the sound of their crying and yelping, every heart is wrung with pity, but Yvain is joyful; Isolt is going away and Yvain is leading her! The hideous cortège disappears beyond the city."

"But God has received her into His mercy" and as He has delivered Tristan, so He will deliver the queen. He allows Tristan, who is in ambush with his squire, to tear her from the lepers; and the two lovers bury themselves in the forest of Morois. Then, in the presence of this double miracle, the idea is thrust upon you and you realize that, for the poet, it is not the deed which proves the crime, it is the judgment, the judgment pronounced by God Himself. But King Marc, in his wrath, does not feel so, and he lays a price upon the head of the fugitives. They wander in the depths of the wild forest, amidst great hardships, tracked like wild animals, and they scarcely dare come back at night to the lodging of the night before. They eat nothing but the flesh of deer and long for the taste of salt and of bread. Their thin faces grow pale and their garments hang in rags. They love and they do not suffer. Beneath the tall friendly trees, they lead a life "stern and hard" and delicious; but they still protest their innocence, and when Ogrin, the old hermit, whom they meet in the forest, exhorts them to repentance, they declare that God Himself holds them in His keeping. More and more we feel that the whole story is built upon a naïvely subtle conception of justice, and at the same time, also, upon the innocent duplicity of the lovers, upon their "bel mentir," Tristan perhaps counting, in case of a judiciary duel, upon his physical strength and upon his prowess to manifest his innocence.

For a long time Marc persists in his anger, but now the day is drawing near when he, in his turn, shall feel with the lovers, with the humble people of Tintagel, and with the poet, that God alone is judge of their innocence or crime.

"Seigneurs, it was upon a summer's day, in the time of the harvest, a little after Pentecost, and the birds were singing in the dew of the approaching dawn. Tristan went out from the hut, girded on his sword, prepared his bow, Arc-Qui-ne-faut, and went away alone to hunt in the woods * * * When he came back from the chase, tired with the great heat, he took the queen within his arms.

"'Beloved, where have you been?' she asked.

"'Chasing a deer who has tired me completely. See how the sweat runs down my limbs, I would fain lie down and sleep.'

"Beneath the hut built of green branches, and strewn with fresh grasses, Isolt lies down first. Tristan throws himself beside her and lays his naked sword between their bodies. For their good fortune, they have not laid off their garments. Upon her finger, the queen wears the golden ring with beautiful emeralds that Marc gave her on the day of their betrothal; her fingers have become so thin that the ring nearly falls off. Thus they sleep, one of Tristan's arms beneath the head of his loved one and the other thrown about her beautiful body, in close embrace; but their lips do not touch.

There is not a breath of wind stirring, and not a leaf that trembles. Through the roof of green foliage, a ray of sunlight falls upon the face of Isolt, making it to shine like ice.

"Now a forester has found a place in the wood where the grasses were crushed; the lovers had slept there the night before, but he does not recognize the imprint of their bodies, and following the tracks, comes to their dwelling. He sees who are sleeping there, recognizes them, and flees, fearful of Tristan's terrible awaking."

He flees even to Tintagel, two leagues from there, and, taking the king aside, tells him how, in a hut in the forest, he has surprised the queen and Tristan, sleeping in each other's arms.

"'Come quickly, if you wish to wreak your vengeance.'

"'Go and wait for me,' replies the king, 'on the outskirts of the forest, at the foot of the Red Cross. Do not speak to any one of what you have seen; I will give you gold and silver, as much as you can carry away.'

"Marc causes his horse to be saddled, girds on his sword, and, without any retainers, escapes from the city. As he rides on, alone, he remembers the night when he had seized his nephew; what tenderness Isolt the Beautiful, with the fair white face, had then shown to Tristan! If he takes them now, he will punish these great sins, he will avenge himself upon those who have dishonored him * * * At the Red Cross he finds the forester.

"'Go before me; lead me straight and quickly.'

"The dark shade of the great trees envelops them. The king follows the spy. He trusts his good sword, which has formerly dealt many a noble blow. Ah! if Tristan awakes, one of the two, and God alone knows which, will lie dead upon the ground. At length the forester whispers softly, 'King, we draw near.' He holds the king's stirrup and ties the reins of the horse to the branches of a green apple tree. They approach nearer still and suddenly, in a sunlit clearing, they see the flowering hut.

"The king unties his mantle with golden strings, throws it off, and his splendid body stands free and bold. He draws his sword from its scabbard and says once more in his heart that he wishes to die if he does not kill them. The forester has followed him, and the king makes a sign for him to go back.

"He enters alone into the hut, his sword bare, and he brandishes it * * * Ah! what sorrow if he strikes the blow! But he sees that their lips do not touch and that a bare sword lies between them.

"'God,' he says to himself, 'what do I see here? Should I kill them? If they loved each other with a wicked love, they who have lived so long together in the forest, would they have placed a naked sword between them? If they loved wickedly, would they rest so purely? No, I will not kill them; it would be a great sin to strike them; and if I should awake this sleeper and one of us should die, it would be talked of for long ages, and to our great shame. But I will do something so that when they wake, they shall know that I have found them sleeping, that I did not seek their death, and that God has had mercy upon them.'

"The sunlight, filtering through the leaves, burned upon the white face of Isolt; the king took his gloves adorned with ermine. 'It was she,' he thought, 'who brought them to me not so long ago from Ireland!' He laid them among the branches, to close the hole through which the sunlight entered, then he slowly drew off the ring with the emerald stones that, in days gone by, he had given to the queen; he had to press a little upon it before he could pass it over her finger then, now her fingers were so thin that the ring came off without an effort, and in its place the king slipped the ring which Isolt had formerly brought to him. Then he took up the sword that separated the lovers; that, too, he recognized,—it had been notched in Morholt's skull,—he laid his own in its place, went out from the hut, jumped into his saddle, and said to the forester:—

"'Fly now, and save thy body, if thou canst!'

"Now Isolt had a vision in her sleep. She was beneath a rich tent in the midst of a great wood. Two lions threw themselves upon her and fought to have possession of her * * * she uttered a cry and awoke * * * the gloves adorned with white ermine fell upon her breast. At her cry, Tristan jumped to his feet, sought to pick up his sword, and recognized that of the king by its golden handle. And the queen sees upon her finger the ring she had given Marc."

During this scene, at the time the bare sword met his glance, what passed in Marc's heart? As before, the night when he had surprised the lovers, he had received indications of their crime, but not proofs; just as they had appealed to the judgment of God and did not dispense with it, so this bare sword was a sign of their chastity, appealing, in its turn, to a regular judgment. Did Marc, at this moment, admit as possible, their innocence? or rather, making himself in his turn the accomplice of their duplicity, in the tender weakness of his heart and in order to take back the queen, did he only pretend to believe in it? We do not know, but this glove that he left amid the branches of the hut is the sign that henceforth he, too, shares the idea of the lovers and of the poet: he is ready, not to pardon, but to judge.

It is judgment, indeed, not pardon, that Tristan ceaselessly demands. In a letter which he dictates to Ogrin, the hermit, and which is addressed to the king, he repeats that he has not loved Isolt with a guilty love, that he was forced and constrained to carry her away into the forest in order to save her life, that God has manifested his innocence by two miracles, and that he is ready to uphold what he says against any comer in judiciary battle. Marc, indeed, organizes the judgment. At the White Lands, Tristan solemnly presents himself for combat. There is no champion found to uphold the accusation, either because every one recognizes the protection of God visibly extended to Tristan and the queen, or because the barons, fearing Tristan's strength and participating in their turn in the "bel mentir" of the lovers, pretend to believe them innocent. From that time on, Tristan is not pardoned, but justified. For want of an accuser he is absolved, and Marc is juridically at peace with himself and his barons; he may take back the queen and his love is an accomplice of his justice.

Is it not true that all this long series of adventures is entirely built upon very particular moral and social postulates? a very specific conception of justice? Suppose the idea were destroyed that the lovers, held by the power of the philtre, are innocent, or that they can juridically appear so, that God absolves them, that they have nothing to fear from a judgment, that the proofs of the deed stand for nothing, then in a trice, the whole romance appears ridiculous and incoherent. Marc is a mere Dandin and the admirable scene of the gloves serves only to bring out his stupid good nature. Ogrin, the venerable hermit, is only a pander; the romance itself is only a mockery of the idea upon which the men of the Middle Ages built their whole system of justice. Is it not true that all these scenes can have been invented only in feudal times, at the very moment when, the method of the judiciary duel being still in high favor, men were, nevertheless, beginning, almost unconsciously perhaps, to admit that a little strategy and strength might often help one of the champions? Is it not true that we have here something *primary*, before which there had been nothing and after which there could be nothing but a pitiful deformation? On the one hand, we cannot take these scenes and try to bring them back to a more archaic type; let any one attempt it, and see the ruin he will make! On the other hand, they cannot be made over to fit a later age, in any way whatsoever; two posterior poets, Thomas and Gottfried von Strassburg, tried to do it, the idea of the judgment of God being already for them something weak and untenable; but all this part of the story, of which they have striven hard to preserve some fragments (the betrayal by the dwarf, the life in the forest, and the episode of the gloves), is in their versions a lamentable and ridiculous failure. All the episodes of the treason of the dwarf, the lovers being sent to the pyre, the tears of the people of Tintagel, the intervention of Dinas, the seneschal, the leap from the chapel, the scene with the lepers, the life in the forest of Morois, the rôle of Ogrin, the hermit, the scene of the gloves, Tristan's message to Marc, the assembly at the White Lands, and the surrender of the queen to the hands of Marc, all these episodes follow one another, imply one another, and mutually uphold each other; each is beautiful and luminous with the beauty and the light of all the others. They owe their existence to one common leaven, to this conception of justice which the poet sets forth and develops through them, and for whose sake alone they exist, to serve as its dramatic illustration. Each is one of the terms of a series to which the assembly of the White Lands alone gives a meaning and conclusion. It follows, then, that all these episodes, written each for the other, must have been composed at one single time by one single poet. We may suppose as many lost intermediaries as we wish between this poet and Béroul, but this part at least, the remoulders thus supposed have not dared to remould, and in it we reach the primitive.

V.

But have we not exposed ourselves to a grave objection, by having here attached so much importance to the feudal belief in the judgment of God, behind which Tristan takes shelter and which serves to give unity to the poem? "Is not this," some one may object, "an artifice or resource which indicates a *late* rather than a primitive state of the poem? is it not a sort of justification of the lovers, by a juridical trick, attempted as an *after-thought?* is it not more probably the invention of a man unfitted to understand the earlier state of the legend, in which love would not take refuge behind the law, but would find its justification in itself, in its own fatal power, and in the heavy sacrifices it imposes upon its victims?" To reply to this, we should have now to show that between this part of the poem and all the others, there are manifold relations of such sort that the apparent discordances resolve into one intimate and profound harmony, and this would be a long undertaking. All the preceding observations have led us to place at the foundation of the French and Germanic tradition, not an amorphous vulgate, made up of a mechanical assemblage of scattered narrations, but a regular poem, all the parts of which, created in relation one to another, were bound together by a strong synergy, one and complex. Nevertheless, we cannot doubt but that some one may oppose our views, till now based principally on logical deductions, with other logical combinations. It is enough for us to have proposed here a hypothesis, born of the observation of the facts, which does not meet with any obstacles in the facts, and to have presented it favorably, perhaps, to the attention of criticism. It will remain a hypothesis, we know, so long as we shall be forced to see so dimly this archetype, of which we can give here only a suggestion to the reader.

Since the five romances upon which depend all the known texts (those by Béroul, Eilhart, Thomas, the romance in French prose, and the poem of the "Folie Tristan") all proceed from it, directly or indirectly, but independently of each other, a comparison of the differences in these five versions will allow us to restore it. By means of a philological operation the mechanism of which it would take too long to describe here, it will be reborn in all its archaic grace, more beautiful than all the romances derived from it,—the primitive poem, at once harsh and delicious, voluptuous and cruel, grave and charming, and with an extraordinary, passionate, and sorrowful exaltation. We must imagine the author of this archetype, doubtless an Anglo-Norman, as living in an early period, and his work was doubtless the venerable contemporary of the "Pèlerinage de Charlemagne" or the "Chanson de Roland." Before him there must certainly have been, in the Celtic country, scattered stories of Tristan, that gave the first impetus to his genius; but these stories would have lived obscurely and have fallen into oblivion but for him, who, alone, gave to them an unforeseen value and meaning; it was through him alone that the legend of the fatal love, stronger than law, stronger than honor, came into being and had life, and this love, being absolute, created a sort of mysterious legitimacy for itself. After him, there were only the remouldings of his poem, very beautiful, assuredly. But what do the works of Thomas and Gottfried von Strassburg represent? They are the reduction to the tone of court poetry, the transposition into the "precieux" manner, of a poem originally foreign to the "precieux" and courtly mind. Charming and exquisite as they are when they embellish and soften the inventions of the primitive poet, these remoulders are great only when they preserve them without daring to touch them. The primitive poet alone was the sovereign poet. The theory according to which a legend, slowly elaborated by thousands of poetic hearts, is the fruit of the collaboration of divers peoples and of manifold generations of bards, has, indeed, a certain romantic nobility. Yet there is another sight no less inspiring: that of a man who, by the power of his heart and of his imagination, starting from a few legendary ideas received from outside, creates heroes that will live, creates the "geste" which is to stir the hearts of men throughout long centuries. Then, too, what matters it whether this sight be the more beautiful or not, sentimentally? It is the more beautiful, only if it is the truer.

Roger Sherman Loomis (essay date 1913)

SOURCE: "A Survey of Tristan Scholarship After 1911," in *Tristan and Isolt: A Study of the Sources of the Romance,* Vol. II. Reprint. Burt Franklin, 1960, pp. 565-587.

[*In the following essay, Loomis comments on the critical reception Gertrude Schoepperle's 1913 study of the Tristan legend received, and discusses the origin, development, and transmission of the legend.*]

REVIEWS

The reviews of Miss Schoepperle's *Tristan and Isolt* were, broadly speaking, highly favorable. Her critique of Bédier's reconstruction of the *poème primitif* in his edition of Thomas's *Tristan* on the basis of its assumed logical structure and consistency was generally accepted. So, too, was her rejection of his thesis that Béroul, Thomas, Eilhart, the *Folie,* and the Prose Romance were all derived from a French poem of the early twelfth century, created at one stroke by a single author of genius. Her array of parallels between the surviving Tristan texts, on the one hand, and motifs, situations, and stories in circulation at the time, on the other, was taken as evidence that there was a far more important body of tradition in the romance than Bédier had recognized, even though Kelemina and others questioned the validity of particular examples which she adduced.

Most of the reviewers were impressed by the array of analogues culled from Irish literature, and especially by the similarity to the Tristan romance presented by the Irish saga of Diarmaid and Grainne, which, though most of the texts are late, could be traced back to the tenth century, and which told a tragic tale of the compulsive love of a hero for his royal uncle's wife, and of their flight to the forest. Miss Schoepperle's contention that this formed the nucleus from which developed the great medieval romance was received favorably by most critics, not only because of the basic resemblance in plot but also because it afforded an explanation of the curious episodes of the sword separating the two lovers in their forest retreat and of the splashing water. Joseph Loth was almost, if not quite, alone in asserting that adultery and elopement were too commonplace in life and fiction to prove dependence of the romance on the saga.

Not all reviewers were ready to accept Miss Schoepperle's contention that Eilhart's French source, the *estoire,* could be taken as the source of Thomas's poem, Kelemina and Nitze being among the sceptics. Huet and Ferdinand Lot questioned the dating of the *estoire* in the last quarter of the twelfth century, both arguing that the courtly elements were not necessarily attributable to so late a date, and Lot pointing out that it was inconsistent with the dating of Thomas's *Tristan* before Chrétien's *Cligès.* Miss Schoepperle's belief that it was Mathilda, daughter of Henry II and Eleanor of Poitou, who confided a manuscript of the *estoire* to Eilhart von Oberge on her return from England to Saxony in 1185, and that this furnishes a *terminus a quo* for the composition of his translation was challenged and is now pretty generally rejected.

On the whole, the response of scholars to Miss Schoepperle's *Tristan* may be summed up in the concluding words of Joseph Loth:

> L'étude des sagas irlandaises se recommandait d'ellemême; elle pouvait assurer la celticité de traits de moeurs, d'épisodes même qui prêtaient à la discussion. A ce point de vue, les recherches de Miss Schoepperle sont des plus méritoires. . . . Les analyses des diverses versions du roman sont également faites avec la plus grande conscience, et ajoutent notablement à l'oeuvre de M. Bédier. Les remarques ingénieuses abondent. En somme, le travail de Miss Schoepperle est un véritable mine de renseignements, un répertoire indispensable non seulement à tous ceux qui s'intéressent aux romans arthuriens, mais encore à ceux qui s'occupent du moyen âge et des questions de Folklore.

THE DATING AND AUTHORSHIP OF TEXTS

The theory of Bédier that the reference of Bernard de Ventadour to Tristan as the suffering lover of Yzeut could be dated approximately 1154, though unacceptable to Miss Schoepperle, was upheld by Deister as a probability, but has again been vigorously challenged by Delbouille.

The dating and the provenance of Eilhart von Oberge's *Tristrant* are still the subject of debate. The editor of the surviving fragments, Wagner, argued that the dialect was that of the Middle Rhine, not of Lower Saxony, and that the poem must have been written about 1170, and in these views he was supported by Van Dam and Ranke. But Wesle in W. Stammler's *Deutsche Literatur des Mittelalters, Verfasserlexikon,* I (1933), cols. 520-4, was not convinced. In any case the poet must have lived earlier than the official of the court of Brunswick with the same name, of whom records survive.

Similar uncertainty exists as to whether the Béroul fragment was composed by one or two poets. Muret in his edition for the Société des Anciens Textes Français maintained that the first part, which corresponded in substance to Eilhart and which extended to vs. 2754, was the work of a jongleur named Béroul, who twice referred to himself, and that the rest of the poem was added by an anonymous author, who not only contradicted his predecessor violently but also used another source and exhibited certain differences of spirit. Later Muret conceded the possibility of a single author, and has had many followers in this opinion. But Miss Schoepperle, though she did not commit herself, distinguished between the two parts, and recently Raynaud de Lage has adduced strong arguments from the versification, the introduction of new characters, and the absence of the mannerisms of oral recitation in the second part, to render nearly certain the division of the poem between two authors. Only the latter part, then, can be assigned, on the basis of the reference in line 3849 to the epidemic which the Crusaders suffered at Acre in 1191, to a period after that date, and the first section may well be twenty or thirty years older.

Though the *terminus a quo* of Thomas's poem still remains fixed at 1155, owing to the certainty of his borrowing from Wace's *Brut,* the *terminus ad quem* is still an open question. A large number of scholars have accepted the arguments of Gaston Paris and Bédier that Chrétien wrote his *Cligès* as a sort of counterblast to Thomas's *Tristan* and that he imitated a word-play, preserved in Gottfried's adaptation of Thomas, on *l'amer* (love), *l'amer* (bitterness), and *la mer* (sea). But not only did Miss Schoepperle reject the dependence of *Cligès* on Thomas as unproved, but Hoepffner also pointed out that certain of the more specific of Chrétien's allusions to, or imitations of, the Tristan material (such as the golden hair) were inspired by another version than that of Thomas. Jirmounsky, in addition to this argument, showed that the verbal conceit was a commonplace with Latin authors. R. S. Loomis was unable to find before 1195 examples in art of the repetition of the heraldic device on shield, lance, pennon, and *conisance,* which Thomas assigned to Tristan le Nain, and hence concluded that the poem could not be much more than ten years earlier. The latest editor of Thomas, Professor Wind, though leaning toward a date after *Cligès,* does not pronounce a final decision. She agrees with Bédier that the poet's professed ignorance of affairs of love does not mean that he was in holy orders, and accepts the general view that he addressed himself to a courtly circle, perhaps to a royal patron. Jonin, however, believes Thomas was a cleric.

THE NAMES IN THE EARLY TRISTAN ROMANCE

Miss Schoepperle adopted a noncommittal attitude to the evidence offered by the names as to the history of the Tristan legend. Bédier, however, even though he minimized the Celtic elements in that legend and believed that all our early texts were derived from a single French poem which owed little to an earlier tradition, somewhat inconsistently defined several stages in the transmission of the story from Pictland to Anglo-Norman Britain by way of Wales, Cornwall, and Brittany, on the basis of the names. Later scholars have added considerably to our information on the nomenclature. The following is offered as an amplification and rectification of Bédier's scheme.

Pictish: Drustan>Tristan.

Welsh: Esyllt>Iselt, Iseut; March>Mark; Branwen>Brenguen; Kae Hir>Kaherdin (assimilated to Turkish Kahedin); Bleddri>Bleheri>Pelherin; Caradoc>Cariado.

Breton: Rivelen>Rivalen; Rivelen + (French) *reis*>Rouland riis, Kanelengres; Rodald>Roald; Morgan>Morgan; Morald>Morholt, Morhaut; Perinis>Perinis; Donuallen>Donoalent, Denoalan; Godoine>Godoine; Houel>Hoel.

French: Blanchefleur; Guenelon; Orri; Ogrin; Estult le Orgillius.

Of the place-names, some can be identified with certainty. Loenois, Tristan's native land according to Béroul and Eilhart, is Lothian, which then extended from the Firth of Forth to the Tweed; in the Prose *Tristan* it was confused with Leonois, a Breton province. Béroul's Gavoie or Ganoie, whose king was at war with the Scottish king, is Galloway. Carloon or Cuerlion is, of course, Caerleon on Usk. Isneldone, where Perinis found King Arthur, is the Roman fort near Carnarvon, called by the Anglo-Normans "la cité de Snaudone". Tintaguel, needless to say, is the romantic castle of Tintagel. Le Mont in Béroul is St. Michael's Mount, and Loth identified Lancien with the modern parish of Lantyan in Cornwall. Ermonie, mentioned by the English redactor of Thomas as the land of Tristan's father, represents a not uncommon corruption of Armorique, that is, Brittany.

Some identifications are plausible, others mere guesses. The forest of Morrois, to which the lovers retired, may possibly be the wild region of Moray in northern Scotland. The isle of Saint Sanson, where, according to the Prose *Tristan* and Chrétien's *Erec,* the combat with Morholt took place, is probably one of the Scilly Isles of that name, even though this identification puts it far from Tintagel. Béroul surely knew Cornish geography well, but Loth's attempt to place the Blanche Lande, Costentin, the Mal Pas, and Morrois in that county has been met by the reviewers with scepticism. The notion that Leonois, Malory's Lyonesse, was a country lying west of Land's End, which had sunk beneath the Atlantic waves, goes back no farther than the Cornish antiquary Carew in the seventeenth century (*Modern Philology*, L, 162-70).

THE ORIGIN AND DEVELOPMENT OF THE LEGEND

Since Bédier and Miss Schoepperle wrote, much has been added to our knowledge of the origin, development, and transmission of the Tristan legend. Even as early as 1891

Zimmer had discovered in the *Chronicles of the Picts and Scots* (977-995) a certain Drest or Drust, son of Talorcan, who reigned about 780, and he had pointed out the equivalence of this name with the Drystan son of Tallwch, who in Welsh texts was the lover of Esyllt, wife of March. This identification was not only accepted by Bédier and many others, but it was confirmed by Deutschbein's proof that a tale about Drust had been interpolated in the ancient Irish saga, the *Wooing of Emer.* In this interpolation alone the Ulster hero Cuchulainn is accompanied by a certain Drust. The setting is the Hebrides, not far from Pictish territory at the mouth of the Clyde. When Cuchulainn arives at the king's court, he hears wailing and learns that a human tribute is to be given over to warriors from Ireland. He kills them, but is himself wounded. Though others claim credit for the victory, the king's daughter does not believe them, and is able to recognize Cuchulainn as he takes a bath. The king offers her to him as a bride, but he refuses. Once granted that Drust was the original hero of this episode, is it not obvious that here is reflected the Pictish source of the Morholt episode and of the discomfiture of the false claimant? By great good fortune, then, we have preserved to us the outline of the original saga which was attached to Drustan, the Pictish king, the nucleus of the famous romance.

If Sidney Hartland's great study of the legend of Perseus may be relied on, it is probable that the Pictish saga is a descendant of the classical story of Perseus and Andromeda which had drifted far to the northwest. Its localization in this region may possibly have left traces in the geography of the French romances, where Tristan's homeland is Loenois and the forest to which he and Isolt fled was Morrois. Loenois is certainly Lothian, and Morrois is most plausibly identified as the wild region of Moray, the former adjacent to the southern border of Pictland and the latter lying deep within it. Conceivably, therefore, these lands of Tristan's birth and exile may owe their mention in French romance to Drust's original connection with what is now Scotland.

The Pictish saga, besides passing over to Ulster to be incorporated in the Cuchulainn cycle, must have passed southward by way of the Britons of Strathclyde and Cumberland into Wales, and here an extraordinary process of accretion began. The literary remains concerned with Drystan son of Tallwch (except for a very doubtful fragment from the Black Book of Carmarthen which contains the name Diristan) are unfortunately late. Though two Esyllts are listed among the goldentorqued ladies of Arthur's court in *Kulhwch and Olwen* (ca. 1100), Drystan and March son of Meirchiawn are first mentioned in *Rhonabwy's Dream* of the early or middle thirteenth century—strangely enough, among Arthur's counsellors! But there is no proof that the Welsh Drystan material at this stage had been influenced by the French romances, and it is safe to assume that the tradition was considerably older than the texts. Noteworthy is the fact that Drystan, March, and Esyllt are persistently associated with Arthur. In a thirteenth-century ms., Peniarth 16, we read:

Drystan son of Tallwch, who guarded the swine of March son of Meirchyawn, while the swineherd went to ask Esyllt to come to a meeting with him. Arthur was trying to get one pig from among them, either by deceit or by force, but he did not get it.

A later version magnifies Drystan's cleverness and prowess by adding March, Kei, and Bedwyr to Arthur as unsuccessful pig-snatchers. Such evidence as we have, then, indicates that already in the Welsh stage Drystan had been attracted into the Arthurian orbit, that he was noted for exceptional cunning and strength, and that he was involved in an affair with Esyllt, the wife of March.

This love-affair was evidently the most important accretion to the Pictish tale of Drust. As already noted above, it was Miss Schoepperle's great contribution to show that, as developed in the *estoire,* the tragic story of Tristan and Isolt showed a marked affinity to the famous Irish saga of Diarmaid and Grainne and must, in fact, have been derived, even though indirectly, from some version of it. For there was a correspondence in the relationship of the three principal characters, Diarmaid being, like Tristan, the lover of his uncle's wife; there was a similar compulsive force which brought the lovers together; in both stories the lovers dwelt for a long time in the forests, subsisting on game and moving from place to place. Miss Schoepperle clinched the matter by pointing to parallel incidents, the woman's reaction to the water which splashed against her leg, and the placing of a barrier (stone or sword) between the lovers as they slept. Even though the full form of the *Pursuit of Diarmaid and Grainne* has come down to us in no manuscript earlier than the seventeenth century, the saga is mentioned in a tenth-century list, and may be centuries older. Thus the heart of Tristan's love-story is Irish.

If further proof be needed that this saga exerted a powerful influence on the Tristan romance in the Welsh stage, it is provided by the short Welsh tale entitled *Ystoria Trystan.* This evidence was disregarded by Miss Schoepperle, Loth, and Kelemina, apparently because we have no copy earlier than 1550, but Sir Ifor Williams in his *Lectures on Early Welsh Poetry* declared that the verse elements were much older than the linking prose passages, and that the narrative closely resembled the Diarmaid and Grainne tale in Irish. In fact, there are nine points of likeness, some of them very specific details. Significant is the fact that Kae Hir, the Sir Kay of Arthurian romance, appears as the friend of Trystan and asks Esyllt to bestow her handmaid on him, just as Kaherdin appears in Thomas's poem as Tristan's friend and with Isolt's consent wins her handmaid as his mistress. Of course, the equation of Kaherdin with the brother of Isolt of the White Hands must have been made much later in the development of the romance, since, as Miss Schoepperle argued and as we shall see in due course, the second Isolt belongs to the last stages.

Two other Irish love-stories may have had some influence. One is the tragic tale of Deirdre, which has so strongly appealed to modern Irish poets and playwrights. Like the *Elopement of Diarmaid and Grainne,* it tells of the passion of a young hero, Naisi, for the destined bride of an old king, their elopement and wanderings, and the attempts of the king to catch them. At last, they were persuaded to return with an assurance of safety, but Naisi was treacherously killed, Deirdre never smiled again or raised her head from her knee, and a year later crushed her head against a rock. Miss Schoepperle proposed, with good reason, that at a stage before the addition of Tristan's exile and marriage, the romance had a similar ending with the return of the lovers from the forest with an assurance of forgiveness from Mark—an assurance broken when he found the two together. Much less plausible is Thurneysen's attempt to connect the saga of Cano mac Gartnain with the romance of Tristan. To be sure, this too is a tragic tale of a man's love for another's wife, but except for the fact that the husband's name is Marcan, there is little resemblance. The only certain major Irish influence on Tristan is that of Diarmaid and Grainne.

There are, however, quite a few elements which show enough similarity to motifs or situations in Irish literature to be judged of Celtic origin, but whether derived ultimately from Ireland or derived from similar materials current in Wales or Cornwall or even in Brittany, it is often difficult to determine. According to Cormac's *Glossary* (ca. 900) King Finn had a fool who spied on Finn's wife and revealed her infidelity to his master. Béroul and Eilhart give a roughly similar account of King Mark's dwarf who spied on Tristan and Isolt. Miss Schoepperle cited several instances from Irish literature of chips of wood cast into a stream to convey a message, but none of them corresponds closely enough in the attendant circumstances to be accepted definitely as the source. The same may be said of the analogues she cited for Tristan's carving a message on a hazel rod and laying it on the road where Isolt was to pass, as described in Marie de France's *Chèvrefeuille.* So, too, the voyage of Tristan in a rudderless boat in the hope of healing may well be a Celtic feature, but there is no precise parallel in Irish.

Two episodes, treated by Miss Schoepperle, though they have analogues in Irish, are more closely paralleled in Welsh. Mark, according to Béroul, had the ears of a horse and managed to keep the secret until his confidant, the dwarf, told it to a bush in the hearing of the barons. Essentially the same story was related of March in a Welsh manuscript of the sixteenth century and in the folklore of the Lleyn peninsula as late as 1882. The so-called incident of "the harp and the rote", which involves the abduction of Isolt by a stranger as a result of Mark's rash promise and her rescue by Tristan, is unquestionably Celtic, with analogues in Irish and Arthurian romance, but it comes close enough to the episode of the rash boon in *Pwyll* to render it fairly certain that it was absorbed directly from a variant version of the *mabinogi.* Indeed, as an illustration of Tristan's resourcefulness and skill in music, "the harp and the rote" belongs with the other evidence for Tristan's reputation among the Welsh for cunning—a reputation which in all likelihood was responsible for his later fame as a master of venery.

If one may hazard a reconstruction of the Welsh saga of Drystan, it had little to say of his parentage and boyhood, for it is significant that in the French romances his father's name is Breton and his mother's name French, and his birthplace and early home is Brittany. Probably the story began with his arrival at a royal court and followed the outline of the Pictish tale of Drustan. It continued on the pattern of the Irish saga of Diarmaid and Grainne, the princess of the Pictish tale being carried over and taking the role of Grainne. Drystan, Esyllt, and March were substituted for Diarmaid, Grainne, and Finn. There was no potion exercising its compulsive force on the lovers simultaneously, and though Esyllt may have put a spell on Drystan so that he eloped with her to the forest, he rejected her embraces and placed a stone between them each night. Only after the incident of the splashing water did he yield. After successfully eluding the efforts of March to catch them, the lovers were finally persuaded by the intervention of Arthur to return to the court, but they continued to meet surreptitiously, and, though often suspected, managed to deceive or outwit March. Finally, March discovered them together and murdered Drystan. Esyllt died in her lover's arms or committed suicide. Into some such composite framework minor incidents were fitted—the betrayal of March's secret deformity, "the harp and the rote", Kae Hir's intrigue with Esyllt's maid, and perhaps others from the fund of current non-Celtic fiction. Needless to say, in this oral stage every *cyvarwydd* told the saga with individual and sometimes wide variations from the outline sketched above; some, probably, emphasized the romantic aspect and the lovers' fidelity; other what one might call the *fabliau* elements of bedroom comedy and successful dupery.

Mrs. Bromwich has suggested that in Welsh tradition March's court was in Glamorgan; in any case when the legend traveled south, the centre of the action was moved to Tintagel on the coast of Cornwall, where the ruins ever since have sheltered memories of the famous lovers. This new localization and the choice of the isle of St. Sanson as the site of the combat with Morholt are the only novelties which we can attribute with considerable plausibility to the passage of the legend through Cornwall at this early stage. The alternative situation of Mark's court at Lancien, modern Lantyan, which we find in the first part of Béroul, may well represent a genuine local tradition picked up by the poet, who was certainly acquainted with the country, but since it has left no traces in any other version, it could hardly have enjoyed much currency, and Loth's other geographical speculations, based on Béroul, have been properly received with scepticism.

This elaborate legend of Tristan passed on to Brittany to undergo further change and expansion. Between 1035 and 1045 a lord of Vitré named Triscan or Tristan attained a certain celebrity because of his quarrels with the Duke of Brittany, and his father was named Rivalon or Rivelon. It can hardly be a coincidence that Thomas transferred Tristan's homeland from Loonois to Brittany, assigned him a seneschal with the Breton name of Roald, described

his war with the Duke of that land, and, in agreement with Eilhart, called his father Rivalon. Whether this Triscan or Tristan of Vitré and other Triscans of the same period were named after the Welsh Trystan or not, it is hard to say, but it seems fairly clear that the names were confused and that the hero of the French romances derived his father's name and inherited his war with the Duke of Brittany from the historic baron of Vitré. The Breton influence on the early part of the romance and the lack of specifically Celtic ingredients render it most likely that the affair of Rivalon and Blanchefleur, their deaths, and the upbringing of their orphan son by the faithful Roald were innovations, lacking a traditional basis. Probably some ingenious Breton, struck by the similarity of the name Tristan to the French adjective *triste,* invented a new etymology for the name and gave the birth-story a sombre cast.

Three elements in the Tristan romances have counterparts in modern Breton folklore. The story of King Mark's equine ears, current in Finistère in 1794 and for a century afterwards, was presumably imported as a component part of the legend from Wales. On the other hand, the death of the hero on hearing the lie about the sail, which forms the conclusion of the romance in Thomas and Eilhart, bears a close resemblance to a folktale collected on the islands of Ouessant and Molène some fifty years ago and was probably a native contribution. So, too, was Tristan's combat with the dragon which, Van Hamel has shown, is paralleled in modern Breton folklore. This folktale, an offshoot of the Perseus and Andromeda legend, was apparently combined in Brittany with the other version of which Drust was the hero, thus giving us two combats in which Tristan, though victorious, was left severely poisoned, and employing both the discomfiture of the false seneschal by means of the dragon's tongue from the Breton version and the recognition in the bath from the Pictish version.

Tristan's boast of his mistress and its justification by her beauty and even that of her handmaids, as they ride by, form an episode which was classified by Miss Schoepperle as a wide-spread folktale and such it is in modern times; but it may be claimed as a Breton addition, perhaps a Breton invention, since the earliest forms are found in the Breton *lais* of *Lanval* and *Graelent.* Moreover, the corresponding Italian folktales, as Levi has shown, derive from Breton originals through the fourteenth-century *cantare* of *Liombruno* and its many printed editions.

The curious episode of the *Salle aux Images,* the subterranean hall which Tristan had built and where he resorted secretly to caress the statue of Isolt, bears so marked a resemblance to Geoffrey of Monmouth's tale of the subterranean chamber which King Locrine had made and where he was wont to visit secretly his mistress Estrildis that we may feel sure of some relationship between the two narratives. Though the name Estrildis might suggest that Geoffrey had borrowed the story from a Welsh tale of Esyllt, Drystan's mistress, it is hard to see how the episode would have fitted into the saga when, as yet, Drystan had no jealous wife. One may be rightly cautious in accepting Geoffrey's statement that his source was a book brought from Brittany, yet considerable material did come to him from across the Channel, and the odds favor a common Breton source, more or less remote, for both versions of the clandestine visits to a mistress in a subterranean chamber.

Miss Schoepperle was able to cite Oriental parallels for such *fabliau* themes as the Tryst under the Tree and the Ambiguous Oath, but she did not assert Oriental derivation. Though these themes were coupled with Celtic motifs, such as the chips on the stream, the presumption is that they were not absorbed into the legend till a late stage, perhaps when Breton story-tellers wandered abroad and added to their repertoire fresh stories of jealous husbands, wayward wives, and tricky lovers.

The most important discovery concerning the latter part of the Tristan romance was made by Samuel Singer, who proved that the idea of a second Isolt, the unconsummated marriage, and the offended brother of the bride were taken over from the famous Arabic love-story of Kais and Lobna. Through what channels it had passed before it came to Brittany, no one can say, but that this pathetic plot was incorporated at the Breton stage can hardly be doubted when one considers the geography and the personages. The Arab romance afforded, moreover, examples of a rarefied passion which, when ascribed to Tristan, raised him high above more earthy lovers. Like Kais, Tristan, when separated from his lady, marries another woman for the ultraromantic reason that she bears the same name. Like Kais, he is encouraged to do so by her brother. Like Kais, he cannot bring himself to consummate the marriage and thus gives offense to her relatives. Like Kais, Tristan, in Eilhart, is buried with his first love in one grave.

Thus the Celtic and Arabic tales had come from the West and the East to unite and form a harmonious whole which was singularly adapted to the expression in narrative form of the new cult of idealized extramarital passion of which the troubadours of Provence were the lyrical mouthpiece. For Isolt, as for Grainne, the claims of her husband were as naught beside the claims of love. For Tristan, as for Kais, the claims of his wife were as naught beside the claims of love. It seems probable that at this stage, if not earlier, Tristan as an ideal lover could no longer be depicted as hanging back, like Diarmaid, before the advances of an infatuated woman, and the potion was introduced to bring about a mutual and overpowering attraction. The episode of the separating sword, however, survived as a relic of the older story and as testimony to Tristan's original resistance to Esyllt's overtures.

It was in Brittany, then, that the legend of Tristan and Isolt was expanded into a tragic love-story on a scale comparable to that of Paris and Helen. Though it included much that was episodic and unessential and much that was hardly above the level of farce, the main structure was grandiose and certain situations afforded opportunities for lofty treatment, of which Thomas and Gottfried von Strassburg took full advantage.

BLEHERIS

Before the romance came into the hands of the poets, it was an oral tradition. To this fact there is ample testimony. Béroul himself refers scornfully (vs. 1265) to the *conteor;* Peter of Blois testifies that the *histriones* moved their audiences to tears by their fables of Arthur, Gawain, and Tristan. Bédier quoted the significant passage in which Renart, the fox, disguised as a "jongleur breton", asserts his knowledge of lais concerning Tristan and "Dame Iset". Marie de France asserts that she has heard the lai of the Honeysuckle as well as finding it in writing. Thomas is explicit: "Entre ceus qui solent cunter Et del cunte Tristran parler, Il en cuntent diversement: Oï en ai de plusur gent." Indeed, the poets themselves expected to have their stories recited, as is proved by the addresses of Béroul and Thomas to a listening audience. Thomas goes on to invoke, in favor of his statement that Kaherdin accompanied Tristan to Britain, the authority of one Breri, who knew the deeds of all the kings and counts who have been in Britain. Bédier and Miss Schoepperle held that this reference was merely a device to cover the poet's departure from a common tradition, and they may well be right; but even so, the existence of Breri is not disproved. Others have accepted Breri's existence, but have sought to identify him either with a historical bishop named Bleddri (983-1022), or with a landowner of South Wales of the same name, who may have acted as an interpreter between the Welsh and the Normans in the first third of the twelfth century. Both identifications are pure guesses, and are refuted by the fact that Giraldus Cambrensis, about 1194, referred to that famous *fabulator,* Bledhericus, who came a little before his time. A *fabulator* or *fableor* was a professional story-teller, not an official interpreter or a wealthy landowner, and 1022 is over a century before Giraldus' birth about 1147. Further testimony comes from the Second Continuation of Chrétien's *Perceval* (formerly ascribed to Wauchier), where we read that Bleheris, who was born and brought up in Wales, told a tale of Gawain and a dwarf knight to the Count of Poitiers, who loved it more than any other. Chrétien de Troyes and Eilhart unconsciously reveal an association in their minds between this Bleheris and Tristan, for the first lists Bliobleheris and Tristan together in *Erec,* and the second introduces a minor character under the name of Pleherin. Finally, the author of the so-called *Elucidation,* prefixed to Chrétien's Perceval, mentions a knight of Arthur's Blihos Bleheris, who knew such good tales that no one tired of listening to him. All this testimony, conscious and unconscious, converges to prove that there was a renowned Welsh *conteur* named Bleddri and that he included in his repertoire tales of Tristan. His visit to Poitiers seems to be confirmed by the fact that two troubadours connected with that household, Bernard de Ventadour and Cercamon, refer familiarly to Tristan as a lover. Kellermann's attempt to dispose of this singularly concordant evidence because the manuscripts vary as to the forms of the name Bleheris and because it was mistakenly attached to a knight of Arthur's court should not be taken too seriously.

If we do recognize the validity of the evidence, we must come to some further conclusions. Bleheris must have been fluent in French in order to be understood at the court of Poitou and to win a reputation on the Continent. His stories must have been derived mainly from the Breton rather than from his native tradition. There is no need to suppose with Brugger that he ever composed in verse; the common medium of the *conteurs* was prose. He must have possessed rare histrionic gifts, for he alone of all the reciters of Arthurian tales has left us his name. Whether we should also ascribe to him a share, small or large, in co-ordinating the mass of materials which made up the Breton heritage and in producing the romance of Tristan substantially as we know it from Eilhart, is a question imposible to answer.

THE EARLY POETS AND THEIR PATRONS

According to a hypothesis developed by R. S. Loomis, the influence of Bleheris on the court of Poitou may be detected not only in the alluions of the troubadours to Tristan but also in the fact that scions of that house in the latter half of the century seem to have favored poets who dealt with the theme, briefly or at length. The daughter of Eleanor of Poitou by Louis VII of France, Marie de Champagne, was, for a time at least, the patroness of Chrétien de Troyes, who tells us that he had written a poem on King Mark and Iseut la Blonde. Eleanor's second husband, Henry II of England, is usually identified with the noble king to whom Marie de France dedicated her lais, including *Le Chèvrefeuille*. The Anglo-Norman Thomas, surely a court poet, may have written for Eleanor's circle, since he described the caparison of Tristan's steed as red embroidered with golden lions and this device was probably that of the royal house. Whether this interest on the part of the descendants of the Counts of Poitou was primarily due to the posthumous influence of Bleheris, may be questioned, for, as we have seen, the romance of Tristan must have largely taken shape before his time and there were other *fabulatores* who could make their audiences weep over Tristan's sufferings. In any case, the interest of this same royal house continued into the thirteenth century. King John's regalia included in 1207 a *soi-distant* "sword of Tristram", and there is a fair probability that the Chertsey Tiles which illustrate Thomas's poem were commissioned by Henry III a few years before his death. Edward I before his accession owned a version of the Prose *Tristan,* which came into the hands of Rusticien de Pise. It should be added, of course, that Eleanor of Poitou and her descendants were not the only regal enthusiasts for the Tristan story, but, strange to say, I can find no others recorded before 1339, when Pedro IV of Aragon bought a manuscript of *Meliadus,* a history of Tristan's father.

THE EPISODIC POEMS

Levi argued cogently against the thesis that the Breton lais formed a new type which was created solely by Marie de France, and that all examples of later date were mere imitations of her work. He proved the popularity of Marie's *Chèvrefeuille* by citing many allusions. There has been a spirited debate as to the interpretation of this poem. Mrs. Frank, though she overlooks Miss Schoepperle's treatment of the subject, nevertheless agrees that Tristan carved on the hazel rod not only his name but also a message summarized in vss. 63-78, and she cited examples of inscriptions on wooden tablets and wands. She is supported by the Norse translation and by the statement in the poem itself that the Queen "knew all the letters" on the rod,—a strange remark if there were only the letters of Tristan's name. Spitzer, however, regards this as too prosaic an interpretation of the text and argues that the symbolism of the hazel and the honeysuckle was readily divined by the Queen and that there was no need for Tristan to spell it out. Le Gentil very rightly contends that this theory, though attractive, imputes more subtlety to Marie than the poem itself justifies.

Hoepffner, in his edition of the Berne *Folie Tristan,* abandoned his earlier view that this poem and the Oxford *Fólie* were derived from a common source, and maintained with solid reasons that the latter was an adaptation of the former in order to harmonize it with Thomas's poem and to arrange in chronological sequence the allusions of Tristan to the past history of his amour.

VARIOUS EPISODES

Vinaver in his article on the love potion supports Miss Schoepperle's theory that Eilhart and Béroul represent the original tradition which limited the efficacy of the philtre to three or four years, but he suggests that the abatement of its power was merely an illusion in the minds of the lovers. Vinaver also points out, as does M. Marx in his more recent article on the wakening of passion in the lovers, that in Thomas's account they were already enamored of each other before they drank the potion. To Vinaver this seems a deliberate alteration by Thomas of an earlier tradition represented by Eilhart, whereas Marx finds here a vestige of the original version, taken over from a lai.

In another article Marx treats the discovery of the lovers in the forest and notes that according to Béroul King Mark, when convinced by the separating sword of their innocence, leaves his own in its place, substitutes a ring for that which Iseut wears, and places his glove so that it will shield her face from the rays of the sun. Though maintaining that there are analogues for such actions in Irish sagas, Marx believes that they represent a triple claim—investiture by sword, ring, and glove—and that the king thereby asserts symbolically his right to the loyalty of his nephew and his wife.

Ranke in the Schoepperle memorial studies called attention to the fact that the two scenes connected with the ambiguous oath carved on the French ivory casket at Leningrad were immediately preceded by another depicting Tristan and Isolt lying naked in bed together. Eilhart sheds no light on this concatenation since he has nothing to say of the equivocal oath, and neither Béroul II nor Thomas describes an assignation at which the lovers were observed while in bed, and which caused Isolt to resort to the compurgation by oath. Ranke argued from the casket that there must have been such an assignation in the text followed by the carver since otherwise this bedroom scene would have no specific literary basis. Ranke's case would be stronger if there were in the carving any indication of the presence of an observer.

Miss Newstead, taking full account of Miss Schoepperle's findings regarding the chips in the stream and of Krappe's study of the dwarf, has given an excellent analysis of the whole complex of material which went into the Tryst beneath the Tree.

CONCLUSION

In the last ten years various ambitious attempts have been made to account for the rise and development of the tragic romance of Tristan, among them Mergell's *Tristan und Isolde* (Mainz, 1949) and James Carney's *Studies in Irish Literature and History* (Dublin, 1955), pp. 189-242, but their results are highly speculative. Miss Schoepperle's work remains, after more than forty years, the most solid foundation for research in this vast and fascinating field.

Gertrude Schoepperle (essay date 1913)

SOURCE: "Courtly Elements in the *Estoire:* Its Date," in *Tristan and Isolt: A Study of the Sources of the Romance,* Vol. I. Reprint. Burt Franklin, 1960, pp. 112-83.

[*In the following excerpt, Schoepperle examines the treatment of love in the* estoire *(the French source believed by some critics to be the source of extant versions, including the Germanic and English versions), and argues that the appearance of courtly and immoral elements in some portions of the legend indicate that these episodes were composed during the second half of the twelfth century, when the "cult of unlawful love" was in vogue.*]

. . . B. COURTLY ELEMENTS IN THE *ESTOIRE.*

1. INTRODUCTION.

It is not to the *most* primitive traits in the *estoire,* it is to the *least* primitive ones, that we would turn in our endeavor to determine its date. Let us proceed by this method.

The early portion of the poem implies the condemnation of adultery, whereas in the narrative that follows the return from the forest[1] the fundamental conception is courtly and unmoral[2]. It implies the cult of unlawful love characteristic of the latter half of the twelfth century.

If we examine carefully the incidents of the latter part of the *estoire,* we find that several of them present the favorite situations of the conventional courtly lyrics of that period. Others present problems of courtly love in the same manner. Others imply the currency of the notions of cour-

tesy and the conceptions of Arthur and his knights which then first came into vogue. These conventional situations appear in the Tristan story in too developed a form for us to believe that the narrative was composed before they were universally familiar. Their relation to the biography as a whole is too vital for us to look upon them as the interpolations of this or that version. It is impossible to imagine that it is to the Tristan poet we owe their introduction into French literature. The appearance of these traits in the *estoire* can be accounted for in only one way: the series of incidents from the return from the forest to the death of Tristan must have been composed under the influence of the courtly literature which came into vogue during the time of Eleanor.

2. KAHERDIN AND CAMILLE: THE PASTOURELLE.

In order to measure justly the significance of the traits which seem to associate the *estoire* with the movement of which the lyric types of which we have spoken are a part, it will be necessary to analyze in some detail the incidents in which *motifs* familiar in the lyrics occur.

On his first return to Cornwall from Brittany, Tristan is accompanied by his wife's brother Kaherdin. While Tristan is with Isolt, his companion courts her maid Camille[3].

It is usual in the romances and the *chansons de geste* for the lady to offer her maid to the companion of her lover. In the numerous examples we have found of this occurrence, the maid submits with all docility[4]. In Tristan, Camille resists. The passage that follows is strikingly similar to the type of courtly lyric known as the *pastourelle.* These *pastourelles,* of which we have numerous examples from the latter part of the twelfth and the thirteenth centuries, relate the following incident[5]:

A knight, wandering musing through the fields at sunrise, meets a pretty young shepherdess weaving a garland of flowers. He descends from his horse and, without much ceremony, demands her favor.

He is usually successful, by dint of persuasion or force, in gaining his desire. In some cases the shepherdess pretends to yield to his importunities, but, when he thinks he has only to enjoy his success, she escapes him by some ruse, and, slipping from his hands, taunts him with his defeat.

Kaherdin addresses Camille as the gallant of the *pastourelle* addresses the shepherdess. With a person of her station he is confident of his success and loses no time in coming to the point[6]:

> 'do begunde der hêre Kehenîs
> zu Gymêlen minne sûchen,
> do enwolde sie es nicht rûchen.
> îdoch en lîz her des nît,
> ez wêre ir leit adir lîp,
> vaste he ir ane lach.'

Camille is shocked at his precipitation. She reminds him that she is not a peasant girl that he should ask her to yield to so short a siege[7]:

'wâ tût ir hen ûwirn sin?
jâ sêt ir wol daz ich nicht bin
eine gebûrinne
daz ir mich bittet umme minne
in sô gar korzir zît:
ich wêne ir ein gebûr sît.
wie mochte ez anders geschîn?'

She declares that if Kaherdin had been five years in her service, obedient to all her commands, he would not yet have received this favor[8]:

'hêtet ir ouch vunf jâr
zu allem mîme bote stân,
dennoch wêrez ungetân
des ir gewûgit wedir mich'.

Kaherdin is thus informed that Camille is no *pastoure*. She is to be wooed as a lady is to be wooed, with patience and prayers, with subtleties and reserves, and won by slow and painful steps that are recognized stages of initiation.

Camille, like the shepherdess, escapes Kaherdin by a ruse[9] and in her raillery of him the next morning, there is the light mischievous note characteristic of the *pastourelle*[10].

'"wiste ich nechtin daz ir sô
togentlîchen kundet legin,
ich hête ûch nicht vorzegin
so getâner dinge:
daz ir mich bâtet umme minne,
ich hête es ûch wol irloubit.
des was vorleide nâ irtoubit"
Kehenis dâ ûf der stete.
swer sîne ôren ersnete,
kein blûttropfe wêre komen ûz.
he wêre gerne ze hûs!'

As the *pastourelle* expresses it[11]:

'Et il demeure com musart.
l'ame de lui soit la honie
quant la bele li eschapa.'

3. KAHERDIN AND GARGEOLAIN: THE MAL MARIÉE.

Kaherdin's *amour* with Gargeolain, in spite of its tragic ending, is dealt with in the same light tone as the adventure with Camille.

The elements of the situation are conventional in the *chanson de mal mariée*: the lady has promised, before her marriage, to give herself to her young lover. The husband hears this promise and swears to prevent its fulfilment. He locks up his wife and keeps guard over her day and night. The lady laments her fate; she holds an interview from the parapet with her lover below, and succeeds, in spite of her husband, in fixing a rendezvous. The poet reflects on the wickedness and folly of the husband[12].

In Tristan, Bedenis, the husband of Gargeolain, is a noble lord distinguished in knightly exercises and especially devoted to hunting[13]:

'ein schônez wîp her habete,
die was Garîôle genant.
der hûte der wîgant
sô freislîchen sêre,
daz her sîn selbes êre
dâ mete hâte gekrenkit.'

Bedenis' anxiety is, however, not surprising[14]: his wife, like the lady of the lyric, had promised that before she would accept her husband she would grant Kaherdin her love if he would come to her. Bedenis had overheard this and had at once built three moats and three walls around his castle. Keeping these locked and the keys always in his own hands, he saw to it that no one had access to his wife. One day when the husband is hunting, the lover rides under the battlements and gets speech with his lady. They curse the *jalous* who keeps them from each other. Kaherdin reminds her of what she had promised to grant him before she would take her husband. She declares that she is still ready to give him her favor; she has always loved him; she would gladly have granted him his wish before, and she is of the same mind still, if he can devise a way to approach her. In spite of the difficulties, Kaherdin finds a way.

The ladies in the *chansons de mal mariée* are in a similar situation. We quote but one example[15]:

'En un vergier lez une fontenele,
dont clere est l'onde et blanche la gravele,
siet fille a roi, sa main a sa maxele:
en sospirant son douz ami rapele.
    "ae cuens Guis amis!
    la vostre amors me tout solaz et ris.

Cuens Guis amis, com male destinee!
mes pere m'a a un viellart donee,
qui en cest mes m'a mise et enserree:
n'en puis eissir a soir n'a matinee."
    ae cuens Guis amis!
    la vostre amors me tout solaz et ris.

Li mals mariz en oi la deplainte,
entre el vergier, sa corroie a desceinte:
tant la bati q'ele en fu perse et tainte.
entre ses piez por pou ne l'a estainte.
    ae cuens Guis amis!
    la vostre amors me tout solaz et ris.'

There is no attempt to regard the relation of Kaherdin and Gargeolain from a moral point of view. The poet considers the jealous husband justly served when his wife betrays him and he comments thus on attempting to constrain women to faithfulness by force[16]:

'mich wundert, wes he denkit
der sînes wîbes hûtet,
wen stât ir ir gemûte
nicht williglîchen dar,
sô mag he nimmer sie bewarn
mit allen sînen sinnen.
wen, wil sie einen minnen,
sie tût ez âne sînen dang,
es were korz adir lang.'

The poet's criticism in the *chanson de mal mariée* is invariably the same[17]:

> 'dame qui a mal mari
> s'el fet ami
> n'en fet pas a blasmer.'

The lady's attitude is unambiguous[18]:

> 'li jalous
> envious
> de cor rous
> morra,
> et li dous
> savourous
> amourous
> m'avra.'

The situation not infrequently becomes part of the courtly narrative poems from the middle of the twelfth century. In Marie de France's *Guigemar,* for example, there is a lady similar to Gargeolain[19]:

> 'Li sire, ki la mainteneit
> mult fu vielz huem et femme aveit,
> une dame de halt parage,
> franche, curteise, bele e sage.
> Gelus esteit a desmesure.'

The thirteenth century Provençal romance *Flamenca* sustains throughout more than eight thousand lines the mood of moral *insouciance* which we find in the lyric. Here the husband, like Bedenis, is represented as a handsome and amiable young knight, who after his marriage becomes the most intolerable *jalous*. He immures his wife in the castle, allows no one to go out or to come in, and carries the keys himself. Like Gargeolain, his wife betrays him without compunction[20].

It would be difficult to deny that in these adventures of Kaherdin, the Tristan poet may have appropriated his theme from popular poetry. If we affirm that he did not, however, we are forced to suppose that he introduced for the first time into the range of courtly literature, the themes of the *pastourelle* and the *mal mariée*. It is easier to suppose that the incidents in Tristan, with their conventional features and moral irresponsibility, are part of the same literary movement as the *pastourelles* and *chansons de mal mariée* of the latter part of the twelfth and thirteenth centuries. We are personally inclined to interpret them as due to the influence of an already developed courtly lyric.

4. ISOLT'S REPENTANCE: THE CHANSON A PERSONNAGES.

There is a third incident in the *estoire* that corresponds to a conventional type of thirteenth century lyric.

It is the account of Isolt's repentance for her cruelty to Tristan. Breri has told her that Tristan failed to turn his horse, although adjured in her name to do so. Tristan's denial of the charge has fallen on deaf ears. Isolt persists in believing the accusation. Her lover makes a desperate ef-

fort to regain her favor, seeking to approach her disguised as a leper, but she orders him driven away with blows, and laughs at his humiliation. Some months afterward she is stricken with remorse for this sin against her lover. As a penance she puts on a hair shirt and wears it next her skin night and day. She vows that she will not put it off until Tristan comes to her[21]:

> 'ich enkunne nicht genesin,
> he wil mir denne gnêdig wesin;
> ich bin sicherlîchen tôd,
> he en helfe mir schîre ûz der nôd.'

She sends a messenger to Tristan, imploring him to forgive her and come to her[22].

> 'daz wil sie nû immermêre
> bûzen, swie dû gebûtest:
> daz meiste teil der lûte
> brichet unde bûzzet echt,
> wen gnade ist bezzir denne recht.
> sie sûchit dîne genâde,
> ire trûwe saltû entphâhen
> swaz sie dir hât zu leide getân,
> des wil sie dir zu bûzze stân
> nâch gnâdin und nach rechte,
> sie enmag dir nicht vechtin,
> sie enwil sîn nicht geruchen:
> sie wil genâde sûchen,
> wen daz recht ist ir zu swâr.
> ab sie dir daz entbîten tar,
> sie entbûtet dir iren dinist
> und allez daz dir lîp ist,
> daz sie daz alles gerne tû
> und entbûtit dir dar zû,
> daz sie dir zu êrin
> treget ein hemede hêrîn
> allir nêhist irem lîbe.
> wiltu sie nû lenger mîden,
> sô wert ir nimmir leides bûz.
> hêre, ich sûche dînen fûz
> daz du schîre kumest dâr sî sî:
> sô wirt sie allir sorgin vrî.'

In the *chanson à personnages* the lady has discouraged the lover by her severity and he has at last left her to seek a new love[23]. She loves him now, and in her turn learns the anguish of unrequited affection. She implores him to forgive the wrong she has done him. She repents her cruelty. She is dying for love of him. She reminds him that the path to heaven is the forgiveness of injuries. She encourages herself by the reflection that a drop of water will finally wear away a stone.

The characteristic note is given in this refrain:

> 'Qu'en dirai?
>   Forssenée
> fui, plus que desvée
> quant le refusai.
>   G'en ferai
> droit a son plesir
> s'il m'en daigne oïr. . . .
> Chançon, va sanz delaier

à celui qui tant m'agrée:
por Deu li pri et requier
viengne a moi sanz demorée:
en sa merci me metrai,
tost avrai
pès trovée
se il li agrée,
que je trop mal trai.
  g'en ferai
[droit a son plesir,
s'il m'en daigne oïr.]'

The man covers her with reproaches and recommends her to seek another lover. In one version he is finally touched by her tenacity.

We have a narrative fragment representing a similar theme in the biography of the troubadour Guillem de Balaun[24].

Here it is the lover who, for a whim, is angry with his lady. She humiliates herself before him, coming to his inn to seek his pardon, and is driven away, as Tristan is driven away by Isolt, with blows. Later the knight repents of his cruelty and begs her forgiveness through an intermediary. He declares himself willing to perform any penance to prove his sincerity. Where Isolt puts on a hair shirt, this penitent cuts off his finger nail. The two lovers are at last reconciled and love each other thereafter the more. It is possible that this, like many passages in the troubadour biographies, is founded on lost lyrics of the poet in question.

The courtly poets of the twelfth and thirteenth centuries seem to have been interested in the question of how far the lover should suffer humiliation for love's sake. In Crestien's *Charrette*[25], Guinevere withdraws her favor from Lancelot because she has heard that he hesitated an instant to mount the ignominious cart which offered him a possible means to serve her. Lancelot does not know how he has offended, but he accepts his punishment with entire submission. It is enough for him that it is his lady who lays it upon him. She continues to put his unquestioning devotion to the test. According to her command he is by turns ignominiously cowardly and surpassingly courageous. She rewards him when she has at last tested him to her satisfaction. At no point do we find either the lover or the poet permitting himself to question or criticize her conduct.

In the *estoire,* as we have seen, Tristan is represented as less submissive. Isolt's cruelty is not accepted by him without question. When she seeks his forgiveness, confessing her wrong and imploring mercy in all humility, he sternly refuses her. It is only after long supplication that he is moved[26].

In several late romances we find the poet thus taking revenge for his sex[27]. In one, the *Chevalier au Perroquet,* the hero has submitted to his lady's command to bear himself with cowardice at the tourney, but when she summons him that night to reward him, he covers her with insults and reproaches. He even goes so far as to beat her and drag her by the hair.

5. FOR ISOLT'S SAKE.

Not without significance for the date of the *estoire* are the numerous instances in the latter part of the romance in which the poet uses the phrases *dorch Isalden willen* and *dorch Tristrandes willen.*

Gawain adjures Tristan *for Isolt's sake* to confess if it was he who overthrew *Delakors schevalier (chevalier de la cour?).* Tristan acknowledges the exploit. He declares that if he were to die for it, he would never refuse a request made in these terms[28].

'geselle, ich habez jâ getân:
swes man mich vrâgin î began
dorch willen mîner vrauwin,
daz lâze ich offinbêrlîch schauwin.
ich hele des dorch keine nôt
solde ich dar umme ligen tôt.'

Gawain responds that it is an honor to her that he has done this for her sake[29].

'gnâde mûze sie des hân,
mîne vrauwe die koninginne,
daz dû dorch ire minne
mir dese ding hâst vorjên.'

Tristan boasts to Kaherdin that *for his sake,* Isolt the Queen shows more favor to his dog than Isolt of Brittany shows to him[30].

'jâ helt eine vrauwe baz
ein hundelîn dorch mînen willen
obir lût und stille
den mich ûwir swestir hât getân.'

Kaherdin sees the dog borne in state in the queen's train. Tristan explains that it is for his sake[31].

'den vûret die koningîn
alsus dorch mînen willin.'

When Isolt gives her maid to Kaherdin the night that he comes with Tristan to the Blanche Lande, she says that it is for Tristan's sake[32].

'ich wil ûch zu nacht lîen
eine behegelîche amîen
dorch Tristrandes willen.'

When Breri sees the squires in the distance he calls to them, thinking one of them is Tristan, to turn for the sake of Isolt[33].

'Dô bat her in umme kêrin
dorch der koninginne êre,
ab sie im wêre lîp.'

Isolt is very angry when she hears that Tristan has failed to comply with a request made in these terms[34]:

'''zu lest manete ich in dô
daz he dorch ûch wolde kêren.'. . .
dô môgete die vrauwe [gar] sêre

daz he nicht wolde wedir kêrin
dorch iren willen[35]. . . .
enbôt sie dem helde sân,
her hête gar obele getân
daz he nicht umme kârte
dô Pleherîn rîf sô harte.
und in dorch mich kêren bat[36].'

Tristan protests his innocence and reiterates his principle[37]:

'swer mich des dorch sie bête,
und ab her tûsent ritter hête,
ich kêrte im undir die ougen.'

When Perenis returns to tell him that Isolt is still convinced of his guilt, he repeats that he never has refused and never will refuse a request made in her name[38].

'des sî sie sicher und gewis,
daz ich des nî nicht gelîz,
swes man mich bat adir hîz
dorch mîner vrauwin willen tûn.
ez wêre ouch nû ze vrû,
ab ich des nû nicht entête,
swes man mich dorch sie bête.'

When Isolt repents her cruelty, she puts on a hair shirt next her skin as penance for his sake[39].

'daz tûn ich dorch den willen sîn'.

Her messenger conjures Tristan to return to her for her sake[40].

'hêre, dû salt dar komen
dorch mîner vrauwin lîbe . . .
und dorch die grôze arebeit
die mîn vrauwe nâch dir hât.'

Tristan has been insensible to every other plea, he cannot resist this. He bids the messenger tell his lady for his sake to take off the hair shirt[41].

'und sage der werdin vrauwen dîn
daz sie dorch den willen mîn
daz hêrîn hemede ûz tû.'

When Tristan, returning to Cornwall in his pilgrim disguise, is recognized by a friend, and begged to take part in the court games, he refuses. His friend knows a way, however, to gain his consent. He asks him to do it for the queen's sake[42].

'ich wil dich es betin alsô hô
daz du ez âne zwîvel tûn mûst:
ich bete dich daz dû es tûst
dorch der koninginne willen.'

When Tristan sends the messenger to beg Isolt to come to Brittany to heal him, he tells him to remind her of all Tristan has done for her sake. At sight of the ring which he sends as a token, Isolt for Tristan's sake leaves all to follow his messenger[43].

'sie lîz dorch den willen sîn
ir koninglîche êre
und entrachtete ir nicht mêre[44].'

The poet takes for granted among his audience a complete familiarity with the notion that the appeal in the name of his lady is all powerful to influence the lover[45]. This idea has an important influence on the narrative. The presence of it in the *estoire* is attested not only by the German poem, but by Thomas and the *Folie*[46].

6. THE ARTHURIAN KNIGHTS.

The treatment of Arthur and his knights[47] in the *estoire* implies an audience already acquainted with Kay and Gawain in the stereotyped rôles in which we find them in French Arthurian romance. Gawain is the mirror of courtesy, the faithful friend, the most distinguished of Arthur's knights. His prowess is familiar to the hearers, and his affection is the highest tribute that can be given a hero. The humorous treatment of Kay is a similar indication that this figure also had become conventional.

It is hardly possible that in an episode of such secondary importance, so loosely related to the main story, the Tristan poet should have created two of the most striking figures in Arthurian romance. We must suppose these figures already familiar to the audience through Geoffrey of Monmouth's *Historia* and French romances inspired by it[48].
. . .

Notes

1. cf. Bédier II, 265-306.

2. In the story of Brangien's fatal carelessness, of Tristan's broken faith to Mark, of the lovers' hopeless struggle against themselves, the long agony of desire, their reckless hazards, their hair breadth successes and their shameful defeats—in these there is something of the high seriousness of tragedy. Their appeal is to one age as to another. Kaherdin's *amours*, on the other hand, are the creation of the season. They are in the tone of *badinage* characteristic of the *pastourelles* and *chansons de mal mariée*. Produced under the same influences are the incidents in which Tristan is adjured *dorch Isalden willen*.

3. *OX* 6255-6805.

4. cf. infra, Ch. V.

5. K. Bartsch, *Romances et pastourelles françaises,* Leipzig 1870, Bks. II and III.—For studies of the *pastourelle* see A. Jeanroy, *Les origines de la póesie lyrique en France,* Paris 1904, p. 1-43; G. Paris, *Journal des Savants* 1891-2, p. 674-88, 729-42, 155-67, 407-29.

6. *OX* 6672-8.

7. *OX* 6679-86.

8. *OX* 6690-94.

9. Isolt commands Camille to yield to Kaherdin, but gives her a magic pillow. The moment this is put un-

der his head he falls asleep, and does not awaken until she withdraws it the next morning. cf. Ch. II R; Ch. V, infra.

10. *OX* 6794-6805.

11. Bartsch, *op. cit.,* p. 194, No. 68.

12. cf. Jeanroy, *op. cit.* p. 84-102, *La chanson dramatique;* cf. Bartsch, *op. cit.* p. 13, No. 9; p. 30, No. 35; p. 35, No. 38; p. 41, No. 41; p. 48, No. 47; p. 50, No. 49; p. 52, No. 51; p. 57, No. 56 etc.

13. *OX* 7872-8; cf. chapter II, U X.

14. *OX* 7865-8135; 9033-9190.

15. Bartsch, *op. cit.* p. 13, No. 9.

16. *OX* 7878-87.

17. Bartsch p. 51, No. 49; p. 81, No. 64.

18. Bartsch p. 52, No. 51.

19. *Die Lais der Marie de France,* ed. K. Warnke, Halle 1900, No. 1, *Guigemar,* ll. 209-17.

20. P. Meyer, *Le Roman de Flamenca*², Paris 1901.

21. *OX* 7181-4.

22. *OX* 7252-79.

23. Jeanroy p. 97-9; citation, *op. cit.,* 499-501.

24. Raynouard, *Choix des poésies originales des Troubadours,* Paris 1820, V, 180 ff.

25. ed. Foerster, *Der Karrenritter* (Halle 1899), 3955 ff.

26. cf. Bédier II, 270 ff. and bibliography.

27. *Hist. Litt.* XXX, 107.

28. *OX* 5123-9.

29. *OX* 5130-4.

30. *OX* 6244-8.

31. *OX* 6506-8.

32. *OX* 6711-4.

33. *OX* 6841-4.

34. *OX* 6862-4.

35. *OX* 6885-8.

36. *OX* 6889-94.

37. *OX* 6903-6.

38. *OX* 6950-7.

39. *OX* 7170.

40. *OX* 7292-8.

41. *OX* 7363-6.

42. *OX* 7788-91.

43. *OX* 9265-84.

44. *OX* 9338-41. Cf. also 8830-2, 8835, 8910-2.

45. cf. Bédier I, 342.

46. Bédier II, 276-80; Schoepperle, *Rom.* XL, 86-8. *Sur un vers de la Folie Tristan de Berne (Je ai sailli et lanciez jons,* l. 184).

47. *OX* 5016-5462.

48. cf. Golther, *op. cit.* 1907, p. 73. . . .

Henry Goddard Leach (essay date 1921)

SOURCE: "Tristan in the North," in *Angevin Britain and Scandinavia.* Reprint. Kraus Reprint Co., 1975, pp. 169-98.

[*In the following essay, Leach examines the characteristics of the Scandinavian version of the Tristan legend, which was derived from Thomas's Anglo-Norman version of the late twelfth century.*]

> Ðeim var ekki skapað
> Nema að skilja.
>
> *Tristrams Kvæði*

In the north-west part of Iceland there is a fjord which until modern times bore the name of Trostansfjord. It lies in a district where many names of Celtic origin have survived since the time when they were first bestowed in the ninth century by Celto-Scandinavian colonists from Ireland and the islands north and west of the Scottish coast. Now in the lists of the Pictish kings of the sixth to the eighth century the name Drostan appears frequently. It is, therefore, by no means unlikely that the name of an heroic Drostan was floated across the waves to Iceland a thousand years ago, and remained there through the centuries to preserve the fame of the obscure Pictish king, who, like the equally obscure Arthur and Roland, was destined to become an immortal hero of romance.

How do we know that Drostan the Pict was he whom we have come to know as Tristan of Lyonesse?[1] In the royal Pictish line the name Drostan usually occurs after that of Talorc, and this lends a strong probability to the supposition that these Drostans were sons of Talorcs. Curiously enough, when Tristan appears in the Welsh triads he is called Drystan the son of Tallwch, and most scholars have accepted his identity with one of these kings of the Picts.

Tristan's appearance in Welsh literature is slight and not altogether dignified, but he seems to have attained early renown there as a lover and as a master of tricks and ruses. In the triads he is mentioned as one of the three diadem-bearers of the Isle of Britain; as one of the three peers of Arthur's court; as one of the three masters of machines; as one of the three lovers—the lover of "Essylt, wife of March"; and finally as one of the three great swineherds of the Isle of Britain. His distinction as a swineherd seems to have consisted in his ability to circumvent the wiles and force of certain illustrious cattle-raiders, for this is the story that is told of him:—"Drystan, son of Tallwch, tended the swine of Marc, son of Meirchyon, while the swineherd went with a message to Essylt. Arthur, March, Kei, and Bedwyr came all four, but they were not able to take a single sow, neither by craft nor by force nor by theft." This character as a great lover and as master of primitive strategy Tristan maintained throughout mediæval literature.

The Tristan legend was by no means the sole possession of the Welsh; it belonged to the whole Celtic fringe. While Marie de France and the continuator of Béroul assign his birthplace to South Wales, another twelfth-century poet, Thomas, speaks of South Brittany as his home and of a castle Kanoel, probably at the mouth of the Loire. Furthermore, when the story of Tristan's combat with a monster from over the seas and of his wound which could not be healed except by a kinsman of the monster, came to be rationalized, the monster became the brother-in-law of the king of Ireland, and the monster's mysterious home, only to be reached by abandoning oneself to the seas, became the well-known port of Dublin. But it is chiefly with Cornwall that Tristan is forever associated. Not only was there a tradition in the eighth century of a King Mark of Cornwall, not only do the names of Tristan and Isolt cling forever to

> The wind-hollowed heights and gusty bays
> Of sheer Tintagel, fair with famous days;

but also it has been shown that a few other places mentioned in Béroul's version can be identified with places in Cornwall. Lancien, the Mal Pas, the Blanche Lande can be pointed out with some show of probability today, and popular tradition still finds Lyonesse in the sunken country which lies under the ocean between Land's End and the Scilly Isles.

Though the story of Tristan was not introduced into Ireland, for no allusion is made to it in mediæval Irish literature, yet since the ancient literature of Wales and Scotland preserved to us is scanty, and we have nothing native from Cornwall or Brittany, we must look to the Irish sagas for parallels to the legend of Tristan. Several incidents—such as the rudderless boat, the voyage for healing, the splashing water, the signal chips in the stream, and the carved branch or twig on the highway—are typical features found in Irish tales. Irish, too, is the theme of elopement and forest life, for not only do we find it in the elopement of Diarmaid with Grainne, and of the Sons of Usnach with Deirdre, but it constitutes a whole category of Irish romance. Moreover, Diarmaid and Grainne are driven into each other's arms by fate, the one by the influence of a love-spot, the other through a *geis* or taboo. So the love-potion, which may have been substituted by an English or French poet for a less familiar Celtic charm, is the compelling force in the tragedy of Tristan and Isolt.

When this somewhat barbaric but picturesque and powerful tale was told by Welsh and Breton minstrels at the courts of England and Normandy, which were permeated by the middle of the twelfth century by the pagan idealism

and the fantastic code of love evolved in Provence, the English and Norman romancers saw that here was a supreme opportunity. It was one of them doubtless who composed, in accordance with this amatory creed, a French poem, called the *estoire,* removing from the hero's career any casual amours that may have been associated with it, in order to make Tristan the lover of Isolt and Isolt alone, and introducing Isolt of Brittany in order to show that even the marriage bond and the desire of the flesh could not break his faith to Isolt of Ireland.

From the stock of the *estoire* the romance of Tristan forks into two main branches. One flourished mainly in France and Italy, and includes the version of Béroul, (a Norman poem written about 1165 and continued later), and that of Eilhart von Oberg (1185-1189). The other was dominant in England, Germany, and Scandinavia. It derives from the *Tristan* of Thomas, an Anglo-Norman, who probably was attached to the court of Henry II and wrote about 1175. Of his poem 3,144 lines survive from the latter part, representing only about a sixth of the whole. But his work attained such celebrity that we are able to reconstruct the rest from three mediæval redactions: the English *Sir Tristrem,* a poor jingling thing, written about 1300; the magnificent German romance of Gottfried von Strassburg, dating from the early thirteenth century; and the fairly close translation in Norwegian prose, made by Brother Robert in 1226.[2]

Before going on to a discussion of Robert's version we shall do well to review the story as he tells it.

> Tristram, nephew of Mark, king of England, spent his youth in Brittany. Coming to Mark's court at Tintagel in Cornwall, he won his uncle's affection by his prowess and his harping. At this time there sailed to Tintagel a mighty warrior named Morhold, who demanded an annual tribute for the king of Ireland. Tristram slew Morhold in single combat on an island, receiving a poisoned wound, from which he suffered without relief. Setting out to sea in search of cure, he was driven by wind and wave to Ireland, where he gave an assumed name, and was healed by Morhold's sister, the queen. To her beautiful daughter, Isond, he gave instruction in writing and harping.
>
> After his return to England, Tristram's enemies urged upon King Mark to take to wife the Princess Isond of Ireland, and to send Tristram on the perilous quest. So he went the second time in a new disguise and freed the land of a fire-breathing dragon. While Isond was healing his wounds, she discovered his identity and wished at first to avenge Morhold. On second thought she spared him, and won her father's approval of Tristram's suit on behalf of King Mark.
>
> On the voyage to England, by a fatal mistake, Tristram and Isond drank together the love-potion intended for King Mark. During the bridal night, Bringvet, the maid, took Isond's place beside the king. Tristram and Isond, under the compelling influence of the potion, continued to satisfy their love in secret. At last the lovers were betrayed to King Mark, who, however, doubted the evidence of his eyes, and exacted from Isond a test of

chastity. Before the assembled court she swore an ambiguous oath and bore without injury the red-hot iron. Notwithstanding, Tristram forsook England for a time, sending back to the queen a fairy dog to console her. He returned again, and now Mark, although convinced of the lovers' guilt, compassionately allowed them to leave the court and live in the woods together. Here he discovered them sleeping in a grotto, a naked sword between them, and, once more persuaded of their innocence, he invited them back to court. But not for long; again detected, Tristram fled to the Continent.

Here he married, against his will, Isodd, daughter of the Duke of Brittany, whose name reminded him of Isond the queen, but, faithful to Isond his love, he did not consummate his marriage. At this her brother Kardin took umbrage, until he went with Tristram in disguise to England, and there saw the beauty of Isond and fell in love with her attendant. Soon the two knights were obliged to flee back to Brittany, and here Tristram was injured in war by a poisoned sword and lay at the point of death. Tristram knew that only Isond in England could heal his wound. Secretly he sent Kardin across the sea with a ring as token. His envoy succeeded, and Isond accompanied Kardin back. Long they were delayed by storm and becalmed outside the harbor. Kardin had agreed with Tristram that if he were successful, his sails would be white and blue, but if Isond did not come, he would hoist black sails. Now the sails were glistening blue and white.

Isodd, Tristram's wife, came to him. "Dearest," she said, "Kardin is come; I see his ship."

Tristram asked her about the sails. But she had overheard the agreement and told Tristram that the sails were black. Tristram groaned; "three times he called Isond's name and the fourth time he gave up his spirit."

Isond, arriving too late, died with her arms about his neck. "And it is said that Tristram's wife buried Tristram and Isond on opposite sides of the church, so that they should be separated even in death. But it came to pass that an oak grew out of the grave of each, so high that the branches intertwined above the church, showing how great a love had been between them."

It is to the source of the Norse translation, to the poem of Thomas the Englishman, that we chiefly owe the psychological refinement and the profound passion that have made the tale of Tristan and Isolt immortal. What was tragic Thomas heightened, what was brutal he refined, and he produced a poem of chivalry and courtesy worthy to be read before Eleanor of Aquitaine or her troubadour son, Richard the Lion Heart. He was little concerned with mere adventure and intrigue, but he cared much for description of courtly life and subtle analysis of emotion. Thomas is almost as delicately and profusely analytical of sentiment as Richardson seven centuries later. Yet for all his preciosity, this twelfth century poet is fresh and ardent. Though like Crestien de Troyes and other French poets, Thomas was influenced by the conventions of courtly love, his native genius burns and glows through the bars of formalism.

M. Bédier in his admirable critique of Brother Robert's translation, says, "That which he most willingly suppressed of his original is the poetry." This is true if we understand by poetry only those pages of sentimental analysis so characteristic of Thomas. A comparison of surviving passages from Thomas with the Norwegian text shows that when Robert does translate he is so faithful that if both were rendered into English, they would be nearly identical. Robert adds very little of his own, the exceptions being the list of Norwegian exports quoted in a previous chapter, a short prayer put into the mouth of the dying Isond, and the little romantic touch at the end about the oaks entwining their branches over the lovers' graves. The omissions, however, are considerable, and reduce the saga by about a half. One passage of reflection and introspection totaling 143 lines is matched in Robert by a blank. Tristan's revulsion of feeling upon his wedding night, when he catches a glimpse of Isolt's ring, and his long mental conflict is condensed to this:—"This night I must sleep here as beside my wedded wife: I cannot separate from her now, because I have married her in the hearing of many witnesses, and I am not able to live with her as a husband, unless I break my troth and abase my honor. However, let come what will." It sounds like a school edition of *Clarissa Harlowe*.

Has Robert lost or gained by his ruthless pruning? It is by no means easy to pass judgment. We have lost many a long passage of dissected passion, and a laboring of the problems of the triangle in its many phases. Though of intense interest to the student of mediæval manners and psychology, these retards are somewhat too technical and prolonged to be of universal and permanent value. They do not possess the magic simplicity with which the sagas treat the emotions and which renders them eternal. On the other hand, Brother Robert has performed too drastic an operation. No one who reads his summary account of the drinking of the potion can help feeling that he has cut away not only the excrescence but also the living flesh of the romance. Though Robert runs no risk of boring the reader, he has fallen into the equal peril of playing only upon the superficial interest of action.

Who was this saga-man, this Robert, who first planted the rose of romance in the stony garden of the North? Of rigid facts we have no more about him than about his contemporary who translated the same poem into German, Gottfried von Strassburg. We know only that Friar Robert came to be promoted to the dignity of abbot, and afterwards translated for King Hákon another romance, the *Elie de Saint-Gilles*. *Elis Saga* states simply that "Abbot Robert translated, and King Hákon son of King Hákon bade him translate this Norse book." The work is undated.

It will be observed that neither in *Elis Saga* nor in *Tristram* does Robert make mention of his foreign source. Apparently he takes no pride in being able to understand the *valskumál*; the *Norræn* rendering is the achievement. This brings up the question: Was Robert a Norwegian at all? Was he not rather one of those numerous English clerics who crossed the seas to enter monasteries in the North?

The style of his two sagas does not betray the secret—they could have been composed either by a native Norwegian or a foreigner well versed in his adopted language. His name, however, is an important argument for English nationality. It is not Norwegian but Anglo-Norman. In its present form the name is a French adaptation of the German Hrodebert—"illustrious in council," or "illustrious in glory." It occurs in Anglo-Saxon records of the eleventh century, before the Conquest, but in nearly every instance the bearer is definitely known to be a Norman. After the Conquest the name was widespread in England, and not least among the clergy: Fountains Abbey had three abbots named Robert, before 1400. In 1200, as we have seen, Robert son of Sunnolf was taking a cargo to Norway. In Norway, however, the name Robert is not recorded before the time of the two translations containing that signature, and it does not occur again until the fourteenth century, when it appears several times in Norwegian diplomas, in most cases late in the century and borne by clerics. Significant for Robert's English origin is the fact that *Tristram* and *Eli* spell the translator's name in the foreign French form popularized by the Normans in England.

A man with a Norman name, a literary clerk, a friend of King Hákon, an abbot: where then was his abbey? The foundation whose members were in closest contact with the Norwegian court, and were likewise most frequently employed for English diplomatic service, was the abbey of Lysa, a day's journey south of the royal residence in Bergen. Clerks of Lysa served as ambassadors to England in 1217, 1218, 1221, 1229, and again as late as 1280. Lysa, like Hovedö, was an English foundation and continued, as we have seen, close to the mother country. From the decade before *Tristram* was translated, the printed English Rolls supply no less than nine writs concerning ships or monks from Lysa. As for the abbots of Lysa, the first abbot in the second half of the twelfth century was certainly an Englishman, and a later abbot, Richard, about 1265, appears also to have been of that nation, if we may judge from his continued intimacy with Henry III. About 1246 the sister institution of Hovedö had an English abbot, Lawrence. Now the records of Lysa supply us with no abbot from 1194 to 1265. Robert would fill admirably part of the gap.

Robert wrote his *Tristram* at the time when communication between Norway and England—clerical, diplomatic, commercial—had reached highwater mark. What an amazing array of voyages during the twelve months of 1225, the year before the *Tristram* was completed! In that summer the king's uncle, Duke Skúli, sent his ship over to Lynn on trade. Hákon himself presented a brace of hawks to Henry III, while the latter reciprocated with a welcome present of grain to Hákon, sent through the archdeacon of Bergen. On August 30, King Henry notified his bailiffs at Lynn, that, despite all previous ordinances, he had given Hákon's subjects permission to take eight thousand bushels of corn out of the country, and bade them not hinder the Norwegians when they came to Lynn to buy goods. Not content with this, Henry—or the guardians of the young king—wrote again, on the following day, to the officials of Lynn to receive in a friendly way the men and merchants of Norway, this protection to last three years.

Askeld, archdeacon of Bergen, and Friar William of Lysa were in England this summer, also John Steel, a leading Norwegian noble and a friend of the king, went to England on business, with a shipload of goods, and proceeded for a vigil to the shrine of Becket. In England he met Peter of Housesteads, the newly elected archbishop of Nidaros, on his way back from the pope. Steel left the prelate in England and sailed for Norway late in the summer. At sea he met King Hákon himself and heartened him with the news of Peter's elevation. This evidence of one year's activities is very striking when we consider that it is gathered from the scattered and imperfect records that have been preserved through seven centuries.

No wonder that at a time of such intimacy between the two countries, Anglo-Norman romances were being translated into Norse. What was happening meanwhile in the internal affairs of Norway? Does history throw any direct light upon the circumstances under which *Tristrams Saga* was written? In 1225, the young king was twenty-one years old and his life was a rich composite of romance and adventure. In the early months of that year he was fighting in Sweden. After Easter he sailed north to Bergen for his wedding with his cousin, the Lady Margaret, Skúli's daughter. According to Sturla, "the liegemen and the best yeomen all over the Gula-thing were bidden. *There came, too, many learned clerks.* The bridal was set for Trinity Sunday, and lasted five nights, with an honorable feast, as was intended. The king treated all the men in the Yule-hall; but the queen was up in the summer-hall, and the women with her; *but the cloister-men were all by themselves in one room, and five abbots were over that company.*" So the monks were merry at Hákon's festival. Was it not natural that to celebrate his wedding the young king should have commissioned Brother Robert to translate an Anglo-Norman love-story?

But which? The answer was almost inevitable. The royal house of Anjou seem to have had a special predilection for the romance of Tristan. Thomas himself probably wrote for the favor of Henry II and Eleanor. Eleanor's daughters, Marie de Champagne and Mathilda of Saxony, both were the patrons of poets who wrote of Tristan. King John numbered among his regalia "Tristram's sword," and there is reason to believe that a magnificent tile pavement formerly laid down at Chertsey Abbey, depicting scenes from Thomas' poem, was commissioned by Henry III in his last years. Hákon, who took the Angevin court for his model, must have known the romance well. There could be no more logical consequence of all the circumstances than that the *Tristan* of Thomas should have been translated into Norse in 1226.

The history of the Tristan legend in the Scandinavian North does not end with Robert's Norwegian version. Like most Northern romances, *Tristrams Saga* is preserved to us in Icelandic copies only, and one can never be sure how much the Icelandic scribes may have tampered with the text. From Iceland also we have quite another *Tristrams Saga,*[3] preserved in a fifteenth-century parchment somewhat older, as it happens, than the earliest existing copies of Robert's romance. That this later saga rests upon an imperfect memory of Robert's *Tristram,* not upon an independent version of the story, is proved by the fact that, while there are many alterations and much new material is added, the saga reproduces several incidents which are recorded only by Thomas and his translators and no episodes which are characteristic only of the Béroul group of romances. The general outline of the events of the Norwegian saga is there, only greatly condensed, the one hundred and twelve printed pages of Robert being compressed into thirty-eight.

> The Icelandic author pretends to a greater knowledge of Tristram's ancestry than the English poet. In fact, one-fourth of the saga elapses before the birth of the hero—a proportion quite consistent with the methods of the classical Icelandic family sagas. The names are bungled: Mark is called Morodd, Morhold is called Engres, while the unfortunate Irishman who falsely boasted of having slain the fire-breathing dragon is quite naturally confused with Kay, the vainglorious seneschal of Arthurian romance. Again, Brittany has moved into Spain, which nation is at war with Russia; the sword splinter is lodged in Tristram instead of in Morhold and leads to his discovery by Isodd on the first voyage to Ireland. The dragon-slaying is also telescoped into the first voyage, and there is a remarkable tale of how Tristram killed all his crew when they landed in Ireland. On the return voyage the love potion is not forgotten, but Bringven has advanced to the dignity of Isodd's foster-mother, "daughter of Carl Cusen." The lovers are in no hurry about going to King Morodd; they conveniently delay three months. King Morodd is more courteous and magnanimous than even Thomas intended, for he offers the princess to Tristram, insisting that it is more fitting that she be his bride.

> The king married her, nevertheless, and events ensued which aroused his increasing suspicion. One night, returning from church, he found Tristram and Isodd abed together: so he sent them off to a cave. Here Isodd said, "What else is there to do but enjoy one's self in the cave?" "No," said Tristram, "let us each go to his own side of the cave." The king, of course, was listening. Eventually Tristram went to Spain, and there married "the dark Isodd." At first he was constant to "the fair Isodd," but at length he yielded to nature and after three years a child named Kalegras was born. Tristram died in Jakobland, and the saga faithfully recounts the incident of the black and white sails. In keeping with Icelandic saga tradition the saga-man adds an account of the hero's family after his death. Tristram's uncle, after this sorrowful dénouement, sent for Kalegras, Tristram's son, and had him declared king over England. He married a daughter of the German Emperor and had a daughter and two sons, about whom there is a long saga. King Morodd penitently went to Jerusalem, where he ended his days in a monastery.

This boorish account of Tristram's noble passion has very properly been called a rustic version in distinction from Robert's court translation. In refinement of style it is as far below Robert as the French prose romance falls short of Thomas. As a tale for the winter fireside, however, the na-

tive Icelandic account was more homely than Robert's, and its popularity is attested by the greater number of manuscripts preserved.

One incident of the Tristan story finds a parallel at the end of *Grettis Saga.*[4] It is the episode of Isolt's ambiguous oath of wifely fidelity. According to Robert's translation, Isond, on her way to take the oath, had to cross a river by boat. On the other side Tristram was waiting in the disguise of a pilgrim. At her request the supposed pilgrim carried her from the boat to the dry land, where he stumbled and fell on her. Therefore she was able to swear that no man had come near her except Mark and the pilgrim, and bore the hot iron without peril.

In the rustic Icelandic account, the boat does not figure; instead, Isodd comes riding, her horse sticks in a ditch, Tristram in the guise of a beggar pulls her out, and she manages to step over him.

In two respects—the disguise as a beggar, and the muddy ditch—the Icelandic saga corresponds to the Spes incident at the end of *Grettis Saga.* The history of Grettir, Iceland's most famous outlaw, slain in 1031, concludes with an account which seems rather less than more historical, describing how the hero was avenged two years later.

> Thorbiörn, Grettir's slayer, fled to Byzantium—Miklagarth, "the Great City"—and took service in the Varangian guard. Thorsteinn, Grettir's brother, followed and slew him in the presence of the Varangians. He was arrested but released at the instance of a rich Byzantine woman, Spes, who fell in love with him. Her husband surprised them together, but Spes protested her innocence and offered to affirm it by oath. On the day appointed Spes proceeded to the church, accompanied by many noble ladies. There had been heavy rains, the road was wet, and they had to cross a large pool of water before getting to the church. Many poor people were gathered there, ready apparently to carry a parcel or earn an honest coin. Among them was a large-limbed beggar, supported by crutches, who proceeded to carry Spes across the puddle, but stumbled and fell with her at the edge. However, she gave him some money. Going into the church, she took oath that she had given gold to no man and had suffered fleshly defilement of no man except the beggar and her husband. The beggar was, of course, her lover, Thorsteinn.

The story is better told here than in the other Scandinavian accounts, because the saga in which it is found is a work of greater literary merit. It is natural to suppose that the Spes episode is a tag supplied after the Tristram story became familiar in the North. It must be remembered, however, that *Grettis Saga* is largely historical, and that the incident is told of an Icelander who entered the Varangian service at Byzantium in 1033. Instead of supposing the whole a fabrication, one may possibly hold that the report of Thorsteinn's strategies was actually brought from the Great City with the history of Grettir's revenge; not that the trick was historically performed, but that a merry Byzantine tale was associated with a Northman in the Varangian guard. One version of the unfaithful wife's ambiguous oath was actually current there at this time in the popular Byzantine romance of the loves of *Clitophon and Leucippe*. If this surmise is sound, we have in *Grettis Saga* another example of the oral transmission of stories from the Great City suggested in a later chapter. This does not exclude the possibility that the continuator of *Grettir* knew also Robert's *Tristram* and that it colored his account of Thorsteinn.

More interesting, however, than the Spes episode in *Grettis Saga*, is the appearance, in another Icelandic saga, of the framework upon which a large portion of the Tristan story is built. So completely are the characters distorted that, upon first reading, the saga gives one only the vague impression of having been met with before, either in childhood or in dreams. Betrothal by proxy, indeed, is common enough in mediæval literature and need awake little curiosity. But when, on closer scrutiny, we find that, in this new romance, the proxy-wooing is joined by a sea voyage to the motif of the substituted bride, as nowhere in literature save here and in *Tristan,* we realize that there must be some connection between the two. Probability becomes certainty when we reach, later in the story, a journey for the healing that can come only from a relative of the enemy. Yet the narration of these themes is so different from that in Tristan's career as we know it, so much more radically different from Robert's saga than the rustic *Tristram,* or than the Oriental *Tyodel* from its Breton lay, that we seem to have here, not a readaptation of *Tristrams Saga,* but the survival of a Tristan tradition earlier than the twelfth-century *estoire.*

Although this saga, the romance of Harald Hringsbani[5]— Harald who slew his father Hring—has never been published, it was as much read in Iceland, to judge from the number of paper manuscripts, as the genuine *Tristram*. And the romance has sufficient antiquity to command respect. There are two accounts of Harald Hringsbani. The earlier of these exists only in *rímur,* based, we presume, on a lost saga. Here the geography of the Tristan story is distorted to such an extent that England takes the place of Ireland as the home of the bride across the sea, while the realm of the abused king is Denmark. In the later version, represented by both prose and metrical accounts, even England disappears, giving room to Constantinople—a consequence of the vogue of Byzantine romance.

> The scene of the *rímur* opens in Denmark, which was ruled by King Hring, "over-king over twenty kings." When his queen died, his son Harald urged him to cease sorrowing and take a young bride. Hring accordingly commissioned the prince to secure for him the hand of Signy, daughter of Erik, king of England. Harald and his retinue sailed in state, their silken sails shot with gold. At the English court they were banqueted, Erik readily granted Hring's suit, and the proxy wooer set sail with the bride. They had, however, conceived an ardent passion for each other and were very unhappy as they approached Denmark. At this juncture appeared Odin in disguise, who is represented as a promoter of strife. He offered a solution which was adopted. A farm-

er's daughter, likewise named Signy, was persuaded to change places with the bride. But Odin came in another disguise to the king and told him he had been deceived. Hring then tried to burn his son in his hall, but he escaped and offered to leave the land. Hring insisted on revenge and was slain in battle by Harald.

> In violent grief over his hard fate, Harald with his warriors set sail over the raging sea. In the course of his adventures he overthrew in single combat a champion named Hermod. Harald was wounded, however, and the dying man declared that no one had power to heal that wound but his sister, who loved Hermod above all things, and would treat his slayer with shame. Harald sent his followers back to Denmark and went forth alone in search of cure. For a twelvemonth he wandered, until he came upon Hertrygg, the Greek emperor, Hermod's sister's son, out to avenge his uncle. Disguised as a beggar, Harald tricked the Byzantine into swearing brotherhood, on condition that he deliver Harald. Compelled by his oath, Hertrygg took Harald to Constantinople as his guest and, by a ruse, persuaded his mother to perform the cure.

> In the end Harald and the real Signy reign over Denmark, and Hertrygg and the substituted bride over Byzantium.

The *rímur* are for the most part bald in their treatment of details. Their kennings are strained to the limit and inferior in conception. When the action, however, is unravelled from the cipher code of *rímur* metrics, it proves to be straight-forward and dramatic. Only essentials are preserved. In this respect *Haralds Rímur Hringsbana* bears a stylistic resemblance to the English *Sir Tristrem.*

The later version of the Hringsbani romance retains the above outlines until the king's death. But England is not mentioned; instead, Signy is the daughter of King Dag of Constantinople. The healing is quite different; the injunction about the relative is removed and the cure performed by a canny dwarf. Harald has adventures with monsters in Asia, and ends his days happily as king of Byzantium. This saga, though distorted, preserves some earlier features, no doubt more completely than the condensed *rímur.* Among them are passages as beautiful as any in *Tristan;* for example, the portion describing the wooing by proxy in Byzantium, and the subsequent voyage:

> He tried to console her, but she wept all the more. So he took her alone into a cabin and said, "Now tell me the cause of your grief, and I will help it if I can." "You alone can relieve me," she said, "you knew my desire before." "Do not speak so," said Harald: "that I cannot do, and so it needs must be." "Never," she cried, "if I can avoid it, will I behold your father with my eyes! It is pleasanter for me to sink into the sea and never more to see the sun, and this I will do; but though you will all be turned from me, yet will I continue to love you, as my life."

Thus has the tragedy of Tristan of Leonois become the tragi-comedy of Harald prince of Denmark. The setting is Scandinavian, and some of the incidents, such as the "burning in," are Norse. Other features are more or less suggestive of Tristan tradition; there are two maidens named Signy, as two named Isond; Mariadok, the accuser of Tristram, is paralleled by the disguised Odin who reveals the deception to Hring; the single combat, the parts taken by Hermod and Morholt, the sisters of the slain, and the sea voyage in search of healing are identical; Hertrygg performs services similar to those of Kardin, Tristram's friend; both are enamoured of the substituted bride. It is, however, the combination of the three basic themes of proxy-betrothal, substitution in bride-bed, and quest of cure that certainly connects Harald with Tristan. These motifs appear singly in other Icelandic tales. But it is only the unique union of the three themes that locks the chain of evidence identifying the Danish-Byzantine prince with his Pictish prototype.

From what stage of Tristan tradition, then, was the Hringsbani story derived? Surely not from Robert's translation. For the dissonances are greater than the harmonies. We are loath to concede such sweeping changes even to the cumulative imagination of habitually exact Icelandic recitation. How much more like is the Spes episode in *Grettla!* Where is the love potion that even the rustic version retains? Where is that other Isolt who was remembered for centuries in the popular ballads of Iceland? In *Hringsbani* the substituted bride continues her rôle; in *Tristram* she is a temporary expedient. And the incident of wound and the voyage of healing is quite out of its setting and attached to another lady later in the story. When once the herbs of healing had been placed in the hands of the lady sought in marriage, could this triple knot of tragedy—cure, proxy-wooer, and substitution—once tied, ever have been disentangled by an Icelandic redactor?

It is easier to suppose that the romance of *Harald Hringkiller* is descended from a stage in the Tristan tradition earlier than that in the romances derived from the so-called *estoire*, before the love-potion was introduced, or the voyage of healing led to the first Isolt, or Tristan wedded Isolt of the White Hands. The Icelandic story may possibly represent a simpler, unquestioning form of the tale, when the leech was the second Isolt—a stage in the tradition before some poet placed all the skeins in the hands of his heroine Isolt of Ireland, leaving it to that other Isolt only to serve as a foil to the transcendent beauty of her rival and to try in the furnace Tristan's fidelity.

Hringsbani, moreover, is not the only disguise in which Tristan has come to the North independently of Brother Robert's saga. The other versions arrived, not *via* England and Norway, but through Germany and Denmark, and in more recent times.[6] There are, for example, two Danish prose romances. One of them, first printed in 1857, is a translation of the German prose romance based upon Eilhart von Oberg's *Tristrant* and first printed at Augsburg in 1484. The other Danish account appeared in Copenhagen as early as 1792 and has since been published many times. It also professes to be translated from German and bears the strange title "A Tragical History of the Noble and Val-

iant Tristrand, Son of the Duke of Burgundy, and the Beautiful Indiana, Daughter of the Grand Mogul, Emperor of India." The contents are as extraordinary as the title. Although *Tristrand and Indiana* follows the German prose *Tristrant* in outline, the hero is the only character who keeps his original name; the countries, too, are all changed, and many details are altered. The German original, now lost, was perhaps intended as a political satire. This version was printed also in Norway, while in Iceland it was made the subject of *rímur* by the poet Sigurd Breidfjörd (1798-1846).

Tristan has lived on in Scandinavia in the life of the people, in ballad and folk-tale[7] as well as in written sagas and *rímur*. Unlike the Icelandic ballads, the Tristram ballads of the Færoes and Denmark do not agree with any existing versions of a Tristan romance, and are apparently based on faint popular reminiscences. The name Isalt-Isolt, instead of Isond-Isodd of the sagas, points to German influence. The hero is called Tistrum or Tistram. The three Danish ballads—all different in theme—contain little in accord with the Tristan romances except that they are love stories. Apparently the names Tistrum and Isalt had become synonyms in the popular imagination for any two lovers. The curious Færoe ballad of true love, however, has slightly more in common with the real Tristan:

> Tistram and Lady Isin loved each other, but his parents wished to separate them. They sent him with a letter to the king of France: he should either give him his daughter in marriage or take his life. Tistram refused to be faithless to Lady Isin, and was accordingly hanged. In revenge Lady Isin sailed to France, devastated the country, and took her lover's body down from the gallows; then her own heart broke.

The rustic Icelandic *Tristrams Saga* had fallen upon a happy designation for the two Isodds: Mark's queen was *Isodd Bjarta,* Isodd the fair, and she of Brittany *Isodd Svarta,* Isodd the dark. The same terms are used by an Icelandic ballad on Tristan's death. Again they are employed in an Icelandic fairy tale entitled *Isól Fair and Isól Dark.* The tale itself, however, is quite independent of the Tristan tradition.

In artistic merit all other ballads about Tristan yield to the Icelandic *Tristrams Kvæði*. Based upon Robert, it confines its action to the end of the story, telling in lines of naïve beauty the hero's last illness and the hurried voyage of Isodd to save him. For eighteen days she was delayed on the voyage before fair wids drove her to port. Then the other Isodd went in to her dying husband.

> These words she spake, Isodd the dark,
>   When she had gone within;
> "Black are the sails upon the ship
>   Which here is lying in."

Then comes the refrain:

> For them it was fated only to sever.

> These words she spake, Isodd the dark,
>   She said that they were true:

"Black are the sails upon the ship,
  But are not blue."

Thereat Tristram turned to the wall and died.

They anchored the ship
  Off the black strand,
They bore Isodd the fair
  First to the land.

Long, long was the way
  And narrow the street,
Ever heard she bells a-ringing
  And song so sweet.

Into the church went Isodd;
  A hundred men she led,
Priests were chanting in procession
  Around the dead.

Twice Isodd looked down upon Tristram's body while "the priests stood round on the church floor with candle lights," and then she gave up her life on his bier. With the same restrained pathos the ballad describes their burial. This ballad of a later age may well have been sung upon the shores of the Icelandic fjord which kept intact the name of that first Drostan, the Pictish king. And the refrain which follows each verse shows how completely the simple Icelandic farmers realized the tragic undertone of the song. *Đeim var ekki skapaað, nem að skilja*—"For them it was fated only to sever."

Notes

1. On the Tristan story, see J. Bédier, Le Roman de Tristan par Thomas, Paris, 1902-1905; W. Golther, Tristan und Isolde in den Dichtungen des Mittelalters und der Neuen Zeit, Leipzig, 1907; G. Schoepperle, Tristan and Isolt, A Study of the Sources of the Romance, London and Frankfurt a. M., 1913.

2. Tristrams Saga ok Ísondar, edited by E. Kölbing, Heilbronn, 1878.

3. The Icelandic Tristrams Saga is edited by G. Brynjúlfsson in Annaler för Nordisk Oldkyndighed, Copenhagen, 1851, pp. 1-160. For *rímur,* see same, pp. 159-160.

4. For the Grettis Saga, see Chapter XIII.

5. For the Hringsbani analogue, see H. G. Leach and G. Schoepperle, Haraldssaga Hringsbana and the Tristan and Svanhild Romances (Publications of the Society for the Advancement of Scandinavian Study, II, 1916, 264 ff).

6. For the late Danish folkbook versions of Tristan, see Golther, Tristan und Isolde, 1907, pp. 247-254.

7. For Tristan ballads, see Grundtvig and Olrik, Danmarks Gamle Folkeviser, Ridderviser, III, 29-46; Grundtvig, Íslenzk Fornkvæði, I, No. 23; V. U. Hammershaimb, Færösk Anthologi, I, No. 26; G. Brynjúlfsson, Saga af Tristram ok Ísond, Copenhagen, 1878, pp. 339-370. For folk-tales, see J. Árnason, Íslenzka Þjóðsögur, II, 315-326.

William Henry Schofield (essay date 1921)

SOURCE: "The Matter of Britain," in *English Literature from the Norman Conquest to Chaucer,* Macmillan, 1921 pp. 201-14.

[*In the following excerpt, Schofield compares the versions of the Tristan legend written by the Anglo-Norman poet Thomas and the Norman Béroul and offers a discussion of Thomas's version, including commentary on the poet's form and style.*]

. . . It is appropriate that our study of the Tristram stories should follow directly that of the Breton lays, for in no legendary cycle is the influence of this form of Celtic material more manifest. Several of the most charming episodes in which the famous lovers appear are easily detachable from their surroundings and reveal a previous existence in the form of isolated lays. And, indeed, Marie de France records an incident in Tristram's life based on an earlier lay, the composition of which is ascribed to the hero himself. The good knight, after a year's exile from court, gives way to his longings and returns secretly to Cornwall, where he hides himself in the forest near Ysolt's abode. He carves a message on a piece of wood and puts it in the road where he knows she is to pass. In this he declares that he cannot live without her: it is with them as with the honeysuckle and the hazel, which, once intertwined, no one can separate without destroying both.

This lay, written down by Marie in England, was previously recorded in English under the name *Gotelef* (honeysuckle), and is perhaps connected with an Anglo-Saxon lyric, not attached to Tristram, *The Lover's Message.* England, indeed, can well claim the credit of preserving, if not of originating, the absorbing tale of Tristram's love. Not only have we positive statements that it was current among the English, and put by them into poetic form; we know also that it was written down in French by two Norman poets, one of whom we are pretty certain was born in England, while the other may have lived there. And it is on one or the other of these two versions that almost all the later forms are based. The two poets were of different dispositions and wrote in a different spirit. The *Tristan* of Thomas presents us with what has been termed the English, or Germanic, version of the story; that of Béroul, the French, or Breton. Thus all poems about our hero may suitably be treated in two groups. A characteristic difference between them consists in the fact that while the French group represents King Mark as reigning over Cornwall alone and as contemporary with Arthur, in the English Arthur has already passed away and Mark is king both of Cornwall and England.

Thomas's poem is but partially preserved in fragments (in Anglo-Norman handwriting) discovered in England, Germany, and Italy—some 3000 lines in all—only about one-sixth of the work, but sufficient to allow a just estimate of the author's style. The defect, however, is partly remedied by the existence of two early translations of the work. Its scope is easily determined from the faithful, if abridged, version made in Old Norse prose in 1226 by a friar Robert for King Hákon, that insatiable reader of French romance. Its style is more apparent in the translation by an admirable German poet, Gottfried von Strassburg, made early in the thirteenth century. Gottfried did not succeed in nearly 20,000 verses in bringing his work to an end. The last third of the story was added later by two other poets (Ulrich von Türheim and Heinrich von Freiberg), who, working independently of each other, utilised the French version, and record some incidents of which the source is lost. Nowhere is the story of Tristram so well preserved as in this composite German version. Thence Wagner got the inspiration for his noble music-drama on the theme. Towards the end of the thirteenth century, Thomas's version was also used as the basis of a Middle English poem, *Sir Tristram,* which was first edited, with extensive introduction and illustration, by Sir Walter Scott. Before 1200 an interesting short poem called *La Folie Tristan* was composed in England. The author represents the hero, dressed as a fool, recalling the experiences of his life, and by this device gives a fairly complete review of the episodes of the legend.

On the other hand, forming the so-called French group, we have a long fragment by the Norman Béroul; then, a lost poem, which was translated into German, *c.* 1180, by Eilhart von Oberg, closely resembling Béroul's account in the beginning but with a unique conclusion, especially valuable because the French original has disappeared; and finally, an immense prose romance, a conglomerate of all sorts of material factitiously joined together in the course of the thirteenth century. Crestien de Troyes and an author called La Chièvre also wrote episodic poems on Tristram, both of which are lost. Crestien's patronesses undoubtedly had a repugnance for compromise in love; and since Ysolt favoured her uxorious husband while adoring another, Crestien may not have presented her in a favourable light. It was from the French version, in the degenerate form of the prose romance, that Malory drew a large part of his famous work.

We now return to Thomas, who may be said to represent the highest achievement of any English poet in the twelfth century. Gaston Paris, whose words always carry with them the weight of a great authority, has made an illuminating comparison between Thomas and his contemporary Crestien, as follows:

> Genius of different kinds appeals to us in these two poets. The Frenchman endeavours especially to make his narrative interesting, amusing even, to please the society for which it is intended; he is "social," truly worldly; he smiles at the adventures he relates, and skilfully lets it appear that he is not taken in by them; he strives to give to his style a constant elegance, a uniform polish, wherein sparkle here and there words pointed by wit; above all, he wishes to please, and thinks of his public more than of his subject. The Englishman feels with the heroes of his tale; his heart participates in their griefs and joys; he searches the hidden recesses of their souls; his style, embarrassed and often obscure when he narrates adventures that do not thoroughly interest him, becomes living and full of *nuances* when he tries to express the inner feelings, which alone touch him; he writes for himself, and for those who have the same emotional needs as he, much more than for a public sensitive above all to the talent of the narrator and indifferent to the subject of the narrative. It is unfortunate that we cannot compare the *Tristan* of Crestien and that of Thomas; we can at least imagine the difference which the two works would present: the poet of Champagne would show us gracefully poised on a brilliant stand, and carved by a skilled and delicate hand, the cup from which the two lovers drank the drink of love; the Anglo-Norman poet has emptied it, and we feel still trembling in his lines the frenzy that filled his heart.

Tristram was celebrated in early saga, before he was connected with Arthur, as a hero of extraordinary and varied accomplishment, as a warrior and hunter, as well as a lover. He is, moreover, the most famous of all the harpers of romance. Over and over again he is pictured at the royal court making melodious music, and therewith singing lays so full of tenderness and passion that the breasts of his auditors swelled with emotion. It was thus that he stimulated the affection of Ysolt, the beautiful princess of Ireland, to whom he journeyed overseas as a stranger for the healing of his wounds. Thus he won her favour when together they sat in the quiet bower of her palace, and he taught her so skilfully the mysteries of his art that soon her hands became proficient like his, and struck the chords with the same power to ravish the senses and fill with delight. So, in words that haunt the memory, Thomas describes Ysolt later in her loneliness singing to her harp the lay of Guiron and his lady, who suffered even more than she and Tristram from the evil contrivance of foes.

> La dame chante doucement,
> La vois acorde a l'estrument;
> Les mains sont beles, li lais bons,
> Douce la vois et bas li tons.

These words exhale the sweetest perfume of romance, under the influence of which we are prone to free ourselves from workaday principles of behaviour, and abandon the conventional standards of commonplace life. Were it but a passing or a frivolous passion that the two cherished, we should be shocked by the flagrant violation of domestic honour that it entailed. But we have a deep conviction of the inevitability of it all. The burden of Tristram's song when with Ysolt of the White Hands in Brittany sums up the whole tragedy of the true lovers' life:

> Ysolt ma drue, Ysolt m'amie,
> En vus ma mort, en vus ma vie.

Here, we feel, is an attachment over which the subjects had no control: from the magic beaker they drank down death together with rapturous love. As Thomas says:

> Tristrans murut pur sue amur
> E la bele Ysolt pur tendrur.

The story of Tristram and Ysolt is too well known to require a detailed analysis. But a few passages from Thomas's poem (in Miss Weston's felicitous translation of Gottfried's version) may be quoted here. The first pictures the lovers, banished from court and dwelling alone in a solitary retreat, where all nature ministers to their joy.

"In the dewy morning they gat them forth to the meadow where grass and flowers alike had been refreshed. The glade was their pleasure-ground—they wandered hither and thither, hearkening each other's speech, and waking the song of the birds by their footsteps. Then they turned them to where the cold clear spring rippled forth, and sat beside its stream, and watched its flow, till the sun grew high in the heavens, and they felt its heat. Then they betook them to the linden: its branches offered them a welcome shelter, the breezes were sweet and soft beneath its shade, and the couch at its feet was decked with the fairest grass and flowers.

"There they sat side by side, those true lovers, and told each other tales of those who ere their time had suffered and died for love. They mourned the fate of the sad Queen Dido; of Phyllis of Thrace; and Biblis, whose heart brake for love. With such tales did they beguile the time. But when they would think of them no more, they turned them again to their grotto and took the harp, and each in their turn sang to it softly lays of love and longing; now Tristram would strike the harp while Isolt sang the words, then it would be the turn of Isolt to make music while Tristram's voice followed the notes. Full well might it be called the Love Grotto."

Thither King Mark is led, even as Guingamor to his joyful meeting with his fairy mistress, by the hunt of the mysterious stag that lures him ever on in apparently fruitless pursuit. He is rewarded by seeing the queen, "more beautiful than a fairy," for whom he could not but yearn. Stealthily the king nears the bower where he knows the lovers to be, and climbs to the little window high in the wall. A tenderly moving sight meets his eyes. There they lay, the entranced pair, on a crystal couch, a naked sword between them.

"He gazed on his heart's delight, Isolt, and deemed that never before had he seen her so fair. She lay sleeping, with a flush as of mingled roses on her cheek, and her red and glowing lips apart, a little heated by her morning wandering in the dewy meadow and by the spring. On her head was a chaplet woven of clover. A ray of sunlight from the little window fell upon her face, and as Mark looked upon her he longed to kiss her, for never had she seemed so fair and so lovable as now. And when he saw how the sunlight fell upon her he feared lest it harm her, or awaken her, and so he took grass and leaves and flowers, and covered the window therewith, and spake a blessing on his love, and commended her to God, and went his way, weeping."

No doubt the "fair adventure" of the love-grotto was the subject of an independent lay, and the same is perhaps the case with the two following episodes in the hero's life. In each we detect a parallel to the general situation already noted in the Franklin's Tale, the indefinite boon granted rashly and fulfilled with sorrow.

To the court of Cornwall comes one day an Irish knight, a former lover of Ysolt, in the guise of a minstrel. After meat, the king bids him show his skill on the lute, and promises him whatever reward he shall ask. Thus requested, the knight begins at once. He sings the king's favourite lays, one after the other, and then craves his boon. When he names it, there is consternation at court, for in his arrogance he claims the queen. Rather than be forsworn, Mark hands over to him the fair Ysolt, and she must needs follow him to the seashore, where his boat lies ready to depart when the tide shall rise. Fortunately, before then news of the event reaches Tristram, who makes his way hastily to the haven-side. Harp in hand, he approaches the tent where the queen sits weeping bitterly. At the request of the knight he plays the lay of Dido to banish the lady's sorrow. He plays so sweetly that the notes enter Ysolt's heart, and her captor too listens eagerly. The water rises, but they heed not—so insinuating are the sounds. Finally, the tide runs so strong that they can only reach the boat on horseback, and Ysolt insists on being borne by the minstrel. Once in Tristram's arms she is, of course, free, and the traitorous Irish knight must return home, ashamed and sorrowful.

The second tale is permeated with the mysterious magic of the Otherworld. It tells how Tristram won from Duke Gilan of Wales his little dog Petit-Criu, "a fairy dog, that had been sent to the Duke from the land of Avalon, as love-token, by a fay."

"No tongue could tell the marvel of it; 'twas of such wondrous fashion that no man might say of what colour it was. If one looked on the breast and saw nought else, one had said 'twas white as snow, yet its thighs were greener than clover, and its sides, one red as scarlet, the other more yellow than saffron. Its underparts were even as azure, while above 'twas mingled so that no one colour might be distinguished; 'twas neither green nor red, white nor black, yellow nor blue, and yet was there somewhat of all these therein; 'twas a fair purple brown. And if one saw this strange creature of Avalon against the lie of the hair there would be no man wise enough to tell its colour, so manifold and so changing were its hues.

"Around its neck was a golden chain, and therefrom hung a bell, which rang so sweet and clear that when it began to chime Tristram forgot his sadness and his sorrow, and the longing for Isolt that lay heavy on his heart. So sweet was the tone of the bell that no man heard it but he straightway forgot all that aforetime had troubled him. . . .

"Tristram stretched forth his hand and stroked the dog, and it seemed to him that he handled the softest silk, so fine and so smooth was the hair to his touch. And the dog neither growled nor barked nor showed any sign of ill-temper, however one might play with it; nor, as the tale goes, was it ever seen to eat or drink.

"When the dog was borne away, Tristram's sorrow fell upon him as heavy as before, and to it was added the thought how he might by any means win Petit-Criu, the fairy dog, for his lady the queen, that thereby her sorrow and her longing might be lessened. Yet he could not see how this might be brought about either by craft or by prayer, for he knew well that Gilan would not have parted with it for his life. This desire and longing lay heavy on his heart, but he gave no outward sign of his thought."

Now the Duke was in perpetual fear of a giant magician, Argan, and he promises Tristram whatever he may ask of him, if he will rid him of his terrible foe. This the hero accomplishes after a fierce fight, and then demands the fairy dog as his reward. The Duke pleads with him to take anything else, but when Tristram insists, he yields. "Alas! my lord Tristram," he says, "if that be indeed thy will, I will keep faith with thee and do thy pleasure. Neither craft nor cunning am I minded to use. Though it be greatly against my will, yet what thou desirest, that shall be done."

Tristram, overjoyed, sends the precious dog, hidden cunningly in a lute, to the queen, explaining how he had won it, at great peril to his life, for her sake. At first she had it ever with her, and it brought her great comfort. The bell's wonderful sweet chime made her forget her grief. But when she bethought herself that while she thus rejoiced her lover was in sorrow, she upbraided herself bitterly. The bell she tore from the dog's neck, and no longer had it power to sooth a downcast heart. Yet Ysolt was now the better pleased, for she would not be comforted when Tristram was sad.

Thomas wrote in simple, flowing, octosyllabic couplets, the usual metre of French romances. A much more complicated, and to our ears much less pleasing, metre characterises the Northern English poem *Sir Tristram,* which is based on his poem. This work was obviously written with hearers, not readers, especially in mind. It has all the marks of being prepared for recitation by a minstrel at a public gathering.

The opening stanza, which will serve to illustrate the metre, gives us some would-be indication of the source of the work.

> I was a[t Erceldoun,]
> With Thomas spoke I there;
> There heard I read in roun (private),
> Who Tristram got and bore;
> Who was king with crown,
> And who him fostered (of) yore,
> And who was bold baron
> As their elders were.
>   By yere
> Thomas tells in town
> These adventures, as they were.

From this passage it would appear that one Thomas of Erceldoun was accustomed to tell in public the adventures of Sir Tristram, and that our author had the advantage of conversing with him in private on the same matter. This Thomas had a remarkable fictitious career. He was called "Rhymer," and apparently justified the name. His personality is hazy; but there seems to be good evidence to attest his existence as an historical person living towards the close of the thirteenth century. In a very interesting balladromance, dating from about 1400, he is said to have gone, like Launfal, to dwell with the queen of fairyland, whose favour he had won. She, however, is said to have conducted him after a while back to this world, and before leaving him here to have granted him the gift of soothsaying, and told him much of future events. On this account he very soon was associated with Merlin, and for centuries a great deal of influential prophetical literature was current under his name. Indeed, it is said that the "Whole Prophecie" of Merlin, Thomas Rymour, and others, which was collected and issued as early as 1603, continued to be printed as a chap-book down to the beginning of the nineteenth century, when few farm-houses in Scotland were without it. There is no evidence, however, that this Thomas had anything to do with the composition of *Sir Tristram.* It can never be proved, of course, that he did not write a poem on that hero; but it seems highly probable that he was connected with the particular poem before us only because of the identity of his name with that of the Anglo-Norman author of the original version, it being well understood that the popularity of the poem would be appreciably increased by reference to so distinguished an authority as the prophet of Erceldoun.

Robert of Brunne, in his chronicle written *c.* 1340, is thought to bear witness to the fact that *Sir Tristram* was attributed to Thomas of Erceldoun even in his time. In an important passage, in which he reproaches those who used such artificial metres and strange phraseology that the common people could hardly understand what they meant, he says:

> I see in song, in sedgeyng tale,
> Of Erceldoun and of Kendale,
> None them say as they them wrought,
> And in their saying it seemeth nought.

Thereupon follows directly a plain reference to the English poem, which is apparently contrasted with the work of the original author Thomas (neither of Erceldoun nor of Kendale), though this is not the inference usually drawn from the passage:

> That mayst thou hear in Sir Tristrem,
> Over gests it has the (e)steem,
> Over all that is or was.
> If men it said as made Thomas;
> But I hear it no man so say,
> That of some couplet some is away;
> So their fair saying herebeforn,
> So their travail near forlorn.
> They say it for pride and nobley,
> That none were such as they;
> And all that they would overwhere,
> All that ilk will now forfare.
> They said in so quaint English,
> That many a one wots not what it is.

The last lines may be taken to refer to the *Sir Tristram* we are discussing, which is certainly written in a very complicated metre, and so succinctly that it but ill reproduces the couplets of the earlier version. It would have required a great poet to move quite unhampered by the clogs of rhyme that this peculiar stanza imposed. Not satisfied, however, with these restrictions, the English writer laboured for alliterative effects. No one, then, will be surprised to learn that frequently he sacrificed the sense of the story, to say nothing of the general impression, to his enforced display of clever artifice. The whole story, moreover, he cut down so recklessly that it is at times almost unintelligible. Gottfried took nearly 20,000 lines to reproduce about two-thirds of Thomas's poem. The English minstrel disposed of the whole in about 3500. In contrast to the "quaint English" and elaborate stanza in which the story is obscured and disfigured, Robert places Thomas's irreproachable version in couplets. And rightly so. The Anglo-Norman poem, simple and clear, reveals in the author a very high degree of poetic power. Truly, Robert had reason to say that "over all gests" the story of Tristram was worthy to be esteemed "if men it said as Thomas made it." But such a remark would in truth have been unwarranted if it applied to the English poem. The author was a clever rhymer, and some passages of his work have much vigour, but had not the adventures of Tristram been well known before, from French narratives current in England, this poem would not have sufficed to spread his fame.

We have no other English treatment of the Tristram story until we come to Malory's redaction of one version of the late French prose romance. Here is a hotch-potch of miscellaneous adventures, many of which have nothing to do with the central theme and serve only to prolong the tale. Echoes of classical antiquity, reminiscences of the Bible, bits of popular tradition, independent works of different cycles are to be discovered in the vast accumulation. But above all it is noticeable how the costuming has changed. The manners and dress of the heroes and heroines are those of the late days of chivalry. Tristram is a vastly different personage from what he was even in the time of Thomas. He is now a conventional knighterrant, who spends his time going about from one tourney to another, ever on the lookout for adventure. In the earlier stories, Arthur and his knights have practically no part to play. Now, one at least of them surely appears on every page, and no uninformed reader would for a moment suspect that Tristram was a hero once quite independent of Arthur, and that his thoroughgoing connection with the Round Table is to be found only in late compilations, which departed far too freely from trustworthy tradition, in order to gratify the taste of an uncritical Continental audience whose appetite for familiar adventures appears to have been insatiate.

Inasmuch as Malory drew almost one-third of his *Morte Darthur* (mostly to be found in the eighth, ninth, and tenth books) from the French prose *Tristan,* a word concerning his method may be in place here. There is so great diversity in the various manuscripts of a prose romance that it is well-nigh impossible to state just what process was followed in any particular instance. But in general it may be said that from a common archetype scribes developed divergent versions, each of which, being repeatedly copied, was differently altered by different sorts of men to answer different purposes. There appears to have been a "vulgate," and an "enlarged" *Tristan,* the former going under the name of a supposed "Luces de Gast," the latter under that of an equally fictitious "Hélie de Boron." It was from some manuscript of the vulgate version that Malory drew his story. Here, more than anywhere else, save only in the Quest of the Holy Grail, he abstains from "reducing."

We claim the immortal legend of Tristram and Ysolt as peculiarly ours, not only because it was formed in its present shape in England, being a possession of our composite race before and after the Conquest, but also because it is localised in Britain; and, as is well known, all nations cling to the traditions of the country in which they have settled, even though to come into power they had to dispossess those to whom these traditions rightly belonged. Mark was a king of Cornwall, and that, it seems, in history, before he became the legendary husband of Ysolt. His castle was at Tintagel on the Cornish coast. Tristram, originally a Pictish or Scandinavian hero, was probably born in Anglesey and lived in Wales. One Ysolt was a princess of Ireland, the other of Brittany. In these neighbouring lands the action passes almost exclusively, and the hero traverses the dangerous waters between with as much equanimity as any Norse viking whose home was on the sea. The people among whom the Tristram story grew up were as familiar with ocean as with land pathways.

The saga certainly originated in heathen times, when Christianity had not softened the minds of men; in a barbarous epoch when people lived a rough, uncivilised life in rude simplicity; in a time when chivalrous warfare was undreamed of, when heroes fought on foot, using as weapons arrows speeded by the cross-bow, or javelins thrown by hand. If we stop to think of it, the manners and customs of the court of the Cornish king are seen to be often barbarous and savage. No Christian sentiments govern the hearts of the characters. Might is right; cunning is praiseworthy; passions are unbridled, and impulses unrestrained. The primordial instincts of men and women are seen unveiled.

Tristram and Ysolt are the most illustrious lovers of British, perhaps of any romance. Wherein do they differ typically from those of other lands? In this, that the whole of their lives moves about the pivot of their mutual devotion. With them both love is a persistent, uncontrollable, supreme passion. It is the end that justifies every means, the cause of an uninterrupted ecstasy that renders death at any moment as welcome as life. The heroines of classical story never moved their lovers to the same overmastering passion, never controlled their destinies by the same mysterious charm. In the grave *chansons de geste* love was little welcome: women played no dominant rôle in the careers of the stern warriors of Charlemagne, ever engaged in manly conflict for communal gain. In the North, on the other hand, there is in tensity and passion in abundance. There the women share the greatest joys of the men; they stimulate, incite, enter into the struggle themselves. Yet theirs was self-sacrifice that asked no return, devotion that demanded no favour. Life was too real for music, time too precious for reverie. Men were not men, they felt, who waited on luxurious ease. With Guthrun blood is thicker than any amorous philtre. Without a scruple she deceives her husband to get revenge for her brother's death, but not to indulge a guilty love. The prototypes of the Northern heroines are the strong, impetuous, warlike goddesses of Valhalla, clad in birnie, and pointing with flashing spear to the scene of strife; those of the Celtic lady-loves are the exquisitely beautiful, richly attired, marvellously subtle queens of a joyour Otherworld, who fascinate and soothe.

It is not possible here to trace the history of the Tristram legend either in internal growth or in dissemination. It is well to remember, however, that there was no one in the Middle Ages in Western Europe who did not know it in some form. All the great mediæval poets and those of the Renaissance evince their profound appreciation of its charm. In our own time, Tennyson, Matthew Arnold, and Swinburne in England, Wagner in Germany, and others in many places, have reawakened it to power.

We may leave the hero with the presentation of one aspect of his character that Malory exalted. It will indicate another reason why he was beloved in England, and show how the stories of Arthur affected the conceptions of the nobility.

> And so Tristram learned to be a harper passing all other, that there was none such called in no country, and so in harping and on instruments of music he applied him in his youth for to learn. And after, as he growed in might and strength, he laboured ever in hunting and hawking, so that never gentleman more that ever we heard tell of. And as the book saith, he began good measures of blowing of beasts of venery and beasts of chase, and all manner of vermains; and all these terms we have yet of hawking and hunting. And therefore the book of venery, of hawking and hunting, is called the book of Sir Tristram. Wherefore, as me seemeth, all gentlemen that bear old arms ought of right to honour Sir Tristram for the goodly terms that gentlemen have and use, and shall to the day of doom, that thereby in a manner all men of worship may dissever a gentleman from a yeoman, and from a yeoman a villain. For he that gentle is will draw unto him gentle taches, and to follow the custom of noble gentlemen.

A. G. van Hamel (essay date 1924)

SOURCE: "Tristan's Combat with the Dragon," in *Revue Celtique*, Vol. 41. Reprint. Kraus Reprint Ltd., 1966, pp. 331-49.

[*In the following essay, van Hamel studies the details of the dragon-slaying episode in the Tristan legend and compares these elements as they appear in different versions of the legend.*]

When Tristan and his men, in quest of the Princess of the Swallow's Hair, have reached the Irish coast and lie in the harbour, they learn that the country is being devastated by a fiery dragon, and that the king has promised his daughter and the half of his kingdom to the man who will slay the monster. The next day the hero sets out alone and accomplishes the deed. He cuts out the dragon's tongue as a trophy. Overcome by his burns, he lies down in a brook and falls asleep. An impostor, the king's seneschal, desires the royal bride for himself. First he makes sure that the monster is dead, and then, under the impression that it has also killed its slayer, he rides off with the head to the court and proclaims himself as winner of the king's daughter. The next day the princess sets out herself to investigate the scene of the combat. The wounded Tristan is discovered and carried to the town. Here she recognises him as the slayer not only of the dragon but of the Morold, her uncle. However, both the king and his daughter are willing to pardon him because of the slaying of the dragon. The claim of the seneschal, who is challenged to battle by Tristan, is proved to be false, the hero being able to produce the monster's tongue. The impostor now leaves the court in disgrace. Tristan proffers his sue for Isolt on behalf of king Mark of Cornwall, and the Irish king readily accepts it[1].

The episode of the slaying of the dragon has long been recognised as one of the many folk-elements, which underly the Tristan romance[2]. The natural conclusion would be that the champion wins the bride for himself, but this has been changed in accordance with the altruistic character of Tristan's quest. The story, as it is told in Tristan and Isolt, belongs to a particular group of folk-tales of the Perseus-type, owing to the character of the impostor, which gives the trait of the hero's cutting out the monster's tongue a deeper significance. This character, as Gertrude Schoepperle remarks, is known in other folk-tales, which are also represented in Celtic popular tradition.

In a recently published collection of Breton folk-lore[3] the story occurs even in a more elaborate form, and here it illustrates once more the well-known fact, that the reputation of Brittany for its exact and careful preservation of primitive lore is well-deserved. In a good many cases, I think, Breton traditions are superior even to those of Ireland. Besides, this is not the first instance of a popular element of the Tristan romance being retraced in Brittany[4]. A particular interest attaches to this coincidence, although the day has not yet arrived to make out the nature of the connection.

In the Breton version here alluded to[5] the story forms a portion of a longer tale entitled *Ar Zarpant milliguet*. Here the dragon is a monster with six heads. Every day it receives a human being for its prey, in order to prevent it from further devastations. On the day of the hero's arrival the king's eldest daughter will be sacrificed. Immediately the hero presents himself before the king, who promises him his daughter, if he should succeed in delivering her. The princess is on her knees before the serpent's hole. Her unknown champion (who is only a boy) sees the monster emerging from its subterranean abode. In the combat, which ensues, he receives great help from his horse, his dog and his iron helmet, and at last he separates the dragon's six heads from the body with his sword. He cuts out the six tongues, wraps them up in his handkerchief and makes off for an inn near by, in order to prepare himself to appear before the king. A disgusting dwarf, distorted and warped, who dwells not far from the palace (his name is Beg-lor)[6], has witnessed the bloody scene. He takes the six heads in his hand, dips his knife in the gore, and announces at the palace that he has killed the dragon. Reluctantly the king declares himself prepared to fulfill his promise, and the princess, though disbelieving the claimant's remonstrances, can only obey. Owing to the dwarf's orders the hero is refused admittance to the king's presence. Thus he is obliged to devise a stratagem. When the banquet has commenced, he tells his dog to penetrate into the hall, to lick the maiden's hand, and then to overthrow the table with all the dishes upon it. The faithful animal does as it is told, and the same scene is repeated on a second and a third day. Twice the dog escapes, but the third time it is caught, and its master is dragged before the king. Now he makes himself known as the rightful pretender to the seat next the princess, and supports his claim against the usurper by producing the six tongues, which appear to fit exactly into the six mouths. In vain the false bridegroom attempts to disappear, and his crime is expiated on the gallows. But the successful dragon-slayer becomes the king's son-in-law.

The above summary shows once more that in Celtic popular tradition stories of the same type as that of Tristan's dragon fight are known. It could not be held that this folk-tale should have drawn its material from any poetic or prose version of the Tristan story. It preserves several traits, which no doubt are ancient, and which all our versions of Tristan and Isolt ignore. Among these I reckon the hero's youthful age, the large number of heads of the monster, the part played by the helpful animals at the combat, and by the faithful dog at the banquet.

Other stories of the same type have been noted down in Brittany[7] and in other Celtic countries as well[8]. A striking variant is preserved in Lorraine[9]. In all these the monster emerges at regular periods and claims a living oblation, which it has been promised in order that it may refrain from further devastations. The youth arrives on the day when the king's daughter will be sacrificed. The number of the dragon's heads varies from one to six or seven, and the slaying takes from one to three days. An important incident is the recognition of the hero, who either modestly retires or falls asleep after the combat. It occurs in two variants. In one of these there is an impostor, or even three, and everything happens as in the tale quoted above. This is the version of all the Breton variants; it has been retraced by E.S. Hartland in a large number of versions of our story all over the world. The other variant knows of no impostor. Here the hero falls asleep on the third day and the princess takes from him either a lock of hair or a shoe, or both. When afterwards the king orders his men to search the country for the unknown champion, he is easily recognised by means of one of these tokens. It is clear that

a connection exists between these two variants of the recognition scene and the number of days of the combat. The princess only realises the necessity of keeping the hero's shoe or cutting off a lock of hair, when she has come to know his habit of disappearing after his day's work on a previous occasion. On the other hand the impostor draws his sinister courage from the hero's unnoticed and ephemerical appearance.

In all the folk-tales an introduction has been prefixed to the story of the dragon fight; its object is to account for the supernatural power, with which the youthful hero is invested. Of this introduction two principal versions may be distinguished. In the first he possesses himself of a magic sword, or even armour, which he finds in a giants' hoard. The other version derives his heroic character from a supernatural birth and represents his mother as having eaten a wonderful fish, which is sometimes styled "The Queen of Fishes". Of these the former is not sufficient in itself, for the sword can only be won by killing the giants, and thus supernatural power is required even at this stage of the story. Thus the fight with the giants involves a preliminary introduction, where the hero makes friends with a supernatural being, mostly an animal, which imparts to him the necessary magical qualities.

From the two Irish representatives of the introduction I distinguish these versions as the Speckled bull-version and the White salmon-version. In the Irish tale called *An tarbh breac* the boy is being ill treated by a stepmother, who sends him out to look after the cattle but leaves him without food. Among the herd there is a speckled bull. It nourishes the boy from its horn. When the stepmother becomes aware of this, she determines on having the animal killed. She does not succeed, however, but at the same time the bull has to leave the place. It takes the boy with it, and when they find themselves in safety in the woods, it tells him, as soon as it will have been killed in a fight with another bull, to strip it of a part of its skin and thus make a girdle, which will preserve him in all subsequent dangers. It is this girdle which afterwards enables the hero to overcome the giants and win the magic sword.

The *Speckled bull* version occurs in other variants of our story also. In the Breton folk-tale given by Luzel we find a supernatural animal called the "Murlu", which supports the boy, who is the son of the king of France and his second wife, in his three days' struggle with the giants. Afterwards the Murlu is transformed into a beautiful horse; it carries the boy to the place of the dragon fight and quenches the monster's fire by vomiting large gushes of water. At the end the Murlu makes itself known to the hero as a transformation of his father's first wife, who had attempted to seduce his mother when, disguised as a young page, she first came to the kings court; she had died of grief because of her lack of success, and her punishment consisted in remaining in animal shape, until the day when she should succeed in marrying the young prince to a lady he would have saved from a dragon.

Notwithstanding the complicated form, in which the *Speckled bull* version occurs in this story, it shows the same fundamental conception as the Irish tale, and we may gather from it that here also the speckled bull, although it is not explicitly stated, must, be considered as a transformation animal. Other evidence confirms this view. In an Irish story of an altogether different type[10], where the King of Greece's sword has to be won in order to fight a giant, the speckled bull's part is played by a white horse, which gives exactly the same advice as the speckled bull: *bain an croiceann díom*. The true nature of this horse is revealed by the helpful horse in a Breton folktale, which makes itself known as the hero's grandfather[11]. An interesting variant of the group of tales discussed here is supplied by the Egyptian legend of the *Two Brothers*[12], where āa good many of the elements which constitute the Celtic tales (such as the helpful bull, the false queen, etc.) may be discerned, though differently connected.

The *White Salmon*—version of the introduction in its simplest form is very perspicuous. The supernatural power, which the hero displays in fighting the dragon, is accounted for by a supernatural birth. The hero's mother has been denied the blessings of maternity during many years of matrimony until, by the intercession of supernatural powers, a child is born, which afterwards becomes a hero. This trait is quite common even in newly-made stories[13].

The Wonderful Fish presents itself in two different ways. Either it is caught by the father, who is a fisherman, and reveals its secret only when its life is threatened (thus in *Ar Zarpant Milliguet* and *Le Fils du Pêcheur*), or the father consults a wizard as to how to get an heir, and is told to go fishing and make his wife eat the Wonderful Fish he will catch (*An Bradán Geal*). In the former variant the fish provides the future hero at the same time with a set of animal friends, who, deriving their life force from the same source, will remain devoted to him and support him in all dangers. In *Ar Zarpant Milliguet* the fish tells the father to give the water, in which it is boiled, to the bitch, the bones to the mare, and to plant the three big thorns that will be found in its interior in the garden. Thus are born on the same day three boys, three cubs and three colts, and in the garden three lances spring up. In *Le Fils du Pêcheur* the same thing happens. *An Bradán Geal* puts it differently. Here the wizard strictly forbids that anyone should partake of the fish but the mother. The cook, however, desirous to taste of her own hands' work, puts a little piece of fish into her mouth, and within a year she gives birth to a boy at the same moment as her mistress.

Thus in some versions the supernatural birth from the Wonderful Fish is connected with another well-known folk-element, that of the Helpful Animals, which, however, is not necessarily implied. The Life Brother, on the other hand, who in *An Bradán Geal* is born from the cook, occurs in all tales of this type and may be regarded as an essential element of the Wonderful Fish formula. In *Ar Zarpant Milliguet* and *Le fils du Pêcheur* the hero has two brothers from the outset, and the close connection, which exists between the three owing to their common birth, is expressed by the symbol of the Life Liquid, which the

parting brother leaves in the others' hands. The hero of *An Bradán Geal* tells his brother to go out into the garden every morning and observe the colour of the water in the well; as long as it has the colour of honey, he will be thriving well, but as soon as things turn against him, there will be the colour of blood upon it. In the same way in *Ar Zarpant Milliguet* the boys, on bidding farewell to the paternal home, leave a pitcher, filled with water, behind them; when there is something wrong with them, the water will become dark. The father of *Le Fils du Pêcheur* is told by the Wonderful Fish to preserve its blood in three vials, one of whom he is to give to each of his three sons; as soon as danger threatens them, the blood will boil. Similar traits are found in many other folktales[14].

As it has been argued before, an introduction conveying the hero's supernatural power, was attracted by the story of the dragon fight, but the special character of origin of this power was in no way determined by it. The Sword of the Giants, preceded by the *Speckled Bull* formula, and the *White Salmon* formula would suit equally well. For the structure of the story as a whole, however, the prefixion of the latter introduction had another consequence, which tended to sever it farther from the *Speckled Bull* variant. The Life Brother and the Life Liquid, both original elements of the *White Salmon* formula, play no part in the dragon fight, what shows the secondary character of the combination. Still it cannot be imagined, that they should be devoid of all interest for the further development of the story as a whole. We shall have to look for a connection outside the dragon fight.

The versions that open with the *White Salmon* formula, followed by the story of the dragon fight, have a sequel, which is lacking in those that have the *Speckled Bull* introduction, and which does bear a connection to the elements in discussion. This sequel is found in its simplest from in the Irish tale of *An Bradán Geal*. Soon after his marriage with the princess, whom he has delivered from the dragon, the hero sees a stag entering the room by the window and leaving it again on the opposite side. He saddles his horse and sets out to hunt it, accompanied by his dog and his hawk. At the falling of night he discovers a house, which is inhabited by a witch. She wants him to tie up the animals with a magic withe, and then she starts wrestling with him. When he is overcome, she touches him and his animals with a magic wand and changes them all into grey stones. On that very moment his Life Liquid turns dark as blood, and his Life Brother starts to trace him. When he gets to the court, they all take him for his brother and express their surprise, that he has been the first knight to return safely from the hunt of the enchanted stag. He does not reveal his identity and the next day, when the stag again crosses the room, he undertakes the hunt. The witch desires him to fasten up his animals, but the throws the withes into the fire. Then she attacks him, but with the help of the animals he masters her; wrings the wand from her, and delivers his brother and his three animals by touching them with it. At last the witch is turned into a stone.

Ar Zarpant Milliguet has exactly the same sequel, but for a few discrepancies owing to the differences in the introduction. Here the number of the brothers amounts to three, so that two of them have to be petrified before the third can perform the delivering act. Here the hunt is not introduced by the appearance of the enchanted stag—which, of course, has to be regarded as a transformation animal under the evil power of the witch,—but when looking from his window on the day after his marriage, the hero perceives a magic wood, which he enters hunting notwithstanding his wife's supplication. Here he discovers the witch and her hut after having passed through a terrible thunderstorm, which recalls that of *Owein and Lluned*. Of the brothers' animals only their dogs are mentioned and it is not expressly stated, that these are the dogs with whom each of them is connected by conception from the Wonderful Fish, but it may be surmised that the real character of the dogs must be explained in this way and that also the horses are understood.

In the Lorraine version *Le fils du pêcheur* the magic wood is replaced by a burning castle. This must be an innovation of this particular tale, as the burning castle belongs to a different type of story and has nothing to do with the hunt of the enchanted stag[15].

If this sequel of the Enchanted Hunt, which is found in all versions with the *White Salmon* introduction, is originally and essentially connected with it, the same question may be asked as to the Helpful Animals. It has already been pointed out that supernatural conception from a fish does not necessarily imply the birth of helpful animals of the same origin. The Irish version *An Bradán Geal* lacks the helpful animals altogether in the introduction, whereas they do appear here in the sequel. Thus the helpful animals were neither implied by the introduction, nor attracted by the dragon fight, where they play no part, but by the enchanted hunt. But even here they are only of an accidental character. In *An Bradán Geal,* when the second brother delivers the hero out of the power of the witch, he is assisted by his three helpful hunting animals. But *Ar Zarpant Milliguet* omits the horse entirely from the sequel, and assigns no active part to the dog in the wrestle with the witch; the magic lance, which was also engendered by the wonderful fish, appears to be forgotten at the end, and is superseded by a firearm, and but for the witch's transforming the dog and the firearm into stones, we should not be aware of anything supernatural in either of them. The Lorraine version given by Cosquin puts it exactly in the same way, but here the transformation object is a tuft of grass, Thus it would seem that, once the hero had been equipped for the enchanted hunt with hunting animals, which could assume more or less the character of helpful animals, a closer relation between him and his animal friends could easily be established, by deriving their birth from the identical supernatural power, emanating from the wonderful fish. But at the same time the helpful animals are essential neither to the Wonderful Fish nor to the Enchanted Hunt formula.

This conclusion is confirmed by the observation that helpful animals are sometimes utilised in altogether different connections. In one of the versions of our tale taken down by Luzel in Brittany[16], the hero is assisted by helpful animals in all his difficulties, but here they are no hunting animals owing to the absence of the enchanted hunt. The hero meets a bear, a fox and a hare, who lend him their services first in overcoming a set of robbers, then in delivering a princess from a dragon, and finally in exposing the impostor. In this version the hero has no supernatural birth, what is decisive for the character of the helpful animals also. Helpful animals are found in many folktales and in various forms. They borrow their special character in each case from the possibilities afforded by the story into which they are introduced.

The helpful animals, once they have found their way into a story framed out of various elements, will easily find a part to play in each of these. The more remarkable is the fact that they figure but rarely in the dragon fight. The version given by Luzel in *Mélusine* is almost unique in this respect. In the dragon fight the folktale raises itself unconsciouly to the level of the epic, and shrinks before impairing the hero's character by lending him any supernatural aid. Exactly the same fact may be noticed in those variants, which have the *Speckled Bull* introduction in stead of the Wonderful Fish formula. Here also the speckled bull retires, when the heroic deeds commence, and it is only in the Breton *Murlu* story, that the Murlu, rather awkwardly and to great detriment of the epic character of the whole, takes an active part in the combat by vomiting water and thus quenching the monster's flames.

Only where the dragon fight is extended with the scene of an impostor, who attempts to profit from the hero's fatigue and secure the royal bride for himself by presenting the monster's heads to the King, the helpful animals come in regularly. The impostor is not an essential element of the dragon fight, in the Irish version *An Bradán Geal* he is not alluded to. But in a great many tales of the *Perseus* type he is well-known[17]. The hero either retires or falls asleep after the combat. The impostor, who is mostly a charcoal-burner (or three charcoal-burners), passes and finds the monster's heads, without noticing that the tongues have been cut out. The king finds himself under the obligation to accept him as his son-in-law, though reluctantly, and the wedding-feast begins. At this moment the helpful animals come in. In *Ar Zarpant Milliguet* the dog provides for his master an opportunity to appear before the king and present the dragon's tongues, by surrendering itself into the hands of the king's servants on the third day, after having overthrown the dining table twice before. Cosquin's Lorraine version puts it in much the same way: the dog penetrates into the hall twice over, and the third time it is pursued by the king himself who thus detects the hero.

In the two Breton versions given by Luzel the development is slightly different, owing to the preceding traits. In the *Murlu* story the Murlu appears in the hall and transforms itself into a beautiful queen, who discloses the impostor's lies. In the *Mélusine* version the hare and the fox venture themselves into the hall on the first and second day to tell the princess that the hero is coming to claim her for his rightful bride. On the third day the bear takes him on its back and forces a way to the king's presence, where the hero produces the dragon's tongues and challenges the impostor to battle. he impostor never accepts the challenge and expiates his crime on the pyre or the gallows.

Of the impostor scene the same thing may be said as of the helpful animals. It is in no way essential to the dragon fight and adapts itself to the trend of each particular tale. In some versions it is altogether lacking. Sometimes the hero disappears because of his utter fatigue owing to his many wounds and burns, sometimes he retires out of modesty. The character of the impostor is not fixed and the incidents connected with the recognition vary. The whole scene is but a digression, which does not contribute to the development of the story. Still it seems possible to account for its introduction into so many folktales of the *Perseus* type. It was attracted not so much by an artistic desire of contrast between the ideal hero and the wicked world, as by the psychological necessity to place the hero's identity in the king's eyes beyond all doubt. Once it has been contested and successfully maintained, it remains unquestionable.

Hence it is in no way surprising, that with a similar object other episodes were introduced into tales, where the impostor is unknown. Thus in the Irish version *An Tarbh Breac* the struggle with the monster lasts three days, and on the third day, when the princess has come to know the hero's habit of vanishing after his difficult work, she snatches a shoe from him, which enables her afterwards to retrace her deliverer. In the same way *An Bradán Geal* makes the hero befriend himself with the princess on two subsequent days, after he has loosened her fetters and expressed his desire to await the monster by her side. At the falling of night, when the dragon has remained invisible, he makes away of a sudden, promising to return on the morrow. Thus, when on the third day he falls asleep on her bosom, she cuts off a lock of his hair, and later on, when the dragon has been killed and the hero is ready to vanish again, she manages to hold one of his shoes. Now she possesses two tokens, which will serve afterwards as a means of recognition.

The episode of the combat with the dragon, as it occurs in Tristan and Isolt, has preserved the main characteristics of the folktale from which it was borrowed, though a few details were modified in order to raise it to the level of a chivalresque romance. Both the introduction and the sequel are absent, as well as all the other traits connected with them. One would even hesitate to see in Tristan's horse a rest of the hero's helpful horse from the folktale, as the animal, far from protecting his master against the monster's flames, succumbs at the inception of the fight.

In Tristan's dragon fight, besides, the princess is not going to be sacrificed by her countrymen to the monster as a tribute, but the king will present her as a reward to the slayer of the devastating dragon. Thus the hero is not so much the deliverer of the maiden as of the country. The impostor, of course, could not remain a charcoal-burner or a dwarf, but was raised to a courtier's rank, though in Eilhart's relation his original character is by no means eclipsed. In order to escape from the impostor's snares the princess rides out the day after the combat and discovers the exhausted hero herself. Thus a connection is established between the hero and the heroïne, what was a necessity, since the hero does not deliver her with his own hands. The healing episode, which ensues, is in accordance with the character of Isolt in the romance.

The most conspicuous, however, of all details in the whole episode of the romance are the two recognition scenes, where Isolt identifies the dragon-slayer first with Tantris, then with Tristan. Tantris was the wounded harper, whom she had healed on his previous visit to Ireland, Tristan the slayer of her uncle, the Morold. It will be noticed, that the two recognition scenes occur only in the redaction of Tristan and Isolt by Thomas. The older redaction, represented by the fragment of Béroul and Eilhart von Oberge's *Tristan,* only mentions the latter, owing to the fact that here the hero, after his first voyage for healing to Ireland, has not been admitted to Isolt's presence, but is only presented with a powerful plaster, which she prepares for him.

There is a controversy between prof. Bédier and the much regretted Miss Schoepperle on this subject[18]. Miss Schoepperle has shown[19] that in the French Prose Romance, which along with Eilhart is our only existing authority for this part of the Béroul version, the whole dragon combat is an interpolation. Hence this version knew only of a recognition with Tristan, the slayer of Morold. Thus it becomes questionable whether the recognition scene with Tantris, and the meeting in person of Tantris and Isolt during the voyage for healing, by which this recognition is implied, must be assigned to the original Tristan romance (the *Estoire*), or not.

From a logical point of view Miss Schoepperle can only be right in answering this question in the negative. Tristan sets out to win for his under the Princess of the Swallow's Hair, who needs must be unknown to him. If Tristan, after the slaying of Morold and the first voyage to Ireland as Tantris, recovers his health by Isolt's personal care, the quest of the Princess of the Swallow's Hair is deprived of its original significance. Hence it may be argued that the *Estoire* knew of no meeting of Isolt and Tantris (or Pro, as he is called by Eilhart), and consequently of no recognition as Tantris after the dragon fight. According to Miss Schoepperle only one recognition of the hero can be accepted for the *Estoire* after the slaying of the dragon, namely that as Tristan, the killer of Morold, from the missing fragment in his blade.

Miss Schoepperle admits, that some uncertainty in this part of the narrative is not surprising. It arose from the mixing together of two inconsistent elements, the voyage for healing and the quest of the Princess of the Swallow's Hair. The *Estoire* discarded the contradiction by representing Isolt as preparing a plaster for Tristan, but not seeing him personally at the court. Thomas, on the other hand, who rejected the swallow and the golden hair as childish, made Tantris appear at the Irish court and recover his health by Isolt's personal attendance, what involved another recognition scene after the dragon combat.

Now even this original uncertainty would justify us in questioning the *Estoire's* demand for logic as it is proposed by Miss Schoepperle. Something may be said in behalf of prof. Bédier's case too. In Thomas and his followers we find two recognition scenes, one arising from the previous encounter of Tantris and Isolt, and the other from the missing fragment in the hero's blade. Of these only one, namely the second, occurs in Eilhart and, it may be assumed, Béroul. What is more likely to have happened, the discarding of one by Béroul, or its invention by Thomas?

The invention of the recognition as Tantris could easily be accounted for, once the healing by Isolt in person was there, and it was, no doubt, attracted by it. But would an original version represent the hero as crossing to Ireland, as the only place on earth where his health could be recovered, without his encountering at the same time the princess that was to heal him? If we find one version where such a meeting occurs, and another where it is lacking, is it not more probable that the former preserves the original tradition, even if a want of logic must be waived, and that the latter has endeavoured to establish the missing order?

The solution of the problem depends on the interpretation of Tristan's island combat with Morold. The king of Ireland claims a tribute from Cornwall and sends Morold, his wife's brother, to levy it. However, Morold is killed by Tristan, and his corpse is taken to Ireland, where a fragment of Tristan's blade is found in it. Afterwards the hero, who has been wounded with Morold's envenomed sword, finds healing in Ireland and his identity is not discovered. But on a later quest for a bride for his king he is recognised owing to the failing fragment of his sword.

Miss Schoepperle points out that this story is founded upon a popular tradition. Consequently it must be considered apart from all relations which the persons that play a part in it bear to each other or to the Tristan romance. Morold, though represented as the king's brother-in-law, is originally not a human being[20]. Monster's levying tribute are well-known in folktales[21]. As a rule the annual tribute consists of a young man or maid, and is only stopped when the king's daughter herself is being threatened by the monster and an unknown hero delivers her. After the combat the hero has his wounds dressed by her, but then escapes, until he is recognised by a token. These tales constitute a division of the Perseus legend[22] and are closely related to the tales analysed in the present paper.

In the Morold episode all these elements occur, and but for the relations existing between the different persons, caused by its being adapted to the Tristan romance, it would not be difficult to recognise them. Morold has become a man, though many of his supernatural traits remain, and the brother of the Irish queen. At the same time the place of the delivered princess that was to attend the hero and recognise him after his escape by a fragment of his blade, was taken by Isolt of Ireland. That, however, these two were originally not one and the same person, still appears from the fact that the lady that heals the hero's wounds is not Isolt the princess but her mother, Isolt the queen. Thus the Morold story was linked to the love romance of Tristan and Isolt by what may be styled a partial identification of the heroïnes. A similar process is adopted at a later stage of the romance. During his exile in Brittany a commonplace romantic trait is attached to the person of Tristan. He supports Kaherdin, who finds himself in a great strain, and thus wins his friend's sister as his wife. This lady also bears the name of Isolt, and by this outer symbol the combination of this episode with the rest of the romance acquires a very intimate character.

In fact, three conceptions were interwoven in the *Estoire* to account for the winning of Isolt by Tristan:

1. The princess is intended as a tribute to Morold, who is, however, slain by Tristan. She heals his wounds, but he escapes. Afterwards he is recognised by a token. This token, as we have seen already, is mostly a lock of hair or a shoe. But according to the tastes of chivalry, which prevail in the romance of Tristan, a fragment of the blade, which is discovered in the monster's corpse, is put in stead.

2. A swallow drops a golden hair in the court and the king vows to marry the lady to whom it belongs. The quest is accomplished by one of his heroes.

3. The hero slays a dragon and exposes an impostor by producing the tongue. Thus he wins the bride.

Of these three conceptions the first, which, in fact, is but a variant of the third, was more or less curtailed in order to make it consistent with the story as a whole: the princess is no longer intended as a tribute for the Morold. This modification, as all other alterations in the subject-matter of the story, was caused by the localisation of both the Morold's and the princess' home in Ireland and the establishing of a blood relation between Morold and Isolt. The lady claimed as a tribute was now eliminated from the story and only a few traits were left, which betray her original presence, namely the healing of Tristan by the Irish queen, and the recognition from the missing fragment of his blade. Another of these traits is that Mark after the Morold combat makes Tristan his heir, what in the underlying folktale doubtless implied the giving of his daughter as a wife.

The further modifications involved by the interweaving of the three conceptions as explained above, are the following.

1. The healing of Tristan has been split up. It is started, although in vain, in Cornwall, that is the country delivered from tribute, and finished in Ireland, the residence of the princess that takes the place of the lady saved by the hero.

2. A voyage for healing must be introduced. The curing lady is the queen and the hero meets the future heroïne only to teach her harping. In a branch of the tradition, namely in the Béroul-Eilhart version, this meeting was omitted and superseded by the sending of a plaster, in order to avoid contradiction with the formula of the Princess of the Swallow's Hair.

3. Isolt regards Tristan as her enemy, because he has slain her uncle. Thus a conflict is created in her, as he is at the same time the deliverer of her country from the fiery dragon.

4. The various recognitions must get a fixed place, which is not inconsistent with the general trend of the romance. The recognition of Tristan as the slayer of the dragon by his being able to produce the monster's tongue preserves its original position immediately after the exploit. The recognition of Tristan as the slayer of Morold by the lost fragment of the blade is deferred until after the dragon combat, thus causing the tragic conflict in Isolt already referred to. A third recognition (as Tantris) survives in that part of the tradition, which has not discarded the encounter of Tristan and Isolt during the voyage for healing. Here, on the other hand, the formula of the Princess of the Swallow's Hair was deliberately left out, since it was not an unknown bride the hero went to win for his lord, but the lady to whose tender care he owed the recovery from his wounds, inflicted by the Morold.

Of all these modifications the original enmity, arising from the blood relation between Isolt and Morold, was by far the most important. It engendered the tragical conflict in Isolt, which is the most outstanding characteristic of this portion of the romance. The author of the *Estoire* was fully aware of the necessity to credit Tristan with as much good-will in Isolt's eyes as he could possibly accumulate. The dragon fight was already there, but this was more to the country's benefit than Isolt's. So Tristan was made the princess' beloved harping teacher during his previous visit, but even so there was Morold's blood on his hands. Nothing but the love potion could wipe it off. In the scenes preceding Isolt's leaving Ireland in Tristan's company a contradiction remains, which strikes every reader's eyes. The sudden change in the princess can be explained from obedience to her parents, but on the side of the king and queen, who resent the slaying of Morold so strongly, it remains puzzling. Here the way in which the *Estoire* was patched up, peeps through. But for the blood relation between Morold and the Irish royal house everything would be quite natural. In the underlying folktale, of course, the Morold never levied tribute in behalf of a foreign king, but on his own account. It was this new-established blood relation which gave birth to a well-devised tragical conflict, but to a rather awkward contradiction at the same time.

Notes

1. The scene does not occur in the fragment of Béroul. See *Eilhart von Oberge*, 1598-2264.

2. See Gertrude Schoepperle, *Tristan and Isolt*, I, 203 sqq.

3. *E Korn an Oaled*, livet ha renket gant an aotrou Jézégou, Quimper, 1923. J. M. Guivarc'h.

4. Cf. *Revue Celtique*, 37, 323 sqq. (the co'our of the sail on the returning hero's ship).

5. *E Korn an Oaled*, p. 239 sqq.

6. "Eur paourkeaz reuzeudijk, tort, luch, kamm, pikouzet, eun druez a welet."

      Revue Celtique, XLI.

7. See *Mélusine*, I, 57; *Revue des traditions populaires*, IX, 172 sq.; F. M. Luzel, *Contes populaires de Basse-Bretagne*, II, 296 suiv.

8. Irish: *An tarbh breac* (ed. Dublin, Gill and Son); *Brian 7 Aodh an braddiu gbil* (ed. Athlone, Cumann Clodhadóireachta). A Scotch variant is cited by E. S. Hartland, *The legend of Perseus*, I, 37, where variants from all other parts of the world will also be found.

9. See E. Cosquin, *Contes populaires de Lorraine*, no. 5. (*Le fils du pécheur*); cf. also no. 37.

10. *Sgéaluidhe fíor na seachimhaine*, ed. by An Craoibhín Aoibhinn, Dublin, 1911, Gill and Son, p. 48 sqq.

11. "*Me, va mabig, eo da dad-koz*": Jézégou, *E korn an oaled*, p. 107.

12. Quoted by Andrew Lang, *Myth, ritual and religion*, II, 318 sqq.

13. Cf. the story of Daniel O'Connell's birth in Lady Gregory's *Kiltartan History Book*, p. 23 sq.

14. See, for instance, the Egyptian story quoted by Andrew Lang.

15. Cf. the tale quoted above from *Sgéaluidhe fíor na seachtmhaine*, where both the enchanted hunt and the burning castle occur independently from each other.

16. See *Mélusine*, I, 57.

17. See E. S. Hartland, *The legend of Perseus*, vol. III, appendix, table C.

18. See J. Bédier, *Le Roman de Tristan*, II, 210 sqq. and G. Schoepperle, *Tristan and Isolt*, I, 84 sqq.

19. See also Röttiger, *Der heutige Stand der Tristanforschung*, Hamburg, 1897.

20. See Eilhart von Oberge, *Tristan*, l. 351 sqq.

21. For instances see G. Schoepperle, *op. cit.*, II, 326 sqq. The connection with the Irish *fomoire* must be rejected.

22. See E. S. Hartland, *Legend of Perseus*, III, 1-95.

Roger Sherman Loomis (essay date 1927)

SOURCE: "Problems of the Tristan Legend," in *Romania*, Vol. 53, 1927, pp. 82-102.

[*In the following essay, Loomis examines several areas of critical disagreement regarding the Tristan legend: the in-*

fluence of the Welshman Bleheris on the development of the legend, the relation of the legend to the Irish tale of Diarmaide and Grainne, and the dating of Thomas's poem.]

Readers of *Romania* are aware that in vol. LI M. Ferdinand Lot attacked with some severity the theory, proposed by Miss Weston and elaborated by myself, that a certain Welshman Bleheris was to be regarded as an important figure in the development of Arthurian romance[1]. Giraldus Cambrensis, Thomas, the author of *Tristan,* Pseudo-Wauchier, and Wauchier de Denain, all refer to this Bleheris though under somewhat different forms of the name; and there are other less certain references to a Blihos Bleheris and a Master Blihis, who may be identical with him. M. Lot maintains that of these six authors, only Giraldus and Thomas speak from authentic knowledge. In particular he disputes the credibility of Wauchier's statement that Bleheris was born and brought up in Wales and told tales to a Count of Poitiers, who loved "l'estoire" more than any other did. This and the remaining allusions to Bleheris he regards as disingenuous inventions, having no basis in fact beyond what was derived from the reading of Giraldus Cambrensis.

Now it is the chief value of M. Lot's article, in my opinion, that he has led us to perceive that when an author refers, as Wauchier does, vaguely to a Count of Poitiers, there was probably some one outstanding Count of Poitiers whom he had in mind and whom his readers would recognize. Dr. Brugger has argued that the noble in question is Henry Fitzempress, who for two years before his accession to the throne of England in 1154 enjoyed the title of Count of Poitou[2]. But no one fifty years or more later would have referred to Henry by the title, and he would not have been understood if he had. William VIII of Poitou, whom Miss Weston[3], Prof. Levi[4], and I have urged as the probable patron of Bleheris, may be questioned on similar grounds, though he cannot be altogether rejected. The only count of Poitiers who was celebrated at the end of the twelfth century as a personality and a patron of arts was William VII, the famous troubadour. Miss Weston[5] and Prof. Singer[6] preceded M. Lot in this identification, but it is M. Lot's argument which compels me to agree in his conclusion: "Wauchier de Denain, s'il a pensé à un conte de Poitiers en particulier, a dû songer à Guillaume VII"[7].

But M. Lot is doubtful after all whether any historic figure lies behind the allusion, and denies strenuously that Wauchier had any historic basis for the association of count and conteur. He proposes a new and ingenious theory: Wauchier had read Giraldus Cambrensis' *Descriptio Kambriae,* in which the famous *fabulator* Bledhericus is mentioned, and had also read the romance of *Joufrois,* in which he found a jongleur-loving Count of Poitiers. He merely put two and two together. Taken by itself, the theory is possible. But search M. Lot's article for proofs of the influence of either of these works on Wauchier, and there is none. How, then, does M. Lot arrive at certainty in

the matter? Having pointed out that two editions of the *Descriptio* appeared in 1194 and between 1213 and 1215 respectively, he continues[8]: "L'une ou l'autre *a donc pu* être connue de Wauchier de Denian, dont l'activité littéraire couvre le premier tiers du XIIIᵉ siècle. Entreprenant d'écrire une suite au *Perceval le Gallois* de Chrétien de Troyes, Wauchier *était porté* à se procurer et à lire une description du pays de Galles (Cambria). Y voyant invoquée l'autorité d'un 'famosus fabulator' il *a pris* tout naturellement ce personnage comme garantie de ses propres récits, obéissant à la préoccupation du temps d'invoquer des autorités pour les histoires, surtout quand elles étaient de pure fantaisie." In brief, the argument is simply: Wauchier could have read Giraldus: *ergo* he did. What color of plausibility the theory possesses it derives from the assumed falsity of all citations of authority by medieval historians and romancers. But this premise would also force us to believe that Layamon did not draw upon Wace because he cites him, and would work havoc with other known derivations. When M. Lot comes to the question of *Joufrois,* he is so carried away by his hypothesis that he exclaims[9]: "Gageons que Wauchier de Denain venait de lire le roman de *Joufroís* au moment où il écrivait la continuation de *Perceval.*" But again M. Lot fails to bring anything more than his enthusiasm to prove that what was possible was a fact. Of positive evidence for M. Lot's view there is not a trace.

We come to the alternative theory which M. Lot rejects, namely, that Wauchier reports a reliable tradition that Bleheris told his tales to a certain Count of Poitiers. This theory enjoys the support of scholars like Miss Weston, Levi, Brugger, Nitze, and Brown. It deserves a serious refutation. M. Lot's attack is contained in these two sentences[10]: "Les deux seuls personnages qui ont connu, et de réputation seulement, Breri-Bledhericus, Thomas et Giraud de Barry, sont l'un un Anglo-Normand, l'autre un Gallo-Normand. Imaginer que la réputation d'un 'fabulator' gallois ait pu passer sur le continent ´par la voie orale et lui survivre longtemps, c'est supposer un fait dont il n'y a aucun autre exemple." True enough. But the word "réputation" begs the whole question at issue. It assumes that Bleheris did not *in person* cross to France, the very point which M. Lot is called upon to demonstrate. But instead of a demonstration he offers us a neat example of *petitio principii.*

There is nothing in his argument to convince anyone who does not presuppose that medieval citations of authority are uniformly spurious and that Welsh nationality precludes any share in the propagation of Arthurian romance on the Continent. There is for me something hard to understand in M. Lot's position. For many years in the pages of *Romania*[11], he has demonstrated the presence of Welsh elements, particularly proper names, in French romances of the Round Table, and in the very issue in which he attacks Bleheris, he propounds that Lancelot himself owes his name to the Welsh Llenlleawc[12]. More than that, he has stoutly denied that Wace and others who refer to the propagators of Arthurian legends as *Bretons* or *Britones* could mean any but Welshmen, though he admits that the words themselves as applied to contemporaries usually meant Bretons, and though the words *Gallois* or *Wallenses* are never applied to the conteurs[13]. Bleheris is the only Welshman, clearly specified as a transmitter of the Arthurian legend. Yet M. Lot gags at Bleheris. Why? Because there is no other example of a Welshman who enjoyed such a reputation on the Continent. In other words, simply because he was a Welshman! This argument will appeal least of all to those who accept M. Lot's own articles in *Romania,* and who see no reason why a French-speaking Welshman, of whom there must have been many by the year 1100, should not have crossed to the Continent and made himself famous as a conteur.

If M. Lot in the first part of his article seems to have mistaken a possibility for a certainty, in the end he has mistaken an impossibility for a probability. Granting as he does that Giraldus had authentic knowledge of a real Bledhericus, M. Lot attempts to determine what he did to make himself famous since he could not have charmed the Count of Poitiers with his tales. M. Lot concludes that Bledhericus was not a storyteller at all, but a serious historian, and recommends that students of early British history search for surviving traces of his work. He is tempted to identify him with a certain Bledri or Blethery, Bishop of Landaff from 983-1022[14]. It is obvious that these suggestions are in flat contradiction to Giraldus' words, which qualify him as a *fabulator.* In the first part of his article M. Lot consistently implies that the term means a professional reciter of tales: his argument turns on this interpretation. In 1896 he wrote[15]: "Breri n'est pas un barde; c'est un conteur (*fabulator*), et c'est par cette dernière classe qu'était conservée l'épopée celtique en Galles et en Irlande." Now how can one maintain that Giraldus, a learned and well-informed cleric, who would certainly have known if this Bledhericus had written serious history, referred to him by so derogatory a term as *fabulator*[16]? One might as easily suppose that a Supreme Court Justice, author of erudite treatises on the law, should be described in his obituary merely as a famous writer of detective stories. It is also unlikely that Giraldus would say of one who flourished nearly 175 years before his time that "tempora nostra *paulo* praevenit". Of this expression M. Lot once held that "it may mean anything from ten to a hundred years; we might say that Bonaparte lived a little before our time[17]". Perhaps, but hardly the Young Pretender, Charles Edward. There is a gap of 172 years between the publication of the *Descriptio Kambriae* and the death of Bishop Bledri. In sum, if M. Lot attributes any authority to Giraldus' words, he cannot with consistency surmise that Bledhericus was a bishop, who wrote a Latin history of Britain.

This latter hypothesis M. Lot bases on Thomas's well-known statement that Breri knew "les gestes e les cuntes de tuz les reis, de tuz les cuntes ki orent esté en Bretaigne". Adopting Golther's interpretation[18], M. Lot declares[19]: "Il n'y a pas de doute: pour Thomas 'Breri' est un historien qui possède à fond l'histoire de 'Bretagne'". Are then the words *geste* and *cunte* limited in meaning to learned his-

tory, and are counts and kings of Britain mentioned only between the covers of Latin chronicles? None should know better than the distinguished author of *Étude sur le Lancelot en Prose* that such is not the case. Yet on this premise his deduction rests. As a matter of fact, Thomas's description of Breri is in entire accord with Giraldus. A famous conteur of Arthurian themes would inevitably be one who knew the *gestes* and *cuntes* of Uther, Leodegan, Lot, Pelles, Erec, Galeschin, and the multitudinous kings and nobles whose wars, loves, and adventures make up the cycle of the Table Round. M. Lot continues: "L'œuvre de Breri est nécessairement en latin, non en gallois, d'abord parce que cette dernière langue était inconnue de Thomas, et que même s'il l'avait possédée, il n'aurait pas renvoyé ses lecteurs à un auteur écrivant en un idiome impénétrable, ensuite parce que Giraud de Barry, reproduisant quelques lignes de Bledhericus, fait une citation latine, non une traduction." Here are three reasons given, the first of which is withdrawn in the next breath, the second is quite contrary to probability, since if Thomas was trying to milerad his readers, as M. Lot believes, he would, more likely than not, employ a reference his readers could not check up, and the third is a statement for which I find no warrant in the text. How does M. Lot know that Giraldus is not translating Bledhericus' remarks from the Welsh? Though I am among the first to acknowledge the great contribution M. Lot has made to historic and literary science, I frankly confess that his conclusions regarding Bleheris seem founded on false premises and misinterpreted evidence. Those scholars who are moved by his appeal to search for the Latin works of Bishop Bledri have my sympathy.

Thus far I have dealt only with M. Lot's own opinions. Let me pass to his criticism of my views. In the first paragraph on p. 401 he gives a very fair summary of my conclusions. "Ce fait capital que l'amour courtois a trouvé son véhicule narratif dans la matière de Bretagne doit, dans une large mesure, être mis sur le compte de Bleheri." But in the next paragraph he attributes to me this fantastic thesis: "Si les concepts de l'amour courtois, inconnus de l'antiquité, ont pu naître chez nous, c'est grâce au pollen fécondant transporté du Galles." May I refer the reader to these sentences in my article[20]: "The theories with which the Midi was aflame and which the troubadours celebrated in lyric form, Bleheris exemplified in his burning tale of Tristram and Ysolt." "It seems probable then that the legend of this hero was known in Brittany early in the eleventh century; that there the story of Ysolt of the White Hands was invented and developed; and that it was this already expanded legend that Bleheris knew and brought to Poitiers." The reader may judge how accurately M. Lot has reproduced my views.

Having held up to ridicule this distorted version of my conclusions, he dismisses them with scarcely any discussion of the facts on which I felt it necessary to found them. Let me review the evidence briefly[21]. Thomas cites Breri particularly as an authority on the Tristan legend. In Crestien's *Erec* a knight Bliobleheris, whose name is sometimes confused in MSS. with Bleheris, is mentioned as sitting next to Tristan. In Eilhart's *Tristant* there is a minor character Pleherin, whose name, M. Lot admits, may easily be derived from Bleheris. It seems not unreasonable to conclude that though Thomas alone had any clear conception of Bleheris' relation to the Tristan legend, Crestien vaguely connected the names, and Eilhart or his source, when put to it to supply a name, used one that was familiar in the Tristan tradition. To object that the association in the latter cases is incorrect and unintentional shows little understanding of the human mind. Modern psychology has demonstrated the importance of just such uncontrolled associations. Let us suppose that a folklorist, visiting an Irish village in quest of stories, should learn from one old man that his version of the exploits of Diarmaid was backed by the authority of a famous reciter of tales, by the name of Barrett, a real person who had died some time before. A second old man in telling a tale of Diarmaid introduces the name of Barrett as that of a minor character. A third old man in the course of another narrative mentions together the name of Diarmaid and a somewhat distorted form of the name Barrett. Would not the folklorist, knowing that Barrett had actually lived and told such stories as these, be justified in concluding that the unconscious linking of Diarmaid and Barrett in the minds of the last two men was not an accident but a definite corroboration of the statement of the first old man?

The coincidence in the testimony of Thomas, Crestien, and Eilhart becomes even more striking when one realizes that while two early Tristan romances, those of Thomas and Eilhart, suggest derivation from a tradition going back to Bleheris, most of the other early evidence on the Tristan story outside of Wales points more or less directly towards Eleanor of Poitou, granddaughter of that count of Poitiers, the presumptive patron of Bleheris[22]. Of the poets who treated the Tristan legend or allude to it, Crestien wrote at the court of Eleanor's daughter, Marie de Champagne; Thomas and Marie de France must have been in or close to Eleanor's own entourage; Bernard de Ventadour and Cercamon we know were in intimate association with the gay young countess. Five threads, therefore, connect the Tristan legend with one reared in the court of Poitou. "Especially noteworthy is the fact that Tristan is first mentioned in Continental literature by two troubadours immediately associated with" Eleanor and the court of Poitou. It is this body of evidence, so curiously corroborative of Wauchier's statement, of which M. Lot, in attacking my theory, says not a word. Without offering the slightest explanation for the familiarity of Bernard de Ventadour and Cercamon with the Tristan legend in the decade 1150-1160, before any Northern French author, he declares that the journey of Bleheris to Poitiers is a "chimaera bombinans in vacuo".

There is still another group of facts which militates against M. Lot's theory and with which he must deal. He has failed to realize the significance of Miss Weston's chapter on the Chastel Orguellous, of which the Bleheris citation is merely a part. She there points out that Wauchier seems

to be drawing on a series of disconnected though sometimes admirable tales, and refers to them as the *branches* of a *grand conte*. He appeals to his audience in the manner of reciters, and proposes that they say a pater-noster for the soul of a certain man of Loudun. There are also the significant lines[23]: "Puis vous ferez le vin doner; Tant m'orrez dire e conter. Seingneurs, la branche se depart Du grant conte, se Dieu me gart. Des or orrez comment il fu. De ce qu'avez atendu: Cil de Loudon [variant Lodun] racontera Que ce riche romans dira." Of this Dr. Brugger remarks acutely: "*Cil de Loudon* is no doubt a minstrel, who was a remanieur of Bledri's Gawain compilation . . . He was a native of Loudun near Poitiers[24]". If M. Lot's interpretation be applied here, we must believe that Wauchier was so anxious to impose on his readers of the thirteenth century and on the Celtists of the twentieth that he deliberately sprinkled through his verses the mannerisms of the conteurs, invented besides the visit of Bleheris to Poitiers an anonymous minstrel from Loudun near Poitiers, and asked for a paternoster for the soul of the mythical minstrel. It seems to me that M. Lot requires more of our credulity than Wauchier.

In the *Zeitschrift für Französische Sprache*, XLVII, 162, Dr. Brugger also has dealt with the Bleheris problem, and with many of his points I agree. For him Bleheris was a figure as important as Crestien de Troyes in the evolution of Arthurian romance. He also rejects from consideration Bledri ap Cadivor, a Welsh chieftain, as identical with the *fabulator*. But there are points on which we differ. He goes farther than I in taking literally the specific indebtedness which Wauchier acknowledges to Bleheris, and presumably accepts the other passage in which the Welshman's authority is invoked.

Personally I am not confident that he was the source of Thomas and Wauchier in more than a general sense. The intervening steps of oral tradition would inevitably produce considerable changes. Dr. Brugger refers to Bleheris as "Dichter", but there is no evidence to show that he was anything but a reciter of prose tales. His identification of the Count of Poitiers with Henry Fitzempress I reject for reasons already given. I also regret that I am among those whom he suspects of not reading his work because they do not accept his arguments regarding Blihos Bleheris. Of this knight who appears in the *Elucidation* prefixed to the *Conte del Graal,* one reads that "si tres bons contes savoit que nus ne se peust lasser de ses paroles escouter". Miss Weston and other scholars have been struck by the singular appropriateness of these lines in case there were a confusion of Bleheris and Blihos Bleheris. Dr. Brugger, however, produces a list of knights who recounted their adventures, and argues that they are conteurs in the same sense as Blihos Bleheris. I have looked through the list, but none conveys the same clear implication that he had a repertory of tales stored in his memory (not merely a knowledge of his own adventures) and that people were in the habit of listening to him for hours at a time. These are the attributes of Blihos Bleheris, and the reason Miss Weston's suggestion has had so many adherents is because these are the attributes of a professional conteur. Since the writer of the *Elucidation* knew of Master Blih[er]is as an authority on Arthurian tradition, it is quite possible that he knew other facts about him, which by a strange confusion he attached to the knight. If Dr. Brugger should note in an American novel of today an Italian count named Emilio Caruso, who had such a soul-stirring voice that no one who heard him could forget it, would he not recognize a reminiscence of the famous operatic singer? Or would he maintain that because the real Caruso was not named Emilio and was not a count, and because other counts had been known to sing, the description of Emilio was not suggested by Enrico?

One cannot be too literal-minded in investigations of material so nebulous, transmitted by men so little serious as these conteurs must have been. Does not Crestien rage at their capacity for mutilating the stories they tell in the presence of kings and counts[25]? These broken and distorted hints, these confused echoes of the facts are not to be wondered and caviled at, but rather to be expected. If they form a consistent pattern, we can only congratulate ourselves on our luck. Such a pattern we seem to possess in the case of Bleheris and his work.

Another debated problem in the realm of Tristan studies is the relation of the Continental legend to the insular and to the Irish saga of Diarmaid and Grainne. Miss Schoepperle first urged that the central situation of the French romances had its source in the Irish saga. M. Joseph Loth poured over the theory the vials of his sarcasm[26]. It would be superfluous for me to go over the ground, for any reader can turn to the parallels which Miss Schoepperle adduced for the splashing water and the separating sword, the latter feature being comprehensible only by reference to the different conditions of the Irish story[27]. But I may bring forward a new bit of evidence which proves the Welsh Tristan legend to be even more profoundly indebted to the same Irish saga than the French.

In the very year before M. Loth denied any connection between the French romance and Irish *aithed,* he had published the Welsh *Ystoria Trystan*[28]. Let me point out ten obvious resemblances between this charming tale and the Irish *Pursuit of Diarmaid and Grainne*[29].

1. The relationship of the characters is identical. Diarmaid is the lover of his uncle's wife, as is Trystan.

2. Both pairs of lovers escape to the forest.

3. In the Irish tale, Muadhan, who became Diarmaid's attendant, "dressed a bed of soft rushes and of birch tops" for the lovers[30]. In the Welsh, immediately after the mention of Trystan's page, we read "A couch of leaves was made for them."

4. The lovers in both tales are surrounded in the wood by the vengeful husband and his allies[31].

5. Both ladies are terrified. When Diarmaid hears the warning shouts, he wakes Grainne, but refuses to flee. "Fear and great dread seized Grainne when she heard that[32]." Compare with this: "When Esyllt heard the talking around the wood, she trembled between the two hands of Trystan."

6. The friends of the lover refuse to harm him. Oisin and Oscar, for instance, cry: "Come out to us, and none will dare to do thee harm, hurt, or damage[33]." When Trystan, sword in hand, attempts to break through, March's allies said: "'Shame upon us if we interfere with him.'"

7. The hero passes unscathed through the troops of his foe. When Diarmaid is told "Here are Fionn . . . and four hundred hirelings with him; . . . and if thou wouldst come out to us, we would cleave thy bones asunder," he "arose with an airy high exceeding light bound, by the shafts of his javelins, . . . and went a great way out beyond Fionn and beyond his people without their knowledge[34]." Trystan likewise "met March ap Meirchion, and then March said, 'I will kill myself in order to kill him.' . . . Thereupon Trystan went through the three battalions uninjured."

8. The wronged husband summons a king to his aid. Fionn summons the king of Alba[35] and March summons Arthur.

9. Finally a friend comes to the lover and arranges a reconciliation. Aonghus makes peace between Diarmaid and Fionn, King Cormac playing an important part[36]. So Gwalchmai persuades Trystan to return to Arthur, who makes peace between him and March.

10. The lovers are allowed to remain together. In the Irish, Diarmaid and Grainne for a time before the ultimate tragic ending settle in Rath Grainne[37]. The Welsh tale also gives them to each other but forever. Called on to decide whether Trystan or March should enjoy Esyllt, Arthur adjudged her to one while the leaves were on the wood and to the other while the leaves were not on the wood, and gave March the choice. He chose the leafless season; whereupon Esyllt blessed the holly, the ivy and the yew, which kept their leaves throughout their lives, and thus made her Trystan's as long as he lived.

As far back as 1903 Mr. John asked the question[38]: "Are we to trace any connection with the tale of Demeter and Persephone? And if so what is the connection, that of primitive community of myth or of late borrowing?" In 1883 Gaston Paris in a distinguished article proved that the abduction of Guinevere by Meleagant was a variant of the Persephone myth and certainly not a late borrowing[39]. In 1924 I proved that the abduction of Winlogee (Guinevere) on the Modena sculpture (1099-1106) originated in an Irish tale of the abduction of Blathnat by Curoi, and of her rescue by Cuchulinn, the sun-hero, after a battle lasting from Nov. 1 to the middle of spring[40]. Now Blathnat is a diminutive meaning Little Flower, and Grainne is also a diminutive meaning Little Grain[41]. There is abundant evidence, as I show in my *Celtic Myth and*

Arthurian Romance, that the Irish worshipped a vegetation goddess under many names. The goddess Tea, worshipped at Tara, was descended from Ith, "Grain", and was married to Eremon, the "Plowman[42]". All this creates a probability that Grainne is a romanticised vegetation goddess[43]. And it is hard to avoid the conclusion that the mythological suggestions which crop up in the story of Esyllt, Grainne's counterpart, are survivals of the original significance of the *Elopement of Diarmaid and Grainne,* which have been effaced in the extant late forms of the very ancient Irish legend.

There can be no shadow of doubt that this legend of Diarmaid and Grainne is the model for the Welsh *Ystoria Trystan*[44], since the opposite relationship is out of the question. There is also reason to suppose that the Welsh tale, in some form or other, has furnished in turn at least one episode to the French romance, the love of Kaherdin for Ysolt's handmaid. In the Welsh we read[45] that Kae Hir (the Tall) was in love with Golwg Hafddydd (Summer Day Visage), Esyllt's attendant. He goes to Esyllt and tells her of Trystan's escape. She blesses him and says that he will obtain a golden mistress. He replies that he desires no golden mistress but Golwg. Whereupon she declares that Golwg shall be his. According to Eilhart's *Tristrant*[46], based of course on a French poem, Kehenis woos Gymele, Isalde's maid, but she scorns him. But Isalde says: "For Tristan's sake, I will give you one of my maids to bear you company. Choose Brangene or Gymele as may please you, and I will bid her be with you tonight." Kehenis asks for Gymele, but she by the use of a magic pillow prevents the satisfaction of his passion that night. Thomas relates the same story about Kaherdin and Bringvain, but adds that after two tantalizing nights the lover finally has his desire[47]. Can the bestowal of Esyllt's maid on her lover's friend, which appears in both stories, be regarded as fortuitous especially when the friend's name in Welsh is Kae Hir and in the French Kaherdin, a corruption probably due to assimilation to the Turkish name Kahedin or Kaardin[48]?

The conclusion is unavoidable that the Irish elopement tale of Diarmaid and Grainne formed the nucleus of the Welsh and French Tristan legends. It is also clear that some Welsh accretions to that nucleus, which are lost to us in their Celtic form, are probably imbedded in the French romances. But we must not believe that these Welsh materials passed directly into France through the agency of Bleheris. Dr. Brugger prudently warns us[49]: "His Cymric descent indicates little or nothing as to the origin of his narrative materials." Neither can we believe that the Anglo-Normans had any considerable share in the transmission, since the *Waldef* passage which so largely influenced Gaston Paris has been questioned by M. Bédier and altogether rejected by other scholars[50]. The Welsh legend must have passed through a Cornish stage, for most of the Continental versions make the injured husband king of Cornwall, and all lay certain crucial scenes in Tintagel or its neighborhood. I am far from subscribing, however, to M. J. Loth's theory of the Cornish origin and immediate transmission of the legend from Cornwall to France[51]. The in-

troduction of Lancien and the chapel of Saint Samson seem to me late localizations, made after French conteurs had begun to cater to audiences in England. At least, these details cannot have deep roots in tradition since Béroul is the only poet who knows them. There are signs that the legend had taken root in Brittany as early as 1000, since M. Bédier pointed out a considerable number of Breton names in the romance[52] and we have records of three historic Bretons by the name of Tristan before 1050[53]. One of them, a lord of Vitré, seems to have influenced the legend in turn. Curiously enough, he was the son of a Rivallon or Ruivallon[54], and since the account of these two real persons in the *Chronique de Vitré* is quite uncontaminated by the romance and bears all the earmarks of genuine history, it is highly probable that the hero's father, in Gottfried and Eilhart, owes his name to a reminiscence of Ruivallon lord of Vitré. M. Bédier pointed out that in the name "Rouland riis" which the same figure bears in *Sir Tristrem* there is a corruption of Rivallon[55]. M. Muret and Dr. Brugger in turn, noting how closely R and K resemble each other in manuscript, suggested that "Rouland riis" was related to the name which the Norse Saga and Gottfried give to Tristan's father, "Kanelengres[56]". All these suggestions lead to the conclusion that the original form was "Rivalon" or "Riuelen reis[57]". This could have produced easily both "Rouland riis" and "Kanelengres". When Gottfried says, "Sin rehter name was Riwalin, sin anam was Kanelengres, . . . kunec uber daz lant ze Lohnois[58]", he is putting together two versions of the same fact; namely that Tristan's father was Riualen, king (*reis*) of Loonois. On the name Loonois I accept the theory proposed by M. Lot[59] and conclusively demonstrated by Dr. Brugger in his admirable article[60], and it points, together with the name of Tristan himself, toward the region of Lothian and a Pictish king as the starting points of the legend. The names which *Sir Tristrem* and Gottfried assign to Tristran's fatherland, Ermonie and Parmenie, seem to me certainly corruptions of Armorique, since it is a dependency of the Duke of Brittany, and since Hertz has shown that the transformation of Armorica into Armenia occurs more than once in documents[61]. Gottfried, then, in the statement quoted above was combining the ancient tradition which made Tristan's father king of Lothian with the later Breton tradition which confused him with Ruivallon, father of the historic Tristan, lord of Vitré and vassal of the Duke of Brittany.

That the development of the Second Ysolt theme took place mainly in Brittany seems clear from the localization, the presence of such names as Carhaix, Nantes, Hoel, a second Rivalin, etc. The suggestion for the Second Ysolt may have come, as M. Lot pointed out[62], from Wales, for two Esyllts are mentioned together in *Kilhwch,* though whether these are really two distinct personages or simply the same person with two epithets, as are so many in the same list, we cannot determine. That the story of the First Ysolt still retains a vestige of the Irish tradition that Diarmaid for a long time spurned Grainne Miss Schœpperle demonstrated in her discussion of the separating sword. But the Second Ysolt, once created, could take over this humiliating part of the tradition, and we find the incident of the splashing water attached to her. This and the motif of the black and white sails are the only Celtic traits which Miss Schœpperle could discover connected with the Second Ysolt[63]. And this is natural enough, for Prof. Singer has made the highly significant discovery[64] that the story of the Second Ysolt and her brother Kaherdin follows in all essentials the Arabic story (dated 687) of Kais and Lobna,—a fact which gives added point to the substitution of Turkish Kaherdin for Welsh Kae Hir. All this development I believe took place on Breton soil, so consistently is the background Breton.

That the Bretons used alien material cannot be regarded as incredible ever since Prof. Kittredge demonstrated the use of the classic tale of Orpheus in the Breton lai of *Sir Orfeo*[65]. Nor is it hard to conceive that a Welshman should have adopted a Breton version of the Tristan romance. Geoffrey of Monmouth, contemporary of Bleheris, and like him "nes e engenuis en Gales", employed as the foundation of the *Historia Regum Britanniae* a book which he attests was brought from Brittany and which the internal evidence of proper names shows to have contained insular Arthurian tradition in Bretonized form[66]. It is quite on the cards, then, that a Welsh conteur should have gone to Brittany for his materials.

Needless to say, a legend which now included the romantic Irish *aithed*, with its motif of the deserted husband, and also the romantic Arabic story, with its motif of the spurned wife, lent itself perfectly to illustrate the theories of courtly love. It would seem to be the most momentous of the achievements of Bleheris that he brought this tale to the court of William VII at the crucial time. There could not have been a more perfect narrative vehicle for the spirit of the age than this composite romance. Told with some of the colorful detail characteristic of contemporary Welsh prose and with the dramatic fire which the great conteurs possessed, the story must have been moving indeed. If the passionate Eleanor of Poitou heard it in her girlhood, as seems probable, from the lips of Bleheris himself, if is not unnatural that we should find traces of the romance wherever her influence was felt, and that Thomas, when he wished to assure his readers of the authenticity of his version, should refer to Breri as his warrant.

A curious link between Eleanor and the *Tristan* of Thomas is found in a poem of Ramon Vidal de Bezaudu, describing the marriage of Eleanor's daughter to Alfonso of Aragon in 1170[67]. In the *Modern Language Review*, XVII, 24-8, I proved that Thomas must have assigned to his hero the cognizance of a gold lion on a red field, and that it was probably intended as a piece of heraldic flattery to some patron of the English royal house. Now the poem in question says that Eleanor's daughter wore a mantle of ciclatoun: "Vermelhs ab lista d'argen fo, E y hac un levon d'aur devis." If there was any doubt whether this was a device adopted early by Henry II and his family, it must dissolve before this quotation. Thomas certainly had a patron in Henry, Eleanor, or one of their children.

The heraldry of Thomas is significant not only for his court connections but also for his date. In the same article, I proved that his poem must have contained the detail of the gold lions embroidered on Tristan's horse-trappings. In his later description of the gigantic Tristan le Nain, Thomas says that his shield, lance, pennon, and "conisance" were all blazoned *or de vair fretté*[68]. There can be no doubt that when Thomas wrote, a very elaborate repetition of the heraldic device was fashionable. The earliest known example of heraldic housings is 1178[69]; and the earliest representation of such a multiplied armory known to me is in the *De Rebus Siculis* of Petrus de Ebulo which cannot be earlier than 1195[70]. Allowing a margin of ten years, we arrive at the year 1185, and until earlier instances of this armorial protusion are brought to my attention, I shall consider that as early a date as our evidence on this point will allow.

This conclusion does not square with the date which Gaston Paris and M. Bédier have endowed with the weight of their authority, namely before 1170[71]. They argued that Crestien's *Cliges,* written in that year at latest, is manifestly a counter-blast to some Tristan romance very like that of Thomas, and that Crestien's use of the word-play on *amer-mer-l'amer* is conclusive proof that he took it from Thomas. The argument is indeed weighty, but cannot be regarded as conclusive since it is disputed by Foerster, Wilmotte, Miss Schœpperle, Ranke, and Kelemina[72]. Granting as I do that Crestien is the borrower, I nevertheless am not convinced that his source was necessarily Thomas. The whole course of this article has shown that Bleheris established a tradition, saturated with the ideals of courtly love which Crestien attacks in *Cligès*. Very probably there were versions of the romance before 1170 which Crestien and Thomas both used. Nor is it out of the question that the word-play on *mer-amer-l'amer* was in their common source[73].

I believe it now possible to state quite definitely the steps in the growth of the Tristan legend. It will be seen that in general the steps approximate those traced by M. Bédier in his masterly edition of Thomas.

1. The Pictish king Drostan son of Talorc, his kingdom of Loonois, and the forest of Morois.

2. The Welsh legend of Trystan mab Tallwch, largely modeled on the Irish *Aithed* of Diarmaid and Grainne, which still retained traces of mythic significance. Association with Arthur.

3. The localization in Cornwall (ante 1000).

4. Localization of *enfances* and conclusion in Brittany. Development of Second Ysolt. Remodeling of conclusion on basis of Arabic tale.

5. Transmission of tale to the court of Poitou by the Welshman Bleheris before 1137, and establishment of fixed tradition. Infusion of courtly love element.

6. Spread of story in two main forms: the Bleheris tradition represented by Eilhart, Béroul, Thomas; a Breton tradition largely independent of Bleheris, represented by the *Prose Tristan*[74].

Notes

1. For extensive bibliography of the Bleheris problem see *Modern Philology,* XXII, 123 n.

2. *ZfSL,* XXXI[2], 158-60.

3. *Romania,* XXXIV, 100.

4. E. Levi, *I lais e la leggenda di Tristano,* 69.

5. J. L. Weston, *Legend of Sir Perceval,* I, 294.

6. *Abhandlungen der Preussischen Akademie der Wissenschaften, ph. hist. Kl.,* 1918, No. 13, p. 10.

7. *Romania,* LI, 404.

8. *Ibid.,* 402 f.

9. *Romania,* LI, 404.

10. *Ibid.,* 402.

11. *Romania,* XXIV, 321-330, 497-528, XXV, 1-32, XXVII, 529-73, XXVIII, 1-48, 321-47, XXX, 13-21.

12. *Romania,* LI, 423.

13. For discussion and meaning of words Breton, Brito, etc. cf. A. B. Hopkins, *Influence of Wace,* 114 ff.

14. The identification was first made in J. L. Weston, *Legend of Sir Perceval,* I, 294 f.

15. *Romania,* XXV, 23.

16. Cf. on these conteurs Huet's article in *Moyen Age,* XXVIII, 234; Wauchier's continuation of the *Conte del Graal,* ed. Potvin, vv. 28373 ff. The tone of Wace, Crestien, and Wauchier towards these conteurs is decidedly supercilious.

17. *Folklore,* XVIII, 285.

18. W. Golther, *Tristan und Isolde,* 139 ff.

19. *Romania,* LI, 406.

20. *MLN,* XXXIX, 325, 327.

21. *Ibid.,* 320 f.

22. *MLN,* 322 f. Prof. Ranke has kindly referred me to the following work which shows that Eilhart had no connection with Eleanor's daughter Matilda of Saxony, but wrote in the Rhineland: Kurt Wagner, edition of Eilhart, Teil I, 11.

23. *Op. cit.,* I, 239, 242 f.

24. *Modern Philology,* XXII, 185 n.

25. *Erec,* vv. 22-5.

26. *Rev. Celt.,* XXXV, 380 ff. Cf. *Comptes rendus de l'Acad. des Inscr.,* 1924, 122 f.

27. G. Schoepperle, *Tristan and Isolt,* II, 413 ff., 430 f.

28. *Rev. Celt.,* XXXIV, 377. I quote, however, from the edition of T. P. Cross, *Studies in Philology,* XVII, 93 ff.

29. For bibliography of this tale, cf. Schoepperle, *op. cit.,* 599, n. 2, 415 n.

30. *Transactions of the Ossianic Soc.,* III, 79.

31. *Ibid.,* 66.

32. *Ibid.,* 67.

33. *Ibid.,* 71.

34. *Ibid.,* 75.

35. *Ibid.,* 163 ff.

36. *Ibid.,* 169 ff.

37. *Trans. of Oss. Soc.,* 171.

38. *Transactions of the Guild of Graduates,* University of Wales, 1903, 17.

39. *Romania,* XII, 508.

40. *Romanic Rev.,* XV, 266.

41. Thurneysen, *Irische Helden und Königsagen,* 28; *Handbuch des Altirischen,* I, 169.

42. *Proceedings of the Royal Irish Academy,* XXXIV, C, 300.

43. Just as Blathnat's lover Cuchulinn has many solar traits, so Diarmaid is often called Diarmaid «of the Bright Face», «with the Fiery Face», and a modern folktale calls him Son of the Monarch of Light. Cf. *Folklore,* XVII, 452 n.

44. The Diarmaid story is certainly as old as the tenth century (Schoepperle, II, 393), whereas the *Ystoria Trystan* first occurs in a MS. of 1550.

45. *Studies in Philology,* XVII, 106.

46. Eilhart's *Tristrant,* ed. F. Lichtenstein, 294 ff.

47. Thomas, *Tristan,* ed. Bédier, I, 340.

48. *ZfrP,* XLII, 482.

49. *ZfSL,* XLVII, 169.

50. Thomas, *Tristan,* II, 316; *ZfSL,* XXXII[2], 138; *Bonner Studien z. Eng. Phil.,* IV, xxiii; L. Hibbard, *Med. Romance in England,* 102.

51. J. Loth, *Contribution à l'étude des romans de la Table Ronde,* 60 ff. Cf. the reviews in *Romania,* XLIII, 121; *Romanic Review,* III, 431; and the notices *ZfSL,* XLVII, 227; Bruce, *Evolution of Arthurian Romance,* I, 184, n. 58.

52. Thomas, *Tristan,* ed. Bédier, II, 122 f. Note also that Moraldus appears in a Breton document of about 1075. Cf. H. Morice, *Mémoires pour servir de preuves,* I, col. 436.

53. *MLN,* XXXIX, 326 f.

54. Pierre le Baud, *Chronique de Vitré* (bound with *Histoire de Bretagne,* Paris, 1638), 7; *Rev. de Bretagne,* XVIII, 435-9.

55. Thomas, *Tristan,* éd. Bédier, I, 3 n.

56. *Romania,* XXVII, 610; *Archiv für das Studium,* CXXIX, 138.

57. Rivelen appears in a Breton document of the first half of the eleventh century, and Riwellenus in 1123. Cf. H. Morice, *Mémoires pour servir de preuves,* I, col. 337, 546. This proves how unreliable M. Loth is on his own ground, for in *Contributions,* 100, we read: «L'affaiblissement de *-on* en *-en* est, en somme, tardif en armoricain; à part Roallen (p. 295, en 1080) et Graalend, p. 750, en 1124-1125, je n'en vois guère d'exemple avant le xɪvᵉ siècle.»

My explanation of the name Kanelengres seems decidedly more natural than the tours de force of Brugger, *Archiv für das Studium,* CXXIX, 138 ff, of Zimmer, *ZfSL,* XIII, 96-99, and of Loth, *Contributions,* 105 f.

58. Vv. 320-25.

59. *Romania,* XXV, 16 f.

Romania, LIII.

60. *Modern Philology,* XXII, 159.

61. *Tristan und Isolde,* tr. W. Hertz, ed. 3, 490.

62. *Romania,* XXV, 29 f. Cf. Thomas, *Tristan,* ed. Bédier, II, 115 n.

63. Schoepperle, *Tristan and Isolt,* 414, 438; *Rev. Celt.,* XXXVII, 323.

64. *Abhandlungen der Preussischen Akad. der Wissenschaften, phil. hist. Kl.,* 1918, No. 13, p. 9. The story is in Hammer-Purgstall, *Literaturgeschichte der Araber,* II, 412.

65. *American Journal of Philology,* VII, 176 ff.

66. R. S. Loomis, *Celtic Myth and Arthurian Romance* (Columbia University Press, 1927), 344 f.

67. Mila y Fontanals, *De los trovadores Obras,* II, 133 n.

68. Vv. 2182-4.

69. E. Bertaux, *L'art dans l'Italie méridionale,* I, 493. On this date cf. *Nuovi Studi Medievali,* vol. II (1906), p. 104 ss.

70. Ed. E. Rota, pl. 36, 39; ed. G. B. Siragusa, pl. 36, 39.

71. *Journal des Savants,* 1902, 347-5; Thomas, *Tristan,* ed. Bédier, II, 53-5.

72. Foerster, *Cliges*[3], lvi-lviii; Wilmotte, *L'évolution du roman français, Bulletin de l'Acad: roy. de Belg.,* 1903, no. 7, 67; Schoepperle, *op. cit.,* I, 179; F. Ranke, *Tristan und Isolt;* J. Kelemina, *Geschichte der Tristansage,* 105.

73. Prof. Nitze has generously called it to my attention that the *mer-amer* word-play occurs independently in the seventeenth century and in Robert de Boron's *Joseph.*

74. Cf. Schoepperle, *op. cit,* II, 439-6.

Eugène Vinaver (essay date 1927)

SOURCE: "The Love Potion in the Primitive Tristan Romance," in *Medieval Studies in the Memory of Gertrude Schoepperle Loomis.* Reprint. Slatkine Reprints, 1974, pp. 75-86.

[*In the following essay, Vinaver reviews the critical debate surrounding the nature of the origin of the extant versions of the Tristan legend. He also examines the treatment of the love potion motif found in the various versions of the legend.*]

In his epoch-making introduction to the poem of Thomas, M. Bédier inserted a reconstruction of the original Tristan poem. He gave there the following version of the episode of the love potion:

«Quand le temps du départ fut venu, la reine d'Irlande prépara un breuvage puissant, et le confia secrètement à Brangien qui devait accompagner Iseut en Cornouailles. C'était un filtre d'amour . . . Telle en était la vertu que ceux qui le boiraient ensemble devaient s'aimer à jamais»[1].

M. Bédier acknowledges that his reconstruction of the last sentence quoted is based on the versions of Thomas, the French Prose Romance and the Oxford *Folie* all of which describe the influence of the love potion as *unlimited,* and is contradicted by the poems of Eilhart and Béroul, in which the influence of the love draught is limited to a certain period. The poet suggests that if the lovers did not see each other for half a day during the first four years they would fall ill; if they did not see each other for a week they would die[2]. But after four years the influence of the potion would become slightly leess potent and the lovers might part[3]. In the extant fragment of the poem of Béroul the scene of the giving of the potion by the Irish Queen is missing, but in the episode of the lovers' return from the forest Béroul says that after a certain period (three years according to Béroul) the love potion abated[4].

M. Bédier thought that the limitation of the efficacy of the « vin herbé» which occurs in Eilhart and Béroul was due not to the author of the primitive Tristan romance, but to a later imitator whose work was the source of Béroul and Eilhart. In M. Bédier's view the primitive poet to whom we owe the world's greatest love story could not have reduced the *motif* of the love potion to a mere piece of witchcraft devoid of symbolié value. He could not, indeed, have conceived of the Tristan romance as a «story of a triennial intoxication». In consequence, M. Bédier assumes that Eilhart and Béroul proceed from a common original which is not the primitive romance. «Un poète» he says, «l'auteur de ce roman que devaient imiter Eilhart et Béroul, connaissait la version selon laquelle le philre garde un pouvoir indéfini . . . Il a voulu affranchir autant que possible ses héros de cette sorcellerie. Il a observé que dans l'*estoire* les amants passent plusieurs années ensemble se voyant journellement, avant la grande séparation. Alors, non sans ingéniosité, il a inventé la donnée que reproduit Eilhart d'Oberg: par la force du «boire», Tristan et Iseut s'aimeront de tous leurs sens leur vie durant; pendant les quatre premières années, s'ils sont séparés une seule demi-journée, tous deux tomberont en langueur; si la séparation dure une semaine, tous deux mourront; mais au bout de quatre ans s'ils s'aiment toujours, ils peuvent pourtant supporter d'être séparés»[5].

Writing in 1907, Professor W. Golther suggested that M. Bédier's theory was incorrect and that Eilhart and Béroul derived directly from the first romance of Tristan, «Da nach meiner Ansicht Eilhart und Berol selbständig je für sich, nicht durch eine gemeinsame Zwischenstufe hindurch auf den alten Roman zurückgehen, so muss jeder von ihnen gemeinsam überlieferte Zug fürs Urgedicht angesprochen werden. So gehört nach meiner Auffassung auch die zwar lebenslängliche, in ihrer unwiderstehlichen Kraft jedoch auf drei Jahre beschränkte Wirkung des Trankes schon zum alten Roman»[6].

The problem of the love potion *motif* in the primitive Tristan romance received a new and thorough treatment in the admirable work of the late Miss Gertrude Schoepperle: «Tristan and Isolt. A Study of The Sources of the Romance»[7] Miss Schoepperle disputed M. Bédier's reconstruction of the episode of the love potion and insisted, as Prof. Golther had done, upon the authenticity of the Béroul-Eilhart version. «It seems unjustifiable», she suggested, «to suppose that Thomas has preserved the version of the *estoire* in the treatment of the potion when we have evidence that he has altered it in every other important particular in which he differs from the other redactora»[8].

Miss Schoepperle further contends that Thomas would not have been in sympathy with a conception which condemned the relation of the lovers as criminal and made their repentance the cause of their return. «It was almost inevitable», says Miss Schoepperle, «that he should alter such a version in accordance with his own attitude toward love, an attitude less naive, less ascetic, more impregnated with the courtly ideals of his time. In his version the return from the forest is not due to the abatement of the influence of the potion and the repentance of the lovers. On the contrary the two lovers give up the life together only when forced by Mark».

It is to be regretted that Miss Schoepperle confined herself to the statement of facts without attempting to justify her theory on literary grounds and to answer the criticisms of her predecessor. M. Bédier. In the following few pages an attempt will be made both to develop Miss Schoepperle's critical argument and to suggest some account of the literary aspects of the problem.

It cannot be gainsaid that if Thomas's source contained anything like the Eilhart-Béroul version of the love potion *motif* he would certainly alter it. He would do so not only because that version contradicted his attitude toward love in general, but because it did not fit in with his particular presentation of love in the story of Tristan. Indeed, Thomas's touch in remodelling the story shows itself, first and foremost, in the diminishing of the supernatural. The drama has to proceed from a source that is not beyond human knowledge. Consequently, the love potion is merely a means by which a spontaneous, a human bond of love is strengthened. It cannot be resorted to as the ultimate justification of the relationship of the lovers, as is the case in Béroul and Eilhart. This is particularly obvious from the fact that in Thomas the love between Tristan and Iseult is prior to the episode of the love potion. Thomas's faithful translator, the Norwegian friar Robert, tells that when «Isond the maid came to Tristran to talk to him she beheld his beautiful face with enamoured eyes»[9]. The occurrence of similar traits in Gottfried (9994-10037) has led a recent investigator, M. Piquet, to conclude: « Il est certain que la donnée ancienne qui fait naître l'amour dans le cœur des deux jeunes gens seulement après le philtre ne paraît pas respectée par Thomas chez qui l'éclosion de ce sentiment a lieu avant la fameuse méprise»[10]. But there is hardly any doubt that having altered his original in this point Thomas was bound to omit the reference to the magic virtues of the potion in the scene of the lover's return from the forest.

Two other texts call for attention in consideration of the problem: the French Prose Romance of Tristan and the poem of the *Folie Tristan,* both of which represent the «unlimited» version of the *motif* of the love potion.

It is easy enough, however, to show that the version of the *Folie* does not in the least affect our argument. The *Folie* of the Douce MS in the Bodleian Library is a derivative of Thomas and has no direct connection with the primitive Tristan poem[11]. The *Folie* of Bern alone may be regarded as a derivative of that poem. But in the Bern *Folie* there is no evidence whatsoever that the author was using a version different from that of Eilhart and Béroul Here is his description of the love philtre (318-322):

> Cil boivres fu faiz a envers
> De plusors herbes mout divers,
> Je muir por li, ele nel sant
> N'est pas parti oniemant,
> Car je suis Tristanz qui mar fu.

These lines merely indicate that the influence of the love potion did not terminate, but whether it abated partially, as in Eilhart, or remained unchanged throughout, as in Thomas, the *Folie* does not say.

As regards the French Prose Romance which, too, may seem to support the theory of the «unlimited» version, two possibilities are open: first, it may have been influenced by the version of Thomas and, second, « the author may», as Miss Schoepperle thought, «have omitted independently, with his characteristic freedom, the limitation of the influence of the potion, the repentance of the lovers, and the voluntary return from the forest—traits that were no doubt as shocking to him as they were to Thomas»[12]. The second hypothesis may be correct, but in view of its conjectural character we should prefer to choose as a starting point of the argument the first supposition, namely that the Prose Romance is directly dependent on the poem of Thomas. It may, indeed, be gleaned from the works of previous investigators that there are points of isolated agreement between Thomas and the Prose Romance, which cannot be explained by mere coincidence. M. Muret, Professor W. Golther and W. Röttiger have pointed out that the episode of «the harp and the rote» in Thomas (Gottfried, 13101-

13453; *Sir Tristrem,* 1809-1925; *Saga,* XLIX-LI) corresponds to a passage in the Prose Romance (MS. Bibl. Nat. fr. 756, f° 65 ff.) relating to the story of Iseult's being carried away by Palomides[13]. W. Röttiger and E. Löseth have traced the details about the garden scene in the Prose Romance to Thomas's version of the episode[14]. It is not improbable that the explanation of Tristan's name by the adjective *triste* was borrowed by the prose writer from Thomas[15]. Lastly, it would appear that the description of Tristan's hesitation before his marriage with the second Iseult («la bataille des deux Yseltes») which occurs in all the MSS. of the Prose Romance[16] is traceable to Thomas's lengthy discourse on the subject[17].

The French Prose Romance, inasmuch as it represents the old Tristan tradition, would thus appear to be a derivative of both the «archetype» and the poem of Thomas. But if the prose writer had under his eyes two versions of the story, one which confined the strongest efficacy of the love potion to a certain period, and made the potion actually control the whole story, and the other which assigned to the potion the part of a mere symbol, it was only too natural that he should choose the latter. For, just as in Thomas, in the Prose Romance the love potion is entirely relegated to the background. It has pratically no effect upon the events of the story, since Tristan and Iseult love each other *before* drinking the potion. Besides, their love being represented as a model of chivalrous « amour», it was impossible for the author to make it abate, even if one of his sources had done so.

For these reasons, it would not seem to be correct to base a reconstruction of the love potion *motif* either on Thomas, or on the French Prose Romance or indeed on the Oxford *Folie,* and it is impossible to escape the conclusion that the Eilhart-Béroul version represents in this point the primitive romance.

Apart from the general problem with which we are concerned here, it might be interesting to remember the manner in which the idea of the limited efficacy of the love potion is introduced in Béroul. In a passage relating to the lovers' return from the forest the poet says (2133-8):

> Seignors, du vin de qoi il burent
> Avez oi, por qoi il furent
> En si grant paine lonc tens mis;
> *Mais ne savez, ce m'est a vis,*
> *A conbien fu determinez*
> *Li loucuendris, li vin herbez.*

The last three lines suggest that this is the first announcement of the limited efficacy of the love potion in Béroul, and that Béroul did not mention that virtue of the potion in the scene of the lovers' departure from Cornwall. Nor does Eilhart's description of the potion in the scene of the departure go beyond the statement that during the first four years, if the lovers were separated for half a day, they would fall ill; if for a week, they would die:

> vîr jâr sie abir phlegetin
> sô grôzir lîbe beide,
> daz sie sich nicht gescheidin

> mochtin einen halbin tag.
> swedir daz ander nicht en sach
> alle tage, daz wart siech:
> von dem tranke hâten sie sich lîp.
> ab sie wêrin eine wochen
> von ein ander ungesprochen,
> sie musten beide wesin tôt:
> der trang was sô getemperôt,
> von also grôzir sterke.
> daz mogit ir wol gemerkin!

(Eilhart, 2288-2300).

It is not unlikely that (as the concluding line seems to suggest) all this description is anticipated from a later section of the story which corresponds to Eilhart's lines 4730-4739 and forms a direct continuation of the passage just quoted. This is another way of saying that in the primitive Tristan poem there would be no reference to the limited nature of the ïnfluence of the love potion until the episode of the return from the forest. It is there that the author must have explained to his readers for the first time «a combien fu determinez» the magic philtre which the lovers drank.

The theory that the Eilhart-Béroul version of the love potion *motif* represents the original Tristan romance may be substantiated not only on textual but on literary grounds, for it suggests the only adequate interpretation of the general meaning of the story and of the methods of the author.

There is in the romance of Tristan a remarkable simplicity of the tragic conception. It is the tragedy born by the all-powerful love, that is stronger than honour, stronger than blood and stronger than death, and that comes into clash with the immense, vast world of rights and duties, human and divine. But the whole essence and the greatest beauty of the tragedy in Tristan lies in the fact that it is a conflict in which the lovers never refuse to recognize the rightfulness of the law that causes their misfortune.

If an actual struggle had been possible, if Tristan and Iseult could openly have fought the forces against them, how much simpler the story would have been: there would have been no «vie aspre et dure», no hardships such as those through which they lived in the forest of Morrois. But they cannot flee from the world of suffering, they cannot openly challenge their rivals and they never think of escaping to a happier land. There is in Béroul a passage which for tragic intensity has no parallel in the story. It is when Tristan begins to feel that he must restore Iseult to king Mark and says: «So now I cry to God the Lord who is the King of the world, and beg him to give me strength to yield back Iseult to King Mark»[18].

It is a remarkable feature of the story of Tristan that it is controlled entirely by that fundamental tragic theme, which is so immensurably stronger than the lovers themselves. Like the rudderless boat in which Tristan was set adrift, they never move of their own volition—they obey some supernatural element, which, like the waves, throws them from rock to rock, sends them joys and sorrows and finally releases them from their earthly chains. They are unable not only to control the elemental force which causes their joy and their death, but even to understand it. And it is through the love potion only, through the medium of its magic qualities that the poet could possibly suggest to his heroes a fitting explanation of their story.

In the scene with the hermit Tristan swears: «S'el m'aime, c'est pas la poison»[19], and Iseult replies: «Por Deu omnipotent, il ne m'aime pas, ne je lui, fors par un herbé que je bui, et il en but: ce fut pechiez»[20]. The lovers constantly think themselves acting under a spell. And in order to enable them to interpret in that way the whole tragedy, it was essential to make them think that even when they leave the forest of Morrois and submit to the king, they are forced to do so by the power of magic. This accounts for the idea of the partial abatement of the love potion, a *motif* which thus appears to be an indispensable element of the tragedy. For where could Tristan find strength to restore Iseult to the king, if he did not believe that the potion which had made him mad released him now from part of its spell? And when the time came to part, and it began to seem to the lovers that they must leave Morrois, they thought it was the love potion that came to abate.

Thus, in the original story the influence of the love potion is not *actually* limited: its limitation is merely an illusion of the lovers, an instance of the author's naïve method of making them unconscious of their tragedy. The «vin herbé» is a poison in the eyes of the lovers, but it never ceases to be a symbol of unchangeable love in those of the poet. Indeed, in the concluding lines of the story he restores to the potion its full symbolic value. After the death of the lovers[21], King Mark brought their bodies back to Cornwall and had their tombs built on the right and left of a chantry. But in one night there sprang from the tomb of Tristan a green and leafy briar, strong in its branches and in the scent of its flowers. It climbed the chantry and took root again by Iseult's tomb. Thrice did king Mark command to cut it down, but thrice it grew again as blooming and as strong. The people told the marvel to the king and he forbade to cut the briar any more. It was the potion, says Eilhart, that did this thing.

Notes

1. *Le Roman de Tristan par Thomas*. S. A. T. F., T. II, p. 133.

2. Cf. Eilhart von Oberge, ed. Lichtenstein, lignes 2279-2299.

3. Cf. *ibid.*, 4730-4742.

4. *Le Roman de Tristan par Béroul et un anonyme*, éd. E. Muret, S. A. T. F., pp. 67-68.

5. *Op. cit.*, 238.

6. W. Golther, *Tristan und Insolde in den Dichtungen des Mitelalters und der Neuen Zeit*, Leipzig, 1907, p. 59.

7. Frankfurt an London, 1913.

8. *Op. cit.*, I, 76.

9. Cf. *Tristrams Saga ok Isondar*, ed. Kölbing, ch. XLIII. Cf. also ch. XLVI (. . . En Tristram huggadi hana med miklu blidlaeti).

10. F. Piquet, *L'originalité de Gottfried de Strasburg*, p. 208.

11. M. Bédier mentions (*Les deux poèmes de la Folie Tristan*, ed. J. Bédier, S. A. T. F., pp. 2-3) that «l'auteur de la *Folie Tristan* d'Oxford résume le roman de Thomas avec une grande fidélité . . . Il le rappelle parfois à s'y méprendre». The arguments recently advanced by E. Hoepffner (*Ztschr. f. rom. Phil.*, XXXIX, 698) do not suffice to make out the case for a direct dependence of the Oxford *Folie* on the « archetype».

12. *Op. cit.*, I, 82. Miss Schoepperle also advanced the hypothesis that «the Prose Romance preserves a version independent of the *estoire*». In my view, which I am compelled by want of space to indicate but briefly, all the four points in the Prose Romance for which Miss Schoepperle claimed an independent origin (Tristan's childhood, his quest of Iseult, their return from the forest, and their death) derive from a version common to all the other authorities but altered in accordance with the methods of the prose writer.

13. Cf. E. Muret, *Eilhart d'Oberg et sa source française*, Romania, XVI, 310; W. Golther, *Die Sage von Tristan und Isolde*, München, 1887, p. 58; W. Röttiger, *Der heutige Stand der Tristanforschung*, Hamburg, 1897, p. 30.

14. Cf. E. Löseth, *Le roman en prose de Tristan, le roman de Palamède et la compilation de Rusticien de Pise*, 1890, §§ 284-286. W. Röttiger, *op. cit.*, pp. 32-33.

15. Cf. E. Löseth, *op. cit.*, § XX.

16. *Ibid.*, § 58.

17. LI. 447-640.

18. Béroul, 2185-8.

19. *Ibid.*, 1384.

20. *Ibid.*, 1412-15,

21. MS. Bibl. Nat. fr. 103, f° 383a.

James Douglas Bruce (essay date 1928)

SOURCE: "Tristan," in *The Evolution of Arthurian Romance From the Beginnings Down to the Year 1300*, Vol. I. Reprint. Peter Smith, 1958, pp. 152-91.

[*In the following essay, Bruce maintains that most modern critics agree that a "single primitive Tristan romance" is the source of all extant versions. Bruce then surveys those versions, and discusses the plot of the Tristan legend and its similarity to the Irish Diarmaid and Grainne legend.*]

In one important respect the study of the story of Tristan is easier than is the case with that of Lancelot: there is substantial agreement among authorities on the subject that all the mediaeval romances and shorter poems concerning this hero go back to a lost French romance[1] of a considerably earlier date than any on the subject that is now in existence. The close relation of the incidents in the various extant versions of the story, despite individual divergencies, was explained by scholars of the last generation as due to the fact that the writers all drew from the same body of lays or prose tales which were supposed to be current orally,[2] but the conviction gradually forced itself on the minds of students of the *Tristan* romances that the resemblances in question were really due to a common original—a definite romance, now lost.[3] This solution of the problem was given scientific demonstration by Bédier in the Second Volume (1905) of his great edition of Thomas' *Tristan*,[4] and substantially the same results were reached independently by W. Golther in his *Tristan und Isolde* (1907), which, though published two years later, had been written before the appearance of Bédier's work. The conclusions of Bédier and Golther have been disputed by a few scholars, as will be observed from the notes below, but, in general, we may say that the existence of a single primitive Tristan romance (*Ur-Tristan,* as German scholars call it) from which all extant versions are ultimately derived is one of the few matters of Arthurian discussion on which students are definitely agreed.[5] Bédier has reconstructed the narrative of this primitive *Tristan* by the comparative method, and so has Golther. Their respective reconstructions do not differ in essentials, so that the task of the Tristan student at the present time consists mainly in the study of the sources of this hypothetical romance, as reconstructed by these scholars.

The materials which form the basis of these reconstructions are. 1. The *Tristan*-poem of the Anglo-Norman poet, Thomas, composed somewhere between 1155 and 1170.[6] 2. The fragments of a French poem which is, at least in part, by a poet of Normandy named Béroul,[7] coupled with the Middle High German poem on Tristan by Eilhart von Oberge.[8] Both belong to the closing years of the twelfth century and both draw evidently from the same source—a lost derivative of the primitive *Tristan*.[9] 3. Portions of the French prose *Tristan* which, in its earliest form, is dated by Löseth (p. XXIV) between 1215 and 1230 and by Bédier (II, 309) about 1230.[10] 4. Two short French poems each called *La Folie Tristan:* One (the Oxford version) was the production of an Anglo-Norman poet of the last quarter of the twelfth century, the other (Berne version) of a poet of North-Eastern France, probably of the early thirteenth century.[11]

The problem of reconstruction was rendered more difficult by the fact that only fragments of Thomas's poem in its original French form have come down to modern times, and so this poem itself, in the missing portion, had first to be reconstructed from the versions in foreign languages which are known to be based upon it—viz: the Scandinavian prose *Tristan* saga, Gottfried von Strassburg's *Tristan,* the Middle English Sir *Tristrem,* the *Folie Tristan* of the Oxford MS., and the Italian *La Tavola Ritonda.*[12] This task has been accomplished in masterly fashion by Bédier in the First Volume of his edition of Thomas's *Tristan,* so that we have here a solid basis for the reconstruction of the primitive poem.

In the discussion of the sources of this hypothetical romance, from which the whole mediaeval tradition concerning Tristan flows,[13] it will be necessary, as in previous cases, to indicate briefly the succession of episodes which made up the romance. The reconstructions of Bédier (II, 194 ff.) and Golther (pp. 40 ff.) do not differ very materially.[14] The following succinct outline which is based on the former, represents, then, in essentials, with virtual certainty, the content of the lost French romance:

Tristan was the son of Rivalen, King of Loenois (in some versions, Armonie or Parmanie) in Great Britain and of Blanchefleur, sister of Marc, King of Cornwall. Blanchefleur dies in the act of giving birth to Tristan, whose name[15] was suggested by the affliction that accompanies his birth. A knight, named Gorvenal, instructed the young Tristan in the accomplishments of knighthood, and when his charge was fifteen years old, they set out for Cornwall and arrive at Marc's court. Although Tristan does not disclose his identity, he becomes a favorite at court. In the course of time an opportunity arises which enables him to show his prowess. A great knight called Morholt, brother-in-law of the Irish king, comes from Ireland to exact the tribute of every third child of fifteen years old, but he was ready to settle the matter with any suitable Cornish champion. The Cornish knights hold back, but Tristan undertakes the combat, after having first had himself knighted. The duel takes place on the isle of Saint-Samson and only the combatants are present. Morholt is mortally wounded, but escapes to his boat with a fragment of Tristan's sword in his head. He expired before he could reach Ireland; nevertheless, his niece, Iseult, daughter of the Irish king, kept the fragment of Tristan's sword.

Tristan, too, had been wounded in the combat and his condition grows constantly worse. In despair, he finally has himself put in a boat which is pushed out to sea.[16] He carries his harp with him. The boat drifts to the Irish coast, and the king, hearing Tristan playing on his harp, takes him ashore, and Iseult, who is skilled in the healing art, cures him. He calls himself Tantris, and so eludes identification. He then returns to Cornwall.

King Marc had always refused to marry, but one day a swallow brings to his hall some strands of a woman's hair as beautiful as gold. The king thought that he could rid himself of the importunities of his courtiers by declaring that he was willing to marry the woman to whom this hair belonged, but no one else. Tristan goes forth to discover the unknown beauty and is borne by chance to Ireland.

The king's officer is sent to slay him, but Tristan pretends that he is a merchant and secures a delay. A dragon was then devastating Ireland and the king promises his daughter's hand to any man that would kill the monster. Tristan accomplishes this and cuts out the dragon's tongue as a token of his victory. He falls afterwards into a swoon and the king's seneschal, stealing the dragon's tongue, represents himself as the victor.[17] Iseult knows, however, that the seneschal is a coward, suspects some deceit, goes forth with her mother to look into the matter and finds Tristan. Aided by her mother, she heals him, but Tristan, perceiving her golden hair, sees that she is the woman for whom he is looking. She, however, observes that the fragment taken from the dead Morholt's head fits exactly a gap in Tristan's sword. She would have informed on him, despite his prayers, but she knew that she would then be compelled to marry the treacherous seneschal. The deceit of this man is disclosed and the Irish king pardons Tristan, who asks for Iseult's hand on behalf of his uncle. Iseult is sent to Marc under the charge of Tristan. Then follows the incident of the fatal love-potion. Iseult's mother had prepared it, to render perpetual the love of her daughter and Marc, but, through an accident on the voyage, Bringvain (Brangien), Iseult's female attendant, gives it to Tristan and Iseult, so that they are united in an undying passion.[18] Accordingly, on Iseult's wedding night, Bringvain takes her place with Marc and she remains with her lover.[19]

Fearing that Bringvain would betray the deception practised on Marc, Iseult engages two men to murder her. By a clever allegory the girl touches the hearts of these men and they spare her. They report to Iseult that they have executed their commission, but she exhibits such remorse that they tell her the truth.

One day an Irish harper plays at court on condition that Marc will grant anything he wishes. It turns out that he wishes Iseult, and Marc, though reluctant, is constrained to comply with his promise. The Irishman takes the queen to his ship, but Tristan returns at this moment from the forest and goes to seek Iseult. He tells her captor that he can quiet her distress with his rote.[20] He gains time in this way, wins the Irishman's confidence, and finally manages to carry off Iseult, flinging back the taunt, as he goes, that the Irishman has won her with his harp, but that he has won her back with his rote.[21]

The lovers now continue their intrigue, but Audret (Andret), another nephew of Marc's, who hates Tristan, spies on the pair, and, assisted by a wicked dwarf, endeavors to ruin them. Tristan communicates with his mistress by sending inscribed pieces of wood down a stream which flows through Iseult's chamber. They have all sorts of escapes. Once Marc is hidden in a tree above them, listening to them, but they observe his shadow in a spring and give their conversation such a turn that he is deceived. They are, however, finally detected. Tristan is sleeping in the same chamber with the king and queen. The king by design leaves the chamber and Tristan wishes to join Iseult. The dwarf has strewn the floor between them with meal,

so that Tristan's tracks may be shown, but, seeing the snare, Tristan springs over to Iseult's bed. He had lately been wounded, however, and the exertion broke his wound. The blood accordingly stained both his bed and Iseult's and their guilt was divulged. Tristan escapes, but Marc, who at first had determined to burn his wife, later decides to give her up to a band of lepers. Her lover, however, rescues her from this fate and they fly to the forest and spend two years there in the enjoyment of each other's love. One day Marc, in hunting, came upon them asleep in their hut, but Tristan's sword lay between them, which convinced him of their innocence.[22] On awakening, the lovers observe signs that Marc had been there (his sword and his glove) and fly deeper into the forest.

The forest-life, however, becomes no longer bearable, and Tristan and Iseult agree to part. Tristan threw a letter into Marc's chamber, inquiring whether he would take her back. By another letter Marc signified his willingness to do so, provided Tristan left the kingdom.

Tristan now goes to Arthur's court, but with Gawain's help has another meeting with his mistress. Arthur hunts near Tintagel and Marc has to receive him and his followers, including Tristan. To guard Iseult from Tristan, he has sharp blades set near her bed. Tristan is wounded by them, but, in order to protect him, his companions feign a fight, get wounded with the same blades, and so it is impossible the next day to convict him. The king now compels Iseult to make a public declaration of her innocence. To confirm her veracity, she will have to endure the test of holding a red-hot iron in her hand. On the way to the place where the test is to be made Iseult is borne across a ford by Tristan disguised as a beggar. She swears afterwards that no one but the king and this man had touched her. The people do not see into the real significance of this oath, but it enables the queen to go through the test unharmed.[23]

Tristan next goes to Brittany and helps Duke Hoel of Carhaix in his war with a rival. The latter has a daughter named Iseult (Iseult of the White Hands she is called) and she is wedded to Tristan, but the marriage remains merely nominal, the husband's mind still dwelling on Iseult of Cornwall. The wife lets her brother Kaherdin know this. Tristan tells this brother of the love of Iseult of Cornwall for him and they go then to Cornwall together, where Tristan has a secret meeting with Iseult. Afterwards, however, through a misunderstanding, Iseult is out of humor with him because of a supposed act of cowardice on his part. Disguised as a leper, he seeks an interview with her to explain, but although she recognizes him, she has him beaten away. He returns, therefore, to Brittany and becomes really the husband of the other Iseult. Iseult of Cornwall now feels remorseful in regard to her lover and even puts on haircloth. On hearing the news of this, Tristan again comes from Brittany—meets her in secret—the next day bears off the prize in some sports, but is detected by accident and escapes. At a later time, however, having been much altered in appearance because of his sufferings from a wound which he had received in war, he goes back to Cornwall, disguised as a madman, and carries on his clandestine *amours* with Iseult, until he is finally detected and returns to Brittany.

Kaherdin carries on an intrigue with the wife of Bedenis. In the fight that follows on account of this affair he is killed and Tristan severely wounded. Tristan sends to Iseult of Cornwall to come and cure him. It is agreed that the ship on its return shall hoist a white sail, if it brings her—otherwise a black sail. She comes, but Tristan's wife is jealous and reports that the sail is black. At this the hero dies, and when Iseult of Cornwall arrives, she too expires upon his body. Marc at last learns how the lovers were bound together by the fatal potion and has them buried side by side. Rose-bushes spring up out of the two graves and intertwine their branches.

Now, the investigations of Miss Gertrude Schoepperle[24] have made it virtually certain that the starting-point of this long and romantic narrative is a Celtic *Aithed*[25] (elopement story), similar to the Old Irish story of *Diarmaid and Grainne*.[26] In this Irish story, too, the hero (Diarmaid), under the influence of passion, violates the obligations of friendship and loyalty and flies with the wife of his uncle and king to the forest. They are pursued from place to place and have to endure all sorts of hardships. *Diarmaid and Grainne* is preserved only in such varying fragmentary and corrupt versions[27] that it is difficult to compare the story with that of Tristan in detail, and the difficulty is still further enhanced by the fact that these versions are so largely lyrical. The central *motif*, however, is the same in the two stories, so that the derivation of the latter from the former or some similar *Aithed* seems to be an acceptable conclusion.[28] It is, doubtless, due to this origin that the Tristan of the Old French poems still differs so greatly from the conventional hero of the French romances of chivalry—Gawain, for example, whose main function is to exemplify the knightly virtues of prowess and courtesy in their highest manifestations. Tristan's nimbleness of hand and foot, his forest cunning, his skill in elementary feats of strength (leaping, putting the stone) are all surviving traits of a more primitive type. Apart, however, from the numerous accretions to the central theme and the coloring of French chivalrous society which the whole story has received, it must be acknowledged that the Celtic tale, even in respect to this central theme, has undergone a transformation in the hands of the French romancers, who developed it into what is, perhaps, the greatest love-story in literature. The transformation, indeed, is so great that some scholars have been disposed to deny any Celtic influence at all in the shaping of the love-story. In particular, it has been objected that the conflict of passion and law which constitutes the tragedy of the lovers in the romance could not have been of Celtic origin, since the dissolution of the marriage tie was easy among the Celts[29] and the idea of womanly modesty and virtue had little force among the Celtic populations in the period with which we are concerned.[30] There is a measure of truth in the first of these objections, for the moral reprobation of adultery is not emphasized in these Celtic tales, which reflect a more primitive condition of society than the French romances, but the parallelism with *Diarmaid and Grainne,* or even with the more celebrated story of the love of Naisi and Deirdre, wife of Conchobar,[31] is too striking to be accidental. All three of these tales, with their forest setting to a drama of adultery, in which the principal actors are a hero, his uncle (a king), and the latter's wife, bear unmistakably, it would seem, the stamp of the same mint. A recognition of this fact, however, does not conflict with the view that, after all, the tragedy of Tristan and Iseult, which, through the romances, has impressed itself on the imagination of the modern world so deeply, owes its strength, mainly, to the changes which the French poets wrought in the Celtic tradition. Leaving aside the addition of the story of Iseult of Brittany to the original *Aithed* and other accretions that heighten, in a variety of ways, the interest of the legend, one may note among these changes the discardal of the bizarre paganism of the Old Irish tale with its duplicate *motifs* of the hero's love-spot and the heroine's *geis*[32]—both based on forms of superstition that are too primitive to win the interest or sympathy of modern society—and the substitution in the romances of the incident of the love-drink, shared by the two lovers, which has the double advantage of a unified *motif* and of the hallowed familiarity of classical associations. But, above all, the power of the story in the French romances is due to the initial scene of Tristan and Iseult's love-story (the scene of the love-potion), with its definite symbolism that dominates the rest of the narrative—the symbolism of a passion against which no human convention can stand—to the elaboration of the forest scenes, to the true and vivid picture of the passion that constantly draws the hero back to the heroine, contrary to the obligations of kinship and personal loyalty, and, despite every variety of obstacle, not permitting him to forget her even in the embraces of another woman. The Celtic texts, such as *The Reproach of Diarmaid* and *Death of Diarmaid,* have a beauty of their own that testifies to a more intimate contact with the life of nature, but the French romances are manifestly the products of a higher civilization[33] and a more strongly sustained narrative art.

Granting, now, the Celtic origin[34] of this famous love-story of Tristan and Iseult of Cornwall, it remains to fix as far as possible, the history of its growth before it reached the French romancers and the share which the different regions, inhabited by the Celts, had in this process. The task is one which has long enlisted the energies of the ablest students of the *matière de Bretagne.*

As is customary in cases where the records are so scanty, scholars have turned to the nomenclature[35] of the story in the search for light regarding the question just mentioned. In his well-known studies of Arthurian names,[36] the late Professor Zimmer endeavored to establish the Pictish origin of the hero's name, and that scholar's identification[37] was all but universally accepted, even by those who had been engaged in the bitterest controversies with him.[38] In the Irish chronicles of the Picts we have in the eighth century a *Talorcan filius Drostan* and a *Drest filius Talorcan.*[39] Now, Celtic scholars are agreed that *Drostan* is the same as *Drest (Drust),* with a common Celtic suffix added, and that *Tristan* is derived from *Drostan.*[40] It has been shown, however, that *Drust (Drest* and its derivatives) is not confined to the Picts, as Zimmer maintained, but belongs to the general nomenclature of the Brythonic Celts, although commonest among the Picts.[41] As far, then, as the name alone is concerned, we could not infer anything positively as to the ultimate origin of the story. It might have belonged to any branch of the Brythonic Celts. Nevertheless, there are sufficient reasons, I believe, for regarding Tristan as, in the first instance, a Pict. First of all, the name, although not confined to the Picts, is much commoner among them than among the other Celts. Furthermore, all the chief versions of the story represent the hero's father as ruling *Loonois (Loenois)* and the region in which he and Iseult lead their forest-life as *Morois.* Now, despite mistaken identifications in the romances, themselves, it seems most probable that *Loonois* is the Scottish *Lothian* and *Morois (Morrois)* the Scottish *Murray*—so two districts that were undeniably inhabited by the Picts.[42]

The fame of Tristan began, then, as we may assume, with the Picts, probably merely as a character in heroic saga, with no love-story attached; but did it pass through Wales[43] and, perhaps, Cornwall on its way to the French, and, if so, what accertions did it receive in those regions? The principal evidence bearing on the Welsh side of the question is that which is offered by the Triads. In one of these (Loth's *Mabinogion,* II, 231) Tristan is called one of the three chief diadem-wearers of Britain; in another (*ibid,* p. 238) he is one of the three machine-masters of Britain: in still another, (*ibid,* p. 260), he is one of the three lovers of Britain. Lastly, in a fourth triad (*ibid,* pp. 247 f.), he is one of the three great swine-herds of Britain, but he is, at the same time, the lover of Marc's wife, apparently. He keeps Marc's swine, whilst the regular swine-herd goes on a message to Essyllt, as she is here called; Arthur, Marc, Kay and Bedivere could not get a single hog from him, whether by ruse, violence, or theft. Furthermore, in the *Dream of Rhonabwy,* a prose tale of the *Mabinogion* collection, he appears (*Drystan mab Tallwch*) among Arthur's counsellors. This tale is certainly not earlier than the middle of the twelfth century and it may have been influenced by the French poems. The triads, enumerated above, are found only in a MS. of the fourteenth century, when the French romances had spread the fame of Tristan throughout Europe, and if we were dependent entirely on them, it would be impossible to say whether, in representing the hero as a lover of Marc's wife, they were really reflecting native tradition. After he became known through the French romances, it would be only natural that native writers should weave still other stories about him and his famous mistress. This seems certainly the origin of the pretty tale[44] in which Arthur is called on to judge between Marc and Tristan as to the possession of Iseult. It includes a metrical dialogue[45] of mutual compliment between Tristan and Gawain (Gwalchmai), the latter's object being to induce his friend to meet Arthur.

The following considerations, however, seem to show that the conception of Tristan as the lover of Iseult originated either in Wales or, more probably, in Cornwall. The mistress of Tristan is in all versions represented as the wife of Marc (Mark), King of Cornwall. Now *Mark* is common as a Germanic name, but it is also given as the name of a king of Cornwall in the sixth century in the life of the saint, Paulus Aurelianus. It is said of this saint in his Latin biography, which was written by Wrmonoc, a monk of Landevennec (in Brittany) in 884, that his fame reached the ears of King Marc—"otherwise Quonomorius".[46] Quonomorius, it may be observed, is a Celtic name occurring elsewhere. On the other hand, *Marc* means *horse* in the Celtic languages. In the *Tristan* poem by Béroul, King Marc is represented as having the ears of a horse, which he tries to conceal, and we have here, doubtless, a trait of Cornish tradition[47] which came to Béroul through the primitive *Tristan.* Moreover, Marc's seneschal, Dinas of Lidan, bears a name of Welsh[48] or Cornish[49] origin, which, to be sure, as it appears in the French poems, rests on a misunderstanding, since *Dinas Lidan* in these languages means "large fortress." In the poem the proper name (perhaps, *Dinan*) or title, which must have stood in the original Celtic source, has dropped out.[50] This character, it should be remembered, has an intimate connection with the legend and his name is, therefore, significant of the origin of the romance, or, at least, of the episodes in which he plays a part.

As regards the name of the heroine, Iseult, this has been usually regarded as of Germanic origin, and, accordingly, seemed to conflict with the theory of the Welsh or Cornish, or, indeed, Celtic origin of the love-story. *Iswalda, Ishild* (parallel to *Brunehild, Richild*) have been suggested as Germanic equivalents.[51] Zimmer disputed the Celtic character of the name, *Essylt,* which is given to Marc's wife in the Welsh triads, and derived it from the Anglo-Saxon *Ethylda.*[52] This accorded with his view that the triads about Tristan and Essylt do not reflect a native tradition.[53] The Cornish place-name, *Ryt-Eselt* ("Eselt's ford"), which is found in an Anglo-Saxon charter of the year 967,[54] proves, however, that this name could be Cornish as well as Welsh. The matter is too technical for a layman to pass judgment on, but, on the whole, the argument in favor of the Celtic origin of the name appears to carry with it the weight of probability, and it seems, furthermore, mere pedantry to lay stress on the fact that the French *Iselt (Iseut)* is not quite exact in its phonetic correspondence to Welsh *Essylt* or Cornish *Eselt.*[55] Foreign names are seldom caught correctly and the difference, after all, is very slight. This difficulty seems, then, to offer no serious obstacle to the acceptance of the Welsh or Cornish origin of the love-saga.

As between Wales and Cornwall, the evidence would seem to point rather to the latter as the region in which the great love-story of Tristan and Iseult first took shape. Indeed, but for the rôle of an intermediary between Pictland and Cornwall—regions far apart—which we are compelled to assume, there would be no reason to attribute to Wales any part at all in the development of the legend. The wronged husband, as we have seen, bore a Cornish name, and was very likely an actual Cornish king. As Loth has pointed out,[56] his Lancien was identical with the *Lantien (Lantyan)* of our own day, a village on the river Fowey, and the parish in which this village is situated is still called Saint Sampson's—that is to say, still bears the same name as the church where, according to Béroul (l. 2977), Marc and Iseult performed their devotions.[57] In the neighborhood there is a place of the name of *Kilmarth,* a corruption for *Kilmarch* ("Marc's retreat"). Taking into consideration the evidence of these place-names, to say nothing of some others, suggested by Loth, which are more open to question,[58] and the fact that the *Tristan* poems distinctly locate the story in Cornwall, there can be no doubt that Cornwall had a main share in the formation of the legend. It would appear that the fame of a character, originally Pictish, had spread through Wales and Cornwall, and that in the latter, owing to circumstances over which time has drawn an impenetrable veil, that character became the hero of this crowning love-story of the Middle Ages.

Apart from the Pictish, Welsh and Cornish elements already noted, an analysis of the Tristan tradition[59] reveals still further Breton and French names, which point to the conclusion that both of these people likewise had a hand in the final shaping of the story, before it reached the author of the lost romance which was the common source of the extant Tristan poems. For instance, the names of Rivalin, Tristan's father, and Hoel, his father-in-law, are unmistakably Breton, whereas Blanchefleur, the name of his mother, and Petiteru, that of his marvellous dog, are evidently French. It is plain, then, that the Bretons acted as intermediaries in the transmission of the story from Great Britain to the French. The fact that one of the hero's parents bears a French name, the other a Breton name, is especially significant.[60] The inventor of this part of the legend must have been familiar with both languages and he was, doubtless, a Breton from the bi-lingual zone. According to Bédier, it was the Breton jongleurs who were drawn to Great Britain by the Norman occupation that brought the story of the lovers home with him across the channel, but since the researches of Loth have shown that there was certainly, to say the least of it, an early localization of this story in Cornwall, it would seem likely that it was transmitted directly from Cornwall to Brittany by the ordinary processes of oral tradition.[61]

Accepting, in general, the theory that the essential feature of the Tristan legend—the love-motif—was Celtic, and that it reached the French poets in the manner that has been described, I will conclude with an examination of those elements in the story which we may regard as later accretions.

It has always been recognized that the various stratagems by which the lovers elude the vigilance of King Marc were not characteristically Celtic and were probably brought into the story at a comparatively late stage. Thus the incident of the blades by which Tristan is wounded, with the subsequent trick to deceive the husband, has been shown to be a modification of a story as old as Heroda-

tus—the tale of the thief who robs a king's treasury.[62] Iseult's oath that no one has touched her save Marc and the beggar (really the disguised Tristan) is likewise a widespread folk-lore *motif.* For instance there is a close parallel to the incident in the Icelandic Grettissaga (end of thirteenth century).[63] Take also the episode in which Marc, concealed in a tree, listens to the lovers, who, becoming aware of his presence, change their conversation so as to deceive him. This was manifestly suggested by the peartree story, so well known to folklorists and immortalized by Chaucer in the *Merchant's Tale.* The *motifs,* to be sure, are not the same, for in the pear-tree tale the lovers persuade the husband that the disgraceful scene which he has witnessed was the result of optical illusion. Nevertheless, the situation is so similar—the husband hidden in the tree and the lovers beneath—that we may safely accept the *Tristan* episode as a mild adaptation of that story.

More important than these matters is the question of the origin of the opening and concluding divisions of the romance—Tristan's birth and childhood, on the one hand, and the story of Iseult of Brittany, on the other. There is no indication of these features of the romance in the scanty Welsh tradition, and there can be hardly a doubt that both episodes are later developments in the story—doubtless, inventions of the author of the lost primitive French *Tristan.* In the *chansons de geste,* nearly all the great heroes had *enfances,* including occasionally some romantic narrative concerning their parents, so that when the legend of Tristan passed into the hands of a poet familiar with French epical tradition, Tristan, too, was provided with a set of youthful adventures. The name, for which the hero's tragical fate suggested a connection with French *triste,* set the poet's imagination to work, and we have as a result the sorrowful birth of the character. Then for the last division of the romance—the elements here also seem plain. The man loved by two wives was one of the common themes of mediaeval romance, *Eliduc,* the lay by Marie de France, being perhaps the most famous example of it. Combine with this, now, the classical legend of *Oenone,* the jealous wife of Paris, who is skilled in the healing art, but refuses to save her wounded husband, from jealousy of her rival Helen, and we have the essentials of the concluding episode in our romance,[64] beginning with the expulsion of Tristan after his second detection with Iseult.

To be sure, Iseult of Cornwall retains the knowledge of the healing art which she had evidently possessed already in the Celtic legend, so in this respect the conditions required that she, rather than her rival, should resemble the nymph of the classical legend, but the general situation is obviously the same, and I see no reason for rejecting Golther's identification of the stories. On the other hand, with equal confidence we may accept the *motif* of the white and black sails as derived from the legend of Theseus, in which the hero's father, Aegeus, perished in consequence of his son's forgetfulness in regard to this same signal. Servius's commentary on the *Aeneid,* doubtless, made this incident the common property of the Middle Ages.[65]

It will be observed that even the central theme of the primitive French *Tristan,* as outlined above, is a much more complex affair than the Irish *Aitheda* (*Diarmaid und Grainne* etc.), from which we have derived it. We have, in addition to the *motifs* of the *Aitheda,* the combat with Morholt, the two voyages to Ireland, the first of which involves the hero's healing at the hands of an enemy and the second his quest for the princess of the beautiful hair, the part played by Bringvain, besides the series of incidents, in which the lovers evade detection. Now, the combat with the Irish champion, Morholt, and the voyage for healing manifestly belong together, and, inasmuch as the name of this strange champion seems Celtic,[66] we may accept both combat[67] and voyage as of Celtic origin, although the idea of a wound which can be healed only by an enemy is by no means confined to the Celts.[68] It has been suggested that this episode reflects early historical conditions, when the Pictish population of Scotland were being subjugated by Irish invaders.[69] This would seem to be a plausible conjecture, and if Tristan was, indeed, in the beginning, a Pictish hero, no incident is so likely to have belonged to him in that character as that of this combat and its sequel. The second voyage in which Tristan goes forth on his indeterminate search for the unknown golden-haired princess, owes its suggestion, too, no doubt, to a favorite class of Celtic tales—the *Imrama* (tales of fantastic voyages),[70] one of which in its Christianized form, the legend of St. Brendan, enjoyed a wide-spread popularity in the Middle Ages throughout Western Europe. In the episode of the *Tristan* under consideration, however, the object of the voyage has no parallel in these Celtic tales,[71] and the *imram motif* seems plainly combined with that of a hero's quest of a bride for a king,[72] and in a specific form which is apparently unknown to the Celts—the search for the girl, the strands of whose hair have been brought to the king by a bird.[73] A distinguished scholar, indeed, once regarded this adaptation of the well-known fairy-tale of the Fair Maid with the Golden Locks as the fundamental theme of the Tristan legend,[74] but the fairy tale in question, beautiful as it is, is too gossamerlike ever to have suggested the most passionate love-story in literature, and, since the publication of Miss Schoepperle's researches, we may safely regard this adaptation as merely a later embellishment—introduced, no doubt, by a French poet—of what is, in itself, a secondary element in the legend, the second voyage to Ireland.[75]

Notes

1. Owing to its archaic character and, the (in many respects) rude civilization which it depicted Bédier, II, 314, dates this lost romance back "jusq' aux premiers temps de la conquête de l'Angleterre par les Normands", which must mean, at the latest, the early years of the twelfth century. Golther, p. 73, however, objects that the introduction of Arthur and his knights proves that it must have been written after Geoffrey's *Historia,* which dates from about 1136, had made these characters familiar figures—more specifically, between 1140 and 1150. Indeed, Golther, p. 34, was inclined to believe that the adultery of a nephew

with his uncle's wife in this primitive *Tristan* was imitated from the similar relations of Mordred, Arthur, and Guinevere in Geoffrey's work, as Muret, *Romania,* XVI, 322 (1887) had already suggested. Miss Schoepperle, p. 183, dates the lost romance "very shortly" before the extant redactions, none of which, according to her, antedate the last decades of the twelfth century.

Bédier, II, 154 f., accepts 1154 as the date of Bernart de Ventadour's lyric which contains the earliest allusion to Tristan and Iseult, and hence as the *terminuœs ad quem* of the primitive *Tristan,* but Miss Schoepperle, pp. 112 ff., has shown that the true date of composition of this lyric is wholly uncertain, and, consequently, that it cannot be used for dating the lost archetype of our Tristan poems. Her own late dating of this archetype (pp. 120 ff.) is based on the observation that it contained *motifs* that did not become current until the latter half of the twelfth century: 1. A girl who eludes an importunate lover (Kaherdin-Camille episode), imitated, according to Miss Schoepperle, from the *pastourelles;* 2. Two lovers deceive a jealous husband, despite all his precautions (Kaherdin-Gargeolain), imitated from the *chansons de mal mariée.* 3. Notions that are rooted in the *amour courtois* (cp., already, Muret, *Romania,* XVI, 360), such as the extravagant tests of humiliation to which a lady puts her lover and the idea that a lover must do anything, if appealed to in the name of his lady-love. 4. The stereotyped characters of Arthur, Kay and Gawain, which show the influence of the Arthurian romances. In Eilhart ll. 5047 ff. especially, I may add, show unmistakably this influence. They describe as accurately as possible the plan of the regular Arthurian romances.

F. Lot's criticism (*Romania,* XLIII, 128 f.) of these points has invalidated, I think, so late a dating of the primitive *Tristan* as Miss Schoepperle's (which, besides, would be impossible, if Thomas' poem were written about 1170), but it seems to me that the evidence, especially under the above heading, is sufficient to prove that this lost archetype was not earlier than the romances of antiquity 1155-1165). G. Huet, *Moyen Age,* 2 e. série, XVIII, 380 ff. (1914), has added Iseult's love-monologue (Eilhart, 2398 ff.) to Miss Schoepperle's illustrations of the *amour courtois.* The matter is not susceptible of determination, but it seems most likely that ideas of the *amour courtois* were in the archetype, since they are found in all the extant versions. The same thing applies to the Arthurian connections of these versions. To be sure, in the case of Thomas, this connection is very slender, consisting entirely of Arthur's encounters with two giants (Bédier, I, 290 ff., 307), which really stand outside of the Tristan adventures and may very well have been borrowed directly from Geoffrey's *Historia,* Book X, ch. 3 or Wace's *Brut,* ll. 11634 ff. In Béroul, ll, 3706 ff. *et passim,* and Eilhart, ll. 5231 ff., Arthurian characters are more intimately connected with the narrative, and Lot, *op. cit.,* pp. 131 f., argues that the episode in Eilhart was expressly introduced by the author for the purpose of imparting novelty to the story. This, of course, is possible.

In his "Tristan bei Cercamon?", *Zs. f. rom. Ph.,* XLI, 219 ff. (1921), C. Appel, detects an allusion to Tristan in a poem of this Provençal poet. He assigns the poem to the period, 1150-1160, and contends that this is the earliest extant allusion to Tristan. The evidence, however, is too uncertain.

2. So R. Heinzel, *Zs. f. d. A.* XIV, 272 ff. (1869), W. Golther, *Die Sage von Tristan und Isolde,* pp. 30 ff. *et passim* (Munich 1887), F. Novati, *Studj di filologia romanza,* II, 390 (1887), G. Paris, *Manuel,* pp. 99 ff. (1888). For historical surveys of *Tristan* studies, cp. Bédier, II, 168 ff. and Golther, 1 ff.

3. In his review of Röttiger's Program in *Romania,* XXVII, 608ff. (1898), E. Muret makes Chrétien's lost poem and Thomas the sources (one or the other) of all extant Tristan versions. E. Brugger, *Zs. f. frz. Spr. u. Litt.* XX, 134, note (1898) suggested a single source (undefined). Golther, however, *ibid.* XXII[1], 23 (1900), was the first to work out a definite scheme, based substantially on the hypothesis of a single source (Chrétien). In his later work Golther gives up Chrétien as the author of the *Ur-Tristan.*

In the *Journal des Savants* for 1902, p. 301, note 2, G. Paris expressed the belief that all French Tristan poems go back to a lost English poem, itself incomplete. In that case, the story of Tristan and Iseult would have passed from the Cornish (or Welsh) to the English and from the English to the French. For a discussion of this hypothesis and the reasons which led Paris to adopt it see Bédier II, 314 ff. In so far as these reasons are connected with Paris's general theory of the Anglo-Norman origin of the Arthurian romances, I have dealt with them elsewhere. For the rest, I will add to what Bédier says on the subject that the testimony of the unpublished French poem *Waldef* (eleventh or twelfth century) as to the existence of an early English *Tristan (Tristram)* is, on the face of it, valueless, since in the same line the author of this poem speaks of an early English original for the French *Bruit (Brut).* The line of works entitled *Brut,* however, all go back to Geoffrey of Monmouth (cf. Gaimar, Wace etc.) and have, of course, nothing to do with any earlier English works. Cp. on this subject Golther, *Zs. f. frz. Spr. u. Litt.* XXIX[2], 151· ff. (1906) and Brugger, *ibid.* XXXII[2], 136 ff. (1907), and, above all, R. Immelmann in his edition of the fifteenth century Latin *Waldef* romance, *Johannes Bramis' Historia Regis Waldei,* pp. XXX ff. (Bonn, 1912). The argument from the *Waldef* which Paris had already cited, *Romania* XV, 597 (1886), XVIII, 510 (1889), in connection with the discussion of Tristan's origin, was adopted, also, by W. Hertz, *Tristan und Isolde von Gottfried von Strassburg,* pp. 477 f.—so, too, apparently by W. H. Schofield, *English Literature from the Norman Conquest to Chau-cer,* p. 202 (New York, 1906). Schofield here goes so far as to connect the incident of Tristan's sending his message to Iseult by the chips on the stream with the Anglo-Saxon lyric which is usually entitled "*The Husband's Message.*"

4. Also in a popular article in the now defunct *International Quarterly* (March-June, 1904).

5. It would seem natural to identify this *Ur-Tristan* with the lost poem "del roi Marc et d' Iseut la blonde" which Chrétien, in the list of his works, *Cliges,* ll. 1 ff., tells us that he wrote, and, as a matter of fact, Foerster, *Cliges*[3], p. LXVIII, argues that the two are identical. But its connection in this list with Chrétien's tales from Ovid (certainly compositions of the poet's youth) shows that the lost poem was an early work. Now, the *Ur-Tristan* was evidently a masterpiece and superior in construction and in poetical content to even the maturest romances from Chrétien's pen, so that it is inconceivable that it was one of Chrétien's compositions. Golther, p. 74, very properly raises this objection to the theory of the identity and adds with less force that Chrétien is not likely to have had the knowledge of English conditions that the *Ur-Tristan* (as reconstructed by Bédier and himself, with a high degree of probability) implies. Foerster, *loc. cit.,* tries to meet Golther's objection, with the supposition that Chrétien had before him a still earlier *Tristan* poem *(Ururtristan)* and that the merits of construction may have come to him from his original.

In the *Journal des Savants* for 1902, pp. 299 ff., G. Paris has argued that Chrétien did not write a full poem on the story of Tristan and Iseult, but merely a brief one, dealing with some episode in which Marc and Iseult figured. Novati, *Studj di filologia romanza,* II, 411 and Röttiger, *Der heutige Stand der Tristanforschung,* pp. 28 f. (1897) had already discerned a significance in the absence of Tristan's name from Chrétien's allusion to his lost poem. Paris's hypothesis is based on the consideration that in all the literature of the Middle Ages there is no allusion to a Tristan poem by Chrétien. We have, however, no episodic poems from Chrétien's pen, and it seems to me more likely that he planned a long poem on Tristan and Iseult, but failed to complete it, as he later failed to complete his *Lancelot* (to say nothing of the *Perceval*)—only in the case of this earlier composition he never put his work into circulation, recognizing it as immature.—In Paul's *Grundriss der germanischen Philologie* II, 1, 459 (1890) J. te Winkel conjectures that there was a (lost) Dutch translation of Chrétien's *Tristan,* but gives no reasons for this conjecture.

In the *Roman de Renard,* Branch II, there is an allusion to a lost Tristan poem by a certain La Chievre and in a *conte dévot* (Foerster *Festschrift,* Halle, 1902) there is a similar allusion to this lost poem—only its author's name is here given in the Picard form, Li Kievres. The poem, of whose contents we know nothing, was probably composed in the twelfth century and its author should, doubtless, be identified with the lyric poet, Robert La Chievre of Rheims. On these subjects cp. Gröber's *Grundriss,* Band II, Abteilung I, pp. 494, 671, and G. Paris, *op. cit.* p. 299.

In l. 2119 of his *Tristan,* Thomas appeals to "Breri" as his authority for representing that Tristan sent Kaherdin, and not Governal, as his messenger to Iseult on a certain occasion. G. Paris, *Romania,* VIII, 425 ff. (1879) identified this "Breri" with "famosus ille fabulator Bledhericus, qui tempora nostra paulo praevenit", of Giraldus Cambrensis, *Descriptio Kambriae,* ch. XVII, in Vol. VI (London, 1868) of that writer's Works edited for the Rolls Series by J. F. Dimock. As Paris, himself, however, says, Thomas does not hereby imply that he is using a book by Breri, but is merely appealing to the authority of a person of that name who is said to know more about British history than anybody else. "Breri" and "Bledhericus" are, indeed, probably the same name and Paris's identification of the persons concerned is *a priori* admissible. The identification was favored, also, by H. Zimmer, *Göttingische Gelehrte Anzeigen* for Oct. 1, 1890, p. 805, note, and *Zs. f. frz. Spr. u. Litt.,* XIII[1], 84, (1891). Nevertheless, Thomas's appeal to Breri is, no doubt, merely one of the innumerable instances in mediaeval literature of a writer's bolstering up his narrative by the citation of fictitious authorities. He puts off on Breri the responsibility for innovations in the story which are really, his own. Cp. Muret, *Romania,* XVII, 608 f. For a full discussion of the Breri question cp. Bédier, II, 95 ff. He lists p. 95, note 1, the chief previous discussions of the subject. Add J. L. Weston, *Romania,* XXXIII, 334 ff. (1904), who identifies Thomas's Breri with the Bleheris (Blihos-Bleheris) of the additions made to Chrétien's *Perceval*—also, W. Golther, *Tristan und Isolde,* pp. 139 f. (Leipzig, 1907), who points out that Thomas, in the passage referred to above, cites Breri as a great authority on British history, yet, as a matter of fact, derives all his knowledge of that history from Wace. Very important is L. Foulet, "Thomas and Marie in their relation to the conteurs," MLN, XXIII, 205 ff. (1908). Foulet shows that Thomas's reference to the "conteurs", to whose varying accounts he opposes the authority of Breri, is really a "meaningless mannerism", copied from Marie de France, and does not imply any knowledge of oral traditions concerning Tristan.

We shall have to return to this mysterious Breri in the discussion of the continuations to Chrétien's *Perceval.*

6. The upward limit is fixed by the author's use of Wace's *Brut,* the lower by his influence on Chrétien's *Cliges.* F. Lot, *Romania,* XXVII, 42 (1898), called attention to the first point, G. Paris, *Journal des Savants* for July, 1902, pp. 354ff. to the latter. For a full discussion of the subject cp. Bédier, I,

37ff. M. Wilmotte, *L'évolution du roman francais,* p. 67 (Brussels, 1903) and W. Foerster, *Cliges*[3], pp. LXVIff. (Halle, 1910) have disputed Paris's proofs as to the priority of Thomas's *Tristan* over the *Cliges,* on the ground that Chrétien and Thomas may have been drawing from a common source (one of the lost Tristan poems), in the cases where Paris assumes imitation of the latter by the former. The question is difficult to decide, but it seems to me that Thomas would hardly have appropriated from a predecessor so distinctive a play on words as *amer: mer.*

The limits of date would be still further narrowed, if we could accept S. Singer's contention, "Thomas, Tristan, und Benoit de Saint Maure," *Zs. f. rom. Phil.* XXXIII, 729ff. (1909), that the *Roman de Troie* influenced Thomas's *Tristan;* for the former was written about 1165. Singer compares especially the description of the loves of Rivalen and Blanchefleur, Bédier, I, 12ff., with those of Achilles and Polyxena, *R. de Troie,* 17554ff. But the matter is too indefinite, and the passage in Thomas, just named, may be imitated from some other romance embodying the new spirit of the *amour courtois.* Singer, himself, compares, also, Gottfried, ll, 16478ff. (which goes back, doubtless, to Thomas) with *Eneas,* 9885ff. (eye belongs to love, hand to grief).

Traces of the influence of the *Disciplina Clericalis* in Thomas throw no light on the subject of date, since the author of that work, Petrus Alfonsi, flourished in the early part of the twelfth century. Cp., on this influence, A. Hilka, "Der Tristanroman des Thomas und die Disciplina Clericalis," *Zs. f. frz. Spr. u. Litt.,* XLV[1], 38ff. (1917).

That Thomas was not identical with the poet of the same name who wrote *Horn et Rimenhild* has been shown by W. Söderhjelm, "Sur l'identité du Thomas, auteur de Tristan, et du Thomas, auteur de Horn", *Romania,* XV, 175ff. (1886). The identification of our Anglo-Norman Thomas with Thomas of Erceldoune is, of course, merely the individual fancy of the author of the English *Sir Tristrem.*

Novati, *Studj di filologia romanza,* II, 403, note 3, conjectures that Thomas, author of *Tristan,* was an ecclesiastic. There is no means of deciding the matter, but the conjecture hardly seems probable.

7. The poem has been preserved in the unique MS. 2171 of the Bibliothèque Nationale and was edited by H. von der Hagen in Vol. II of his edition of Gottfried von Strassburg (Breslau, 1823) and by F. Michel in his edition of the Tristan fragments I, 1ff. (London and Paris, 1835). The authoritative editions, however, are E. Muret's 1. *Le roman de Tristan par Béroul et un anonyme* (Paris, 1903, for the Société des Anciens Textes Français) and 2. *Béroul, le roman de Tristan, poème du XII*e *siècle* (Paris, 1913, in *Les Classiques français du moyen age*). Ll. 1268 and 1790, the poet calls himself *Berox* (nominative form). Down to l. 2754 the narrative accords closely with

that of Eilhart. Not so with ll. 3028-4485 (end), nor with ll. 2767-3031, which latter connects the two principal divisions of the poem. In his first edition of Béroul (Paris, 1903) Muret, pp. LXVff., concluded with G. Paris and others that Béroul II (ll. 3028-4485) was by a different hand from Béroul I (ll. 1-2754) and that the two were connected by still a third hand. Beroul II, he observes, is grosser and more barbarous, is not marked by the same literary knowledge or influences of chivalrous courtesy. In his second edition (Paris, 1913) he repeats this opinion, though with some hesitation (pp. VIIIff.), being affected, it would seem, by Bédier's view (*Légendes Épiques,* III, 399), that the whole of the Béroul fragment is by one person. Heinzel (*Zs. f. d. Altertum,* XIV) had maintained, as no one would now, that it consisted of nineteen different lays by different authors. Bédier's view seems to me, the most likely.—The Béroul *Tristan* was undoubtedly addressed to an audience of lower social position than Thomas's poem. It is a jongleur's version. There is nothing, however, to support the view, formerly held, that it was older than Thomas.

The upward limit of date for Beroul II, is fixed by an allusion (l. 3853) to the epidemic of leprosy which raged among the crusaders at Acre, 1190-1. This part of the poem probably falls in the last decade of the twelfth century. Muret (p. LXIV of his first edition) assumes that Beroul I was not earlier than 1165 or 1170. There is no evidence, however, to prove that this part of the poem was not composed substantially at the same time as Béroul II, granting even that the two parts were by different authors.

8. Edited by Franz Lichtenstein (Strassburg, 1877). In the extant MSS. Eilhart's poem has been subjected to changes. On this subject cp. especially E. Muret, "Eilhart d'Oberg et sa source française", *Romania,* XVI, 287ff. (1887) and G. Schoepperle, II, 476ff. Between these two discussions E. Gierach, "Zur Sprache von Eilhart's Tristrant", *Prager Deutsche Studien,* IV (1908), had shown that the Czech version of Eilhart did not have the importance for the reconstruction of Eilhart's text that Knieschek and Muret attributed to it. Knieschek translated the Czech version into German, *Zs. f. d. Altertum,* XXVIII, 261ff.

Eilhart composed his poem probably between 1185 and 1189. Cp. Gierach, *op. cit.* pp. 254f. When Muret, *Romania,* XVI, 361f., suggests that the author of his source was Li Kievres, this is pure conjecture.

Recently a fragmentary twelfth century MS. of Eilhart's *Tristrant*—now in the (formerly) Royal Library at Berlin—has been discovered. It contains 461 lines, corresponding to ll. 7061ff. of Lichtenstein's edition, and has been edited by H. Degering. "Neue Funde aus dem zwölften Jahrhundert: Ein Bruchstück der Urfassung von Eilharts Tristrant", PBB, XLI, 513ff. (1916).

9. Like Golther, p. 59, Miss Gertrude Schoepperle, *Romania,* XXXIX, 277ff. (1910) and *Tristan and Isolt,* pp. 72ff. (Frankfort and London, 1913), disputes the existence of this hypothetical intermediate derivative (the *y* of Bédier's stemma) and derives both Eilhart and Béroul direct from the primitive *Tristan* poem. In my review of her book, MLN, XXIX, 213ff. (1914), however, I have pointed out the improbability of her derivation. So, too, Nitze, JEGc Ph. XIII, 444ff. (1914). Muret, in his review of Golther's book, *Zs. f. frz. Spr. u. Litt.,* XXXVII[2], 167ff. (1911), has adopted Golther's and Miss Schoepperle's conclusions in regard to this matter, but adds no new arguments. *Ibid.* he contends that the author of the primitive *Tristan* merely combined Celtic (insular) traditions concerning Tristan.

Bédier's reconstruction has been criticised by Jakob Kelemina, *Untersuchungen zur Tristansage* (Leipzig, 1910), and by Muret and Miss Schoepperle *loc. cit.*—also, by R. Zenker in his "Zum Ursprung der Tristansage," *Zs. f. rom. Ph.,* XXXV, 715ff. (1911)—especially, pp. 728ff.—and again in *Romanische Forschungen,* XXIX, 328ff. (1911). Kelemina and Miss Schoepperle complain that the French scholar does not sufficiently recognize cross influences between the extant versions, and Zenker offers the same criticism, though in milder terms Zenker, accordingly, does not accept the lost primitive *Tristan* poem as the sole source of Eilhart and the prose *Tristan.* What he says of the partial dependence of the prose on Béroul and Thomas is, doubtless, true. A romance on Tristan, written so late as the prose (circa 1220) could hardly escape such influences.—Kelemina, on the other hand, denies altogether the possibility of reconstructing an *Ur-Tristan* and takes the ground that already in the pre-literary period of the development of the *Tristan* legend there were two lines of tradition, corresponding roughly to the Béroul and Thomas forms of the story, respectively. His theory, however, has found no adherents.

10. The passages in question are preserved only in MS. 103 (Bibl. Nat.) and are printed by Bédier, II, 321ff. See, also, his article, "La mort de Tristan et d'Iseut d'après le manuscrit fr. 103 de la Bibliothèque Nationale comparé au poème allemand d'Eilhart d'Oberg," *Romania,* XV, 481ff. (1886). The relation of these passages, however, to the primitive *Tristan* is somewhat uncertain. They were late modifications, doubtless, of the prose *Tristan* under the influence of a poetic version—but of which one? According to W. Röttiger, *Der heutige Stand der Tristanforschung,* p. 26 (Hamburg, 1897), it was a compilation similar to the source of Eilhart and Béroul. Miss Schoepperle, I, 10, conjectures, on the other hand, that the episodes were drawn from the source of the primitive *Tristan,* which seems, however, very improbable.

It should be noted that G. Paris once held the opinion (cp. *Romania,* XV, 602), that an imitation (presumably in prose) of Chrétien's *Tristan* constituted the nucleus of the prose *Tristan*. His subsequent theory, however, that Chrétien composed only a brief episodic poem concerning Tristan implies a withdrawal of his earlier opinion. In his discussion of the subject Röttiger, *op. cit.*, pp. 28f., had already expressed himself unfavorably as to the dependence of the prose romance on Chrétien. Löseth, in his analysis of the prose *Tristan*, p. XXV, regards that work as based largely on the lost poem of Chrétien.

For the closeness of the prose-romance to Eilhart-Béroul cp. Heinzel, *Zs. f. d. Altertum*, XIV, 354, Brakelmann, *Zs. f. d. Phil.*, XVIII, 87, Muret, *Romania*, XVI, 292.

11. The two *Folie Tristan*'s have the same general design: Tristan gains access to Marc's court by disguising himself as a madman and in this disguise gradually reveals himself to Iseult by recalling the various incidents of their love-affair. Both poems were first edited by Francisque Michel in his *Tristan: recueil de ce qui reste des poemes relatifs a ses aventures*, from the Berne MS. (No. 354 of the Berne Library), I, 215ff., and the Bodleian MS. (Douce d 6) II, 89ff. (1835). The second of these versions was, also, edited by H. Morf, *Romania*, XV. 558ff. (1886). The standard edition of both poems now, however, is that of J. Bédier, *Les deux poèmes de la Folie Tristan*, 1ff. (Paris, 1907, for the Société des Anciens Textes Français). The Oxford *Folie* is plainly dependent on Thomas; that of Berne is closely related to Béroul, but, according to Bédier, pp. 82f. not directly dependent. On the subject see, still further, W. Lutoslawski, "Les Folies de Tristan," *Romania*, XV, 511ff. (1886) and E. Hoepffner, "Das Verhältnis der Berner *Folie Tristan* zu Berols Tristandichtung," *Zs. f. rom. Ph.* XXXIX, 62ff. (1917), and "Die Berner und die Oxforder Folie," *ibid.*, XXXIX, 551ff. (1918), 672ff. (1919). According to Hoepffner, the Berne version follows closely an hypothetical lost poem (X), derived from Béroul. On the other hand, the author of the Oxford version, he thinks, recast this, using very fully in the process Thomas's poem and aiming at the production of a romance in the courtly style. *Ibid.* XL, "Die Folie Tristan und die Odyssee", Hoepffner has discussed the *motif* in the French *Folies* as compared with the similar one in the Odyssey.

A similar episode to that of these two poems is found in the prose *Tristan* (cp. Bédier's edition of Thomas, I, 372ff.), in Eilhart, ll. 8695ff., in Ulrich von Turheim's and Heinrich von Freyberg's continuations to Gottfried von Strassburg.

For a discussion of the affiliations of all the various versions, see W. Lutoslawski's above-mentioned article and Bédier, II, 287ff. Bédier's stemma (p. 296) is preferable to Lutoslawski's (p. 287). Somewhat different is W. Golther, p. 219, note 1.

Tristan appears elsewhere in other disguises—namely, as *1.* leper, Thomas, ll. 1773ff. *2.* penitent, *ibid.*, ll, 2061ff. *3.* minstrel, Gerbert's continuation to

Chrétien's *Perceval, Romania*, XXXVI, 497ff. *4.* monk, Middle High German poem (based, no doubt, on a lost French original), *Tristan als Mönch*, edited by H. Paul, *Sitzungsberichte der Münchener Akademie der Wissenschaften* for 1895, pp. 317ff., from the two extant MSS. of the thirteenth century. The author, it seems, was an Alsatian.

As Golther, p. 29, has remarked, these stories of Tristan seeking his lady-love in various disguises were probably due, in the first instance, to the influence of the legend of Solomon.

12. Of Thomas's French original only 3144 lines, all told, are extant. Following are the works on which reconstructions of the remainder of Thomas's poem have to be based: *1.* The Old Norse prose saga (dating from 1226), edited by Brynjulfson, *Saga af Tristram ok Isondar* (Copenhagen, 1878) and E. Kölbing *Tristrams Saga ok Isondar* (Heilbronn, 1878). *2.* Gottfried von Strassburg's poem, *Tristan* (early thirteenth century), which has been often edited (cp. list in Golther p. 165, note 1)—last by K. Marold (Leipzig, 1912). Marold furnishes the best text, but the commentary has not appeared. A. Bossert, *Tristan et Iseult, poème de Gotfrit de Strasbourg, comparé à d'autres poèmes sur le même sujet* (Paris, 1865), was the first to show that Gottfried's poem was based on Thomas. For the best studies of the relation of the German poet to his original see W. Hertz, *Tristan und Isolde*,[5] pp. 473f. (Stuttgart and Berlin, 1907), F. Piquet, *L'originalité de Gottfried de Strasbourg* (Lille, 1905) and Bédier, II, 76ff. (1905).

Of minor importance are the articles in a controversy on this subject in Pfeiffer's *Germania* between O. Glöde (who claims greater independence for Gottfried) and E. Kölbing: cp. that journal, Glöde XXXIII, 17ff. (1888), XXXV, 344f. (1890) and Kölbing, XXXIV, 187ff. (1889). *3.* The English *Sir Tristrem* (probably, end of the thirteenth century) edited by E. Kölbing (Heilbronn, 1882) and by G. P. McNeill (Edinburgh, 1886, for the Scottish Text Society). *4.* *La Folie Tristan* (Oxford MS.), edited by Bédier (Paris, 1907). *5.* *La Tavola Ritonda* (thirteenth century), edited by F. L. Polidori, 2 vols. (Bologna, 1864-5). Chapters 63-67 are based on Thomas's poem for this part of the narrative (Marc spies upon Tristan and Iseult from the pine-tree, but is observed, etc.). On this subject see E. G. Parodi, *Il Tristano Riccardiano*, pp. LXXXIIff. (Bologna, 1896) and Bédier, II, 91. The text edited by Parodi is the chief source of *La Tavola Ritonda*.

13. In the Middle Ages no branch of the *matière de Bretagne*, perhaps, won such popularity as the story of Tristan and Iseult. For allusions to the same in mediaeval literature cp. L. Sudre, "Les allusions à la légende de Tristan dans la littérature du moyen age," *Romania*, XV, 534ff. (1886) and Bedier, II, 397ff. For allusions in Italian literature cp., more particularly, A. Graf, "Appunti per la storia del ciclo brettone," *Giornale Storico della Letteratura Italiana*, V,

81ff. and *Miti, leggende e superstizioni nel medio evo,* II, 339ff. (Turin, 1893), and, above all, Elvira Sommer-Tolomei, La leggenda di Tristano in Italia," *Rivista d'Italia* for July, 1910, pp. 73ff. P. 127 of the last-named article, some additional minor contributions to the subject of Tristan and Iseult in Italy are named. The fourteenth century Italian poem, *La Morte di Tristano,* is still unpublished. For an account of it see G. Bertoni, *Fanfulla della Domenica,* nos. 43, 46, 48 (Rome, 1915). It is of popular origin.—For similar allusions in Spanish literature see A. Bonilla y San Martin, *Libro del esforçado cauallero Don Tristan de Leonis,* pp. XXVIff. (Madrid, 1912).

For the literature of allusions to Tristan and Iseult in German writings of the Middle Ages cp. Golther p. 211, note 1.

The popularity of the Tristan romances (especially the Eilhart-Béroul tradition) is reflected, also, in the use which is made of them in the decorative arts (apart from miniatures in MSS.). Examples of such use are found in all the principal European countries,—particularly, from the fourteenth century. For the literature of this subject see Hertz, pp. 475f., 541, Golther, pp. 408ff. and, above all, R. S. Loomis in "A Sidelight on the *Tristan* of Thomas," *Modern Language Review,* X, 304ff. (1915)—an article which corrects Bédier's reconstruction of Thomas in three minor details—and "Illustrations of Medieval Romance on Tiles from Chertsey Abbey," *University of Illinois Studies in Language and Literature,* Vol. II, No. 2 (1916). The tiles in question are both the earliest (circa 1270) and the finest specimens of decorative illustrations drawn from the *Tristan* romances. In the second of his above-mentioned studies, Loomis gives plates (with identifications and discussions) of the tiles (34, in all). They are based on Thomas. In this same study he gives, also, full indications of the very extensive literature on the subject of the *Tristan* romances in the decorative arts. Cp. now, also, the same scholar's articles: "The Tristran and Perceval Caskets," RR, VIII, 196ff. (1917) and "Notes on the *Tristan* of Thomas," MLR, XIV, 38ff. (1919). The first describes a *Tristan* casket in the Hermitage Museum at Petrograd; the second makes additions to the author's previous articles—also, some corrections.

Of especial interest is Pio Rajna's description of two coverlets (dating from about 1400) embroidered with figures from the legend of Tristan. See his article "Intorno a due antiche coperte con figurazioni tratte dalle storie di Tristano," *Romania,* XLII, 517ff. (1913). The legends accompanying the figures are in the Sicilian dialect and the ultimate source of the scenes is the prose *Tristan,* the immediate source some Italian version of that romance. The plates in Rajna's article reproduce the figures in the coverlets.

Localizations from the Tristan poems in Dublin and its vicinity from as early as the twelfth century are noted in letters to *The Athenaeum* for Feb 21 and April 26, 1913. Cp., too, the issues for May 10 and 17, 1913. The writers naively cite these localizations as proofs of the actual existence of the characters concerned. "Chapelizod" (= Iseult's Chapel), as the name of a village near Dublin, persists even to this day.

From the romances, the name, *Tristan,* passed into the general nomenclature of France, England, etc. Students of the romances appear to have overlooked the fact that *Tristan* is recorded as a French surname as early as 1207. In that year a person of this name, whose Christian name seems to have been *Arnoul,* bought a property in the neighborhood of Soissons. More distinguished than himself was one of his sons, Pierre Tristan, (Tristran)—or in Latin, Petrus Tristanides—who saved the life of Philip Augustus in the battle of Bouvines (1214). Cp. *Oeuvres de Rigord et de Guillaume le Breton,* I, 282 (2 vols., Paris, 1882-1885), edited by H. F. Delaborde for the Société de l'Histoire de la France. We have, also, a record of Pierre's purchasing a piece of property in 1207—from the convent of St. Magloire de Paris. On the other hand, he was still living in 1249. Since he was of age in 1207, he could hardly have been born later than 1185 and his father, who bore the same name, is not likely to have been born later than 1165. If he (Arnoul), in turn, inherited the surname from *his* father, we should have *Tristan* occurring as the proper name of an actual person in the first half of the twelfth century. I see no way, however, of determining which of Pierre's progenitors was the first to assume the surname. For abundant documentary evidence relating to this family cp. Henri Stein: "Pierre Tristan, chambellan de Philippe Auguste et sa famille," *Bibliothèque de l'École des Chartes,* LXXVII, 135ff. (1918). Stein does not mention the legendary Tristan in connection with the family.

14. For an enumeration of the differences cp. Golther, pp. 59ff. I have given my reasons, MLN, XXIX, 214ff. for not accepting with Golther (p. 59) and Miss Schoepperle (pp. 75ff.) certain features of Eilhart and Béroul as belonging to the lost Tristan poem: In these poems (as against Thomas) there is an abatement in the influence of the love-potion after the lapse of three (Béroul) or four (Eilhart) years, whereupon the lovers confess to a hermit (Ogrin) in the forest and on his advice it is agreed that Iseult shall return to Marc. Marc takes her back, but banishes Tristan. In the earliest form of the story, however, the efficacy of the love-potion obviously could not have been limited as to time and it is not so limited in Thomas (nor in the prose *Tristan*), so that it is highly improbable that in the intermediate version (the primitive Tristan poem) there was any such limitation. It is principally on account of these views regarding this feature and the changes in the narrative that are corollary to it that Golther (p. 103) and Miss Schoepperle (pp. 72ff.) consider the narrative of Eil-

hart as differing very slightly from that of the lost Tristan poem.

Another point in which Eilhart's narrative shows degradation is in dropping the *motif* of jealousy, which is necessary to explain the conduct of Iseult of Brittany at the end of the story, in the incident of the sails. Miss Schoepperle, pp. 96ff. and in the *Zs. f. d. Ph.*, XLIII, 453ff. (1911) "Isolde Weisshand am Sterbebette Tristan's," argues that she is jealous in Eilhart, too, but the argument does not convince.

Altogether, Bédier's stemma of the *Tristan* versions seems to me to be the soundest that has yet been offered.

15. Cp. French *triste* = sad.

16. In the primitive *Tristan,* the hero, when he started on his voyage, evidently had no fixed destination in view. According to F. Piquet, *"L'originalité de Gottfried de Strasbourg,"* pp. 165ff. (Lille, 1905), Thomas modified this and made Ireland his destination from the beginning. For a refutation of this opinion, however, cp. R. S. Loomis, MLR, XIV, 39ff. (1919).

17. For parallels in folk-tales to this incident of the false seneschal cp. Bolte and Polivka's *"Anmerkungen zu den Kinder- und Hausmärchen der Brüder Grimm,"* I, 547ff. (Leipzig, 1913).

18. Miss Schoepperle, "The Love-Potion in Tristan and Isolt," *Romania*, XXXIX, 277ff. (1910), tries to show that the *motif* of the love-potion here is Celtic. I agree, however, with Bédier, II, 163ff. and Golther, p. 34, that it was introduced into the legend by a French poet from classical sources.

For the variant forms of the name of Iseult's attendant in the different mediaeval versions of the *Tristan* story, cp. W. Hertz's *Tristan und Isolde von Gottfried von Straßburg*[5], p. 527 (Stuttgart and Berlin, 1907). It is hardly open to doubt that *Bringvain* was the form used by Thomas, although in our extant MSS. of his poem, the name sometimes appears in an altered form. See on the subject W. Golther, *Zs. f. rom. Ph.* XII, 352. According to G. Paris, *Romania*, XVIII, 323, *Brenwain* was the form employed in the source (or sources) of the *Tristan* romances. This is, however, purely hypothetical, and I have thought it better to use in an outline even of the *Ur-Tristan* the form of the name which is virtually assured for Thomas. There is no agreement as yet in regard to the etymology of this name.

19. For parallels to this *motif* in folk-tales and literature cp., especially, Hertz, *Tristan und Isolde*[5], pp. 533 ff., and P. Arferth, *Das Motiv von der untergeschobenen Braut* (Rostock Diss. 1897).

20. The rote was a kind of violin, it seems.

21. Miss Schoepperle, II, 417 ff., has shown that this incident, doubtless, formed a feature of the *Tristan* saga in its original Celtic form. In the *Archiv für das Studium der neueren Sprachen*, CXXIX, 375 ff.

(1912), Brugger had already contended that the incident was of Celtic origin. He cites examples from the Welsh tales, *Kulhwch and Olwen* and *Pwyll Prince of Dyvet*—also, from the Irish story of Mongan, son of Manawyddan. It is very questionable, however, whether the *don-motif* in Arthurian romance is so exclusively of Celtic origin as Brugger believes.

22. For this common folk-tale *motif* cp. Hertz, *Tristan und Isolde,* pp. 551 ff., B. Heller, *Romania*, XXXVI, 36 ff., XXXVII, 162 f., and Bolte and Polivka, I, 554 f.

23. For numerous parallels in Oriental literature to this *motif* cp. J. J. Meyer's *Isolde's Gottesurteil in seiner erotischen Bedeutung,* (Berlin, 1914). For some additional examples see Golther's review of Meyer's book in the *Deutsche Literaturzeitung*, March 14, 1914, and Miss Schoepperle, pp. 223 ff. Miss Schoepperle gives references to articles and books on the *motif,* in general. Bédier II, 265, expresses some uncertainty as to whether this episode was in the *estoire.* He, also, rejects the beautiful incident, told in some of the versions, concerning the dog, Petitcrû, presented by the King of Scotland to Tristan and by him, in turn, to Iseult. The sound of a magic bell hung about the creature's neck had the power of dispelling grief, but Iseult would not be happy, whilst her lover was sorrowful, so she broke the bell.

24. Later Mrs. R. S. Loomis. See her fine study, *Tristan and Isolt, a Study of the Sources of the Romance,* 2 vols. Frankfort and London, 1913. The pagination of the volumes is continuous.

25. For a list of this class of Celtic tales cp. Schoepperle, II, 393 f. The *Aitheda* are not to be confounded with tales headed *Aided (Death)*, which recount the deaths of heroes and heroines. Cp. the long list of the latter in G. Dottin's catalogue of Irish epic literature, *Revue Celtique*, XXXIII, 1 ff. (1912).

26. J. F. Campbell identified the story of Tristan and Iseult with that of Diarmaid and Grainne in his *Popular Tales of the West Highlands,* IV, 240 (4 Vols. London, 1890-1893). Miss Schoepperle seems to have overlooked this.

27. For an account of these versions, which range from the tenth century to the present time, see the two articles by J. H. Lloyd, O. J. Bergin and G. Schoepperle in the *Revue Celtique:* "The Reproach of Diarmaid," XXXIII, 41 ff. (1912), and "The Death of Diarmaid," *Ibid.,* 157 ff. We have here, also, editions and translations of some of the most important texts. Cp., also, on the subject Miss Schoepperle's *Tristan and Isolt,* II, 395 ff.

28. It must be confessed that in the *Diarmaid and Grainne* texts the passion displayed is mainly on the part of the heroine. Cp. for instance, *The Reproach of Diarmaid,* just cited, where the hero bewails to the heroine the misfortunes which she has brought on him. In still other versions (cp. *Revue Celtique*,

XXXIII, 49 and Miss Schoepperle, II, 402) he resists her advances for a long time. On the other hand (cp. *Rev. Celt., loc. cit.*), in some of these versions Grainne is unfaithful to Diarmaid with a stranger who visits their cave.

29. Cp. Bédier's edition of Thomas's *Tristan*, II. 163 ff. Bédier appeals especially to the Welsh law on the subject in the so-called Laws of Howel the Good (ninth and tenth centuries). In his reply to Bédier, *Revue Celtique*, XXX, 270 ff. (1909), Loth has attenuated, in some measure, the force of that scholar's argument.

30. Cp. the posthumous article of H. Zimmer, cited above: "Der Kulturgeschichtliche Hintergrund in den Erzählungen der alten irischen Heldensage," *Sitzungsberichte der königlichen preussischen Akademie der Wissenschaften*," pp. 174 ff. (Berlin 1911), where he collects some extraordinary instances of shameless immodesty on the part of women in the Irish heroic sagas. Loth observes in reply, *Revue Celtique*, XXXIII, 260, note (1912), "Quant aux faits de divergondage qu'il cite ils ne prouvent pas plus contre les moeurs des Celtes que la conduite des personnages de l'Olympe contre les moeurs des anciens Grecs." Loth, *ibid.*, refutes Zimmer's idea that this supposed immodesty was a concomitant of the matriarchal system which was in vogue among the Picts.

31. The *Aithed* of these two characters is preserved, in one of its versions, in the *Book of Leinster* (a MS. written before 1150). For editions and translations cp. Miss Schoepperle, II, 411, note 1. There are convenient English translations of this Irish saga in A. H. Leahy, *Heroic Romances of Ireland*, I, 95, (2 vols., London, 1905-6) and Eleanor Hull, *The Cuchullin Saga*, pp. 123 ff. (London, 1898).

32. Cp. Miss Schoepperle, II, 401 f. on this subject. The "love-spot" was a mark on a man's person that rendered him irresistible to women. "The *geis* is a peculiarly Irish taboo which any individual seems to have been at liberty to impose upon any other, and which, if disregarded, entailed moral degradation and swift retribution." D'Arbois de Jubainville observed, however, *Revue Celtique*, XV, 406, note 1 (1894), that the Irish *geis* differs from the spell which the love-potion exercises in the French *Tristan* romances, inasmuch as one was free to disregard the former—only the punishment inevitably followed.

33. It has been remarked that the whole character of this great love-story, with its *dreieckiges Verhältnis* (husband, wife and lover), is manifestly French, and, consequently, could only have entered into the Tristan tradition after the French writers began to handle the theme. But adultery has been a favorite theme of romances, both written and oral, in all parts of the world. The Irish *Aitheda* show how common it was in Celtic romances. Nevertheless, as said above, the conflict of passion and law which is at the basis of the tragedy of Tristan and Iseult in the French ro-

mances is characteristic of a more advanced stage of civilisation than that which produced the Irish sagas. There are some admirable remarks on this subject by H. D'Arbois de Jubainville, *Revue Celtique*, XV, 407 f. (1894). It was the growing power of women in the twelfth century, who now inherited fiefs, that gave their quality to such heroines as Iseult.

I may remark, in passing, that, owing to the idea of fate, which the Tristan legend seems to show, Egidio Gorra has suggested that the primitive story concerning this hero was of classical origin. Cp. his article "Tristano," pp. 577 ff. of the *Studj letterari e linguistici dedicati a Pio Rajna, nel quarantesimo anno del suo insegnamento* (Milan, 1911). This is true, doubtless, of the love-potion feature of our extant texts, but one cannot make such an assertion of the story as a whole. Gorra's article is purely subjective throughout and adds nothing to our knowledge of the evolution of the legend.

34. Bédier, II, 155 ff., has noted the following details in various Tristan poems as being too primitive for a French knight of the twelfth century, and hence, as of Celtic origin: *1*. In the Tristan episode, ll. 453-662 of the *Donnei des Amanz (Amorous dialogue of lovers)*, edited by G. Paris, *Romania*, XXV, 497 ff. (1896). According to Paris (pp. 531, 534), the poem, which is a mediaeval "debate", and not a romance, was written in England towards the end of the twelfth century. The lover (a cleric, it seems), urging his lady-love to yield to his suit cites the example of various heroines of romance—among others, Iseult—and, in connection therewith, tells a story not found elsewhere in the *Tristan* romances, viz. how Tristan, returning to Cornwall from Brittany, signaled his presence to Iseult from a garden near Marc's palace by imitating various birds. From childhood, the poet says (ll. 475 ff.), Tristan had been able to imitate any bird in the forest. The episode is one of the most vigorous things in the literature of the Tristan legend, and Paris is, no doubt, right in regarding it (p. 536) as based on an earlier short poem concerning Tristan. One may agree, too, with Bédier (*loc. cit.*) that the power of the hero to imitate birds exactly belongs to a different state of society from that which prevailed among the knights and barons of the twelfth century. But the episode, as is acknowledged even by G. Paris (p. 537), who is inclined to believe that it is essentially of Celtic origin, shows unmistakable dependence on Béroul, and so the trait in question is, in all probability, secondary. Besides, Miss Schoepperle, II, 288 ff., has shown that the power of imitating birds was a not uncommon accomplishment of French minstrels in the twelfth and thirteenth century. It would be, then, quite natural for one of the guild to attribute to the hero of a poem he was composing this trick under the circumstances of the above-mentioned episode, especially as we find one of them in the *Folie Tristan*, ll. 184 f., ascribing to him other juggler's tricks. Cp. Schoepperle, II, 290 ff. *2*. In Béroul, ll.

1752f. Tristan has a bow that never fails to hit the mark. For a similar bow, however, in English tradition, much earlier than Béroul cp. the example from Geffrai Gaimar, *Lestorie des Engles,* ll. 4409 ff. (edited for the Rolls Series in 1888 by T. D. Hardy and E. Martin), cited by E. Muret in his edition of Béroul, p. IX, and Miss Schoepperle, II, 316 f. The traitor, Eadric, is there said to have slain Edmund, King of England, in 1016 with such a bow. *3.* Mark's horselike ears which he has to conceal under his hair, Béroul, ll. 1306 ff. As stated above, this is, doubtless, Celtic, although similar to the Midas legend. *4.* Tintagel, *Folie Tristan* ll. 129 ff. (Douce MS.), disappears twice a year. Occurring in only one version, the detail may well be the fancy of the individual poet.

There is nothing distinctively Celtic in vanishing castles, which are common in fairy-tales the world over. I agree with Miss Schoepperle, II, 325, note 2, that the Irish parallels to this and the next detail No. 5, cited by D'Arbois de Jubainville, *Revue Celtique,* XXII, 133 (1901) and approved by Bédier, ll. 156 ff., are really no parallels. In the *Folie Tristan* (Douce MS.), ll. 301 ff., Tristan, playing the rôle of a fool, says that he has a hall of glass up in the air. What I have said of No. 4 applies here, too. On the subject of glass-houses cp. W. O. Sypherd, *Studies in Chaucer's House of Fame,* pp. 85 f. Publications of the Chaucer Society (London, 1907).

Besides these five features, Bédier has conjectured, also, a Celtic origin for two others, though less positively: 1. In both Thomas (cp. Bédier, I, 194 ff.) and Eilhart, ll. 3504 f., and hence, one may say, certainly in their common (lost) source, Tristan communicates with Iseult by writing on bits of wood which he drops into a stream that flows through or past Iseult's chamber. Kuno Meyer, *Zs. f. rom. Ph.* XXVI, 716 f. (1902) and XXVIII, 353 f. (1904), first cited indubitable parallels to this from Irish sagas, with examples of streams flowing through houses in Wales and Southern Scotland even at the present day. See, also, Miss Schoepperle, pp. 303 ff., for examples drawn from the saga of Dairmaid and Grainne, which, as we have seen, is so closely akin to that of Tristan and Iseult. It seems certain that this detail descended to the Tristan poems from the original Celtic saga, although streams running through houses, despite K. Meyer, *Zs. f. rom. Ph.* XXVIII, 353, note 2, are not confined to Celtic regions. Cp. Miss Schoepperle, II, 302, notes 1 and 2. To the examples which she discusses I may add one from the version of the Alexander saga called *Historia de Preliis,* III, 22 (tenth century). It is cited by A. Hilka, Vollmöller's *Jahrbuch,* Teil II, p. 86, note 89. Here a stream flows under Candace's palace. 2. The incident of the blades which Marc places by Iseult's bed and by which Tristan is wounded. Here thirty or forty guests are represented as sleeping in the chamber of their host. This trait belongs, as Bédier remarks, to a primitive state of society. This is true, but that society need not have been Celtic, for we find the same thing in the actual customs, as well as folktales, of other regions too.— Cp. Schoepperle, I, 215 ff. The trick, by which, Tristan, with the aid of Arthur's knights, evades detection (they all wound themselves, so that no one can say who is really the guilty person) is merely a variant of the tale of the Masterthief, which, from Herodotus, Book II, Ch. 121, down, is found in innumerable variants. For the literature of the subject see Schoepperle, I, 214, note 3. On this particular episode, cp. G. Huet, "Sur un épisode du Tristan d'Eilhart d'Oberg," *Romania,* XXXVI, 50 ff. (1907).

35. For variants of Tristan, Iseult, Marc and the other names in the Tristan romances, cp. W. Hertz, *Tristan und Isolde,* pp. 479 ff. Hertz, however, is mistaken (pp. 483 f.) in accepting the supposed discovery of the name "Tristan" in a document of the year, 807 (from Langenargen on Lake Constance). The name there is really "Cristan". Cp. F. Lot, *Romania,* XXXV, 596 f. Hertz, *ibid.,* discusses there (pp. 482 f.) other Tristans in mediaeval romances—likewise, other Iseults (pp. 487 f.).

In his "Tristan on the Continent before 1066", MLN, XXIV, 37 f. (1909) F. M. Warren points out in early documents relating to South Italy instances of the occurrence of names (of Normans) which he identifies with *Tristan,* viz. *Trostayne* in *Ystoire de li Normant* (early fourteenth century), translated from the lost chronicle (written in Latin about 1075) of Amatus of Monte Cassino; *Torstainus, Tristainus* (also, names of Normans in South Italy) in the part of the Latin chronicle of Monte Cassino by Leo de Marsico (died 1115), which ends towards the year 1075, *Trostenus (Tristaynus), Trostaynus,* in the continuation (carried down to 1139) of the same chronicle by Peter the Deacon. We may have here, however, MS. corruptions of the common Norman name *Turstin* (from Old Norse *Thorsstein),* which is found in Domesday Book and (as *Tursten)* in *Rotuli Scaccarii Normanniae,* p. LVII (2 vols., London, 1840). In Ordericus Vitalis's *Historiae Ecclesiasticae Libri Tredecim* we find twelve different men of this name *(Turstinus).* Cp. the edition by A. Le Prevost, V, 477 (5 vols., Paris, 1838-1855. Société de l'Histoire de France). It occurs many times as *Tosteins (Tostains)* in Wace's *Roman de Rou,* II, 166, *et passim* (edited by H. Andresen, 2 vols. Heilbronn, 1877-1879). In the form of *Toustain* the name is still met with in Normandy. The variant *Tristaynus* would then be due to the influence of the *Tristan* of our romances. Warren thinks that the forms which he has cited represent Celtic *Drostan* and that they reached Normandy through Brittany. As he remarks, however, this would not necessarily imply that the legend accompanied the name.

36. *Zs. f. frz. Spr. u. Litt.* XIII[1], 1 ff. (1891).

37. *Ibid.* pp. 58 ff.

38. So by F. Lot, *Romania,* XXV, 15 (1896), who goes so far as to say that this is Zimmer's sole serious

contribution to the question of the origin of the Arthurian romances.

39. Cp. Zimmer, *op. cit*, p. 71.

40. That is to say, by weakening of the radical vowel under conditions of light stress. The examples of *Tristan (Trystan)* from Celtic documents, cited by Zimmer, p. 72 of the above-mentioned article, show that there is no need of assuming the influence of French *triste,* as is sometimes done, to explain the change of form.

Zimmer still further maintained that the *Trystan mab Tallwch* of a Welsh triad, which we shall soon discuss, was merely a Welsh rendering of a Pictish *Drostan mac Talorg.* J. Loth, however, the eminent Celtic authority, who argues, as we shall see, that the story of Tristan and Iseult is a Cornish legend, which reached the French poets through the Welsh, has proved, *Revue Celtique,* XXXII, 409 (1911), that there is no phonetic correspondence between *Tallwch* and *Talorg:* the names are not identical. On the other hand, as it seems to me, *Tallwch* is so close in sound to *Talorg* that we may reasonably accept it as an inexact rendering of the latter. It is significant that the name, *Tallwch,* is not found elsewhere in Welsh records.

41. Loth further contends that *Dristan,* the form nearest to the French name, which is actually found in Welsh documents of about 1100, cannot even be Cornish, that it is only possible in Welsh and, still further, that, since in pronunciation this *i* had the sound of an umlauted *o,* the French must have derived the name from written and not oral sources. (on these subjects cp. *loc. cit.* and the reprint of the same in his *Contributions à l'étude des romans de la table ronde* pp. 16 ff. In *Romania,* XIX, 455 ff. he had already contended that Welsh (Cornish) *Drystan* was independent of the Gaelic and the French *Iseult* came from Welsh Essylt). I confess, however, that this distinction seems to me somewhat wire-drawn. It would be easy for anyone who was not familiar with the name to catch imperfectly the pronunciation, *Drostan* or *Trostan,* and write it down, *Tristan.* Indeed, there would be nothing very surprising if a person, hearing even the Cornish or Breton pronunciation of the name, *Drostan,* were to record it inaccurately as *Tristan.*

On the names, *Tristan* and *Iseult,* see, still further, E. Windisch, *Das Keltische Brittanien bis zu Kaiser Arthur,* pp. 213 ff. (Leipzig, 1912).

42. This interpretation was first proposed by F. Lot, *Romania,* XXV, 16 ff. (1896). J. Loth, *Revue Celtique,* XXXIII, 280 ff. (1912), identifies *Morois* with a manor in Cornwall named *Moresc* (now, St. Clement's), in the neighborhood of Truro; but, as A. Smirnov has pointed out in his excellent review of Loth's *Contributions à l'étude des romans de la table ronde, Romania,* XLIII, 121 (1914), Moresc, as a place-name, occurs frequently in other Celtic regions. Besides, as he says, the situation of the Cornish Mo-

resc does not fit well with the requirements of the *Tristan* narrative. For my own part, I would add that Loonois and Morois evidently belong together and that they are both explained satisfactorily on Lot's theory, whereas Loth, *op. cit.,* pp. 286 f., is unable to explain the former at all, under his new theory. In the *Annales de Bretagne,* XI, 479 (1895-6) he had accepted the identification of *Loonois* with *Loonia (Lothian).*

43. The question would be hardly arguable, if the Welsh *Tristan* fragments from the Black Book of Carmarthen which J. Loth has edited and translated, *Revue Celtique,* XXXIII, 403 ff. (1912), really date from the first half of the twelfth century, as he thinks. These fragments are excessively obscure, but the second one would appear to relate to Kaherdin, brother of Iseult of Brittany. Now the story of Iseult of Brittany seems plainly a French addition to the Tristan romance, as set forth above, but the date assigned by Loth to these fragments would be too early for French influence.

44. Arthur decided that one should possess her, whilst the leaves were on the wood, the other, whilst they were off, the husband to have the choice. Mark chose the second alternative, because the nights are longer in that season, but Iseult joyfully pointed out that the holly, the ivy and the yew were never without leaves—hence Mark lost her forever.

This tale, the earliest MS. of which dates from about 1550, was first edited by J. Gwenogvryn Evans in the *Report on Manuscripts in the Welsh language* (Historical Manuscripts Commission), Vol. I, Part II, (London, 1899) and Vol. II, Part I (1902). It has since been edited (as *Ystoria Tristan),* with translation, by J. Loth, *Revue Celtique,* XXXV, 365 ff. (1913), and by T. P. Cross, under the title of "A Welsh Tristan Episode," [University of North Carolina] *Studies in Philology,* XVII, 93 ff. (1920). Cp., too, W. Golther, *Tristan und Isolde,* pp. 238 f. for an outline of the tale, which he quotes from I. B. John's paper on it in the *Transactions of the Guild of Graduates,* pp. 14 ff. (Cardiff, 1904). Loth gives, also, an account of the story in the *Comptes Rendus de l'Académie des Inscriptions et Belles-Lettres, Bulletin de Mars-Avril,* 1913, pp. 92 ff.

Bédier does not include this tale in his discussion (in his Introduction) of the different versions of the Tristan legend. Evans claimed that it was the story of Tristan in its earliest form and Windisch, *Das Keltische Brittanien bis zu Kaiser Arthur,* p. 285 (Leipzig, 1912), unwarily accepted this claim, but Loth has refuted it in his edition, pp. 377 ff.

45. These verses, which belong to the species of poetry called *Englynion* (epigrams) in Welsh, were known to scholars long before the rest of the tale in which they occur. Cp. Golther, *op. cit.,* p. 239. Cross, p. 93, cites another Welsh dialogue between Tristan and Gwalchmai, similar to this.

46. F. Lot, *Romania,* XXV, 19 f. (1896), shows that Wrmonoc's sources were certainly insular, and he is probably right in regarding Marc (Quonomorius) as an actual person. For other occurrences of *Marc* as a Celtic name, cp. Miss Schoepperle, II, 271, note 3.

47. In a note, however, to A. le Braz's *La Légende de la Mort,* II, 97 (new ed. Paris, 1902), G. Dottin derives it from the story of Midas and cites it as an instance of the adaptation of a classical legend by the Celts.

48. Cp. F. Lot, *Romania,* XXIV, 337.

49. Cp. J. Loth, *Revue Celtique,* XXXIII, 288 f.

50. Loth, *loc cit.* p. 290, points out that "Dinas" cannot be Armorican. "Pendennis" (whence the name of Thackeray's hero), name of a place in Cornwall, was originally "Pen-dinas"—"chief fortress". On *Dinas* and its diminutive, *dinan,* cp., still further, E. Phillimore, *Y Cymmrodor,* XI, 38 f., 42 ff. (1892). The last is frequent as a suffix in place-names, though disguised in spelling as—*dinam,*—*dinham,* e. g. Cardinham in Cornwall, which Phillimore wrongly identifies with the Arthurian *Caradigan.* Cp. Lot, *Romania,* XXX, 19 f.

51. Cp. Muret, *Romania,* XVII, 606, and G. Paris, *ibid.* XVIII, 423.

52. *Zs. f. frz. Spr. u. Litt.,* XIII[1], 73 ff. (1891). F. Lot, *Romania,* XXV, 18 f. (1896) was inclined to accept Zimmer's view.

53. So, too, D'Arbois de Jubainville, *Revue Celtique,* XV, 408 (1894), and Golther, *Tristan und Isolde,* pp. 237 ff. (1907).

54. Cp. J. Loth, *Revue Celtique,* XXXII, 414 ff. (1911). He argues that *Iseult (Iselt)* is Celtic in origin.

55. Loth, *ibid.,* XXXII, 420, declares quite positively that Armorican participation in transmitting the name of Iseult to the French is, on phonetic grounds, out of the question.

56. Cp. *Revue Celtique,* XXXIII, 270 f. (1912). It appears in Domesday Book as *Lantien (Lanthien).* This name for Marc's capital is found only in Béroul, ll. 1155 *et passim,* and in Gerbert's continuation to Chrétien's *Perceval,* in the episode which Bédier and Miss Weston have published, *Romania* XXXV, 497 ff. (1906), under the title of *Tristan menestrel.* The latter derived it from Béroul, no doubt. It is safe to assume that Béroul, in turn, derived it from the (lost) primitive Tristan poem.

In the *Comptes Rendus* of the Académie des Inscriptions et Belles-Lettres, *Bulletin de Decembre, 1916,* pp. 592 f., Loth points out that a gate entering Lantyan Wood is still called Mark's Gate.

57. According to the *Folie Tristan,* prose *Tristan* and Chrétien's *Erec,* Tristan and the Morholt fight on an island of St. Sampson, off the coast of Cornwall. In the *Bulletin* cited in the previous note, pp. 589 ff., Loth cites a charter of May 20, 1301, to prove that an island once existed at the mouth of the Fawe. This isle he identifies with the Isle of St. Sampson.

58. Namely, of *Tristan's Leap* with *Bodrigan's Leap* (south of Lantien), *Mal Pas* with *Malpas* (near Truro, on the Truro river), *Blanche Lande* with *Blaunchelound* (not far from Malpas and recorded as early as 1306), now called *Nansavallan.* Cp. *Revue Celtique,* XXXIII, 274 ff. (1912) and the above-cited *Bulletin,* 590. The first of these identifications, however, is hardly more than a guess. As for the last two, A. Smirnov, *Romania,* XLIII, 121 ff., has raised objections which appear to me worthy of serious attention: The two names are common in the Middle Ages; Arthur, coming to Lantien from Wales, would not pass by Blanche Lande; and, besides, the names occur in episodes that do not appear to belong to the story of Tristan in its original form.

Loth, *Revue Celtique,* XXXIII, 287 f. (1912) also proposes to emend *Parmenie* (name of the kingdom of Tristan's father in Gottfried) to *Hermenie* and identify it with the manor named in Domesday Book *Hoimenen* (now *Harmony*). But it is not likely that a manor should be called a kingdom. The alternative identification which he suggests, viz. with *Henmoniu,* is not open to the same objection, but this, too, is pure speculation.

It is to be observed, finally, that the Cornish names, *Malpas; Blanche Lande, Mark's Gate,* may be due to attempts at localization of the Tristan story, suggested by the romances. As early as the twelfth century such localizations of the story as we have seen, were made about Dublin, and one of them, *Chapelizod* (name of a village near Dublin), has persisted to this day. Cp. letters on the subject in *The Athenaeum* Feb. 21 (p. 26), May 10, 17, 1913. The writers naively cite these localizations as proofs of the actual existence of the characters concerned, but they are, of course, like the localizations of the Romeo and Juliet story at Verona, which are all recent and based on Shakespeare's play.

59. Cp. Bédier, II, 122 f.

60. I am assuming here that *Riwelin (Riwelen)*—which is Breton (cp. Zimmer, *Zs. f. frz. Spr. u. Litt.,* XIII[1], 58ff.)—was the name of Tristan's father in the legend in the form in which it first became known to the French. This is the name of the hero's father in Eilhart and Gottfried. The early part of Thomas's *Tristan* is lost, but, doubtless, Gottfried derived the name from Thomas. In the prose romance, the character is called *Meliadus.* This, however, is certainly a late substitution. He is surnamed, still further, *Kanelangres* by Thomas. Brugger, in his article, "Zum Tristan-Roman", *Archiv für das Studium der neueren Sprachen,* CXXIX, 134ff. (1912) tries to prove that *Kanelangres* is a mere corruption of *Talergen* (diminutive of *Talorch,* the name of the eighth century Pictish king, whose son was named *Drust-Tristan*), but his argument is not convincing. The

name still awaits a satisfactory explanation. Cp. Bédier, I, 2, note 2.

61. This is, on the whole, the most likely hypothesis, and Golther (p. 70) has accepted it as such. But he believes that the Tristan legend was among both Welsh and Bretons, mere heroic saga, not a love-story and that the love *motif* was first introduced by the French. Indeed, he sees in the Tristan story the influence of Geoffrey of Monmouth and the narrative of the infidelity of Arthur's wife with his nephew, Mordred. But, as I have observed above, the balance of probabilities seems against this supposition.

62. Cp. G. Huet, "Sur un épisode du Tristan d'Eilhart d'Oberg" *Romania,* XXXVI, 50ff. (1907) and G. Schoepperle, I, 213ff. (1913). The latter gives, p. 214, note 3, the previous literature of the subject.

63. Cp. Golther, p. 28.

64. The author of the primitive French *Tristan* poem, doubtless, transferred to Iseult of Brittany some traits that originally belonged to Iseult of Cornwall. Cp., especially, the incident of the water which splashes up under the latter's dress and which, she says, is bolder than Tristan has been. Miss Schoepperle, II, 415, points out that this incident occurs, also, in the Diarmaid and Grainne saga—so that we may accept it as attached to the original of Iseult of Cornwall in the Celtic *Aithed.*

65. This was pointed out by Bédier, II, 138f. To be sure, Brugger, *Archiv für das Studium der neueren Sprachen,* CXXX, 124ff. (1913), disputes Bédier's conclusion. He cites especially (pp. 132ff.) a Gaelic parallel (a tale written down by J. G. Campbell) as proving the Celtic origin of the incident. But the Gaelic story is not recorded before the nineteenth century and may very well be, itself, derived from the Theseus legend. Miss Schoepperle, *Revue Celtique,* XXXII, 185f., and in her *Tristan* book, II, 437f. (1913) is more cautious than Brugger. The fact that the white and black sail *motif* is here combined with a classical *motif* (that of Paris and Oenone) points strongly, in my judgment, to the conclusion that it, too, is of classical origin.

66. The question one must acknowledge, is doubtful, since the name is not found in Celtic, nor in exactly this form, indeed, anywhere outside of the *Tristan* poems. *Mor,* however, means "sea" in the Celtic languages, and Loth, *Revue Celtique,* XXXII, 420, note 1, (1011) has derived *Morholt* tentatively from an hypothetical Old Celtic *morispolto* = "sea-splitter". Miss Schoepperle, II, 331, note 1, seems to me to have misunderstood Muret, *Romania,* XVII, 606 (1888) when she imputes to him the idea (which is really Golther's, p. 17) that Morholt's name was connected with that of the Fomori (giants or marine monsters in Irish saga). Muret merely means that originally Morholt was one of these Celtic giants. Like Miss Schoepperle, *loc. cit.,* I cannot regard the story from the Cuchullin saga (Cuchullin frees a prin-

cess who has been offered as a tribute to the Fomorians) which Deutschbein, *Beiblatt zu Anglia,* XV, 16ff. (1904) and *Studien zur Sagengeschichte Englands,* 172f. (Cöthen, 1906) cites, as having any historical connection with the Morholt episode.

Morhold occurs as a Germanic name in eighth century documents (Cp. E. Foerstemann, *Altdeutsches Namenbuch,* col. 1118), but the similarity is probably accidental.

67. That the combat should take place on an island was once regarded as a Scandinavian (Viking) feature of the story, another example of the *holmgang.* Cp. Golther, p. 16. Miss Schoepperle, however, has shown that island-combats were stock features of the Old French romances and that the combat in the *Tristan* does not conform to the rules of the *holmgang.* Cp. her paper in the Radcliffe College Monographs, No. 15, (1910) and her *Tristan and Isolt,* II, 338ff.

68. For examples from different parts of the world see Schoepperle, II, 377ff.

69. Golther, *Tristan und Isolde,* pp. 15f. (1907).

70. For a discussion of the *Imrama* see A. C. L. Brown, *Iwain,* 566ff. For MSS. and editions cp. G. Dottin, *Revue Celtique,* XXXIII, 26 (1912).

71. Cp. Schoepperle, I, 188ff.

72. Miss Schoepperle, I, 188, note 3, gives a very full list of such stories in the various literatures.

73. Miss Schoepperle's list, just cited, contains no Celtic tale with this particular feature.

74. Cp. W. Golther, "Die Jungfrau mit den goldenen Haaren", *Studien zur Litteraturgeschichte, Michael Bernays gewidmet von Schülern und Freunden,* p. 173 (Hamburg and Leipzig, 1893)—also, Reinhold Köhler, "Tristan und Isolde und das Märchen von der goldhaarigen Jungfrau und von den Wassern des Todes und des Lebens", *Germania,* XI, 389ff. (1866)—reprinted in Köhler, *Kleinere Schriften,* II, 328ff. (Berlin, 1900). For additional notes on the theme cp. Felix Liebrecht, *Germania,* XII (1867), and Köhlers *Kleinere Schriften,* I, 511.

75. This ends our discussion of the *Tristan* romances; for the endeavor of Zenker to connect the saga of this hero with the Persian epic of Wis and Ramin has been generally pronounced a failure. Cp. his *Die Tristansage und das persische Epos von Wis und Ramin* (Erlangen, 1910)—also, *Zs. f. rom. Ph.,* XXXV, 715ff. (1912). Zenker, p. 326, cites Hermann Ethe, *Die höfische und romantische Poesie der Perser,* p. 38 (Hamburg, 1887), as the first to call attention to the resemblance of the stories. So, too, W. Hertz, *Tristan und Isolde von Gottfried von Strassburg,* p. 478 (Stuttgart and Berlin, 1907).

On other Tristans, besides the famous hero, see W. Hertz, ibid. pp. 482ff. Of most interest, perhaps, is the "Tristanz qui onques ne rist," who figures in a number of romances, cited, *loc. cit.,* by Hertz—first of all, in Chrétien's *Erec,* 1, 1713, in the well-known list of Arthur's knights. It has been customary to regard this character as drawn from oral tradition, but he was, unquestionably, the invention of a Frenchman—no doubt, a French poet—to whom the similarity of *Tristan* and *triste* suggested the nickname. It occurred to the author of *L'Atre Perillos* to make him play the part of a host (cp. 1. 5392) in a brief episode of that poem—otherwise (in Chrétien and the other romancers), he is a mere name. My own belief is that the character is an invention for the nonce of Chrétien's, who was put to it to make out the long list of knights in the above-mentioned passage and who, consequently, fabricated this new character, like some other characters in the list. He derived the name primarily, of course, from the renowned lover of Iseult, and the accompanying nickname was supplied to him, partly, by an obvious play on words, and, partly, by the necessity of finding a rhyme to *sist.*

Grace Frank (essay date 1948)

SOURCE: "Marie de France and the Tristram Legend," in *PMLA,* Vol. 63, No. 2, June, 1948, pp. 405-11.

[*In the following essay, Frank maintains that the* Chievre-fueil, *a lay by Marie de France, was derived from longer versions of the Tristram (Tristan) legend.*]

Chievrefueil, the shortest and perhaps the most charming of the lays by Marie de France, has troubled critics because, unlike her other poems, it seems to lack clarity. Is it not fair to assume, however, that in this instance the usual limpidity and forthrightness of Marie's narrative style may have been clouded by her modern interpreters, rather than by Marie herself? I hope to show that to her mediæval audience the lovely lines of *Chievrefueil* presented no difficulties whatsoever, needed no esoteric subtleties for their understanding, and that their Old Norse translator as well as the scribes of both our surviving manuscripts readily comprehended Marie's lucid phrases.

The crux of the difficulty, it seems to me, lies in a needlessly realistic scepticism regarding lines 51 ff. Marie tells us (and I translate as literally as possible from Warnke's third edition of 1925):

> [Tristram] cut a hazel tree in half, split it quite square. After he had prepared the staff, he wrote his name with his knife. If the Queen becomes aware of it, she who was wont to take very careful notice, she will certainly recognize the staff of her lover when she sees it. Another time it had happened that she had thus perceived it. This was the sum of the writing that he had sent and said to her [or, according to MS. S, *This was the sum of the writing which was on the staff of which I speak*]: that he had long been there and waited and stayed in order to spy out and learn how he might see her, for he

could not live without her. It was with the two of them just as it was with the honeysuckle which attached itself to the hazel: when the honeysuckle has twined there and taken firm hold and twisted itself completely around the trunk of the tree, together they can well survive, but if anyone wishes to separate them afterwards, the hazel quickly dies and the honeysuckle in like fashion. My fair lady, thus it is with us: nor you without me, nor I without you.

> The Queen came riding. She looked a little in front of her, saw the stick, observed it well, knew all the letters there.

Now to our modern scholars it seems improbable that so long a message could have been written upon a wooden tablet. Miss Rickert remarks: "We cannot suppose Tristram wrote out in full the message of which the 'import' fills seventeen lines. Even if it had been possible, Yseult could not have read it as she rode along, nor was there any need for her to do so, as the branch served merely to indicate Tristram's whereabouts." With this general conception—that the message was not on the staff—Sudre, Foulet and Spitzer would agree. Miss Rickert thinks the message was probably conveyed by the symbolism of the hazel and the honeysuckle. Sudre and Foulet, stressing the words *escrit* and *mandé,* believe Tristram's name alone was on the hazel tablet and that a written communication had been sent the Queen by her lover a few days earlier, the message whose import or substance Marie gives us. Spitzer, who accepts the notion that Tristram's name alone appeared upon the tablet, suggests that the Queen, inspired solely by love, read beneath the literal surface of the bark to its spiritual core and thus divined her lover's message, murmuring to herself the words she seemed to hear him speak to her, "comme si elle les avait entendus de la bouche de Tristan."[1]

But are we not being too prosaically literal-minded when we reject the possibility that Tristram cut his message upon the hazel tree? Foulet, before rejecting this possibility as *invraisemblable,* clearly sees its intrinsic likelihood: "Où se trouvait cet 'escrit qu'il li aveit mandé et dit'? Il semble bien, à suivre l'ordre des événements tel qu'il nous est donné dans le récit, que ce dut être sur le bâton." For my part, if Marie writes of werewolves, magic potions, speaking hinds, birds that turn into knights, ships that sail themselves, a fairy mistress who appears and disappears at will, I do not ask how such things can be. Tristram might carve a message whose import fills twice seventeen lines and I should not question Marie's poetic right to have him do so.

Nor, I venture to think, would the length of Tristram's xylographic message have disturbed any mediæval audience, however literal-minded. For in England where Marie lived, in Celtic lands from whence some parts of the Tristram legend came, and on the continent where it spread, rune sticks, letters graven on wood, wands and squared staves with poems and other inscriptions upon them were no novelty. The Old English "Lover's [or, Husband's] Message," a poem of fifty-five lines, speaks of itself as engraved on wood. It is well known that Irish love poems and other inscriptions (some of which were planted in paths to give messages) were carved on tablets of wood, and references to wands and squared staves with ogham inscriptions are frequent in Irish literature. According to *Egil's Saga,* the *Sonatorrek,* a poetic lament of some 200 lines, was taken down on a *Kefli,* or rune stick, and runes carved on various kinds of wood and trees are frequently mentioned in the *Sagas* and *Edda.*[2] A famous instance of a letter carved on wood occurs in the story of Hamlet as recorded by Saxo Grammaticus in his *Danish History,* Book III. I cite his words in the translation of Elton and Powell, p. 113: "Two retainers of Feng then accompanied him, bearing a letter graven on wood—a kind of writing material frequent in old times." By Marie's day such tablets may well have seemed archaic and mention of them might have served to give her lay the flavor of the *tens anciënur* which she so frequently evokes in her poems. In any case, inscribed staves were known to her and to her contemporaries, and were surely known to her sources.

For, this whole passage—Tristram's cutting the hazel and writing upon it with his knife in order to apprise the Queen of his presence—bears a striking resemblance to an episode in the Tristram legend which has been preserved for us in no less than five different versions: those of Eilhart von Oberge, Gottfried von Strassburg, the Old Norse *Saga,* the Oxford *Folie Tristan,* and the English *Sir Tristrem.* In the Oxford *Folie* (784-86) Tristram recalls to the Queen the ruse by which he had she were wont to meet, the chips fashioned by his knife and thrown into the stream as "signs between us when it pleased me to come to you":

> de mun canivet cospels fis
> k'erent enseignes entre nus
> quant me plaiseit venir a vus.

In the versions of this episode by Eilhart and Gottfried and in the English *Sir Tristrem* these cutting bear inscriptions. In Eilhart's poem Tristram carves a cross with five branches (3346 ff.); in Gottfried's, he carves the initials *T* and *I* on each tablet (14427 ff.). But in *Sir Tristrem* it is actually runes that he writes upon them (2049 ff.):

> Bi water he sent adoun
> Liȝt linden spon:
> He wrot hem al wiþ roun;
> Ysonde hem knewe wel sone;
> Bi þat Tristrem was boun,
> Ysonde wist his bone
> To abide.

These light linden chips carved with *roun,* the initialed olive *spaene* of Gottfried, the decorated cuttings of Eilhart (dar an sal gemâlet sîn / ein crûce mit vunf orten), the *lokarspónu* of the Old Norse *Saga* (chapter LIV [77]), and the *cospels* of the Oxford *Folie* all serve the same purpose of advising Iseut of Tristram's desire to see her. "Ysonde hem knewe wel sone," says the English version; "swen sie daz crûce vinde, / sô bin ich bî der linde," says Eilhart; and Bédier summarizes the whole episode in his recon-

struction of Thomas as follows: "Chaque fois donc que Tristan voulait se rencontrer avec Isolt, il jetait les copeaux au ruisseau qui courait le long de la tour du château . . . : par cette ruse Isolt connaissait aussitôt son désir de sa venue au rendez-vous."[3]

Now when Marie writes:

> Se la reïne s'aparceit,
> ki mult grant guarde s'en perneit,
> de sun ami bien conuistra
> le bastun quant el le verra;
> altre feiz li fu avenu
> que si l'aveit aparceü,
>
> [55-60]

is she not alluding to this episode in her sources?

> Plusur le m'unt cunté e dit
> e jeo l'ai trové en escrit
> de Tristram e de la reïne . . .

The curious means by which Tristram and the Queen were wont to communicate with each other probably appealed to her imagination, and from the wooden chips inscribed by Tristram to tell Iseut of his eagerness to meet her, Marie elaborated her fanciful hazel tablet with its beautiful, poetic message.

Accordingly, whether or not Marie—or her sources—had rune sticks or ogham tablets in mind, I am convinced that she thought of Tristram's words as carved upon the hazel wood he had prepared. She gives us the "sume de l'escrit" (61), paraphrasing at first and then quoting directly. If the message were conceived as written in a secret or cryptic alphabet, her reason for telling us its substance and her reference to the Queen's knowledge of "tutes les letres" (82) would have special significance. But in any case I see no reason for rejecting the obvious inference of our texts or for regarding the length of Tristram's words to the Queen as precluding their appearance on the *bastun* which he had *paré* to receive them.

It is evident that the simple interpretation here proposed was that of the scribe of MS. S. He says deliberately: "This was the sum of the writing that was upon the stick." And, although it has not been remarked before, I believe, the Old Norse translator of Marie, who follows a manuscript related to H, is here even more explicit than S.[4] I translate his words as literally as possible:

> Then he cut down a hazel tree and made it four-edged with his knife and cut his name on the stick. If it so happen that the Queen sees the stick, then she will be reminded of her lover, because it had so happened to her another time. Now it was inscribed on the stick that Tristram had waited for her there a long time and listened around in order to ask about her and find out in what way he might see her, for he can in no wise live without her. "So it is with us," he said, "as with the honeysuckle which twines around the hazel. . . ."

Now the Queen came riding and saw the stick which stood in the way and she took the stick and read that which was cut on it. . . .[5]

There can be no question but that for the Norse translator the whole message was inscribed upon the tablet.

At the end of her poem Marie justifies its title, *Chievrefueil,* in lines that again have troubled some of our modern scholars because they refuse to believe that Tristram's words could have appeared upon the *bastun.* Marie says (107-16):

> Because of the joy which he had had from his love whom he had seen and because of that which he had written [or, according to MS. S, *Because of the joy which he had had from his love whom he had seen by means of the staff which he had inscribed*], just as he had said it to the Queen,[6] in order to remember the words, Tristram, who well knew how to play the harp, made of these a new lay. I shall name it briefly: the English call it *Gotelef,* the French, *Chievrefueil.*

Clearly, the title of the lay must refer to the words about the honeysuckle which Tristram used to the Queen, addressing her as his "bele amie." Sudre and Foulet think these words occurred in a written communication sent her some days before the meeting. But this interpretation seems to me to be awkwardly prosaic and to spoil the finely woven pattern of the poem by assuming, as it does, a message that has been undramatically delivered off-stage. Spitzer, on the other hand, believes Tristram made his lay about words divined by the Queen as belonging to her lover, words apparently made into a lay by that lover to record her divination of his message.[7] Surely this interpretation violates both the letter and the spirit of the text:

> Pur la joie qu'il ot eüe
> de s'amie qu'il ot veüe
> e pur ceo qu'il aveit escrit, [S: par le baston qu'il ot escrit]
> si cum la reïne l'ot dit,
> pur les paroles remembrer,
> Tristram ki bien saveit harper,
> en aveit fet un nuvel lai.

The emphasis throughout this passage is on Tristram and the pronoun *il.* It is his joy, his mistress whom he has seen, the words he wrote (on the *baston,* says S) which are to be recorded, and obviously, because of the title of the lay, *The Honeysuckle,* the words addressed to the Queen that he would remember exactly are his lovely image of interlaced vine and tree, his beautiful identification of their life and death with the love that exists between himself and his *bele amie:*

> Bele amie, si est de nus:
> Ni vus sens mei, ni mei sens vus.

In short, then, I believe that *Chievrefueil,* a little gem of synthesis, compression and clean-cut narration, derives from one of the longer versions of the Tristram legend. Marie tells us of a single meeting between the lovers and,

like any good writer of short stories, she makes this one significant scene embrace the past and foreshadow the future. Her originality consists in letting us share the emotions of her hero before the meeting, and she does this by embroidering most poetically upon a theme found in her sources, the fragments of wood that served the lovers as secret messengers before their rendezvous. Upon such a tablet Tristram engraves the words about hazel and honeysuckle in which he so vividly embodies his love for Iseut and his feeling that separation must spell death for both of them. In order to remember these words and to express the joy he experienced in meeting his mistress by having written them, he made a lay called *The Honeysuckle.* And Marie concludes:

> Dit vus en ai la verité
> del lai que j'ai ici cunté.

Notes

1. See Edith Rickert, *Marie de France: Seven of her Lays done into English* (New York, 1901), p. 193; L. Sudre, *Romania,* XV (1886), 551; L. Foulet, *ZRP,* XXXII (1908), 278-80; L. Spitzer, *Romania,* LXIX (1946), 80 ff., who cites a biblical exegesis of *Genesis,* XXX, 37, by Macé de la Charité to support the contrast he finds in Marie between *letre* and *sume=écorce* and *moelle.* For Spitzer's interpretation see also note 7, below.

2. On runes in general see the works of Helmut Arntz, *Bibliographie der runenkunde* (Leipzig, 1937), *Die Runenschrift* (Halle, 1938). For runes in England, see *The Cambridge History of English Literature,* I, chapt. 2. "The Lover's Message" is in *The Exeter Book,* II, ed. W. S. Mackie, *EETS,* CXCIV (1934), 192. For Irish material, Douglas Hyde's *A Literary History of Ireland* (1901), chapt. XI, is convenient (cf. especially p. 111); see also *Revue Celtique,* XIII (1892), 220. In the *Egil's Saga* note especially chapters 44, 72, 78 and cf. *The Lay of Sigrdrífa, The Sayings of Hór, The Lay of Skírnir,* etc. Note that it is the *coldre* itself which Tristram cuts *par mi,* and that he splits the tree and squares it to make his *bastun.* Most modern critics imply diminutives which are not in the text. Incidentally, the European hazel, *Corylus Avellana,* may attain considerable size and has a tough, pliant, close-textured wood much used in the Middle Ages for making bows and crossbows, and, as is well known, the O.F. *baston* might be a very big stick indeed.

3. See Bédier, *Le Roman de Tristan par Thomas,* SATF (1902), I, 194 ff. The Old Norse version is here almost like Bédier's. For it and the English *Sir Tristrem* see Eugen Kölbing's editions, *Die Nordische und die Englische Version der Tristan-Sage* (Heilbronn, 1878, 1882). Eilhart was edited by Franz Lichtenstein in *Quellen und Forschungen* (1877), XIX; Gottfried's *Tristan,* by Karl Marold in *Teutonia,* VI (Leipzig, 1906). For the *Folie Tristan d'Oxford,* see Bédier's edition (SATF, 1907) or Hoepffner's (1938).

4. Warnke and Rudolf Meissner, *Die Strengleikar* (Halle, 1902), p. 205, agree in positing a close relationship between MS. H and the Norse version.

5. For the Old Norse version I have used the text in *Leit eg suður til landa,* ed. Einar Òl. Sveinsson (Reykjavík, 1944), pp. 112-4. I should like to express here my warm thanks to Professor Stefán Einarsson for his aid in translating it and for many other helpful suggestions.

6. Because of the meaning and the emphasis throughout the passage on Tristram, I believe, with Warnke (p. 268) and G. Cohn (*ZFSL* 24[2], 1902, p. 15) that *la reïne* in the phrase *si cum la reïne l'ot dit* is a dative. Grammatically, there is no objection to Foulet's translation (sur la demande de la reine), although nothing has heretofore been said of this request, nor to the Old Norse translation (remembering the words she spoke), nor to Miss Rickert's (for remembrance of her words), nor to Spitzer's (comme la reine le lui avait dit). But if one adopts the interpretation that the words to be remembered are the Queen's, then the line must refer to the Queen's conversation in the forest (et ele li dist son plaisir, etc.) and not to the lines beginning *Bele amie* or to the words about the honeysuckle which give the lay its title. In any case, it must be the passage about the honeysuckle that is to be commemorated in a lay so called, and these are the words that Tristram wrote (on the tablet).

7. See *op. cit.,* p. 84: "Il n'y avait sur la baguette de coudrier comme *letre* que le nom 'Tristan,' c'était à Iseut de découvrir le sens du message, et c'est l'amour seul qui, Tristan le sait, aiguisera l'intelligence de l'amante, au point de lui faire découvrir l'image du coudrier et du chèvrefeuille . . . et de lui faire murmurer les deux beaux vers finaux, comme si elle les avait entendus de la bouche de Tristan. . . ." And pp. 87-8: "A cause de la joie de Tristan d'avoir réussi à voir son amie par le message de la baguette, joie que la reine lui avait exprimée lors de leur rendez-vous, et pour conserver les paroles telles qu'elle les lui avait dites, Tristan. . . ."

Helaine Newstead (essay date 1956)

SOURCE: "The Tryst beneath the Tree: An Episode in the Tristan Legend," in *Romance Philology,* Vol. 9, No. 3, February, 1956, pp. 269-84.

[In the following essay, Newstead traces the literary history of the "tryst episode" of the Tristan legend, finding that it originated in three Celtic stories before it developed in various forms in Welsh, Breton, and French tales.]

The modern reader, schooled to appreciate the legend of Tristan and Isolt as a tale of tragic and overwhelming passion, may be startled to realize that the episode most familiar to the medieval public was no moment of exalted romance but rather a scene of audaciously successful deception. The lovers, meeting secretly beneath a tree, discover King Mark hidden in the branches above them and evade the trap by a series of lies improvised to deceive him. No episode in the *matière de Bretagne* is more often represented in medieval art. The scene was painted on castle walls and ceilings, embroidered on cloister hangings and table coverings, carved in wood, stone, and ivory, on mirrorbacks, combs, salt-cellars, hanaps, caskets, corbels, and misericords.[1] Some of these pictorial versions even preserve traits not elsewhere recorded.[2] The written sources, too, are marked by a diversity of detail that confirms the iconographic evidence of popular taste for the episode.

This astonishing vogue reminds us that it was the narrative power of the Tristan legend as much as any other quality that enthralled the medieval public. The treatment of the tryst episode in the literary sources is vividly dramatic, exploiting in varied ways the opportunities for suspense in the situation. Although the narrative framework remains constant, the variations in the different versions show that the plot is a product of tradition. To analyze these variations and to explore the complex literary history of the episode is to gain insight into the processes that created one of the most famous tales of the Middle Ages.

According to Eilhart's romance,[3] the separation of the lovers caused them such suffering after Tristan's banishment from court that Isolt, through her emissary Brangain, implored him to devise some way of meeting. He sent word that Isolt would find him under a linden in the orchard whenever she saw on the stream flowing through her chamber a branch followed by a piece of bark carved with a five-pointed cross. This signal enabled them to enjoy many secret nocturnal meetings. Meanwhile, Tristan's enemies employed a dwarf who could read the stars to learn whether the lovers still saw each other. The dwarf reported that indeed Tristan possessed the queen, and offered to prove it to the king or forfeit his head. Accordingly, the king announced that he would be absent on a hunting excursion for a week, and then secretly followed the dwarf to the linden. Soon after they had climbed the tree and were hidden in its foliage, Tristan arrived and sent the branch and the carved bark down the stream. Then the bright moonlight revealed, to his consternation, the shadows of the two spies on the water. As the queen hastened to the rendezvous, he remained seated by the stream, gesturing backward, so that she caught sight of the spies and understood the situation. He pretended to have arranged the interview to ask her help in restoring him to the king's favor. Feigning indignation, she refused because of the shame he had brought upon her. She departed in simulated fury, spurning his plea to intercede with the king to return his pledges so that he could leave the kingdom honorably. This display of animosity so thoroughly convinced the king of their innocence that the dwarf would have been slain on the spot if he had not fled. Next morning when the remorseful king entreated Isolt to prevent Tristan's departure, she angrily refused, relenting only after he promised to allow Tristan to associate freely with her and even to sleep in the royal bedchamber. He publicly declared his belief in Tristan's innocence, and the lovers were reunited.

The extant fragments of Béroul's poem begin with this episode, which in the main agrees with Eilhart's version. Nevertheless, there are differences. Though the dwarf is the instigator,[4] King Mark is alone in the tree,[5] which is a pine (vss. 404, 415) by a fountain (vs. 351).[6] Since the opening of the episode is lost,[7] there is naturally no reference to the lovers' signal on the stream or to the king's announced departure for the hunt. The hunt, however, may have been part of Béroul's account, as a later passage suggests:

> Et plusors foiz les ont veüz
> El lit roi Marc gesir toz nus.
> Quar, quant li rois en vet al bois,
> Et Tristran dit: "Sire, g'en vois";
> Puis se remaint, entre en la chanbre,
> Iluec grant piece sont ensenble

(vss. 593-598).

Thomas's French text of this episode is also lost, but other versions based upon it enable us to reconstruct its outlines. In the Norse prose translation of Thomas[8] we read that the king, observing the visible suffering of the parted lovers, resolved to trap them together. He announced his departure on a hunting expedition of six weeks and took leave of the queen. Now, Tristan used to cut chips from a wand so skilfully that they floated upon the water like foam, and whenever he wished to meet Isolt he would cast them as a signal into the brook that flowed past her chamber. As he was carving the chips, a dwarf from the castle delivered what purported to be a message from Isolt to visit her during the absence of the whole court. But Tristan, suspecting trickery, refused because of his illness. When the dwarf reported this failure to the king hidden in the castle, they planned another attempt to surprise the lovers, for the dwarf explained why Tristan was carving the chips. That night the king hid himself in the tree in the orchard, where the lovers were accustomed to meet. When Isolt saw the chips floating on the stream, she hastened to the rendezvous under the tree, and Tristan crossed the garden from another direction. At that moment in the bright moonlight he saw the shadow of the king on the ground. Isolt caught sight of it, too, and feigned anger and resentment against Tristan so successfully that, when they parted, the suspicions of the royal spy in the tree were quieted.

The Norse translation is sadly abbreviated. The entire dialogue between the lovers in the garden is summarized in one sentence, and there are obvious gaps in the story, such as the sudden appearance of the dwarf as *agent provocateur* and collaborator of the king, and his unexplained familiarity with the lovers' signal.[9] For these reasons critics in general have tended to distrust the *Saga* text as an accurate representative of Thomas's version, and to rely instead upon Gottfried and the English *Sir Tristrem* in this episode.[10] Gottfried introduces the dwarf as a court favor-

ite employed by Meriadoc to spy upon the lovers and to persuade the king to banish Tristan.[11] After the separation, the dwarf observes one meeting of the lovers at the fountain and discovers how the chips are used to summon Isolt. Gottfried also explains that Brangain taught Tristan the ingenious signal (vss. 14,417-14,501). In Gottfried's version, too, the dwarf mounts the tree with the king (vss. 14,598-14,612).

The English *Sir Tristrem* is too muddled to be a reliable guide to the content of Thomas's poem. Yet, since it agrees with Gottfried that the dwarf surprised the lovers in the orchard,[12] it is probable that this element belonged to the original. In another stanza, misplaced in the manuscript, Meriadoc proposes the hunting excursion as a trap for the lovers, an incident that must have occurred just before the dwarf's visit to Tristan with the false message.[13] Otherwise, *Sir Tristrem* offers only dubious support for the other features of Gottfried's account, and there is no sound objective reason for considering Gottfried in these respects a more authentic representative of Thomas than the *Saga*.[14] A study of the literary traditions underlying the episode will help to clarify the relationships of the different versions.

One of the most distinctive features of all forms of the story is the lovers' unusual method of communication, the signal of the chips on the stream. Tristan cut them so artfully, according to the Norse *Saga*, that no man ever saw their equal, for they floated like foam upon the water and no current could damage them. Isolt could therefore identify these unique whittlings when they passed before her in the water, and so she knew when Tristan was ready to meet her. A similar version appears in *Sir Tristrem* (vss. 2047-2054):

> Tristrem was in toun,
> In boure Ysonde was don.
> Bi water he sent adoun
> Liȝt linden spon:
> He wrot hem al wiþ roun;
> Ysonde hem knewe wel sone;
> Bi þat Tristrem was boun,
> Ysonde wist his bone;

and in the Oxford *Folie Tristan* (vss. 784-794):

> De mun cnivet les cospels fis
> K'erent enseignes entre nus,
> Quant me plaiseit venir a vus.
> Une funteine iloc surdeit
> Ki de . . . (?) la chambre curreit.
> En l'ewe jetai les cospels,
> Aval les porta li rusels.
> Quant vëiez la doleüre,
> Si vëiez ben a dreiture
> Ke jo i vendreie la nuit
> Pur envaiser par mun deduit.

The device is far more elaborate in Eilhart and Gottfried, presumably to explain how Isolt recognized its meaning as a signal.

Whether or not the simpler form in the *Saga, Sir Tristrem,* and the Oxford *Folie* is due to the processes of abridgment and condensation,[15] it is unquestionably closer than the more rationalized versions to the Irish parallels collected by Gertrude Schoepperle.[16] These Irish stories are especially significant because they concern Finn, one of the Celtic prototypes of King Mark. In all the Irish examples, distinctively fashioned chips floating down a stream enable Finn to identify and locate their maker. A ninth-century tale relates that after a pursuit of seven years Finn slew Ferchess at a certain pool "when he found the chips carried down by the river which Ferchess had set free."[17] According to another story current in the tenth century, when Oisin was abducted by enemies, he cut a chip from a spear shaft and cast it into a stream which eventually bore it to Finn. At once he recognized it as Oisin's work.[18] Perhaps the most significant example appears in *The Pursuit of Diarmaid and Grainne,* a saga which exercised a potent influence on the early forms of the Tristan legend.[19] In the three versions of this incident, Diarmaid cut shavings which were carried down a stream. When Finn saw them floating in the water, he recognized the characteristic workmanship of Diarmaid, for "there was none in Ireland that could do the like."[20] Although this tradition is preserved only in late documents,[21] there is no reason to deny its authenticity. Since the two texts from the ninth and tenth centuries show that the motif was already part of the legend of Finn, it could not have been introduced from the Tristan story into the oral versions of *Diarmaid and Grainne.*

In these Irish stories the chips on the stream are used not as a signal between lovers but as an identification of a hidden enemy. Yet, despite the different circumstances, the analogies with the Tristan episode are striking. Like Diarmaid, Tristan carves such extraordinary chips that no one has ever seen their equal; like Diarmaid's, they are recognized by their workmanship when they float on the water past someone located at a distance downstream. Since Tristan has inherited many other traditions of the Irish Diarmaid[22] and since the motif of the chips on the stream is no mere commonplace of fiction,[23] it seems evident that the Irish tradition is the ultimate source of the motif in the Tristan episode.

How did it come to be changed into a signal between the lovers? In *Diarmaid and Grainne,* which otherwise contributed much to the history of the lovers, the incident of the chips on the stream serves as an introduction to the death of the hero, and the pair are together at the time. A closer parallel to the situation in the Tristan episode, however, is provided by another celebrated Irish saga, *The Tragic Death of Curoi.*[24] Blathnat, the wife of Curoi, arranged a tryst with her paramour Cuchulainn: she poured milk into the river that flowed downstream to the Ulstermen, as a signal to Cuchulainn to come to her and put into action their plan to kill Curoi.[25] As in the Tristan episode, the lovers are separated, a tryst is prepared, and the signal is conveyed by a substance cast into a stream.[26] No drastic change was necessary to substitute the chips on the stream

for the milk in the Curoi story and to adapt it to the circumstances, if not the purpose, of Cuchulainn's famous tryst with Blathnat.[27]

But at what stage in the development of the Tristan legend did this felicitous blending take place? The saga of Diarmaid and Grainne shows no influence from the Curoi legend since the late oral versions do not associate the chips on the stream with a clandestine meeting of the lovers. The story of Blathnat's treachery, however, was well known in Wales. The late Professor Gruffydd has shown its profound effect upon the legend of Blodeuwedd in the Mabinogi of *Math Vab Mathonwy,*[28] one of the Four Branches, composed in its extant redaction early in the second half of the eleventh century.[29] Like Blathnat, Blodeuwedd conspired with her lover to slay her husband; when she learned the only way to kill him, she sent a message to her lover to be "under the lee of the hill which is now called Bryn Cyfergyr. That was on the bank of Cynfael river."[30] Although unfortunately her method of communication with her lover is not specified, the river plays an essential part in the scheme, for only on its bank can the victim be slain. The tryst, therefore, takes place on the river bank. The widespread influence upon the *matière de Bretagne* of the saga of Curoi, Blathnat, and Cuchulainn[31] and its demonstrable relationship to the Welsh legend of Blodeuwedd indicate that it was a Welsh redactor of the Tristan legend who first combined the motifs of the tryst and the chips on the stream. In the story of Blodeuwedd the meeting of the lovers on the banks of a stream approaches the Tristan episode more closely than it does the Irish source, in which Cuchulainn storms the fortress of Curoi in response to Blathnat's summons. In another Welsh tradition preserved in a poem by Dafydd ap Gwilym, Blodeuwedd is said to be the daughter or granddaughter of a lord of Môn (Anglesey) named Meirchion.[32] Although Dafydd wrote in the fourteenth century,[33] Professor Gruffydd considered the story of Blodeuwedd in this poem substantially the version current in Wales and independent of the Mabinogi.[34] The name Meirchion, of course, is the patronymic of King Mark in Wales. The occurrence of this name in the legend of Blodeuwedd may be nothing more than an interesting coincidence. Yet it is a hint, however fragile, that the setting of the tryst and the lovers' signal borne by the stream may have entered the Tristan legend from the story of Blodeuwedd, the Welsh counterpart of the Irish Blathnat.

There is nothing in these Celtic traditions that corresponds to the figure of the spying dwarf and his rôle as informer, but a suggestive parallel appears in another story about Finn, preserved in *Cormac's Glossary,* an Irish text of the ninth or early tenth century.[35] Although neither Diarmaid nor Grainne is mentioned, the tale merits careful consideration because it is unquestionably early in date and because Finn is presented as a betrayed husband. According to this Irish text,[36] Finn had as his Fool Lomna the Coward. One day Finn went on a hunting excursion, but Lomna remained at home. While he was walking outside, he found Coirpre lying with Finn's wife. The woman warned Lomna to conceal his discovery, but it was grievous to him to betray Finn. Lomna therefore cut an ogham on a four-cornered rod, and when Finn comprehended this cryptic message, he became disgusted with the woman. Realizing then that Lomna had betrayed her, she summoned her lover to kill the Fool. Coirpre cut off Lomna's head and took it away with him. When Finn found the headless corpse, he put his thumb into his mouth and by *teinm laeda* discovered the identity of the victim.[37] Setting out in pursuit, Finn tracked Coirpre and his warriors to a hut; Lomna's head was on a spit near the fire. Twice Coirpre attempted to distribute food to his men without offering any to the head, and each time the head spoke in protest. Coirpre put the head outside, but still it spoke. Then Finn came up and slew them.

First, it must be noted that this story is a composite of two traditions about Lomna—one about his discovery of the faithless wife, the other about his severed head. In the ninth-century saga *The Destruction of Da Derga's Hostel,*[38] Lomna the Fool in a long dialogue reports what he observes in the Hostel and prophesies the manner of his own death just as it occurs at the beginning of the great battle: the gatekeepers of the Hostel cut off his head, and thrice it is flung inside and thrice cast out.[39] The story of Lomna's severed head, therefore, evidently belongs to an independent tradition,[40] as do his epithets Lomna the Fool and Lomna the Coward.[41] Separated from this tradition, the story of Finn runs as follows: during Finn's absence on a hunt, his Fool discovers the infidelity of Finn's wife; fearing the consequences of outright disclosure since the woman is aware of his knowledge, yet unwilling to betray his master by keeping silence, he solves the dilemma by conveying the information to Finn through a cryptic ogham message cut on a four-cornered rod. Afterwards when the woman learns from Finn's behavior that the Fool has betrayed her, she has him killed by her paramour, who takes flight. Finn pursues and kills him.

The rôle of the Fool, as A. H. Krappe pointed out,[42] closely resembles that of the dwarf in the Tristan legend. Just as Lomna enjoys the confidence of Finn, so the dwarf is presented as a court favorite and the companion of the king. Like Lomna, too, the dwarf discovers the meeting of the lovers and informs the king. In both stories also the real or pretended absence of the husband on a hunting excursion plays a prominent part. In the Irish tale the Fool makes his fateful discovery during Finn's absence on a hunt. So in Thomas's romance the dwarf surprises the lovers in the garden after the king's announced departure on a hunt. Eilhart, too, retains the hunting expedition, though only as a preliminary to the king's concealment in the tree.

Finally, there are strong indications of a tradition that the dwarf, like Lomna, was decapitated. According to Eilhart, the dwarf promises to offer proof to the king or lose his head (vss. 3422-3423):

> her sprach "ne si daz wâr niet,
> sô heizzet mir mîn hôbit abe slân!"

And afterwards the king prepares to behead him as the penalty for his failure to prove the lovers' guilt (vss. 3615-3617):

> dô zoug der koning ûz sîn swert
> und hête gerne daz getwerg
> ûf dem boime ze tôde geslân.[43]

In Béroul's version, at a later point in the action (vss. 1305-1347), the king actually strikes off the dwarf's head because he betrayed a secret. Although this secret concerned an embarrassing physical characteristic of King Mark, it is significant that, like Finn's Fool, the dwarf in Béroul's poem was decapitated because he revealed a dangerous discovery that he had been warned to conceal. Thus the dwarf suffers the same fate as the Irish Lomna; but since the headless corpse in the Irish story could not be identified, Lomna was evidently no dwarf. It would have been natural, however, for the redactors of the Tristan legend to imagine the Fool of the Celtic story as a dwarf because in their own experience court fools were often dwarfs.[44]

The story of Finn and his Fool, then, accounts for a number of features in the tryst episode: the king's departure on a hunt, the dwarf's activities as confidential adviser and informer, and the references to his decapitation. Since the motif of the chips on the stream is not derived from the same Celtic tradition as the spying dwarf, certain difficulties would naturally arise from their combination. For example, the curious scene in Thomas's romance of the dwarf's visit to Tristan as he is carving the chips is an obvious attempt to link the two motifs by explaining how the dwarf knew the time of the tryst.[45] Eilhart's version solves the problem by endowing the dwarf with supernatural powers that enable him to learn whatever is required for the next step in the action. One version is not necessarily dependent upon the other; they merely represent different ways of blending two separate traditions.[46]

The most striking feature of the tryst episode, however, is neither the dwarf nor the signal. It is rather the clever escape of the lovers from apparently inevitable detection by the king lurking in the tree above them. The distinctive tree with its hidden observer seems to have been contributed by the immensely popular fabliau, of Oriental origin, known as the Enchanted Tree. Versions and adaptations of this story are so common in both Orient and Occident that it must have been easily accessible when the Tristan legend was circulating on the Continent. One version current in the twelfth century is the Latin tale *Lidia,* composed about 1175 but based on an earlier French source.[47] In this form of the fabliau (vss. 461-556), Lidia, the wife of Duke Decius, was enamored of a knight named Pirrus ("Pear Tree"). As a demonstration of her devotion and cleverness, she promised that her husband should surprise them together without believing his eyes. Accordingly, she pretended to be ill, and accompanied by Decius and Pirrus, she went to a neighboring orchard to be refreshed in the shade of a pear tree. At the duke's suggestion, Pirrus climbed the tree to gather fruit. Suddenly he cried out that Decius and his wife were offending his modesty by their lewd behavior. Lidia explained to the astounded Decius that the tree created strange optical illusions because it was enchanted. The duke climbed the tree to see for himself. Meanwhile the lovers made the pretended illusion a reality. Decius, watching from the branches, was amazed at the spectacle, but the lovers persuaded him that the tree was to blame, and he ordered it cut down.

As in the tryst episode, the deceived husband, stationed in a tree, observes the compromising behavior of his wife and her lover, but is nevertheless induced to repudiate the evidence of his senses; and the incident occurs in a similar setting (*Lidia*, vss. 493-496): "There was an orchard surrounded by waters, renowned for the shade of trees and productive of ripe fruits. In the midst flowed a fountain, shadowed by the branches of a pear tree." The action and the motivation, to be sure, are quite different, but once Tristan and Isolt realize the presence of Mark in the tree, they collaborate as vigorously as did Lidia and her lover to convince the observer of their innocence. In *Lidia* the scheme succeeds partly because of the preliminary trick played by the lovers, which has no counterpart in the Tristan episode, and partly because of her bold lies (vss. 551-554): "As I told you, O Duke, it is the fault of the tree; perhaps it wil delude others, too. Its guilt remains; since so evil an illusion darknes it, let the pear tree be cut down."[48]

A more remarkable parallel to the action of the tryst episode appears in a similar fabliau, an Oriental tale that reached Western Europe through the famous Arabic book of *Kalilah and Dimnah,* of Hindu-Persian origin. The wife in this tale extricates herself entirely by a brilliantly improvised discourse that convinces her spying husband of her devotion to him. A Latin version of the story preserved in the *Directorium vitae humanae* of John of Capua (*ca.* 1265) represents a form known in Western Europe in the twelfth century and probably earlier.[49] According to this story, a certain carpenter, informed that his fair wife was entertaining a lover, refused to believe it unless he saw it with his own eyes. Announcing his departure on a journey, he bade her farewell, but secretly returned and concealed himself beneath the bed. She sent for her lover, and they ate, drank, and told stories until they went to bed. All that happened the carpenter saw and heard from his hiding-place; nevertheless, he fell asleep. His wife caught sight of his protruding foot and woke her lover, saying, "I know that my husband is under the bed; now I want you to ask me in a loud voice whom I love more, you or my husband. When I refuse, insist until I tell you." In answer to the repeated question, she replied, "Why do you ask this of me? Do you think that anyone is as dear and beloved to me as my husband? We women do not care for our lovers in this way; once we have satisfied our desire, they are no more to us than the rest of the world. But a husband is better to a woman than father and mother and brothers and sisters, for he works and thinks only of her. Therefore cursed be any woman who does not cherish her husband's

life more than her lover's." This eulogy so charmed the carpenter that he fell asleep again, confident of his wife's utter devotion. He awoke next morning after the lover's departure, and kissed and embraced her. "Now lie there and rest," he said, "for you did not sleep last night. If I had not wished to disturb you, I would have killed that wicked wretch and given you peace from him."[50]

As in the Tristan episode, a suspicious husband, determined to learn the truth for himself, pretends to depart on a journey but in reality conceals himself to observe the assignation. While the wife entertains her lover, she discovers the spy by chance, and with the aid of her paramour delivers an impromptu discourse for the benefit of the listener that proclaims her single-minded devotion to her husband. Like King Mark, the deluded husband next morning manifests his complete acceptance of her words. In structure this fabliau corresponds to the Tristan episode more closely than does the story of the Enchanted Tree, for the deception of the husband is not prearranged, and the wife pretends, like Isolt, to be unaware of his presence. The major differences are the setting of the assignation in the house and the observation post of the spy under the bed.

The two fabliaux, both popular in Arabic sources and both familiar in twelfth-century Europe, are so alike in plot that the more picturesque setting of the Enchanted Tree could have been easily shifted to the story of the Carpenter's Wife. Such modifications were freely made: for example, in a variant of the Enchanted Tree, "Le Prestre qui abevete,"[51] the setting is a peasant's cottage and the observation post an opening in the door. And a modern Italian variant[52] combines both features: a monk peering through a window pretends to see the couple behaving scandalously beneath a tree. In any event, the fabliau of the Carpenter's Wife in the setting of the Enchanted Tree accounts for all the essential features in the escape of Tristan and Isolt from detection during their tryst beneath the tree that hides the spying king. Both fabliaux were known in Western Europe early enough to have become part of the Tristan legend. In the absence of evidence that they enjoyed any popularity in Celtic-speaking territory, it is likely that they entered the legend at an early stage in its circulation on the Continent, probably in a French version close to the Arabic sources. The presence of this fabliau material in all versions of the legend and the skilful blending with the Celtic traditions in the first part of the episode lead to the same conclusion.[53]

We shall probably never know exactly what inspired the introduction of Oriental fabliau themes into this episode. In the Celtic sources for the motifs of the spying dwarf and the chips on the stream, a tree forms no part of the setting. How then did it become the focal point of the action? Perhaps the Oriental material replaced a Celtic incident in which a tree figured prominently but which for some reason proved to be unsuitable as the legend developed. Two incidents of this kind, curiously enough, are attached to Finn. One, in a text of the eighth or early ninth century,[54] relates how Finn banished a servant loved by a maiden whom he desired for himself; the servant fled into the forest and concealed himself wearing a "hood of disguise" in the branches of a tree. Finn pursued him in the forest, came to the tree, and identified him by the supernatural power of *imbas*.[55] The other story, appearing in numerous versions, is part of the saga of Diarmaid and Grainne. Diarmaid conceals himself in the branches of a yew tree; Finn and Oisin play chess below, and Diarmaid throws down a berry to show Oisin the correct moves to win; Finn thus discovers his presence.[56] It would have been natural for an Irish story-teller to link this tradition with the two similar stories of Finn's identification of Lomna's headless corpse and his recognition of the chips on the stream, which, as we have seen, furnished the substance of the first half of the Tristan episode. If the three tales were combined, perhaps as illustrations of Finn's special attributes as a seer,[57] and if as a group they were absorbed into the Celtic traditions that eventually became the episode of the Tryst beneath the Tree, they explain the otherwise baffling emphasis upon the tree and the man hidden in its foliage.

When these tales of Finn were later reshaped in Wales into a story of a clandestine meeting between the lovers, most of Finn's encounter with the enemy in the tree would have had to be abandoned. But the tree was retained and probably transferred to the incident of the dwarf's discovery of the lovers, a development which would explain why in Thomas's version the dwarf surprises them from the branches of the tree, and why, in Eilhart's, he climbs into the tree with the king. The motif of the spying dwarf in the tree would have been enough to attract the Oriental fabliau of the deceived husband who watches his wife and her lover from a similar vantage point. The Celtic tryst also contained another element, the husband's departure on a journey, which, though common in stories of marital deception, would have facilitated the assimilation of the Oriental tale of the Carpenter's Wife adapted to the setting of the Enchanted Tree.

Although there are regrettable gaps in our evidence, especially for the intermediate Welsh and Breton versions of the episode, this explanation accounts for the otherwise capricious introduction of Oriental themes alien in source and spirit. If the tradition of Finn's encounter with an enemy hidden in a tree furnished the initial suggestion for the adaptation of the Oriental material, it also follows that the episode of the Tryst beneath the Tree is based upon a trio of similar stories that demonstrate Finn's supernatural gifts of knowledge. By *teinm laeda* he recognizes the headless corpse of Lomna; by *imbas* he identifies the chips of Ferchess[58] and the man in the tree wearing a "hood of disguise." Now, it is a striking fact that three supernatural powers are attributed to Finn in *The Youthful Exploits of Finn:*[59] *teinm laeda, imbas forosnai,* and *dichetal do chennaib.* These names also occur together in *Cormac's Glossary* as three ways of acquiring hidden or prophetic knowledge[60] and again in the *Triads of Ireland* as the three qualities necessary for a poet.[61] Since these powers, though

obscure in meaning,[62] were traditionally associated with Finn, it would have been entirely natural to link together three stories exemplifying his use of them.

With these clues it is possible to trace the literary history of the episode. The Tryst beneath the Tree seems to have originated in three stories about Finn. The first, Finn and Lomna, contributed the spying informer and the departure of the husband on a hunting expedition. The second recounted Finn's identification of a distant person by the characteristic workmanship of whittlings floating past him on a stream. In the third story, Finn recognized an enemy concealed in the tree above him. Certain forms of the second and third include Diarmaid as well as Finn and suggest that this group of stories became part of the legend of Tristan in Wales when it absorbed other elements of the saga of Diarmaid, Grainne, and Finn.

In Wales the three stories underwent drastic remodeling, possibly because Finn's divinatory powers had lost their significance in that stage of development. Under the influence of *The Death of Curoi,* another Irish saga well known in Wales, the group of incidents was fitted into the framework of a lovers' tryst. The Irish Blathnat sent a signal down a stream to her lover Cuchulainn to launch a prearranged attack upon her defenseless husband. Blathnat's Welsh counterpart Blodeuwedd summoned her lover, who was waiting downstream, to join her on the bank of the river in order to accomplish the destruction of her husband. Although her method of communicating with her paramour is not recorded, his location downstream and the significance of the river bank as the only place where the husband could be killed indicate that she used the flowing water as Blathnat did to signal her accomplice. Once this pattern was established in the Tristan legend, the Irish tradition of Diarmaid's distinctive whittlings became the lovers' signal. In Wales, too, the story of Finn and the man in the tree seems to have been adapted to the circumstances of the tryst by locating in the tree the spy derived from the Lomna story and transferring the recognition of his presence to the lovers. How did this Welsh version of the tryst end? Probably, following the action of Finn and Lomna, it ended with the slaying of the spy by the lover,[63] for the death of the informer appears to be an integral part of the Celtic Tristan tradition.

The Welsh tale that reached the Bretons, we may assume, related how the lovers arranged to meet secretly whenever Tristan sent his distinctively carved whittlings downstream as a signal to Isolt; how the dwarf, when the king was away on a hunt, accidentally observed a tryst from the branches of the tree in which he was concealed, and so discovered their ingenious system of communication; and how Tristan, perceiving his presence, beheaded him. The adaptation of the Oriental fabliau material to this Celtic story resulted in important changes. The spying dwarf in the tree becomes subordinate in interest to the spying husband of the fabliau who observes his wife and her lover from the branches of a tree. Other details are modified in accordance with the plot of the Carpenter's Wife. Instead of departing unsuspiciously on a hunting expedition, the husband now baits a trap for his wife by pretending to set out on a journey. And the lovers, like their Oriental counterparts, extricate themselves with such verbal virtuosity that the eavesdropping husband is utterly deluded.

These features became standardized in all versions of the episode, but the rôle of the dwarf is not treated with the same uniformity. In Thomas's romance his activities as a spy are presented in a preliminary incident; Eilhart's version fuses them with the king's, so that both characters watch from the tree simultaneously. The death of the dwarf, attributed in the Celtic story to the lover, is now assigned to the husband. This element of the story was either deferred, as in Béroul's account, or reduced to a threat against the dwarf's life, according to Eilhart, or simply ignored, as in the other versions.

There can be no doubt that the fabliau material greatly strengthened the Celtic plot, heightening the drama of the situation by placing the king in the tree as a spy and prolonging the suspense by the lovers' dialogue improvised to deceive the eavesdropper. The fabliaux are clearly adapted to the purpose of the tryst episode; only certain features are selected that develop the dramatic qualities inherent in the Celtic plot. It was surely a creative imagination that perceived the possibilities in these ribald tales, otherwise so remote in atmosphere from the world of Tristan and Isolt. Perhaps the fabliau themes were introduced into the Celtic plot by Bleheris himself, the most renowned *conteur* of the *matière de Bretagne,* whose version of the Tristan legend Thomas regarded as authoritative.[64] Bleheris flourished between 1100 and 1140,[65] and he recited his *contes* at the court of Poitou before his patron, probably the famed troubadour count, William VII, who died in 1127.[66] The facts dovetail neatly: the Arabic versions of the Enchanted Tree and the Carpenter's Wife were known in the West by the early twelfth century,[67] and Poitou, close to the centers of Arabic culture, was a place where Bleheris could have become acquainted with the two tales of successful deception. Whether or not Bleheris himself made the momentous adaptation of the Oriental fabliau material to the Celtic plot, it seems certain that this final step in the development of the episode occurred on the Continent in the early years of the twelfth century. The court of Poitou, hospitable alike to Oriental and Celtic story during this period, provided the necessary conditions. If Bleheris was indeed the first to borrow from Arabic sources to enrich the Celtic tradition of the lovers' tryst, he well deserved his reputation as a *conteur* of genius.

Notes

1. R. S. Loomis and L. H. Loomis, *Arthurian Legends in Medieval Art* (New York, 1938), pp. 50-69 and corresponding plates.

2. *Ibid.,* pp. 59, 67, 68 f., 69.

3. Eilhart von Oberge, [*Tristrant*], ed. F. Lichtenstein (Strassburg, 1877), vss. 5277-5772.

4. Béroul, *Le Roman de Tristan,* ed. E. Muret (4th ed.; Paris, 1947), vss. 265-272:

> "Las!" fait li rois, "or ai veü
> Que li nains m'a trop deceü.
> En cest arbre me fist monter,
> Il ne me pout plus ahonter.
> De mon nevo me fist entendre
> Mençonge, porqoi ferai pendre.
> Por ce me fist metre en aïr,
> De ma mollier faire haïr."

5. *Ibid.,* vss. 348-351:

> "Ne sai qui hui nos vout traïr,
> Mais li rois Marc estoit en l'arbre,
> Ou li perrons estait de marbre.
> Je vi son onbre en la fontaine."

6. This particular combination appears only in Béroul and the Italian *Novellino* (tr. E. Storer [London, n.d.], pp. 134-158, No. LXV) among the literary sources, and in the St. Floret mural and the carving on the Bamberg comb (Loomis, p. 69). In *Le Donnei des Amants* (*Rom.,* XXV [1896], 508), the lovers meet on another occasion "a la funtaine suz le pin."

7. The text begins with the arrival of the queen and her dialogue with Tristan.

8. *Tristrams Saga ok Ísondar (Die nordische und die englische Version der Tristan-Sage,* I), ed. E. Kölbing (Heilbronn, 1878), Chaps. LIV-LV. Cf. Thomas, *Le Roman de Tristan,* ed. J. Bédier (Paris, 1902-05), I, 191-203.

9. The Oxford *Folie* (ed. E. Hœpffner [2d ed.; Strasbourg, 1943], vss. 777-816), which is based upon Thomas, gives different details. Tristan cut the chips in the garden beneath the "espin" by the fountain. Although the dwarf reports the intended tryst to the king there is no parallel to the scene between Tristan and the dwarf.

10. See, for example, Bédier's criticism, I, 191, n. 1: "Nulle part le traducteur scandinave n'a si brutalement malmené son modèle que dans les deux chapitres qui vont suivre [Chaps. LIV, LV]. Il y a pratiqué des coupures si maladroites qu'il a presque atteint à l'inintelligibilité du poète anglais"; *ibid.,* I, 200, n. 1; *Tristrams Saga,* ed. Kölbing, pp. xciii-ciii; F. Piquet, *L'Originalité de Gottfried de Strasbourg* (Lille, 1905), pp. 253-259; J. Gombert, *Eilhart von Oberge und Gottfried von Strassburg* (Rotterdam, 1927), pp. 103-111.

11. Gottfried von Strassburg, *Tristan und Isolde,* ed. F. Ranke (Berlin, 1930), vss. 14,235-15,046.

12. *Sir Tristrem. (Die nordische und die englische Version der Tristan-Sage,* II), ed. E. Kölbing (Heilbronn, 1882), vss. 2058-2068.

13. *Ibid.,* vss. 2036-2046.

14. There is, however, much subjective evidence on both sides of the question. See references in n. 10 above.

15. Cf. Bédier, I, 193, n. 4; G. Schoepperle, *Tristan and Isolt* (Frankfurt and London, 1913), I, 149 f.

16. *Ibid.,* II, 301-305.

17. K. Meyer, *Fianaigecht,* Royal Irish Academy, Todd Lecture Series, XVI (1910), 39, xxi.

18. *The Rennes Dindsenchas,* ed. W. Stokes, *RC,* XV (1894), 446. A metrical version of this tale in the Book of Leinster is dated by Meyer in the tenth century, *Fianaigecht,* p. xxiii. Cf. *The Metrical Dindshenchas,* ed. E. Gwynn, Royal Irish Academy, Todd Lecture Series, X (1913), Part III, 242-253.

19. Schoepperle, II, 391-470.

20. The three variants are printed in Schoepperle, II, 303 f. Cf. also *RC,* XXXIII (1912), 157-180.

21. *RC,* XXXIII, 157-159.

22. Schoepperle, II, 397-417; J. D. Bruce, *Evolution of Arthurian Romance* (2d ed.; Göttingen and Baltimore, 1928), I, 171-186.

23. The language of signs occurs frequently as a motif in Oriental fiction, but not in the specific form found in the Irish tales and the Tristan legend. Cf. references cited in Somadeva, *The Ocean of Story,* tr. C. H. Tawney, ed. N. M. Penzer (London, 1924-28), VI, 247-251. For example, in the *Hemacandra* (tr. W. Hertel, pp. 95-98), a youth sends a nun with a message to Durgila. She drives the nun away with harsh words and strikes her on the back so that the imprint of her hand is visible on the nun's white robes. The youth, when he sees the mark of the five-fingered hand on the back, understands that Durgila has set a rendezvous for the fifth night of the dark half of the month. In a similar way she discloses to him the place of their meeting.

24. This saga appears in numerous versions in Irish: cf. R. Thurneysen, *Die irische Helden- und Königsage* (Halle, 1921), pp. 431-446; W. J. Gruffydd, *Math Vab Mathonwy* (Cardiff, 1928), pp. 265 f. R. I. Best's translation of the version in the Yellow Book of Lecan, published with his edition of the text in *Eriu,* II (1905), 18-35, has been reprinted in T. P. Cross and C. H. Slover, *Ancient Irish Tales* (New York, 1936), pp. 328-332.

25. Cross and Slover, p. 329.

26. F. Lot, *Rom.,* XXIV (1895), 322, and G. Henderson, *Bricriu's Feast* (London, 1899), p. 145, noted the resemblance to the Tristan legend. Miss Schoepperle, II, 302, n. 2, mentions the parallel but underestimates its value.

27. Dr. Roland Blenner-Hassett informs me that in his boyhood near Tralee there was a local legend about a Queen Scotia, who cast chips into a stream to summon her lover to rescue her from her abductor. This is the very region in which *The Death of Curoi* is localized; the river Findglais which carried the signal between Blathnat and Cuchulainn flows into the Bay of Tralee (Thurneysen, p. 431). Cf. also *The Metrical Dindshenchas,* Royal Irish Academy, Todd Lecture Series, X (1913), 523, on Findglais, and *ibid.,* XII (1935), 100, on Scota, wife of Mil. A modern Irish folk tale version of Curoi's death from Kerry, Munster, is printed in K. Müller-Lisowski, *Irische Volksmärchen* (Jena, 1923), pp. 9-13.

28. *Math Vab Mathonwy,* pp. 253-271, 356.

29. *The Mobinogion,* tr. G. and T. Jones (Everyman's Library; London, 1949), p. xix.

30. *Ibid.,* p. 71. On the derivation of the name Blodeuwedd and its relationship to the Irish Blathnat, see Gruffydd, pp. 263 f.

31. R. S. Loomis, *Arthurian Tradition and Chrétien de Troyes* (New York, 1949), Index, s.vv. Blathnat, Blodeuwedd, Curoi, Cuchulainn.

32. David Bell in his edition and translation of the poem (Dafydd ap Gwilym, *Fifty Poems* [London, 1942], pp. 282-285) renders the line "Merch i arglwydd, ail Meirchion" as: 'My father was son to Meirchion.' Gruffydd, p. 254, translates it with the line following: 'I am a daughter of a lord of Môn [Anglesey], a second Meirchion.'

33. Bell, pp. 1-11.

34. *Math Vab Mathonwy,* pp. 254 f.

35. On the date of *Cormac's Glossary,* see Thurneysen, pp. 19 f. Meyer, *Fianaigecht,* p. xix, dates it in the ninth century.

36. W. Stokes, *Transactions of the Philological Society, 1891-94,* pp. 176-179. The text is also printed by Meyer, *Fianaigecht,* pp. xix f.

37. T. F. O'Rahilly, *Early Irish History and Mythology* (Dublin, 1946), pp. 336-340, discusses the meaning of *teinm laeda* and concludes that it signified literally 'chewing of the pith' and originally referred to Finn's practice of chewing his thumb for divinatory purposes. Cf. also R. D. Scott, *The Thumb of Knowledge* (New York, 1930), pp. 3-44, 96-117, and O'Rahilly, p. 327, n. 4.

38. *Togail Bruidne Da Derga,* ed. Eleanor Knott (Dublin, 1936). A translation by Stokes, with some omissions, is printed in Cross and Slover, pp. 93-126. For dating, discussion, and analysis of the text, see Thurneysen, pp. 621 f.

39. *Togail Bruidne Da Derga,* ed. Knott, pp. 22, 42; Thurneysen, pp. 643 f., 649; Cross and Slover, p. 122.

40. Although Dr. Knott, p. 83, n. to l. 615, doubts that the name of Lomna appeared in the original tale, it is unquestionably part of the ninth-century redaction. O'Rahilly, p. 283, n. 1, believes that the tradition of Lomna's speaking head in *Cormac's Glossary* is mythological.

41. Cf. *Togail Bruidne Da Derga,* ed. Knott, p. 21, ll. 713-715, which has been thus translated: "'An evil

utterance has routed thee, O Lomna,' said Ingcel. 'You are a worthless warrior and they know you.'"

42. *RF,* XLV (1931), 95-99.

43. A scene on a wooden casket of the fourteenth century, probably carved in England, depicts Mark about to slay the dwarf (Loomis, *Arthurian Legends in Medieval Art,* p. 67, fig. 129).

44. Cf. Schoepperle, I, 244-249.

45. Bédier, I, 197 n., is led by the inconsistencies to accept Eilhart's version as the original which Thomas modified to eliminate any trace of magic.

46. Since Béroul's poem also endows the dwarf with astrological powers (vss. 320-336), Gottfried's critical rejection of this version, as Bédier surmised (I, 192, 197 n.), may well have been based on a similar passage in Thomas:

> ein getwere was in dem hove da,
> daz selbe solte namen han
> Melot petit von Aquitan
> und kunde ein teil, also man giht,
> umbe verholne geschiht
> an dem gestirne nahtes sehen.
> ine wil aber nihtes von im jehen,
> was alse ichz von dem buoche nim.
> nun vinde ich aber niht von im
> an dem waren maere,
> wan dez ez kündic waere,
> listic unde rederich

(ed. Ranke, vss. 14,238-14,249).

But the Irish parallel does not support his argument that Thomas modified a source which presented the dwarf as an astrologer. It is more likely, as Gottfried's comment implies, that he was following the "true story" in which the dwarf learned about the rendezvous as Lomna did, by direct observation.

47. G. Cohen, *La "Comédie" latine en France au XIIe siècle* (Paris, 1931), I, 213-246. This is evidently the source of Boccaccio's tale, *Decameron,* VII, 9. For analogues see A. C. Lee, *The Decameron, Its Sources and Analogues* (London, 1909), pp. 236-244. J. D. Bruce, *Evolution,* I, 187, suggested the "Pear Tree Story" as the source of the episode; but, as Mrs. Dempster has pointed out (W. F. Bryan and G. Dempster, *Sources and Analogues of the Canterbury Tales* [Chicago, 1941], pp. 341-356), one must distinguish between those versions, like Chaucer's *Merchant's Tale,* in which the blind husband's sight is restored, and the others, like *Lidia,* where the deceived husband's vision is normal. Cf. Bédier, *Les Fabliaux* (4th ed.; Paris, 1925), pp. 269 f.

48. In view of the wide circulation of the tryst episode, are the partial resemblances in *Lidia* to be explained by the influence of the romance upon the fabliau? Such an explanation is hardly acceptable since *Lidia* includes many important elements lacking in the episode which are present in versions of the fabliau that

could not possibly have been affected by the Tristan legend. For example, in the French fabliau "Le Prestre qui abevete" (Montaiglon and Raynaud, *Recueil général et complet des fabliaux* [Paris, 1872-90], III, 54-57), the observation post is not a tree but an opening in the door of a peasant's cottage. Another analogue close to *Lidia* but quite outside the orbit of the Tristan legend is an Arabic tale, in R. Basset, *Mille et un contes, récits et légendes arabes* (Paris, 1924-26), II, 150-152.

49. John of Capua, *Directorium vitae humanae,* ed. J. Derenbourg, Bibliothèque de l'Ecole des Hautes Études, Sciences philologiques et historiques, LXXII (1889), xiii-xvii, 185-187. On the literary history of *Kalilah and Dimnah,* see Tawney and Penzer, *The Ocean of Story,* V, Appendix I.

50. The *Panchatantra* version of this tale (ed. T. Benfey [Leipzig, 1859], Book III, No. 11, pp. 258-262) is more remote from the Tristan episode. The wife explains to her lover, for the benefit of her eavesdropping husband, that she had invited him in order to save her husband's life, for the goddess had revealed to her that he would die unless she could remain chaste in the arms of a stranger.

51. Montaiglon and Raynaud, *Recueil . . . des fabliaux,* III, 54-57.

52. F. Liebrecht, *Zur Volkskunde* (Heilbronn, 1879), p. 135; R. Basset, II, 150-152.

53. Even the detail of the reflection in the water may be derived from a tale similar to one in Marie de France's *Fables,* ed. K. Warnke (Halle, 1898), No. XLIV, in which a wife, to convince her husband that he has not seen her in bed with another man, shows him his reflection in a vessel of water. Since he sees himself in the water but is not actually there, he must never trust the evidence of his eyes, which always lie. The detail in the Tristan episode may have been borrowed from such a story, which was familiar in the twelfth century, as Marie's version proves. Other Oriental parallels have been suggested for the tryst episode, but they are more distant than the two fabliaux discussed above. The Persian tale of the prince of Sind, which R. Zenker, *RF,* XXIX (1911), 366 (following Hertz) and Miss Schoepperle, I, 212, considered significant, is hardly a parallel. The prince feigns madness to protect himself from his brother; as he prays one night by a tree, the moonlight reveals the shadow of his brother's spy in the tree, and he resumes his pretended madness. Here, of course, the presence of a spy in a tree is providentially revealed by moonlight, but not to lovers who are meeting secretly. There is also no indication that this story was known in Western Europe in the twelfth century, as the two fabliaux undoubtedly were. The Sanskrit tales from the *Panchatantra* and the *Cukasaptati,* cited by Miss Schoepperle, I, 212, are analogues of the Carpenter's Wife, but more remote from the Tristan episode than the version in *Kalilah and Dim-*

nah. Cf. n. 50 above and *Cukasaptati,* ed. R. Schmidt (Kiel, 1894), No. 25, p. 45 and No. 19, p. 35.

54. K. Meyer, *Fianaigecht,* p. xviii.

55. "Finn and the Man in the Tree," ed. K. Meyer, *RC,* XXV (1904), 344-349. On *imbas forosnai,* see O'Rahilly, *Early Irish History and Mythology,* pp. 323, 339 f.

56. *Duanaire Finn,* ed. G. Murphy, *Irish Texts Society,* XXVIII (1933), 402-409; Cross and Slover, pp. 200-203; *RC,* XXXIII (1912), 175, l. 50 and n. 5; J. F. Campbell, *Popular Tales of the West Highlands* (Edinburgh, 1860-62), III, 56-59; J. G. Campbell, *The Fians* (London, 1891), p. 77.

57. Both *teinm laeda* and *imbas forosnai* are illustrated in these stories. Finn identifies the chips of Ferchess by *imbas forosnai.* On Finn as seer, cf. O'Rahilly, pp. 316-340.

58. K. Meyer, *Fianaigccht,* p. 39.

59. *RC,* V (1881-83), 201; Cross and Slover, p. 365.

60. O'Rahilly, pp. 323-340.

61. *The Triads of Ireland,* ed. K. Meyer, Royal Irish Academy, Todd Lecture Series, XIII (1906), 17, No. 123.

62. O'Rahilly's discussion, pp. 323-340, sheds little light on the third power, *dichetal do chennaib.* Cf. Scott, *The Thumb of Knowledge,* pp. 258-263.

63. Cf. Krappe, *RF,* XLV, 98 f.

64. Bédier, I, vss. 2113-2123.

65. Loomis, *RR,* XXXII (1941), 16-19; *MLN,* XXXIX (1924), 319-329; J. van Dam, *Neoph.,* XV (1929), 30-34.

66. F. Lot, *Rom.,* LI (1925), 406; S. Singer, *Abh. der Preuss. Akad. der Wiss., phil.-hist. Klasse,* 1918, No. 13, pp. 8-10; *Neoph.,* XV, 101; Loomis, *RR,* XXXII, 18 f.; A. R. Nykl, *Hispano-Arabic Poetry and its Relations with the Old Provençal Troubadours* (Baltimore, 1946), pp. 373-396; R. Menéndez Pidal, *Poesía árabe y poesía europea* (2d ed.; Buenos Aires [1943]), pp. 9-66.

67. J.-T. Welter, *L'Exemplum dans la littérature religieuse et didactique du moyen âge* (Paris, 1927), p. 99. The *Disciplina clericalis,* for example, which contains thirty-four Arabic tales, was composed about 1110.

Helaine Newstead (essay date 1958)

SOURCE: "King Mark of Cornwall," in*Romance Philology,* Vol. 11, No. 3, February, 1958, pp. 240-53.

[*In the following essay, Newstead evaluates the significance of the role of King Mark of Cornwall in the Tristan romances, observing that the character figures prominently in the stories, as does the setting of many incidents in the King's castle at Tintagel.*]

In the dramatic action of the Tristan romances King Mark is almost as important as the lovers themselves. Tristan, as the son of his sister, is bound to him by close ties of kinship, and the hero's first spectacular exploit is the liberation of Mark's kingdom of Cornwall from the annual human tribute demanded by the Irish champion Morholt. Many of the subsequent plots, counter-plots, stratagems, and thrilling escapes that characterize the story are initiated by Mark's uncertain temper towards the lovers, his continual vacillation between belief in their innocence and suspicion of their guilt.[1] His prominence in the story and the setting of many incidents in his castle at Tintagel have generally been interpreted as evidence of Cornish influence in the Tristan legend, but there is wide disagreement about its nature, extent, and significance.[2] Since King Mark is so closely identified with Cornwall in the Tristan romances, a fresh study of the traditions attached to him may shed some light on this perplexing problem.

The oldest extant document to mention King Mark is the Latln *Vita* of St. Paul Aurelian, composed in 884 by Wrmonoc, a monk of the Abbey of Landévennec in Brittany.[3] After the saint had performed many good works as a disciple of St. Illtud in south Wales[4]

> fama eius regis Marci peruolat ad aures quem alio nomine Quonomorium uocant. Qui eo tempore amplissime producto sub limite regendo moenia sceptri, uir magnus imperiali potentiae atque potentissimus habebatur, ita ut quatuor linguae diuersarum gentium uno eius subiacerent imperio.[5]

The saint declined Mark's invitation to become his bishop and later quarreled with him over a bell that the king refused to relinquish. Then St. Paul Aurelian, after a sojourn with his sister in western Cornwall, departed for Brittany. Long afterwards, just as he was relating the story of his dispute with Mark to a kinsman on the isle of Batz off the Breton coast, Mark's bell miraculously turned up in the interior of a huge fish.

Although Mark's kingdom is not explicitly identified in the *Vita,* the itinerary of the saint—from south Wales, to Mark's realm, to western Cornwall, and then to Brittany—is commonly understood to imply Cornwall; but as Mrs. Bromwich has pointed out after a judicious review of the facts,[6] it is more probable that the ninth-century hagiographer intended to refer to a location in south Wales nearer St. Paul Aurelian's home in Glamorgan. Because of the usual but doubtful assumption that the *Vita* presents Mark as king of Cornwall, much has been made of the alternative name Quonomorius given to him in the text. On a sixth-century stone at Castle Dôr near Fowey in Cornwall, the same name, in the form Cunomor, is inscribed. Although the first part of the inscription is very much worn and has been deciphered in diverse ways, the most recent reading of the whole is:

DRUSTAUS HIC IACIT / CVNOMORI FILIUS.[7]

If Cunomor is equated with King Mark and Drustaus (for Drustanus) interpreted as a sixth-century form of Tristan's name, the inscription would seem to commemorate Tristan son of Cunomor or Mark. But what is the real basis for this sensational argument?

In the first place, the identification of King Mark with Quonomorius rests on this single passage in the *Vita;* nowhere else does Wrmonoc use the alternative name to refer to the king.[8] On the other hand, a tyrant Conomor is a familiar figure in the biography of St. Paul Aurelian's fellow-student St. Samson,[9] and since Wrmonoc knew the *Vita* of St. Samson and elsewhere drew upon it,[10] he might easily have borrowed Quonomorius from the same source as an appropriate name for one who had offended St. Paul Aurelian, just as other Breton hagiographers considered it necessary to include a hostile encounter between their subjects and Conomor.[11] As F. Lot has remarked, "Conomor est un croquemitaine que les Vies de saints s'empruntent les unes aux autres pour donner du pathétique au récit."[12] The historic Coonomor, who lived probably in the sixth century,[13] appears to have been well known on the Continent, but there is no indication that he enjoyed a comparable vogue in the British Isles. The Castle Dôr inscription, then, merely means that a person named Cunomor lived in Cornwall; it does not prove that he was a Cornish king or the historic original of King Mark.

Similarly, all the evidence points away from Cornwall to the derivation of the legendary Tristan from a Pictish king named Drust son of Talorc, who ruled in northern Scotland about 780 A.D.[14] Drust (diminutive Drostan) son of Talorc appears in Welsh as Drystan or Trystan son of Tallwch, an almost exact equivalent in sound. Since Drystan son of Tallwch is linked in the Welsh triads[15] with Esyllt, the wife of his uncle March son of Meirchion, he is clearly identified with the Tristan of the romances. Furthermore, a fragment of the Pictish saga of Drust is preserved in a tenth-century recension of the Irish *Wooing of Emer,* an interpolated episode that strikingly parallels Tristan's deliverance of Cornwall from the demand for human tribute and his later rescue of the princess Isolt.[16] In the light of these facts, the Drustaus of the Castle Dôr inscription, whoever he may have been, must be rejected as the historic original of the hero.[17] No literary source, moreover, assigns the name Cunomor to Tristan's father or kinsman. Unless a more substantial connection can be demonstrated between the Tristan legend and Cornish archaeology, the value of the Castle Dôr stone in the context of the romances remains negligible.

The *Vita* of St. Paul Aurelian indicates that King Mark was a contemporary of the saint in the sixth century. He may, however, have ruled in south Wales rather than in Cornwall, and Wrmonoc in the ninth century may have learned of him from his south Welsh sources.[18] In any event, the only certain inference to be drawn from the passage in the *Vita* is that by the second half of the ninth century King Mark had achieved legendary renown. His fame could have been no recent growth if he was considered to belong to that distant past when St. Paul Aurelian traveled in Wales and Cornwall before settling in Brittany.

In Welsh tradition King Mark is known as March son of Meirchion.[19] In the *Dream of Rhonabwy*[20] March son of Meirchion is mentioned twice: once as the leader of an army and a cousin german of King Arthur, and again in a list of Arthur's counselors, among whom is also Drystan son of Tallwch.[21] A Welsh triad informs us that March son of Meirchion was one of the three fleet owners of the Isle of Britain.[22] Another triad relates how Drystan son of Tallwch, one of the three great swineherds of Britain, guarded the swine of March son of Meirchion while the swineherd delivered a message to Esyllt. Arthur, March, Kei, and Bedwyr failed, despite their best efforts, to carry off a single animal.[23]

Although the *Dream of Rhonabwy* and the triads are recorded in manuscripts of the thirteenth and fourteenth centuries, these four references represent native Welsh tradition independent of any known version of the French romances.[24] What can we learn from them? First of all, they confirm the tradition of Mark's fame, which also appears in a hagiographic source. Both Welsh texts, moreover, link him with Tristan and Arthur. In the *Dream of Rhonabwy* he is Arthur's cousin, and both Mark and Tristan are among the counselors of Arthur. These facts indicate that Welsh tradition established the close relationship of Tristan and Mark[25] and also connected them with King Arthur and two of his warriors, Kei and Bedwyr.

The association of Mark and Arthur is natural if we recall that important traditions of Arthur's birth and last battle were localized in Cornwall.[26] According to Geoffrey of Monmouth (ca. 1136),[27] the begetting of Arthur took place in Tintagel, the very castle which in the Tristan legend in Mark's principal stronghold. The connection of both monarchs with Tintagel undoubtedly cemented their relationship and stimulated the *conteurs* to interweave their histories.

Since King Mark was the legendary ruler of Cornwall, his court would inevitably be located at Tintagel, which had become the residence of the earls of Cornwall shortly after the Norman Conquest.[28] The spectacular landscape of Tintagel, with its chasm and ruined walls,[29] exercised a potent spell upon the *conteurs*. In their hands it became the setting for the clandestine interviews of Tristan and Isolt and for the illicit amour of Igerne and Uter Pendragon. To Geoffrey of Monmouth and Wace, Tintagel was an impregnable stronghold on a lofty cliff protected by the sea and impenetrable to Uter Pendragon except with the aid of Merlin's wizardry. The author of *Perlesvaus* (ca. 1210) gravely explains that the sin of Uter and Igerne caused the chasm and the ruin of the castle, and thus describes the impressive approach to Tintagel:

. . . e cevauchierent a grant esploit, tant que il vinrent
en.i. terre mout diverse, qui n'ert gaires hantee de gent;
e troverent.i. petit chastel en.i. destor. I[l] vinrent cele
part, e virent que tot li clos, donc li chastel estoit avi-
ronnez, estoit fondus dusqu'en abisme, ne n'estoit
homme terriens qui aprochier i peüst de cele part. Mais
il i avoit.i. molt bele entree e.i. porte gramde e larje par
onc on i entroit. Il esgarderent la dedenz, e virent.i.
chapele qui molt estoit bele e riche, e par dejoste.i.
grant sale, e avoit.i. tor au cief de la sale mout ancienne.[30]

The Oxford text of the *Folie Tristan* preserves a charming
local tradition that vividly conveys the power of the
legend-haunted castle to stir the imagination. To the Cornish peasantry of the twelfth century it was a "chastel faé"
that vanished twice a year:

> E si fu jadis apelez
> Tintagel li chastel faëz,
> Chastel faé fu dit a droit,
> Car dous faiz l'an [il] se perdeit.
> Li païsant distrent pur veir
> Ke dous faiz l'an nel pot l'en veir,
> Hume del païs ne nul hom,
> Ja grant guarde ne prengë hom.
> Une en ivern, autre en esté,
> So dient la gent del vingné.[31]

The same tradition seems to have persisted into quite recent times in Cornwall,[32] inspired, no doubt, by the mists
that often enshroud the entire headland so that it is actually invisible a short distance away.

Since Tintagel was King Mark's principal court, presumably it was the site of the tribute episode, although Gottfried von Strassburg is the only source to name it specifically.[33] A curious story in the *Vulgate Lancelot,* however,
not only associates the motif of human tribute with Tintagel but also suggests that it circulated in a form independent of the Tristan material. According to this story, Galeschin delivered a castle named Pintagoel, whose lord was
obliged to surrender a child from each household and a
third of his land to a *grant vilain.*[34] Since an analogue,
likewise in the *Vulgate Lancelot,* names the castle Tinaguel
and its lord "le duc de Cornuaille,"[35] and another analogue
in Malory's Book vi identifies it with "Tyntagyll,"[36] it is
clear that Tintagel is meant. Although the second story in
the *Lancelot* and Malory's variant lack the theme of the
human tribute, a close cognate of all three versions in
Chrétien's *Yvain* preserves it in unmistakable form and
shows that its appearance in the Pintagoel episode is not
fortuitous.[37] In *Yvain,* the king of the "Isle as Puceles" was
forced to deliver an annual tribute of thirty maidens to two
sons of a devil until some valorous knight should succeed
in vanquishing them. Yvain destroyed them and delivered
the castle, here known only as "Le Chastel de Pesme Avan-
ture." The Pintagoel story, therefore, embodies a tradition
that Tintagel was oppressed by a demand for human tribute, and since nothing in the cognates suggests the slightest influence from the Tristan romances, it may well represent a local legend. If such a story about human tribute

was independently attached to Tintagel, the similarity of
theme would explain how Tristan's first important adventure came to be localized there and geographically separated from its normal sequel, the rescue of the princess.

Tintagel is King Mark's stronghold in all versions of the
Tristan legend except Béroul's and the episode known as
Tristan the Minstrel, included in Gerbert de Montreuil's
continuation of *Le Conte del Graal.*[38] Both texts locate
Mark's court at Lancien,[39] which J. Loth identified with
Lantyan, now a village on the river Fowey in the parish of
St. Samson's, Cornwall.[40] Béroul also mentions a church
of Saint Sanson (vss. 2973, 2994) apparently in or near
Lancien, which was attended by Mark and Isolt; and the
parish church of the modern Lantyan is dedicated to the
same saint. Loth's identification is therefore certainly correct, but the localization adopted by Béroul and Gerbert
seems to be an arbitrary departure from the traditional setting introduced by some *conteur* familiar with the region,
perhaps by Béroul or his immediate source.[41] Nowhere
else, so far as I am aware, is Lancien a place of legendary
import in the *matière de Bretagne.* In any case, Béroul
also mentions Tintagel as Mark's court (vs. 3150) and refers (vss. 264, 880) to the evil dwarf who lived in Mark's
household as "le nain de Tintaguel."

If the localization at Lancien represents no particularly archaic trait, it is far otherwise with the second tradition
about King Mark that Béroul alone records. He relates
(vss. 1303-50) that the king had a secret known only to
the dwarf Frocin. One day, when the dwarf was drunk, the
barons asked him why he and the king spoke together so
often and so confidentially. He replied (vss. 1315-26):

> "A celer bien un suen consel
> Mot m'a trové toz jors feel.
> Bien voi que le volez oïr,
> Et je ne vuel ma foi mentir.
> Mais je merrai les trois de vos
> Devant le Gué Aventuros.
> Et iluec a une aube espine,
> Une fosse a soz la racine:
> Mon chief porai dedenz boter
> Et vos m'orrez defors parler.
> Ce que dirai, c'ert du segroi
> Dont je sui vers le roi par foi."

The barons accompanied the dwarf and listened as he announced to the hawthorn bush (vss. 1332-34):

> "Or escoutez, seignor marchis!
> Espine, a vos, non a vasal:
> Marc a orelles de cheval."

When they reported to the king that they knew the secret,
he promptly cut off the dwarf's head.

It is easy to understand why this grotesque story does not
appear in the more courtly and refined versions of the
Tristan romances, in which continuity and a certain consistency of tone are maintained. The free episodic structure
of Béroul's narrative enables him to exploit the broadly

comic implications of the incident and to stress the element of dramatic surprise so effectively that no one is disposed to wonder why Mark's deformity is neither observed nor mentioned again. Although Béroul is the only romancer to include the story, the *conte* of the horse's ears was probably adapted to the legend of King Mark at an early date because in all the Celtic languages his name means 'horse'.[42] Onomastic stories of this kind form a typical category of Celtic narrative,[43] and versions of this particular tale have been collected in Ireland, Wales, and Brittany, usually attached to a personage whose name means 'horse'. The story, of course, is not restricted to these areas, for similar legends were related of King Midas, the emperor Trajan, and Alexander, among others.[44] Béroul's version, however, was derived from a Celtic source. The story flourished so lustily on Celtic soil because Celtic tradition is especially rich in names with an equine meaning.[45]

The earliest version is an Irish saga dated by Kuno Meyer in the tenth century.[46] It relates how King Eochaid (Ir. 'horse') had two horse's ears, and to conceal this blemish he used to retire to the wilderness to be shaved and each time slay the person who performed the operation for him. He had a nephew named Angus but called MacDichoime ('Son of the Unlovely'), who was a keen and splendid youth. He used to shave the warriors, take care of their weapons, and entertain them with musical instruments. Everyone loved him, especially the queen, Eochaid's wife, who desired to lie with him. Rumors of an affair between MacDichoime and the queen reached Eochaid, and the jealous king determined to kill him. With that intention he invited his nephew to the wilderness to shave him, but MacDichoime instead threatened to kill him. Eochaid begged for mercy, offering his nephew a share of the kingdom and the permanent post of royal barber in exchange for the promise to keep the secret of the horse's ears. MacDichoime agreed, but the secret pressed so heavily upon him that he fell into a wasting illness. One day as he passed a moor on his way to a leech, he fell face down on the ground, three streams of blood gushed from his nose and mouth, and he was instantaneously cured. A year later, passing there with the warriors, he found that three saplings had grown on the spot, and he related the story of his miraculous cure to his companions. Afterwards a harper and his company came to the saplings and heard the trees telling each other about Eochaid's ears. The harper, a satirist, decided to use this theme in his performance. When Eochaid heard the harper proclaiming his secret, he ordered the entertainers bound; but after learning that the revelation had been caused by the saplings sprung from his nephew's blood, he released them. He no longer tried to conceal his deformity, and MacDichoime later made a double pipe from the saplings. After Eochaid's death he became king, but he always cherished his pipe.

This remarkable story, which is no folk tale but rather an elaborate literary version, is too early to have been influenced by the French Tristan legend, and it is obviously not the direct source of Béroul. There are, nevertheless, three noteworthy points of resemblance. First, the story of the horse's ears is attached not only to a king whose name, like Mark's, means 'horse', but it is also adapted to a situation in which the king is roused to murderous jealousy by rumors of his queen's amour with his nephew, just as Mark is. This triangular relationship may have been affected by the Irish saga of Diarmaid and Grainne, which was known in Ireland before the tenth century[47] and which, as Miss Schoepperle showed,[48] also influenced the legend of Tristan. The fact that in Béroul the incident of the horse's ears is connected with the loathsome dwarf whose principal function is to arouse the king's suspicions suggests that the tale may have reached Béroul in a composite form similar to the Irish.

In the second place, the name 'Son of the Unlovely' given to the custodian of the secret[49] accords with the appearance of the dwarf in Béroul's poem, who is said (vs. 320) to be "boçu," and in the episode itself is thus described (vs. 1329):

> Li nains fu cort, la teste ot grose.[50]

The alternative name 'Son of the Unlovely' may represent a variant of the story in which the king's nephew is a repulsive character instead of a splendid, handsome youth loved by all; or the epithet may be the result of an attempt to fuse two originally distinct persons.[51]

The third parallel between Béroul and the Irish saga concerns the revelation of the secret. The Irish story displays considerable confusion on this point. In a later but simpler Irish version in the Yellow Book of Lecan (fourteenth and fifteenth centuries), the hero is cured of his malady by divulging his secret to a willow tree, from which a harper afterwards fashions a harp that can produce nothing but the revelatory statement.[52] In the Welsh and Breton folk tales, too, a pipe or a flute is made from reeds growing on the spot, and the musician unwittingly discloses the secret by performing on the instrument. The tenth-century Irish saga preserves a muddled reminiscence of the standard version in the pipe which the king's nephew makes from the saplings, but this instrument plays no part in the action. The harp, on the other hand, is not made from the saplings. The trees are merely overheard by the harper, who then of his own volition determines to repeat the statement in his performance before the king. Now, in Béroul's episode, the secret is similarly overheard by the barons as the dwarf communicates it to the shrubbery, and they deliberately repeat it to the king. It is surely significant that of all the extant versions only Béroul and the tenth-century Irish saga should present this distinctive deviation from the traditional form.

Although Béroul's story rationalizes the supernatural revelation of the secret, its original nature is betrayed by the locale. The place chosen by the dwarf for his meeting with the barons is "le Gué Aventuros / Et iluec a une aube espine." A ford by a hawthorn tree was a typical setting for uncanny marvels, as numerous other examples in Celtic and Arthurian tradition prove.[53] A place of magic and enchantment, it was the haunt of fays and the site of mysterious combats in which the prize was a faery steed. Since there is nothing supernatural in Béroul's account to suggest the appropriateness of such an eerie locality, it must have been a traditional element in the story. Mark's equine characteristics might have inspired the choice of the setting because of the frequent appearance of supernatural horses in stories about fords near hawthorn trees.

Despite the contrast between Béroul's compressed, anecdotal treatment of the tale and the highly developed, conflate form of the Irish text,[54] the remarkable correspondences make it clear that the stories are related. The relationship may be remote and indirect, but it does exist.

Wales and Brittany furnish no text as early as the Irish saga but rather a number of folk-tale versions ranging in date from about 1550 to the end of the nineteenth century. They preserve a simple but fairly complete form of the basic story, which is attached to the name March. Béroul's account, lacking the introductory incidents and other typical features,[55] could not have been their source. These tales, then, testify to the independent circulation in Wales and Brittany of the legend about King Mark's ears.

The earliest is a Welsh tale appended to the genealogy of Iarddur ap Egri, who traced his ancestry back to March ab Meirchion; it was written down in a manuscript copied between 1550 and 1562 (Peniarth MS 134, formerly Hengwrt MS 107). According to this anecdote,[56] March had horse's ears, a secret known only to his barber, who was warned to guard it on pain of losing his head. But the barber fell ill, and a physician, perceiving that he was dying, ordered him to tell it to the ground. The barber recovered, but reeds grew on the spot that received his confidence. Certain pipers of Maelgwn Gwynedd cut these reeds and used them for their instruments.[57] When they had to perform before March, they could elicit nothing but "Horse's ears for March ab Meirchion."

Another Welsh tale, found in the papers of Edward Llwyd and dated 1693,[58] relates that one of Arthur's warriors named March Amheirchion was lord of Castellmarch in Lleyn. To conceal his horse's ears he used to kill each man who shaved him. On the spot where he buried the bodies there grew reeds, which someone cut to make a pipe. Since the pipe would utter nothing but "March Amheirchion has horse's ears," March was ready to slay the piper, but refrained when he himself obtained the same result from the instrument. After he learned where the reeds had grown, he no longer attempted to hide either the murders or his deformity. This tale continued to circulate in the district of Castellmarch: in the summer of 1882, nearly two hundred years later, the aged blacksmith of Aber Soch, near Castellmarch, told the same legend to Sir John Rhys.[59]

These Welsh versions agree with the Irish in the murderous nature of the king with the horse's ears. The Peniarth text, in particular, resembles the Irish saga of the tenth century in the barber's illness and the growth of the communicative plants on the spot where he recovered after being relieved of his secret. The Welsh tales also agree with Béroul in the characterization of the king, for in his story Mark actually murders the dwarf. It is significant, too, that the Welsh tales should name the protagonist March, and that the version of 1693 should link him with King Arthur, a tradition corroborated by independent Welsh sources of much earlier date. In Béroul's poem, King Arthur plays a major rôle and is closely associated with King Mark.[60]

In Brittany the legend is similarly connected with the name March. One version, recorded in 1794, relates how the king of Portzmarch killed all his barbers to prevent them from revealing that he had horse's ears. The intimate friend of the king, after shaving him, was spared only because he promised never to disclose the secret, but he suffered so acutely from repressing it that, on the advice of a wise man, he confided it to the sandy banks of a stream. Three reeds grew in this spot and were later used by bards to make flutes. The flutes could only repeat: "Portzmarch, le roi Portzmarch a des oreilles de cheval."[61] The utterance of the flutes makes it evident that March was part of the king's personal name as well as an element in the place-name. The setting of this version in Plomarch (formerly Portzmarch) and its currency in the region of the bay of Douarnenez, where the Ile Tristan, so called since 1368, is situated, confirm the connection with King Mark of the Tristan legend.[62]

As in Béroul's account, the sole guardian of the secret is an intimate friend of the king. In both, too, the secret is betrayed in a similar place. In Béroul, the location is "le Gué Aventuros," which must be at a stream since a ford can hardly be anywhere else. In the Breton tale, the barber confides to the sandy bank of a stream where reeds grow. The Breton story also agrees with the Welsh tradition in the multiple murders and in the use of reeds to make a pipe or flute, a detail missing in Béroul. It is still more astonishing to find agreements between the Breton variant and the tenth-century Irish saga: in the Irish, the custodian of the secret is also an intimate of the king, his nephew; and a pipe is made from the three saplings that grew in the place of the revelation just as a flute is made from the three reeds in the Breton tale.[63]

In another Breton version[64] the name of the king with the horse's ears, Gwiwarch, also contains the element *march*. Gwiwarch's barber reveals the oppressive secret to a thicket of elder-bushes growing on the bank of a stream, a feature that significantly corresponds to Béroul's "aube espine" beside "le Gué Aventuros." A variant of this tale also supplies a parallel to March's murder of the dwarf, for Gwiwarch killed the barber after his indiscretion. This particular version resembles as well the Welsh tale of 1693: an elderbush grows from the burial place of the slain barber and is used to provide material for the pipe that publicly proclaims the secret.[65] In addition to a number of other Breton variants of the legend, there is in the museum at Quimper a bas-relief of a head with horse's ears that is known locally as the head of King March.[66]

The Celtic variants indicate that a Breton *conte* must have been Béroul's source for the episode, as the following agreements show:

> 1. The king's name is Mark: the Breton stories are attached to the name March in some form.
>
> 2. The custodian of the secret is a confidant of the king, as in the Portzmarch version.
>
> 3. The Gué Aventuros is the site of the revelation; in the Portzmarch version it takes place on the banks of a stream.
>
> 4. The dwarf reveals the secret to an "aube espine" near the "Gué Aventuros"; in the Gwiwarch variant the secret is confided to a thicket of elder-bushes near a stream.
>
> 5. King Mark kills the dwarf after the revelation; King Gwiwarch kills the barber who has betrayed the secret.

This Breton *conte,* which is only partially preserved in Béroul, must have been more elaborate than the folk-tales now extant. These popular Breton tales, nevertheless, display a clear connection with the Welsh forms of the story in the name of the horse-eared king and in the detail, lacking in Béroul, of the flute fashioned from the reeds. The Breton variant, moreover, agrees with the Castellmarch story in the reeds that grow from the burial place of the king's murdered victims. Both the Welsh and the Breton tales also reveal a relationship to the tenth-century Irish saga. It is reasonable to assume, therefore, that the *conte* which found its way into Béroul's poem had been expanded, like the Irish tale, by a story of the king's jealousy aroused by rumors of the queen's amorous dalliance with his nephew. This circumstance probably facilitated its adaptation to the Welsh and Breton versions of the Tristan legend. The cognomen of the king's nephew in the Irish saga, 'Son of the Unlovely', seems to have split off from the original character as the story passed through Wales and Brittany[67] and to have been absorbed into the personality of the hideous dwarf, who is the confidant of King Mark and who exists in Béroul's romance only to stimulate the king's jealous suspicions. The "intimate friend" in the Portzmarch variant strongly implies that the Irish tradition of a close personal relationship between the king and the guardian of his secret was current in Brittany.[68] The Breton *conte* upon which Béroul's episode was based must also have contained the localization at a thorny thicket by a stream, which is preserved in two of the later folk-tales; and it concluded, most probably, with the slaying of the confidant.[69]

The story of King Mark's ears is an ancient tradition, rooted in the Celtic meaning of his name. Attached to an Irish king with the equivalent equine name of Eochaid, it existed in Ireland in a written form dated in the tenth century. But since this saga shows unmistakable signs of conflation, there must also have been earlier versions. The traditions represented in the tenth-century account of Eochaid migrated to Wales, where they became part of the legend of March son of Meirchion, who was already a famous personage of sufficient magnitude to rank with Arthur and Tristan and to be linked with them. In Wales the composite Irish story of the king with horse's ears who also suspected his wife's fidelity was probably attracted into the orbit of the Tristan traditions, although the extant Welsh tales do not afford enough evidence to permit certainty on this point. The version of 1693, at any rate, shows that the story of March, the king with the horse's ears, was connected with Arthur in Wales.

In Brittany the evidence is clearer. The location of the Portzmarch version in the neighborhood of the Ile Tristan strongly implies that the legend of March with the horse's ears was absorbed into the Tristan legend in Brittany. It is reasonably certain, too, that the hideous dwarf as the king's confidant and the custodian of the secret was already established in Breton tradition since his name, Frocin, seems to be of Breton provenance.[70] And, of course, the setting at the Gué Aventuros near a hawthorn was another Breton contribution that invested the story with the weird connotations of this place of faerie.

All these facts point to the derivation of Béroul's episode from a Breton *conte.* If the story also existed as a local legend in Cornwall, it is unlikely to have been introduced into Béroul's poem from that source. In both Wales and Brittany the story of March and his horse's ears lived continuously in popular tradition at least until the end of the nineteenth century and clung tenaciously to a number of place-names with the element *march.* In contrast to this brisk circulation in Wales and Brittany, the story manifests no vitality in Cornwall, even if it was once current there. Of course, Frocin is called "le nain de Tintaguel," but since Tintagel was the traditional site of Mark's court and the dwarf belonged to his household, this localization is no proof of Cornish origin for Béroul's story of Mark's ears.

To judge from the variety of traditions preserved about King Mark, he must have enjoyed an impressive legendary reputation. He is a monarch of great power, according to the biography of St. Paul Aurelian. In Welsh tradition, he is a chief of the army and the navy of Britain, and one of Arthur's counselors. On a less exalted plane, he fails, in spite of Arthur's help, to steal a single pig from Tristan disguised as a swineherd. And he appears in a grotesque, even sinister light in the vigorous tradition current for more than seven centuries in Wales and Brittany that depicts him as a king with horse's ears who murders his barbers to conceal his deformity.

Although Mark was celebrated in Wales and Brittany, his geographical associations in the Tristan legend are unquestionably centered in Cornwall. His castle Tintagel is the setting for a legend of human tribute that circulated in a form untouched by the Tristan traditions. Since a similar story was one of the earliest to be attached to Tristan, the resemblance may have brought the two figures together. The sources of King Mark's legendary identification with Cornwall are thus to be sought not in the obscure monument at Castle Dôr but rather in the storied ruins of Tintagel.

Notes

1. Cf. Béroul, *Le Roman de Tristan,* ed. E. Muret, rev. L. M. Defourques (CFMA; Paris, 1947), vss. 3432 f.:

   Li rois n'a pas coraige entier,
   Senpres est ci et senpres la.

   All references to Béroul's text in this paper are derived from this edition.

2. J. Loth, *Contributions à l'étude des romans de la Table Ronde* (Paris, 1912), Chapter VI, has argued for the Cornish origin of the Tristan legend. Dissenting views have been expressed by E. Brugger, *MP,* XXII (1924), 159-191; A. Smirnov, *Romania,* XLIII (1914), 121-125; R. S. Loomis, *MLN,* XXXIX (1924), 319-329, among others. Cf. also J. D. Bruce, *Evolution of Arthurian Romance,* 2d ed. (Baltimore, 1928), I, 177-185; P. Rickard, *Britain in Medieval French Literature 1100-1500* (Cambridge, 1956), pp. 93-97; R. Bromwich, *Trans. Honourable Society of Cymmrodorion,* 1953 (1955), pp. 46-49, and in *Studies in Early British History,* ed. N. K. Chadwick (Cambridge, 1954), p. 122 n. 6; C. A. Ralegh Radford, *Journal of the Royal Institution of Cornwall,* N.S. 1 (1951), Appendix.

3. The text was edited by C. Cuissard, *RC,* V (1881-83), 413-460. Cf. S. Baring-Gould and J. Fisher, *Lives of the British Saints* (London, 1907-1913), IV, 75-86; J. F. Kenney, *The Sources for the Early History of Ireland* (New York, 1929), I, 176.

4. F. Lot, *Romania,* XXV (1896), 19; L. Gougaud, *Christianity in Celtic Lands,* trans. M. Joynt (London, 1932), pp. 58 f. St. Paul Aurelian lived in the sixth century and founded the diocese of Léon in Brittany.

5. *RC,* V, 431. As Baring-Gould and Fisher point out, *op. cit.,* IV, 77 n. 2, the phrase about bringing peoples of four languages under his domination is borrowed from Bede, *Historia Ecclesiastica,* Book III, Chapter VI.

6. *THSC,* 1953, pp. 47 f.

7. C. A. Ralegh Radford, *op. cit.* This reading is also that of Professor Kenneth Jackson, according to Mrs. Bromwich, *THSC,* 1953, p. 47 n. 70. For different readings of the name and additional information about the stone, cf. R. A. S. Macalister, *Corpus Inscriptionum Insularum Celticarum* (Dublin, 1945-49), I, 465, 466; *Archaeologia Cambrensis,* LXXXIV (1929), 181; *ibid.,* 5. Ser., XII (1895), 53; *Victoria History of the County of Cornwall,* I (London, 1906), 410; H. O. Hencken, *The Archaeology of Cornwall and Scilly* (London, 1932), p. 231; F. Lot, *Romania,* XXV, 20 f.

8. *RC,* V, 445.

9. R. Fawtier, *La Vie de Saint Samson* (BEHE; Paris, 1912), pp. 64-59.

10. *RC,* V, 421; Fawtier, *op. cit.,* pp. 41 f.

11. *Ibid.,* pp. 64-69; F. Lot, *Mélanges d'histoire bretonne* (Paris, 1907), pp. 450-453, 124-127, 253 f.

12. *Ibid.,* p. 127 n. 1.

13. Gregory of Tours, *Opera,* Part I: *Historia Francorum,* ed. W. Arndt (Hanover, 1885), Book IV, Chapter IV; cf. Fawtier, *op. cit.,* p. 69.

14. H. Zimmer, *ZFSL,* XIII (1891), 65-72; J. Bédier, ed., Thomas, *Le Roman de Tristan* (SATF; Paris, 1902-05), II, 105-108; A. O. Anderson, *Early Sources of Scottish History* (Edinburgh, 1922), I, cxiii-cxxviii; H. M. Chadwick, *Early Scotland* (Cambridge, 1949), pp. 1-49; R. Bromwich, *THSC,* 1953, pp. 35-39. Even Loth, in Académie des Inscriptions, *Comptes rendus,* 1924, p. 128, accepts the derivation of Tristan from the Pictish Drust.

15. J. Loth, *Les Mabinogion* (Paris, 1913), II, 284. Tallwch is not a native Welsh name, and it occurs only as Drystan's patronymic. Since the French romances assign entirely different names to Tristan's father, Tallwch cannot possibly be derived from French sources.

16. M. Deutschbein, *Beiblatt zur Anglia,* XV (1904), 16-21; Bromwich, *THSC,* 1953, pp. 38-43.

17. *Ibid.,* p. 48; Rickard, *op. cit.,* p. 94.

18. Bromwich, *THSC,* 1953, pp. 48 f. Cf. Lot, *Romania,* XXV, 20.

19. Mrs. Bromwich, *op. cit.,* p. 48, suggests that Mark's father may have been King Meirchiawn of Glamorgan, who gave lands to St. Illtud in the early sixth century. J. Rhys, *Hibbert Lectures, 1886* (London, 1888), pp. 271, 650, considered the name Meirchion a kind of reduplication of March.

20. M. Richards, *Breudwyt Ronabwy* (Cardiff, 1948), p. xxxix; Bromwich, in *Studies in Early British History,* pp. 116 f. On traditional material in this tale see R. S. Loomis, *Wales and the Arthurian Legend* (Cardiff, 1956), pp. 96-101.

21. Loth, *Les Mabinogion,* I, 361 f., 373.

22. Peniarth 16, No. 14, ed. R. Bromwich, *Bulletin of the Board of Celtic Studies,* XII (1946), 1-15; this collection of triads is dated in the thirteenth century, *Studies in Early British History,* p. 111 n. 3. The same triad is No. 31 in the Red Book of Hergest collection (fourteenth century), Loth, *Les Mabinogion,* II, 255, 223-226.

23. *Ibid.,* II, 270 f. The Peniarth 16 version (No. 26) is the same except that Kei and Bedwyr are not mentioned. Cf. Bromwich, *THSC,* 1953, pp. 33 f.; J. Bédier, *Tristan,* II, 115.

24. On the triads as native Welsh tradition see Bromwich, *THSC,* 1953, pp. 34 f. and *Studies in Early British History,* pp. 114-118.

25. Another triad (Loth, *Les Mabinogion,* II, 284, No. 81) makes Trystan the nephew of March and the lover of Esyllt, the wife of March, but it is perhaps wise not to rely too heavily upon this triad because, unlike the others, it includes no details that could not

have been derived from the French romances. Trystan, March, Arthur, Kei, and Esyllt also appear together in the *Ystorya Trystan*, ed. Ifor Williams, *Bull. Board of Celtic Studies*, V (1930), 115-129; cf. Bromwich, *THSC*, 1953, pp. 54 f; H. Newstead, *PMLA*, LXV (March 1950), 291-294.

26. R. S. Loomis, *Arthurian Tradition and Chrétien de Troyes* (New York, 1949), pp. 14 f.; *MP*, XXXIII (1936), 231.

27. *Historia Regum Britanniae*, ed. A. Griscom (New York, 1929), pp. 424-426.

28. H. Jenner, *Journal of the Royal Institution of Cornwall*, XXII Part 2 (1927), 191 f.; C. G. Harper, *The Cornish Coast (North)*, (London, 1910), p. 112.

29. Although the early history of Tintagel is obscure, there is little doubt that the promontory was the site of buildings from early times. The formation of the land, which produced the great chasm and caused landslips, would make ruins almost inevitable. The present ruins may date only from Norman times, but there were surely ruins of earlier buildings. Cf. Jenner, *op. cit.*, pp. 190-195; J. Kinsman, *Journal of the British Archaeological Association*, XXXIII (1877), 170-175.

30. *Perlesvaus*, ed. W. A. Nitze and T. A. Jenkins (Chicago, 1932-37), I, 280 f.; II, 319 f.

31. *La Folie Tristan d'Oxford*, ed. E. Hœpffner, 2d ed. (Strasbourg, 1943), vss. 131-140, and p. 19.

32. C. G. Harper, *The Cornish Coast (North)*, p. 116.

33. Gottfried von Strassburg, *Tristan und Isold*, ed. F. Ranke (Berlin, 1930), vs. 6018.

34. *Vulgate Version of the Arthurian Romances*, ed. H. O. Sommer (Washington, 1908-13), IV, 107: "Et il li auoit iure auant & fait tele seurte comme lui plot quil li donroit ce quil li demanderoit. Et il li demanda de cascune meson de sa terre. vn. enfant por lui seruir tant com il li plairoit. et le tierc de toute sa terre." The form Pintagoel is cited *ibid.*, IV, 109 n. 2.

35. *Ibid.*, V, 214 n. 3.

36. Sir Thomas Malory, *Works*, ed. E. Vinaver (Oxford, 1947), I, 272. Here Tyntagyll is associated not with Mark and the Tristan legend but with the begetting of Arthur. The principal story underlying these analogues is discussed by Loomis, *Arthurian Tradition*, pp. 322 f.

37. *Ibid.*, pp. 320-326. Chrétien de Troyes, *Yvain*, Textausgabe ed. W. Foerster, 2d ed. (Halle, 1926), vss. 5256-5770. Cf. also A. Pauphilet, *Le Legs du Moyen Age* (Melun, 1950), p. 123, who has also noted the parallel with Tristan.

38. Gerbert de Montreuil, *La Continuation de Perceval*, ed. Mary Williams (CFMA; Paris, 1922), I, vss. 3309 ff.; also ed. J. L. Weston and J. Bédier, *Romania*, XXXV (1906), 497-530, with useful notes.

39. Béroul, vss. 1155, 2359, 2394, 2438, 2453; Gerbert, vss. 3642, 3844, 3855, 3880.

40. J. Loth, in Académie des Inscriptions, *Comptes rendus*, 1916, pp. 589-593; Bromwich, *THSC*, 1953, pp. 32, 59 f.; Rickard, *op. cit.*, pp. 95-100.

41. Cf. Loomis, *MLN*, XXXIX, 328; Brugger, *MP*, XXVI (1928), 11 f.

42. G. Schoepperle, *Tristan and Isolt* (Frankfurt and London, 1913), II, 269-272; C. Foulon, *Bulletin philologique et historique* 1951-52 (1953), pp. 31-40; Bromwich, *THSC*, 1953, p. 36.

43. W. J. Gruffydd, *Math vab Mathonwy* (Cardiff, 1928), pp. 155, 335-339.

44. For references to other occurrences in folk tales, see Stith Thompson, *Motif-Index of Folk-Literature*, rev. ed., III (Bloomington, Indiana, 1956), F 511.2.2; T. P. Cross, *Motif-Index of Early Irish Literature* (Bloomington, Indiana, 1952), p. 274; J. J. Jones, *Aberystwyth Studies*, XII (1932), 21-33; W. Stokes, *RC*, II (1873-75), 198; W. Crooke, *Folk-Lore*, XXII (1911), 196 f.

45. For a discussion of these names see T. F. O'Rahilly, *Early Irish History and Mythology* (Dublin, 1946), p. 61.

46. K. Meyer, *Otia Merseiana*, III (1903), 46-54; trans. into German by K. Müller-Lisowski, *Irische Volksmärchen* (Jena, 1923), pp. 1-5.

47. Schoepperle, *op. cit.*, II, 397-400; Bromwich, *THSC*, 1953, p. 51.

48. *Op. cit.*, II, 391-446; Bromwich, *THSC*, 1953, pp. 51-54. James Carney, *Studies in Irish Literature and History* (Dublin, 1955), pp. 189-242, considers the Diarmaid saga and other Irish *aitheda* derivatives of the "primitive" Tristan story.

49. The text reads, *Otia Merseiana*, III, 50: "His name was Angus; however, he was not called so, but MacDichoime, for Dichoime (i.e., Unlovely) was his mother's name, and from her the son was so called. For the mother was a good woman, though she was unlovely."

50. Not all Celtic dwarfs were ugly. See Schoepperle, *op. cit.*, I, 241-249; Loomis, *Arthurian Tradition*, pp. 139-145, discusses beautiful, high-minded dwarfs in Celtic and Arthurian fiction.

51. On the fusion of characters see Loomis, *Arthurian Tradition*, pp. 50 f.

52. W. Stokes, *RC*, II, 197-199; trans. in M. Dillon, *The Cycles of the Kings* (Oxford, 1946), pp. 9 f. This story is attached to Labraid Lorc, apparently identical with Labraid Loingsech. The name has no connection with horses. On Labraid Loingsech, cf. O'Rahilly, *Early Irish History and Mythology*, pp. 110-117. The story of Labraid Lorc was repeated by Keating, who seems to be the source of the numerous folk-tale versions collected in modern Ireland (Dillon, *op. cit.*, p. 10 n. 1). At least Keating is doubtless the source of the versions printed by Patrick

Kennedy, *Legendary Fictions of the Irish Celts* (London, 1866), pp. 248-254, for the narrator said (p. 248) that he had heard a schoolmaster read this story in the history of Ireland. For another version and additional references, see G. Dottin, trans., *Contes et légendes d'Irlande* (Le Havre, 1901), pp. 201 f.

53. Loomis, *Arthurian Tradition,* pp. 129 f.

54. The harp and the pipe are obvious duplicates in function. Similarly, the king's nephew, who is said to be skilled in music and who fashions a pipe out of the saplings, is probably a doublet of the harper. The growth of the saplings from the blood of the nephew also suggests another version in which the king actually killed him.

55. Schoepperle, *op. cit.,* II, 270; R. S. Loomis, *Comparative Literature,* II (1950), 291.

56. Historical MSS Commission, *Report on MSS in the Welsh Language,* ed. J. Gwenogvryn Evans, I Part 2 (London, 1899), 834. The Welsh text is printed on p. 837; an English version is given by J. Rhys, *Celtic Folklore, Welsh and Manx* (Oxford, 1901), II, 572 f.

57. Maelgwn Gwynedd is a prominent figure in Welsh tradition: see Loth, *Les Mabinogion,* "Index des noms propres," s.v. Maelgwn de Gwynedd; Bromwich, in *Studies in Early British History,* p. 91 n. 3. His pipers are introduced into this tale probably because tradition recorded a similar experience of theirs: Taliesin placed the bards and minstrels of Maelgwn Gwynedd under a spell so that all that they could do was to pout their lips and play "Blerwm, blerwm" upon their lips with their fingers (*The Mabinogion,* trans. C. Guest, Everyman ed., pp. 272f.). This furnishes a simple but excellent illustration of the syncretic methods customarily used by Welsh story-tellers.

58. J. Rhys, *Y Cymmrodor,* VI (1883), 181-183; *Celtic Folklore,* I, 233 f.

59. *Ibid.,* I, 232, 197; II, 572-574.

60. Béroul, "Index des noms propres," s.v. Artur.

61. *RC,* XIII (1892), 485, quoted from J. Cambry, *Voyage dans le Finistère . . . en 1794 et 1795* (Paris, 1799), II, 287. Cf. P. Sébillot, *Le Folk-lore de France* (Paris, 1904-07), III, 527.

62. On the Ile Tristan, see Loth, *Contributions,* p. 108; *RC,* XXXII (1911), 413; Loth, *Chrestomathie bretonne* (Paris, 1890), p. 235; Brugger, *MP,* XXII, 182.

63. An incomplete Breton version located near Portzall (*Revue des traditions populaires,* I [1886], 327 f.) tells of a chieftain who lived alone and slew the barbers who came to shave him. One youth discovered the secret, and to avoid the fate of the others, he cut off the chieftain's head. This recalls the situation in the Irish saga in which, after the king's nephew has discovered the secret, he threatens to cut off Eochaid's head to save his own life.

64. Sébillot, *Folk-lore de France,* III, 432.

65. *Loc. cit.*

66. *Revue des traditions populaires,* VII (1892), 356-359; C. Foulon, *Bulletin philologique et historique,* 1951-52 (1953), p. 37.

67. On the common phenomenon of fission of characters see Loomis, *Arthurian Tradition,* pp. 51-54.

68. In the Irish version from the Yellow Book of Lecan the hero is merely a widow's son, and there is no hint of any relationship between him and the king.

69. For another Irish parallel to the decapitation of the dwarf see A. H. Krappe, *RF,* XLV (1931), 95-99; H. Newstead, *RPh.,* IX (1956), 275-278.

70. Schoepperle, *op. cit.,* I, 242.

FURTHER READING

Bibliography

Shirt, David J. *The Old French Tristan Poems: A Bibliographical, Guide.* London: Grant and Cutler Ltd., 1980, 186 p.

Bibliographic listing in which the works are grouped by author or version of the legend (i.e., the Beroul fragment, the Thomas fragment, etc.), and are divided into several categories, including manuscript and critical editions; translations; textual comment and exegesis; authorship; literary context; feudal context; moral context; narrative structure; and style.

Criticism

Brégy, Katherine. "Tristram, The Perennial Hero of Romance." *The Catholic World* CXXVII, No. 760 (July 1928): 385-94.

Reviews the plot of the legend in its various versions and describes the story as "sealed indelibly by a pagan sense of Fate," a characteristic which accounts for the tale's immortality.

Cox, Sir George W. and Eustace Hinton Jones. "Sir Tristrem." *Popular Romances of the Middle Ages,* pp. 123-39. New York: Henry Holt and Company, 1880.

Recounts the legend of Tristan and Isolde.

Gardner, Edmund G. "The 'Tristano Riccardiano'." *The Arthurian Legend in Italian Literature,* pp. 64-84. London: J. M. Dent and Sons Ltd., 1930.

Examination of what is likely the earliest Arthurian romance in Italian, *Tristan Riccardiano,* written at the end of the thirteenth or beginning of the fourteenth century. Gardner compares this story to the extant French versions of the Tristan legend.

Loomis, Roger Sherman. "Bleheris and the Tristram Story." *Modern Language Notes* XXXIX, No. 6 (June 1924): 319-29.

>Studies the role of the Welshman Bleheris in the transmission of the Tristan legend.

Newstead, Helaine. "Kaherdin and the Enchanted Pillow: An Episode in the Tristan Legend." *PMLA* 65, No. 2 (March 1950): 290-312.

>Analyzes the story of Kaherdin, Tristan's wife's brother, and his love affair with Isolde's maid. The tale is found in the versions of the Tristan tale by Eilhart and Thomas.

———. "The Origin and Growth of the Tristan Legend." *Arthurian Literature in the Middle Ages: A Collaborative History,* edited by Roger Sherman Loomis, pp. 122-33. Oxford: Clarendon Press, 1959.

>Offers a synopsis of the legend, observes the consistency among the legend's various versions, and discusses the transmission of and additions to the legend by its various authors.

Owen, D. D. R. "Love and Fate: Tristan and Ysolt." *Noble Lovers,* pp. 75-100. London: Phaidon Press Limited, 1975.

>Offers an overview of the legend, its transmission, and its development.

Vinaver, Eugène. "The Prose *Tristan.*" *Arthurian Literature in the Middle Ages: A Collaborative History,* edited by Roger Sherman Loomis, pp. 339-47. Oxford: Clarendon Press, 1959.

>Examines the French prose version of the Tristan legend dating from the early- to mid-thirteenth century, *Le Roman de Tristan de Léonois.* Vinaver focuses particularly on the way in which the prose version of the legend deviates from the conventions of Arthurian romance.

Whitehead, Frederick. "The Early Tristan Poems." *Arthurian Literature in the Middle Ages,* edited by Roger Sherman Loomis, pp. 134-44. Oxford: Clarendon Press, 1959.

>Reviews the authors and dates of the extant versions of the Tristan and Isolde legend and provides an overview of the critical discussion surrounding the origins of the romance.

How to Use This Index

The main references

Calvino, Italo
1923-1985 .... CLC **5, 8, 11, 22, 33, 39,**
73; SSC 3

---

list all author entries in the following Gale Literary Criticism series:

BLC = *Black Literature Criticism*
CLC = *Contemporary Literary Criticism*
CLR = *Children's Literature Review*
CMLC = *Classical and Medieval Literature Criticism*
DA = *DISCovering Authors*
DAB = *DISCovering Authors: British*
DAC = *DISCovering Authors: Canadian*
DAM = *DISCovering Authors: Modules*
    DRAM: Dramatists Module; *MST: Most-Studied Authors Module;*
    MULT: Multicultural Authors Module; *NOV: Novelists Module;*
    POET: Poets Module; *POP: Popular Fiction and Genre Authors Module*
DC = *Drama Criticism*
HLC = *Hispanic Literature Criticism*
LC = *Literature Criticism from 1400 to 1800*
NCLC = *Nineteenth-Century Literature Criticism*
NNAL = *Native North American Literature*
PC = *Poetry Criticism*
SSC = *Short Story Criticism*
TCLC = *Twentieth-Century Literary Criticism*
WLC = *World Literature Criticism, 1500 to the Present*

The cross-references

See also CANR 23; CA 85-88;
obituary CA116

---

list all author entries in the following Gale biographical and literary sources:

AAYA = *Authors & Artists for Young Adults*
AITN = *Authors in the News*
BEST = *Bestsellers*
BW = *Black Writers*
CA = *Contemporary Authors*
CAAS = *Contemporary Authors Autobiography Series*
CABS = *Contemporary Authors Bibliographical Series*
CANR = *Contemporary Authors New Revision Series*
CAP = *Contemporary Authors Permanent Series*
CDALB = *Concise Dictionary of American Literary Biography*
CDBLB = *Concise Dictionary of British Literary Biography*
DLB = *Dictionary of Literary Biography*
DLBD = *Dictionary of Literary Biography Documentary Series*
DLBY = *Dictionary of Literary Biography Yearbook*
HW = *Hispanic Writers*
JRDA = *Junior DISCovering Authors*
MAICYA = *Major Authors and Illustrators for Children and Young Adults*
MTCW = *Major 20th-Century Writers*
SAAS = *Something about the Author Autobiography Series*
SATA = *Something about the Author*
YABC = *Yesterday's Authors of Books for Children*

Literary Criticism Series
Cumulative Author Index

Anaximander c. 610B.C.-c.
546B.C. .... **CMLC 22**

Anaya, Rudolfo A(lfonso) 1937- ...... **CLC 23;**
DAM MULT, NOV; HLC 1
See also AAYA 20; CA 45-48; CAAS 4;
CANR 1, 32, 51; DLB 82, 206; HW 1;
MTCW 1, 2

Andersen, Hans Christian
1805-1875 .... **NCLC 7, 79; DA; DAB;**
DAC; DAM MST, POP; SSC 6; WLC
See also CLR 6; DA3; MAICYA; SATA
100; YABC 1

Anderson, C. Farley
See Mencken, H(enry) L(ouis); Nathan,
George Jean

Anderson, Jessica (Margaret) Queale
1916- .... **CLC 37**
See also CA 9-12R; CANR 4, 62

Anderson, Jon (Victor) 1940- . **CLC 9; DAM**
POET
See also CA 25-28R; CANR 20

Anderson, Lindsay (Gordon)
1923-1994 .... **CLC 20**
See also CA 125; 128; 146; CANR 77

Anderson, Maxwell 1888-1959 .... **TCLC 2;**
DAM DRAM
See also CA 105; 152; DLB 7, 228; MTCW
2

Anderson, Poul (William) 1926- .... **CLC 15**
See also AAYA 5, 34; CA 1-4R, 181; CAAE
181; CAAS 2; CANR 2, 15, 34, 64; CLR
58; DLB 8; INT CANR-15; MTCW 1, 2;
SATA 90; SATA-Brief 39; SATA-Essay
106

Anderson, Robert (Woodruff)
1917- .... **CLC 23; DAM DRAM**
See also AITN 1; CA 21-24R; CANR 32;
DLB 7

Anderson, Sherwood 1876-1941 ..... **TCLC 1,**
10, 24; DA; DAB; DAC; DAM MST,
NOV; SSC 1; WLC
See also AAYA 30; CA 104; 121; CANR
61; CDALB 1917-1929; DA3; DLB 4, 9,
86; DLBD 1; MTCW 1, 2

Andier, Pierre
See Desnos, Robert

Andouard
See Giraudoux, (Hippolyte) Jean

Andrade, Carlos Drummond de CLC 18
See also Drummond de Andrade, Carlos

Andrade, Mario de 1893-1945 .... **TCLC 43**

Andreae, Johann V(alentin)
1586-1654 .... **LC 32**
See also DLB 164

Andreas-Salome, Lou 1861-1937 ... **TCLC 56**
See also CA 178; DLB 66

Andress, Lesley
See Sanders, Lawrence

Andrewes, Lancelot 1555-1626 .... **LC 5**
See also DLB 151, 172

Andrews, Cicily Fairfield
See West, Rebecca

Andrews, Elton V.
See Pohl, Frederik

Andreyev, Leonid (Nikolaevich)
1871-1919 .... **TCLC 3**
See also CA 104; 185

Andric, Ivo 1892-1975 .... **CLC 8; SSC 36**
See also CA 81-84; 57-60; CANR 43, 60;
DLB 147; MTCW 1

Androvar
See Prado (Calvo), Pedro

Angelique, Pierre
See Bataille, Georges

Angell, Roger 1920- .... **CLC 26**
See also CA 57-60; CANR 13, 44, 70; DLB
171, 185

Angelou, Maya 1928- .... **CLC 12, 35, 64, 77;**
BLC 1; DA; DAB; DAC; DAM MST,
MULT, POET, POP; PC 32; WLCS
See also AAYA 7, 20; BW 2, 3; CA 65-68;
CANR 19, 42, 65; CDALBS; CLR 53;
DA3; DLB 38; MTCW 1, 2; SATA 49

Anna Comnena 1083-1153 .... **CMLC 25**

Annensky, Innokenty (Fyodorovich)
1856-1909 .... **TCLC 14**
See also CA 110; 155

Annunzio, Gabriele d'
See D'Annunzio, Gabriele

Anodos
See Coleridge, Mary E(lizabeth)

Anon, Charles Robert
See Pessoa, Fernando (Antonio Nogueira)

Anouilh, Jean (Marie Lucien Pierre)
1910-1987 .... **CLC 1, 3, 8, 13, 40, 50;**
DAM DRAM; DC 8
See also CA 17-20R; 123; CANR 32;
MTCW 1, 2

Anthony, Florence
See Ai

Anthony, John
See Ciardi, John (Anthony)

Anthony, Peter
See Shaffer, Anthony (Joshua); Shaffer, Peter (Levin)

Anthony, Piers 1934- .... **CLC 35; DAM POP**
See also AAYA 11; CA 21-24R; CANR 28,
56, 73; DLB 8; MTCW 1, 2; SAAS 22;
SATA 84

Anthony, Susan B(rownell)
1916-1991 .... **TCLC 84**
See also CA 89-92; 134

Antoine, Marc
See Proust, (Valentin-Louis-George-
Eugene-) Marcel

Antoninus, Brother
See Everson, William (Oliver)

Antonioni, Michelangelo 1912- .... **CLC 20**
See also CA 73-76; CANR 45, 77

Antschel, Paul 1920-1970
See Celan, Paul
See also CA 85-88; CANR 33, 61; MTCW
1

Anwar, Chairil 1922-1949 .... **TCLC 22**
See also CA 121

Anzaldua, Gloria (Evanjelina) 1942-
See also CA 175; DLB 122; HLCS 1

Apess, William 1798-1839(?) .... **NCLC 73;**
DAM MULT
See also DLB 175; NNAL

Apollinaire, Guillaume 1880-1918 .. **TCLC 3,**
8, 51; DAM POET; PC 7
See also CA 152; MTCW 1

Appelfeld, Aharon 1932- ... **CLC 23, 47; SSC**
42
See also CA 112; 133; CANR 86

Apple, Max (Isaac) 1941- .... **CLC 9, 33**
See also CA 81-84; CANR 19, 54; DLB
130

Appleman, Philip (Dean) 1926- .... **CLC 51**
See also CA 13-16R; CAAS 18; CANR 6,
29, 56

Appleton, Lawrence
See Lovecraft, H(oward) P(hillips)

Apteryx
See Eliot, T(homas) S(tearns)

Apuleius, (Lucius Madaurensis)
125(?)-175(?) .... **CMLC 1**
See also DLB 211

Aquin, Hubert 1929-1977 .... **CLC 15**
See also CA 105; DLB 53

Aquinas, Thomas 1224(?)-1274 ..... **CMLC 33**
See also DLB 115

Aragon, Louis 1897-1982 .. **CLC 3, 22; DAM**
NOV, POET
See also CA 69-72; 108; CANR 28, 71;
DLB 72; MTCW 1, 2

Arany, Janos 1817-1882 .... **NCLC 34**

Aranyos, Kakay
See Mikszath, Kalman

Arbuthnot, John 1667-1735 .... **LC 1**
See also DLB 101

Archer, Herbert Winslow
See Mencken, H(enry) L(ouis)

Archer, Jeffrey (Howard) 1940- ...... **CLC 28;**
DAM POP
See also AAYA 16; BEST 89:3; CA 77-80;
CANR 22, 52; DA3; INT CANR-22

Archer, Jules 1915- .... **CLC 12**
See also CA 9-12R; CANR 6, 69; SAAS 5;
SATA 4, 85

Archer, Lee
See Ellison, Harlan (Jay)

Arden, John 1930- .... **CLC 6, 13, 15; DAM**
DRAM
See also CA 13-16R; CAAS 4; CANR 31,
65, 67; DLB 13; MTCW 1

Arenas, Reinaldo 1943-1990 . **CLC 41; DAM**
MULT; HLC 1
See also CA 124; 128; 133; CANR 73; DLB
145; HW 1; MTCW 1

Arendt, Hannah 1906-1975 .... **CLC 66, 98**
See also CA 17-20R; 61-64; CANR 26, 60;
MTCW 1, 2

Aretino, Pietro 1492-1556 .... **LC 12**

Arghezi, Tudor 1880-1967 .... **CLC 80**
See also Theodorescu, Ion N.
See also CA 167; DLB 220

Arguedas, Jose Maria 1911-1969 .... **CLC 10,**
18; HLCS 1
See also CA 89-92; CANR 73; DLB 113;
HW 1

Argueta, Manlio 1936- .... **CLC 31**
See also CA 131; CANR 73; DLB 145; HW
1

Arias, Ron(ald Francis) 1941-
See also CA 131; CANR 81; DAM MULT;
DLB 82; HLC 1; HW 1, 2; MTCW 2

Ariosto, Ludovico 1474-1533 .... **LC 6**

Aristides
See Epstein, Joseph

Aristophanes 450B.C.-385B.C. .... **CMLC 4;**
DA; DAB; DAC; DAM DRAM, MST;
DC 2; WLCS
See also DA3; DLB 176

Aristotle 384B.C.-322B.C. .... **CMLC 31; DA;**
DAB; DAC; DAM MST; WLCS
See also DA3; DLB 176

Arlt, Roberto (Godofredo Christophersen)
1900-1942 .... **TCLC 29; DAM MULT;**
HLC 1
See also CA 123; 131; CANR 67; HW 1, 2

Armah, Ayi Kwei 1939- ..... **CLC 5, 33, 136;**
BLC 1; DAM MULT, POET
See also BW 1; CA 61-64; CANR 21, 64;
DLB 117; MTCW 1

Armatrading, Joan 1950- .... **CLC 17**
See also CA 114; 186

Arnette, Robert
See Silverberg, Robert

Arnim, Achim von (Ludwig Joachim von
Arnim) 1781-1831 ..... **NCLC 5; SSC 29**
See also DLB 90

Arnim, Bettina von 1785-1859 .... **NCLC 38**
See also DLB 90

Arnold, Matthew 1822-1888 ..... **NCLC 6, 29,**
89; DA; DAB; DAC; DAM MST,
POET; PC 5; WLC
See also CDBLB 1832-1890; DLB 32, 57

Arnold, Thomas 1795-1842 .... **NCLC 18**
See also DLB 55

Baker, Elliott 1922- .... **CLC 8**
    See also CA 45-48; CANR 2, 63
Baker, Jean H. TCLC 3, 10
    See also Russell, George William
Baker, Nicholson 1957- .... **CLC 61; DAM POP**
    See CA 135; CANR 63; DA3; DLB 227
Baker, Ray Stannard 1870-1946 .... **TCLC 47**
    See also CA 118
Baker, Russell (Wayne) 1925- .... **CLC 31**
    See also BEST 89:4; CA 57-60; CANR 11, 41, 59; MTCW 1, 2
Bakhtin, M.
    See Bakhtin, Mikhail Mikhailovich
Bakhtin, M. M.
    See Bakhtin, Mikhail Mikhailovich
Bakhtin, Mikhail
    See Bakhtin, Mikhail Mikhailovich
Bakhtin, Mikhail Mikhailovich
    1895-1975 .... **CLC 83**
    See also CA 128; 113
Bakshi, Ralph 1938(?)- .... **CLC 26**
    See also CA 112; 138
Bakunin, Mikhail (Alexandrovich)
    1814-1876 .... **NCLC 25, 58**
Baldwin, James (Arthur) 1924-1987 . **CLC 1, 2, 3, 4, 5, 8, 13, 15, 17, 42, 50, 67, 90, 127; BLC 1; DA; DAB; DAC; DAM MST, MULT, NOV, POP; DC 1; SSC 10, 33; WLC**
    See also AAYA 4, 34; BW 1; CA 1-4R; 124; CABS 1; CANR 3, 24; CDALB 1941-1968; DA3; DLB 2, 7, 33; DLBY 87; MTCW 1, 2; SATA 9; SATA-Obit 54
Bale, John 1495-1563 .... **LC 62**
    See also DLB 132
Ballard, J(ames) G(raham) 1930- . **CLC 3, 6, 14, 36; DAM NOV, POP; SSC 1**
    See also AAYA 3; CA 5-8R; CANR 15, 39, 65; DA3; DLB 14, 207; MTCW 1, 2; SATA 93
Balmont, Konstantin (Dmitriyevich)
    1867-1943 .... **TCLC 11**
    See also CA 109; 155
Baltausis, Vincas
    See Mikszath, Kalman
Balzac, Honore de 1799-1850 ... **NCLC 5, 35, 53; DA; DAB; DAC; DAM MST, NOV; SSC 5; WLC**
    See also DA3; DLB 119
Bambara, Toni Cade 1939-1995 ...... **CLC 19, 88; BLC 1; DA; DAC; DAM MST, MULT; SSC 35; WLCS**
    See also AAYA 5; BW 2, 3; CA 29-32R; 150; CANR 24, 49, 81; CDALBS; DA3; DLB 38; MTCW 1, 2; SATA 112
Bamdad, A.
    See Shamlu, Ahmad
Banat, D. R.
    See Bradbury, Ray (Douglas)
Bancroft, Laura
    See Baum, L(yman) Frank
Banim, John 1798-1842 .... **NCLC 13**
    See also DLB 116, 158, 159
Banim, Michael 1796-1874 .... **NCLC 13**
    See also DLB 158, 159
Banjo, The
    See Paterson, A(ndrew) B(arton)
Banks, Iain
    See Banks, Iain M(enzies)
Banks, Iain M(enzies) 1954- .... **CLC 34**
    See also CA 123; 128; CANR 61; DLB 194; INT 128
Banks, Lynne Reid CLC 23
    See also Reid Banks, Lynne
    See also AAYA 6

Banks, Russell 1940- .... **CLC 37, 72; SSC 42**
    See also CA 65-68; CAAS 15; CANR 19, 52, 73; DLB 130
Banville, John 1945- .... **CLC 46, 118**
    See also CA 117; 128; DLB 14; INT 128
Banville, Theodore (Faullain) de
    1832-1891 .... **NCLC 9**
Baraka, Amiri 1934- . **CLC 1, 2, 3, 5, 10, 14, 33, 115; BLC 1; DA; DAC; DAM MST, MULT, POET, POP; DC 6; PC 4; WLCS**
    See also Jones, LeRoi
    See also BW 2, 3; CA 21-24R; CABS 3; CANR 27, 38, 61; CDALB 1941-1968; DA3; DLB 5, 7, 16, 38; DLBD 8; MTCW 1, 2
Barbauld, Anna Laetitia
    1743-1825 .... **NCLC 50**
    See also DLB 107, 109, 142, 158
Barbellion, W. N. P. TCLC 24
    See also Cummings, Bruce F(rederick)
Barbera, Jack (Vincent) 1945- .... **CLC 44**
    See also CA 110; CANR 45
Barbey d'Aurevilly, Jules Amedee
    1808-1889 .... **NCLC 1; SSC 17**
    See also DLB 119
Barbour, John c. 1316-1395 .... **CMLC 33**
    See also DLB 146
Barbusse, Henri 1873-1935 .... **TCLC 5**
    See also CA 105; 154; DLB 65
Barclay, Bill
    See Moorcock, Michael (John)
Barclay, William Ewert
    See Moorcock, Michael (John)
Barea, Arturo 1897-1957 .... **TCLC 14**
    See also CA 111
Barfoot, Joan 1946- .... **CLC 18**
    See also CA 105
Barham, Richard Harris
    1788-1845 .... **NCLC 77**
    See also DLB 159
Baring, Maurice 1874-1945 .... **TCLC 8**
    See also CA 105; 168; DLB 34
Baring-Gould, Sabine 1834-1924 ... **TCLC 88**
    See also DLB 156, 190
Barker, Clive 1952- .... **CLC 52; DAM POP**
    See also AAYA 10; BEST 90:3; CA 121; 129; CANR 71; DA3; INT 129; MTCW 1, 2
Barker, George Granville
    1913-1991 .... **CLC 8, 48; DAM POET**
    See also CA 9-12R; 135; CANR 7, 38; DLB 20; MTCW 1
Barker, Harley Granville
    See Granville-Barker, Harley
    See also DLB 10
Barker, Howard 1946- .... **CLC 37**
    See also CA 102; DLB 13, 233
Barker, Jane 1652-1732 .... **LC 42**
Barker, Pat(ricia) 1943- .... **CLC 32, 94**
    See also CA 117; 122; CANR 50; INT 122
Barlach, Ernst (Heinrich)
    1870-1938 .... **TCLC 84**
    See also CA 178; DLB 56, 118
Barlow, Joel 1754-1812 .... **NCLC 23**
    See also DLB 37
Barnard, Mary (Ethel) 1909- .... **CLC 48**
    See also CA 21-22; CAP 2
Barnes, Djuna 1892-1982 .... **CLC 3, 4, 8, 11, 29, 127; SSC 3**
    See also CA 9-12R; 107; CANR 16, 55; DLB 4, 9, 45; MTCW 1, 2
Barnes, Julian (Patrick) 1946- .... **CLC 42; DAB**
    See also CA 102; CANR 19, 54; DLB 194; DLBY 93; MTCW 1
Barnes, Peter 1931- .... **CLC 5, 56**
    See also CA 65-68; CAAS 12; CANR 33, 34, 64; DLB 13, 233; MTCW 1

Barnes, William 1801-1886 .... **NCLC 75**
    See also DLB 32
Baroja (y Nessi), Pio 1872-1956 ..... **TCLC 8; HLC 1**
    See also CA 104
Baron, David
    See Pinter, Harold
Baron Corvo
    See Rolfe, Frederick (William Serafino Austin Lewis Mary)
Barondess, Sue K(aufman)
    1926-1977 .... **CLC 8**
    See also Kaufman, Sue
    See also CA 1-4R; 69-72; CANR 1
Baron de Teive
    See Pessoa, Fernando (Antonio Nogueira)
Baroness Von S.
    See Zangwill, Israel
Barres, (Auguste-) Maurice
    1862-1923 .... **TCLC 47**
    See also CA 164; DLB 123
Barreto, Afonso Henrique de Lima
    See Lima Barreto, Afonso Henrique de
Barrett, (Roger) Syd 1946- .... **CLC 35**
Barrett, William (Christopher)
    1913-1992 .... **CLC 27**
    See also CA 13-16R; 139; CANR 11, 67; INT CANR-11
Barrie, J(ames) M(atthew)
    1860-1937 .... **TCLC 2; DAB; DAM DRAM**
    See also CA 104; 136; CANR 77; CDBLB 1890-1914; CLR 16; DA3; DLB 10, 141, 156; MAICYA; MTCW 1; SATA 100; YABC 1
Barrington, Michael
    See Moorcock, Michael (John)
Barrol, Grady
    See Bograd, Larry
Barry, Mike
    See Malzberg, Barry N(athaniel)
Barry, Philip 1896-1949 .... **TCLC 11**
    See also CA 109; DLB 7, 228
Bart, Andre Schwarz
    See Schwarz-Bart, Andre
Barth, John (Simmons) 1930- ... **CLC 1, 2, 3, 5, 7, 9, 10, 14, 27, 51, 89; DAM NOV; SSC 10**
    See also AITN 1, 2; CA 1-4R; CABS 1; CANR 5, 23, 49, 64; DLB 2, 227; MTCW 1
Barthelme, Donald 1931-1989 ... **CLC 1, 2, 3, 5, 6, 8, 13, 23, 46, 59, 115; DAM NOV; SSC 2**
    See also CA 21-24R; 129; CANR 20, 58; DA3; DLB 2; DLBY 80, 89; MTCW 1, 2; SATA 7; SATA-Obit 62
Barthelme, Frederick 1943- ...... **CLC 36, 117**
    See also CA 114; 122; CANR 77; DLBY 85; INT 122
Barthes, Roland (Gerard)
    1915-1980 .... **CLC 24, 83**
    See also CA 130; 97-100; CANR 66; MTCW 1, 2
Barzun, Jacques (Martin) 1907- ...... **CLC 51**
    See also CA 61-64; CANR 22
Bashevis, Isaac
    See Singer, Isaac Bashevis
Bashkirtseff, Marie 1859-1884 .... **NCLC 27**
Basho
    See Matsuo Basho
Basil of Caesaria c. 330-379 .... **CMLC 35**
Bass, Kingsley B., Jr.
    See Bullins, Ed
Bass, Rick 1958- .... **CLC 79**
    See also CA 126; CANR 53, 93; DLB 212
Bassani, Giorgio 1916- .... **CLC 9**
    See also CA 65-68; CANR 33; DLB 128, 177; MTCW 1

Benet, Stephen Vincent 1898-1943 . **TCLC 7; DAM POET; SSC 10**
See also CA 104; 152; DA3; DLB 4, 48, 102; DLBY 97; MTCW 1; YABC 1

Benet, William Rose 1886-1950 .... **TCLC 28; DAM POET**
See also CA 118; 152; DLB 45

Benford, Gregory (Albert) 1941- ..... **CLC 52**
See also CA 69-72; 175; CAAE 175; CAAS 27; CANR 12, 24, 49; DLBY 82

Bengtsson, Frans (Gunnar) 1894-1954 .... **TCLC 48**
See also CA 170

Benjamin, David
See Slavitt, David R(ytman)

Benjamin, Lois
See Gould, Lois

Benjamin, Walter 1892-1940 .... **TCLC 39**
See also CA 164

Benn, Gottfried 1886-1956 .... **TCLC 3**
See also CA 106; 153; DLB 56

Bennett, Alan 1934- .... **CLC 45, 77; DAB; DAM MST**
See also CA 103; CANR 35, 55; MTCW 1, 2

Bennett, (Enoch) Arnold 1867-1931 .... **TCLC 5, 20**
See also CA 106; 155; CDBLB 1890-1914; DLB 10, 34, 98, 135; MTCW 2

Bennett, Elizabeth
See Mitchell, Margaret (Munnerlyn)

Bennett, George Harold 1930-
See Bennett, Hal
See also BW 1; CA 97-100; CANR 87

Bennett, Hal CLC 5
See also Bennett, George Harold
See also DLB 33

Bennett, Jay 1912- .... **CLC 35**
See also AAYA 10; CA 69-72; CANR 11, 42, 79; JRDA; SAAS 4; SATA 41, 87; SATA-Brief 27

Bennett, Louise (Simone) 1919- ...... **CLC 28; BLC 1; DAM MULT**
See also BW 2, 3; CA 151; DLB 117

Benson, E(dward) F(rederic) 1867-1940 .... **TCLC 27**
See also CA 114; 157; DLB 135, 153

Benson, Jackson J. 1930- .... **CLC 34**
See also CA 25-28R; DLB 111

Benson, Sally 1900-1972 .... **CLC 17**
See also CA 19-20; 37-40R; CAP 1; SATA 1, 35; SATA-Obit 27

Benson, Stella 1892-1933 .... **TCLC 17**
See also CA 117; 155; DLB 36, 162

Bentham, Jeremy 1748-1832 .... **NCLC 38**
See also DLB 107, 158

Bentley, E(dmund) C(lerihew) 1875-1956 .... **TCLC 12**
See also CA 108; DLB 70

Bentley, Eric (Russell) 1916- .... **CLC 24**
See also CA 5-8R; CANR 6, 67; INT CANR-6

Beranger, Pierre Jean de 1780-1857 .... **NCLC 34**

Berdyaev, Nicolas
See Berdyaev, Nikolai (Aleksandrovich)

Berdyaev, Nikolai (Aleksandrovich) 1874-1948 .... **TCLC 67**
See also CA 120; 157

Berdyayev, Nikolai (Aleksandrovich)
See Berdyaev, Nikolai (Aleksandrovich)

Berendt, John (Lawrence) 1939- ...... **CLC 86**
See also CA 146; CANR 75, 93; DA3; MTCW 1

Beresford, J(ohn) D(avys) 1873-1947 .... **TCLC 81**
See also CA 112; 155; DLB 162, 178, 197

Bergelson, David 1884-1952 .... **TCLC 81**

Berger, Colonel
See Malraux, (Georges-)Andre

Berger, John (Peter) 1926- .... **CLC 2, 19**
See also CA 81-84; CANR 51, 78; DLB 14, 207

Berger, Melvin H. 1927- .... **CLC 12**
See also CA 5-8R; CANR 4; CLR 32; SAAS 2; SATA 5, 88

Berger, Thomas (Louis) 1924- .. **CLC 3, 5, 8, 11, 18, 38; DAM NOV**
See also CA 1-4R; CANR 5, 28, 51; DLB 2; DLBY 80; INT CANR-28; MTCW 1, 2

Bergman, (Ernst) Ingmar 1918- ...... **CLC 16, 72**
See also CA 81-84; CANR 33, 70; MTCW 2

Bergson, Henri(-Louis) 1859-1941 . **TCLC 32**
See also CA 164

Bergstein, Eleanor 1938- .... **CLC 4**
See also CA 53-56; CANR 5

Berkoff, Steven 1937- .... **CLC 56**
See also CA 104; CANR 72

Bermant, Chaim (Icyk) 1929- .... **CLC 40**
See also CA 57-60; CANR 6, 31, 57

Bern, Victoria
See Fisher, M(ary) F(rances) K(ennedy)

Bernanos, (Paul Louis) Georges 1888-1948 .... **TCLC 3**
See also CA 104; 130; DLB 72

Bernard, April 1956- .... **CLC 59**
See also CA 131

Berne, Victoria
See Fisher, M(ary) F(rances) K(ennedy)

Bernhard, Thomas 1931-1989 ..... **CLC 3, 32, 61**
See also CA 85-88; 127; CANR 32, 57; DLB 85, 124; MTCW 1

Bernhardt, Sarah (Henriette Rosine) 1844-1923 .... **TCLC 75**
See also CA 157

Berriault, Gina 1926-1999 .... **CLC 54, 109; SSC 30**
See also CA 116; 129; 185; CANR 66; DLB 130

Berrigan, Daniel 1921- .... **CLC 4**
See also CA 33-36R; CAAE 187; CAAS 1; CANR 11, 43, 78; DLB 5

Berrigan, Edmund Joseph Michael, Jr. 1934-1983
See Berrigan, Ted
See also CA 61-64; 110; CANR 14

Berrigan, Ted CLC 37
See also Berrigan, Edmund Joseph Michael, Jr.
See also DLB 5, 169

Berry, Charles Edward Anderson 1931-
See Berry, Chuck
See also CA 115

Berry, Chuck CLC 17
See also Berry, Charles Edward Anderson

Berry, Jonas
See Ashbery, John (Lawrence)

Berry, Wendell (Erdman) 1934- ... **CLC 4, 6, 8, 27, 46; DAM POET; PC 28**
See also AITN 1; CA 73-76; CANR 50, 73; DLB 5, 6; MTCW 1

Berryman, John 1914-1972 ... **CLC 1, 2, 3, 4, 6, 8, 10, 13, 25, 62; DAM POET**
See also CA 13-16; 33-36R; CABS 2; CANR 35; CAP 1; CDALB 1941-1968; DLB 48; MTCW 1, 2

Bertolucci, Bernardo 1940- .... **CLC 16**
See also CA 106

Berton, Pierre (Francis Demarigny) 1920- .... **CLC 104**
See also CA 1-4R; CANR 2, 56; DLB 68; SATA 99

Bertrand, Aloysius 1807-1841 .... **NCLC 31**

Bertran de Born c. 1140-1215 .... **CMLC 5**

Besant, Annie (Wood) 1847-1933 ..... **TCLC 9**
See also CA 105; 185

Bessie, Alvah 1904-1985 .... **CLC 23**
See also CA 5-8R; 116; CANR 2, 80; DLB 26

Bethlen, T. D.
See Silverberg, Robert

Beti, Mongo CLC 27; BLC 1; DAM MULT
See also Biyidi, Alexandre
See also CANR 79

Betjeman, John 1906-1984 ...... **CLC 2, 6, 10, 34, 43; DAB; DAM MST, POET**
See also CA 9-12R; 112; CANR 33, 56; CDBLB 1945-1960; DA3; DLB 20; DLBY 84; MTCW 1, 2

Bettelheim, Bruno 1903-1990 .... **CLC 79**
See also CA 81-84; 131; CANR 23, 61; DA3; MTCW 1, 2

Betti, Ugo 1892-1953 .... **TCLC 5**
See also CA 104; 155

Betts, Doris (Waugh) 1932- ...... **CLC 3, 6, 28**
See also CA 13-16R; CANR 9, 66, 77; DLBY 82; INT CANR-9

Bevan, Alistair
See Roberts, Keith (John Kingston)

Bey, Pilaff
See Douglas, (George) Norman

Bialik, Chaim Nachman 1873-1934 .... **TCLC 25**
See also CA 170

Bickerstaff, Isaac
See Swift, Jonathan

Bidart, Frank 1939- .... **CLC 33**
See also CA 140

Bienek, Horst 1930- .... **CLC 7, 11**
See also CA 73-76; DLB 75

Bierce, Ambrose (Gwinett) 1842-1914(?) .... **TCLC 1, 7, 44; DA; DAC; DAM MST; SSC 9; WLC**
See also CA 104; 139; CANR 78; CDALB 1865-1917; DA3; DLB 11, 12, 23, 71, 74, 186

Biggers, Earl Derr 1884-1933 .... **TCLC 65**
See also CA 108; 153

Billings, Josh
See Shaw, Henry Wheeler

Billington, (Lady) Rachel (Mary) 1942- .... **CLC 43**
See also AITN 2; CA 33-36R; CANR 44

Binyon, T(imothy) J(ohn) 1936- .... **CLC 34**
See also CA 111; CANR 28

Bion 335B.C.-245B.C. .... **CMLC 39**

Bioy Casares, Adolfo 1914-1999 ... **CLC 4, 8, 13, 88; DAM MULT; HLC 1; SSC 17**
See also CA 29-32R; 177; CANR 19, 43, 66; DLB 113; HW 1, 2; MTCW 1, 2

Bird, Cordwainer
See Ellison, Harlan (Jay)

Bird, Robert Montgomery 1806-1854 .... **NCLC 1**
See also DLB 202

Birkerts, Sven 1951- .... **CLC 116**
See also CA 128; 133; 176; CAAE 176; CAAS 29; INT 133

Birney, (Alfred) Earle 1904-1995 .. **CLC 1, 4, 6, 11; DAC; DAM MST, POET**
See also CA 1-4R; CANR 5, 20; DLB 88; MTCW 1

Biruni, al 973-1048(?) .... **CMLC 28**

Bishop, Elizabeth 1911-1979 ..... **CLC 1, 4, 9, 13, 15, 32; DA; DAC; DAM MST, POET; PC 3**
See also CA 5-8R; 89-92; CABS 2; CANR 26, 61; CDALB 1968-1988; DA3; DLB 5, 169; MTCW 1, 2; SATA-Obit 24

Buell, John (Edward) 1927- .... **CLC 10**
See also CA 1-4R; CANR 71; DLB 53

Buero Vallejo, Antonio 1916-2000 ... **CLC 15, 46**
See also CA 106; CANR 24, 49, 75; HW 1; MTCW 1, 2

Bufalino, Gesualdo 1920(?)- .... **CLC 74**
See also DLB 196

Bugayev, Boris Nikolayevich 1880-1934 .... **TCLC 7; PC 11**
See also Bely, Andrey
See also CA 104; 165; MTCW 1

Bukowski, Charles 1920-1994 ... **CLC 2, 5, 9, 41, 82, 108; DAM NOV, POET; PC 18**
See also CA 17-20R; 144; CANR 40, 62; DA3; DLB 5, 130, 169; MTCW 1, 2

Bulgakov, Mikhail (Afanas'evich) 1891-1940 . **TCLC 2, 16; DAM DRAM, NOV; SSC 18**
See also CA 105; 152

Bulgya, Alexander Alexandrovich 1901-1956 .... **TCLC 53**
See also Fadeyev, Alexander
See also CA 117; 181

Bullins, Ed 1935- .... **CLC 1, 5, 7; BLC 1; DAM DRAM, MULT; DC 6**
See also BW 2, 3; CA 49-52; CAAS 16; CANR 24, 46, 73; DLB 7, 38; MTCW 1, 2

Bulwer-Lytton, Edward (George Earle Lytton) 1803-1873 .... **NCLC 1, 45**
See also DLB 21

Bunin, Ivan Alexeyevich 1870-1953 .... **TCLC 6; SSC 5**
See also CA 104

Bunting, Basil 1900-1985 ..... **CLC 10, 39, 47; DAM POET**
See also CA 53-56; 115; CANR 7; DLB 20

Bunuel, Luis 1900-1983 .. **CLC 16, 80; DAM MULT; HLC 1**
See also CA 101; 110; CANR 32, 77; HW 1

Bunyan, John 1628-1688 ... **LC 4; DA; DAB; DAC; DAM MST; WLC**
See also CDBLB 1660-1789; DLB 39

Burckhardt, Jacob (Christoph) 1818-1897 .... **NCLC 49**

Burford, Eleanor
See Hibbert, Eleanor Alice Burford

Burgess, Anthony -1993 .... **CLC 1, 2, 4, 5, 8, 10, 13, 15, 22, 40, 62, 81, 94; DAB**
See also Wilson, John (Anthony) Burgess
See also AAYA 25; AITN 1; CDBLB 1960 to Present; DLB 14, 194; DLBY 98; MTCW 1

Burke, Edmund 1729(?)-1797 .... **LC 7, 36; DA; DAB; DAC; DAM MST; WLC**
See also DA3; DLB 104

Burke, Kenneth (Duva) 1897-1993 ... **CLC 2, 24**
See also CA 5-8R; 143; CANR 39, 74; DLB 45, 63; MTCW 1, 2

Burke, Leda
See Garnett, David

Burke, Ralph
See Silverberg, Robert

Burke, Thomas 1886-1945 .... **TCLC 63**
See also CA 113; 155; DLB 197

Burney, Fanny 1752-1840 .... **NCLC 12, 54**
See also DLB 39

Burns, Robert 1759-1796 . **LC 3, 29, 40; DA; DAB; DAC; DAM MST, POET; PC 6; WLC**
See also CDBLB 1789-1832; DA3; DLB 109

Burns, Tex
See L'Amour, Louis (Dearborn)

Burnshaw, Stanley 1906- .... **CLC 3, 13, 44**
See also CA 9-12R; DLB 48; DLBY 97

Burr, Anne 1937- .... **CLC 6**
See also CA 25-28R

Burroughs, Edgar Rice 1875-1950 . **TCLC 2, 32; DAM NOV**
See also AAYA 11; CA 104; 132; DA3; DLB 8; MTCW 1, 2; SATA 41

Burroughs, William S(eward) 1914-1997 .. **CLC 1, 2, 5, 15, 22, 42, 75, 109; DA; DAB; DAC; DAM MST, NOV, POP; WLC**
See also AITN 2; CA 9-12R; 160; CANR 20, 52; DA3; DLB 2, 8, 16, 152; DLBY 81, 97; MTCW 1, 2

Burton, Sir Richard F(rancis) 1821-1890 .... **NCLC 42**
See also DLB 55, 166, 184

Busch, Frederick 1941- .... **CLC 7, 10, 18, 47**
See also CA 33-36R; CAAS 1; CANR 45, 73, 92; DLB 6

Bush, Ronald 1946- .... **CLC 34**
See also CA 136

Bustos, F(rancisco)
See Borges, Jorge Luis

Bustos Domecq, H(onorio)
See Bioy Casares, Adolfo; Borges, Jorge Luis

Butler, Octavia E(stelle) 1947- .... **CLC 38, 121; BLCS; DAM MULT, POP**
See also AAYA 18; BW 2, 3; CA 73-76; CANR 12, 24, 38, 73; CLR 65; DA3; DLB 33; MTCW 1, 2; SATA 84

Butler, Robert Olen (Jr.) 1945- .... **CLC 81; DAM POP**
See also CA 112; CANR 66; DLB 173; INT 112; MTCW 1

Butler, Samuel 1612-1680 .... **LC 16, 43**
See also DLB 101, 126

Butler, Samuel 1835-1902 . **TCLC 1, 33; DA; DAB; DAC; DAM MST, NOV; WLC**
See also CA 143; CDBLB 1890-1914; DA3; DLB 18, 57, 174

Butler, Walter C.
See Faust, Frederick (Schiller)

Butor, Michel (Marie Francois) 1926- .... **CLC 1, 3, 8, 11, 15**
See also CA 9-12R; CANR 33, 66; DLB 83; MTCW 1, 2

Butts, Mary 1892(?)-1937 .... **TCLC 77**
See also CA 148

Buzo, Alexander (John) 1944- .... **CLC 61**
See also CA 97-100; CANR 17, 39, 69

Buzzati, Dino 1906-1972 .... **CLC 36**
See also CA 160; 33-36R; DLB 177

Byars, Betsy (Cromer) 1928- .... **CLC 35**
See also AAYA 19; CA 33-36R, 183; CAAE 183; CANR 18, 36, 57; CLR 1, 16; DLB 52; INT CANR-18; JRDA; MAICYA; MTCW 1; SAAS 1; SATA 4, 46, 80; SATA-Essay 108

Byatt, A(ntonia) S(usan Drabble) 1936- ...... **CLC 19, 65, 136; DAM NOV, POP**
See also CA 13-16R; CANR 13, 33, 50, 75; DA3; DLB 14, 194; MTCW 1, 2

Byrne, David 1952- .... **CLC 26**
See also CA 127

Byrne, John Keyes 1926-
See Leonard, Hugh
See also CA 102; CANR 78; INT 102

Byron, George Gordon (Noel) 1788-1824 .... **NCLC 2, 12; DA; DAB; DAC; DAM MST, POET; PC 16; WLC**
See also CDBLB 1789-1832; DA3; DLB 96, 110

Byron, Robert 1905-1941 .... **TCLC 67**
See also CA 160; DLB 195

C. 3. 3.
See Wilde, Oscar (Fingal O'Flahertie Wills)

Caballero, Fernan 1796-1877 .... **NCLC 10**

Cabell, Branch
See Cabell, James Branch

Cabell, James Branch 1879-1958 .... **TCLC 6**
See also CA 105; 152; DLB 9, 78; MTCW 1

Cabeza de Vaca, Alvar Nunez 1490-1557(?) .... **LC 61**

Cable, George Washington 1844-1925 .... **TCLC 4; SSC 4**
See also CA 104; 155; DLB 12, 74; DLBD 13

Cabral de Melo Neto, Joao 1920- ... **CLC 76; DAM MULT**
See also CA 151

Cabrera Infante, G(uillermo) 1929- . **CLC 5, 25, 45, 120; DAM MULT; HLC 1; SSC 39**
See also CA 85-88; CANR 29, 65; DA3; DLB 113; HW 1, 2; MTCW 1, 2

Cade, Toni
See Bambara, Toni Cade

Cadmus and Harmonia
See Buchan, John

Caedmon fl. 658-680 .... **CMLC 7**
See also DLB 146

Caeiro, Alberto
See Pessoa, Fernando (Antonio Nogueira)

Cage, John (Milton, Jr.) 1912-1992 . **CLC 41**
See also CA 13-16R; 169; CANR 9, 78; DLB 193; INT CANR-9

Cahan, Abraham 1860-1951 .... **TCLC 71**
See also CA 108; 154; DLB 9, 25, 28

Cain, G.
See Cabrera Infante, G(uillermo)

Cain, Guillermo
See Cabrera Infante, G(uillermo)

Cain, James M(allahan) 1892-1977 .. **CLC 3, 11, 28**
See also AITN 1; CA 17-20R; 73-76; CANR 8, 34, 61; DLB 226; MTCW 1

Caine, Hall 1853-1931 .... **TCLC 97**

Caine, Mark
See Raphael, Frederic (Michael)

Calasso, Roberto 1941- .... **CLC 81**
See also CA 143; CANR 89

Calderon de la Barca, Pedro 1600-1681 .... **LC 23; DC 3; HLCS 1**

Caldwell, Erskine (Preston) 1903-1987 .. **CLC 1, 8, 14, 50, 60; DAM NOV; SSC 19**
See also AITN 1; CA 1-4R; 121; CAAS 1; CANR 2, 33; DA3; DLB 9, 86; MTCW 1, 2

Caldwell, (Janet Miriam) Taylor (Holland) 1900-1985 .. **CLC 2, 28, 39; DAM NOV, POP**
See also CA 5-8R; 116; CANR 5; DA3; DLBD 17

Calhoun, John Caldwell 1782-1850 .... **NCLC 15**
See also DLB 3

Calisher, Hortense 1911- ..... **CLC 2, 4, 8, 38, 134; DAM NOV; SSC 15**
See also CA 1-4R; CANR 1, 22, 67; DA3; DLB 2; INT CANR-22; MTCW 1, 2

Callaghan, Morley Edward 1903-1990 ...... **CLC 3, 14, 41, 65; DAC; DAM MST**
See also CA 9-12R; 132; CANR 33, 73; DLB 68; MTCW 1, 2

Callimachus c. 305B.C.-c. 240B.C. .... **CMLC 18**
See also DLB 176

Calvin, John 1509-1564 .... **LC 37**

Calvino, Italo 1923-1985 .... **CLC 5, 8, 11, 22, 33, 39, 73; DAM NOV; SSC 3**
See also CA 85-88; 116; CANR 23, 61; DLB 196; MTCW 1, 2

Castro (Ruz), Fidel 1926(?)-
See also CA 110; 129; CANR 81; DAM
MULT; HLC 1; HW 2

Castro, Guillen de 1569-1631 .... **LC 19**

Castro, Rosalia de 1837-1885 ... **NCLC 3, 78;**
DAM MULT

Cather, Willa -1947
See Cather, Willa Sibert

Cather, Willa Sibert 1873-1947 ...... **TCLC 1,**
11, 31, 99; DA; DAB; DAC; DAM
MST, NOV; SSC 2; WLC
See also Cather, Willa
See also AAYA 24; CA 104; 128; CDALB
1865-1917; DA3; DLB 9, 54, 78; DLBD
1; MTCW 1, 2; SATA 30

Catherine, Saint 1347-1380 .... **CMLC 27**

Cato, Marcus Porcius
234B.C.-149B.C. .... **CMLC 21**
See also DLB 211

Catton, (Charles) Bruce 1899-1978 . **CLC 35**
See also AITN 1; CA 5-8R; 81-84; CANR
7, 74; DLB 17; SATA 2; SATA-Obit 24

Catullus c. 84B.C.-c. 54B.C. .... **CMLC 18**
See also DLB 211

Cauldwell, Frank
See King, Francis (Henry)

Caunitz, William J. 1933-1996 .... **CLC 34**
See also BEST 89:3; CA 125; 130; 152;
CANR 73; INT 130

Causley, Charles (Stanley) 1917- .... **CLC 7**
See also CA 9-12R; CANR 5, 35; CLR 30;
DLB 27; MTCW 1; SATA 3, 66

Caute, (John) David 1936- .... **CLC 29; DAM**
NOV
See also CA 1-4R; CAAS 4; CANR 1, 33,
64; DLB 14, 231

Cavafy, C(onstantine) P(eter)
1863-1933 ...... **TCLC 2, 7; DAM POET**
See also Kavafis, Konstantinos Petrou
See also CA 148; DA3; MTCW 1

Cavallo, Evelyn
See Spark, Muriel (Sarah)

Cavanna, Betty **CLC 12**
See also Harrison, Elizabeth Cavanna
See also JRDA; MAICYA; SAAS 4; SATA
1, 30

Cavendish, Margaret Lucas
1623-1673 .... **LC 30**
See also DLB 131

Caxton, William 1421(?)-1491(?) .... **LC 17**
See also DLB 170

Cayer, D. M.
See Duffy, Maureen

Cayrol, Jean 1911- .... **CLC 11**
See also CA 89-92; DLB 83

Cela, Camilo Jose 1916- .... **CLC 4, 13, 59,**
122; DAM MULT; HLC 1
See also BEST 90:2; CA 21-24R; CAAS
10; CANR 21, 32, 76; DLBY 89; HW 1;
MTCW 1, 2

Celan, Paul **CLC 10, 19, 53, 82; PC 10**
See also Antschel, Paul
See also DLB 69

Celine, Louis-Ferdinand **CLC 1, 3, 4, 7, 9,**
15, 47, 124
See also Destouches, Louis-Ferdinand
See also DLB 72

Cellini, Benvenuto 1500-1571 .... **LC 7**

Cendrars, Blaise 1887-1961 ...... **CLC 18, 106**
See also Sauser-Hall, Frederic

Cernuda (y Bidon), Luis
1902-1963 .... **CLC 54; DAM POET**
See also CA 131; 89-92; DLB 134; HW 1

Cervantes, Lorna Dee 1954-
See also CA 131; CANR 80; DLB 82;
HLCS 1; HW 1

Cervantes (Saavedra), Miguel de
1547-1616 .. **LC 6, 23; DA; DAB; DAC;**
DAM MST, NOV; SSC 12; WLC

Cesaire, Aime (Fernand) 1913- . **CLC 19, 32,**
112; BLC 1; DAM MULT, POET; PC
25
See also BW 2, 3; CA 65-68; CANR 24,
43, 81; DA3; MTCW 1, 2

Chabon, Michael 1963- .... **CLC 55**
See also CA 139; CANR 57

Chabrol, Claude 1930- .... **CLC 16**
See also CA 110

Challans, Mary 1905-1983
See Renault, Mary
See also CA 81-84; 111; CANR 74; DA3;
MTCW 2; SATA 23; SATA-Obit 36

Challis, George
See Faust, Frederick (Schiller)

Chambers, Aidan 1934- .... **CLC 35**
See also AAYA 27; CA 25-28R; CANR 12,
31, 58; JRDA; MAICYA; SAAS 12;
SATA 1, 69, 108

Chambers, James 1948-
See Cliff, Jimmy
See also CA 124

Chambers, Jessie
See Lawrence, D(avid) H(erbert Richards)

Chambers, Robert W(illiam)
1865-1933 .... **TCLC 41**
See also CA 165; DLB 202; SATA 107

Chamisso, Adelbert von
1781-1838 .... **NCLC 82**
See also DLB 90

Chandler, Raymond (Thornton)
1888-1959 .... **TCLC 1, 7; SSC 23**
See also AAYA 25; CA 104; 129; CANR
60; CDALB 1929-1941; DA3; DLB 226;
DLBD 6; MTCW 1, 2

Chang, Eileen 1920-1995 .... **SSC 28**
See also CA 166

Chang, Jung 1952- .... **CLC 71**
See also CA 142

Chang Ai-Ling
See Chang, Eileen

Channing, William Ellery
1780-1842 .... **NCLC 17**
See also DLB 1, 59, 235

Chao, Patricia 1955- .... **CLC 119**
See also CA 163

Chaplin, Charles Spencer
1889-1977 .... **CLC 16**
See also Chaplin, Charlie
See also CA 81-84; 73-76

Chaplin, Charlie
See Chaplin, Charles Spencer
See also DLB 44

Chapman, George 1559(?)-1634 .... **LC 22;**
DAM DRAM
See also DLB 62, 121

Chapman, Graham 1941-1989 .... **CLC 21**
See also Monty Python
See also CA 116; 129; CANR 35

Chapman, John Jay 1862-1933 .... **TCLC 7**
See also CA 104

Chapman, Lee
See Bradley, Marion Zimmer

Chapman, Walker
See Silverberg, Robert

Chappell, Fred (Davis) 1936- .... **CLC 40, 78**
See also CA 5-8R; CAAS 4; CANR 8, 33,
67; DLB 6, 105

Char, Rene(-Emile) 1907-1988 .... **CLC 9, 11,**
14, 55; DAM POET
See also CA 13-16R; 124; CANR 32;
MTCW 1, 2

Charby, Jay
See Ellison, Harlan (Jay)

Chardin, Pierre Teilhard de
See Teilhard de Chardin, (Marie Joseph)
Pierre

Charlemagne 742-814 .... **CMLC 37**

Charles I 1600-1649 .... **LC 13**

Charriere, Isabelle de 1740-1805 ..**NCLC 66**

Charyn, Jerome 1937- .... **CLC 5, 8, 18**
See also CA 5-8R; CAAS 1; CANR 7, 61;
DLBY 83; MTCW 1

Chase, Mary (Coyle) 1907-1981 .... **DC 1**
See also CA 77-80; 105; DLB 228; SATA
17; SATA-Obit 29

Chase, Mary Ellen 1887-1973 .... **CLC 2**
See also CA 13-16; 41-44R; CAP 1; SATA
10

Chase, Nicholas
See Hyde, Anthony

Chateaubriand, Francois Rene de
1768-1848 .... **NCLC 3**
See also DLB 119

Chatterje, Sarat Chandra 1876-1936(?)
See Chatterji, Saratchandra
See also CA 109

Chatterji, Bankim Chandra
1838-1894 .... **NCLC 19**

Chatterji, Saratchandra -1938 .... **TCLC 13**
See also Chatterje, Sarat Chandra
See also CA 186

Chatterton, Thomas 1752-1770 ..... **LC 3, 54;**
DAM POET
See also DLB 109

Chatwin, (Charles) Bruce
1940-1989 . **CLC 28, 57, 59; DAM POP**
See also AAYA 4; BEST 90:1; CA 85-88;
127; DLB 194, 204

Chaucer, Daniel -1939
See Ford, Ford Madox

Chaucer, Geoffrey 1340(?)-1400 .. **LC 17, 56;**
DA; DAB; DAC; DAM MST, POET;
PC 19; WLCS
See also CDBLB Before 1660; DA3; DLB
146

Chavez, Denise (Elia) 1948-
See also CA 131; CANR 56, 81; DAM
MULT; DLB 122; HLC 1; HW 1, 2;
MTCW 2

Chaviaras, Strates 1935-
See Haviaras, Stratis
See also CA 105

Chayefsky, Paddy **CLC 23**
See also Chayefsky, Sidney
See also DLB 7, 44; DLBY 81

Chayefsky, Sidney 1923-1981
See Chayefsky, Paddy
See also CA 9-12R; 104; CANR 18; DAM
DRAM

Chedid, Andree 1920- .... **CLC 47**
See also CA 145

Cheever, John 1912-1982 ..... **CLC 3, 7, 8, 11,**
15, 25, 64; DA; DAB; DAC; DAM
MST, NOV, POP; SSC 1, 38; WLC
See also CA 5-8R; 106; CABS 1; CANR 5,
27, 76; CDALB 1941-1968; DA3; DLB
2, 102, 227; DLBY 80, 82; INT CANR-5;
MTCW 1, 2

Cheever, Susan 1943- .... **CLC 18, 48**
See also CA 103; CANR 27, 51, 92; DLBY
82; INT CANR-27

Chekhonte, Antosha
See Chekhov, Anton (Pavlovich)

Chekhov, Anton (Pavlovich)
1860-1904 ..... **TCLC 3, 10, 31, 55, 96;**
DA; DAB; DAC; DAM DRAM, MST;
DC 9; SSC 2, 28, 41; WLC
See also CA 104; 124; DA3; SATA 90

Chernyshevsky, Nikolay Gavrilovich
1828-1889 .... NCLC 1

Cherry, Carolyn Janice 1942-
See Cherryh, C. J.
See also CA 65-68; CANR 10

Cherryh, C. J. CLC 35
See also Cherry, Carolyn Janice
See also AAYA 24; DLBY 80; SATA 93

Chesnutt, Charles W(addell)
1858-1932 .. TCLC 5, 39; BLC 1; DAM
MULT; SSC 7
See also BW 1, 3; CA 106; 125; CANR 76;
DLB 12, 50, 78; MTCW 1, 2

Chester, Alfred 1929(?)-1971 .... CLC 49
See also CA 33-36R; DLB 130

Chesterton, G(ilbert) K(eith)
1874-1936 . TCLC 1, 6, 64; DAM NOV,
POET; PC 28; SSC 1
See also CA 104; 132; CANR 73; CDBLB
1914-1945; DLB 10, 19, 34, 70, 98, 149,
178; MTCW 1, 2; SATA 27

Chiang, Pin-chin 1904-1986
See Ding Ling
See also CA 118

Ch'ien Chung-shu 1910- .... CLC 22
See also CA 130; CANR 73; MTCW 1, 2

Child, L. Maria
See Child, Lydia Maria

Child, Lydia Maria 1802-1880 .. NCLC 6, 73
See also DLB 1, 74; SATA 67

Child, Mrs.
See Child, Lydia Maria

Child, Philip 1898-1978 .... CLC 19, 68
See also CA 13-14; CAP 1; SATA 47

Childers, (Robert) Erskine
1870-1922 .... TCLC 65
See also CA 113; 153; DLB 70

Childress, Alice 1920-1994 .. CLC 12, 15, 86,
96; BLC 1; DAM DRAM, MULT,
NOV; DC 4
See also AAYA 8; BW 2, 3; CA 45-48; 146;
CANR 3, 27, 50, 74; CLR 14; DA3; DLB
7, 38; JRDA; MAICYA; MTCW 1, 2;
SATA 7, 48, 81

Chin, Frank (Chew, Jr.) 1940- ...... CLC 135;
DAM MULT; DC 7
See also CA 33-36R; CANR 71; DLB 206

Chislett, (Margaret) Anne 1943- ...... CLC 34
See also CA 151

Chitty, Thomas Willes 1926- .... CLC 11
See also Hinde, Thomas
See also CA 5-8R

Chivers, Thomas Holley
1809-1858 .... NCLC 49
See also DLB 3

Choi, Susan CLC 119

Chomette, Rene Lucien 1898-1981
See Clair, Rene
See also CA 103

Chomsky, (Avram) Noam 1928- ..... CLC 132
See also CA 17-20R; CANR 28, 62; DA3;
MTCW 1, 2

Chopin, Kate TCLC 5, 14; DA; DAB; SSC
8; WLCS
See also Chopin, Katherine
See also AAYA 33; CDALB 1865-1917;
DLB 12, 78

Chopin, Katherine 1851-1904
See Chopin, Kate
See also CA 104; 122; DAC; DAM MST,
NOV; DA3

Chretien de Troyes c. 12th cent. - . CMLC 10
See also DLB 208

Christie
See Ichikawa, Kon

Christie, Agatha (Mary Clarissa)
1890-1976 .... CLC 1, 6, 8, 12, 39, 48,
110; DAB; DAC; DAM NOV
See also AAYA 9; AITN 1, 2; CA 17-20R;
61-64; CANR 10, 37; CDBLB 1914-1945;
DA3; DLB 13, 77; MTCW 1, 2; SATA 36

Christie, (Ann) Philippa
See Pearce, Philippa
See also CA 5-8R; CANR 4

Christine de Pizan 1365(?)-1431(?) .... LC 9
See also DLB 208

Chubb, Elmer
See Masters, Edgar Lee

Chulkov, Mikhail Dmitrievich
1743-1792 .... LC 2
See also DLB 150

Churchill, Caryl 1938- .... CLC 31, 55; DC 5
See also CA 102; CANR 22, 46; DLB 13;
MTCW 1

Churchill, Charles 1731-1764 .... LC 3
See also DLB 109

Chute, Carolyn 1947- .... CLC 39
See also CA 123

Ciardi, John (Anthony) 1916-1986 . CLC 10,
40, 44, 129; DAM POET
See also CA 5-8R; 118; CAAS 2; CANR 5,
33; CLR 19; DLB 5; DLBY 86; INT
CANR-5; MAICYA; MTCW 1, 2; SAAS
26; SATA 1, 65; SATA-Obit 46

Cicero, Marcus Tullius
106B.C.-43B.C. .... CMLC 3
See also DLB 211

Cimino, Michael 1943- .... CLC 16
See also CA 105

Cioran, E(mil) M. 1911-1995 .... CLC 64
See also CA 25-28R; 149; CANR 91; DLB
220

Cisneros, Sandra 1954- . CLC 69, 118; DAM
MULT; HLC 1; SSC 32
See also AAYA 9; CA 131; CANR 64; DA3;
DLB 122, 152; HW 1, 2; MTCW 2

Cixous, Helene 1937- .... CLC 92
See also CA 126; CANR 55; DLB 83;
MTCW 1, 2

Clair, Rene CLC 20
See also Chomette, Rene Lucien

Clampitt, Amy 1920-1994 .... CLC 32; PC 19
See also CA 110; 146; CANR 29, 79; DLB
105

Clancy, Thomas L., Jr. 1947-
See Clancy, Tom
See also CA 125; 131; CANR 62; DA3;
DLB 227; INT 131; MTCW 1, 2

Clancy, Tom CLC 45, 112; DAM NOV, POP
See also Clancy, Thomas L., Jr.
See also AAYA 9; BEST 89:1, 90:1; MTCW
2

Clare, John 1793-1864 ... NCLC 9, 86; DAB;
DAM POET; PC 23
See also DLB 55, 96

Clarin
See Alas (y Urena), Leopoldo (Enrique
Garcia)

Clark, Al C.
See Goines, Donald

Clark, (Robert) Brian 1932- .... CLC 29
See also CA 41-44R; CANR 67

Clark, Curt
See Westlake, Donald E(dwin)

Clark, Eleanor 1913-1996 .... CLC 5, 19
See also CA 9-12R; 151; CANR 41; DLB 6

Clark, J. P.
See Clark Bekedermo, J(ohnson) P(epper)
See also DLB 117

Clark, John Pepper
See Clark Bekedermo, J(ohnson) P(epper)

Clark, M. R.
See Clark, Mavis Thorpe

Clark, Mavis Thorpe 1909- .... CLC 12
See also CA 57-60; CANR 8, 37; CLR 30;
MAICYA; SAAS 5; SATA 8, 74

Clark, Walter Van Tilburg
1909-1971 .... CLC 28
See also CA 9-12R; 33-36R; CANR 63;
DLB 9, 206; SATA 8

Clark Bekedermo, J(ohnson) P(epper)
1935- .. CLC 38; BLC 1; DAM DRAM,
MULT; DC 5
See also Clark, J. P.; Clark, John Pepper
See also BW 1; CA 65-68; CANR 16, 72;
MTCW 1

Clarke, Arthur C(harles) 1917- .... CLC 1, 4,
13, 18, 35, 136; DAM POP; SSC 3
See also AAYA 4, 33; CA 1-4R; CANR 2,
28, 55, 74; DA3; JRDA; MAICYA;
MTCW 1, 2; SATA 13, 70, 115

Clarke, Austin 1896-1974 ... CLC 6, 9; DAM
POET
See also CA 29-32; 49-52; CAP 2; DLB 10,
20

Clarke, Austin C(hesterfield) 1934- .. CLC 8,
53; BLC 1; DAC; DAM MULT
See also BW 1; CA 25-28R; CAAS 16;
CANR 14, 32, 68; DLB 53, 125

Clarke, Gillian 1937- .... CLC 61
See also CA 106; DLB 40

Clarke, Marcus (Andrew Hislop)
1846-1881 .... NCLC 19

Clarke, Shirley 1925- .... CLC 16

Clash, The
See Headon, (Nicky) Topper; Jones, Mick;
Simonon, Paul; Strummer, Joe

Claudel, Paul (Louis Charles Marie)
1868-1955 .... TCLC 2, 10
See also CA 104; 165; DLB 192

Claudius, Matthias 1740-1815 .... NCLC 75
See also DLB 97

Clavell, James (duMaresq)
1925-1994 .. CLC 6, 25, 87; DAM NOV,
POP
See also CA 25-28R; 146; CANR 26, 48;
DA3; MTCW 1, 2

Cleaver, (Leroy) Eldridge
1935-1998 . CLC 30, 119; BLC 1; DAM
MULT
See also BW 1, 3; CA 21-24R; 167; CANR
16, 75; DA3; MTCW 2

Cleese, John (Marwood) 1939- .... CLC 21
See also Monty Python
See also CA 112; 116; CANR 35; MTCW 1

Cleishbotham, Jebediah
See Scott, Walter

Cleland, John 1710-1789 .... LC 2, 48
See also DLB 39

Clemens, Samuel Langhorne 1835-1910
See Twain, Mark
See also CA 104; 135; CDALB 1865-1917;
DA; DAB; DAC; DAM MST, NOV; DA3;
DLB 11, 12, 23, 64, 74, 186, 189; JRDA;
MAICYA; SATA 100; YABC 2

Clement of Alexandria
150(?)-215(?) .... CMLC 41

Cleophil
See Congreve, William

Clerihew, E.
See Bentley, E(dmund) C(lerihew)

Clerk, N. W.
See Lewis, C(live) S(taples)

Cliff, Jimmy CLC 21
See also Chambers, James

Cliff, Michelle 1946- .... CLC 120; BLCS
See also BW 2; CA 116; CANR 39, 72;
DLB 157

Clifton, (Thelma) Lucille 1936- .... **CLC 19,**
66; BLC 1; DAM MULT, POET; PC
17
See also BW 2, 3; CA 49-52; CANR 2, 24,
42, 76; CLR 5; DA3; DLB 5, 41; MAI-
CYA; MTCW 1, 2; SATA 20, 69
Clinton, Dirk
See Silverberg, Robert
Clough, Arthur Hugh 1819-1861 ... **NCLC 27**
See also DLB 32
Clutha, Janet Paterson Frame 1924-
See Frame, Janet
See also CA 1-4R; CANR 2, 36, 76; MTCW
1, 2; SATA 119
Clyne, Terence
See Blatty, William Peter
Cobalt, Martin
See Mayne, William (James Carter)
Cobb, Irvin S(hrewsbury)
1876-1944 .... **TCLC 77**
See also CA 175; DLB 11, 25, 86
Cobbett, William 1763-1835 .... **NCLC 49**
See also DLB 43, 107, 158
Coburn, D(onald) L(ee) 1938- .... **CLC 10**
See also CA 89-92
Cocteau, Jean (Maurice Eugene Clement)
1889-1963 .... **CLC 1, 8, 15, 16, 43; DA;**
DAB; DAC; DAM DRAM, MST, NOV;
WLC
See also CA 25-28; CANR 40; CAP 2;
DA3; DLB 65; MTCW 1, 2
Codrescu, Andrei 1946- .... **CLC 46, 121;**
DAM POET
See also CA 33-36R; CAAS 19; CANR 13,
34, 53, 76; DA3; MTCW 2
Coe, Max
See Bourne, Randolph S(illiman)
Coe, Tucker
See Westlake, Donald E(dwin)
Coen, Ethan 1958- .... **CLC 108**
See also CA 126; CANR 85
Coen, Joel 1955- .... **CLC 108**
See also CA 126
The Coen Brothers
See Coen, Ethan; Coen, Joel
Coetzee, J(ohn) M(ichael) 1940- ...... **CLC 23,**
33, 66, 117; DAM NOV
See also CA 77-80; CANR 41, 54, 74; DA3;
DLB 225; MTCW 1, 2
Coffey, Brian
See Koontz, Dean R(ay)
Coffin, Robert P(eter) Tristram
1892-1955 .... **TCLC 95**
See also CA 123; 169; DLB 45
Cohan, George M(ichael)
1878-1942 .... **TCLC 60**
See also CA 157
Cohen, Arthur A(llen) 1928-1986 ...... **CLC 7,**
31
See also CA 1-4R; 120; CANR 1, 17, 42;
DLB 28
Cohen, Leonard (Norman) 1934- ...... **CLC 3,**
38; DAC; DAM MST
See also CA 21-24R; CANR 14, 69; DLB
53; MTCW 1
Cohen, Matt(hew) 1942-1999 .... **CLC 19;**
DAC
See also CA 61-64; 187; CAAS 18; CANR
40; DLB 53
Cohen-Solal, Annie 19(?)- .... **CLC 50**
Colegate, Isabel 1931- .... **CLC 36**
See also CA 17-20R; CANR 8, 22, 74; DLB
14, 231; INT CANR-22; MTCW 1
Coleman, Emmett
See Reed, Ishmael
Coleridge, Hartley 1796-1849 .... **NCLC 90**
See also DLB 96
Coleridge, M. E.
See Coleridge, Mary E(lizabeth)

Coleridge, Mary E(lizabeth)
1861-1907 .... **TCLC 73**
See also CA 116; 166; DLB 19, 98
Coleridge, Samuel Taylor
1772-1834 .... **NCLC 9, 54; DA; DAB;**
DAC; DAM MST, POET; PC 11; WLC
See also CDBLB 1789-1832; DA3; DLB
93, 107
Coleridge, Sara 1802-1852 .... **NCLC 31**
See also DLB 199
Coles, Don 1928- .... **CLC 46**
See also CA 115; CANR 38
Coles, Robert (Martin) 1929- .... **CLC 108**
See also CA 45-48; CANR 3, 32, 66, 70;
INT CANR-32; SATA 23
Colette, (Sidonie-Gabrielle)
1873-1954 . **TCLC 1, 5, 16; DAM NOV;**
SSC 10
See also CA 104; 131; DA3; DLB 65;
MTCW 1, 2
Collett, (Jacobine) Camilla (Wergeland)
1813-1895 .... **NCLC 22**
Collier, Christopher 1930- .... **CLC 30**
See also AAYA 13; CA 33-36R; CANR 13,
33; JRDA; MAICYA; SATA 16, 70
Collier, James L(incoln) 1928- .... **CLC 30;**
DAM POP
See also AAYA 13; CA 9-12R; CANR 4,
33, 60; CLR 3; JRDA; MAICYA; SAAS
21; SATA 8, 70
Collier, Jeremy 1650-1726 .... **LC 6**
Collier, John 1901-1980 .... **SSC 19**
See also CA 65-68; 97-100; CANR 10;
DLB 77
Collingwood, R(obin) G(eorge)
1889(?)-1943 .... **TCLC 67**
See also CA 117; 155
Collins, Hunt
See Hunter, Evan
Collins, Linda 1931- .... **CLC 44**
See also CA 125
Collins, (William) Wilkie
1824-1889 .... **NCLC 1, 18, 93**
See also CDBLB 1832-1890; DLB 18, 70,
159
Collins, William 1721-1759 . **LC 4, 40; DAM**
POET
See also DLB 109
Collodi, Carlo 1826-1890 .... **NCLC 54**
See also Lorenzini, Carlo
See also CLR 5
Colman, George 1732-1794 .... **LC 98**
See Glassco, John
Colt, Winchester Remington
See Hubbard, L(afayette) Ron(ald)
Colter, Cyrus 1910- .... **CLC 58**
See also BW 1; CA 65-68; CANR 10, 66;
DLB 33
Colton, James
See Hansen, Joseph
Colum, Padraic 1881-1972 .... **CLC 28**
See also CA 73-76; 33-36R; CANR 35;
CLR 36; MAICYA; MTCW 1; SATA 15
Colvin, James
See Moorcock, Michael (John)
Colwin, Laurie (E.) 1944-1992 .... **CLC 5, 13,**
23, 84
See also CA 89-92; 139; CANR 20, 46;
DLBY 80; MTCW 1
Comfort, Alex(ander) 1920- .... **CLC 7; DAM**
POP
See also CA 1-4R; CANR 1, 45; MTCW 1
Comfort, Montgomery
See Campbell, (John) Ramsey
Compton-Burnett, I(vy)
1884(?)-1969 .... **CLC 1, 3, 10, 15, 34;**
DAM NOV
See also CA 1-4R; 25-28R; CANR 4; DLB
36; MTCW 1

Comstock, Anthony 1844-1915 ...... **TCLC 13**
See also CA 110; 169
Comte, Auguste 1798-1857 .... **NCLC 54**
Conan Doyle, Arthur
See Doyle, Arthur Conan
Conde (Abellan), Carmen 1901-
See also CA 177; DLB 108; HLCS 1; HW
2
Conde, Maryse 1937- .... **CLC 52, 92; BLCS;**
DAM MULT
See also BW 2, 3; CA 110; CANR 30, 53,
76; MTCW 1
Condillac, Etienne Bonnot de
1714-1780 .... **LC 26**
Condon, Richard (Thomas)
1915-1996 ...... **CLC 4, 6, 8, 10, 45, 100;**
DAM NOV
See also BEST 90:3; CA 1-4R; 151; CAAS
1; CANR 2, 23; INT CANR-23; MTCW
1, 2
Confucius 551B.C.-479B.C. .. **CMLC 19; DA;**
DAB; DAC; DAM MST; WLCS
See also DA3
Congreve, William 1670-1729 .... **LC 5, 21;**
DA; DAB; DAC; DAM DRAM, MST,
POET; DC 2; WLC
See also CDBLB 1660-1789; DLB 39, 84
Connell, Evan S(helby), Jr. 1924- . **CLC 4, 6,**
45; DAM NOV
See also AAYA 7; CA 1-4R; CAAS 2;
CANR 2, 39, 76; DLB 2; DLBY 81;
MTCW 1, 2
Connelly, Marc(us Cook) 1890-1980 . **CLC 7**
See also CA 85-88; 102; CANR 30; DLB
7; DLBY 80; SATA-Obit 25
Connor, Ralph **TCLC 31**
See also Gordon, Charles William
See also DLB 92
Conrad, Joseph 1857-1924 .... **TCLC 1, 6, 13,**
25, 43, 57; DA; DAB; DAC; DAM
MST, NOV; SSC 9; WLC
See also AAYA 26; CA 104; 131; CANR
60; CDBLB 1890-1914; DA3; DLB 10,
34, 98, 156; MTCW 1, 2; SATA 27
Conrad, Robert Arnold
See Hart, Moss
Conroy, Pat
See Conroy, (Donald) Pat(rick)
See also MTCW 2
Conroy, (Donald) Pat(rick) 1945- ... **CLC 30,**
74; DAM NOV, POP
See also Conroy, Pat
See also AAYA 8; AITN 1; CA 85-88;
CANR 24, 53; DA3; DLB 6; MTCW 1
Constant (de Rebecque), (Henri) Benjamin
1767-1830 .... **NCLC 6**
See also DLB 119
Conybeare, Charles Augustus
See Eliot, T(homas) S(tearns)
Cook, Michael 1933- .... **CLC 58**
See also CA 93-96; CANR 68; DLB 53
Cook, Robin 1940- .... **CLC 14; DAM POP**
See also AAYA 32; BEST 90:2; CA 108;
111; CANR 41, 90; DA3; INT 111
Cook, Roy
See Silverberg, Robert
Cooke, Elizabeth 1948- .... **CLC 55**
See also CA 129
Cooke, John Esten 1830-1886 .... **NCLC 5**
See also DLB 3
Cooke, John Estes
See Baum, L(yman) Frank
Cooke, M. E.
See Creasey, John
Cooke, Margaret
See Creasey, John

Croves, Hal
See Traven, B.

Crow Dog, Mary (Ellen) (?)- .... **CLC 93**
See also Brave Bird, Mary
See also CA 154

Crowfield, Christopher
See Stowe, Harriet (Elizabeth) Beecher

Crowley, Aleister TCLC 7
See also Crowley, Edward Alexander

Crowley, Edward Alexander 1875-1947
See Crowley, Aleister
See also CA 104

Crowley, John 1942- .... **CLC 57**
See also CA 61-64; CANR 43; DLBY 82;
SATA 65

Crud
See Crumb, R(obert)

Crumarums
See Crumb, R(obert)

Crumb, R(obert) 1943- .... **CLC 17**
See also CA 106

Crumbum
See Crumb, R(obert)

Crumski
See Crumb, R(obert)

Crum the Bum
See Crumb, R(obert)

Crunk
See Crumb, R(obert)

Crustt
See Crumb, R(obert)

Cruz, Victor Hernandez 1949-
See also BW 2; CA 65-68; CAAS 17;
CANR 14, 32, 74; DAM MULT, POET;
DLB 41; HLC 1; HW 1, 2; MTCW 1

Cryer, Gretchen (Kiger) 1935- .... **CLC 21**
See also CA 114; 123

Csath, Geza 1887-1919 .... **TCLC 13**
See also CA 111

Cudlip, David R(ockwell) 1933- .... **CLC 34**
See also CA 177

Cullen, Countee 1903-1946 .... **TCLC 4, 37;**
BLC 1; DA; DAC; DAM MST, MULT,
POET; PC 20; WLCS
See also BW 1; CA 108; 124; CDALB
1917-1929; DA3; DLB 4, 48, 51; MTCW
1, 2; SATA 18

Cum, R.
See Crumb, R(obert)

Cummings, Bruce F(rederick) 1889-1919
See Barbellion, W. N. P.
See also CA 123

Cummings, E(dward) E(stlin)
1894-1962 .... **CLC 1, 3, 8, 12, 15, 68;**
DA; DAB; DAC; DAM MST, POET;
PC 5; WLC
See also CA 73-76; CANR 31; CDALB
1929-1941; DA3; DLB 4, 48; MTCW 1,
2

Cunha, Euclides (Rodrigues Pimenta) da
1866-1909 .... **TCLC 24**
See also CA 123

Cunningham, E. V.
See Fast, Howard (Melvin)

Cunningham, J(ames) V(incent)
1911-1985 .... **CLC 3, 31**
See also CA 1-4R; 115; CANR 1, 72; DLB
5

Cunningham, Julia (Woolfolk)
1916- .... **CLC 12**
See also CA 9-12R; CANR 4, 19, 36;
JRDA; MAICYA; SAAS 2; SATA 1, 26

Cunningham, Michael 1952- .... **CLC 34**
See also CA 136

Cunninghame Graham, R. B.
See Cunninghame Graham, Robert
(Gallnigad) Bontine

Cunninghame Graham, Robert (Gallnigad)
Bontine 1852-1936 .... **TCLC 19**
See also Graham, R(obert) B(ontine) Cun-
ninghame
See also CA 119; 184; DLB 98

Currie, Ellen 19(?)- .... **CLC 44**

Curtin, Philip
See Lowndes, Marie Adelaide (Belloc)

Curtis, Price
See Ellison, Harlan (Jay)

Cutrate, Joe
See Spiegelman, Art

Cynewulf c. 770-c. 840 .... **CMLC 23**

Czaczkes, Shmuel Yosef
See Agnon, S(hmuel) Y(osef Halevi)

Dabrowska, Maria (Szumska)
1889-1965 .... **CLC 15**
See also CA 106

Dabydeen, David 1955- .... **CLC 34**
See also BW 1; CA 125; CANR 56, 92

Dacey, Philip 1939- .... **CLC 51**
See also CA 37-40R; CAAS 17; CANR 14,
32, 64; DLB 105

Dagerman, Stig (Halvard)
1923-1954 .... **TCLC 17**
See also CA 117; 155

Dahl, Roald 1916-1990 ...... **CLC 1, 6, 18, 79;**
DAB; DAC; DAM MST, NOV, POP
See also AAYA 15; CA 1-4R; 133; CANR
6, 32, 37, 62; CLR 1, 7, 41; DA3; DLB
139; JRDA; MAICYA; MTCW 1, 2;
SATA 1, 26, 73; SATA-Obit 65

Dahlberg, Edward 1900-1977 .. **CLC 1, 7, 14**
See also CA 9-12R; 69-72; CANR 31, 62;
DLB 48; MTCW 1

Daitch, Susan 1954- .... **CLC 103**
See also CA 161

Dale, Colin TCLC 18
See also Lawrence, T(homas) E(dward)

Dale, George E.
See Asimov, Isaac

Dalton, Roque 1935-1975
See also HLCS 1; HW 2

Daly, Elizabeth 1878-1967 .... **CLC 52**
See also CA 23-24; 25-28R; CANR 60;
CAP 2

Daly, Maureen 1921-1983 .... **CLC 17**
See also AAYA 5; CANR 37, 83; JRDA;
MAICYA; SAAS 1; SATA 2

Damas, Leon-Gontran 1912-1978 .... **CLC 84**
See also BW 1; CA 125; 73-76

Dana, Richard Henry Sr.
1787-1879 .... **NCLC 53**

Daniel, Samuel 1562(?)-1619 .... **LC 24**
See also DLB 62

Daniels, Brett
See Adler, Renata

Dannay, Frederic 1905-1982 . **CLC 11; DAM**
POP
See also Queen, Ellery
See also CA 1-4R; 107; CANR 1, 39; DLB
137; MTCW 1

D'Annunzio, Gabriele 1863-1938 ... **TCLC 6,**
40
See also CA 104; 155

Danois, N. le
See Gourmont, Remy (-Marie-Charles) de

Dante 1265-1321 .... **CMLC 3, 18, 39; DA;**
DAB; DAC; DAM MST, POET; PC
21; WLCS
See also Alighieri, Dante
See also DA3

d'Antibes, Germain
See Simenon, Georges (Jacques Christian)

Danticat, Edwidge 1969- .... **CLC 94**
See also AAYA 29; CA 152; CANR 73;
MTCW 1

Danvers, Dennis 1947- .... **CLC 70**

Danziger, Paula 1944- .... **CLC 21**
See also AAYA 4; CA 112; 115; CANR 37;
CLR 20; JRDA; MAICYA; SATA 36, 63,
102; SATA-Brief 30

Da Ponte, Lorenzo 1749-1838 .... **NCLC 50**

Dario, Ruben 1867-1916 .... **TCLC 4; DAM**
MULT; HLC 1; PC 15
See also CA 131; CANR 81; HW 1, 2;
MTCW 1, 2

Darley, George 1795-1846 .... **NCLC 2**
See also DLB 96

Darrow, Clarence (Seward)
1857-1938 .... **TCLC 81**
See also CA 164

Darwin, Charles 1809-1882 .... **NCLC 57**
See also DLB 57, 166

Daryush, Elizabeth 1887-1977 ...... **CLC 6, 19**
See also CA 49-52; CANR 3, 81; DLB 20

Dasgupta, Surendranath
1887-1952 .... **TCLC 81**
See also CA 157

Dashwood, Edmee Elizabeth Monica de la
Pasture 1890-1943
See Delafield, E. M.
See also CA 119; 154

Daudet, (Louis Marie) Alphonse
1840-1897 .... **NCLC 1**
See also DLB 123

Daumal, Rene 1908-1944 .... **TCLC 14**
See also CA 114

Davenant, William 1606-1668 .... **LC 13**
See also DLB 58, 126

Davenport, Guy (Mattison, Jr.)
1927- .... **CLC 6, 14, 38; SSC 16**
See also CA 33-36R; CANR 23, 73; DLB
130

Davidson, Avram (James) 1923-1993
See Queen, Ellery
See also CA 101; 171; CANR 26; DLB 8

Davidson, Donald (Grady)
1893-1968 .... **CLC 2, 13, 19**
See also CA 5-8R; 25-28R; CANR 4, 84;
DLB 45

Davidson, Hugh
See Hamilton, Edmond

Davidson, John 1857-1909 .... **TCLC 24**
See also CA 118; DLB 19

Davidson, Sara 1943- .... **CLC 9**
See also CA 81-84; CANR 44, 68; DLB
185

Davie, Donald (Alfred) 1922-1995 .... **CLC 5,**
8, 10, 31; PC 29
See also CA 1-4R; 149; CAAS 3; CANR 1,
44; DLB 27; MTCW 1

Davies, Ray(mond Douglas) 1944- ... **CLC 21**
See also CA 116; 146; CANR 92

Davies, Rhys 1901-1978 .... **CLC 23**
See also CA 9-12R; 81-84; CANR 4; DLB
139, 191

Davies, (William) Robertson
1913-1995 .... **CLC 2, 7, 13, 25, 42, 75,**
91; DA; DAB; DAC; DAM MST, NOV,
POP; WLC
See also BEST 89:2; CA 33-36R; 150;
CANR 17, 42; DA3; DLB 68; INT
CANR-17; MTCW 1, 2

Davies, Walter C.
See Kornbluth, C(yril) M.

Davies, William Henry 1871-1940 ... **TCLC 5**
See also CA 104; 179; DLB 19, 174

Da Vinci, Leonardo 1452-1519 ..... **LC 12, 57,**
60

Davis, Angela (Yvonne) 1944- .... **CLC 77;**
DAM MULT
See also BW 2, 3; CA 57-60; CANR 10,
81; DA3

Desai, Kiran 1971- .... **CLC 119**
See also CA 171

de Saint-Luc, Jean
See Glassco, John

de Saint Roman, Arnaud
See Aragon, Louis

Descartes, Rene 1596-1650 .... **LC 20, 35**

De Sica, Vittorio 1901(?)-1974 .... **CLC 20**
See also CA 117

Desnos, Robert 1900-1945 .... **TCLC 22**
See also CA 121; 151

de Stael, Germaine 1766-1817 .... **NCLC 91**
See also Stael-Holstein, Anne Louise Germaine Necker Baronn
See also DLB 119

Destouches, Louis-Ferdinand
1894-1961 .... **CLC 9, 15**
See also Celine, Louis-Ferdinand
See also CA 85-88; CANR 28; MTCW 1

de Tolignac, Gaston
See Griffith, D(avid Lewelyn) W(ark)

Deutsch, Babette 1895-1982 .... **CLC 18**
See also CA 1-4R; 108; CANR 4, 79; DLB 45; SATA 1; SATA-Obit 33

Devenant, William 1606-1649 .... **LC 13**

Devkota, Laxmiprasad 1909-1959 . **TCLC 23**
See also CA 123

De Voto, Bernard (Augustine)
1897-1955 .... **TCLC 29**
See also CA 113; 160; DLB 9

De Vries, Peter 1910-1993 ..... **CLC 1, 2, 3, 7, 10, 28, 46; DAM NOV**
See also CA 17-20R; 142; CANR 41; DLB 6; DLBY 82; MTCW 1, 2

Dewey, John 1859-1952 .... **TCLC 95**
See also CA 114; 170

Dexter, John
See Bradley, Marion Zimmer

Dexter, Martin
See Faust, Frederick (Schiller)

Dexter, Pete 1943- .. **CLC 34, 55; DAM POP**
See also BEST 89:2; CA 127; 131; INT 131; MTCW 1

Diamano, Silmang
See Senghor, Leopold Sedar

Diamond, Neil 1941- .... **CLC 30**
See also CA 108

Diaz del Castillo, Bernal 1496-1584 .. **LC 31; HLCS 1**

di Bassetto, Corno
See Shaw, George Bernard

Dick, Philip K(indred) 1928-1982 ... **CLC 10, 30, 72; DAM NOV, POP**
See also AAYA 24; CA 49-52; 106; CANR 2, 16; DA3; DLB 8; MTCW 1, 2

Dickens, Charles (John Huffam)
1812-1870 .... **NCLC 3, 8, 18, 26, 37, 50, 86; DA; DAB; DAC; DAM MST, NOV; SSC 17; WLC**
See also AAYA 23; CDBLB 1832-1890; DA3; DLB 21, 55, 70, 159, 166; JRDA; MAICYA; SATA 15

Dickey, James (Lafayette)
1923-1997 .... **CLC 1, 2, 4, 7, 10, 15, 47, 109; DAM NOV, POET, POP**
See also AITN 1, 2; CA 9-12R; 156; CABS 2; CANR 10, 48, 61; CDALB 1968-1988; DA3; DLB 5, 193; DLBD 7; DLBY 82, 93, 96, 97, 98; INT CANR-10; MTCW 1, 2

Dickey, William 1928-1994 .... **CLC 3, 28**
See also CA 9-12R; 145; CANR 24, 79; DLB 5

Dickinson, Charles 1951- .... **CLC 49**
See also CA 128

Dickinson, Emily (Elizabeth)
1830-1886 ..... **NCLC 21, 77; DA; DAB; DAC; DAM MST, POET; PC 1; WLC**
See also AAYA 22; CDALB 1865-1917; DA3; DLB 1; SATA 29

Dickinson, Peter (Malcolm) 1927- .. **CLC 12, 35**
See also AAYA 9; CA 41-44R; CANR 31, 58, 88; CLR 29; DLB 87, 161; JRDA; MAICYA; SATA 5, 62, 95

Dickson, Carr
See Carr, John Dickson

Dickson, Carter
See Carr, John Dickson

Diderot, Denis 1713-1784 .... **LC 26**

Didion, Joan 1934- .... **CLC 1, 3, 8, 14, 32, 129; DAM NOV**
See also AITN 1; CA 5-8R; CANR 14, 52, 76; CDALB 1968-1988; DA3; DLB 2, 173, 185; DLBY 81, 86; MTCW 1, 2

Dietrich, Robert
See Hunt, E(verette) Howard, (Jr.)

Difusa, Pati
See Almodovar, Pedro

Dillard, Annie 1945- .. **CLC 9, 60, 115; DAM NOV**
See also AAYA 6; CA 49-52; CANR 3, 43, 62, 90; DA3; DLBY 80; MTCW 1, 2; SATA 10

Dillard, R(ichard) H(enry) W(ilde)
1937- .... **CLC 5**
See also CA 21-24R; CAAS 7; CANR 10; DLB 5

Dillon, Eilis 1920-1994 .... **CLC 17**
See also CA 9-12R; 182; 147; CAAE 182; CAAS 3; CANR 4, 38, 78; CLR 26; MAICYA; SATA 2, 74; SATA-Essay 105; SATA-Obit 83

Dimont, Penelope
See Mortimer, Penelope (Ruth)

Dinesen, Isak -1962 .. **CLC 10, 29, 95; SSC 7**
See also Blixen, Karen (Christentze Dinesen)
See also MTCW 1

Ding Ling CLC 68
See also Chiang, Pin-chin

Diphusa, Patty
See Almodovar, Pedro

Disch, Thomas M(ichael) 1940- ... **CLC 7, 36**
See also AAYA 17; CA 21-24R; CAAS 4; CANR 17, 36, 54, 89; CLR 18; DA3; DLB 8; MAICYA; MTCW 1, 2; SAAS 15; SATA 92

Disch, Tom
See Disch, Thomas M(ichael)

d'Isly, Georges
See Simenon, Georges (Jacques Christian)

Disraeli, Benjamin 1804-1881 ... **NCLC 2, 39, 79**
See also DLB 21, 55

Ditcum, Steve
See Crumb, R(obert)

Dixon, Paige
See Corcoran, Barbara

Dixon, Stephen 1936- .... **CLC 52; SSC 16**
See also CA 89-92; CANR 17, 40, 54, 91; DLB 130

Doak, Annie
See Dillard, Annie

Dobell, Sydney Thompson
1824-1874 .... **NCLC 43**
See also DLB 32

Doblin, Alfred TCLC 13
See also Doeblin, Alfred

Dobrolyubov, Nikolai Alexandrovich
1836-1861 .... **NCLC 5**

Dobson, Austin 1840-1921 .... **TCLC 79**
See also DLB 35; 144

Dobyns, Stephen 1941- .... **CLC 37**
See also CA 45-48; CANR 2, 18

Doctorow, E(dgar) L(aurence)
1931- .... **CLC 6, 11, 15, 18, 37, 44, 65, 113; DAM NOV, POP**
See also AAYA 22; AITN 2; BEST 89:3; CA 45-48; CANR 2, 33, 51, 76; CDALB 1968-1988; DA3; DLB 2, 28, 173; DLBY 80; MTCW 1, 2

Dodgson, Charles Lutwidge 1832-1898
See Carroll, Lewis
See also CLR 2; DA; DAB; DAC; DAM MST, NOV, POET; DA3; MAICYA; SATA 100; YABC 2

Dodson, Owen (Vincent)
1914-1983 .... **CLC 79; BLC 1; DAM MULT**
See also BW 1; CA 65-68; 110; CANR 24; DLB 76

Doeblin, Alfred 1878-1957 .... **TCLC 13**
See also Doblin, Alfred
See also CA 110; 141; DLB 66

Doerr, Harriet 1910- .... **CLC 34**
See also CA 117; 122; CANR 47; INT 122

Domecq, H(onorio Bustos)
See Bioy Casares, Adolfo

Domecq, H(onorio) Bustos
See Bioy Casares, Adolfo; Borges, Jorge Luis

Domini, Rey
See Lorde, Audre (Geraldine)

Dominique
See Proust, (Valentin-Louis-George-Eugene-) Marcel

Don, A
See Stephen, SirLeslie

Donaldson, Stephen R. 1947- .... **CLC 46; DAM POP**
See also CA 89-92; CANR 13, 55; INT CANR-13

Donleavy, J(ames) P(atrick) 1926- .... **CLC 1, 4, 6, 10, 45**
See also AITN 2; CA 9-12R; CANR 24, 49, 62, 80; DLB 6, 173; INT CANR-24; MTCW 1, 2

Donne, John 1572-1631 .... **LC 10, 24; DA; DAB; DAC; DAM MST, POET; PC 1; WLC**
See also CDBLB Before 1660; DLB 121, 151

Donnell, David 1939(?)- .... **CLC 34**

Donoghue, P. S.
See Hunt, E(verette) Howard, (Jr.)

Donoso (Yanez), Jose 1924-1996 ... **CLC 4, 8, 11, 32, 99; DAM MULT; HLC 1; SSC 34**
See also CA 81-84; 155; CANR 32, 73; DLB 113; HW 1, 2; MTCW 1, 2

Donovan, John 1928-1992 .... **CLC 35**
See also AAYA 20; CA 97-100; 137; CLR 3; MAICYA; SATA 72; SATA-Brief 29

Don Roberto
See Cunninghame Graham, Robert (Gallnigad) Bontine

Doolittle, Hilda 1886-1961 . **CLC 3, 8, 14, 31, 34, 73; DA; DAC; DAM MST, POET; PC 5; WLC**
See also H. D.
See also CA 97-100; CANR 35; DLB 4, 45; MTCW 1, 2

Doppo, Kunikida 1869-1908 .... **TCLC 99**
See also DLB 180

Dorfman, Ariel 1942- ...... **CLC 48, 77; DAM MULT; HLC 1**
See also CA 124; 130; CANR 67, 70; HW 1, 2; INT 130

Duncan, Robert (Edward)
1919-1988 .... **CLC 1, 2, 4, 7, 15, 41, 55;
DAM POET; PC 2**
See also CA 9-12R; 124; CANR 28, 62;
DLB 5, 16, 193; MTCW 1, 2
Duncan, Sara Jeannette
1861-1922 .... **TCLC 60**
See also CA 157; DLB 92
Dunlap, William 1766-1839 .... **NCLC 2**
See also DLB 30, 37, 59
Dunn, Douglas (Eaglesham) 1942- .... **CLC 6,
40**
See also CA 45-48; CANR 2, 33; DLB 40;
MTCW 1
Dunn, Katherine (Karen) 1945- .... **CLC 71**
See also CA 33-36R; CANR 72; MTCW 1
Dunn, Stephen 1939- .... **CLC 36**
See also CA 33-36R; CANR 12, 48, 53;
DLB 105
Dunne, Finley Peter 1867-1936 ...... **TCLC 28**
See also CA 108; 178; DLB 11, 23
Dunne, John Gregory 1932- .... **CLC 28**
See also CA 25-28R; CANR 14, 50; DLBY
80
**Dunsany, Edward John Moreton Drax
Plunkett** 1878-1957
See Dunsany, Lord
See also CA 104; 148; DLB 10; MTCW 1
Dunsany, Lord -1957 .... **TCLC 2, 59**
See also Dunsany, Edward John Moreton
Drax Plunkett
See also DLB 77, 153, 156
du Perry, Jean
See Simenon, Georges (Jacques Christian)
Durang, Christopher (Ferdinand)
1949- .... **CLC 27, 38**
See also CA 105; CANR 50, 76; MTCW 1
Duras, Marguerite 1914-1996 . **CLC 3, 6, 11,
20, 34, 40, 68, 100; SSC 40**
See also CA 25-28R; 151; CANR 50; DLB
83; MTCW 1, 2
Durban, (Rosa) Pam 1947- .... **CLC 39**
See also CA 123
Durcan, Paul 1944- .... **CLC 43, 70; DAM
POET**
See also CA 134
Durkheim, Emile 1858-1917 .... **TCLC 55**
Durrell, Lawrence (George)
1912-1990 .... **CLC 1, 4, 6, 8, 13, 27, 41;
DAM NOV**
See also CA 9-12R; 132; CANR 40, 77;
CDBLB 1945-1960; DLB 15, 27, 204;
DLBY 90; MTCW 1, 2
Durrenmatt, Friedrich
See Duerrenmatt, Friedrich
DuRrenmatt, Friedrich
See Duerrenmatt, Friedrich
Dutt, Toru 1856-1877 .... **NCLC 29**
Dwight, Timothy 1752-1817 .... **NCLC 13**
See also DLB 37
Dworkin, Andrea 1946- .... **CLC 43, 123**
See also CA 77-80; CAAS 21; CANR 16,
39, 76; INT CANR-16; MTCW 1, 2
Dwyer, Deanna
See Koontz, Dean R(ay)
Dwyer, K. R.
See Koontz, Dean R(ay)
Dwyer, Thomas A. 1923- .... **CLC 114**
See also CA 115
Dye, Richard
See De Voto, Bernard (Augustine)
Dylan, Bob 1941- .... **CLC 3, 4, 6, 12, 77**
See also CA 41-44R; DLB 16
E. V. L.
See Lucas, E(dward) V(errall)
Eagleton, Terence (Francis) 1943- .. **CLC 63,
132**
See also CA 57-60; CANR 7, 23, 68;
MTCW 1, 2

Eagleton, Terry
See Eagleton, Terence (Francis)
Early, Jack
See Scoppettone, Sandra
East, Michael
See West, Morris L(anglo)
Eastaway, Edward
See Thomas, (Philip) Edward
Eastlake, William (Derry)
1917-1997 .... **CLC 8**
See also CA 5-8R; 158; CAAS 1; CANR 5,
63; DLB 6, 206; INT CANR-5
Eastman, Charles A(lexander)
1858-1939 .... **TCLC 55; DAM MULT**
See also CA 179; CANR 91; DLB 175;
NNAL; YABC 1
Eberhart, Richard (Ghormley)
1904- .. **CLC 3, 11, 19, 56; DAM POET**
See also CA 1-4R; CANR 2; CDALB 1941-
1968; DLB 48; MTCW 1
Eberstadt, Fernanda 1960- .... **CLC 39**
See also CA 136; CANR 69
**Echegaray (y Eizaguirre), Jose (Maria
Waldo)** 1832-1916 .... **TCLC 4; HLCS 1**
See also CA 104; CANR 32; HW 1; MTCW
1
Echeverria, (Jose) Esteban (Antonino)
1805-1851 .... **NCLC 18**
Echo
See Proust, (Valentin-Louis-George-
Eugene-) Marcel
Eckert, Allan W. 1931- .... **CLC 17**
See also AAYA 18; CA 13-16R; CANR 14,
45; INT CANR-14; SAAS 21; SATA 29,
91; SATA-Brief 27
Eckhart, Meister 1260(?)-1328(?) ... **CMLC 9**
See also DLB 115
Eckmar, F. R.
See de Hartog, Jan
Eco, Umberto 1932- .... **CLC 28, 60; DAM
NOV, POP**
See also BEST 90:1; CA 77-80; CANR 12,
33, 55; DA3; DLB 196; MTCW 1, 2
Eddison, E(ric) R(ucker)
1882-1945 .... **TCLC 15**
See also CA 109; 156
Eddy, Mary (Ann Morse) Baker
1821-1910 .... **TCLC 71**
See also CA 113; 174
Edel, (Joseph) Leon 1907-1997 .. **CLC 29, 34**
See also CA 1-4R; 161; CANR 1, 22; DLB
103; INT CANR-22
Eden, Emily 1797-1869 .... **NCLC 10**
Edgar, David 1948- .. **CLC 42; DAM DRAM**
See also CA 57-60; CANR 12, 61; DLB 13,
233; MTCW 1
Edgerton, Clyde (Carlyle) 1944- ...... **CLC 39**
See also AAYA 17; CA 118; 134; CANR
64; INT 134
Edgeworth, Maria 1768-1849 .... **NCLC 1, 51**
See also DLB 116, 159, 163; SATA 21
Edmonds, Paul
See Kuttner, Henry
Edmonds, Walter D(umaux)
1903-1998 .... **CLC 35**
See also CA 5-8R; CANR 2; DLB 9; MAI-
CYA; SAAS 4; SATA 1, 27; SATA-Obit
99
Edmondson, Wallace
See Ellison, Harlan (Jay)
Edson, Russell CLC 13
See also CA 33-36R
Edwards, Bronwen Elizabeth
See Rose, Wendy
Edwards, G(erald) B(asil)
1899-1976 .... **CLC 25**
See also CA 110
Edwards, Gus 1939- .... **CLC 43**
See also CA 108; INT 108

Edwards, Jonathan 1703-1758 .... **LC 7, 54;
DA; DAC; DAM MST**
See also DLB 24
Efron, Marina Ivanovna Tsvetaeva
See Tsvetaeva (Efron), Marina (Ivanovna)
Ehle, John (Marsden, Jr.) 1925- ...... **CLC 27**
See also CA 9-12R
Ehrenbourg, Ilya (Grigoryevich)
See Ehrenburg, Ilya (Grigoryevich)
Ehrenburg, Ilya (Grigoryevich)
1891-1967 .... **CLC 18, 34, 62**
See also CA 102; 25-28R
Ehrenburg, Ilyo (Grigoryevich)
See Ehrenburg, Ilya (Grigoryevich)
Ehrenreich, Barbara 1941- .... **CLC 110**
See also BEST 90:4; CA 73-76; CANR 16,
37, 62; MTCW 1, 2
Eich, Guenter 1907-1972 .... **CLC 15**
See also CA 111; 93-96; DLB 69, 124
Eichendorff, Joseph Freiherr von
1788-1857 .... **NCLC 8**
See also DLB 90
Eigner, Larry CLC 9
See also Eigner, Laurence (Joel)
See also CAAS 23; DLB 5
Eigner, Laurence (Joel) 1927-1996
See Eigner, Larry
See also CA 9-12R; 151; CANR 6, 84; DLB
193
Einstein, Albert 1879-1955 .... **TCLC 65**
See also CA 121; 133; MTCW 1, 2
Eiseley, Loren Corey 1907-1977 .... **CLC 7**
See also AAYA 5; CA 1-4R; 73-76; CANR
6; DLBD 17
Eisenstadt, Jill 1963- .... **CLC 50**
See also CA 140
Eisenstein, Sergei (Mikhailovich)
1898-1948 .... **TCLC 57**
See also CA 114; 149
Eisner, Simon
See Kornbluth, C(yril) M.
Ekeloef, (Bengt) Gunnar
1907-1968 ... **CLC 27; DAM POET; PC
23**
See also CA 123; 25-28R
Ekelof, (Bengt) Gunnar
See Ekeloef, (Bengt) Gunnar
Ekelund, Vilhelm 1880-1949 .... **TCLC 75**
Ekwensi, C. O. D.
See Ekwensi, Cyprian (Odiatu Duaka)
Ekwensi, Cyprian (Odiatu Duaka)
1921- ...... **CLC 4; BLC 1; DAM MULT**
See also BW 2, 3; CA 29-32R; CANR 18,
42, 74; DLB 117; MTCW 1, 2; SATA 66
Elaine TCLC 18
See also Leverson, Ada
El Crummo
See Crumb, R(obert)
Elder, Lonne III 1931-1996 .... **DC 8**
See also BLC 1; BW 1, 3; CA 81-84; 152;
CANR 25; DAM MULT; DLB 7, 38, 44
Eleanor of Aquitaine 1122-1204 ... **CMLC 39**
Elia
See Lamb, Charles
Eliade, Mircea 1907-1986 .... **CLC 19**
See also CA 65-68; 119; CANR 30, 62;
DLB 220; MTCW 1
Eliot, A. D.
See Jewett, (Theodora) Sarah Orne
Eliot, Alice
See Jewett, (Theodora) Sarah Orne
Eliot, Dan
See Silverberg, Robert
Eliot, George 1819- . **NCLC 4, 13, 23, 41, 49,
89; DA; DAB; DAC; DAM MST, NOV;
PC 20; WLC**
See also CDBLB 1832-1890; DA3; DLB
21, 35, 55

Exley, Frederick (Earl) 1929-1992 .... **CLC 6, 11**
See also AITN 2; CA 81-84; 138; DLB 143; DLBY 81

Eynhardt, Guillermo
See Quiroga, Horacio (Sylvestre)

Ezekiel, Nissim 1924- .... **CLC 61**
See also CA 61-64

Ezekiel, Tish O'Dowd 1943- .... **CLC 34**
See also CA 129

Fadeyev, A.
See Bulgya, Alexander Alexandrovich

Fadeyev, Alexander **TCLC 53**
See also Bulgya, Alexander Alexandrovich

Fagen, Donald 1948- .... **CLC 26**

Fainzilberg, Ilya Arnoldovich 1897-1937
See Ilf, Ilya
See also CA 120; 165

Fair, Ronald L. 1932- .... **CLC 18**
See also BW 1; CA 69-72; CANR 25; DLB 33

Fairbairn, Roger
See Carr, John Dickson

Fairbairns, Zoe (Ann) 1948- .... **CLC 32**
See also CA 103; CANR 21, 85

Fairman, Paul W. 1916-1977
See Queen, Ellery
See also CA 114

Falco, Gian
See Papini, Giovanni

Falconer, James
See Kirkup, James

Falconer, Kenneth
See Kornbluth, C(yril) M.

Falkland, Samuel
See Heijermans, Herman

Fallaci, Oriana 1930- .... **CLC 11, 110**
See also CA 77-80; CANR 15, 58; MTCW 1

Faludy, George 1913- .... **CLC 42**
See also CA 21-24R

Faludy, Gyoergy
See Faludy, George

Fanon, Frantz 1925-1961 ... **CLC 74; BLC 2; DAM MULT**
See also BW 1; CA 116; 89-92

Fanshawe, Ann 1625-1680 .... **LC 11**

Fante, John (Thomas) 1911-1983 ..... **CLC 60**
See also CA 69-72; 109; CANR 23; DLB 130; DLBY 83

Farah, Nuruddin 1945- ...... **CLC 53; BLC 2; DAM MULT**
See also BW 2, 3; CA 106; CANR 81; DLB 125

Fargue, Leon-Paul 1876(?)-1947 .... **TCLC 11**
See also CA 109

Farigoule, Louis
See Romains, Jules

Farina, Richard 1936(?)-1966 .... **CLC 9**
See also CA 81-84; 25-28R

Farley, Walter (Lorimer)
1915-1989 .... **CLC 17**
See also CA 17-20R; CANR 8, 29, 84; DLB 22; JRDA; MAICYA; SATA 2, 43

Farmer, Philip Jose 1918- .... **CLC 1, 19**
See also AAYA 28; CA 1-4R; CANR 4, 35; DLB 8; MTCW 1; SATA 93

Farquhar, George 1677-1707 ... **LC 21; DAM DRAM**
See also DLB 84

Farrell, J(ames) G(ordon)
1935-1979 .... **CLC 6**
See also CA 73-76; 89-92; CANR 36; DLB 14; MTCW 1

Farrell, James T(homas) 1904-1979 . **CLC 1, 4, 8, 11, 66; SSC 28**
See also CA 5-8R; 89-92; CANR 9, 61; DLB 4, 9, 86; DLBD 2; MTCW 1, 2

Farren, Richard J.
See Betjeman, John

Farren, Richard M.
See Betjeman, John

Fassbinder, Rainer Werner
1946-1982 .... **CLC 20**
See also CA 93-96; 106; CANR 31

Fast, Howard (Melvin) 1914- .. **CLC 23, 131; DAM NOV**
See also AAYA 16; CA 1-4R, 181; CAAE 181; CAAS 18; CANR 1, 33, 54, 75; DLB 9; INT CANR-33; MTCW 1; SATA 7; SATA-Essay 107

Faulcon, Robert
See Holdstock, Robert P.

Faulkner, William (Cuthbert)
1897-1962 .... **CLC 1, 3, 6, 8, 9, 11, 14, 18, 28, 52, 68; DA; DAB; DAC; DAM MST, NOV; SSC 1, 35, 42; WLC**
See also AAYA 7; CA 81-84; CANR 33; CDALB 1929-1941; DA3; DLB 9, 11, 44, 102; DLBD 2; DLBY 86, 97; MTCW 1, 2

Fauset, Jessie Redmon
1884(?)-1961 .... **CLC 19, 54; BLC 2; DAM MULT**
See also BW 1; CA 109; CANR 83; DLB 51

Faust, Frederick (Schiller)
1892-1944(?) .... **TCLC 49; DAM POP**
See also CA 108; 152

Faust, Irvin 1924- .... **CLC 8**
See also CA 33-36R; CANR 28, 67; DLB 2, 28; DLBY 80

Fawkes, Guy
See Benchley, Robert (Charles)

Fearing, Kenneth (Flexner)
1902-1961 .... **CLC 51**
See also CA 93-96; CANR 59; DLB 9

Fecamps, Elise
See Creasey, John

Federman, Raymond 1928- .... **CLC 6, 47**
See also CA 17-20R; CAAS 8; CANR 10, 43, 83; DLBY 80

Federspiel, J(uerg) F. 1931- .... **CLC 42**
See also CA 146

Feiffer, Jules (Ralph) 1929- ..... **CLC 2, 8, 64; DAM DRAM**
See also AAYA 3; CA 17-20R; CANR 30, 59; DLB 7, 44; INT CANR-30; MTCW 1; SATA 8, 61, 111

Feige, Hermann Albert Otto Maximilian
See Traven, B.

Feinberg, David B. 1956-1994 .... **CLC 59**
See also CA 135; 147

Feinstein, Elaine 1930- .... **CLC 36**
See also CA 69-72; CAAS 1; CANR 31, 68; DLB 14, 40; MTCW 1

Feldman, Irving (Mordecai) 1928- ..... **CLC 7**
See also CA 1-4R; CANR 1; DLB 169

Felix-Tchicaya, Gerald
See Tchicaya, Gerald Felix

Fellini, Federico 1920-1993 .... **CLC 16, 85**
See also CA 65-68; 143; CANR 33

Felsen, Henry Gregor 1916-1995 ..... **CLC 17**
See also CA 1-4R; 180; CANR 1; SAAS 2; SATA 1

Fenno, Jack
See Calisher, Hortense

Fenollosa, Ernest (Francisco)
1853-1908 .... **TCLC 91**

Fenton, James Martin 1949- .... **CLC 32**
See also CA 102; DLB 40

Ferber, Edna 1887-1968 .... **CLC 18, 93**
See also AITN 1; CA 5-8R; 25-28R; CANR 68; DLB 9, 28, 86; MTCW 1, 2; SATA 7

Ferguson, Helen
See Kavan, Anna

Ferguson, Niall 1967- .... **CLC 134**

Ferguson, Samuel 1810-1886 .... **NCLC 33**
See also DLB 32

Fergusson, Robert 1750-1774 .... **LC 29**
See also DLB 109

Ferling, Lawrence
See Ferlinghetti, Lawrence (Monsanto)

Ferlinghetti, Lawrence (Monsanto)
1919(?)- .... **CLC 2, 6, 10, 27, 111; DAM POET; PC 1**
See also CA 5-8R; CANR 3, 41, 73; CDALB 1941-1968; DA3; DLB 5, 16; MTCW 1, 2

Fern, Fanny 1811-1872
See Parton, Sara Payson Willis

Fernandez, Vicente Garcia Huidobro
See Huidobro Fernandez, Vicente Garcia

Ferre, Rosario 1942- .... **SSC 36; HLCS 1**
See also CA 131; CANR 55, 81; DLB 145; HW 1, 2; MTCW 1

Ferrer, Gabriel (Francisco Victor) Miro
See Miro (Ferrer), Gabriel (Francisco Victor)

Ferrier, Susan (Edmonstone)
1782-1854 .... **NCLC 8**
See also DLB 116

Ferrigno, Robert 1948(?)- .... **CLC 65**
See also CA 140

Ferron, Jacques 1921-1985 .... **CLC 94; DAC**
See also CA 117; 129; DLB 60

Feuchtwanger, Lion 1884-1958 .... **TCLC 3**
See also CA 104; 187; DLB 66

Feuillet, Octave 1821-1890 .... **NCLC 45**
See also DLB 192

Feydeau, Georges (Leon Jules Marie)
1862-1921 .... **TCLC 22; DAM DRAM**
See also CA 113; 152; CANR 84; DLB 192

Fichte, Johann Gottlieb
1762-1814 .... **NCLC 62**
See also DLB 90

Ficino, Marsilio 1433-1499 .... **LC 12**

Fiedeler, Hans
See Doeblin, Alfred

Fiedler, Leslie A(aron) 1917- .. **CLC 4, 13, 24**
See also CA 9-12R; CANR 7, 63; DLB 28, 67; MTCW 1, 2

Field, Andrew 1938- .... **CLC 44**
See also CA 97-100; CANR 25

Field, Eugene 1850-1895 .... **NCLC 3**
See also DLB 23, 42, 140; DLBD 13; MAICYA; SATA 16

Field, Gans T.
See Wellman, Manly Wade

Field, Michael 1915-1971 .... **TCLC 43**
See also CA 29-32R

Field, Peter
See Hobson, Laura Z(ametkin)

Fielding, Henry 1707-1754 ..... **LC 1, 46; DA; DAB; DAC; DAM DRAM, MST, NOV; WLC**
See also CDBLB 1660-1789; DA3; DLB 39, 84, 101

Fielding, Sarah 1710-1768 .... **LC 1, 44**
See also DLB 39

Fields, W. C. 1880-1946 .... **TCLC 80**
See also DLB 44

Fierstein, Harvey (Forbes) 1954- .... **CLC 33; DAM DRAM, POP**
See also CA 123; 129; DA3

Figes, Eva 1932- .... **CLC 31**
See also CA 53-56; CANR 4, 44, 83; DLB 14

Finch, Anne 1661-1720 .... **LC 3; PC 21**
See also DLB 95

Finch, Robert (Duer Claydon)
1900- .... **CLC 18**
See also CA 57-60; CANR 9, 24, 49; DLB 88

Frank, Elizabeth 1945- .... CLC 39
  See also CA 121; 126; CANR 78; INT 126
Frankl, Viktor E(mil) 1905-1997 ...... CLC 93
  See also CA 65-68; 161
Franklin, Benjamin
  See Hasek, Jaroslav (Matej Frantisek)
Franklin, Benjamin 1706-1790 .. LC 25; DA;
    DAB; DAC; DAM MST; WLCS
  See also CDALB 1640-1865; DA3; DLB
    24, 43, 73
Franklin, (Stella Maria Sarah) Miles
    (Lampe) 1879-1954 .... TCLC 7
  See also CA 104; 164
Fraser, (Lady) Antonia (Pakenham)
    1932- .... CLC 32, 107
  See also CA 85-88; CANR 44, 65; MTCW
    1, 2; SATA-Brief 32
Fraser, George MacDonald 1925- ...... CLC 7
  See also CA 45-48, 180; CAAE 180; CANR
    2, 48, 74; MTCW 1
Fraser, Sylvia 1935- .... CLC 64
  See also CA 45-48; CANR 1, 16, 60
Frayn, Michael 1933- .... CLC 3, 7, 31, 47;
    DAM DRAM, NOV
  See also CA 5-8R; CANR 30, 69; DLB 13,
    14, 194; MTCW 1, 2
Fraze, Candida (Merrill) 1945- .... CLC 50
  See also CA 126
Frazer, J(ames) G(eorge)
    1854-1941 .... TCLC 32
  See also CA 118
Frazer, Robert Caine
  See Creasey, John
Frazer, Sir James George
  See Frazer, J(ames) G(eorge)
Frazier, Charles 1950- .... CLC 109
  See also AAYA 34; CA 161
Frazier, Ian 1951- .... CLC 46
  See also CA 130; CANR 54, 93
Frederic, Harold 1856-1898 .... NCLC 10
  See also DLB 12, 23; DLBD 13
Frederick, John
  See Faust, Frederick (Schiller)
Frederick the Great 1712-1786 .... LC 14
Fredro, Aleksander 1793-1876 .... NCLC 8
Freeling, Nicolas 1927- .... CLC 38
  See also CA 49-52; CAAS 12; CANR 1,
    17, 50, 84; DLB 87
Freeman, Douglas Southall
    1886-1953 .... TCLC 11
  See also CA 109; DLB 17; DLBD 17
Freeman, Judith 1946- .... CLC 55
  See also CA 148
Freeman, Mary E(leanor) Wilkins
    1852-1930 .... TCLC 9; SSC 1
  See also CA 106; 177; DLB 12, 78, 221
Freeman, R(ichard) Austin
    1862-1943 .... TCLC 21
  See also CA 113; CANR 84; DLB 70
French, Albert 1943- .... CLC 86
  See also BW 3; CA 167
French, Marilyn 1929- .... CLC 10, 18, 60;
    DAM DRAM, NOV, POP
  See also CA 69-72; CANR 3, 31; INT
    CANR-31; MTCW 1, 2
French, Paul
  See Asimov, Isaac
Freneau, Philip Morin 1752-1832 ... NCLC 1
  See also DLB 37, 43
Freud, Sigmund 1856-1939 .... TCLC 52
  See also CA 115; 133; CANR 69; MTCW
    1, 2
Friedan, Betty (Naomi) 1921- .... CLC 74
  See also CA 65-68; CANR 18, 45, 74;
    MTCW 1, 2
Friedlander, Saul 1932- .... CLC 90
  See also CA 117; 130; CANR 72

Friedman, B(ernard) H(arper)
    1926- .... CLC 7
  See also CA 1-4R; CANR 3, 48
Friedman, Bruce Jay 1930- ...... CLC 3, 5, 56
  See also CA 9-12R; CANR 25, 52; DLB 2,
    28; INT CANR-25
Friel, Brian 1929- .... CLC 5, 42, 59, 115; DC
    8
  See also CA 21-24R; CANR 33, 69; DLB
    13; MTCW 1
Friis-Baastad, Babbis Ellinor
    1921-1970 .... CLC 12
  See also CA 17-20R; 134; SATA 7
Frisch, Max (Rudolf) 1911-1991 ... CLC 3, 9,
    14, 18, 32, 44; DAM DRAM, NOV
  See also CA 85-88; 134; CANR 32, 74;
    DLB 69, 124; MTCW 1, 2
Fromentin, Eugene (Samuel Auguste)
    1820-1876 .... NCLC 10
  See also DLB 123
Frost, Frederick
  See Faust, Frederick (Schiller)
Frost, Robert (Lee) 1874-1963 .. CLC 1, 3, 4,
    9, 10, 13, 15, 26, 34, 44; DA; DAB;
    DAC; DAM MST, POET; PC 1; WLC
  See also AAYA 21; CA 89-92; CANR 33;
    CDALB 1917-1929; CLR 67; DA3; DLB
    54; DLBD 7; MTCW 1, 2; SATA 14
Froude, James Anthony
    1818-1894 .... NCLC 43
  See also DLB 18, 57, 144
Froy, Herald
  See Waterhouse, Keith (Spencer)
Fry, Christopher 1907- .... CLC 2, 10, 14;
    DAM DRAM
  See also CA 17-20R; CAAS 23; CANR 9,
    30, 74; DLB 13; MTCW 1, 2; SATA 66
Frye, (Herman) Northrop
    1912-1991 .... CLC 24, 70
  See also CA 5-8R; 133; CANR 8, 37; DLB
    67, 68; MTCW 1, 2
Fuchs, Daniel 1909-1993 .... CLC 8, 22
  See also CA 81-84; 142; CAAS 5; CANR
    40; DLB 9, 26, 28; DLBY 93
Fuchs, Daniel 1934- .... CLC 34
  See also CA 37-40R; CANR 14, 48
Fuentes, Carlos 1928- .. CLC 3, 8, 10, 13, 22,
    41, 60, 113; DA; DAB; DAC; DAM
    MST, MULT, NOV; HLC 1; SSC 24;
    WLC
  See also AAYA 4; AITN 2; CA 69-72;
    CANR 10, 32, 68; DA3; DLB 113; HW
    1, 2; MTCW 1, 2
Fuentes, Gregorio Lopez y
  See Lopez y Fuentes, Gregorio
Fuertes, Gloria 1918- .... PC 27
  See also CA 178, 180; DLB 108; HW 2;
    SATA 115
Fugard, (Harold) Athol 1932- . CLC 5, 9, 14,
    25, 40, 80; DAM DRAM; DC 3
  See also AAYA 17; CA 85-88; CANR 32,
    54; DLB 225; MTCW 1
Fugard, Sheila 1932- .... CLC 48
  See also CA 125
Fukuyama, Francis 1952- .... CLC 131
  See also CA 140; CANR 72
Fuller, Charles (H., Jr.) 1939- .... CLC 25;
    BLC 2; DAM DRAM, MULT; DC 1
  See also BW 2; CA 108; 112; CANR 87;
    DLB 38; INT 112; MTCW 1
Fuller, John (Leopold) 1937- .... CLC 62
  See also CA 21-24R; CANR 9, 44; DLB 40
Fuller, Margaret
  See Ossoli, Sarah Margaret (Fuller marchesa
    d')
Fuller, Roy (Broadbent) 1912-1991 ... CLC 4,
    28
  See also CA 5-8R; 135; CAAS 10; CANR
    53, 83; DLB 15, 20; SATA 87

Fuller, Sarah Margaret 1810-1850
  See Ossoli, Sarah Margaret (Fuller marchesa
    d')
Fulton, Alice 1952- .... CLC 52
  See also CA 116; CANR 57, 88; DLB 193
Furphy, Joseph 1843-1912 .... TCLC 25
  See also CA 163
Fussell, Paul 1924- .... CLC 74
  See also BEST 90:1; CA 17-20R; CANR 8,
    21, 35, 69; INT CANR-21; MTCW 1, 2
Futabatei, Shimei 1864-1909 .... TCLC 44
  See also CA 162; DLB 180
Futrelle, Jacques 1875-1912 .... TCLC 19
  See also CA 113; 155
Gaboriau, Emile 1835-1873 .... NCLC 14
Gadda, Carlo Emilio 1893-1973 .... CLC 11
  See also CA 89-92; DLB 177
Gaddis, William 1922-1998 ... CLC 1, 3, 6, 8,
    10, 19, 43, 86
  See also CA 17-20R; 172; CANR 21, 48;
    DLB 2; MTCW 1, 2
Gage, Walter
  See Inge, William (Motter)
Gaines, Ernest J(ames) 1933- ...... CLC 3, 11,
    18, 86; BLC 2; DAM MULT
  See also AAYA 18; AITN 1; BW 2, 3; CA
    9-12R; CANR 6, 24, 42, 75; CDALB
    1968-1988; CLR 62; DA3; DLB 2, 33,
    152; DLBY 80; MTCW 1, 2; SATA 86
Gaitskill, Mary 1954- .... CLC 69
  See also CA 128; CANR 61
Galdos, Benito Perez
  See Perez Galdos, Benito
Gale, Zona 1874-1938 .... TCLC 7; DAM
    DRAM
  See also CA 105; 153; CANR 84; DLB 9,
    78, 228
Galeano, Eduardo (Hughes) 1940- . CLC 72;
    HLCS 1
  See also CA 29-32R; CANR 13, 32; HW 1
Galiano, Juan Valera y Alcala
  See Valera y Alcala-Galiano, Juan
Galilei, Galileo 1546-1642 .... LC 45
Gallagher, Tess 1943- ...... CLC 18, 63; DAM
    POET; PC 9
  See also CA 106; DLB 212
Gallant, Mavis 1922- .. CLC 7, 18, 38; DAC;
    DAM MST; SSC 5
  See also CA 69-72; CANR 29, 69; DLB 53;
    MTCW 1, 2
Gallant, Roy A(rthur) 1924- .... CLC 17
  See also CA 5-8R; CANR 4, 29, 54; CLR
    30; MAICYA; SATA 4, 68, 110
Gallico, Paul (William) 1897-1976 ..... CLC 2
  See also AITN 1; CA 5-8R; 69-72; CANR
    23; DLB 9, 171; MAICYA; SATA 13
Gallo, Max Louis 1932- .... CLC 95
  See also CA 85-88
Gallois, Lucien
  See Desnos, Robert
Gallup, Ralph
  See Whitemore, Hugh (John)
Galsworthy, John 1867-1933 .... TCLC 1, 45;
    DA; DAB; DAC; DAM DRAM, MST,
    NOV; SSC 22; WLC
  See also CA 104; 141; CANR 75; CDBLB
    1890-1914; DA3; DLB 10, 34, 98, 162;
    DLBD 16; MTCW 1
Galt, John 1779-1839 .... NCLC 1
  See also DLB 99, 116, 159
Galvin, James 1951- .... CLC 38
  See also CA 108; CANR 26
Gamboa, Federico 1864-1939 .... TCLC 36
  See also CA 167; HW 2
Gandhi, M. K.
  See Gandhi, Mohandas Karamchand
Gandhi, Mahatma
  See Gandhi, Mohandas Karamchand

Gandhi, Mohandas Karamchand
1869-1948 .... **TCLC 59; DAM MULT**
See also CA 121; 132; DA3; MTCW 1, 2

Gann, Ernest Kellogg 1910-1991 ..... **CLC 23**
See also AITN 1; CA 1-4R; 136; CANR 1, 83

Garber, Eric 1943(?)-
See Holleran, Andrew
See also CANR 89

Garcia, Cristina 1958- .... **CLC 76**
See also CA 141; CANR 73; HW 2

Garcia Lorca, Federico 1898-1936 . **TCLC 1, 7, 49; DA; DAB; DAC; DAM DRAM, MST, MULT, POET; DC 2; HLC 2; PC 3; WLC**
See also Lorca, Federico Garcia
See also CA 104; 131; CANR 81; DA3; DLB 108; HW 1, 2; MTCW 1, 2

Garcia Marquez, Gabriel (Jose)
1928- .... **CLC 2, 3, 8, 10, 15, 27, 47, 55, 68; DA; DAB; DAC; DAM MST, MULT, NOV, POP; HLC 1; SSC 8; WLC**
See also AAYA 3, 33; BEST 89:1, 90:4; CA 33-36R; CANR 10, 28, 50, 75, 82; DA3; DLB 113; HW 1, 2; MTCW 1, 2

Garcilaso de la Vega, El Inca 1503-1536
See also HLCS 1

Gard, Janice
See Latham, Jean Lee

Gard, Roger Martin du
See Martin du Gard, Roger

Gardam, Jane 1928- .... **CLC 43**
See also CA 49-52; CANR 2, 18, 33, 54; CLR 12; DLB 14, 161, 231; MAICYA; MTCW 1; SAAS 9; SATA 39, 76; SATA-Brief 28

Gardner, Herb(ert) 1934- .... **CLC 44**
See also CA 149

Gardner, John (Champlin), Jr.
1933-1982 ...... **CLC 2, 3, 5, 7, 8, 10, 18, 28, 34; DAM NOV, POP; SSC 7**
See also AITN 1; CA 65-68; 107; CANR 33, 73; CDALBS; DA3; DLB 2; DLBY 82; MTCW 1; SATA 40; SATA-Obit 31

Gardner, John (Edmund) 1926- ...... **CLC 30; DAM POP**
See also CA 103; CANR 15, 69; MTCW 1

Gardner, Miriam
See Bradley, Marion Zimmer

Gardner, Noel
See Kuttner, Henry

Gardons, S. S.
See Snodgrass, W(illiam) D(e Witt)

Garfield, Leon 1921-1996 .... **CLC 12**
See also AAYA 8; CA 17-20R; 152; CANR 38, 41, 78; CLR 21; DLB 161; JRDA; MAICYA; SATA 1, 32, 76; SATA-Obit 90

Garland, (Hannibal) Hamlin
1860-1940 .... **TCLC 3; SSC 18**
See also CA 104; DLB 12, 71, 78, 186

Garneau, (Hector de) Saint-Denys
1912-1943 .... **TCLC 13**
See also CA 111; DLB 88

Garner, Alan 1934- ..... **CLC 17; DAB; DAM POP**
See also AAYA 18; CA 73-76, 178; CAAE 178; CANR 15, 64; CLR 20; DLB 161; MAICYA; MTCW 1, 2; SATA 18, 69; SATA-Essay 108

Garner, Hugh 1913-1979 .... **CLC 13**
See also CA 69-72; CANR 31; DLB 68

Garnett, David 1892-1981 .... **CLC 3**
See also CA 5-8R; 103; CANR 17, 79; DLB 34; MTCW 2

Garos, Stephanie
See Katz, Steve

Garrett, George (Palmer) 1929- .. **CLC 3, 11, 51; SSC 30**
See also CA 1-4R; CAAS 5; CANR 1, 42, 67; DLB 2, 5, 130, 152; DLBY 83

Garrick, David 1717-1779 .... **LC 15; DAM DRAM**
See also DLB 84

Garrigue, Jean 1914-1972 .... **CLC 2, 8**
See also CA 5-8R; 37-40R; CANR 20

Garrison, Frederick
See Sinclair, Upton (Beall)

Garro, Elena 1920(?)-1998
See also CA 131; 169; DLB 145; HLCS 1; HW 1

Garth, Will
See Hamilton, Edmond; Kuttner, Henry

Garvey, Marcus (Moziah, Jr.)
1887-1940 ...... **TCLC 41; BLC 2; DAM MULT**
See also BW 1; CA 120; 124; CANR 79

Gary, Romain CLC 25
See also Kacew, Romain
See also DLB 83

Gascar, Pierre CLC 11
See also Fournier, Pierre

Gascoyne, David (Emery) 1916- .... **CLC 45**
See also CA 65-68; CANR 10, 28, 54; DLB 20; MTCW 1

Gaskell, Elizabeth Cleghorn
1810-1865 .... **NCLC 70; DAB; DAM MST; SSC 25**
See also CDBLB 1832-1890; DLB 21, 144, 159

Gass, William H(oward) 1924- . **CLC 1, 2, 8, 11, 15, 39, 132; SSC 12**
See also CA 17-20R; CANR 30, 71; DLB 2, 227; MTCW 1, 2

Gassendi, Pierre 1592-1655 .... **LC 54**

Gasset, Jose Ortega y
See Ortega y Gasset, Jose

Gates, Henry Louis, Jr. 1950- .... **CLC 65; BLCS; DAM MULT**
See also BW 2, 3; CA 109; CANR 25, 53, 75; DA3; DLB 67; MTCW 1

Gautier, Theophile 1811-1872 .. **NCLC 1, 59; DAM POET; PC 18; SSC 20**
See also DLB 119

Gawsworth, John
See Bates, H(erbert) E(rnest)

Gay, John 1685-1732 .. **LC 49; DAM DRAM**
See also DLB 84, 95

Gay, Oliver
See Gogarty, Oliver St. John

Gaye, Marvin (Penze) 1939-1984 ..... **CLC 26**
See also CA 112

Gebler, Carlo (Ernest) 1954- .... **CLC 39**
See also CA 119; 133

Gee, Maggie (Mary) 1948- .... **CLC 57**
See also CA 130; DLB 207

Gee, Maurice (Gough) 1931- .... **CLC 29**
See also CA 97-100; CANR 67; CLR 56; SATA 46, 101

Gelbart, Larry (Simon) 1928- .... **CLC 21, 61**
See Gelbart, Larry
See also CA 73-76; CANR 45

Gelbart, Larry 1928-
See Gelbart, Larry (Simon)

Gelber, Jack 1932- .... **CLC 1, 6, 14, 79**
See also CA 1-4R; CANR 2; DLB 7, 228

Gellhorn, Martha (Ellis)
1908-1998 .... **CLC 14, 60**
See also CA 77-80; 164; CANR 44; DLBY 82, 98

Genet, Jean 1910-1986 .. **CLC 1, 2, 5, 10, 14, 44, 46; DAM DRAM**
See also CA 13-16R; CANR 18; DA3; DLB 72; DLBY 86; MTCW 1, 2

Gent, Peter 1942- .... **CLC 29**
See also AITN 1; CA 89-92; DLBY 82

Gentile, Giovanni 1875-1944 .... **TCLC 96**
See also CA 119

Gentlewoman in New England, A
See Bradstreet, Anne

Gentlewoman in Those Parts, A
See Bradstreet, Anne

George, Jean Craighead 1919- .... **CLC 35**
See also AAYA 8; CA 5-8R; CANR 25; CLR 1; DLB 52; JRDA; MAICYA; SATA 2, 68

George, Stefan (Anton) 1868-1933 . **TCLC 2, 14**
See also CA 104

Georges, Georges Martin
See Simenon, Georges (Jacques Christian)

Gerhardi, William Alexander
See Gerhardie, William Alexander

Gerhardie, William Alexander
1895-1977 .... **CLC 5**
See also CA 25-28R; 73-76; CANR 18; DLB 36

Gerstler, Amy 1956- .... **CLC 70**
See also CA 146

Gertler, T. CLC 134
See also CA 116; 121

Ghalib NCLC 39, 78
See also Ghalib, Hsadullah Khan

Ghalib, Hsadullah Khan 1797-1869
See Ghalib
See also DAM POET

Ghelderode, Michel de 1898-1962 ..... **CLC 6, 11; DAM DRAM**
See also CA 85-88; CANR 40, 77

Ghiselin, Brewster 1903- .... **CLC 23**
See also CA 13-16R; CAAS 10; CANR 13

Ghose, Aurabinda 1872-1950 .... **TCLC 63**
See also CA 163

Ghose, Zulfikar 1935- .... **CLC 42**
See also CA 65-68; CANR 67

Ghosh, Amitav 1956- .... **CLC 44**
See also CA 147; CANR 80

Giacosa, Giuseppe 1847-1906 .... **TCLC 7**
See also CA 104

Gibb, Lee
See Waterhouse, Keith (Spencer)

Gibbon, Lewis Grassic TCLC 4
See also Mitchell, James Leslie

Gibbons, Kaye 1960- .... **CLC 50, 88; DAM POP**
See also AAYA 34; CA 151; CANR 75; DA3; MTCW 1; SATA 117

Gibran, Kahlil 1883-1931 .... **TCLC 1, 9; DAM POET, POP; PC 9**
See also CA 104; 150; DA3; MTCW 2

Gibran, Khalil
See Gibran, Kahlil

Gibson, William 1914- .. **CLC 23; DA; DAB; DAC; DAM DRAM, MST**
See also CA 9-12R; CANR 9, 42, 75; DLB 7; MTCW 1; SATA 66

Gibson, William (Ford) 1948- ... **CLC 39, 63; DAM POP**
See also AAYA 12; CA 126; 133; CANR 52, 90; DA3; MTCW 1

Gide, Andre (Paul Guillaume)
1869-1951 . **TCLC 5, 12, 36; DA; DAB; DAC; DAM MST, NOV; SSC 13; WLC**
See also CA 104; 124; DA3; DLB 65; MTCW 1, 2

Gifford, Barry (Colby) 1946- .... **CLC 34**
See also CA 65-68; CANR 9, 30, 40, 90

Gilbert, Frank
See De Voto, Bernard (Augustine)

Gilbert, W(illiam) S(chwenck)
1836-1911 .... **TCLC 3; DAM DRAM, POET**
See also CA 104; 173; SATA 36

Gilbreth, Frank B., Jr. 1911- .... **CLC 17**
See also CA 9-12R; SATA 2

Gilchrist, Ellen 1935- ...... **CLC 34, 48; DAM POP; SSC 14**
See also CA 113; 116; CANR 41, 61; DLB 130; MTCW 1, 2

Giles, Molly 1942- .... **CLC 39**
See also CA 126

Gill, Eric 1882-1940 .... **TCLC 85**

Gill, Patrick
See Creasey, John

Gilliam, Terry (Vance) 1940- .... **CLC 21**
See also Monty Python
See also AAYA 19; CA 108; 113; CANR 35; INT 113

Gillian, Jerry
See Gilliam, Terry (Vance)

Gilliatt, Penelope (Ann Douglass) 1932-1993 .... **CLC 2, 10, 13, 53**
See also AITN 2; CA 13-16R; 141; CANR 49; DLB 14

Gilman, Charlotte (Anna) Perkins (Stetson) 1860-1935 .... **TCLC 9, 37; SSC 13**
See also CA 106; 150; DLB 221; MTCW 1

Gilmour, David 1949- .... **CLC 35**
See also CA 138, 147

Gilpin, William 1724-1804 .... **NCLC 30**

Gilray, J. D.
See Mencken, H(enry) L(ouis)

Gilroy, Frank D(aniel) 1925- .... **CLC 2**
See also CA 81-84; CANR 32, 64, 86; DLB 7

Gilstrap, John 1957(?)- .... **CLC 99**
See also CA 160

Ginsberg, Allen 1926-1997 .... **CLC 1, 2, 3, 4, 6, 13, 36, 69, 109; DA; DAB; DAC; DAM MST, POET; PC 4; WLC**
See also AAYA 33; AITN 1; CA 1-4R; 157; CANR 2, 41, 63; CDALB 1941-1968; DA3; DLB 5, 16, 169; MTCW 1, 2

Ginzburg, Natalia 1916-1991 .... **CLC 5, 11, 54, 70**
See also CA 85-88; 135; CANR 33; DLB 177; MTCW 1, 2

Giono, Jean 1895-1970 .... **CLC 4, 11**
See also CA 45-48; 29-32R; CANR 2, 35; DLB 72; MTCW 1

Giovanni, Nikki 1943- .... **CLC 2, 4, 19, 64, 117; BLC 2; DA; DAB; DAC; DAM MST, MULT, POET; PC 19; WLCS**
See also AAYA 22; AITN 1; BW 2, 3; CA 29-32R; CAAS 6; CANR 18, 41, 60, 91; CDALBS; CLR 6; DA3; DLB 5, 41; INT CANR-18; MAICYA; MTCW 1, 2; SATA 24, 107

Giovene, Andrea 1904- .... **CLC 7**
See also CA 85-88

Gippius, Zinaida (Nikolayevna) 1869-1945
See Hippius, Zinaida
See also CA 106

Giraudoux, (Hippolyte) Jean 1882-1944 .... **TCLC 2, 7; DAM DRAM**
See also CA 104; DLB 65

Gironella, Jose Maria 1917- .... **CLC 11**
See also CA 101

Gissing, George (Robert) 1857-1903 .... **TCLC 3, 24, 47; SSC 37**
See also CA 105; 167; DLB 18, 135, 184

Giurlani, Aldo
See Palazzeschi, Aldo

Gladkov, Fyodor (Vasilyevich) 1883-1958 .... **TCLC 27**
See also CA 170

Glanville, Brian (Lester) 1931- .... **CLC 6**
See also CA 5-8R; CAAS 9; CANR 3, 70; DLB 15, 139; SATA 42

Glasgow, Ellen (Anderson Gholson) 1873-1945 .... **TCLC 2, 7; SSC 34**
See also CA 104; 164; DLB 9, 12; MTCW 2

Glaspell, Susan 1882(?)-1948 . **TCLC 55; DC 10; SSC 41**
See also CA 110; 154; DLB 7, 9, 78, 228; YABC 2

Glassco, John 1909-1981 .... **CLC 9**
See also CA 13-16R; 102; CANR 15; DLB 68

Glasscock, Amnesia
See Steinbeck, John (Ernst)

Glasser, Ronald J. 1940(?)- .... **CLC 37**

Glassman, Joyce
See Johnson, Joyce

Glendinning, Victoria 1937- .... **CLC 50**
See also CA 120; 127; CANR 59, 89; DLB 155

Glissant, Edouard 1928- . **CLC 10, 68; DAM MULT**
See also CA 153

Gloag, Julian 1930- .... **CLC 40**
See also AITN 1; CA 65-68; CANR 10, 70

Glowacki, Aleksander
See Prus, Boleslaw

Gluck, Louise (Elisabeth) 1943- .. **CLC 7, 22, 44, 81; DAM POET; PC 16**
See also CA 33-36R; CANR 40, 69; DA3; DLB 5; MTCW 2

Glyn, Elinor 1864-1943 .... **TCLC 72**
See also DLB 153

Gobineau, Joseph Arthur (Comte) de 1816-1882 .... **NCLC 17**
See also DLB 123

Godard, Jean-Luc 1930- .... **CLC 20**
See also CA 93-96

Godden, (Margaret) Rumer 1907-1998 .... **CLC 53**
See also AAYA 6; CA 5-8R; 172; CANR 4, 27, 36, 55, 80; CLR 20; DLB 161; MAI-CYA; SAAS 12; SATA 3, 36; SATA-Obit 109

Godoy Alcayaga, Lucila 1889-1957 .... **TCLC 2; DAM MULT; HLC 2; PC 32**
See also BW 2; CA 104; 131; CANR 81; HW 1, 2; MTCW 1, 2

Godwin, Gail (Kathleen) 1937- ..... **CLC 5, 8, 22, 31, 69, 125; DAM POP**
See also CA 29-32R; CANR 15, 43, 69; DA3; DLB 6; INT CANR-15; MTCW 1, 2

Godwin, William 1756-1836 .... **NCLC 14**
See also CDBLB 1789-1832; DLB 39, 104, 142, 158, 163

Goebbels, Josef
See Goebbels, (Paul) Joseph

Goebbels, (Paul) Joseph 1897-1945 .... **TCLC 68**
See also CA 115; 148

Goebbels, Joseph Paul
See Goebbels, (Paul) Joseph

Goethe, Johann Wolfgang von 1749-1832 ...... **NCLC 4, 22, 34, 90; DA; DAB; DAC; DAM DRAM, MST, POET; PC 5; SSC 38; WLC**
See also DA3; DLB 94

Gogarty, Oliver St. John 1878-1957 .... **TCLC 15**
See also CA 109; 150; DLB 15, 19

Gogol, Nikolai (Vasilyevich) 1809-1852 . **NCLC 5, 15, 31; DA; DAB; DAC; DAM DRAM, MST; DC 1; SSC 4, 29; WLC**
See also DLB 198

Goines, Donald 1937(?)-1974 . **CLC 80; BLC 2; DAM MULT, POP**
See also AITN 1; BW 1, 3; CA 124; 114; CANR 82; DA3; DLB 33

Gold, Herbert 1924- .... **CLC 4, 7, 14, 42**
See also CA 9-12R; CANR 17, 45; DLB 2; DLBY 81

Goldbarth, Albert 1948- .... **CLC 5, 38**
See also CA 53-56; CANR 6, 40; DLB 120

Goldberg, Anatol 1910-1982 .... **CLC 34**
See also CA 131; 117

Goldemberg, Isaac 1945- .... **CLC 52**
See also CA 69-72; CAAS 12; CANR 11, 32; HW 1

Golding, William (Gerald) 1911-1993 ..... **CLC 1, 2, 3, 8, 10, 17, 27, 58, 81; DA; DAB; DAC; DAM MST, NOV; WLC**
See also AAYA 5; CA 5-8R; 141; CANR 13, 33, 54; CDBLB 1945-1960; DA3; DLB 15, 100; MTCW 1, 2

Goldman, Emma 1869-1940 .... **TCLC 13**
See also CA 110; 150; DLB 221

Goldman, Francisco 1954- .... **CLC 76**
See also CA 162

Goldman, William (W.) 1931- ...... **CLC 1, 48**
See also CA 9-12R; CANR 29, 69; DLB 44

Goldmann, Lucien 1913-1970 .... **CLC 24**
See also CA 25-28; CAP 2

Goldoni, Carlo 1707-1793 .... **LC 4; DAM DRAM**

Goldsberry, Steven 1949- .... **CLC 34**
See also CA 131

Goldsmith, Oliver 1728-1774 . **LC 2, 48; DA; DAB; DAC; DAM DRAM, MST, NOV, POET; DC 8; WLC**
See also CDBLB 1660-1789; DLB 39, 89, 104, 109, 142; SATA 26

Goldsmith, Peter
See Priestley, J(ohn) B(oynton)

Gombrowicz, Witold 1904-1969 .... **CLC 4, 7, 11, 49; DAM DRAM**
See also CA 19-20; 25-28R; CAP 2

Gomez de la Serna, Ramon 1888-1963 .... **CLC 9**
See also CA 153; 116; CANR 79; HW 1, 2

Goncharov, Ivan Alexandrovich 1812-1891 .... **NCLC 1, 63**

Goncourt, Edmond (Louis Antoine Huot) de 1822-1896 .... **NCLC 7**
See also DLB 123

Goncourt, Jules (Alfred Huot) de 1830-1870 .... **NCLC 7**
See also DLB 123

Gontier, Fernande 19(?)- .... **CLC 50**

Gonzalez Martinez, Enrique 1871-1952 .... **TCLC 72**
See also CA 166; CANR 81; HW 1, 2

Goodman, Paul 1911-1972 ..... **CLC 1, 2, 4, 7**
See also CA 19-20; 37-40R; CANR 34; CAP 2; DLB 130; MTCW 1

Gordimer, Nadine 1923- ...... **CLC 3, 5, 7, 10, 18, 33, 51, 70, 123; DA; DAB; DAC; DAM MST, NOV; SSC 17; WLCS**
See also CA 5-8R; CANR 3, 28, 56, 88; DA3; DLB 225; INT CANR-28; MTCW 1, 2

Gordon, Adam Lindsay 1833-1870 .... **NCLC 21**

Gordon, Caroline 1895-1981 . **CLC 6, 13, 29, 83; SSC 15**
See also CA 11-12; 103; CANR 36; CAP 1; DLB 4, 9, 102; DLBD 17; DLBY 81; MTCW 1, 2

Gordon, Charles William 1860-1937
See Connor, Ralph
See also CA 109

Grieg, (Johan) Nordahl (Brun)
1902-1943 .... **TCLC 10**
See also CA 107

Grieve, C(hristopher) M(urray)
1892-1978 ..... **CLC 11, 19; DAM POET**
See also MacDiarmid, Hugh; Pteleon
See also CA 5-8R; 85-88; CANR 33;
MTCW 1

Griffin, Gerald 1803-1840 .... **NCLC 7**
See also DLB 159

Griffin, John Howard 1920-1980 ..... **CLC 68**
See also AITN 1; CA 1-4R; 101; CANR 2

Griffin, Peter 1942- .... **CLC 39**
See also CA 136

Griffith, D(avid Lewelyn) W(ark)
1875(?)-1948 .... **TCLC 68**
See also CA 119; 150; CANR 80

Griffith, Lawrence
See Griffith, D(avid Lewelyn) W(ark)

Griffiths, Trevor 1935- .... **CLC 13, 52**
See also CA 97-100; CANR 45; DLB 13

Griggs, Sutton (Elbert)
1872-1930 .... **TCLC 77**
See also CA 123; 186; DLB 50

Grigson, Geoffrey (Edward Harvey)
1905-1985 .... **CLC 7, 39**
See also CA 25-28R; 118; CANR 20, 33;
DLB 27; MTCW 1, 2

Grillparzer, Franz 1791-1872 .... **NCLC 1;**
SSC 37
See also DLB 133

Grimble, Reverend Charles James
See Eliot, T(homas) S(tearns)

Grimke, Charlotte L(ottie) Forten
1837(?)-1914
See Forten, Charlotte L.
See also BW 1; CA 117; 124; DAM MULT,
POET

Grimm, Jacob Ludwig Karl
1785-1863 .... **NCLC 3, 77; SSC 36**
See also DLB 90; MAICYA; SATA 22

Grimm, Wilhelm Karl 1786-1859 .. **NCLC 3,**
77; SSC 36
See also DLB 90; MAICYA; SATA 22

Grimmelshausen, Johann Jakob Christoffel
von 1621-1676 .... **LC 6**
See also DLB 168

Grindel, Eugene 1895-1952
See Eluard, Paul
See also CA 104

Grisham, John 1955- .... **CLC 84; DAM POP**
See also AAYA 14; CA 138; CANR 47, 69;
DA3; MTCW 2

Grossman, David 1954- .... **CLC 67**
See also CA 138

Grossman, Vasily (Semenovich)
1905-1964 .... **CLC 41**
See also CA 124; 130; MTCW 1

Grove, Frederick Philip TCLC 4
See also Greve, Felix Paul (Berthold
Friedrich)
See also DLB 92

Grubb
See Crumb, R(obert)

Grumbach, Doris (Isaac) 1918- . **CLC 13, 22,**
64
See also CA 5-8R; CAAS 2; CANR 9, 42,
70; INT CANR-9; MTCW 2

Grundtvig, Nicolai Frederik Severin
1783-1872 .... **NCLC 1**

Grunge
See Crumb, R(obert)

Grunwald, Lisa 1959- .... **CLC 44**
See also CA 120

Guare, John 1938- .... **CLC 8, 14, 29, 67;**
DAM DRAM
See also CA 73-76; CANR 21, 69; DLB 7;
MTCW 1, 2

Gudjonsson, Halldor Kiljan 1902-1998
See Laxness, Halldor
See also CA 103; 164

Guenter, Erich
See Eich, Guenter

Guest, Barbara 1920- .... **CLC 34**
See also CA 25-28R; CANR 11, 44, 84;
DLB 5, 193

Guest, Edgar A(lbert) 1881-1959 ... **TCLC 95**
See also CA 112; 168

Guest, Judith (Ann) 1936- .... **CLC 8, 30;**
DAM NOV, POP
See also AAYA 7; CA 77-80; CANR 15,
75; DA3; INT CANR-15; MTCW 1, 2

Guevara, Che CLC 87; HLC 1
See also Guevara (Serna), Ernesto

Guevara (Serna), Ernesto
1928-1967 .... **CLC 87; DAM MULT;**
HLC 1
See also Guevara, Che
See also CA 127; 111; CANR 56; HW 1

Guicciardini, Francesco 1483-1540 ..... **LC 49**

Guild, Nicholas M. 1944- .... **CLC 33**
See also CA 93-96

Guillemin, Jacques
See Sartre, Jean-Paul

Guillen, Jorge 1893-1984 .... **CLC 11; DAM**
MULT, POET; HLCS 1
See also CA 89-92; 112; DLB 108; HW 1

Guillen, Nicolas (Cristobal)
1902-1989 ... **CLC 48, 79; BLC 2; DAM**
MST, MULT, POET; HLC 1; PC 23
See also BW 2; CA 116; 125; 129; CANR
84; HW 1

Guillevic, (Eugene) 1907- .... **CLC 33**
See also CA 93-96

Guillois
See Desnos, Robert

Guillois, Valentin
See Desnos, Robert

Guimaraes Rosa, Joao 1908-1967
See also CA 175; HLCS 2

Guiney, Louise Imogen
1861-1920 .... **TCLC 41**
See also CA 160; DLB 54

Guiraldes, Ricardo (Guillermo)
1886-1927 .... **TCLC 39**
See also CA 131; HW 1; MTCW 1

Gumilev, Nikolai (Stepanovich)
1886-1921 .... **TCLC 60**
See also CA 165

Gunesekera, Romesh 1954- .... **CLC 91**
See also CA 159

Gunn, Bill CLC 5
See also Gunn, William Harrison
See also DLB 38

Gunn, Thom(son William) 1929- .. **CLC 3, 6,**
18, 32, 81; DAM POET; PC 26
See also CA 17-20R; CANR 9, 33; CDBLB
1960 to Present; DLB 27; INT CANR-33;
MTCW 1

Gunn, William Harrison 1934(?)-1989
See Gunn, Bill
See also AITN 1; BW 1, 3; CA 13-16R;
128; CANR 12, 25, 76

Gunnars, Kristjana 1948- .... **CLC 69**
See also CA 113; DLB 60

Gurdjieff, G(eorgei) I(vanovich)
1877(?)-1949 .... **TCLC 71**
See also CA 157

Gurganus, Allan 1947- . **CLC 70; DAM POP**
See also BEST 90:1; CA 135

Gurney, A(lbert) R(amsdell), Jr.
1930- ..... **CLC 32, 50, 54; DAM DRAM**
See also CA 77-80; CANR 32, 64

Gurney, Ivor (Bertie) 1890-1937 ... **TCLC 33**
See also CA 167

Gurney, Peter
See Gurney, A(lbert) R(amsdell), Jr.

Guro, Elena 1877-1913 .... **TCLC 56**

Gustafson, James M(oody) 1925- ... **CLC 100**
See also CA 25-28R; CANR 37

Gustafson, Ralph (Barker) 1909- ..... **CLC 36**
See also CA 21-24R; CANR 8, 45, 84; DLB
88

Gut, Gom
See Simenon, Georges (Jacques Christian)

Guterson, David 1956- .... **CLC 91**
See also CA 132; CANR 73; MTCW 2

Guthrie, A(lfred) B(ertram), Jr.
1901-1991 .... **CLC 23**
See also CA 57-60; 134; CANR 24; DLB
212; SATA 62; SATA-Obit 67

Guthrie, Isobel
See Grieve, C(hristopher) M(urray)

Guthrie, Woodrow Wilson 1912-1967
See Guthrie, Woody
See also CA 113; 93-96

Guthrie, Woody CLC 35
See also Guthrie, Woodrow Wilson

Gutierrez Najera, Manuel 1859-1895
See also HLCS 2

Guy, Rosa (Cuthbert) 1928- .... **CLC 26**
See also AAYA 4; BW 2; CA 17-20R;
CANR 14, 34, 83; CLR 13; DLB 33;
JRDA; MAICYA; SATA 14, 62

Gwendolyn
See Bennett, (Enoch) Arnold

H. D. CLC 3, 8, 14, 31, 34, 73; PC 5
See also Doolittle, Hilda

H. de V.
See Buchan, John

Haavikko, Paavo Juhani 1931- .. **CLC 18, 34**
See also CA 106

Habbema, Koos
See Heijermans, Herman

Habermas, Juergen 1929- .... **CLC 104**
See also CA 109; CANR 85

Habermas, Jurgen
See Habermas, Juergen

Hacker, Marilyn 1942- ...... **CLC 5, 9, 23, 72,**
91; DAM POET
See also CA 77-80; CANR 68; DLB 120

Haeckel, Ernst Heinrich (Philipp August)
1834-1919 .... **TCLC 83**
See also CA 157

Hafiz c. 1326-1389(?) .... **CMLC 34**

Hafiz c. 1326-1389 .... **CMLC 34**

Haggard, H(enry) Rider
1856-1925 .... **TCLC 11**
See also CA 108; 148; DLB 70, 156, 174,
178; MTCW 2; SATA 16

Hagiosy, L.
See Larbaud, Valery (Nicolas)

Hagiwara Sakutaro 1886-1942 ..... **TCLC 60;**
PC 18

Haig, Fenil
See Ford, Ford Madox

Haig-Brown, Roderick (Langmere)
1908-1976 .... **CLC 21**
See also CA 5-8R; 69-72; CANR 4, 38, 83;
CLR 31; DLB 88; MAICYA; SATA 12

Hailey, Arthur 1920- ..... **CLC 5; DAM NOV,**
POP
See also AITN 2; BEST 90:3; CA 1-4R;
CANR 2, 36, 75; DLB 88; DLBY 82;
MTCW 1, 2

Hailey, Elizabeth Forsythe 1938- ..... **CLC 40**
See also CA 93-96; CAAS 1; CANR 15,
48; INT CANR-15

Haines, John (Meade) 1924- .... **CLC 58**
See also CA 17-20R; CANR 13, 34; DLB
212

Irving, John (Winslow) 1942- ... **CLC 13, 23, 38, 112; DAM NOV, POP**
See also AAYA 8; BEST 89:3; CA 25-28R; CANR 28, 73; DA3; DLB 6; DLBY 82; MTCW 1, 2

Irving, Washington 1783-1859 . **NCLC 2, 19; DA; DAB; DAC; DAM MST; SSC 2, 37; WLC**
See also CDALB 1640-1865; DA3; DLB 3, 11, 30, 59, 73, 74, 186; YABC 2

Irwin, P. K.
See Page, P(atricia) K(athleen)

Isaacs, Jorge Ricardo 1837-1895 ... **NCLC 70**

Isaacs, Susan 1943- .... **CLC 32; DAM POP**
See also BEST 89:1; CA 89-92; CANR 20, 41, 65; DA3; INT CANR-20; MTCW 1, 2

Isherwood, Christopher (William Bradshaw) 1904-1986 .. **CLC 1, 9, 11, 14, 44; DAM DRAM, NOV**
See also CA 13-16R; 117; CANR 35; DA3; DLB 15, 195; DLBY 86; MTCW 1, 2

Ishiguro, Kazuo 1954- . **CLC 27, 56, 59, 110; DAM NOV**
See also BEST 90:2; CA 120; CANR 49; DA3; DLB 194; MTCW 1, 2

Ishikawa, Hakuhin
See Ishikawa, Takuboku

Ishikawa, Takuboku
1886(?)-1912 ... **TCLC 15; DAM POET; PC 10**
See also CA 113; 153

Iskander, Fazil 1929- .... **CLC 47**
See also CA 102

Isler, Alan (David) 1934- .... **CLC 91**
See also CA 156

Ivan IV 1530-1584 .... **LC 17**

Ivanov, Vyacheslav Ivanovich
1866-1949 .... **TCLC 33**
See also CA 122

Ivask, Ivar Vidrik 1927-1992 .... **CLC 14**
See also CA 37-40R; 139; CANR 24

Ives, Morgan
See Bradley, Marion Zimmer

Izumi Shikibu c. 973-c. 1034 .... **CMLC 33**
J CLC 25, 58, 65, 123; DAM DRAM; DC 6
See also CA 104; CANR 36, 63; DA3; DLB 232; MTCW 1, 2

J. R. S.
See Gogarty, Oliver St. John

Jabran, Kahlil
See Gibran, Kahlil

Jabran, Khalil
See Gibran, Kahlil

Jackson, Daniel
See Wingrove, David (John)

Jackson, Helen Hunt 1830-1885 .... **NCLC 90**
See also DLB 42, 47, 186, 189

Jackson, Jesse 1908-1983 .... **CLC 12**
See also BW 1; CA 25-28R; 109; CANR 27; CLR 28; MAICYA; SATA 2, 29; SATA-Obit 48

Jackson, Laura (Riding) 1901-1991
See Riding, Laura
See also CA 65-68; 135; CANR 28, 89; DLB 48

Jackson, Sam
See Trumbo, Dalton

Jackson, Sara
See Wingrove, David (John)

Jackson, Shirley 1919-1965 . **CLC 11, 60, 87; DA; DAC; DAM MST; SSC 9, 39; WLC**
See also AAYA 9; CA 1-4R; 25-28R; CANR 4, 52; CDALB 1941-1968; DA3; DLB 6; MTCW 2; SATA 2

Jacob, (Cyprien-)Max 1876-1944 .... **TCLC 6**
See also CA 104

Jacobs, Harriet A(nn)
1813(?)-1897 .... **NCLC 67**

Jacobs, Jim 1942- .... **CLC 12**
See also CA 97-100; INT 97-100

Jacobs, W(illiam) W(ymark)
1863-1943 .... **TCLC 22**
See also CA 121; 167; DLB 135

Jacobsen, Jens Peter 1847-1885 .... **NCLC 34**

Jacobsen, Josephine 1908- .... **CLC 48, 102**
See also CA 33-36R; CAAS 18; CANR 23, 48

Jacobson, Dan 1929- .... **CLC 4, 14**
See also CA 1-4R; CANR 2, 25, 66; DLB 14, 207, 225; MTCW 1

Jacqueline
See Carpentier (y Valmont), Alejo

Jagger, Mick 1944- .... **CLC 17**

Jahiz, al- c. 780-c. 869 .... **CMLC 25**

Jakes, John (William) 1932- . **CLC 29; DAM NOV, POP**
See also AAYA 32; BEST 89:4; CA 57-60; CANR 10, 43, 66; DA3; DLBY 83; INT CANR-10; MTCW 1, 2; SATA 62

James, Andrew
See Kirkup, James

James, C(yril) L(ionel) R(obert)
1901-1989 .... **CLC 33; BLCS**
See also BW 2; CA 117; 125; 128; CANR 62; DLB 125; MTCW 1

James, Daniel (Lewis) 1911-1988
See Santiago, Danny
See also CA 174; 125

James, Dynely
See Mayne, William (James Carter)

James, Henry Sr. 1811-1882 .... **NCLC 53**

James, Henry 1843-1916 ..... **TCLC 2, 11, 24, 40, 47, 64; DA; DAB; DAC; DAM MST, NOV; SSC 8, 32; WLC**
See also CA 104; 132; CDALB 1865-1917; DA3; DLB 12, 71, 74, 189; DLBD 13; MTCW 1, 2

James, M. R.
See James, Montague (Rhodes)
See also DLB 156

James, Montague (Rhodes)
1862-1936 .... **TCLC 6; SSC 16**
See also CA 104; DLB 201

James, P. D. 1920- .... **CLC 18, 46, 122**
See also White, Phyllis Dorothy James
See also BEST 90:2; CDBLB 1960 to Present; DLB 87; DLBD 17

James, Philip
See Moorcock, Michael (John)

James, William 1842-1910 .... **TCLC 15, 32**
See also CA 109

James I 1394-1437 .... **LC 20**

Jameson, Anna 1794-1860 .... **NCLC 43**
See also DLB 99, 166

Jami, Nur al-Din 'Abd al-Rahman
1414-1492 .... **LC 9**

Jammes, Francis 1868-1938 .... **TCLC 75**

Jandl, Ernst 1925- .... **CLC 34**

Janowitz, Tama 1957- .. **CLC 43; DAM POP**
See also CA 106; CANR 52, 89

Japrisot, Sebastien 1931- .... **CLC 90**

Jarrell, Randall 1914-1965 .... **CLC 1, 2, 6, 9, 13, 49; DAM POET**
See also CA 5-8R; 25-28R; CABS 2; CANR 6, 34; CDALB 1941-1968; CLR 6; DLB 48, 52; MAICYA; MTCW 1, 2; SATA 7

Jarry, Alfred 1873-1907 . **TCLC 2, 14; DAM DRAM; SSC 20**
See also CA 104; 153; DA3; DLB 192

Jawien, Andrzej
See John Paul II, Pope

Jaynes, Roderick
See Coen, Ethan

Jeake, Samuel, Jr.
See Aiken, Conrad (Potter)

Jean Paul 1763-1825 .... **NCLC 7**

Jefferies, (John) Richard
1848-1887 .... **NCLC 47**
See also DLB 98, 141; SATA 16

Jeffers, (John) Robinson 1887-1962 .. **CLC 2, 3, 11, 15, 54; DA; DAC; DAM MST, POET; PC 17; WLC**
See also CA 85-88; CANR 35; CDALB 1917-1929; DLB 45, 212; MTCW 1, 2

Jefferson, Janet
See Mencken, H(enry) L(ouis)

Jefferson, Thomas 1743-1826 .... **NCLC 11**
See also CDALB 1640-1865; DA3; DLB 31

Jeffrey, Francis 1773-1850 .... **NCLC 33**
See also DLB 107

Jelakowitch, Ivan
See Heijermans, Herman

Jellicoe, (Patricia) Ann 1927- .... **CLC 27**
See also CA 85-88; DLB 13, 233

Jemyma
See Holley, Marietta

Jen, Gish CLC 70
See also Jen, Lillian

Jen, Lillian 1956(?)-
See Jen, Gish
See also CA 135; CANR 89

Jenkins, (John) Robin 1912- .... **CLC 52**
See also CA 1-4R; CANR 1; DLB 14

Jennings, Elizabeth (Joan) 1926- ...... **CLC 5, 14, 131**
See also CA 61-64; CAAS 5; CANR 8, 39, 66; DLB 27; MTCW 1; SATA 66

Jennings, Waylon 1937- .... **CLC 21**

Jensen, Johannes V. 1873-1950 ...... **TCLC 41**
See also CA 170

Jensen, Laura (Linnea) 1948- .... **CLC 37**
See also CA 103

Jerome, Jerome K(lapka)
1859-1927 .... **TCLC 23**
See also CA 119; 177; DLB 10, 34, 135

Jerrold, Douglas William
1803-1857 .... **NCLC 2**
See also DLB 158, 159

Jewett, (Theodora) Sarah Orne
1849-1909 .... **TCLC 1, 22; SSC 6**
See also CA 108; 127; CANR 71; DLB 12, 74, 221; SATA 15

Jewsbury, Geraldine (Endsor)
1812-1880 .... **NCLC 22**
See also DLB 21

Jhabvala, Ruth Prawer 1927- . **CLC 4, 8, 29, 94; DAB; DAM NOV**
See also CA 1-4R; CANR 2, 29, 51, 74, 91; DLB 139, 194; INT CANR-29; MTCW 1, 2

Jibran, Kahlil
See Gibran, Kahlil

Jibran, Khalil
See Gibran, Kahlil

Jiles, Paulette 1943- .... **CLC 13, 58**
See also CA 101; CANR 70

Jimenez (Mantecon), Juan Ramon
1881-1958 .... **TCLC 4; DAM MULT, POET; HLC 1; PC 7**
See also CA 104; 131; CANR 74; DLB 134; HW 1; MTCW 1, 2

Jimenez, Ramon
See Jimenez (Mantecon), Juan Ramon

Jimenez Mantecon, Juan
See Jimenez (Mantecon), Juan Ramon

Jin, Ha
See Jin, Xuefei

Keynes, John Maynard
1883-1946 .... **TCLC 64**
See also CA 114; 162, 163; DLBD 10;
MTCW 2

Khanshendel, Chiron
See Rose, Wendy

Khayyam, Omar 1048-1131 .... **CMLC 11;
DAM POET; PC 8**
See also DA3

Kherdian, David 1931- .... **CLC 6, 9**
See also CA 21-24R; CAAS 2; CANR 39,
78; CLR 24; JRDA; MAICYA; SATA 16,
74

Khlebnikov, Velimir TCLC 20
See also Khlebnikov, Viktor Vladimirovich

Khlebnikov, Viktor Vladimirovich 1885-1922
See Khlebnikov, Velimir
See also CA 117

Khodasevich, Vladislav (Felitsianovich)
1886-1939 .... **TCLC 15**
See also CA 115

Kielland, Alexander Lange
1849-1906 .... **TCLC 5**
See also CA 104

Kiely, Benedict 1919- .... **CLC 23, 43**
See also CA 1-4R; CANR 2, 84; DLB 15

Kienzle, William X(avier) 1928- ..... **CLC 25;
DAM POP**
See also CA 93-96; CAAS 1; CANR 9, 31,
59; DA3; INT CANR-31; MTCW 1, 2

Kierkegaard, Soren 1813-1855 ..... **NCLC 34,
78**

Kieslowski, Krzysztof 1941-1996 .... **CLC 120**
See also CA 147; 151

Killens, John Oliver 1916-1987 .... **CLC 10**
See also BW 2; CA 77-80; 123; CAAS 2;
CANR 26; DLB 33

Killigrew, Anne 1660-1685 .... **LC 4**
See also DLB 131

Killigrew, Thomas 1612-1683 .... **LC 57**
See also DLB 58

Kim
See Simenon, Georges (Jacques Christian)

Kincaid, Jamaica 1949- .... **CLC 43, 68; BLC
2; DAM MULT, NOV**
See also AAYA 13; BW 2, 3; CA 125;
CANR 47, 59; CDALBS; CLR 63; DA3;
DLB 157, 227; MTCW 2

King, Francis (Henry) 1923- .... **CLC 8, 53;
DAM NOV**
See also CA 1-4R; CANR 1, 33, 86; DLB
15, 139; MTCW 1

King, Kennedy
See Brown, George Douglas

King, Martin Luther, Jr.
1929-1968 .... **CLC 83; BLC 2; DA;
DAB; DAC; DAM MST, MULT;
WLCS**
See also BW 2, 3; CA 25-28; CANR 27,
44; CAP 2; DA3; MTCW 1, 2; SATA 14

King, Stephen (Edwin) 1947- .... **CLC 12, 26,
37, 61, 113; DAM NOV, POP; SSC 17**
See also AAYA 1, 17; BEST 90:1; CA 61-
64; CANR 1, 30, 52, 76; DA3; DLB 143;
DLBY 80; JRDA; MTCW 1, 2; SATA 9,
55

King, Steve
See King, Stephen (Edwin)

King, Thomas 1943- ... **CLC 89; DAC; DAM
MULT**
See also CA 144; DLB 175; NNAL; SATA
96

Kingman, Lee CLC 17
See also Natti, (Mary) Lee
See also SAAS 3; SATA 1, 67

Kingsley, Charles 1819-1875 .... **NCLC 35**
See also DLB 21, 32, 163, 190; YABC 2

Kingsley, Sidney 1906-1995 .... **CLC 44**
See also CA 85-88; 147; DLB 7

Kingsolver, Barbara 1955- .... **CLC 55, 81,
130; DAM POP**
See also AAYA 15; CA 129; 134; CANR
60; CDALBS; DA3; DLB 206; INT 134;
MTCW 2

Kingston, Maxine (Ting Ting) Hong
1940- .... **CLC 12, 19, 58, 121; DAM
MULT, NOV; WLCS**
See also AAYA 8; CA 69-72; CANR 13,
38, 74, 87; CDALBS; DA3; DLB 173,
212; DLBY 80; INT CANR-13; MTCW
1, 2; SATA 53

Kinnell, Galway 1927- ..... **CLC 1, 2, 3, 5, 13,
29, 129; PC 26**
See also CA 9-12R; CANR 10, 34, 66; DLB
5; DLBY 87; INT CANR-34; MTCW 1, 2

Kinsella, Thomas 1928- .... **CLC 4, 19**
See also CA 17-20R; CANR 15; DLB 27;
MTCW 1, 2

Kinsella, W(illiam) P(atrick) 1935- . **CLC 27,
43; DAC; DAM NOV, POP**
See also AAYA 7; CA 97-100; CAAS 7;
CANR 21, 35, 66, 75; INT CANR-21;
MTCW 1, 2

Kinsey, Alfred C(harles)
1894-1956 .... **TCLC 91**
See also CA 115; 170; MTCW 2

Kipling, (Joseph) Rudyard
1865-1936 .... **TCLC 8, 17; DA; DAB;
DAC; DAM MST, POET; PC 3; SSC
5; WLC**
See also AAYA 32; CA 105; 120; CANR
33; CDBLB 1890-1914; CLR 39, 65;
DA3; DLB 19, 34, 141, 156; MAICYA;
MTCW 1, 2; SATA 100; YABC 2

Kirkland, Caroline M. 1801-1864 . **NCLC 85**
See also DLB 3, 73, 74; DLBD 13

Kirkup, James 1918- .... **CLC 1**
See also CA 1-4R; CAAS 4; CANR 2; DLB
27; SATA 12

Kirkwood, James 1930(?)-1989 .... **CLC 9**
See also AITN 2; CA 1-4R; 128; CANR 6,
40

Kirshner, Sidney
See Kingsley, Sidney

Kis, Danilo 1935-1989 .... **CLC 57**
See also CA 109; 118; 129; CANR 61; DLB
181; MTCW 1

Kivi, Aleksis 1834-1872 .... **NCLC 30**

Kizer, Carolyn (Ashley) 1925- ... **CLC 15, 39,
80; DAM POET**
See also CA 65-68; CAAS 5; CANR 24,
70; DLB 5, 169; MTCW 2

Klabund 1890-1928 .... **TCLC 44**
See also CA 162; DLB 66

Klappert, Peter 1942- .... **CLC 57**
See also CA 33-36R; DLB 5

Klein, A(braham) M(oses)
1909-1972 . **CLC 19; DAB; DAC; DAM
MST**
See also CA 101; 37-40R; DLB 68

Klein, Norma 1938-1989 .... **CLC 30**
See also AAYA 2; CA 41-44R; 128; CANR
15, 37; CLR 2, 19; INT CANR-15; JRDA;
MAICYA; SAAS 1; SATA 7, 57

Klein, T(heodore) E(ibon) D(onald)
1947- .... **CLC 34**
See also CA 119; CANR 44, 75

Kleist, Heinrich von 1777-1811 ...... **NCLC 2,
37; DAM DRAM; SSC 22**
See also DLB 90

Klima, Ivan 1931- .... **CLC 56; DAM NOV**
See also CA 25-28R; CANR 17, 50, 91;
DLB 232

Klimentov, Andrei Platonovich
1899-1951 .... **TCLC 14; SSC 42**
See also CA 108

Klinger, Friedrich Maximilian von
1752-1831 .... **NCLC 1**
See also DLB 94

Klingsor the Magician
See Hartmann, Sadakichi

Klopstock, Friedrich Gottlieb
1724-1803 .... **NCLC 11**
See also DLB 97

Knapp, Caroline 1959- .... **CLC 99**
See also CA 154

Knebel, Fletcher 1911-1993 .... **CLC 14**
See also AITN 1; CA 1-4R; 140; CAAS 3;
CANR 1, 36; SATA 36; SATA-Obit 75

Knickerbocker, Diedrich
See Irving, Washington

Knight, Etheridge 1931-1991 . **CLC 40; BLC
2; DAM POET; PC 14**
See also BW 1, 3; CA 21-24R; 133; CANR
23, 82; DLB 41; MTCW 2

Knight, Sarah Kemble 1666-1727 .... **LC 7**
See also DLB 24, 200

Knister, Raymond 1899-1932 .... **TCLC 56**
See also CA 186; DLB 68

Knowles, John 1926- . **CLC 1, 4, 10, 26; DA;
DAC; DAM MST, NOV**
See also AAYA 10; CA 17-20R; CANR 40,
74, 76; CDALB 1968-1988; DLB 6;
MTCW 1, 2; SATA 8, 89

Knox, Calvin M.
See Silverberg, Robert

Knox, John c. 1505-1572 .... **LC 37**
See also DLB 132

Knye, Cassandra
See Disch, Thomas M(ichael)

Koch, C(hristopher) J(ohn) 1932- .... **CLC 42**
See also CA 127; CANR 84

Koch, Christopher
See Koch, C(hristopher) J(ohn)

Koch, Kenneth 1925- .... **CLC 5, 8, 44; DAM
POET**
See also CA 1-4R; CANR 6, 36, 57; DLB
5; INT CANR-36; MTCW 2; SATA 65

Kochanowski, Jan 1530-1584 .... **LC 10**

Kock, Charles Paul de 1794-1871 . **NCLC 16**

Koda Rohan 1867-
See Koda Shigeyuki

Koda Shigeyuki 1867-1947 .... **TCLC 22**
See also CA 121; 183; DLB 180

Koestler, Arthur 1905-1983 ... **CLC 1, 3, 6, 8,
15, 33**
See also CA 1-4R; 109; CANR 1, 33; CD-
BLB 1945-1960; DLBY 83; MTCW 1, 2

Kogawa, Joy Nozomi 1935- ..... **CLC 78, 129;
DAC; DAM MST, MULT**
See also CA 101; CANR 19, 62; MTCW 2;
SATA 99

Kohout, Pavel 1928- .... **CLC 13**
See also CA 45-48; CANR 3

Koizumi, Yakumo
See Hearn, (Patricio) Lafcadio (Tessima
Carlos)

Kolmar, Gertrud 1894-1943 .... **TCLC 40**
See also CA 167

Komunyakaa, Yusef 1947- .... **CLC 86, 94;
BLCS**
See also CA 147; CANR 83; DLB 120

Konrad, George
See Konrad, Gyorgy

Konrad, Gyorgy 1933- .... **CLC 4, 10, 73**
See also CA 85-88; DLB 232

Konwicki, Tadeusz 1926- .... **CLC 8, 28, 54,
117**
See also CA 101; CAAS 9; CANR 39, 59;
DLB 232; MTCW 1

Koontz, Dean R(ay) 1945- .... **CLC 78; DAM NOV, POP**
See also AAYA 9, 31; BEST 89:3, 90:2; CA 108; CANR 19, 36, 52; DA3; MTCW 1; SATA 92

Kopernik, Mikolaj
See Copernicus, Nicolaus

Kopit, Arthur (Lee) 1937- ..... **CLC 1, 18, 33; DAM DRAM**
See also AITN 1; CA 81-84; CABS 3; DLB 7; MTCW 1

Kops, Bernard 1926- .... **CLC 4**
See also CA 5-8R; CANR 84; DLB 13

Kornbluth, C(yril) M. 1923-1958 .... **TCLC 8**
See also CA 105; 160; DLB 8

Korolenko, V. G.
See Korolenko, Vladimir Galaktionovich

Korolenko, Vladimir
See Korolenko, Vladimir Galaktionovich

Korolenko, Vladimir G.
See Korolenko, Vladimir Galaktionovich

Korolenko, Vladimir Galaktionovich
1853-1921 .... **TCLC 22**
See also CA 121

Korzybski, Alfred (Habdank Skarbek)
1879-1950 .... **TCLC 61**
See also CA 123; 160

Kosinski, Jerzy (Nikodem)
1933-1991 .... **CLC 1, 2, 3, 6, 10, 15, 53, 70; DAM NOV**
See also CA 17-20R; 134; CANR 9, 46; DA3; DLB 2; DLBY 82; MTCW 1, 2

Kostelanetz, Richard (Cory) 1940- .. **CLC 28**
See also CA 13-16R; CAAS 8; CANR 38, 77

Kotlowitz, Robert 1924- .... **CLC 4**
See also CA 33-36R; CANR 36

Kotzebue, August (Friedrich Ferdinand) von
1761-1819 .... **NCLC 25**
See also DLB 94

Kotzwinkle, William 1938- ..... **CLC 5, 14, 35**
See also CA 45-48; CANR 3, 44, 84; CLR 6; DLB 173; MAICYA; SATA 24, 70

Kowna, Stancy
See Szymborska, Wislawa

Kozol, Jonathan 1936- .... **CLC 17**
See also CA 61-64; CANR 16, 45

Kozoll, Michael 1940(?)- .... **CLC 35**

Kramer, Kathryn 19(?)- .... **CLC 34**

Kramer, Larry 1935- .. **CLC 42; DAM POP; DC 8**
See also CA 124; 126; CANR 60

Krasicki, Ignacy 1735-1801 .... **NCLC 8**

Krasinski, Zygmunt 1812-1859 .... **NCLC 4**

Kraus, Karl 1874-1936 .... **TCLC 5**
See also CA 104; DLB 118

Kreve (Mickevicius), Vincas
1882-1954 .... **TCLC 27**
See also CA 170; DLB 220

Kristeva, Julia 1941- .... **CLC 77**
See also CA 154

Kristofferson, Kris 1936- .... **CLC 26**
See also CA 104

Krizanc, John 1956- .... **CLC 57**
See also CA 187

Krleza, Miroslav 1893-1981 .... **CLC 8, 114**
See also CA 97-100; 105; CANR 50; DLB 147

Kroetsch, Robert 1927- . **CLC 5, 23, 57, 132; DAC; DAM POET**
See also CA 17-20R; CANR 8, 38; DLB 53; MTCW 1

Kroetz, Franz
See Kroetz, Franz Xaver

Kroetz, Franz Xaver 1946- .... **CLC 41**
See also CA 130

Kroker, Arthur (W.) 1945- .... **CLC 77**
See also CA 161

Kropotkin, Peter (Aleksieevich)
1842-1921 .... **TCLC 36**
See also CA 119

Krotkov, Yuri 1917- .... **CLC 19**
See also CA 102

Krumb
See Crumb, R(obert)

Krumgold, Joseph (Quincy)
1908-1980 .... **CLC 12**
See also CA 9-12R; 101; CANR 7; MAICYA; SATA 1, 48; SATA-Obit 23

Krumwitz
See Crumb, R(obert)

Krutch, Joseph Wood 1893-1970 ..... **CLC 24**
See also CA 1-4R; 25-28R; CANR 4; DLB 63, 206

Krutzch, Gus
See Eliot, T(homas) S(tearns)

Krylov, Ivan Andreevich
1768(?)-1844 .... **NCLC 1**
See also DLB 150

Kubin, Alfred (Leopold Isidor)
1877-1959 .... **TCLC 23**
See also CA 112; 149; DLB 81

Kubrick, Stanley 1928-1999 .... **CLC 16**
See also AAYA 30; CA 81-84; 177; CANR 33; DLB 26

Kueng, Hans 1928-
See Kung, Hans
See also CA 53-56; CANR 66; MTCW 1, 2

Kumin, Maxine (Winokur) 1925- ..... **CLC 5, 13, 28; DAM POET; PC 15**
See also AITN 2; CA 1-4R; CAAS 8; CANR 1, 21, 69; DA3; DLB 5; MTCW 1, 2; SATA 12

Kundera, Milan 1929- . **CLC 4, 9, 19, 32, 68, 115, 135; DAM NOV; SSC 24**
See also AAYA 2; CA 85-88; CANR 19, 52, 74; DA3; DLB 232; MTCW 1, 2

Kunene, Mazisi (Raymond) 1930- ... **CLC 85**
See also BW 1, 3; CA 125; CANR 81; DLB 117

Kung, Hans 1928- .... **CLC 130**
See also Kueng, Hans

Kunitz, Stanley (Jasspon) 1905- .. **CLC 6, 11, 14; PC 19**
See also CA 41-44R; CANR 26, 57; DA3; DLB 48; INT CANR-26; MTCW 1, 2

Kunze, Reiner 1933- .... **CLC 10**
See also CA 93-96; DLB 75

Kuprin, Aleksander Ivanovich
1870-1938 .... **TCLC 5**
See also CA 104; 182

Kureishi, Hanif 1954(?)- .... **CLC 64, 135**
See also CA 139; DLB 194

Kurosawa, Akira 1910-1998 .... **CLC 16, 119; DAM MULT**
See also AAYA 11; CA 101; 170; CANR 46

Kushner, Tony 1957(?)- .... **CLC 81; DAM DRAM; DC 10**
See also CA 144; CANR 74; DA3; DLB 228; MTCW 2

Kuttner, Henry 1915-1958 .... **TCLC 10**
See also CA 107; 157; DLB 8

Kuzma, Greg 1944- .... **CLC 7**
See also CA 33-36R; CANR 70

Kuzmin, Mikhail 1872(?)-1936 ...... **TCLC 40**
See also CA 170

Kyd, Thomas 1558-1594 .... **LC 22; DAM DRAM; DC 3**
See also DLB 62

Kyprianos, Iossif
See Samarakis, Antonis

La Bruyere, Jean de 1645-1696 .... **LC 17**

Lacan, Jacques (Marie Emile)
1901-1981 .... **CLC 75**
See also CA 121; 104

Laclos, Pierre Ambroise Francois Choderlos de 1741-1803 .... **NCLC 4, 87**

La Colere, Francois
See Aragon, Louis

Lacolere, Francois
See Aragon, Louis

La Deshabilleuse
See Simenon, Georges (Jacques Christian)

Lady Gregory
See Gregory, Isabella Augusta (Persse)

Lady of Quality, A
See Bagnold, Enid

La Fayette, Marie (Madelaine Pioche de la Vergne Comtes 1634-1693 .... **LC 2**

Lafayette, Rene
See Hubbard, L(afayette) Ron(ald)

La Fontaine, Jean de 1621-1695 .... **LC 50**
See also MAICYA; SATA 18

Laforgue, Jules 1860-1887 . **NCLC 5, 53; PC 14; SSC 20**

Lagerkvist, Paer (Fabian)
1891-1974 ...... **CLC 7, 10, 13, 54; DAM DRAM, NOV**
See also Lagerkvist, Par
See also CA 85-88; 49-52; DA3; MTCW 1, 2

Lagerkvist, Par SSC 12
See also Lagerkvist, Paer (Fabian)
See also MTCW 2

Lagerloef, Selma (Ottiliana Lovisa)
1858-1940 .... **TCLC 4, 36**
See also Lagerlof, Selma (Ottiliana Lovisa)
See also CA 108; MTCW 2; SATA 15

Lagerlof, Selma (Ottiliana Lovisa)
See Lagerloef, Selma (Ottiliana Lovisa)
See also CLR 7; SATA 15

La Guma, (Justin) Alex(ander)
1925-1985 .... **CLC 19; BLCS; DAM NOV**
See also BW 1, 3; CA 49-52; 118; CANR 25, 81; DLB 117, 225; MTCW 1, 2

Laidlaw, A. K.
See Grieve, C(hristopher) M(urray)

Lainez, Manuel Mujica
See Mujica Lainez, Manuel
See also HW 1

Laing, R(onald) D(avid) 1927-1989 . **CLC 95**
See also CA 107; 129; CANR 34; MTCW 1

Lamartine, Alphonse (Marie Louis Prat) de
1790-1869 . **NCLC 11; DAM POET; PC 16**

Lamb, Charles 1775-1834 ..... **NCLC 10; DA; DAB; DAC; DAM MST; WLC**
See also CDBLB 1789-1832; DLB 93, 107, 163; SATA 17

Lamb, Lady Caroline 1785-1828 ... **NCLC 38**
See also DLB 116

Lamming, George (William) 1927- ... **CLC 2, 4, 66; BLC 2; DAM MULT**
See also BW 2, 3; CA 85-88; CANR 26, 76; DLB 125; MTCW 1, 2

L'Amour, Louis (Dearborn)
1908-1988 ...... **CLC 25, 55; DAM NOV, POP**
See also AAYA 16; AITN 2; BEST 89:2; CA 1-4R; 125; CANR 3, 25, 40; DA3; DLB 206; DLBY 80; MTCW 1, 2

Lampedusa, Giuseppe (Tomasi) di
1896-1957 .... **TCLC 13**
See also Tomasi di Lampedusa, Giuseppe
See also CA 164; DLB 177; MTCW 2

Lampman, Archibald 1861-1899 ... **NCLC 25**
See also DLB 92

Lancaster, Bruce 1896-1963 .... **CLC 36**
See also CA 9-10; CANR 70; CAP 1; SATA 9

Lanchester, John CLC 99

Landau, Mark Alexandrovich
See Aldanov, Mark (Alexandrovich)

Lee, Laurie 1914-1997 .... **CLC 90; DAB; DAM POP**
See also CA 77-80; 158; CANR 33, 73; DLB 27; MTCW 1

Lee, Lawrence 1941-1990 .... **CLC 34**
See also CA 131; CANR 43

Lee, Li-Young 1957- .... **PC 24**
See also CA 153; DLB 165

Lee, Manfred B(ennington)
1905-1971 .... **CLC 11**
See also Queen, Ellery
See also CA 1-4R; 29-32R; CANR 2; DLB 137

Lee, Shelton Jackson 1957(?)- .... **CLC 105; BLCS; DAM MULT**
See also Lee, Spike
See also BW 2, 3; CA 125; CANR 42

Lee, Spike
See Lee, Shelton Jackson
See also AAYA 4, 29

Lee, Stan 1922- .... **CLC 17**
See also AAYA 5; CA 108; 111; INT 111

Lee, Tanith 1947- .... **CLC 46**
See also AAYA 15; CA 37-40R; CANR 53; SATA 8, 88

Lee, Vernon TCLC 5; SSC 33
See also Paget, Violet
See also DLB 57, 153, 156, 174, 178

Lee, William
See Burroughs, William S(eward)

Lee, Willy
See Burroughs, William S(eward)

Lee-Hamilton, Eugene (Jacob)
1845-1907 .... **TCLC 22**
See also CA 117

Leet, Judith 1935- .... **CLC 11**
See also CA 187

Le Fanu, Joseph Sheridan
1814-1873 ..... **NCLC 9, 58; DAM POP; SSC 14**
See also DA3; DLB 21, 70, 159, 178

Leffland, Ella 1931- .... **CLC 19**
See also CA 29-32R; CANR 35, 78, 82; DLBY 84; INT CANR-35; SATA 65

Leger, Alexis
See Leger, (Marie-Rene Auguste) Alexis Saint-Leger

Leger, (Marie-Rene Auguste) Alexis Saint-Leger 1887-1975 .. **CLC 4, 11, 46; DAM POET; PC 23**
See also CA 13-16R; 61-64; CANR 43; MTCW 1

Leger, Saintleger
See Leger, (Marie-Rene Auguste) Alexis Saint-Leger

Le Guin, Ursula K(roeber) 1929- ..... **CLC 8, 13, 22, 45, 71, 136; DAB; DAC; DAM MST, POP; SSC 12**
See also AAYA 9, 27; AITN 1; CA 21-24R; CANR 9, 32, 52, 74; CDALB 1968-1988; CLR 3, 28; DA3; DLB 8, 52; INT CANR-32; JRDA; MAICYA; MTCW 1, 2; SATA 4, 52, 99

Lehmann, Rosamond (Nina)
1901-1990 .... **CLC 5**
See also CA 77-80; 131; CANR 8, 73; DLB 15; MTCW 2

Leiber, Fritz (Reuter, Jr.)
1910-1992 .... **CLC 25**
See also CA 45-48; 139; CANR 2, 40, 86; DLB 8; MTCW 1, 2; SATA 45; SATA-Obit 73

Leibniz, Gottfried Wilhelm von
1646-1716 .... **LC 35**
See also DLB 168

Leimbach, Martha 1963-
See Leimbach, Marti
See also CA 130

Leimbach, Marti CLC 65
See also Leimbach, Martha

Leino, Eino TCLC 24
See also Loennbohm, Armas Eino Leopold

Leiris, Michel (Julien) 1901-1990 ..... **CLC 61**
See also CA 119; 128; 132

Leithauser, Brad 1953- .... **CLC 27**
See also CA 107; CANR 27, 81; DLB 120

Lelchuk, Alan 1938- .... **CLC 5**
See also CA 45-48; CAAS 20; CANR 1, 70

Lem, Stanislaw 1921- .... **CLC 8, 15, 40**
See also CA 105; CAAS 1; CANR 32; MTCW 1

Lemann, Nancy 1956- .... **CLC 39**
See also CA 118; 136

Lemonnier, (Antoine Louis) Camille
1844-1913 .... **TCLC 22**
See also CA 121

Lenau, Nikolaus 1802-1850 .... **NCLC 16**

L'Engle, Madeleine (Camp Franklin)
1918- .... **CLC 12; DAM POP**
See also AAYA 28; AITN 2; CA 1-4R; CANR 3, 21, 39, 66; CLR 1, 14, 57; DA3; DLB 52; JRDA; MAICYA; MTCW 1, 2; SAAS 15; SATA 1, 27, 75

Lengyel, Jozsef 1896-1975 .... **CLC 7**
See also CA 85-88; 57-60; CANR 71

Lenin 1870-1924
See Lenin, V. I.
See also CA 121; 168

Lenin, V. I. TCLC 67
See also Lenin

Lennon, John (Ono) 1940-1980 .. **CLC 12, 35**
See also CA 102; SATA 114

Lennox, Charlotte Ramsay
1729(?)-1804 .... **NCLC 23**
See also DLB 39

Lentricchia, Frank (Jr.) 1940- .... **CLC 34**
See also CA 25-28R; CANR 19

Lenz, Siegfried 1926- .... **CLC 27; SSC 33**
See also CA 89-92; CANR 80; DLB 75

Leonard, Elmore (John, Jr.) 1925- . **CLC 28, 34, 71, 120; DAM POP**
See also AAYA 22; AITN 1; BEST 89:1, 90:4; CA 81-84; CANR 12, 28, 53, 76; DA3; DLB 173, 226; INT CANR-28; MTCW 1, 2

Leonard, Hugh CLC 19
See also Byrne, John Keyes
See also DLB 13

Leonov, Leonid (Maximovich)
1899-1994 .... **CLC 92; DAM NOV**
See also CA 129; CANR 74, 76; MTCW 1, 2

Leopardi, (Conte) Giacomo
1798-1837 .... **NCLC 22**

Le Reveler
See Artaud, Antonin (Marie Joseph)

Lerman, Eleanor 1952- .... **CLC 9**
See also CA 85-88; CANR 69

Lerman, Rhoda 1936- .... **CLC 56**
See also CA 49-52; CANR 70

Lermontov, Mikhail Yuryevich
1814-1841 .... **NCLC 47; PC 18**
See also DLB 205

Leroux, Gaston 1868-1927 .... **TCLC 25**
See also CA 108; 136; CANR 69; SATA 65

Lesage, Alain-Rene 1668-1747 .... **LC 2, 28**

Leskov, Nikolai (Semyonovich)
1831-1895 .... **NCLC 25; SSC 34**

Lessing, Doris (May) 1919- ... **CLC 1, 2, 3, 6, 10, 15, 22, 40, 94; DA; DAB; DAC; DAM MST, NOV; SSC 6; WLCS**
See also CA 9-12R; CAAS 14; CANR 33, 54, 76; CDBLB 1960 to Present; DA3; DLB 15, 139; DLBY 85; MTCW 1, 2

Lessing, Gotthold Ephraim 1729-1781 . **LC 8**
See also DLB 97

Lester, Richard 1932- .... **CLC 20**

Lever, Charles (James)
1806-1872 .... **NCLC 23**
See also DLB 21

Leverson, Ada 1865(?)-1936(?) .... **TCLC 18**
See also Elaine
See also CA 117; DLB 153

Levertov, Denise 1923-1997 .. **CLC 1, 2, 3, 5, 8, 15, 28, 66; DAM POET; PC 11**
See also CA 1-4R, 178; 163; CAAE 178; CAAS 19; CANR 3, 29, 50; CDALBS; DLB 5, 165; INT CANR-29; MTCW 1, 2

Levi, Jonathan CLC 76

Levi, Peter (Chad Tigar)
1931-2000 .... **CLC 41**
See also CA 5-8R; 187; CANR 34, 80; DLB 40

Levi, Primo 1919-1987 . **CLC 37, 50; SSC 12**
See also CA 13-16R; 122; CANR 12, 33, 61, 70; DLB 177; MTCW 1, 2

Levin, Ira 1929- .... **CLC 3, 6; DAM POP**
See also CA 21-24R; CANR 17, 44, 74; DA3; MTCW 1, 2; SATA 66

Levin, Meyer 1905-1981 .... **CLC 7; DAM POP**
See also AITN 1; CA 9-12R; 104; CANR 15; DLB 9, 28; DLBY 81; SATA 21; SATA-Obit 27

Levine, Norman 1924- .... **CLC 54**
See also CA 73-76; CAAS 23; CANR 14, 70; DLB 88

Levine, Philip 1928- .. **CLC 2, 4, 5, 9, 14, 33, 118; DAM POET; PC 22**
See also CA 9-12R; CANR 9, 37, 52; DLB 5

Levinson, Deirdre 1931- .... **CLC 49**
See also CA 73-76; CANR 70

Levi-Strauss, Claude 1908- .... **CLC 38**
See also CA 1-4R; CANR 6, 32, 57; MTCW 1, 2

Levitin, Sonia (Wolff) 1934- .... **CLC 17**
See also AAYA 13; CA 29-32R; CANR 14, 32, 79; CLR 53; JRDA; MAICYA; SAAS 2; SATA 4, 68, 119

Levon, O. U.
See Kesey, Ken (Elton)

Levy, Amy 1861-1889 .... **NCLC 59**
See also DLB 156

Lewes, George Henry 1817-1878 ... **NCLC 25**
See also DLB 55, 144

Lewis, Alun 1915-1944 .... **TCLC 3; SSC 40**
See also CA 104; DLB 20, 162

Lewis, C. Day
See Day Lewis, C(ecil)

Lewis, C(live) S(taples) 1898-1963 .... **CLC 1, 3, 6, 14, 27, 124; DA; DAB; DAC; DAM MST, NOV, POP; WLC**
See also AAYA 3; CA 81-84; CANR 33, 71; CDBLB 1945-1960; CLR 3, 27; DA3; DLB 15, 100, 160; JRDA; MAICYA; MTCW 1, 2; SATA 13, 100

Lewis, Janet 1899-1998 .... **CLC 41**
See also Winters, Janet Lewis
See also CA 9-12R; 172; CANR 29, 63; CAP 1; DLBY 87

Lewis, Matthew Gregory
1775-1818 .... **NCLC 11, 62**
See also DLB 39, 158, 178

Lewis, (Harry) Sinclair 1885-1951 . **TCLC 4, 13, 23, 39; DA; DAB; DAC; DAM MST, NOV; WLC**
See also CA 104; 133; CDALB 1917-1929; DA3; DLB 9, 102; DLBD 1; MTCW 1, 2

Lewis, (Percy) Wyndham
1882(?)-1957 .... **TCLC 2, 9; SSC 34**
See also CA 104; 157; DLB 15; MTCW 2

Lewisohn, Ludwig 1883-1955 .... **TCLC 19**
See also CA 107; DLB 4, 9, 28, 102

Lou, Henri
    See Andreas-Salome, Lou
Louie, David Wong 1954- .... **CLC 70**
    See also CA 139
Louis, Father M.
    See Merton, Thomas
Lovecraft, H(oward) P(hillips)
    1890-1937 ...... **TCLC 4, 22; DAM POP;
    SSC 3**
    See also AAYA 14; CA 104; 133; DA3;
    MTCW 1, 2
Lovelace, Earl 1935- .... **CLC 51**
    See also BW 2; CA 77-80; CANR 41, 72;
    DLB 125; MTCW 1
Lovelace, Richard 1618-1657 .... **LC 24**
    See also DLB 131
Lowell, Amy 1874-1925 .... **TCLC 1, 8; DAM
    POET; PC 13**
    See also CA 104; 151; DLB 54, 140;
    MTCW 2
Lowell, James Russell 1819-1891 ... **NCLC 2,
    90**
    See also CDALB 1640-1865; DLB 1, 11,
    64, 79, 189, 235
Lowell, Robert (Traill Spence, Jr.)
    1917-1977 .... **CLC 1, 2, 3, 4, 5, 8, 9, 11,
    15, 37, 124; DA; DAB; DAC; DAM
    MST, NOV; PC 3; WLC**
    See also CA 9-12R; 73-76; CABS 2; CANR
    26, 60; CDALBS; DA3; DLB 5, 169;
    MTCW 1, 2
Lowenthal, Michael (Francis)
    1969- .... **CLC 119**
    See also CA 150
Lowndes, Marie Adelaide (Belloc)
    1868-1947 .... **TCLC 12**
    See also CA 107; DLB 70
Lowry, (Clarence) Malcolm
    1909-1957 .... **TCLC 6, 40; SSC 31**
    See also CA 105; 131; CANR 62; CDBLB
    1945-1960; DLB 15; MTCW 1, 2
Lowry, Mina Gertrude 1882-1966
    See Loy, Mina
    See also CA 113
Loxsmith, John
    See Brunner, John (Kilian Houston)
Loy, Mina **CLC 28; DAM POET; PC 16**
    See Lowry, Mina Gertrude
    See also DLB 4, 54
Loyson-Bridet
    See Schwob, Marcel (Mayer Andre)
Lucan 39-65 .... **CMLC 33**
    See also DLB 211
Lucas, Craig 1951- .... **CLC 64**
    See also CA 137; CANR 71
Lucas, E(dward) V(errall)
    1868-1938 .... **TCLC 73**
    See also CA 176; DLB 98, 149, 153; SATA
    20
Lucas, George 1944- .... **CLC 16**
    See also AAYA 1, 23; CA 77-80; CANR
    30; SATA 56
Lucas, Hans
    See Godard, Jean-Luc
Lucas, Victoria
    See Plath, Sylvia
Lucian c. 120-c. 180 .... **CMLC 32**
    See also DLB 176
Ludlam, Charles 1943-1987 .... **CLC 46, 50**
    See also CA 85-88; 122; CANR 72, 86
Ludlum, Robert 1927- .... **CLC 22, 43; DAM
    NOV, POP**
    See also AAYA 10; BEST 89:1, 90:3; CA
    33-36R; CANR 25, 41, 68; DA3; DLBY
    82; MTCW 1, 2
Ludwig, Ken **CLC 60**
Ludwig, Otto 1813-1865 .... **NCLC 4**
    See also DLB 129

Lugones, Leopoldo 1874-1938 ...... **TCLC 15;
    HLCS 2**
    See also CA 116; 131; HW 1
Lu Hsun 1881-1936 .... **TCLC 3; SSC 20**
    See also Shu-Jen, Chou
Lukacs, George **CLC 24**
    See also Lukacs, Gyorgy (Szegeny von)
Lukacs, Gyorgy (Szegeny von) 1885-1971
    See Lukacs, George
    See also CA 101; 29-32R; CANR 62;
    MTCW 2
Luke, Peter (Ambrose Cyprian)
    1919-1995 .... **CLC 38**
    See also CA 81-84; 147; CANR 72; DLB
    13
Lunar, Dennis
    See Mungo, Raymond
Lurie, Alison 1926- .... **CLC 4, 5, 18, 39**
    See also CA 1-4R; CANR 2, 17, 50, 88;
    DLB 2; MTCW 1; SATA 46, 112
Lustig, Arnost 1926- .... **CLC 56**
    See also AAYA 3; CA 69-72; CANR 47;
    DLB 232; SATA 56
Luther, Martin 1483-1546 .... **LC 9, 37**
    See also DLB 179
Luxemburg, Rosa 1870(?)-1919 ..... **TCLC 63**
    See also CA 118
Luzi, Mario 1914- .... **CLC 13**
    See also CA 61-64; CANR 9, 70; DLB 128
Lyly, John 1554(?)-1606 .... **LC 41; DAM
    DRAM; DC 7**
    See also DLB 62, 167
L'Ymagier
    See Gourmont, Remy (-Marie-Charles) de
Lynch, B. Suarez
    See Bioy Casares, Adolfo; Borges, Jorge
    Luis
Lynch, B. Suarez
    See Bioy Casares, Adolfo
Lynch, David (K.) 1946- .... **CLC 66**
    See also CA 124; 129
Lynch, James
    See Andreyev, Leonid (Nikolaevich)
Lynch Davis, B.
    See Bioy Casares, Adolfo; Borges, Jorge
    Luis
Lyndsay, Sir David 1490-1555 .... **LC 20**
Lynn, Kenneth S(chuyler) 1923- ...... **CLC 50**
    See also CA 1-4R; CANR 3, 27, 65
Lynx
    See West, Rebecca
Lyons, Marcus
    See Blish, James (Benjamin)
Lyre, Pinchbeck
    See Sassoon, Siegfried (Lorraine)
Lytle, Andrew (Nelson) 1902-1995 ... **CLC 22**
    See also CA 9-12R; 150; CANR 70; DLB
    6; DLBY 95
Lyttelton, George 1709-1773 .... **LC 10**
Maas, Peter 1929- .... **CLC 29**
    See also CA 93-96; INT 93-96; MTCW 2
Macaulay, (Emilie) Rose
    1881(?)-1958 .... **TCLC 7, 44**
    See also CA 104; DLB 36
Macaulay, Thomas Babington
    1800-1859 .... **NCLC 42**
    See also CDBLB 1832-1890; DLB 32, 55
MacBeth, George (Mann)
    1932-1992 .... **CLC 2, 5, 9**
    See also CA 25-28R; 136; CANR 61, 66;
    DLB 40; MTCW 1; SATA 4; SATA-Obit
    70
MacCaig, Norman (Alexander)
    1910- .... **CLC 36; DAB; DAM POET**
    See also CA 9-12R; CANR 3, 34; DLB 27

MacCarthy, Sir(Charles Otto) Desmond
    1877-1952 .... **TCLC 36**
    See also CA 167
MacDiarmid, Hugh **CLC 2, 4, 11, 19, 63; PC
    9**
    See also Grieve, C(hristopher) M(urray)
    See also CDBLB 1945-1960; DLB 20
MacDonald, Anson
    See Heinlein, Robert A(nson)
Macdonald, Cynthia 1928- .... **CLC 13, 19**
    See also CA 49-52; CANR 4, 44; DLB 105
MacDonald, George 1824-1905 .... **TCLC 9**
    See also CA 106; 137; CANR 80; CLR 67;
    DLB 18, 163, 178; MAICYA; SATA 33,
    100
Macdonald, John
    See Millar, Kenneth
MacDonald, John D(ann)
    1916-1986 .. **CLC 3, 27, 44; DAM NOV,
    POP**
    See also CA 1-4R; 121; CANR 1, 19, 60;
    DLB 8; DLBY 86; MTCW 1, 2
Macdonald, John Ross
    See Millar, Kenneth
Macdonald, Ross **CLC 1, 2, 3, 14, 34, 41**
    See also Millar, Kenneth
    See also DLBD 6
MacDougal, John
    See Blish, James (Benjamin)
MacDougal, John
    See Blish, James (Benjamin)
MacEwen, Gwendolyn (Margaret)
    1941-1987 .... **CLC 13, 55**
    See also CA 9-12R; 124; CANR 7, 22; DLB
    53; SATA 50; SATA-Obit 55
Macha, Karel Hynek 1810-1846 .... **NCLC 46**
Machado (y Ruiz), Antonio
    1875-1939 .... **TCLC 3**
    See also CA 104; 174; DLB 108; HW 2
Machado de Assis, Joaquim Maria
    1839-1908 ..... **TCLC 10; BLC 2; HLCS
    2; SSC 24**
    See also CA 107; 153; CANR 91
Machen, Arthur **TCLC 4; SSC 20**
    See also Jones, Arthur Llewellyn
    See also CA 179; DLB 36, 156, 178
Machiavelli, Niccolo 1469-1527 ..... **LC 8, 36;
    DA; DAB; DAC; DAM MST; WLCS**
MacInnes, Colin 1914-1976 .... **CLC 4, 23**
    See also CA 69-72; 65-68; CANR 21; DLB
    14; MTCW 1, 2
MacInnes, Helen (Clark)
    1907-1985 .... **CLC 27, 39; DAM POP**
    See also CA 1-4R; 117; CANR 1, 28, 58;
    DLB 87; MTCW 1, 2; SATA 22; SATA-
    Obit 44
Mackenzie, Compton (Edward Montague)
    1883-1972 .... **CLC 18**
    See also CA 21-22; 37-40R; CAP 2; DLB
    34, 100
Mackenzie, Henry 1745-1831 .... **NCLC 41**
    See also DLB 39
Mackintosh, Elizabeth 1896(?)-1952
    See Tey, Josephine
    See also CA 110
MacLaren, James
    See Grieve, C(hristopher) M(urray)
Mac Laverty, Bernard 1942- .... **CLC 31**
    See also CA 116; 118; CANR 43, 88; INT
    118
MacLean, Alistair (Stuart)
    1922(?)-1987 .. **CLC 3, 13, 50, 63; DAM
    POP**
    See also CA 57-60; 121; CANR 28, 61;
    MTCW 1; SATA 23; SATA-Obit 50
Maclean, Norman (Fitzroy)
    1902-1990 .... **CLC 78; DAM POP; SSC
    13**
    See also CA 102; 132; CANR 49; DLB 206

Marinetti, Filippo Tommaso
1876-1944 .... **TCLC 10**
See also CA 107; DLB 114

Marivaux, Pierre Carlet de Chamblain de
1688-1763 .... **LC 4; DC 7**

Markandaya, Kamala CLC 8, 38
See also Taylor, Kamala (Purnaiya)

Markfield, Wallace 1926- .... **CLC 8**
See also CA 69-72; CAAS 3; DLB 2, 28

Markham, Edwin 1852-1940 .... **TCLC 47**
See also CA 160; DLB 54, 186

Markham, Robert
See Amis, Kingsley (William)

Marks, J
See Highwater, Jamake (Mamake)

Marks-Highwater, J
See Highwater, Jamake (Mamake)

Markson, David M(errill) 1927- .... **CLC 67**
See also CA 49-52; CANR 1, 91

Marley, Bob CLC 17
See also Marley, Robert Nesta

Marley, Robert Nesta 1945-1981
See Marley, Bob
See also CA 107; 103

Marlowe, Christopher 1564-1593 ...... **LC 22,**
47; DA; DAB; DAC; DAM DRAM,
MST; DC 1; WLC
See also CDBLB Before 1660; DA3; DLB
62

Marlowe, Stephen 1928-
See Queen, Ellery
See also CA 13-16R; CANR 6, 55

Marmontel, Jean-Francois 1723-1799 .. **LC 2**

Marquand, John P(hillips)
1893-1960 .... **CLC 2, 10**
See also CA 85-88; CANR 73; DLB 9, 102;
MTCW 2

Marques, Rene 1919-1979 ..... **CLC 96; DAM**
MULT; HLC 2
See also CA 97-100; 85-88; CANR 78;
DLB 113; HW 1, 2

Marquez, Gabriel (Jose) Garcia
See Garcia Marquez, Gabriel (Jose)

Marquis, Don(ald Robert Perry)
1878-1937 .... **TCLC 7**
See also CA 104; 166; DLB 11, 25

Marric, J. J.
See Creasey, John

Marryat, Frederick 1792-1848 .... **NCLC 3**
See also DLB 21, 163

Marsden, James
See Creasey, John

Marsh, Edward 1872-1953 .... **TCLC 99**

Marsh, (Edith) Ngaio 1899-1982 .... **CLC 7,**
53; DAM POP
See also CA 9-12R; CANR 6, 58; DLB 77;
MTCW 1, 2

Marshall, Garry 1934- .... **CLC 17**
See also AAYA 3; CA 111; SATA 60

Marshall, Paule 1929- .. **CLC 27, 72; BLC 3;**
DAM MULT; SSC 3
See also BW 2, 3; CA 77-80; CANR 25,
73; DA3; DLB 33, 157, 227; MTCW 1, 2

Marshallik
See Zangwill, Israel

Marsten, Richard
See Hunter, Evan

Marston, John 1576-1634 .... **LC 33; DAM**
DRAM
See also DLB 58, 172

Martha, Henry
See Harris, Mark

Marti (y Perez), Jose (Julian)
1853-1895 ...... **NCLC 63; DAM MULT;**
HLC 2
See also HW 2

Martial c. 40-c. 104 .... **CMLC 35; PC 10**
See also DLB 211

Martin, Ken
See Hubbard, L(afayette) Ron(ald)

Martin, Richard
See Creasey, John

Martin, Steve 1945- .... **CLC 30**
See also CA 97-100; CANR 30; MTCW 1

Martin, Valerie 1948- .... **CLC 89**
See also BEST 90:2; CA 85-88; CANR 49,
89

Martin, Violet Florence
1862-1915 .... **TCLC 51**

Martin, Webber
See Silverberg, Robert

Martindale, Patrick Victor
See White, Patrick (Victor Martindale)

Martin du Gard, Roger
1881-1958 .... **TCLC 24**
See also CA 118; DLB 65

Martineau, Harriet 1802-1876 .... **NCLC 26**
See also DLB 21, 55, 159, 163, 166, 190;
YABC 2

Martines, Julia
See O'Faolain, Julia

Martinez, Enrique Gonzalez
See Gonzalez Martinez, Enrique

Martinez, Jacinto Benavente y
See Benavente (y Martinez), Jacinto

Martinez Ruiz, Jose 1873-1967
See Azorin; Ruiz, Jose Martinez
See also CA 93-96; HW 1

Martinez Sierra, Gregorio
1881-1947 .... **TCLC 6**
See also CA 115

Martinez Sierra, Maria (de la O'LeJarraga)
1874-1974 .... **TCLC 6**
See also CA 115

Martinsen, Martin
See Follett, Ken(neth Martin)

Martinson, Harry (Edmund)
1904-1978 .... **CLC 14**
See also CA 77-80; CANR 34

Marut, Ret
See Traven, B.

Marut, Robert
See Traven, B.

Marvell, Andrew 1621-1678 .. **LC 4, 43; DA;**
DAB; DAC; DAM MST, POET; PC
10; WLC
See also CDBLB 1660-1789; DLB 131

Marx, Karl (Heinrich) 1818-1883 . **NCLC 17**
See also DLB 129

Masaoka Shiki TCLC 18
See also Masaoka Tsunenori

Masaoka Tsunenori 1867-1902
See Masaoka Shiki
See also CA 117

Masefield, John (Edward)
1878-1967 ...... **CLC 11, 47; DAM POET**
See also CA 19-20; 25-28R; CANR 33;
CAP 2; CDBLB 1890-1914; DLB 10, 19,
153, 160; MTCW 1, 2; SATA 19

Maso, Carole 19(?)- .... **CLC 44**
See also CA 170

Mason, Bobbie Ann 1940- ... **CLC 28, 43, 82;**
SSC 4
See also AAYA 5; CA 53-56; CANR 11, 31,
58, 83; CDALBS; DA3; DLB 173; DLBY
87; INT CANR-31; MTCW 1, 2

Mason, Ernst
See Pohl, Frederik

Mason, Lee W.
See Malzberg, Barry N(athaniel)

Mason, Nick 1945- .... **CLC 35**

Mason, Tally
See Derleth, August (William)

Mass, William
See Gibson, William

Master Lao
See Lao Tzu

Masters, Edgar Lee 1868-1950 .... **TCLC 2,**
25; DA; DAC; DAM MST, POET; PC
1; WLCS
See also CA 104; 133; CDALB 1865-1917;
DLB 54; MTCW 1, 2

Masters, Hilary 1928- .... **CLC 48**
See also CA 25-28R; CANR 13, 47

Mastrosimone, William 19(?)- .... **CLC 36**
See also CA 186

Mathe, Albert
See Camus, Albert

Mather, Cotton 1663-1728 .... **LC 38**
See also CDALB 1640-1865; DLB 24, 30,
140

Mather, Increase 1639-1723 .... **LC 38**
See also DLB 24

Matheson, Richard Burton 1926- .... **CLC 37**
See also AAYA 31; CA 97-100; CANR 88;
DLB 8, 44; INT 97-100

Mathews, Harry 1930- .... **CLC 6, 52**
See also CA 21-24R; CAAS 6; CANR 18,
40

Mathews, John Joseph 1894-1979 .. **CLC 84;**
DAM MULT
See also CA 19-20; 142; CANR 45; CAP 2;
DLB 175; NNAL

Mathias, Roland (Glyn) 1915- .... **CLC 45**
See also CA 97-100; CANR 19, 41; DLB
27

Matsuo Basho 1644-1694 .... **LC 62; DAM**
POET; PC 3

Mattheson, Rodney
See Creasey, John

Matthews, (James) Brander
1852-1929 .... **TCLC 95**
See also DLB 71, 78; DLBD 13

Matthews, Greg 1949- .... **CLC 45**
See also CA 135

Matthews, William (Procter, III)
1942-1997 .... **CLC 40**
See also CA 29-32R; 162; CAAS 18; CANR
12, 57; DLB 5

Matthias, John (Edward) 1941- .... **CLC 9**
See also CA 33-36R; CANR 56

Matthiessen, F(rancis) O(tto)
1902-1950 .... **TCLC 100**
See also CA 185; DLB 63

Matthiessen, Peter 1927- ... **CLC 5, 7, 11, 32,**
64; DAM NOV
See also AAYA 6; BEST 90:4; CA 9-12R;
CANR 21, 50, 73; DA3; DLB 6, 173;
MTCW 1, 2; SATA 27

Maturin, Charles Robert
1780(?)-1824 .... **NCLC 6**
See also DLB 178

Matute (Ausejo), Ana Maria 1925- .. **CLC 11**
See also CA 89-92; MTCW 1

Maugham, W. S.
See Maugham, W(illiam) Somerset

Maugham, W(illiam) Somerset
1874-1965 ... **CLC 1, 11, 15, 67, 93; DA;**
DAB; DAC; DAM DRAM, MST, NOV;
SSC 8; WLC
See also CA 5-8R; 25-28R; CANR 40; CD-
BLB 1914-1945; DA3; DLB 10, 36, 77,
100, 162, 195; MTCW 1, 2; SATA 54

Maugham, William Somerset
See Maugham, W(illiam) Somerset

Maupassant, (Henri Rene Albert) Guy de
1850-1893 . **NCLC 1, 42, 83; DA; DAB;**
DAC; DAM MST; SSC 1; WLC
See also DA3; DLB 123

Maupin, Armistead 1944- ..... **CLC 95; DAM**
POP
See also CA 125; 130; CANR 58; DA3;
INT 130; MTCW 2

Minus, Ed 1938- .... CLC 39
See also CA 185

Miranda, Javier
See Bioy Casares, Adolfo

Miranda, Javier
See Bioy Casares, Adolfo

Mirbeau, Octave 1848-1917 .... TCLC 55
See also DLB 123, 192

Miro (Ferrer), Gabriel (Francisco Victor)
1879-1930 .... TCLC 5
See also CA 104; 185

Mishima, Yukio 1925-1970 .... CLC 2, 4, 6, 9,
27; DC 1; SSC 4
See also Hiraoka, Kimitake
See also DLB 182; MTCW 2

Mistral, Frederic 1830-1914 .... TCLC 51
See also CA 122

Mistral, Gabriela
See Godoy Alcayaga, Lucila

Mistry, Rohinton 1952- .... CLC 71; DAC
See also CA 141; CANR 86

Mitchell, Clyde
See Ellison, Harlan (Jay); Silverberg, Robert

Mitchell, James Leslie 1901-1935
See Gibbon, Lewis Grassic
See also CA 104; DLB 15

Mitchell, Joni 1943- .... CLC 12
See also CA 112

Mitchell, Joseph (Quincy)
1908-1996 .... CLC 98
See also CA 77-80; 152; CANR 69; DLB
185; DLBY 96

Mitchell, Margaret (Munnerlyn)
1900-1949 . TCLC 11; DAM NOV, POP
See also AAYA 23; CA 109; 125; CANR
55; CDALBS; DA3; DLB 9; MTCW 1, 2

Mitchell, Peggy
See Mitchell, Margaret (Munnerlyn)

Mitchell, S(ilas) Weir 1829-1914 .... TCLC 36
See also CA 165; DLB 202

Mitchell, W(illiam) O(rmond)
1914-1998 .. CLC 25; DAC; DAM MST
See also CA 77-80; 165; CANR 15, 43;
DLB 88

Mitchell, William 1879-1936 .... TCLC 81

Mitford, Mary Russell 1787-1855 ... NCLC 4
See also DLB 110, 116

Mitford, Nancy 1904-1973 .... CLC 44
See also CA 9-12R; DLB 191

Miyamoto, (Chujo) Yuriko
1899-1951 .... TCLC 37
See also CA 170, 174; DLB 180

Miyazawa, Kenji 1896-1933 .... TCLC 76
See also CA 157

Mizoguchi, Kenji 1898-1956 .... TCLC 72
See also CA 167

Mo, Timothy (Peter) 1950(?)- ... CLC 46, 134
See also CA 117; DLB 194; MTCW 1

Modarressi, Taghi (M.) 1931- .... CLC 44
See also CA 121; 134; INT 134

Modiano, Patrick (Jean) 1945- .... CLC 18
See also CA 85-88; CANR 17, 40; DLB 83

Moerck, Paal
See Roelvaag, O(le) E(dvart)

Mofolo, Thomas (Mokopu)
1875(?)-1948 .. TCLC 22; BLC 3; DAM
MULT
See also CA 121; 153; CANR 83; DLB 225;
MTCW 2

Mohr, Nicholasa 1938- .... CLC 12; DAM
MULT; HLC 2
See also AAYA 8; CA 49-52; CANR 1, 32,
64; CLR 22; DLB 145; HW 1, 2; JRDA;
SAAS 8; SATA 8, 97; SATA-Essay 113

Mojtabai, A(nn) G(race) 1938- ..... CLC 5, 9,
15, 29
See also CA 85-88; CANR 88

Moliere 1622-1673 ..... LC 10, 28; DA; DAB;
DAC; DAM DRAM, MST; DC 13;
WLC
See also DA3

Molin, Charles
See Mayne, William (James Carter)

Molnar, Ferenc 1878-1952 .. TCLC 20; DAM
DRAM
See also CA 109; 153; CANR 83

Momaday, N(avarre) Scott 1934- ...... CLC 2,
19, 85, 95; DA; DAB; DAC; DAM
MST, MULT, NOV, POP; PC 25;
WLCS
See also AAYA 11; CA 25-28R; CANR 14,
34, 68; CDALBS; DA3; DLB 143, 175;
INT CANR-14; MTCW 1, 2; NNAL;
SATA 48; SATA-Brief 30

Monette, Paul 1945-1995 .... CLC 82
See also CA 139; 147

Monroe, Harriet 1860-1936 .... TCLC 12
See also CA 109; DLB 54, 91

Monroe, Lyle
See Heinlein, Robert A(nson)

Montagu, Elizabeth 1720-1800 .... NCLC 7

Montagu, Elizabeth 1917- .... NCLC 7
See also CA 9-12R

Montagu, Mary (Pierrepont) Wortley
1689-1762 .... LC 9, 57; PC 16
See also DLB 95, 101

Montagu, W. H.
See Coleridge, Samuel Taylor

Montague, John (Patrick) 1929- ..... CLC 13,
46
See also CA 9-12R; CANR 9, 69; DLB 40;
MTCW 1

Montaigne, Michel (Eyquem) de
1533-1592 .... LC 8; DA; DAB; DAC;
DAM MST; WLC

Montale, Eugenio 1896-1981 ... CLC 7, 9, 18;
PC 13
See also CA 17-20R; 104; CANR 30; DLB
114; MTCW 1

Montesquieu, Charles-Louis de Secondat
1689-1755 .... LC 7

Montgomery, (Robert) Bruce 1921(?)-1978
See Crispin, Edmund
See also CA 179; 104

Montgomery, L(ucy) M(aud)
1874-1942 .... TCLC 51; DAC; DAM
MST
See also AAYA 12; CA 108; 137; CLR 8;
DA3; DLB 92; DLBD 14; JRDA; MAI-
CYA; MTCW 2; SATA 100; YABC 1

Montgomery, Marion H., Jr. 1925- .... CLC 7
See also AITN 1; CA 1-4R; CANR 3, 48;
DLB 6

Montgomery, Max
See Davenport, Guy (Mattison, Jr.)

Montherlant, Henry (Milon) de
1896-1972 ..... CLC 8, 19; DAM DRAM
See also CA 85-88; 37-40R; DLB 72;
MTCW 1

Monty Python
See Chapman, Graham; Cleese, John
(Marwood); Gilliam, Terry (Vance); Idle,
Eric; Jones, Terence Graham Parry; Palin,
Michael (Edward)
See also AAYA 7

Moodie, Susanna (Strickland)
1803-1885 .... NCLC 14
See also DLB 99

Mooney, Edward 1951-
See Mooney, Ted
See also CA 130

Mooney, Ted CLC 25
See also Mooney, Edward

Moorcock, Michael (John) 1939- ...... CLC 5,
27, 58
See also Bradbury, Edward P.
See also AAYA 26; CA 45-48; CAAS 5;
CANR 2, 17, 38, 64; DLB 14, 231;
MTCW 1, 2; SATA 93

Moore, Brian 1921-1999 ... CLC 1, 3, 5, 7, 8,
19, 32, 90; DAB; DAC; DAM MST
See also CA 1-4R; 174; CANR 1, 25, 42,
63; MTCW 1, 2

Moore, Edward
See Muir, Edwin

Moore, G. E. 1873-1958 .... TCLC 89

Moore, George Augustus
1852-1933 .... TCLC 7; SSC 19
See also CA 104; 177; DLB 10, 18, 57, 135

Moore, Lorrie CLC 39, 45, 68
See also Moore, Marie Lorena

Moore, Marianne (Craig)
1887-1972 .... CLC 1, 2, 4, 8, 10, 13, 19,
47; DA; DAB; DAC; DAM MST,
POET; PC 4; WLCS
See also CA 1-4R; 33-36R; CANR 3, 61;
CDALB 1929-1941; DA3; DLB 45;
DLBD 7; MTCW 1, 2; SATA 20

Moore, Marie Lorena 1957-
See Moore, Lorrie
See also CA 116; CANR 39, 83

Moore, Thomas 1779-1852 .... NCLC 6
See also DLB 96, 144

Moorhouse, Frank 1938- .... SSC 40
See also CA 118; CANR 92

Mora, Pat(ricia) 1942-
See also CA 129; CANR 57, 81; CLR 58;
DAM MULT; DLB 209; HLC 2; HW 1,
2; SATA 92

Moraga, Cherrie 1952- .... CLC 126; DAM
MULT
See also CA 131; CANR 66; DLB 82; HW
1, 2

Morand, Paul 1888-1976 .... CLC 41; SSC 22
See also CA 184; 69-72; DLB 65

Morante, Elsa 1918-1985 .... CLC 8, 47
See also CA 85-88; 117; CANR 35; DLB
177; MTCW 1, 2

Moravia, Alberto 1907-1990 .... CLC 2, 7, 11,
27, 46; SSC 26
See also Pincherle, Alberto
See also DLB 177; MTCW 2

More, Hannah 1745-1833 .... NCLC 27
See also DLB 107, 109, 116, 158

More, Henry 1614-1687 .... LC 9
See also DLB 126

More, Sir Thomas 1478-1535 .... LC 10, 32

Moreas, Jean TCLC 18
See also Papadiamantopoulos, Johannes

Morgan, Berry 1919- .... CLC 6
See also CA 49-52; DLB 6

Morgan, Claire
See Highsmith, (Mary) Patricia

Morgan, Edwin (George) 1920- .... CLC 31
See also CA 5-8R; CANR 3, 43, 90; DLB
27

Morgan, (George) Frederick 1922- .. CLC 23
See also CA 17-20R; CANR 21

Morgan, Harriet
See Mencken, H(enry) L(ouis)

Morgan, Jane
See Cooper, James Fenimore

Morgan, Janet 1945- .... CLC 39
See also CA 65-68

Morgan, Lady 1776(?)-1859 .... NCLC 29
See also DLB 116, 158

Morgan, Robin (Evonne) 1941- .... CLC 2
See also CA 69-72; CANR 29, 68; MTCW
1; SATA 80

Morgan, Scott
See Kuttner, Henry

Morgan, Seth 1949(?)-1990 .... **CLC 65**
    See also CA 185; 132
Morgenstern, Christian 1871-1914 .. **TCLC 8**
    See also CA 105
Morgenstern, S.
    See Goldman, William (W.)
Moricz, Zsigmond 1879-1942 .... **TCLC 33**
    See also CA 165
Morike, Eduard (Friedrich)
    1804-1875 .... **NCLC 10**
    See also DLB 133
Moritz, Karl Philipp 1756-1793 .... **LC 2**
    See also DLB 94
Morland, Peter Henry
    See Faust, Frederick (Schiller)
Morley, Christopher (Darlington)
    1890-1957 .... **TCLC 87**
    See also CA 112; DLB 9
Morren, Theophil
    See Hofmannsthal, Hugo von
Morris, Bill 1952- .... **CLC 76**
Morris, Julian
    See West, Morris L(anglo)
Morris, Steveland Judkins 1950(?)-
    See Wonder, Stevie
    See also CA 111
Morris, William 1834-1896 .... **NCLC 4**
    See also CDBLB 1832-1890; DLB 18, 35, 57, 156, 178, 184
Morris, Wright 1910-1998 .. **CLC 1, 3, 7, 18, 37**
    See also CA 9-12R; 167; CANR 21, 81; DLB 2, 206; DLBY 81; MTCW 1, 2
Morrison, Arthur 1863-1945 .... **TCLC 72; SSC 40**
    See also CA 120; 157; DLB 70, 135, 197
Morrison, Chloe Anthony Wofford
    See Morrison, Toni
Morrison, James Douglas 1943-1971
    See Morrison, Jim
    See also CA 73-76; CANR 40
Morrison, Jim CLC 17
    See also Morrison, James Douglas
Morrison, Toni 1931- . **CLC 4, 10, 22, 55, 81, 87; BLC 3; DA; DAB; DAC; DAM MST, MULT, NOV, POP**
    See also AAYA 1, 22; BW 2, 3; CA 29-32R; CANR 27, 42, 67; CDALB 1968-1988; DA3; DLB 6, 33, 143; DLBY 81; MTCW 1, 2; SATA 57
Morrison, Van 1945- .... **CLC 21**
    See also CA 116; 168
Morrissy, Mary 1958- .... **CLC 99**
Mortimer, John (Clifford) 1923- ..... **CLC 28, 43; DAM DRAM, POP**
    See also CA 13-16R; CANR 21, 69; CD-BLB 1960 to Present; DA3; DLB 13; INT CANR-21; MTCW 1, 2
Mortimer, Penelope (Ruth)
    1918-1999 .... **CLC 5**
    See also CA 57-60; 187; CANR 45, 88
Morton, Anthony
    See Creasey, John
Mosca, Gaetano 1858-1941 .... **TCLC 75**
Mosher, Howard Frank 1943- .... **CLC 62**
    See also CA 139; CANR 65
Mosley, Nicholas 1923- .... **CLC 43, 70**
    See also CA 69-72; CANR 41, 60; DLB 14, 207
Mosley, Walter 1952- .... **CLC 97; BLCS; DAM MULT, POP**
    See also AAYA 17; BW 2; CA 142; CANR 57, 92; DA3; MTCW 2
Moss, Howard 1922-1987 ...... **CLC 7, 14, 45, 50; DAM POET**
    See also CA 1-4R; 123; CANR 1, 44; DLB 5

Mossgiel, Rab
    See Burns, Robert
Motion, Andrew (Peter) 1952- .... **CLC 47**
    See also CA 146; CANR 90; DLB 40
Motley, Willard (Francis)
    1909-1965 .... **CLC 18**
    See also BW 1; CA 117; 106; CANR 88; DLB 76, 143
Motoori, Noringa 1730-1801 .... **NCLC 45**
Mott, Michael (Charles Alston)
    1930- .... **CLC 15, 34**
    See also CA 5-8R; CAAS 7; CANR 7, 29
Mountain Wolf Woman 1884-1960 .. **CLC 92**
    See also CA 144; CANR 90; NNAL
Moure, Erin 1955- .... **CLC 88**
    See also CA 113; DLB 60
Mowat, Farley (McGill) 1921- .... **CLC 26; DAC; DAM MST**
    See also AAYA 1; CA 1-4R; CANR 4, 24, 42, 68; CLR 20; DLB 68; INT CANR-24; JRDA; MAICYA; MTCW 1, 2; SATA 3, 55
Mowatt, Anna Cora 1819-1870 ..... **NCLC 74**
Moyers, Bill 1934- .... **CLC 74**
    See also AITN 2; CA 61-64; CANR 31, 52
Mphahlele, Es'kia
    See Mphahlele, Ezekiel
    See also DLB 125, 225
Mphahlele, Ezekiel 1919- .... **CLC 25, 133; BLC 3; DAM MULT**
    See also Mphahlele, Es'kia
    See also BW 2, 3; CA 81-84; CANR 26, 76; DA3; DLB 225; MTCW 2; SATA 119
Mqhayi, S(amuel) E(dward) K(rune Loliwe)
    1875-1945 ...... **TCLC 25; BLC 3; DAM MULT**
    See also CA 153; CANR 87
Mrozek, Slawomir 1930- .... **CLC 3, 13**
    See also CA 13-16R; CAAS 10; CANR 29; DLB 232; MTCW 1
Mrs. Belloc-Lowndes
    See Lowndes, Marie Adelaide (Belloc)
Mtwa, Percy (?)- .... **CLC 47**
Mueller, Lisel 1924- .... **CLC 13, 51**
    See also CA 93-96; DLB 105
Muir, Edwin 1887-1959 .... **TCLC 2, 87**
    See also CA 104; DLB 20, 100, 191
Muir, John 1838-1914 .... **TCLC 28**
    See also CA 165; DLB 186
Mujica Lainez, Manuel 1910-1984 ... **CLC 31**
    See also Lainez, Manuel Mujica
    See also CA 81-84; 112; CANR 32; HW 1
Mukherjee, Bharati 1940- .... **CLC 53, 115; DAM NOV; SSC 38**
    See also BEST 89:2; CA 107; CANR 45, 72; DLB 60; MTCW 1, 2
Muldoon, Paul 1951- .... **CLC 32, 72; DAM POET**
    See also CA 113; 129; CANR 52, 91; DLB 40; INT 129
Mulisch, Harry 1927- .... **CLC 42**
    See also CA 9-12R; CANR 6, 26, 56
Mull, Martin 1943- .... **CLC 17**
    See also CA 105
Muller, Wilhelm NCLC 73
Mulock, Dinah Maria
    See Craik, Dinah Maria (Mulock)
Munford, Robert 1737(?)-1783 .... **LC 5**
    See also DLB 31
Mungo, Raymond 1946- .... **CLC 72**
    See also CA 49-52; CANR 2
Munro, Alice 1931- .... **CLC 6, 10, 19, 50, 95; DAC; DAM MST, NOV; SSC 3; WLCS**
    See also AITN 2; CA 33-36R; CANR 33, 53, 75; DA3; DLB 53; MTCW 1, 2; SATA 29

Munro, H(ector) H(ugh) 1870-1916
    See Saki
    See also CA 104; 130; CDBLB 1890-1914; DA; DAB; DAC; DAM MST, NOV; DA3; DLB 34, 162; MTCW 1, 2; WLC
Murdoch, (Jean) Iris 1919-1999 ... **CLC 1, 2, 3, 4, 6, 8, 11, 15, 22, 31, 51; DAB; DAC; DAM MST, NOV**
    See also CA 13-16R; 179; CANR 8, 43, 68; CDBLB 1960 to Present; DA3; DLB 14, 194, 233; INT CANR-8; MTCW 1, 2
Murfree, Mary Noailles 1850-1922 ... **SSC 22**
    See also CA 122; 176; DLB 12, 74
Murnau, Friedrich Wilhelm
    See Plumpe, Friedrich Wilhelm
Murphy, Richard 1927- .... **CLC 41**
    See also CA 29-32R; DLB 40
Murphy, Sylvia 1937- .... **CLC 34**
    See also CA 121
Murphy, Thomas (Bernard) 1935- ... **CLC 51**
    See also CA 101
Murray, Albert L. 1916- .... **CLC 73**
    See also BW 2; CA 49-52; CANR 26, 52, 78; DLB 38
Murray, Judith Sargent
    1751-1820 .... **NCLC 63**
    See also DLB 37, 200
Murray, Les(lie) A(llan) 1938- .... **CLC 40; DAM POET**
    See also CA 21-24R; CANR 11, 27, 56
Murry, J. Middleton
    See Murry, John Middleton
Murry, John Middleton
    1889-1957 .... **TCLC 16**
    See also CA 118; DLB 149
Musgrave, Susan 1951- .... **CLC 13, 54**
    See also CA 69-72; CANR 45, 84
Musil, Robert (Edler von)
    1880-1942 .... **TCLC 12, 68; SSC 18**
    See also CA 109; CANR 55, 84; DLB 81, 124; MTCW 2
Muske, Carol 1945- .... **CLC 90**
    See also Muske-Dukes, Carol (Anne)
Muske-Dukes, Carol (Anne) 1945-
    See Muske, Carol
    See also CA 65-68; CANR 32, 70
Musset, (Louis Charles) Alfred de
    1810-1857 .... **NCLC 7**
    See also DLB 192
Mussolini, Benito (Amilcare Andrea)
    1883-1945 .... **TCLC 96**
    See also CA 116
My Brother's Brother
    See Chekhov, Anton (Pavlovich)
Myers, L(eopold) H(amilton)
    1881-1944 .... **TCLC 59**
    See also CA 157; DLB 15
Myers, Walter Dean 1937- ..... **CLC 35; BLC 3; DAM MULT, NOV**
    See also AAYA 4, 23; BW 2; CA 33-36R; CANR 20, 42, 67; CLR 4, 16, 35; DLB 33; INT CANR-20; JRDA; MAICYA; MTCW 2; SAAS 2; SATA 41, 71, 109; SATA-Brief 27
Myers, Walter M.
    See Myers, Walter Dean
Myles, Symon
    See Follett, Ken(neth Martin)
Nabokov, Vladimir (Vladimirovich)
    1899-1977 .... **CLC 1, 2, 3, 6, 8, 11, 15, 23, 44, 46, 64; DA; DAB; DAC; DAM MST, NOV; SSC 11; WLC**
    See also CA 5-8R; 69-72; CANR 20; CDALB 1941-1968; DA3; DLB 2; DLBD 3; DLBY 80, 91; MTCW 1, 2
Naevius c. 265B.C.-201B.C. .... **CMLC 37**
    See also DLB 211

Norton, Andre 1912- .... **CLC 12**
See also Norton, Alice Mary
See also AAYA 14; CA 1-4R; CANR 68;
CLR 50; DLB 8, 52; JRDA; MTCW 1;
SATA 91

Norton, Caroline 1808-1877 .... **NCLC 47**
See also DLB 21, 159, 199

Norway, Nevil Shute 1899-1960
See Shute, Nevil
See also CA 102; 93-96; CANR 85; MTCW
2

Norwid, Cyprian Kamil
1821-1883 .... **NCLC 17**

Nosille, Nabrah
See Ellison, Harlan (Jay)

Nossack, Hans Erich 1901-1978 .... **CLC 6**
See also CA 93-96; 85-88; DLB 69

Nostradamus 1503-1566 .... **LC 27**

Nosu, Chuji
See Ozu, Yasujiro

Notenburg, Eleanora (Genrikhovna) von
See Guro, Elena

Nova, Craig 1945- .... **CLC 7, 31**
See also CA 45-48; CANR 2, 53

Novak, Joseph
See Kosinski, Jerzy (Nikodem)

Novalis 1772-1801 .... **NCLC 13**
See also DLB 90

Novis, Emile
See Weil, Simone (Adolphine)

Nowlan, Alden (Albert) 1933-1983 . **CLC 15;
DAC; DAM MST**
See also CA 9-12R; CANR 5; DLB 53

Noyes, Alfred 1880-1958 ...... **TCLC 7; PC 27**
See also CA 104; DLB 20

Nunn, Kem CLC 34
See also CA 159

Nwapa, Flora 1931- .... **CLC 133; BLCS**
See also BW 2; CA 143; CANR 83; DLB
125

Nye, Robert 1939- . **CLC 13, 42; DAM NOV**
See also CA 33-36R; CANR 29, 67; DLB
14; MTCW 1; SATA 6

Nyro, Laura 1947- .... **CLC 17**

Oates, Joyce Carol 1938- .. **CLC 1, 2, 3, 6, 9,
11, 15, 19, 33, 52, 108, 134; DA; DAB;
DAC; DAM MST, NOV, POP; SSC 6;
WLC**
See also AAYA 15; AITN 1; BEST 89:2;
CA 5-8R; CANR 25, 45, 74; CDALB
1968-1988; DA3; DLB 2, 5, 130; DLBY
81; INT CANR-25; MTCW 1, 2

O'Brien, Darcy 1939-1998 .... **CLC 11**
See also CA 21-24R; 167; CANR 8, 59

O'Brien, E. G.
See Clarke, Arthur C(harles)

O'Brien, Edna 1936- ..... **CLC 3, 5, 8, 13, 36,
65, 116; DAM NOV; SSC 10**
See also CA 1-4R; CANR 6, 41, 65; CD-
BLB 1960 to Present; DA3; DLB 14, 231;
MTCW 1, 2

O'Brien, Fitz-James 1828-1862 ..... **NCLC 21**
See also DLB 74

O'Brien, Flann CLC 1, 4, 5, 7, 10, 47
See also O Nuallain, Brian
See also DLB 231

O'Brien, Richard 1942- .... **CLC 17**
See also CA 124

O'Brien, (William) Tim(othy) 1946- . **CLC 7,
19, 40, 103; DAM POP**
See also AAYA 16; CA 85-88; CANR 40,
58; CDALBS; DA3; DLB 152; DLBD 9;
DLBY 80; MTCW 2

Obstfelder, Sigbjoern 1866-1900 .... **TCLC 23**
See also CA 123

O'Casey, Sean 1880-1964 .... **CLC 1, 5, 9, 11,
15, 88; DAB; DAC; DAM DRAM,
MST; DC 12; WLCS**
See also CA 89-92; CANR 62; CDBLB
1914-1945; DA3; DLB 10; MTCW 1, 2

O'Cathasaigh, Sean
See O'Casey, Sean

Occom, Samson 1723-1792 .... **LC 60**
See also DLB 175; NNAL

Ochs, Phil(ip David) 1940-1976 .... **CLC 17**
See also CA 185; 65-68

O'Connor, Edwin (Greene)
1918-1968 .... **CLC 14**
See also CA 93-96; 25-28R

O'Connor, (Mary) Flannery
1925-1964 .... **CLC 1, 2, 3, 6, 10, 13, 15,
21, 66, 104; DA; DAB; DAC; DAM
MST, NOV; SSC 1, 23; WLC**
See also AAYA 7; CA 1-4R; CANR 3, 41;
CDALB 1941-1968; DA3; DLB 2, 152;
DLBD 12; DLBY 80; MTCW 1, 2

O'Connor, Frank CLC 23; SSC 5
See also O'Donovan, Michael John
See also DLB 162

O'Dell, Scott 1898-1989 .... **CLC 30**
See also AAYA 3; CA 61-64; 129; CANR
12, 30; CLR 1, 16; DLB 52; JRDA; MAI-
CYA; SATA 12, 60

Odets, Clifford 1906-1963 ..... **CLC 2, 28, 98;
DAM DRAM; DC 6**
See also CA 85-88; CANR 62; DLB 7, 26;
MTCW 1, 2

O'Doherty, Brian 1934- .... **CLC 76**
See also CA 105

O'Donnell, K. M.
See Malzberg, Barry N(athaniel)

O'Donnell, Lawrence
See Kuttner, Henry

O'Donovan, Michael John
1903-1966 .... **CLC 14**
See also O'Connor, Frank
See also CA 93-96; CANR 84

Oe, Kenzaburo 1935- .... **CLC 10, 36, 86;
DAM NOV; SSC 20**
See also CA 97-100; CANR 36, 50, 74;
DA3; DLB 182; DLBY 94; MTCW 1, 2

O'Faolain, Julia 1932- .... **CLC 6, 19, 47, 108**
See also CA 81-84; CAAS 2; CANR 12,
61; DLB 14, 231; MTCW 1

O'Faolain, Sean 1900-1991 ...... **CLC 1, 7, 14,
32, 70; SSC 13**
See also CA 61-64; 134; CANR 12, 66;
DLB 15, 162; MTCW 1, 2

O'Flaherty, Liam 1896-1984 .... **CLC 5, 34;
SSC 6**
See also CA 101; 113; CANR 35; DLB 36,
162; DLBY 84; MTCW 1, 2

Ogilvy, Gavin
See Barrie, J(ames) M(atthew)

O'Grady, Standish (James)
1846-1928 .... **TCLC 5**
See also CA 104; 157

O'Grady, Timothy 1951- .... **CLC 59**
See also CA 138

O'Hara, Frank 1926-1966 .... **CLC 2, 5, 13,
78; DAM POET**
See also CA 9-12R; 25-28R; CANR 33;
DA3; DLB 5, 16, 193; MTCW 1, 2

O'Hara, John (Henry) 1905-1970 . **CLC 1, 2,
3, 6, 11, 42; DAM NOV; SSC 15**
See also CA 5-8R; 25-28R; CANR 31, 60;
CDALB 1929-1941; DLB 9, 86; DLBD
2; MTCW 1, 2

O Hehir, Diana 1922- .... **CLC 41**
See also CA 93-96

Ohiyesa
See Eastman, Charles A(lexander)

Okigbo, Christopher (Ifenayichukwu)
1932-1967 ... **CLC 25, 84; BLC 3; DAM
MULT, POET; PC 7**
See also BW 1, 3; CA 77-80; CANR 74;
DLB 125; MTCW 1, 2

Okri, Ben 1959- .... **CLC 87**
See also BW 2, 3; CA 130; 138; CANR 65;
DLB 157, 231; INT 138; MTCW 2

Olds, Sharon 1942- ... **CLC 32, 39, 85; DAM
POET; PC 22**
See also CA 101; CANR 18, 41, 66; DLB
120; MTCW 2

Oldstyle, Jonathan
See Irving, Washington

Olesha, Yuri (Karlovich) 1899-1960 .. **CLC 8**
See also CA 85-88

Oliphant, Laurence 1829(?)-1888 .. **NCLC 47**
See also DLB 18, 166

Oliphant, Margaret (Oliphant Wilson)
1828-1897 .... **NCLC 11, 61; SSC 25**
See also DLB 18, 159, 190

Oliver, Mary 1935- .... **CLC 19, 34, 98**
See also CA 21-24R; CANR 9, 43, 84, 92;
DLB 5, 193

Olivier, Laurence (Kerr) 1907-1989 . **CLC 20**
See also CA 111; 150; 129

Olsen, Tillie 1912- .... **CLC 4, 13, 114; DA;
DAB; DAC; DAM MST; SSC 11**
See also CA 1-4R; CANR 1, 43, 74;
CDALBS; DA3; DLB 28, 206; DLBY 80;
MTCW 1, 2

Olson, Charles (John) 1910-1970 .. **CLC 1, 2,
5, 6, 9, 11, 29; DAM POET; PC 19**
See also CA 13-16; 25-28R; CABS 2;
CANR 35, 61; CAP 1; DLB 5, 16, 193;
MTCW 1, 2

Olson, Toby 1937- .... **CLC 28**
See also CA 65-68; CANR 9, 31, 84

Olyesha, Yuri
See Olesha, Yuri (Karlovich)

Ondaatje, (Philip) Michael 1943- .... **CLC 14,
29, 51, 76; DAB; DAC; DAM MST; PC
28**
See also CA 77-80; CANR 42, 74; DA3;
DLB 60; MTCW 2

Oneal, Elizabeth 1934-
See Oneal, Zibby
See also CA 106; CANR 28, 84; MAICYA;
SATA 30, 82

Oneal, Zibby CLC 30
See also Oneal, Elizabeth
See also AAYA 5; CLR 13; JRDA

O'Neill, Eugene (Gladstone)
1888-1953 .... **TCLC 1, 6, 27, 49; DA;
DAB; DAC; DAM DRAM, MST; WLC**
See also AITN 1; CA 110; 132; CDALB
1929-1941; DA3; DLB 7; MTCW 1, 2

Onetti, Juan Carlos 1909-1994 ... **CLC 7, 10;
DAM MULT, NOV; HLCS 2; SSC 23**
See also CA 85-88; 145; CANR 32, 63;
DLB 113; HW 1, 2; MTCW 1, 2

O Nuallain, Brian 1911-1966
See O'Brien, Flann
See also CA 21-22; 25-28R; CAP 2; DLB
231

Ophuls, Max 1902-1957 .... **TCLC 79**
See also CA 113

Opie, Amelia 1769-1853 .... **NCLC 65**
See also DLB 116, 159

Oppen, George 1908-1984 ...... **CLC 7, 13, 34**
See also CA 13-16R; 113; CANR 8, 82;
DLB 5, 165

Oppenheim, E(dward) Phillips
1866-1946 .... **TCLC 45**
See also CA 111; DLB 70

Opuls, Max
See Ophuls, Max

Porter, Peter (Neville Frederick)
1929- .... CLC **5, 13, 33**
See also CA 85-88; DLB 40

Porter, William Sydney 1862-1910
See Henry, O.
See also CA 104; 131; CDALB 1865-1917;
DA; DAB; DAC; DAM MST; DA3; DLB
12, 78, 79; MTCW 1, 2; YABC 2

Portillo (y Pacheco), Jose Lopez
See Lopez Portillo (y Pacheco), Jose

Portillo Trambley, Estela 1927-1998
See also CANR 32; DAM MULT; DLB
209; HLC 2; HW 1

Post, Melville Davisson
1869-1930 .... TCLC **39**
See also CA 110

Potok, Chaim 1929- ... CLC **2, 7, 14, 26, 112;**
DAM NOV
See also AAYA 15; AITN 1, 2; CA 17-20R;
CANR 19, 35, 64; DA3; DLB 28, 152;
INT CANR-19; MTCW 1, 2; SATA 33,
106

Potter, Dennis (Christopher George)
1935-1994 .... CLC **58, 86, 123**
See also CA 107; 145; CANR 33, 61; DLB
233; MTCW 1

Pound, Ezra (Weston Loomis)
1885-1972 .. CLC **1, 2, 3, 4, 5, 7, 10, 13,**
18, 34, 48, 50, 112; DA; DAB; DAC;
DAM MST, POET; PC 4; WLC
See also CA 5-8R; 37-40R; CANR 40;
CDALB 1917-1929; DA3; DLB 4, 45, 63;
DLBD 15; MTCW 1, 2

Povod, Reinaldo 1959-1994 .... CLC **44**
See also CA 136; 146; CANR 83

Powell, Adam Clayton, Jr.
1908-1972 .... CLC **89; BLC 3; DAM**
MULT
See also BW 1, 3; CA 102; 33-36R; CANR
86

Powell, Anthony (Dymoke) 1905- . CLC **1, 3,**
7, 9, 10, 31
See also CA 1-4R; CANR 1, 32, 62; CD-
BLB 1945-1960; DLB 15; MTCW 1, 2

Powell, Dawn 1897-1965 .... CLC **66**
See also CA 5-8R; DLBY 97

Powell, Padgett 1952- .... CLC **34**
See also CA 126; CANR 63

Powell, Talmage 1920-
See Queen, Ellery
See also CA 5-8R; CANR 2, 80

Power, Susan 1961- .... CLC **91**
See also CA 145

Powers, J(ames) F(arl) 1917-1999 ..... CLC **1,**
4, 8, 57; SSC 4
See also CA 1-4R; 181; CANR 2, 61; DLB
130; MTCW 1

Powers, John J(ames) 1945-
See Powers, John R.
See also CA 69-72

Powers, John R. CLC 66
See also Powers, John J(ames)

Powers, Richard (S.) 1957- .... CLC **93**
See also CA 148; CANR 80

Pownall, David 1938- .... CLC **10**
See also CA 89-92; 180; CAAS 18; CANR
49; DLB 14

Powys, John Cowper 1872-1963 ... CLC **7, 9,**
15, 46, 125
See also CA 85-88; DLB 15; MTCW 1, 2

Powys, T(heodore) F(rancis)
1875-1953 .... TCLC **9**
See also CA 106; DLB 36, 162

Prado (Calvo), Pedro 1886-1952 ... TCLC **75**
See also CA 131; HW 1

Prager, Emily 1952- .... CLC **56**

Pratt, E(dwin) J(ohn)
1883(?)-1964 .... CLC **19; DAC; DAM**
POET
See also CA 141; 93-96; CANR 77; DLB
92

Premchand TCLC 21
See also Srivastava, Dhanpat Rai

Preussler, Otfried 1923- .... CLC **17**
See also CA 77-80; SATA 24

Prevert, Jacques (Henri Marie)
1900-1977 .... CLC **15**
See also CA 77-80; 69-72; CANR 29, 61;
MTCW 1; SATA-Obit 30

Prevost, Abbe (Antoine Francois)
1697-1763 .... LC **1**

Price, (Edward) Reynolds 1933- ... CLC **3, 6,**
13, 43, 50, 63; DAM NOV; SSC 22
See also CA 1-4R; CANR 1, 37, 57, 87;
DLB 2; INT CANR-37

Price, Richard 1949- .... CLC **6, 12**
See also CA 49-52; CANR 3; DLBY 81

Prichard, Katharine Susannah
1883-1969 .... CLC **46**
See also CA 11-12; CANR 33; CAP 1;
MTCW 1; SATA 66

Priestley, J(ohn) B(oynton)
1894-1984 .... CLC **2, 5, 9, 34; DAM**
DRAM, NOV
See also CA 9-12R; 113; CANR 33; CD-
BLB 1914-1945; DA3; DLB 10, 34, 77,
100, 139; DLBY 84; MTCW 1, 2

Prince 1958(?)- .... CLC **35**

Prince, F(rank) T(empleton) 1912- .. CLC **22**
See also CA 101; CANR 43, 79; DLB 20

Prince Kropotkin
See Kropotkin, Peter (Alekseievich)

Prior, Matthew 1664-1721 .... LC **4**
See also DLB 95

Prishvin, Mikhail 1873-1954 .... TCLC **75**

Pritchard, William H(arrison)
1932- .... CLC **34**
See also CA 65-68; CANR 23; DLB 111

Pritchett, V(ictor) S(awdon)
1900-1997 ...... CLC **5, 13, 15, 41; DAM**
NOV; SSC 14
See also CA 61-64; 157; CANR 31, 63;
DA3; DLB 15, 139; MTCW 1, 2

Private 19022
See Manning, Frederic

Probst, Mark 1925- .... CLC **59**
See also CA 130

Prokosch, Frederic 1908-1989 ...... CLC **4, 48**
See also CA 73-76; 128; CANR 82; DLB
48; MTCW 2

Propertius, Sextus c. 50B.C.-c.
16B.C. .... CMLC **32**
See also DLB 211

Prophet, The
See Dreiser, Theodore (Herman Albert)

Prose, Francine 1947- .... CLC **45**
See also CA 109; 112; CANR 46; SATA
101

Proudhon
See Cunha, Euclides (Rodrigues Pimenta)
da

Proulx, Annie
See Proulx, E(dna) Annie

Proulx, E(dna) Annie 1935- .. CLC **81; DAM**
POP
See also CA 145; CANR 65; DA3; MTCW
2

Proust, (Valentin-Louis-George-Eugene-)
Marcel 1871-1922 .... TCLC **7, 13, 33;**
DA; DAB; DAC; DAM MST, NOV;
WLC
See also CA 104; 120; DA3; DLB 65;
MTCW 1, 2

Prowler, Harley
See Masters, Edgar Lee

Prus, Boleslaw 1845-1912 .... TCLC **48**

Pryor, Richard (Franklin Lenox Thomas)
1940- .... CLC **26**
See also CA 122; 152

Przybyszewski, Stanislaw
1868-1927 .... TCLC **36**
See also CA 160; DLB 66

Pteleon
See Grieve, C(hristopher) M(urray)
See also DAM POET

Puckett, Lute
See Masters, Edgar Lee

Puig, Manuel 1932-1990 .... CLC **3, 5, 10, 28,**
65, 133; DAM MULT; HLC 2
See also CA 45-48; CANR 2, 32, 63; DA3;
DLB 113; HW 1, 2; MTCW 1, 2

Pulitzer, Joseph 1847-1911 .... TCLC **76**
See also CA 114; DLB 23

Purdy, A(lfred) W(ellington) 1918- ... CLC **3,**
6, 14, 50; DAC; DAM MST, POET
See also CA 81-84; CAAS 17; CANR 42,
66; DLB 88

Purdy, James (Amos) 1923- .... CLC **2, 4, 10,**
28, 52
See also CA 33-36R; CAAS 1; CANR 19,
51; DLB 2; INT CANR-19; MTCW 1

Pure, Simon
See Swinnerton, Frank Arthur

Pushkin, Alexander (Sergeyevich)
1799-1837 . NCLC **3, 27, 83; DA; DAB;**
DAC; DAM DRAM, MST, POET; PC
10; SSC 27; WLC
See also DA3; DLB 205; SATA 61

P'u Sung-ling 1640-1715 .... LC **49; SSC 31**

Putnam, Arthur Lee
See Alger, Horatio Jr., Jr.

Puzo, Mario 1920-1999 .... CLC **1, 2, 6, 36,**
107; DAM NOV, POP
See also CA 65-68; 185; CANR 4, 42, 65;
DA3; DLB 6; MTCW 1, 2

Pygge, Edward
See Barnes, Julian (Patrick)

Pyle, Ernest Taylor 1900-1945
See Pyle, Ernie
See also CA 115; 160

Pyle, Ernie 1900-1945 .... TCLC **75**
See also Pyle, Ernest Taylor
See also DLB 29; MTCW 2

Pyle, Howard 1853-1911 .... TCLC **81**
See also CA 109; 137; CLR 22; DLB 42,
188; DLBD 13; MAICYA; SATA 16, 100

Pym, Barbara (Mary Crampton)
1913-1980 .... CLC **13, 19, 37, 111**
See also CA 13-14; 97-100; CANR 13, 34;
CAP 1; DLB 14, 207; DLBY 87; MTCW
1, 2

Pynchon, Thomas (Ruggles, Jr.)
1937- ...... CLC **2, 3, 6, 9, 11, 18, 33, 62,**
72, 123; DA; DAB; DAC; DAM MST,
NOV, POP; SSC 14; WLC
See also BEST 90:2; CA 17-20R; CANR
22, 46, 73; DA3; DLB 2, 173; MTCW 1,
2

Pythagoras c. 570B.C.-c. 500B.C. . CMLC **22**
See also DLB 176

Q
See Quiller-Couch, SirArthur (Thomas)

Qian Zhongshu
See Ch'ien Chung-shu

Qroll
See Dagerman, Stig (Halvard)

Quarrington, Paul (Lewis) 1953- ..... CLC **65**
See also CA 129; CANR 62

Quasimodo, Salvatore 1901-1968 ..... CLC **10**
See also CA 13-16; 25-28R; CAP 1; DLB
114; MTCW 1

Remarque, Erich Maria
1898-1970 ... **CLC 21; DA; DAB; DAC; DAM MST, NOV**
See also AAYA 27; CA 77-80; 29-32R; DA3; DLB 56; MTCW 1, 2

Remington, Frederic 1861-1909 ..... **TCLC 89**
See also CA 108; 169; DLB 12, 186, 188; SATA 41

Remizov, A.
See Remizov, Aleksei (Mikhailovich)

Remizov, A. M.
See Remizov, Aleksei (Mikhailovich)

Remizov, Aleksei (Mikhailovich)
1877-1957 .... **TCLC 27**
See also CA 125; 133

Renan, Joseph Ernest 1823-1892 .. **NCLC 26**

Renard, Jules 1864-1910 .... **TCLC 17**
See also CA 117

Renault, Mary -1983 .... **CLC 3, 11, 17**
See also Challans, Mary
See also DLBY 83; MTCW 2

Rendell, Ruth (Barbara) 1930- . **CLC 28, 48; DAM POP**
See Vine, Barbara
See also CA 109; CANR 32, 52, 74; DLB 87; INT CANR-32; MTCW 1, 2

Renoir, Jean 1894-1979 .... **CLC 20**
See also CA 129; 85-88

Resnais, Alain 1922- .... **CLC 16**

Reverdy, Pierre 1889-1960 .... **CLC 53**
See also CA 97-100; 89-92

Rexroth, Kenneth 1905-1982 .... **CLC 1, 2, 6, 11, 22, 49, 112; DAM POET; PC 20**
See also CA 5-8R; 107; CANR 14, 34, 63; CDALB 1941-1968; DLB 16, 48, 165, 212; DLBY 82; INT CANR-14; MTCW 1, 2

Reyes, Alfonso 1889-1959 .. **TCLC 33; HLCS 2**
See also CA 131; HW 1

Reyes y Basoalto, Ricardo Eliecer Neftali
See Neruda, Pablo

Reymont, Wladyslaw (Stanislaw)
1868(?)-1925 .... **TCLC 5**
See also CA 104

Reynolds, Jonathan 1942- .... **CLC 6, 38**
See also CA 65-68; CANR 28

Reynolds, Joshua 1723-1792 .... **LC 15**
See also DLB 104

Reynolds, Michael S(hane) 1937- ..... **CLC 44**
See also CA 65-68; CANR 9, 89

Reznikoff, Charles 1894-1976 .... **CLC 9**
See also CA 33-36; 61-64; CAP 2; DLB 28, 45

Rezzori (d'Arezzo), Gregor von
1914-1998 .... **CLC 25**
See also CA 122; 136; 167

Rhine, Richard
See Silverstein, Alvin

Rhodes, Eugene Manlove
1869-1934 .... **TCLC 53**

Rhodius, Apollonius c. 3rd cent.
B.C.- .... **CMLC 28**
See also DLB 176

R'hoone
See Balzac, Honore de

Rhys, Jean 1890(?)-1979 ...... **CLC 2, 4, 6, 14, 19, 51, 124; DAM NOV; SSC 21**
See also CA 25-28R; 85-88; CANR 35, 62; CDBLB 1945-1960; DA3; DLB 36, 117, 162; MTCW 1, 2

Ribeiro, Darcy 1922-1997 .... **CLC 34**
See also CA 33-36R; 156

Ribeiro, Joao Ubaldo (Osorio Pimentel)
1941- .... **CLC 10, 67**
See also CA 81-84

Ribman, Ronald (Burt) 1932- .... **CLC 7**
See also CA 21-24R; CANR 46, 80

Ricci, Nino 1959- .... **CLC 70**
See also CA 137

Rice, Anne 1941- .. **CLC 41, 128; DAM POP**
See also AAYA 9; BEST 89:2; CA 65-68; CANR 12, 36, 53, 74; DA3; MTCW 2

Rice, Elmer (Leopold) 1892-1967 ...... **CLC 7, 49; DAM DRAM**
See also CA 21-22; 25-28R; CAP 2; DLB 4, 7; MTCW 1, 2

Rice, Tim(othy Miles Bindon)
1944- .... **CLC 21**
See also CA 103; CANR 46

Rich, Adrienne (Cecile) 1929- ... **CLC 3, 6, 7, 11, 18, 36, 73, 76, 125; DAM POET; PC 5**
See also CA 9-12R; CANR 20, 53, 74; CDALBS; DA3; DLB 5, 67; MTCW 1, 2

Rich, Barbara
See Graves, Robert (von Ranke)

Rich, Robert
See Trumbo, Dalton

Richard, Keith **CLC 17**
See also Richards, Keith

Richards, David Adams 1950- .... **CLC 59; DAC**
See also CA 93-96; CANR 60; DLB 53

Richards, I(vor) A(rmstrong)
1893-1979 .... **CLC 14, 24**
See also CA 41-44R; 89-92; CANR 34, 74; DLB 27; MTCW 2

Richards, Keith 1943-
See Richard, Keith
See also CA 107; CANR 77

Richardson, Anne
See Roiphe, Anne (Richardson)

Richardson, Dorothy Miller
1873-1957 .... **TCLC 3**
See also CA 104; DLB 36

Richardson, Ethel Florence (Lindesay)
1870-1946
See Richardson, Henry Handel
See also CA 105

Richardson, Henry Handel **TCLC 4**
See also Richardson, Ethel Florence (Lindesay)
See also DLB 197

Richardson, John 1796-1852 .... **NCLC 55; DAC**
See also DLB 99

Richardson, Samuel 1689-1761 ...... **LC 1, 44; DA; DAB; DAC; DAM MST, NOV; WLC**
See also CDBLB 1660-1789; DLB 39

Richler, Mordecai 1931- ...... **CLC 3, 5, 9, 13, 18, 46, 70; DAC; DAM MST, NOV**
See also AITN 1; CA 65-68; CANR 31, 62; CLR 17; DLB 53; MAICYA; MTCW 1, 2; SATA 44, 98; SATA-Brief 27

Richter, Conrad (Michael)
1890-1968 .... **CLC 30**
See also AAYA 21; CA 5-8R; 25-28R; CANR 23; DLB 9, 212; MTCW 1, 2; SATA 3

Ricostranza, Tom
See Ellis, Trey

Riddell, Charlotte 1832-1906 .... **TCLC 40**
See also CA 165; DLB 156

Ridge, John Rollin 1827-1867 ...... **NCLC 82; DAM MULT**
See also CA 144; DLB 175; NNAL

Ridgway, Keith 1965- .... **CLC 119**
See also CA 172

Riding, Laura **CLC 3, 7**
See also Jackson, Laura (Riding)

Riefenstahl, Berta Helene Amalia 1902-
See Riefenstahl, Leni
See also CA 108

Riefenstahl, Leni **CLC 16**
See also Riefenstahl, Berta Helene Amalia

Riffe, Ernest
See Bergman, (Ernst) Ingmar

Riggs, (Rolla) Lynn 1899-1954 ..... **TCLC 56; DAM MULT**
See also CA 144; DLB 175; NNAL

Riis, Jacob A(ugust) 1849-1914 ..... **TCLC 80**
See also CA 113; 168; DLB 23

Riley, James Whitcomb
1849-1916 .... **TCLC 51; DAM POET**
See also CA 118; 137; MAICYA; SATA 17

Riley, Tex
See Creasey, John

Rilke, Rainer Maria 1875-1926 .. **TCLC 1, 6, 19; DAM POET; PC 2**
See also CA 104; 132; CANR 62; DA3; DLB 81; MTCW 1, 2

Rimbaud, (Jean Nicolas) Arthur
1854-1891 . **NCLC 4, 35, 82; DA; DAB; DAC; DAM MST, POET; PC 3; WLC**
See also DA3

Rinehart, Mary Roberts
1876-1958 .... **TCLC 52**
See also CA 108; 166

Ringmaster, The
See Mencken, H(enry) L(ouis)

Ringwood, Gwen(dolyn Margaret) Pharis
1910-1984 .... **CLC 48**
See also CA 148; 112; DLB 88

Rio, Michel 19(?)- .... **CLC 43**

Ritsos, Giannes
See Ritsos, Yannis

Ritsos, Yannis 1909-1990 .... **CLC 6, 13, 31**
See also CA 77-80; 133; CANR 39, 61; MTCW 1

Ritter, Erika 1948(?)- .... **CLC 52**

Rivera, Jose Eustasio 1889-1928 ... **TCLC 35**
See also CA 162; HW 1, 2

Rivera, Tomas 1935-1984
See also CA 49-52; CANR 32; DLB 82; HLCS 2; HW 1

Rivers, Conrad Kent 1933-1968 .... **CLC 1**
See also BW 1; CA 85-88; DLB 41

Rivers, Elfrida
See Bradley, Marion Zimmer

Riverside, John
See Heinlein, Robert A(nson)

Rizal, Jose 1861-1896 .... **NCLC 27**

Roa Bastos, Augusto (Antonio)
1917- .... **CLC 45; DAM MULT; HLC 2**
See also CA 131; DLB 113; HW 1

Robbe-Grillet, Alain 1922- .... **CLC 1, 2, 4, 6, 8, 10, 14, 43, 128**
See also CA 9-12R; CANR 33, 65; DLB 83; MTCW 1, 2

Robbins, Harold 1916-1997 .... **CLC 5; DAM NOV**
See also CA 73-76; 162; CANR 26, 54; DA3; MTCW 1, 2

Robbins, Thomas Eugene 1936-
See Robbins, Tom
See also CA 81-84; CANR 29, 59; DAM NOV, POP; DA3; MTCW 1, 2

Robbins, Tom **CLC 9, 32, 64**
See also Robbins, Thomas Eugene
See also AAYA 32; BEST 90:3; DLBY 80; MTCW 2

Robbins, Trina 1938- .... **CLC 21**
See also CA 128

Roberts, Charles G(eorge) D(ouglas)
1860-1943 .... **TCLC 8**
See also CA 105; CLR 33; DLB 92; SATA 88; SATA-Brief 27

Roberts, Elizabeth Madox
1886-1941 .... **TCLC 68**
See also CA 111; 166; DLB 9, 54, 102; SATA 33; SATA-Brief 27

Roberts, Kate 1891-1985 .... **CLC 15**
See also CA 107; 116

Roberts, Keith (John Kingston)
1935- .... **CLC 14**
See also CA 25-28R; CANR 46
Roberts, Kenneth (Lewis)
1885-1957 .... **TCLC 23**
See also CA 109; DLB 9
Roberts, Michele (B.) 1949- .... **CLC 48**
See also CA 115; CANR 58; DLB 231
Robertson, Ellis
See Ellison, Harlan (Jay); Silverberg, Robert
Robertson, Thomas William
1829-1871 .... **NCLC 35; DAM DRAM**
Robeson, Kenneth
See Dent, Lester
Robinson, Edwin Arlington
1869-1935 ..... **TCLC 5, 101; DA; DAC;
DAM MST, POET; PC 1**
See also CA 104; 133; CDALB 1865-1917;
DLB 54; MTCW 1, 2
Robinson, Henry Crabb
1775-1867 .... **NCLC 15**
See also DLB 107
Robinson, Jill 1936- .... **CLC 10**
See also CA 102; INT 102
Robinson, Kim Stanley 1952- .... **CLC 34**
See also AAYA 26; CA 126; SATA 109
Robinson, Lloyd
See Silverberg, Robert
Robinson, Marilynne 1944- .... **CLC 25**
See also CA 116; CANR 80; DLB 206
Robinson, Smokey **CLC 21**
See also Robinson, William, Jr.
Robinson, William, Jr. 1940-
See Robinson, Smokey
See also CA 116
Robison, Mary 1949- .... **CLC 42, 98**
See also CA 113; 116; CANR 87; DLB 130;
INT 116
Rod, Edouard 1857-1910 .... **TCLC 52**
Roddenberry, Eugene Wesley 1921-1991
See Roddenberry, Gene
See also CA 110; 135; CANR 37; SATA 45;
SATA-Obit 69
Roddenberry, Gene **CLC 17**
See also Roddenberry, Eugene Wesley
See also AAYA 5; SATA-Obit 69
Rodgers, Mary 1931- .... **CLC 12**
See also CA 49-52; CANR 8, 55, 90; CLR
20; INT CANR-8; JRDA; MAICYA;
SATA 8
Rodgers, W(illiam) R(obert)
1909-1969 .... **CLC 7**
See also CA 85-88; DLB 20
Rodman, Eric
See Silverberg, Robert
Rodman, Howard 1920(?)-1985 .... **CLC 65**
See also CA 118
Rodman, Maia
See Wojciechowska, Maia (Teresa)
Rodo, Jose Enrique 1872(?)-1917
See also CA 178; HLCS 2; HW 2
Rodriguez, Claudio 1934- .... **CLC 10**
See also DLB 134
Rodriguez, Richard 1944-
See also CA 110; CANR 66; DAM MULT;
DLB 82; HLC 2; HW 1, 2
Roelvaag, O(le) E(dvart)
1876-1931 .... **TCLC 17**
See also Rolvaag, O(le) E(dvart)
See also CA 117; 171; DLB 9
Roethke, Theodore (Huebner)
1908-1963 .... **CLC 1, 3, 8, 11, 19, 46,
101; DAM POET; PC 15**
See also CA 81-84; CABS 2; CDALB 1941-
1968; DA3; DLB 5, 206; MTCW 1, 2
Rogers, Samuel 1763-1855 .... **NCLC 69**
See also DLB 93

Rogers, Thomas Hunton 1927- .... **CLC 57**
See also CA 89-92; INT 89-92
Rogers, Will(iam Penn Adair)
1879-1935 ... **TCLC 8, 71; DAM MULT**
See also CA 105; 144; DA3; DLB 11;
MTCW 2; NNAL
Rogin, Gilbert 1929- .... **CLC 18**
See also CA 65-68; CANR 15
Rohan, Koda
See Koda Shigeyuki
Rohlfs, Anna Katharine Green
See Green, Anna Katharine
Rohmer, Eric **CLC 16**
See also Scherer, Jean-Marie Maurice
Rohmer, Sax **TCLC 28**
See also Ward, Arthur Henry Sarsfield
See also DLB 70
Roiphe, Anne (Richardson) 1935- .. **CLC 3, 9**
See also CA 89-92; CANR 45, 73; DLBY
80; INT 89-92
Rojas, Fernando de 1465-1541 .... **LC 23;
HLCS 1**
Rojas, Gonzalo 1917-
See also HLCS 2; HW 2
Rojas, Gonzalo 1917-
See also CA 178; HLCS 2
Rolfe, Frederick (William Serafino Austin
Lewis Mary) 1860-1913 .... **TCLC 12**
See also CA 107; DLB 34, 156
Rolland, Romain 1866-1944 .... **TCLC 23**
See also CA 118; DLB 65
Rolle, Richard c. 1300-c. 1349 ...... **CMLC 21**
See also DLB 146
Rolvaag, O(le) E(dvart)
See Roelvaag, O(le) E(dvart)
Romain Arnaud, Saint
See Aragon, Louis
Romains, Jules 1885-1972 .... **CLC 7**
See also CA 85-88; CANR 34; DLB 65;
MTCW 1
Romero, Jose Ruben 1890-1952 .... **TCLC 14**
See also CA 114; 131; HW 1
Ronsard, Pierre de 1524-1585 . **LC 6, 54; PC
11**
Rooke, Leon 1934- . **CLC 25, 34; DAM POP**
See also CA 25-28R; CANR 23, 53
Roosevelt, Franklin Delano
1882-1945 .... **TCLC 93**
See also CA 116; 173
Roosevelt, Theodore 1858-1919 ..... **TCLC 69**
See also CA 115; 170; DLB 47, 186
Roper, William 1498-1578 .... **LC 10**
Roquelaure, A. N.
See Rice, Anne
Rosa, Joao Guimaraes 1908-1967 ... **CLC 23;
HLCS 1**
See also CA 89-92; DLB 113
Rose, Wendy 1948- .. **CLC 85; DAM MULT;
PC 13**
See also CA 53-56; CANR 5, 51; DLB 175;
NNAL; SATA 12
Rosen, R. D.
See Rosen, Richard (Dean)
Rosen, Richard (Dean) 1949- .... **CLC 39**
See also CA 77-80; CANR 62; INT
CANR-30
Rosenberg, Isaac 1890-1918 .... **TCLC 12**
See also CA 107; DLB 20
Rosenblatt, Joe **CLC 15**
See also Rosenblatt, Joseph
Rosenblatt, Joseph 1933-
See Rosenblatt, Joe
See also CA 89-92; INT 89-92
Rosenfeld, Samuel
See Tzara, Tristan
Rosenstock, Sami
See Tzara, Tristan

Rosenstock, Samuel
See Tzara, Tristan
Rosenthal, M(acha) L(ouis)
1917-1996 .... **CLC 28**
See also CA 1-4R; 152; CAAS 6; CANR 4,
51; DLB 5; SATA 59
Ross, Barnaby
See Dannay, Frederic
Ross, Bernard L.
See Follett, Ken(neth Martin)
Ross, J. H.
See Lawrence, T(homas) E(dward)
Ross, John Hume
See Lawrence, T(homas) E(dward)
Ross, Martin
See Martin, Violet Florence
See also DLB 135
Ross, (James) Sinclair 1908-1996 ... **CLC 13;
DAC; DAM MST; SSC 24**
See also CA 73-76; CANR 81; DLB 88
Rossetti, Christina (Georgina)
1830-1894 . **NCLC 2, 50, 66; DA; DAB;
DAC; DAM MST, POET; PC 7; WLC**
See also DA3; DLB 35, 163; MAICYA;
SATA 20
Rossetti, Dante Gabriel 1828-1882 . **NCLC 4,
77; DA; DAB; DAC; DAM MST,
POET; WLC**
See also CDBLB 1832-1890; DLB 35
Rossner, Judith (Perelman) 1935- . **CLC 6, 9,
29**
See also AITN 2; BEST 90:3; CA 17-20R;
CANR 18, 51, 73; DLB 6; INT CANR-
18; MTCW 1, 2
Rostand, Edmond (Eugene Alexis)
1868-1918 .... **TCLC 6, 37; DA; DAB;
DAC; DAM DRAM, MST; DC 10**
See also CA 104; 126; DA3; DLB 192;
MTCW 1
Roth, Henry 1906-1995 ..... **CLC 2, 6, 11, 104**
See also CA 11-12; 149; CANR 38, 63;
CAP 1; DA3; DLB 28; MTCW 1, 2
Roth, Philip (Milton) 1933- ... **CLC 1, 2, 3, 4,
6, 9, 15, 22, 31, 47, 66, 86, 119; DA;
DAB; DAC; DAM MST, NOV, POP;
SSC 26; WLC**
See also BEST 90:3; CA 1-4R; CANR 1,
22, 36, 55, 89; CDALB 1968-1988; DA3;
DLB 2, 28, 173; DLBY 82; MTCW 1, 2
Rothenberg, Jerome 1931- .... **CLC 6, 57**
See also CA 45-48; CANR 1; DLB 5, 193
Roumain, Jacques (Jean Baptiste)
1907-1944 ...... **TCLC 19; BLC 3; DAM
MULT**
See also BW 1; CA 117; 125
Rourke, Constance (Mayfield)
1885-1941 .... **TCLC 12**
See also CA 107; YABC 1
Rousseau, Jean-Baptiste 1671-1741 ...... **LC 9**
Rousseau, Jean-Jacques 1712-1778 .... **LC 14,
36; DA; DAB; DAC; DAM MST; WLC**
See also DA3
Roussel, Raymond 1877-1933 .... **TCLC 20**
See also CA 117
Rovit, Earl (Herbert) 1927- .... **CLC 7**
See also CA 5-8R; CANR 12
Rowe, Elizabeth Singer 1674-1737 ..... **LC 44**
See also DLB 39, 95
Rowe, Nicholas 1674-1718 .... **LC 8**
See also DLB 84
Rowley, Ames Dorrance
See Lovecraft, H(oward) P(hillips)
Rowson, Susanna Haswell
1762(?)-1824 .... **NCLC 5, 69**
See also DLB 37, 200
Roy, Arundhati 1960(?)- .... **CLC 109**
See also CA 163; CANR 90; DLBY 97

Simpson, Louis (Aston Marantz)
1923- ...... **CLC 4, 7, 9, 32; DAM POET**
See also CA 1-4R; CAAS 4; CANR 1, 61; DLB 5; MTCW 1, 2

Simpson, Mona (Elizabeth) 1957- .... **CLC 44**
See also CA 122; 135; CANR 68

Simpson, N(orman) F(rederick)
1919- .... **CLC 29**
See also CA 13-16R; DLB 13

Sinclair, Andrew (Annandale) 1935- . **CLC 2, 14**
See also CA 9-12R; CAAS 5; CANR 14, 38, 91; DLB 14; MTCW 1

Sinclair, Emil
See Hesse, Hermann

Sinclair, Iain 1943- .... **CLC 76**
See also CA 132; CANR 81

Sinclair, Iain MacGregor
See Sinclair, Iain

Sinclair, Irene
See Griffith, D(avid Lewelyn) W(ark)

Sinclair, Mary Amelia St. Clair 1865(?)-1946
See Sinclair, May
See also CA 104

Sinclair, May 1863-1946 .... **TCLC 3, 11**
See also Sinclair, Mary Amelia St. Clair
See also CA 166; DLB 36, 135

Sinclair, Roy
See Griffith, D(avid Lewelyn) W(ark)

Sinclair, Upton (Beall) 1878-1968 ..... **CLC 1, 11, 15, 63; DA; DAB; DAC; DAM MST, NOV; WLC**
See also CA 5-8R; 25-28R; CANR 7; CDALB 1929-1941; DA3; DLB 9; INT CANR-7; MTCW 1, 2; SATA 9

Singer, Isaac
See Singer, Isaac Bashevis

Singer, Isaac Bashevis 1904-1991 .. **CLC 1, 3, 6, 9, 11, 15, 23, 38, 69, 111; DA; DAB; DAC; DAM MST, NOV; SSC 3; WLC**
See also AAYA 32; AITN 1, 2; CA 1-4R; 134; CANR 1, 39; CDALB 1941-1968; CLR 1; DA3; DLB 6, 28, 52; DLBY 91; JRDA; MAICYA; MTCW 1, 2; SATA 3, 27; SATA-Obit 68

Singer, Israel Joshua 1893-1944 .... **TCLC 33**
See also CA 169

Singh, Khushwant 1915- .... **CLC 11**
See also CA 9-12R; CAAS 9; CANR 6, 84

Singleton, Ann
See Benedict, Ruth (Fulton)

Sinjohn, John
See Galsworthy, John

Sinyavsky, Andrei (Donatevich)
1925-1997 .... **CLC 8**
See also CA 85-88; 159

Sirin, V.
See Nabokov, Vladimir (Vladimirovich)

Sissman, L(ouis) E(dward)
1928-1976 .... **CLC 9, 18**
See also CA 21-24R; 65-68; CANR 13; DLB 5

Sisson, C(harles) H(ubert) 1914- .... **CLC 8**
See also CA 1-4R; CAAS 3; CANR 3, 48, 84; DLB 27

Sitwell, Dame Edith 1887-1964 ..... **CLC 2, 9, 67; DAM POET; PC 3**
See also CA 9-12R; CANR 35; CDBLB 1945-1960; DLB 20; MTCW 1, 2

Siwaarmill, H. P.
See Sharp, William

Sjoewall, Maj 1935- .... **CLC 7**
See also Sjowall, Maj
See also CA 65-68; CANR 73

Sjowall, Maj
See Sjoewall, Maj

Skelton, John 1463-1529 .... **PC 25**

Skelton, Robin 1925-1997 .... **CLC 13**
See also AITN 2; CA 5-8R; 160; CAAS 5; CANR 28, 89; DLB 27, 53

Skolimowski, Jerzy 1938- .... **CLC 20**
See also CA 128

Skram, Amalie (Bertha)
1847-1905 .... **TCLC 25**
See also CA 165

Skvorecky, Josef (Vaclav) 1924- ...... **CLC 15, 39, 69; DAC; DAM NOV**
See also CA 61-64; CAAS 1; CANR 10, 34, 63; DA3; DLB 232; MTCW 1, 2

Slade, Bernard CLC 11, 46
See also Newbound, Bernard Slade
See also CAAS 9; DLB 53

Slaughter, Carolyn 1946- .... **CLC 56**
See also CA 85-88; CANR 85

Slaughter, Frank G(ill) 1908- .... **CLC 29**
See also AITN 2; CA 5-8R; CANR 5, 85; INT CANR-5

Slavitt, David R(ytman) 1935- ..... **CLC 5, 14**
See also CA 21-24R; CAAS 3; CANR 41, 83; DLB 5, 6

Slesinger, Tess 1905-1945 .... **TCLC 10**
See also CA 107; DLB 102

Slessor, Kenneth 1901-1971 .... **CLC 14**
See also CA 102; 89-92

Slowacki, Juliusz 1809-1849 .... **NCLC 15**

Smart, Christopher 1722-1771 .. **LC 3; DAM POET; PC 13**
See also DLB 109

Smart, Elizabeth 1913-1986 .... **CLC 54**
See also CA 81-84; 118; DLB 88

Smiley, Jane (Graves) 1949- ...... **CLC 53, 76; DAM POP**
See also CA 104; CANR 30, 50, 74; DA3; DLB 227; INT CANR-30

Smith, A(rthur) J(ames) M(arshall)
1902-1980 .... **CLC 15; DAC**
See also CA 1-4R; 102; CANR 4; DLB 88

Smith, Adam 1723-1790 .... **LC 36**
See also DLB 104

Smith, Alexander 1829-1867 .... **NCLC 59**
See also DLB 32, 55

Smith, Anna Deavere 1950- .... **CLC 86**
See also CA 133

Smith, Betty (Wehner) 1896-1972 .... **CLC 19**
See also CA 5-8R; 33-36R; DLBY 82; SATA 6

Smith, Charlotte (Turner)
1749-1806 .... **NCLC 23**
See also DLB 39, 109

Smith, Clark Ashton 1893-1961 .... **CLC 43**
See also CA 143; CANR 81; MTCW 2

Smith, Dave CLC 22, 42
See also Smith, David (Jeddie)
See also CAAS 7; DLB 5

Smith, David (Jeddie) 1942-
See Smith, Dave
See also CA 49-52; CANR 1, 59; DAM POET

Smith, Florence Margaret 1902-1971
See Smith, Stevie
See also CA 17-18; 29-32R; CANR 35; CAP 2; DAM POET; MTCW 1, 2

Smith, Iain Crichton 1928-1998 .... **CLC 64**
See also CA 21-24R; 171; DLB 40, 139

Smith, John 1580(?)-1631 .... **LC 9**
See also DLB 24, 30

Smith, Johnston
See Crane, Stephen (Townley)

Smith, Joseph, Jr. 1805-1844 .... **NCLC 53**

Smith, Lee 1944- .... **CLC 25, 73**
See also CA 114; 119; CANR 46; DLB 143; DLBY 83; INT 119

Smith, Martin
See Smith, Martin Cruz

Smith, Martin Cruz 1942- .... **CLC 25; DAM MULT, POP**
See also BEST 89:4; CA 85-88; CANR 6, 23, 43, 65; INT CANR-23; MTCW 2; NNAL

Smith, Mary-Ann Tirone 1944- .... **CLC 39**
See also CA 118; 136

Smith, Patti 1946- .... **CLC 12**
See also CA 93-96; CANR 63

Smith, Pauline (Urmson)
1882-1959 .... **TCLC 25**
See also DLB 225

Smith, Rosamond
See Oates, Joyce Carol

Smith, Sheila Kaye
See Kaye-Smith, Sheila

Smith, Stevie CLC 3, 8, 25, 44; PC 12
See also Smith, Florence Margaret
See also DLB 20; MTCW 2

Smith, Wilbur (Addison) 1933- .... **CLC 33**
See also CA 13-16R; CANR 7, 46, 66; MTCW 1, 2

Smith, William Jay 1918- .... **CLC 6**
See also CA 5-8R; CANR 44; DLB 5; MAI-CYA; SAAS 22; SATA 2, 68

Smith, Woodrow Wilson
See Kuttner, Henry

Smolenskin, Peretz 1842-1885 .... **NCLC 30**

Smollett, Tobias (George) 1721-1771 ... **LC 2, 46**
See also CDBLB 1660-1789; DLB 39, 104

Snodgrass, W(illiam) D(e Witt)
1926- .... **CLC 2, 6, 10, 18, 68; DAM POET**
See also CA 1-4R; CANR 6, 36, 65, 85; DLB 5; MTCW 1, 2

Snow, C(harles) P(ercy) 1905-1980 ... **CLC 1, 4, 6, 9, 13, 19; DAM NOV**
See also CA 5-8R; 101; CANR 28; CDBLB 1945-1960; DLB 15, 77; DLBD 17; MTCW 1, 2

Snow, Frances Compton
See Adams, Henry (Brooks)

Snyder, Gary (Sherman) 1930- . **CLC 1, 2, 5, 9, 32, 120; DAM POET; PC 21**
See also CA 17-20R; CANR 30, 60; DA3; DLB 5, 16, 165, 212; MTCW 2

Snyder, Zilpha Keatley 1927- .... **CLC 17**
See also AAYA 15; CA 9-12R; CANR 38; CLR 31; JRDA; MAICYA; SAAS 2; SATA 1, 28, 75, 110; SATA-Essay 112

Soares, Bernardo
See Pessoa, Fernando (Antonio Nogueira)

Sobh, A.
See Shamlu, Ahmad

Sobol, Joshua CLC 60

Socrates 469B.C.-399B.C. .... **CMLC 27**

Soderberg, Hjalmar 1869-1941 ...... **TCLC 39**

Sodergran, Edith (Irene)
See Soedergran, Edith (Irene)

Soedergran, Edith (Irene)
1892-1923 .... **TCLC 31**

Softly, Edgar
See Lovecraft, H(oward) P(hillips)

Softly, Edward
See Lovecraft, H(oward) P(hillips)

Sokolov, Raymond 1941- .... **CLC 7**
See also CA 85-88

Solo, Jay
See Ellison, Harlan (Jay)

Sologub, Fyodor TCLC 9
See also Teternikov, Fyodor Kuzmich

Solomons, Ikey Esquir
See Thackeray, William Makepeace

Solomos, Dionysios 1798-1857 .... **NCLC 15**

Solwoska, Mara
See French, Marilyn

Stephen, Sir Leslie
See Stephen, SirLeslie
Stephen, Virginia
See Woolf, (Adeline) Virginia
Stephens, James 1882(?)-1950 .... **TCLC 4**
See also CA 104; DLB 19, 153, 162
Stephens, Reed
See Donaldson, Stephen R.
Steptoe, Lydia
See Barnes, Djuna
Sterchi, Beat 1949- .... **CLC 65**
Sterling, Brett
See Bradbury, Ray (Douglas); Hamilton,
Edmond
Sterling, Bruce 1954- .... **CLC 72**
See also CA 119; CANR 44
Sterling, George 1869-1926 .... **TCLC 20**
See also CA 117; 165; DLB 54
Stern, Gerald 1925- .... **CLC 40, 100**
See also CA 81-84; CANR 28; DLB 105
Stern, Richard (Gustave) 1928- ... **CLC 4, 39**
See also CA 1-4R; CANR 1, 25, 52; DLBY
87; INT CANR-25
Sternberg, Josef von 1894-1969 .... **CLC 20**
See also CA 81-84
Sterne, Laurence 1713-1768 .. **LC 2, 48; DA;**
DAB; DAC; DAM MST, NOV; WLC
See also CDBLB 1660-1789; DLB 39
Sternheim, (William Adolf) Carl
1878-1942 .... **TCLC 8**
See also CA 105; DLB 56, 118
Stevens, Mark 1951- .... **CLC 34**
See also CA 122
Stevens, Wallace 1879-1955 ...... **TCLC 3, 12,**
45; DA; DAB; DAC; DAM MST,
POET; PC 6; WLC
See also CA 104; 124; CDALB 1929-1941;
DA3; DLB 54; MTCW 1, 2
Stevenson, Anne (Katharine) 1933- .. **CLC 7,**
33
See also CA 17-20R; CAAS 9; CANR 9,
33; DLB 40; MTCW 1
Stevenson, Robert Louis (Balfour)
1850-1894 . **NCLC 5, 14, 63; DA; DAB;**
DAC; DAM MST, NOV; SSC 11; WLC
See also AAYA 24; CDBLB 1890-1914;
CLR 10, 11; DA3; DLB 18, 57, 141, 156,
174; DLBD 13; JRDA; MAICYA; SATA
100; YABC 2
Stewart, J(ohn) I(nnes) M(ackintosh)
1906-1994 .... **CLC 7, 14, 32**
See also CA 85-88; 147; CAAS 3; CANR
47; MTCW 1, 2
Stewart, Mary (Florence Elinor)
1916- .... **CLC 7, 35, 117; DAB**
See also AAYA 29; CA 1-4R; CANR 1, 59;
SATA 12
Stewart, Mary Rainbow
See Stewart, Mary (Florence Elinor)
Stifle, June
See Campbell, Maria
Stifter, Adalbert 1805-1868 .. **NCLC 41; SSC**
28
See also DLB 133
Still, James 1906- .... **CLC 49**
See also CA 65-68; CAAS 17; CANR 10,
26; DLB 9; SATA 29
Sting 1951-
See Sumner, Gordon Matthew
See also CA 167
Stirling, Arthur
See Sinclair, Upton (Beall)
Stitt, Milan 1941- .... **CLC 29**
See also CA 69-72
Stockton, Francis Richard 1834-1902
See Stockton, Frank R.
See also CA 108; 137; MAICYA; SATA 44

Stockton, Frank R. TCLC 47
See also Stockton, Francis Richard
See also DLB 42, 74; DLBD 13; SATA-
Brief 32
Stoddard, Charles
See Kuttner, Henry
Stoker, Abraham 1847-1912
See Stoker, Bram
See also CA 105; 150; DA; DAC; DAM
MST, NOV; DA3; SATA 29
Stoker, Bram 1847-1912 .... **TCLC 8; DAB;**
WLC
See also Stoker, Abraham
See also AAYA 23; CDBLB 1890-1914;
DLB 36, 70, 178
Stolz, Mary (Slattery) 1920- .... **CLC 12**
See also AAYA 8; AITN 1; CA 5-8R;
CANR 13, 41; JRDA; MAICYA; SAAS
3; SATA 10, 71
Stone, Irving 1903-1989 . **CLC 7; DAM POP**
See also AITN 1; CA 1-4R; 129; CAAS 3;
CANR 1, 23; DA3; INT CANR-23;
MTCW 1, 2; SATA 3; SATA-Obit 64
Stone, Oliver (William) 1946- .... **CLC 73**
See also AAYA 15; CA 110; CANR 55
Stone, Robert (Anthony) 1937- ... **CLC 5, 23,**
42
See also CA 85-88; CANR 23, 66; DLB
152; INT CANR-23; MTCW 1
Stone, Zachary
See Follett, Ken(neth Martin)
Stoppard, Tom 1937- .. **CLC 1, 3, 4, 5, 8, 15,**
29, 34, 63, 91; DA; DAB; DAC; DAM
DRAM, MST; DC 6; WLC
See also CA 81-84; CANR 39, 67; CDBLB
1960 to Present; DA3; DLB 13, 233;
DLBY 85; MTCW 1, 2
Storey, David (Malcolm) 1933- . **CLC 2, 4, 5,**
8; DAM DRAM
See also CA 81-84; CANR 36; DLB 13, 14,
207; MTCW 1
Storm, Hyemeyohsts 1935- ..... **CLC 3; DAM**
MULT
See also CA 81-84; CANR 45; NNAL
Storm, Theodor 1817-1888 .... **SSC 27**
Storm, (Hans) Theodor (Woldsen)
1817-1888 .... **NCLC 1; SSC 27**
See also DLB 129
Storni, Alfonsina 1892-1938 . **TCLC 5; DAM**
MULT; HLC 2
See also CA 104; 131; HW 1
Stoughton, William 1631-1701 .... **LC 38**
See also DLB 24
Stout, Rex (Todhunter) 1886-1975 ..... **CLC 3**
See also AITN 2; CA 61-64; CANR 71
Stow, (Julian) Randolph 1935- ... **CLC 23, 48**
See also CA 13-16R; CANR 33; MTCW 1
Stowe, Harriet (Elizabeth) Beecher
1811-1896 .... **NCLC 3, 50; DA; DAB;**
DAC; DAM MST, NOV; WLC
See also CDALB 1865-1917; DA3; DLB 1,
12, 42, 74, 189; JRDA; MAICYA; YABC
1
Strabo c. 64B.C.-c. 25 .... **CMLC 37**
See also DLB 176
Strachey, (Giles) Lytton
1880-1932 .... **TCLC 12**
See also CA 110; 178; DLB 149; DLBD
10; MTCW 2
Strand, Mark 1934- .... **CLC 6, 18, 41, 71;**
DAM POET
See also CA 21-24R; CANR 40, 65; DLB
5; SATA 41
Straub, Peter (Francis) 1943- . **CLC 28, 107;**
DAM POP
See also BEST 89:1; CA 85-88; CANR 28,
65; DLBY 84; MTCW 1, 2
Strauss, Botho 1944- .... **CLC 22**
See also CA 157; DLB 124

Streatfeild, (Mary) Noel
1895(?)-1986 .... **CLC 21**
See also CA 81-84; 120; CANR 31; CLR
17; DLB 160; MAICYA; SATA 20; SATA-
Obit 48
Stribling, T(homas) S(igismund)
1881-1965 .... **CLC 23**
See also CA 107; DLB 9
Strindberg, (Johan) August
1849-1912 .... **TCLC 1, 8, 21, 47; DA;**
DAB; DAC; DAM DRAM, MST; WLC
See also CA 104; 135; DA3; MTCW 2
Stringer, Arthur 1874-1950 .... **TCLC 37**
See also CA 161; DLB 92
Stringer, David
See Roberts, Keith (John Kingston)
Stroheim, Erich von 1885-1957 ..... **TCLC 71**
Strugatskii, Arkadii (Natanovich)
1925-1991 .... **CLC 27**
See also CA 106; 135
Strugatskii, Boris (Natanovich)
1933- .... **CLC 27**
See also CA 106
Strummer, Joe 1953(?)- .... **CLC 30**
Strunk, William, Jr. 1869-1946 ...... **TCLC 92**
See also CA 118; 164
Stryk, Lucien 1924- .... **PC 27**
See also CA 13-16R; CANR 10, 28, 55
Stuart, Don A.
See Campbell, John W(ood, Jr.)
Stuart, Ian
See MacLean, Alistair (Stuart)
Stuart, Jesse (Hilton) 1906-1984 ... **CLC 1, 8,**
11, 14, 34; SSC 31
See also CA 5-8R; 112; CANR 31; DLB 9,
48, 102; DLBY 84; SATA 2; SATA-Obit
36
Sturgeon, Theodore (Hamilton)
1918-1985 .... **CLC 22, 39**
See also Queen, Ellery
See also CA 81-84; 116; CANR 32; DLB 8;
DLBY 85; MTCW 1, 2
Sturges, Preston 1898-1959 .... **TCLC 48**
See also CA 114; 149; DLB 26
Styron, William 1925- .... **CLC 1, 3, 5, 11, 15,**
60; DAM NOV, POP; SSC 25
See also BEST 90:4; CA 5-8R; CANR 6,
33, 74; CDALB 1968-1988; DA3; DLB
2, 143; DLBY 80; INT CANR-6; MTCW
1, 2
Su, Chien 1884-1918
See Su Man-shu
See also CA 123
Suarez Lynch, B.
See Bioy Casares, Adolfo; Borges, Jorge
Luis
Suassuna, Ariano Vilar 1927-
See also CA 178; HLCS 1; HW 2
Suckling, John 1609-1641 .... **PC 30**
See also DAM POET; DLB 58, 126
Suckow, Ruth 1892-1960 .... **SSC 18**
See also CA 113; DLB 9, 102
Sudermann, Hermann 1857-1928 .. **TCLC 15**
See also CA 107; DLB 118
Sue, Eugene 1804-1857 .... **NCLC 1**
See also DLB 119
Sueskind, Patrick 1949- .... **CLC 44**
See also Suskind, Patrick
Sukenick, Ronald 1932- .... **CLC 3, 4, 6, 48**
See also CA 25-28R; CAAS 8; CANR 32,
89; DLB 173; DLBY 81
Suknaski, Andrew 1942- .... **CLC 19**
See also CA 101; DLB 53
Sullivan, Vernon
See Vian, Boris
Sully Prudhomme 1839-1907 .... **TCLC 31**
Su Man-shu TCLC 24
See also Su, Chien

Summerforest, Ivy B.
See Kirkup, James
Summers, Andrew James 1942- .... **CLC 26**
Summers, Andy
See Summers, Andrew James
Summers, Hollis (Spurgeon, Jr.)
1916- .... **CLC 10**
See also CA 5-8R; CANR 3; DLB 6
Summers, (Alphonsus Joseph-Mary Augustus) Montague
1880-1948 .... **TCLC 16**
See also CA 118; 163
Sumner, Gordon Matthew CLC 26
See also Sting
Surtees, Robert Smith 1803-1864 .. **NCLC 14**
See also DLB 21
Susann, Jacqueline 1921-1974 .... **CLC 3**
See also AITN 1; CA 65-68; 53-56; MTCW
1, 2
Su Shih 1036-1101 .... **CMLC 15**
Suskind, Patrick
See Sueskind, Patrick
See also CA 145
Sutcliff, Rosemary 1920-1992 .... **CLC 26;**
DAB; DAC; DAM MST, POP
See also AAYA 10; CA 5-8R; 139; CANR
37; CLR 1, 37; JRDA; MAICYA; SATA
6, 44, 78; SATA-Obit 73
Sutro, Alfred 1863-1933 .... **TCLC 6**
See also CA 105; 185; DLB 10
Sutton, Henry
See Slavitt, David R(ytman)
Svevo, Italo 1861-1928 ...... **TCLC 2, 35; SSC**
25
See also Schmitz, Aron Hector
Swados, Elizabeth (A.) 1951- .... **CLC 12**
See also CA 97-100; CANR 49; INT 97-
100
Swados, Harvey 1920-1972 .... **CLC 5**
See also CA 5-8R; 37-40R; CANR 6; DLB
2
Swan, Gladys 1934- .... **CLC 69**
See also CA 101; CANR 17, 39
Swanson, Logan
See Matheson, Richard Burton
Swarthout, Glendon (Fred)
1918-1992 .... **CLC 35**
See also CA 1-4R; 139; CANR 1, 47; SATA
26
Sweet, Sarah C.
See Jewett, (Theodora) Sarah Orne
Swenson, May 1919-1989 ...... **CLC 4, 14, 61,**
106; DA; DAB; DAC; DAM MST,
POET; PC 14
See also CA 5-8R; 130; CANR 36, 61; DLB
5; MTCW 1, 2; SATA 15
Swift, Augustus
See Lovecraft, H(oward) P(hillips)
Swift, Graham (Colin) 1949- ...... **CLC 41, 88**
See also CA 117; 122; CANR 46, 71; DLB
194; MTCW 2
Swift, Jonathan 1667-1745 ..... **LC 1, 42; DA;**
DAB; DAC; DAM MST, NOV, POET;
PC 9; WLC
See also CDBLB 1660-1789; CLR 53;
DA3; DLB 39, 95, 101; SATA 19
Swinburne, Algernon Charles
1837-1909 .... **TCLC 8, 36; DA; DAB;**
DAC; DAM MST, POET; PC 24; WLC
See also CA 105; 140; CDBLB 1832-1890;
DA3; DLB 35, 57
Swinfen, Ann CLC 34
Swinnerton, Frank Arthur
1884-1982 .... **CLC 31**
See also CA 108; DLB 34
Swithen, John
See King, Stephen (Edwin)
Sylvia
See Ashton-Warner, Sylvia (Constance)

Symmes, Robert Edward
See Duncan, Robert (Edward)
Symonds, John Addington
1840-1893 .... **NCLC 34**
See also DLB 57, 144
Symons, Arthur 1865-1945 .... **TCLC 11**
See also CA 107; DLB 19, 57, 149
Symons, Julian (Gustave)
1912-1994 .... **CLC 2, 14, 32**
See also CA 49-52; 147; CAAS 3; CANR
3, 33, 59; DLB 87, 155; DLBY 92;
MTCW 1
Synge, (Edmund) J(ohn) M(illington)
1871-1909 . **TCLC 6, 37; DAM DRAM;**
DC 2
See also CA 104; 141; CDBLB 1890-1914;
DLB 10, 19
Syruc, J.
See Milosz, Czeslaw
Szirtes, George 1948- .... **CLC 46**
See also CA 109; CANR 27, 61
Szymborska, Wislawa 1923- .... **CLC 99**
See also CA 154; CANR 91; DA3; DLB
232; DLBY 96; MTCW 2
T. O., Nik
See Annensky, Innokenty (Fyodorovich)
Tabori, George 1914- .... **CLC 19**
See also CA 49-52; CANR 4, 69
Tagore, Rabindranath 1861-1941 ... **TCLC 3,**
53; DAM DRAM, POET; PC 8
See also CA 104; 120; DA3; MTCW 1, 2
Taine, Hippolyte Adolphe
1828-1893 .... **NCLC 15**
Talese, Gay 1932- .... **CLC 37**
See also AITN 1; CA 1-4R; CANR 9, 58;
DLB 185; INT CANR-9; MTCW 1, 2
Tallent, Elizabeth (Ann) 1954- .... **CLC 45**
See also CA 117; CANR 72; DLB 130
Tally, Ted 1952- .... **CLC 42**
See also CA 120; 124; INT 124
Talvik, Heiti 1904-1947 .... **TCLC 87**
Tamayo y Baus, Manuel
1829-1898 .... **NCLC 1**
Tammsaare, A(nton) H(ansen)
1878-1940 .... **TCLC 27**
See also CA 164; DLB 220
Tam'si, Tchicaya U
See Tchicaya, Gerald Felix
Tan, Amy (Ruth) 1952- . **CLC 59, 120; DAM**
MULT, NOV, POP
See also AAYA 9; BEST 89:3; CA 136;
CANR 54; CDALBS; DA3; DLB 173;
MTCW 2; SATA 75
Tandem, Felix
See Spitteler, Carl (Friedrich Georg)
Tanizaki, Jun'ichiro 1886-1965 ... **CLC 8, 14,**
28; SSC 21
See also CA 93-96; 25-28R; DLB 180;
MTCW 2
Tanner, William
See Amis, Kingsley (William)
Tao Lao
See Storni, Alfonsina
Tarantino, Quentin (Jerome)
1963- .... **CLC 125**
See also CA 171
Tarassoff, Lev
See Troyat, Henri
Tarbell, Ida M(inerva) 1857-1944 . **TCLC 40**
See also CA 122; 181; DLB 47
Tarkington, (Newton) Booth
1869-1946 .... **TCLC 9**
See also CA 110; 143; DLB 9, 102; MTCW
2; SATA 17
Tarkovsky, Andrei (Arsenyevich)
1932-1986 .... **CLC 75**
See also CA 127

Tartt, Donna 1964(?)- .... **CLC 76**
See also CA 142
Tasso, Torquato 1544-1595 .... **LC 5**
Tate, (John Orley) Allen 1899-1979 .. **CLC 2,**
4, 6, 9, 11, 14, 24
See also CA 5-8R; 85-88; CANR 32; DLB
4, 45, 63; DLBD 17; MTCW 1, 2
Tate, Ellalice
See Hibbert, Eleanor Alice Burford
Tate, James (Vincent) 1943- ..... **CLC 2, 6, 25**
See also CA 21-24R; CANR 29, 57; DLB
5, 169
Tauler, Johannes c. 1300-1361 ...... **CMLC 37**
See also DLB 179
Tavel, Ronald 1940- .... **CLC 6**
See also CA 21-24R; CANR 33
Taylor, Bayard 1825-1878 .... **NCLC 89**
See also DLB 3, 189
Taylor, C(ecil) P(hilip) 1929-1981 .... **CLC 27**
See also CA 25-28R; 105; CANR 47
Taylor, Edward 1642(?)-1729 ...... **LC 11; DA;**
DAB; DAC; DAM MST, POET
See also DLB 24
Taylor, Eleanor Ross 1920- .... **CLC 5**
See also CA 81-84; CANR 70
Taylor, Elizabeth 1912-1975 ..... **CLC 2, 4, 29**
See also CA 13-16R; CANR 9, 70; DLB
139; MTCW 1; SATA 13
Taylor, Frederick Winslow
1856-1915 .... **TCLC 76**
Taylor, Henry (Splawn) 1942- .... **CLC 44**
See also CA 33-36R; CAAS 7; CANR 31;
DLB 5
Taylor, Kamala (Purnaiya) 1924-
See Markandaya, Kamala
See also CA 77-80
Taylor, Mildred D. CLC 21
See also AAYA 10; BW 1; CA 85-88;
CANR 25; CLR 9, 59; DLB 52; JRDA;
MAICYA; SAAS 5; SATA 15, 70
Taylor, Peter (Hillsman) 1917-1994 .. **CLC 1,**
4, 18, 37, 44, 50, 71; SSC 10
See also CA 13-16R; 147; CANR 9, 50;
DLBY 81, 94; INT CANR-9; MTCW 1, 2
Taylor, Robert Lewis 1912-1998 .... **CLC 14**
See also CA 1-4R; 170; CANR 3, 64; SATA
10
Tchekhov, Anton
See Chekhov, Anton (Pavlovich)
Tchicaya, Gerald Felix 1931-1988 .. **CLC 101**
See also CA 129; 125; CANR 81
Tchicaya U Tam'si
See Tchicaya, Gerald Felix
Teasdale, Sara 1884-1933 .... **TCLC 4; PC 31**
See also CA 104; 163; DLB 45; SATA 32
Tegner, Esaias 1782-1846 .... **NCLC 2**
Teilhard de Chardin, (Marie Joseph) Pierre
1881-1955 .... **TCLC 9**
See also CA 105
Temple, Ann
See Mortimer, Penelope (Ruth)
Tennant, Emma (Christina) 1937- .. **CLC 13,**
52
See also CA 65-68; CAAS 9; CANR 10,
38, 59, 88; DLB 14
Tenneshaw, S. M.
See Silverberg, Robert
Tennyson, Alfred 1809-1892 ... **NCLC 30, 65;**
DA; DAB; DAC; DAM MST, POET;
PC 6; WLC
See also CDBLB 1832-1890; DA3; DLB
32
Teran, Lisa St. Aubin de CLC 36
See also St. Aubin de Teran, Lisa
Terence c. 184B.C.-c. 159B.C. ...... **CMLC 14;**
DC 7
See also DLB 211

Teresa de Jesus, St. 1515-1582 .... **LC 18**

Terkel, Louis 1912-
See Terkel, Studs
See also CA 57-60; CANR 18, 45, 67; DA3;
MTCW 1, 2

Terkel, Studs **CLC 38**
See also Terkel, Louis
See also AAYA 32; AITN 1; MTCW 2

Terry, C. V.
See Slaughter, Frank G(ill)

Terry, Megan 1932- .... **CLC 19; DC 13**
See also CA 77-80; CABS 3; CANR 43;
DLB 7

Tertullian c. 155-c. 245 .... **CMLC 29**

Tertz, Abram
See Sinyavsky, Andrei (Donatevich)

Tesich, Steve 1943(?)-1996 .... **CLC 40, 69**
See also CA 105; 152; DLBY 83

Tesla, Nikola 1856-1943 .... **TCLC 88**

Teternikov, Fyodor Kuzmich 1863-1927
See Sologub, Fyodor
See also CA 104

Tevis, Walter 1928-1984 .... **CLC 42**
See also CA 113

Tey, Josephine **TCLC 14**
See also Mackintosh, Elizabeth
See also DLB 77

Thackeray, William Makepeace
1811-1863 ...... **NCLC 5, 14, 22, 43; DA;
DAB; DAC; DAM MST, NOV; WLC**
See also CDBLB 1832-1890; DA3; DLB
21, 55, 159, 163; SATA 23

Thakura, Ravindranatha
See Tagore, Rabindranath

Tharoor, Shashi 1956- .... **CLC 70**
See also CA 141; CANR 91

Thelwell, Michael Miles 1939- .... **CLC 22**
See also BW 2; CA 101

Theobald, Lewis, Jr.
See Lovecraft, H(oward) P(hillips)

Theodorescu, Ion N. 1880-1967
See Arghezi, Tudor
See also CA 116; DLB 220

Theriault, Yves 1915-1983 .... **CLC 79; DAC;
DAM MST**
See also CA 102; DLB 88

Theroux, Alexander (Louis) 1939- .... **CLC 2,
25**
See also CA 85-88; CANR 20, 63

Theroux, Paul (Edward) 1941- ..... **CLC 5, 8,
11, 15, 28, 46; DAM POP**
See also AAYA 28; BEST 89:4; CA 33-36R;
CANR 20, 45, 74; CDALBS; DA3; DLB
2; MTCW 1, 2; SATA 44, 109

Thesen, Sharon 1946- .... **CLC 56**
See also CA 163

Thevenin, Denis
See Duhamel, Georges

Thibault, Jacques Anatole Francois
1844-1924
See France, Anatole
See also CA 106; 127; DAM NOV; DA3;
MTCW 1, 2

Thiele, Colin (Milton) 1920- .... **CLC 17**
See also CA 29-32R; CANR 12, 28, 53;
CLR 27; MAICYA; SAAS 2; SATA 14,
72

Thomas, Audrey (Callahan) 1935- .... **CLC 7,
13, 37, 107; SSC 20**
See also CA 21-24R; CAAS 19;
CANR 36, 58; DLB 60; MTCW 1

Thomas, Augustus 1857-1934 .... **TCLC 97**

Thomas, D(onald) M(ichael) 1935- . **CLC 13,
22, 31, 132**
See also CA 61-64; CAAS 11; CANR 17,
45, 75; CDBLB 1960 to Present; DA3;
DLB 40, 207; INT CANR-17; MTCW 1,
2

Thomas, Dylan (Marlais)
1914-1953 ... **TCLC 1, 8, 45; DA; DAB;
DAC; DAM DRAM, MST, POET; PC
2; SSC 3; WLC**
See also CA 104; 120; CANR 65; CDBLB
1945-1960; DA3; DLB 13, 20, 139;
MTCW 1, 2; SATA 60

Thomas, (Philip) Edward
1878-1917 .... **TCLC 10; DAM POET**
See also CA 106; 153; DLB 98

Thomas, Joyce Carol 1938- .... **CLC 35**
See also AAYA 12; BW 2, 3; CA 113; 116;
CANR 48; CLR 19; DLB 33; INT 116;
JRDA; MAICYA; MTCW 1, 2; SAAS 7;
SATA 40, 78

Thomas, Lewis 1913-1993 .... **CLC 35**
See also CA 85-88; 143; CANR 38, 60;
MTCW 1, 2

Thomas, M. Carey 1857-1935 .... **TCLC 89**

Thomas, Paul
See Mann, (Paul) Thomas

Thomas, Piri 1928- .... **CLC 17; HLCS 2**
See also CA 73-76; HW 1

Thomas, R(onald) S(tuart) 1913- ...... **CLC 6,
13, 48; DAB; DAM POET**
See also CA 89-92; CAAS 4; CANR 30;
CDBLB 1960 to Present; DLB 27; MTCW
1

Thomas, Ross (Elmore) 1926-1995 .. **CLC 39**
See also CA 33-36R; 150; CANR 22, 63

Thompson, Francis Clegg
See Mencken, H(enry) L(ouis)

Thompson, Francis Joseph
1859-1907 .... **TCLC 4**
See also CA 104; CDBLB 1890-1914; DLB
19

Thompson, Hunter S(tockton)
1939- ... **CLC 9, 17, 40, 104; DAM POP**
See also BEST 89:1; CA 17-20R; CANR
23, 46, 74, 77; DA3; DLB 185; MTCW
1, 2

Thompson, James Myers
See Thompson, Jim (Myers)

Thompson, Jim (Myers)
1906-1977(?) .... **CLC 69**
See also CA 140; DLB 226

Thompson, Judith **CLC 39**

Thomson, James 1700-1748 ... **LC 16, 29, 40;
DAM POET**
See also DLB 95

Thomson, James 1834-1882 .... **NCLC 18;
DAM POET**
See also DLB 35

Thoreau, Henry David 1817-1862 .. **NCLC 7,
21, 61; DA; DAB; DAC; DAM MST;
PC 30; WLC**
See also CDALB 1640-1865; DA3; DLB 1,
223

Thornton, Hall
See Silverberg, Robert

Thucydides c. 455B.C.-399B.C. ..... **CMLC 17**
See also DLB 176

Thumboo, Edwin 1933- .... **PC 30**

Thurber, James (Grover)
1894-1961 .... **CLC 5, 11, 25, 125; DA;
DAB; DAC; DAM DRAM, MST, NOV;
SSC 1**
See also CA 73-76; CANR 17, 39; CDALB
1929-1941; DA3; DLB 4, 11, 22, 102;
MAICYA; MTCW 1, 2; SATA 13

Thurman, Wallace (Henry)
1902-1934 .... **TCLC 6; BLC 3; DAM
MULT**
See also BW 1, 3; CA 104; 124; CANR 81;
DLB 51

Tibullus, Albius c. 54B.C.-c.
19B.C. .... **CMLC 36**
See also DLB 211

Ticheburn, Cheviot
See Ainsworth, William Harrison

Tieck, (Johann) Ludwig
1773-1853 .... **NCLC 5, 46; SSC 31**
See also DLB 90

Tiger, Derry
See Ellison, Harlan (Jay)

Tilghman, Christopher 1948(?)- .... **CLC 65**
See also CA 159

Tillich, Paul (Johannes)
1886-1965 .... **CLC 131**
See also CA 5-8R; 25-28R; CANR 33;
MTCW 1, 2

Tillinghast, Richard (Williford)
1940- .... **CLC 29**
See also CA 29-32R; CAAS 23; CANR 26,
51

Timrod, Henry 1828-1867 .... **NCLC 25**
See also DLB 3

Tindall, Gillian (Elizabeth) 1938- ...... **CLC 7**
See also CA 21-24R; CANR 11, 65

Tiptree, James, Jr. **CLC 48, 50**
See also Sheldon, Alice Hastings Bradley
See also DLB 8

Titmarsh, Michael Angelo
See Thackeray, William Makepeace

Tocqueville, Alexis (Charles Henri Maurice
Clerel, Comte) de 1805-1859 . **NCLC 7,
63**

Tolkien, J(ohn) R(onald) R(euel)
1892-1973 .. **CLC 1, 2, 3, 8, 12, 38; DA;
DAB; DAC; DAM MST, NOV, POP;
WLC**
See also AAYA 10; AITN 1; CA 17-18; 45-
48; CANR 36; CAP 2; CDBLB 1914-
1945; CLR 56; DA3; DLB 15, 160;
JRDA; MAICYA; MTCW 1, 2; SATA 2,
32, 100; SATA-Obit 24

Toller, Ernst 1893-1939 .... **TCLC 10**
See also CA 107; 186; DLB 124

Tolson, M. B.
See Tolson, Melvin B(eaunorus)

Tolson, Melvin B(eaunorus)
1898(?)-1966 .... **CLC 36, 105; BLC 3;
DAM MULT, POET**
See also BW 1, 3; CA 124; 89-92; CANR
80; DLB 48, 76

Tolstoi, Aleksei Nikolaevich
See Tolstoy, Alexey Nikolaevich

Tolstoy, Alexey Nikolaevich
1882-1945 .... **TCLC 18**
See also CA 107; 158

Tolstoy, Count Leo
See Tolstoy, Leo (Nikolaevich)

Tolstoy, Leo (Nikolaevich)
1828-1910 .. **TCLC 4, 11, 17, 28, 44, 79;
DA; DAB; DAC; DAM MST, NOV;
SSC 9, 30; WLC**
See also CA 104; 123; DA3; SATA 26

Tomasi di Lampedusa, Giuseppe 1896-1957
See Lampedusa, Giuseppe (Tomasi) di
See also CA 111

Tomlin, Lily **CLC 17**
See also Tomlin, Mary Jean

Tomlin, Mary Jean 1939(?)-
See Tomlin, Lily
See also CA 117

Tomlinson, (Alfred) Charles 1927- .... **CLC 2,
4, 6, 13, 45; DAM POET; PC 17**
See also CA 5-8R; CANR 33; DLB 40

Tomlinson, H(enry) M(ajor)
1873-1958 .... **TCLC 71**
See also CA 118; 161; DLB 36, 100, 195

Tonson, Jacob
See Bennett, (Enoch) Arnold

Toole, John Kennedy 1937-1969 ..... **CLC 19,
64**
See also CA 104; DLBY 81; MTCW 2

Unsworth, Barry (Forster) 1930- .... **CLC 76, 127**
See also CA 25-28R; CANR 30, 54; DLB 194

Updike, John (Hoyer) 1932- . **CLC 1, 2, 3, 5, 7, 9, 13, 15, 23, 34, 43, 70; DA; DAB; DAC; DAM MST, NOV, POET, POP; SSC 13, 27; WLC**
See also CA 1-4R; CABS 1; CANR 4, 33, 51; CDALB 1968-1988; DA3; DLB 2, 5, 143, 227; DLBD 3; DLBY 80, 82, 97; MTCW 1, 2

Upshaw, Margaret Mitchell
See Mitchell, Margaret (Munnerlyn)

Upton, Mark
See Sanders, Lawrence

Upward, Allen 1863-1926 .... **TCLC 85**
See also CA 117; 187; DLB 36

Urdang, Constance (Henriette) 1922- .... **CLC 47**
See also CA 21-24R; CANR 9, 24

Uriel, Henry
See Faust, Frederick (Schiller)

Uris, Leon (Marcus) 1924- .... **CLC 7, 32; DAM NOV, POP**
See also AITN 1, 2; BEST 89:2; CA 1-4R; CANR 1, 40, 65; DA3; MTCW 1, 2; SATA 49

Urista, Alberto H. 1947-
See Alurista
See also CA 45-48, 182; CANR 2, 32; HLCS 1; HW 1

Urmuz
See Codrescu, Andrei

Urquhart, Guy
See McAlmon, Robert (Menzies)

Urquhart, Jane 1949- .... **CLC 90; DAC**
See also CA 113; CANR 32, 68

Usigli, Rodolfo 1905-1979
See also CA 131; HLCS 1; HW 1

Ustinov, Peter (Alexander) 1921- .... **CLC 1**
See also AITN 1; CA 13-16R; CANR 25, 51; DLB 13; MTCW 2

U Tam'si, Gerald Felix Tchicaya
See Tchicaya, Gerald Felix

U Tam'si, Tchicaya
See Tchicaya, Gerald Felix

Vachss, Andrew (Henry) 1942- .... **CLC 106**
See also CA 118; CANR 44

Vachss, Andrew H.
See Vachss, Andrew (Henry)

Vaculik, Ludvik 1926- .... **CLC 7**
See also CA 53-56; CANR 72; DLB 232

Vaihinger, Hans 1852-1933 .... **TCLC 71**
See also CA 116; 166

Valdez, Luis (Miguel) 1940- .. **CLC 84; DAM MULT; DC 10; HLC 2**
See also CA 101; CANR 32, 81; DLB 122; HW 1

Valenzuela, Luisa 1938- .... **CLC 31, 104; DAM MULT; HLCS 2; SSC 14**
See also CA 101; CANR 32, 65; DLB 113; HW 1, 2

Valera y Alcala-Galiano, Juan 1824-1905 .... **TCLC 10**
See also CA 106

Valery, (Ambroise) Paul (Toussaint Jules) 1871-1945 ... **TCLC 4, 15; DAM POET; PC 9**
See also CA 104; 122; DA3; MTCW 1, 2

Valle-Inclan, Ramon (Maria) del 1866-1936 .... **TCLC 5; DAM MULT; HLC 2**
See also CA 106; 153; CANR 80; DLB 134; HW 2

Vallejo, Antonio Buero
See Buero Vallejo, Antonio

Vallejo, Cesar (Abraham) 1892-1938 .. **TCLC 3, 56; DAM MULT; HLC 2**
See also CA 105; 153; HW 1

Valles, Jules 1832-1885 .... **NCLC 71**
See also DLB 123

Vallette, Marguerite Eymery 1860-1953 .... **TCLC 67**
See also CA 182; DLB 123, 192

Valle Y Pena, Ramon del
See Valle-Inclan, Ramon (Maria) del

Van Ash, Cay 1918- .... **CLC 34**

Vanbrugh, Sir John 1664-1726 .... **LC 21; DAM DRAM**
See also DLB 80

Van Campen, Karl
See Campbell, John W(ood, Jr.)

Vance, Gerald
See Silverberg, Robert

Vance, Jack CLC 35
See also Vance, John Holbrook
See also DLB 8

Vance, John Holbrook 1916-
See Queen, Ellery; Vance, Jack
See also CA 29-32R; CANR 17, 65; MTCW 1

Van Den Bogarde, Derek Jules Gaspard Ulric Niven 1921-1999 .... **CLC 14**
See also CA 77-80; 179; DLB 19

Vandenburgh, Jane CLC 59
See also CA 168

Vanderhaeghe, Guy 1951- .... **CLC 41**
See also CA 113; CANR 72

van der Post, Laurens (Jan) 1906-1996 .... **CLC 5**
See also CA 5-8R; 155; CANR 35; DLB 204

van de Wetering, Janwillem 1931- ... **CLC 47**
See also CA 49-52; CANR 4, 62, 90

Van Dine, S. S. TCLC 23
See also Wright, Willard Huntington

Van Doren, Carl (Clinton) 1885-1950 .... **TCLC 18**
See also CA 111; 168

Van Doren, Mark 1894-1972 .... **CLC 6, 10**
See also CA 1-4R; 37-40R; CANR 3; DLB 45; MTCW 1, 2

Van Druten, John (William) 1901-1957 .... **TCLC 2**
See also CA 104; 161; DLB 10

Van Duyn, Mona (Jane) 1921- ...... **CLC 3, 7, 63, 116; DAM POET**
See also CA 9-12R; CANR 7, 38, 60; DLB 5

Van Dyne, Edith
See Baum, L(yman) Frank

van Itallie, Jean-Claude 1936- .... **CLC 3**
See also CA 45-48; CAAS 2; CANR 1, 48; DLB 7

van Ostaijen, Paul 1896-1928 .... **TCLC 33**
See also CA 163

Van Peebles, Melvin 1932- .... **CLC 2, 20; DAM MULT**
See also BW 2, 3; CA 85-88; CANR 27, 67, 82

Vansittart, Peter 1920- .... **CLC 42**
See also CA 1-4R; CANR 3, 49, 90

Van Vechten, Carl 1880-1964 .... **CLC 33**
See also CA 183; 89-92; DLB 4, 9, 51

Van Vogt, A(lfred) E(lton) 1912-2000 .... **CLC 1**
See also CA 21-24R; CANR 28; DLB 8; SATA 14

Varda, Agnes 1928- .... **CLC 16**
See also CA 116; 122

Vargas Llosa, (Jorge) Mario (Pedro) 1936- .... **CLC 3, 6, 9, 10, 15, 31, 42, 85; DA; DAB; DAC; DAM MST, MULT, NOV; HLC 2**
See also CA 73-76; CANR 18, 32, 42, 67; DA3; DLB 145; HW 1, 2; MTCW 1, 2

Vasiliu, Gheorghe 1881-1957
See Bacovia, George
See also CA 123; DLB 220

Vassa, Gustavus
See Equiano, Olaudah

Vassilikos, Vassilis 1933- .... **CLC 4, 8**
See also CA 81-84; CANR 75

Vaughan, Henry 1621-1695 .... **LC 27**
See also DLB 131

Vaughn, Stephanie CLC 62

Vazov, Ivan (Minchov) 1850-1921 . **TCLC 25**
See also CA 121; 167; DLB 147

Veblen, Thorstein B(unde) 1857-1929 .... **TCLC 31**
See also CA 115; 165

Vega, Lope de 1562-1635 .... **LC 23; HLCS 2**

Venison, Alfred
See Pound, Ezra (Weston Loomis)

Verdi, Marie de
See Mencken, H(enry) L(ouis)

Verdu, Matilde
See Cela, Camilo Jose

Verga, Giovanni (Carmelo) 1840-1922 .... **TCLC 3; SSC 21**
See also CA 104; 123

Vergil 70B.C.-19B.C. .... **CMLC 9, 40; DA; DAB; DAC; DAM MST, POET; PC 12; WLCS**
See also Virgil
See also DA3; DLB 211

Verhaeren, Emile (Adolphe Gustave) 1855-1916 .... **TCLC 12**
See also CA 109

Verlaine, Paul (Marie) 1844-1896 .. **NCLC 2, 51; DAM POET; PC 2, 32**

Verne, Jules (Gabriel) 1828-1905 ... **TCLC 6, 52**
See also AAYA 16; CA 110; 131; DA3; DLB 123; JRDA; MAICYA; SATA 21

Very, Jones 1813-1880 .... **NCLC 9**
See also DLB 1

Vesaas, Tarjei 1897-1970 .... **CLC 48**
See also CA 29-32R

Vialis, Gaston
See Simenon, Georges (Jacques Christian)

Vian, Boris 1920-1959 .... **TCLC 9**
See also CA 106; 164; DLB 72; MTCW 2

Viaud, (Louis Marie) Julien 1850-1923
See Loti, Pierre
See also CA 107

Vicar, Henry
See Felsen, Henry Gregor

Vicker, Angus
See Felsen, Henry Gregor

Vidal, Gore 1925- ...... **CLC 2, 4, 6, 8, 10, 22, 33, 72; DAM NOV, POP**
See also AITN 1; BEST 90:2; CA 5-8R; CANR 13, 45, 65; CDALBS; DA3; DLB 6, 152; INT CANR-13; MTCW 1, 2

Viereck, Peter (Robert Edwin) 1916- .... **CLC 4; PC 27**
See also CA 1-4R; CANR 1, 47; DLB 5

Vigny, Alfred (Victor) de 1797-1863 .. **NCLC 7; DAM POET; PC 26**
See also DLB 119, 192

Vilakazi, Benedict Wallet 1906-1947 .... **TCLC 37**
See also CA 168

Villa, Jose Garcia 1904-1997 .... **PC 22**
See also CA 25-28R; CANR 12

Wambaugh, Joseph (Aloysius, Jr.) 1937- .... **CLC 3, 18; DAM NOV, POP**
See also AITN 1; BEST 89:3; CA 33-36R; CANR 42, 65; DA3; DLB 6; DLBY 83; MTCW 1, 2

Wang Wei 699(?)-761(?) .... **PC 18**

Ward, Arthur Henry Sarsfield 1883-1959
See Rohmer, Sax
See also CA 108; 173

Ward, Douglas Turner 1930- .... **CLC 19**
See also BW 1; CA 81-84; CANR 27; DLB 7, 38

Ward, E. D.
See Lucas, E(dward) V(errall)

Ward, Mary Augusta
See Ward, Mary Augusta

Ward, Mary Augusta 1851-1920 ... **TCLC 55**
See also DLB 18

Ward, Peter
See Faust, Frederick (Schiller)

Warhol, Andy 1928(?)-1987 .... **CLC 20**
See also AAYA 12; BEST 89:4; CA 89-92; 121; CANR 34

Warner, Francis (Robert le Plastrier) 1937- .... **CLC 14**
See also CA 53-56; CANR 11

Warner, Marina 1946- .... **CLC 59**
See also CA 65-68; CANR 21, 55; DLB 194

Warner, Rex (Ernest) 1905-1986 ...... **CLC 45**
See also CA 89-92; 119; DLB 15

Warner, Susan (Bogert) 1819-1885 .... **NCLC 31**
See also DLB 3, 42

Warner, Sylvia (Constance) Ashton
See Ashton-Warner, Sylvia (Constance)

Warner, Sylvia Townsend 1893-1978 .... **CLC 7, 19; SSC 23**
See also CA 61-64; 77-80; CANR 16, 60; DLB 34, 139; MTCW 1, 2

Warren, Mercy Otis 1728-1814 ..... **NCLC 13**
See also DLB 31, 200

Warren, Robert Penn 1905-1989 .. **CLC 1, 4, 6, 8, 10, 13, 18, 39, 53, 59; DA; DAB; DAC; DAM MST, NOV, POET; SSC 4; WLC**
See also AITN 1; CA 13-16R; 129; CANR 10, 47; CDALB 1968-1988; DA3; DLB 2, 48, 152; DLBY 80, 89; INT CANR-10; MTCW 1, 2; SATA 46; SATA-Obit 63

Warshofsky, Isaac
See Singer, Isaac Bashevis

Warton, Thomas 1728-1790 ..... **LC 15; DAM POET**
See also DLB 104, 109

Waruk, Kona
See Harris, (Theodore) Wilson

Warung, Price 1855-1911 .... **TCLC 45**

Warwick, Jarvis
See Garner, Hugh

Washington, Alex
See Harris, Mark

Washington, Booker T(aliaferro) 1856-1915 ...... **TCLC 10; BLC 3; DAM MULT**
See also BW 1; CA 114; 125; DA3; SATA 28

Washington, George 1732-1799 .... **LC 25**
See also DLB 31

Wassermann, (Karl) Jakob 1873-1934 .... **TCLC 6**
See also CA 104; 163; DLB 66

Wasserstein, Wendy 1950- .. **CLC 32, 59, 90; DAM DRAM; DC 4**
See also CA 121; 129; CABS 3; CANR 53, 75; DA3; DLB 228; INT 129; MTCW 2; SATA 94

Waterhouse, Keith (Spencer) 1929- . **CLC 47**
See also CA 5-8R; CANR 38, 67; DLB 13, 15; MTCW 1, 2

Waters, Frank (Joseph) 1902-1995 .. **CLC 88**
See also CA 5-8R; 149; CAAS 13; CANR 3, 18, 63; DLB 212; DLBY 86

Waters, Roger 1944- .... **CLC 35**

Watkins, Frances Ellen
See Harper, Frances Ellen Watkins

Watkins, Gerrold
See Malzberg, Barry N(athaniel)

Watkins, Gloria Jean 1952(?)-
See hooks, bell
See also BW 2; CA 143; CANR 87; MTCW 2; SATA 115

Watkins, Paul 1964- .... **CLC 55**
See also CA 132; CANR 62

Watkins, Vernon Phillips 1906-1967 .... **CLC 43**
See also CA 9-10; 25-28R; CAP 1; DLB 20

Watson, Irving S.
See Mencken, H(enry) L(ouis)

Watson, John H.
See Farmer, Philip Jose

Watson, Richard F.
See Silverberg, Robert

Waugh, Auberon (Alexander) 1939- .. **CLC 7**
See also CA 45-48; CANR 6, 22, 92; DLB 14, 194

Waugh, Evelyn (Arthur St. John) 1903-1966 .. **CLC 1, 3, 8, 13, 19, 27, 44, 107; DA; DAB; DAC; DAM MST, NOV, POP; SSC 41; WLC**
See also CA 85-88; 25-28R; CANR 22; CD-BLB 1914-1945; DA3; DLB 15, 162, 195; MTCW 1, 2

Waugh, Harriet 1944- .... **CLC 6**
See also CA 85-88; CANR 22

Ways, C. R.
See Blount, Roy (Alton), Jr.

Waystaff, Simon
See Swift, Jonathan

Webb, Beatrice (Martha Potter) 1858-1943 .... **TCLC 22**
See also CA 117; 162; DLB 190

Webb, Charles (Richard) 1939- .... **CLC 7**
See also CA 25-28R

Webb, James H(enry), Jr. 1946- ...... **CLC 22**
See also CA 81-84

Webb, Mary Gladys (Meredith) 1881-1927 .... **TCLC 24**
See also CA 182; 123; DLB 34

Webb, Mrs. Sidney
See Webb, Beatrice (Martha Potter)

Webb, Phyllis 1927- .... **CLC 18**
See also CA 104; CANR 23; DLB 53

Webb, Sidney (James) 1859-1947 .. **TCLC 22**
See also CA 117; 163; DLB 190

Webber, Andrew Lloyd CLC 21
See also Lloyd Webber, Andrew

Weber, Lenora Mattingly 1895-1971 .... **CLC 12**
See also CA 19-20; 29-32R; CAP 1; SATA 2; SATA-Obit 26

Weber, Max 1864-1920 .... **TCLC 69**
See also CA 109

Webster, John 1579(?)-1634(?) ... **LC 33; DA; DAB; DAC; DAM DRAM, MST; DC 2; WLC**
See also CDBLB Before 1660; DLB 58

Webster, Noah 1758-1843 .... **NCLC 30**
See also DLB 1, 37, 42, 43, 73

Wedekind, (Benjamin) Frank(lin) 1864-1918 .... **TCLC 7; DAM DRAM**
See also CA 104; 153; DLB 118

Weidman, Jerome 1913-1998 .... **CLC 7**
See also AITN 2; CA 1-4R; 171; CANR 1; DLB 28

Weil, Simone (Adolphine) 1909-1943 .... **TCLC 23**
See also CA 117; 159; MTCW 2

Weininger, Otto 1880-1903 .... **TCLC 84**

Weinstein, Nathan
See West, Nathanael

Weinstein, Nathan von Wallenstein
See West, Nathanael

Weir, Peter (Lindsay) 1944- .... **CLC 20**
See also CA 113; 123

Weiss, Peter (Ulrich) 1916-1982 .. **CLC 3, 15, 51; DAM DRAM**
See also CA 45-48; 106; CANR 3; DLB 69, 124

Weiss, Theodore (Russell) 1916- ... **CLC 3, 8, 14**
See also CA 9-12R; CAAS 2; CANR 46; DLB 5

Welch, (Maurice) Denton 1915-1948 .... **TCLC 22**
See also CA 121; 148

Welch, James 1940- ..... **CLC 6, 14, 52; DAM MULT, POP**
See also CA 85-88; CANR 42, 66; DLB 175; NNAL

Weldon, Fay 1931- . **CLC 6, 9, 11, 19, 36, 59, 122; DAM POP**
See also CA 21-24R; CANR 16, 46, 63; CDBLB 1960 to Present; DLB 14, 194; INT CANR-16; MTCW 1, 2

Wellek, Rene 1903-1995 .... **CLC 28**
See also CA 5-8R; 150; CAAS 7; CANR 8; DLB 63; INT CANR-8

Weller, Michael 1942- .... **CLC 10, 53**
See also CA 85-88

Weller, Paul 1958- .... **CLC 26**

Wellershoff, Dieter 1925- .... **CLC 46**
See also CA 89-92; CANR 16, 37

Welles, (George) Orson 1915-1985 .. **CLC 20, 80**
See also CA 93-96; 117

Wellman, John McDowell 1945-
See Wellman, Mac
See also CA 166

Wellman, Mac 1945- .... **CLC 65**
See also Wellman, John McDowell; Wellman, John McDowell

Wellman, Manly Wade 1903-1986 ... **CLC 49**
See also CA 1-4R; 118; CANR 6, 16, 44; SATA 6; SATA-Obit 47

Wells, Carolyn 1869(?)-1942 .... **TCLC 35**
See also CA 113; 185; DLB 11

Wells, H(erbert) G(eorge) 1866-1946 . **TCLC 6, 12, 19; DA; DAB; DAC; DAM MST, NOV; SSC 6; WLC**
See also AAYA 18; CA 110; 121; CDBLB 1914-1945; CLR 64; DA3; DLB 34, 70, 156, 178; MTCW 1, 2; SATA 20

Wells, Rosemary 1943- .... **CLC 12**
See also AAYA 13; CA 85-88; CANR 48; CLR 16; MAICYA; SAAS 1; SATA 18, 69, 114

Welty, Eudora 1909- ...... **CLC 1, 2, 5, 14, 22, 33, 105; DA; DAB; DAC; DAM MST, NOV; SSC 1, 27; WLC**
See also CA 9-12R; CABS 1; CANR 32, 65; CDALB 1941-1968; DA3; DLB 2, 102, 143; DLBD 12; DLBY 87; MTCW 1, 2

Wen I-to 1899-1946 .... **TCLC 28**

Wentworth, Robert
See Hamilton, Edmond

Werfel, Franz (Viktor) 1890-1945 ... **TCLC 8**
See also CA 104; 161; DLB 81, 124

Wilhelm, Katie Gertrude 1928-
See Wilhelm, Kate
See also CA 37-40R; CANR 17, 36, 60;
MTCW 1

Wilkins, Mary
See Freeman, Mary E(leanor) Wilkins

Willard, Nancy 1936- .... **CLC 7, 37**
See also CA 89-92; CANR 10, 39, 68; CLR
5; DLB 5, 52; MAICYA; MTCW 1; SATA
37, 71; SATA-Brief 30

William of Ockham 1285-1347 ..... **CMLC 32**

Williams, Ben Ames 1889-1953 ..... **TCLC 89**
See also CA 183; DLB 102

Williams, C(harles) K(enneth)
1936- .... **CLC 33, 56; DAM POET**
See also CA 37-40R; CAAS 26; CANR 57;
DLB 5

Williams, Charles
See Collier, James L(incoln)

Williams, Charles (Walter Stansby)
1886-1945 .... **TCLC 1, 11**
See also CA 104; 163; DLB 100, 153

Williams, (George) Emlyn
1905-1987 .... **CLC 15; DAM DRAM**
See also CA 104; 123; CANR 36; DLB 10,
77; MTCW 1

Williams, Hank 1923-1953 .... **TCLC 81**

Williams, Hugo 1942- .... **CLC 42**
See also CA 17-20R; CANR 45; DLB 40

Williams, J. Walker
See Wodehouse, P(elham) G(renville)

Williams, John A(lfred) 1925- ..... **CLC 5, 13;**
BLC 3; DAM MULT
See also BW 2, 3; CA 53-56; CAAS 3;
CANR 6, 26, 51; DLB 2, 33; INT
CANR-6

Williams, Jonathan (Chamberlain)
1929- .... **CLC 13**
See also CA 9-12R; CAAS 12; CANR 8;
DLB 5

Williams, Joy 1944- .... **CLC 31**
See also CA 41-44R; CANR 22, 48

Williams, Norman 1952- .... **CLC 39**
See also CA 118

Williams, Sherley Anne 1944-1999 . **CLC 89;**
BLC 3; DAM MULT, POET
See also BW 2, 3; CA 73-76; 185; CANR
25, 82; DLB 41; INT CANR-25; SATA
78; SATA-Obit 116

Williams, Shirley
See Williams, Sherley Anne

Williams, Tennessee 1911-1983 . **CLC 1, 2, 5,**
7, 8, 11, 15, 19, 30, 39, 45, 71, 111; DA;
DAB; DAC; DAM DRAM, MST; DC
4; WLC
See also AAYA 31; AITN 1, 2; CA 5-8R;
108; CABS 3; CANR 31; CDALB 1941-
1968; DA3; DLB 7; DLBD 4; DLBY 83;
MTCW 1, 2

Williams, Thomas (Alonzo)
1926-1990 .... **CLC 14**
See also CA 1-4R; 132; CANR 2

Williams, William C.
See Williams, William Carlos

Williams, William Carlos
1883-1963 .... **CLC 1, 2, 5, 9, 13, 22, 42,**
67; DA; DAB; DAC; DAM MST,
POET; PC 7; SSC 31
See also CA 89-92; CANR 34; CDALB
1917-1929; DA3; DLB 4, 16, 54, 86;
MTCW 1, 2

Williamson, David (Keith) 1942- ..... **CLC 56**
See also CA 103; CANR 41

Williamson, Ellen Douglas 1905-1984
See Douglas, Ellen
See also CA 17-20R; 114; CANR 39

Williamson, Jack **CLC 29**
See also Williamson, John Stewart
See also CAAS 8; DLB 8

Williamson, John Stewart 1908-
See Williamson, Jack
See also CA 17-20R; CANR 23, 70

Willie, Frederick
See Lovecraft, H(oward) P(hillips)

Willingham, Calder (Baynard, Jr.)
1922-1995 .... **CLC 5, 51**
See also CA 5-8R; 147; CANR 3; DLB 2,
44; MTCW 1

Willis, Charles
See Clarke, Arthur C(harles)

Willy
See Colette, (Sidonie-Gabrielle)

Willy, Colette
See Colette, (Sidonie-Gabrielle)

Wilson, A(ndrew) N(orman) 1950- .. **CLC 33**
See also CA 112; 122; DLB 14, 155, 194;
MTCW 2

Wilson, Angus (Frank Johnstone)
1913-1991 . **CLC 2, 3, 5, 25, 34; SSC 21**
See also CA 5-8R; 134; CANR 21; DLB
15, 139, 155; MTCW 1, 2

Wilson, August 1945- ... **CLC 39, 50, 63, 118;**
BLC 3; DA; DAB; DAC; DAM
DRAM, MST, MULT; DC 2; WLCS
See also AAYA 16; BW 2, 3; CA 115; 122;
CANR 42, 54, 76; DA3; DLB 228;
MTCW 1, 2

Wilson, Brian 1942- .... **CLC 12**

Wilson, Colin 1931- .... **CLC 3, 14**
See also CA 1-4R; CAAS 5; CANR 1, 22,
33, 77; DLB 14, 194; MTCW 1

Wilson, Dirk
See Pohl, Frederik

Wilson, Edmund 1895-1972 .. **CLC 1, 2, 3, 8,**
24
See also CA 1-4R; 37-40R; CANR 1, 46;
DLB 63; MTCW 1, 2

Wilson, Ethel Davis (Bryant)
1888(?)-1980 .... **CLC 13; DAC; DAM**
POET
See also CA 102; DLB 68; MTCW 1

Wilson, John 1785-1854 .... **NCLC 5**

Wilson, John (Anthony) Burgess 1917-1993
See Burgess, Anthony
See also CA 1-4R; 143; CANR 2, 46; DAC;
DAM NOV; DA3; MTCW 1, 2

Wilson, Lanford 1937- .... **CLC 7, 14, 36;**
DAM DRAM
See also CA 17-20R; CABS 3; CANR 45;
DLB 7

Wilson, Robert M. 1944- .... **CLC 7, 9**
See also CA 49-52; CANR 2, 41; MTCW 1

Wilson, Robert McLiam 1964- .... **CLC 59**
See also CA 132

Wilson, Sloan 1920- .... **CLC 32**
See also CA 1-4R; CANR 1, 44

Wilson, Snoo 1948- .... **CLC 33**
See also CA 69-72

Wilson, William S(mith) 1932- .... **CLC 49**
See also CA 81-84

Wilson, (Thomas) Woodrow
1856-1924 .... **TCLC 79**
See also CA 166; DLB 47

Winchilsea, Anne (Kingsmill) Finch Counte
1661-1720
See Finch, Anne

Windham, Basil
See Wodehouse, P(elham) G(renville)

Wingrove, David (John) 1954- .... **CLC 68**
See also CA 133

Winnemucca, Sarah 1844-1891 ..... **NCLC 79**

Winstanley, Gerrard 1609-1676 .... **LC 52**

Wintergreen, Jane
See Duncan, Sara Jeannette

Winters, Janet Lewis **CLC 41**
See also Lewis, Janet
See also DLBY 87

Winters, (Arthur) Yvor 1900-1968 .... **CLC 4,**
8, 32
See also CA 11-12; 25-28R; CAP 1; DLB
48; MTCW 1

Winterson, Jeanette 1959- .... **CLC 64; DAM**
POP
See also CA 136; CANR 58; DA3; DLB
207; MTCW 2

Winthrop, John 1588-1649 .... **LC 31**
See also DLB 24, 30

Wirth, Louis 1897-1952 .... **TCLC 92**

Wiseman, Frederick 1930- .... **CLC 20**
See also CA 159

Wister, Owen 1860-1938 .... **TCLC 21**
See also CA 108; 162; DLB 9, 78, 186;
SATA 62

Witkacy
See Witkiewicz, Stanislaw Ignacy

Witkiewicz, Stanislaw Ignacy
1885-1939 .... **TCLC 8**
See also CA 105; 162

Wittgenstein, Ludwig (Josef Johann)
1889-1951 .... **TCLC 59**
See also CA 113; 164; MTCW 2

Wittig, Monique 1935(?)- .... **CLC 22**
See also CA 116; 135; DLB 83

Wittlin, Jozef 1896-1976 .... **CLC 25**
See also CA 49-52; 65-68; CANR 3

Wodehouse, P(elham) G(renville)
1881-1975 .... **CLC 1, 2, 5, 10, 22; DAB;**
DAC; DAM NOV; SSC 2
See also AITN 2; CA 45-48; 57-60; CANR
3, 33; CDBLB 1914-1945; DA3; DLB 34,
162; MTCW 1, 2; SATA 22

Woiwode, L.
See Woiwode, Larry (Alfred)

Woiwode, Larry (Alfred) 1941- ... **CLC 6, 10**
See also CA 73-76; CANR 16; DLB 6; INT
CANR-16

Wojciechowska, Maia (Teresa)
1927- .... **CLC 26**
See also AAYA 8; CA 9-12R; 183; CAAE
183; CANR 4, 41; CLR 1; JRDA; MAI-
CYA; SAAS 1; SATA 1, 28, 83; SATA-
Essay 104

Wojtyla, Karol
See John Paul II, Pope

Wolf, Christa 1929- .... **CLC 14, 29, 58**
See also CA 85-88; CANR 45; DLB 75;
MTCW 1

Wolfe, Gene (Rodman) 1931- .... **CLC 25;**
DAM POP
See also CA 57-60; CAAS 9; CANR 6, 32,
60; DLB 8; MTCW 2; SATA 118

Wolfe, George C. 1954- .... **CLC 49; BLCS**
See also CA 149

Wolfe, Thomas (Clayton)
1900-1938 ...... **TCLC 4, 13, 29, 61; DA;**
DAB; DAC; DAM MST, NOV; SSC
33; WLC
See also CA 104; 132; CDALB 1929-1941;
DA3; DLB 9, 102; DLBD 2, 16; DLBY
85, 97; MTCW 1, 2

Wolfe, Thomas Kennerly, Jr. 1930-
See Wolfe, Tom
See also CA 13-16R; CANR 9, 33, 70;
DAM POP; DA3; DLB 185; INT
CANR-9; MTCW 1, 2

Wolfe, Tom **CLC 1, 2, 9, 15, 35, 51**
See also Wolfe, Thomas Kennerly, Jr.
See also AAYA 8; AITN 2; BEST 89:1;
DLB 152

Wolff, Geoffrey (Ansell) 1937- .... **CLC 41**
See also CA 29-32R; CANR 29, 43, 78

Wolff, Sonia
See Levitin, Sonia (Wolff)

Zamyatin, Evgeny Ivanovich
  1884-1937 .... **TCLC 8, 37**
  See also CA 105; 166

Zangwill, Israel 1864-1926 .... **TCLC 16**
  See also CA 109; 167; DLB 10, 135, 197

Zappa, Francis Vincent, Jr. 1940-1993
  See Zappa, Frank
  See also CA 108; 143; CANR 57

Zappa, Frank CLC 17
  See also Zappa, Francis Vincent, Jr.

Zaturenska, Marya 1902-1982 ..... **CLC 6, 11**
  See also CA 13-16R; 105; CANR 22

Zeami 1363-1443 .... **DC 7**

Zelazny, Roger (Joseph) 1937-1995 . **CLC 21**
  See also AAYA 7; CA 21-24R; 148; CANR
  26, 60; DLB 8; MTCW 1, 2; SATA 57;
  SATA-Brief 39

Zhdanov, Andrei Alexandrovich
  1896-1948 .... **TCLC 18**
  See also CA 117; 167

Zhukovsky, Vasily (Andreevich)
  1783-1852 .... **NCLC 35**
  See also DLB 205

Ziegenhagen, Eric CLC 55

Zimmer, Jill Schary
  See Robinson, Jill

Zimmerman, Robert
  See Dylan, Bob

Zindel, Paul 1936- ..... **CLC 6, 26; DA; DAB;
  DAC; DAM DRAM, MST, NOV; DC 5**
  See also AAYA 2; CA 73-76; CANR 31,
  65; CDALBS; CLR 3, 45; DA3; DLB 7,
  52; JRDA; MAICYA; MTCW 1, 2; SATA
  16, 58, 102

Zinov'Ev, A. A.
  See Zinoviev, Alexander (Aleksandrovich)

Zinoviev, Alexander (Aleksandrovich)
  1922- .... **CLC 19**
  See also CA 116; 133; CAAS 10

Zoilus
  See Lovecraft, H(oward) P(hillips)

Zola, Emile (Edouard Charles Antoine)
  1840-1902 .... **TCLC 1, 6, 21, 41; DA;
  DAB; DAC; DAM MST, NOV; WLC**
  See also CA 104; 138; DA3; DLB 123

Zoline, Pamela 1941- .... **CLC 62**
  See also CA 161

Zoroaster 628(?)B.C.-551(?)B.C. ... **CMLC 40**

Zorrilla y Moral, Jose 1817-1893 .... **NCLC 6**

Zoshchenko, Mikhail (Mikhailovich)
  1895-1958 .... **TCLC 15; SSC 15**
  See also CA 115; 160

Zuckmayer, Carl 1896-1977 .... **CLC 18**
  See also CA 69-72; DLB 56, 124

Zuk, Georges
  See Skelton, Robin

Zukofsky, Louis 1904-1978 ... **CLC 1, 2, 4, 7,
  11, 18; DAM POET; PC 11**
  See also CA 9-12R; 77-80; CANR 39; DLB
  5, 165; MTCW 1

Zweig, Paul 1935-1984 .... **CLC 34, 42**
  See also CA 85-88; 113

Zweig, Stefan 1881-1942 .... **TCLC 17**
  See also CA 112; 170; DLB 81, 118

Zwingli, Huldreich 1484-1531 .... **LC 37**
  See also DLB 179

Literary Criticism Series
Cumulative Topic Index

This index lists all topic entries in Gale's *Classical and Medieval Literature Criticism, Contemporary Literary Criticism, Literature Criticism from 1400 to 1800, Nineteenth-Century Literature Criticism,* and *Twentieth-Century Literary Criticism.*

CMLC Cumulative Nationality Index

CMLC Cumulative Title Index

Ab urbe condita libri (Livy) **11**:310-86
"Abdallah-the-Hunter" **2**:63
"Abdallah-the-Mariner" **2**:42, 63
Abhijñāna-śakuntala (Kalidasa) **9**:82, 86-7, 89-97, 100-02, 108-13, 127, 130-34, 136-39
Ablbi ne Doleas (Horace) **39**:259
"Aboulhusn ed Duraj and the Leper" **2**:40
About Gods (Cicero)
    See *De natura deorum*
About the Burning of the City (Lucan)
    See *De Incendio Urbu*
Abraham (Hroswitha of Gandersheim) **29**:101-03, 112, 115, 119, 139, 147-48, 163, 174, 176, 178, 189, 192, 198
"Abu Kasem's Slippers" **2**:32-5
Academics (Cicero) **3**:193,202
The Academics; or, A History and Defense of the Beliefs of the New Academy (Cicero)
    See *Academics*
Acharnae (Aristophanes) **4**:44, 62, 69, 76, 87, 94, 97-99, 105-06, 108-10, 113, 123-28, 131-33, 135, 137, 142-43, 149, 151-52, 157, 159-60, 162-63, 165-66
The Acharnians (Aristophanes)
    See *Acharnae*
The Acharnians (Euripides) **23**:175
Acontius (Callimachus) **18**:7-9, 42, 43
Ad Atticum (Cicero) **3**:186-87, 200
Ad Brutum (Cicero) **3**:200
Ad familiares (Cicero) **3**:200
Ad filium (Cato) **21**:28, 39, 46, 48-9
Ad helviam matrem de consolatione (Seneca) **6**:382, 410
Ad Leptinem (Demosthenes)
    See *Against Leptines*
Ad Marciam (Seneca) **6**:382
Ad Martyras (Tertullian)
    See *To the Martyrs*
Ad Nationes (Tertullian)
    See *To the Heathen*
Ad P. Lentulum (Cicero) **3**:186
Ad Polybium de consolatione (Seneca) **6**:382
Ad Q. fratrem (Cicero) **3**:200
Ad Quosdam Sapientes Huius Libri Fautores (Hroswitha of Gandersheim) **29**:100
Ad Scapulam (Tertullian)
    See *To Scapula*
Ad Simplicium (Augustine) **6**:9
Ad Uxorem (Tertullian)
    See *To His Wife*
Adam
    See *Ordo Representacionis Ade*
Addictus (Lucian) **32**:15
Address to Polla (Lucan) **33**:422
Address to the Heathen (Tertullian)
    See *To the Heathen*
Address to the Newly Baptised (Clement of Alexandria) **41**:20-1, 76
Adelphi (Terence)
    See *Adelphoe*
Adelphoe (Terence) **14**:301, 303-04, 306-07, 309, 313-14, 316, 320-21, 332-37, 339-40,

347-49, 352, 357-60, 362-66, 368, 370-71, 374-77, 381, 383-85, 387, 394, 397
Adelphoi (Menander) **9**:270
Adv. Haereses (St. Irenaeus)
    See *Adversus haereses*
"Advaita Vedanta" (Sankara) **32**:332, 342, 344
Adversus haereses (St. Irenaeus) **42**:228-29, 234-35, 237, 259-62, 264-66, 268-69, 271, 279, 284, 286-88, 290-92
Adversus Helvidium (Jerome) **30**:108, 131
Adversus Hermogenem (Tertullian)
    See *Against Hermogenes*
Adversus Iovinianum (Jerome)
    See *Adversus Jovinianum*
Adversus Jovinianum (Jerome) **30**:57, 76, 108, 131
Adversus Marcionem (Tertullian)
    See *Against Marcion*
Adversus Rufin (Jerome) **30**:118, 120-21
Adversus Valentinians (Tertullian)
    See *Against the Valentiniams*
The Aeneid (Vergil) **9**:294-447; **40**:140, 146, 149, 154, 163, 172, 175, 178, 199-200, 204, 208, 216, 249
Aeolus (Euripides) **23**:117, 203
Aesopia (Aesop)
    See *Aesop's Fables*
Aesop's Fables (Aesop) **24**:4-5, 12, 14-15, 17-18, 32-33, 44, 56, 63-65, 70, 74, 77, 82-83
De aeternitate mundi (Aquinas) **33**:108
Africa (Petrarch) **20**:212, 214, 226, 235-39, 245, 251, 260, 308, 326-27, 333
"After Being Separated for a Long Time" (Li Po) **2**:132
Against Androtion (Demosthenes) **13**:148-9, 156, 163-4, 169, 171, 184
Against Aphobus (Demosthenes) **13**:163, 184
Against Apion (Josephus)
    See *Contra Apionem*
Against Aristocrates (Demosthenes) **13**:148, 156-8, 164, 169, 189
Against Aristogiton (Demosthenes) **13**:149
Against Callicles (Demosthenes) **13**:168
Against Catilina (Cicero)
    See *In Catilinam*
Against Conon (Demosthenes) **13**:144
Against Eratosthenes (Demosthenes) **13**:179
"Against Eunomius" (Basil of Caesaria) **35**:87, 120
Against Hermogenes (Tertullian) **29**:311-12, 362, 368, 371, 373
Against Jovinian (Jerome)
    See *Adversus Jovinianum*
Against Judaisers (Clement of Alexandria) **41**:21
Against Leptines (Demosthenes) **13**:137, 148-51, 156, 163-4, 169-71, 197
Against Marcion (Tertullian) **29**:311-12, 316, 329-30, 362-64, 366, 371-73, 384
Against Medias (Demosthenes)
    See *Against Midias*
Against Midias (Demosthenes) **13**:140, 149, 165, 169

Against Neaera (Demosthenes) **13**:169
Against Onetor (Demosthenes) **13**:163, 168, 184
Against Praxeas (Tertullian) **29**:311-12, 371-72
Against Praxiphanes (Callimachus) **18**:36-7, 48
Against Superstitions (Seneca) **6**:330, 342
Against the Academicians (Augustine)
    See *Contra academicos*
Against the Gentiles (Josephus)
    See *Contra Apionem*
Against the Greeks (Josephus)
    See *Contra Apionem*
Against the Heresies (St. Irenaeus)
    See *Adversus haereses*
Against the Jews (Tertullian) **29**:311-12
Against the Megarians (Epicurus) **21**:165
Against the Physicists (Epicurus) **21**:165
Against the Valentiniams (Tertullian) **29**:311-12, 330, 372
Against Theophrastus (Epicurus) **21**:71, 165
Against Timocrates (Demosthenes) **13**:146-8, 156, 163-4, 169
Agamemnon (Aeschylus) **11**:85-6, 101-02, 104-05, 107-08, 110-11, 113, 116-20, 126, 128, 132-34, 136, 138-42, 148, 150-55, 158, 162-63, 165, 167, 171, 175-76, 179-82, 184-85, 187, 190-91, 194-97, 200-07, 217, 220-22
Agamemnon (Seneca) **6**:339, 343, 363, 366-69, 377-81, 389, 407, 409, 414, 417, 431-32, 440, 442, 447
Agesilaus (Xenophon) **17**:329, 330, 331, 339, 340, 349, 350, 352, 353, 354, 355, 359, 362, 374
Agnes (Hroswitha of Gandersheim) **29**:123
De agricultura (Cato) **21**:17, 26-30, 39, 41-50, 54-7
Ahwal al-Nafs (Avicenna) **16**:166
Ai Ying (Yuan) **36**:92-93
"Ailas e que'm miey huelh" (Sordello) **15**:367
Aitia (Callimachus) **18**:6-9, 11, 18, 22-4, 30, 32, 34-8, 42, 44, 48-50, 53, 62-4, 68
Aitnaiai (Aeschylus) **11**:217
Akharnes (Aristophanes)
    See *Acharnae*
"Al poco giorno e al gan cerchio d'ombra" (Petrarch) **20**:283
"Alâ Ed-Dîn Abu Esh-Shamât" **2**:43
"Alas for Ying!" (Yuan)
    See *Ai Ying*
Alcestis (Euripides) **23**:113-14, 121-24, 127, 129-31, 150, 156-60, 162, 171-74, 177, 180, 185, 188, 207
De Alchimia (Albert the Great)
    See *Libellus de Alchimia*
Alcibiades (Plato)
    See *Alcibiades I*
Alcibiades I (Plato) **8**:218, 305-06, 311, 356
Alcibiades II (Plato) **8**:250, 305, 311
Alcibiades Major (Plato)
    See *Alcibiades I*
Alcmaeon at Corinth (Euripides) **23**:173, 176
Alexander (Euripides) **23**:176

Title Index

Title Index

Title Index

Title Index

Title Index

Title Index

Title Index